W9-CKJ-756

The **Rough Guide** to

California

written and researched by

J.D. Dickey, Nick Edwards,
Charles Hodgkins and Paul Whitfield

ROUGH GUIDES

www.roughguides.com

Contents

Epicurean California
colour section
following p.216

Exploring the outdoors
colour section
following p.360

West Coast sounds
colour section
following p.600

◀◀ Joshua Tree National Park ◀ Newport Beach

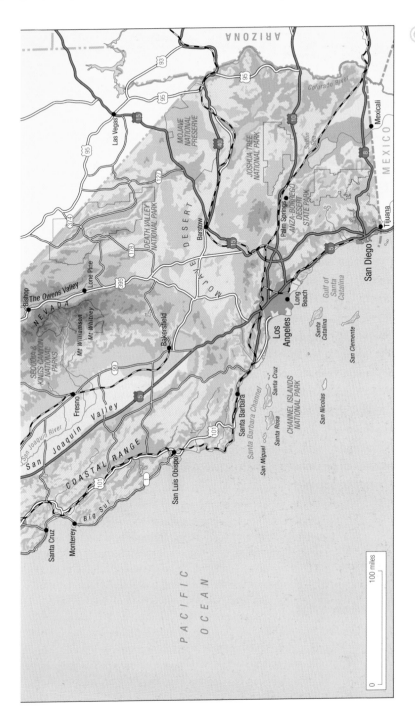

Introduction to

California

Few regions of the world have been as idealized and mythologized as California – and yet it seldom fails to live up to the hype. The glamour, surf beaches and near-endless sun of LA and the Southern California coast are rightly celebrated, but from here you're only a few hours' drive from majestic snowy mountains, Wild West ghost towns, barren deserts pocked with Joshua trees and even ski resorts. Up the coast, boutique wine regions mix with primeval forests, wild seascapes and the sophistication of San Francisco and the Bay Area. This amazing variety is packed into just 160,000 square miles of North America's West Coast. That's an area nearly twice the size of Great Britain, and yet California only ranks as the third largest state in the union, after Alaska and Texas.

California represents the ultimate "now" society: urban life is lived in the fast lane, conspicuous consumption is often paramount, and, in some circles, having the right hairstyle, wardrobe, tan and income is everything. The supposed superficiality of California is just one side of the coin, however, created in equal measure by outsiders and Californians themselves – by San Franciscans contemptuous of LA's position as entertainment, theme-park and beach-culture capital of America, and by Angelenos with a disregard for San Francisco as an outpost of snooty yuppies with pretensions to hipster, and hippy, culture. While there may be plenty of such elements in both towns, the full range of cultures and communities of California cannot be reduced to any one stereotype – there's simply too much going on here.

Beyond the main centres, the atmosphere and environment change dramatically, the saturated cities giving way to dense groves of ancient trees, primitive rock carvings left by Native Americans, and eerie ghost towns. The sheer grandeur of the landscape is hard to beat – anywhere. The Pacific crashes on barely accessible coastlines teeming with sea lions. The snow-capped granite spires and cliffs of the Sierra Nevada harbour gentle meadows where bears roam free. Raging snowmelt rivers carve deep canyons lined by thick forest of cedar and fir. Often, just a few miles away, you're into desert landscapes dotted with abandoned mines and, if you time it right, blazing fields of golden California poppies.

Fact file

- California's "Golden State" nickname is perpetuated by the golden poppy, or *Eschsholtzia californica*, which appears all over California each spring and is the state flower.

- California raised the flags of Spain, England, Mexico and the short-lived Bear Republic before it was admitted to the Union on September 9, 1850, as the thirty-first state.

- Each year, California becomes home to more immigrants than any other state, with most settlers hailing from Latin America and Asia, though a smattering come from Europe, Russia and the Middle East. Almost a third of all immigrants to the US settle here.

- The third largest state in the US, California boasts an almost 700-mile coast along the Pacific and around 25,000 square miles of desert. It's also the most populous state, at almost 37 million inhabitants. In 2010, for the first time since the Gold Rush, California-born residents made up the majority of the state's population.

- Based on agriculture and the electronic, aerospace, film and tourism industries, the state's economy is the strongest in the US. Indeed, if it were a country, California's economy would rank as eighth largest in the world. In 2010 there were over 663,000 millionaires in California – more than any other state in the nation.

It's easy to mix up your trip so that a morning spent whitewater rafting might be followed by an afternoon of wine tasting, before you watch the sun go down on a West Coast beach. The rigours of a long hike in the mountains can be eased by a wallow in some hot springs. And it can all be linked on a classic road trip; few are better than the one outlined in the box on p.12.

Despite its focus on the here and now, California does have a fascinating past. Hunter-gathering Native American tribes had the place largely to themselves until Spanish missionaries up from modern-day Mexico started building a string of missions from 1770. Contact was minimal and on a small scale until the Gold Rush of the 1840s and 1850s – a period which gave California its "Golden State" moniker. People of all social and political stripes flocked to California, a pattern that has continued ever since and which has undoubtedly contributed to making this one of America's most polarized states, home to right-wing bastions like Orange County and San Diego and yet also a principal source of America's most dynamic left-wing movements: environmentalism, women's lib, and gay and immigrant rights. Some of the fiercest protests of the 1960s took root here, and in many ways this is still the heart of liberal America, as California continues to set the standard for the rest of the country (if not the world) regarding progressive action and social tolerance.

Put simply, this is a place that can be all things to all people. Whatever you want California to be, you'll find it somewhere; and no matter what you expect, it'll always surprise you.

People are drawn to California year-round for its wonderfully diverse landscapes, fascinating sights and the extremes that make this the US's most enticing state – our favourites are listed below. For our definitive list of the Californian highlights you really shouldn't miss, see pp.14–24.

Activities
Rafting the Kern River, Kernville. See p.311.
Hiking Half Dome, Yosemite National Park. See p.352.
Riding the Giant Dipper roller coaster, Santa Cruz. See p.423.
Skiing and boarding, Squaw Valley, Lake Tahoe. See p.585.
Cycling in Napa and Sonoma valleys. See p.608.

Natural wonders
Kelso Dunes, Mojave National Preserve. See p.259.
Mono Lake, Lee Vining. See p.297.
Sequoia and Kings Canyon national parks. See p.322.
Lassen Volcanic National Park. See p.657.
Mount Shasta. See p.668.

Festivals
Pageant of the Masters, Laguna Beach. See p.133.
Doo-dah Parade, Pasadena. See p.142.
Hardly Strictly Bluegrass, San Francisco. See p.437.
Pumpkin Festival, Half Moon Bay. See p.532.
Jumping Frog Jubilee, Angels Camp. See p.570.

Beaches
Leo Carrillo State Park, north of Malibu. See p.81.
Tourmaline Surfing Park, San Diego. See p.190.
Pfeiffer Beach, Big Sur. See p.403.
Stinson Beach, Marin County. See p.541.
Sand Harbor, Lake Tahoe. See p.590.

Foodie destinations
LA burger joints. See p.134.
Palm Springs. See p.232.
Gourmet Ghetto, Berkeley. See p.541.
San Francisco. See p.476.
Yountville, Napa Valley. See p.611.

Offbeat attractions
Watts Towers, LA. See p.91.
Salvation Mountain, Salton Sea. See p.245.
Forestiere Underground Gardens, Fresno. See p.317.
Mystery Spot, Santa Cruz. See p.425.
Trees of Mystery, Del Norte County. See p.647.

Historic sites
Hollywood movie palaces, LA. See p.98.
Old Town, San Diego. See p.183.
Bodie Ghost Town, near Mono Lake. See p.300.
Mission San Miguel Arcangel, San Miguel. See p.396.
Johnsville, Plumas County. See p.581.

Where to go

t's worth keeping in mind that distances between the main destinations can be huge, and naturally you won't be able to see everything on one trip. In an area so varied, it's hard to pick out specific highlights, and much will depend on the kind of holiday you're looking for. You may well start off in **Los Angeles**, far and away the biggest and most stimulating California city: a maddening collection of freeways and beaches, seedy suburbs and high-gloss neighbourhoods, and extreme lifestyles. From here you can head south to **San Diego**, with its broad, welcoming beaches and a handy position close to the Mexican border, or inland to the California **deserts**, notably **Death Valley** – as its name suggests, a barren, inhospitable landscape of volcanic craters and windswept sand dunes that in summer becomes the hottest place on earth. An alternative is to make the steady journey up the **Central Coast**, a gorgeous run following the shoreline north of LA through some of the state's most dramatic scenery, and taking in some of its liveliest small towns, particularly Santa Barbara and Santa Cruz.

The Central Coast marks the transition from Southern to Northern California – a break that's more than just geographical. **San Francisco**, California's other defining metropolis, is quite different from LA: the coast's oldest, most European-styled city, it's set compactly over a series of steep hills, with wooden Victorian houses tumbling down to water on both sides. From here you have access to some of the state's most extraordinary scenery, not least in the national parks to the east, especially **Yosemite**, where powerful waterfalls cascade

▲ Yosemite National Park

into a sheer glacial valley that's been immortalized by Ansel Adams – and countless others – in search of the definitive landscape photograph. Yosemite is the highlight of the Sierra Nevada mountains; south from here are the vast national parks of **Sequoia** and **Kings Canyon**, and north an interesting mix of quaint towns like Nevada City and resorts such as **Lake Tahoe**.

North of San Francisco, the population thins and the landscape changes yet again. The climate is wetter up here, the valleys that much greener and flanked by a jagged coastline shadowed by mighty **redwoods**, the tallest trees in the world. Though many visitors choose to venture no further than the Napa Valley and Sonoma **Wine Country** and the Russian River Valley on weekend forays from the city, it's well worth taking time out to explore the state's northernmost regions, which are split distinctly in two. The coastline is simultaneously rugged and serene, guarded by towering redwoods; the interior, meanwhile, dominated by majestic **Mount Shasta**, is a volcano-scarred wilderness that's as different from the stereotype of California as you could imagine.

On shaky ground

With an estimated 500,000 tremors detected annually in the state, California is a seismic time bomb, bisected by the most famous faultline in the world, the **San Andreas**, which runs loosely from San Francisco to Los Angeles and marks the junction of the Pacific and North American tectonic plates. Given its fearsome reputation, though, it's not the most active fault at the moment – that honour goes to one of its connected faults, known as the **Hayward**.

Despite the 1906 **San Francisco earthquake**'s notoriety, it wasn't actually the quake itself that levelled the city, but a careless homeowner cooking breakfast on a gas stove at the time; the ensuing fire raged for four days, razed 28,000 buildings, and left at least 3000 dead. Since then, there have been several significant quakes, most recently in 1989, when San Francisco again shook during the **Loma Prieta**, named after its epicentre close to Santa Cruz and responsible for the horrifying collapse of a double-decker freeway, and in 1994, when the **Northridge** quake tore through the north side of LA, rupturing freeways and flattening an apartment building.

Of course, everyone's waiting for the so-called **Big One**, a massive earthquake that, it's feared, could wipe out Los Angeles or San Francisco. Speculation has intensified recently, since experts have pegged the interval between major ruptures in the southern reaches of the San Andreas at 140 years: the last such quake was Fort Tejon in 1857.

The classic California road trip

With a couple of weeks at your disposal and an ambition to see a cross section of the best California has to offer you can't go too far wrong with this city, coast, wine, mountain and desert loop starting in LA (though equally feasible from San Francisco or even Las Vegas).

Los Angeles Get your fix of Tinseltown and beach culture.

The Central Coast Drive slowly up Hwy-1 with stops at Santa Barbara, Hearst Castle, Santa Cruz and along the wild Big Sur Coast.

San Francisco Sample the best of the Bay Area with a side trip to the Sonoma and Napa valley wineries.

Gold Country Swing east into the quaint old gold towns of the Sierra foothills.

Yosemite Gaze slack-jawed at the magnificent scenery and visit the stupendously big sequoias of California's finest national park.

Owens Valley Photograph the otherworldly tufa towers in Mono Lake and the world's oldest trees in the bristlecone pine forests of the White Mountains.

Death Valley Experience the barren landscapes of the hottest place on earth.

Joshua Tree Freakish trees, sensual boulders and the howl of the coyote make camping in this national park a real treat.

Palm Springs Sip a cocktail by the pool in a Mid-century Modern resort and take in a celebrity tour.

Los Angeles Last chance to wrap up your shopping.

When to go

California's climate is as varied as its landscape: in **Southern California**, count on endless days of sunshine from May to October, and warm, dry nights – though LA's notorious **smog** is at its worst when temperatures are highest, in August and September.

Along the **coast**, mornings can be hazily overcast, especially in May and June, though you'll still tan – or burn – under grey skies. In winter temperatures drop somewhat, but, more importantly, weeks of rain can cause massive mudslides that wipe out roads and hillside homes. Inland, the **deserts** are warm in winter and unbearably hot (49°C is not unusual) in summer; desert nights can be freezing in winter, when it can even snow. For serious white stuff, head to the **mountains**, where hiking trails at the higher elevations are covered with snow from November to June: skiers can take advantage of well-groomed slopes among the Sierra Nevada mountains and around Lake Tahoe.

The coast of **Northern California** is wetter and cooler than the south, its summers tempered by sea breezes and fog, and its winters mild but damp. **San Francisco**, because of its exposed position at the tip of a peninsula, can be chilly all year, with summer fog often rolling in and chasing off what may have started off as a pleasant day. Head across the bay to Oakland, though, and you'll be back in the sun.

Average temperatures and rainfall

	Jan	Apr	Jul	Oct
Death Valley				
max/min (°F)	66/39	89/62	115/86	92/61
max/min (°C)	19/4	32/17	46/30	33/16
rain (inches/mm)	0.4/10	0.1/3	0.0/0	0.1/3
Eureka				
max/min (°F)	55/41	57/44	63/53	61/48
max/min (°C)	13/5	14/7	17/12	16/9
rain (inches/mm)	5.9/150	2.9/74	0.2/5	2.4/61
Lake Tahoe				
max/min (°F)	41/15	53/26	79/40	62/26
max/min (°C)	5/-9	12/-3	26/4	17/-3
rain (inches/mm)	6.9/175	2.5/64	0.5/13	2.2/56
Los Angeles				
max/min (°F)	68/48	73/54	84/65	79/60
max/min (°C)	20/9	23/12	29/18	26/16
rain (inches/mm)	3.3/84	0.8/20	0.0/0	0.4/10
San Diego				
max/min (°F)	66/50	69/56	76/66	74/61
max/min (°C)	19/10	21/13	24/19	23/16
rain (inches/mm)	2.3/58	0.8/20	0.0/0	0.4/10
San Francisco				
max/min (°F)	56/43	64/48	71/55	70/52
max/min (°C)	13/6	17/9	22/13	21/11
rain (inches/mm)	4.5/114	1.2/31	0.0/0	1.0/25

things not to miss

It's not possible to see everything that California has to offer in one trip – and we don't suggest you try. What follows is a selective taste of the state's highlights, from its bustling beaches to its deserted Gold Rush outposts. They're arranged in five colour-coded categories to help you find the very best to see, do and experience. All highlights have a page reference to take you straight into the Guide, where you can find out more.

01 Big Sur Page **400** • Bask in the secluded beauty of Big Sur's approximately ninety miles of rocky cliffs and crashing waves along the Pacific.

02 **Santa Monica Mountains** Page **118** • The verdant canyons and rocky crags of this range of low mountains, bordering the northern edge of Los Angeles, provide an escape for humans and refuge for wildlife.

04 **Surfing** See *Exploring the outdoors colour section* • From the gargantuan waves at Mavericks to the hot-dogging longboard heaven of Malibu, California's consummate pastime can be enjoyed year-round on beaches all along its coast.

03 **Lava Beds National Monument** Page **675** • The eerie black volcanic landscape and massive network of nearly 750 lava tubes are also the site of some grim history.

05 **Hearst Castle** Page **393** • Of all California's lavish dreams, none quite rivals William Randolph Hearst's monument to himself, which boasts a Mudejar cathedral facade.

06 **Cruising the Sunset Strip** Page **109** • The Sunset Strip has long been a choice LA hangout, jammed with groovy bars and clubs, swanky hotels and towering billboards selling all manner of vices.

07 **Mexican food** Page **40** • Duck into a roadside taquería or burrito joint to enjoy one of the state's signature cuisines.

08 **Tufa towers of Mono Lake** Page **299** • See the fluffy, sandcastle-like tufa spires that have frothed up from below the surface of this fast-shrinking body of water.

09 Sequoia National Park

Page **322** • The trees after which this park is named are some of the world's biggest – and oldest – living things.

10 Skiing and snowboarding

Pages **584** & **295** • Hit California's celebrated slopes, home to unbeatable downhill skiing and snowboarding.

11 Red Rock Canyon

Page **253** • Once used as a backdrop in Spielberg's *Jurassic Park*, the canyon's rock formations present a panoply of aboriginal carvings.

12 **San Francisco Pride** Page **495** • In late June, the San Francisco Pride parade takes over the streets of San Francisco's Castro district in exuberant fashion.

13 **Yosemite Valley** Page **340** • There's much stunning geology up and down the state but nothing surpasses Yosemite Valley, where El Capitan and Half Dome are just two of the awe-inspiring monoliths that await you.

14 La Jolla Page **190** • A glittering oceanside enclave where the San Diego elite reside in period revival mansions and where day-trippers come for the striking scenery, beachside coves and quality museums.

15 The Mojave National Preserve Page **259** • The Mojave Desert can be shocking in its extremes – some of the imposing sand dunes of the preserve rise as high as 4000ft above sea level.

16 Bodie Ghost Town Page **300** • Well past its 1880s gold-mining heyday, when it was the second largest town in the state, Bodie is now an intriguing time-capsule of some 150 atmospheric wooden buildings.

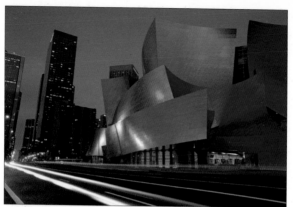

17 Disney Hall Page **85** • Although Frank Gehry's architectural marvel was designed in 1987, sixteen years passed before it was finally built and today this inspired sculptural creation serves as the monumental home of the LA Philharmonic.

18 Riding a cable car Page **439** • No visit to San Francisco is complete without a ride on a cable car, the best means of scaling the hills and enjoying the views.

19 Klamath Basin National Wildlife Refuge Page **679** • Each year, travellers from the avian world rest up in the gigantic sanctuary of the Klamath Basin before resuming their journeys along the Pacific Flyway.

20 Redwood National Park Page **645** • The tallest trees in the world – some close to 380ft high – preside over this dramatic national park, home to Roosevelt elk, black bears and serene hiking trails.

22 Hiking Mount Whitney Page **282** • Climb the tallest mountain in the continental US, which sits right on the edge of Sequoia National Park.

21 Balboa Park Page **179** • San Diego's staggering collection of museums, lush greenery and evocative Spanish Colonial buildings provides a wealth of opportunities for exploration.

23 **Salvation Mountain** Page **245** • This only-in-California creation is a kaleidoscopic mound of concrete, hay bales and vast quantities of paint, peppered liberally with Biblical quotes.

24 **Rafting on the Kern River** Page **312** • The Kern River offers some of the most appealing whitewater rafting anywhere in the States.

25 **Whale-watching** Page **371** • Springtime is your best chance of seeing grey whales during their annual migration in the Pacific.

26 **The Chinese Theatre** Page **98** • A cherished relic of the 1920s, LA's Chinese Theatre recalls the glory years of Hollywood cinema, both with its Art Deco interior and the celebrity hand- and footprints pressed into the pavement outside.

27 **Ride the Coast Starlight** Page **33** • While most visitors take to the highways, the best way to see the hundred-mile-long coast between Santa Barbara and San Luis Obispo is by rail.

28 **Golden Gate Park** Page **473** • A long strip of green stretching from San Francisco's Haight-Ashbury neighbourhood to the Pacific Ocean, this urban oasis is packed with museums, gardens and live music.

29 **Cholla Cactus Garden** Page **245** • One of the high points of any trip to Joshua Tree National Park is this cactus garden, part of a circular hike that takes in the unique "jumping" cholla.

Basics

Basics

Getting there

The second largest state in the continental US, California presents an easy target for both domestic and international visitors. All the main airlines operate daily scheduled flights to San Francisco and Los Angeles from all over the world, and the state is easily accessible by road or rail too. California is a year-round destination but fares tend to be highest over summer (June–September) and around Christmas.

Flights from the UK and Ireland

Nonstop flights from Britain to California are with BA, AA and Virgin from London to Los Angeles and San Francisco (both 11hr). Flights are often advertised as "direct" because they keep the same flight number but actually land elsewhere first. The first place the plane lands is your point of entry into the US, which means you'll have to collect your bags and go through customs and immigration formalities there, even if you're continuing on to California on the same plane. Many other routings involve a change of aircraft.

Britain remains one of the best places in Europe to obtain flight **bargains**, though fares vary widely according to season, availability and inter-airline competition. Fares, including taxes, start from £500–700 return, depending on the season.

Aer Lingus fly direct from Dublin to Los Angeles and San Francisco with refuelling stops in Boston or Chicago. Expect to pay €550 to €1000. Flights via London may cost less, but you pay slightly more tax.

"**Open-jaw**" tickets can be a good idea, allowing you to fly into LA, for example, and back from San Francisco for little or no extra charge. This makes a convenient option for those who want a **fly-drive** deal, which gives cut-rate (and sometimes free) car rental when you buy an air ticket. Many airlines also offer **air passes**, which allow foreign travellers to fly between a given number of US cities for one discounted price.

Packages – fly-drive, flight-accommodation deals and guided tours – can work out cheaper than arranging the same trip yourself, especially for a short-term stay. The obvious drawbacks are the loss of flexibility and the fact that most schemes use hotels in the mid-range bracket, but there is a wide variety of options available.

Flights from the US and Canada

Most domestic flights are likely to take you to one of the following international airports: **Los Angeles** (airport code LAX), **San Francisco** (SFO), **Oakland** (OAK), **San Jose** (SJO) or **San Diego** (SAN). Some flights use smaller airports in the vicinity of those metropolitan areas and you can also fly direct to one of the minor cities such as Sacramento, Redding or Reno (in Nevada) for the Lake Tahoe region.

Flying is the most convenient and sometimes the cheapest way to travel within North America. Round-trip prices midweek in summer on the major airlines start at around $350 from New York and other eastern seaboard cities, $400 from Midwest cities, and $500 from Toronto and Montréal. What makes more difference than your choice of carrier are the conditions governing the ticket – whether it's fully refundable, the time and day, and, most importantly, the **time of year** you travel.

> One word of **warning**: it's not a good idea to buy a **one-way** ticket to the States. US immigration officials usually take them as a sign that you aren't planning to go home and you are unlikely to be allowed even to board your flight, let alone enter the US.

Four steps to a better kind of travel

At Rough Guides we are passionately committed to travel. We feel strongly that only through travelling do we truly come to understand the world we live in and the people we share it with – plus tourism has brought a great deal of **benefit** to developing economies around the world over the last few decades. But the extraordinary growth in tourism has also damaged some places irreparably, and of course **climate change** is exacerbated by most forms of transport, especially flying. This means that now more than ever it's important to **travel thoughtfully and responsibly**, with respect for the cultures you're visiting – not only to derive the most benefit from your trip but also to preserve the best bits of the planet for everyone to enjoy. At Rough Guides we feel there are four main areas in which you can make a difference:

• Travel with a purpose, not just to tick off experiences. Consider **spending longer** in a place, and getting to know it and its people.

• Give thought to how often you **fly**. Try to avoid short hops by air and more harmful night flights.

• Consider **alternatives to flying**, travelling instead by bus, train, boat and even by bike or on foot where possible.

• Make your trips **"climate neutral"** via a reputable carbon offset scheme. All Rough Guide flights are offset, and every year we donate money to a variety of charities devoted to combating the effects of climate change.

In addition to the big-name scheduled airlines, a few lesser-known carriers run no-frills flights, which can prove to be very good value, especially if you have a flexible schedule and can put up with a few delays; try **JetBlue** or **Frontier Airlines**, for example, who can often get you across the country and back for around $200.

Flights from Australia, New Zealand and South Africa

If you are coming from Australia or New Zealand, there's very little price difference between airlines and no shortage of flights, either via the Pacific or Asia, to Los Angeles and San Francisco. Most flights crossing the Pacific are nonstop, with twelve to fourteen hours' travel time between Auckland/Sydney and LA, though some include stopovers in Honolulu and a number of the South Pacific islands. If you go via Asia (a slightly more roundabout route that can work out a little cheaper), you may have to spend the best part of a day (or a night), in the airline's home city.

Travelling from **Australia**, fares to LA and San Francisco from eastern cities cost the same, while from Perth they're about Aus$400 more. Flights from Sydney or Melbourne to LA and San Francisco range between Aus$1800 and Aus$3000, depending on the season, with airline specials sometimes reducing that to around Aus$1500. Seat availability on most international flights out of Australia and New Zealand is limited, so it's best to book at least several weeks ahead.

From **New Zealand**, most flights are Auckland–LA; add about NZ$200 for Christchurch and Wellington. Prices vary depending on availability, but range between NZ$2000 and NZ$2800. Flights into San Francisco are a similar price.

Travel to California is not particularly cheap from **South Africa**; prices are about the same out of Cape Town or Johannesburg but several hundred rand more from Durban and other smaller cities. Return flights, mostly via Europe, New York or Washington DC, cost ZAR10,000–20,000.

Round-the-world tickets

No matter what continent you are starting from, if you intend to take in California as part of a world trip, a **round-the-world (RTW)** ticket offers the greatest flexibility and can work out far more economical than booking separate flights. The most US-oriented are the 28 airlines making up the Star Alliance network (www.staralliance.com), which offers three to fifteen stopovers worldwide, with a total trip length from ten days to a year. Another option is One World (including Qantas, American, and British Airways; www.oneworld.com), which bases its rates on the number of continents visited, allowing three to six possible stopovers in each. RTW tickets from London are often the best value: expect to pay around £2000 for a basic itinerary, more like £3000 for something quite comprehensive. Set aside around Aus$3700–5000 from Australia, NZ$3800–4800 from New Zealand, and ZAR22000–30000 from South Africa. If you're starting in the UK, consider the Escapade group (Virgin, Singapore Air and Air New Zealand; www.thegreatescapade.com), who offer more limited routing possibilities but great prices, starting under £1000.

Trains

If you are willing to pay for extra creature comforts and have the time and inclination to take in some of the rest of the US on your way to California, then riding Amtrak (1-800/872-7245, www.amtrak.com) may be just the ticket. The most spectacular train journey of all has to be the **California Zephyr**, which runs all the way from Chicago to San Francisco (53hr; departs 2pm daily) via the exquisitely scenic Rockies west of Denver and the mighty Sierra Nevada, as it traces the route of the first transcontinental railroad. It actually terminates in Emeryville, where you change onto a bus for the twenty-minute ride into San Francisco. Two other useful services are the **Texas Eagle** (3 weekly; 66hr), which also starts in Chicago and travels through chunks of the Midwest and Southwest before eventually arriving in Los Angeles, and the **Coast Starlight** (see p.33), which covers all of the West Coast between Seattle and Los Angeles.

Amtrak **fares** can be more expensive than flying, though **off-peak discounts**, special deals and passes (all detailed on the website) can make the train an economical and appealing choice. If you want to travel in a bit more comfort, costs rise quickly – **sleeping compartments**, which include meals, small toilets, and showers, start at around $190 per night for one or two people.

Buses

Bus travel is the most tedious and time-consuming way to get to California but can save you a lot of money if you don't mind the discomfort. **Greyhound** (1-800/231-2222 and 214/849-8100, www.greyhound.com, www.discoverypass.com) is the sole long-distance operator and has an extensive network of destinations in California. The best reason to go Greyhound is if you're planning to visit a number of other places en route; Greyhound's **Discovery Pass** is good for unlimited travel within a certain time frame (see box, p.34).

An alternative, in every sense, is the San Francisco-based **Green Tortoise** bus company; see p.34 for details.

Airlines, agents and operators

Airlines

Aer Lingus www.aerlingus.com
Air Canada www.aircanada.com
Air New Zealand www.airnewzealand.com
American Airlines www.aa.com
British Airways www.ba.com
EgyptAir www.egyptair.com
Frontier Airlines www.flyfrontier.com
JetBlue www.jetblue.com
Qantas www.qantas.com
Singapore Airlines www.singaporeair.com
South African Airways www.flysaa.com
Thai Airways www.thaiair.com
United Airlines www.united.com
Virgin Atlantic Airways www.virgin-atlantic.com

Agents and operators

UK and Ireland

American Holidays Northern Ireland 028/9051 1840, Republic of Ireland 01/673 3840; www.american-holidays.com. Package tours to the US, including California, from Ireland.
Bon Voyage UK 0800/316 3012, www.bon-voyage.co.uk. Flight-plus-accommodation deals all over California.
Contiki Travel UK 0845/075 0990, www.contiki.co.uk. West Coast coach tours aimed at 18–35-year-olds willing to party.

Flight Centre UK 0844/800 8660, ☏www
.flightcentre.co.uk. Near-ubiquitous high-street
agency offering some of the lowest fares around.
Kuoni UK ☏1306/747 002, ☏www.kuoni.co.uk.
Flight-plus-accommodation-plus-car deals featuring
the big cities, beaches and national parks. Special
deals for families.
North South Travel UK ☏01245/608 291,
☏www.northsouthtravel.co.uk. Friendly,
competitive travel agency, offering discounted fares
worldwide. Profits are used to support projects in
the developing world, especially the promotion of
sustainable tourism.
STA Travel UK ☏0871/230 0040, ☏www
.statravel.co.uk. Worldwide specialists in independent
travel; also student IDs, travel insurance, car rental,
rail passes and more. Good discounts for students
and under-26s.
Trailfinders UK ☏0845/058 5858, Ireland
☏01/677 7888; ☏www.trailfinders.com. One
of the best-informed and most efficient agents for
independent travellers.
TrekAmerica UK ☏0844/576 1393, ☏www
.trekamerica.com. Touring adventure holidays, usually
small groups in well-equipped 4WD vans.
USIT Northern Ireland ☏028/9032 7111, Republic
of Ireland ☏01/602 1906, ☏www.usit.ie. Ireland's
premier student travel centre, which can also find
good non-student deals.
Virgin Holidays UK ☏0844/557 5825, ☏www
.virginholidays.co.uk. Packages to a wide range of
California destinations.

US and Canada

Abercrombie & Kent ☏1-800/554-7016,
☏www.abercrombiekent.com. Well-tailored,
somewhat upmarket tours worldwide with a handful
in California.
Adventure Center ☏1-800/228-8747, ☏www
.adventurecenter.com. Hiking and soft-adventure
specialists.
Backroads ☏1-800/462-2848, ☏www
.backroads.com. Cycling, hiking and multisport tours.
Mountain Travel Sobek ☏1-888/687-6235,
☏www.mtsobek.com. Hiking tours in the California
mountains.
REI Adventures ☏1-800/622-2236, ☏www.rei
.com. Climbing, cycling, hiking, cruising, paddling and
multisport tours.
STA Travel ☏1-800/781-4040, ☏www.statravel
.com. Nationwide student agency that also does good
deals for older travellers.
Travel CUTS Canada ☏1-866/246-9762, US
☏1-800/592-2887; ☏www.travelcuts.com.
Canadian youth and student travel firm.

Australia, NZ and South Africa

Flight Centre Australia ☏133 133, ☏www
.flightcentre.com.au; New Zealand ☏800/243 544,
☏www.flightcentre.co.nz; South Africa ☏0860/400
727, ☏www.flightcentre.co.za. High-street agency
frequently offering some of the lowest fares around.
STA Travel Australia ☏13 4782, ☏www.statravel
.com.au; New Zealand ☏0800/474 400, ☏www
.statravel.co.nz. A major player in student, youth and
budget travel with branches in many universities.
Trailfinders Australia ☏1300/780 212, ☏www
.trailfinders.com.au. Knowledgeable staff skilled at
turning up odd itineraries and good prices.
Travel.com.au Australia ☏1300/130 483, ☏www
.travel.com.au. Efficient, online and retail (in Sydney)
travel agency offering good fares, hotels and car rental.

Getting around

Although distances can be great, getting around California is seldom much of a
problem. Certainly, things are always easier if you have a car – particularly in the
isolated rural areas – but between the major cities there are good bus links and a
reasonable train service.

By car

Throughout much of the state, driving is by far
the easiest way to get around. Los Angeles,
for example, sprawls for so many miles in all
directions that your hotel may be fifteen or
twenty miles from the sights you came to see.
Away from the cities, points of interest are
much harder to reach without your own

City-to-city distances (in miles)

	Los Angeles	Sacramento	San Diego	San Francisco
Bakersfield	115	272	231	297
Eureka	694	314	800	272
Los Angeles	-	387	116	412
Monterey	335	185	451	116
Palm Springs	111	498	139	523
Redding	551	164	667	223
Sacramento	387	-	503	87
San Diego	116	503	-	528
San Francisco	412	87	528	-
San Jose	367	114	483	45
Santa Barbara	95	406	211	337

transport; most national and state parks are only served by infrequent public transport as far as the main visitor centre, if that much. What's more, if you are planning on doing a fair amount of camping, renting a car can save you money by allowing access to less expensive, out-of-the-way campgrounds.

Drivers under 25 years old who wish to rent a car may encounter problems, and will probably get lumbered with a higher than normal insurance premium – and if you're under 21, it's unlikely you'll be permitted to rent at all. Car rental companies will also expect you to have a **credit card**. The likeliest tactic for getting a good deal is to phone the major firms' toll-free numbers (see box above) and ask for their best rate – most will try to beat the offers of their competitors, so it's worth haggling.

In general, the lowest **rates** are available at the airport branches – $150–180 is roughly the minimum for a week's rental. Always be sure to get free unlimited mileage and be aware that leaving the car in a different city than the one in which you rent it will incur a **drop-off charge** that can be $200 or more.

However, many companies do not charge drop-off fees within California itself, so check before you book if you're planning a one-way drive. If you intend to venture outside California, enquire if there are any limitations; some companies don't allow travel beyond Nevada or into Mexico, while others simply ramp up their insurance charges, which are typically $14–18 per day.

When you rent a car, read the small print carefully for details on the **Collision Damage Waiver (CDW)** – sometimes called a Liability Damage Waiver (LDW) or a Physical Damage Waiver (PDW) – a form of insurance which usually isn't included in the initial rental charge. Americans who have their own car-insurance policy may already be covered (check before you leave home), but foreign visitors should definitely consider taking this option. It specifically covers the car that you are driving, as you are in any case insured for damage to other vehicles. Smaller companies may offer low-cost CDW that still leaves you liable for, say, the first $500 of any claim. Before stumping up for their optional Personal Accident Coverage

Road conditions

The California Department of Transportation (CalTrans) operates a toll-free **24-hour information line** (☎1-800/427-7623) giving up-to-the-minute details of road conditions throughout the state. Simply input the number of the road ("5" for I-5, "299" for Hwy-299, etc) and a recorded voice will tell you about any relevant weather conditions, delays, detours, snow closures, and so on. From out of state, or without a touch-tone phone, road information is available on ☎916/445-1534. You can also check online at ⊛www.dot.ca.gov.

(or similar), consult your travel insurance policy, which may cover you for a certain amount of rental vehicle excess, eliminating the need for this extra cost. Alternately, your **credit card company** may cover your rental when you use its card for the transaction; however, policies can vary widely, depending on the company, and there may be strict limitations on the liability coverage offered, with collision coverage even less common.

One variation on renting is a **driveaway**. Companies operate in most major cities, and are paid to find drivers to take a customer's car from one place to another. The company will normally pay for your insurance and your first tank of gas; after that, you'll be expected to drive along the most direct route and to average a set number of miles a day. Many driveaway companies are keen to use foreign travellers, so if you can convince them you are a safe bet they'll take something like a $300 deposit, which you get back after delivering the car in good condition. It makes obvious sense to get in touch in advance, to spare yourself a week's wait for a car to turn up. Look under "Automobile transporters and driveaway companies" in the *Yellow Pages* or on the internet and phone around for the latest offers, or check through the database on ⓦwww.movecars.com.

Car rental companies

Advantage ☎1-800/777-5500, ⓦwww
.advantage.com
Alamo ☎1-800/462-5266, ⓦwww.alamo.com
Avis ☎1-800/230-4898, ⓦwww.avis.com
Budget ☎1-800/527-0700, ⓦwww.budget.com
Dollar ☎1-800/800-3665, ⓦwww.dollar.com
Enterprise ☎1-800/261-7331, ⓦwww
.enterprise.com
Hertz ☎1-800/654-3131, ⓦwww.hertz.com
National ☎1-800/227-7368, ⓦwww
.nationalcar.com
Payless ☎1-800/729-5377, ⓦwww.payless
carrental.com
Rent-A-Wreck ☎1-800/944-7501, ⓦwww
.rentawreck.com
Thrifty ☎1-800/847-4389, ⓦwww.thrifty.com

Driving for foreign visitors

Most visitors can **drive** in the US on their own driver's licence if they've also obtained an International Driving Permit from their home country. The most important difference between driving in the US and in other countries is that in the US you need to **drive on the right**. Once you have rented a vehicle, you'll find that **gas** (petrol) is fairly cheap compared to Europe, though California is one of the more expensive states for it; a self-serve US gallon (3.8 litres) of **unleaded** costs $3 or more, depending on the location of the gas station. In California, most gas stations are self-service and you always have to prepay; full-service pumps, where available, often charge upwards of 30¢ extra per gallon.

There are several **types of roads**. The best for covering long distances quickly are the wide, straight and fast interstate highways, usually at least six-lane motorways and always prefixed by "I" (eg I-5). Even-numbered interstates usually run east–west and those with odd numbers north–south. Drivers **change lanes** frequently; in California, you are also permitted to stay in the fast lane while being overtaken on the inside, although common courtesy dictates that slower drivers stay to the right. A grade down, and broadly similar to British dual carriageways and main roads, are the **state highways** (eg Hwy-1) and the **US highways** (eg US-395). In rural areas, you'll also find much smaller county or rural roads, sometimes topped with dirt or gravel, or even more challenging forest service roads, for which you may need a four-wheel-drive vehicle.

If your car **breaks down** at night while on a major street, activate the emergency lights to signal a police officer for assistance. During the day, find the nearest phone book and call for a tow truck. Should you be forced to stop your car on a freeway, pull over to the right shoulder – never the left – and activate your emergency lights. Wait for assistance from a patrol officer in your vehicle, while strapped in by a seatbelt, or on a safe embankment nearby.

By train

California is well covered by the Amtrak **rail** network (☎1-800/872-7245, ⓦwww.amtrak .com), thanks to the number of routes available and the Amtrak Thruway buses that bring passengers from the many rail-less parts of the state to the trains. The train is more expensive than Greyhound — for example, $56 one way between Los Angeles and San Francisco (by way of Oakland or Santa Barbara and a bus connection) — but most major cities are connected and the carriages rarely crowded, though delays can be frequent since Amtrak shares rail lines with commercial freight carriers.

Probably the prettiest route is the **Coast Starlight**, which runs between Seattle and Los Angeles and passes some of the most attractive scenery in the state, from an evening trip around Mount Shasta to coastal views between San Luis Obispo and Santa Barbara. Shorter in-state routes include the **Pacific Surfliner**, which connects San Diego to San Luis Obispo; **Capitol Corridor**, from Sacramento to San Jose; and the **San Joaquin**, connecting Oakland to Bakersfield across the San Joaquin Valley. Other routes – Southwest Chief, Sunset Limited, Texas Eagle – connect to places such as Chicago, Texas and New Orleans.

If California is part of wider travels, it may be worth investing in one of Amtrak's rail passes (see box, p.34).

By bus

If you're travelling on your own and making a lot of stops, **buses** are the cheapest way to get around. The only long-distance service is **Greyhound**, which links all major cities and many smaller towns. Out in the country, buses are fairly scarce, sometimes appearing only once a day; as a result, you'll need to plot your route with care. But along the main highways, buses run around the clock to a fairly full timetable, stopping only for meal breaks (almost always fast-food dives) and driver changeovers.

The maximum **speed limit** in California is 70mph, with lower signposted limits – usually around 35–55mph – in urban areas, and 20mph near schools when children are present. If given a ticket for **speeding**, your case will come to court and the size of the fine will be at the discretion of the judge; $200 is a starting point. If the **police** do flag you down, don't get out of the car, make any sudden movements, or reach into the glove compartment, as they may think you have a gun. Simply sit still with your hands on the wheel; when questioned, be polite and don't attempt to make jokes.

As for other possible violations, US law requires that any **alcohol** be carried unopened in the boot (US "trunk") of the car, and **driving under the influence (DUI)** is a very serious offence (see p.54). At intersections, one rule is crucially different from many other countries: you can turn right on a red light (having first come to a halt) if there is no traffic approaching from the left, unless there is a "no turn on red" sign; otherwise red means stop. Stopping is also compulsory, in both directions, when you come upon a school bus disgorging passengers with its lights flashing, and not doing so is regarded as a serious infraction. Blinking red lights should be treated as a stop sign (as should devices at an intersection where stoplights are temporarily disabled), and blinking yellow lights indicate that you should cross the intersection with caution, but do not need to come to a complete stop. And at any intersection with more than one **stop sign**, cars proceed in the order in which they arrived; if two vehicles arrive simultaneously, the one on the right has right of way. Three other rules to be aware of: it is illegal to park within ten feet of a **fire hydrant** anywhere in the US; when **parking on a hill** in California, your wheels need to be angled towards the kerb if you're parked downhill, and if you're parked uphill, your wheels need to be angled towards the left; and California motorcycles are allowed "lane-splitting" – riding the line between cars in traffic – an unnerving experience for drivers not used to seeing choppers passing a few inches away.

It used to be that any sizeable community had a Greyhound station; now in some places, the post office or a gas station doubles as the bus stop and ticket office, and in many others the bus service has been cancelled altogether. Note that advance reservations, either in person at the station or on the toll-free number, are useful for getting cheaper tickets but do not guarantee a seat, so it's still wise to arrive in good time and join the **line** at busy stations.

Fares average 10¢ a mile, which can add up quickly; for example, $42 one way from Los Angeles to San Francisco. Though long-distance travel by bus is inefficient, it's the best deal if you plan to visit a lot of places, and Greyhound's **Discovery Pass** (see box below) can work out to be good value. To plan your route, pick up the free route-by-route **timetables** from larger stations, or consult Greyhound's website.

Bear in mind that fair distances can be covered for very little money – if also very slowly – using **local buses**, which connect neighbouring districts. It's possible, for example, to travel from San Diego to Los Angeles using Metrolink and Coaster systems for around $10–20, but it'll take all day and at least three changes of bus to do it. And of course, there's always the hippyish **Green Tortoise** (☎1-800/867-8647, ⊛www.greentortoise.com), which offers seasonal trips to sights like the redwoods, Yosemite, Mono Lake and Joshua Tree National Monument (most multi-day trips $150–500), and also runs every Sunday from June to early October between San Francisco and LA on the **Hostel Hopper** route ($42 one way).

By plane

Air travel is obviously the quickest way of getting around California, and less expensive than you may think. Airlines with a strong route structure in the state include Alaska, American, Delta, Northwest, Southwest and United. At **off-peak times**, flights between Los Angeles and San Francisco can cost as little as $65 one way, though they will require

Rail and bus passes

Amtrak Rail Passes

The two Amtrak **rail passes** that cover California are mainly useful if you're on an extended tour of the state and have plenty of time to explore your destinations.

The **USA Rail Pass** covers varying time periods; the longer the period, the more "segments" (individual train rides) you're allowed for travel within the US. For 15 days, eight segments are offered ($389); 30 days gets you 12 segments ($579); and 45 days allows 18 segments ($749). Alternatively, the **California Rail Pass** ($159) covers any seven days of travel in a 21-day window for routes such as the Pacific Surfliner and San Joaquin, or the in-state portion of national routes such as the Coast Starlight, Southwest Chief, etc. Many trains fill quickly, so it's worth making reservations well ahead.

For all information on Amtrak **fares and schedules** in the US, use the toll-free number ☎1-800/872-7245, or use the reservation facility on their website ⊛www .amtrak.com; do not phone individual stations.

Greyhound Discovery Passes

The **Greyhound Discovery Pass**, available to all, offers unlimited travel within a set time limit. A seven-day pass costs $239, fifteen days for $339, thirty days for $439, and the longest, a sixty-day pass, is $539. Order through ⊛www.discoverypass .com, or see the online list of international vendors. The first time you use your pass, the ticket clerk will date it (which becomes the commencement date of the pass), and you will receive a ticket that allows you to board the bus. Repeat this procedure for every subsequent journey. Greyhound's nationwide toll-free **information service** (☎1-800/231-2222) can give you routes and times, plus phone numbers and addresses of local terminals. You can also make reservations at the same number.

FAMOUS ATTRACTIONS
AT AMAZING PRICES

San Francisco CityPASS

Southern California CityPASS

Hollywood CityPASS

7-Day, Unlimited-Use Cable Car & Muni Transportation Passport

California Academy of Sciences

Blue & Gold Fleet Bay Cruise

Aquarium of the Bay

San Francisco Museum of Modern Art

Your choice of Exploratorium or de Young Museum & Legion of Honor

3-Day Park Hopper to Disneyland₂ Park and Disney California Adventure™ Park

Universal Studios Hollywood™

SeaWorld San Diego

Your choice of San Diego Zoo or San Diego Zoo Safari Park

2-hour Starline Movie Stars' Homes Tour

Madame Tussauds Hollywood

Red Line Behind-the-Scenes Tour

Your choice of Kodak Theatre Guided Tour or The Hollywood Museum in the Historic Max Factor Building

Only $69
A $130.30 Value
(Child 5 -12 $44)

Only $276
A $391 Value
(Child 3 -9 $229)

Only $59
A $103.90 Value
(Child 3 -11 $39)

SOLD AT THESE ATTRACTIONS • BUY IT AT THE FIRST ONE YOU VISIT

citypass.com (888) 330-5008
Pricing and programs are subject to change.

CityPASS is also available in **Atlanta Boston Chicago Houston New York Philadelphia Seattle Toronto**

booking 21 days in advance. If you're flying between other cities, such as Sacramento and San Jose or Santa Barbara and San Diego, bear in mind that a stopover at LAX or SFO may be necessary, even if it means flying twice the distance.

Cycling

In general, **cycling** is a cheap and healthy method of getting around all the big **cities**, though hilly San Francisco will test your legs. Even Los Angeles has its appeal, mostly along the beaches and in the mountains. Some cities have cycle lanes and local buses equipped to carry bikes, strapped to the outside. In **rural areas**, certainly, there's much scenic and largely level land, especially around Sacramento and the Wine Country.

Bikes can be **rented** for $20–30 a day, and $120–175 a week from most bike stores; local visitor centres will have details. Apart from the coastal fog, which tends to clear by midday, you'll encounter few **weather** problems (except perhaps sunburn), but remember that the further north you go, the lower the temperatures and the more frequent the rains become.

For **long-distance cycling**, a route avoiding the interstates – on which cycling is illegal – is essential, and it's also wise to cycle **north to south**, as the wind blows this way in the summer and can make all the difference between a pleasant trip and a journey full of acute leg aches. Be particularly careful if you're planning to cycle along Hwy-1 on the Central Coast since, besides heavy traffic, it has tight

Hitchhiking

Hitchhiking in the US is generally a **bad idea**. We do not recommend it, though it is practiced commonly enough by hikers seeking access to Sierra trailheads and in certain parts of Northern California. In Southern California, standing anywhere near a highway is an invitation to a quick death.

curves and dangerous precipices, and is prone to fog.

If you're camping as well as cycling, look out for **hiker/biker campgrounds** (around $3–5 per person per night), which are free of cars and RVs, dotted across California's state parks and beaches. Sites are allotted on a first-come, first-served basis, and all offer water and toilet facilities but seldom showers. For more information, call ☎1-800/444-7275 (⊛www.reserveamerica .com) or check with Hostelling International – USA (details on p.38), the Adventure Cycling Association (☎1-800/755-2453, ⊛www.adventurecycling.org), or the Sierra Club (see box, p.46).

Accommodation

Accommodation standards in California – as in the rest of the US – are high and costs will inevitably form a significant proportion of your budget. You can pare costs down by sleeping in hostels, though outside the main cities these are rare. Groups of two and up will find it only a little more expensive to stay in the plentiful motels and hotels, many of which will increase the rate only slightly for a third or fourth adult, reducing costs considerably. By contrast, the solo traveller will have a hard time of it: "singles" are usually double rooms at an only slightly reduced rate.

However, with the exception of the budget interstate motels, there's rarely such a thing as a set rate for a room, most applying **seasonal** and often **weekend** rates. A basic motel in a seaside or mountain resort may more than double its prices according to the season, while a big-city hotel which charges $200 per room during the week will often slash its tariff at the weekend when all the business types have gone home.

Since cheap accommodation in the cities, on the popular sections of the coast and close to the major national parks is snapped up fast, **book ahead** whenever possible. **Reservations** are only held until 5 or 6pm unless you've told the hotel you'll be arriving late.

Wherever you stay, you'll be expected to **pay in advance**, at least for the first night and perhaps for further nights too, particularly if it's **high season** – generally summer, but most likely winter in desert and ski areas. Payment can be in cash or travellers' cheques, though it's more common to give your credit card number and sign for everything when you leave.

Hotels and motels

Hotels and **motels** are essentially the same thing, although motels tend to congregate along the main approach roads to cities, around beaches and by the main road junctions in country areas. High-rise hotels predominate along the popular sections of the coast and are sometimes the only accommodation in city centres.

In general, there's a uniform standard of comfort everywhere, with all rooms featuring one or more double or queen beds, plus bathroom, cable TV, phone, fridge, a coffee-maker and maybe a microwave. The budget places will be pretty basic and possibly run down but an extra $10–15 will get you more space, modern fittings and better facilities, such as a swimming pool and/or gym. Most hotels (and the better motels) provide a **complimentary breakfast**. Sometimes this will be no more than a cup of coffee and a soggy Danish pastry, but it can also be a

Accommodation price codes

Throughout this book, **accommodation** has been price-coded according to the cost, excluding tax, of the **least expensive double room in high season**; we have given individual prices for hostel beds and campgrounds, plus a price code if double rooms are also available.

In **resort areas** you can expect places to jump into the next highest category on Friday and Saturday nights. Almost all lodging (except state- and federally run campgrounds) is subject to additional **hotel taxes**, which are generally around ten percent more than the quoted price, but may soar to twenty percent.

❶ **$60 and under** The cheapest motels in unfashionable small towns and desert areas. Also cabins at some campgrounds.

❷ **$61–80** No-frills motel rooms – with bathroom, TV, phone, coffee-maker and perhaps a pool – in an unpopular location.

❸ **$81–100** You'll get a fairly high-standard chain motel or even decent hotel or cheap B&B in desert and country areas but in resorts and cities you can expect only a basic motel or cheap hotel room, perhaps with shared bathroom.

❹ **$101–130** Mid-range chain hotels (with fitness room, hot tub and on-site restaurant) in cheaper parts of the state, and well-appointed motels (perhaps with hot tub and laundry) in more popular areas. Most of the least expensive country B&Bs start in this category.

❺ **$131–160** & ❻ **$161–200** Good-quality hotels and comfortable B&Bs everywhere except in the most expensive resort areas and cities, where standards will be lower. At the upper end you're getting into real luxury, with antique-furnished rooms, gourmet breakfasts and lavish attention to detail.

❼ **$201–250** & ❽ **$251–300** Top-quality city hotels with concierge and a range of bars and restaurants or an exclusive resort where privacy and pampering take priority. Expect extraordinary accommodation and outstanding service.

❾ **$301 and over** Services as you might expect from a place in price code 8, but in super-luxury hotels or unique locations such as a historic landmark – *The Ahwahnee* in Yosemite Valley, for example.

---

sit-down affair likely to comprise fruit, cereals, muffins and toast. In the pricier places, you may also be offered made-to-order omelettes.

Enormous roadside signs make finding cheap hotels and motels pretty simple and you'll soon become familiar with the numerous **chains**, such as Econolodge, Days Inn and Motel 6. For mid-priced options try Best Western, Howard Johnson, Travelodge and Ramada, though if you can afford to pay this much there's normally somewhere with more character to stay. When it's worth blowing a wad of cash on somewhere really atmospheric we've said as much in the Guide. Bear in mind that the most upscale establishments have all manner of services which may appear to be free but for which you'll be expected to **tip** generously in a style commensurate with the hotel's status.

Discounts and reservations

During **off-peak periods**, many motels and hotels struggle to fill their rooms and it's worth **haggling** to get a few dollars off the asking price. Staying in the same place for more than one night will bring further reductions, and motels in particular offer worthwhile discounts (usually ten percent) for seniors and members of various organizations, particularly the American Automobile Association (AAA). Members of sister motoring associations in other countries may also be entitled to such discounts. You could also pick up the many **discount coupons** which fill tourist information offices and look out for the free *Traveler Discount Guide*. Read the small print, though – what appears to be an amazingly cheap room rate sometimes turns out to be a per-person charge for two people sharing and limited to midweek.

Bed and breakfasts

Staying at a **bed and breakfast** in California is mostly a mid-range to luxury option. Typically, the bed-and-breakfast inns, as they're usually known, are restored buildings and grand houses in the smaller cities and more rural areas, although the big cities also have a few, especially San Francisco. Even the larger establishments tend to have no more than ten rooms, often without TV and phone but with plentiful flowers, stuffed cushions and a homely atmosphere. Others may just be a couple of furnished rooms in someone's home, or an entire apartment where you won't even see your host. Victorian and Romantic are dominant themes; while selecting the best in that vein, we've also gone out of our way to find those that don't conform.

While always including a huge and wholesome **breakfast** (five courses is not unheard of), prices vary greatly: anything from $80 to $300 depending on location and season. Most fall between $100 and $180 per night for a double, a little more for a whole apartment. Bear in mind, too, that they are frequently booked well in advance and even if they're not full, the cheaper rooms may already be taken.

As well as the B&Bs listed in this guide, there are hundreds more throughout the state, many of them listed on various **accommodation websites** such as B&B Travel (ⓦwww.bbtravel.com), the California Association of B&B Inns (ⓦwww.cabbi.com) and B&B Inns of North America (ⓦwww.inntravels.com).

Hostels

At an average of little over $20 per night per person (a little higher in San Francisco and at Santa Monica in LA), **hostels** are clearly the cheapest accommodation option in California other than camping. There are two main kinds of hostel-type accommodation in the US: the internationally affiliated Hostelling International – USA hostels, and a growing number of independent hostels aligned with assorted umbrella organizations.

Altogether California has around twenty **Hostelling International – USA** hostels (**HI** in accommodation reviews; ⓦwww.hiusa.org), mostly in major cities and close to popular hiking areas, including national and state parks. Most urban hostels have 24-hour access, while rural ones may have a curfew and limited daytime hours. HI hostels don't allow sleeping bags, though they provide sheets as a matter of course. Few hostels provide meals but most have **cooking** facilities. Alcohol and smoking are banned.

Dorm rates at HI hostels range from $20 to $28 for members. **Membership** is international, though people typically join in their home country (see below for contacts), which will cost the equivalent of $20–30 annually. Non-members pay an additional $3 per night for the first six nights at an HI hostel, at which point membership is granted – a cheaper option than joining upfront. Particularly if you're travelling in high season, it's advisable to make **reservations**, either by contacting the hostel directly or booking online at least 48 hours in advance. There's also the IBN booking service (ⓦwww.hihostels.com), which helps you book certain big-city and gateway hostels through your home organization. San Diego, LA and San Francisco hostels can be booked this way.

Independent hostels now number around fifty and are concentrated in the big cities. They're usually a little less expensive than their HI counterparts, and have fewer rules, but the quality is not as consistent; some can be quite poor, while others are wonderful. In popular areas, especially LA, San Francisco and San Diego, they compete fiercely for your business with airport and train station pick-ups, free breakfasts and free bike rental. There is often no curfew and, at some, a party atmosphere

CouchSurfing

An increasing number of travellers are using the web-based international hospitality network known as CouchSurfing, whereby travellers contact locals via their online profile to arrange a stay in their home. Apart from the obvious benefit of free accommodation, the scheme has been lauded as a valuable means of cultural exchange. There are thousands of hosts in California; to find out more, see ⓦwww.couchsurfing.org.

is encouraged at barbeqnes and keg parties. Their independent status may be due to a failure to measure up to the HI's strict criteria, yet often it's simply because the owners prefer not to be tied down by HI regulations.

Keep in mind that hostels are often shoestring organizations, prone to changing address or closing down altogether. Similarly, new ones appear each year; check the noticeboards of other hostels for news or consult hostel websites, particularly ⓦwww.hostels.com.

Campgrounds

California **campgrounds** range from the primitive – a flat piece of ground that may or may not have a pit toilet and water tap – to others that are more like open-air hotels, with shops, restaurants and washing facilities. In major cities, campgrounds tend to be inconveniently sited on the outskirts, if they exist at all.

When camping in national and state **parks**, as well as **national forests**, you can typically expect a large site with picnic table and fire pit, designed to accommodate up to two vehicles and six people. It is usually a short walk to an outhouse and drinking water. Note that sites fill up quickly and it's worth reserving well in advance (see below for contact details).

Campgrounds outside the parks are often less busy, and the facilities are usually marginally better; some of the more basic campgrounds in isolated areas will often be empty whatever time of year you're there.

Prices vary accordingly, ranging from nothing for the most basic plots, up to $35 a night for something comparatively luxurious, and more like $35–45 if you want to hook your RV up to electricity, water, sewage and cable TV. For comprehensive listings of these, check out ⓦwww.californiacamp grounds.org and Kampgrounds of America (ⓦwww.koa.com). Often rural campgrounds have no one in attendance (though a ranger may stop by), and if there's any charge at all you'll need to pay by posting the money in the slot provided.

Look out too for **hiker/biker** or **walk-in** campgrounds (see p.36), which, at around $5 per person per night, are much cheaper than most sites but only available if you are travelling without a motorized vehicle. For **backcountry camping**, see p.47.

Camping reservation contacts

National Forests and National Parks
☎1-877/444-6777, ⓦwww.recreation.gov
State Parks California State Parks Reservations
☎1-800/444-7275, ⓦwww.parks.ca.gov

Eating and drinking

It's not too much of an exaggeration to say that in California – its cities, at least – you can eat whatever you want, whenever you want. On every main street, a mass of restaurants, fast-food places and coffee shops vie for your business. Be warned, though, that in rural areas you might go for days finding little more than diners and cheap Mexican joints.

California's cornucopia stems largely from its being one of the most agriculturally rich parts of the country. Junk food is as common as anywhere else in the US but the state also produces its own range of high-quality produce, often organic. You'll rarely find anything that's not fresh, be it a bagel or a

spinach-in-Mornay-sauce croissant, and even fast food won't necessarily be rubbish.

California is also one of the most **health-conscious** states in the country and the supermarket shelves are chock-full of products which, if not fat-free, are low-fat, low-sodium, low-carb, zero-transfat, caffeine-free and dairy-free. The same ethic runs through the menus of most restaurants, though you needn't worry about going hungry: portions are universally huge and what you don't eat can always be "boxed up" for later consumption – no shame involved even in a high-class establishment.

Breakfast

For the price, on average $6–10, **breakfast** is the best-value and most filling meal of the day. Go to a diner, café or coffee shop, all of which serve breakfast until at least 11am, with some diners serving them all day.

The breakfasts themselves are pretty much what you'd find all over the country. **Eggs** are served in a variety of styles, usually with some form of **meat** – ham, bacon or sausages – and generally accompanied by toast or a muffin. **Waffles**, **pancakes** or **French toast** are typically consumed swamped in butter with lashings of sickly-sweet maple syrup, though you may be offered **fruit**.

Lunch and snacks

Between 11am and 3pm you should look for the excellent-value **lunchtime set menus** on offer – Chinese, Indian and Thai restaurants frequently have help-yourself buffets for $7–10, and many Japanese restaurants give you a chance to eat sushi much more cheaply ($8–12) than usual. Most Mexican restaurants are exceptionally well priced at any hour: you can get a good-sized lunch for $5–8. In Northern California, watch out for seafood restaurants selling **fish'n'chips**: the fish is breaded and then fried, and the chips are chunky chipped potatoes rather than matchstick French fries. A plateful is about $8. Look as well for **clam chowder**, a thick, creamy shellfish soup commonly served for $5–6, sometimes using a hollowed-out sourdough cottage loaf as a bowl for a dollar or so more.

As you'd expect, there's also **pizza** ($12–16 for a basic two-person pie) available from chains like *Pizza Hut*, *Round Table* and *Shakey's*, or from local, more personalized restaurants. Delis usually serve a broad range of salads from about $5, ready-cooked meals for $6–9 and a range of **sandwiches** which can be meals in themselves: huge French rolls filled with a custom-built combination of meat, cheese and vegetables.

Bagels are also everywhere, filled with anything you fancy. **Street stands** sell hot dogs, burgers, tacos or a slice of pizza for around $3–4 and most shopping malls have ethnic fast-food stalls, often pricier than their equivalent outside, but usually edible and filling. There are **Mexican** chains too, like *El Pollo Loco*, *Del Taco* and *Taco Bell*, which sell swift tacos and burritos from $1 up. And of course the burger chains are as ubiquitous here as anywhere in the US: best to seek out the few *In-n-Out* franchises if possible, with the burgers all made to order and as delicious as you'll find.

Restaurants

Even if it often seems swamped by the more fashionable regional and ethnic cuisines, traditional **American cooking** – juicy burgers, steaks, fries and salads (invariably served before the main dish) – is found all over California. Cheapest of the food chains is the California-wide *Denny's*, although you'll rarely need to spend much more than $12 for a filling feast anywhere.

By contrast, though, it's **California cuisine**, geared towards health and aesthetics, that's raved about by foodies on the West Coast – and rightly so. Restaurants serving California cuisine build their reputation by word of mouth; if you can, ask a local enthusiast for recommendations or simply follow our suggestions, especially in Berkeley, the recognized birthplace of California cuisine. Meals usually cost at least $30 per head, and often a lot more. See the *Epicurean California* colour section for a full description.

Although technically ethnic, **Mexican** food is in effect an indigenous cuisine, especially in Southern California. What's more, day or night, it's the cheapest type of food to eat: even a full dinner with a beer or margarita will be over $15 only at the more upmarket establishments. Californian Mexican food makes more use of fresh vegetables and fruit than in Mexico but the essentials are the same: lots of rice and pinto beans, often served refried (ie boiled, mashed and fried), plus chopped veg and a choice of meat. The accompanying **tortilla**, a thin maize or flour-dough pancake, comes in various forms: wrapped around the food and eaten by hand (a **burrito**); filled and folded (a **taco**); rolled, filled and baked (an enchilada); or fried flat and topped with a stack of food (a **tostada**). One of the few options for vegetarians is the **chile relleno**, a mild green pepper stuffed with cheese, dipped in egg batter and fried. Veggie burritos, filled with beans, rice, lettuce, avocado, cheese and sour cream are another option.

Other ethnic cuisines are plentiful, too. **Chinese** and **Indian** restaurants are everywhere and can often be as cheap as Mexican if you go for the buffet lunches and dinners, often less than $10. **Thai**, **Korean**, **Vietnamese** and **Indonesian** food is also available and generally fairly cheap. Moving upscale, you find **Italian**, which can be pricey once you explore specialist Italian regional cooking, and **French**, which is seldom cheap and rarely found outside the larger cities. Expect to pay $20–40 per head.

Drinking

In freeway-dominated Los Angeles, the traditional neighbourhood bar is as rare as the traditional neighbourhood. There are exceptions, but LA bars tend to be either extremely pretentious or extremely seedy, neither good for long bouts of social drinking. On the other hand, the San Francisco Bay Area is consummate boozing territory, still with a strong contingent of old-fashioned bars that are fun to spend an evening in. Elsewhere in the state you'll find the normal array of watering holes.

To buy and consume alcohol in California, you need to be 21 and bars almost always have someone at the door **checking ID**: you'll probably need to be into your thirties before getting waved through automatically. Alcohol can be bought and consumed any time between 6am and 2am, seven days a week in bars, clubs and many restaurants. Some **restaurants** only have a beer and wine licence, and many allow you to bring your own bottled wine, where the corkage fee will be $10–15. You can buy beer, wine or spirits more cheaply and easily in supermarkets, many delis and, of course, liquor stores.

American **beers** fall into two distinct categories: wonderful and tasteless. The latter are found everywhere: light, fizzy brands such as Budweiser, Miller, Coors and so on; the alternative is a fabulous range of **microbrewed beers**. Head for one of the

Winery tours

California is justly known around the country and indeed the world as a wine-producing powerhouse. You can learn a lot about California wine by taking a **winery tour** at any number of the state's boutique vintners or calling in for a tasting; many places offer these free or for $5–10, but some charge over $20 for rare vintages.

See the *Epicurean California* colour section for more on the region's celebrated wines, and where to taste them.

many listed brewpubs and you'll find handcrafted beers such as crisp pilsners, wheat beers, full-bodied ales and stouts on tap, at prices not much above those of the national brews. Bottled microbrews, like Chico's hoppy Sierra Nevada Pale Ale and the bitter San Francisco-brewed Anchor Steam Beer, are sold throughout the state, while Red Tail Ale is found throughout Northern California. Expect to pay $5 for a pint of draught beer, about the same for a bottle of imported beer.

A decent glass of **wine** in a bar or restaurant costs $6–8, a bottle $20–30 (perhaps more in LA and San Francisco). Buying from a supermarket is better still – a decent bottle can be purchased for as little as $7–8.

Cocktails are extremely popular, especially during **happy hour** (usually any time between 5pm and 7pm), when drinks may have a couple of dollars knocked off and there may be some finger food thrown in too. Varieties are innumerable, sometimes specific to a single bar or cocktail lounge, and they cost $4–15, though typically around $7–8.

Increasingly an alternative to drinking dens, **coffee shops** play a vibrant part in California's social scene and are havens of high-quality coffee far removed from the stuff served in diners and convenience stores. In larger towns and cities, cafés will boast of the quality of the roast and offer a full array of espressos, cappuccinos, lattes and the like, served straight, iced, organic or flavoured with syrups. Herbal teas and light snacks are often also on the menu.

The media

Like the rest of the country, California has a welter of media for an English- and Spanish-speaking public. The quality and level of parochialism varies but you'll never be short of a paper to read, radio channel to tune in to, or TV station to watch.

Newspapers

Every major urban centre in California has its own newspaper, from the politically obsessed *Sacramento Bee* to the Hollywood hype of the *Los Angeles Times*. You'll also be able to pick up *USA Today*, the moderate if rather toothless national daily, while such East Coast stalwarts as the *New York Times*, the *Washington Post* and the *Wall Street Journal* should be available in most towns and upscale hotels, with a slight price premium.

As in any North American town, the best place to turn for **entertainment listings** – not to mention an irreverent take on local government and politics – is one of the many freesheets available on most street corners – *LA Weekly*, *SF Weekly*, etc. Since clubs and bars open and close so frequently, they're the best source of up-to-date listings available. We've noted local titles in relevant towns throughout the text; many have online editions too.

Radio

Owned by faceless multimedia conglomerates, the majority of California's radio stations won't tell you anything particularly useful or insightful about the state – unless you're a fan of zealous political ranting, round-the-clock sports coverage or, more helpfully, traffic reports. It's best to skip most speciality stations on the AM frequency – although AM chat shows, with their often angry callers and hosts can be hilarious and illuminating, if not in the intended sense. On FM, you'll find the usual mix of rock, pop, Latin, country and hip-hop, peppered by ads. Many stations have astonishingly limited playlists – songs will often be played half a dozen times a day. You could also tune in to satellite radio, which comes with most rental cars and typically includes fewer ads.

If you're struggling to find satisfying local news, a safe harbour is **National Public Radio (NPR)**, the listener-funded talk station with a refreshingly sober take on news and chat (FM frequencies vary). To check for local frequencies for the World Service log on to the BBC (@www.bbc.co.uk /worldservice), Radio Canada (@www.rcinet .ca) or the Voice of America (@www .voanews.com).

Television

In California, you'll have access to all the usual stations: from major networks like ABC, CBS and NBC, to smaller netlets like CW and MyNetwork. Expect talk shows in the morning, soaps in the afternoon, and big-name comedies and dramas during primetime. If it's all too commercial-heavy, there's always PBS, the rather earnest, ad-free alternative, which fills its schedule with news, documentaries and imported period dramas. The precise channel numbers vary from area to area.

There's a wider choice on **cable**, including CNN and MTV, as well as the Discovery and History channels, plus **premium channels** like HBO and Showtime, which are often available on hotel TV systems, showing original series and blockbuster movies.

Festivals and public holidays

Someone is always celebrating something in California, although apart from national holidays, few festivities are shared throughout the entire state. Instead, there is a multitude of local events: art and craft shows, county fairs, ethnic celebrations, music festivals, rodeos, sandcastle-building competitions, and many others of every kind.

Among California's major annual events are the **gay and lesbian freedom** parades held in June in LA and, particularly, San Francisco (see p.142 & p.495); the **Academy Awards** in LA in early March (see p.142); and the world-class **Monterey Jazz Festival** in September (see p.417). In addition, the tourist board can provide full lists, or you can just phone the visitor centre in a particular region ahead of your arrival and ask what's coming up.

The biggest and most all-American of the national festivals and holidays is **Independence Day** on the fourth of July, when Americans commemorate the signing of the Declaration of Independence in 1776 by getting drunk, saluting the flag, and blowing things up with fireworks. **Halloween** (October 31) lacks any such patriotic overtones and is not a public holiday despite being one of the most popular yearly flings. Traditionally, kids run around the streets banging on doors and collecting pieces of candy, but in bigger cities Halloween has grown into a massive gay celebration: in West Hollywood in LA and San Francisco's Castro district, the night is marked by mass cross-dressing, huge block parties and general debauchery. More sedate is **Thanksgiving**, on the last Thursday in November, which is essentially a domestic affair, when relatives return to the familial nest to stuff themselves with roast turkey, and (supposedly) fondly recall the first harvest of Pilgrims and Native Americans in Massachusetts. **Christmas** is another family occasion and is celebrated much as it is in other countries – preceded, of course, by a commercial onslaught.

Local festivals are detailed throughout the Guide. For a detailed rundown of events in LA, see p.142; for San Francisco, see p.437.

Public holidays

On the national **public holidays** listed below, banks, government offices and many museums are likely to be closed all day. Small stores, as well as some restaurants and clubs, are usually closed as well, but shopping malls, supermarkets and department and chain stores increasingly remain open, regardless of the holiday. Most parks, beaches and cemeteries stay open during holidays, too.

Public holidays

New Year's Day Jan 1
Martin Luther King's Birthday observed third Mon in Jan
Presidents' Day third Mon in Feb
Memorial Day last Mon in May
Independence Day July 4
Labor Day first Mon in Sept
Columbus Day second Mon in Oct
Veterans Day Nov 11
Thanksgiving fourth Thurs in Nov
Christmas Dec 25

Sports and outdoor pursuits

Nowhere in the country do competitive sports have a higher profile than in California. The big cities generally have at least one team in each of the major professional sports – football, baseball and basketball – and support teams in soccer, volleyball, ice hockey, wrestling and even roller derby. And in California, where being physically fit and adventurous often appears to be a condition of state citizenship, the locals are passionate about outdoor pursuits; the most popular include hiking, surfing, cycling and skiing.

California's landscape is another enormously compelling reason to visit, with some of the most fabulous **backcountry and wilderness areas** in the US, coated by dense forests and capped by great mountains. While there are huge areas reachable only on foot, the excellent road system makes much of it easily accessible, aided by spacious and beautiful campgrounds right where you need them. Unfortunately, it isn't all as wild as it once was, and the more popular areas can get pretty crowded.

Spectator sports

For foreign visitors, American sports can appear something of a mystery; one unusual feature is that in all the major sports the divisions are fixed, apart from the occasional expansion, so there is no fear of relegation to lower leagues. Another puzzle is the passion for **intercollegiate sports** – college and university teams, competing against one another in the Pacific-10 Conference, usually with an enthusiasm fuelled by local rivalries. In Los Angeles, USC and UCLA have an intense and high-powered sporting enmity, with fans on each side as vociferous as any European soccer crowd, and in the San Francisco Bay Area, the rivalry between UC Berkeley and Stanford is akin to that of Britain's Oxford and Cambridge.

Football

Professional football in America attracts the most obsessive and devoted fans of any sport, during its short season from September until the **Super Bowl** at the end of January.

The game lasts for four fifteen-minute quarters, with a fifteen-minute break at half-time. But since time is only counted when play is in progress, matches can take at least three hours to complete, mainly due to interruptions for TV advertising.

All major teams play in the National Football League (**NFL**; Ⓦwww.nfl.com), the sport's governing body, which divides the teams into two conferences of equal stature, the National Football Conference (**NFC**) and the American Football Conference (**AFC**). In turn, each conference is split into four divisions, North, East, South and West. For the end-of-season play-offs, the best team in each of the eight divisions, plus two wildcards from each conference, fight it out for the title.

The California teams are the **Oakland Raiders**, who were the last California team to reach the Super Bowl in 2003; the **San Diego Chargers**, who have performed best in recent seasons and had the third best record in the NFL in 2009–11; and the **San Francisco 49ers**, who have recently been letting down the team's history of five Super Bowl wins.

Tickets usually cost at least $60 for professional games and can be very hard to come by, while college games can be as low as $10 and are more readily available – check at the respective campuses detailed in the Guide.

Booking tickets

Oakland Raiders ☎1-800/724-3377, Ⓦwww.raiders.com
San Diego Chargers ☎1-877/242-7437, Ⓦwww.chargers.com
San Francisco 49ers ☎1-800/746-0764, Ⓦwww.sf49ers.com

Baseball

Baseball is often called "America's pastime", though its continuing steroids scandals have somewhat tarnished its old-time image. Despite this, the sport's stars continue to earn a lot of publicity, not to mention money.

Games are played – 162 each in the regular season – almost every day from April to September, with the division and league championship play-offs, followed by the **World Series** (the best-of-seven match-up between the American and National League champions), lasting through October.

All major-league (W www.mlb.com) baseball teams play in either the **National League** or the **American League**, each of equal stature and split into three divisions: East, Central and West. For the end-of-season play-offs and the World Series, the best team in each of the six divisions plus a second-place wildcard from each league fight it out for the title. In 2010 the unfancied San Francisco Giants finally lifted the curse that had been hanging over them since they relocated from New York by winning the World Series against the Texas Rangers.

California's other major-league clubs are the **Oakland Athletics (A's)**, **Los Angeles Dodgers** and **San Diego Padres**. There are also numerous minor-league clubs, known as "farm teams" because they supply the top clubs with talent. **Tickets** cost $10–70, and are generally available on the day of the game.

Booking tickets

Los Angeles Angels of Anaheim T 1-888/796-4256, W angelsbaseball.com
Los Angeles Dodgers T 1-866/363-4377, W dodgers.com
Oakland Athletics T 1-877/493-2255, W oaklandathletics.com
San Diego Padres T 1-877/374-2784, W padres.com
San Francisco Giants T 1-877/483-4849, W sfgiants.com

Basketball

Basketball is one of the few professional sports that is also actually played by many ordinary Americans, since all you need is a ball and a hoop. The men's professional game is governed by the National Basketball Association (**NBA**; W www.nba.com), which oversees a season running from November until the play-offs in June. Games last for an exhausting 48 minutes of actual playing time, around two hours-total.

The women's professional game is run by the **WNBA** (W www.wnba.com); the season goes through the summer.

California's professional men's basketball teams consist of the **Los Angeles Lakers**, the **Golden State Warriors** (who play in Oakland), the **Sacramento Kings** and the **Los Angeles Clippers**. The Lakers are the historically most successful team and have won five of the championships since the millennium, including 2009 and 2010, while the Warriors made an unexpected run to the second round of the play-offs in 2007. LA's **UCLA** once dominated the college game, winning national championships throughout the 1960s; they emerged to win again in 1995. **USC**, **UC Berkeley** and **Stanford** also field perpetually competitive intercollegiate teams, the last being the predominant force in the Pac-10 athletic conference in recent years.

Local **women's basketball teams** are the Sparks in LA and Monarchs in Sacramento; **tickets** (beginning at about $10) are much more reasonable than the $50-plus for a decent seat at the men's game.

Tickets for NBA teams

Golden State Warriors T 1-888/479-4667, W www.nba.com/warriors
Los Angeles Clippers T 1-888/895-8662, W www.nba.com/clippers
Los Angeles Lakers T 1-800/462-2849, W www.nba.com/lakers
Sacramento Kings T 916/928-3650, W www.nba.com/kings

Tickets for WNBA teams

Los Angeles Sparks T 310/330-2434, W www.wnba.com/sparks
Sacramento Monarchs T 916/419-9622, W www.wnba.com/monarchs

Ice hockey

Despite California's sun-and-sand reputation, **ice hockey** enjoys considerable popularity in the state, although most of the players are imported from more traditionally hockey-centric regions in Canada, Eastern Europe and Scandinavia. The domestic title is the **Stanley Cup**, contested by the play-off winners of the two **NHL** (National Hockey League; @www.nhl.com) conferences (Eastern and Western).

The season runs from October to the play-offs in May and June – amazingly for such a fast and physical sport, each team plays several times a week.

California boasts three NHL teams which manage to draw considerable crowds. The **San Jose Sharks** sell out nearly every game and regularly reach the play-offs, while the **Anaheim Mighty Ducks** came from nowhere to reach the Stanley Cup final in 2003 and win it in 2007. The **Los Angeles Kings** complete the trio. **Tickets** start at about $25–30.

Booking tickets

Anaheim Mighty Ducks ☎1-877/945-3946, @www.mightyducks.com
Los Angeles Kings ☎1-888/546-4752, @www.lakings.com
San Jose Sharks ☎1-800/755-5050, @www.sj-sharks.com

Soccer

In the main, the traditional American sports rule, but **soccer** has been gaining some ground, especially as a participation sport for youngsters of both sexes. At the professional level, the successful US bid to host the 1994 World Cup led to the establishment of **Major League Soccer** (MLS; @www.mlsnet.com) in 1996, where sixteen teams are divided into two conferences. The game continues to get injections of exposure, most notably with the signing of world-famous English star David Beckham by the Los Angeles Galaxy in 2007.

The **Los Angeles Galaxy**, **San Jose Earthquakes** and Carson-based **Chivas USA** all play in the Western Conference of the MLS. The Galaxy have had some success in recent seasons, winning the MLS Cup in 2002 and 2005. They just failed to reach the 2010 final though, despite having Beckham in their ranks.

The season runs through the summer and tickets cost $15–50.

Booking tickets

Chivas USA ☎1-877/244-8271, @www.cdchivasusa.com
Los Angeles Galaxy ☎1-877/342-5299, @www.lagalaxy.com
San Jose Earthquakes ☎1-877/782-5301, @www.sjearthquakes.com

Outdoor pursuits

When and where to enjoy the most popular outdoor activities is detailed in the relevant chapters, along with listings of guides and facilities. As well as the activities below, other options include both fresh and saltwater **fishing** – it's usually easier if you have your own gear but it can be rented in some places – and **horseriding**. Prices vary more widely than for other activities, ranging from $50 to $100 for rides that might not differ all that much in length, so it's a good idea to seek out the best deals.

Hiking

California offers virtually unlimited **hiking** opportunities, from coastal trails through dense forest paths to some stunning mountain ranges that are bound to test your stamina. All you need, of course, is stout footwear and to be prepared for the possibility of some drastic changes in the weather.

No special permits are required for **day-hikes**. Simply arrive at the trailhead of your choice with the appropriate gear – map, raincoat, comfortable boots, etc – and head off into the wilderness. **Overnight trips** usually require **wilderness permits** (see box opposite), which operate on a quota system in popular areas in peak periods. If there's a specific hike you want to take, obtain your permit well ahead of time (at least two weeks, or more for popular hikes). Before completing the form for your permit, be sure to ask a park ranger for weather conditions and general information about the hike you're undertaking.

In California, the San Francisco-based grassroots environmental organization the **Sierra Club** (☎415/977-5500, @www.sierraclub.org) offers a range of backcountry hikes into otherwise barely accessible parts of the High Sierra wilderness, with food and

State and national parks

The US's protected backcountry areas fall into a number of potentially confusing categories. Most numerous are California **state parks** (W www.parks.ca.gov), which include beaches, historic parks and recreational areas, not necessarily in rural areas. Typically you pay for parking rather than entry, with daily fees usually $4–12; you are unlikely to save money by buying the **Annual Day-Use Pass** ($125) available online and at most parks.

National parks – such as Yosemite, Death Valley and Joshua Tree – generally charge entry fees of $15–20 per car (valid seven days). These are supplemented by the smaller **national monuments** (generally $5), like Devils Postpile, with just one major feature. If you plan on visiting a few of these, invest in the **America the Beautiful Annual Pass** ($80 from any national park entrance), which grants both driver and passengers (or if cycling or hiking, the holder's immediate family) twelve months' access to all the federally run parks and monuments, historic sites, recreation areas and wildlife refuges across the country.

California's eighteen **national forests** cover twenty percent of the state's surface area. Most of them border the national parks and are less tightly regulated. The federal government also operates **national recreation areas**, often huge hydro dams where you can jet-ski or windsurf free of the necessarily restrictive laws of the national parks. Campgrounds and equipment-rental outlets are always abundant. Excellent free **ranger programmes** – guided walks, video presentations and campfire talks – are held throughout the year.

All the above forms of protected land can contain **wilderness areas**, which aim to protect natural resources in their most native state. In practice, this means there's no commercial activity at all; buildings, motorized vehicles and bicycles are not permitted, nor are firearms or pets. Overnight camping is allowed, but **wilderness permits** (usually free) must be obtained from the land management agency responsible. In California, Lava Beds, Lassen, Death Valley, Sequoia and Kings Canyon, Joshua Tree, Pinnacles, Point Reyes and Yosemite all have large wilderness areas – 94 percent of Yosemite, for example – with only the regions near roads, visitor centres and buildings designated as less stringently regulated "front country".

guide provided. The tours are mostly in the summer, and are heavily subscribed, making it essential to book at least three months in advance: check the website for availability and to make reservations. You can expect to pay around $700 for seven days and will also have to pay $39 to join the club.

Hikes covered in the Guide are given with length and estimated walking time for a healthy, but not especially fit, adult. State parks have graded trails designed for people who drive to the corner store, so anyone used to walking and with a moderate degree of fitness will find their ratings conservative.

Backcountry camping

When **camping rough**, check that fires are permitted before you start one; in times of high fire danger, campfire permits (available free from park rangers) may be necessary even for cooking stoves. Stoves are preferable to using local materials, since in some places firewood is scarce, although you may be allowed to use deadwood. No open fires are allowed in wilderness areas, where you should also try to camp on previously used sites. Where there are no toilets, **bury human waste** at least four inches into the ground and a hundred feet from the nearest water supply and camp. Always **pack out what you pack in** (or more if you come across some inconsiderate soul's litter), and avoid the old advice to burn rubbish; wildfires have been started in this way. **Water** should be boiled for at least five minutes, or cleansed with an iodine-based purifier (such as Potable Aqua) or a giardia-rated filter, available from camping and sports shops.

Finally, don't use **soaps or detergents** (even special ecological or biodegradable soaps) anywhere near lakes and streams; people using water purifiers or filters downstream won't thank you at all. Instead carry water at least a hundred feet (preferably two hundred) from the water's edge before washing.

For more information on camping logistics, see p.39.

Equipment

Choose your tent wisely. Many Sierra sites are on rock with only a thin covering of soil, so driving pegs in can be a problem; freestanding dome-style tents are therefore

Outdoor dangers and wildlife

You'll probably meet many kinds of **wildlife** and come upon unexpected **hazards** on your travels through non-urban California, but only a few are likely to cause problems. For more on California wildlife in general, see p.696 of Contexts.

Acute Mountain Sickness With much of the High Sierra above ten thousand feet, altitude sickness is always a possibility. Only those planning to bag one of the 14,000-foot peaks are likely to suffer much more than a slight headache, but it pays to **acclimatize** slowly. Limit your exertions for the first day, drink plenty of fluids, eat little and often, and note any nausea, headaches or double vision.

Bears Bear encounters are rare, and virtually unknown outside national parks and forests. If you do meet one, it will be a black bear – the last California grizzly was shot in 1922. To reduce the likelihood of an unwanted encounter, make noise as you walk. If you see a bear before it detects you (they've got fairly poor eyesight but an acute sense of smell), give it a wide berth; but if a bear visits your camp, scare it off by yelling and banging pots and pans. The bear isn't interested in you but in your food, and you should do everything you safely can to prevent them from getting it – bears who successfully raid campsites can become dependent on human food and will be shot. Campgrounds in areas where bears are common come equipped with steel **bear lockers** for storing food when not preparing or eating it. In the backcountry, you are increasingly required to store food within a hard plastic **bear-resistant food canister**. These can be purchased ($50–80) or rented (usually $5 per trip) from camp stores in Yosemite and Sequoia and Kings Canyon national parks. Hanging or counterbalancing food in a tree is a disaster, as Sierra bears either chew through the supporting rope or even send a cub along a branch. And finding a suitable tree after a long day's hike is tricky. Finally, never feed a bear or get between a mother and her cubs. Cubs are cute; irate mothers are not.

Cacti Keep an eye out for the eight-foot **cholla** (pronounced "choy-uh"), or "jumping cholla", because of the way segments seem to jump off and attach themselves to you if you brush past. Don't use your hands to get them off – you'll just spear all your fingers. Instead, use a stick or comb to flick off the largest piece and remove the remaining spines with tweezers. The large pancake pads of prickly pear cactus are also worth avoiding: in addition to the larger spines, they have thousands of tiny, hair-like stickers that are almost impossible to remove. You should expect a day of painful irritation before they begin to wear away. For more on desert flora and fauna, see p.702.

Campground critters Ground squirrels, chipmunks and raccoons are usually just a nuisance, though they carry diseases and you should avoid contact. Only the **alpine marmot** is a real pest, as it likes to chew through radiator hoses and car electrics to reach a warm engine on a cold night. Before setting off in the morning from high-country trailheads, check under the hood for gnawed components; boots and rucksacks also can fall prey to marmot scrutiny.

Drowning Fast-flowing meltwater rivers are the single biggest cause of death in Kings Canyon and are a danger elsewhere in the Sierra Nevada. The riverbanks are preferable. Go for one with a large area of mosquito netting and a removable flysheet: tents designed for harsh European winters can get horribly sweaty once the California sun rises. In fact, travelling in summer you may seldom use a flysheet, as it rarely rains and little dew settles in the night.

Most developed campgrounds are equipped with fire rings with some form of grill for cooking, but many people prefer a **Coleman stove**, powered by white gas (a kind of super-clean gasoline). Both stoves and white gas (also used for MSR backcountry stoves) are widely available in camping stores. Other camping stoves are less common.

strewn with large, slippery boulders – keep well clear unless you are specifically there for river activities.

Giardia This water-borne protozoan causes an intestinal disease, symptoms of which are chronic diarrhoea, abdominal cramps, fatigue and loss of weight. To avoid catching it, never drink directly from rivers and streams, no matter how clear and inviting they may look (you never know what unspeakable acts people – or animals – further upstream have performed in them).

Mosquitoes Common around water, these insects are more pesky than dangerous. Cover up around dusk and carry insect repellent or candles scented with citronella to keep them at bay.

Mountain lions Count yourself lucky if you see one of these magnificent beasts (also known as cougars, panthers and pumas), as they are being hard hit by urban expansion into former habitats (from deserts to coastal and subalpine forests). Avoid walking by yourself, especially after dark, when lions tend to hunt. Make noise as you walk, wield a stick, and keep children close to you. If you encounter one, **don't run**. Instead, face the lion and make yourself appear larger by raising your arms or holding your coat above you, and it will probably back away. If not, throw rocks and sticks in its vicinity. If it attacks, fight back. Its normal prey doesn't do this and it will probably flee.

Poison oak Recognized by its shiny configuration of three dark-green-veined leaves (turning red or yellow in the autumn) that secrete an oily juice, this twiggy shrub or climbing vine is found in open woods or along stream banks throughout much of California. It's highly **allergenic**, so avoid touching it. If you do, washing with strong soap usually helps, though you are better off applying an oil-removal product such as Tecnu as soon after contact as possible. In extreme cases, see a doctor.

Rattlesnakes In the desert areas and drier foothills up to around 6000ft you may come across rattlesnakes, which seldom attack unless provoked: do not tease or try to handle them. When it's hot, snakes lurk in shaded areas under bushes and around wood debris, old mining shafts and piles of rocks. When it's cooler, they sun themselves out in the open, but they won't be expecting you and, if disturbed, may attack. When hiking, you'll be far better served by **strong boots** and long trousers than sandals and shorts. Not only do they offer some protection in case of attack, but firm footfalls send vibrations through the ground, giving ample warning of your approach. Walk heavily and you're unlikely to see anything you don't want to.

Rattlesnake **bites** are rarely fatal, but you might suffer severe tissue damage. If bitten, try to remain calm and still, keep the bitten limb below the heart and send someone for medical help. Do not tourniquet, cut or suck the bitten area.

Scorpions They're generally non-aggressive, but they are extremely venomous and easily disturbed.

Ticks When hiking in the foothills you should periodically check your clothes for ticks – pesky, bloodsucking, burrowing insects that are known to carry Lyme disease. If you have been bitten, and especially if you get flu-like symptoms, get advice from a park ranger.

Equipment using butane and propane – Camping Gaz and, to a lesser extent, EPI gas, Scorpion and Optimus – is often unavailable outside of major camping areas: stock up when you can. If you need methylated spirits for your Trangia, go to a hardware store and ask for denatured alcohol.

Airlines often have a complete ban on transporting fuel and gas canisters, and are extremely reluctant to transport stoves. Liquid fuel bottles and fuel pumps for MSR and similar stoves (even if empty, washed out and virtually odourless) are routinely confiscated at check-in, so fly-in visitors are better off bringing a gas burner and buying canisters once they arrive.

Watersports

Surfing is probably the best-known California pastime, immortalized in the songs of the Beach Boys. The California coast up to a little north of San Francisco, especially the southern half, is dotted with excellent surfing beaches. Some of the finest places to catch a wave, with or without a board, are at Tourmaline Beach near San Diego, Huntington Beach and Malibu in Los Angeles, along the coast north of Santa Barbara and at Santa Cruz – where there's a small but worthy surfing museum. See the *Exploring the outdoors* colour section for more. **Windsurfing** is more commonly practiced on lakes and protected inland lagoons, as the ocean is usually too rough, and again there are plenty of places to rent a board or get lessons.

California also has some of the world's best **rafting** rivers, most of which cascade off the western side of the Sierra Nevada. The majority are highly seasonal, normally rafted from mid-April to the end of June. Rivers and rapids are classed according to a grading system, ranging from a Class I, which is designed to be easy, to a Class VI, which is dicing with death. Trips can be as short as a couple of hours, taking in the best a river has to offer (or just the most accessible section), or extend up to several days, allowing more time to hike up side canyons, swim or just laze about on the bank. You might expect to pay around $90 for a four- to six-hour trip, up to $160–200 a day for longer outings, including food and camping equipment

rental. **Kayaking** is another popular water-based activity, both on the many rivers and, increasingly, in the ocean. Equipment rental starts at around $20 per hour, and can exceed $70 for longer, guided day-trips.

Cycling

Cycling is an extremely popular outdoor activity, with California home to some highly competitive, world-class road races, particularly around the Wine Country. The heavy-duty, all-terrain **mountain bike** was invented in Marin County, designed to tackle the slopes of Mount Tamalpais, and there are now countless trails that weave throughout California's beautiful backcountry. Special mountain-bike parks, most operating in summer only, exploit the groomed, snow-free runs of the Sierra ski bowls of Lake Tahoe and Mammoth. In such places, and throughout California, you can rent bikes for $25–50 a day. See p.35 for more on general cycling.

Winter sports

Skiing and **snowboarding** are also wildly popular, with downhill resorts all over eastern California – where it snows heavily most winters. In fact, the Sierra Nevada Mountains offer some of the best skiing in the US, particularly around Lake Tahoe (see p.582), where the 1960 Winter Olympics were held. You can rent equipment for about $30–40 a day, plus another $40 to $70 a day for lift tickets. A cheaper option is **cross-country skiing**, or ski-touring. A number of backcountry ski lodges in the Sierra Nevada offer a range of rustic accommodation, equipment rental and lessons, from as little as $20 a day for skis, boots and poles, up to about $200 for an all-inclusive weekend tour.

Mountaineering

During the summer months, when the snows have melted and laid bare the crags of California's peaks, there is also a thriving **mountaineering** community, especially around Mount Shasta in the far north and in parts of the High Sierras. If you are not very experienced and do not have your own equipment, you can hire just about anything you might possibly need and get expert advice, lessons or a guided expedition.

Shopping

Not surprisingly, the richest state in the land of rampant consumerism is something of a shopper's paradise and, especially in the two major metropolises, you'll be able to find just about anything your heart may desire. That said, California cannot really boast a wealth of intrinsically Californian souvenirs to take home, beyond the obvious mini Golden Gate Bridges and ironic LA snowglobes found in the tackier tourist shops. Details of specific shopping locations are given in the relevant Guide chapters.

Remember that a **sales tax** is added to virtually everything you buy except for groceries and prescription drugs; it is seldom included in the quoted price. The base rate starts around 8 percent but can escalate nearly up to 10 percent, especially in Southern California.

Malls

Visitors to California, especially on their first visit to the US, cannot fail to be impressed by the ubiquitousness of the ultimate American shopping venue, the mall. Whether these are of the **"strip mall"** variety, strung out along major arteries on the edges of most towns, or showpiece complexes in desirable neighbourhoods, they unabashedly glorify commercialism and consist mostly of well-known multinational chains. The summit of consumer excess is Rodeo Drive in Beverly Hills, where the Hollywood stars go to shop. Many chic designers have flagship boutiques on the strip, and appointment-only menswear merchant Bijan, at no. 420, claims to be the most expensive shop in the world, with the average suit costing $50,000.

Arts and crafts

California is home to many **artists** and their paintings, sculptures and other creations can easily be found, both in big-city galleries and in smaller communities with a reputation for creativity, such as Mendocino. Being original artworks, these will set you back a fair amount, maybe even thousands of dollars, depending on how established the artist is. Quaint gift shops selling attractive items from all over the world also abound

and are a good source of souvenirs and presents, even if they are not specifically local. Some places, such as the Gold Country towns and Redwood Country, do offer more indigenous goods, as do the few Native American reservations.

Books and music

There is a strong intellectual tradition in the state, which shows in its manifold quality **bookshops**. The most famous browsing territory is around UC Berkeley but all the large cities and quite a few small towns offer lots of reading material. Likewise, the state that spawned psychedelia and other musical trends is rich in **music shops**, both for listening material and quality instruments. The three branches of Amoeba Records in Berkeley, San Francisco and LA are among the biggest and best in the world. Areas strong on books and music also tend to inspire related alternative shopping possibilities, with anti-establishment and political T-shirts, posters and so on readily available.

Food and drink

One fine tradition that has survived since more rustic times is the **farmers' market**, examples of which pop up regularly in the metropolitan areas, as well as in the state's smaller towns. It can come as a pleasant surprise to stumble on a street full of stalls selling fresh country fare in the middle of Downtown Oakland, for example. Most concentrate solely on consumable goods but the larger ones may have a few gift stalls as well.

California's famous **wineries** are not only great for tastings (see pp.606–613) – you

Clothing and shoe sizes

Women's dresses and skirts

American	4	6	8	10	12	14	16	18
British	8	10	12	14	16	18	20	22
Continental	38	40	42	44	46	48	50	52

Women's blouses and sweaters

American	6	8	10	12	14	16	18
British	30	32	34	36	38	40	42
Continental	40	42	44	46	48	50	52

Women's shoes

American	5	6	7	8	9	10	11
British	3	4	5	6	7	8	9
Continental	36	37	38	39	40	41	42

Men's suits

American	34	36	38	40	42	44	46	48
British	34	36	38	40	42	44	46	48
Continental	44	46	48	50	52	54	56	58

Men's shirts

American	14	15	15.5	16	16.5	17	17.5	18
British	14	15	15.5	16	16.5	17	17.5	18
Continental	36	38	39	41	42	43	44	45

Men's shoes

American	7	7.5	8	8.5	9.5	10	10.5	11	11.5
British	6	7	7.5	8	9	9.5	10	11	12
Continental	39	40	41	42	43	44	44	45	46

can also take away a couple of bottles for a special occasion or even get a case shipped interstate or abroad, though complicated laws mean not all companies are allowed to do so. Meanwhile, other seasonal and speciality **produce** proliferates in certain locales, such as olives in Corning and artichokes in Moss Landing.

Travel essentials

Costs

California is one of the pricier US states in which to travel. While car rental, gas, clothes and consumer goods are usually cheaper than in Western Europe and Australasia, the benefit is often less than it seems once you've factored in the additional **sales and hotel tax** (see box, p.51 & p.37) or added the cost of rental-car insurance. Eating and drinking seem a bargain (and fast-food joints are), but in more upscale establishments you'll be adding close to 25 percent to your expected total to cover taxes and **tips** (see p.54).

For museums and similar attractions, the prices we quote are generally for adults; you can assume that **children** (typically aged from 5 to 12 or 14) get in for half or up to three-quarters of the adult fee. Generally youth and **student cards** are of little benefit; take it if you have one, but don't make any special effort to get one.

Daily costs vary enormously, and the following estimates are per person for two people travelling together. If you are on a tight budget, using public transport, camping or staying in hostels, and cooking most of your own meals, you could scrape by on $50 a day. A couple renting a car, staying in budget motels, and eating out a fair bit are looking at more like $100 per person. Step up to comfortable B&Bs, nicer restaurants and a few whale-watching trips and shows, and you can easily find yourself spending $250 a day.

Crime and personal safety

Though California isn't trouble-free, you're unlikely to have any run-ins if you stick to the tourist-friendly confines of the major cities, or most rural areas. The lawless reputation of Los Angeles is far in excess of the truth; at night, though, a few areas – notably Compton, Inglewood and East LA – are off-limits. San Francisco, too, has its pockets of crime and decay, especially around the South of Market area. But by being careful, planning ahead and taking care of your possessions, you should be able to avoid any problems.

Foreign visitors should carry some form of **photo ID** – preferably a passport – at all times. For US residents, other photo ID such as a driver's licence will suffice.

Mugging and theft

If you're unlucky enough to get mugged, just hand over your money; resistance is generally not a good idea. After the crime occurs, report it immediately to the police at ☏911 so you can later attempt to recover your loss from an insurance provider – unlikely, but worth a try. One prime spot to be mugged is at an ATM outside the tourist areas, where you may be told to make the maximum withdrawal and hand it over. Needless to say, you should treat ATM use with the strictest caution and not worry about looking paranoid.

Also, keep a record of the numbers of your **travellers' cheques** separately from the actual cheques; if you lose them, ring the issuing company. They'll ask you for the cheque numbers, the place you bought them, when and how you lost them, and whether it's been reported to the police. All being well, you should get the missing cheques reissued within a couple of days.

If your **passport** is stolen (or if you lose it), call your country's consulate (see p.55) and pick up or have sent to you an application form, which you must submit with a notarized photocopy of your ID and a reissuing fee, often at least $30.

Though crimes committed against tourists driving **rental cars** are rare, you should still exercise common sense. Keep doors locked and hide valuables out of sight, either in the boot (trunk) or the glove compartment, and leave any valuables you don't need for your journey back in your hotel safe.

Breaking the law

Aside from speeding or parking violations, one of the most common ways visitors accidentally break the law is through **jaywalking**, or crossing the road against red lights or away from intersections. Fines can be stiff, and the police will definitely not take sympathy on you if you mumble that you "didn't think it was illegal".

Alcohol laws provide another source of irritation to visitors, particularly as the law prohibits drinking spirits, wine or beer in most public spaces like parks and beaches, and, most frustrating of all to European tourists, alcohol is officially off-limits to anyone under 21. Some try to get around this with a phony driver's licence, even though getting caught with a **fake ID** will put you in jeopardy, particularly if you're from out of the country. Driving under the influence, or **drink driving**, is aggressively punished throughout the state, with loss of licence, fines and potential jail time for those caught failing the Breathalyzer test. The current limit is a blood-alcohol level of .08, or three drinks within a single hour for a 150-pound person.

Some locals chance **marijuana possession** for amounts under an ounce, though it can get foreign visitors thrown out of the country – or into jail for larger amounts or for any other narcotics.

Other infringements include **insulting a police officer** (ie arguing with one) and **riding a bicycle at night** without proper lights and reflectors.

Culture and etiquette

One point of eternal discussion is **tipping**. Many workers in service industries get paid very little and rely on tips to bolster their income. Unless you've had abominable service (in which case you should tell the management), you really shouldn't leave a bar or restaurant without leaving a tip of at least **fifteen percent**, and about the same should be added to taxi fares. A hotel porter deserves roughly $1 for each bag carried to your room; a coat-check clerk should receive the same per coat. When paying by credit card you're expected to add the tip to the total bill before filling in the amount and signing.

Smoking is a much frowned upon activity in California, which has banned it in all indoor public places, including bars and restaurants, and some cities have even banned it on beaches and in outdoor spaces. In fact, you can spend weeks in the state barely ever smelling cigarette smoke. Nevertheless, cigarettes are sold in virtually any food shop, drugstore and bar, and also from the occasional vending machine.

Electricity

The US operates on 110V at 60Hz and uses two-pronged plugs with the flat prongs parallel. Foreign devices will need both a plug adapter and a transformer, though laptops and phone chargers usually automatically detect and cope with the different voltage and frequency.

Entry requirements

Basic requirements for entry to the US are detailed (and should be frequently checked for updates) on the US State Department website ⓦtravel.state.gov.

Under the Visa Waiver Program (VWP), if you're a citizen of the UK or most other European states, Australia, New Zealand, Japan, or other selected countries (36 in all), and visiting the US for less than ninety days, at a minimum you'll need an onward or return ticket, a visa waiver form, and a Machine Readable Passport (MRP). The **I-94W Nonimmigrant Visa Waiver Arrival/Departure Form** can be provided by your travel agency or embassy, or you can get the form online at the US Customs website, ⓦwww.cbp.gov. The same form covers entry across the US borders with Canada and Mexico (for non-Canadian and non-Mexican citizens). Under no circumstances are visitors who have been admitted under the Visa Waiver Program allowed to extend their stays beyond ninety days. If you're in the Visa Waiver Program and intend to work, study or stay in the country for more than ninety days, you must apply for a **regular visa** through your local US embassy or consulate.

Canadian citizens should have their passports on them when entering the country. If you're planning to stay for more than ninety days you'll need a **visa**. Without the proper paperwork, Canadians are barred from working in the US.

Citizens of all other countries should contact their local US embassy or consulate for details of current entry requirements, as they are often required to have both a valid passport and a nonimmigrant visitor's visa, and additional information may be required, depending on the home country and its current relationship with the US government.

For further information or to get a **visa extension** before your time is up, contact the nearest US Citizenship and Immigration Service office, whose address will be at the front of the phone book under the Federal Government Offices listings. You can also contact the National Customer Service Center at ℡1-800/375-5283 or ⓦwww .uscis.gov/contact_us.

US Customs

Upon your entry to the US, Customs officers will relieve you of your customs declaration form, which you receive on incoming planes, on ferries and at border crossing points. It asks if you're carrying any fresh foods and if you've visited a farm in the last month.

As well as food and anything agricultural, it's prohibited to carry into the country any articles from such places as North Korea, Iran, Syria or Cuba, as well as obvious no-nos like protected wildlife species and ancient artefacts. Anyone caught sneaking drugs into the country will not only face prosecution but be entered in the records as an undesirable and probably denied entry for all time. For **duty-free allowances** and other information regarding Customs, call ℡202/354-1000 or visit ⓦwww .customs.gov.

US embassies and consulates abroad

Australia

Canberra (embassy) 21 Moonah Place, Yarralumla ACT 2600 ℡02/6214 5600, ⓦcanberra .usembassy.gov
Melbourne 553 St Kilda Rd, VIC 3004 ℡03/9526 5900
Perth 16 St George's Terrace, 13th Floor, WA 6000 ℡08/9202 1224
Sydney MLC Centre, Level 10, 19–29 Martin Place, NSW 2000 ℡02/9373 9200

Canada

Ottawa (embassy) 490 Sussex Drive, ON K1N 1G8 ℡613/238-5335, ⓦcanada.usembassy.gov
Calgary 615 Macleod Trail SE, Room 1000, AB T2G 4T8 ℡403/266-8962
Halifax Wharf Tower II, 1969 Upper Water St, Suite 904, NS B3J 3R7 ℡902/429-2480
Montréal 1155 St Alexandre St, QC H3B 1Z1 ℡514/398-9695, ⓦmontreal.usconsulate.gov
Québec City 2 Place Terrasse Dufferin, QC G1R 4T9 ℡418/692-2095, ⓦquebec.usconsulate.gov
Toronto 360 University Ave, ON M5G 1S4 ℡416/595-1700, ⓦtoronto.usconsulate.gov
Vancouver 1095 W Pender St, 21st Floor, BC V6E 2M6 ℡604/685-4311, ⓦvancouver .usconsulate.gov
Winnipeg 201 Portage Ave, Suite 860, MB R3B 3K6 ℡204/940-1800, ⓦwinnipeg.usconsulate.gov

Ireland

Dublin (embassy) 42 Elgin Rd, Ballsbridge 4 ℡01/668 8777, ⓦdublin.usembassy.gov

New Zealand

Wellington (embassy) 29 Fitzherbert Terrace, Thorndon ℡04/462 6000, ⓦnewzealand .usembassy.gov
Auckland 3rd Floor, Citibank Building, 23 Customs St ℡09/303 2724

South Africa

Pretoria (embassy) 877 Pretorius St 0083 ℡12/431 4000, ⓦsouthafrica.usembassy.gov

UK

London (embassy) 24 Grosvenor Square, W1A 1AE ℡020/7499 9000, visa hotline ℡09042/450 100, ⓦlondon.usembassy.gov
Belfast Danesfort House, 223 Stranmillis Rd, Belfast BT9 5GR ℡028/9038 6100
Edinburgh 3 Regent Terrace, EH7 5BW ℡0131/556 8315

Consulates in California

Australia

Los Angeles 2049 Century Park E, 31st Floor, CA 90067 ℡310/229-4800, ⓦwww.dfat.gov .au/missions
San Francisco 575 Market St, Suite 1800, CA 94105-2815 ℡415/536-1970

Canada

Los Angeles 550 S Hope St, 9th Floor, CA 90071-2627 ℡213/346-2700, ⓦwww.dfait-maeci.gc.ca

San Diego 402 W Broadway, 4th Floor, CA 92101 ⊤619/615-4287
San Francisco 580 California St, 14th Floor, CA 94104 ⊤415/834-3180

South Africa

Los Angeles 6300 Wilshire Blvd, Suite 600, CA 90048 ⊤323/651-0902, ⓕ323/651-5969, ⓦwww.link2southafrica.com

UK

Los Angeles 11766 Wilshire Blvd, Suite 1200, CA 90025 ⊤310/481-0031, ⓦwww.britainusa .com/la
San Francisco 1 Sansome St, Suite 850, CA 94101 ⊤415/617-1300, ⓦwww.britainusa.com/sf

Gay and lesbian travellers

California's easy-going attitude is evident in its vibrant gay and lesbian scene. The heart of gay California (and perhaps of gay America) is San Francisco, which has been almost synonymous with gay life since World War II, when suspected homosexuals, purged by the military at their point of embarkation, stayed put rather than going home to face stigma and shame. This, and the advent of gay liberation in the early 1970s, nurtured a community with powerful political and social connections.

San Francisco's gay, lesbian, bisexual and transgender scene is easy to find (see p.494), but there are also strong communities in Los Angeles (see p.156; centred in **West Hollywood)**, **Palm Springs** and **Santa Cruz** (see p.428). Be aware, though, that outside major urban centres and particularly in the deserts of interior California, attitudes may be more conservative and openness about your sexuality may provoke hostility in locals.

Health

Foreign travellers should be comforted that if you have a serious accident while you're in California, emergency services will get to you sooner and charge you later. For an **ambulance**, dial toll-free ⊤911 from any phone. If you need urgent medical attention but are able to get to the hospital without an ambulance, head for the hospital's walk-in emergency room. For your nearest hospital or dental office, check with your hotel or dial information at ⊤411.

Should you need to see a **doctor**, lists can be found in the *Yellow Pages* or on the web under "Clinics" or "Physicians and Surgeons". Be aware that even consultations are costly, usually around $100 each visit, payable in advance. Keep receipts for any part of your medical treatment, including prescriptions, so that you can claim against your insurance once you're home.

For minor ailments, stop by a local **pharmacy**. Foreign visitors should note that many medicines available over the counter at home – codeine-based painkillers, for one – are **prescription-only** in the US. Bring additional supplies if you're particularly brand-loyal.

By far the most common tourist illness in California is **sunburn**: south of Santa Barbara and in the state's interior, the summer sun can be fierce, so plenty of protective sunscreen (SPF 30) is a must. Surfers and swimmers should also watch for strong currents and **undertows** at some beaches: we've noted in the text where the water can be especially treacherous. Note that despite the media's frenzied circling around stories of **sharks**, these are extremely rare.

Insurance

The US has no national healthcare system and, while major healthcare legislation passed in 2010, this won't be enforced for many years, and the law itself is a bit of a patchwork. All foreign visitors would do well to take out an **insurance** policy before travelling to cover against theft, loss and illness or injury. Before paying for a new policy, however, it's worth checking whether you are already covered – some all-risks home insurance policies may cover your possessions when overseas, and many private medical schemes include coverage abroad.

After exhausting the possibilities above, you might want to contact a **specialist travel insurance** company. A typical travel insurance policy usually provides cover for the loss of baggage, tickets, and – up to a certain limit – cash or cheques, as well as cancellation or curtailment of your journey.

Rough Guides travel insurance

Rough Guides has teamed up with WorldNomads.com to offer great **travel insurance** deals. Policies are available to residents of over 150 countries, with cover for a wide range of **adventure sports**, 24hr emergency assistance, high levels of medical and evacuation cover and a stream of **travel safety information**. Roughguides.com users can take advantage of their policies online 24/7, from anywhere in the world – even if you're already travelling. And since plans often change when you're on the road, you can extend your policy and even claim online. Roughguides.com users who buy travel insurance with WorldNomads.com can also leave a positive footprint and donate to a community development project. For more information go to ⊛**www.roughguides.com/shop**.

Most of them exclude so-called dangerous sports unless an extra premium is paid: in America, this can mean scuba diving, white-water rafting and windsurfing. Many policies can be changed to exclude coverage you don't need – for example, sickness and accident benefits can often be excluded or included at will. If you do take medical coverage, ascertain whether benefits will be paid as treatment proceeds or only after return home, and if there is a 24-hour medical emergency number. When securing **baggage coverage**, make sure that the per-article limit – typically under £500 – will cover your most valuable possession. If you need to make a claim, you should keep receipts for medicines and medical treatment, and in the event you have anything stolen, you must obtain an official theft report from the police.

Internet

The spread of **wireless hotspots** all over the state means anyone travelling with a laptop or PDA enabled for wi-fi should have no trouble getting connected, often at fast speeds. At some cafés you'll need to use your credit card to sign up for a service, though many other cafés have unsecured access or will give you the password when you buy a coffee or muffin. Many libraries have free wi-fi and internet terminals, as do lots of motels and restaurants. With the advent of wireless, the former **internet cafés** (with a dozen or more machines usually charged at around $5 an hour) have largely been superseded.

⊛www.kropla.com gives details of how to enable your laptop for wireless use when abroad.

Laundry

The larger hotels provide a laundry service at a price. Cheaper motels and hostels may have self-service laundry facilities, but in general you'll be doing your laundry at a **laundromat**. Found all over the place, they're usually open fairly long hours and have a powder-dispensing machine and another to provide change. A typical wash and dry costs $4–6.

Mail

Post offices are usually open Monday to Friday from 9am to 5pm (with larger branches also open Saturday from 9am–1pm), and there are blue **mailboxes** on many street corners. **Ordinary mail** within the US costs 44¢ for letters weighing up to an ounce; addresses must include the **zip code**, which can be found at ⊛www .usps.com. The return address should be written in the upper left corner of the envelope. **Airmail** from California to Europe generally takes about a week. Postcards cost 28¢ or 44¢, depending on size.

Letters can be sent c/o **General Delivery** (what's known elsewhere as **poste restante**) to the one relevant post office in each city, but must include the zip code and will only be held for thirty days before being returned to sender – so make sure there's a return address on the envelope. If you're receiving mail at someone else's address, it should include "c/o" and the regular occupant's name, or it may be returned.

Rules on sending **parcels** are very rigid: packages must be sealed according to the instructions given at ⊛www.usps.com. To send anything out of the country, you'll need a green **customs declaration form**, available from the post office. Postal rates for airmailing a parcel weighing up to 1lb to Europe, Australia and New Zealand are $15–18.

Maps

Rough Guides produce an excellent double-sided, rip-proof map of California, which has all the sights and most useful campgrounds marked. With that, the maps in this book, and free maps supplied by local tourist offices, you can't go far wrong.

Rand McNally produces good low-cost foldout maps of the state, and its *Road Atlas* covers the whole country plus Mexico and Canada, and is a worthwhile investment if you're travelling further afield. For **driving or cycling** through rural areas, the *California Atlas & Gazetteer* (published by DeLorme) and *Benchmark California Road and Recreation Atlas* are valuable companions, with detailed city plans, marked campgrounds, and national park and forest information.

The **American Automobile Association** (Ⓦwww.aaa-calif.com) has offices in most large cities and provides excellent free maps and travel assistance to its members, and members, of affiliated organizations elsewhere.

Hikers should visit ranger stations in parks and wilderness areas, which sell good-quality local topographic maps for around $6–10. Camping stores generally have a good selection, too. The *National Geographic/Trails Illustrated* topographic maps are particularly good and cover such destinations as Sequoia and Kings Canyon, Yosemite, Death Valley and Joshua Tree national parks, and Santa Monica Mountains National Recreation Area.

Money

US banknotes ($1, $5, $10, $20, $50 and $100) are all the same size so be sure to check what you are handing over. All bills except the dollar have been revamped in recent years with colour-shifting inks, watermarks and other security features to foil counterfeiters. The dollar is made up of 100 cents with coins of 1 cent (known as a penny, and regarded as worthless), 5 cents (a nickel), 10 cents (a dime) and 25 cents (a quarter). Quarters are very useful for buses, vending machines, parking meters and telephones, so always carry plenty. For current **exchange rates**, see Ⓦwww .xe.com.

If you don't already have a **credit card**, you should think seriously about getting one before you set off. For many services, it's simply taken for granted that you'll be paying with plastic. When renting a car (or even a bike) or checking into a hotel, you may well be asked to show a credit card to establish your credit worthiness – even if you intend to settle the bill in cash. **Visa** and **MasterCard** are the most widely used, and **Diners Club**, **American Express** and **Discover** less so. When paying with a credit card, you'll sometimes be required to show supporting photo ID, so be sure to carry your driver's licence or passport.

It is worth carrying a second major credit card as a backup, but you may feel more comfortable with a wad of **US dollar travellers' cheques**, which will be replaced if lost or stolen. You should have no problem using the better-known cheques, such as those from American Express and Visa, in the same way as cash in shops, restaurants and gas stations. Be sure to have plenty of the $10 and $20 denominations for everyday transactions, and don't be put off by "no checks" signs, which usually refer to personal cheques.

With cards and travellers' cheques, you may never need to visit **banks**, which are generally open from 9am until 5pm Monday to Thursday and 9am to 6pm on Friday, and sometimes on Saturday morning. Some banks in major towns will change major **foreign currency**, but it is far better to buy US dollars before you arrive. Credit card **cash advances** and debit card withdrawals are easy at abundant **ATMs**, though there is sometimes a transaction fee of $2–4.

Opening hours

Public holidays (see p.43) may shut down certain businesses altogether and otherwise throw a wrench into your well-laid travel plans. Beyond this, regular opening hours are more predictable, and though listed for each attraction in the Guide, most operate according to the same general schedule.

As a general rule, most **museums** are open Tuesday to Saturday (occasionally Sunday, too) from 10am until 5 or 6pm, with somewhat shorter hours on the weekends. Many museums will also stay open late one evening a week – usually Thursday, when ticket prices are sometimes reduced. Government **offices**, including post offices, are open during regular business hours, typically 8 or 9am until 5pm, Monday to Friday (though some post offices are open Saturday morning). Most **shops** are open daily from 10am until 5 or 6pm, while speciality stores can be more erratic, usually opening and closing later in the day, from noon to 2pm until 8 or 9pm, and remaining shuttered for two days of the week. **Malls** tend to be open from 10am until 7 or 8pm daily, though individual stores may close before the mall does. For visitor centre opening hours, see "Tourist information"; for banks, see "Money".

While some diners stay open 24 hours, the more typical **restaurants** open daily around 11am or noon for lunch and close at 9 to 10pm. Places that serve breakfast usually open early, between 6 to 8am, serve lunch later, and close in the early or mid-afternoon. Dance and live music **clubs** often won't open until 9 or 10pm, and many will serve alcohol until 2am and then either close for the night or stay open until dawn without serving booze. **Bars** that close at 2am may reopen as early as 6am to grab bleary-eyed regulars in need of a liquid breakfast.

Some tourist attractions, visitor centres, motels and campgrounds are only open during the traditional **tourist season**, from Memorial Day to Labor Day, though California's benign weather extends that considerably, and the desert areas have their peak season through the winter.

Phones

With excellent reception in all but the remotest areas, taking your **mobile phone** ("cell" or "cell phone" in US parlance) to California makes a lot of sense. Ask your provider to confirm that your phone will work on US frequencies (most do these days) and get it set up for international use. **Roaming** rates can be pretty high and if you're planning to make a lot of calls it may work out cheaper to **buy a phone** in California, though the lower cost is counterbalanced by the need to tell all your friends your new phone number. Basic, new phones can be picked up for as little as $30; it is probably most convenient to go for a pre-pay service, which you can top up as you go.

Public phones are less plentiful than they used to be. Local calls mostly cost 50¢, and any number prefixed by 1-800/, 1-888/, 1-877/ or 1-866/ is free (as well as from landlines, though mobile phones will incur normal charges). Some numbers covered by the same area code are considered so far apart that calls between them count as non-local ("zone calls") and cost much more. Pricier still are long-distance calls (ie to a different area code and preceded by a 1), for which you'll need plenty of change. Rates are much cheaper using **phone cards** – typically in denominations of $5, $10 and $20 – bought from general stores and some hostels. There are many brands, some quoting long-distance rates as low as 5¢ a minute, but beware of the 50¢ connection fee only mentioned in the fine print. Making telephone calls from **hotel rooms** is usually more expensive ($1–2 each) than from a payphone, though many hotels offer free local calls from rooms – ask when you check in.

Calling home from California

Note that the initial zero is omitted from the area code when dialling the UK, Ireland, Australia and New Zealand from abroad.

Australia 00 + 61 + city code

Canada 1 + area code

New Zealand 00 + 64 + city code

UK and Northern Ireland 00 + 44 + city code

Republic of Ireland 00 + 353 + city code

South Africa 00 + 27 + city code

Useful numbers

Emergencies ☎911
Directory information ☎411
Directory enquiries for toll-free numbers ☎1-800/555-1212
Long-distance directory information ☎1- (area code)/555-1212
International operator ☎00

One of the most convenient ways of phoning home from California is via a **telephone charge card** from your phone company back home. Calls made from most hotel, public and private phones will be charged to your account. Since most major charge cards are free to obtain, it's certainly worth getting one at least for emergencies; but bear in mind that rates aren't necessarily cheaper than calling from a public phone.

Photography

With fabulous scenery and great light much of the time, California is a photographer's paradise. Bring plenty of digital memory or be prepared to periodically visit photo shops and burn your images onto CD. As ever, try to shoot in the early morning and late afternoon when the lower-angled light casts deeper shadows and gives greater depth to your shots. Wildlife is also more active at these times.

It is never a good idea to take photos of **military installations** and the like, and with the current heightened security, airports, ports and harbours, and some government buildings may be considered sensitive.

Senior travellers

Establishments vary in their definition of **seniors**: in some places it's over-55s, in others over-65s. Seniors can regularly find **discounts** of anywhere from ten to fifty percent at movie theatres, museums, hotels, restaurants, performing arts venues, and the occasional shop. On Amtrak, seniors can get a 15 percent discount on most regular fares. On Greyhound the discount is around five to ten percent. If heading to a national park, don't miss the Senior Pass, which, when bought at a park for a mere $10, provides a lifetime of free entry to federally operated recreation sites, as well as half-price discounts on concessions such as boat launches and camping. California residents can apply for a Golden Bear Pass ($5; ⓦwww.parks.ca.gov), which allows complimentary parking at all state-operated facilities, though it doesn't cover boating fees, camping and the like.

Time

California runs on Pacific Standard Time (PST), which is eight hours behind GMT, and jumps forward an hour in summer (the second Sunday in March to the first Sunday in November). During most of this eight-month daylight saving period, when it is noon Monday in California it is 3pm in New York, 8pm in London, 5am Tuesday in Sydney, and 7am Tuesday in Auckland.

Tourist information

California's official tourism website (ⓦwww .visitcalifornia.com) is a reasonable starting point for information. Much of the same material is available in its free tourism information packet, which can be ordered online, by calling ☎1-877/225-4367, or by contacting California Tourism, PO Box 1499, Sacramento, CA 95812-1499 (☎916/444-4429 or 1-877/225-4367).

Visitor centres go under a variety of names, but they all provide detailed information about the local area. Typically they're open Monday to Friday 9am to 5pm and Saturday 9am to 1pm, except in summer, when they may be open seven days a week from 8am or 9am until 6pm or later. In the US, visitor centres are often known as the "Convention and Visitors Bureaus" (CVB), while in small towns many operate under the auspices of the **Chamber of Commerce**, which promotes local business interests. You'll also find small visitor centres in airports, where there's usually a free phone system connecting to leading hotels.

Park visitor centres should be your first destination in any national or state park. Staff are usually outdoors experts, and can offer invaluable advice on trails, current conditions, and the full range of outfitting or adventure specialists. These are also the places to go to obtain national park permits and, where applicable, permits for fishing or backcountry camping.

Travelling with children

There's plenty to occupy kids in California, from theme parks to miles of beachfront. **Hotels** and motels will usually allow kids under a certain age (often 12) to stay for free in the same room as their parents; most will add extra cots at nominal charges.

Restaurants often try hard to lure parents in with their kids. Most of the national chains offer high chairs and a special menu, packed with huge, cheap (if not necessarily healthy) meals like mini-burgers and macaroni and cheese. Most large cities have natural history museums or aquariums, and quite a few have hands-on children's **museums**. Virtually all museums and tourist attractions offer reduced rates for kids. Contact the California Office of Tourism (☎1-877/225-4367, ⓦwww.visitcalifornia.com) for excellent, free brochures that can answer most questions.

Getting around

Under-2s fly free on domestic routes, and usually for ten percent of the adult fare on international flights – though that doesn't necessarily mean they get their own seat. Kids aged from 2 to 12 may be entitled to reduced-price tickets, though recent airline-industry economic troubles have reduced perks like these to a large degree.

Most families choose to travel **by car**, but if you're hoping to enjoy a driving holiday with your kids, it's essential to plan ahead. Don't set unrealistic targets, pack plenty of sensible snacks and drinks, plan to stop every couple of hours, arrive at your destination well before sunset, and avoid travelling through big cities during rush hour. Note that when **renting a car** the company is legally obliged to provide free car seats for kids.

Travelling **by bus** (see p.33) may be the cheapest way to go, but it's also the most uncomfortable for kids. Babies and toddlers can travel (on your lap) for free, whereas children aged 2 to 12 get a 25 percent discount off the standard fare.

Even if you discount the romance of the rails, **train travel** is the best option for long journeys – not only does everyone get to enjoy the scenery, but you can get up and walk around, relieving pent-up energy. Most cross-country trains have sleeping compartments, which may be quite expensive but are a great adventure. Children's discounts are slightly better than on buses or planes, with babies and toddlers riding free and kids from 2 to 12 half-price.

Travellers with disabilities

Under the Americans with Disabilities Act (ADA), all public buildings have to be **wheelchair accessible** and provide suitable toilet facilities, almost all street corners have dropped kerbs, public telephones are specially equipped for hearing-aid users, and most public transport has accessibility aids such as subways with elevators and buses that "kneel" to let riders board. Even movie theatres are now required to allow people in wheelchairs to have a reasonable, unimpeded view of the screen. Most hotel and motel chains offer accessible **accommodation**, with new standards of access that meet or, in some cases, exceed the requirements of the ADA, by building new facilities, retrofitting older hotels, and providing special training to all employees. However, the situation may be more problematic at B&Bs built a century ago, where a narrow stairway may be the only option.

Information

The **California Office of Tourism** (ⓦwww .visitcalifornia.com) has lists of handicapped facilities at accommodation and attractions. **National organizations** facilitating travel for people with disabilities include SATH, the Society for the Advancement of Travelers with Handicaps (☎212/447-7284, ⓦwww .sath.org), a nonprofit travel-industry grouping made up of travel agents, tour operators, and hotel and airline management; contact them in advance so they can notify the appropriate members. **Mobility International USA** (☎541/343-1284, ⓦwww.miusa.org) answers transport queries and operates an exchange programme for people with disabilities.

Access-Able (Ⓣ303/232-2979, Ⓦwww.access-able.com) is an information service that assists travellers with disabilities by putting them in contact with other people with similar conditions.

Getting around

Major car-rental firms can provide vehicles with hand controls for drivers with leg or spinal disabilities, though these are typically available only on the pricier models. Parking regulations for disabled motorists are now uniform: licence plates for the disabled must carry a three-inch-square international access symbol, and a placard bearing this symbol must be hung from the car's rear-view mirror.

American **airlines** must by law accommodate customers with disabilities, and some even allow attendants of those with serious conditions to accompany them for a reduced fare. Almost every **Amtrak train** includes one or more cars with accommodation for disabled passengers, along with wheelchair assistance at train platforms, adapted on-board seating, free travel for guide dogs, and discounts on fares, all with 24 hours' advance notice. Passengers with hearing impairment can get information by calling Ⓣ1-800/523-6590 (TDD) or checking out Ⓦwww.amtrak.com.

By contrast, travelling by **Greyhound** and **Amtrak Thruway** bus connections is often problematic. Buses are not equipped with platforms for wheelchairs, though there is intercity assistance with boarding, and disabled passengers may be able to get priority seating. Call Greyhound's ADA customer assistance line for more information (Ⓣ1-800/752-4841, Ⓦwww.greyhound.com).

The great outdoors

Disabled citizens or permanent residents of the US can obtain the **America the Beautiful Access Pass**, a free lifetime entrance pass to federally operated parks, monuments, historic sites, recreation areas and wildlife refuges. It also provides a fifty percent discount on fees charged for facilities such as camping, boat launching and parking. The pass is available from the National Park Service (Ⓦwww.nps.gov/fees_passes.htm) and must be picked up in person from the areas described. The **Disabled Discount Pass** ($3.50; Ⓦwww.parks.ca.gov) offers half-price concessions on parking and camping at state-run parks, beaches and historic sites.

Guide

Guide

Los Angeles

OREGON · IDAHO

NEVADA

UTAH

ARIZONA

PACIFIC OCEAN

MEXICO

N

0   100 miles

CHAPTER 1   # Highlights

* **Disney Hall** A marvellous piece of sculptural art masquerading as a (spectacular) concert hall, which has been described as resembling anything from broken eggshells to origami. See p.85

* **Musso and Frank Grill** This classically dark and moody watering-hole has long been a favourite hangout for movie stars of the Golden Age and today's brattier celebrities. See p.98

* **Golden Triangle/Rodeo Drive** For high-end consumers (and avid window-shoppers), this compact section of Downtown Beverly Hills, featuring jewellery, fashion and beauty boutiques, is the main reason to visit Los Angeles. See p.109

* **Getty Center** A colossal, Modernist arts centre, the Getty is stuffed with treasures of the Old World and is set on a hillside providing a great view of the metropolis. See p.112

* **Pacific Coast Highway** This sinewy stretch of Highway 1 winds around coastal cliffs and legendary beaches from Santa Monica to Malibu, where the views are stunning. See p.113

* **Rose Parade** If you are here on New Year's Day, check out this Pasadena procession of grand floral floats and marching bands, culminating in a momentous football game. See p.142

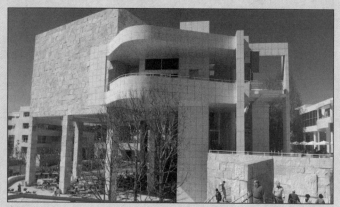

▲ The Getty Center

Los Angeles

OS ANGELES spreads across its great desert basin in an eye-popping array of fast-food joints, palm trees, movie studios and swimming pools. Bordered by snowcapped mountains and the Pacific Ocean, it's stitched together by an intricate network of freeways crossing a thousand square miles of widely varying architecture, social strata and cultures. It's an extremely visual place, colourful and brash in myriad ways – a crazy quilt of small-town, suburban and urban life – and the second largest city in the US.

The entertainment industry has been hyping the place ever since filmmakers arrived a century ago, attracted by a climate that allowed them to film outdoors year-round, plenty of open land on which to build elaborate sets, nearby landscapes varied enough to mimic just about anywhere in the world, and of course, the ever-popular lures of cheap labour, low taxes and lax government. Since then, the money and glitz of Hollywood have enticed countless thousands of would-be actors, writers, designers and other budding artistes and celebrities to cast their lot in this hard-edged glamour town, their triumphs and failures becoming intrinsic to the city's towering myths. So, too, has the threat of sudden disaster: floods, fires and earthquakes are facts of life here, and the coexistence of both extremes – spectacle and tragedy – lends a perilous, unhinged personality to the city.

Some history

Originally settled by Chumash and Tongva peoples about a thousand years before the arrival of Spanish settlers in 1781, Los Angeles was named for the Spanish phrase for **"Our Lady Queen of the Angels"**. Not surprisingly, it later became a link in Junípero Serra's lengthy chain of 21 Franciscan missions (see p.686), as well as a staging ground for Spanish military expeditions. In 1821, Mexico gained control of California, and the entire terrain was subdivided into huge **ranchos** under the control of politically powerful land bosses, only to be swallowed up again during the Mexican–American War in 1847 by the US, which did everything it could to eradicate the society and government created by Spain and Mexico.

Up until the Civil War, LA was a small town comprising white American immigrants, poor Chinese labourers and wealthy Mexican ranchers, with a population of less than fifty thousand. It wasn't until the completion of the **transcontinental railroad** in the 1870s that the city really began to grow, doubling in population every ten years, with hundreds of thousands coming to live in what was billed as a Mediterranean-style paradise for clean living and, ironically from today's viewpoint, healthy air. Ranches were broken up into innumerable suburban lots, and scores of new towns, like San Pedro and Santa Monica, sprang up. Meanwhile, land speculators marketed an enduring image of Los Angeles,

LOS ANGELES

Bakersfield ▲

SAN FERNANDO

Bob Hope/
Burbank
Airport

118 SIMI VALLEY – SAN FERNANDO VALLEY FREEWAY

23

SIMI VALLEY

NORTHRIDGE

CANOGA PARK

San Fernando Valley

VAN NUYS

NORTH
HOLLYWOOD

BURBANK

ENCINO

VENTURA FREEWAY

NORTH HOLLYWOOD

SHERMAN
OAKS

MULHOLLAND DRIVE

HOLLYWOOD &
VINE

MALIBU CREEK
STATE PARK

MULHOLLAND HIGHWAY

TOPANGA
STATE PARK

BEL AIR

HOLLYWOOD
W HOLLYWOOD

SANTA MONICA MOUNTAINS

WESTWOOD

Getty Center

BRENTWOOD

BEVERLY HILLS

UCLA

LACMA

SANTA MONICA
MOUNTAINS NRA

WILSHIRE &
WESTERN

MALIBU

PACIFIC
PALISADES

PACIFIC COAST HIGHWAY

SANTA
MONICA

SANTA MONICA BLVD

CRENSHAW

Point Dume

Santa Monica Pier

VENICE

CULVER
CITY

SANTA MONICA FREEWAY

Venice Boardwalk

Marina
del Rey

INGLEWOOD

LAX

Santa Monica
Bay

EL
SEGUNDO

MARINE
AVENUE

Manhattan Beach

Hermosa Beach

Redondo Beach

PALOS
VERDES
PENINSULA

PALOS VERDES DRIVE

N

Orange Line Light Rail
Gold Line Light Rail
Red Line Subway
Blue Line Light Rail
Green Line Light Rail
Station

O

P A C I F I C

0   10 miles

Ventura & Santa Barbara ◀

Santa Catalina Island ▼

TUJUNGA

ANGELES NATIONAL FOREST

FOOTHILL FREEWAY

LA CANADA
FLINTRIDGE

San Gabriel Valley

Rose
Bowl

PASADENA

MONROVIA

GLENDALE

GLENDALE FWY

VENTURA FREEWAY

134

2

210

FOOTHILL FREEWAY

210

Hollywood Sign

GOLDEN STATE FREEWAY

PASADENA FREEWAY

OLD PASADENA

SAN MARINO

AZUSA AVE

WEST COVINA

210

LOS
FELIZ

110

HUNTINGDON DR

19

101

SILVER
LAKE

SOUTH
PASADENA

Huntington
Library &
Gardens

ARCADIA

605

10

HIGHLAND PARK

WILSHIRE &
VERMONT

MID-
WILSHIRE

Union Station

MONTEREY
PARK

EL MONTE

SAN BERNARDINO FREEWAY

SEVENTH STREET/
METRO CENTER

DOWNTOWN

60

Exposition
Park

EAST LA

60

POMONA FREEWAY

SOUTH
CENTRAL
LA

VERNON

5

HARBOR FREEWAY

SLAUSON AVENUE

710 FREEWAY

SAN GABRIEL RIVER

WHITTIER

42

MANCHESTER AVENUE

SAN GABRIEL RIVER FREEWAY

ROSEMEAD BOULEVARD

SANTA FE
SPRINGS

LA HABRA

Watts Towers

WATTS

CENTURY FREEWAY

105

WILMINGTON

IMPERIAL HIGHWAY

90

HAWTHORNE

GARDENA

91

COMPTON

605/105 FREEWAY
INTERCHANGE

ARTESIA FREEWAY

FULLERTON

Nixon
Library

REDONDO BEACH FWY

LAKEWOOD

91

BUENA
PARK

RIVERSIDE FREEWAY

91

TORRANCE

SAN DIEGO FREEWAY

LAKEWOOD BLVD

605

CARSON ST

LINCOLN AVENUE

57

55

Long Beach
Airport

SANTA ANA FREEWAY

WILMINGTON

SEPULVEDA

BOULEVARD

405

LOS ALAMITOS

Knott's Berry
Farm

ANAHEIM

Disneyland

1

PACIFIC COAST HIGHWAY

19

LONG BEACH PLAZA

LONG BEACH

GARDEN GROVE

Crystal Cathedral

5

22

SAN PEDRO

Queen Mary

LA HARBOR

SEAL
BEACH

405

GARDEN GROVE FREEWAY

ORANGE
COUNTY

Cabrillo
Marine Aquarium

1

BEACH BOULEVARD

SAN DIEGO FREEWAY

HARBOR BLVD

COSTA-MESA FREEWAY

55

IRVINE

405

Huntington Beach

PACIFIC COAST HIGHWAY

John Wayne
Airport

OCEAN

Newport Beach

Balboa
Peninsula

73

Laguna Beach

Palm Springs & Ontario Airport

San Diego

LA area codes

Because the Los Angeles metro region has thirteen telephone **area codes** – ☎213, ☎310, ☎323, ☎424, ☎562, ☎626, ☎657, ☎661, ☎714, ☎805, ☎818, ☎909 and ☎949 – we have included the code before each number.

epitomized by the family-size suburban house (with a swimming pool and two-car garage) set amid the orange groves in a glorious land of sunshine.

More **boom years** followed World War II, when veterans, some of them African American, bought government-subsidized houses and found well-paying jobs in the mushrooming defense and aeronautics industries or with oil, steel and car companies. Along with heavy manufacturing, the entertainment and real-estate sectors drew ever-increasing numbers of people from around the country, and LA's population exploded, eventually eclipsing Chicago as the nation's second-largest metropolis.

After the Cold War, though, Southern California was hit hard by cutbacks in defense spending, particularly in the aeronautics industry. Unemployment reached a peak of ten percent in the early 1990s, resulting in a spike in crime and a pervasive paranoia in the suburbs. The **riots of 1992** (see p.90) exacerbated tensions, which were only increased by two of earthquakes and various floods and fires in Southern California during the same period.

Nonetheless, **Latino immigration** continued to increase dramatically, especially to Santa Ana and Garden Grove, and once-entrenched white suburbanites sought new refuges in distant "edge cities" like Rancho Cucamonga and Palmdale. Even in South Central, long the centre of African-American culture in the city, massive demographic upheaval took place as traditional black neighbourhoods became largely Latino, with many of those newcomers arriving from some of the most impoverished regions of Central America. The most visible symbol of the newfound power of LA's Hispanic community was the 2005 election of Antonio Villaraigosa as mayor.

Although LA is still strong in entertainment, light manufacturing and shipping – the port of LA and Long Beach handles more than sixty percent of the ocean-going cargo coming to the West Coast – times have otherwise been tough in recent years. Following the **economic turmoil** that began in the US in 2007–2008, Los Angeles saw local unemployment climb to around 12 percent, the bottom drop out of the local real-estate market, and government services cut back dramatically. However, crime has tailed off from its 1990s highs and the city is safer than it's been in decades, making LA a great place to visit despite the troubled times.

Arrival

However you **arrive** in Los Angeles, and especially if you're not driving, you're faced with a seemingly unending sprawl that can be a source of bewilderment even for those who've lived in it for years. Nonetheless, this ungainly beast of a city can be managed and even navigated, if not necessarily tamed.

By plane

All international and most domestic **flights** use Los Angeles International Airport (**LAX**) sixteen miles southwest of Downtown LA (☎310/646-5252, ⓦwww.los-angeles-lax.com). **Shuttle bus A** is for intra-airport connections (carrier-to-carrier), while buses B and C serve their respective parking lots round the clock, with parking lot C being the place to board city buses (the citywide MTA and individual lines to Santa Monica, Culver City and Torrance) – see box, p.74. To travel between LAX and Downtown's Union Station, the UCLA campus in Westwood (at parking structure 32 on Kinross Ave), or the private Van Nuys Airport, the **LAX Flyaway** service (℡1-866/435-9529, Ⓦwww.lawa.aero/flyaway) uses buses in freeway carpool lanes to provide the most direct airport access on public transport; buses leave every thirty minutes and run around the clock, except at Westwood, where the service runs from 6am–10pm ($5–7 one way).

Another way into town is to take a shuttle service such as **SuperShuttle** (℡1-800/258-3826, Ⓦwww.supershuttle.com) and **Prime Time Shuttle** (℡1-800/733-8267, Ⓦwww.primetimeshuttle.com), which run all over town; fares depend on your destination but start at around $15 for travel to Downtown and the Westside (or up to $40 for more outlying areas), with a journey time of between thirty and sixty minutes. Shuttles run around the clock from outside the baggage reclaim areas, and you should never have to wait more than about fifteen minutes.

Taxis charge at least $35 to West LA, $40 to Hollywood, around $100 to Disneyland, and a flat $46.50 to Downtown from LAX; a $2.50 surcharge applies for all trips starting from LAX (all airport trips are a minimum of $17.50). For more information check out Ⓦwww.taxicabsla.org. Using the **Metro** system to get to your destination from LAX is difficult. The nearest light-rail train, the **Green Line**, stops miles from the airport, and the overall journey involves two time-consuming transfers (very difficult with luggage) before you even arrive in Downtown Los Angeles. If you'd like to try anyway, a shuttle service ($1.50) leaves from the lower level of the terminal to access the Metro stop at Aviation Station.

If you're arriving from elsewhere in the US or from Mexico, you can land at one of the **smaller airports** in the LA area: Burbank's Bob Hope Airport (℡818/840-8840, Ⓦwww.burbankairport.com), convenient for the Valley and Hollywood; Long Beach (℡562/570-2619, Ⓦwww.longbeach.gov/airport), good for the South Bay; Ontario (℡909/937-2700, Ⓦwww.lawa.org/ont), only useful for the eastern suburbs; and Costa Mesa's John Wayne Airport (℡949/252-5200, Ⓦwww.ocair.com), the best way to get to Orange County and Disneyland. These are similarly well served by car rental firms; if you want to use public transport, phone the MTA Regional Information Network on arrival (℡1-800/266-6883, Ⓦwww.mta.net), and tell them where you are and where you want to go.

By train and bus

Arriving in LA by **train**, you'll be greeted with the expansive Mission Revival architecture of Union Station, on the north side of Downtown at 800 N Alameda St (℡213/624-0171), from which you can reach Metrorail and Metrolink lines and also access the nearby Gateway Transit Centre, which offers connections to bus lines. Amtrak trains also stop at outlying stations in the LA area; for all listings, call Amtrak (℡1-800/872-7245, Ⓦwww.amtrak.com).

The main **Greyhound** bus terminal, at 1716 E 7th St (℡213/629-8401, Ⓦwww.greyhound.com), is in a seedy section of Downtown, though access is restricted to ticket holders and it's safe enough inside. The website has details of other metropolitan stops but only the Downtown terminal is open around the clock.

By car

The main routes by **car** into Los Angeles are the interstate highways, all of which pass through Downtown. I-10, the San Bernardino Freeway, US-60, the Pomona Freeway, and I-210, the Foothill Freeway, head in through the eastern suburbs;

from the north and south, I-5 connects LA to Northern California. Of the non-interstate routes into the city, US-101, the scenic route from San Francisco, cuts across the San Fernando Valley and Hollywood into Downtown; Hwy-1, or the Pacific Coast Highway (PCH), follows the coast of California and takes surface streets through Santa Monica, the South Bay and Orange County; and the San Diego Freeway, I-405, is used as a Westside alternative to I-5.

Information

The Convention and Visitors Bureau (CVB) operates two **visitor centres**, Downtown and in Hollywood; other LA areas have their own bureaus (see box below).

All centres offer free **maps** of their areas, but if you're in LA for a while, you may want to invest in the latest edition of the hefty, spiral-bound *LA County Thomas Guide* ($19.95), and *Thomas Guide to Los Angeles and Orange Counties* ($34.95), sold at most bookstores. As the city's definitive road atlas, they're used by tourists and locals alike to navigate the bewildering maze of LA streets. There are also Thomas Guides for most neighboring counties if you're venturing further afield.

Of the city's many **free papers**, the fullest and most useful are the *LA Weekly* (🌐www.laweekly.com) and *Orange County Weekly* (🌐www.ocweekly.com), featuring news, reviews and listings with an alternative bent. Numerous local papers covering individual neighbourhoods are available all over the city, especially in cafés, record stores and bookshops.

City transport

However you're getting around LA, you should allow plenty of time to reach your destination. The confusing entanglements of freeways and the gridlock common during rush hours (or any hours) can make car trips lengthy slogs – and the fact that most local buses stop on every other corner hardly makes bus travel a speedy option.

Driving

Not surprisingly, the best way to get around LA is to **drive**. Despite the traffic being bumper-to-bumper much of the day, the **freeways** are the only way to cover long distances with any efficiency. The system, however, can be confusing, especially since each stretch can have two or three names (often derived from their

---

Visitor centres in and around LA

Anaheim/Disneyland 800 W Katella Ave ☎714/991-8963, 🌐www.anaheimoc.org

Beverly Hills 239 S Beverly Drive ☎1-800/345-2210, 🌐www.beverlyhillscvb.com

Downtown LA 685 S Figueroa St ☎213/689-8822, 🌐www.discoverlosangeles.com

Hollywood Hollywood & Highland mall, 6801 Hollywood Blvd ☎323/467-6412

Long Beach 1 World Trade Center, 3rd Floor ☎562/436-3645, 🌐www.visit longbeach.com

Pasadena 300 E Green St ☎626/795-9311, 🌐www.pasadenacal.com

Santa Monica 1920 Main St ☎310/393-7593, 🌐www.santamonica.com

West Hollywood Pacific Design Center, 8687 Melrose Ave #M38 ☎310/289-2525, 🌐www.visitwesthollywood.com

eventual destination, however far away) as well as a number. Out of an unbeliev-able four-level interchange known as "The Stack", four major freeways fan out from Downtown: the Hollywood Freeway (US-101) heads northwest through Hollywood into the San Fernando Valley; the Santa Monica Freeway (I-10) connects the northern edge of South Central LA with Santa Monica; the Harbor Freeway (I-110) runs south to San Pedro (heading northeast it's called the Pasadena Freeway); and the Santa Ana Freeway (I-5) passes Disneyland and continues to Orange County and San Diego. **Other area freeways** include the San Diego Freeway (I-405), following the coast through West LA and the South Bay (but not actually reaching San Diego); the Ventura Freeway (Hwy-134), linking Burbank, Glendale and Pasadena to US-101 in the San Fernando Valley; the Long Beach Freeway (I-710), a truck-heavy route connecting East LA and Long Beach; the Foothill Freeway (I-210), skirting the suburbs at the base of the San Gabriel Mountains; and the San Gabriel River Freeway (I-605), linking those suburbs with Long Beach. For **shorter journeys**, especially between Hollywood and West LA, the wide avenues and boulevards are a better – and sometimes the only – option.

Car rental

All the major **car rental** companies have branches in the city (check the internet or the *Yellow Pages* for the nearest office or call one of the numbers listed on p.32), and most have their main office close to LAX, linked to each terminal by a free shuttle bus.

    Parking is a particular challenge Downtown, along Melrose Avenue's trendy Westside shopping zone, on central Hollywood Boulevard, in Downtown Beverly Hills, in West Hollywood near the Sunset Strip, and throughout Westwood – which is notorious for its legions of traffic wardens and expensive short-term parking. Anywhere else is less troublesome, but watch out for restrictions – some lampposts boast as many as four placards listing do's and don'ts.

Public transport

The bulk of LA's public transport is operated by the LA County Metropolitan Transit Authority (**MTA** or **"Metro"**). Its massive **Gateway Transit Center**, east of Union Station on Chavez Avenue at Vignes Street, serves many thousands of daily commuters travelling by Metrorail, Metrolink, Amtrak and the regional bus systems. The Centre comprises **Patsaouras Transit Plaza**, where you can hop on a bus; the glass-domed **East Portal**, where you can connect to a train; and the 26-storey **Gateway Tower**, where you can find an MTA customer service office (Mon–Fri 6am–6.30pm; ☎1-800/266-6883, ⓦwww.mta.net) on the ground floor.

Metrorail and Metrolink

LA's **Metrorail** subway and light-rail system encompasses seven major lines, though extensions are planned in coming years. The **Orange Line** crosses the San Fernando Valley and links Canoga Park with North Hollywood, where it connects to the northern terminus for the underground **Red Line**, heading south under the Hollywood Hills to connect Central Hollywood and Downtown (stopping at the Gateway Transit Centre, as do all Downtown routes). The **Purple Line** subway covers the last part of the same ground, from Vermont Avenue to Union Station, but also extends a short distance west to Western Avenue. Of more use to residents than tourists, the **Green Line** runs between industrial El Segundo (where you can pick up an LAX shuttle at Aviation Station; see p.71) and colourless Norwalk in South LA. The **Blue Line** leaves Downtown and heads overland through South Central to Long Beach, while the more appealing **Gold Line**, another light-rail route, connects Downtown with northeast LA, Highland Park and Old Pasadena,

MTA bus routes

MTA **buses** fall into the route categories shown below. Whatever bus you're on, if travelling alone, especially at night, sit up front near the driver.

#1–99 local routes to and from Downtown

#100–199 east–west routes between other areas

#200–299 north–south routes between other areas

#300–399 limited-stop routes (usually rush hours only)

#400–499 express routes to and from Downtown

#500–599 express routes between other areas

#600–699 special service routes (for sports events and the like)

#700–799 Metro Rapid service

#800–899 Metrorail subways and light rail

#900–999 Metrorail express buses

Major LA bus services

From LAX bus center to:

Beverly Hills Santa Monica line #3 or Culver City line #6 to Metro #720

Culver City Culver City line #6

Downtown #42, #439

Hollywood Santa Monica line #3 to Metro #4 or #304

Long Beach #232

Santa Monica Santa Monica line #3

Watts Towers #117

West Hollywood Santa Monica line #3 to Metro #4 or #304

From Downtown along:

Beverly Blvd #14, #714

Sunset Blvd #2, #302

Melrose Ave #10

Olympic Blvd #28

Santa Monica Blvd #4, #704

Venice Blvd #33

Wilshire Blvd #20, #720

From Downtown to:

Beverly Hills #14, #20, #714, #720

Burbank Studios #96

Exposition Park #81

Forest Lawn Cemetery, Glendale #90, #91

Getty Centre #2 or #302, then transfer at UCLA to #761

Hermosa Beach/Redondo Beach #130

Hollywood #2, #302

Huntington Library #79

Long Beach #60

Orange County, Knott's Berry Farm, Disneyland #460

Santa Monica #4, #20, #720

Venice #33, #333

before ending at drab Sierra Madre; another section of the Gold Line recently opened to service East LA from Downtown. Finally, the **Silver Line** uses express buses, like those on the Orange Line, to reach the San Gabriel Valley. The **Expo Line** light rail is due to open by late 2011 and connect Downtown LA with Culver City, parallelling the I-10 freeway. **Fares** are $1.50 one way, with day-passes available for $6. Trains run daily from 5am to 12.30am, about every five minutes during peak hours and every ten to fifteen minutes at other times. No smoking, eating or drinking is allowed on board.

Metrolink commuter trains (☎1-800/371-5465 or visit ⓦwww.metrolink trains.com) ply primarily suburban-to-Downtown routes on weekdays, which can be useful if you find yourself in any such far-flung districts, among them places in Orange, Ventura, Riverside and San Bernardino counties. The system reaches as far as Oceanside in San Diego County, where you can connect to that region's Coaster and Sprinter commuter rail (see p.167 & p.170). One-way fares range from $5 to $14.

Buses

Car-less Angelenos not lucky enough to live near a train route have to settle for **buses**. Although initially bewildering, the MTA network is really quite simple: the main routes run east–west (eg between Downtown and the coast) and north–south (eg between Downtown and the South Bay). With a bit of planning you should have few real problems – though always allow plenty of time.

Free brochures and information on bus routes are available from MTA offices. Buses on the major arteries between Downtown and the coast run roughly every 15 to 25 minutes between 5am and 2am; other routes, and the **all-night services** along the major thoroughfares, are less frequent, sometimes only hourly. At night, be careful not to get stranded Downtown waiting for connecting buses.

The standard **one-way fare** is $1.50, but **express buses** (a limited commuter service) and any others using a freeway are usually $2.20–2.90. Put the correct money (coins or notes) into the slot when getting on. If you're staying a while, you can save some money with a **weekly** or **monthly pass**, which cost $20 and $75 respectively, and also give reductions at selected shops and travel agents. Finally, "EZ Transit" passes give you the option of travelling on MTA and DASH buses, as well as Metrorail trains, for a flat $84 per month.

Several red **Metro Rapid** buses run throughout the region, offering a modified service along the #700–799 lines. There are also the mini **DASH** buses, which operate through the LA Department of Transportation, or LADOT (☎808-2273 for area codes 213, 310, 323 and 818; ⓦwww.ladottransit.com), with a flat fare of 25¢ for broad coverage throughout Downtown and very limited routes elsewhere in the city. The LADOT also operates quick, limited-stop routes called **commuter express**, though these cost a bit more (90¢–$4 depending on distance).

Other **local bus services** include those for Orange County (OCTD; ☎714/636-7433, ⓦwww.octa.net), Long Beach (LBTD; ☎562/591-2301, ⓦwww.lbtransit .org), Culver City (☎310/253-6500, ⓦwww.culvercity.org/bus) and Santa Monica (☎310/451-5444, ⓦwww.bigbluebus.com).

Taxis

You can find **taxis** at most terminals and major hotels. Among the more reliable companies are Independent Taxi (☎1-800/521-8294), Checker Cab (☎1-800/300-5007), Yellow Cab (☎1-800/200-1085) and United Independent Taxi (☎1-800/411-0303). Fares start at $2.85, plus $2.70 for each mile (or 30¢ per 37 seconds of waiting time), with a $2.50 surcharge if you're picked up at LAX. The driver won't know every street in LA but will know the major ones; ask for the

Guided tours of LA

One quick and easy way to see LA is on a **guided tour**. The mainstream tours carry large busloads of visitors to the major tourist sights; specialist tours usually carry smaller groups and are often quirkier and better value; and media studio tours are available on day-trips by most of the mainstream operators, though you'll save money by turning up on your own.

Some of your best bets for touring Downtown and other spots are the walking tours offered by the LA Conservancy (Sat 10am; 2hr 30min; $10; ☎213/623-2489, ⓦlaconservancy.org), which typically set off from Pershing Square Downtown and concentrate on various aspects of the city's architecture, history and culture. **Architours** (☎323/294-5821, ⓦwww.architours.com) offers walking, driving and custom tours of the art and architecture highlights of the city; most last for 2–3 hour and cost $68–75. Also appealing, Neon Cruises, 501 W Olympic Blvd, Downtown (June–Nov; $55; ☎213/489-9918, ⓦwww.neonmona.org), are three-hour-long, eye-popping evening tours of LA's best remaining neon art, one Saturday a month, sponsored by the Museum of Neon Art.

One type of trek to avoid are the uninspired bus tours that focus on the homes of the stars (ie, their ivy-covered security gates) and advertise their overpriced services around central Hollywood. For some insight into how a film or TV show is made, or just to admire the special effects, there are guided **studio tours** at Warner Bros (see p.127), NBC (p.128), Sony, Paramount (p.99) and Universal (p.128), all near Burbank except for Sony, in Culver City, and Paramount, in Hollywood. On a related note, if you want to be part of the **audience** in a TV show, Hollywood Boulevard, just outside the Chinese Theatre, is the spot to be: TV company reps regularly appear handing out free tickets, and they'll bus you to the studio and back. All you have to do once there is be willing to laugh and clap on cue.

---

nearest junction and give directions from there. If you encounter problems, call ☎1-800/501-0999, or visit ⓦwww.taxicabsla.org.

Cycling

Cycling in LA may sound perverse, but in some areas it can be one of the better ways of getting around. There is an excellent **beach bike path** between Santa Monica and Redondo Beach, and another from Long Beach to Newport Beach, as well as many equally enjoyable inland routes, notably around Griffith Park and the grand mansions of Pasadena. For maps and information, contact the LA office of the state's Department of Transportation, known as CalTrans, 100 S Main St (Mon–Fri 8am–5pm; ☎213/897-3656, ⓦwww.dot.ca.gov), or the LA Department of Transportation, 100 S Main St, 9th Floor (☎213/972-4962, ⓦwww.bicyclela.org).

Walking and hiking

Although some people are surprised to find pavements in LA, let alone pedestrians, **walking** is in fact the best way to see much of Downtown and districts like central Hollywood, Pasadena, Beverly Hills, Santa Monica and Venice. You can enjoy guided **hikes** through the wilds of the Santa Monica Mountains and Hollywood Hills free of charge every weekend with a variety of organizations, including the Sierra Club (☎213/387-4287, ⓦwww.angeles .sierraclub.org), the State Parks Department (☎818/880-0350, ⓦwww.parks .ca.gov) and the Santa Monica Mountains National Recreation Area (☎805/370-2301, ⓦwww.nps.gov/samo).

Accommodation

Since LA has 100,000-plus rooms, finding **accommodation** is easy, and the city has something for everyone, from budget motels to world-class resorts. **Motels** and the bottom-end hotels start at about $50 for a double, but many are situated in seedy or out-of-the-way areas; any decent motel or hotel will cost at least $70. **B&Bs** are still uncommon in central LA, and tend to be quite expensive, often fully booked, and sited in out-of-the-way places. A handful of **hostels** are dotted all over the city, many in good locations, though at some stays are limited to a few nights and at others a nonstop party atmosphere prevails. Surprisingly, there are a few **campgrounds** on the edge of the metropolitan area (see box, p.81) – along the beach north of Malibu and in the San Gabriel Mountains, for example – but you'll need a car to get to them.

LA is so big that if you want to see it all without constantly having to cross huge expanses, it makes sense to divide your stay between several **districts**. Downtown has both chic hotels and basic dives; Hollywood has similar options, with roadside motels providing cheap and adequate rooms; more salubrious West Hollywood, West LA, Santa Monica, Venice and Malibu are predominantly mid-to-upper-range territory, with the odd hostel here and there. It's only worth staying in Orange County, thirty miles southeast of Downtown, if you're aiming for Disneyland or are travelling along the coast.

Hotels are listed here by **neighbourhood**. In case you're arriving on a late flight, or leaving on an early one, we've also included a few places near the airport: cheap hotels near LAX are blandly similar and generally around $70, but most have complimentary transportation to and from the terminals.

Downtown and around
See the map on p.82.

Hilton Checkers 535 S Grand ☎213/624-0000, ⓦwww.hiltoncheckers.com. One of the great LA hotels, with modern furnishings in historic 1920s architecture, and attractive rooms, gym, rooftop deck with pool and spa, and swanky *Checkers* restaurant. ➐

Kyoto Grand 120 S Los Angeles St ☎213/629-1200, ⓦwww.kyotograndhotel.com. Sleek, Japanese-styled business hotel with gym, beauty salon and straightforward rooms, plus three decent restaurants. An authentic Japanese garden is another plus. ➏

Los Angeles Athletic Club 431 W 7th St ☎213/625-2211, ⓦwww.laac.com. While still home to an exclusive club, the top three floors make up a hotel with 72 nicely furnished rooms and nine expensive suites, all with free wi-fi and flat-screen TVs; a real plus is free use of the club's gym equipment, handball and basketball courts, plus a whirlpool and sauna. ➏

Millennium Biltmore 506 S Grand Ave ☎213/624-1011, ⓦwww.thebiltmore.com. Neoclassical 1923 architecture combined with modern luxury, with a health club modelled on a Roman bathhouse, cherub-and-angel decor, and a view overlooking Pershing Square. ➐

Omni Los Angeles 251 S Olive St at 4th St ☎213/617-3300, ⓦwww.omnilosangeles.com. Fancy, Bunker Hill hotel with plush rooms with internet access, swimming pool and weight room. Adjacent to MOCA and the Music Center. ➏

Westin Bonaventure 404 S Figueroa St ☎213/624-1000, ⓦwww.westin.com. Modernist luxury hotel with five glass towers that resemble cocktail shakers, a six-storey atrium with a "lake", and elegant cone-shaped rooms. A breathtaking exterior elevator ride ascends to a rotating cocktail lounge. ➏

Hollywood
See the map on p.94.

Holiday Inn Express 2005 N Highland Ave ☎323/850-8151, ⓦwww.hiexpress.com. Massive and well placed, near the heart of Hollywood Boulevard and the Chinese Theatre. Clean and modern rooms with flat-screen HDTVs and internet access; other amenities include pool, spa, gym and business centre. ➐

Hollywood Celebrity 1775 Orchid Ave ☎323/850-6464 or 1-800/222-7017, ⓦwww.hotelcelebrity.com. Good choice on the affordable boutique scene, with a great location in central Hollywood and rooms with charming furnishings, free breakfast and free high-speed internet. ➏

Hollywood Roosevelt 7000 Hollywood Blvd, between Highland and La Brea ⊕ 323/466-7000, ⓦ www.hollywoodroosevelt.com. The first hotel built for the movie greats in 1927. The place reeks of atmosphere, with boutique rooms, cabanas and suites, plus a jacuzzi, fitness room and swimming pool. However, many of the old-fashioned rooms can be a bit cramped for modern travellers. ❽

Orchid Suites 1753 Orchid Ave ⊕ 1-800/537-3052, ⓦ www.orchidsuites.com. Roomy, if spartan, suites with cable TV, kitchenette, laundry room and heated pool. Very close to the most popular parts of Hollywood and adjacent to the massive Hollywood & Highland mall. ❺

Renaissance Hollywood 1755 N Highland Blvd ⊕ 323/856-1200, ⓦ www.renaissancehollywood .com. The centrepiece of the Hollywood & Highland mall, with arty, boutique-style rooms and suites and a prime location in the heart of Tinseltown. The upscale chain lodging in the centre of the district guarantees you'll pay top dollar for a room. ❽

West Hollywood
See the map on pp.104–105.

Chateau Marmont 8221 Sunset Blvd ⊕ 323/656-1010, ⓦ www.chateaumarmont.com. Iconic, Norman Revival hotel, which resembles a dark castle or Hollywood fortress and has hosted all manner of celebrities. A bit worn these days, though, despite the glamour. Come for the history, but don't expect any kind of deal; rooms start at $370. ❾

Elan Hotel Modern 8435 Beverly Blvd ⊕ 323/658-6663, ⓦ www.elanhotel.com. Good-value boutique hotel located in a busy shopping zone just north of the Beverly Center mall. Rooms are smartly appointed, with free wi-fi, breakfast, and wine and cheese in the later afternoon. Also with fitness centre and spa. ❼

Grafton on Sunset 8462 Sunset Blvd ⊕ 323/654-4600, ⓦ www.graftononsunset.com. Mid-level boutique hotel with attractive furnishings and CD and DVD players, iPod docks and flat-screen TVs, plus a pool and fitness centre. ❼

Le Montrose 900 Hammond St ⊕ 310/855-1115, ⓦ www.lemontrose.com. West Hollywood hotel with Art Nouveau styling, featuring rooftop tennis courts, pool and jacuzzi. Most rooms are suites with full amenities such as kitchenettes, balconies and fireplaces. ❽

Ramada Plaza West Hollywood 8585 Santa Monica Blvd ⊕ 310/652-6400, ⓦ www .ramadaweho.com. Clean and comfortable rooms with high-speed internet, a pool and a gym. Very popular with gay travellers and a local hub of social activity. ❻

Beverly Hills
See the map on p.104.

Beverly Hills Hotel 9641 Sunset Blvd ⊕ 1-800/283-8885, ⓦ www.beverlyhillshotel.com. The classic Hollywood resort, with a bold colour scheme and Mission-style design, and surrounded by its own exotic gardens. Features marbled bathrooms, VCRs, jacuzzis and other such luxuries, as well as the famed *Polo Lounge* restaurant. ❾

Beverly Hilton 9876 Wilshire Blvd ⊕ 1-800/922-5432, ⓦ www.hilton.com. This prominent, geometric white hotel at the corner of Wilshire and Santa Monica boulevards has a pool and gym, plus in-room plasma TVs, boutique decor and balconies. Also has one of the few remaining *Trader Vic's* bars. ❽

Maison 140 140 S Lasky Drive ⊕ 310/281-4000, ⓦ www.maison140.com. High-profile place for hipsters, boasting nicely furnished rooms with CD and DVD players and internet access, plus salon, bar, fitness room and complimentary breakfast. ❼

Peninsula Beverly Hills 9882 Little Santa Monica Blvd ⊕ 310/551-2888 or 1-800/462-7899, ⓦ beverlyhills.peninsula.com. Luxury celebrity digs featuring ultra-chic rooms, suites and villas thick with graceful furnishings, along with pool, sun deck, cabanas, rooftop gardens and whirlpool. A room will set you back $495; more than double that for suites. ❾

West LA
See the map on pp.104–105.

Avalon 9400 W Olympic Blvd ⊕ 310/277-5221, ⓦ www.avalonbeverlyhills.com. A hipster-oriented hotel with cosy rooms and modern furnishings, along with in-room CD players, balconies and internet access (for a fee). The poolside bar is where the young elite go to pose. ❼

Bel Air 701 Stone Canyon Rd ⊕ 1-800/648-1097, ⓦ www.hotelbelair.com. The nicest hotel in LA bar none – and the only business in Bel Air – in a lushly overgrown canyon. Go for a beautiful brunch by Swan Lake if you can't afford the rooms. Currently being remodelled, it's due to reopen in summer 2011, with room rates likely to start at $500 per night. ❾

Beverly Laurel 8018 Beverly Blvd ⊕ 323/651-2441. The coffee shop, *Swingers*, attracts the most attention here; the motel has nice retro 1960s touches, though the rooms are plain. Good location, not far from the Fairfax District and Beverly Hills. ❻

Farmer's Daughter 115 S Fairfax Ave ⊕ 323/937-3930 or 1-800/334-1658, ⓦ www.farmersdaughterhotel.com. Conveniently located across from (naturally) the Farmers Market, this is a newly renovated boutique property with internet access, DVD players, flat-screen TVs and elements of Midwestern kitsch. ⑦

Sky Hotel 2352 Westwood Blvd ⊤310/475-4551, ⒲www.skyhotella.com. Good-value choice with simple boutique furnishings, rooms with high-speed internet, iPod stations and plasma TVs, gym and business centre. Continental breakfast included. ⑥

Santa Monica, Venice and Malibu

See the map on p.114.

Ambrose 1255 20th St, Santa Monica ⊤310/315-1555, ⒲www.ambrosehotel .com. Excellent choice for inland Santa Monica with Craftsman-styled decor and boutique rooms that have internet access and include continental breakfast. ⑧

Cal Mar 220 California St, Santa Monica ⊤310/395-5555, ⒲www.calmarhotel.com. Good for its central location, and the garden suites have CD/DVD players and dining rooms, kitchens and balconies. There's a heated pool, fitness room and airport shuttle too. ⑦

Casa Malibu Inn 22752 Pacific Coast Hwy, near Malibu ⊤310/456-2219. Located opposite Carbon Beach and featuring superb, well-appointed rooms – facing a courtyard garden or right on the beach – with great modern design and some rooms with fireplace, jacuzzi and balcony. ⑦

Channel Road Inn 219 W Channel Rd, Pacific Palisades ⊤310/459-1920, ⒲www.channel roadinn.com. B&B rooms in a romantic getaway nestled in lower Santa Monica Canyon (northwest of the city of Santa Monica), with ocean views, a hot tub and free bike rental. Enjoy complimentary grapes and champagne in the sumptuous rooms, each priced according to its view. ⑧

Fairmont Miramar 101 Wilshire Blvd, Santa Monica ⊤310/576-7777, ⒲www.fairmont.com. Swanky hotel that's a fixture near the north end of the Promenade, with designer-furnished suites and tropical-flavoured bungalows (upwards of $500), plus a pool, salon, spa and fitness centre, and fine views over the Pacific. One of the best luxury choices in town. ⑨

Shutters on the Beach 1 Pico Blvd at Appian Way, Santa Monica ⊤1-800/334-9000, ⒲www.shutters onthebeach.com. This white-shuttered luxury resort south of the pier is the seafront home to the stars. Amenities include hot tubs (with shuttered screens), pool, spa, sundeck, ground-floor shopping and ocean views, all for the price of $485. ⑨

Venice Beach House 15 30th Ave, Venice ⊤310/823-1966, ⒲www.venicebeachhouse.com.

A quaint B&B in a 1915 Craftsman house, with nine comfortable rooms and suites finished with lush period appointments and named for famous guests – Charlie Chaplin, Abbot Kinney, etc – and, true to the name, right next to the beach. ⑥

Venice on the Beach 2819 Ocean Front Walk ⊤310/437-4103, ⒲www.veniceonthebeachhotel .com. Groovy beachside spot whose simply furnished rooms have microwaves, fridges and internet access; some come with patios by the sands. Two-night minimum stay at weekends. Excellent value for the area. ⑥

The South Bay and Harbor Area

Beach House at Hermosa 1300 Strand, Hermosa Beach ⊤310/374-3001, ⒲www.beach-house .com. The height of luxury in the South Bay, offering two-room suites with fireplaces, wet bars, balconies, hot tubs, stereos and refrigerators, with many rooms overlooking the ocean. On the beachside concourse of the Strand. ⑨

Portofino Hotel and Yacht Club 260 Portofino Way, Redondo Beach ⊤310/379-8481, ⒲www .hotelportofino.com. Serviceable suite-hotel by the ocean. The best choices are the well-furnished, comfortable two-room suites with hot tubs and nice views over the elite playground of King Harbor. ⑧

Varden 335 Pacific Ave ⊤562/432-8950, ⒲www.thevardenhotel.com. A 1920s building modernized with sleek white contemporary decor and cosy rooms with free wi-fi, flat-screen TVs and boutique touches. The location a block from Pine Avenue also makes this a great choice. ⑤

Westin Long Beach 333 E Ocean Blvd, Long Beach ⊤562/436-3000, ⒲www.westin.com. A solid bet for bayside luxury at affordable prices (cheaper when booked online), right by the conference centre, with a spa, fitness centre and pool. ⑦

The San Gabriel and San Fernando valleys

Amarano 322 N Pass Ave ⊤818/842-8887, ⒲www.thegraciela.com. Smart boutique hotel whose stylish rooms have plasma TVs, DVD and CD players, iPod docks and free wi-fi. There's also a pool, gym, sauna and rooftop sundeck with jacuzzi. ⑦

Artists Inn 1038 Magnolia St, South Pasadena ⊤1-888/799-5668, ⒲www.artistsinns.com. Themed B&B with ten rooms and suites (some with spas) honouring famous painters and styles. Best of all is the Italian Suite, with an antique tub and sun porch. Located just two blocks from a Gold Line Metro stop. ⑥

Langham Huntington 1401 S Knoll Ave, Pasadena ⊤626/568-3900, ⒲pasadena.langhamhotels.com.

Landmark 1906 hotel on an imposing hilltop with spacious grounds, ponds and courtyards, expansive rear lawn and terrific San Gabriel Valley views. The elegant rooms are a bit on the small side, though they offer (paid) wi-fi, CD players and flat-screen TVs. **7**

Safari Inn 1911 W Olive St, Burbank ☎818/845-8586, ⊛www.safariburbank.com. A classic mid-century motel, renovated but still loaded with Pop-architecture touches. Amenities include a pool, fitness room, Burbank airport shuttle and in-room fridges, with some suites also available. **4**

Disneyland and around

Courtyard by Marriott 7621 Beach Blvd, Buena Park ☎714/670-6600, ⊛www.courtyard.com /snabp. The best bet for visiting Knott's Berry Farm, with in-room fridges and internet access, plus free parking, pool, spa, bar and restaurant. **4**

Disneyland Hotel 1150 W Cerritos Ave, Anaheim ☎714/956-6400, ⊛disneyland.disney.go.com. A thousand cookie-cutter rooms in a huge, monolithic pile – but still, an irresistible stop for many. Also with pools, faux beach and interior shopping. The Disneyland monorail stops outside, though park admission is separate. The most fun of three similarly overpriced ($350 and up) Disney hotels. **9**

Park Place Inn 1544 S Harbor Blvd, Anaheim ☎714/776-4800, ⊛www.parkplaceinnand minisuites.com. Best Western chain hotel across from Disneyland, with some mini-suites with fridges and microwaves, plus pool, sauna, jacuzzi and continental breakfast. **5**

Pavilions 1176 W Katella Ave, Anaheim ☎714/776-0140, ⊛www.pavilionshotel.com.

Convenient chain hotel offering basic rooms with fridges and microwaves, as well as a pool, spa, sauna, and shuttle to Disneyland. **3**

The Orange County Coast

Best Western Regency Inn 19360 Beach Blvd, Huntington Beach ☎714/962-4244, ⊛www .bestwesterncalifornia.com. A few miles from the beach, but still worth it for clean and reliable rooms, pool, jacuzzi and continental breakfast. **4**

Hilton Waterfront Beach Resort 21100 Pacific Coast Hwy, Huntington Beach ☎714/845-8000, ⊛www.waterfrontbeachresort.hilton.com. A towering high-rise with nicely furnished rooms and the added attractions of private balconies, serpentine pool, spa, and rentals of everything from surfboards to rollerblades; rooms have views of gardens or ocean and cost upwards of $300, with big savings to be found in low season. **9**

Ritz-Carlton Laguna Niguel Pacific Coast Hwy at 1 Ritz-Carlton Drive ☎949/240-2000, ⊛www.ritzcarlton.com/resorts/laguna_niguel. A stunning Ritz-Carlton, this one perhaps the best in town for its oceanside beauty (on the cliffs overlooking the sea around Dana Point) and rooms and suites chock-full of luxury. The high-end amenities – swanky decor, pool, spa, racquet club, etc – are everything you'd expect if paying $425 a night. **9**

Surf and Sand Resort 1555 S Coast Hwy, Laguna Beach ☎1-888/869-7969, ⊛www.surfandsand resort.com. Among the best of the coast's hotels, with terrific oceanside views, easy beach access and luxurious rooms and suites with balconies. Rates begin at $500. **9**

Hostels

Hostels offer dorm beds for around $18–28, depending on whether you're a member of their organization. Many hostels also offer cut-rate singles and doubles for $45–90. You can expect little more from your stay than a clean, safe bed, somewhere to lock your valuables, and a typically colourful crowd of visitors.

Banana Bungalow 5920 Hollywood Blvd ☎1-888/977-5077, ⊛www.bananabungalow .com. See map, p.94. Large, popular hostel, just east of the heart of Hollywood, with airport shuttles, internet, tours to Venice Beach and theme parks, and in-room kitchens and many other amenities. Dorms $25–27, doubles **3**–**4**. There's a similarly priced branch in West Hollywood at 603 N Fairfax Ave (☎323/655-2002).

HI–Anaheim/Fullerton 1700 N Harbor Blvd at Brea, Fullerton ☎714/738-3721, ⊛www.hihostels .com. Convenient and comfortable, five miles north

of Disneyland on the site of a former dairy farm. The hostel's excellent facilities include a grass volleyball court, golf driving range and picnic area. There are only twenty dorm beds, so reservations are a must. $25.

HI–LA/Santa Monica 1436 2nd St at Broadway, Santa Monica ☎310/393-9913, ⊛www .hilosangeles.org. See map, p.114. A few blocks from the beach and pier, the building was LA's Town Hall from 1887 to 1889, and retains its historic charm, with a pleasant inner courtyard, internet café, movie room – and 260 beds ($39). Reservations essential in summer.

LA area campgrounds

Reserve America (☎1-800/444-7275, ⊛www.reserveamerica.com) processes reservations at many of the **campgrounds** listed below and can look for an alternative if your chosen site is full. It charges $8 per reservation per night up to a maximum of eight people per site, including one vehicle.

Bolsa Chica Campground ☎714/846-3460 or 1-800/444-7275. Facing the ocean in Huntington Beach, also near a thousand-acre wildlife sanctuary and birders' paradise, with fishing opportunities as well. $50–65 for campers with a self-contained vehicle. No tent camping.

Crystal Cove State Park 8471 Pacific Coast Hwy, north of Laguna Beach ☎949/494-3539 or 1-800/444-7275. Two thousand acres of woods and nearly four miles of coastline (rich with tide pools) make this tent-camping park a good choice for all manner of hiking, horseriding, snorkelling, scuba diving and surfing. $25. Also with restored vintage beach cottages (dorm-style $33–98, private $125–191; ⊛www.crystalcovebeachcottages.com), often reserved months in advance.

Leo Carrillo State Park Northern Malibu ☎818/706-1310 or 1-800/444-7275. Pronounced "ca-REE-oh", near one of LA's best surfing beaches, with campsites in sight of the ocean, 25 miles northwest of Santa Monica on the Pacific Coast Hwy. $35.

Malibu Creek State Park 1925 Las Virgenes Rd, in the Santa Monica Mountains ☎818/706-8809 or 1-800/444-7275. A rustic campground in a park which can become crowded at times. Sixty sites in the shade of huge oak trees, almost all with fire pits, solar-heated showers, and flush toilets. One-time location for TV show *M*A*S*H*. $35.

Point Mugu State Park 9000 W Pacific Coast Hwy ☎818/880-0363 or 1-800/444-7275. On the northwestern edge of the Santa Monica Mountains, this park has five miles of shoreline, with sand dunes and canyons, and the waters are good for surfing and fishing. $25–35.

San Clemente State Beach Campground 3030 Avenida del Presidente, two miles south of San Clemente ☎714/492-7146 or 1-800/444-7275. A prime spot for hiking, diving and surfing, around an area that was once home to Richard Nixon's "Western White House". $35–60.

HI–LA/South Bay 3601 S Gaffey St #613, San Pedro ☎310/831-8109, ⊛www.hihostels.com. Sixty beds in old US Army barracks, with a panoramic view of the Pacific Ocean. Ideal for seeing San Pedro, Palos Verdes and the Harbor Area. Oct–May only open to groups of 20 or more. Dorms $25, rooms ❶

Hollywood International Hostel 6820 Hollywood Blvd ☎1-800/557-7038, ⊛www.hollywoodhostels.com. See map, p.94. Centrally located, with game room, gymnasium, patio garden, kitchen and laundry. Offers tours of Hollywood, theme parks, Las Vegas and Tijuana. Dorms $17, rooms ❶

Orange Drive Manor 1764 N Orange Drive, Hollywood ☎323/850-0350, ⊛www.orangedrivehostel.com. See map, p.94. Centrally located hostel (right behind the Chinese Theater), offering tours to film studios, theme parks and homes of the stars. Dorm beds $25–35, rooms ❸–❹

Orbit Hotel and Hostel 7950 Melrose Ave, West Hollywood ☎1-877/672-4887, ⊛www.orbithotel.com. See map, p.104. Retro 1960s hotel and hostel with sleek Day-Glo furnishings and modern decor, offering complimentary breakfast, movie screening room, patio, café, private baths in all rooms, and shuttle tours. Dorms $22–28, rooms ❷–❹

Stay Hotel 636 S Main St, Downtown ☎213/213-7829, ⊛www.stayhotels.com. See map, p.82. Lodging near a dicey section of the Old Bank District, offering internet access and some rooms with DVD players, but mostly no-frills accommodation, with rooms with and without private bath. Dorm beds $25, rooms ❷

USA Hostels – Hollywood 1624 Schrader Ave ☎1-800/524-6783, ⊛www.usahostels.com. See map, p.94. A block south of the centre of Hollywood Boulevard, near major attractions, and with a games room, private baths, bar, internet access and garden patio, as well as airport and train shuttles. Dorm beds $36–39, rooms ❹

Downtown LA

Rich with greatly varying social, economic and ethnic groups, the square mile (surrounded by the 10, 110 and 101 freeways) that makes up **DOWNTOWN LA** has, in the space of a few blocks, adobe buildings and Mexican market stalls, Japanese shopping plazas and avant-garde art galleries, high-rise corporate towers and antique movie palaces. Much of it can be seen on foot, starting with LA's historic and governmental heart at the **Civic Center**, crossing into the skyscraper-dominated **Bunker Hill**, continuing past the street vendors, flea markets and theatres of **Broadway**, and finally, checking out the lively **Fashion District**.

Downtown can easily be seen in a day, and if your feet get tired you can hop aboard the **DASH buses** that run every five to ten minutes through key areas, costing only 25¢. Car parks can be expensive; street parking is a good alternative, except on Bunker Hill, where the meters cost at least $2 per hour. Downtown is the hub of the MTA networks and easily accessible by public transport, especially around the grand colossus of Union Station.

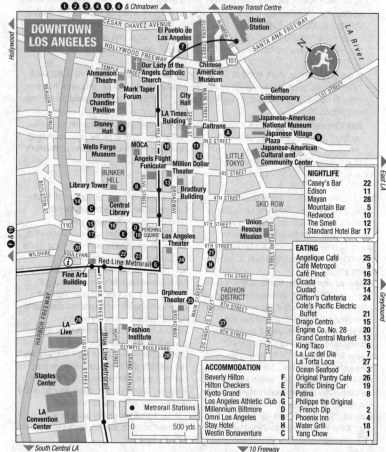

DOWNTOWN LOS ANGELES

NIGHTLIFE

Casey's Bar	22
Edison	11
Mayan	28
Mountain Bar	5
Redwood	10
The Smell	12
Standard Hotel Bar	17

EATING

Angelique Café	25
Café Metropol	9
Café Pinot	16
Cicada	23
Ciudad	14
Clifton's Cafeteria	24
Cole's Pacific Electric Buffet	21
Drago Centro	15
Engine Co. No. 28	20
Grand Central Market	13
King Taco	6
La Luz del Dia	7
La Torta Loca	27
Ocean Seafood	3
Original Pantry Café	26
Pacific Dining Car	19
Patina	8
Philippe the Original French Dip	2
Phoenix Inn	4
Water Grill	18
Yang Chow	1

ACCOMMODATION

Beverly Hilton	F
Hilton Checkers	E
Kyoto Grand	A
Los Angeles Athletic Club	G
Millennium Biltmore	D
Omni Los Angeles	B
Stay Hotel	H
Westin Bonaventure	C

● Metrorail Stations

0   500 yds

El Pueblo de Los Angeles and around

Just across US-101 from the seat of local government at the Civic Center, you can get a glimpse of LA's early frontier days at **El Pueblo de Los Angeles**, 845 N Alameda St (daily 9am–5pm; free). The site of the original, late eighteenth-century Spanish settlement of Los Angeles, its few remaining early buildings evoke a strong sense of LA's Hispanic origins – the rest is filled in with period replicas and a few modern buildings with Spanish Colonial-style facades. Las Angelitas, a docent group, offers regular free tours of this and Olvera Street (Tues–Sat 10am, 11am & noon; ☏213/628-1274, Ⓦwww.lasangelitas.org), which begin at the business office next to the Old Plaza Firehouse on the plaza's south end; there are also tour brochures available at the plaza's central information desk at 130 Paseo de la Plaza or in the Sepulveda House. The church here, **La Placita**, 535 N Main St (daily 6.30am–8pm; ☏213/629-3101, Ⓦwww.laplacita.org), is the city's oldest and has long served as a sanctuary for Central American refugees. If you'd like to take part in one of the church **Masses**, they occur three or four times daily, with twelve Eucharist services on Sunday. The early nineteenth-century **Avila Adobe**, 10 Olvera St, is touted as the oldest structure in Los Angeles (from 1847), although it was almost entirely rebuilt out of reinforced concrete following the 1971 Sylmar earthquake. Inside are two museums (daily 9am–4pm; free) covering the rise and restoration of the pueblo and a sanitized history of LA's unquenchable demands for a water supply. Across the street, the **Sepulveda House**, 125 Paseo de la Plaza (daily 9am–4pm; free), is a quaint 1887 Eastlake Victorian and El Pueblo's visitor centre, with rooms highlighting different eras in Hispanic cultural history and an informative free film on the history of LA.

The ethnic museums and Olvera Street

Along with its Mexican heritage, the pueblo also features the remnants of Chinese, Italian and even French settlements. Of particular note, the **Chinese American Museum**, 425 N Los Angeles St (Tues–Sun 10am–3pm; $5), details the local history of Chinese settlement, society and culture. Artefacts from the nineteenth and twentieth centuries, such as revealing letters, photos and documents, are displayed along with a smattering of contemporary art and a re-created Chinese herb shop circa 1900. Also worth a look is the city's first **firehouse** (Tues–Sun 10am–3pm; free) – later a boarding house and saloon – which has a small but intriguing roomful of fire-fighting gear and dates back to 1884; and the **Italian Hall**, due to open in 2011 as the **Italian American Museum** (Ⓦitalianhall.org), just south of the Chinese American Museum, which will house artefacts and mementos of a community that flourished here in the early twentieth century. **Olvera Street**, which runs north from the plaza (daily 10am–7pm; free; Ⓦwww.olvera-street.com), is a curious attempt at restoration, a pseudo-Mexican village market comprising about thirty old-looking buildings. Taken over for numerous festivals throughout the year, the street is at its best on such communal occasions, and regularly features strolling mariachi bands, Aztec- and Mexican-themed processions, and various dancers and artisans.

Union Station and Chinatown

Across from Olvera Street at 800 N Alameda St, **Union Station** is a striking mix of monumental Art Deco and Mission Revival architecture, finished in 1939. Although the building is no longer the evocative point of locomotive arrival and departure it once was, Amtrak and commuter rail still stop here (see p.73), and the structure itself is in fine condition, with a spacious vaulted lobby, heavy wooden benches and intact Art Deco signs. The station famously doubled as the gloomy police headquarters in the film *Blade Runner*.

What is now **Chinatown** was established by 1938 along North Broadway and North Spring Street following its residents' abrupt transplant from the site of Union Station. It's not the bustling affair you'll find in a number of other US cities, unless it's Chinese New Year, when there's a parade of dragons and firework celebrations. Apart from the many good restaurants here (see p.141), official culture consists of a handful of small shopping malls, where you can pick up an assortment of lanterns, teapots and jade jewellery – aimed more at tourists than residents. (To get a truer sense of contemporary Chinese culture, visit Alhambra or Monterey Park, lively ethnic suburbs located just beyond LA's eastern boundary.)

The Civic Center

South of the Santa Ana Freeway from Olvera Street, most of the **Civic Center** is a collection of plodding bureaucratic office buildings. One exception is the strangely futuristic glass walls and steel panels of the **Caltrans Building**, 100 S Main St (Mon–Fri 8am–5pm; free), an ultra modern glass-and-aluminium office for state freeway planners that helped its designer, Thom Mayne, win the 2005 Pritzker Prize, architecture's highest honour. More traditional, a block north, is LA's famous Art Deco **City Hall**, known to the world through LAPD badges seen in TV shows ever since *Dragnet*, and until 1960 the city's tallest structure. You can get a good look inside on free **tours**, which include its 28th-storey, 360-degree observation deck (Mon–Fri 9am–4pm; free).

On the south side of the Civic Center plaza, the **Los Angeles Times**, 202 W 1st St, provides free, twice-monthly tours of the building (hours vary; by reservation only at ℡213/237-5757, Ⓦwww.latimes.com), offering a glimpse of how the West Coast's biggest newspaper is put together.

Little Tokyo and the Geffen Contemporary

East of the Civic Center, the colourful shopping precinct of **Little Tokyo** is centred on the Japanese American Cultural and Community Center, 244 S San Pedro St, whose **Doizaki Gallery** (Tues–Fri noon–5pm, Sat & Sun 11am–4pm; free) shows traditional and contemporary Japanese drawing and calligraphy, along with costumes, sculptures and other associated art forms. Located between the two and easy to miss, the stunning **James Irvine Garden** (daily 9am–5pm; free), with a 170-foot stream running along its sloping hillside, was carved out of a flat lot to become the "garden of the clear stream", and makes the site seem a world away from LA's expanse of asphalt and concrete. The most active part of Little Tokyo is **Japanese Village Plaza** (most stores daily 9am–6pm), a touristy outdoor mall near First Street and Central Avenue lined with sushi bars and shops. Across the road at 369 E 1st St, the **Japanese American National Museum** (Tues–Sun 11am–5pm, Thurs until 8pm; $9; ℡213/625-0414, Ⓦwww.janm.org) houses exhibits on everything from origami to traditional furniture and folk craftwork to the internment of Japanese-Americans during World War II.

Near the museum is the **Geffen Contemporary**, 152 N Central Ave (same hours, contact details and prices as the Museum of Contemporary Art, see opposite, to which a ticket also entitles same-day entrance), set in a converted police garage, designed by Frank Gehry. An alternative exhibition space to its more mainstream sibling, the Geffen presents huge installation pieces, architecture retrospectives and other big shows with a voracious need for space.

Bunker Hill

Until a century ago the area south of the Civic Center, **BUNKER HILL**, was LA's most elegant neighbourhood, its elaborate Victorian mansions and houses connected by funicular railroad to the growing business district down below on Spring Street. These structures were all wiped out by 1960s urban renewal and replaced with a forest of glossy high-rises.

To reach them, the **Angels Flight** funicular – restored in 2010 – is a bright and colourful reminder of a long-departed era. You can board the train just north of the intersection of Hill and Fourth streets for a mere quarter. At the top rise the austerely modern office-blocks of the **Financial District**, whose fifty-storey towers have shops and restaurants at their base – outmoded shopping malls intended to provide street life for the brokers and traders, and about as dreary as you might expect. One of the few notable structures is the **Gas Company Tower**, 555 W 5th St, a metallic blue building whose crown symbolizes a natural-gas flame on its side.

The Museum of Contemporary Art

Based at the California Plaza, a billion-dollar complex of offices and luxury condos, the **Museum of Contemporary Art (MOCA)**, 250 S Grand Ave (Mon & Fri 11am–5pm, Thurs 11am–8pm, Sat & Sun 11am–6pm; $10, students $5, free Thurs; ☎213/626-6222, ⊛www.moca.org), was designed by showman architect Arata Isozaki, its silhouette offering an array of geometric red shapes recognizable from TV advertisements filmed here.

Much of the gallery is used for temporary exhibitions and the bulk of the **permanent collection** is mid-twentieth-century American, particularly from the Abstract Expressionist period, including work by Franz Kline and Mark Rothko. You'll also find plenty of Pop Art, in Robert Rauschenberg's junk collages, Claes Oldenburg's papier-mâché hamburgers and fast food, and Andy Warhol's print-ad black telephone. Aside from more recent highlights like Alexis Smith's quirky collages, Charles Ray's Amazonian mannequins and Martin Puryear's anthropomorphic wooden sculptures, the museum is also strong on **photography**, exhibiting Diane Arbus, Larry Clark, Robert Frank, Lee Friedlander and Cindy Sherman. Much of the museum is used for **temporary exhibitions**, which may include the likes of Donald Judd's prefabricated metal boxes and Ed Kienholz's perverse assemblage art, or you can explore some of the city's up-and-coming names.

The theatre on the lower floor of MOCA hosts some multimedia shows and performances, as well as lectures and seminars. The best time to visit the museum is during an evening concert in summer, when entry is free, and **jazz and classical concerts** are played outdoors under the red pyramids. At other times, a ticket to MOCA also entitles you to same-day entrance to Downtown's Geffen Contemporary (see opposite), and to the branch at the Pacific Design Center (see p.108) out in West Hollywood.

Disney Hall and Our Lady of the Angels

Just north of the museum, around the stodgy music and theatre establishments of the Music Center, 135 Grand Ave, **Disney Hall**, First Street at Grand Avenue, is LA's finest jewel of modern architecture, a Frank Gehry-designed, 2300-seat acoustic showpiece whose titanium exterior resembles something akin to colossal broken eggshells. The LA Philharmonic (see "Performing arts and film", p.153) is based here, and with the hall's rich, warm acoustics and features such as a colossal, intricate pipe organ, it may be the best place to hear music in the city, perhaps in all of California. Hours and days vary for the free 60-minutes **tours**, which run between 10am and 2pm most days of the month (☎213/972-4399, ⊛musiccenter .org/visit).

One long block north of Disney Hall stands LA's other Modernist colossus, the $200-million **Our Lady of the Angels** Catholic church, 555 W Temple St

(Mon–Fri 6.30am–6pm, Sat 9am–6pm, Sun 7am–6pm; free tours Mon–Fri 1pm; ⓣ213/680-5200, ⓦwww.olacathedral.org). The church, the centrepiece of the local archdiocese, is a truly massive structure in its own right – eleven concrete storeys tall and capable of holding three thousand people. The interior is the highlight, featuring tapestries of saints, giant bronze doors, ultra-thin alabaster screens for diffusing light, a grand marble altar, and $30 million worth of art and furnishings.

Southwest of MOCA

Southwest of MOCA, the **Wells Fargo History Museum**, 333 Grand Ave (Mon–Fri 9am–5pm; free), sits at the base of the Wells Fargo Center. It tells the history of Wells Fargo & Co, the current banking colossus that was founded in Gold Rush California, and displays among other things photographs, a two-pound chunk of gold, a re-created assay office from the nineteenth century and an original Concord stagecoach.

A block away, the shining glass tubes of the **Westin Bonaventure Hotel**, 404 S Figueroa St (see p.77), have become one of the city's most unusual landmarks since the late 1970s. The structure features a flurry of ramps, elevators, concrete columns and catwalks in a soaring atrium. Make sure to ride in the glass elevators that run up through the atrium and climb the outside walls, giving views over much of Downtown and beyond.

A short distance away, the **Richard J. Riordan Central Library**, 630 W 5th St (Mon–Thurs 10am–8pm, Fri & Sat 10am–6pm, Sun 1–5pm), was built in 1926 but was renamed for LA's billionaire mayor of the 1990s; its lower floors form a pedestal for the squat central tower, which is topped by a brilliantly coloured pyramid roof. Across Fifth Street, the **Library Tower** is the tallest office building west of Chicago. Now owned by US Bank (which has named the tower after itself, to little public notice), the cylindrical tower features Lawrence Halprin's huge **Bunker Hill Steps** at its base, supposedly modelled after the Spanish Steps in Rome.

Broadway and around

Downtown's north–south axis of **Broadway** once formed the core of Los Angeles's most fashionable shopping and entertainment district, brimming with movie palaces and department stores. Today it's a bustling Hispanic community, whose vendors operate out of hundred-year-old buildings, the salsa music and street culture making for one of the city's most electric environments. The indoor **Grand Central Market** (daily 9am–6pm), on Broadway between Third and Fourth, provides a good taste of modern Broadway – everything from apples and oranges to *carne asada* and pickled pig's feet. Across the street, the 1893 **Bradbury Building** (lobby open Mon–Sat 9am–5pm; free) has a magnificent sunlit atrium surrounded by wrought-iron balconies, open-cage elevators set around a narrow court, and elaborate staircases at either end; scenes from both *Blade Runner* and *Citizen Kane* were filmed here. Tourists are only permitted in the lobby, but it's worth a look for the great view up. (Los Angeles Conservancy tours often begin here; see p.76.)

Broadway was first known for its **Theater District**, and it still constitutes one of the last remaining urban pockets of classic cinema architecture in the country – though none of the structures shows movies regularly. Several are noteworthy, though: next to the Grand Central Market, the opulent 1918 **Million Dollar Theater**, 307 S Broadway, its whimsical terracotta facade mixing buffalo heads with bald eagles in typical Hollywood Spanish Baroque style, was originally built by theatre magnate Sid Grauman, who went on to build the Egyptian and Chinese theatres in Hollywood. The **Los Angeles Theater**, 615 S Broadway, is considered the best movie palace in the city and one of the finest in the country. Its plush lobby behind the triumphal arch facade is lined by marble columns supporting an intricate mosaic ceiling, while the 1800-seat auditorium is enveloped by trompe l'oeil murals and lighting effects. Like the Million Dollar, it's no longer open to the public for regular screenings, but a June programme called **Last Remaining Seats** draws huge crowds to both of them and the nearby **Orpheum Theatre**, 842 S Broadway, to watch revivals of classic Hollywood films (tickets $20, often with live entertainment; call ☏213/623-2489 or visit Ⓦwww.laconservancy.org for details).

A few other architectural gems stand out within a few blocks of Broadway. The **Millennium Biltmore Hotel** (see p.77) stands over the west side of Pershing Square two blocks west of Broadway, its three brick towers rising from a Renaissance Revival arcade along Olive Street and its grand old lobby (the original main entrance) offering an intricately painted Spanish-beamed ceiling. A block south, the Art Deco **Oviatt Building**, 617 S Olive St, features elevators with hand-carved oak panelling designed and executed by Parisian craftsman René Lalique. Also striking is the intricate 1928 design of the building's exterior, especially its grand sign and looming clock above. Finally, three more blocks west, the **Fine Arts Building**, 811 W 7th St (Mon–Fri 8.30am–5pm; free), is notable for its grand entry arch featuring gargoyles and griffins, intricate Romanesque Revival styling, and an eye-catching lobby where you'll find medieval-style carvings and the occasional art exhibit.

Spring Street and the Fashion District

A block **east** of Broadway, **Spring Street**, between Fourth and Seventh streets, was once the axis of the city's commerce and banking in the early twentieth century, but was abandoned in the 1980s. In the last decade, however, it has re-emerged as a centre for upmarket loft housing. Behind these Neoclassical facades you can find a handful of interesting nightclubs, galleries and theatres, though one impediment to the neighbourhood's revival is its closeness to **Skid Row**, just a few blocks east, supposedly the largest concentration of homeless people in the US.

The other major attraction in the area is the welter of commercial activity in the **Fashion District** (most businesses Mon–Sat 10am–5pm; ☏213/488-1153, Ⓦwww.fashiondistrict.org), bounded by Los Angeles and San Pedro streets and Seventh and Ninth avenues, where you can pick up decent fabric for as little as $2 per yard. Highlights include the **California Market Center**, at Ninth and Los Angeles streets (typically Mon–Fri 9am–5pm; ☏213/630-3600, Ⓦwww.californiamarketcenter.com), which fills three million square feet and seemingly has just as many visitors; the **Flower Market**, 766 Wall St (Mon, Wed & Fri 8am–noon, Tues, Thurs & Sat 6am–noon; entry $2, Sat $1), which has a voluminous selection of blooms that you can buy for a fraction of the prices charged elsewhere; and **Santee Alley** (between Maple Ave and Santee St, running from Olympic Blvd to 12th St), a chaotic market thick with hundreds of vendor shops and stalls selling everything from the cheapest sunglasses to smart suits – LA's pint-sized version of New York's Canal Street.

The Fashion Institute and further south

To the west near Grand Hope Park, the **Fashion Institute of Design and Merchandising**, 919 S Grand Ave (Tues–Sat 10am–4pm; free; ☏1-800/624-1200, Ⓦwww.fashionmuseum.org), features items drawn from its collection of ten thousand pieces of costume and apparel – French gowns, Russian jewels, quirky shoes and so on. The main draw is the **"Art of Motion Picture Costume Design"** show that runs from February to April – roughly Oscar time – displaying colourful outfits that may include anything from Liz Taylor's *Cleopatra* garb to the spacey get-ups from *Star Wars*.

Finally, three blocks to the southwest, the **LA Convention Center**, 1201 S Figueroa St, and the **Staples Center**, 865 S Figueroa St, are sleek modern structures that have led the way for the redevelopment of the area, but otherwise offer little of interest beyond conventions and Lakers games. Just north of the Staples Center is a retail behemoth called **LA Live** (℗213/763-6030, Ⓦwww .nokiatheatrela.com/lalive.php), a $2.5-billion shopping and entertainment complex that features theatres, sports facilities and broadcast studios, upper-end hotels, a central plaza, a museum devoted to the Grammy Awards, a bowling alley, and numerous arcades, restaurants and clubs.

Around Downtown

The area **around Downtown** is united by little more than freeways and large distances separating the major points of interest, though there's quite a bit worth seeing. The districts immediately northwest of Downtown, **Angelino Heights** and **Echo Park**, are where the upper crust of LA society lived luxuriously in the late nineteenth and early twentieth centuries in stylish Victorian houses (now either preserved or decrepit). Directly south of Downtown, the walled-off **USC campus** has a smattering of sights, and neighbouring **Exposition Park** features acres of gardens and several excellent museums. Beyond here, the vast urban bleakness of **South Central LA** has a few isolated spots of interest; it's generally a place to visit with caution or with someone who knows the area, though it's safe enough in daytime around the main drags. More appealing is colourful **East LA**, the largest Mexican-immigrant enclave outside Mexico, a buzzing district of markets, shops and street-corner music.

Angelino Heights and Echo Park

LA's first suburb, **Angelino Heights**, just northwest of Downtown off US-101, was laid out in the flush of a property boom at the end of the 1880s on a pleasant hilltop. Though the boom soon went bust, around a dozen of the elaborate houses that were built here, especially along **Carroll Avenue**, have survived and been restored, their wraparound verandas, turrets and pediments set appealingly against the Downtown skyline. The best of the lot is the **Sessions House**, no. 1330, a Queen Anne masterpiece with Moorish detail, decorative glass and a circular "moon window". On the first Saturday of the month, you can take a two-and-a-half-hour tour of the neighbourhood with the LA Conservancy (10am; $10; reserve at ℗213/623-2489, Ⓦwww.laconservancy.org).

At the foot of the hill, to the west of Angelino Heights, **Echo Park** is a small oasis of palm trees and lotus blossoms set around a lake. In the large white **Angelus Temple** on the northern side of the lake, the evangelist **Aimee Semple McPherson** used to preach sermons to five thousand people in the 1920s, with thousands more listening in on the radio. You can rent a rowing boat or paddleboat (typically $10 per hour) from vendors along Echo Park Avenue, running along the eastern edge of the lake. The park also appeals for its funky, **bohemian atmosphere**, with countless affordable (for LA) bungalows and apartments around the park housing the city's next generation of artists, musicians and filmmakers.

Wilshire Boulevard and around

Wilshire Boulevard leaves Downtown between Sixth and Seventh streets as the main route across 25 miles of Los Angeles to Santa Monica's beachside Palisades Park. The large plot of land west of the Westlake district, **MacArthur Park**, has a Red Line Metrorail connection, scattered patches of green, and a seemingly idyllic lake – though drug-dealing is still a popular activity and the park should be strictly avoided after dark. Nearby, at 403 S Bonnie Brae St, the **Grier-Musser Museum** (Wed–Sat noon–4pm; $6) provides a glimpse of the luxurious decor and stylish architecture of the nineteenth century, with six rooms overflowing with all manner of Victorian bric-a-brac and precious furnishings.

Half a mile west of MacArthur Park, the **Bullocks Wilshire** department store, 3050 Wilshire Blvd, is a stunning monument to 1920s Los Angeles and the most complete and unaltered example of Zigzag Art Deco architecture in the city. The building is now the law library of adjacent **Southwestern University**; to enquire about visiting during special events, visit ⓦwww.swlaw.edu/campus/building.

Two blocks south of Wilshire, between Vermont and Western, **Koreatown** is home to the largest concentration of Koreans outside Korea and five times bigger than Chinatown and Little Tokyo combined. In reality, the comparison is unfair, for Koreatown is an active residential and commercial district, not just a tourist sight, and boasts as many bars, theatres, community groups, banks and shopping complexes as it does restaurants. To check out the community's art and culture, the **Korean Cultural Centre**, in the Miracle Mile at 5505 Wilshire Blvd (Mon–Fri 9am–5pm, Sat 10am–1pm; free; ☏323/936-7141, ⓦwww.kccla.org), has a museum displaying photographs, antiques and craftwork from Korea and the local immigrant community, and rotating exhibitions of fine art, folk work and applied crafts, plus theatrical performances.

The USC campus

The **USC campus** (University of Southern California), a few miles south of Downtown along Figueroa Street, is an enclave of wealth in one of the city's poorer neighbourhoods, South Central LA. USC, or the "University of Spoiled Children", is one of the most expensive universities in the country, carefully walled off from the rough neighbourhood that surrounds it. Though sizeable, the campus is reasonably easy to get around. You might find it easiest to take the free fifty-minute **walking tour** (four tours daily; book on ☏213/740-6605, ⓦwww .usc.edu). Without a guide, a good place to start is in the **Doheny Library**, between Childs Way and Trousdale Parkway (hours vary; often Mon–Thurs 9am–8pm, Fri & Sat 9am–5pm, Sun noon–5pm; ☏213/740-2924), an inviting 1932 Romanesque Revival structure where you can pick up a campus map and browse a large stock of overseas newspapers and magazines.

USC's art collection is housed in the **Fisher Gallery**, 823 Exposition Blvd (Tues–Sat noon–5pm; free; ☏213/740-4561, ⓦfisher.usc.edu), focusing on a wide range of art, from international and multicultural to avant-garde and contemporary. The **Helen Lindhurst Fine Arts Gallery**, room 103 in Watt Hall, 850 W 37th St (Mon–Thurs 9am–7pm, Fri 9am–4.30pm; free; ☏213/740-2787), holds contemporary and experimental works from student and regional artists. If music is more to your interest, the **Bovard Auditorium**, 3551 Trousdale Parkway (☏213/740-4211), is one of five concert venues on campus that hosts regular performances by students, faculty and guest performers. The campus is also home to the **School of Cinematic Arts**, a mainstream rival to the UCLA film school in Westwood. You can sometimes catch a classic or foreign flick at the nearby **Eileen Norris Cinema**, south of the Cinema School at 3507 Trousdale Parkway.

Between USC and Exposition Park, sports fans may want to stop at the **Coliseum**, 3939 S Figueroa St. The site of the 1932 and 1984 Olympic Games hosts home games for the dominant USC football team, one of the top squads in the country, which allows them to charge a minimum of $75 per game (℡213/740-GOSC, Ⓦwww.usctrojans.com). Otherwise, the imposing grand arch on the facade and muscular, headless commemorative statues create enough interest to make the place worth a look.

Exposition Park

Across Exposition Boulevard from the USC campus, **Exposition Park** incorporates lush landscaped gardens and a number of decent museums off 3800 S Figueroa St, at 700 State Drive (parking $8). One of the highlights, the **California Science Center** (daily 10am–5pm; free) has scores of quirky displays aimed at making the world of science more fun for youngsters. Displays include a walk-in periscope, an imitation earthquake and a demonstration wind tunnel; three of the museum's attractions – a "high-wire" bicycle, motion simulator and rock-climbing wall – cost $7 jointly. In the same complex, an **IMAX Theater** (tickets $8.25, kids $5) plays a range of kid-oriented documentaries on a gigantic curved screen. Nearby, the **Air and Space Gallery** (same hours as Science Center) is marked by a sleek jet stuck to its facade and offers a series of satellites and telescopes, and a slew of aeroplanes and rockets hanging from above.

To the south, head for the stimulating **California African-American Museum**, 600 State Drive (Tues–Sat 10am–5pm, Sun 11am–5pm; free; ℡213/744-7432, Ⓦwww.caamuseum.org), which has diverse temporary exhibitions on the history and culture of black people in the Americas, as well as a good range of painting and sculpture from local and national artists. Not far away, the **Natural History Museum of Los Angeles County**, 900 Exposition Blvd (daily 9.30am–5pm; $9), is an explosion of Spanish Revival architecture with echoing domes, travertine columns and a marble floor. Foremost among the exhibits is a tremendous stock of dinosaur bones and fossils, and some individually imposing skeletons (usually casts) including the crested duckbilled dinosaur, the skull of a Tyrannosaurus Rex, and the astonishing frame of a Diatryma – a huge prehistoric bird incapable of flight. More contemporary (relatively speaking) bones of Ice Age-era ground sloths, mammoths, lions and the like are sometimes on view – many of them dug out of the muck of the La Brea Tar Pits, where the Page Museum is a satellite of this one (see p.108). In the fascinating pre-Columbian Hall are Maya pyramid murals and the complete contents of a reconstructed Mexican tomb. Topping the whole place off is the gem collection, several breathtaking roomfuls of crystals, and an enticing display of three hundred pounds of gold, safely protected from prying fingers. On a sunny day, spare some time for walking through Exposition Park's **Rose Garden**, 701 State Drive (mid-March to Dec daily 9am–dusk; free; ℡213/765-5397). The flowers are at their most fragrant in April and May, when the bulk of the visitors come by to admire the 16,000 rose bushes and the charm of their setting.

South Central LA

Lacking the scenic splendour of the coast, the glamour of West LA and the history of Downtown, **SOUTH CENTRAL LA** comprises such notable neighbourhoods as **Watts**, **Compton** and **Inglewood**, but hardly ranks on the tourist circuit – especially since it burst onto the world's TV screens as the focal point of the April 1992 **riots**. A big, elliptical chunk reaching from the southern edge of Downtown to the northern fringe of the Harbor Area, most LA visitors go out of their way to avoid the district, but there are a handful of sights that may be worth your while during daylight hours, most of them in the revived **West Adams** district just south of, and paralleling, the I-10 freeway.

The Watts Towers

The district of **Watts**, on the eastern side of South Central, achieved notoriety as the scene of the six-day **Watts Riots** of August 1965. There is one valid reason to come here: to see the internationally famous, Gaudí-esque **Watts Towers**, 1765 E 107th St (30min tours every half-hour Thurs & Fri 11am–3pm, Sat 10.30am–3pm, Sun 12.30–3pm; $7; ☎213/847-4646), one of Southern California's most important visual landmarks. Constructed from iron, stainless steel, old bedsteads and cement, and decorated with fragments of bottles and around 70,000 crushed seashells, these striking pieces of street art were built by Simon Rodia, who had no artistic training but laboured over the towers' construction from 1921 to 1954, refusing offers of help and unable to explain either their meaning or why he was building them. Once finished, he left the area, refused to talk about the towers, and faded into obscurity. One especially good time to come is during a late September weekend that hosts the Saturday **Day of the Drums Festival** and Sunday **Watts Towers Jazz Festival**, both signature events in the city.

Compton and Inglewood

Despite its fame as the home of many of LA's rappers – NWA, for example, sang venomously of its ills on their album *Straight Outta Compton* – not to mention tennis phenoms Serena and Venus Williams, **Compton** is not a place where strangers should attempt to sniff out the local music or sports scenes. History buffs secure in their cars, however, might enjoy a stop for the free conducted tours at the **Dominguez Ranch Adobe**, 18127 S Alameda St (Sun & Wed 1, 2 & 3pm; ☎310/603-0088, ⓦdominguezrancho.org), a restored mission that chronicles the social ascent of its founder, Juan José Dominguez – one of the soldiers who left Mexico with Padre Junípero Serra's expedition to found the California missions – whose long military service was acknowledged in 1782 by the granting of 75,000 acres of land (long since subdivided into tiny modern parcels). The six main rooms of the 1826 adobe are on display with their original furnishings, or at least replicas of them, and are well worth a look for anyone intrigued by the pre-American period in California.

Closer to LAX, on the other side of the Harbor Freeway, drab **Inglewood** is home to the **Hollywood Park Racetrack** (☎310/419-1549, ⓦwww .hollywoodpark.com), a landscaped track with lagoons and tropical vegetation. Nearer to the 405 freeway, two gems of Pop architecture are worth a look: **Randy's Donuts**, 805 Manchester Blvd, an iconic fast-food drive-through operation that's famed for its giant rooftop donut, and **Pann's**, a mile north at La Tijera and Centinela boulevards, one of the last true pop-modern coffee shops around, with a pitched roof, big neon sign, exotic plants and wealth of primary colours. If you have a taste for more historic architecture, check out the **Centinela Adobe**, just south of *Pann's* at 7636 Midfield Ave (Sun 2–4pm; free), an 1834 structure whose earthen bricks were made at the site, and which is loaded with period antiques and Victorian furnishings.

West Adams

The charming **West Adams** neighbourhood, along Adams Boulevard from Crenshaw Boulevard to Hoover Street, was one of LA's few racially mixed neighbourhoods in the early part of the twentieth century, and still boasts some terrific architecture from that era. Known in the Twenties and Thirties as **"Sugar Hill"**, it was also one of the spots where silent-screen movie stars tended to live, though many of the grand houses and mansions have since become religious institutions. Busby Berkeley's estate, the 1910 **Guasti Villa**, 3500 W Adams Blvd, is a graceful Renaissance Revival creation that might fit nicely in Italy but is now home to a New Age spiritual institute. Nearby, the **Lindsay House**, no. 3424, a terracotta curiosity with a heavy stone facade and unique tilework, has become the Our Lady of Bright Mount, a Polish Catholic church. Elsewhere, the **South Seas House**, 2301 W 24th St (Mon–Fri 8am–10pm, Sat 10am–4pm), is a community centre that you can visit to sample the place's odd 1902 blend of Victorian and Polynesian architecture, and the **Britt Mansion**, 2115 W Adams, is a 1910 Neoclassical gem with grand white columns and adjoining gardens. It's now home to the sports organization LA84, whose library boasts a large selection of books on athletics (Mon–Fri 10am–5pm; free).

The finest building in the area is the French Renaissance **William Clark Memorial Library**, 2520 Cimarron St (Mon–Fri 9am–4.45pm; free), with its elegant symmetry, yellow-brick walls, formal gardens and grand entrance hall. As millionaire heir to a copper fortune, founder of the LA Philharmonic, and a US Senator from Montana, Clark amassed this great collection before donating it to UCLA, which continues to oversee it as a non-circulating library. Besides rare volumes by Pope, Fielding, Dryden, Swift and Milton, plus a huge set of letters and manuscripts by Oscar Wilde, the library includes four Shakespeare folios, a group of works by Chaucer, and copies of key documents in American history pertaining to the Louisiana Purchase and the like.

East LA

Of the many Hispanic neighbourhoods all over LA, one of the longest standing is **East LA**, beginning two miles east of Downtown. There was a Mexican population here long before white settlers came, and from the late nineteenth century onward millions more arrived, coming chiefly to work on the land. As the white inhabitants moved west towards the coast, the Mexicans stayed, creating a vast Spanish-speaking community that's one of the most historic in the country.

There are few specific "sights" in East LA. The best plan is just to turn up on a Saturday afternoon – the liveliest part of the week – and stroll along **Cesar Chavez Avenue**, formerly Brooklyn Avenue, going eastward from Indiana Street, checking out the wild pet shops, with free-roaming parrots and cases of boa constrictors, and **botanicas shops**, where you can browse amid the shark's teeth, dried devilfish and plastic statuettes of Catholic saints, and buy magical herbs, ointments or candles after consulting the shopkeeper and explaining (in Spanish) what ails you. Only slightly less exotic fare can be found in **El Mercado de Los Angeles**, 3425 E 1st St (daily 10am–8pm), an indoor market somewhat similar to Olvera Street (see p.83) but much more authentic. An indoor warren of vendor stalls sell *botanicas*, clothing, Latin American food and arts-and-crafts pieces; on the top floor, where the restaurants are located, mariachi bands play until well after midnight every day.

Guadalupe, the Mexican image of the Virgin Mary, appears in mural art all over East LA, nowhere better than at the junction of Mednik and Cesar Chavez avenues. Lined with blue tile, it now forms an unofficial shrine where worshippers place fresh flowers and candles. If sufficiently moved by the spirit, continue on to the mausoleum of **New Calvary Cemetery**, 4201 E Whittier Ave (daily 8am–5pm, spring & summer closes 6pm), rich with Corinthian columns and pilasters, an Egyptian-pyramid roof and a few Byzantine domes, plus some sculpted angels thrown in for good measure. Beyond its exterior panache, the cemetery is also the resting place of rich, old-time Angelenos like oil magnate Edward Doheny, jazz great Jelly Roll Morton, and movie stars like Lionel and Ethel Barrymore, and Lou Costello.

Highland Park

Two miles north of Downtown, **Highland Park** has a handful of exuberantly detailed Victorian houses, eight of them brought together from around the city to form **Heritage Square**. This fenced-off ten-acre park at 3800 Homer St (Fri–Sun noon–5pm; $10) uncomfortably sites a railway station next to an octagonal house next to a Methodist church, and although the buildings are interesting enough, the park's freeway-adjacent home is a less-than-ideal spot to escape into a Victorian world of buggies and gingerbread.

Just beyond the next freeway exit, at 200 E Ave 43, the **Lummis House** (Fri–Sun noon–4pm; free) is the well-preserved home of **Charles F. Lummis**, a publicist who was at the heart of LA's nineteenth-century boom. An early champion of civil rights for Native Americans, and one who worked to save and preserve many of the missions, Lummis built his home as a cultural centre where the literati of the day would meet to discuss poetry and the art and architecture of the Southwest. He built it in an ad hoc mixture of Mission and Medieval styles, naming it *El Alisal* after the many large sycamore trees that shade the gardens, and constructing the thick walls out of rounded granite boulders taken from the nearby riverbed and the beams over the living room from old telephone poles. The solid-wood front doors are similarly built to last, reinforced with iron and weighing tonnes, while the plaster-and-tile interior features rustic, hand-cut timber ceilings and home-made furniture, all a fitting reflection of its rugged owner, one of the few individuals to reach LA by walking – from Cincinnati.

Lastly, one of the city's most historic museums, the **Southwest Museum of the American Indian**, rising castle-like below Mount Washington at 234 Museum Drive (☎323/221-2164), was founded in 1907 to house tribal artefacts from all over North America. However, seemingly endless seismic renovation has kept the collection off-limits until 2013 at the earliest (see ⓦ theautry.org for the latest details).

Hollywood

Ever since movies and their stars became international symbols of the good life, **HOLLYWOOD** has been a magnet to millions of tourists on celebrity-seeking pilgrimages and an equal number of hopefuls drawn by the prospect of riches and glory.

In reality, successful Hollywood residents actually spent little time here – leaving as soon as they could afford to for the privacy of the hills or coast. Even as early as the 1930s Hollywood had developed into a gritty district rife with prostitution and petty thievery, and subsequent decades only accelerated the decline. Although the area continues to be a secondary centre for the film business, with abundant technical service companies like prop shops and equipment suppliers, all the big film companies (other than Paramount) relocated long ago to places like Burbank, leaving Hollywood to decay. Things have brightened up in the past few years, however, with public and private capital financing the construction of new tourist plazas and shopping malls – places which, with their focus on the golden age of movie making, try to take the tarnish off the Hollywood myth once more.

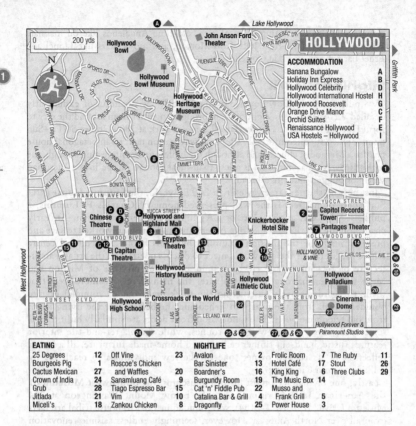

EATING		NIGHTLIFE					
25 Degrees	12	Avalon	2	Frolic Room	7	The Ruby	11
Bourgeois Pig	1	Bar Sinister	13	Hotel Café	17	Stout	26
Cactus Mexican	27	Boardner's	16	King King	6	Three Clubs	29
Crown of India	24	Burgundy Room	19	The Music Box	14		
Grub	28	Cat 'n' Fiddle Pub	22	Musso and			
Jitlada	21	Catalina Bar & Grill	4	Frank Grill	5		
Miceli's	18	Dragonfly	25	Power House	3		

Off Vine	23
Roscoe's Chicken and Waffles	20
Sanamluang Café	9
Tiago Espresso Bar	15
Vim	10
Zankou Chicken	8

Approaching from Downtown via Sunset Boulevard, **East Hollywood** offers the first taste of the district, an assortment of cheap housing and low-rent businesses with a few interesting sights scattered here and there, among them **Los Feliz**, which has become a trendy place to live and socialize, with a number of eye-catching Modernist homes glittering above in the hills. Further west, **Central Hollywood** is a compact zone loaded with movie history and swamped by an eccentric street mix of social derelicts and starstruck tourists along the legendary stretch of Hollywood Boulevard. To the north, the slopes of the Santa Monica Mountains contain **Griffith Park** – several thousand acres offering rugged hiking trails and busy sports and picnic grounds – and the **Hollywood Hills**, whose exclusive homes perched on snaking driveways are the most tangible reminders of the wealth generated in the city, and the brand-name celebrities that own them.

East Hollywood: Silver Lake and Los Feliz

Off the radar screen of most visitors, **EAST HOLLYWOOD** finds its focus near the eastern intersection of Hollywood and Sunset boulevards, a rough stretch that represents the "real" LA with its blend of working-class Latinos, bohemian artists and musicians of all stripes, and assorted punks and prostitutes. Even here, the perimeter neighbourhoods bordering the hills are highly sought after, the streets around Beachwood Avenue have evolved into popular places to live and hang out, and upscale Mediterranean-style homes clutter the hillside.

A history of Hollywood

Strangely enough, Hollywood started life in the 1880s as a **temperance colony**, created to be a sober, God-fearing alternative to raunchy Downtown LA, eight miles away by rough country road. In 1911 residents were forced, in return for a regular water supply, to become an LA suburb. The film industry, then gathering momentum on the East Coast, needed a place with cheap labour, low taxes, compliant government, guaranteed sunshine and a diverse assortment of natural backdrops to stand in for any worldwide location, and most importantly, a distant spot to dodge Thomas Edison's patent trust, which tried to restrict filmmaking nationwide. Southern California was the perfect spot. A few offices affiliated with Eastern film companies appeared Downtown in 1906 and the first true studios opened in nearby Silver Lake, but independent hopefuls soon discovered the cheaper rents on offer in Hollywood. Soon, the first **Hollywood studio** opened in 1911 (the long-vanished Nestor Studio, at the corner of Sunset and Gower), and within three years the place was packed with filmmakers – many of them, like **Cecil B. DeMille**, who shared his barn-converted office space with a horse, destined to be the big names of the future.

The industry expanded fast, bringing riches and fame – with momentum provided by the overnight success of DeMille's *The Squaw Man*, filmed inside the former barn itself, which is now the **Hollywood Heritage Museum**, 2100 N Highland Blvd (Wed–Sun noon–4pm; $7), exhibiting interesting antiques and treasures from the silent era. Yet movie making was far from being a financially secure business, and it wasn't until the release of D.W. Griffith's **The Birth of a Nation** in 1914 that the power of film was demonstrated. The film's racist account of the Civil War and Reconstruction caused riots outside cinemas and months of critical debate in the newspapers, and for the first time drew the middle classes to movie houses – despite the exorbitant $2 ticket price. It also perfected the narrative style and production techniques that gradually became standard in classic Hollywood cinema.

Modern Hollywood took shape from the 1920s on, when film production grew more specialized, the "**star system**" was perfected, and many small companies either went bust or were incorporated into one of the handful of bigger studios that came to dominate filmmaking. The **Golden Age** of the studio system peaked from the 1930s through the late 1940s, when a Supreme Court ruling put an end to studio monopolies owning their own exhibitors and theatres. Despite lean years from the later 1950s until the 1970s, and the onslaught of competition from television and other sources, Hollywood slowly rebounded. These days, the studios have become profitable adjuncts to global media empires, the industry relies on $200-million spectacles aimed at teenage boys to keep its accounts balanced, and the creative spark has mostly migrated to cable television. Whatever the structure or quality of the business, though, the film industry's enduring success is in making slick, unchallenging flicks that sell – from Rhett Butler romancing Scarlett O'Hara to Yoda duelling with a light sabre.

Four blocks north of Sunset, **Silver Lake** was once home to some of Hollywood's first studios, since converted into restaurants and galleries, or at least warehouses and storage units. Walt Disney opened his first studio in 1926 at 2719 Hyperion Ave (now demolished), and the Keystone Kops were dreamed up in Mack Sennett's studio at 1712 Glendale Blvd (now a storage facility), when the area was known as **Edendale**, and where just a single sound studio now remains. Otherwise there are no official "sights" in Silver Lake, except for a collection of interesting Modernist houses in the hills designed by the likes of Richard Neutra and R.M. Schindler and highlighted by John Lautner's **Silvertop**, 2138 Micheltorena St (best viewed from 2100 Redcliff Drive), with its projecting roofs and balconies, wraparound glass windows and sweeping concrete curves. Architecture buffs can take an in-depth look at these and other top-notch works around town through Architecture Tours LA (daily 9.30am & 1.30pm; $75 per person; book on ☎323/464-7868, ⓦwww.architecturetoursla.com).

The district is also known for its gay bars, quirky dance clubs and leftist bookstores that represent a hint of what central Hollywood looked like before the redevelopment dollars began to flow. The full effect is on display during the **Sunset Junction Street Fair** in August (☎323/661-7771, ⓦwww.sunset junction.org), a social carnival known for its loud music, ethnic food and vintage clothing stalls, which draw everyone from ageing hippies with their families to a pierced and tattooed crowd looking for a little raucous amusement.

Nearby **Los Feliz** is the home of the **American Film Institute** campus, Los Feliz Boulevard at Western Avenue, whose **Louis B. Mayer Library** (Mon, Tues & Thurs 9am–5pm, Wed 9am–7pm, Sat 10am–4pm; free) holds 14,000 books, 5000 scripts, and all manner of archives on classic and contemporary movies. Further south, the **Hollyhock House**, on a small hill close to the junction of Vermont Avenue at 4800 Hollywood Blvd (tours Wed–Sun 12.30–3.30pm; $7), was the first of architect Frank Lloyd Wright's contributions to LA. Covered with Maya motifs and stylized, geometric renderings of the hollyhock flower, the house, completed in 1921, is an intriguingly obsessive dwelling, whose original furniture (now replaced by detailed reconstructions) continued the conceptual flow.

Another Wright building, the 1924 **Ennis House**, looms over Los Feliz at 2655 Glendower Ave. One of four of his local structures to feature "textile" concrete blocks, its temple-like pre-Columbian appearance has added atmosphere to dozens of film and TV productions, from Vincent Price's *The House on Haunted Hill* to Ridley Scott's *Blade Runner*. Recent renovations have kept the house from collapsing, but it's not open to the public – though you can get a very close look as Glendower winds around it. Further into the hills, Richard Neutra's **Lovell House**, 4616 Dundee Drive, is a set of sleek, white rectangles and broad window bands that looks quite contemporary for a 1929 building, making it one of LA's landmarks of early Modernism. More garish is the **Sowden House**, 5121 Franklin Ave, a pink box with concrete jaws designed by Frank Lloyd Wright's son Lloyd. It's not open for tours, though it and other homes in the area can be viewed (at least from the outside) on a trip sponsored by Architecture Tours LA (see above).

Central Hollywood

The few short blocks of **CENTRAL HOLLYWOOD** contain the densest concentration of celebrity glamour and film mythology in the world. The decline that blighted the area from the early 1960s is slowly receding in the face of prolonged efforts by local authorities, from increasing police patrols to inviting all manner of new malls to take root here. Nevertheless the place still gets hairy after dark away from the main tourist zones, when petty thieves go hunting for the odd purse or wallet. The contrasting qualities of freshly polished nostalgia, corporate hype and deep-set seediness also make Hollywood one of LA's most diverse areas – and one of its best spots for bar-hopping and clubbing, with a range of affordable options.

Hollywood Boulevard and around

HOLLYWOOD BOULEVARD is, of course, the axis of all the accumulated movie lore, and if you follow it west, the first notable sight is the junction of **Hollywood and Vine**, where, during the early studio era (1910s–20s), the rumour spread that any budding star had only to parade around this junction to be spotted by big-name film producers or directors (the major studios were all concentrated nearby), who nursed coffees behind the windows of neighbouring restaurants. The crossing soon earned quite the reputation, though its actual contribution to elevating nobodies into stars was practically nil. For a commemoration of the era and this legend, proceed underground to the local **Red Line** subway stop, which is decorated with all sorts of film-related geegaws and memorabilia.

Much of the pavement along this stretch of Hollywood Boulevard is marked by the brass nameplates of the **Walk of Fame** (officially beginning at Hollywood and Vine). The laying of the plates began in 1960, instigated by the local chamber of commerce, which set about honouring the big names in radio, television, movies, music and theatre to boost tourism. Local newspapers announce induction ceremonies for such worthies, and selected stars have to part with several thousand dollars for the privilege of being included: among them are Marlon Brando (1717 Vine St), Marlene Dietrich (6400 Hollywood Blvd), Michael Jackson (6927 Hollywood Blvd), Elvis Presley (6777 Hollywood Blvd) and Ronald Reagan (6374 Hollywood Blvd).

Vine Street and Ivar Avenue

Other Hollywood icons can be found just off the Walk: at 1750 N Vine St, for one, the **Capitol Records Tower** resembles a stack of 45rpm records and served as the music company's headquarters until it was sold to a developer in 2006. Nearby, at 6233 Hollywood Blvd, the **Pantages Theater** (T 323/468-1770) has one of the city's greatest interiors, a melange of Baroque styling that sees mainly touring stage productions. Also in the vicinity, the bulky **Knickerbocker Hotel**, 1714 Ivar Ave, now a care home, was where the widow of legendary escapologist Harry Houdini conducted a rooftop seance in an attempt to assist her late spouse in his greatest escape of all. During the 1930s and 1940s, a number of lesser names jumped from its high windows; in the 1950s the likes of Elvis Presley and Jerry Lee Lewis stayed here. Further south on Ivar, between Sunset and Hollywood boulevards, the popular **Hollywood Farmers' Market** (Sun 8am–1pm) offers a hundred vendors selling a variety of produce, from local citrus fruits and avocados to more exotic specimens like cherimoyas.

The Hollywood sign

The famed **Hollywood sign** began life on the slopes of Mount Lee in 1923 as a billboard for the **Hollywoodland** development and originally contained its full name; however, in 1949 when a storm knocked down the "H" and damaged the rest of the sign, the "land" part was removed and the rest became the familiar symbol of the area and of the entertainment industry. Unfortunately, the current incarnation has literally lost its radiance: it once featured 4000 light bulbs that beamed the district's name as far away as LA Harbor, but a lack of maintenance and an abundance of thievery put an end to that practice.

The sign has also gained a reputation as a suicide spot, ever since would-be movie star Peg Entwistle terminated her career and life here in 1932, aged 24 – no mean feat, with the sign being as difficult to reach then as it is now. Less fatal mischief has been practised by students of nearby Caltech, who on one occasion renamed the sign for their school, while other defacers have included USC, UCLA, the US Navy and Fox Television. Because of this sullied history, there's no public road to the sign (Beachwood Drive comes nearest, but ends at a closed gate) and you'll incur minor cuts and bruises while scrambling to get anywhere near. In any case, infrared cameras and radar-activated zoom lenses have been installed to catch graffiti writers, and innocent tourists who can't resist a closer peek are also liable for a steep fine. For a much simpler look, see ⓦwww.hollywoodsign.org.

The Egyptian Theatre and around

Back on Hollywood Boulevard, the **Musso and Frank Grill,** no. 6667 (see p.147), is a 1919 restaurant and bar that has been a fixture since the days of silent cinema, where writers, actors and studio bosses would meet (and still do, occasionally) to slap backs, cut deals and drink potent lunches. A block away, the **Egyptian Theatre,** 6712 Hollywood Blvd, was the site of the very first Hollywood premiere (*Robin Hood,* an epic swashbuckler starring Douglas Fairbanks Sr) in 1922. Financed by impresario Sid Grauman, the Egyptian was a glorious fantasy in its heyday, modestly seeking to re-create the Temple of Thebes, with usherettes dressed as Cleopatra. It has since been lovingly restored by the American Cinematheque film foundation, and now plays an assortment of classics, documentaries, avant-garde flicks and foreign films to small but appreciative crowds (tickets around $11). Tourists are encouraged to check out a short documentary, presented hourly, chronicling the rise of Hollywood as America's movie capital (Sat & Sun 11.40am; $10; ⓣ323/461-2020 ext 3, ⓦwww.egyptiantheatre.com). Much less appealing, the eastern corners of the Hollywood and Highland intersection feature a handful of overpriced tourist traps – wax museum, oddities gallery, world-record exhibits – worthwhile only for the easily amused.

The Kodak and Chinese theatres

West of the Egyptian, the **Hollywood & Highland** complex, on the northwest side of the eponymous intersection, was the spur to much recent development, its chain retailers making central Hollywood safe again for corporate America and its specially designed **Kodak Theatre** (30min tours daily 10.30am–4pm; $15; ⓣ323/308-6300, ⓦwww.kodaktheatre.com), annually hosting the Oscars. Still, despite its eye-catching Pop architecture – a replica of the Babylonian set from the 1916 D.W. Griffith spectacular *Intolerance,* with super-sized columns, elephant statues and colossal archway – it's still no better than your average suburban mall.

One site that the mall has nearly swallowed up is the **Chinese Theatre,** 6925 Hollywood Blvd (ⓣ323/464-8111, ⓦwww.manntheatres.com/chinese), which has been expanded into a multiplex and its main auditorium restored to its gloriously kitschy origins. This was another of Sid Grauman's showpieces from the early days of the movie biz, an odd version of a classical Asian temple, replete with dubious Chinese motifs and upturned dragon-tail flanks, and the lobby's Art Deco splendour and the grand chinoiserie of the auditorium make for interesting viewing. For $12 you can take in a tour of a theatre, complete with a look at VIP

Hollywood impressions at the Chinese Theatre

Opened in 1927 as a lavish setting for premieres of swanky new productions, the **Chinese Theatre** was for many decades *the* spot for movie first nights, and the public crowded behind the rope barriers in the thousands to watch the movie aristocrats arriving for the screenings. The main draw, of course, has always been the assortment of **cement handprints and footprints** embedded in the theatre's forecourt. The idea came about when actress Norma Talmadge accidentally – though some say it was a deliberate publicity stunt – trod in wet cement while visiting the construction site with owner Sid Grauman, who had established a reputation for creating garish movie palaces with gloriously vulgar designs based on exotic themes. The first formally to leave their marks were Mary Pickford and Douglas Fairbanks Sr, who ceremoniously dipped their digits when arriving for the opening of **King of Kings,** and the practice continues today. It's certainly fun to work out the actual dimensions of your favourite film stars, and to discover if your hands are smaller than Julie Andrews' or your feet bigger than Rock Hudson's.

seating, a lounge and balconies for the glitterati who attend premieres of big-budget spectaculars. Afterwards, linger in the theatre's forecourt to see the handprints and footprints left in cement by Hollywood's big names (see box opposite). You'll probably encounter hundreds of other sightseers, as well as celebrity impersonators – Elvis, Marilyn and *Star Wars* characters among them – low-rent magicians, smiling hawkers and assorted oddballs vying for your amusement and money.

The El Capitan Theatre and the Hollywood Roosevelt

The **El Capitan Theatre**, no. 6834, is a colourful 1926 movie palace, with Baroque and Moorish details and a wild South Seas-themed interior of sculpted angels and garlands, plus grotesque sculptures of strange faces and creatures. Twice restored in recent years, the theatre also has one of LA's great signs, a multicoloured profusion of flashing bulbs and neon tubes, and now hosts Disney movies as well as the TV talk show of frat-house humourist Jimmy Kimmel (TV tickets at ☏866/546-6984, movie tickets at Ⓦwww.elcapitantickets.com). A few doors down, the **Hollywood Roosevelt**, 7000 Hollywood Blvd, was movieland's first luxury hotel (see p.78). Opened in the same year as the Chinese Theatre, it fast became the meeting place of top actors and screenwriters, its *Cinegrill* restaurant feeding and watering the likes of W.C. Fields, Ernest Hemingway and F. Scott Fitzgerald, and has since been sumptuously restored into one of the more elegant redoubts of old Tinseltown.

The Hollywood History Museum

Just south of Hollywood Boulevard, the **Hollywood History Museum**, 1660 Highland Blvd (Wed–Sun 10am–5pm; $15; Ⓦwww.thehollywoodmuseum .com), exhibits on its four levels the fashion, art design, props and special effects taken from a broad swath of movie history, including the latest Hollywood spectaculars. However, even though it's located in America's film capital, it has less a feel of a museum than a hotchpotch of castoffs in an overstuffed attic. Indeed, the museum pales in comparison to the much more comprehensive and informative Paley Centre for Media in Beverly Hills (see p.109), and Hollywood still awaits its definitive movieland museum.

Along Sunset Boulevard

Paralleling Hollywood Boulevard to the south is another famous stretch nearly as steeped in movie legend, **Sunset Boulevard**, which runs all the way from Downtown through Hollywood and into West Hollywood, where it becomes the colourful Sunset Strip (and beyond that runs for miles to the Pacific Ocean). At no. 6360, the huge, white **Cinerama Dome** was built in 1963 to exhibit giant three-projector films on a curved screen and is now part of a larger retail complex of theatres, shops and restaurants called ArcLight (☏323/464-1478, Ⓦwww.arclightcinemas.com). Luckily, you can still see (single-projector) blockbusters in the dome on a large, curved screen – as fun and engaging a cinematic experience as any in LA. South of the Dome are the grand gates of **Paramount Studios**, south entrance at 5555 Melrose Ave (2hr tours Mon–Fri 10am, 11am, 1pm & 2pm; $35; book on ☏323/956-1777), though the original entrance – which Gloria Swanson rode through in *Sunset Boulevard* – is now inaccessible. The tour isn't quite up to the standard of Universal's theme-park madness or Warner Bros' close-up journey, but if you want to poke around soundstages and a mildly interesting backlot (and have plenty of cash to spare), it may be worth it. Back on Sunset Boulevard, the Spanish Revival-style building at no. 6525 was, from the 1920s until the 1950s, known as the **Hollywood Athletic Club**. Another of Hollywood's legendary watering-holes, the likes of Charlie Chaplin, Clark Gable and Tarzan himself (Johnny Weismuller) lounged beside its Olympic-sized pool, while Johns Barrymore and Wayne held olympic drinking parties in the apartment levels above, with the Duke himself prone to chucking billiard balls at passing automobiles below. Nowadays the club opens only for special parties and events.

Continuing west, **Crossroads of the World**, 6672 Sunset Blvd, when finished in 1936, was one of LA's major tourist attractions and one of the first modern malls anywhere. The central plaza supposedly resembles a ship, surrounded by shops designed with Tudor, French, Italian and Spanish motifs – the idea being that the shops are the ports into which the shopper would sail (the boutiques have since been replaced with media production offices). Further on, the **Guitar Center**, 7425 Sunset Blvd, a musical-instrument store, features handprints of your favourite guitar gods embedded in the manner of the movie stars' at the Chinese Theatre, in this case with performers from AC/DC to ZZ Top; and the 1918 **Charlie Chaplin Studios**, just south of Sunset at 1416 N La Brea Ave, exhibits a bit of whimsical, Tudor-style architecture. Now owned by the Jim Henson Company, the complex is not open to the public but does feature a statue of Kermit the Frog dressed as Chaplin's most famous character.

Hollywood Forever

Not surprisingly for a town obsessed with marketing and PR, even the cemeteries are renamed to draw the crowds. Thus the former Hollywood Memorial Park has been reincarnated as **Hollywood Forever**, a few blocks below Sunset at 6000 Santa Monica Blvd (daily dawn–dusk; free). Overlooked by the famous water tower of neighboring Paramount Studios, the cemetery displays myriad tombs of dead celebrities, most notably in its southeastern corner, where a cathedral mausoleum includes, at no. 1205, the resting place of **Rudolph Valentino**. In 1926, ten thousand people packed the cemetery when the celebrated screen lover died aged just 31, and to this day on each anniversary of his passing (23 August), at least one "Lady in Black" will likely be found mourning – a tradition that started as a publicity stunt in 1931 and has continued ever since. Appropriately enough, the current Lady in Black also serves as a cemetery guide, and her regular **tours** are great opportunities to find out more about the famous and forgotten names buried here (2hr; $12; to book, contact Ⓔinfo@cemeterytour.com, Ⓦcemeterytour.com).

The most pompous grave belongs to **Douglas Fairbanks Sr**, who, with his wife Mary Pickford (herself buried at Forest Lawn Glendale), did much to introduce nouveau-riche snobbery to Hollywood. Even in death Fairbanks keeps a snooty distance from the pack, his ostentatious memorial (complete with pond) only reachable by a shrub-lined path from the mausoleum. More visually appealing, on the south side of Fairbanks' memorial lake stands the appropriately black bust of **Johnny Ramone**, showing the punk pioneer rocking out with dark, mop-top intensity. Further west, **Mel Blanc**, "the man of a thousand voices" – among them Bugs Bunny, Porky Pig, Tweety Bird and Sylvester – has an epitaph that simply reads "That's All, Folks".

Griffith Park

Built on land donated by Gilded Age mining millionaire Griffith J. Griffith, vast **GRIFFITH PARK**, between Hollywood and the San Fernando Valley (daily 5am–10.30pm, mountain roads close at dusk; free; Ⓣ323/913-4688), offers gentle greenery and rugged mountain slopes, a welcome respite from the chaos of LA. Above the landscaped flat sections, the hillsides are rough and wild, marked only by foot and bridle paths, leading into desolate but unspoiled terrain that gives great

Activities in Griffith Park

The steeper parts of Griffith Park, which blend into the foothills of the Santa Monica Mountains, offer a variety of **hiking trails**, with some 55 miles in the park overall. You can get maps at the park centres at 4400 and 4730 Crystal Springs Rd (daily during daylight hours; ☏323/664-6611). Near the latter ranger station you can **rent bikes** at Spokes 'n Stuff (summer Mon–Fri 2–6pm, Sat & Sun 10.30am–dusk; $10/hr cash only; ☏323/653-4099), good for touring the upper trails and canyons as well as the easier lower slopes. The highest point in the area – the summit of Mount Hollywood – is a good hike for those in shape, but there are plenty of lesser jaunts too. If you'd rather go horseriding, the **Sunset Ranch**, 3400 N Beachwood Drive, provides one- or two-hour rides through the area for $25 and $40 (daily 9am–4pm; ☏323/469-5450, ⊛www.sunsetranchhollywood.com), and the **LA Equestrian Center**, just across the LA River at 480 Riverside Drive, offers rides for $20 per hour or evening rides for $40 (daily 5am–9pm; ☏818/840-8401, ⊛www.la-equestriancenter.com). The park also holds basketball and tennis courts, a swimming pool, a golf course and a baseball field, among other things; call ☏323/913-4688 for information on these sites.

views over the LA basin and out towards the ocean. The only thing marring the landscape is the occasional **wildfire**, the most recent of which, in May 2007, burned out well-loved spots like Dante's View. So be alert if you arrive at the height of summer.

There are four **main entrances**. Western Canyon Road, north of Los Feliz Boulevard, enters the park through the **Ferndell** – as the name suggests, a lush glade of ferns, from which numerous trails run deeper into the park – and continues up to the **Griffith Observatory**, 2800 E Observatory Rd (Tues–Fri noon–10pm, Sat & Sun 10am–10pm; free; ☏213/473-0800, ⊛www.griffithobservatory.org), familiar from its use as a backdrop in *Rebel Without a Cause* and numerous low-budget sci-fi flicks. This astronomical icon now presents an array of high-tech exhibits for young and old alike – highlighted by the twelve-inch Zeiss refracting telescope, the trio of solar telescopes for viewing sunspots and solar storms, and other assorted, smaller telescopes set up on selected evenings for inspecting the firmament at your own pace. A full range of modern exhibits covers the history of astronomy and human observation, including a camera obscura and a 150-foot timeline of the universe. For planetarium shows (Tues–Fri 12.45pm–8.45pm, Sat & Sun 10.45am–8.45pm; $7) you'll need to reserve a space at the observatory.

Descending from the observatory on Vermont Canyon Road (effectively the continuation of Western Canyon Road) brings you to a small **bird sanctuary** set within a modest-sized wooded canyon. Across the road is the **Greek Theatre** (☏323/665-5857, ⊛www.greektheatrela.com), an open-air amphitheatre that seats nearly five thousand beneath its quasi-Greek columns for big-name rock, jazz and country music concerts during the summer.

The **northern end** of the park, over the hills in the San Fernando Valley, is best reached directly by car from the Golden State Freeway, although you can take the park roads (or explore the labyrinth of hiking trails) that climb the park's hilly core past some of its wildlife lurking in the brush. In the **recreation centre**, Los Feliz Boulevard at Riverside Drive, are various sports facilities, as well as an old-fashioned **carousel** (11am–5pm: summer daily, rest of year Sat & Sun; free) with 68 sprightly horses first carved in 1926, and a rather sizeable organ. Caged animals, meanwhile, are plentiful in the **LA Zoo**, 5333 Zoo Drive (daily 10am–5pm; $13), one of the biggest zoos in the country and home to a thousand creatures, divided by continent. Despite this, it's still not terribly impressive, especially in comparison to its San Diego counterpart (see p.183). Elsewhere, the **Travel Town Museum**,

5200 Zoo Drive (Mon–Fri 10am–4pm, Sat & Sun 10am–6pm; free), is a lot full of creaky locomotives and antique trucks, plus a miniature train ($2.50) to keep the little ones occupied. Bounding Griffith Park's northwest rim, **Forest Lawn Hollywood Hills**, 6300 Forest Lawn Drive (daily 8am–5pm), is a cemetery of the stars that, while not quite as awe-inspiringly vulgar as its Glendale counterpart, is no less pretentious, with memorials to such figures as Buster Keaton, Marvin Gaye, Charles Laughton, Liberace and Jack Webb.

Museum of the American West

The **Museum of the American West**, near the junction of the Ventura and Golden State freeways at 4700 Western Heritage Way (Tues–Fri 10am–4pm, Sat & Sun 11am–5pm; $9; ☎323/667-2000, ⒲theautry.org), was founded by Gene Autry, the "singing cowboy" who cut more than six hundred discs beginning in 1929, starred in blockbuster Hollywood Westerns during the 1930s and 1940s, became even more of a household name through his TV show in the 1950s, and died in 1999 after a very lengthy career. The **collection** – from buckskin jackets and branding irons to Frederic Remington's sculptures of early twentieth-century Western life and the truth about the shootout at the OK Corral – is a serious and credible attempt to explore the mindset and culture of those who colonized the West. The museum includes engaging sections on native peoples, European exploration, nineteenth-century pioneers, the Wild West, Asian immigrants, and, of course, Hollywood's versions of all of the above.

The Hollywood Hills

Apart from offering the chance to see the endlessly flat expanse of the LA basin, the views from the **HOLLYWOOD HILLS** feature the most opulent selection of properties to be found in California. Around these canyons and slopes, which run from Hollywood itself into Benedict Canyon above Beverly Hills, mansions are so commonplace that only the half-dozen full-blown castles really stand out.

  Mulholland Drive, named after LA's most renowned hydro-engineer, runs along the crest, providing magnificent vistas of the Los Angeles basin and the San Fernando Valley at night, when both spread out like sparkling grids for many miles below. The architectural highlights include the **Chemosphere**, 776 Torreyson Drive, a giant UFO house hovering above the canyon on a long pedestal, designed by quirky architect John Lautner and now home to irreverent publisher Benedikt Taschen, and **Case Study House #21**, 9038 Wonderland Park Ave, Pierre Koenig's hillside glass-and-steel box, part of the influential Case Study Program that tried to bring Modernism to the middle class in the Forties and Fifties. Koenig's other notable home, **Case Study House #22**, also known as the Stahl House, 1635 Woods Drive, has an even more spectacular layout, famously perched above a cliff, and including a swimming pool. Best of all, the house is on view for occasional tours ($26–40; ☎208/331-1414, ⒲www.stahlhouse.com). Unfortunately, most of the area's other houses are hidden away, and there's no real way to explore in depth without your own car, a copy of the latest Thomas Guide map and, if possible, a detailed guide to LA architecture.

Lake Hollywood

Hemmed in among the hills between Griffith Park and the Hollywood Freeway, **Lake Hollywood** is a small piece of open country in the heart of the city. The clear, calm waters, actually a reservoir intended for drought relief, are surrounded by clumps of pines in which squirrels, lizards and a few scurrying skunks and coyotes easily outnumber humans. You can't get too near the water, as metal fences protect it from the public, but the footpaths that encircle it are pleasant for a stroll, especially for a glimpse of the stone bears' heads that decorate the reservoir's curving front wall.

You can only reach the lake by car. Although opening and closing times vary widely throughout the year, the **access road** is generally open from 6.30am until 7.30pm. To get to it, go north on Cahuenga Boulevard past Franklin Avenue and turn right onto Dix Street, left into Holly Drive and climb to Deep Dell Place; from here it's a sharp left on Weidlake Drive. Follow the winding little street to the main gate.

The Hollywood Bowl

Near the Hollywood Freeway at 2301 N Highland Ave, the **Hollywood Bowl** is a natural amphitheatre that's better known for its bandshell, which is an open-air auditorium that opened in 1921 and has since become something of an icon for outdoor stages. The Beatles played here in the mid-1960s, but the Bowl's principal function is as the occasional summer home of the Los Angeles Philharmonic, which gives evening concerts from July to September (T 323/850-2000, W www.hollywoodbowl.com). More about the Bowl's history can be gleaned from the video inside the **Hollywood Bowl Museum** near the entrance (mid-June to Sept Tues–Sat 10am to showtime, Sun 4pm–showtime; Oct to mid-June Tues–Fri 10am–5pm; free). It's worth a visit if you have any affection for the grand old structure, which has gone through many different incarnations and composition materials, from concrete and fibreglass to steel and even cardboard (for acoustics). With a collection of musical instruments from around the world, the museum also features recordings of notable symphonic moments in the Bowl's history and architectural drawings by Lloyd Wright, Frank's son, who contributed a design for one of the many shells. The fifth and newest of these dates from the summer of 2004.

West LA

What is loosely called the Westside of Los Angeles begins immediately beyond Hollywood in **WEST LA** – which contains some of the city's most expensive neighbourhoods. Bordered by the Santa Monica Mountains to the north and the Santa Monica Freeway to the south, and Hollywood and the beach cities to the respective east and west, this swath of the city best embodies the stylish images that the city projects to the outside world.

One of the best reasons to come to West LA is the impressive collection of the **LA County Museum of Art (LACMA)**, on the eastern perimeter of the **Fairfax District**, forming the centrepiece of **Museum Row** (sitting at the west end of the classic 1930s auto-oriented shopping strip known as the Miracle Mile). West of Fairfax Avenue and north of Beverly Boulevard, **West Hollywood** is known for its art and design, and considerable gay community, loaded with posey restaurants and boutiques, and is surprisingly low-key except for a giant design centre at its core. **Beverly Hills**, a little further west, is less friendly but more affluent: you may need an expense account to buy a sandwich but it's a matchless place to indulge in window-shopping on the way to the more roundly appealing **Westwood**. The main activity in this low-rise, Spanish Revival, pedestrianized area has always been movies – seeing them rather than making them. The adjacent **UCLA campus** is home to a number of galleries and museums, with a lively student atmosphere. The **Sepulveda Pass** forms the western edge of West LA and leads to the essential **Getty Center**, positioned high above the LA basin.

THE WESTSIDE

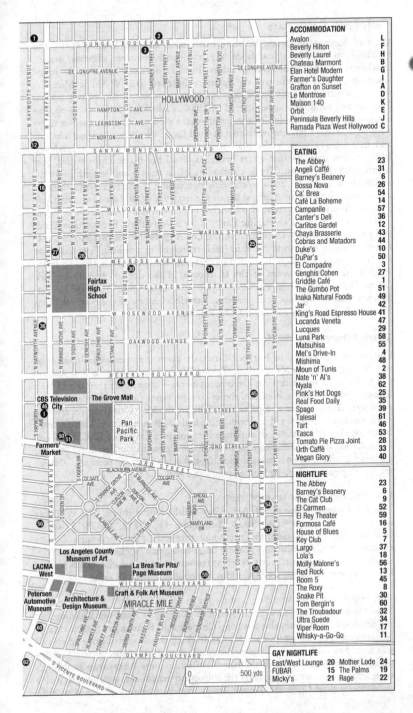

ACCOMMODATION

Avalon	L
Beverly Hilton	F
Beverly Laurel	H
Chateau Marmont	B
Elan Hotel Modern	G
Farmer's Daughter	I
Grafton on Sunset	A
Le Montrose	D
Maison 140	K
Orbit	E
Peninsula Beverly Hills	J
Ramada Plaza West Hollywood	C

EATING

The Abbey	23
Angeli Caffé	31
Barney's Beanery	6
Bossa Nova	26
Ca' Brea	54
Café La Boheme	14
Campanile	57
Canter's Deli	36
Carlitos Gardel	12
Chaya Brasserie	43
Cobras and Matadors	44
Duke's	10
DuPar's	50
El Compadre	3
Genghis Cohen	27
Griddle Café	1
The Gumbo Pot	51
Inaka Natural Foods	49
Jar	42
King's Road Espresso House	41
Locanda Veneta	29
Lucques	58
Luna Park	55
Matsuhisa	4
Mel's Drive-In	48
Mishima	2
Moun of Tunis	38
Nate 'n' Al's	25
Nyala	35
Pink's Hot Dogs	39
Real Food Daily	61
Spago	46
Talesai	53
Tart	28
Tasca	33
Tomato Pie Pizza Joint	40
Urth Caffé	
Vegan Glory	

NIGHTLIFE

The Abbey	23
Barney's Beanery	6
The Cat Club	9
El Carmen	52
El Rey Theater	59
Formosa Café	16
House of Blues	5
Key Club	7
Largo	37
Lola's	18
Molly Malone's	56
Red Rock	13
Room 5	45
The Roxy	8
Snake Pit	30
Tom Bergin's	60
The Troubadour	32
Ultra Suede	34
Viper Room	17
Whisky-a-Go-Go	11

GAY NIGHTLIFE

East/West Lounge	20	Mother Lode	24
FUBAR	15	The Palms	19
Micky's	21	Rage	22

Fairfax Avenue

Between Santa Monica and Wilshire boulevards, **Fairfax Avenue** is still the backbone of the city's Jewish culture, rich with temples, yeshivas, kosher butcher shops and delis. From Wilshire, Fairfax continues north to the long-standing wooden structures of the **Farmers' Market**, 6333 W 3rd St (Mon–Fri 9am–9pm, Sat 9am–8pm, Sun 10am–7pm; free), a rabbit warren of restaurants, bakeries and produce stands. Started in 1934 as a little agricultural co-op, the market has since expanded to the point where it's a social phenomenon in its own right, always buzzing with tourists and locals who come to meet and eat, and increasingly shop – the mall next door, **The Grove**, is a three-level, $100-million colossus that offers branches of all the major chain stores. Just north, **CBS Television City** is a sprawling black cube – and something of an architectural eyesore – but a worthwhile destination if you're in town to sit in an audience for a sitcom, game show or the network's *Late Late Show with Craig Ferguson* (apply for tickets at Ⓦwww.cbs.com or call ☎818/295-2700). To the east on Third Street, **Pan Pacific Park**, 7600 Beverly Blvd, has sports facilities and a jogging path, as well as the affecting **Los Angeles Holocaust Monument**, featuring six black-granite columns (each representing a million Jews killed by the Nazis) inscribed with the events of that horrific period from 1933 to 1945. By 2011 the new **Museum of the Holocaust** is also due to open in the park (Mon–Thurs 10am–4pm, Fri 10am–2pm, Sun noon–4pm; ☎323/651-3704, Ⓦwww.lamoth.org), and will present the terrible history of the Nazi era using interactive technology and multimedia exhibits.

The Miracle Mile

On the southern end of the Fairfax District, the premier property development of the 1930s, the **Miracle Mile**, stretched along Wilshire eastward to La Brea Avenue and is still lined with faded Art Deco monuments – none better than the **El Rey Theatre**, 5515 Wilshire Blvd, a thriving concert venue (see p.150) with a flashy neon sign. At the corner of Fairfax and Wilshire, the **May Company** department store was built in 1934 and has been compared to an oversized, golden perfume bottle ever since; its main contemporary function is as the site of **LACMA West**, an exhibition annexe to the larger museum down the road (same details as LACMA, see below), which, when it isn't showing big-ticket blockbusters, presents children's art – with pieces made to be jumped on, played with and laughed at.

LA County Museum of Art

The **LA County Museum of Art**, 5905 Wilshire Blvd (Mon, Tues & Thurs noon–8pm, Fri noon–9pm, Sat & Sun 11am–8pm; $12; ☎323/857-6000, Ⓦwww.lacma.org), is one of the largest museums west of the Mississippi. Since its creation in 1965, the museum's homely beige-and-green blocks have attracted the scorn of architecture critics, but its recent renovation and expansion makes it more like the proper venue for art exhibitions it should have been all along.

The Hammer and Ahmanson buildings

Most big-budget temporary exhibitions take place in the **Hammer Building**, on the north side of the site, also featuring **Chinese and Korean art** such as ancient lacquerware trays, hanging scrolls, bronze drinking vessels, glazed stone bowls and jade figurines, covering nearly seven thousand years of East Asian history. Contiguous with the second floor of the Hammer Building, the **Ahmanson Building**'s central attractions are undoubtedly the **European art rooms**, which begin with a good overview of Greek and Roman art and continue into the medieval era with religious sculptures and ecclesiastical ornamentation, notably a series of stone carvings of the Passion cycle. The Renaissance and Mannerist eras are represented by compelling works such as Paolo Veronese's *Two Allegories of Navigation*, great Mannerist figures filling the frame from an imposing low angle; El Greco's *The Apostle Saint Andrew*, an uncommonly reserved portrait; and Titian's *Portrait of Giacomo Dolfin*, a carefully tinted study by the great colourist. Northern European painters are well represented by Hans Holbein's small, resplendent *Portrait of a Young Woman with White Coif*, a number of Frans Hals pictures of cheerful burghers, and Rembrandt's probing *Portrait of Marten Looten*.

The Art of the Americas Building
Counterclockwise at the site, the **Art of the Americas Building** is home to the museum's collection of **American art**, ranging from the landscapes and portraits of the early American period up to the homegrown Impressionism and social realism of the turn of the nineteenth century. Although the collection is rotated, typical highlights include the work of John Singleton Copley (the regal *Portrait of a Lady*), Winslow Homer (the dusty realism of the *Cotton Pickers*), Albert Pinkham Ryder (the murky, alluring landscape of *The River*) and Thomas Eakins (the writhing, nude *Wrestlers*). Better than most of the pre-modern paintings on display, though, is the impressive assortment of American and Western **furniture**, and a striking selection of Central and South American art, the highlight of which is the **Fearing Collection**, consisting of funeral masks and sculpted guardian figures from pre-Columbian Mexico.

The Broad Contemporary Art Museum
Heading west, **modern art** is showcased in the **Broad Contemporary Art Museum**, which houses some of the West Coast's largest pieces of art. Among the more prominent are works by abstract expressionists like Mark Rothko and Franz Kline, as well as the splashy, colourful paintings of Sam Francis. Less celebrated, but just as appealing, are Mariko Mori's hypnotic video presentation *Miko No Inori*; Bill Viola's *Slowly Turning Narrative*, a huge, rotating projection screen displaying discordant images; and Ed Kienholz's *Back Seat Dodge '38*, looking just as perverse as it did in the 1960s when it caused political outrage. Other eye-openers are by Cindy Sherman, whose self-portrait photographs are stacked four and five high in one huge gallery; Jeff Koons, whose various pop-culture-kitsch pieces are centred on a huge blue-metallic "balloon animal"; and Richard Serra, whose giant, rusted, curving steel walls have the entire ground floor all to themselves. Just north, the new **Resnick Pavilion**, a huge, glass-and-marble showpiece designed by Renzo Piano, houses flexible open galleries to accommodate works of any size.

The Pavilion for Japanese Art and Bing Center
Finally, on the eastern side of the site, the **Pavilion for Japanese Art** was created by iconoclastic architect Bruce Goff to re-create the effects of traditional shoji screens, filtering varying levels and qualities of light through to the interior. Displays include painted screens and scrolls, ceramics and lacquerware, viewable on a ramp spiralling down to a small, ground-floor waterfall that trickles pleasantly amid the near-silence of the gallery. Across from the Pavilion, the **Leo S. Bing Theater** in the **Bing Center** presents a regular series of film programmes that focus on classic Hollywood, art-house and foreign favourites ($11; ☏323/857-6010).

Other Museum Row attractions
Just east of LACMA, the **La Brea Tar Pits**, a large pool of smelly tar ("la brea" in Spanish), are one of LA's most familiar natural formations. Tens of thousands of

years ago during the last Ice Age, primeval creatures from tapirs to mastodons tried to drink from the thin layer of water covering the tar in the pits, only to become stuck fast and preserved for modern science. Millions of bones belonging to the animals (and one set of human bones) have been found here, with some of them reconstructed in the **George C. Page Museum** (daily 9.30am–5pm; $7), where you can spot the skeletons of your favourite extinct creatures, from giant ground sloths to menacing sabre-toothed tigers. Across the street, the **Craft and Folk Art Museum**, 5814 Wilshire Blvd (Tues–Fri 11am–5pm, Sat & Sun noon–6pm; $5; Ⓦwww.cafam.org), has a small selection of handmade objects – rugs, pottery, clothing and so on – with rotating exhibitions featuring the likes of handmade tarot cards, ceramic folk art and highly detailed Asian textiles. Further west, the **Architecture + Design Museum**, 6032 Wilshire Blvd (Tues–Fri 11am–5pm, Sat & Sun noon–6pm; $5; Ⓣ323/932-9393, Ⓦwww.aplusd.org), puts on rotating exhibits of the latest trends in art, photography and architecture.

South of LACMA, across from LACMA West at 6060 Wilshire Blvd, the **Petersen Automotive Museum** (Tues–Sun 10am–6pm; $10; Ⓣ323/930-2277, Ⓦwww.petersen.org) offers three floors loaded with all kinds of vehicles, with periodic exhibits on topics like the golden age of custom cars in the 1950s and 1960s and "million-dollar" vehicles like the 1919 Bentley and 1961 Ferrari. The ground floor takes you on a journey through the city's vehicular past, from crude early twentieth-century flivvers and hot rods that raced on dangerous wooden tracks, to a classic 1930s gas station, post-World War II gas guzzlers, and so on.

West Hollywood

Between Fairfax Avenue and Beverly Hills, **WEST HOLLYWOOD** is synonymous with social tolerance and upmarket trendiness, with a sizeable gay contingent. **Santa Monica Boulevard** is the district's main drag, with flashy dance clubs and designer clothing stores, with the hub of social activity around the intersection with San Vicente Boulevard.

Melrose Avenue

Four blocks south is **Melrose Avenue**, LA's trendiest shopping street, which in its heyday was an eccentric world of its own, thick with underground art galleries, palm readers and head shops. Since the 1990s, though, a crush of designer shops, salons and restaurants has been gaining ground at the expense of the quirkier tenants, though there are still enough curiosities and eye-popping boutiques to make for an interesting stroll. The west end of Melrose is a rather snooty precinct, with furniture shops and art galleries spread out around the hulking, bright-blue glassy pile of the **Pacific Design Center** (Mon–Fri 9am–5pm; Ⓣ310/657-0800, Ⓦwww.pacificdesigncenter.com), a design marketplace at 8687 Melrose Ave near San Vicente Boulevard, known as the "Blue Whale" for the way it dwarfs its low-rise neighbours, along with its counterparts, two geometric red-and-green superblocks. The centre also features a branch of the **Museum of Contemporary Art** (Tues–Fri 11am–5pm, Sat & Sun 11am–6pm; free; Ⓣ310/289-5223, Ⓦwww.moca.org), focusing on architecture and design with a sleek, modern bent, and often participating in exhibitions with the Downtown MOCA and Geffen Contemporary (see p.85 & p.84).

The stylistic extremes of Melrose Avenue are also reflected in the area's domestic architecture. The 1922 **Schindler House**, 835 N Kings Rd (Wed–Sun 11am–6pm; $7), was for years the blueprint of California Modernist architecture, designed by master architect R.M. Schindler with sliding canvas panels meant to be removed in summer, exposed roof rafters and open-plan rooms facing onto outdoor terraces. Now functioning as the **MAK Center for Art and Architecture**, the house plays host to a range of avant-garde music, art, film and design exhibitions (T 323/651-1510, W www.makcenter.org). Four blocks west of the Schindler House, **La Cienega Boulevard** ("the swamp" in Spanish) holds a mixture of LA's best and priciest restaurants and art galleries, and passes the huge **Beverly Center** shopping mall at 8500 Beverly Blvd – a looming fortress of brown plaster that is nonetheless the city's main consumer icon, and teenager central at weekends.

Further south, on the Beverly Hills border at 333 S La Cienega, the Academy of Motion Picture Arts and Sciences' **Margaret Herrick Library** (Mon, Thurs & Fri 10am–6pm, Tues 10am–8pm) holds a hoard of film memorabilia and scripts inside a Moorish-style building that was once a water-treatment plant.

Sunset Strip

Above West Hollywood, the roughly two-mile-long conglomeration of restaurants, plush hotels and nightclubs on Sunset Boulevard has long been known as the **Sunset Strip**. It came to national fame in the 1960s when a scene developed around the landmark *Whisky-a-Go-Go* club, which featured seminal rock bands such as Love and Buffalo Springfield, as well as the manic theatrics of Jim Morrison and The Doors. Although no longer rock central for indie bands – look for that around Echo Park and Silver Lake – there are still enough clubs to keep music tourists occupied for a night or two. Others come to the strip just to see the enormous **billboards**: fantastic commercial murals animated with eye-catching gimmicks, movie ads with names of celebrities in gargantuan letters, and half-naked models hawking the trendiest brands of perfume, jewellery, clothing and spirits.

Greta Garbo was only one of many stars to visit the huge Norman castle that is the **Chateau Marmont** hotel, towering over the east end of Sunset Strip at no. 8221. Built in 1927 as luxury apartments, this stodgy block of white concrete has long been a Hollywood favourite for its elegant private suites and bungalows (see p.78). The rock scene is focused further west around the clubs **Whisky-a-Go-Go**, no. 8901, and **Roxy**, no. 9009, both of which still offer shows from some of the loudest and angriest rock and punk bands, with the Johnny Depp-owned **Viper Room**, no. 8852, and the **Key Club**, no. 9039, also providing a thrill for indie rock and DJ sets in the same area.

Beverly Hills

Probably the most famous small city in the world, **Beverly Hills** has, through its relentless PR machine, made itself internationally synonymous with free-spending wealth and untrammelled luxury, if not necessarily good taste. The town divides into two distinct halves, separated by Santa Monica Boulevard. To the south is the flashy **Golden Triangle** business district, which fills the wedge between Santa Monica and Wilshire boulevards, ground zero for window-shopping and gawking at major and minor celebrities. **Rodeo Drive** cuts through the triangle in a two-block-long, concentrated showcase of the most expensive names in international fashion. It's a dauntingly stylish area, each boutique trying to outshine the rest, crowned by the tourist trap of **Two Rodeo** at Wilshire, a faux-European shopping alley that is the height of pretentious kitsch, its phony cobblestone street hiding a car park below. For a complete overview of the shopping scene, including Rodeo Drive and beyond, take a 40-minutes trip on the **Beverly Hills Trolley** (Sat & Sun 11am–4pm; also July, Aug & Dec Tues–Sun same hours; $5), which offers tourists a glimpse of the town's highlights, departing hourly from the corner of Rodeo Drive and Dayton Way. Even more enjoyable is the **Paley Center for Media**, 465 N Beverly Drive (Wed–Sun noon–5pm; $10, kids $5; T 310/786-1000, W www.paleycenter.org), which features a collection of more than 140,000 TV and radio programmes and presents rotating exhibits on famous characters from the twentieth century, and the best of radio and TV sitcoms, dramas and thrillers.

Above Santa Monica Boulevard is the upmarket part of residential Beverly Hills, its gently curving drives converging on the florid pink-plaster **Beverly Hills Hotel**, on Sunset Boulevard at Rodeo Drive (see p.109). Built in 1913 to attract wealthy settlers to what was then a town of just five hundred people, the hotel's social cachet makes its *Polo Lounge* a prime spot for movie execs to power-lunch. In the verdant canyons and foothills above Sunset, a number of palatial estates lie hidden away behind landscaped security gates. **Benedict Canyon Drive** climbs up from the hotel near many of them, including Harold Lloyd's **Green Acres**, 1740 Green Acres Place, where the actor lived for forty years. With its secret passageways and large private screening room, the home survives intact, though the grounds, which contained a waterfall and a nine-hole golf course, have since been broken up into smaller lots. One of the few estates in the area that is open to the public is the wooded **Virginia Robinson Gardens**, 1008 Elden Way (tours Tues–Fri 10am & 1pm; $10, by appointment only at ☏310/276-5367), which holds six acres of over a thousand plant varieties, including some impressive Australian king palm trees.

The biggest house in Beverly Hills, 50,000-square-foot **Greystone Mansion**, was once the property of oil titan Edward Doheny and is rarely open (except for political fundraisers and filming movies and music videos). The grounds, however, are now maintained as a public park by the city as **Greystone Park** (daily 10am–5pm; free), at 905 Loma Vista Drive, where you can admire the mansion's limestone facade and intricately designed chimneys, then stroll through the sixteen-acre park, with its koi-filled ponds and expansive views of the LA sprawl.

Century City and around

The bland high-rise boxes of **Century City**, just west of Beverly Hills, were erected during the 1960s on what was the backlot of the 20th Century-Fox film studio. The district's main focus, as is so often the case in LA, is a large shopping mall, the **Century City Shopping Center**, 10250 Santa Monica Blvd, loaded with upscale boutiques and department stores and one of the better moviehouses for current films. To the southwest, the still-functional **20th Century-Fox** studios are strictly off-limits and don't offer tours.

Less frivolously, just east of Century City below Beverly Hills, the affecting **Beit HaShoa Museum of Tolerance** (hours vary, often Mon–Fri 10am–5pm, Sun 11am–5pm; $15; ☏310/553-8403, ⓦwww.museumoftolerance.com), an extraordinary interactive resource centre that shows the story of Fascism and the genocide of Jews and other atrocities in contemporary world history. Among other exhibits, it leads the visitor through multimedia re-enactments outlining the rise of Nazism to a harrowing conclusion in a replica gas chamber.

Westwood and UCLA

Just west of Beverly Hills, on the north side of Wilshire Boulevard, **WESTWOOD** is one of LA's more user-friendly neighbourhoods, a grouping of low-slung Spanish Revival buildings that went up in the late 1920s under the name **Westwood Village**, along with the nearby campus of the nascent University of California, Los Angeles (UCLA), which had moved from East Hollywood. Because of its ease for pedestrians, the neighbourhood has limited and expensive street parking; for minimum frustration, find a cheap car park and dump your vehicle there for a few hours while you explore.

Broxton Avenue, Westwood's main drag, has plenty of small shops and diners. The spire at the end of the street, at 961 Broxton Ave, belongs to the Art Deco-style 1931 Fox Village theatre (☎310/248-6266), which, together with the neon-signed Bruin across the street (☎310/208-8998), is sometimes used by movie studios for sneak previews of films to gauge audience reaction.

Inside one of the towers on the corner with Westwood Boulevard, art lovers shouldn't miss a trip to the UCLA Hammer Museum, 10899 Wilshire Blvd (Tues–Sat 11am–7pm, Thurs closes 9pm, Sun 11am–5pm; $7, kids free, Thurs free to all; ☎310/443-7000, ⓦhammer.ucla.edu). The minor Rembrandts and Rubenses may be less than stunning, but make sure to seek out the impressive early-American works of Gilbert Stuart, Thomas Eakins and John Singer Sargent, and a range of insightful, sometimes risk-taking, modern and avant-garde temporary exhibitions. Across Wilshire from the museum, at the end of the driveway behind the tiny Avco movie theatre at 1218 Glendon Ave, you'll find oil magnate Hammer's speckled marble tomb sharing the tiny cemetery of Westwood Village Memorial Park (daily 8am–5pm) with the likes of movie stars Peter Lorre, Burt Lancaster and Dean Martin, jazz drummer Buddy Rich, and, to the left of the entrance in the far northeast corner, Marilyn Monroe, who rests under a lipstick-covered plaque. You can also see some of these stars on the radiant mural inside the Crest Theater, 1262 Westwood Blvd (☎310/474-7866, ⓦwww .westwoodcrest.com), also notable for its brash neon sign.

The UCLA campus

On the northern side of Westwood, the UCLA campus comprises a group of lovely Romanesque Revival and more angular modern buildings spread across well-landscaped grounds. It's worth a wander if you've time to kill, particularly for a couple of good exhibition spaces. Before embarking on your exploration, pick up a map from various information kiosks scattered around campus. A good place to start is the Mathias Botanical Garden, 405 Hilgard Ave (Mon–Sat 8am–4pm, summer Mon–Fri closes at 5pm; free), a bucolic glade on the east side of the university where you can pick your way along sloping paths through the redwoods and fern groves, past small waterfalls splashing into lily-covered ponds. Just north, the Powell Library (hours vary, often Mon–Thurs 7.30am–11pm, Fri 7.30am–6pm, Sat 9am–5pm, Sun 1–10pm; ⓦwww.library.ucla.edu) has a spell-binding interior with lovely Romanesque arches, columns and stairwell, and an array of medieval ornament to complement its ecclesiastical feel. The highlight is the dome above the reading room, where Renaissance printers' marks are inscribed, among them icons representing such pioneers as Johann Fust and William Caxton. At the northern end of campus, the large Franklin D. Murphy Sculpture Garden (always open; free) has seventy works by such major names as Jean Arp, Henry Moore, Henri Matisse and Jacques Lipchitz, as well as other notable works including Rodin's *Walking Man*, a stark nude composed of only a torso and legs; Gaston Lachaise's Amazonian *Standing Woman*, a proud, if grotesque, 1932 sculpture; and George Tsutakawa's *OBOS-69*, an odd example of fountain art resembling abstracted TV sets.

Just to the east, UCLA's film school has produced filmmakers like Francis Ford Coppola, Alison Anders and Alex Cox. The school oversees the massive store-house of the UCLA Film and Television Archive, a treasure-trove of more than 220,000 items, among them classic, foreign and art movies, and a wide range of old TV shows. To check out the collection, make an appointment at 46 Powell Library (where the archive's items are kept), or by calling ☎310/206-5388 (Mon–Fri 9am–5pm) or visiting ⓦwww.cinema.ucla.edu. The archive also presents regular screenings of films in the Billy Wilder Theater in the courtyard of the

Hammer Museum (see p.111; $9; ⊤310/206-8013). Also worth a look is the **Fowler Museum of Cultural History**, Bruin Walk at Westwood Plaza (Wed–Sun noon–5pm, Thurs closes 8pm; free), which offers an immense range of multicultural art – including ceramics, religious icons, paintings and musical instruments. The museum's highlights include a worldwide selection of native masks, more than ten thousand textile pieces from different cultures, and an extensive collection of African and Polynesian art and various folk designs. For a more contemplative experience, travel just north of campus to UCLA's **Hannah Carter Japanese Garden**, 10619 Bellagio Rd (Tues, Wed & Fri 10am–3pm; free; by appointment only at ⊤310/794-0320 or ⓦwww.japanesegarden.ucla.edu), an idyllic spot featuring magnolias, Japanese maples, and traditional structures and river rocks brought directly from Japan. Adding to the calming Zen feel are a pagoda, a teahouse, quaint bridges, and assorted gold and stone Buddhas.

The Getty Center

The gap through the Santa Monica Mountains known as the **Sepulveda Pass** is best known for the 405 freeway that cuts through it. Starting at Sunset Boulevard just northwest of UCLA, the pass divides several of LA's most exclusive residential zones. The most famous, to the east, is **Bel Air**, a hillside community that boasts one of the most exquisite hotels in the LA region, the *Bel Air* (see p.78).

Further northwest, Getty Center Drive leads up to the monumental **Getty Center** (Tues–Thurs & Sun 10am–5.30pm, Fri & Sat 10am–9pm; free, parking $15; ⊤310/440-7300, ⓦwww.getty.edu), a gleaming 110-acre complex that towers over the city as oil baron J. Paul Getty once towered over his competitors. By bus, take MTA line #761 from UCLA after taking line #2 or #302 from Downtown, or line #720 from Santa Monica; if you come by car, there's a car park at the base of the hill. Either way, a tram ride can get you up to the complex – a slow ride that features fine vistas of the metropolis, which you can also get by hoofing it up the slope alongside the track.

Designed by arch-modernist **Richard Meier**, the Center was built for about $1 billion and was a decade in the making, constructed from classical travertine. Although the Getty Foundation shelled out a ten-figure sum for the Center, it still has billions in reserve and must, by law, spend hundreds of millions each year from its endowment. Thus, it plays an elephantine role on the international art scene and can freely outbid its competitors for anything it wants.

Decorative arts

Getty started building his massive collection in the 1930s, storing much of it in his house until the Getty Museum opened in 1974 on a bluff overlooking the Pacific Ocean. That site has now reopened as the **Getty Villa**, a showcase for the foundation's antiquities (see p.118). As the main museum's collection is, not surprisingly, determined by the enthusiasms of Getty himself, there's a formidable array of ornate furniture and **decorative arts**, with clocks, chandeliers, tapestries and gilt-edged commodes, designed for the French nobility from the reign of Louis XIV, filling several overwhelmingly opulent rooms.

Painting

Getty was much less interested in **painting** – although he did scoop up a very fine stash. Here you'll find such worthies as Andrea Mantegna's stoic but affecting *Adoration of the Magi*, Correggio's *Head of Christ*, and Titian's *Venus and Adonis*, depicting in muted colours the last moments between the lovers before the latter is gored by a wild boar. The finest works from the seventeenth century are **Flemish** and **Dutch**. Among the highlights are Rubens' *Entombment*, a pictorial essay supporting the Catholic doctrine of transubstantiation; Hendrik ter Brugghen's *Bacchante with an Ape*, showing a drunken libertine clutching a handful of grapes, an action mirrored by his pet monkey; and a trio of Rembrandts: *Daniel and Cyrus before the Idol Bel*, in which the Persian king tries foolishly to feed the bronze statue he worships, *An Old Man in Military Costume*, the exhausted, uncertain face of an old soldier, and the great portrait of *Saint Bartholomew*.

The Getty Center is also known for bidding on **Impressionist** works; as such, these acquisitions read like a roll-call of late nineteenth-century French artists: a portrait of *Albert Cahen d'Anvers* by Renoir, the inevitable Monet haystacks, and one of Degas' ballet dancers. Van Gogh's *Irises* is also on view, the Getty Trust snatching up the vivid floral icon for an unknown price. Other significant works from the **nineteenth century** include *Bullfight* by Goya, in which the bull stares triumphantly at a group of unsuccessful matadors; J.M.W. Turner's frenzied *Ships at Sea, Getting a Good Wetting*, all hazy colours that look surprisingly modern and abstract; and Caspar David Friedrich's elegant and understated *A Walk at Dusk*, a Romantic painting of a man bowing before a stone cairn during twilight. Also fascinating is the museum's excellent collection of medieval **illuminated manuscripts**, depicting Biblical scenes such as the Passion cycle as well as notable saints. Exquisitely drawn letters introduce chapters from Scripture and maintain their radiance to this day, especially when lit from behind in a dark, dramatic gallery.

Photographs, sculpture and drawings

Elsewhere in the museum, there's an extensive and highly absorbing collection of **photographs** by Man Ray, Laszlo Moholy-Nagy and other notables, along with a respectable assortment of **sculpture** from the seventeenth to the nineteenth centuries. The museum also boasts a wide collection of **drawings**. Among the best are Albrecht Dürer's meticulous *Study of the Good Thief*, a portrait of the crucified criminal who was converted on the cross; his *Stag Beetle*, precise enough to look as if the bug were crawling on the page itself; Giovanni Piranesi's dramatic image of a ruined, but still monumental, *Ancient Port*; and William Blake's bizarre watercolour of *Satan Exalting over Eve*, an expressionless devil hovering over his prone captive.

Santa Monica Bay

Set along a twenty-mile white-sand beach and home to some of LA's finest stores, restaurants and galleries, the small communities that line the **Santa Monica Bay** have little of the smog or searing heat that can make the rest of the metropolis unbearable. The entire area is well served by public transport and near enough to the airport, plus there's a wide array of accommodation, making it a good base for seeing the rest of LA.

Santa Monica, lined by palm-tree-shaded bluffs above the Pacific Ocean, is the oldest, biggest and best known of the towns, a self-consciously healthy and liberal community that has attracted a large contingent of British expats. Directly south, **Venice**'s beachfront boardwalk brings together a lively mixture of street performers, roller skaters and casual voyeurs, while its remaining network of canals gives a hint of what the place looked like a hundred years ago.

North from Santa Monica along the Pacific Coast Highway, **Pacific Palisades** is close to two main sights: **Will Rogers State Park**, holding the home and museum of one of the legends of the American West, and the spectacular **Getty Villa**, a treasure house of antiquities in the form of a Roman hillside villa. A few miles further along the coast road, **Topanga Canyon** offers more hiking, with a surprisingly wild set of trails leading into the deep, wooded canyons and sculptured rock

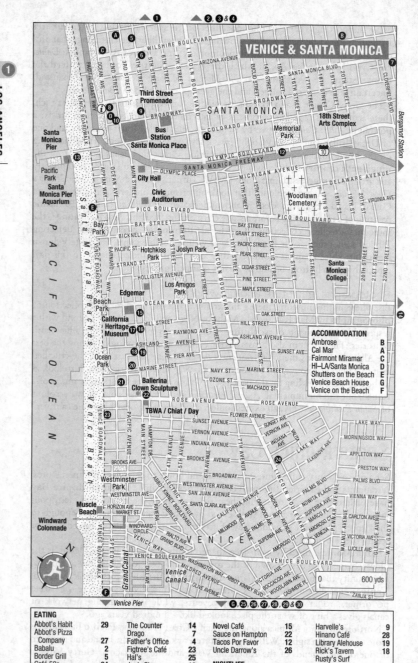

VENICE & SANTA MONICA

ACCOMMODATION

Ambrose	B
Cal Mar	A
Fairmont Miramar	C
HI–LA/Santa Monica	D
Shutters on the Beach	E
Venice Beach House	G
Venice on the Beach	F

EATING

Abbot's Habit	29	The Counter	14	Novel Café	15	Harvelle's	9
Abbot's Pizza		Drago	7	Sauce on Hampton	22	Hinano Café	28
Company	27	Father's Office	4	Tacos Por Favor	12	Library Alehouse	19
Babalu	2	Figtree's Café	23	Uncle Darrow's	26	Rick's Tavern	18
Border Grill	5	Hal's	25			Rusty's Surf	
Café 50s	24	Joe's Pizza	10	**NIGHTLIFE**		Ranch	13
Café Luxxe	3	Melisse	4	Beechwood	30	Ye Olde King's	
Chaya Venice	21	Musha	6	Circle Bar	20	Head	8
Chinois on Main	16	Norm's	11	Finn McCool's	17	Zanzibar	1

outcrops of the Santa Monica Mountains. **Malibu**, at the top of the bay, twenty miles from Santa Monica and the northern and westernmost edge of the LA region, is studded with beach-colony houses owned by those who are famous enough to need privacy and rich enough to afford it, despite the constant threat of hillside wildfires. However, you don't have to be a millionaire to enjoy its fine surfing beaches, or the birds, seals and whales that seasonally migrate offshore.

Santa Monica

For a lot of Westsiders, **SANTA MONICA** represents the impossible dream – a low-key, tolerant beachside town with a relaxed air and easy access to the rest of the city. Of course, many of its upper-crust homes may be just as expensive as those found in Beverly Hills or West LA, but what it lacks in affordability it makes up for in humility. Friendly and unpretentious, Santa Monica is a great spot to visit, a compact, accessible bastion of oceanside charm.

Lying across Centinela Avenue from West LA, Santa Monica splits into three distinct portions. The **town** itself, holding a fair chunk of Santa Monica's history and its day-to-day business, is mostly inland but is more interesting closer to the coastal bluffs. Just to the west there's the **pier** and **beach**, while **Main Street**, running south from close to the pier towards Venice, is a style-conscious quarter, with designer restaurants and fancy shops. You can easily travel between these areas on the **Tide Ride** (every 15min; Sat noon–8pm, Sun noon–10pm; ☎310/451-5444), which costs a mere 50 cents to hit all the highlights.

The Town

Santa Monica reaches nearly three miles inland, but most of its attractions lie within a few blocks of the beach. Make your first stop the **Visitor Information Office**, 1400 Ocean Ave (daily: summer 9am–5pm; winter 10am–4pm; ☎310/393-7593, ⓦwww.santamonica.com), in a kiosk just south of Santa Monica Boulevard in **Palisades Park**, the famous, cypress-tree-lined strip that runs along the top of the bluffs and makes for striking views of the surf below. The visitor centre's handy free map includes the routes of the Santa Monica Big Blue Bus system, a useful Westside complement to the MTA network (☎310/451-5444, ⓦwww.bigbluebus.com).

Two blocks east of Ocean Boulevard, between Wilshire and Broadway, the **Third Street Promenade** is a pedestrian stretch that's one of LA's most densely touristed, especially on summer weekends. It's fun to hang out in the cafés, bars and clubs, or play a game of pool, and the promenade can be really busy at night, when huge numbers of tourists and locals jostle for space with sidewalk poets and swinging jazz bands under the watchful eyes of water-spewing **dinosaur sculptures** draped in ivy. The mall is anchored at its southern end by **Santa Monica Place**, which has been newly remodelled as a lively outdoor retail complex with access to the Promenade.

Santa Monica has a number of fine **galleries** selling works by emerging local and international artists. Near the intersection of 26th Street and Cloverfield Boulevard, **Bergamot Station**, the city's aesthetic hub at 2525 Michigan Ave, is a collection of former tramcar sheds housing around thirty small art galleries (most open Tues–Fri 10am–6pm; free). Many of LA's latest generation of artists have shown here, and the highlight is, of course, the **Santa Monica Museum of Art**, in Building G-1 (Tues–Sat 11am–6pm; $5; ☎310/586-6488, ⓦwww.smmoa .org), a good space to see some of the most engaging and curious work on the local scene, in temporary exhibitions ranging from simple painting shows to complex, space-demanding installations. If you want to check out more art, the **18th Street Arts Complex**, further inland at 1639 18th St (Mon–Fri 11am–5.30pm;

T 310/453-3711, W www.18thstreet.org), is a hip and modern centre for various types of art, much of it experimental.

There are few other worthwhile sights inland. On the northern border, **San Vicente Boulevard**'s grassy tree-lined strip is a joggers' freeway, while south of San Vicente, the flashy restaurants and boutiques of **Montana Avenue** are somewhat overpriced and underwhelming. Fans of big-name architect Frank Gehry will no doubt want to check out one of the first structures that made his reputation, the artist's own **Gehry House**, 22nd Street at Washington Avenue (not open to the public), a deconstructivist fantasy with assorted structural ideas thrown together and bundled up with concrete walls and metal fencing.

Santa Monica Pier and around

Jutting out into the bay at the foot of Colorado Avenue, the **Santa Monica Pier** is a great example of an old-fashioned, festive beach-town hub, with a giant helter-skelter and a restored 1922 wooden **carousel** (March–Sept Mon–Thurs 11am–5pm, Fri–Sun 11am–7pm; Oct–Feb Mon & Thurs 11am–5pm, Fri–Sun 11am–7pm; $2 a ride, kids 50¢), with more than forty colourful hand-carved horses. Although the familiar thrill rides of **Pacific Park** (hours vary, often summer daily 11am–11pm, Sat & Sun closes 12.30am; unlimited rides $21) may catch your eye, it's still a rather overpriced attempt to lure back the suburban families – you're better off saving your money for a real theme-park. Better yet, visit the **Santa Monica Pier Aquarium**, below the pier at 1600 Ocean Front Walk (Tues–Fri 2–6pm, Sat & Sun 12.30–6pm; $5, kids free), where you can find out about marine biology and touch sea anemones and starfish.

Just south of the pier, Santa Monica has its own miniature version of Venice's Muscle Beach: a workout area loaded with rings, bars and other athletic equipment for would-be bodybuilders and fitness fans. The adjacent **International Chess Park** is a fancy name for a serviceable collection of chessboards that attracts a range of players from rank amateurs to slumming pros. Finally, a **bike path** begins at the pier and heads twenty miles south, a stretch that ranks as one of the area's top choices for cycling.

Main Street

Five minutes' walk from the pier, **Main Street** is an enticing collection of boutiques, bars and restaurants that forms one of the most popular shopping strips on the Westside. Beyond this, though, there's not much to do or see. One of the few actual sights, the **California Heritage Museum**, 2612 Main St (Wed–Sun 11am–4pm; $5; T 310/392-8537, W www.californiaheritagemuseum.org), hosts temporary displays on California cultural topics, from old fruit-box labels to modern skateboards, and has permanent exhibits on regional pottery, furniture, quilts and decorative arts. There are also several noteworthy buildings on and around Main Street, including the angular grey volumes and strange geometry of Frank Gehry's **Edgemar** shopping development, at no. 2415, a deliberately awkward construction whose chain-link fencing and sheet-metal design bring to mind an abstract sculpture.

Venice

Immediately south of Santa Monica, connected by Main Street, **Venice** was laid out in the marshlands of Ballona Creek in 1905 by developer **Abbot Kinney** as a romantic replica of the northern Italian city. Intended to attract artists to sample its pseudo-European air, this twenty-mile network of canals and waterfront homes never really caught on, although a later remodelling into a low-grade version of Coney Island postponed its demise for a few decades. These days, a few shards of the original plan survive, and the bohemian atmosphere has since worked to draw in the artistic community Kinney was targeting. Main Street, for instance, is home to the offices of advertising firm **TBWA/Chiat/Day**, just south of Rose Street and marked by Claes Oldenburg's huge pair of binoculars at the entrance to the Frank Gehry-designed offices. Just to the north, the frightening **Ballerina Clown**, a gargantuan sculpture by Jonathan Borofsky, looms over a nearby intersection, its stubbly clown head and lithe body making for an unforgettably disturbing combination.

Windward Avenue is the district's main artery, running from the beach into what was the Grand Circle of the canal system – now paved over – and the original Romanesque arcade, around the intersection with Pacific Avenue, is alive with health-food shops, trinket stores and rollerblade rental stands. Here and there colourful giant **murals** depict everything from a shirtless Jim Morrison (1811 Ocean Front Walk) to Botticelli's Venus on rollerskates (Windward at Speedway Ave). The remaining **canals** are just a few blocks south, accessed on Dell Avenue between Washington and Venice boulevards, where the original quaint little bridges survive. A short distance inland, much of **Abbot Kinney Boulevard** is a fine stretch for hanging out, sipping a latte, deciphering modern art and having a bite in a smart restaurant.

Still, it's **Venice Beach** that draws most people to the town, and nowhere else does LA parade itself quite so openly, colourfully and aggressively as it does along the **Venice Boardwalk**, a wide pathway also known as Ocean Front Walk. Year-round at weekends and every day in summer it's packed with jugglers, fire-eaters, Hare Krishnas, rasta guitar players and, of course, teeming masses of tourists. West of Windward is **Muscle Beach**, a legendary weightlifting centre where serious hunks of muscle pump serious iron, and high-flying gymnasts swing on the adjacent rings and bars. The Venice Beach Recreation Center, 1800 Ocean Front Walk (ⓣ310/399-2775, ⓦwww.laparks.org/venice), has information on the activities and contests that take place here. Rollerbladers, skateboarders, volleyball players and cyclists are ubiquitous throughout the area, and there are **rental shacks** along the beach for picking up skates, surfboards or bikes.

Incidentally, be warned that Venice Beach at night can be a dangerous place, and walking on the beach after dark is illegal in many stretches.

Pacific Palisades

The district of **Pacific Palisades**, rising on the bluffs two miles north of Santa Monica Pier, has a few places of interest among the suburban ranch houses, as a handful of the most influential buildings of postwar LA were constructed here. The **Eames House**, for example, at 203 Chautauqua St, was fashioned out of prefabricated industrial parts in 1947 as part of the Case Study Program. Only the grounds and exterior are viewable (Mon–Fri 10am–4pm, Sat 10am–3pm; free; by appointment at ⓣ310/459-9663, ⓦwww.eamesfoundation.org).

Will Rogers State Historic Park

A mile east along Sunset Boulevard is **Will Rogers State Historic Park** (daily: summer 8am–dusk; winter 8am–6pm; free; parking $12; ⓣ310/454-8212), the home and ranch of the Depression-era cowboy philosopher and journalist **Will Rogers**. At the time he was one of America's most popular figures, renowned for saying that he "never met a man he didn't like". The ranch-style house serves as an informal **museum**, filled with cowboy gear and Native American art (free tours Thurs & Fri 11am, 1pm & 2pm, Sat & Sun on the hour 10am–4pm). The surrounding 200-acre park has miles of foot and bridle paths, the most appealing being the three-mile trek up to **Inspiration Point**, where you can enjoy magnificent vistas of the Pacific and the sweeping curve of Santa Monica Bay. Closer to the ranch, visitors can drop by the **polo grounds** where matches take place during the spring and summer (April–Oct Sat 2–5pm, Sun 10am–1pm).

The Getty Villa

Just west of Sunset Boulevard's intersection with PCH, the **Getty Villa**, 17985 PCH (Wed–Mon 10am–5pm; free, parking $15 or take Metro Bus #534; by reservation only at ⓣ310/440-7300, ⓦwww.getty.edu), was originally the location of the full Getty Center, until that site was reconstructed on a West LA hilltop (see p.112) and this one underwent significant renovation. It now serves as the Getty Foundation's spectacular showcase for its wide array of Greek and Roman antiquities. Modelled after a Roman country house buried by Mount Vesuvius in 79 AD, the villa is built around its own fetching gardens, one an expansive courtyard complex surrounding a long, shallow pool and peppered with black, faintly menacing replicas of stern-looking Roman heads, the other a pleasant herb garden that shows the kinds of plants used for cooking two millennia ago.

Inside, the rooms are grouped in themes ranging from religious and mythic to theatrical to martial. Highlights include the *Getty Kouros*, a rigidly posed figure of a boy that conservators openly admit could be a later forgery, as well as Athenian vases, many of them the red-ground variety, ancient *kylikes*, or drinking vessels, and ceremonial amphorae, or vases given as prizes in athletic contests. Not to be missed is a wondrous Roman-era *skyphos*, a fragile-looking blue vase decorated with white cameos of Bacchus and his friends, properly preparing for a bacchanalia. Keep in mind that because of the dubious provenance of some of the collection's holdings (dating from the days when valuable art was routinely shipped out of the Mediterranean region with little oversight), the Italian government recently forced the Getty to send up to forty priceless items back to the Old World. Despite this, there's more than enough statues, vases, vessels, sculptures and oddments to keep you occupied, and the site well merits a full afternoon of exploration.

The Santa Monica Mountains and Topanga

With hillsides covered in golden poppies and wildflowers, 150,000 acres of the mountains north of PCH and the adjacent seashore have been protected as the **Santa Monica Mountains National Recreation Area**. Park rangers offer free guided hikes throughout the mountains most weekends (ⓣ818/597-9192), and there are self-guided trails through the canyon's **Topanga State Park**, off Old Topanga Canyon Road at the crest of the mountains, with spectacular views over the Pacific. To find out more, contact the visitor centre in neighbouring Thousand Oaks, 401 W Hillcrest Drive (daily 9am–5pm; ⓣ805/370-2301, ⓦwww.nps.gov/samo).

The nearby community of **Topanga** was, in the 1960s, a well-known proving ground for West Coast rock music. Few real bohemians are left, however, and most of the moneyed residents just affect an enlightened, pseudo-hippy style. Before leaving the area, don't miss **Red Rock Canyon**, off Old Topanga Canyon Road at 23601 Red Rock Rd, a stunning red-banded sandstone gorge and state park whose colourful rock formations, surrounding gardens and river wildlife give you a good reason to leave your car behind and go exploring.

Malibu and around

Everyone has heard of **MALIBU**, and while its upscale Hollywood image is not so very far from the truth, you might not think so on arrival. The succession of ramshackle surf shops and fast-food stands scattered along both sides of PCH around the graceful Malibu Pier don't exactly reek of money, but the secluded estates just inland are as valuable as any in the entire country.

Facing south by the pier, **Surfrider Beach** is a major surfing nexus, first gaining recognition when the sport was brought over from Hawaii and mastered by Southern California pioneers. The waves are best in late summer, when storms off

Mexico cause them to reach upwards of eight feet – not huge for serious pros, but big enough for amateurs. Adjoining the beach is a nature reserve and lagoon good for birdwatching, along with seasonal guided tours that showcase, among other things, the sea life in the marshes and tide pools (information at ⊤310/456-8432). Nearby is the **Adamson House**, 23200 PCH (grounds 8am–sunset, house tours Wed–Fri 10.30am–3.30pm, Sat 10.30am–3pm; $5; ⓦwww.adamsonhouse.org), a stunning, historic Spanish Colonial-style home featuring opulent decor and colourful tilework.

Much of **Malibu Creek State Park** (daily dawn–dusk; ⊤818/880-0367), at the crest of Malibu Canyon Road along Mulholland Drive, used to belong to 20th Century-Fox studios, which filmed many Tarzan pictures here and used the chaparral-covered hillsides to simulate South Korea for the TV show *M*A*S*H*. The 4000-acre park includes a large lake, some waterfalls, and nearly fifteen miles of hiking trails, making it crowded on summer weekends but fairly accessible and pleasant the rest of the time (for camping, see box, p.81). The **Paramount Ranch**, near Mulholland Drive at 2813 Cornell Rd (daily 8am–5pm), is another old studio backlot, with a fake railroad crossing, cemetery and Western movie set used for, among other things, the interminable TV drama *Dr Quinn, Medicine Woman*. Finally, **Ramirez Canyon Park**, north of Point Dume and PCH at 5750 Ramirez Canyon Rd (tours Wed 1–4pm; $35; by reservation only at ⊤310/589-2850, ⓦwww .lamountains.com), is a 22-acre complex of houses and gardens that Barbra Streisand donated to the Santa Monica Mountains Conservancy in 1993. Amid extensive flower, herb and fruit gardens, you can get a glimpse into her former properties, constructed in styles ranging from Art Nouveau to Craftsman to Art Deco.

The beaches

Five miles up the coast from Malibu Pier, **Zuma Beach** (most beaches below daily 7am–10pm) is the largest of the LA County beaches, easily connected to the San Fernando Valley by Kanan Dume Road. Adjacent **Point Dume State Beach**, below the bluffs, is more relaxed, and the rocks here are also a good place to look out for seals and migrating grey whales in winter, as the point above – best accessed by car or a longish path – juts out into the Pacific at the northern lip of Santa Monica Bay. **El Matador State Beach**, about 25 miles up the coast from Santa Monica, is about as close as you can get to the private-beach seclusion enjoyed by the stars, thanks to its northern location and an easily missable turn off PCH. Another five miles along the highway, where Mulholland Drive reaches the ocean, **Leo Carrillo** ("ca-REE-oh") **State Park** marks the northwestern border of LA County. The mile-long sandy beach is divided by Sequit Point, a small bluff that has underwater caves and a tunnel you can pass through at low tide, and is also one of LA's best campgrounds (see p.81). You can also camp five miles further on, at **Point Mugu State Park**, where there are some good walks through mountain canyons, and pitches right on the beach.

The South Bay and LA Harbor

South of Venice, the charmless high-rise condos of Marina del Rey and the faded resort town of Playa del Rey offer little to interest visitors. Heading south of LAX, however, is an eight-mile strip of beach towns – **Manhattan Beach**, **Hermosa Beach** and **Redondo Beach**, collectively known as the **SOUTH BAY** – which are quieter, smaller and more insular than the Westside beach communities.

Visible all along this stretch of the coast, the large green peninsula of **Palos Verdes** is an upmarket residential area, while the rough-hewn working town of

San Pedro is sited on the LA Harbor, which with its municipal LA and Long Beach sections is the busiest cargo port in the country, and still growing. On the other side of the Harbor, **Long Beach** is best known as the resting place of the *Queen Mary* – even though it's also the region's second-largest city, with nearly half a million people – while inland are a pair of historically interesting sites in otherwise bland **Wilmington**. Perhaps the most enticing place in the area is **Santa Catalina Island**, twenty miles offshore and easily reached by ferry. It's almost completely conserved wilderness, with many unique forms of plant and animal life and just one main town, **Avalon**.

Manhattan, Hermosa and Redondo beaches

Along the South Bay cities' shared beach boardwalk, known as **The Strand** (which ends at Redondo Beach), the joggers and roller skaters are more likely to be locals than tourists. Each city has at least one municipal pier and a beckoning strip of white sand, with most oceanside locations equipped for surfing and beach volleyball. A major **international surf festival** across all three towns takes place at the end of July (Ⓦwww.surffestival.org), a good time to see California leisure life at its finest.

The most northerly city, **Manhattan Beach**, is a likeable place with a healthy, well-to-do air, home mainly to white-collar workers whose upper-middle-class stucco homes tumble towards the beach. These days, Manhattan Beach's pier is used mainly for strolling, but is also the site of the accurately named Roundhouse, sitting at the end, which encloses a fine **aquarium** (Mon–Fri 3pm–dusk, Sat & Sun 10am–dusk; $2), a mildly interesting spot where you can look at crabs, eels, lobsters, squid and – in their own "touch tank" – tide-pool creatures like anemones and sea stars.

To the south, **Hermosa Beach**, across Longfellow Avenue, has a lingering bohemian feel of the Sixties and Seventies in certain spots, and features a lively beachside strip, most energetic near the foot of the pier on 12th Street. Packed with restaurants and clubs, the area has long been a major hangout for hedonists of all stripes. A good time to come is during the **Fiesta Hermosa** (Ⓦwww.fiestahermosa .com), a three-day event held over Memorial Day and Labor Day that's good for fun music (including surf rock), tasty food and displays of regional arts and crafts.

Despite some decent strips of sand and fine views of Palos Verdes' stunning greenery, **Redondo Beach**, south of Hermosa, is much less inviting than its relaxed neighbour. Condos and hotels line the beachfront, and the yacht-lined King's Harbor is off-limits to curious visitors.

Palos Verdes

A great green hump marking LA's southwest corner, **Palos Verdes** is a rich enclave holding a number of gated communities, but can be enjoyable for the bluffs and coves along its protected coastline. One of these, **Abalone Cove**, reached from a car park at 5970 Palos Verdes Drive S (Mon–Fri noon–4pm, Sat & Sun 9am–4pm; free, parking $5), boasts rock and tide pools, and offshore kelp beds with rock scallops, sea urchins and, of course, abalone. While you're in the area, don't miss **Wayfarer's Chapel**, 5755 Palos Verdes Drive S (daily 10am–5pm), designed by Frank Lloyd Wright's son and now LA's ultimate spot for weddings, the redwood grove around the chapel symbolically growing and weaving itself into the glass-framed structure. A few miles further on, just before the end of Palos Verdes Drive, **Point Fermin Park** is a small tip of land poking into the ocean at LA's southernmost point. The squat wooden **lighthouse** here (tours usually on the hour Tues–Sun 1–4pm; donation; Ⓣ310/241-0684, Ⓦwww.pointferminlighthouse.org) is an

1874 Eastlake structure with a cupola that once contained a 6600-candlepower light which beamed 22 miles out to sea; a whale-watching station lets you read up on the winter migrations. Below the bluff, the excellent **Cabrillo Marine Aquarium**, 3720 Stephen White Drive (Tues–Fri noon–5pm, Sat & Sun 10am–5pm; $5; parking $1 per hour), displays a diverse collection of marine life that has been imaginatively and instructively assembled: everything from predator snails, octopuses and jellyfish to larger displays on otters, seals and whales.

About ten miles inland on the peninsula and not really close to anything else worth seeing, the curious **South Coast Botanic Garden**, 26300 Crenshaw Blvd (daily 9am–5pm; $8), was once the site of a huge landfill stuffed with 3.5 tonnes of rubbish, but has since been covered over and turned into a charming array of themed gardens filled with cacti, ferns, bromeliads, several types of palm trees, and even a small French-style garden. The only hint of its former life is its undulating terrain, evidence of the refuse slowly shifting below the surface.

San Pedro

Three miles north of the Cabrillo Aquarium, the scruffy harbour district of **San Pedro** was a small fishing community until the late nineteenth century, when the construction of the LA Harbor nearby brought a huge influx of foreign labour. Many of these immigrants, and their descendants, never left the place, lending a striking ethnic mix to the town. A good chunk of the district's nautical history is revealed in the **Maritime Museum**, on the harbour's edge at the foot of Sixth Street (Tues–Thurs 10am–5pm, Fri noon–5pm, Sat 10am–5pm; $3), housed in the former Municipal Ferry Building. It now holds art and artefacts from the glory days of San Pedro's fishing and whaling industries, among other collections, with displays on everything from old-fashioned clipper-ship voyages to contemporary diving expeditions. Further north, the **SS Lane Victory**, in Berth 94 off Swinford Street (daily 9am–3pm; $3; ☎310/519-9545, ⓦwww.lanevictory.org), is a huge, ten-thousand-tonne cargo ship that was built in the shipyard in 1945 and operated in Korea and Vietnam. Tours take you through its many cramped spaces, including the engine and radio rooms, crew quarters, galley and bridge.

Four blocks west of the Maritime Museum, old Downtown San Pedro is focused on the restored, opulent **Warner Grand Theatre**, 478 W 6th St (☎310/548-7672, ⓦwww.warnergrand.org), a terrific 1931 Zigzag Moderne moviehouse and performing arts centre with dark geometric details, grand columns and sunburst motifs, a style that almost looks pre-Columbian. Nearby, the **San Pedro Trolley** (Fri–Sun noon–9.30pm; $1) a collection of three classic 1908 Pacific Electric Red Cars (two replica trolleys, one restored), links most of the city's major attractions, running alongside Harbor Boulevard and connecting the SS *Lane Victory* with the Cabrillo Marina at 22nd Street.

Wilmington

Between San Pedro and Long Beach soar two tall road bridges, giving aerial views of huge facilities thick with oil wells and docks. Just inland, the community of **Wilmington** is the site of the Greek Revival **Banning House**, 401 E Main St (guided tours Tues–Thurs 12.30–2.30pm, Sat & Sun 12.30–3.30pm; $5; ☎310/548-7777, ⓦwww.banningmuseum.org), the opulent Victorian home of mid-nineteenth-century entrepreneur Phineas Banning, "the father of Los Angeles transportation", whose 23-room house remains an engaging spot to visit, full of opulent Victorian touches (chandeliers, elegant place-settings and the like) and several restored carriages and stagecoaches kept in an outside barn. While you're in the area, be sure to visit the **Drum Barracks and Civil War Museum**,

1052 Banning Blvd (tours Tues–Thurs 10am & 11.30am, Sat & Sun 11.30am & 1pm; $5; ℡310/548-7509, ⊛www.drumbarracks.org), the Civil War-era federal staging-point for attacks in the Southwest against Confederates and, later, Indians. The sole remaining building houses a collection of military antiques and memorabilia, such as a 34-star US flag and assorted guns, muskets and weaponry, including an early prototype of a machine gun.

Long Beach

Combined with San Pedro, **LONG BEACH** is home to one of the largest ports in the world – making it the point of entry for the majority of goods shipped (and then trucked) to the Western US. It's fairly upmarket near the water, with office buildings, a conference centre, hotels, a shopping mall, and some of the best-preserved early twentieth-century buildings on the coast. Few are better than the **Villa Riviera**, 800 E Ocean Blvd, a fourteen-story Gothic Revival apartment block, with high dormers on a pitched copper roof, pointed octagonal turret and narrow ground-level archways.

Running from Magnolia Avenue to Alamitos Boulevard and Ocean Boulevard to Tenth Street, Downtown Long Beach offers an array of boutiques, antique dealers and diners, many of them around a three-block strip known as **The Promenade**, lined with touristy restaurants and stores that can get busy on weekend nights. To the south, Shoreline Village is a waterfront entertainment belt that used to feature carnival rides and a carousel until the 1940s, but is now mostly a ragtag collection of shops and restaurants. One sight worth a stop is the intriguing, though pricey, **Aquarium of the Pacific** (daily 9am–6pm; $21, kids $13), which exhibits more than eleven thousand marine species, from the familiar sea lions and otters, tide-pool creatures and assorted ocean flora, to the more exotic leopard sharks and giant Japanese spider crabs.

A mile east, the **Long Beach Museum of Art**, 2300 Ocean Blvd (Tues–Sun 11am–5pm; $7), is home to local art and tasteful displays of early Modernist furniture and sculpture. Several blocks north of the ocean, the **Museum of Latin American Art**, 628 Alamitos Ave (Wed, Fri, Sat & Sun 11am–5pm, Thurs 11am–9pm; $9; ℡562/437-1689, ⊛www.molaa.com), is LA's only major museum devoted solely to Latino art. Showcasing artists from Mexico to South America, the collection includes big names like Diego Rivera and José Orozco, as well as newcomers working within contexts that range from social criticism to magical realism.

The Queen Mary

Long Beach's most famous attraction is, of course, the mighty ocean-liner **Queen Mary** (daily 10am–6pm; $25 self-guided tours, kids $12; ⊛www.queenmary .com). Now a luxury hotel, with somewhat overpriced rooms for what you get ($130), the ship offers exhibits that include extravagantly furnished lounges and luxurious first-class cabins, and a wealth of gorgeous Art Deco details in its glasswork, geometric decor and chic streamlining; there are also shops and

---

Long Beach whale-watching trips

Between November and March, more than fifteen thousand whales cruise the **"Whale Freeway"** past Long Beach on their annual migration to and from winter breeding and berthing grounds in Baja California. Harbor Breeze, at Rainbow Harbor next to the Aquarium of the Pacific (℡562/432-4900, ⊛www.longbeachcruises.com), operates good two-hour whale-watching trips for $40 per adult, $25 per child.

restaurants, and even a wedding chapel. There are various add-ons to the basic tour, themed around ghosts, spycraft, scavenger hunts and more, boosting the price by $30. One of the more peculiar sights alongside the ship is a Foxtrot-class **submarine** (same hours; $11, or joint ticket $33) that was until 1994 used in the service of the Soviet, and then Russian, navy, carrying a payload of 22 nuclear weapons and powered by clunky diesel engines.

Santa Catalina Island

The enticing island of **Santa Catalina**, twenty miles offshore from Long Beach, is mostly preserved wilderness, but does have substantial charm and offers a nice break from the metropolis. Indeed, with cars largely forbidden, the two thousand islanders walk, ride bikes or drive golf carts. **Ferry** trips run several times daily from Long Beach, and cost $65–70 for a round trip. Operators include Catalina Express, from Long Beach (☎1-800/481-3470, ⓦwww.catalinaexpress.com), and, from Newport Beach, Catalina Flyer (☎800/834-7744, ⓦwww.catalina -flyer.com).

The island's one town, **Avalon**, can be fully explored on foot in an hour, with maps issued by the Chamber of Commerce at the foot of the ferry pier (☎310/510-1520, ⓦwww.catalinachamber.com). Begin at the sumptuous Art Deco **Avalon Casino**, 1 Casino Way, a 1920s structure that still shows movies and features mermaid murals, gold-leaf ceiling motifs, an Art Deco ballroom and a small **museum** (daily 10am–4pm, Jan–March closed Thurs; $5) displaying Native American artefacts from Catalina's past and explaining Hollywood's use of the island as a film location. Roughly three miles southwest of Avalon, the **Wrigley Memorial and Botanical Garden**, 1400 Avalon Canyon Rd (daily 8am–5pm; $5), displays all manner of endemic flora and fauna on forty acres. **Santa Catalina Island Company** (☎310/510-8687, ⓦwww.visitcatalinaisland.com) offers tours of the Avalon Casino ($19–30), bus trips through the outback ($43–120), and harbour cruises and glass-bottom-boat rides ($18–42), while **Catalina Adventure Tours** provides slightly cheaper versions of the same ($17–64; ☎310/510-2888, ⓦwww.catalinaadventuretours.com).

The most interesting **hotel** is the *Zane Grey Pueblo*, 199 Chimes Tower Rd (☎310/510-0966, ⓦwww.zanegreypueblohotel.com; ⑥), which has sixteen rooms overlooking the bay or mountains, with an enticing off-season (Nov–April) weekday rate of $75. If you have plenty of spending money, the *Inn on Mt Ada*, 398 Wrigley Rd (☎1-800/608-7669, ⓦwww.innonmtada.com; ⑨, from $415), is the final word in Catalina luxury. The only budget option is **camping**: *Hermit Gulch* is the closest site to Avalon, and the busiest. Four other sites in Catalina's interior – *Blackjack*, *Little Harbor*, *Parsons Landing* and *Two Harbors* (all $14 per person, kids $7) – are much more distant, but also roomier. Book at ☎310/510-8368 or ⓦwww.scico.com/camping.

The San Gabriel and San Fernando valleys

Running north of central LA, beyond the crest of the hills, lie two long, expansive valleys that start close to one another a few miles north of Downtown and span outwards in opposite directions – east to the deserts around Palm Springs, west to Ventura on the Central Coast. To the east, the **SAN GABRIEL VALLEY** was settled by farmers and cattle ranchers as foothill communities, which grew into prime resort towns, luring many here around the turn of the last century. **Pasadena**, the largest of the modest cities, holds many elegant period houses, as well as the fine **Norton Simon Museum** and the **Old Pasadena** outdoor shopping mall, with restaurants, cinemas and other activities. Above Pasadena, the southern slopes of the San Gabriel Mountains are great spots for hiking and rough camping, though you'll nearly always need a car to get to the trailheads. South of Pasadena, WASP-ish **San Marino** is dominated by the **Huntington Library and Gardens**, a stash of art and literature ringed by botanical gardens that in itself is worth a trip to the valley.

North of Downtown LA and spreading west, the **SAN FERNANDO VALLEY** is, to most Angelenos, simply "the Valley": a sprawl of tract homes, mini-malls, fast-food drive-ins, and car-parts shops that has more of a middle-American feel than anywhere else in LA. For most people, the main reason to come out here is to tour the movie studios in **Burbank** and **Universal City**. Elsewhere, **Forest Lawn Cemetery** is a prime example of graveyard kitsch that's hard to imagine anywhere except in LA, and exciting **Magic Mountain** easily outdoes Disneyland for death-defying rides.

Pasadena

In the 1880s, wealthy East Coast tourists who came to California looking for the good life found it in **PASADENA**, ten miles north of LA and connected via the I-10 (Pasadena) Freeway. A century later the Downtown area underwent a major renovation, with modern shopping centres slipped in behind 1920s facades, but the historic parts of town have not been forgotten. Maps and booklets detailing self-guided tours of city architecture and history are available from the **Pasadena Visitors Bureau**, 171 S Los Robles Ave (Mon–Fri 9am–5pm, Sat 10am–4pm; ℡626/795-9311, Ⓦwww.pasadenacal.com). The town's most notable attraction, the New Year's Day **Tournament of Roses**, began in 1890 to celebrate and publicize the mild Southern California winters, and now attracts more than a million visitors every year to watch its marching bands and elaborate flower-emblazoned floats (see box, p.142). Also fascinating is the **Tournament House**, 391 S Orange Grove Blvd (tours Feb–Aug Thurs 2 & 3pm; free; ℡626/449-4100), a pink 1914 Renaissance Revival mansion that's well worth a look for its grand manor and surrounding gardens – containing up to 1500 types of rose.

Earthquake Central: The San Fernando Valley

The devastating 6.7-magnitude **earthquake** that shook LA on the morning of January 17, 1994, was one of the biggest disasters in US history. Fifty-five people were killed, two hundred more suffered critical injuries, and the economic cost was estimated at $8 billion. One can only guess how much higher these totals would have been had the quake hit during the day, when the many collapsed stores would have been crowded with shoppers and the freeways full of commuters. The quake, with its epicentre in the San Fernando Valley community of **Northridge**, eclipsed LA's previous worst earthquake in modern times, the 6.6-magnitude temblor of February 1971, which had its epicentre in Sylmar – also in the Valley.

In the unlikely event a sizeable earthquake strikes when you're in LA, protect yourself under something sturdy, such as a heavy table or a doorframe, and well away from windows or anything made of glass. In theory, all the city's new buildings are "quake-safe", though as the 1994 quake recedes in memory, the retrofitting of older buildings seems to diminish in perceived importance. So when the inevitable "Big One" – a quake in the 8-plus-range – arrives, no one knows exactly what will be left standing.

Old Pasadena and around

Between Fair Oaks and Euclid avenues along Colorado Boulevard, the historic shopping precinct of **Old Pasadena** draws visitors for its fine restaurants, galleries and theatres, and is accessible by light-rail connection on the Metro Gold Line (see p.73). Downtown Pasadena's most prominent architectural work and its municipal centrepiece, **Pasadena City Hall**, 100 N Garfield Ave (Mon–Fri 9am–5pm; ☎626/744-7073), is one of several city buildings in Mediterranean Revival styles, in this case Spanish Baroque, with a large, tiled dome and imperious facade with grand arches and columns. The local preservation society, **Pasadena Heritage**, offers periodic tours of this and other city landmarks – including an excellent 90-minutes overview of Old Pasadena on the first Saturday of the month (9am; $10; book on ☎626/441-6333, ⓦwww.pasadenaheritage.org).

Just to the east of City Hall, a replica Chinese imperial palace houses the **Pacific Asia Museum**, 46 N Los Robles Ave (Wed–Sun 10am–6pm; $9), which is modelled after a Chinese imperial palace, with a sloping tiled roof topped with ceramic-dog decorations, inset balconies and dragon-emblazoned front gates. It includes thousands of historical treasures and everyday objects from Korea, China and Japan, including decorative jade and porcelain, various swords and spears, and a large cache of paintings and drawings. Just around the corner, at 490 E Union St, the three-storey **Pasadena Museum of California Art** (Wed–Sun noon–5pm; $7; ☎626/568-3665, ⓦwww.pmcaonline.org) focuses on the many aspects of the state's art world since it became part of the Union in 1850, in all kinds of media from painting to digital.

The Norton Simon Museum

The excellent **Norton Simon Museum**, 411 W Colorado Blvd (Wed–Mon noon–6pm, Fri until 9pm; $8, students free; ☎626/449-6840, ⓦwww.norton simon.org), merits at least an afternoon to wander through its spacious galleries. The core of the massive collection is **Western European painting**. Highlights include Dutch paintings of the seventeenth century – notably Rembrandt's vivacious *Titus, Portrait of a Boy* and Frans Hals' quietly aggressive *Portrait of a Man* – and Italian Renaissance work from Botticelli, Raphael, Giorgione, Bellini and others. There's also a good sprinkling of French Impressionists and post-Impressionists: Monet's *Mouth of the Seine at Honfleur*, Manet's *Ragpicker* and a Degas capturing the extended yawn of a washerwoman in *The Ironers*, plus works by Cézanne, Gauguin and Van Gogh.

Unlike the Getty Museum, the Norton Simon also boasts a solid collection of Modernist greats, from Georges Braque and Pablo Picasso to Roy Lichtenstein and Andy Warhol, with figures such as Robert Irwin, Richard Diebenkorn, Ed Kienholz and Ed Ruscha adding a California bent. As a counterpoint to the Western art, the museum has a fine collection of **Asian art**, including many highly polished Buddhist and Hindu figures, some inlaid with precious stones, and many drawings and prints – the highlight being Hiroshige's masterful series of coloured woodblock prints, showing nature in quiet, dusky hues.

Arroyo Seco

The residential pocket northwest of the junction of the 134 and 210 freeways, known as **Arroyo Seco**, or "dry riverbed" in Spanish, features some of LA's best architecture. Orange Grove Boulevard leads you into the neighbourhood from central Pasadena and takes you to the **Pasadena Museum of History**, 470 W Walnut St at Orange Grove Blvd (Wed–Sun noon–5pm; $5, kids free; ☎626/577-1660, ⓦwww.pasadenahistory.org), which has fine displays on Pasadena's history and tasteful gardens, but is most interesting for the on-site **Feynes Mansion** (tours by appointment at ☎626/577-1660; $4). Decorated with its original 1905 furnishings and paintings, this elegant Beaux Arts mansion was once the home of the Finnish Consulate. But it's the **Gamble House**, nearby at 4 Westmoreland Place (hour-long tours every 20–30min Thurs–Sun noon–3pm; $10, kids free; reserve at ☎626/793-3333, ⓦwww.gamblehouse.org), that really appeals, a 1908 Craftsman masterpiece combining elements from Swiss chalets and Japanese temples in a romantic, sprawling shingled house. The area around the Gamble House holds at least eleven other houses attributed to the two brothers (the firm of Greene & Greene) who designed it, including Charles Greene's own house at 368 Arroyo Terrace (closed to the public).

Incongruously sited just to the north, the 104,000-seat **Rose Bowl** is out of use for most of the year but is home to a very popular **flea market** on the second Sunday of the month ($8, reserve tickets on ☎323/560-7469, ⓦwww.rgcshows .com) and, in the autumn, the place where the UCLA football team plays its home games (tickets at ☎310/825-2101, ⓦwww.uclabruins.com).

Into the foothills

On the other side of the Foothill Freeway (I-210), **Descanso Gardens**, 1418 Descanso Drive (Fri–Mon 9am–5pm, summer also Tues–Thurs 9am–8pm; $8, kids $3; ☎818/949-4200, ⓦwww.descansogardens.org), in the nearby city of La Cañada Flintridge, concentrates all the plants you might see in the mountains into 155 acres of landscaped park, especially brilliant in the spring when all the camellias, tulips, lilies and daffodils are in bloom. From La Cañada, the winding **Angeles Crest Highway** (Hwy-2) heads up into the mountains above Pasadena, an area once dotted with resort hotels and wilderness camps. The highway leads up to Mount Wilson, high enough to be the major siting spot for TV broadcast antennae, and with a small **museum** (April–Nov 10am–4pm; $1; free tours Sat & Sun 1pm) near the 100-inch telescope of the 1904 Mount Wilson Observatory.

The Huntington Library and Gardens

South of Pasadena, **San Marino** is a dull, upper-crust suburb with little of interest beyond the fantastic **Huntington Library, Art Collections and Botanical Gardens**, off Huntington Drive at 1151 Oxford Rd (Mon & Wed–Fri noon–4.30pm, Sat & Sun 10.30am–4.30pm; $15 weekdays, $20 weekends; ☎626/405-2100, ⓦwww.huntington.org), based on the collections of Henry Huntington, who owned and operated the Pacific Electric Railway Company, which controlled the Red Car line that helped make Huntington the largest landowner in the state. In later years he moved to this estate and devoted himself full-time to buying rare books and manuscripts.

You can pick up a self-guided walking tour from the bookstore and information desk in the covered pavilion. The **Library**, right off the main entrance, has a two-storey exhibition hall containing rare manuscripts and books, among them a Gutenberg Bible, a folio edition of Shakespeare's plays and the **Ellesmere Chaucer**, a circa-1410 illuminated manuscript of *The Canterbury Tales*. Displays around the walls trace the history of printing and of the English language from medieval manuscripts to a King James Bible, from Milton's *Paradise Lost* and Blake's *Songs of Innocence and Experience* to first editions of Swift, Dickens, Woolf and Joyce.

The recently renovated **Huntington Gallery**, a grand mansion done out in Louis XIV carpets and later French tapestries, has works by Van Dyck and Constable and the stars of the whole collection – Gainsborough's *Blue Boy* and Reynolds' *Mrs Siddons as the Tragic Muse*. More striking, perhaps, are Turner's *Grand Canal, Venice*, awash in hazy sunlight and gondolas, and Blake's *Satan Comes to the Gates of Hell*, which is quite the portrait of Old Nick, in this case battling Death with spears.

Elsewhere, the **Scott and Erburu Galleries** display paintings by John Singleton Copley, Frederic Church, Benjamin West, Edward Hopper and Mary Cassatt, Wild West drawings and sculpture, and work by the architects Greene & Greene. The acres of beautiful themed **gardens** surrounding the buildings include a Desert Garden with the world's largest collection of desert plants, including twelve acres of cacti; lush rose, palm and subtropical gardens; a sculpture garden full of Baroque statues; and a Japanese garden dotted with koi ponds, cherry trees and "moon bridges". While strolling through these assorted wonders, you might also call in on Huntington and his wife, buried in a neo-Palladian **mausoleum** at the northwest corner of the estate.

Along Foothill Boulevard

Parallel to the Foothill Freeway, **Foothill Boulevard** was once best known as part of Route 66, and nowadays leads to the town of **Arcadia**, whose **LA County Arboretum**, 301 N Baldwin Ave (daily 9am–4.30pm; $5), contains many impressive gardens and waterfalls, flocks of peacocks and, of course, a great assortment of trees arranged according to their native continents. The fanciful white Victorian manor along a palm-treed lagoon was famously used in the 1970s TV show *Fantasy Island*.

Southwest of Arcadia in small **San Gabriel** stands the valley's original settlement, the church and grounds of **Mission San Gabriel Arcangel**, 428 S Mission Drive (daily 9am–4.30pm; $5), established here in 1771 by Junípero Serra and the current building finished in 1812. Despite decades of damage by earthquakes and the elements, the church and grounds have been repaired and reopened, their old winery, cistern, kitchens, gardens and antique-filled rooms giving some sense of mission-era life.

Forest Lawn Cemetery

Jumping many miles west, to the opposite side of the San Gabriel Valley, **Glendale** is best known for its branch of **Forest Lawn Cemetery**, 1712 S Glendale Ave (daily 8am–5pm; free), its pompous landscaping and pious artworks attracting celebrities by the dozen. It's best to climb the hill and see the cemetery in reverse from the **Forest Lawn Museum**, whose hotchpotch of historical bric-a-brac includes coins from ancient Rome, Viking relics, medieval armour and a mysterious sculpted Easter Island figure – the only one on view in the US. Next door to the museum, the **Hall of the Crucifixion-Resurrection** houses the biggest piece of Western religious art in the world: *The Crucifixion* by Jan Styka – an oil painting nearly 200ft tall and 45ft wide – though you're only allowed to see it during the unveiling every hour on the hour.

From the museum, the terraced gardens lead down past sculpted replicas of the greats of classical European art, and on to the **Freedom Mausoleum**, home to a handful of the cemetery's better-known graves. Just outside the mausoleum's doors, Errol Flynn lies in an unspectacular plot, rumoured to have been buried with six bottles of whisky at his side, while nearby is the grave of Walt Disney, who wasn't frozen, as urban legend would have it. Inside the mausoleum itself you'll find Clara Bow, Nat King Cole, Jeanette MacDonald and Alan Ladd, all close to each other on the first floor. To the left, heading back down the hill, the **Great Mausoleum** is notable for the tombs of Clark Gable and Jean Harlow.

The Burbank studios

On the eastern edge of the San Fernando Valley, dull **Burbank** is the place where many movie studios relocated from Hollywood long ago. Although you can't get into Disney, **Warner Bros**, Warner Boulevard at Hollywood Way, does offer worthwhile "insider" tours of its sizeable facilities and active backlot (Mon–Fri 8.30am–4pm; $48; ☎818/972-8687, Ⓦwww2.warnerbros.com/vipstudiotour). **NBC**, 3000 W Alameda St (box office Mon–Fri 9am–4pm; $8; ☎818/840-3537), allows 75-minute tours of the largest production facility in the US, and gives you the chance to be in the audience for the taping of a TV programme (phone ahead for free tickets) such as Jay Leno's *Tonight Show*.

The largest of the backlots belongs to **Universal Studios**, whose high-priced four-hour "tours" (hours vary, often summer daily 8am–10pm; rest of year daily 10am–6pm; two-day minimum ticket $69, kids $59; ☎818/508-9600, Ⓦwww.universalstudioshollywood.com) are more like a trip around an amusement park than a visit to a film studio, with the first half featuring a tram ride through a make-believe set where you can see the house from *Psycho* and the shark from *Jaws*, experience a San Francisco-style earthquake, have a close encounter with King Kong and watch Wild West actors performing stunts and holding gunfights. Elsewhere, the other theme rides are based on the studio's TV franchises (*The Simpsons Ride*, a wacky trip into the Krustyland theme-park-within-a-theme-park) and films such as *Jurassic Park* (close encounters with prehistoric plastic), *Terminator 2* (a 3-D movie with robot stuntmen), and *Shrek 4-D* (a motion simulator, plus a 3-D movie). You never actually get to see any filming, though.

North of the Valley and beyond

At the north end of the Valley, the San Diego, Golden State and Foothill freeways join together at I-5. Just east of the junction, **Mission San Fernando Rey de España**, 15151 San Fernando Mission Blvd (daily 9am–4.30pm; donation), has a good collection of historic pottery, furniture and saddles, and a replica of an old-time blacksmith's shop. Up the road in nearby Sylmar, the wondrous **Nethercutt Collection**, 15200 Bledsoe St (tours only Thurs–Sat 10am & 1.30pm; free; by reservation at ☎818/364-6464, Ⓦwww.nethercuttcollection.org), is a storehouse for all kinds of Wurlitzer organs, old-time player-pianos, cosmetic paraphernalia, Tiffany stained glass and classic French furniture; there are also two dozen antique cars on view from the 1920s and 30s. Even more worthwhile, however, is the adjoining **Nethercutt Museum** (Tues–Sat 9am–4.30pm; free), a stunning showroom filled with 130 collectors' vintage automobiles such as Packards, Mercedes, Bugattis and especially the Duesenbergs, splendid machines driven by movie stars in the Jazz Age.

Just north of the freeway junction in the town of **Santa Clarita**, the **William S. Hart Ranch and Museum**, 24151 San Fernando Rd (summer Wed–Sun 11am–4pm; winter Wed–Fri 10am–1pm, Sat & Sun 11am–4pm; free), holds a fine assemblage of Western history, featuring native artworks, Remington sculptures, displays of spurs, guns and lariats, Tinseltown costumes and authentic cowhand clothing, all housed in a Spanish Colonial mansion on a surrounding 265-acre ranch once owned by the silent-era cowboy actor. Continuing north, Hwy-14 splits off east to the Mojave Desert, while I-5 heads on past Valencia to **Six Flags Magic Mountain**, Magic Mountain Parkway at I-5 (hours vary, often summer daily 10am–10pm; winter Sat & Sun 10am–8pm; $60, kids $35, $15 parking; Ⓦwww.sixflags.com/parks/magicmountain), which has some of the wildest roller coasters and rides in the world – highlights include the Viper, a huge orange monster with seven loops; the Goliath, full of harrowing 85mph dips; and Tatsu, which sends you through the requisite loops while strapped in face-down at a 90-degree angle. The adjacent water park, **Hurricane Harbor** (same hours; $30, kids $20), provides aquatic fun if you don't mind getting splashed by throngs of giddy pre-adolescents.

Inland Orange County

Although **ORANGE COUNTY** has long been emblematic of insular white suburbia, the reality is now a bit different. Certain sections of the county have a tolerant, even progressive, bent, especially in the inland part of the region, and Hispanics and Asians increasingly populate cities like Anaheim, Garden Grove, Santa Ana and Westminster. For most visitors, however, Orange County means **Disneyland**; even though it only exists on roughly one square mile of land, it continues to dominate the **Anaheim** area. Elsewhere, the thrill rides at **Knott's Berry Farm** provide a cheaper alternative; the **Crystal Cathedral** is an imposing reminder of the potency of the US evangelical movement; and the **Richard Nixon Library and Birthplace** is a good spot to find out about the illustrious life and career of Tricky Dick.

Disneyland

In the early 1950s, illustrator and filmmaker **Walt Disney** conceived a theme park where his internationally famous cartoon characters – Mickey Mouse, Donald Duck, Goofy and the rest – would come to life, animated quite literally, and his fabulously successful company would rake in even more money. **DISNEYLAND**, 1313 Harbor Blvd (hours vary, usually summer daily 8am–1am; winter Mon–Fri 10am–6pm, Sat 9am–midnight, Sun 9am–10pm; $72, $62 kids, parking $14; ⊤714/781-4565, ⓦwww.disneyland.com), is still world-renowned as one of the defining hallmarks of American culture, a theme-park phenomenon with the emphasis strongly on family fun.

The main park

Not including the newer California Adventure annexe (see p.130), the Disneyland admission price includes all the rides, although during peak periods you might have to wait in line for hours – lines are shortest when the park opens, so choose a few top rides and get to them very early.

From the front gates, **Main Street** leads through a scaled-down, camped-up replica of a bucolic Midwestern town, filled with souvenir shops and diners, toward **Sleeping Beauty's Castle**, a pseudo-Rhineland palace recently reopened to fascinating effect, with narrow corridors and stairs leading to brightly coloured, three-dimensional scenes from the classic Disney cartoon. **New Orleans Square**, nearby, contains the two best rides in the park: the Pirates of the Caribbean, a boat trip through underground caverns, singing along with drunken pirates, and the Haunted Mansion, a riotous "doom buggy" tour in the company of the house spooks. In **Adventureland**, the antiquated Jungle Cruise has "tour guides" making crude puns about the fake animatronic beasts creaking amid the scenery,

---

Disneyland practicalities

Disneyland is about 45 minutes by **car** from Downtown LA on the Santa Ana Freeway (I-5). By **train** from Downtown, it's a thirty-minute journey to Fullerton, from where OCTD buses will drop you at Disneyland or Knott's Berry Farm. By **bus**, MTA #460 from Downtown takes about ninety minutes, and Greyhound takes 45 minutes to get to Anaheim, from where it's an easy walk to the park.

As for **accommodation**, most people try to visit Disneyland just for the day and spend the night somewhere else. If you want to stay, see the options on p.80. If the fast food available in the park doesn't appeal, the listings on p.136 suggest some of the more palatable options.

and **Indiana Jones Adventure**, a giddy journey down skull-encrusted corridors in which you face fireballs, burning rubble, venomous snakes and, inevitably, a rolling-boulder finale.

Less fun are the neighbouring areas of **Critter Country** and **Frontierland**, where the main attraction, Big Thunder Mountain Railroad, is a drab, slow-moving coaster. Splash Mountain at least has the added thrill of getting drenched by a log-flume ride, and Tom Sawyer Island has been re-themed around Disney's movie franchise *Pirates of the Caribbean*: you can poke around the spooky Dead Man's Grotto for hidden treasure, and explore the skeletons littered through a shipwreck at Smuggler's Cove. Continuing counterclockwise around the park, **Fantasyland** shows off the cleverest, but also the most senti-mental, aspects of the Disney imagination: Peter Pan, a fairytale flight over London, and It's a Small World, a tour of the world's continents in which animated dolls warble the same cloying song over and over. For tots who just can't get enough saccharine, there's **Toontown**, thick with slow-moving bumper cars and other kiddie amusements.

Fantasyland mercifully gives way to **Tomorrowland**, Disney's vision of the future, where the Space Mountain rollercoaster zips through the pitch-blackness of outer space; the late Michael Jackson is celebrated in the *Captain EO Tribute*, a 17-minute 3-D film juiced up with special effects; and the Finding Nemo Submarine Voyage picks up where its predecessor, 20,000 Leagues Under the Sea, left off, giving you a quick underwater tour of notable aquatic scenes from the hit movie.

The California Adventure

The **California Adventure** is technically a separate park but is connected to the main one in architecture and style – although it's much less popular. Aside from its slightly more exciting rollercoasters and better food, the California Adventure is really just another "land" to visit, albeit a much more expensive one – you'll have to shell out another $72, or $97 for a two-day pass that covers both.

There's a handful of highlights. Grizzly River Run is a fun giant-inner-tube ride, splashing through plunges and "caverns"; Soarin' Over California is an exciting trip on a mock-experimental aircraft that buzzes through hairpin turns and steep dives; and the **Pacific Pier** zone has a slew of old-fashioned carnival rides – from California Screamin', a sizeable roller coaster, to the Ferris-like Mickey's Fun Wheel – that only faintly recall the wilder, harder-edged midways of California's past. There's also a rather tame zone devoted to Tinseltown, **Hollywoodland**, which, aside from a few theatres and special-effects displays, features the Tower of Terror, a shock-drop ride in a haunted hotel.

Knott's Berry Farm

If you're a bit fazed by the excesses of Disneyland, you might prefer the more down-to-earth **Knott's Berry Farm**, four miles northwest, off the Santa Ana Freeway at 8039 Beach Blvd (hours vary, usually summer Sun–Thurs 9am–11pm, Fri & Sat 9am–midnight; winter Mon–Fri 10am–6pm, Sat 10am–10pm, Sun 10am–7pm; $55, kids $24; ⓦ www.knotts.com), whose rollercoasters are far more exciting than anything at its rival. Although there are ostensibly six themed lands here, you should spend most or all of your time in just half of them: **Fiesta Village**, home to the Jaguar, a high-flying coaster that spins you around the park concourse; **Ghost Town**, with fun wooden coasters and log flumes; and the **Boardwalk**, which is all about heart-thumping thrill rides. Knott's also has its own adjacent water park, **Soak City USA** (June–Sept only, hours vary but generally daily 10am–5pm or 6pm; $26, kids $20), offering fourteen drenching rides of various heights and speeds.

Around Disneyland

To the south of Disneyland, the giant **Crystal Cathedral**, just off the Santa Ana Freeway on Chapman Avenue (tours Mon–Sat 9am–3.30pm; free), is a famous Philip Johnson design of tubular space-frames and plate-glass walls that forms part of the vision of evangelist Robert Schuller. More worthwhile, in the nearby city of **Santa Ana**, is the splendid **Bowers Museum of Cultural Art**, 2002 N Main Street (Tues–Sun 10am–4pm; $18 weekdays, $20 weekends), which features anthropological treasures from early Asian, African, Native American and pre-Columbian civilizations. Showcasing artefacts as diverse as ceramic Maya icons, handcrafted baskets from native Californians and Chinese funerary sculpture, the museum is an essential stop for anyone interested in civilizations outside the West. North of Disneyland, bland **Fullerton** is the site of the **Muckenthaler Cultural Center**, 1201 W Malvern Ave (Wed–Sun noon–4pm; free; ℡714/738-6595, ⓦthemuck.org), located in an attractive 1924 Renaissance Revival mansion and hosting a wide range of international multicultural art, with Native American art and textiles, African craftwork and jewellery, and contemporary Korean ceramics being only a few of the highlights.

The Richard Nixon Presidential Library and Museum

In freeway-caged **Yorba Linda**, about eight miles northeast of Disneyland, the **Richard Nixon Presidential Library and Museum**, 18001 Yorba Linda Blvd (Mon–Sat 10am–5pm, Sun 11am–5pm; $10), exhibits items such as the presidential limousine, campaign relics and the little house where the future president was born. In 2007 control over the site was given to the federal government, and access to the Watergate tapes and other crucial documents from Nixon's era has become more open. Also on view is the **World Leaders Gallery** of Nixon's heyday, with Mao, Brezhnev and de Gaulle among them, cast in bronze and arranged in rigid poses, and a re-creation of the **East Room** of the White House. You can also get up close to the **helicopter** he used as president – and when he was whisked away from the White House after resigning in disgrace. Nixon's grave is also on site.

The Orange County Coast

On the **ORANGE COUNTY COAST**, a string of towns from the edge of the LA Harbor Area to the borders of San Diego County 35 miles south, swanky condos line the sands and the ambience is easy-going and affluent. As the names of the main towns suggest – **Huntington Beach**, **Newport Beach** and **Laguna Beach** – there are few reasons beyond sea and sand to come here. The other place that merits a stop is just inland at **San Juan Capistrano**, site of the best kept of all the California missions. Further on, there's little to see before you reach adjoining San Diego County, but the campground at **San Clemente** provides the only cheap accommodation along the southern part of the coast (see p.81).

The fastest way to **travel** from LA to San Diego skips the coast by passing through Orange County on the inland San Diego Freeway, the 405. The coastal cities, though, are linked by the more appealing **Pacific Coast Highway (PCH)**, part of Hwy-1. OCTD bus #1 rumbles along PCH regularly during the day, though Greyhound largely avoids this part of Orange County. Amtrak's Pacific Surfliner route connects Downtown LA (or Disneyland) to San Juan Capistrano and San Clemente, though you can travel all the way along the coast from LA to San Diego using local buses for about $6–8 – but you should allow a full day for the journey. A slightly pricier but more worthwhile option is the Metrolink commuter train line (see p.73), which not only connects Downtown LA with Orange County down to San Clemente, but continues on to Oceanside in San Diego County, from where you can pick up that region's Coaster and connect to Downtown San Diego.

Huntington Beach

Huntington Beach is a compact town of engaging single-storey cafés and beach stores grouped around the foot of a long pier, off PCH at Main Street – also the place where the **Surfers Walk of Fame** commemorates the sport's towering figures. Otherwise the beach is the sole focus: it was here that California surfing began, imported from Hawaii in 1907. You can check out the **International Surfing Museum**, 411 Olive Ave (Mon–Fri noon–5pm, Sat & Sun 11am–6pm; free), which features exhibits on such surfing legends, historic posters from surfing contests, and an array of traditional, contemporary and far-out boards.

Several miles north, nature lovers won't want to miss the **Bolsa Chica State Ecological Reserve**, PCH at Warner Avenue, a sizeable wetland preserve. Taking a one-and-one-half-mile loop tour will get you acquainted with some of the current avian residents of this salt marsh, including a fair number of herons, egrets and grebes, and even a few peregrine falcons and endangered snowy plovers. Self-guided tours are free, and guided tours are available on the first Saturday of the month (9–10.30am; $1; groups need to reserve on ☎714/840-1575, ⓦwww.amigosdebolsachica.org).

Newport Beach and Corona Del Mar

Ten miles south of Huntington, **Newport Beach**, with its bevy of yachts and yacht clubs, is upmarket even by Orange County standards. Although there are hardly any conventional "sights" in town, the place to hang out is on the thin **Balboa Peninsula**, along which runs the three-mile-long strand. The most youthful and boisterous section is about halfway along, around **Newport Pier** at the end of 20th Street. North of here, beachfront homes restrict access, but to the south, around the **Balboa Pier**, is a tourist-friendly area with a marina from which you can escape to Santa Catalina Island (see p.123). Away from the peninsula, Newport Beach is home to the **Orange County Museum of Art**, 850 San Clemente Drive (Wed–Sun 11am–5pm, Thurs until 8pm; $10, free on Thurs; ☎949/759-1122, ⓦwww.ocma.net), one of the county's few modern art institutions on a par with its LA rivals. Its collection focuses on contemporary work from California artists like Lari Pittman, Ed Ruscha and Ed Kienholz, and there are periodical retrospectives of great twentieth-century figures as well as Southern Californian up-and-comers.

A few miles along PCH from Newport, **Corona Del Mar** is worth a short stop for the **Sherman Library and Gardens**, 2647 E PCH (daily 10.30am–4pm; $3), devoted to the horticulture of the Southwest and raising many vivid blooms in its botanical gardens, including cacti, orchids, roses and an array of herbs. Between here and Laguna Beach lies an unspoiled three-mile-long coastline, protected as **Crystal Cove State Park**, which also holds two thousand acres of rugged inland terrain good for hiking, horseriding and biking, on trails that cross hilly peaks and ravines – it's perfect to explore on foot, far from the crowds, and offers good beachside accommodation (see p.81).

Laguna Beach

Six miles south of Crystal Cove, nestled among the crags around a small sandy strip, **Laguna Beach** has a relaxed and tolerant feel among its inhabitants, who range from millionaires to middle-class gays and lesbians, and offers a flourishing arts scene in the many streetside galleries. PCH passes right through the centre of town, a few steps from the small main **beach**. One of the few conventional attractions is the excellent **Laguna Art Museum**, 307 Cliff Drive (daily 11am–5pm; $15; ☎949/494-8971, ⓦwww.lagunaartmuseum.org), which holds fine exhibitions drawn from its stock of Southern California art from the 1900s to the present.

About two and a half miles inland from Downtown Laguna Beach is a sight not to be missed by lovers of sea life: the **Pacific Marine Mammal Center**, 20612 Laguna Canyon Rd (daily 10am–4pm; free), a rehabilitation centre that lets you watch as underweight, injured or otherwise threatened seals and sea lions are nursed back to health.

San Juan Capistrano

Further south, and three miles inland along the I-5 freeway, most of the small town of **San Juan Capistrano** is built in a Spanish Colonial style derived from **Mission San Juan Capistrano**, Ortega Highway at Camino Capistrano in the centre of town (daily 8.30am–5pm; $9), a short walk from the Amtrak stop. The seventh of California's missions, it was founded by Junípero Serra in 1776; soon after, the **Great Stone Church** was erected, the ruins of which are the first thing you see as you walk in – it was destroyed by an earthquake soon after its 1812 completion. The mission **chapel** is small and narrow, set off by a sixteenth-century altar from Barcelona. In a side room, the tiny chapel of **St Pereguin** is kept warm by the heat from the dozens of candles lit by miracle-seeking pilgrims who arrive here from all over the US and Mexico. Other restored buildings include the kitchen, smelter and workshops used for dyeing, weaving and candle making.

The city is further noted for its **swallows**, popularly thought to return here from their winter migration on March 19. They sometimes do arrive on this day, but are much more likely to show up as soon as the weather is warm enough, and when there are enough insects on the ground to provide a decent homecoming banquet.

Laguna Beach festivals

Laguna hosts a number of large summer **art festivals** over six weeks in July and August. The best known is the **Pageant of the Masters**, in which participants pose in front of a painted backdrop to portray a famous work of art. It's surprisingly impressive and takes a great deal of preparation – something reflected in the prices: $15–150 for shows that sell out months in advance. You may, however, be able to pick up cancellations on the night (shows begin at 8.30pm; ☎1-800/487-3378, ⓦwww.foapom.com). The pageant is combined with the **Festival of the Arts** (daily 10am–11.30pm; $7; contact information as above), held at the same venue and featuring the work of 150 local artists.

The excitement of both festivals waned in the 1960s, when a group of hippies created the alternative **Sawdust Festival**, 935 Laguna Canyon ad (July & Aug daily 10am–10pm; $7.75, season pass $15; ☎949/494-3030, ⓦwww.sawdustart festival.org), in which local artists set up makeshift studios to demonstrate their skills. It is now just as established, but easier to get into than the other two.

San Clemente

Five miles south of San Juan Capistrano down I-5, **San Clemente** is a pretty little town, its streets contoured around the hills, lending it an almost Mediterranean air. It's also home to some of Orange County's better surfing beaches, especially toward the south end of town, and has a reasonable campground, too (see p.81). It's here, around the city's southern tip, that San Clemente had a brief glimmer of fame when President Richard Nixon convened his **Western White House** here from 1969 to 1974. The 25-acre estate is located off of Avenida del Presidente and is visible from the beach – you can't get any closer than this.

Eating

Whatever you want to eat and however much you want to spend, LA's **restaurants** leave you spoiled for choice. **Cheap food** is, of course, plentiful here, ranging from historic diners to street-corner coffee shops to trusty burger shacks. Almost as common and just as cheap, **Mexican food** is the closest thing you'll get to an indigenous LA cuisine. Many of the city's **higher-end restaurants** serve superb food in consciously cultivated surroundings, driving up their prices on the back of a good review, and typically specializing in French, Italian, Japanese or **California cuisine** – the latter the signature style of top-notch LA eating, blending French-styled cuisine with fresh local ingredients in an eclectic, harmonious brew.

For **cafés**, see p.145; for specialist **food shops**, bakeries and grocery stores, see p.158.

Delis, diners and stands

Affordable food is everywhere in LA, at its best in the many small and stylish **delis** and **diners** that serve soups, omelettes, sandwiches and burgers; it's easy to eat this way constantly and never have to spend much more than $10 for a full meal. There are, of course, the franchise fast-food joints on every street, though the local **hamburger** and **taco stands** (many open 24hr) are always much better – some of them, such as *Pann's* near Inglewood, catering to fans of old-fashioned Formica diners, with their neon signs, boomerang roofs and classic steak-and-eggs breakfasts.

Downtown and around
See the map on p.82.

Clifton's Cafeteria 648 S Broadway. Classic 1930s cafeteria with bizarre decor: redwood trees, waterfall and mini-chapel. The food is traditional meat-and-potatoes American, and cheap, too.

Cole's Pacific Electric Buffet 118 E 6th St. In the same seedy spot for 102 years, this is LA's oldest restaurant – and recently restored. The decor and food haven't changed much, and the rich, hearty French-dip sandwiches are still loaded with steak, pastrami or brisket – a dish invented at this very spot.

Grand Central Market 317 S Broadway. Plenty of tacos, deli sandwiches and Chinese food, plus a few more exotic items, like pigs' ears and lamb sweetbreads. A fun, cheap place to eat.

Langer's Deli 704 S Alvarado St. Offers more than twenty ways of eating what is easily LA's best pastrami sandwich. Open daylight hours only in a dicey spot; kerbside pick-up available.

Original Pantry Café 877 S Figueroa St. Hearty portions of meaty American cooking – chops and steaks, mostly – in this diner owned by former mayor Dick Riordan. Breakfast is the best option (available 24hr).

Philippe the Original French Dip 1001 N Alameda St. 1908 sawdust café that serves up the eponymous sandwich with turkey, ham, lamb, pork or beef – an amazingly good and filling treat for less than $6.

Hollywood
See the maps on p.94 & p.104.

25 Degrees 7000 Hollywood Blvd, inside *Hollywood Roosevelt Hotel*. The top gourmet burger joint in town, where you can pack your home-made burger with fried eggs, avocado, prosciutto, pesto, even artisan cheeses, along with more traditional toppings. 24hr daily.

DuPar's 6333 W 3rd St. A long-standing LA institution, located in the Farmers' Market, which draws a whole host of old-timers for its gut-busting comfort food, from chicken pot pie to cheeseburgers to fruit pies.

Fred 62 1854 N Vermont Ave, Los Feliz. Designed like something out of the 1950s, this diner offers stylish, affordable California-cuisine twists on familiar staples like salads, burgers and fries, and a tempting array of pancakes and omelettes.

Mel's Drive-In 8585 Sunset Blvd. Calorie-packed milkshakes, fries and, of course, burgers make this 24hr diner an essential stop if you've got the late-night munchies.

Pink's Hot Dogs 709 N La Brea Ave. Depending on your taste, these monster hot dogs – topped with anything from bacon and chilli cheese to pastrami and Swiss cheese – are lifesavers or gut bombs. Open till 2am, or 3am at weekends.

Roscoe's House of Chicken and Waffles 1514 N Gower St. This diner attracts all sorts for its fried chicken, greens and thick waffles.

Tommy's 2575 Beverly Blvd. One of the prime LA spots for big, greasy, tasty burgers and scrumptious fries – and, many would say, the best. Located right off the 101 freeway in a somewhat grim section of East Hollywood. 24hr daily.

West LA and Beverly Hills
See the map on p.104.

The Apple Pan 10801 W Pico Blvd. Grab a spot at the counter and enjoy freshly baked apple pie and nicely greasy hamburgers. An old-time joint that opened just after World War II.

Barney's Beanery 8447 Santa Monica Blvd. Hundreds of bottled beers and hot dogs, hamburgers and bowls of chilli served in a hip, grungy environment. Angelenos can be divided up by those who love or hate the place – everyone knows it.

Canter's Deli 419 N Fairfax Ave. Huge sandwiches and excellent kosher soups served by waitresses in pink uniforms and running shoes. Open 24hr. Live music nightly in *Canter's* adjoining "Kibbitz Room" till 1.40am.

Duke's 8909 Sunset Blvd. A favourite of visiting rock musicians, this coffee shop with staples like steak and eggs and omelettes also attracts a motley crew of night owls and bleary-eyed locals who've managed to hang on till daybreak.

Hole in the Wall Burger Joint 11058 Santa Monica Blvd. Trendy handcrafted burgers that you can create from a bevy of nouveau ingredients – cranberry mayo, pretzel buns, zucchini pickles, fried eggs, etc. Prices start at $10. Cash only.

John o' Groats 10516 W Pico Blvd. Excellent breakfasts and lunches (mostly staples like bacon and eggs, oatmeal, and waffles), but come outside of the morning rush hour. A full breakfast will set you back $15–20.

Nate 'n' Al's 414 N Beverly Drive. The best-known deli in Beverly Hills, popular with movie people and one of the few reasonably priced places in the vicinity. Get there early to grab a booth.

Santa Monica, Venice and Malibu
See the map on p.114.

Benito's Taco Shop 11614 Santa Monica Blvd. Tacos rolled up in a flour tortilla and served with beef, pork or fish, for just a few bucks. Most combos are around $5, making this a good spot to gulp and run. 24hr daily.

Café 50s 838 Lincoln Blvd, Venice. Grubby little diner that's nonetheless kept going for years because of its tasty eats – pancakes, French toast, milkshakes – and rock'n'roll jukebox.

The Counter 2901 Ocean Park Blvd, Santa Monica. Choose from the likes of smoked bacon, guacamole, horseradish mayo, garlic aioli, goat's cheese and dozens of other toppings to create your own delightful, if pricey, burger.

Father's Office 1018 Montana Ave, Santa Monica. If you're interested in celebrity-spotting as in chowing down, this chic burger joint is a good spot for its upmarket offerings with top-notch prices.

Norm's 1601 Lincoln Blvd, Santa Monica. One of the last remaining classic diners, this local chain has 15 other LA branches and serves breakfasts and lunches for around $7. Great Googie architecture and open 24hr.

24-hour eats

25 Degrees Hollywood. See p.135.
Bob's Big Boy Burbank. See p.136.
Canter's Deli West LA. See p.135.
Fred 62 Los Feliz. See p.135.
Mel's Drive-In Hollywood. See p.135.

Norm's Santa Monica. See p.135.
Original Pantry Café Downtown. See p.135.
Pacific Dining Car Downtown. See p.138.
Tommy's Hollwood. See p.135.

Rae's Diner 2901 Pico Blvd, Santa Monica. Solid 1950s diner with heavy comfort food. Its turquoise-blue facade and interior have been seen in many films, notably *True Romance*.

LAX and the South Bay and Harbor Area

Johnny Reb's 4663 N Long Beach Blvd, Long Beach. The waft of BBQ ribs, catfish and hush puppies alone may draw you to this prime Southern spot, where the portions are large and the prices cheap.

Pann's 6710 La Tijera Blvd, Inglewood. One of the all-time great Googie diners, where you can't go wrong with the classic burgers or biscuits and gravy.

Pier Bakery 100 Fisherman's Wharf #M, Redondo Beach. A small but satisfying menu with jalapeño-cheese bread, churros and cinnamon rolls. Probably the best food in this touristy area.

Randy's Donuts 805 W Manchester Ave, Inglewood. This Pop Art fixture is hard to miss, thanks to the colossal donut sitting on the roof. Excellent for its piping-hot treats, which you can pick up at the drive-through on your way to or from LAX.

The San Gabriel and San Fernando valleys

Art's Deli 12224 Ventura Blvd, Studio City. Longtime deli favorite, with a good range of hefty, scrumptious sandwiches and soups like the good ol' chicken-noodle.

Bob's Big Boy 4211 W Riverside Drive, Burbank. The classic chain diner, fronted by the plump burger lad, and a veritable Pop-architecture classic, saved from demolition through the efforts of preservationists. Open 24hr.

Dr Hogly-Wogly's Tyler Texas Bar-B-Q 8136 Sepulveda Blvd, Van Nuys. You could be in for a long wait for some of the best chicken, sausages,

ribs and beans in LA, despite the long drive to the middle of nowhere.

Fair Oaks Pharmacy and Soda Fountain 1526 Mission St, South Pasadena ☎626/799-1414. Restored soda fountain with many old-time drinks like lime rickeys, root beer floats, milkshakes and egg creams – a historic 1915 highlight along the former Route 66.

Porto's Bakery 315 N Brand Blvd, Glendale. Top-notch café serving Cuban flaky pastries and sandwiches, rum-soaked cheesecakes, muffins, Danishes, croissants, tarts and cappuccino.

Wolfe Burgers 46 N Lake Ave, Pasadena. Knockout gyros, chilli, tamales and burgers – a long-standing Valley favourite.

Orange County

Angelo's 511 S State College Blvd, Anaheim. Straight out of *Happy Days*, a drive-in complete with roller-skating car-hops, neon signs, vintage cars and, incidentally, good burgers.

Heroes 125 W Santa Fe Ave, Fullerton. The place to come if you're starving after hitting the theme parks. Knock back one of the 100 beers available or chow down on hamburgers, chilli, ribs or meatloaf.

Mimi's Café 1400 S Harbor Blvd, Anaheim. Huge servings, low prices and solid breakfasts and lunches. Part of a sizeable chain in Los Angeles and Orange counties, and popular in both.

Ruby's 1 Balboa Pier, Newport Beach. The first and finest of the retro-streamline 1940s diners in this chain – in a great location at the end of Newport's popular pier. Mostly offers the standard fare of burgers, fries and soda.

Zinc Café 344 Ocean Ave, Laguna Beach. A popular breakfast spot offering simple soup-and-salad meals and other vegetarian fare, with some tasty desserts.

Mexican and Latin American

LA's **Mexican** restaurants offer some of the city's best dishes, serving tasty and filling meals for as little as $5. **Caribbean** food is less visible but, when sought out, can be quite rewarding, especially in its Cuban incarnation. The cuisine of the rest of **Latin America** includes a mix of flavours and spices from Central American countries like Honduras and Nicaragua, and a tasty blend of local seafood and native Peruvian cuisine (aka "Peruvian seafood").

Downtown
See the map on p.82.

El Taurino 2306 W 11th St. Tacos, burritos and especially tostadas are the draw at this popular and authentic eatery – where the green and red salsas burn all the way down.

King Taco 2904 N Broadway. The most centrally located diner in a chain of ultra-cheap shops around Downtown (this one north of Chinatown), with many varieties of savoury tacos, tamales, quesadillas and burritos.

La Luz del Dia 107 Paseo de la Plaza. Authentic Mexican eatery on Olvera St that's worth seeking out for its fiery burritos, enchiladas and stews, served in sizeable enough portions to make you sweat with a smile.

La Torta Loca 855 Santee St. With tasty $2 tacos, scrumptious Cuban burritos, various quesadillas, and dozens of cheap and filling tortas, this Cuban joint deserves a lengthy stop if you're anywhere near the Fashion District.

Hollywood
See the maps on p.94 & p.104.

Cactus Mexican 950 Vine St. A good spot to keep the evening going while you're club-hopping with delicious quesadillas and burritos.

El Compadre 7408 W Sunset Blvd. With potent margaritas, live mariachi bands and cheap Mexican standards, this is a gourmand's delight.

El Floridita 1253 N Vine St. Despite the uninspiring strip-mall facade, this is a lively Cuban restaurant where the dancefloor swings on the weekends. The menu features solid standards like plantains, croquetas and yucca, all affordably priced.

Mario's Peruvian Seafood Restaurant 5786 Melrose Ave. Delicious and authentic Peruvian fare: supremely tender squid and rich and flavourful mussels, among many other good choices.

Yuca's 2056 N Hillhurst Ave. A hidden jewel serving considerable burritos, Yucatan pork, and beef tacos alfresco, and which despite its small size has garnered a national following.

West LA
See the map on p.104.

Bamboo 10835 Venice Blvd, Culver City. In a section of West LA full of enticing ethnic restaurants, this one stands out for its chicken curry dishes, paella with swordfish and spicy Caribbean-style pizza, as well as its reasonable prices.

Bossa Nova 685 N Robertson Blvd. Fascinating Brazilian eatery with a menu that includes South American staples (shrimp croquettes, fried yucca, etc) and more unexpected items such as chicken skewers, filet mignon and pasta.

Carlitos Gardel 7963 Melrose Ave. Seriously rich and tasty Argentine cuisine – heavy on the beef and spices, with sausages and garlic adding to the kick.

Monte Alban 11927 Santa Monica Blvd. Forget the tacky mini-mall setting and focus on the fine, affordable selection of *mole* sauces and Mexican staples that make any trip here worthwhile.

Versailles 10319 Venice Blvd. Busy and noisily authentic Cuban restaurant with excellent fried plantains, paella and black beans and rice. Also nearby at 1415 S La Cienega Blvd (☎310/289-0392).

Santa Monica, Venice and Malibu
See the map on p.114.

Babalu 1002 Montana Ave, Santa Monica. The pancakes at this pan-ethnic, Caribbean-influenced restaurant are delightful, as are the sweet-potato tamales, fried plantains, mango shrimp and crab enchiladas.

Border Grill 1445 4th St, Santa Monica. Good place to sup on shrimp, pork, plantains and other Latin American-flavoured dishes, with excellent desserts, too.

Marix Tex-Mex Playa 118 Entrada Drive, Pacific Palisades. Flavourful fajitas and big margaritas in this rowdy beachfront cantina.

Tacos por Favor 1406 Olympic Blvd. Uninspired-looking from the outside, but this humble eatery has some of the city's best chow, including great tacos and tortas, and hefty burritos that are easy on your wallet – but not your waistline.

The South Bay and Harbor Area

By Brazil 1615 Cabrillo Ave, Torrance. Hearty and affordable Brazilian fare, mostly grilled chicken and beef dishes; worth a visit to inland Torrance for a taste.

El Pollo Inka 1100 PCH, Hermosa Beach. Good Peruvian-style chicken, catfish, and hot and spicy soups to make your mouth water.

The San Gabriel and San Fernando valleys

Don Cuco 3911 W Riverside Drive, Burbank. Top-notch quesadillas, spicy soups, burritos and potent margaritas are the prime draws at this small Burbank eatery.

Izalco 10729 Burbank Blvd, North Hollywood. Salvadoran cuisine presented with grace and style, from plantains and pork ribs to corn cakes and pupusas.

La Estrella 502 N Fair Oaks Ave, Pasadena. Delicious old favourite for Mexican cuisine, where you can get great tacos, burritos, ceviche and tostadas at inexpensive prices.

American and California cuisine

American cuisine – with its steaks, ribs, baked potatoes and salads – has a low profile in faddish LA, although it's available almost everywhere and may even cost less than $15 for a blowout. More prominent – and more expensive, at upwards of $20 per entrée – is **California cuisine**, based on fresh local ingredients, more likely grilled than fried, and stylishly presented with a nod to nouvelle **French** cuisine.

Downtown

See the map on p.82.

Angelique Café 840 S Spring St. A marvellous Continental eatery in the middle of the Fashion District, where you can sit on the quaint patio and dine on well-crafted pastries for breakfast or tasty sandwiches, rich casseroles and fine salads for lunch.

Café Metropol 923 E 3rd St. The area may still be industrial, but this arty eatery is worth a visit for its hearty panini, salads, pizza and pasta.

Café Pinot 700 W 5th St ☎ 213/239-6500. Located next to the LA Public Library, this elegant restaurant offers a touch of French style in its nouvelle California cuisine, and is good for risotto, tuna Niçoise, lamb loin and steak.

Engine Co. No. 28 644 S Figueroa St ☎ 213/624-6996. This long-time favourite features expensive grilled steaks and seafood, plus lamb shank and chicken pot pie, served with great fries in a renovated 1912 fire station.

Pacific Dining Car 1310 W 6th St ☎ 213/483-6000. Would-be English supper club, here since 1921, located inside an old railroad carriage where the Downtown elite used to cut secret deals. Open 24hr for very expensive and delicious steaks. Breakfast is the best value.

Patina 141 S Grand Ave ☎ 213/972-3331. Fancy, ultra-swanky Disney Hall branch of one of LA's top restaurants, where you can devour Maine lobster, Jidori chicken and foie-gras ravioli, among other supreme dishes on the menu, if you're prepared to drop a wad of cash.

Water Grill 544 S Grand Ave ☎ 213/891-0900. One of the top-priced, top-notch spots for munching on California cuisine with the focus on seafood, prepared in all manner of colourful ways – such as mint bass ceviche, or big-eye tuna with pomegranate couscous.

Hollywood

See the maps on p.94 & p.104.

The Abbey 692 N Robertson Blvd ☎ 310/289-8410. A popular spot for excellent, all-American food and drink, with a positive, upbeat vibe and sizeable lounge with convivial atmosphere.

Griddle Café 7916 Sunset Blvd. The postmodern Hollywood version of a diner, where the pancakes, chilli and omelettes come with various outlandish toppings (Oreos, breakfast cereal, etc), and the cheesecake French toast will make you cheer.

Grub 911 Seward St. A fine spot for affordable comfort food, especially for breakfast: cinnamon-vanilla French toast, chorizo burritos and inventive omelettes. Flavourful soups, chilli and salads are on the lunch menu.

Off Vine 6263 Leland Way. Dine on eclectic Cal cuisine – Cornish game hen with cornbread, turkey breast with jalapeño relish – in a renovated but still funky Craftsman bungalow.

Providence 5955 Melrose Ave ☎ 323/460-4170. Near the top of the LA pricey-restaurant scale, and for good reason: the place is swarming with foodies, who come for the black sea bass, foie-gras ravioli, lump blue crab and plenty of other tremendous choices.

vermont 1714 N Vermont Ave ☎ 323/661-6163. One of the better Cal-cuisine eateries in the area. The entrées are predictable enough – roasted chicken, crab cakes, ravioli, etc – but the presentation is effective and, on occasion, inspired.

West LA and Beverly Hills

See the map on p.104.

Café La Boheme 8400 Santa Monica Blvd, West Hollywood ☎ 323/848-2360. The dark-red, brothel-like decor is matched by the mix of Cal-cuisine flavours enlivening the pasta, risotto and steak dishes.

Cut 9500 Wilshire Blvd, Beverly Hills ☏ 310/276-8500. Since this steakhouse, with chef Wolfgang Puck at the helm, was designed by Richard Meier, it looks like the Getty Center cafeteria. Nonetheless, if you like (and can afford) steaks that cost up to $100, Kobe short ribs, and Maine lobster, this is the place.

The Gumbo Pot 6333 W 3rd St in the Farmers' Market. Delicious, dirt-cheap Cajun food in a busy setting; try the gumbo yaya (chicken, shrimp and sausage) or the fruit-and-potato salad.

Jar 8225 Beverly Blvd ☏ 323/655-6566. An upper-end steakhouse featuring all the usual red-meat fare – prime rib, T-bone, even a pot roast – with an inspired Cal-cuisine flair.

Lucques 8474 Melrose Ave ☏ 323/655-6277. Expensive but tasty restaurant that doles out comfort food for the culinary elite – spiced lamb ribs, wild mushroom lasagne and grilled cornbread are but a few of the dishes you might find on the rotating menu.

Luna Park 672 S La Brea Ave. Reliable Cal-cuisine spot that serves up soup and sandwiches for lunch, and anything from short ribs to flat-iron steak to jalapeño grits for dinner.

Spago 176 N Cañon Drive, Beverly Hills ☏ 310/385-0880. Flagship restaurant that helped nationalize Cal cuisine (in a different location), and still good for supping on Wolfgang Puck's latest concoctions, among them designer pizzas.

Tart 115 S Fairfax Ave, in the *Farmer's Daughter* hotel. Some imaginative offerings – fried chicken with honey, sweet-potato hash, crispy alligator, etc – make this mid-priced California-cuisine spot a worthwhile stop for adventurous eaters.

Santa Monica, Venice and Malibu

See the map on p.114.

Hal's 1349 Abbot Kinney Blvd, Venice ☏ 310/396-3105. Popular restaurant in a hip shopping area in Venice, with a range of well-done American standards, including marinated steaks, turkey burgers and salmon dishes.

Melisse 1104 Wilshire Blvd, Santa Monica ☏ 310/395-0881. Top of the line in some people's minds for LA dining, this California-French restaurant offers a fixed-price $105 menu that may include duck breast with cherries, Sonoma sausage or seafood.

Sauce on Hampton 259 Hampton Drive. It's all about organic eats at this Venice diner that crosses a lot of culinary boundaries – ahi tuna wraps, prosciutto sandwiches and meatloaf are among the creative, inexpensive offerings.

Uncle Darrow's 2560 S Lincoln Blvd, Venice. A bit south of the main beach action, but worth a stop if you like down-home Cajun and Creole dishes like tasty catfish and gumbos.

Italian, Spanish and Greek

LA has a good number of restaurants specializing in regional **Italian** cooking, and the phenomenon of **designer pizza** features toppings such as duck, shiitake mushrooms and other exotic ingredients. It doesn't come cheap, of course. A pasta dish in the above-average Italian restaurant can cost upwards of $15–20, and the least-elaborate designer pizza will set you back $10. **Spanish** food and tapas bars have also become popular, and pricey. In contrast, if you want **Greek** food, you'll have to look hard – restaurants are good but uncommon.

Downtown and around

See the map on p.82.

Cicada 617 S Olive St ☏ 213/488-9488. Lodged in the stunning Art Deco Oviatt Building, this Northern Italian restaurant offers fine pasta, fish and steak entrées.

Ciudad 445 S Figueroa St. Ceviche and paella are some of the highlights of this colourful Mexican-influenced Spanish spot, where the live Latin music competes with the delicious food for your attention.

Drago Centro 525 S Flower St ☏ 213/228-8998. Hard to go wrong with this delicious upscale Italian fare, from panini and small plates under $10 to a fabulous four-course meal for $48. *Molto bene.*

Papa Cristos 2771 W Pico Blvd. Consider venturing to a grim neighbourhood near the 10 freeway to sample the authentic delights at this Greek joint, where you can munch on delicious gyros and *spanakopita* or enjoy a hearty meal of lamb chops or roast chicken without spending more than $10.

Hollywood

See the maps on p.94 & p.104.

Angeli Caffè 7274 Melrose Ave. Refreshingly simple pizzas – baked in a wood-burning oven – make this a worthwhile stop, as do its tasty frittatas and croquettes.

Miceli's 1646 N Las Palmas Ave. Generous, old-style pizzas that come laden with gooey cheese and plenty of tomato sauce. It's hardly nouvelle cuisine, but you'll be too busy scarfing it down to notice.

Palermo 1858 N Vermont Ave. As old as Hollywood, and with as many devoted fans, who flock here for the rich Southern Italian pizzas, cheesy decor and cheapish red wine.

Tomato Pie Pizza Joint 7751 Melrose Ave. A great place to grab a slice, with the usual staples, plus pies with pesto, eggplant parmigiana, hot wings, and breakfast-style eggs and cheese on top. Also serves decent pastas, subs and salads.

West LA

See the map on p.104.

Ca' Brea 346 S La Brea Ave ☎323/938-2863. One of LA's best-known, and best, choices for Italian cuisine, and especially good for *ossobuco* and risotto. Getting in is difficult, so reserve ahead and expect to pay a bundle (upwards of $70 per person without drinks).

Campanile 624 S La Brea Ave ☎323/938-1447. Incredible but very expensive Northern Italian food – if you can't afford a dinner, try the dessert or the best bread in Los Angeles at the adjacent La Brea Bakery.

Cobras and Matadors 7615 Beverly Blvd ☎323/932-6178. Expensive tapas restaurant just down the street from Pan Pacific Park, where you can sample all your favourite Castilian delights in a hushed, dramatic setting.

Locanda Veneta 8638 W 3rd St ☎310/274-1893. Scrumptious ravioli, risotto, veal and carpaccio – you can't go wrong at one of LA's culinary hotspots.

Tasca 8108 W 3rd St ☎323/951-9890. A great choice for upper-end tapas, with faves like *arancini*, braised short ribs and baby octopus, along with a nice selection of salads and wines.

Santa Monica, Venice and Malibu

See the map on p.114.

Abbot's Pizza Company 1407 Abbot Kinney Blvd, Venice. Named after the old-time founder of the district, this home of the bagel-crust pizza allows your choice of Alfredo (creamy white sauce), tomato, or two kinds of pesto sauce.

Drago 2628 Wilshire Blvd, Santa Monica ☎310/828-1585. One of the better of LA's super-chic Italian eateries, offering meat and pasta dishes with eclectic ingredients and sauces.

Joe's Pizza 111 Broadway, Santa Monica. New Yorkers can quit complaining about LA pizza at this mini-chain based, naturally, in New York. Features the requisite crispy, thin pizza prepared with aplomb.

Valentino 3115 Pico Blvd, Santa Monica ☎310/829-4313. Some call this the best Italian cuisine in the US, served up in classy surroundings with great flair. Fixed-price menus for $55 and $70 per person.

The South Bay and Harbor Area

Alegria Cocina Latina 115 Pine Ave, Long Beach ☎562/436-3388. Tapas, gazpacho and a variety of *platos principales* served with sangría on the patio, and to the beat of live flamenco at weekends. Good location near the harbour in Downtown Long Beach.

L'Opera 101 Pine Ave ☎562/491-0066. Very swanky Italian dining – mixed with a fair bit of California-cuisine style – in a historic old building near the centre of Long Beach's Downtown activity.

La Sosta Enoteca 2700 Manhattan Ave, Hermosa Beach ☎310/318-1556. Among the best options for Italian fare in the South Bay, with an array of excellent pasta, risotto and seafood choices, as well as supreme wine and desserts.

The San Gabriel and San Fernando valleys

Avanti Café 111 N Lake Ave, Pasadena ☎626/577-4688. A lip-smacking place to get your (affordable) gourmet pizza fix, with toppings ranging from seafood, glazed apple, prosciutto and duck sausage to good old pepperoni, sausage and anchovies.

Café Santorini 64–70 W Union St, Pasadena ☎626/564-4200. A fine mix of Greek and Italian food – capellini, *souvlaki* and risotto, among other treats. Located in a relaxed plaza and offering some patio dining.

Panzanella 14928 Ventura Blvd, Sherman Oaks ☎818/784-4400. Some of the best Italian cuisine in LA, taking culinary styles from central Italy and adding a dash of California creativity, while staying true to the simple, delicious character of traditional pasta, rice and beef dishes.

Japanese, Chinese and other Asian cuisine

LA has many fine **sushi** bars and **dim sum** restaurants, where you can easily eat your way through more than $30. Lower-priced outlets tend to be Downtown, where you can get a fair-sized meal for half that price. There are also a good number of excellent **Thai, Vietnamese** and **Korean** places – for which you can expect to pay around $15 per meal, or around $40 or more for top-notch Korean spots.

Downtown and around

See the map on p.82.

Dong Il Jang 3455 W 8th St, Koreatown. Cosy little Korean restaurant where the meat is cooked at your table and the food is consistently good, especially the grilled chicken, kimchi fried rice and roasted *gui* prime rib. Tempura dishes and a sushi bar are an added draw.

Ocean Seafood 750 N Hill St. Busy Cantonese restaurant serving inexpensive and excellent food – dim sum, crab, shrimp and duck are among many standout choices.

Pho 2000 215 N Western Ave. One of several Koreatown restaurants specializing in hot, spicy bowls of the Vietnamese soup *pho*: cheap, authentic and succulent, drawing a loyal crowd of regulars.

Phoenix Inn 301 Ord St, Chinatown. Newly renovated and ready to tempt your taste buds, with an array of noodle soups, hot pots, fried noodles and tofu items. The seafood, duck and sliced prime rib are also worth a try.

Yang Chow 819 N Broadway, Chinatown. Solid Chinese restaurant, where you can't go wrong with the Szechuan beef or any shrimp dish.

Hollywood

See the map on p.94.

Chan Darae 1511 N Cahuenga Blvd. Terrific Thai food, and the locals know it, with a full range of scrumptious staples such as *tom yum* soup and pad thai.

Jitlada 5233 Sunset Blvd. In a dreary mini-mall, but the spicy chicken, squid, oxtail curry, papaya salad, and fishball and other seafood curries more than make up for the setting. Affordable prices, too.

Sanamluang Café 5176 Hollywood Blvd. You can't beat the cheap, excellent and plentiful noodles, or the squid salad and spicy shrimp soup, at this nearly-all-night Thai eatery.

Singapore's Banana Leaf 6333 W 3rd St, in the Farmers' Market. A fine little hole-in-the-wall where you can sample Malaysian cuisine at its spiciest and most tasty, with nice curry soups, satay and tandoori dishes.

Vim 5132 Hollywood Blvd. Authentic Thai and Chinese food at low prices. Especially good are the seafood soup and that old favorite, pad thai.

West LA

See the map on p.104.

Chaya Brasserie 8741 Alden Drive, Beverly Hills ☎310/859-8833. Pan-Asian bistro with moderate-to-expensive prices and a chic clientele

that munches on delicious soy-glazed black cod, sushi rolls and big-eye tuna tartare, along with steak and pasta. Merits a splurge.

Genghis Cohen 740 N Fairfax Ave. Familiar Chinese dishes with a Yiddish touch: the menu abounds with culinary puns. The Szechuan beef, dumplings and kung pao chicken are among the tastiest offerings.

Matsuhisa 129 N La Cienega Blvd ☎310/659-9639. The biggest name in town for sushi, charging the highest prices. Essential if you're a raw-fish aficionado with a wad of cash; combo lunches from $20–25, or fixed-price meals offered from $75–120.

Mishima 8474 W 3rd St. Great miso soup, soft-shell crab salad and udon and soba noodles, at very affordable prices at this popular Westside restaurant.

Mori Sushi 11500 W Pico Blvd. A quietly stylish spot that resists trendiness, but still offers up some of the city's finest sushi, generally delicious and always fresh.

Talesai 9198 Olympic Blvd, Beverly Hills. Excellent curried seafood, satays and Cal-cuisine-leaning noodle dishes served to knowing gourmets in a drab strip-mall.

Santa Monica, Venice and Malibu

See the map on p.114.

Chaya Venice 110 Navy St, Venice ☎310/396-1179. Elegant mix of Japanese and Mediterranean foods in an arty sushi bar, with plenty of Cal-cuisine elements, excellent service and a suitably snazzy clientele.

Chinois on Main 2709 Main St, Santa Monica ☎310/392-9025. Expensive Wolfgang Puck restaurant, skilfully mixing nouvelle French and Chinese cuisine with dash for a ravenous yuppie crowd.

Dragon Palace 2832 Santa Monica Blvd. Hot shredded beef, pan-fried noodles, spicy shrimp and scallops and General Tso's Chicken are among the treats at this engaging Chinese diner.

Musha 424 Wilshire Blvd, Santa Monica. Among the top choices on the LA sushi scene, this spot prepares fish with striking invention and culinary precision; try the sashimi, the lobster roll or the *ponzu duck*.

The San Gabriel and San Fernando valleys

Ocean Star 145 N Atlantic Blvd, Monterey Park. One of the prime names in a city bursting with

LA's festivals

January

1 Tournament of Roses in Pasadena ☎626/795-9311, ⓦwww.tournamentofroses .com. A parade of floral floats and marching bands along a five-mile stretch of Colorado Boulevard. Coincides with the annual Rose Bowl football game.

February

early to mid Chinese New Year ☎213/617-0396, ⓦwww.lachinesechamber.org. Three days of dragon-float street parades, tasty food and cultural programmes, based in Chinatown, Monterey Park and Alhambra.

mid Mardi Gras. Floats, parades, costumes, and lots of singing and dancing at this Latin fun-fest, with traditional ceremonies on Olvera Street Downtown (☎213/625-7074) and campy antics in West Hollywood (☎310/289-2525).

March

early The Academy Awards ☎310/247-3000, ⓦwww.oscars.org. Presented at the Kodak Theatre in the Hollywood & Highland mall (see p.150). Bleacher seats are available to watch the stars arrive.

17th St Patrick's Day ☎213/689-8822, ⓦwww.discoverlosangeles.com. Parade along Colorado Boulevard in Old Town Pasadena, and another in Hermosa Beach. No parade but freely flowing green beer in the "Irish" bars along Fairfax Avenue.

April

mid Long Beach Grand Prix ☎562/981-2600, ⓦwww.gplb.com. Some of auto-racing's best drivers and souped-up vehicles zoom around Shoreline Drive south of Downtown in the city's biggest annual event.

late California Poppy Festival ☎661/723-6075, ⓦwww.poppyfestival.com. North of LA, Lancaster's huge poppy reserve of 1800 acres draws big crowds to see its eye-blinding, fiery orange colours that appear every spring.

late Fiesta Broadway ☎310/914-0015, ⓦwww.fiestabroadway.la. Lively music from Hispanic pop singers and tasty Mexican food are the highlights of this street fair along Broadway Downtown.

May

early Doo-dah Parade ☎626/590-1134, ⓦwww.pasadenadoodahparade.info. Absurdly costumed characters marching through East Pasadena are the main attraction at this immensely popular event, which began as a spoof of the Tournament of Roses parade.

5 Cinco de Mayo ☎213/628-1274, ⓦwww.olvera-street.com/html/fiestas.html. Spirited parade along Olvera Street; several blocks Downtown are blocked off for Latino music performances. There are also celebrations in most LA parks.

June

mid LA Pride ☎323/969-8302, ⓦwww.lapride.org. Parade on Santa Monica Blvd in West Hollywood. Carnival atmosphere, hundreds of vendors, and an all-male drag football cheerleading team.

mid Playboy Jazz Festival ☎213/450-1173, ⓦwww.playboyjazzfestival.com. Renowned event held at the Hollywood Bowl, with a line-up of traditional and non-traditional musicians and groups.

July

4 Independence Day ☎562/435-3511 in Long Beach, or ☎323/848-6530 for West Hollywood's Plummer Park. The *Queen Mary* in Long Beach hosts a particularly large fireworks display, as well as colourful entertainment. Fireworks displays in many places in LA.

first weekend after 4 Lotus Festival ⊤213/413-1622. An Echo Park celebration featuring pan-Pacific food, music and, of course, the resplendent lotus blooms around the lake.

late Central Avenue Jazz Festival ⊤213/473-2309, ⓦwww.centralavejazz.org. Celebration of both jazz and blues by big names and lesser-known performers, held on Central Avenue between 42nd and 43rd streets in South Central.

August

early International Surf Festival ⊤310/802-5413, ⓦwww.surffestival.org. Tournament and celebration in the South Bay that provides an exciting three-day spectacle, which also includes volleyball matches, lifeguard races, sand soccer and sandcastle design.

mid Long Beach Jazz Festival ⊤562/424-0013, ⓦwww.longbeachjazzfestival.com. At the Rainbow Lagoon park in Downtown Long Beach, relax and enjoy famous and local performers.

late Sunset Junction Street Fair ⊤323/661-7771, ⓦwww.sunsetjunction.org. A spirited neighbourhood party – always one of LA's most enjoyable fetes – along Sunset Boulevard in Silver Lake, with live music, ethnic food and a carnivalesque atmosphere.

September

early LA's birthday ⊤213/625-5045, ⓦwww.olvera-street.com. A civic ceremony and assorted street entertainment around El Pueblo de Los Angeles to mark the founding of the original pueblo in 1781.

early Long Beach Blues Festival ⊤562/985-7000, ⓦwww.kkjz.org/events. Hear the region's and the country's top blues performers at this annual event at Cal State University at Long Beach.

late Watts Towers Day of the Drum/Jazz Festival ⊤213/487-4646. Two days of free music – a wealth of African, Asian, Cuban and Brazilian drumming – with the towers as the striking backdrop. Taking place the same weekend, at the same place, the Jazz Festival is the most long-standing such event in LA.

October

mid to late Los Angeles Bach Festival. Revel in the Baroque master's music at the First Congregational Church, just north of Lafayette Park in Westlake (⊤213/385-1345, ⓦwww.fccla.org).

31 Halloween. A wild parade in West Hollywood, with all manner of bizarre outfits and characters on display (⊤310/289-2525). Or you can opt for the Halloween-themed events on the *Queen Mary* (⊤562/435-3511).

November

2 Dia de los Muertos ⊤213/625-5045, ⓦwww.olvera-street.com. The "Day of the Dead", celebrated authentically throughout East LA and more blandly for tourists on Olvera Street. Mexican traditions, such as picnicking on the family burial spot and making skeleton puppets, are faithfully upheld.

end Hollywood Christmas Parade ⊤323/469-2337, ⓦwww.thehollywoodchristmas parade.com. The first and best of the many Yuletide events, with a cavalcade of mind-boggling floats, marching bands and famous and quasi-famous names from film and TV.

December

early to late Griffith Park Light Festival ⊤323/913-4688 ext 9. Tremendous spectacle along Crystal Springs Road in the park, with tunnels of light, thematic displays and representations of familiar LA sights like the Hollywood sign. A hugely popular draw.

early Holiday Boat Parade ⊤310/670-7130, ⓦwww.mdrboatparade.org. Marina del Rey is the site for this ocean-going display of brightly lit watercraft, supposedly the largest boat parade in the West.

excellent Chinese diners, in this case specializing in dim sum, with the fried shrimp, dumplings and salty chicken among the highlights. It's very popular, too.

Saladang 363 S Fair Oaks Ave, Pasadena. Don't miss out on the pad thai, curry and salmon at this chic spot, or the spicy noodles that would pass muster anywhere. The restaurant's annexe,

Saladang Song offers even spicier Thai concoctions.

Shiro 1505 Mission St, South Pasadena. One of the few top-notch restaurants in South Pasadena. The pricey seafood – particularly the catfish and salmon carpaccio – is the highlight of the extensive menu.

Indian, Sri Lankan and Middle Eastern

Indian and **Sri Lankan** food is popular in LA, with menus embracing a mix of traditional and uniquely Californian dishes. **Middle Eastern** places encompass a good range of Levantine cookery, but tend toward the traditional. Most of the Indian and Middle Eastern restaurants are in Hollywood or West LA and fall into a fairly mid-range price bracket – around $15 for a full meal, less for a vegetarian Indian dish.

Hollywood

See the maps on p.94 & p.104.

Crown of India 6755 Santa Monica Blvd. Despite the drab neighbourhood around it, the tikka masala, vindaloo, korma and naans at this authentic spot are consistently first-rate and moderately priced.

Moun of Tunis 7445 Sunset Blvd. Mouthwatering Tunisian fare presented in huge, multi-course meals, heavy on the spices and rich on the exotic flavours – plus regular belly-dancing.

Zankou Chicken 5065 Sunset Blvd. The best-value place in town for a Middle Eastern meal (and part of a citywide chain), with delicious garlicky chicken cooked on a rotisserie and made into a sandwich, plus all the traditional salads – tabouli, hummus and more.

West LA

See the map on p.104.

Koutoubia 2116 Westwood Blvd. Good Moroccan lamb, couscous, lentil soup and seafood, in a comfortable environment enlivened by belly-dancing.

Nyala 1076 S Fairfax Ave. One of several Ethiopian favourites along Fairfax, serving staples like *doro wat* (marinated chicken) and *kitfo* (chopped beef with butter and cheese) with the delightfully spongy *injera* bread.

Samosa House 11510 W Washington Blvd, Culver City. Indian vegetarian fare that appeals for its range of flavourful choices, as well as for its inexpensive dishes – especially the $8 fixed-price meal. Connected to its own ethnic market.

Shamshiri 1712 Westwood Blvd, West LA. Top Iranian restaurant in the area, offering delicious kebabs, pilafs and exotic sauces at moderate prices.

The San Gabriel and San Fernando valleys

Azeen's 110 E Union St, Pasadena. Esteemed, stylish haunt for rich and flavourful Afghani cuisine such as kebabs, meat pastries and dumplings, an appealing mix of Persian and Indian culinary styles.

Carousel 304 N Brand Ave, Glendale. A Lebanese charmer in Downtown Glendale, chock-full of Levantine cultural artefacts and deliciously authentic food, from roasted chicken and quail to several different kinds of kebab.

Vegetarian and wholefood

As you might expect, LA has many **wholefood** and **vegetarian** restaurants, most of them on the consciousness-raised Westside. Some veggie places can be good value, but watch out for the ones that flaunt themselves as a New Age experience – these can be three times as much. Otherwise, for a picnic try the area's **farmers' markets**, advertised in the press.

West LA

See the map on p.104.

A Votre Sante 13016 San Vicente Blvd, Brentwood. Scrambled tofu and fried vegetables are on the menu – along with veggie and turkey burgers – at this mid-priced Westside chain.

Inaka Natural Foods 131 S La Brea Ave. Located in the trendy La Brea district and featuring vegetarian and macrobiotic food, including some tasty soups, with a Japanese theme.
Real Food Daily 414 N La Cienega Blvd. Tempeh burgers, hemp bread and various soups and salads draw a good crowd at this vegan restaurant, which also operates a branch at 514 Santa Monica Blvd, Santa Monica.
Vegan Glory 8393 Beverly Blvd. Although the name overstates its case a little, this is still appealing, affordable vegan fare with a pan-Asian influence, everything from pad thai and pan-fried soy "chicken" to papaya salad and spicy curries.

Santa Monica, Venice and Malibu

See the map on p.114.
Figtree's Café 429 Ocean Front Walk, Venice. Tasty veggie food and grilled fresh fish on a sunny patio just off the Boardwalk. Health-conscious yuppies come in droves for breakfast.
Inn of the Seventh Ray 128 Old Topanga Rd, Topanga Canyon. The ultimate New Age restaurant in a supremely New Age area, serving vegetarian and other wholefood meals in a relatively secluded environment. Excellent desserts, too.

Cafés

Cafés in LA don't quite carry the same cultural cachet as they do in San Francisco, but they are good spots for socializing, whiling away the hours and surfing the web. And the people you see conspicuously writing on their laptops are less likely to be budding novelists than would-be screenwriters plotting bloody action flicks over soy-milk lattes. Well-trafficked areas like Melrose Avenue, West Hollywood and Santa Monica are loaded with spots to grab a caffeinated jolt, as well as tea, food and even alcohol in some cases.

Abbot's Habit 1401 Abbot Kinney Blvd, Venice. See map, p.114. Prototypical coffee house for Venice – rich, tasty coffee and home-made snacks and desserts, assorted artwork on the walls, occasional music and spoken-word events, and a friendly neighbourhood vibe.
Bourgeois Pig 5931 Franklin Ave, Hollywood. See map, p.94. Self-consciously hip environment and overpriced cappuccinos – you really pay for the artsy atmosphere, but the agreeable java and colourful people-watching make it worthwhile.
Cacao Coffee 11609 Santa Monica Blvd, West LA. Fun and friendly joint with all kinds of kitsch and retro-Tiki bric-a-brac, and good snacks and coffee served to an amenable crowd of regulars.
Café Luxxe 925 Montana Ave, Santa Monica. See map, p.114. Some of the best espressos, macchiatos and cappuccinos in town draw loyal customers to this smallish place, which stands out on a busy strip thick with chain coffee-grinders.
Coffee Table 2930 Rowena Ave, Silver Lake. Casual, unpretentious space with affordable coffees and relaxed surroundings. Good for breakfast, too.

King's Road Espresso House 8361 Beverly Blvd, West Hollywood. See map, p.104. Pavement café in the centre of a busy shopping strip, with good breakfasts and lunches. Popular with the hipster crowd as well as a few tourist interlopers.
Novel Café 2507 Main St, Santa Monica. See map, p.114. Used books and high-backed wooden chairs set the tone; good coffees, teas and pastries hit the spot, along with free wi-fi, making for a good place to linger.
Stir Crazy 6903 Melrose Ave. Cozy haunt that provides a glimpse of what this stretch of Melrose used to be like before the chain retailers moved in – with mellow attitudes, decent java and free wi-fi.
Tiago Espresso Bar 7080 Hollywood Blvd, Hollywood. See map, p.94. Located near the corner of La Brea Avenue, this spot offers a good range of coffee, tea and mate, and four hours of wireless access with food or drink purchase.
Urth Caffè 8565 Melrose Ave. See map, p.104. Customers at this high-priced tea-and-java vendor tend towards navel-gazing and celebrity-watching, but the coffees are certainly tasty enough, and the atmosphere is pleasant and fairly well-scrubbed. Also at 267 S Beverly Drive, Beverly Hills, and 2327 Main St, Santa Monica.

Nightlife

Nightlife in LA can be among the best in the country, with many options for serious drinking, partying and debauchery. Weekend nights are the busiest at **bars and clubs**, but during the week things are often cheaper. Where they exist, cover charges range widely, depending on the night and the establishment (often $5–20). Except at all-ages, alcohol-free clubs, the minimum age is 21, and it's normal for ID to be checked, so bring photo ID. LA also has an overwhelming choice of **live music** venues, offering everything from punk to salsa; see p.149.

Bars

As you'd expect, LA's **bars** reflect their locality: a clash of artists, grizzled old-timers and financial whiz kids Downtown; serious hedonists and leather-clad rockers in Hollywood; movie-star wannabes and self-proclaimed producers in West LA; a mix of tourists, locals and British expats in Santa Monica; and a more oddball selection in Venice. A few hard-bitten bars are open the legal maximum hours (from 6am until 2am daily), though the busiest hours are between 9pm and midnight. During **happy hour**, usually from 5 to 7pm or 4 to 6pm, drinks are cheap and sometimes half-price.

Downtown and around

See the map on p.82.

Casey's Bar 613 S Grand Ave. Old-time Irish pub with white floors and dark wood-panelled walls, and friendly, rousing ambience, making it something of a local institution.

Edison 108 W 2nd St. One of LA's best uber-chic bars, with stunning antique industrial decor, retro lounge music, upmarket food, a nice (though pricey) range of cocktails and a smart dress code.

HMS Bounty 3357 Wilshire Blvd. An authentic dive experience, this grungy bar, advertising "Food and Grog", is a hotspot for hipsters and grizzled old-timers – they come for the dark ambience, cheap and potent drinks, and kitschy nautical motifs.

Mountain Bar 475 Gin Ling Way. Since it's hidden in a nook in Chinatown, this bar is hard to find off Bamboo Lane, but if you want a colourful, Asian-themed environment to knock back your cheap, no-name alcohol, this is the spot. There's also a happening club scene downstairs and live music above.

Redwood 316 W 2nd St. Solid choice for serious drinking and cheap all-American grub since 1943, now remade into a "pirate bar" featuring skull-and-crossbones decor and patrons kitted out like Blackbeard.

Standard Hotel Bar 550 S Flower St. The poseur pinnacle in Downtown LA, this is an alcohol-fuelled playpen where the silk-shirted-black-leather-trousers crowd goes to hang in red metallic "pods" with waterbeds and sprawl out on a rooftop Astroturf lawn, with modern corporate towers looming overhead.

Hollywood

See the maps on p.94 & p.104.

Boardner's 1652 N Cherokee Ave. Former historic dive bar now remodelled into sleek, yuppie-friendly confines for tasteful drinking (and a decent happy hour) with an impressively dark and luminous design. Also offers regular electronica, indie rock and burlesque shows.

Burgundy Room 1621 Cahuenga Blvd. A classic place to get down and dirty with the old Hollywood dive-bar vibe, with a cramped interior, gloomy lighting, stiff drinks, a growling crowd of regulars, decent DJs and a rocking jukebox.

Cat 'n' Fiddle Pub 6530 Sunset Blvd. A boisterous but comfortable pub with darts, British food, English beers on tap and live jazz on Sun nights. See also p.151.

Dresden Room 1760 N Vermont Ave. One of the neighbourhood's classic bars, perhaps best known for its evening show (Tues–Sun 9pm), in which the husband-and-wife lounge act of Marty and Elayne take requests from the crowd of old-timers and hipsters.

Formosa Café 7156 Santa Monica Blvd. Started in 1925 as a watering hole for Charlie Chaplin's adjacent United Artists studios, this creaky old spot is still alive with the ghosts of Bogie and Marilyn. Drink the potent spirits, but stay away from the insipid food.

Frolic Room 6245 Hollywood Blvd. This classic LA bar decorated with Hirschfeld cartoons of celebrities offers affordable drinks and a dark, authentic old-time ambience. Right by the Pantages Theater.

Good Luck Bar 1514 Hillhurst Ave. A hip Los Feliz retro-dive, this hangout is popular for its cheesy

Chinese decor and drinks straight from the heyday of *Trader Vic's*. Located near the intersection of Sunset and Hollywood blvds.

Little Temple 4519 Santa Monica Blvd. This Silver Lake bar is themed around moody Asian decor, and with the mood lighting, tasty cocktails like the coconut martini, and an expressive, schmoozy clientele, it draws the smarter bar-hoppers around town.

Musso and Frank Grill 6667 Hollywood Blvd. If you haven't had a drink in this landmark bar (located in the centre of the district), you haven't been to Hollywood. It also serves pricey diner food.

Power House 1714 N Highland Ave. Enjoyable, long-standing rockers' watering hole just off Hollywood Blvd; few people get here much before midnight.

Smog Cutter 864 N Virgil Ave. Dive bar that attracts a mix of boozers and smirking Gen-Xers. Don't miss the karaoke scene, which, like the drinks, can be pleasantly mind-numbing.

Stout 1544 N Cahuenga Blvd. A truly stout brick cube of a place that's known for its inventive burgers and microbrewed beer – both quite good, and its thirty brews on tap and 4am closing time provide its true watering-hole bona fides.

Tiki Ti 4427 W Sunset Blvd. Cocktail bar packed with kitschy pseudo-Polynesian decor and no more than a handful of patrons – it's pretty cozy inside.

West LA

See the map on p.104.

The Arsenal 12012 W Pico Blvd. Lively place that offers fine pub food (notably the salt-and-pepper calamari), a dancefloor with pop and hip-hop sounds, and tasty cocktails, mostly under $10.

Barney's Beanery 8447 Santa Monica Blvd. Well-worn poolroom/bar, stocking hundreds of beers, with a solid, rock'n'roll-hedonist history. It also serves all-American, rib-stuffing food; see p.135.

El Carmen 8138 W 3rd St. Faux dive-bar with a south-of-the-border theme pushed to the extreme, with black-velvet pictures of Mexican wrestlers, steer horns, stuffed snakes and much tongue-in-cheek grunge, as well as signature margaritas and a good range of tequilas.

Lola's 945 N Fairfax Ave. It has beer and wine, but martinis are the theme at this swanky joint, with more than 50 interesting, inventive choices on offer, from the Big Banana to the Caramel Apple to the Garlic Mashed Potato.

Molly Malone's Irish Pub 575 S Fairfax Ave. Self-consciously authentic Irish bar, from the food (corned-beef sandwiches, burgers and other belly-fillers) to the music – mostly grinding rock and Celtic folk – to the shamrocks in the foaming Guinness.

Red Rock 8782 Sunset Blvd. Energetic watering-hole with a wide array of beers on tap and a similarly broad assortment of customers, everyone from bleary-eyed club kids to slumming preppies.

Snake Pit 7529 Melrose Ave. One of the better bars along the Melrose shopping strip, small and not too showy, with a mix of jaded locals and tourists who come to slurp down tropical concoctions.

Tom Bergin's 840 S Fairfax Ave. Old-time drinking joint from 1936, a great place for Irish coffee (supposedly invented here), Irish beer and of course, Irish whiskey.

Santa Monica, Venice and Malibu

See the map on p.114.

Beechwood 822 Washington Blvd, Venice. Smart modern design with a few Asian touches, plus tasty Cal cuisine and a mid-priced beer and cocktail menu, attracting a young, chic crowd.

Encounter 209 World Way, at LAX. A strange bar that lurks in the upper reaches of the boomerang concrete "Theme Building" in the LAX parking lot. Believe it or not, it's worth a visit to sample the potent, if pricey, Day-Glo drinks (though not the food) and watch the jets land.

Finn McCool's 2700 Main St, Santa Monica. Despite the dubious name, this is a worthwhile Irish pub with a tasty selection of Emerald Isle brews and neo-Celtic artwork, plus hefty platters of traditional food that require a pint of Guinness to consume properly.

Hinano Café 15 Washington Blvd, Venice. Low-attitude chill bar by the beach – an untouristy place for a drink, with pool tables, good and cheap burgers, shambling decor and a mostly local crowd.

Library Alehouse 2911 Main St, Santa Monica. Presenting the choicest brews from West Coast microbreweries and beyond, this is a good spot to select from a range of well-known and obscure labels while munching on a decent selection of food.

Rick's Tavern 2907 Main St, Santa Monica. Dark and rowdy neighbourhood joint off the Main Street shopping strip, with sports on TV and boisterous regulars on the bar stools.

Ye Olde King's Head 116 Santa Monica Blvd, Santa Monica. British-heavy joint with jukebox, dartboards and signed photos of all your favourite rock dinosaurs; don't miss the steak-and-kidney pie, afternoon tea, or fish and chips.

The San Gabriel and San Fernando valleys

Clearman's North Woods 7247 N Rosemead Blvd, San Gabriel. A kitsch-lover's delight with fake snow on the outside and moose heads on the inside; a great place for devouring steaks and throwing peanut shells on the floor.

The Colorado 2640 E Colorado Blvd, Pasadena. A bright spot along a bleak Pasadena stretch. Salty bartenders, cheap drinks and a couple of pool tables amid a hunting-themed decor.

Cozy's Bar and Grill 14048 Ventura Blvd, Sherman Oaks. Listen to an excellent range of blues musicians or come by any time to throw darts, shoot pool or knock back a few. A friendly, laidback spot with a devoted clientele.

Ireland's 32 13721 Burbank Blvd, Van Nuys. One of San Fernando Valley's better spots for quaffing Irish drafts, powering down traditional stews and chops, and soaking in a fair amount of Emerald Island decor, shamrocks and all.

Magnolia 492 S Lake Ave, Pasadena. Stylish lounge that's chic and modern, with pricey cocktails, but offers enough of a retro-speakeasy atmosphere – dramatic lights, striking decor, well-groomed patrons – to create a buzz.

Clubs

The **clubs** of LA range from posey hangouts to industrial noise cellars. The more image-conscious joints are like singles bars, with everybody claiming to be a rock musician or a movie producer. Some of the hottest clubs are usually the most transient, especially those catering to the house, ambient, techno or hip-hop scenes, disappearing within a few months of being branded by the media as an "essential stop" for club-hoppers; always check the *LA Weekly* before setting out.

Most of the top clubs are either in Hollywood or West Hollywood. Beverly Hills is a lifeless yuppie desert; Downtown is home to a handful of itinerant clubs operating above and below board; Santa Monica has a smattering of compelling spots; and the San Fernando Valley's more rough-and-ready scene is usually confined to the weekends. For gay and lesbian clubs, see p.156.

Downtown and around

See the map on p.82.

Jewel's Catch One 4067 W Pico Blvd. Sweaty barn catering to a mixed crowd of gays and straights and covering two wild dancefloors. A longtime favourite for club-hoppers of all sorts. Especially busy Fri–Mon, though located in the middle of nowhere.

Mayan 1038 S Hill St. Formerly a groovy pre-Columbian-style movie palace, now hosting Latin rhythms and nonstop disco, salsa and house tunes on three floors.

Hollywood and West Hollywood

See the maps on p.94 & p.104.

The Abbey 692 N Robertson Blvd. West Hollywood party central: a crazy, busy club scene in the heart of gay WeHo that nonetheless caters to a mixed crowd for its great people-watching, go-go dancers and buzzing atmosphere.

Arena 6655 Santa Monica Blvd. Work up a sweat to funk, hip-hop, Latin and house sounds on a massive dancefloor inside a former ice factory. Gay-friendly scene, playing host to ever-changing club nights.

Avalon 1735 N Vine St. Major dance club spinning old-school faves, along with the usual techno and house, with the occasional big-name DJ dropping in. Prices are among the most expensive in town.

Bar Sinister 1652 N Cherokee. Sprightly dance beats most nights of the week, then memorably spooky Goth music and anemic-looking vampire types on Sat. Connected to *Boardner's* bar (see p.94).

Dragonfly 6510 Santa Monica Blvd. Unusual decor, two large dance rooms and a mix of house and disco club nights and live music.

King King 6555 Hollywood Blvd. A solid Hollywood bet for live dance music, with house, funk, rap and retro-pop.

The Ruby 7070 Hollywood Blvd. A wide range of feverish dance nights Thurs–Sun, everything from retro-kitsch to grinding industrial to perky house and garage.

Three Clubs 1123 N Vine St. Dark, perennially trendy bar and club where the usual crowd of hipsters drops in for retro, rock and funk music, and gets pleasingly plastered. Colourless exterior and lack of good signage makes the joint even hipper.

Ultra Suede 661 N Robertson Blvd, West Hollywood. See map, p.104. Heavy on modern techno-pop, played to a mixed gay and straight crowd. The neighbouring *Factory* draws much of the same crowd.

West LA
Carbon 9300 Venice Blvd ☎310/558-9302. Though hardly located near anywhere you'd want to be, this is a good spot for eclectic nightly DJs, whose turntables glow with Latin, retro, jungle, drum'n'bass, hip-hop, soul and rock beats, depending on the night.

Santa Monica
See the map on p.114.
Circle Bar 2926 Main St. Old-fashioned dive that mainly draws a crowd of high-fiving party dudes who get plastered on the pricey but potent drinks and struggle to keep the beat on the dancefloor.
The Gaslite 2030 Wilshire Blvd. Though it features a small dancefloor, the real appeal of this hip, kitschily decorated club is its karaoke. Santa

Monicans rush to this place on weekends – so get there early if you want to take to the mic.
Zanzibar 1301 5th St. DJs spin sounds with a house, hip-hop and soul bent, but also with a bit of reggae, funk and bossa nova thrown in on selected nights.

The San Gabriel and San Fernando valleys
Bigfoot Lodge 3172 Los Feliz Blvd. On the far side of East Hollywood in dreary Atwater, but a prime draw for its nightly DJs, who set feet stomping with retro-pop and rock tunes, with glam, goth and rockabilly thrown in as well.
Coda 5248 Van Nuys Blvd, Sherman Oaks. Fairly hip for the Valley, and not as posey as you might think, drawing locals for its blend of rap, pop and retro.
Verdugo 3408 Verdugo Rd, South Glendale. Cramped and crowded venue not far from Forest Lawn that offers a great taste of the local scene, with regular DJ nights, good brews and a lively crowd.

Live music venues

Since the nihilistic punk bands of thirty years ago distanced the city from its spaced-out cocaine-cowboy image, LA's **rock** and **pop** scene has been second to none. The old **punk** scene has been revitalized with up-and-coming bands, and heavy metal can be found here and there. **Hip-hop** is also prevalent, whether mixed in dance music by Westside DJs or in its more authentic form in the inner city (best avoided by out-of-towners). Surprisingly, **country music** is fairly common, and the valleys are hotbeds of bluegrass and swing. There's also **jazz**, best in the few genuinely authentic downbeat dives, while Latin **salsa** music can be found in a few Westside clubs.

There are always plenty of big names on tour, from major artists to independents, and an enormous number of venues. Most open at 8 or 9pm; headline bands are usually onstage between 11pm and 1am. Cover (or ticket) prices range widely from $5 to $75. You'll need to be 21 and will likely be asked for ID. As ever, *LA Weekly* is the best source of **listings**.

Major venues
Cerritos Center for the Performing Arts 12700 Center Court Drive ☎1-800/300-4345, ⓦwww .cerritoscenter.com. North of Long Beach, a top draw for mainstream country, gospel, classical, pop and jazz acts – usually nothing too quirky or adventurous.
Gibson Amphitheatre 100 Universal City Plaza ☎818/622-4440, ⓦwww.hob.com/venues /concerts/universal. A big but acoustically excellent auditorium with regular rock shows. Located on the Universal Studios lot.
Greek Theatre 2700 N Vermont Ave, Griffith Park ☎323/665-1927, ⓦwww.greektheatrela.com.

Outdoor, summer-only venue (May–Oct) hosting mainstream rock and pop acts and seating for five thousand. Parking can be a mess, so come early.
Grove of Anaheim 2200 E Katella Ave ☎714/712-2700, ⓦwww.thegroveofanaheim.com. Orange County concert space aimed at showcasing old-time performers and mid-level entertainers in soul, country, pop, rock and jazz.
Hollywood Palladium 6215 Sunset Blvd, Hollywood ☎323/962-7600. Once a big-band dance hall, with an authentic 1940s interior, now a home to all manner of hard rock, punk and rap outfits.

Honda Center 2695 E Katella Blvd, Anaheim ⊤714/704-2400, ⊛www.hondacenter.com. A 19,000-seat sports arena that draws the usual big-ticket events in music and entertainment, with a smaller "Theater" configuration for less mainstream rock groups.

Kodak Theatre 6801 Hollywood Blvd, Hollywood ⊤323/308-6300, ⊛www.kodaktheatre.com. Part of the colossal Hollywood & Highland mall, a media-ready theatre partly designed to host the Oscars, as well as major and minor pop acts and special events.

Nokia Theatre 777 Chick Hearn Court ⊤714/763-6030, ⊛www.nokiatheatrelalive.com. Grand auditorium that's part of the colossal LA Live complex (see p.88). To pay off the overhead, the theatre only books the safest pop, children's, country and rock acts.

Staples Center 865 S Figueroa St, Downtown ⊤213/742-7340, ⊛www.staplescenter.com. Big, glassy sports arena (home to the LA Lakers and Clippers) that's also a good showcase for Top 40 rock and pop acts.

Wiltern Theater 3790 Wilshire Blvd, Mid-Wilshire ⊤323/388-1400, ⊛www.wiltern.com. A striking, blue Zigzag Art Deco movie palace, renovated and converted into a top performing space for standard pop acts as well as edgy alternative groups.

Rock and pop

The Cat Club 8911 Sunset Blvd, West Hollywood ⊤310/657-0888. See map, p.104. Hard, meaty jams every night of the week, with the focus on rock, punk and rockabilly, often courtesy of lip-snarling cover bands.

The Echo 1822 Sunset Blvd ⊤213/413-8200. Like the name says, an Echo Park club with scrappy indie-rock bands playing in a dark, intense little hole for a crowd of serious hipsters. A good place to catch what's bubbling up on the underground music scene.

El Rey Theater 5515 Wilshire Blvd, Mid-Wilshire ⊤323/936-4790. See map, p.104. Although not as famous as its Sunset Strip counterparts, this rock and alternative venue is possibly the best spot to see explosive new bands and still-engaging oldsters.

Hotel Café 1623 N Cahuenga Blvd, Hollywood ⊤323/461-2040. See map, p.94. Comfortable spot for acoustic acts and singer-songsmiths, as well as indie bands. Usually has the best line-up in town for this sort of thing.

The Joint 8771 Pico Blvd, West LA ⊤310/275-2619. A dark, small neighbourhood venue with assorted punk screamers and occasionally decent rock and alternative groups.

Key Club 9039 Sunset Blvd ⊤310/274-5800. See map, p.104. A hotspot in the liveliest section of the strip, attracting a young, hip group for its regular concerts in the rock, punk and metal vein, with occasional lighter fare as well. Also has DJ and club nights.

Largo at the Coronet Theatre, 366 N La Cienega Blvd, West LA ⊤323/855-0350. See map, p.104. Offers some compelling live acts, often of the acoustic singer-songwriter variety, with the odd rock or comedy show as well.

The Lighthouse 30 Pier Ave, Hermosa Beach ⊤310/376-9833. Adjacent to the beach, this old-time favourite offers rock, jazz and reggae as well as karaoke and occasional comedy.

The Music Box 6126 Hollywood Blvd ⊤323/464-0808. See map, p.94. A charming, renovated old theatre that began life in 1926 and still hosts theatrical productions, but more typically alternative rock and dance acts.

Room 5 143 N La Brea Blvd, West LA ⊤323/938-2504. See map, p.104. This intimate venue is a good spot to catch a live set by a singer-songwriter, small acoustic band, or other low-decibel performer.

The Roxy 9009 Sunset Blvd, West LA ⊤310/276-2222. See map, p.104. Among the top showcases for the music industry's new signings, intimate and with a great sound system, on the western – but still frenetic – end of the strip. Punk and hip-hop dominate.

The Smell 247 S Main St, Downtown ⊤213/625-4325. See map, p.82. A funky, grungy space, with strange decor, frenetic rock and punk music, and a grim location.

Spaceland 1717 Silver Lake Blvd, Silver Lake ⊤323/661-4380. Doesn't have the national rep of places like the Roxy and Whisky, but you're unlikely to find a better spot in LA to catch up-and-coming rockers and other acts, including punk and alternative musicians.

The Troubadour 9081 Santa Monica Blvd, West Hollywood ⊤310/276-6168. See map, p.104. An old 1960s mainstay that's been through a lot of incarnations in its fifty years. Used to be known for folk and country rock, then metal, now for various flavours of indie rock.

The Viper Room 8852 Sunset Blvd, West Hollywood ⊤310/358-1881. See map, p.104. Great live acts, a famous owner – Johnny Depp – and a headline-hitting past. Expect almost any musician to show up onstage.

Whisky-a-go-Go 8901 Sunset Blvd, West Hollywood ⊤310/652-4202. See map, p.104. Legendary spot in the 1960s, and still important for LA's rising music stars. Mainly hard rock and metal, though you might catch an alternative act now and then.

Country and folk

Boulevard Music 4136 Sepulveda Blvd, Culver City ☎310/398-2583. This unglamorous music store manages to host some fairly interesting folk acts on weekends, from roots country to delta blues, with plenty of international groups too.

Cowboy Palace Saloon 21635 Devonshire St, Chatsworth ☎818/341-0166. Worth a trip to this distant corner of the San Fernando Valley for down-home helpings of tub-thumping country-and-western concerts and Sunday BBQs.

Kulak's Woodshed 5230 Laurel Canyon Blvd, North Hollywood ☎818/766-9913, ⊛kulakswoodshed.com. Nightly shows in a cramped but colourful space, ranging from country, folk and spoken-word to performance art and poetry. You need to be a member to enter ($5 fee); join via the website.

McCabe's 3101 W Pico Blvd, Santa Monica ☎310/828-4497. LA's premier acoustic-guitar shop; long the scene of some excellent and unusual folk and country shows, with the occasional alternative act thrown in as well.

Rusty's Surf Ranch 256 Santa Monica Pier ☎310/393-7437. See map, p.114. Offers not only surf music – and displays of old-time long boards – but also rock, pop, folk and even karaoke. Always a popular spot for tourists, near the end of the pier.

Viva Fresh Cantina 900 Riverside Drive, Burbank ☎818/845-2425. A Mexican restaurant on the far side of Griffith Park, where you can hear some of LA's most engaging country, bluegrass and honky-tonk artists performing nightly.

Jazz and blues

Babe & Ricky's Inn 4339 Leimert Blvd, South Central ☎323/295-9112. Long a top spot for blues on Central Ave, this premier music hall continues to attract quality, nationally known acts at its Leimert Park location.

The Baked Potato 3787 Cahuenga Blvd W, North Hollywood ☎818/980-1615. A small but near-legendary contemporary jazz spot, where many reputations have been forged.

Café Boogaloo 1238 Hermosa Ave, Hermosa Beach ☎310/318-2324. One of the better spots in the South Bay for blues, along with occasional New Orleans jazz and swing, and DJ dance sets.

Catalina Bar & Grill 6725 Hollywood Blvd, Hollywood ☎323/466-2210. See map, p.94. A jazz institution with plenty of style and atmosphere, filling meals and potent drinks. It can get pricey, though.

Cat 'n' Fiddle Pub 6530 Sunset Blvd, Hollywood ☎323/468-3800. An English-style pub with jazz on Sun from 7 until 11pm; no cover. See also p.94.

Fais Do-Do 5247 W Adams Blvd, South Central ☎323/954-8080. West Adams club in a dicey section of town that appeals for its broad sweep – live bands playing New Orleans-flavoured jazz and ragtime, DJs spinning old-school funk and soul, and oddball chamber music and other unusual entertainment.

Grand Star Jazz Club 943 Sun Mun Way, Downtown ☎213/626-2285. Solid Chinatown haunt for live jazz and blues, plus some hip-hop and funk thrown in as well. Also features DJs spinning breakbeats and other dance tunes.

Harvelle's 1432 4th St, Santa Monica ☎310/395-1676. See map, p.114. A stellar blues joint near the Third Street Promenade, for more than 70 years offering different performers nightly and a little funk, R&B and burlesque thrown in too.

House of Blues 8430 Sunset Blvd, West Hollywood ☎323/848-5100. See map, p.104. Over-commercialized mock sugar-shack, with good but pricey live acts. Very popular with tourists – it's the flagship of a national chain. Cover can reach $40 or more.

Jax 339 N Brand Blvd, Glendale ☎818/500-1604. A combination restaurant and performance space where you can take in a good assortment of jazz sounds, from traditional to contemporary.

The Mint 6010 W Pico Blvd, south of Mid-Wilshire ☎323/954-9400. A small, intense spot that's off the beaten path but worth the ramble to hear the latest in the city's avant-jazz sounds, as well as singer-songwriters.

Vibrato Grill and Jazz 2930 Beverly Glen Circle, West LA ☎310/474-9400. You're not going to find anything too challenging at this Bel Air club, but for traditional and smooth jazz sounds, it might fit the bill.

Salsa

El Cid 4212 W Sunset Blvd ☎323/668-0318. Silver Lake is the place to enjoy some good tapas and Mexican food as well as move to the sounds of salsa, flamenco and other Latin rhythms.

El Floridita 1253 N Vine St, Hollywood ☎323/871-8612. Decent Mexican and Cuban food complements a fine line-up of Cuban and salsa artists, who play on weekends and jam on other nights.

Luminarias 3500 Ramona Blvd, Monterey Park, East LA ☎323/268-4177. Hilltop restaurant with regular live salsa reckoned to be as good as its Mexican food.

Mama Juana's 3707 Cahuenga Blvd West, Studio City ☎818/505-8636. Spanish/Mexican restaurant that also serves up nightly helpings of live salsa, merengue and other Latin-flavoured tunes.

Zabumba 10717 Venice Blvd, Culver City ☎310/841-6525. In a colourful building amid drab surroundings, this venue is more bossa nova Brazilian than straight salsa, but it's still great, and very lively.

Performing arts and film

LA's range of **performing arts** is increasingly broad and impressive, with national-calibre groups and performers appealing to audiences well beyond Southern California. LA boasts a world-class conductor and orchestra for **classical music**, along with less-familiar entities like chamber-music groups, and the fields of **opera** and **dance** are represented by several fine companies. **Theatre** is always a growth industry, with more than a thousand shows annually, plenty of actors to draw from, and a burgeoning audience for both mainstream and fringe productions. **Comedy** is a big draw, too, and is one of the prime entertainment options that first-time visitors seek out. Not surprisingly, though, it's **film** that is still the chief cultural staple of the region.

Classical music, opera and dance

The Los Angeles Philharmonic and LA Opera are the major names for **classical music** and **opera** in the city, and perform regularly, while smaller groups appear more sporadically. Check the press, especially the *LA Times*, for details, and expect to pay from $15 to $120 for most concerts, more for really big names. **Dance** performances tend to be grouped around major events, so check cultural listings or call the venues listed below for seasonal information.

Major venues

Disney Hall 1st St at Grand Ave, Downtown ☎323/850-2000, Ⓦwww.laphil.com. LA's most renowned cultural attraction (along with the Getty Centre), which hosts the LA Philharmonic in a striking Frank Gehry design.

The Dorothy Chandler Pavilion In the Music Centre, 135 N Grand Ave, Downtown ☎213/972-7211 or 972-7460, Ⓦwww.musiccenter.org. Long-standing warhorse of the arts community, used by LA Opera and other top names.

The Hollywood Bowl 2301 N Highland Ave, Hollywood ☎323/850-2000, Ⓦwww.hollywoodbowl.org. A famed bandshell (see p.103) that hosts the LA Philharmonic and summer open-air concerts, usually of the pops variety.

Japan America Theatre 244 S San Pedro St, Little Tokyo ☎213/680-3700, Ⓦwww.jaccc.org. Intriguing theatrical, dance and performance works drawn from Japan and the Far East, mixing traditional and contemporary styles.

John Anson Ford Theater 2850 Cahuenga Blvd, Hollywood ☎323/461-3673, Ⓦwww.fordamphitheater.org. An open-air venue that has eclectic productions by local classical and operatic groups as well as sporadic pop and rock concerts.

Pasadena Dance Theatre 1985 Locust St, Pasadena ☎626/683-3459, Ⓦwww.pasadenadance.org. One of the San Gabriel Valley's most prominent dance venues, hosting diverse groups throughout the year.

Segerstrom Concert Hall 615 Town Center Drive, Costa Mesa ☎714/556-2787, Ⓦwww.ocpac.org. A polished-glass-and-steel marvel that's part of the Orange County Performing Arts Center complex, which also presents dance, theatre and other high-culture offerings in sleekly modern style.

The Shrine Auditorium 665 W Jefferson, South Central LA ☎213/749-5123; box office at 655 S Hill St. Huge, 1926 Moorish curiosity that hosts touring pop acts, choral gospel groups and countless award shows.

Thornton School of Music On the USC campus, South Central ☎213/740-6935, Ⓦwww.usc.edu/schools/music. A fine array of venues, from 90–1200 seats, for sonatas, concertos and other works (usually Sept–May).

UCLA Center for the Performing Arts ☎310/825-4401, Ⓦwww.uclalive.org. Coordinates a wide range of companies in music, theatre and dance (Sept–June), and runs a fine dance series, often with an experimental bent.

Zipper Concert Hall 200 S Grand Ave, Downtown ☎213/621-2200. Part of the esteemed performing-arts Colburn School across from Disney Hall, this warm and modern facility hosts a broad range of troupes, from dance to classical, and chamber music.

Groups and institutions

Da Camera Society Rotating venues ☎213/477-2929, Ⓦwww.dacamera.org. This organization's "Chamber Music in Historic Sites" provides a great opportunity to hear chamber works in stunning settings, from grand churches to private homes, including Doheny Mansion near USC. Ticket prices vary.

LA Opera Music Center, 135 N Grand Ave, Downtown ☏ 213/972-8001, ⓦ www.losangeles opera.com. Stages productions between September and June, from epic *opera seria* to lighter operettas. The mainstream heavyweight in town.

Long Beach Opera Rotating venues ☏ 562/432-5934, ⓦ www.longbeachopera.org. Despite being eight years older than the LA Opera, this alternative company presents the freshest and edgiest work in town, from lesser-known pieces by old masters to craggy newer works by local composers and librettists.

Los Angeles Ballet Rotating venues; office at 11755 Exposition Blvd, West LA ☏ 310/998-7782, ⓦ www.losangelesballet.org. Features a Nov–May programme with standards like the *Nutcracker* and a good number of new and modern works.

Los Angeles Chamber Orchestra Rotating venues ☏ 213/622-7001 ext 215, ⓦ www.laco .org. Presents a range of chamber works, not all canonical, from different eras. Prices vary widely.

Los Angeles Master Chorale At Disney Hall and rotating venues, 135 N Grand Ave, Downtown ☏ 213/972-2782, ⓦ www.lamc.org. Classic canonical works, along with newer commissions and experimental pieces, are showcased by this choral institution.

Los Angeles Philharmonic At Disney Hall, 1st St and Grand Ave, Downtown ☏ 323/850-2000, ⓦ www.laphil.org. The big name in the city performs throughout the year, and conductor Gustavo Dudamel always provides a rousing programme, from powerful Romantic works to modern pieces, with an accent on Latin American works.

Pacific Symphony Orchestra Orange County Performing Arts Center, 615 Town Center Drive, Costa Mesa ☏ 714/755-5788, ⓦ www.pacific symphony.org. Suburban orchestra that draws big crowds for its stylish performances of canonical works, performed in Segerstrom Concert Hall.

Pasadena Symphony At Ambassador Auditorium, 131 St John Ave ☏ 626/793-7172, ⓦ www .pasadenasymphony-pops.org. Veering between the standard repertoire and more contemporary pieces, this esteemed symphony also offers a pops symphony that plays on the Rose Bowl lawn, west of Downtown.

Southwest Chamber Music Rotating venues ☏ 1-800/726-7147, ⓦ www.swmusic.org. A nationally recognized troupe that offers a wide range of music, from medieval to modern (Oct–May). Venues include the Norton Simon Museum and the Huntington Library.

Comedy

LA has a wide range of **comedy** clubs. While rising stars and beginners can be spotted on the "underground" open-mic scene, most of the famous comics, both stand-up and improv, appear at the more established clubs in Hollywood, West LA or the valleys. These venues usually have a bar (and a two-drink minimum) and put on two shows per evening, generally starting at 8pm and 10.30pm – the later one being more popular.

Acme Comedy Theatre 135 N La Brea Ave, Hollywood ☏ 323/525-0202, ⓦ www.acmecomedy .com. A fancy venue with sketch and improv comedy, as well as variety shows and theme-comedy performances.

bang 457 N Fairfax Ave, Hollywood ☏ 323/653-6886, ⓦ www.bangstudio.com. One-person shows and long-form improvisation are the specialities at this small theatre/comedy club, with the popular shows running on weekends.

Comedy & Magic Club 1018 Hermosa Ave, Hermosa Beach ☏ 310/372-1193, ⓦ www.comedy andmagicclub.info. Notable South Bay comedy space where Jay Leno sometimes tests material. Tickets can run up to $30, depending on the performer.

The Comedy Store 8433 W Sunset Blvd, West LA ☏ 323/656-6228, ⓦ www.thecomedy store.com. LA's premier comedy showcase and

popular enough to be spread over three rooms – which means there's usually space, even at weekends.

Groundlings Theatre 7307 Melrose Ave, West LA ☏ 323/934-4747, ⓦ www .groundlings.com. Pioneering venue where only the gifted survive, with furious improv events and high-wire comedy acts that can inspire greatness or groans.

Ha Ha Café 5010 Lankershim Blvd, North Hollywood ☏ 818/508-4995, ⓦ www.hahacafe .com. Amateur and a few professional comedians face off for your amusement nightly at this combination comedy club and café space.

The Ice House 24 N Mentor Ave, Pasadena ☏ 626/577-1894, ⓦ www.icehousecomedy.com. The comedy mainstay of the Valley, very established and safe; often amusing, with plenty of old warhorses and the occasional big name.

The Improv 8162 Melrose Ave, West LA ☎ 323/651-2583, ⊛ www.improv.com. Long-standing brick-walled joint that spawned a national chain. Still known for hosting some of the best acts working in both stand-up and improv. One of LA's top comedy spots – so book ahead.

Improv Olympic West 6366 Hollywood Blvd ☎ 323/962-7560, ⊛ west.ioimprov.com. A spot for those who like their improv drawn out and elaborate, with comedy routines more like short theatre pieces than a set of wacky one-liners. $5–10.

The Laugh Factory 8001 Sunset Blvd, West Hollywood ☎ 323/656-1336, ⊛ www .laughfactory.com. Stand-ups of varying reputations, with the odd big name and regular ensemble shows.

Second City Studio Theater 6560 Hollywood Blvd, Hollywood ☎ 323/464-8542, ⊛ www.second city.com. Groundbreaking comedy troupe with numerous branches in LA, hosting nightly improv and sketch comedy sometimes built around lengthy routines and theme performances.

Theatre

From huge Broadway shows to tiny avant-garde productions, LA has a very active **theatre** scene. While the bigger venues host a predictable array of musicals and classics with an all-star cast of celebrities, more than a hundred small theatres with fewer than a hundred seats can be found around the city, enabling a vast network of fringe or little-known writers, actors and directors to showcase their talent. **Tickets** are less expensive than you might expect: a big show will set you back at least $40–50, or up to $100–125 for some blockbusters (matinees are cheaper), with smaller shows around $10 to $20.

Major theatres

The Actors' Gang 9070 Venice Blvd, Culver City ☎ 310/838-GANG, ⊛ www.theactors gang.com. A cross between a major and an alternative theatre; having fewer than a hundred seats keeps it cosy, though it does host the odd spectacular production that features semi-famous names from film or TV.

Ahmanson Theatre Music Center, 135 N Grand Ave, Downtown ☎ 213/628-2772, ⊛ www .taperahmanson.com. A two-thousand-seat theatre hosting colossal travelling shows from Broadway. If you've seen a major production advertised on TV and on the sides of buses, it's probably playing here.

Alex Theatre 216 N Brand Blvd, Glendale ☎ 818/243-3622, ⊛ www.alextheatre.org. Gloriously restored movie palace bedecked with green-and-yellow decor and neon spire, hosting a fine range of musical theatre, dance, comedy and film.

Freud Playhouse In MacGowan Hall at UCLA, Westwood ☎ 310/825-2101, ⊛ www.uclalive.org. A nearly 600-seat venue that features a mix of mainstream and contemporary pieces – plus risk-taking experimental works.

Geffen Playhouse 10886 Le Conte Ave, Westwood ☎ 310/208-5454, ⊛ www.geffenplayhouse.com. A five-hundred-seat, quaint Spanish Revival building that often hosts one-person shows. There's a decidedly Hollywood connection, evident in the crowd-pleasing nature of many of the productions.

Mark Taper Forum 135 N Grand Ave, Downtown ☎ 213/628-2772, ⊛ www.taperahmanson.com. Mainstream theatre in the three-quarter round, with a mix of classic and contemporary works. Located in the Music Center.

Pantages Theater 6233 Hollywood Blvd, Hollywood ☎ 323/468-1770, ⊛ www.nederlander.com/wc. Quite the stunner: an exquisite, atmospheric Art Deco theater in the heart of historic Hollywood, hosting major touring Broadway productions.

Pasadena Playhouse 39 S El Molino Ave, Pasadena ☎ 626/356-7529, ⊛ www.pasadena playhouse.org. A grand old space that provides enjoyably mainstream entertainment. Actors are often a mix of youthful professionals and ageing TV and movie stars.

South Coast Repertory 655 Town Center Drive, Costa Mesa ☎ 714/708-5555, ⊛ www.scr.org. Orange County's major entry for theatre, with well-executed performances of the classics on the main stage, and edgier works by new writers on the smaller second stage.

Fringe theatres

The Complex 6476 Santa Monica Blvd, Hollywood ☎ 323/465-0383, ⊛ www .complexhollywood.com. A group of alternative companies revolving around five small theatres, where you're likely to see any number of dynamic productions.

Highways 1651 18th St, Santa Monica ☎ 310/315-1459, ⊛ www.highwaysperformance.org. Located in the 18th Street Arts Complex, an adventurous performance space that offers a range of topical drama and politically charged productions, with a strong bent toward the subversive.

Hudson Theaters 6539 Santa Monica Blvd, Hollywood ⊤ 323/856-4252, ⓦ www.hudson theater.com. Socially conscious "message" plays alternate with more satirical, comedic works at this venue for upcoming actors. Complex consists of three stages, plus a café and art gallery.

Open Fist Theatre 1625 N La Brea Ave, Hollywood ⊤ 323/882-6912, ⓦ www.openfist.org. As you might expect from the name, biting and edgy works are often the focus at this small theatre company, employing a limited cast of spirited unknowns.

Powerhouse Theater 3116 2nd St, Santa Monica ⊤ 213/674-6682, ⓦ www.powerhouse theatre.com. Cosy venue not far from Venice, worth visiting for the adventurous and risk-taking experimental shows.

Stages Theater Center 1540 N McCadden Place, Hollywood ⊤ 323/465-1010, ⓦ www.stagestheatrecenter.com. With three stages offering twenty to one hundred seats, this is an excellent place to catch a wide range of comedies and dramas, including re-stagings of canonical works and contemporary productions as well.

Steve Allen Theater 4773 Hollywood Blvd ⊤ 323/666-4268, ⓦ www.steveallentheater.com. An intriguing East Hollywood grab bag of entertainment, ranging from vaudeville-style productions, underground theatre and one-person comedy shows, to vintage and oddball films, experimental music, variety shows and cartoons.

Theatre West 3333 Cahuenga Blvd West, Hollywood ⊤ 323/851-7977, ⓦ www.theatrewest .org. A classic venue that's always a good spot to see inventive, sometimes odd, productions with a troupe of excellent young up-and-comers.

Theatricum Botanicum 1419 N Topanga Canyon Blvd, Topanga Canyon ⊤ 310/455-3723, ⓦ www .theatricum.com. Terrific spot in the Santa Monica Mountains showing a range of classic (often Shakespearean) and modern plays in an idyllic outdoor setting.

Film

Major feature **films** are often released in LA months (or years) before they play anywhere else, and a huge number of cinemas show both the new releases and the classics – with fewer screens showing independent and foreign movies. Tickets cost $11–13. (Theatres not regularly open to the public, such as many movie palaces Downtown, aren't listed.)

Mainstream film

AMC Century 15 In the Century City mall, 10250 Santa Monica Blvd, Century City ⊤ 310/289-4AMC. One of the best places to see new films in LA. The theatres are somewhat boxy, but if you're after crisp projection, booming sound and comfy seating, there are few better choices.

Arclight 6360 Sunset Blvd, Hollywood ⊤ 323/464-4226, ⓦ www.arclightcinemas.com. All-reserved seats in 14 theatres, top-of-the-line projection, good sightlines, wide seats and – best of all – the iconic Cinerama Dome, a white hemisphere that has the biggest screen in California.

Bruin 948 Broxton Ave, Westwood ⊤ 310/208-8998. Dashing 1930s moviehouse that's a city landmark for its wraparound marquee and sleek Moderne styling.

Chinese 6925 Hollywood Blvd, Hollywood ⊤ 323/464-8111. With its forecourt thick with tourists and wild chinoiserie design, this Hollywood icon shows relentlessly mainstream films, but is still worthy of all the postcard images (see p.98).

Egyptian 6712 Hollywood Blvd, Hollywood ⊤ 323/466-3456. Has showings of revival, experimental and art films, and has been lovingly restored as a kitschy masterpiece of the Egyptian Revival – all grand columns, winged scarabs and mythological gods (see p.98).

El Capitan 6834 Hollywood Blvd, Hollywood ⊤ 323/467-7674. Whether or not you enjoy the typically kiddie-oriented fare offered here – thanks to its Disney ownership – the twice-restored splendour of this classic Hollywood movie palace is bound to impress.

Majestic Crest 1262 Westwood Blvd, Westwood ⊤ 310/474-7866. A riot of neon and flashing lights outside, with glowing murals of Old Hollywood inside. Often shows Disney flicks, in one of the last single-screen cinemas in LA.

Regal 14 at LA Live 800 W Olympic Blvd, Downtown ⊤ 1-877/835-5734. Between parking and a movie ticket, it'll cost you $20 just to see a Hollywood flick here, but if you want huge screens, booming Dolby sound and plenty of 3-D/special effects wizardry, there are few better spots in the city.

Village 961 Broxton Ave, Westwood ⊤ 310/248-6266. One of the best places to watch a movie in LA, with a giant screen, fine seats and good balcony views, and a frequent spot for Hollywood premieres. The marvellous 1931 exterior features a white spire.

Art-house and revival

Aero 1328 Montana Ave, Santa Monica ☎310/466-3456. American Cinematheque presents an eclectic programme of classic and art-house movies in this fine old venue from 1940.

Bing At the LA County Art Museum, 5905 Wilshire Blvd, Mid-Wilshire ☎323/857-6010. Offers engaging retrospectives of actors and directors, as well as evening programmes of classic, indie, foreign, art-house and revival cinema.

Cinefamily 611 N Fairfax Ave, south of West Hollywood ☎323/655-2510. Boasting some of the most inspired movie-buff showings in town, this vintage theatre presents silent films (with live accompaniment), and cult, foreign, avant-garde and long-forgotten flicks, along with more familiar classics and indie films.

The Landmark 10850 W Pico Blvd, West LA ☎310/470-0492. Huge, 12-screen multiplex with comfortable furnishings including couches, excellent sound and projection. One of the top venues for un-Hollywood fare in LA.

New Beverly Cinema 7165 Beverly Blvd, Mid-Wilshire ☎323/938-4038. Worthwhile for its

excellent art films and revival screenings, with some imaginative double bills.

Nuart 11272 Santa Monica Blvd, West LA ☎310/281-8223. Shows rarely seen classics, documentaries and edgy foreign-language films, and is the main option for independent filmmakers testing their work. Sometimes offers brief December previews of Oscar contenders.

Old Town Music Hall 140 Richmond St, El Segundo ☎310/322-2592. An old-fashioned spot to see historic movies, with accompanying organ or piano music on some nights.

Sunset 5 8000 Sunset Blvd, West Hollywood ☎323/848-3500. This art-house complex sits on the second floor of the Sunset Plaza outdoor mall and shows a good assortment of edgy independent flicks.

Vista 4473 Sunset Drive, Hollywood ☎323/660-6639. A nicely renovated moviehouse with very eclectic offerings – from mindless action flicks to micro-budgeted indie productions – located near the intersection of Sunset and Hollywood boulevards.

🏃 **Warner Grand** 478 W 6th St, San Pedro ☎310/548-7672. Restored 1931 Zigzag Moderne masterpiece with dark geometric details, great columns and sunburst motifs – a style that almost looks pre-Columbian. Now a repertory cinema and performance hall.

Gay and lesbian LA

Although nowhere near as big as that of San Francisco, LA's **gay and lesbian scene** is almost as well established. The best-known area is the city of **West Hollywood**, which is synonymous with the (affluent, white) gay lifestyle, with the epicentre where Santa Monica Boulevard meets San Vicente Boulevard. **Silver Lake**, especially along Hyperion and Sunset boulevards, has much more of a vibrant ethnic and working-class mix. Surprisingly, perhaps, even Orange County has its pockets of gay and lesbian culture, centred mainly on the upscale confines of **Laguna Beach**.

Gay couples will find themselves accepted at most LA **hotels**, but the most well-known gay establishment is the *Ramada Plaza West Hollywood* (see p.76).

Bars and clubs

Akbar 4356 Sunset Blvd ☎323/665-6810. A curious blend of patrons – manual labourers and bohemians, old-timers and newbies – frequent this cosy, unpretentious watering-hole. Also presents occasional dance events.

🏃 **Arena** 6655 Santa Monica Blvd, Hollywood ☎323/462-0714. See map, p.104. Many clubs under one roof, large dancefloors throbbing to funk, house and hi-NRG grooves, and sometimes with live bands and mind-blowing drag shows (see also p.148).

East/West Lounge 8851 Santa Monica Blvd. See map, p.104. Friendly spot in the hub of West Hollywood with somewhat pricey drinks, but a chic atmosphere, good range of cocktails and decent food. Pavement seating offers great people-watching.

FUBAR 7994 Santa Monica Blvd ☎323/654-0396. See map, p.104. If you recognize the acronym, you'll know what you're in for at this high-energy club, a popular scene that offers regular dance events, plus Friday-night drag shows and a Wednesday-night lesbian night – rare in LA.

Micky's 8857 Santa Monica Blvd ☎310/657-1176. See map, p.104. Lively, pulsating scene with a full range of club nights, including the usual Seventies and Eighties dance-pop, thundering house and hip-hop beats, and drag shows.

Mother Lode 8944 Santa Monica Blvd ☎310/659-9700. See map, p.104. Strong drinks and wild dancing to house and garage music make this one of the more colourful and frenetic of WeHo's clubs.

The Palms 8572 Santa Monica Blvd, West Hollywood ☎310/652-6188. See map, p.104. Mostly house and dance nights at West Hollywood's most established lesbian bar, which increasingly caters to a mixed crowd.

Rage 8911 Santa Monica Blvd, West Hollywood ☎310/652-7055. See map, p.104. Very flashy gay men's club and neighbourhood favourite, playing the latest house to a long-established crowd.

Shopping

Shopping in LA is an art – besides the run-of-the-mill chain retailers you'll find anywhere, there are big **department stores** and mega-sized **malls** where most of the hardcore shopping goes on, and of course **Rodeo Drive**, two blocks of the world's most exclusive shopping. Trendy boutiques line **Melrose Avenue** in Hollywood, and **Third Street** and **La Brea Avenue** in West LA. **Old Town Pasadena** boasts a few more upmarket chains, and the few blocks above Prospect on Vermont Avenue in **Los Feliz** are home to some of the underground's groovier shops.

Department stores and malls

Each of LA's neighbourhoods has a collection of ordinary **stores** and **mini-malls**. A step up from these in price and quality are **department stores**, which are often included within massive **malls** and resemble self-contained city suburbs, around which Angelenos do the bulk of their serious buying.

Beverly Center 8500 Beverly Blvd, West Hollywood. Seven acres of boutiques, Macy's and Bloomingdale's, all in one complex that resembles a giant brown concrete bunker – built over a parking garage, with active (off-limits) oil wells on its western side.

Century City Marketplace 10250 Santa Monica Blvd, Century City. An outdoor mall with one hundred upscale shops and one of the better food courts around. The place to come to see stars do their shopping, and a spot to catch a first-run movie in excellent surroundings at the AMC Century 15 Theaters.

Del Amo Fashion Square Hawthorne Blvd at Carson St, Torrance. The South Bay's own super-mall, one of the country's largest, with Sears, Macy's and JCPenney, and a wealth of mid-level retailers and shoppers.

The Grove 6301 W 3rd St, Mid-Wilshire. A giant, open-air mega-structure by the Farmers' Market; has all the usual chain retailers, restaurants and movie theatres, and a more stylish design than the typical "dumb-box" construction found elsewhere.

Hollywood & Highland At the intersection of Hollywood and Highland blvds in Hollywood. Colossal mega-mall with a design inspired by an ancient film set, but offering the same old corporate boutiques and trendy shops, and a cineplex connected to the Chinese Theatre.

Paseo Colorado E Colorado Blvd at S Los Robles Ave, Pasadena. Two levels of (mostly chain) stores with street-front entrances, an open-air design that invites strolling, and several levels of condos built above it all.

Santa Monica Place Broadway at 2nd St, Santa Monica. Old Frank Gehry-designed mall that was radically reconfigured into an open-air design in 2010. Sits at the south end of the Third Street Promenade, and is anchored by Bloomingdale's and Nordstrom.

South Coast Plaza 3333 Bristol St, north of 405 freeway, Costa Mesa. Orange County's main super-mall, one of the most profitable malls in North America, with nearly three hundred shops and huge crowds of locals and tourists. Includes Macy's, Saks Fifth Avenue and Nordstrom, plus many top-name designer boutiques.

Third Street Promenade Between Broadway and Wilshire Blvd, Santa Monica. Major outdoor mall, packed on weekend evenings with mobs scurrying about to get to bookstores, boutiques, restaurants and cinemas; see also p.115.

Westside Pavilion Pico Blvd at Westwood Blvd, West LA. Postmodern shopping complex centre with Nordstrom and Macy's; the former western side of the mall has been converted into The Landmark theatres.

Food and drink

Since eating out in LA is so common, you may never have to shop for **food** at all. But if you're preparing a picnic or want to indulge in a spot of home cooking, there are plenty of places to stock up. Many **delis** are open round the clock; some **supermarkets** are open 24 hours, or at least until 10pm; and there are also **ethnic groceries** and more expensive **gourmet markets**.

Bakeries and desserts

Diamond Bakery 335 N Fairfax Ave, West LA. In the heart of the Fairfax District, this great old Jewish bakery provides a good number of traditional favourites, including *babka*, *challah*, *mandelbrot* and *rugelach*, and a legendary pumpernickel bread.

Doughboy's Café and Bakery 8136 W 3rd St, Mid-Wilshire. Tasty pizzas, pancakes, scones and sandwiches are available for midday meals, but the real highlight of this Westside bakery is the bread: rich, hearty loaves with interesting ingredients like walnuts, olives and various cheeses.

Fosselman's 1824 W Main St, Alhambra. Reason alone to visit this San Gabriel Valley town: what many Angelenos regard as the area's best ice cream, a long-standing (91 years) seller of creamy concoctions, highlighted by the macadamia crunch and burgundy cherry.

Gourmet Cobbler Factory 33 N Catalina Ave, Pasadena. Bakery selling a range of yummy, fruity cobblers, from blackberry to apple and peach, pecan and sweet potato. Occupies a prime spot near Old Pasadena.

La Brea Bakery 624 S La Brea Ave, West LA. Perhaps LA's best bakery, selling everything from cheap sourdough rolls to thick, heavy breads made with olives, cherries and cheese. Connected to the equally appealing *Campanile* restaurant (see p.140).

Porto's Bakery 315 N Brand Blvd, Glendale. Tasty baked goods and desserts, along with flaky Cuban pastries, cheesecakes soaked in rum, muffins, Danishes, croissants and tortes.

Viktor Benes Continental Pastries 13455 Maxella Ave, Marina del Rey. This is the place to go for freshly baked bread, coffee cakes, Danish pastries and various chocolate-oriented treats, and its appreciative local fans know it.

Delis and grocery stores

Bay Cities Italian Deli 1517 Lincoln Blvd, Santa Monica. An excellent, centrally located deli and retailer with an Italian focus. Offers piles of fresh pasta, meat, home-made pasta, spices and sauces, along with many imports, desserts, espresso and terrific lunchtime sandwiches.

The Cheese Store of Beverly Hills 419 N Beverly Drive, Beverly Hills. More than four hundred types of cheese from all over the world, including every kind produced in the US, with many of them suspended invitingly over your head. Typically high prices to match.

Jeff's Gourmet Kosher Sausage Factory 8930 W Pico Blvd, West LA. A top-notch vendor of well-crafted sausages, from merguez to jalapeño to Polish to veal bratwurst and Cajun chicken.

Olson's Deli 5560 Pico Blvd, Mid-Wilshire. Herring, meatballs and assorted sausages at this Swedish grocer, one of the few Scandinavian food retailers in LA and definitely worth a try.

Say Cheese 2800 Hyperion Ave, Silver Lake. A distinctive array of French and other international cheeses, priced moderately to steeply. The delicious sandwiches may be your best bet.

Vallarta Supermarket 10950 Sherman Way, Burbank. San Fernando Valley chain focusing on foodstuffs from Latin America, including special chillis and spices, with an on-site *taqueria* that doles out delicious and inexpensive food.

Books

LA's **bookstores**, like those of other cities, have been in trouble in recent years. The chain stores and other major players in town (namely, Book Soup) have ridden out the lean years, but others haven't done so well – going out of business in a matter of weeks. What follows are the best of the survivors.

Book Soup 8818 W Sunset Blvd, West Hollywood. Great selection, right on Sunset Strip. Narrow, winding aisles stuffed pell-mell with books, strong in entertainment, travel and photography.

Brand Book Shop 231 N Brand Blvd, Glendale. Valley used-bookseller with a broad range of liberal-arts titles and particular strengths in entertainment, history and politics.

Distant Lands 56 S Raymond Ave, Pasadena. Well-stocked travel bookstore in Old Pasadena, with some fairly hard-to-find titles, as well as maps and travel gear. Also hosts the occasional public speaker and globe-trotting slide show.

Hennessey and Ingalls 214 Wilshire Blvd, Santa Monica. An impressive range of art and architecture books makes this bookstore the best in LA in its field, though many of the volumes are quite expensive.

Iliad Bookshop 5400 Cahuenga Blvd, San Fernando Valley. Easily one of LA's best used booksellers, and meriting a trip out to North Hollywood. Features a broad selection of affordable titles, including some you probably won't find anywhere else.

Larry Edmunds Book Shop 6644 Hollywood Blvd. Many stacks of books, a large number of them out of print, are offered on every aspect of film and theatre, with movie stills and posters. Located at the centre of tourist-oriented Hollywood.

Samuel French Theatre & Film Bookshop 7623 Sunset Blvd, West Hollywood. LA's broadest selection of theatre books is found in this local institution, along with a good collection of movie-and media-related titles.

Taschen 354 N Beverly Drive, Beverly Hills. Fun, edifying and weird titles that focus on everything

from Renaissance art to Americana kitsch to fetish photography. Cheap volumes on both familiar and obscure subjects. Also right outside the Farmers' Market, 6333 W 3rd St, Mid-Wilshire.

Traveler's Bookcase 8375 W 3rd St, Mid-Wilshire. A bookseller with a limited but well-chosen selection of travel guides, maps and publications, along with a fine array of literary travel stories, novels, trip diaries and personal memoirs and essays.

Vroman's 695 E Colorado Blvd, Pasadena. One of the San Gabriel Valley's major retailers, offering a good selection with a café. Although there are no real bargains, other, smaller used bookstores can be found within a few blocks.

Wacko 4633 Hollywood Blvd, Hollywood. Although also great for its eclectic gift selection, this East Hollywood favourite stocks an excellent array of titles leaning toward the alternative: art and architecture, bizarre fetishes, alternative history, music guides, and conspiracy theories and assorted rants.

Music

While CDs are the dominant format in LA's **record stores**, vinyl fans will be happy to find LPs here and there, thanks in equal parts to diehard collectors and the constant need for "scratching" by club DJs.

Amoeba Music 6400 W Sunset Blvd, Hollywood. A vast selection of titles – supposedly numbering around half a million – on CD, tape and vinyl, which you can listen to at booths throughout the store. Also presents occasional in-store live music.

Backside Records Though oriented toward DJs and the vinyl-minded, this store stocks both LPs and CDs with a broad range of electronica, plus some jazz, rap and soul. Also with a wide selection of apparel for young dudes.

Counterpoint 5911 Franklin Ave, Hollywood. A terrific smorgasbord of used vinyl, CDs, movies on cassette and DVD, books and even antique 78 records. Also connected to its own underground art gallery.

Fingerprints 4612 E 2nd St, Long Beach. Fine indie outfit in the South Bay, offering

alternative-leaning CD and vinyl, plus in-store performances from local rockers.

Freakbeat Records 13616 Ventura Blvd, Sherman Oaks. One of the Valley's biggest dealers in CDs and vinyl, the store has plenty to browse over (and listen to), from vintage 1960s surf pioneers to latter-day punk nihilists, with cheap prices, too.

Record Surplus 11609 W Pico Blvd, West LA. Massive LP collection of surf music, ancient rock'n'roll, Sixties soundtracks, and unintentionally hilarious spoken-word recordings. Prices are excellent, with many CDs offered for low prices.

Rockaway Records 2395 Glendale Blvd, Silver Lake. Great place to come for both used CDs and LPs, as well as DVDs. Also offers old magazines, posters and memorabilia. Just east of the Silver Lake reservoir.

Listings

Beach information Weather conditions for the northern beaches from Santa Monica to Malibu ☎310/457-9701, ⊚www.watchthewater.org, or around the South Bay ☎310/379-8471.

Currency exchange Outside of banking hours, exchange offices are scattered inconveniently throughout town. Most reliable are those at LAX; hours vary by terminal (often daily until 11pm; ☎310/649-2801).

Dental treatment The cheapest place is USC School of Dentistry, 925 W 34th St (☎213/740-1576, ⊛dentistry.usc.edu), on the USC Campus, costing $50–200 and up. Be prepared to wait all day. You can also get emergency treatment at the LA Dental Society, 3660 Wilshire Blvd #1152 (☎213/380-7669, ⊛www.ladental.com).

Directory inquiries Local ☎411 (free call at pay phones); long distance ☎1, then area code, then 555-1212.

Driving The California Department of Transportation (CalTrans; ☎1-800/427-7623, ⊛www.dot.ca.gov/hq/roadinfo) gives up-to-the-minute details of road conditions throughout the state. Road information is also available on ☎916/445-1534, and on the web at ⊛maps.google.com (with traffic overlay) or www.sigalert.com. The AAA of Southern California (2601 S Figueroa St, South Central LA ☎213/741-3686, ⊛www.calif.aaa.com) has maps, guides and information on getting around by car.

Emergencies ☎911 for fire, police and medical emergencies. For less urgent needs: police ☎1-877/275-5273.

Hospitals The following have 24-hour emergency departments: Cedars-Sinai Medical Center, 8700 Beverly Blvd, Beverly Hills (☎310/423-3277, ⊛www.csmc.edu); Good Samaritan Hospital, 1225 Wilshire Blvd, Downtown (☎213/977-2121, ⊛www.goodsam.org); UCLA Medical Center, 10833 Le Conte Ave, Westwood (☎1-800/825-2631, ⊛www.uclahealth.org).

Internet Available in internet cafés, many city libraries and sit-down terminals near flight gates at LAX. Outside of libraries, expect to pay around 10–30¢/min.

Libraries Downtown's Central Library is the city's finest (see p.86), with branches throughout LA. Other cities also have good main libraries, notably Beverly Hills, 444 N Rexford Drive (☎310/288-2244, ⊛www.bhpl.org), and Santa Monica, 601 Santa Monica Blvd (☎310/458-8600, ⊛www.smpl.org).

Mexican Tourist Office and Consulate 2401 W 6th St, 5th floor, Downtown (☎1-800/446-3942, ⊛www.visitmexico.com).

Newspapers USC and UCLA have libraries with overseas newspapers. European papers are on sale at World Book and News, 1652 N Cahuenga Blvd (☎323/465-4352), in Hollywood.

Pharmacies Late hours at Horton & Converse, 11600 Wilshire Blvd, West LA (until 9pm; ☎310/478-0801), and Kaiser Permanente's West LA hospital, 6041 Cadillac Ave (24hr; ☎323/857-2151).

Post office The main Downtown post office is at 900 N Alameda St (Mon–Fri 8am–5.30pm, Sat 8am–4pm; ☎213/617-4404), north of Union Station. Zip Code is 90012.

Smog LA's air quality can often be very poor and, especially in the valleys in late summer, sometimes dangerous. An air-quality index is published daily in the *LA Times*; if the air is really bad, warnings are issued on TV, radio and in newspapers. For more information contact the South Coast Air Quality Management District (☎1-800/288-7664, ⊛www.aqmd.gov).

Taxes LA sales tax is 9.75 percent; hotel tax variable, generally 14–16 percent.

Travel details

Amtrak trains

Los Angeles to: Anaheim (10 daily; 40min); Fullerton (for Disneyland; 10 daily; 35min); Oceanside (10 daily; 1hr 50min); Oxnard (6 daily; 1hr 35min); Palm Springs (2 daily; 2hr 35min); Sacramento (1 daily; 14hr); San Bernardino (1 daily; 1hr 45min); San Diego (12 daily; 2hr 40min); San Francisco (6 daily; 9–12hr, with bus connection); San Juan Capistrano (10 daily; 1hr 20min); Santa Barbara (6 daily; 2hr 35min); Tucson (2 daily; 9hr 30min); Ventura (6 daily; 1hr 50min).

Greyhound buses

Los Angeles to: Bakersfield (12 daily; 2hr 45min); Las Vegas (13 daily; 6–8hr); Palm Springs (4 daily; 2–3hr); Phoenix (10 daily; 7–9hr); Sacramento (8 daily; 7–10hr); San Diego (20 daily; 2hr 30min–3hr); San Francisco (12 daily; 8–13hr); Santa Barbara (4 daily; 2–3hr); Santa Cruz (4 daily; 9hr); Tucson (10 daily; 10–13hr).

San Diego and around

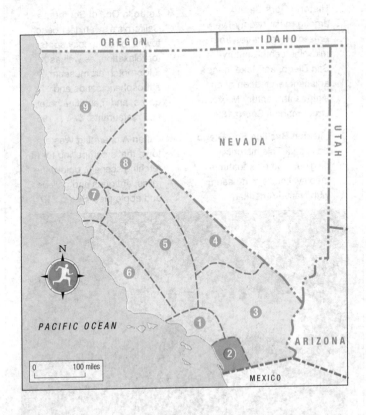

CHAPTER 2   # Highlights

* **Balboa Park** The museum centrepiece of San Diego, a 1400-acre green space loaded with history, science and art, and crowned with the city's popular zoo. See p.179

* **Old Town State Historic Park** Stroll among these twenty-five preserved structures from mid-nineteenth-century San Diego, and take in the adjacent re-creation of an eighteenth-century Mexican street market. See p.183

* **Mission Basilica San Diego de Alcalá** This historic religious complex features medieval stalls, a museum with Native American craftworks and the state's oldest cemetery. See p.185

* **Mission Beach** The most free-spirited of the city's surfing beaches, with acres of bronzed flesh and bikini babes, chaotic bars and even carnival rides. See p.189

* **La Jolla** One of Southern California's swankiest beach towns, offering cosy spots for relaxation, as well as a top-notch art museum, atmospheric sands and coves, and many fine hotels and restaurants. See p.190

* **Julian** A charming Western town that's compelling for its fetching scenery, gold-mine relics, antiques and galleries, and apple pies. See p.210

▲ Mission Basilica San Diego de Alcalá

San Diego and around

Lacking much of the urban chaos, social vitality and pop-cultural energy of its neighbouring megalopolis to the north, **San Diego** and its surrounding county nonetheless fundamentally represent the Southern California good life – an area of nouveau-riche luxury, sun-and-surf hedonism and the family-oriented fun of zoos, parks and aquariums. Surpassed long ago by Los Angeles in the race to become the region's essential city, San Diego was for a time considered an insignificant blot between LA and Mexico, home only to right-wing pensioners and cloistered suburbanites. Although that stereotype still has a measure of truth, San Diego also boasts considerable charm. With its gracefully curving bay, appealing oceanside vistas, a clutch of fine museums in Balboa Park and the large-scale tourist attractions of San Diego Zoo and SeaWorld, it's an excellent place to while away a weekend, or even a week, with glorious weather for much of the year.

Outside San Diego County's urban centre, you can find a host of compelling destinations. The **North County** includes small, enticing coastal communities from the northern edge of San Diego itself to the Camp Pendleton marine base, as well as the vineyards and avocado groves that reach east into wilder mountain country. Beyond the beach towns, you can explore the forests and state parks via hiking trails and obscure backroads.

Countless Mexicans stream into Southern California, above and below the official radar. Many are hotel and restaurant workers, but first- and especially second-generation immigrants are gradually becoming integrated into less menial levels of the workforce. However, unlike in LA, where Latino newcomers are flexing their political muscle, those of San Diego County are largely ghettoized, still viewed by the white gentry with suspicion. Not surprisingly, then, the urban goal for many migrants isn't the more convenient San Diego, but its big brother two hours north.

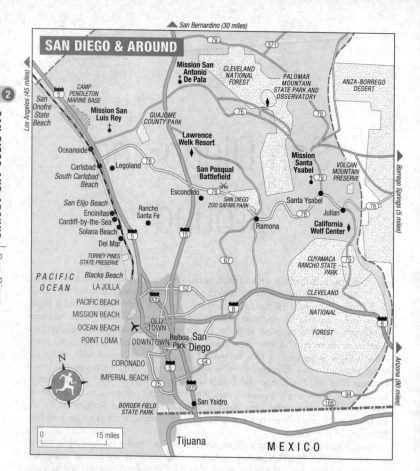

Map: SAN DIEGO & AROUND

San Bernardino (30 miles)

Los Angeles (45 miles)

Borrego Springs (5 miles)

Arizona (90 miles)

CAMP PENDLETON MARINE BASE
San Onofre State Beach
Mission San Luis Rey
Mission San Antonio De Pala
CLEVELAND NATIONAL FOREST
PALOMAR MOUNTAIN STATE PARK AND OBSERVATORY
ANZA-BORREGO DESERT
GUAJOME COUNTY PARK
Lawrence Welk Resort
Mission Santa Ysabel
VOLCAN MOUNTAIN PRESERVE
Oceanside
Carlsbad
Legoland
South Carlsbad Beach
San Pasqual Battlefield
Escondido
SAN DIEGO ZOO SAFARI PARK
Santa Ysabel
San Elijo Beach
Encinitas
Rancho Santa Fe
Julian
California Wolf Center
Cardiff-by-the-Sea
Solana Beach
Ramona
Del Mar
TORREY PINES STATE PRESERVE
CUYAMACA RANCHO STATE PARK
PACIFIC OCEAN
Blacks Beach
LA JOLLA
CLEVELAND
PACIFIC BEACH
MISSION BEACH
NATIONAL
OCEAN BEACH
OLD TOWN
FOREST
POINT LOMA
DOWNTOWN
Balboa Park
San Diego
CORONADO
IMPERIAL BEACH
BORDER FIELD STATE PARK
San Ysidro
N
0   15 miles
Tijuana
MEXICO

San Diego

Basking in the sun, but tempered by ocean breezes, **SAN DIEGO** is an ideal family holiday resort, with most tourists coming for its terrific beaches, major attractions like the San Diego Zoo and SeaWorld, and excellent museums in Balboa Park. More enterprising visitors may wish to explore the city's historic Downtown, namely the Gaslamp Quarter, whose building style ranges from true historic preservation to pseudo-historic kitsch.

The traditional image of San Diegans as conformist, affluent and Republican is true to a large extent – San Diego has as much in common with Salt Lake City or Phoenix as it does with Los Angeles or San Francisco. However, there are also a few unexpected undercurrents, from the emergence and tolerance of a vibrant gay scene in Hillcrest to increasing numbers of liberal students and professionals. The presence of three **college campuses** – SDSU, UCSD and USD – has also helped the city lose some of its rigid character. Still, its insularity remains – the city is notorious as having one of the most corrupt political cultures in the nation, with ongoing scandals involving bribes, municipal kickbacks and all manner of secret wheeling-and-dealing.

But travellers will hardly notice this darker side while enjoying the long white beaches, sunny weather and bronzed bodies – giving rise to the city's nickname, "Sandy Ego". Paradoxically, though, for such a sunny place throughout the year, San Diego is susceptible to extended periods of overcast skies and light rain when you'd least expect it – the so-called "June Gloom" that's caused by a climatic anomaly and leaves visitors scratching their heads as they trudge through damp beach sands.

Some history

The first European to land on California soil, Portuguese adventurer and Spanish agent Juan Rodríguez Cabrillo, put ashore at Point Loma, ten miles from today's Downtown San Diego, in 1542. White settlement didn't begin until two centuries later, however, with the building in 1769 of a Catholic mission – the first in California – and a military garrison on a site overlooking San Diego Bay. Later conflict between land-holding *Californios* and the fresh waves of settlers from the East led to America's capture of San Diego in 1847, in the midst of the Mexican–American War. However, the city missed out on the new mail route to the West and was plagued by a series of droughts through the 1860s, causing many bankruptcies and economic problems. Although the transcontinental Santa Fe Railroad link was short-lived – repeated flooding forced the terminus to be moved north to Los Angeles, depriving San Diego of direct rail service to the East – its establishment resulted in an economic boom through the 1880s. In 1915 came the first of two international expositions in Balboa Park, which were to establish San Diego's nationwide reputation.

In part because of its lack of direct railway access to the East Coast, the city has long been overshadowed by Los Angeles in trade and economic significance, though it has used its strategic seaside location to become a martial stronghold. During World War II, the US Navy took advantage of the city's sheltered bays, and much of San Diego's economy came to be dominated by the military.

However, it is San Diego's reputation as an ocean-oriented "resort city" that provides much of its modern relevance (at least to those not in uniform). Although it has a formidable population of more than a million people, making it the seventh-largest city in the US, for most tourists it's synonymous only with getting tanned, yachting around the bay, surfing a killer break, and hanging out at the zoo – all worthwhile pursuits to be sure, but intrepid visitors will find that there's much more to San Diego if staying longer than just a few days.

Arrival and information

Motorists can easily reach the city centre from three interstate **highways**: I-5, the main artery from Los Angeles and the rest of California, follows the coast and the northern parts of the central city, hits Downtown (with I-805 as a bypass that skirts it), and heads on to Mexico; from the east, I-8 comes from Arizona and runs by Old Town before terminating in Ocean Beach; and I-15 arrives from inland San Diego County and cuts through the city's northern and eastern suburbs.

All forms of **public transport** drop you in or near the heart of Downtown San Diego. Amtrak **trains** on the Pacific Surfliner route from LA use the Santa Fe Railroad Depot, close to the western end of Broadway at 1050 Kettner Blud

(☎1-800/872-7245), while the Greyhound **bus** terminal is six blocks east at Broadway and First Avenue (☎619/239-6737). Lindbergh Field **airport** (aka San Diego International; ☎619/400-2400, ⓦwww.san.org) is only two miles from Downtown, and is connected to it by buses #923 ($2.25) and #992 ($2.50); services start at 5am and finish around 11pm to midnight. **Taxis** to Downtown cost $10–12 one way, and some hotels offer guests a free **airport limo** service; alternatively, **shuttle services** such as EZ Ride (☎1-800/777-0585, ⓦwww .ezrideshuttle.com) and SuperShuttle (☎1-800/258-3826, ⓦwww.supershuttle .com) can take you Downtown for $5–10 one way. The main **car rental** firms have desks at the airport.

A good first stop in the city is the **International Visitor Information Center**, near the bay at 1040 W Broadway (summer 9am–5pm, winter until 4pm; ☎619/236-1212, ⓦwww.seeyouinsandiego.com), which has maps and information; there's another outlet in La Jolla at 7966 Herschel Ave (summer daily 10am–6pm, rest of year hours vary; ☎619/236-1212). For eating and entertainment **listings**, the free, weekly *San Diego Reader* (ⓦwww.sandiegoreader .com) can be found in many shops, bars and clubs; the entertainment section of the *San Diego Union-Tribune* (ⓦentertainment.signonsandiego.com) is also useful.

City transport

Despite its size, **getting around** San Diego without a car is slow but not too difficult, whether you use buses, the light-rail-like San Diego Trolley, or a rented bike. Travelling can be harder at night, with most public transport routes closing down around 11pm or midnight. The transport system won't break anyone's budget, especially with longer-term tickets and passes reducing costs over a few days or weeks. **Taxis** are also an affordable option: the average fare is anywhere from $5 for a jaunt around Downtown, to $10 for Coronado, to $20–25 to get up to the more northerly beaches (Ocean, Mission or Pacific).

Buses

The overarching **bus** system within San Diego County, the Metropolitan Transit System (☎1-619/595-4555, ⓦwww.sdmts.com), is the most convenient and accessible means of public transport in the region. Typical one-way fares are

Useful San Diego bus routes

The following buses connect **Downtown San Diego** with the surrounding area:
Balboa Park #1, #3, #7, #120
Coronado #901, #904
East San Diego #1, #7, #10, #13, #15, #955, #965
Hillcrest #1, #3, #10, #83, #120
Imperial Beach #901, #933, #934
La Jolla #30
Mission Bay/Mission Beach #8, #9
Ocean Beach #35, #923
Old Town #8, #9, #10, #28, #30, #35, #44, #105
Pacific Beach #8, #9, #27, #30
Point Loma peninsula #28

$2.25–2.50, and $5–10 for the most lengthy journeys into rural terrain; the exact fare is required when boarding (dollar bills are accepted). Alternatively, invest in the **Day Tripper Transit Pass** for one- to four-day visits ($5, $9, $12 and $15 respectively), available from the Transit Store (see below). Transfers are often free, but those made onto express buses or between transport systems (bus to trolley, bus to Coaster, etc) will require the price of the higher fare. Service is reliable and frequent, particularly Downtown, which is known on route maps and timetables as "Centre City". If you're headed anywhere in the North County, you'll take Breeze Buses operated by North County Transit District (fares $2; ☎1-800/266-6883, ⓦwww.gonctd.com).

The **Transit Store**, at First and Broadway (Mon–Fri 9am–5pm; ☎619/234-1060), has local bus timetables, free regional transport guides and travel passes. If you know your point of departure and destination, you can get automated bus information on ☎619/685-4900.

The trolley

Complementing county bus lines is the **San Diego Trolley**, often called the "Tijuana Trolley" because it travels sixteen miles from the Santa Fe Railroad Depot to the US–Mexico border in San Ysidro – a 45-minute trip. One-way tickets are $2.50, and Day Tripper packages are also available (see above). One-way tickets should be bought from the machines at trolley stops, which also offer return tickets. Of the three routes, the **Blue Line** is the more visitor-oriented, starting with Old Town and heading south to Little Italy and Downtown San Diego, then on to the Mexican border. From the transfer station at Imperial and 12th, the trolley's **Orange Line** usefully loops around Downtown, but offers little else of interest to visitors, darting out toward the eastern suburbs. The newer **Green Line** also reaches these suburbs, starting at Old Town, but is really only useful for visitors headed to Mission San Diego or Qualcomm Stadium. Trolleys leave every fifteen minutes during the day (starting around 5am); the last service back from San Ysidro leaves at 1am, so an evening of south-of-the-border revelry and a return to San Diego the same night is quite possible.

The Coaster and Sprinter

North San Diego County is linked to Downtown via a commuter light-rail system called **The Coaster**, which includes eight stops from Oceanside through Carlsbad, Encinitas, Solana Beach, Sorrento Valley and Old Town, ending up at the Santa Fe Railroad Depot. On weekdays, eleven trains run southbound, with the same number returning northbound (and an extra two trains on Friday night), while six trains make the trip on Saturdays. Fares range from $5 to $6.50 one way, $2.50 to $3.25 for seniors, and $14 for a day-pass (☎1-800/262-7837,

---

Old Town Trolley Tour

Not to be confused with the San Diego Trolley, the **Old Town Trolley Tour** (☎619/298-8687, ⓦwww.historictours.com/sandiego) is a two-hour narrated trip around San Diego's most popular spots, including Downtown, Balboa Park, the San Diego Zoo, Old Town and Coronado, aboard an open-sided motor-driven carriage. If you're short of time, the tour is a simple way to cover a lot of ground quickly. You can buy **tickets** ($34, kids $17) on the bus and hop on and off all day (summer 9am–5pm, winter until 4pm) at any of the stops. Leaflets detailing the various routes are found in hotel lobbies and at visitor centres.

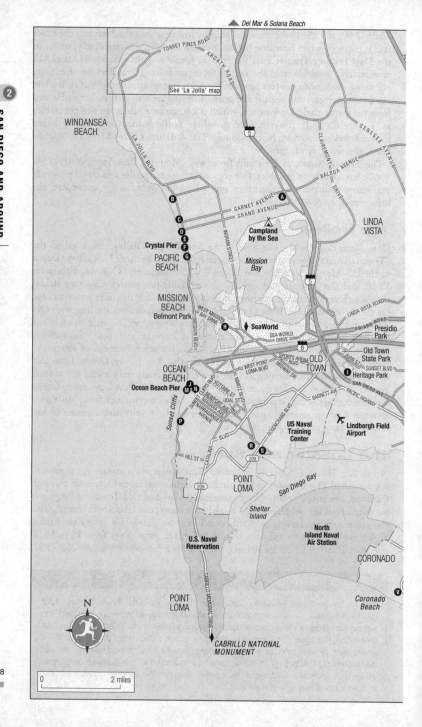

TORREY PINES ROAD

ARDATH ROAD

See 'La Jolla' map

WINDANSEA
BEACH

LA JOLLA BLVD

GENESEE AVENUE

CLAIREMONT DRIVE

BALBOA AVENUE

GARNET AVENUE   **A**
GRAND AVENUE

B

C

D
E
Crystal Pier **F**
G

PACIFIC
BEACH

INGRAM STREET

Campland
by the Sea

Mission
Bay

LINDA
VISTA

MISSION
BEACH
Belmont Park

WEST MISSION
BAY DRIVE

MISSION BLVD

SeaWorld

SEA WORLD
DRIVE

LINDA VISTA ROAD

FRIARS ROAD

Presidio
Park

Old Town
State Park

H

SPORTS ARENA
BLVD

OLD
TOWN

JUAN ST

SUNSET BLVD

Heritage Park **I**

SAN DIEGO AVE

OCEAN
BEACH

Ocean Beach Pier

Sunset Cliffs

J
M
L

SUNSET CLIFFS BLVD
VOLTAIRE ST
UDAL ST
NEWPORT AVE
NARRAGANSETT AVENUE
NIAGARA AVE

WEST POINT
LOMA BLVD

MIDWAY DR

NIMITZ BLVD

BARNETT AVE

PACIFIC HIGHWAY

ROSECRANS BLVD

US Naval
Training
Center

✈ Lindbergh Field
Airport

P

CATALINA BLVD

HILL ST

R
S

209

POINT
LOMA

San Diego Bay

Shelter
Island

CABRILLO MEMORIAL DRIVE

209

U.S. Naval
Reservation

North
Island Naval
Air Station

CORONADO

V

POINT
LOMA

Coronado
Beach

CABRILLO NATIONAL
MONUMENT

N

0   2 miles

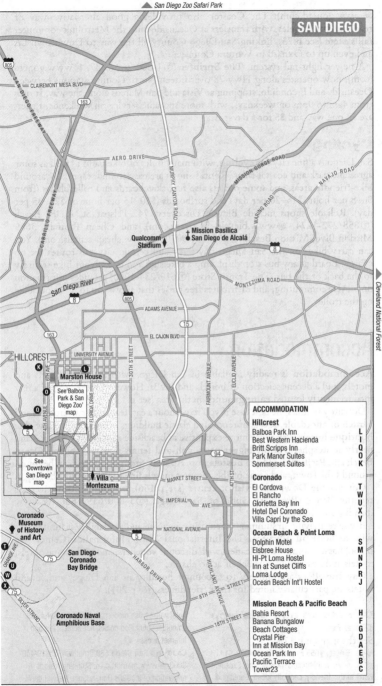

SAN DIEGO Zoo Safari Park

SAN DIEGO

SAN DIEGO AND AROUND

Cleveland National Forest

CLAIREMONT MESA BLVD
SAN DIEGO FREEWAY
805
163
AERO DRIVE
MURPHY CANYON ROAD
MISSION GORGE ROAD
NAVAJO ROAD
WARING ROAD
Mission Basilica
San Diego de Alcalá
Qualcomm Stadium
8
MONTEZUMA ROAD
San Diego River
8
805
ADAMS AVENUE
163
EL CAJON BLVD
15
HILLCREST
UNIVERSITY AVENUE
FAIRMOUNT AVENUE
EUCLID AVENUE
K
6th AVE
Marston House
30TH STREET
L
See 'Balboa Park & San Diego Zoo' map
O
FLORIDA DRIVE
Q
4th AVENUE
5
94
47th ST
See 'Downtown San Diego' map
MARKET STREET
Villa Montezuma
IMPERIAL AVE
Coronado Museum of History and Art
NATIONAL AVENUE
T
5
O
San Diego-Coronado Bay Bridge
75
HARBOR DRIVE
HIGHLAND AVENUE
W
U
8TH STREET
X
75
Coronado Naval Amphibious Base
SILVER STRAND
18TH AVENUE

ACCOMMODATION

Hillcrest
Balboa Park Inn	L
Best Western Hacienda	I
Britt Scripps Inn	Q
Park Manor Suites	O
Sommerset Suites	K

Coronado
El Cordova	T
El Rancho	W
Glorietta Bay Inn	U
Hotel Del Coronado	X
Villa Capri by the Sea	V

Ocean Beach & Point Loma
Dolphin Motel	S
Elsbree House	M
HI-Pt Loma Hostel	N
Inn at Sunset Cliffs	P
Loma Lodge	R
Ocean Beach Int'l Hostel	J

Mission Beach & Pacific Beach
Bahia Resort	H
Banana Bungalow	F
Beach Cottages	G
Crystal Pier	D
Inn at Mission Bay	A
Ocean Park Inn	E
Pacific Terrace	B
Tower23	C

Imperial Beach

Ⓦwww.gonctd.com). The Coaster also provides a good alternative way of reaching Los Angeles, with transfers at Oceanside onto the Metrolink commuter rail system (see p.73), linking San Diego County all the way to Downtown LA and even up to Oxnard in Ventura County.

A newer light-rail system, **The Sprinter** (Ⓣ1-800/262-7837, Ⓦwww.gonctd .com), now operates along Hwy 78 over fifteen North County stations between Oceanside and Escondido, stopping at Vista and San Marcos along the way. It runs from 4am to 9pm on weekdays, with more sporadic service on weekends; tickets are $2 one way and $5 for a day-pass.

Cycling

San Diego is a fine city for **cycling**, with many miles of bike paths as well as some agreeable park and coastal rides. **Rental shops** are easy to find, especially around bike-friendly areas, and some outlets also rent skateboards and rollerblades (from $6–8 per hour, $15–20 per day) and surfboards ($10–15 per hour or $25–35 per day). Reliable shops include Bicycle Discovery, 742 Felspar St, Pacific Beach (Ⓣ858/272-1274, Ⓦwww.bicycle-discovery.com), and Cheap Rentals, 3689 Mission Blvd, Mission Beach (Ⓣ858/488-9070, Ⓦwww.cheap-rentals.com). You can carry bikes on the San Diego Bay ferry and certain city bus routes for no charge. Board at any bus stop displaying a bike sign and fasten your bike securely to the back of the bus. The Transit Store (Ⓣ619/234-1060) provides information on bicycle commuting, and distributes free passes that allow you to take your bike on the trolley.

Accommodation

Accommodation is readily available in San Diego, with abundant hotels and motels, and a decent selection of hostels and B&Bs. However, there are just a few inconveniently located **campgrounds** in the area (see p.173).

Downtown offers the best base if you're without a car, featuring two **hostels** and a batch of affordable **hotels** in renovated classic buildings – along with a few chic **boutique hotels**. Prices are more expensive at beachside **motels** and hotels – and nearly stratospheric at the bigger-name golf-and-tennis resorts – though Ocean Beach and Pacific Beach have **hostels**, too. Another group of motels can be found around Old Town, and some of the cheapest motels line the roads into the city.

Contact the Downtown visitor centre (see p.166) for **B&B** information, or try the Bed & Breakfast Guild of San Diego (Ⓣ1-800/619-7666, Ⓦwww .bandbguildsandiego.org).

If you're arriving in summer, when prices increase and availability is limited, it's wise to **book in advance**. The International Visitor Information Center (see p.166) has accommodation leaflets with discount vouchers, and will phone hotels, motels and hostels on your behalf at no charge.

Gay travellers are unlikely to encounter hostility in San Diego, and several hotels are particularly noted for their friendliness (see p.201).

Downtown and Gaslamp Quarter

See the map on p.175.

Bristol 1055 First Ave Ⓣ619/232-6141, Ⓦwww.thebristolsandiego.com. Excellent value at this friendly, centrally located boutique hotel with stylish modern decor and tasteful amenities, plus iPod docks, flat-screen TVs and internet access. Ⓖ

Courtyard San Diego 530 Broadway Ⓣ619/446-3000, Ⓦwww.marriott.com. Stunning historic renovation of a 1920s Renaissance Revival bank, now home to tasteful rooms and suites, and loaded with beautiful period detail in the lobby and even a conference room in a one-time bank vault. A cheaper branch, recently renovated and with free wi-fi, is six miles east of Mission Bay at 8651 Spectrum Center Blvd (℡858/573-0700). ❻

Horton Grand 311 Island Ave at Third Ave ℡1-800/542-1886, ⓦ www.hortongrand.com. This classy amalgam of two century-old hotels has fireplaces in most of the rooms and balconies in some, plus a restaurant and piano bar. Somewhat minimal amenities for such a historic spot, though. ❼

Indigo 509 Ninth Ave ℡619-727-4000, ⓦ www .hotelsandiegoDowntown.com. Smart boutique digs in the Gaslamp Quarter at a new property that offers the usual upscale amenities – gym, free wi-fi – plus special touches such as local art on the walls and rooftop terrace bar with a fire pit. ❽

La Pensione 606 W Date St at India St ℡619/236-8000, ⓦ www.lapensionehotel.com. Good-value hotel within walking distance of the city centre. Minimalist-modernist rooms are small but equipped with wi-fi, microwaves, fridges and cable TV, and there's an on-site laundry. ❹

Manchester Grand Hyatt One Market Place at Harbor Drive ℡619/232-1234, ⓦ www.manchester grand.hyatt.com. The most prominent hotel along the waterfront, a pair of gleaming white slabs of luxury with all the top-notch amenities: pool, spas, health club, several restaurants and lounges, and rooms with expansive views of the bay. Popular with business travellers. ❼

Omni San Diego 675 L St ℡619/231-6664, ⓦ www.omnihotels.com. Sleek modern high-rise in the Gaslamp Quarter and linked to Petco Park by skybridge; rooms come with internet access and good city or bay views, and some with flat-screen TVs and DVD players. There's also a gym, pool and spa, and several fine restaurants. ❽

Solamar 435 Sixth Ave ℡619/819-9500, ⓦ www .hotelsolamar.com. Tasteful and modern boutique hotel central to the Gaslamp Quarter, whose rooms have internet access, flat-screen TVs and CD and DVD players, and which also offers spa and gym. Suites with jacuzzis add to the hip appeal. ❽

The U.S. Grant 326 Broadway ℡1-800/237-5029, ⓦ www.usgrant.net. Across from Horton Plaza, this has been Downtown's poshest address since 1910, with grand Neoclassical design, chandeliers, marble floors, and cosy but comfortable rooms with internet access and more capacious suites. The elegant ballrooms and swanky conference rooms are also worth a peek. ❽

Westgate 1055 Second Ave ℡1-800/522-1564, ⓦ www.westgatehotel.com. Centrally sited hotel near Horton Plaza with a stylish lobby (almost to the point of kitsch), elegant rooms furnished with balconies and antiques, and CD and DVD players. Also with spa and gym. ❼

Old Town, Hillcrest and Balboa Park

See the map on pp.168–169.

Balboa Park Inn 3402 Park Blvd, Hillcrest ℡619/298-0823, ⓦ www.balboaparkinn.com. Spanish Colonial, gay-oriented B&B within walking distance of Balboa Park and the museums. The 26 themed suites (with oceanside, Impressionist and Tarzan motifs, to name a few) come with free breakfast, microwaves and mini-fridges. Prices vary, depending on the size and the level of kitsch. ❺

Best Western Hacienda 401 Harney St ℡619/298-4707, ⓦ www.bestwesterncalifornia .com. Most decent hotels around Old Town are of the chain variety, and this is among the best, featuring mock Spanish Colonial design, free wi-fi, pool, jacuzzi, gym and clean, modern rooms – plus free airport shuttle. ❻

Britt Scripps Inn 406 Maple St ℡1-888/881-1991, ⓦ www.brittscripps.com. Fetching Victorian inn located in a marvellously restored 1887 Queen Anne mansion near Balboa Park, with nine plush rooms offering antiques, free wi-fi, flat-screen TV and some modern boutique touches, too. ❽

Park Manor Suites 525 Spruce St, near Balboa Park ℡1-800/874-2649, ⓦ www.parkmanorsuites .com. This renovated apartment complex is a hundred years old. The stately hotel suites feature kitchens and pleasant, large sitting areas, and continental breakfast and wi-fi are free. ❻

Sommerset Suites 606 Washington St, Hillcrest ℡1-800/962-9665, ⓦ www.sommersetsuites.com. Well-equipped suites offering balconies or patios, with kitchens, pool, spa, internet access and breakfast. One of the better deals in the area. ❻

Coronado

See the map on pp.168–169.

El Cordova 1351 Orange Ave, Coronado ℡1-800/229-2032, ⓦ www.elcordovahotel.com. One of the better deals in pricey Coronado, comprising Spanish Colonial buildings from 1902 arranged around lovely gardens. There's a pool, and many rooms have kitchenettes. Rooms vary hugely in price, from cheap and basic units to grandly elegant suites. ❼

El Rancho 370 Orange Ave ℡619/435-2251, ⓦ www.elranchocoronado.com. One of the cheapest deals on this side of the water: a small, clean motel with ten units offering basic decor, but equipped with free wi-fi, microwaves and fridges. ❺

Glorietta Bay Inn 1630 Glorietta Blvd ⊕619/435-3101, ⊛www.gloriettabayinn.com. Striking 1908 Edwardian mansion that's since been converted into swanky modern rooms and suites, all with internet access, iPod docks, DVD players and HDTVs, and some with kitchenettes and balconies. The place drips with period detail, from the antique chandeliers to the grand piano. Breakfast included. Prices dip considerably on weekdays. ⑧

Hotel del Coronado 1500 Orange Ave ⊕1-800/468-3533, ⊛www.hoteldel.com. The luxurious spot that put Coronado on the map and is still the area's major tourist sight (see p.187) – millions have been poured into the complex in renovations, and the striking rooms and suites, expansive bay views, and old-fashioned Victorian charm from 1888 still give the place plenty of appeal. ⑨

Villa Capri by the Sea 1417 Orange Ave ⊕1-800/231-3954, ⊛www.villacapribythesea .com. Old-style motel-like accommodation that offers fourteen suites with kitchens, internet access, VCR and a homely feel in a classic 1950s structure with some modern style inside. The pool and the central location by the beach are other big pluses. ⑥

Ocean Beach and Point Loma
See the map on pp.168–169.

Dolphin Motel 2912 Garrison St ⊕866/353-7897, ⊛www.dolphin-motel.com. The epitome of the roadside motel, in this case offering small, clean rooms with queen beds, free wi-fi and a good location roughly between Ocean Beach and Point Loma, within easy reach of the airport. Off-season rates can drop as low as $50. ③

Elsbree House 5054 Narragansett Ave, Ocean Beach ⊕619/226-4133, ⊛www.bbinnob.com. Retro New England-style shingled B&B with close access to the beach. The five rooms and one suite have free wi-fi, and a decent breakfast is included. Three-night minimum stay in summer. ⑦

Inn at Sunset Cliffs 1370 Sunset Cliffs Blvd, Point Loma ⊕1-866/786-2543, ⊛www.innatsunset cliffs.com. Perched on a precipice above the ocean, this property has a range of rooms, from entry-level suites with poolside access or kitchens to more elaborate digs with jacuzzis, luxury decor and stunning oceanside views. ⑥

Loma Lodge 3202 Rosecrans St, Ocean Beach ⊕1-800/266-0511, ⊛www.lomalodge.com. Among the best-value places in the area, this is a decent motel with pool and complimentary breakfast; good for exploring the peninsula, but not that close to the beach. ③

Mission Beach and Pacific Beach
See the map on pp.168–169.

Bahia Resort 998 W Mission Bay Drive, Mission Beach ⊕1-800/576-4229, ⊛www.bahiahotel.com. Prime beachside accommodation with expansive ocean views, watersport rentals, pool and jacuzzi. Rooms vary, from cosy and pleasant options in a palm-garden setting to pricier bayside suites. Wi-fi and fridges included. ⑦

Beach Cottages 4255 Ocean Blvd, Mission Beach ⊕858/483-7440, ⊛www.beachcottages.com. Beside the beach, three blocks south of the pier, this relaxing spot offers a wide range of accommodation, from simple motel units to more elaborate cottages. Most have kitchenettes; all have fridges. Motel rooms ⑥, studios ⑥, cottages and apartments ⑨

Crystal Pier 4500 Ocean Blvd, Pacific Beach ⊕1-800/748-5894, ⊛www.crystalpier.com. Beautiful deluxe cottages built in the 1920s and situated right on the pier. All rooms are suites with private decks, and most have kitchenettes. It can get pricey (upwards of $350 per night), but you stay literally on the water. Most rooms are booked many months in advance. ⑨

Inn at Mission Bay 4545 Mission Bay Drive ⊕858/483-4222, ⊛www.innatmissionbay.com. If you're headed to SeaWorld (3 miles away), you'll need to save your money for the sky-high tickets – and with that in mind, this is a cheap choice whose basic motel rooms have internet access, fridges and microwaves, plus access to a heated pool and continental breakfast. ③

Ocean Park Inn 710 Grand Ave, Pacific Beach ⊕858/483-5858, ⊛www.oceanparkinn.com. Another solid beachfront choice, offering free wi-fi, microwaves, fridges and breakfast, plus a pool and spa. Nothing too flashy, but the central location on the boardwalk is a very good draw. ⑦

Pacific Terrace 610 Diamond St, Pacific Beach ⊕858/581-3500, ⊛www.pacificterrace.com. Entrancing, chic accommodation on the beach, with rooms offering kitchenettes, fridges, internet access and sea-facing balconies, and suites with the full range of swanky amenities. From $399. ⑨

Tower23 4551 Ocean Blvd, Pacific Beach ⊕1-866/869-3723, ⊛www.tower23hotel.com. Named after a lifeguard tower, this is among the most chic of San Diego's boutique hotels, offering rooms with flat-screen TVs, internet access and designer furnishings, and even more stylish suites that come with balconies, cabanas and whirlpool tubs. ⑧

La Jolla

See the map on p.191.

Bed & Breakfast Inn at La Jolla 7753 Draper Ave ☎1-800/582-2466, ⓦwww.innlajolla.com. Designed in 1913 by early modernist Irving Gill, this is a collection of fifteen themed rooms – topped by the $425-a-night Irving Gill Penthouse, inexplicably decorated in Victoriana – with tranquil gardens and great service. It's close to the beach and art museum, too. ⑥

Empress 7766 Fay Ave ☎858/454-3001, ⓦwww.empress-hotel.com. A good range of rooms and suites at this centrally located property, where the larger units also have jacuzzis and there's internet access, continental breakfast, gym, spa and sauna. ⑦

Grande Colonial 910 Prospect St ☎1-888/530-5766, ⓦwww.thegrandecolonial.com. A 1920s landmark in the heart of La Jolla and a short walk from the cove. The cosy but elegant rooms have boutique furnishings and free wi-fi, and there's a handful of larger suites, and excellent package deals. ⑥

La Jolla Inn 1110 Prospect St ☎1-888/855-7829, ⓦwww.lajollainn.com. Charming lodge, well priced for the area, with ocean views (for a few dollars more), fridges, balconies, internet access and complimentary breakfast. The inn offers studios as well. ⑦

La Valencia 1132 Prospect St ☎1-800/451-0772, ⓦwww.lavalencia.com. This radiant pink favourite of Hollywood celebs in the 1920s is a slightly less glamorous spot today, but no less plush, with capacious rooms and suites and elaborate villas. All boast beautiful decor, nice amenities and good sea or garden views, plus there's an on-site pool, spa and fitness centre. ⑧

Parisi 1111 Prospect St ☎1-858/454-1511, ⓦwww.hotelparisi.com. Top-shelf boutique hotel with a New Age twist, offering feng shui design and rooms with balconies, designer furnishings, spas, CD and DVD players, and some ocean views. If all this luxury still doesn't relax you, there's a full complement of aromatherapy, acupuncture and meditation to properly align your chakras. ⑧

Hostels

Banana Bungalow 707 Reed Ave, Pacific Beach ☎858/273-3060 or 1-800/546-7835, ⓦwww .bananabungalow.com. See map, p.168. Friendly if scruffy place with beach access, offering volleyball, BBQ cookouts and a lively atmosphere. There's free breakfast, internet access and a communal kitchen too. Take bus #30 from Downtown then it's a five-minute walk. Dorm beds $20–25, rooms ❸

HI-Point Loma Hostel 3790 Udall St, Ocean Beach ☎619/223-4778, ⓦwww.sandiegohostels .org. See map, p.168. Well-run and friendly, located a few miles from the beach and six miles from Downtown. The hostel features a large kitchen, free breakfast, a patio and weekly bonfires. Dorm beds $20–31, rooms ❷

HI-San Diego Downtown Hostel 521 Market St at Fifth, Downtown ☎619/525-1531, ⓦwww .sandiegohostels.org. See map, p.175. Centrally located, especially good for the Gaslamp Quarter and Horton Plaza. Free breakfast and high-speed internet, plus a library, kitchen, and various organized trips to Tijuana and other places. Dorm beds $28–31, rooms ❸

Ocean Beach International Hostel 4961 Newport Ave, Ocean Beach ☎619/223-7873 or 1-800/339-7263, ⓦwww.californiahostel.com. See map, p.168. Lively spot a block from the beach, offering barbecues, bike and surfboard rentals, airport transport and nightly movies. Free wi-fi, sheets, showers and continental breakfast. Dorm beds $16–24.

USA Hostels – San Diego 726 Fifth Ave between F and G sts, Downtown ☎1-800/438-8622, ⓦwww.usahostels.com/sandiego/. See map, p.175. This well-placed hostel on the edge of the Gaslamp Quarter is a converted 1890s building, with six to eight beds per room. Sheets, breakfast and wi-fi included, plus organized tours to Tijuana, make this one of the city's best hostels. Dorm beds $28–31, rooms ❸

Campgrounds

Of the city's half-dozen **campgrounds**, very few accept tents. The best-placed of these is *Campland on the Bay*, 2211 Pacific Beach Drive (☎1-800/422-9386, ⓦwww.campland.com), where a basic site starts at $41, though larger, more elaborate sites with more amenities can run to $400. *Campland* boasts a number of pools and hot tubs, as well as a marina, activity rentals and a general store. For a more serene alternative, San Elijo State Beach, Route 21 south of Cardiff-by-the-Sea, offers fishing, hiking, swimming and wi-fi, and sites run from $35 to $55. For reservations, call ☎1-800/444-7275 or visit ⓦwww .reserveamerica.com.

The City

Like most other major cities in California, San Diego is set along a wide, curving bay, its climate among the most agreeable in the country and its atmosphere friendly and relaxed. Its hedonism is on display mainly at the beaches, and elsewhere there's a persistently conservative air. It shares with LA many of the same extremes of rich and poor, oceanside and inland, respectively, with most of the prime-time tourist draws on or within a few miles of the water.

San Diego divides into several easily defined sections, the most prominent of which is **Downtown**, where anonymous high-rise banks and hotels cluster around the epicentre of the Horton Plaza mall. There are older, often renovated structures from San Diego's earlier boom days in the **Gaslamp Quarter**, home to a number of worthwhile cafés and bars, making it the focus of the weekend party scene. A few miles northeast, the well-maintained oasis of **Balboa Park** contains many of the city's major museums, set in splendid Spanish Revival buildings from the 1920s, and the ever-popular San Diego Zoo, and is perfectly suited for strolls and picnics through acres of carefully tended gardens and natural greenery. Just northwest of Downtown, **Old Town** is a somewhat isolated enclave where the first white settlement developed near the site of the original San Diego Mission, an area now featuring an array of shops and theme restaurants intended to evoke the style of Old Mexico; it's easily accessible via trolley, and makes for a few good hours of wandering. Other districts near Downtown don't have any specific sights, but can be worth a visit nonetheless. The most prominent of these is **Hillcrest**, whose eclectic mix of yuppies, gays, bohemians and artists makes it one of the best areas for dining and nightlife.

If you're mainly interested in pure relaxation, simple beach-bumming or a golf-and-tennis weekend, the **seaside towns** are the obvious first choice; each of them, from **Ocean Beach** to **Pacific Beach** to **Mission Beach**, has its own style and social scene, but all boast the same appealing sands and waves, perfect for volley-ball, surfing and other sports throughout the year. Finally, the aquatic diversions of the **SeaWorld** theme park, within easy reach of Downtown, are good for a half-day trip – or longer if you really want to get your money's worth from the steep admission price.

Downtown San Diego

Loosely bordered by the arc of San Diego Bay and the I-5 freeway, **DOWNTOWN** is, for those not headed straight to the beach, the nexus of San Diego and the best place to start a tour of the city. Kick-started in the late 1970s, various preservation and restoration projects have improved many of the area's older buildings, resulting in pockets of stylishly renovated turn-of-the-century architecture, while there are numerous postmodern corporate towers left over from the boomtown Eighties and Nineties – giving the skyline a mildly dated look. Although Downtown is largely safe by day, at night it can be unwelcoming and deserted in spots. Unless you're with a local or someone who knows their way around, after-dark activities are best confined to the popular and well-policed Gaslamp Quarter.

Along Broadway

Broadway slices through the centre of Downtown and is most lively between Fourth and Fifth avenues, where the pedestrian traffic is a mix of shoppers, sailors, yuppies, homeless people and tourists. Although this is far from the free-spirited, somewhat chaotic strip of LA's Broadway (much less New York's), there are still a

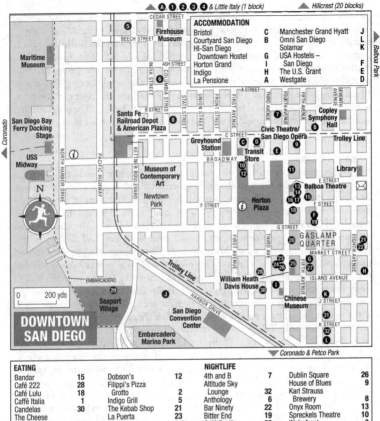

▲ A, 1, 2, 3, 4 & Little Italy (1 block) ▲ Hillcrest (20 blocks)

ACCOMMODATION

Bristol	C	Manchester Grand Hyatt	J
Courtyard San Diego	B	Omni San Diego	L
HI-San Diego		Solamar	K
Downtown Hostel	G	USA Hostels –	
Horton Grand	I	San Diego	F
Indigo	H	The U.S. Grant	E
La Pensione	A	Westgate	D

DOWNTOWN SAN DIEGO

0 — 200 yds

EATING				NIGHTLIFE			
Bandar	15	Dobson's	12	4th and B	7	Dublin Square	26
Café 222	28	Filippi's Pizza		Altitude Sky		House of Blues	9
Café Lulu	18	Grotto	2	Lounge	32	Karl Strauss	
Caffè Italia	1	Indigo Grill	5	Anthology	6	Brewery	8
Candelas	30	The Kebab Shop	21	Bar Ninety	22	Onyx Room	13
The Cheese		La Puerta	23	Bitter End	19	Spreckels Theatre	10
Shop	20	Las Hadas	24	Café Sevilla	25	Waterfront	3
Confidential	16	Rei Do Gado	11	Casbah	4		
Croce's	17	Taka	27	Croce's	17		
de' Medici	14	Upstart Crow	29	Dizzy's	31		

few points of interest here and there. From the west, if you roll into town by train or trolley, you'll be dropped off at the tall Spanish Colonial archways of the **Santa Fe Railroad Depot**, which were built to welcome visitors to the 1915 Panama–California International Exposition in Balboa Park.

The Museum of Contemporary Art and around

Adjacent to the depot, and partially located in its former baggage building, is the **Museum of Contemporary Art**, or MCA San Diego, 1001 Kettner Blvd (Thurs–Tues 11am–5pm; $10; ℗858/454-3541, ⓦwww.mcasd.org), which is the essential first stop for art in Southern California outside of LA. Its permanent collection focuses on American works, Pop Art and the indigenous art of Mexico, and also offers the usual mainline retrospectives of Abstract Expressionism, Minimalism, Conceptual Art and various other totems of modern art. But its temporary shows are the real draw, often involving irreverent imagery drawn from the intersection of pop-culture surrealism, ethnic subcultures and socioeconomic issues. The complex comprises two adjoining buildings: the depot's old halls,

175

preserved (if slightly altered) as the **Jacobs Building** – now showcasing various installation and multimedia pieces that would be too huge to display elsewhere – and the much newer metal, concrete and glass box of the **Copley Building**, which presents rotating exhibitions. (The museum also has a La Jolla branch; see p.190.) With the bayfront just to the west, the depot's old historic-revival architecture provides a dramatic contrast to the contours of the neighbouring **American Plaza**, a high-rise complex left over from the boom of the late twentieth century, which encompasses a central terminal of the San Diego Trolley. The plaza still has a certain chic, if dated, appeal, and is connected to One America Plaza, the city's tallest building at 34 storeys, with a rather drab postmodern look.

Horton Plaza

For livelier postmodernism, further east, many visitors linger around the fountains on the square outside **Horton Plaza**, between First and Fourth avenues south of Broadway (Mon–Sat 10am–9pm, Sun 11am–7pm), a giant mall of more than a hundred stores and San Diego's de facto city centre. Planned in 1977 and completed in 1985, Horton Plaza's quick success caused local real-estate prices to soar and condo development to surge, and gave shopping-mall developer **Jon Jerde** the green light to stamp his neon-bedecked, pop-art-flavoured design on malls across the country. The complex's whimsical style is inevitably a colossal tourist draw, and though there's nothing on the shopping front you won't find in every other American mall, the 21-foot-tall **Jessop Clock**, on level one, is the one inescapable highlight, an intriguing antique from the California State Fair of 1907. If the mall is the primary reason you came to San Diego, make a weekend of it by staying at the swanky *Westin* hotel within the complex.

On the eastern edge of the mall, the striking **Balboa Theatre**, 850 Fourth Ave (☎619/570-1100, ⓦwww.sandiegotheatres.org), is one of the city's marvellous old moviehouses and a gem of historic restoration, built in an appealing Spanish Revival style in 1924 and presenting a range of theatre, film, dance and music events. Further along, the **Central Library**, 820 E St (Mon & Wed noon–8pm, Tues, Thurs & Fri 9.30am–5.30pm, Sun 1–5pm), has an extensive reference section where you can pore over California magazines and newspapers. The functional site serves its purpose, though a flashy new Downtown library will open in 2013 near Petco Park, at 330 Park Blvd. Tucked away on the third floor, the **Wangenheim Room** (Mon–Fri 1.30–4.30pm) holds the fascinating collection of early twentieth-century patrician Julius Wangenheim. Among its many treasures are Babylonian cuneiform tablets, palm-leaf books from India, silk scrolls from China, and many more global curios documenting the history of the written word.

Little Italy and the Firehouse Museum

If you have plenty of time to explore, another interesting diversion is the **Firehouse Museum**, six blocks north of Broadway at 1572 Columbia St (Thurs & Fri 10am–2pm, Sat & Sun 10am–4pm; $3), which is situated in San Diego's oldest firehouse and displays firefighting equipment, paraphernalia and uniforms, as well as archaic hand-pumps, cranks and sirens, and photographs recalling some of San Diego's most horrific conflagrations and the horses and firefighters who had to battle them. The museum is located in the **Little Italy** district (ⓦwww.little italysd.com), one of the city's historic ethnic neighbourhoods, which today is mostly worth visiting for its restaurants and occasional festivals. The late-May Sicilian Festival (ⓦwww.sicilianfesta.com) and mid-October Festa are among the highlights – both featuring the spicy, delicious food of the Old World.

The Gaslamp Quarter

South of Broadway, the **GASLAMP QUARTER** occupies a sixteen-block area running south to K Street, bordered by Fourth and Seventh avenues. The core of San Diego when it was still a frontier town, the district – known then as **Stingaree** after a stingray found in San Diego Bay – was rife with prostitution, opium dens and street violence, a chaotic scene that played out beneath the wrought-iron balconies and Victorian gingerbread of the nineteenth-century piles lining the street. The area predictably decayed until its revitalization in the late 1970s under an intensive urban-renewal campaign, after which it started to mutate into the heavily tourist-oriented zone it is today, and the target for many visitors for after-hours drinking and debauchery.

What remaining flophouses and dive bars there are make a dramatic contrast with the nearby yuppie-centric cafés, antique stores and art galleries – all under the glow of ersatz "gas lamps" powered by electricity. There are any number of worthwhile restaurants, bars and clubs here to keep you occupied and well lubricated, and the district's relatively high police profile is designed to keep the area clean and safe, and to keep the tourists coming. The flow of visitors increases whenever there's a game at **Petco Park**, Seventh Avenue at Harbor Drive (Ⓦsandiego.padres.mlb.com), which has an attractive open-air layout that's done much to revitalize this part of Downtown and draws plenty of Padres baseball fans, but limited parking. If you're coming to a game, make an early trip on the Blue Line trolley that stops just outside – around game time it resembles a rail-bound journey into deepest tourist hell.

The William Heath Davis House

The square where the Gaslamp Quarter walking tour starts (see box below) is within the grounds of the **William Heath Davis House**, 410 Island Ave (Tues–Sat 10am–6pm, Sun 9am–3pm; $5; Ⓣ619/233-4692), whose owner founded modern San Diego and built his saltbox-style home here in 1850, believing that a waterfront location would stimulate growth (the fledgling city had previously been located a few miles inland and to the north – the site of Old Town San Diego; see p.183). Although Davis was initially wrong and swiftly had to leave the city, eventually dying penniless, the more influential Alonzo Horton (namesake of the city's signature mall) did manage to fulfil some of his goals for waterfront growth in later years. Copious with photographs, each room of the house commemorates a different period with its decor, and should be fascinating to anyone with an interest in Southern California history.

Architecture of the Gaslamp Quarter

The Gaslamp Quarter is intriguing to explore, not least for the scores of late nineteenth-century buildings – rich with period detail and styles from Eastlake to Queen Anne, with some Spanish Colonial and Baroque Revival touches as well – in various stages of renovation. Few are better than the grandiose **Louis Bank of Commerce**, 835 Fifth Ave, an eye-popping Victorian confection from 1888 replete with carved wooden-and-terracotta bay windows, a sheet-metal frieze across the front, and a pair of squat, colourful little towers on top. In its early years it was variously home to an ice-cream parlour, a brothel and an oyster bar run by Wyatt Earp. This classic building is best examined – and the area's general history gleaned – during a two-hour **walking tour** (Sat 11am; $10; Ⓣ619/233-4692, Ⓦwww.gaslamp quarter.org/tours). Beginning at the small cobbled square at Fourth and Island avenues, you'll hear about the exploits of gunslingers like Earp, the more colourful of the town's Victorian-era prostitutes, and other assorted miscreants who made Stingaree the dynamic town it once was.

The Horton Grand Hotel

Opposite the William Heath Davis House is the **Horton Grand Hotel** (see p.171), created in the mid-1980s by cobbling together two older hotels, the **Grand Horton** and the **Brooklyn Kahle Saddlery** – where Wyatt Earp lived for seven years in the early twentieth century. Dating back to the 1880s, the hotels were carefully dismantled and moved about four blocks from their original sites. In the lobby of the *Horton Grand*, the small **Chinese Historical Museum** (Tues–Sat 10.30am–4pm, Sun noon–4pm; $2; ℡619/338-9888, Ⓦwww.sdchm.org) is a reminder of the once-thriving Chinatown area, where railroad labourers and their families lived, and offers a series of artefacts, from household items to small sculptures to paintings and calligraphy, that give some sense of life in the era. The museum also hosts monthly **walking tours** of Asian-American history in the district, covering eight blocks (second Sat 11am; 1hr 30min; $2; same contact as museum).

Villa Montezuma

Half a mile east of the Gaslamp Quarter, at 1925 K Street, the site of **Villa Montezuma** (Ⓦwww.villamontezuma.org) is one of the more unusual entries on the National Register of Historic Places. Ignored by most visitors to San Diego, possibly due to its location, the villa is a florid show of Victoriana, with a rich variety of onion domes and all manner of loopy eccentricities. Known to some as the "haunted house", it was built for **Jesse Shepard** – composer, pianist, author and all-round aesthete – and financed by a group of culturally aspiring San Diegans in 1887. The glorious stock of furniture remains, as do many ornaments and oddments and the dramatic stained-glass windows. It's a place that well reflects Shepard's introspective nature and interest in spiritualism – he claimed that his musical gifts were a result of his "channelling" the spirits of great composers of the past. The Villa was closed for renovation at the time of writing; check the website for updates about its reopening.

The bayfront

The streets south of the Gaslamp Quarter are now occupied by expensive condos and the **San Diego Convention Center**, a $165-million complex with a sail-like roof resembling the yachts in the nearby marina. Continuing north along San Diego's appealing, curved **bayfront**, the pathway of the **Embarcadero** runs a mile or so along the bay, curling around to the western end of Downtown; along this stretch, the expansive green lawn of **Embarcadero Marina Park South** provides some summertime amusement in its concert series (see p.198). Although the route is favoured by strollers, joggers and kite-flyers, some tourists get no further than **Seaport Village** (daily 10am–9pm), a predictable array of trinket shops, mid-range boutiques and diners, though nothing worth detaining you more than half an hour. Beyond this, you can clamber aboard for a tour of the **USS Midway**, 910 N Harbor Drive (daily 10am–5pm, last admission 4pm; $18), which is permanently docked here to show off its formidable collection of naval hardware and weapons to the public. Although touring the innards of an old-time aircraft carrier may not be for everyone, for those with a taste for naval combat from World War II to the first Gulf War (the life cycle of the ship), the experience is a memorable one, enhanced by the presence of flight simulators and a handful of old-time planes parked at the site.

Other, much older, ships can be visited further north at the **Maritime Museum**, 1492 Harbor Drive (daily 9am–9pm, winter closes 8pm; $12; ℡619/234-9153), highlighted by a collection of nine boats such as the 1863 **Star of India**, the world's oldest iron sailing ship still afloat, which began its career hauling cargo and

▲ Hillcrest

**BALBOA PARK &
SAN DIEGO ZOO**

N

Zoo Entrance ⊠ ⊠

San Diego Zoo

PARK BOULEVARD

ZOO PLAZA

Spanish Village
Arts and Crafts Center

Botanical
Building

Natural History
Museum

Desert and
Rose Gardens

San Diego
Museum of Art

Sculpture
Garden

Globe
Theatres

Museum of Man

Timken
Museum of Art

◄ Hillcrest

E L   P R A D O

PLAZA DE
PANAMA

PLAZA DE
BALBOA

San Diego Art Institute

163

Mingei
International
Museum

ⓘ

House of
Hospitality

Casa de
Balboa

Reuben H. Fleet
Science Center

Palm
Canyon

Japanese
Friendship
Garden

Model
Railroad
Museum

Museum of
Photographic
Arts

San Diego
Historical Society
Museum

Spreckels Organ Pavilion
(Open Air Theater)

Marie Hitchcock
Puppet Theater

House of Pacific
Relations

Centro
Cultural
de la Raza

Automotive
Museum

PAN AMERICAN
PLAZA

Hall of
Champions

Air and Space
Museum

Gymnasium

Starlight
Bowl

0   200 yds

▼ Downtown

then working-class immigrants. Other vessels include the **Californian**, a modern replica of an 1847 cutter that served as a federal law boat patrolling the Pacific during the Gold Rush; the **HMS Surprise**, a replica of an eighteenth-century, 24-gun frigate, built for the film *Master and Commander*; and a creaky Soviet diesel submarine, the **B-39**, which was only decommissioned in the 1990s, well into the nuclear-sub era. On the *Pilot*, a 1914 commercial pilot boat, you can take a half-hour cruise on the bay for an extra $3 on top of museum admission; an excursion on board the *Californian* or yacht *America* will cost from $42 to $2100, depending on length of trip. Since most of these craft are seaworthy, some may be cruising around elsewhere when you come to visit; call ahead to make sure the boat you're interested in will be on view.

Balboa Park and the San Diego Zoo

A healthy walk away, less than two miles northeast of Downtown, the 1400 sumptuous acres of **BALBOA PARK** feature one of the largest collections of museums in the US, marked by a verdant landscape of trees, gardens, promenades and Spanish Colonial buildings – and of course, the ever-popular **San Diego Zoo**.

Balboa Park practicalities

Within easy reach of Downtown on **buses** #1, #3, #7 and #120, Balboa Park is large but fairly easy to navigate on foot – if you get tired, the free **Balboa Park tram** runs frequently between the main museum groupings and the car parks.

If you're planning on spending a lot of time in Balboa Park, the cheapest way to see the museums is to buy the $45 **Balboa Park Passport**, which allows admission to the park's fourteen museums and is valid for a week, although you can visit each once only. This passport, along with a $70 option that includes the San Diego Zoo, is available at all the museums and at the **visitor centre** (daily 9.30am–4.30pm; ☎619/239-0512, ⓦwww.balboapark.org), located in the **House of Hospitality** on the Prado. This is the best place to find information about each individual museum, and to buy the useful Balboa Park map and guide. If you're interested in a basic hour-long **tour** of the park, drop by the House on Saturdays at 10am, or for a more architecture-oriented journey, come by on the first Wednesday of the month at 9.30am; for a history and garden tour, visit at 1pm on Sundays and Tuesdays. All walks are free.

A desolate stretch of cacti and scrubland until 1898, the park began to take shape when one Kate Sessions began cultivating nurseries and planting trees in lieu of rent. The first buildings were erected for the 1915 Panama–California International Exposition, held to celebrate the opening of the Canal, and memories of its success lingered well into the Depression, until in 1935 another building programme was organized for the California–Pacific International Exposition. Five years later the park was in such sparkling condition that Orson Welles decided to film insert shots of Charles Foster Kane's monumental Xanadu enclave for the film *Citizen Kane*, and today the park's allure hasn't diminished much, making it one of the essential stops on any trip to Southern California.

Most of the major museums flank **El Prado**, the park's pedestrian-oriented east–west axis, which encompasses the charming Plaza de Panama at the heart of the park, and is best explored from the west via Laurel Street and the Cabrillo Bridge.

The Museum of Man and around

Approaching from the west, the first institution you'll come to will be the handsome neo-Baroque folly of the **Museum of Man** (daily 10am–4.30pm; $10), which, among other things, offers demonstrations of Mexican loom-weaving, replicas of huge Maya stones, interesting Native American artefacts, Egyptian relics, and bowls, toys, garments and other items from the Kumeyaay people native to the region. Just to the north, theatre buffs will want to drop in on **The Old Globe** complex (see p.201), which was built in 1935 for the exposition and now features a trio of theatres putting on plays by Shakespeare and other playwrights. Just across El Prado to the east, the **San Diego Art Institute**, 1439 El Prado (Tues–Sat 10am–4pm, Sun noon–4pm; $3; ☎619/236-0011, ⓦwww.sandiego-art.org), is a sporadically interesting venue for the works of its members, showcasing everything from pedestrian pieces by artists-in-training to unexpectedly fascinating mixed-media and curious installation art. New shows for regional artists open monthly. Next door, the **Mingei International Museum** (Tues–Sun 10am–4pm; $7; ☎619/239-0003, ⓦwww.mingei.org) has a rotating collection of folk art, featuring everything from jewellery from China to Mexico, to golden Kazakh artefacts, to functional pop sculpture in the form of vases, mugs and plates.

The San Diego Museum of Art

Adorned with fountains, the lovely **Plaza de Panama** is immediately adjacent, and on its north side lies the **San Diego Museum of Art** (Tues–Sat 10am–5pm, Sun noon–5pm; $12; ☏619/232-7931, ⓦwww.sdmart.org), with a heavily ornamented facade in the style of a Spanish cathedral. It's the main venue for any big shows that come through town – collections from Egypt, China and Russia (to name a few) that usually charge a $5–10 premium beyond the admission price. In the permanent collection, there's a solid stock of European paintings from the Renaissance to the nineteenth century, among them some lesser works by Giorgione, Veronese and Van Dyck; the highlights are some agreeable Rembrandts and Halses, and El Greco's charismatic *Penitent St Peter*. The biggest surprises are found amid the exquisitely crafted pieces in the Asian section, mainly from China and Japan but with smaller works from India and Korea. The **Sculpture Court and Garden** offers free exploration at any time, with a number of important works by artists like Henry Moore, Louise Nevelson, David Smith and Alexander Calder.

The Timken Museum of Art and around

Just to the east, the **Timken Museum of Art** (Tues–Sat 10am–4.30pm, Sun 1.30–4.30pm; closed Sept; free) stands out for its squat, drab, modern design. Most of the works – from the early Renaissance to the Impressionist era – are fairly minor. Still, portraits by Hals, David, Van Dyck and Rubens stand out, as does Rembrandt's moving incarnation of *St Bartholomew*, while Veronese's *Madonna and Child with St Elizabeth* is the highlight of the small Italian collection. More appealing for many will be the museum's stirring collection of Russian religious icons, showcasing the imposing wood-panelled *Last Judgment*, arranged in a strict, five-storey hierarchy like a business office for the afterlife.

North of the Timken Museum, the wood-ribbed **Botanical Building** (Fri–Wed 10am–4pm; free) dates back to the 1915 Exposition and features more than two thousand regional and tropical plants – making for a nice break from all the museums, along with the other seven themed gardens scattered throughout the park. On the south side of the Timken, the Spanish Baroque-flavoured **House of Hospitality** hosts the visitor centre (daily 9.30am–4.30pm; see box opposite).

Casa de Balboa

Just to the east, **Casa de Balboa** is home to three museums that are mainly of interest to enthusiasts. The **Museum of Photographic Arts** (Tues–Sun 10am–5pm, Thurs until 9pm; $8; ☏619/238-7559, ⓦwww.mopa.org) offers a fine permanent collection dating back to the daguerreotype and includes the work of Matthew Brady, Alfred Stieglitz, Paul Strand and other big names; rotating exhibits typically showcase the work of local and historical artists, with a bent toward popular culture.

The **San Diego Historical Society Museum** (Tues–Sun 10am–5pm; $5; ☏619/232-6203, ⓦwww.sandiegohistory.org) holds galleries that chart the booms that have elevated San Diego from scrubland into the seventh largest city in the US within 150 years, and the architectural and historical background of Balboa Park.

The **Model Railroad Museum** (Tues–Fri 11am–4pm, Sat & Sun 11am–5pm; $5) displays tiny, elaborate replicas of cityscapes, deserts and mountains, as well as the little trains that chug through them. Aficionados of miniature railways might also enjoy the park's pint-sized **antique railroad** that takes you on a half-hour trip around the grounds on open-air "rail cars" (Sat & Sun 11am–4.30pm, closes 6.30pm in summer; $2).

Around Park Boulevard

Continuing east, near the Park Boulevard end of El Prado, the **Reuben H. Fleet Science Center** (hours vary, often Mon–Thurs 9.30am–5pm, Fri & Sat 9.30am–8pm, Sun 9.30am–6pm; $10, kids $8.75, or $14.50 and $11.75 including an IMAX film; ☎619/238-1233, ⓦwww.rhfleet.org) presents an assortment of child-oriented exhibits of varying interest, loaded with flashing buttons, high-tech gizmos, wacky sounds and goofy effects, and focusing on the glitzier, more rudimentary aspects of contemporary science, as well as the IMAX theatre and motion simulator.

More impressive and appealing, though, is the **Natural History Museum**, on the north side of El Prado at its eastern end (daily 10am–5pm; $17), which features a great collection of fossils, a curious array of stuffed creatures, hands-on displays of minerals, and entertaining exhibits on dinosaurs and crocodiles. The more scholarly topics – such as the controversial links between birds and late-period, chicken-sized dinos – are interspersed with crowd-pleasing exhibits on menacing T-Rexes and other kid-friendly topics.

A short walk behind the Natural History building, the **Spanish Village Arts and Crafts Center** (daily 11am–4pm; free; ☎619/233-9050, ⓦwww.spanish villageart.com) dates from the California Pacific 1935 Expo and features the work of some three hundred craftspeople in three dozen different studios and galleries, where you can watch them practice their skills at painting, sculpture, photography, pottery and glass-working. If you continue north from here you'll find yourself at the gates of the San Diego Zoo (see opposite).

The Pan American Plaza and around

El Prado holds most of the park's highlights, and only if you have a significant amount of time (or are a car, aeroplane or sports enthusiast) should you venture further south, in the direction of **Pan American Plaza**. At the outset, the **Palm Canyon**, two acres holding some 450 palms, and the **Japanese Friendship Garden**, with the familiar bonsai, koi, and Zen garden, are pleasantly appealing, if missable, but the **Spreckels Organ Pavilion** (concerts Sun 2pm; free; ⓦwww.sosorgan.com) is definitely worth a look as the home of one of the world's largest pipe organs, with no fewer than 4500 pipes. Also compelling are the **Marie Hitchcock Puppet Theater** (Wed–Sun 11am, 1pm & 2.30pm; $5, kids $3; ☎619/544-9203, ⓦwww.balboaparkpuppets.com), in the nearby Pacific Palisades building, with lively productions involving fairy tales and ventriloquists, and the **Automotive Museum** (daily 10am–5pm; $8), offering a host of classic cars and motorcycles, from old-time Model Ts and fancy Rolls Royces to more obscure models like the 1912 Flying Merkle cycle and the 1948 Tucker Torpedo – one of only fifty left.

At the southern end of Pan American Plaza, the cylindrical **Air and Space Museum** (daily 10am–5.30pm, winter closes 4.30pm; $16.50; ☎619/234-8291, ⓦwww.sandiegoairandspace.org) showcases the history of aviation with seventy planes like the Spitfire, Hellcat, and the mysterious spy plane Blackbird; special exhibits can tack an extra $10 on to admission. Heading back north, on the west side of the Plaza is the **Starlight Bowl** (☎619/544-7827, ⓦwww.starlight theatre.org), a long-standing performance space for local operettas and musicals, while the **Hall of Champions** (daily 10am–4.30pm; $8) is a sports museum stuffed with memorabilia from baseball to skateboarding, mainly of interest if you have a thing for old jerseys, helmets and trading cards.

The San Diego Zoo

The **San Diego Zoo** (daily: mid-June to early Sept 9am–9pm; early Sept to mid-June 9am–5pm; one-day ticket $37, kids $27; ⊕619/231-1515, ⓦwww .sandiegozoo.org), immediately north of the main museums in Balboa Park, is one of the city's biggest and best-known attractions, and the premier zoo in the country. As zoos go, it undoubtedly deserves its reputation, with more than four thousand animals from eight hundred different species, as well as some pioneering techniques for keeping them in captivity: animals are restrained in "psychological cages", with moats or ridges rather than bars. It's an enormous place, and you can easily spend a full day or more here, checking out major sections devoted to the likes of chimps and gorillas, sun and polar bears, lizards and lions, flamingos and pelicans, and habitats such as the rainforest. There's also a **children's zoo** in the park, with walk-through birdcages and an animal nursery. Take a **guided bus tour** early on to get an idea of the layout, or survey the scene on the vertiginous **Skyfari**, an overhead tramway (both rides included in admission price). Bear in mind, though, that many of the creatures get sleepy in the midday heat and retire behind bushes to take a nap. Moreover, the giant **pandas** Bai Yun, Gao Gao and four others spend a lot of time sleeping or being prodded by biologists in the park's Giant Panda Research Station.

Regular **admission** covers entry to the main zoo and children's zoo, while a $70 ticket (kids $50) also admits you to the San Diego Zoo Safari Park near Escondido (see p.209). Truly motivated tourists will enjoy all of the above, as well as admission to SeaWorld (see p.189), for the rather staggering sum of $121 (kids $99).

Hillcrest

North of Downtown and on the northwest edge of Balboa Park, **Hillcrest** is a lively and arty area, thanks to the wealthy liberals who've moved into the district in recent decades and the general sprucing-up of the place. Altogether, it feels rather more disconnected from the culture of San Diego in a way that, say, Haight-Ashbury in San Francisco or West Hollywood in LA do not. Perhaps its most familiar local characteristic is as the centre of the city's **gay community**, with a handful of gay-oriented hotels (see p.171) and some colourful street life around University and Fifth, where the district's signature sign is prominently displayed. Hillcrest also has a cache of interesting cafés and restaurants (see p.194) and an appealing collection of Victorian homes. Among these, and the only conventional "attraction" in the area, is the **Marston House**, 3525 Seventh Avenue (Fri–Sun 10am–5pm; $8), a 1905 Craftsman charmer whose rustic Arts and Crafts design little resembles the later modernist work of its co-architect Irving Gill. Nonetheless, it has a warmly elegant late-Victorian feel, and is well worth a look for anyone with an interest in houses of the era.

Old Town

Old Town State Historic Park, or just **OLD TOWN**, commemorates San Diego from the 1820s through the 1870s. Featuring 25 structures, some of them original **adobes**, this is one of the core historic sites of the region. In 1769, Spanish settlers chose what's now **Presidio Hill** as the site of the first of California's missions. After their military service, as the soldiers began to leave the mission and the presidio, or fortress, they settled at the foot of the hill. This settlement was the birthplace of San Diego, later to be administered by Mexican officials and afterwards by migrants from the eastern US. The area was preserved in 1968 and is still a good place to get a sense of the city's Hispanic roots away from its modern high-rises.

Old Town practicalities

Old Town is somewhat out in the middle of nowhere, isolated from anything else worthwhile in town. Luckily, eight **bus lines** connect with it (see p.166) and the Blue Line trolley and Coaster **trains** from Downtown make the place conveniently accessible; **by car**, take I-5 and exit on Old Town Avenue, following the signs. Alternatively, from I-8 turn off onto Taylor Street and left onto Juan Street; signs should prevent any confusion.

The old buildings themselves are generally **open** 10am to 5pm and free (exceptions are noted below), though state budget cuts have made the hours for some buildings more erratic – call ahead if there's something you really want to see. Most things in the park that aren't historical – the stores and restaurants – open around 10am and close at 9 or 10pm. Though rife with tacky gift shops in places, the park is enjoyable enough on a Sunday afternoon, with occasional free Latin music and folk dancing. As for **food**, several stalls serve fresh tortillas, and there are various Mexican restaurants that are well worth a try (see p.194).

The best time to be here is during the afternoon, when you can enter the more interesting adobes with an excellent, free **walking tour**, leaving at 11am and 2pm from the **visitor centre** (daily 10am–5pm; ☏619/220-5422, ⓦwww.oldtownsand iegoguide.com or www.oldtownsandiego.org), located inside the **Robinson-Rose House**, a replica of a lawyer's 1853 home, which also housed a newspaper and railroad office.

Exploring Old Town

A number of the historic structures in the park are well preserved and display many of their original furnishings. One of the more significant structures is the **Casa de Estudillo** on Mason Street, built by the commander of the presidio, José Maria de Estudillo, in 1827, and inherited by his son, the city treasurer and tax assessor. The chapel in this most elaborate of the original adobes served as the setting for the wedding in Helen Hunt Jackson's overblown, though highly influential, romance about early California, *Ramona*. Next door, the **Casa de Bandini** was the home of the politician and writer Juan Bandini and acted as the social centre of San Diego during the mid-nineteenth century. After the United States took control of California, the house became the **Cosmopolitan Hotel**, considered among the finest in the state, its many elegant period appointments still visible in the dining room; the site later became a grocery, pickle cannery and Mexican restaurant. Of somewhat less appeal are the **San Diego Union Building**, showing the 1868 print room and editor's office, where the city's newspaper began in 1868, and the **Seeley Stables**, the reconstruction of a stable and barns for an 1880s stage line to LA, which houses various carriages and buggies left over from the era. The **Wells Fargo History Museum** (daily 10am–5pm; free), one in the bank's national chain of Wild West museums, showcases some old telegraphs, an overland coach, and assorted coins, maps and assay supplies – housed in the Colorado House, a replica of an 1851 hotel and saloon.

The Thomas Whaley Museum and around

Just beyond the park gates at 2476 San Diego Ave, the **Thomas Whaley Museum** (summer daily 10am–10pm; rest of year hours vary; $6, $10 after 7pm) was the first brick building in California and the home of Thomas Whaley, a New York entrepreneur drawn by the Gold Rush. It displays furniture and photos from his time, as well as a reconstruction of a courtroom from 1869, when the building housed the county courthouse. Oddly enough, the place has been officially stamped by the US Department of Commerce as haunted, possibly by one of the occupants of the neighbouring **El Campo Santo Cemetery**. Once the site of public executions, it contains tombs that read like a Who's Who of late nineteenth-century San Diego, though the cemetery (Spanish for "holy field") is most renowned for being haunted by the ghost of "Yankee Jim" Robinson, hanged in 1852 by a kangaroo court for the "capital crime" of stealing a rowboat. More crime is on display around the corner at the **Sheriffs Museum** (Tues–Sat 10am–4pm; free), which starts its timeline in the early American period and continues to the present day, showing the way in which county law enforcers have acted to control street crime with guns, batons and helicopters, and the response of criminals with guns, knives and brass knuckles.

Heritage Park

Just north on Juan Street, **Heritage Park** is a collection of several Victorian buildings, gathered from around the city and preserved. They're now mostly shops and offices, and include the agreeable 1889 **Temple Beth Israel** and a few cottages and Victorian structures that were once home to the town sheriff, the doctor, and a cousin of General Sherman. The view of the harbour from the park is worth the climb, as is the walk along Conde Street, which lets you peer into the atmospheric, sculpture-filled interior of the **Old Adobe Chapel**, dating from the 1850s, used as a place of worship until 1917 and restored twenty years later.

The park presents regular **"living history"** exhibitions, when docents appear in period clothing, and often in period character, to discuss the various aspects of the early town. Some of their historic jobs and activities are demonstrated: anything from hammering horseshoes in a blacksmith's shop to printing the newspaper to making coffins. Events are more common in the summertime (often Wed & Sat 10am–4pm); contact the visitor centre (see box opposite) for information.

Presidio Hill

The Spanish Colonial building that now sits atop **Presidio Hill** is only a 1929 approximation of the original 1769 mission – moved in 1774 – but contains the intriguing **Junípero Serra Museum**, 2727 Presidio Drive (Sat & Sun 10am–5pm; $5; ☎619/297-3258), which holds Spanish furniture dating back to the sixteenth century, along with weapons, diaries and documents pertaining to the leading Catholic missionary of California. The museum also lionizes the yeoman struggles of a few devoted historians to preserve the area's Spanish past in the face of dollar-hungry developers. The **Mormon Battalion Memorial Visitor Center**, nearby at 2510 Juan St (daily 9am–9pm; free), presents artefacts, paintings and multimedia about the 500-troop, 2000-mile saga of the Mormon Battalion March during the Mexican–American War – the longest US military infantry march in history, slogging more than halfway across the continent from Council Bluffs, Iowa, to San Diego.

Mission Basilica San Diego

Outside the Serra Museum, the striking **Serra Cross** serves as a modern marker on the site of the original 1769 mission. To find the later site of the mission, you'll need to travel six miles north to 10818 San Diego Mission Rd, where the **Mission Basilica San Diego de Alcalá** (daily 9am–4.45pm; donation; ☎619/283-7319, ⦿www.missionsandiego.com) was relocated in 1774 to be closer to a water source and fertile soil and further from conflict with Native Americans – which still didn't prevent Padre Luis Jayme, California's first Christian martyr, from being clubbed to death a year later. Though most of the mission site was fully reconstructed in 1931, the church dates from 1813 and still hosts a working parish, offering confession, weddings, baptisms and daily masses.

Walk through the dark and echoey church – the fourteenth-century stalls and altar were imported from Spain – to the **garden**, where two small crosses mark the graves of Native American neophytes, making this California's oldest cemetery. A small **museum** holds a collection of Native American crafts and articles from the mission, including the crucifix held by Junípero Serra at his death in 1834. Despite claims that his missionary campaign was one of kidnapping, forced baptisms and virtual native slavery, Serra was summarily beatified in 1998 during a Vatican ceremony.

The beaches

For many visitors, San Diego's renowned **beaches** are reason alone to visit. If you're after seclusion, you've come to the wrong place, but the beaches do live up to their reputation for top-notch sunbathing, surfing and swimming, and if you have any other aim you'll probably be disappointed – unless, of course, you're here for SeaWorld.

Directly southwest of Downtown across San Diego Bay, **Coronado** is a plush, well-heeled settlement, best known as the site of a large naval base and a famous resort hotel. Just beyond, and much less upscale, **Imperial Beach**'s chief draw is simply the peace of its sands, and, if you have an equestrian bent, its nearby horse-riding trails.

Across the bay to the north, the rugged **Point Loma Peninsula** marks the entrance to San Diego Bay, with oceanside trees along its spine and a craggy shoreline often dotted by easily explored tide pools – though offering little opportunity for sunbathing. **Ocean Beach**, further north at the end of the I-8 freeway, was once known to be quite freewheeling, though its hedonism has diminished in recent decades. Some of Ocean Beach's former vitality has migrated to **Mission Beach**, eight miles northwest of Downtown, and the adjoining, and slightly more salubrious, **Pacific Beach** – "PB" – linked by a beachside walkway. Both towns make up a peninsula that provides the western edge of **Mission Bay**, known best as the site of the colossal tourist draw of **SeaWorld**, several miles inland. To see the area at its most chic, travel a few miles further north up the coast to **La Jolla**, whose coastline of caves and coves is matched by short, clean streets lined with coffee bars, art galleries and a stylish art museum.

Coronado

Across San Diego Bay from Downtown, the bulbous isthmus of **CORONADO** is a well-scrubbed resort community with the **North Island Naval Air Station** at its western end, which encompasses a group of eight US military facilities – one of the reasons you're apt to see so many sailors and soldiers in town. Although Coronado has an interesting, vaguely New England air, with an assortment of cosy "saltbox" houses, the town is of limited interest, save for a historic hotel and the long, thin beach – a natural breakwater for the bay – that runs south. Although you could trek way down to the base of the peninsula, a much simpler way to get here is on the **San Diego Bay ferry** (daily 9am–10pm; $3.50 each way; ℡619/234-1111, ⓦwww.sdhe.com), which leaves Broadway Pier on the hour, returning on the half-hour. Tickets are available on the pier at **San Diego Harbor Excursion**, 1050 N Harbor Drive, which offers many other cruises, including a water taxi around the bay ($7), one- to two-hour harbour cruises ($20–25) and whale-watching expeditions ($30–35). From the ferry landing on First Street, shuttle bus #904 runs the mile up Coronado's main street, Orange Avenue, to the *Hotel del Coronado*; alternatively, use bus #901 from Downtown, which also runs to Imperial Beach. By road, you cross the two-mile-long **Coronado Bridge**, its struts decorated with enormous murals depicting Hispanic life, best seen from the park under the bridge in the district of Barrio Logan.

The town of Coronado grew up around the **Hotel del Coronado**, 1500 Orange Ave (see p.172), a Victorian whirl of turrets and towers erected as a health resort in 1888. Using Chinese labourers who worked round-the-clock shifts, the hotel was built to appeal to well-heeled enthusiasts of healthy living, as well as rich hypochondriacs. Through the lobby and courtyard, a small basement **museum** (free) details the history of the "Del", including its most notable moment, when Edward VIII (then Prince of Wales) met Coronado housewife Wallis Warfield Simpson here in 1920, which eventually led to their marriage and his abdication of the British throne. Also not to be missed is the tablecloth signed by Marilyn Monroe and the rest of the cast who filmed Billy Wilder's *Some Like It Hot* here in 1958, when it doubled as a ritzy Miami Beach resort. Outside are the sands upon which Monroe memorably flirted with Tony Curtis as he pretended to be a yachting playboy with a Cary Grant accent. Somewhat less memorably, the hotel was the site of the 1980 cult film *The Stuntman*, starring Peter O'Toole. A guided, hour-long historical **tour** (Tues 10.30am & Fri–Sun 2pm; $15) takes in many of these highlights as it wends its way around the hotel, beginning in the lobby. Reservations can be made through the **Coronado Visitor Center**, 1100 Orange Ave (Mon–Fri 9am–5pm, Sat & Sun 10am–5pm; ⊤619/437-8788, Ⓦwww.coronadovisitorcenter.com), which also provides much useful information on the area.

The centre is on the same site as the **Coronado Museum of History and Art** (Mon–Fri 9am–5pm, Sat & Sun 10am–5pm; $4; Ⓦwww.coronadohistory.org), with displays chronicling the town's early pioneers and first naval aviators, as well as its history of yachting, architecture and ferries. For a look at the historical and architectural importance of the buildings in town, the museum offers hour-long **tours** (Wed 2pm; $10; call the Visitor Center to book).

Silver Strand State Beach to the Mexican border

Heading south from the *Hotel del Coronado* (bus #901), follow Silver Strand Boulevard to the seven-mile-long isthmus of the **Silver Strand**, some of which is given over to military training facilities, at least until you come to **Silver Strand State Beach** (daily 8am–dusk), a pleasant spot to rollerblade or bike, or get into the local spirit by surfing or jet skiing. There are camping facilities, but for RVs only ($35 per night). At the end of Silver Strand Boulevard, **Imperial Beach** is a full half-hour south of Downtown San Diego, nearly at the Mexican border at the far southwest corner of the US. It offers excellent conditions for surfing, and is the site of the **US Open Sandcastle Competition** (late July; 9am–4pm; free; Ⓦwww.usopensandcastle.com), one of the nation's largest such events, where you're apt to see anything from sea monsters and fairytale figures to sandy skyscrapers and the face of Elvis – at least until the next high tide. Also worth a look is the beachside **farmers' market** near the pier, 10 Evergreen St (April–Oct Fri 2–7.30pm; Nov–March Fri 1–6pm), which has a good array of produce and children's activities on offer. Nearby **Border Field State Park** (daily 9.30am–5pm; ⊤619/575-3613) was named for the place where surveyors from the US and Mexico agreed on an international boundary after their war in 1848; the site is commemorated with a memorial and monumental column at **Friendship Park**

(Ⓦwww.friendshippark.org), which ironically has recently been walled off with the creation of a second international boundary fence. To gain access to the site that claims to honour US–Mexican fraternity, you must have government-issued ID and not get too close to the inner fence that divides the two countries.

To return to Coronado from Imperial Beach, take bus #901; to head back to San Diego, take bus #933 or #934 to the Blue Line trolley and head north through dreary Chula Vista and National City.

Ocean Beach

Ruled by the Hell's Angels in the 1960s, **OCEAN BEACH**, six miles northwest of Downtown via bus #35 or #923, is a fun and relaxed beach town that big-moneyed interests have been trying to develop for decades, with limited success. While the single-storey adobe dwellings that were home to several generations of Portuguese fishing families as recently as the 1980s have virtually disappeared, the odour of overdevelopment has otherwise been kept at bay, at least near the shore, where a 30ft building height limit does much to keep things under control. Indeed, the quaint, old-time streets and shops near the coast have preserved some of their ramshackle appeal and funky character. The two big hangouts include the main drag of **Newport Street**, where backpackers populate the snack bars, surf and skate rental shops, and other San Diegans come for the myriad antique malls, and **Voltaire Street**, which, true to its name, has a good range of independent-minded local businesses. There is often good surf, and the beach itself can be quite fun – especially at weekends, when the local party scene cranks up. Ocean Beach has one of the state's longest **piers**, at 2000ft, meant mainly for fishing and strolling. Where Voltaire Street meets the waves, you can visit Ocean Beach's other major attraction, **Dog Beach**, the only sand-strip in the area where pooches are allowed to frolic without leashes – great for canines, if not necessarily for small children. South of the pier rise the dramatic **Sunset Cliffs**, a prime spot for twilight vistas, though notoriously unstable – more than a few people have tumbled over the edge following an afternoon of excess on the beach.

Point Loma

South of Ocean Beach, the hilly green peninsula of **POINT LOMA** is mostly owned by the US Navy, which keeps it attractive, unspoiled and largely inaccessible. To get here from Downtown, take bus #28. After a long, tedious ride to the point's southern extremity, you reach **Cabrillo National Monument** (daily 9am–5pm; seven-day pass $5 per vehicle, $3 per pedestrian or cyclist; Ⓣ619/557-5450, Ⓦwww.nps.gov/cabr), the spot where captain Juan Rodríguez Cabrillo and his crew became the first Europeans to land in California in 1542, though they quickly reboarded their vessel and sailed off. In the American era, the site was recognized for its military value, and various abandoned gun emplacements and fortifications now dot the landscape, left over from the first half of the twentieth century.

The monument's startling vistas, across to Downtown and along the coast to Mexico, easily repay the journey here. After enjoying the view, you can explore the marine life in the many tide pools around the shoreline, reached on a clearly marked **nature walk** beginning near the monument. Also nearby, the visitor centre has information on the history and wildlife of the point, and lies near the **Old Point Loma Lighthouse** (daily 9am–5pm; free), whose historical tours lead you past replica Victoriana and equipment from the 1880s. The structure's main purpose was ultimately unfulfilled: soon after it was built, it was discovered that its beacon would be obscured by fog, and another lighthouse was erected at a lower elevation.

On the southwest-facing cliffs of the lighthouse, a sheltered viewing station with telescopes makes it easy to see the November-to-March **whale migration**, when scores of grey whales pass by on their journey between the Arctic Ocean and their breeding waters off Baja California.

Mission Bay and SeaWorld

Heading northwest from Downtown toward the coast (or along Sunset Cliffs Blud from Ocean Bay), you pass through a drab, cheerless zone – frequented by sailors for its strip clubs and by tourists for its cheap hotels – before reaching **MISSION BAY**, whose mud flats quickly become landscaped lagoons and grassy flatlands crowded with watersports fanatics. The long, circuitous walking and biking concourse that covers much of the 27 miles of shoreline is especially nice. The other source of Mission Bay's popularity is, of course, the formidable amusement park **SEAWORLD** (hours vary, often mid-June to Labor Day 9am–dusk; rest of year 10am–dusk; $69, children $59, parking $12; ℡1-800/257-4268, ⓦwww.seaworld.com), the San Diego branch of an entertainment colossus that stretches from California to Texas to Florida, which you can reach by taking SeaWorld Drive off I-5 or bus #9 (but not #9A) from Downtown. In spite of the steep entrance fee, SeaWorld is San Diego's most popular attraction for its undeniable kid-friendly appeal. Adults may find experiencing the local sea-life by whale-watching and snorkelling more rewarding, and a lot cheaper. The park's entry price demands that you allow a full day to make it worthwhile; for $121 (kids $99) you can also get admission to the San Diego Zoo (see p.183).

Highly regimented, SeaWorld has numerous exhibits and events, including the killer-whale shows that make up "Believe – the Shamu Show" (where you shouldn't sit in the first fourteen rows unless you're prepared to be soaked by belly flops from a high-flying orca) and "Shamu Rocks!", an unfortunate pairing of whales with flashing lights and rock music; and various seal and dolphin shows that seem a bit less threatening. Elsewhere, "Forbidden Reef" is stocked with moray eels and stingrays; "Wild Arctic" has walruses, beluga whales and polar bears; "Shark Encounter" features sharks circling menacingly around visitors walking through a submerged viewing tunnel; and there are assorted aquariums, tide pools and sites devoted to penguins, flamingos and catfish. Some of the park's other attractions, however, have devolved into the sort of standard-issue theme-park fare that includes the likes of giant-inner-tube rides, motion simulators and sky trams – if you've come here for this sort of diversion, you're better off just sticking to Disneyland.

Mission Beach and Pacific Beach

The biggest-name public beaches in San Diego are **MISSION BEACH**, the peninsula that separates Mission Bay from the ocean, and its northern extension, **PACIFIC BEACH**. If you aren't up for sunbathing, you can always nurse a beer at one of the many beachfront bars while observing the toasty sands overrun with scantily clad babes and surfboard-clutching dudes. Or you could rollerblade or bike down **Ocean Front Walk**, the concrete boardwalk running the length of both beaches, and the fastest way to travel when summer traffic is bumper-to-bumper on Mission Boulevard.

After much effort, city authorities have mostly succeeded in curbing the hedonism and drunken debauchery long associated with this classic slice of

Southern California beachlife. The family-friendly highlight is **Belmont Park**, near the southern end of Ocean Front Walk at 3146 Mission Blvd (hours vary, often Mon–Thurs 11am–8pm, Fri–Sun 11am–10pm; most rides $2–6, or full park pass for $20; ☎858/228-9283, ⓦwww.belmontpark.com). The two main attractions, both from 1925, are the **Giant Dipper** rollercoaster, one of the few of its era still around, and the **Plunge**, once the largest saltwater plunge in the world, and the setting for famous celluloid swimmers Johnny Weismuller and Esther Williams. Of the newer draws, **FlowRider** ($20 per hour) is a simulated-wave pool that allows you to get a vague sense of what surfing and wakeboarding are like without having to venture into the ocean, while the more intense **FlowBarrel** ($40 per hour) is a 10ft-high wave, for people who have a little more familiarity with actual surf. Beyond the main draws, the park offers an assortment of lesser carnival thrills, trinket stores, a pricey fitness centre and countless seaside snack joints.

Following Mission Boulevard north, you cross from the spirited amusements of Mission Beach into the more sedate Pacific Beach, where expensive oceanside homes with tidy lawns suggest haute-bourgeois refinement, though there's still plenty to enjoy and the district is the best place to stay of the San Diego beach towns (see p.172). The beach around Crystal Pier is a decent spot to lie in the sun, while **Garnet Avenue**, running inland from the pier, is lined by funky eating joints, bars and clubs. For many, though, Pacific Beach is synonymous with **surfing**, and is one of the prime strips of coastline in the area specifically marked for it. A mile north of the pier, **Tourmaline Surfing Park**, La Jolla Boulevard at Tourmaline Street (☎619/221-8900), or "Turmo", is regularly pounded by heavy waves and is reserved exclusively for the sport, as well as for windsurfing – no swimmers are allowed. If you don't have a board, a good alternative is a few miles north, **Windansea Beach**, a favourite surfing hotspot that's also fine for swimming and hiking alongside the oceanside rocks and reefs.

La Jolla and around

"A nice place – for old people and their parents", wrote Raymond Chandler of **LA JOLLA** (pronounced "la hoya") in the 1950s, though that didn't stop him from moving here (his former house is at 6005 Camino de la Costa) and setting much of his final novel *Playback* in the town, renaming it "Esmeralda". Since then, La Jolla has been infused with new money, and its opulence is now less stuffy and more welcoming. The main section, around Prospect Street and Girard Avenue, has spotless pavements flanked by crisply trimmed grass, and the many upscale art galleries sit alongside chic cafés and swanky boutiques.

The Town

Although it's fairly expensive, La Jolla is worth a visit at least once to savour the elegance of the place – don't miss the ornate pink **La Valencia Hotel**, 1132 Prospect St, frequented by Hollywood's elite in the Thirties and Forties (see p.173). On a quieter section of the same thoroughfare, the La Jolla site of the **Museum of Contemporary Art**, 700 Prospect St (Thurs–Tues 11am–5pm; $10; ☎858/454-3541, ⓦwww.mcasandiego.org), has a huge, rotating stock of works from 1955 onwards. Minimalism, Pop Art and California works are in evidence, bolstered by strong temporary shows involving installations, sculpture and multi-media – ultimately a collection of work no less daring or fascinating than that presented by the museum's Downtown counterpart. There is also an outdoor **sculpture garden**, with fabulous views of the Pacific surf crashing against the rocks below the building's huge windows.

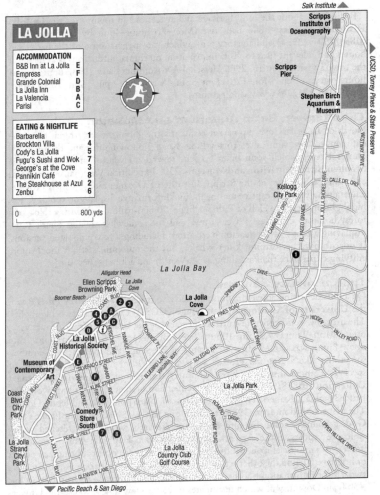

The museum building was once the home of **Ellen Scripps**, a local philanthropist who injected her seemingly endless wealth into La Jolla through the first half of the twentieth century. She commissioned early-modernist architect Irving Gill (who built several distinctive buildings in La Jolla and San Diego, including the Marston House; see p.183) to design her house, and today the Scripps name is still almost everywhere, notably in the tasteful **Ellen Scripps Browning Park**, on the seaward side of the museum, where the fine views and grassy layout ensure its popularity as a wedding location. Where the park meets the coast is the start of **La Jolla Cove** (daily 9am–dusk), a craggy and beautiful expanse marked off as an ecological reserve, whose clear waters make it perfect for snorkelling or scuba diving. However, surfing is banned, and you should keep your hands off the officially protected aquatic flora and fauna, no matter how enticing it looks. One problem, however, is access: parking spaces can be notoriously difficult to find in high season.

To find out about the local heritage and attractions in town, visit the **La Jolla Historical Society**, 7846 Eads Ave (Mon–Fri noon–4pm; by appointment at ☎858/459-5335, @lajollahistory.org), which can suggest some of the better old houses and relevant sites to visit. Information on similar attractions is available at the town's **visitor centre**, 7966 Herschel Ave (summer daily 10am–6pm; winter hours vary, often Mon–Fri 11am–5pm, Sat 10am–6pm, Sun 10am–4pm; ☎619/236-1212, @www.sandiego.org).

The Stephen Birch Aquarium and Museum

North of La Jolla Cove, upmarket residential neighbourhoods stretch from the cliff tops to the main route, Torrey Pines Road. Following this and then La Jolla Shores Drive, which soon branches left, several uneventful miles precede the **Stephen Birch Aquarium and Museum**, 2300 Expedition Way (daily 9am–5pm; $12, kids $8.50), part of the Scripps Institute of Oceanography, which provides entertaining views of captive marine life and informative displays on ecology. The highlights include the Hall of Fishes, a huge, 70,000-gallon tank with a thick kelp forest home to countless sea creatures, and the somewhat smaller Shark Reef, displaying a range of the fearsome creatures, including a few pint-sized versions. It doesn't have performing killer whales, but the museum is still a much more edifying experience than anything at SeaWorld, and a lot cheaper, too.

The university campus

On a hillside setting above the museum and also reached from Torrey Pines Road, the **University of California, San Diego (UCSD)** campus has two highlights. The first, the weird concrete-buttress spectacle of the **Geisel Library** (hours vary, often Mon–Thurs 7.30am–10pm, Fri 7.30am–6pm, Sat 10am–6pm, Sun noon–8pm), was named after the creator of Dr Seuss, and looks it – resembling something like a ziggurat crossed with a UFO. Elsewhere, there's a range of specially commissioned outdoor sculptures throughout campus in the **Stuart Collection** (☎858/534-2117, @stuartcollection.ucsd.edu), including works by Bruce Nauman, Robert Irwin, John Baldessari, Nam June Paik and Jenny Holzer. The first acquisition, from 1983, is still among the best: Niki de Saint Phalle's **Sun God**, a chunky, colourful bird on a concrete arch, whose outstretched wings welcome visitors to the car park opposite Peterson Hall, and which acts as the university's unofficial icon, routinely decorated in garish outfits during key events or holidays. To find the other sculptures, pick up a leaflet from one of the campus's two visitor information booths. Without a car, you can reach the campus on bus #30 from Downtown, which terminates its route a few miles away at the University Town Centre transport centre.

Torrey Pines State Preserve

As it leaves campus, La Jolla Shores Drive meets North Torrey Pines Road. A mile north of the junction, Torrey Pines Scenic Drive, branching left, provides the only access (via a steep path) to **Torrey Pines City Beach Park** – almost always called **Blacks Beach** – the region's premier, though unofficial, clothing-optional beach and one of the top **surfing** beaches in Southern California, known for its huge barrelling waves during big swells.

The beach lies within the southern part of the **Torrey Pines State Preserve** (daily 8am–sunset; no food or drink permitted; ☎858/755-2063, @www .torreypine.org), best entered a few miles further north, which protects the country's rarest species of pine, the Torrey Pine – one of two surviving stands. Thanks to salty conditions and stiff ocean breezes, the pines contort their ten-foot frames into a variety of tortured, twisted shapes that can be viewed at close quarters from the **Guy Fleming Trail**, a loop two-thirds of a mile long that starts near the beachside car park. The **visitor centre** (May–Sept daily 9am–6pm; Oct–April daily 10am–4pm) will tell you all about the pines, especially if your visit coincides with a guided nature tour (Sat & Sun 10am & 2pm). A three-quarter-mile **beach trail** leads from the centre down to Flat Rock and a popular beach, great for sunbathing and picnics, though no picnicking is allowed on the cliffs above the beach. Continuing beyond the preserve will lead you into the North County town of Del Mar (see p.203).

Eating

San Diego offers good **food** at reasonable prices, as well as places to push the boat out if you're feeling extravagant. Although the range isn't quite as wide as LA's, you'll find everything from old-time coffee shops and snack places (see p.196) to stylish restaurants to ethnic eateries at moderate prices.

Restaurants

Mexican food is much in evidence, especially in **Old Town**, while the **Gaslamp Quarter** has the greatest concentration of tourist-friendly restaurants and bars, which are especially crazy on weekend nights and heavy on the all-American food like ribs and burgers. **Little Italy**, on the northern fringes of Downtown, appeals for its handful of decent restaurants, and more bohemian **Hillcrest** has a number of spots to hang out and chow down. The **beach towns**, heavy on seafood and California cuisine, get more expensive the further north you go.

Downtown and Little Italy

See the map on p.175.

Bandar 825 Fourth Ave ☎619/238-0101. Tasty Persian place that tempts the palate with kebabs, lamb shank and stuffed grape leaves, as well as more inventive dishes like chicken tenderloin with barberry rice.

Cafè 222 222 Island Ave at Second Ave ☎619/236-9902. Hip café serving some of the city's best breakfasts and lunches, with excellent pancakes, French toast, and pumpkin-and-peanut-butter waffles, and inventive twists on traditional sandwiches and burgers (including vegetarian), at reasonable prices.

Candelas 416 Third Ave ☎619/702-4455. A Gaslamp Quarter restaurant offering pricey Mexican fare with inventive combinations of seafood and meat dishes with a California-cuisine influence – try the ceviche, prawns with sashimi, or Serrano ham-stuffed chicken breast.

Confidential 901 Fourth Ave ☎619/696-8888. Curious Gaslamp choice for tapas in a trendy modern setting; the small plates are intriguing, if pricey, from lobster-bisque "shooters" to honey-rum-glazed duck, to "deconstructed" pizza broken down to its bare elements. Essential for adventurous eaters.

Croce's 802 Fifth Ave ☎619/233-4355. Delicious choices such as rack of lamb, risotto and duck confit make this one of the pricier eateries in this area, and the Sunday jazz brunch is always a popular event; see also p.199.

de' Medici 815 Fifth Ave ☎619/702-7228. Upscale Italian fare that draws plenty of suits for the tasty Old World-style food such as scampi Vesuvio, langostino lobster, king crab legs, and saltimbocca.

Dobson's 956 Broadway Circle ☎619/231-6771. An elegant restaurant in an old two-tier building, loaded with business types in power ties. The cuisine leans toward Continental, from crab hash and oyster salad to flatiron steak and rack of lamb.

Filippi's Pizza Grotto 1747 India St, Little Italy ☎619/232-5094. A good spot for affordable favourites like thick, chewy pizzas and pasta dishes, including a fine lasagne. Meals are served in a small room at the back of an Italian grocery.

Indigo Grill 1536 India St, Little Italy ☎619/234-6802. Among the most upscale of Little Italy's restaurants, this one appeals for its experimental California cuisine like Indian corn pudding with squash and plantains, blueberry-glazed rack of lamb, jalapeño *pappardelle* and meringue "fire cake" – though main courses can be expensive at dinner.

La Puerta 560 Fourth Ave ☏619/696-3466. Cheap beers and good tequila provide the right refreshment for knocking back some of the city's best tacos, burritos and tortas, with a mean guacamole to boot. Inexpensive prices and a convivial atmosphere – and it's open till 1am daily.

Las Hadas 558 Fourth Ave ☏619/232-1720. Latin American favourite with a good range of affordable dishes, from ceviche and coconut shrimp to lobster taquitos and chipotle ribs. The carne asada fries are also a rib-stuffing treat.

Rei Do Gado 939 Fourth Ave ☏619/702-8464. Brazilian-style barbecue, delivered in a grand buffet atmosphere. You pick what you want from an array of meat skewers – piping hot and ready to devour.

Taka 555 Fifth Ave ☏619/338-0555. Excellent sushi and hot and cold appetizers – as well as sashimi and noodles – in a modern atmosphere with a fair mix of hipsters and families.

Hillcrest

Celadon 3671 Fifth Ave ☏619/297-8424. Quality mid-priced Thai eats at this local favourite, offering a mix of staples and more inventive fare – from spicy chilli rice and Bangkok summer salad to tasty "jungle" curry and red duck curry.

Crest Café 425 Robinson Ave ☏619/295-2510. If you're in the mood for cheap diner-style fare, this is the spot – with satisfying salads, burgers, pancakes and desserts. The salmon scramble, meatloaf and flatiron chimichurri steak are also worth a try.

El Cuervo Taco Shop 110 W Washington St ☏619/295-9713. Long-standing cheap and tasty Mexican joint that can hit the spot after a day at Balboa Park – featuring good carne asada, burritos and shrimp, as well as more exotic offerings like beef-tongue tacos.

Ichiban 1449 University Ave ☏619/299-7203. Altogether scrumptious Japanese cuisine, featuring good rolls, bento boxes, soups and sushi in a popular setting. The combo platters are well-priced, and the sushi's half-price during happy hour (Mon–Fri 3–7pm). Cash only.

Luche Libre 1810 W Washington St ☏619/296-8226. Mexican wrestling-themed taco house that's known for its fat burritos, stuffed with marinated shrimp, steak and avocado, chipotle steak and fries, and bacon-wrapped hot dogs – to make sure you get your full daily cholesterol dose.

🏃 **Marketplace Deli** 2601 Fifth Ave ☏619/239-8361. Just south of Hillcrest near the entrance to Balboa Park, this is a winner for its prime pizzas and sandwiches, and especially the Reuben, with pastrami, sauerkraut and cheese

on rye bread. Also offers good tuna melts and pasta salads, at easy-to-swallow prices.

Taste of Thai 527 University Ave ☏619/291-7525. Terrific Thai staples – spicy noodles, marinated shrimp, curry dishes and pad thai – for reasonable prices in the centre of Hillcrest; expect a wait at weekends.

Old Town

Berta's 3928 Twiggs St ☏619/295-2343. Solid south-of-the-border restaurant, offering well-priced, authentic cooking from all over Latin America. The affordable and tasty dishes include empanadas, seafood soups and paella.

Casa Guadalajara 4105 Taylor St ☏619/295-5111. Serviceable Mexican fare that includes a wide range of choices, such as grilled chicken, shrimp diablo and *mole* enchiladas. Moderately priced and open till 11pm at weekends.

Dos Brasas 1890 San Diego Ave ☏619/291-6527. This place won't do your arteries any favours, but for hefty, succulent burritos – for breakfast or otherwise – you could do a lot worse. Try the carne asada, chorizo burrito or Mexican cheeseburger.

Jack and Giulio's 2391 San Diego Ave ☏619/294-2074. Although not too many diners come to this part of town seeking Italian food, this comfy, affordable spot fits the bill for those who do. Take in the lasagne or gnocchi, or pay a little more for top-notch scampi, steak and veal.

🏃 **Old Town Mexican Café** 2489 San Diego Ave ☏619/297-4330. Among the better Mexican diners in Old Town, where the crowds queue up for the likes of pozole soup and carne asada tacos; apart from at breakfast, you'll probably have to wait for a table.

Coronado

Burger Lounge 922 Orange Ave ☏619/435-6835. Continuing the Southern California trend of nouveau burger joints, this spot offers grass-fed beef patties and the usual fries and rings to go with them, for around $10–12 a meal.

Chez Loma 1132 Loma Ave ☏619/435-0661. Aromatic and delicious selection of French cuisine, especially strong on old favourites, though with nouvelle influences too. Good for its roasted duck, sea scallops, lobster crepes and filet mignon tartare. Most main dishes are $25–30.

Miguel's Cocina 1351 Orange Ave ☏619/437-4237. Delicious fish (and swordfish) tacos, burritos, calamari rellenos and margaritas make this Mexican eatery worth seeking out. The related *Miguelito's*, 1142 Adella Ave in Coronado (☏619/437-8578), offers a similar menu.

Peohe's 1201 1st St ☎619/437-4474. One of Coronado's top choices for fine dining, a restaurant whose supreme bayside views of Downtown are matched only by its pricey but delicious bourbon pork chops, lobster tail, truffle risotto, Pacific fire shrimp and assorted steaks.

Primavera 932 Orange Ave ☎619/435-0454. Swanky and scrumptious Italian cuisine that's among the best in town. There's pasta and risotto for those a little lighter in the wallet and fine *ossobuco*, steak and lamb chops for the big spenders.

Tartine 1106 1st St ☎619/435-4323. Appealing French bistro that has a range of delicious sandwiches with prosciutto, gorgonzola, eggplant and more, along with soups, salads, and main dishes like duck, mussels and flatiron steak. Good desserts and breakfasts too – and all for affordable prices.

Ocean Beach and Point Loma

Hodad's 5010 Newport Ave, Ocean Beach ☎619/224-4623. In business in one spot or another for over 40 years, this is one place in town you can get a damn fine burger, whether it comes straight up or includes cheese, tuna or veggies. Fries and rings complete a meal at this cheap, very popular spot.

Old Venice 2910 Canon Ave, Point Loma ☎619/222-5888. Upscale, romantic atmosphere at this moderately priced café and bar. Great for pizza, pasta, seafood and salads – no real surprises here, just hearty Italian favourites.

Ortiz's Taco Shop 3704 Voltaire St, Point Loma ☎619/222-4476. Among the best tortas, burritos, enchiladas and tacos you're likely to find in a beach town, with cheap prices, authentic recipes and enough oomph to get you revved up for a day on the waves.

Point Loma Seafoods 2805 Emerson St ☎619/223-1109. Mid-priced counter serving up San Diego's freshest fish in a basket, with good platters and seafood cocktails, along with mean crabcake and scallop sandwiches. This justly popular joint is packed at weekends; don't even try to find an adjacent parking spot.

Ranchos Cocina 1830-H Sunset Cliffs Blvd, Ocean Beach ☎619/226-7619. A healthy, affordable joint with well-made staples like enchiladas, burritos and quesadillas – many combining Tex-Mex, Spanish and even Aztec elements. A number of vegan options, too. There's a second location, with an attached market, near Hillcrest at 3910 30th St (☎619/574-1288).

South Beach Bar and Grill 5059 Newport Ave #104, Ocean Beach ☎619/226-4577. A relaxed and friendly place known for its excellent fish tacos, including versions with mahi mahi, wahoo, shark and oysters, plus seafood tostadas, steamed mussels and other marine dishes.

Mission Beach and Pacific Beach

Enoteca Adriano 4864 Cass St, Pacific Beach ☎858/490-0085. Italian wine bar that, aside from its *primo vino*, happens to have terrific pasta as well, including gnocchi and *pappardelle*, and a redoubtable chicken saltimbocca, all for moderate prices.

The Fishery 5040 Cass St, Pacific Beach ☎858/272-9985. Good range of seafood for varying prices at this straightforward fish house, where you can get your fill of oysters, jumbo lump crabcake and ceviche tostadas, as well as shrimp or swordfish tacos.

Kono's 704 Garnet Ave, Pacific Beach ☎858/483-1669. A solid choice for breakfast or lunch on the boardwalk, with hefty portions of eggs, potatoes, toast and sandwiches, and especially plump burgers and burritos – all at affordable prices. Adjacent to Crystal Pier.

Sportsmen's Seafood 1617 Quivira Rd, Mission Beach ☎619/224-3551. For the serious fish-lover, this is a combo diner/market where the catch of the day is laid out before your eyes. A no-frills environment with cheap and delicious fare – highlighted by great fish'n'chips, cioppino (fish stew) and fish sandwiches.

World Famous 711 Pacific Beach Drive, Pacific Beach ☎858/272-3100. Lobster tacos, prime rib hash, crab and shrimp enchiladas, and bread-pudding French toast make this place a popular, affordable lunchtime spot, which also has solid breakfasts and decent pasta and steak dinners.

Zanzibar 976 Garnet Ave, Pacific Beach ☎858/272-4762. A great place to chill out, especially on the back patio, with inexpensive omelettes, pizzas, burritos, sandwiches, smoothies, coffees and desserts. Breakfast is served all day – a major plus.

La Jolla

See the map on p.191.

Barbarella 2171 Avenida de la Playa ☎858/454-7373. Eclectic eatery that serves up a hearty menu of omelettes and frittatas, pizza and pasta, risotto and seafood, and even burgers and fries. Justifiably popular with the swells as well as the proles.

Brockton Villa 1235 Coast Blvd ☎858/454-7393. Mid-priced California cuisine, featuring nice views of the ocean, and a good, changing menu, typically including seafood, rack of lamb, steak and pasta. Also features inventive choices for breakfast, like crab Ipanema with spicy coconut-tomato sauce and carne asada eggs Benedict.

Cody's La Jolla 8030 Girard Ave ☏858/459-0040.You can sit on the patio and catch a glimpse of La Jolla Cove at this innovative California cuisine spot, with good buttermilk pancakes, sage sausage, eggplant sandwiches and scrumptious burgers. A little more expensive than comparable breakfast-and-lunch spots, but worth it.

Fugu's Sushi and Wok 915 Pearl St ☏858/456-1414. Pan-Asian fare including expensive but tasty sushi and sashimi, and more hit-or-miss Chinese dishes such as Mongolian chicken and kung pao salmon, as well as affordable salads and bentos and a nice range of sake.

George's at the Cove 1250 Prospect St ☏858/454-4244. Longtime local favourite split into

three sections – the chic *Ocean Terrace*, with nice views and mid-range salmon, steak, pasta and seafood dishes; a bar and bistro with decent salads and sandwiches; and the pricey *California Modern*, with creative dishes such as lobster stew, halibut ceviche and duck breast with foie gras.

The Steakhouse at Azul 1250 Prospect St ☏858/454-9616. With magnificent views of the Pacific and a range of delicious steak and seafood, this supreme eatery provides one of the city's best, most evocative culinary experiences... which you'll be paying off for months to come.

Zenbu 7660 Fay Ave ☏858/454-4540. Hip, pricey sushi bar where you can enjoy delicious salmon rolls, sashimi and swordfish steak – as well as rolls like the "Jackie Chan", with crab, tuna and cucumber, and "Wind-N-Sea", an odd combination of eel, avocado and banana.

Cafés

Of the city's many decent cafés, Pacific Beach boasts the best selection, which, aside from the usual espresso drinks and pastries, may also offer wi-fi and quirky art on the walls, as well as snacks and light meals – sandwiches, pizza and deli favourites.

Café Lulu 419 F St, Downtown. See map, p.175. Hipster joint with eye-catching, mildly exotic decor, and hookah pipes (from $20). Also a good selection of coffees and late-night food at weekends.

Café Mono 3833 Mission Blvd, Mission Beach. A rare coffee joint that, along with delicious espressos and the rest, has excellent food as well, including great sandwiches and salads, tasty *gelato* and continental-style pastries.

Caffè Calabria 3933 30th St, Hillcrest. Serious coffee for serious coffee drinkers, with some fine espresso and French and Italian roasts from their own roasted beans, which you can also buy to take home. Also offers good pastries and panini.

Caffè Italia 1704 India St, Little Italy ☏619/234-6767. Sandwiches, salads and great coffee, espresso and desserts, including good *gelato*, served in a sleek modern interior or outside. Cash only.

The Cheese Shop 627 Fourth Ave ☏619/232-2303. Scrumptious deli sandwiches stuffed with different meats, from lamb to salami to pork loin. The roast beef and pastrami are good choices, as well as the old favourite grilled-cheese.

Claire de Lune 2906 University Ave, Hillcrest ☏619/688-9845. The prototypical coffee house, with good java, tea and sandwiches, comfy seating and occasional live music. No wi-fi, though.

The Eggery 4150 Mission Blvd, Mission Beach ☏858/274-3122. A coffee shop with imagination,

serving breakfast – omelettes, eggs Benedict, pancakes and other favourites – for decent prices, along with espresso and cocktails. Be prepared to wait at weekends.

Gelato Vero Caffè 3753 India St, at the southern end of Hillcrest. San Diego isn't known for its ice cream, but you can get it here – from *straciatella* to *tiramisú* to a bevy of fruit flavours – along with good espresso.

Jungle Java 5047 Newport Ave, Ocean Beach. If sipping espresso and munching on pastries while shopping for plants sounds like a good idea, this is the place for you – another of this city's quirky shops, with a good range of teas and coffees to go with your ferns and creepers.

The Kebab Shop 630 Ninth Ave ☏619/525-0055. Cheap Turkish joint that's a great place to get your fill of lamb, chicken and falafel kebabs, or enjoy a shawarma sandwich or some tasty rotisserie meat.

Pannikin Café 7467 Girard Ave, La Jolla. See map, p.191. Modest spot that feels warm and lived-in, where you can knock back a java, read the paper and enjoy a sandwich, with none of the attitude you might find elsewhere.

Upstart Crow 835 W Harbor Drive, Downtown ☏619/232-4855. See map, p.168. This coffee bar fused with a bookstore offers a lively cross-section of customers, great coffee, well-chosen reading material and free Saturday-night jazz performances.

Nightlife

San Diego has a respectable range of **bars** throughout much of the city, with the Gaslamp Quarter being a good place to get dressed up for cocktails or for pure sports-bar swilling, while the beach communities offer a more rowdy atmosphere, abetted by plenty of beer and loud music. Many bars put on a happy hour from around 4pm to 6pm to lure in the punters. Decent **clubs** are a bit harder to find – Hillcrest is notable for its gay-oriented spots (see p.202), while more chi-chi spots can be found in the Gaslamp.

When it comes to **live music**, San Diego has a number of good choices Downtown and in the Gaslamp, as well as a smattering along the coast. For listings, pick up the free *San Diego Reader* (Ⓦwww.sandiegoreader.com), buy the *San Diego Union-Tribune* (Ⓦwww.signonsandiego.com) or seek out the youth-oriented *Slamm/San Diego CityBeat* (Ⓦwww.sdcitybeat.com) at some of the live music venues listed below. **Cover charges** at venues range from nothing to $20, unless a big-name act is playing or a major DJ is spinning.

Bars

The Alibi 1403 University Ave, Hillcrest ☏619/295-0881. The place to hit when you just want to get drunk – a classic dive bar with potent drinks, pool tables, occasional live acts and grungy but cosy decor.

Altitude Sky Lounge 660 K St, at *Marriott Gaslamp Hotel*, Downtown. See map, p.168. With great views of Downtown, Petco Park and the bay, this rooftop bar is also good for knocking back colourful cocktails and lounging on the plush furniture with other out-of-towners.

Blind Lady Ale House 3416 Adams Ave, a few miles northeast of Hillcrest. This brewhouse is fantastic for its scrumptious pizzas and huge array of beers, from IPAs to porters, browns and bocks, with plenty of international labels thrown in too.

Coronado Brewing Company 170 Orange Ave, Coronado. A solid choice if you want tantalizing handcrafted brews with names like Hoppy Daze, Mermaid's Red Ale and Idiot IPA, served alongside basic pasta, seafood and burgers.

Counterpoint 830 25th St, south of Balboa Park. With its cheap happy hour (eg house wine $3) and wide selection of microbrewed beers, this is a chic choice for civilized drinking, and the tasty sandwiches, pizzas and snacks add to the appeal.

Dublin Square 554 Fourth Ave, Downtown. See map, p.168. Get your fill of leek soup, shepherd's pie and grilled potato "boxty" as you quaff Irish beer and spirits here. Even the breakfast steak is marinated in Guinness, and the chocolate cake is given a whisky boost.

Gallagher's 5046 Newport Ave, Ocean Beach ☏619/222-5300. Good-time Irish pub with plenty of high spirits, rib-stuffing food and regular live music and DJs, plus all your favourite Emerald Isle brews, whisky and cocktails – great after a day on the sands.

Karl Strauss Brewery & Grill 1157 Columbia St at B, Downtown. See map, p.168. Part of a local chain with a reasonable selection of hearty ales and lagers brewed on the premises, and an adequate array of bar food.

Kensington Club 4079 Adams Ave, Kensington District, north of Hillcrest ☏619/284-2848. "The Ken" – a great divey joint for beer, wine and cocktails, but also for wide-ranging live music, from thumping dance DJs to head-banging rockers.

Live Wire 2103 El Cajon Blvd, just east of Hillcrest. A great place to groove with the rocking jukebox and get hammered on imported and local beers. There's also pinball, pool, and a funky, sub-bohemian atmosphere to wet your whistle.

Red Fox Room 2223 El Cajon Blvd, just east of Hillcrest. This old-style piano bar with good steaks offers a merry, sloshy crowd of regulars and a convivial atmosphere that draws nostalgic types of all ages.

Sunshine Company 5028 Newport Blvd, Ocean Beach. A friendly neighbourhood joint within easy reach of the water that's good for sampling the spirit(s) of Ocean Beach, loading up on beer and bar food, and mixing with the surfer dudes and hipsters.

Waterfront 2044 Kettner Blvd. A mixed bag of working-class boozers and slumming hipsters are drawn to this old-time Little Italy joint for burgers, fish'n'chips and bar food, and a festive atmosphere. An essential stop to see the real drinker's San Diego.

Clubs

Bar Dynamite 1808 W Washington St, Mission Hills ☎619/295-8743. Located between Hillcrest and the airport, this is a good draw for house, hip-hop, reggae and other danceable beats, with a friendly, mixed crowd and less attitude than the Gaslamp clubs.

Bar Ninety 804 Market St, Downtown ☎619/550-5825. See map, p.168. In some ways a typical So-Cal scene, but not quite as posey as it can get in San Diego – offering fun, stylish decor, cheap drinks, adequate pub grub and sushi rolls, and regular DJs to get you moving.

Bitter End 770 Fifth Ave, Downtown ☎619/338-9300. See map, p.168. Three-storey venue in the Gaslamp, complete with lower-level dancefloor, martini bar, and upstairs VIP lounge, for the sophisticated poseur who doesn't mind paying a bundle for an appletini.

Café Sevilla 555 Fourth Ave, Downtown ☎619/233-5979. See map, p.168. Traditional Spanish cuisine and tapas upstairs, hip Latin American-style club downstairs, with salsa and Spanish dance grooves to dance to, and flamenco performances to keep you entertained.

Club Sabbat 3780 Park Blvd, east of Hillcrest ☎619/795-8578. Located in the *Flame* lounge, this twice-monthly club night sees a lively black-clad crowd moving to classic and modern dark beats – goth, industrial, darkwave and anything else that makes you want to crawl back to the thirteenth century.

Onyx Room 852 Fifth Ave, Gaslamp Quarter ☎619/235-6699. See map, p.168. Groovy bar with lush decor, where you can knock back a few cocktails, then hit the back room for live jazz and dance tunes. The chic lounge upstairs has pricier drinks and bigger attitudes.

Thrusters Lounge 4633 Mission Blvd, Pacific Beach ☎858/483-6334. Cosy bar and club where the hip-hop and dance beats come hard and heavy, and jazz and rock make occasional appearances as well.

Whistle Stop Bar 2236 Fern St, South Park ☎619/284-6784. Sited on the east side of Balboa Park, this hip and lively bar presents a wide range of theme nights, from weekend DJs to Sunday "knitting jams" to movie matinees.

Major venues

Copley Symphony Hall 750 B St, Downtown ☎619/235-0804, ⓦwww.sandiego symphony.org.

Cricket Wireless Amphitheatre 2050 Entertainment Circle, Chula Vista ☎619/671-3600, ⓦwww.livenation.com.

Embarcadero Marina Park South Off Marina Park Way near Seaport Village ☎619/659-5300.

Palomar Starlight Theatre At Pala Casino Resort on Hwy 76 ☎1-877/946-7252, ⓦwww.palacasino .com/entertainment.

San Diego Sports Arena 3500 Sports Arena Blvd, Mission Bay ☎619/224-4171, ⓦwww.san diegoarena.com.

Viejas Arena On San Diego State University campus, 5500 Canyon Crest Drive ☎619/594-6947, ⓦwww.as.sdsu.edu/viejas_arena.

Rock and punk

4th and B 345 B St, Downtown ☎619/231-4343, ⓦwww.4thandb.com. See map, p.168. One of the city's premier venues for metal, funk and hip-hop, with pretty good sightlines and atmosphere, and a mix of energetic up-and-comers and well-established old-timers.

Brick by Brick 1130 Buenos Ave, Mission Bay ☎619/675-5483, ⓦwww.brickbybrick.com. Aggressively cool lounge that's one of the better-nown indie spots around town, attracting a broad mix of indie rock, metal, hip-hop and burlesque acts.

Casbah 2501 Kettner Blvd, Downtown ☎619/232-4355, ⓦwww.casbahmusic .com. If you're up for a night of hipstering, this is a good spot to begin – a grungy joint that nevertheless hosts a solid, varying roster of blues, funk, reggae, rock and indie bands. Despite the cramped interior, it's popular with locals.

House of Blues 1055 Fifth Ave, Downtown ☎619/299-2583, ⓦwww.hob.com. See map, p.168. The heavyweight on the local concert scene, drawing big-name rock and pop acts. The environment's a little too well scrubbed – as are the bands – but you can sometimes see a good show here.

Ruby Room 1271 University Ave, Hillcrest ☎619/299-7372. Good-time lounge that serves up cheap brews in convivial company and presents the odd rock'n'roll or burlesque show.

Soda Bar 3615 El Cajon Blvd, several miles northeast of Hillcrest ☎619/255-7224. Sited in a dicey neighbourhood, but this modest lounge provides a sense of what's bubbling under the SD music scene, with all kinds of rock, punk, metal and oddball acts on view, plus karaoke.

Winston's Beach Club 1921 Bacon St, Ocean Beach ☎619/222-6822, ⓦwww.winstonsob .com. A former bowling alley turned semi-dive bar, this local club has rock bands most nights, with occasional reggae and comedy acts as well.

Pop, folk and eclectic

Bar Pink 3829 30th St, east of Hillcrest
℡619/564-7194, ⊛www.barpink.com. Loaded with pink elephant decor to the point of nausea, this lounge has nightly music ranging from hip-hop-spinning DJs and various local rockers and thrashers, to oddball art-music hybrids that make more sense once you've had a few cocktails.

Belly Up Tavern 143 S Cedros Ave, Solana Beach ℡858/481-9022, ⊛www.bellyup.com. Mid-sized hall that plays host nightly to an eclectic range of live music – anything from grizzled rockers to salsa spectaculars and tub-thumping DJs.

Humphrey's by the Bay 2421 Shelter Island Drive, Point Loma ℡619/220-8497, ⊛www .humphreysconcerts.com. Also including a restaurant, this mainstream concert venue draws a range of mellow, agreeable pop, blues, jazz, country, folk and lite-rock acts, often of national calibre.

Lestat's West 3433 Adams Ave, a few miles northeast of Hillcrest ℡619/282-0437, ⊛www .lestats.com. Connected to a 24hr coffee house, this performance venue presents nightly entertainment, from open mics and comedy showcases to indie rock, singer-songwriters and even belly-dancing. A must for fans of the eclectic.

Queen Bee's 3925 Ohio St, east of Hillcrest ℡619/255-5147, ⊛queenbeesd.com. The definition of eclectic, this all-ages venue hosts various rock and indie bands, but also offers tango and salsa classes, open-mic and rap nights, poetry and spoken-word shows, and arty performances that don't fit into a single category. Worth a look for the curious.

Spreckels Theatre 121 Broadway, Downtown ℡619/234-8397, ⊛www.spreckels.net. See map, p.168. Former moviehouse, now converted into an elegant venue for pop and lite-rock acts, as well as comedy, world beat, jazz, and speakers on popular topics.

Jazz and blues

Anthology 1337 India St, Downtown ℡619/595-0300, ⊛www.anthologysd.com. See map, p.168. Pricey supper club that also serves up tasty helpings of nightly jazz, blues and funk, with the occasional big bands, cabaret and over-the-hill rockers thrown in for good measure.

Croce's Jazz Bar 802 Fifth Ave, Downtown ℡619/233-4355, ⊛www.croces.com. See map, p.168. Classy jazz in the back room of a decent restaurant (see p.193), with a solid roster of traditional, cool and smooth acts, and occasionally more adventurous performers as well.

Dizzy's 344 Seventh Ave, Downtown ℡858/270-7467, ⊛www.dizzysjazz.com. See map, p.168. As the name suggests, this joint is devoted to straight-up jazz and little else – literally, because the place is as spartan as they come, forcing you to focus on the music instead of chatting over dinner and cocktails.

Performing arts and film

The **performing arts** in San Diego are represented by both provincial and national-quality venues, depending on the medium. **Theatre** is variable, but can often be quite good. While LA's huge talent pool of actors gives it a leg up on San Diego, the smaller city still can impress with quality productions, some of them inspired. **Comedy**, however, rather pales in comparison here to the other major California cities, with just a few engaging options. **Classical music** and **opera**, by contrast, have much to recommend them, though prices are predictably steeper than for other performing arts fare. Finally, San Diego has a handful of charming venues for classic, revival and art **films**, with the first-run multiplexes thicker on the ground, usually devoted to the latest Tinseltown product.

Classical music and opera

California Center for the Arts 340 N Escondido Blvd, Escondido ℡760/839-4138, ⊛www .artcenter.org. Soprano recitals, violin sonatas and chamber music concerts, as well as the odd jazz, off-Broadway and comedy performance.

La Jolla Athenaeum 1008 Wall St ℡858/454-5872, ⊛www.ljathenaeum.org. A delightful, esteemed music and arts library that has regular performances of music (mainly jazz and classical), as well as a nice art gallery.

Tickets

Depending on availability, **half-price tickets** bought on the day for theatre and classical music events are available from Arts Tix, Broadway at Third Avenue, at Broadway Circle (Tues–Thurs 11am–6pm, Fri & Sat 10am–6pm, Sun 10am–5pm; ☎619/497-5000, ⓦwww.sdartstix.com). Full-price advance sales are also available, and on Saturday, half-price tickets are issued for Sunday performances. Otherwise, tickets for major shows can be purchased from the venue directly or through operators such as Ticketmaster (☎619/220-8497, ⓦwww.ticketmaster.com); check the local papers for times and venues.

La Jolla Music Society ☎858/459-3728, ⓦwww.ljms.org. Makes regular appearances at the Sherwood Auditorium, among other venues, and also puts on regular classical performances and jazz or dance ensembles.

Mandeville Center On the UCSD campus, north of La Jolla ☎858/534-3230, ⓦmandeville.ucsd.edu. Offers jazz, classical and world music throughout the year, as well as dance performances and choral groups.

Museum of Contemporary Art Downtown at 1100 Kettner Blvd, or in La Jolla at Sherwood Auditorium, 700 Prospect St ☎858/454-3541, ⓦwww.mcasd.org. Occasional performances of jazz and classical tunes, as well as more avant-garde offerings.

San Diego Lyric Opera Birch North Park Theatre, east of Hillcrest at 29th and University Ave

☎619/239-8836, ⓦwww.lyricoperasandiego.org. Presents a bevy of frothy, toe-tapping operetta favourites from Strauss to Weill, plus Broadway musical revivals.

San Diego Opera Based at the Civic Theatre, 1200 Third Ave, Downtown ☎619/533-7000, ⓦwww.sdopera.com. Puts on four annual productions of familiar fare (Mozart, Puccini, Verdi, etc) and frequently boasts top international guest performers during its Jan–May season.

San Diego Symphony Copley Symphony Hall, 750 B St, Downtown ☎619/235-0804, ⓦwww.sandiegosymphony.com. Presents a full schedule of Classical- and Romantic-era warhorses, with some lite-pop (and mainstream pop) concerts to please the crowds. Performances are in a beautifully renovated 1929 movie palace.

Comedy

The **comedy** scene in San Diego can barely be called a scene, with most jokes cracked (periodically) at venues like the California Center for the Arts (see p.199) or *Winston's Beach Club* (see p.198), or at *Humphrey's by the Bay* (see p.199). The few dedicated comedy joints are rather far flung, and tickets are generally $10–20.

Comedy Palace 8878 Clairemont Mesa Blvd ☎858/573-9067. Located out near Miramar Air Force Base, this is definitely comedy on the fringe – at least geographically – with a fairly tame showcase of local comics on the rise. Tickets are often free, but admission requires a food-and-drink minimum purchase.

Comedy Store South 916 Pearl St, La Jolla ☎858/454-9176, ⓦcomedystorelajolla.com. San Diego branch of the national chain, whose comics

aren't quite up to the standard of those in Hollywood (see p.153), but are good enough for a snicker or two.

National Comedy Theatre At Marquis Theatre, 3717 India St, Mission Hills ☎619/295-4999, ⓦwww.nationalcomedy.com. A good bet for improvisational comedy – involving much audience participation and berserk antics from a cast of hungry up-and-comers.

Theatre

There's a thriving **theatre** scene in San Diego, with several mid-sized venues and many smaller fringe venues putting on quality shows. Tickets are over $50 for a major production, or $10–25 for a night on the fringe. The *San Diego Reader* (ⓦwww.sandiegoreader.com) carries full listings.

Balboa Theatre 850 Fourth Ave, Downtown ☎619/570-1100, ⓦwww.sdbalboa.org. Grandly restored Spanish Revival moviehouse from 1924 that has a range of classical pops, operetta, musicals, film, dance and more.
Cygnet Theatre 4040 Twiggs St, Old Town ☎619/337-1525, ⓦwww.cygnettheatre.com. Though few venture to Old Town for theatre, this smallish venue provides a good reason, hosting a range of twentieth-century classics and more contemporary productions in an intimate showcase for some of the area's better dramatic and comedic talent.
La Jolla Playhouse UCSD campus, 2910 La Jolla Village Circle ☎858/550-1010, ⓦwww.lajolla playhouse.org. Splashy modern complex that hosts a range of productions, typically a mix of off-Broadway favourites and contemporary dramatic and musical shows.
North Coast Repertory Theatre 987 Lomas Sante Fe Drive, Solana Beach ☎858/481-1055, ⓦwww .northcoastrep.org. Merits a break from the beach, with raucous comedies and affecting dramas, and many local and world premiere productions.

The Old Globe 1363 Old Globe Way, Balboa Park ☎619/234-5623, ⓦwww.theoldglobe.org. As you'd expect from the name, a fine showcase for the works of the Bard, but also featuring more current entertainment, including off-Broadway favourites, revivals and children's plays.
San Diego Civic Theatre 202 C St, Downtown ☎619/570-1100, ⓦwww.sandiegotheatres.org. Three-thousand seater geared towards mainstream entertainment, mainly off-Broadway touring shows and musical revivals.
San Diego Repertory Theatre At Lyceum Stage, 79 Horton Plaza, Downtown ☎619/544-1000, ⓦwww.sdrep.org. A key San Diego theatre that presents consciousness-raising productions of the political and cultural variety, along with a mix of classics and travelling musicals.
Sushi Performance and Visual Art 390 11th Ave, Downtown ☎619/235-8466, ⓦsushiart.org. Avant-garde troupe whose shows are sometimes pretentious, often groundbreaking, sometimes chilling, but rarely boring.

Film

San Diego has many **cinemas**, most of them offering the usual Hollywood blockbusters. Scan the newspapers for full listings; admission is usually $7–11. For more adventurous programmes – foreign-language films, monochrome classics or cult favourites – try the Landmark Cinemas around town: The Ken, 4061 Adams Ave (☎619/283-5909), the Hillcrest Cinemas, 3965 Fifth Ave (☎619/819-0236), or the La Jolla Village Cinemas, 8879 Villa La Jolla Drive (☎858/453-7831). For an entirely different experience, the IMAX films at the Reuben H. Fleet Science Center (☎619/238-1233; see p.182) offer the kids an eye-popping selection of nature films and special-effects reels on a giant curved screen. Finally, as a nostalgic alternative, the South Bay Drive-Inn, 2170 Coronado Ave, near Imperial Beach (☎619/423-2727, ⓦwww.southbaydrivein.com), is one of the few venues of its kind left in Southern California, offering three outdoor screens showing mainstream flicks for $7 per person.

Gay and lesbian San Diego

Although central San Diego is generally welcoming to visitors of all orientations, several hotels and bed and breakfasts are noted for their friendliness toward **gay and lesbian** travellers: the *Balboa Park Inn* (see p.171) and *Park Manor Suites* (see p.171) are both estimable choices. Hillcrest is the heart of San Diego's gay scene. The primary source of gay and lesbian news and events is the free weekly *Gay & Lesbian Times* (ⓦwww.gaylesbiantimes.com), distributed through gay bars and clubs, many of the city's cafés and gay-run businesses. You can learn more by contacting the **Lesbian and Gay Men's Community Center**, 3909 Centre St, Hillcrest (Mon–Fri 9am–10pm, Sat 9am–7pm; ☎619/692-2077, ⓦwww .thecentersd.org), which has served the community for decades.

Gay bars and clubs

Baja Betty's 1421 University Ave, Hillcrest ☎619/269-8510. Festive joint that draws the crowds for its decent Mexican food, cheap drinks and themed dance nights.

Bourbon Street 4612 Park Blvd, University Heights ☎619/291-4043. A chic gay crowd gathers nightly at this convivial bar and grill north of Hillcrest, also featuring karaoke events, dance parties, DJs and other spectacles.

Brass Rail 3796 Fifth Ave, Hillcrest ☎619/298-2233. High-energy dancing every night at this longstanding neighbourhood hangout, with a mixed gay and straight crowd, and disco, house and Eighties music pumping from the speakers.

Chee-Chee Club 929 Broadway, Downtown. Rumpled dive bar with a casual atmosphere and mixed crowd of grizzled regulars, and a bit less attitude than at some of the Hillcrest clubs.

Flicks 1017 University Ave, Hillcrest ☎619/297-2056. Popular drinking joint that plays music videos on large screens and offers pinball, pool and occasional comedy as well.

Lips 3036 El Cajon Blvd, northeast of Hillcrest ☎619/295-7900. Drag Central in San Diego, with regular performances from smart-aleck queens and chic divas alike. Signature events include drag karaoke and bingo, and a curious Sunday Gospel Brunch as well.

Rich's 1051 University Ave, Hillcrest ☎619/295-2195. Originally a mainly gay club, *Rich's* now attracts numerous straights for the heavy dance grooves at weekends and frenzied environment. Cover charge most nights.

Urban Mo's 308 University Ave, Hillcrest ☎619/491-0400. The former *Hamburger Mary's*, and still an epicentre for drinking in the area, this is a restaurant and bar that features assorted drink specials and dance parties, plus regular drag events.

Listings

Beach and surf conditions ☎619/221-8884, ⓦwww.surfingsandiego.com.

Disabled assistance Accessible San Diego (☎858/279-0704, ⓦwww.accessandiego.org); Access to Independence of San Diego, 8885 Rio San Diego Drive (☎619/293-3500, TDD ☎/293-7757, ⓦaccesstoindependence.org).

Driving The AAA of Southern California, for maps, guides and information, is at 2440 Hotel Circle North (☎619/233-1000, ⓦwww.aaa-calif.com).

Emergencies ☎911.

Flea market The huge Kobey's Swap Meet takes place at the San Diego Sports Arena, 3500 Sports Arena Blvd (Fri–Sun 7am–3pm; 50¢ admission Fri, $1 weekends; ☎619/226-0650, ⓦwww.kobeyswap.com).

Hospitals For non-urgent treatment, the cheapest place is the Beach Area Family Health Center, 3705 Mission Blvd, Mission Beach (Mon–Wed & Fri 8.30am–5.30pm, Thurs 9am–6pm; ☎619/515-2444, ⓦwww.fhcsd.org).

Internet The Central Library, 820 E St, has free access (see p.176), as do various cafés.

Left luggage At the Greyhound terminal (see p.166) and, for ticketed train and trolley travellers, at the Santa Fe Depot.

Pharmacy 24-hour pharmacy at Walgreens, 3005 Midway Drive, north of the airport (☎619/221-0834), and 3222 University Ave, east of Hillcrest (☎619/528-1793).

Post offices 815 E St, Downtown (Mon–Fri 9am–5pm; Zip code 92101; ☎1-800/275-8777).

Sports Baseball's San Diego Padres (☎619/795-5000, ⓦsandiego.padres.mlb.com) play at Petco Park, at the edge of the Gaslamp Quarter, while football's Chargers (☎1-877/242-7434, ⓦwww.chargers.com) play at Qualcomm Stadium in Mission Valley.

Taxes Sales tax is 8.75 percent; hotel tax is 10.5 percent, or 12.5 percent for hotels with more than 70 rooms.

North San Diego County

Away from the city itself, **North San Diego County** runs from small communities to more rugged undeveloped country, where camping out and following forest and desert trails are surprisingly appealing for an area so close to a metropolis. **Transport** around the region is straightforward. By car, I-5 skirts the coast and I-15 runs a little deeper inland, while I-8 heads east from San Diego towards the southern part of the Anza-Borrego Desert State Park (see p.246). East of I-15, a network of smaller roads reach the scattered rural communities. The San Diego Coaster runs from Downtown San Diego up to Oceanside, from where you can transfer to LA's Metrolink commuter rail system, and the Sprinter covers the distance between Oceanside and Escondido along Hwy-78. There are also frequent Greyhound buses and Amtrak trains between LA and San Diego.

The North County coast

The towns of the **North County coast** stretch forty miles north from San Diego to the Camp Pendleton marine base, which divides the county from the outskirts of Los Angeles. As they get further from the coast and closer to inland military installations, the communities generally become more working class and less bourgeois, but by and large attract a mix of tight-lipped business commuters, beach-bumming surfer dudes and crewcut-sporting tough guys. The main attraction is, of course, the coast itself: miles of excellent beaches with great opportunities for swimming and surfing.

Del Mar

On the northern edge of the city of San Diego, the tall bluff that contains Torrey Pines State Preserve (see p.192) marks the southern boundary of **DEL MAR**. The town is known mainly for its **Del Mar Racetrack**, which has been going strong for almost 75 years, originally founded by investors including Bing Crosby and Jimmy Durante. It's still one of the most revered and popular tracks in the country, staging horse races between late July and early September (☎858/755-1141, ⓦwww.dmtc .com). The town's other main event is the **San Diego County Fair** (☎858/755-1161, ⓦwww.sdfair.com), held throughout June until Independence Day at the San Diego County Fairgrounds. It's an old-fashioned event with barbecues, kiddie games and livestock shows, though it's mixed with a fair amount of contemporary events, including film screenings, low-key concerts by pop acts and lite-rockers, and the occasional haunted-house visit (in late September or October).

If you want to hit the track or the fair overnight, you can stay in style at *L'Auberge Del Mar*, 1540 Camino del Mar (☎858/259-1515, ⓦwww.lauberge delmar.com; ⓪), loaded with chic restaurants, tennis courts and swanky rooms and cabanas by the pool, and offering top-notch spa and massage services, too. If the $300 room rate seems a little steep, the *Clarion Carriage House Del Mar Inn*, 720 Camino del Mar (☎858/755-9765, ⓦwww.clarionhotel.com; ⓪), is a good budget alternative, with clean and simple rooms, pool, continental breakfast and free wi-fi.

Beyond this, Del Mar is a place to **eat** and **shop**. *Pacifica Del Mar*, 1555 Camino Del Mar (☎858/792-0476), offers a tasty, upper-end combination of fresh seafood, California cuisine and prime ocean views; for about the same prices, but right on the ocean with some lovely sea views, *Jake's Del Mar*, 1660 Coast Blvd (☏858/755-1002), is good for its seafood and chowders, as well as steaks, burgers and Asian dishes such as wasabi ahi and sashimi.

Solana Beach

SOLANA BEACH, the next town north from Del Mar, was the first US city to ban smoking from its coastline. It has some striking oceanside views from Solana Beach County Park (also known as "Pillbox" or "Fletcher Cove"), which offers good diving and surfing opportunities, and the town makes a reasonable place for an overnight stop. There's a smattering of antique shops, galleries and watersports outlets, as well as the North Coast Repertory Theatre, 987 Lomas Sante Fe Drive (see p.201), and the ⅍ *Belly Up Tavern*, 143 S Cedros Ave (☏858/481-9022), the best options for smart entertainment (theatre and indie rock, respectively) before you get to the LA metroplex. Standard-issue **motels** line the coastal road, or you can stay a few miles inland at the chic *Rancho Valencia Resort*, 5921 Valencia Circle (☏858/756-1123, ⓦwww.ranchovalencia.com; ⓞ), an upscale golf-and-tennis outpost with fine dining, spa services and lush rooms starting at $700, or more affordably at *Courtyard by Marriott*, 717 S Hwy-101 (☏858/792-8200, ⓦwww .marriott.com; ⓞ), not far from the waterside, with pool, gym, hot tub and high-speed internet.

For **food**, make sure to drop in on *Nobu*, 315 S Coast Hwy (☏858/755-7787), for sushi and sashimi – among the best in the region – in a stretch dominated by more conventional seafood diners; and *Pizza Nova*, 945 Lomas Santa Fe Drive (☏858/259-0666), a North Coast outpost of the excellent regional chain, with toppings like gorgonzola and pear, or salmon, onion and goat's cheese, among more conventional choices.

If you're driving, take a quick, four-mile detour inland along Hwy-8, passing the town of **Rancho Santa Fe**, an ultra-upscale small community with a distinctive flavour of 1920s and 1930s Spain, whose architecture is enforced by an all-powerful "Art Jury" that rigidly disallows any deviation from the prevailing quaintness.

Encinitas

The major flower-growing centre of **ENCINITAS** is at its best during the spring, when its blooms of floral colour are most radiant. It's no surprise that an Indian guru, Paramahansa Yogananda, chose the town as the headquarters of the Self-Realization Fellowship; created in the guru's honour, **Swami's Beach** is one of the best spots for surfing along this part of the coast. The fellowship's serene **Meditation Gardens**, around the corner at 215 K St (Tues–Sat 9am–5pm, Sun noon–5pm; free), are open to all, and revolve around an ecumenical philosophy with spiritual themes. Nearby are the similarly relaxing **San Diego Botanic Gardens**, 230 Quail Gardens Drive (daily 9am–5pm; $12), which hosts thirty different gardens, rich in bamboo, California endemics, palms and selections of foliage from each continent. Also compelling is **San Elijo Lagoon Ecological Reserve**, 2710 Manchester Ave, one of the biggest remaining coastal wetlands in the state, a thousand acres rich with endemic plants, fish and birds – and based around marshes, scrubland and chaparral – which you can explore on seven miles of hiking trails (nature walks available Sat 10am).

Surfing opportunities are numerous, and you can practice your longboard skills at Leucadia Surf School (☏760/635-7873, ⓦwww.leucadiasurfschool.com), an esteemed outfit that offers two-hour group or private lessons for $65 and $120, respectively, on Moonlight Beach, with boards and wetsuits included.

Practicalities

The **visitor centre** is at 859 2nd St (Mon–Fri 10am–4pm, Sat 10am–2pm; T760/753-6041, Wwww.encinitaschamber.com). Encinitas offers some nice **places to stay**, such as the *Inn at Moonlight Beach*, 105 N Vulcan Ave (T760/561-1755, Wwww.innatmoonlightbeach.com; ❼), which offers four rooms and suites with tasteful decor, free wi-fi and good breakfasts, or the *Ocean Inn*, 1444 N Coast Hwy (T1-800/546-1598, Wwww.oceaninnhotel.com; ❸), which has basic rooms with microwaves and fridges, and complimentary wi-fi and breakfast. Otherwise, there's the landscaped **campground** at San Elijo Beach State Park (T1-800/444-7275, Wwww.reserveamerica.com; $35), near **Cardiff-by-the-Sea** just to the south, whose name comes from the whim of its founder's British wife.

Dining options consist of the usual seafood restaurants along the highway and a slew of diners; what stands out are places such as *Trattoria I Trulli*, 830 S Coast Hwy, Encinitas (T760/943-6800), whose mid-priced California-style Italian cuisine with fresh and delicious ingredients is well worth a try; the fabulous, though more expensive, *Q'ero*, 564 S Coast Hwy, Encinitas (T760/753-9050), whose Peruvian and Latin American cuisine leans heavily toward seafood, steak and lamb, with prime grilled prawns, quinoa salad and empanadas; and *Ki's*, 2591 S Coast Hwy-101, Cardiff (T760/436-5236), which appeals for its salads, seafood wraps, smoothies and pasta, with a number of vegetarian and vegan choices.

Carlsbad

Surfers are the main visitors to **South Carlsbad State Beach**, which has a busy cliff-top campground (see p.206), as well as opportunities for swimming, fishing and scuba diving. The beach marks the edge of upscale **CARLSBAD**, whose cutesy, pseudo-Teutonic architecture derives from the early 1880s belief that water from a local spring had the same invigorating qualities as the waters of Karlsbad, a spa town in Bohemia (now part of the Czech Republic). "Carlsbad" thus became a health resort, promoted by pioneer-turned-entrepreneur John Frazier, whose bronze image overlooks the (now dry) original springs near Carlsbad Boulevard and Carlsbad Village Drive.

One of several local lagoons that are good for birdwatching (grebes, terns, coots and pelicans), the **Buena Vista Lagoon** is a nature reserve of over two hundred acres, which also offers plenty of opportunities for strolling on the paths around it. The Audubon Society, 2202 S Coast Hwy (T760/439-2473, Wwww.bvaudubon.org), has more information and hosts regular guided walks. Also appealing are the fifty acres of blooms in the **Flower Fields**, 5704 Paseo del Norte (March to early May daily 9am–6pm; $10; T760/431-0352, Wwww.theflowerfields.com), with plots of roses, poinsettias and other eye-catching seasonal blossoms. Otherwise, the most popular attraction in Carlsbad these days is the odd theme-park of **Legoland California** (exit Cannon Road off the I-5; summer daily 10am–8pm, winter hours vary; $67, kids $57, parking $12; T760/918-5346, Wwww.legoland.com), where kids are encouraged to climb on larger-than-life Lego bricks, make their way through colourful mazes, ride the Coastersaurus rollercoaster and other pint-sized thrill rides, spray water cannons from boats in Splash Battles, operate miniature cars and ships, and view assorted places built on a minuscule scale – among them New Orleans, Las Vegas, Washington DC and the coastline of Southern California. There's also a newer **water park and aquarium** open similar hours (joint ticket: $87 adults, $77 kids).

Practicalities

The **visitor centre**, 5934 Priestly Drive (Mon–Fri 9am–5pm, Sat 10am–4pm; T760/931-8400, Wwww.carlsbad.org), offers a look at the town's curious local history. **Accommodation** can be pricey, though South Carlsbad State Beach has a **campground**, for RVs only (☏1-800/444-7275, ⊛www.reserveamerica.com; $35 inland, $50 beachfront). One of the less expensive hotels is the *Carlsbad Inn Beach Resort*, 3075 Carlsbad Blvd (☏760/434-7020, ⊛www.carlsbadinn.com; ❽), whose rooms come with DVD players, kitchenettes, spas and fireplaces (and all with free wi-fi), with more expensive suites and condos available with wide views of the Pacific. Otherwise, you can try the *Grand Pacific Palisades* resort, across from the Flower Fields at 5805 Armada Drive (☏760/827-3200, ⊛www.grand pacificpalisades.com; ❼), whose rooms feature balconies or patios, CD and DVD players, and which boasts a pool, sauna, games room and three spas. Good places to **eat** include *Fidel's Norte*, 3003 Carlsbad Blvd (☏760/729-0903), one of the better and more authentic spots for Mexican food, from the usual enchiladas to more exotic fare like cactus in chilli and tomato sauce; and *The Armenian Café*, 3126 Carlsbad Blvd (☏760/720-2233), where the American and Middle Eastern dishes come at affordable prices. For a really hearty meal, though, check out *Tip Top Meats*, 6118 Paseo del Norte, a butcher's and deli whose hefty fare features the likes of German bratwurst, stuffed cabbage and smoked Polish sausages.

Oceanside

The most northerly town on the coast of San Diego County, **Oceanside**, five miles north of Carlsbad, is dominated by the huge **Camp Pendleton** marine base, though its Downtown is charming and its beaches are beautiful, embellished by the fetching town **pier** that extends nearly two thousand feet into the waves. Oceanside is also the major transport hub for North County (Amtrak, Greyhound, the Coaster, the Sprinter and Metrolink trains to LA pass through), and the easiest place from which to reach Mission San Luis Rey (see below).

The town's prime attractions include the **California Surf Museum**, 223 N Coast Hwy (daily 10am–4pm, Thurs until 8pm; free), with displays on some of the top local surfers and boards that tackled the most wicked breaks, and some of the most inventive board designers who gave shape to that quintessential California icon. The **Oceanside Museum of Art**, 704 Pier View Way (Tues–Sat 10am–4pm, Sun 1–4pm; $8; ☏760/721-2787, ⊛www.oma-online.org), is also of interest, partially housed in a spartan but elegant Irving Gill design from the early twentieth century (the striking modern structure is a more recent addition), with a fine range of contemporary art from glassworks to photography to multimedia, typically shown in rotating exhibits.

Oceanside is mostly given over to chain **hotels**, but one of the exceptions is the *Southern California Beach Club*, 121 S Pacific St (☏1-877/477-7368, ⊛www .southerncalifbeachclub.com; ❻–❽), which offers a variety of properties for rent, from one-bedroom studios to two-bedroom condos, with kitchens, balconies, DVD players and wi-fi typically included. For **eating**, try the *Hill Street Café and Gallery*, 524 S Coast Hwy, an old Victorian house offering great coffee, cakes, sandwiches and salads, including some vegetarian options, with local art on the walls; or *333 Pacific*, at 333 N Pacific St (☏760/433-3333), offering well-made cocktails and dishes such as tuna tacos, seafood stews, hand rolls and sashimi, as well as delicious steaks.

Mission San Luis Rey and around

Four miles inland from Oceanside along Hwy-76, **Mission San Luis Rey**, 4050 Mission Ave (daily 10am–4pm; $6; ☏760/757-3651, ⊛www.sanluisrey.org), founded in 1798 by Padre Laséun, was the largest of the California missions and once the centre for three thousand Native American converts. Franciscan monks still inhabit the mission, and there's a **museum** and a serene, candle-lit **chapel**. Even if you don't go inside, look around the foundations of the guards' barracks immediately outside the main building and, across the road, the remains of the mission's ornate **sunken gardens**, once *lavanderías* where the inhabitants did their washing. If you're sufficiently inspired, you can even **stay** here; overnight visits with dinner cost $85.

Beyond the mission, push on another four miles to **Guajome County Park**, 3000 Guajome Lake Road (daily 9.30am to an hour before dusk; vehicles $5, camping $24), which has five miles of trails and picnic tables and playgrounds, but whose centrepiece is a twenty-room adobe **rancho**, 2210 N Santa Fe Avenue (Sat & Sun 10.30am–2.30pm; donation; ☎760/724-4082, ⓦ www.historyand culture.com/guajome), an arcaded Spanish Colonial gem that's popular for weddings. The structure was erected in the mid-nineteenth century for, naturally, newlyweds Cave Couts and Ysidora Bandini, socialites who later entertained celebrities like Helen Hunt Jackson – who, according to legend, based the title character of *Ramona*, her sentimental tale of Indian life in the mission era, on Ysidora's maid. After Couts' death in 1874, Ysidora tried to maintain the place but over the years it became dilapidated, until it was finally bought and restored by the county.

Hwy-76 continues inland to Mission San Antonio de Pala and Palomar Observatory (see p.209). Along the coast beyond Oceanside, the US military keeps its territory relatively undeveloped, creating a vivid impression of how stark the land was before commercialization took hold. The uncluttered **San Onofre State Beach** (daily dawn–dusk) has camping near sandstone bluffs (☎1-800/444-7275, ⓦ www.reserveamerica.com; $35) and is popular with surfers, thanks to its slow-rolling waves. The **Trestles** area here is host to all manner of world-renowned surfers and international competitions during the year; however, it's only accessible by a 1.5-mile hiking trail. Beyond is the town of San Clemente and the southern edge of Orange County, itself the fringe of the LA metropolis.

Inland North County

Unlike the coast, **inland North County** has no sizeable towns and is mostly given over to farming, with a terrain of dense forests, deep valleys and mile-high mountain ranges. Besides a few reminders of the ancient indigenous cultures, remnants from the mission era, and a few settlements, it's best to make for the area's state parks and enjoy some leisurely countryside walks, or venture further east to the dramatic Anza-Borrego Desert (see p.246).

Escondido and around

Spanish for "hidden", **ESCONDIDO** is one of the region's fastest-growing spots, where retirees and ex-urbanites mix with hip younger folk, well away from most of San Diego County's tourist traffic. It's about forty miles north of San Diego on I-15, and is the terminus of the Sprinter rail service (one way $2, day-pass $5; ☎1-800/262-7837, ⓦ www.gonctd.com), which links to Oceanside, from where you can access the entire coast of the state on public transport.

The town is worth a look for its **Heritage Walk** in Grape Day Park, offering a glimpse of several restored Victorian buildings (Thurs–Sat 1–4pm; free): an old-fashioned blacksmith's, the first city library, a rustic barn, a pair of windmills and an antique train depot. There's also a 1925 railroad car with an elaborate scale model of the train that previously linked Escondido to Oceanside. For more information, check out the **History Center**, 321 N Broadway (same hours; $3; ℡760/743-8207, ⊛www.escondidohistory.org). Nearby, the **California Center for the Arts**, 340 N Escondido Blvd (Tues–Sat 10am–4pm, Sun 1–5pm; $5; ℡760/839-4120, ⊛www.artcentre.org), has a surprisingly good contemporary art museum, showcasing a range of traditional media as well as avant-garde, installation, multimedia and video-art exhibitions, and two theatres that present comedy, musicals and dance performances along with live jazz, classical and world music. Both the history and arts centres border **Grape Day Park** (daily dawn–dusk), with a swimming pool, horseshoe pits and a rose garden, but most notable for its vineyard-themed playground, where children can frolic on oversized leaves and vines and slide through a tunnel of giant grapes.

Finally, no trip to Escondido would be complete without a stop at the eye-opening **Queen Califia's Magical Circle**, Bear Valley Parkway at Mary Lane, in Kit Carson Park (Tues–Sun dawn–dusk; free), Niki de Saint Phalle's bizarre, strangely delightful art garden based around nine of her more fanciful mosaic sculptures, including such oddments as hissing snake heads and gilded humans riding multicoloured birds.

Around Escondido

Five miles south of Escondido amid stunning scenery, the **Orfila Winery**, 13455 San Pasqual Valley Rd (daily 10am–6pm, tours at 2pm; ℡760/738-6500 ext 22, ⊛www.orfila.com), offers tastings of wine ($10) produced by a former Napa Valley vintner, as well as tours of the handsome facility. Eight miles north of town off I-15 (no public transport) is the one of the Escondido area's biggest attractions, the **Lawrence Welk Resort**, 8860 Lawrence Welk Drive (℡1-800/932-9355, ⊛www.welkresort.com; ❼), a thousand-acre holiday complex of golf courses, spas, swimming pools, villas, and the Welk Dinner Theater, where you can enjoy anything from forgotten Broadway stars to a Beatles tribute band. Rising from accordion-playing unknown to musical juggernaut, TV bandleader Welk was the inventor of "champagne music" – basically waltzes and polkas with a touch of sanitized swing – during the playing of which bubbles would float through the air around his band. Displayed around the theatre lobby, the Welk hagiography follows the peculiar career of the thick-accented, native North Dakotan who most people assumed was an immigrant fresh from central Europe.

Practicalities

The **visitor centre**, 360 N Escondido Blvd (Mon–Fri 9am–5pm; ℡1-800/848-3336, ⊛www.sandiegonorth.com), provides information for the entire North County area. Unless you've come to partake in the glories of Lawrence Welk, Escondido is not really a good place to **stay**, with only a few reasonable options of the chain-motel variety. The most reliable of these is the *Best Western Escondido*, 1700 Seven Oaks Rd (℡760/740-1700, ⊛www.bestwestern california.com; ❹), good for its pool, jacuzzi, and rooms with complimentary breakfast and free wi-fi. For **dining**, *Vincent's*, 113 W Grand Ave (℡760/745-3835), is worth seeking out for its tremendous (if pricey) French cuisine, of which the tournedos Merlot, rack of lamb and duck à l'orange are particular highlights. Elsewhere, the *Brigantine Escondido*, 421 W Felicita Ave (℡760/743-4718), doles out good, expensive surf'n'turf and has a fine oyster bar, too. As for **drinking**, *Stone Brewing World Bistro*, 1999 Citracado Parkway, presents a range of some of the country's best microbrews, including such tasty offerings as Arrogant Bastard Ale, Stone Ruination IPA and the Sublimely Self-Righteous Ale.

North from Escondido

Hwy-S6 leads fifteen miles north from Escondido to **Mission San Antonio de Pala Asistencia** (daily 10am–5pm; donation; ℡760/742-3317), near the junction of Hwy-76 from Oceanside. Built as an outpost of Mission San Luis Rey in 1816, it lay in ruins until the Cupa Indians were ousted from their tribal home at the turn of the twentieth century and moved to this site, where the mission was revived to serve as their church. Although the current buildings are just replicas of the originals, they do offer an eerie atmosphere, with an evocative cemetery, lovely gardens and a **museum** which contains artefacts created by the native Pala people and dating back to the days of the original mission.

The enormous, half-million-acre **Cleveland National Forest** (℡858/673-6180, ⓦwww.r5.fs.fed.us/cleveland), east from the mission on Hwy-76, is home to fifteen **campgrounds** ($14–32) and stretches south almost to the Mexican border. There are plenty of trails to explore in the Palomar, Trabuco and Descanso sections of the forest, most of them running from one to ten miles, with the exception of the daunting **Pacific Crest Trail**, which covers a hundred miles here – a fraction of its full 2650-mile length as it heads from Mexico to Canada. Otherwise, there's a nice range of activities available in the park, from fishing to scenic drives, but be careful during the summer or excessively hot and dry periods – Cleveland National Forest is known for its significant potential for **wildfires**. For more information on activities, safety and current conditions, contact the **ranger stations** in the region's small towns: Trabuco District, 1147 E 6th St, Corona (℡951/736-1811), Palomar District, 1634 Black Canyon Rd, Ramona (℡760/788-0250), or Descanso District, 3348 Alpine Blvd, Alpine (℡619/445-6235). Alternatively, contact the forest headquarters in San Diego, at 10845 Rancho Bernardo Rd (℡858/673-6180).

Less-hearty backpackers tend to prefer the 1900-acre **Palomar Mountain State Park** (℡760/742-3462), on Hwy-S7 near the junction of Hwy-S6, for its cooler, higher altitude – some parts rise above five thousand feet – and easier hiking trails. You can camp at *Doane Valley* or *Cedar Grove* ($30; first-come-first-served Dec–March, rest of year by reservation at ℡1-800/444-7275, ⓦwww.reserveamerica .com). Eight miles east of the park on Hwy-S6 sits the two-hundred-inch Hale telescope of CalTech's **Palomar Observatory** (daily 9am–4pm, until 3pm in winter; free), capable of seeing a billion light years into the cosmos. Although visitors aren't able to view the distant galaxies directly, the apparatus is impressive in itself and, at the visitor centre, you can admire the observatory's striking collection of deep-space photographs taken with the powerful lens.

East from Escondido

Ten miles east of Escondido on Hwy-78 (bus #386; Mon–Fri) and thirty miles north of San Diego (no direct bus access from that city), the **San Diego Zoo Safari Park**, 15500 San Pasqual Valley Rd (hours vary, often daily 9am–4pm, summer closes 8pm; $37, kids $27, joint ticket with San Diego Zoo $70, kids $50; parking $10; ℡619/718-3000, ⓦwww.sandiegozoo.org/wap), is the major tourist attraction in the area. It's an 1800-acre enclosure packed with three thousand animals, featuring a sizeable tropical-bird aviary, mock African bush and Kilimanjaro hiking trail, elephant rides, and various films and exhibitions. With lions, tigers, cheetahs, deer and monkeys roaming about, it's a great stop for kids, and merits the cost of the pricey joint ticket with the main zoo. More historically minded visitors may, however, prefer a stop at the **San Pasqual Battlefield**, two miles away at 15808 San Pasqual Valley Rd (Sat & Sun 10am–5pm; free), whose visitor centre details the bloody and tumultuous

1846 battle in the Mexican–American War, which is enthusiastically re-created every year on the Sunday closest to December 6. An outlying historic trail also offers information on the region's ecosystem and native cultures predating the arrival of white colonists.

The terrain becomes increasingly sparse as you press further east along Hwy-78 into a region that's difficult to access without a car. If you're coming this way directly from San Diego, use Hwy-67 and join Hwy-78 at Ramona, eighteen miles from Escondido, and continue east for sixteen miles to **Santa Ysabel**. While unexceptional, this tiny crossroads is enlivened by **Dudley's Bakery**, 30218 Hwy-78, just before the junction with Hwy-79 (Mon 9am–1pm, Thurs–Sun 9am–5pm), famous for its home-baked breads and pastries – among them black olive and basil, and garlic sourdough – at giveaway prices. A mile and a half north of town at 23013 Hwy-79, the small **Mission Santa Ysabel Asistencia** (summer 8am–5.30pm; winter 8am–4pm; donation) is a 1924 replacement of an 1818 original structure. Sitting in moody isolation, the mission has a small modern chapel and a one-room **museum** detailing the history of the site. Outside is an Indian burial ground, and the church continues to serve several local Native American communities.

Julian and around

Seven miles southeast of Santa Ysabel on Hwy-78A, the hamlet of **JULIAN** was amazingly once the second biggest town in the San Diego area, thanks to an 1869 gold discovery here. Its population declined after that, and it faded into small-town obscurity. These days, it's known locally for its formidable cider and apple pies that can draw a fair crowd of weekend visitors. At an elevation of 4000ft, the town provides a temperate base from which to make forays into the Anza-Borrego Desert (see p.246), fewer than ten miles to the east. There are also plenty of antique shops and Western-themed boutiques, and access to worthwhile park sites, wineries, horse rides and scenic drives.

To get a sense of the full scope of history and activities, drop by the visitor centre (see opposite), which has information and photos, and offers a **walking tour** of the local highlights. With its quaint buildings and rustic charm, Julian's appeal centres on its Main Street, but there are numerous old buildings in various states of preservation. The most notable include the Gold Rush-era mining equipment on display at the **Julian Pioneer Museum**, 2811 Washington St (April–Nov Wed–Sun 10am–4pm; donation), featuring antiques and castoffs from the late Victorian era, among them pianos, an old-time buggy, lace craftworks and historic apparel, stuffed animals and Native American relics – all housed in a former brewery-turned-blacksmith-shop.

Around Julian

You can try your hand at mining at **Julian Mining Company**, off Hwy-78 three miles west of Julian (Wed–Fri 11am–3pm; ℡951/313-0166, ⓦwww .julianminingcompany.com), where you can learn to pan for gold ($9) and dig for fossils ($15) – though it's more family-oriented entertainment than a way to strike it rich.

To the north, and rising above Julian off Farmer Road, the 5000-foot-high **Volcan Mountain Wilderness Preserve** (open 24hr; free; ℡760/765-2300, ⓦwww.volcanmt.org) makes for an interesting visit, covering some 25,000 acres. Whether self- or fully guided (April–Oct once a month, on Sat or Sun), the main trek is a five-mile round trip to the summit, from where you can get an excellent overview of the region; shorter trails pass through orchards, oak groves and manzanitas. For a natural experience of a very different kind, visit the **California Wolf Center**, four miles south of Julian at 18457 Hwy-79 ($10; by reservation only at ℗619/234-9653, ⓦwww.californiawolfcenter.org), whose programmes (Sat 2pm & Sun 10am; 1hr 30min) provide a look at the steely-eyed North American gray wolves in their packs and discuss the need to reintroduce them to the wild.

Practicalities

The **visitor centre**, housed in the century-old **Julian Town Hall**, 2129 Main St (daily 10am–5pm; ℗760/765-1857, ⓦwww.julianca.com), has details of attractive local **places to stay**. Among these, the *Julian Gold Rush Hotel*, 2032 Main St (℗1-800/734-5854, ⓦwww.julianhotel.com; ⓞ), is the oldest functioning hotel in the state, opened in 1897 by a freed slave; the pair of rooms, plus a cottage and small house, are decorated in period style, and rates include afternoon tea and a full breakfast. The *Julian Lodge*, 2720 C St (℗1-800/542-1420, ⓦwww.julianlodge.com; ⓞ), is only a replica of a historic hotel, but has a similar country atmosphere and many more rooms at cheaper prices, also offering a buffet-style continental breakfast. However, the most distinctive digs are at the *Shadow Mountain Ranch*, 2771 Frisius Rd (℗760/765-0323, ⓦwww .shadowmountainranch.net; ⓞ), which has a conventional Victorian room and two cottages, as well as a more unusual "Grandma's Attic" done up in lace and satin, a storybook cottage and modern treehouse, and a "Gnome Home" that's even kitscher than it sounds.

Eating options include the *Julian Café*, 2112 Main St, for a good old-time atmosphere and meals, including sandwiches, burgers, chicken pot pie and apple pie, and the ⚘*Julian Pie Company*, 2225 Main St, with three kinds of old-fashioned apple pie, and wonderful fruit-pie combinations using cherries, raspberries, peaches and boysenberries.

Cuyamaca Rancho State Park

The oaks, willows, sycamores and pines of **Cuyamaca Rancho State Park**, nine miles south of Julian and nine miles east of I-8 along Hwy-79 (℗760/765-0755, ⓦwww.cuyamaca.us), are set in landscapes ranging from lush subalpine meadows to stark mountain peaks. However, most of the park's 25,000 acres, including its wilderness area, campgrounds and hiking trails, were damaged in wildfires in 2003. In the years since, an army of volunteers has rebuilt the park's facilities and reconstructed its trails, and nature has done the rest – the park is a marvel of adaptability and revival in the face of natural, cyclical catastrophe. Most of the trails, together stretching some one hundred miles, have now been reopened, as have the **campgrounds** ($30; ℗1-800/444-7275, ⓦwww .reserveamerica.com), though keep in mind that due to ongoing restoration work, some sites may close at short notice and your site may be relocated to another part of the park. Pick up information and maps from the **visitor centre**, 12551 Hwy-79 (Sat & Sun 10am–2pm), sixteen miles south of Julian in the heart of the park. If you're a birdwatcher, check out the excellent on-site **museum** (same hours; free) that gives a rundown of the native wrens, hawks, bluebirds and woodpeckers.

Travel details

Amtrak trains

San Diego to: Anaheim (10 daily; 2hr); Los Angeles Downtown (10 daily; 2hr 45min); Oceanside (10 daily; 50min); San Juan Capistrano (10 daily; 1hr 25min); Santa Barbara (4 daily; 5hr 35min); Solana Beach (10 daily; 35min).

Greyhound buses

San Diego to: Anaheim (4 daily; 2hr 5min); Long Beach (7 daily; 2hr 20min); Los Angeles Downtown (18 daily; 2hr 40min); Oceanside (12 daily; 50min); San Francisco (6 daily; 11–13hr); Santa Barbara (4 daily; 6–7hr).

The deserts

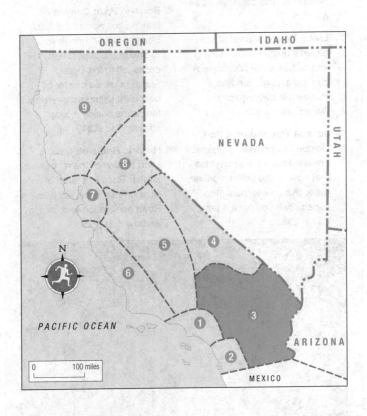

CHAPTER 3 # Highlights

✳ Palm Springs Modernism
Soak up Palm Springs'
Mid-Century Modern
architecture. Take the guided
tour, attend Modernism Week,
stay in a Modernist resort
or just buy the map and
drive around the gems in the
residential districts. See p.224
& p.225

✳ Living Desert Marvel at the
desert's unique flora, fauna
and culture at this combined
zoo, botanic garden and
museum in swanky Palm
Desert. See p.230

✳ Joshua Tree National Park
Unique freaky trees, gorgeous
granite boulders and coyotes
that howl in the warm night air
make this an essential stop,
especially if you have a tent.
See p.238

✳ Salvation Mountain
Surviving on little more than
religious devotion, one man
has produced his personal
monument to God, a bizarrely
colourful synthesis of found
objects, straw bales and
paint. See p.245

✳ Borrego Palm Canyon An
hour's stroll across the Anza-
Borrego Desert brings you
to one of the largest natural
oases left in the United
States, a dense cluster of
over a thousand mop-headed
fan palms beside a crisp
stream. See p.249

✳ Historic Route 66 Trace a
short stretch of the renowned
Mother Road in search of
classic Americana, such as
Roy's gas station and café in
Amboy. See p.256

▲ Joshua Tree National Park

The deserts

The **deserts** of Southern California represent only a fraction of the half a million square miles of North American desert that stretch away eastward into another four states and cross the border into Mexico to the south. Contrary to the monotonous landscape you might expect, California's deserts are a kaleidoscope of light, colour and texture, dotted with everything from ramshackle settlements to swanky resorts. The one thing you can rely on is that, for a large part of the year, they will be uniformly hot and dry. In fact, during the hottest summer months you'd be well advised to give them a miss altogether. And don't count on rain to cool things off – rainfall in this landscape is highly irregular and a whole year's average of three or four inches may fall in a single storm.

Most of the 39,000 square miles that make up the desert are protected in state and national parks, but not all are entirely unspoiled. Vast areas are used by the US government as military bases for training and weapons testing, and many more stretches of fragile ecosystem are damaged by desert fans in off-road vehicles. In spite of this, most of the desert remains a wilderness, and could easily be the highlight of your trip to California. Occupying a quarter of the state, it divides into two distinct regions.

The **Colorado Desert** (or **Low Desert**) in the south stretches down to the Mexican border and east into Arizona, where it continues as the Sonoran Desert. Despite hundreds of miles of beauty and empty highways, most visitors to the region have no intention of getting away from civilization. They're heading for **Palm Springs**, a few square miles overrun with the famous, the star-struck, the aspirational and, above all, the ageing. It is said, not completely in jest, that the average age and average temperature of Palm Springs are about the same – a steady 88. It's the sort of town that fines homeowners who don't maintain their property to a suitable standard. It's the first stopping point east from LA on I-10 and is the hub of the **Coachella Valley**, a residential area that stretches over twenty miles to the southeast along Hwy-111. The valley's farming communities have the distinction of forming part of the most productive irrigated agricultural centre in the world, growing dates, oranges, lemons and grapefruit in vast quantities, though sadly they're steadily giving way to the region's ever-expanding condos and golf courses.

A good-sized budget allows you to make the best of the area's plush resorts and swanky restaurants, but summer accommodation prices are remarkably low, and despite its glossy veneer, there's no shortage of moderately priced things to do: riding the **Palm Springs Aerial Tramway** to the cool of the San Jacinto Mountains, learning about the region's pre-eminent habitat at the **Living Desert** ecological museum and taking a **Celebrity Tour** past the homes of the rich and famous.

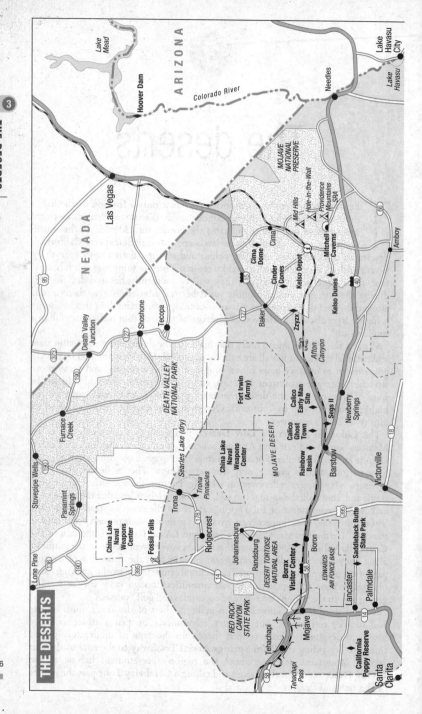

THE DESERTS

ARIZONA

NEVADA

Las Vegas

Lake Mead

Hoover Dam

Colorado River

Needles

Lake Havasu

Lake Havasu City

MOJAVE NATIONAL PRESERVE

Mid Hills

Cima Dome

Cima

Cinder Cones

Kelso Depot

Hole-in-the-Wall

Providence Mountains SRA

Mitchell Caverns

Kelso Dunes

Amboy

Death Valley Junction

Shoshone

Tecopa

Baker

Zzyzx

Afton Canyon

DEATH VALLEY NATIONAL PARK

Furnace Creek

Fort Irwin (Army)

Calico Early Man Site

Segs II

Newberry Springs

Stovepipe Wells

Panamint Springs

China Lake Naval Weapons Center

Searles Lake (dry)

Calico Ghost Town

Rainbow Basin

MOJAVE DESERT

Barstow

Victorville

Lone Pine

China Lake Naval Weapons Center

Fossil Falls

Trona Pinnacles

Trona

Ridgecrest

Johannesburg

Randsburg

DESERT TORTOISE NATURAL AREA

Borax Visitor Center

Boron

EDWARDS AIR FORCE BASE

Saddleback Butte State Park

RED ROCK CANYON STATE PARK

Tehachapi

Tehachapi Pass

Mojave

Lancaster

Palmdale

California Poppy Reserve

Santa Clarita

Exploring the outdoors

The outdoors is one of California's treasures, and the state's fabulous parks and preserves come thick with superlatives. Sequoia National Park holds the largest trees in the world, Death Valley contains the lowest point in the Western Hemisphere, and both are rivalled by the extraordinary domes and spires of Yosemite. This array of astonishing landscapes makes a matchless backdrop for outdoor activities – hiking in summer, skiing and snowboarding in winter, surfing all year, and rock climbing whenever the fancy takes you.

Hitting the slopes

From November to June there's almost always somewhere to **ski or snowboard** in California. Some even claim to have skied every month of the year, but for that you'd have to trudge up to the Sierra crest, and even then you'd only squeeze in a few icy turns.

Most people head for the main **resorts**. The closest major field to LA is Mammoth Mountain in the Owens Valley, a gargantuan and growing area that always seems to be installing new tows and gondolas. With 3000 vertical feet of skiing nicely balanced among beginner, intermediate and advanced slopes (plus terrain parks and halfpipes), you'll not be disappointed. If you're based in the San Francisco Bay Area it's more convenient to head to the cluster of resorts around Lake Tahoe – Heavenly, Homewood and Squaw Valley all deliver the goods (see p.584).

Not all California skiing is downhill. With mile after mile of accessible, snow-covered high country, **cross-country skiing** and **snowshoeing** are affordable and fun. With your own gear you can go just about anywhere in the Sierra Nevada, but for novices, Badger Pass in Yosemite National Park is a great place to start (see p.358).

Cross-country skiing ▲

Surfing at Half Moon Bay ▼

Riding the waves

It's hard to think of California without conjuring up images of bronzed bodies poised atop Pacific breakers, an alluring vision and in many ways a realistic one. With mild temperatures through most of the year and literally hundreds of surf breaks from San Diego to Santa Cruz and beyond, there are endless opportunities for **surfing**.

In recent years the publicity machine has focused on big-wave surfing, much of it pioneered at Mavericks, a reef break off Half Moon Bay south of San Francisco, where winter swells frequently bring beautifully barrelling twenty-footers (see p.531). Only regularly surfed since the early 1990s, it quickly became an institution and has since attracted tow-in surfers who use jet skis to build enough speed to catch the odd fifty-foot monster.

If that's not your scene, there are masses of other appealing breaks. Some, like Malibu, just north of LA, Rincon, up towards Santa Barbara, and Santa Cruz's Steamer Lane, are hugely popular and renowned the world over. Others are secrets, preciously guarded by the local community, though perhaps only a couple of headlands over from the well-known beaches.

Climbing and bouldering

Rock climbers travel the world to test themselves against the granite walls of Yosemite Valley, such an icon of the sport that no climber feels their life is complete without a visit. Some come with quite modest ambitions, but for many the dream is to scale the 3000-foot face of **El Capitan** (see p.346), an imposing monolith that guards the entrance to the valley. Even the easiest routes take most mortals four days (with nights spent sleeping on a kind of camp bed lashed to the rock face), though some superhuman climbers have managed it in just a few hours.

When the mountains are snowbound, climbers head for the **deserts**, particularly **Joshua Tree National Park**, where glorious routes thread their way up rough monzogranite boulders. After a day in the warm spring sun, there's great camaraderie at the *Hidden Valley* campground (see p.244), where everyone gathers for a few beers as the calls of coyotes break the cold night air.

▶ Climbers on El Capitan

A hiker at Zabriskie Point ▲

Kayaking, Lake Tahoe ▼

Excellent hikes

California's national parks, national forests and state parks offer boundless opportunities for **hiking**. Our pick of the trails is below.

Golden Canyon to Zabriskie Point Sample the badlands of Death Valley on this five-mile hike that finishes at one of the finest viewpoints around. Avoid during the heat of high summer; p.274.

John Muir Trail This 211-mile hike from Yosemite Valley to the summit of 14,497-foot Mount Whitney is the pinnacle of Sierra hiking. Most people take about three weeks, sometimes spread over two or three trips; p.340.

Lost Coast Trail Wonderful 24-mile coastal trail well away from civilization and with great camping; p.638.

Mount Shasta For much of the year you'll need crampons and an ice axe to tackle this 14,000-foot volcano. Exhausting but rewarding; p.668.

Pacific Crest Trail For the ultimate challenge, and the widest cross-section of desert and lowland landscapes, consider this mammoth, 2650-mile journey from Mexico into Canada, most of it passing through California.

Best of the rest

California offers plenty of alternative ways of engaging with the outdoors. Why not try **whale-watching** in Point Reyes National Seashore (p.545); **kayaking** on the American River (p.563), **hot-air ballooning** in Napa Valley (p.608); **kiteboarding** at Waddell Beach, Santa Cruz County; **hang-gliding** at Fort Funston, San Francisco (p.531); **whitewater rafting** in Kernville (p.312); or **mountain biking** at Mammoth Mountain (p.293).

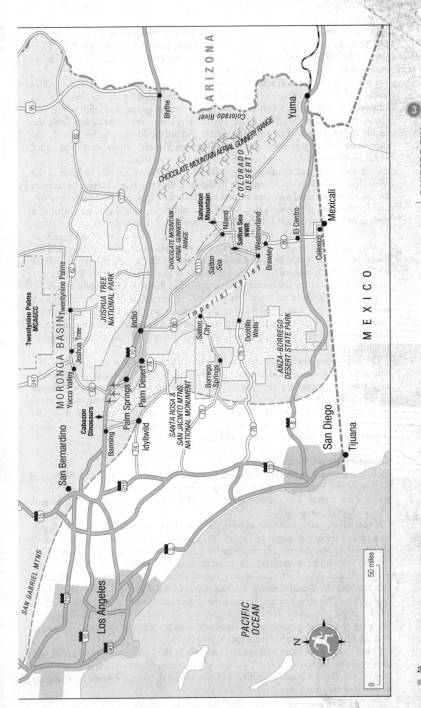

To see the desert at its natural best, head for **Joshua Tree**, one of the most startling of California's national parks and just three hours from LA. A day-trip from Palm Springs would give you a taste, but you really need a couple of days to fully appreciate Joshua Tree's sublime silent landscape, hiking among the weird craggy trees, experiencing the crimson sunsets, then camping out amid the photogenic boulder stacks and the cries of coyotes. In contrast, the undiluted Colorado Desert of the **Imperial Valley** to the south is mostly given over to agricultural land, which you could pass through without realizing anyone lives there. Yet further south, only the highly saline **Salton Sea** and the bizarre **Salvation Mountain** break the arid monotony before you reach the **Anza–Borrego Desert**, whose starkly beautiful vistas are punctuated by several oases and unusual vegetation.

Desolate, silent and virtually lifeless, the **Mojave Desert**, mythic badland of the West, has no equal when it comes to hardship. Called the **High Desert** because its height above sea level averages around two thousand feet, the Mojave is very dry and for the most part deadly flat, dotted here and there with the shaggy form of a Joshua tree and an occasional abandoned miner's shed. Covering the south-central part of the state it forms a barrier between LA and Las Vegas. The Mojave is a land of huge long-haul trucks, rumbling past vast weapons-testing sites, and formed the backdrop for the legion of road movies spawned by the underground film culture in the late 1960s and early 1970s. The desert is also a favourite with bikers and neo-hippies drawn by the barren panorama of sand dunes and mountain ranges.

Although it is short on genuinely compelling attractions, you should linger a little just to see – and smell – what a desert is really like: a vast, impersonal, extreme environment, sharp with its own peculiar fragrance and alive in spring with acres of fiery orange poppies (the state flower of California) and other brightly coloured wildflowers.

The hub of the desert interstates is **Barstow**, often a rest stop on the way to the unnatural neon oasis of **Las Vegas**, just across the border in Nevada. It also works as a base for exploring sections of old **Route 66** and the immense **Mojave National Preserve**. Here you can see spectacular sand dunes, striking rock formations and a huge variety of plant life, including large concentrations of Joshua trees. Much of the preserve rises to about four thousand feet, so it also offers respite from the harshest of the area's heat.

Desert practicalities

Public transport in the desert is poor. Los Angeles connects easily with the major points – Palm Springs, Barstow, Las Vegas – but without your own vehicle you're stuck upon arrival. The region's scant rail and bus services are covered at the end of the chapter (see p.260).

If you have a car, it will need to be in good working order. While the $500 bomb you picked up in LA might be fine for the freeways, don't expect it to cope with the worst of the desert. Three major interstate **highways** cross the desert from west to east. I-15 cuts directly northeast through the middle of the Mojave on its way from Los Angeles to Las Vegas, passing through Barstow where I-40 heads eastwards to the Grand Canyon. I-10 takes you from LA through the Palm Springs and Joshua Tree area, heading into southern Arizona. Some fast, empty secondary roads can get you safely to all but the most remote areas of the desert, but be wary of using the lower-grade roads in between, which are likely to be unmaintained and are often only passable with four-wheel drive.

Other than in the Palm Springs area, **motels** in the California deserts are cheap, and you can generally budget for $40–50 per night. However, even if cost is no object, you'll get a greatly heightened sense of the desert experience by spending some time **camping** out.

The desert is rarely conquered by pioneering spirit alone, and every year people die here, but even in summer, lots of visitors do come to the deserts, when daytime temperatures frequently exceed 120°F (49°C). You'll appreciate travelling here more if you visit during the **cooler months**, from October to May, when daytime temperatures range from the mid-sixties to the low nineties, though night-time temperatures, particularly at high elevations, can drop to below freezing.

Loose, full-length clothing and a wide-brimmed hat will not only help shield you from the sun, but may also prevent bites, stings and scratches from desert flora and fauna, covered in detail on p.48. That said, many people travel the deserts in shorts, T-shirt and sunglasses, and get by quite happily.

Bear in mind too that while the desert may be a danger to man, man is also a danger to the desert. Smog from Los Angeles drifts quickly eastward and you may notice patches of it obscuring vistas here. To reduce your own impact, exercise common sense: remove nothing from the land except your trash and leave only footprints behind.

Driving through
If you're sticking to the main highways, filling your water jugs and gas tank should be all the preparation you need. On steep grades, there is a chance of getting an **overheated engine**. If your car's temperature gauge rises alarmingly, turn the air conditioning off and the heater on full-blast to cool the engine quickly. If this fails and the engine blows, stop with the car facing into the wind and the engine running, pour water over the radiator grille, and top up the water reservoir. Also consider taking along a windshield reflector to keep the car cool when parked.

On less well-travelled routes it could be a long time before anyone comes along. Be sure you have plenty of food and drink and consider carrying an **emergency pack** with flares, a first-aid kit, matches and a compass, a shovel, extra gas and even a tire pump. In an emergency, never leave the car: you'll be harder to find wandering around alone.

Hiking and camping
While heading off on a short walk doesn't require much preparation, **longer hikes** are limited by your inability to carry enough water. The following pointers should help you get back safely.

Register your plans If you get lost, find some shade and wait. So long as you've registered your itinerary, the rangers will eventually come and fetch you. In areas where registration is not required, tell somebody where you are going and your expected time of return.

Take a map and compass And know how to use them.

Hike when it's cool Avoid hiking when the mercury goes over 90°F. Early morning and late afternoon are the best times, though you could even go at night, especially when moonlit.

Take enough water The body loses up to a gallon each day; even when you're not thirsty, you're continually dehydrating and you should keep drinking. On longer walks, take a gallon on full-day hikes, two gallons per day on overnight hikes and don't save it for the walk back. Waiting for thirst, dizziness, nausea or other signs of dehydration before doing anything can be dangerous. If you notice any of these symptoms, or feel weak and have stopped sweating, it's time to get to a doctor.

Take enough food Eat well, packing in the carbohydrates.

Camp safely Never camp in a dry wash. Flash floods can appear from nowhere: an innocent-looking dark cloud can turn a dry wash into a raging river. And don't attempt to cross flooded areas until the water has receded.

Palm Springs and the Coachella Valley

With its manicured golf courses, condominium complexes and thousands of millionaires in residence, **Palm Springs** does not conform to any typical image of the desert. Purpose-built for luxury and leisure, it tends to attract conspicuous consumers and comfort seekers rather than the scruffier desert rats and low-rent retirees of less geographically desirable areas. But though it may seem harder to find the natural attractions and reasonably priced essentials among the glitz, they do exist.

Palm Springs and the adjacent resort towns of the **Coachella Valley** – Cathedral City, Desert Hot Springs, Rancho Mirage, Palm Desert, Indio, Indian Wells and La Quinta – sit in the lushest agricultural pocket of the Colorado Desert, with the massive bulk of the snow-capped San Jacinto Mountains and neighbouring ranges looming over the low-level buildings, casting an instantaneous and welcome shadow over the area in the late afternoon. Meteorologists have noted changes in the humidity of the desert climate around the town, which they attribute to the moisture absorbed from the hundreds of swimming pools – the consummate condo accoutrement, and the only place you're likely to want to be during the day if you come in the hotter months. When scarce water supplies aren't being used to fill the pools or nourish the nearby orchards, each of the Coachella Valley's hundred-plus **golf courses** receives around a million gallons daily to maintain their rolling green fairways.

Lovers of leisure have flocked to Palm Springs since the 1930s, when Hollywood stars were spotted enjoying a bit of mineral rejuvenation out here, and since then it's taken on a celebrity status all of its own – a symbol of good LA living away from the amorphous, smoggy city. Most come for **"The Season"**, the delightfully balmy months from January to May when all the golf and tennis tournaments are held. In recent years it has also become a major **gay** resort (see box opposite), with many exclusively gay – and generally expensive – hotels, bars and restaurants.

Palm Springs wasn't always like this. Before the wealthy settlers moved in, it was the domain of the **Cahuilla**, who lived and hunted around the San Jacinto Mountains to escape the heat of the desert floor. They still own much of the town, and via an odd chequerboard system of land allotment, every other square mile of Palm Springs is theirs and forms part of the **Agua Caliente Indian Reservation** – a Spanish name which means "hot water", referring to the ancient mineral

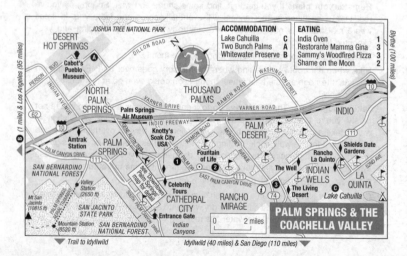

Palm Springs now claims to have overtaken Key West as America's largest **gay resort**, with dozens of exclusively gay clothing-optional inns and hotels flying the rainbow flag. With great weather almost all year round, it is hard to resist working on your tan by the pool all day while regaining your strength for dinner or a night around the clubs and bars.

The local gay press estimate that around forty percent of the town's residents are gay and you'll see evidence all over the place, but nowhere more so than along **Arenas Road**, near South Indian Canyon Drive, which has become something of a gay ghetto. Elsewhere businesses catering to a broader clientele are often gay-run and there's a general sense that the gay and straight communities coexist happily.

That said, in 2003 conservative city officials tried to shut down the event of the gay men's year, the White Party (see p.234), but the election of an openly gay mayor, Ron Oden, in November of that year brought a considerably warmer welcome for the revellers. Lesbians get their turn a couple of weeks earlier during what's known as the Dinah Shore Weekend (see p.234), while later in the year the town hosts the Palm Springs Pride weekend (see p.234).

For information on other events, the local tourist machine puts out the free *Palm Springs Official Gay Visitors Guide*, though you'll get a better insight into the community from the free bi-monthly *The Bottom Line* (Ⓦ www.psbottomline.com) or the weekly *Desert Daily Guide* (Ⓦ www.desertdailyguide.com).

Practicalities

Such is the power of the pink dollar in Palm Springs that virtually all hotels here are gay-friendly, though the Warm Sands district, half a mile southwest of Downtown, contains around thirty exclusively **gay hotels**, most of them hedonistic fun palaces. More resorts populate the Deepwell neighbourhood to the south along San Lorenzo Road and the Las Palmas area on North Palm Canyon Drive. Consult our listings on p.225, or check the town's gay website (Ⓦ www.visitgaypalmsprings.com) for additional suggestions.

Hotel hosts are a mine of information about the trendiest restaurants and bars and will happily point you towards the sort of thing you're after, but restaurants with a strong gay following include *Shame on the Moon*, *Jake's* and *Johannes* (all listed from p.232). For predominantly gay bars and clubs try *Hunter's* and *Toucans Tiki Lounge* (see p.234).

springs on which the town rests. The land was allocated to the tribe in the 1890s, but exact zoning was never settled until the 1940s, by which time the development of hotels and leisure complexes was well under way. The Cahuilla, finding their land built upon, were left with no option but to charge rent, a system that has made them one of the richest of the native tribes in America – and the money continues to pour in, thanks in part to revenue from a new **spa** and the **casinos** of Coachella Valley.

Arrival and information

Palm Springs lies 110 miles east of Los Angeles along the Hwy-111 turnoff from I-10. Arriving by **car**, you'll reach the town on North Palm Canyon Drive (Hwy-111), the main thoroughfare. Amtrak **trains** arrive three times a week from Los Angeles (Sun, Wed & Fri at 5.15pm) and Tucson, Arizona (Sun, Wed & Fri at 4.54am) at a desolate platform three miles north of Palm Springs at North Indian Avenue, just south of I-10. Greyhound **buses** also stop here with daily arrivals from LA and Calexico. A taxi to most accommodation will cost around $20.

Dinosaurs and windmills

After trawling through the dull eastern suburbs of Los Angeles, I-10 throws you a couple of surprises at the San Gorgonio Pass. First up, seventeen miles before Palm Springs, are the Cabazon Dinosaurs (Ⓦwww.cabazondinosaurs.com), two massive fibreglass beasts (claimed to be the world's biggest) flanking the highway. Kids might persuade you to part with $7 to enter the dinosaur museum (with more fibreglass critters) or you could just visit the gift shop in the belly of the 150-foot-long apatosaurus that's full of creationist nonsense about the modernity of dinosaurs.

A mile on, you'll see over three thousand **wind turbines** dotting the valley ahead, their glinting steel arms sending shimmering patterns across the desert floor. Along with Tehachapi Pass (see p.253), this is one of the largest concentrations of windmills in the country, generating enough electricity to service a small city, and the conditions are perfect. The sun beating down on the desert creates a low-pressure zone that sucks air up from the cooler coastal valleys, funnelling it through the San Gorgonio Pass, the only break between two 10,000-foot-plus ranges of mountains. Strong winds often howl for days in spring and early summer, reaching an average speed of between fourteen and twenty miles per hour.

PS Windmill Tours (Ⓣ760/320-1365, Ⓦwww.thebestofthebesttours.com) run two-hour tours (daily 9am, 11.30am & 2pm; $30) making a circuit of the bases of the towers and plying you with facts. Casual observers will be happy just driving by or stopping for a few snaps.

Alaska, American, Delta, United Express and US Airways **fly** into Palm Springs International Airport, 3400 E Tahquitz Canyon Way (Ⓣ760/318-3800), where you can catch bus #24 then transfer to the #111 into town. Tickets are often expensive, and if you're flying to California it is usually cheaper to fly into Los Angeles and rent a car from there.

On the approach to town from I-10 you can't miss the Palm Springs **visitor centre**, 2901 N Palm Canyon Drive (daily 9am–5pm; Ⓣ1-800/347-7746, Ⓦwww .palm-springs.org), installed in a revamped, former gas station designed by Mid-Century Modern leading light Albert Frey. The sweeping roof over the forecourt shades the front of the centre, where helpful staff dispense brochures and sell a couple of handy maps: the *Map of the Stars' Homes* ($5) which details the residences of the famous and the *Palm Springs Modern* map (also $5) which guides you past homes exemplifying the Palm Springs Modern style of architecture (see p.227).

Getting around

Downtown Palm Springs is only a few blocks long and a couple of blocks wide and is manageable on foot. Getting around the rest of the Coachella Valley is possible with the natural-gas-powered **buses** run by SunBus (Ⓣ1-800/347-8628, Ⓦwww.sunline.org), which operate daily from 6am to 8pm (until 11pm on some routes) and charge $1 per ride, plus an extra 25¢ for two transfers (good for two hours after purchase); a day-pass costs $3. While the system is extensive and services fairly frequent, it is never a quick way to get about and you may prefer a **taxi**: call American Cab (Ⓣ760/322-4444).

To get the absolute best out of Palm Springs and the surrounding towns you should think about **car rental**. All the major companies are at the airport and there's a Downtown office of Enterprise at 351 N Palm Canyon Drive (Ⓣ760/327-2699; closed Sun) who have cars from $35 per day.

If you're not planning to stray too far, **rent a bike** or tandem from Bike Palm Springs, 625 N Palm Canyon Drive (Ⓣ760/832-8912, Ⓦwww.bikepsrentals.com;

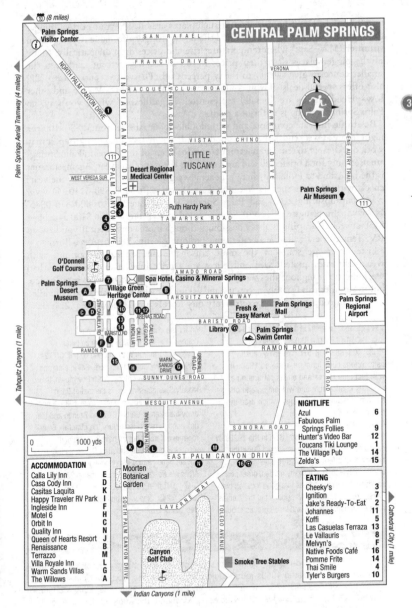

CENTRAL PALM SPRINGS

Palm Springs Visitor Center

(8 miles)

Palm Springs Aerial Tramway (4 miles)

Tahquitz Canyon (1 mile)

SAN RAFAEL

FRANCIS DRIVE

VERONA

RACQUET CLUB ROAD

AVENIDA CABALLEROS

NORTH PALM CANYON DRIVE

INDIAN CANYON DRIVE

VISTA CHINO

SUNRISE WAY

FARRELL DRIVE

GENE AUTRY TRAIL

LITTLE TUSCANY

WEST VEREDA SUR

Desert Regional Medical Center

TACHEVAH ROAD

Ruth Hardy Park

Palm Springs Air Museum

PALM CANYON DRIVE

TAMARISK ROAD

ALEJO ROAD

O'Donnell Golf Course

AMADO ROAD

Spa Hotel, Casino & Mineral Springs

Palm Springs Desert Museum

Village Green Heritage Center

TAHQUITZ CANYON WAY

Fresh & Easy Market

Palm Springs Mall

Palm Springs Regional Airport

N. CAHUILLA RD

ARENAS ROAD

BARISTO ROAD

Library

Palm Springs Swim Center

CALLE EL SEGUNDO

CALLE ENCILIA

BARISTO RD

RAMON RD

RAMON ROAD

EL CIELO ROAD

WARM SANDS DRIVE

GRENFALL ROAD

SUNNY DUNES ROAD

MESQUITE AVENUE

SONORA ROAD

SOUTH INDIAN TRAIL

EAST PALM CANYON DRIVE

Moorten Botanical Garden

SOUTH PALM CANYON DRIVE

LAVERNE WAY

TOLEDO AVENUE

Canyon Golf Club

Smoke Tree Stables

Cathedral City (1 mile)

Indian Canyons (1 mile)

0   1000 yds

NIGHTLIFE

Azul	6
Fabulous Palm Springs Follies	9
Hunter's Video Bar	12
Toucans Tiki Lounge	1
The Village Pub	14
Zelda's	15

ACCOMMODATION

Calla Lily Inn	E
Casa Cody Inn	D
Casitas Laquita	K
Happy Traveler RV Park	I
Ingleside Inn	F
Motel 6	H
Orbit In	C
Quality Inn	N
Queen of Hearts Resort	J
Renaissance	B
Terrazzo	M
Villa Royale Inn	L
Warm Sands Villas	G
The Willows	A

EATING

Cheeky's	3
Ignition	7
Jake's Ready-To-Eat	2
Johannes	11
Koffi	5
Las Casuelas Terraza	13
Le Vallauris	8
Melvyn's	F
Native Foods Café	16
Pomme Frite	14
Thai Smile	4
Tyler's Burgers	10

closed June–Aug), from \$15 for half a day. *Calla Lily Inn* (see p.224) also rent to non-guests year-round (\$10 per hour or \$45 a day; ☏760/323-2453).

Accommodation

Palm Springs was designed for the rich, and big luxury **resorts** and country clubs are everywhere. Comfort and style also come in large doses at smaller and very tasteful hotels. Don't fight it: even if such places are outside your normal budget this is a place to splurge. You may find them surprisingly affordable if you **visit in summer** (May–Sept) when temperatures rise and prices drop dramatically. Many of the bigger places slash their prices by up to seventy percent, and even the smaller concerns give twenty to thirty percent off. The visitor centre (see p.222) also offers special deals. If you couldn't care less about cachet, *Motel 6* and other **low-priced chains** are liberally represented. Regardless of where you stay, no Palm Springs lodging is without a **pool**.

Boutique inns are common, and with double-room rates at around $80–100 per night (more at weekends), they're a good deal. If you're travelling in a group, it may work out cheaper to rent an **apartment/condo**: many of the homes in Palm Springs are used only for a brief spell and are let out for the rest of the year. Again, summer is the best time to look, but there is generally a good supply throughout the year: check with agencies such as Vacation Palm Springs (℡0800/590-3110, ⓦwww.vacationpalmsprings.com) and Palm Springs Rental Agency (℡0800/875-0885, ⓦwww.palmspringsrentals.com). One-bedroom places start around $100 a night or $450 a week. **Camping** is also a possibility though more convenient if you have an **RV**. Tent-carriers will have a better time exploring Joshua Tree or Anza-Borrego.

Listed here are some of the more reasonable and appealing options, with weeknight rates quoted; weekend prices are a price bracket or two higher than weeknights throughout the year. In winter you should always **book in advance**, but in summer this is rarely necessary and asking for a reduced rate is worthwhile.

For an introduction to the **exclusively gay hotels** listed below, see p.221.

Hotels, resorts and B&Bs

Calla Lily Inn 350 S Belardo Rd ℡1-888/888-5787, ⓦwww.callalilypalmsprings.com. Intimate, restored 1950s inn with just nine rooms and suites set around a pool. It's comfortable and welcoming and offers all sorts of summer packages, which drop the rate further. ❻

Casa Cody Inn 175 S Cahuilla Rd ℡760/320-9346, ⓦwww.casacody.com. Built in the 1920s by glamorous Hollywood pioneer Harriet Cody, this historic B&B offers tastefully furnished Southwestern-style rooms, a shady garden, great pool and tasty buffet breakfasts in a good location two blocks from Downtown. All options but the "rooms" have a kitchen. Families and small groups should go for the gorgeous two-bedroom adobe cottage (❽–❾). No weekend price hikes. ❹

Ingleside Inn 200 W Ramon Rd ℡1-800/772-6655, ⓦwww.inglesideinn.com. Set in a serene enclave a couple of blocks from Downtown, this loosely Spanish-style inn is the last of Palm Springs' original hotels, dating from 1935. It once drew the likes of Garbo, Dalí and Brando and still has enough real class to lure the glitterati. Each room is different, but all have a restrained elegance, often with antiques. Of course there are private patios and a lovely pool, and the excellent *Melvyn's Restaurant* is on site (see p.232). ❺

Orbit In 562 W Arenas Rd (℡1-877/996-7248, ⓦwww.orbitin.com; ❺–❼). See box below.

The Orbit In

If you're on the Mid-Century architectural trail or just fancy hanging poolside in your impeccably decorated 1950s-retro studio with private patio, you can't pass up the *Orbit In*, a Modernist nirvana at 562 W Arenas Rd (℡1-877/996-7248, ⓦwww.orbitin.com; ❺–❼). There are two nearly adjacent locations: the super-stylish nine-room *Orbit In* itself designed by Herbert Burns in 1957, with its boomerang bar beside a chilled pool where complimentary Orbitinis are served; and the more secluded 1940s *Hideaway* with lawns, a fire pit and guest kitchen/lounge with photos of the place taken by Julius Shulman in 1948. Cruise town on the free bikes, relax in rooms equipped with DVD and CD player and languish over a continental breakfast. It's adults-only and a two-night stay is required.

Renaissance 888 Tahquitz Canyon Way
ⓣ1-800/228-9290, ⓦwww.marriot.com. Large
hotel that's been recently and stylishly revamped.
Expect all the five-star accoutrements plus elegant
guest rooms and a couple of restaurants. ④–⑤
Villa Royale Inn 1620 S Indian Trail ⓣ1-800/245-
2314, ⓦwww.villaroyale.com. Beautiful inn with
individually designed and exquisitely furnished
rooms and suites, most with jacuzzi, situated
around a pool. In the winter season meals and
drinks are served from the romantic, bougainvillea-
draped *Europa* restaurant. ④
The Willows 412 W Tahquitz Canyon
ⓣ1-800/966-9597, ⓦwww.thewillows
palmsprings.com. The former estate of a US
Secretary of State, whose friends – among them
Clark Gable, Carole Lombard and Albert Einstein –
holed up here during the 1930s. Opulently
decorated rooms, gorgeous lush grounds, a
stunning Mount San Jacinto backdrop, sumptuous
breakfasts and an ideal Downtown location make
this well worth the splurge: starting around $475 in
winter. ⑨

Motels and campgrounds
Happy Traveler RV Park 211 W Mesquite Drive,
Palm Springs ⓣ760/325-8518, ⓦwww.happy
travelerrv.com. RV-only campground with 130 full-
hookup sites and a pool close to the centre of Palm
Springs. $40 per site.
Lake Cahuilla 58075 Jefferson St, La Quinta (see
map p.220); ⓣ760/564-4712, ⓦwww.riverside
countyparks.org. Large campground for tents and
RVs by a 135-acre stocked lake roughly fifteen
miles east of Palm Springs. There are showers, a
dump station for RVs, a summer-only swimming
pool and provision for horses. Electric hookup $22,
tents $15.
Motel 6 660 S Palm Canyon Drive ⓣ760/327-
4200, ⓦwww.motel6.com. The cheapest of the
central motels, with a good pool and outdoor
hot tub. ①

Quality Inn 1269 E Palm Canyon Drive
ⓣ760/323-2775, ⓦwww.qualityinn.com. Modern
motel with spacious grounds, including a nice pool,
exercise room, free wi-fi and a restaurant. ③
Whitewater Preserve 9160 Whitewater Canyon,
17 miles north of Palm Springs and 5 miles north
of I-10 (see map p.220); ⓣ760/325-7222. Basic
tent camping (water and toilets but no showers)
beside a year-round stream on a former trout farm
now run as a nonprofit wildlife preserve. Open all
year. Donations.

Gay accommodation
Casitas Laquita 450 E Palm Canyon Drive, Palm
Springs ⓣ760/416-9999, ⓦwww.casitas
laquita.com. A private women's resort in a rustic
Southwestern-styled compound decorated with
Native American crafts and motifs. All rooms have
kitchen, private bathroom, and TV and CD players;
some come with a fireplace. Breakfast ingredients
are delivered to your room. ⑤
Queen of Hearts Resort 435 Avenida Olancha
ⓣ1-888/275-9903, ⓦwww.queenofheartsps.com.
On the site of Palm Springs' first lesbian hotel, this
renovated resort has just nine rooms around a
great pool, private mist-cooled patio and gorgeous
views of the Santa Rosa Mountains. Some rooms
have kitchens (⑤) and a continental breakfast is
included. ④
Terrazzo 1600 E Palm Canyon Drive ⓣ1-866/837-
7996, ⓦwww.terrazzo-ps.com. An intimate
14-room, clothing-optional men's resort where
comfort and service is such that you'll have trouble
leaving the confines of the hotel. Sumptuous rooms
around the pool, on-site gym and complimentary
sunscreen complete the deal. ⑤
Warm Sands Villas 555 Warms Sands Drive
ⓣ1-800/357-5695, ⓦwww.warmsandsvillas.com.
Renovated with marble floors and king-sized beds
throughout, this men's inn comes with a big
welcome and a generous continental breakfast.
Some rooms have kitchenettes. ⑤

Palm Springs

Much of your time in the Coachella Valley is going to be spent in **Palm Springs**,
home to the majority of the recognized sights. It is a sprawling place but is focused
on a fairly concentrated core.

   Downtown Palm Springs stretches for about half a mile along Palm Canyon
Drive, a wide, bright and modern strip full of boutiques and restaurants that's
engulfed the town's original Spanish village-style structures. With its celebrity
stars embedded in the sidewalk and the neat rows of fan palms along Palm
Canyon Drive, it makes for an attractive stroll through the valley's greatest
concentration of places to eat, many with cooling misters to counteract the
summer heat.

Palm Springs isn't all rampant consumerism, though. It's worth spending time in the **Palm Springs Art Museum** and admiring the architecture of **Little Tuscany** (also known as the Heritage District and "the tennis club district"), just west of North Palm Canyon Drive, where some of the finest small hotels congregate. Further afield, cactus fans should spend an hour at **Moorten Botanical Garden**, while plane buffs are better served at the **Palm Springs Air Museum**.

You'll soon want to stray further, best done by spending half a day riding the **Palm Springs Aerial Tramway** into the San Jacinto Mountains and strolling the easy trails, then returning to explore the palm-filled **Indian Canyons**.

Downtown Palm Springs

Palm Springs owes its very existence to Hollywood, so it's no surprise that South Palm Canyon Drive has a **Walk of Fame** flanked by two life-size bronze statues honouring local leading lights: ex-mayor Sonny Bono stands guard over the junction of Arenas Road, while former resident Lucille Ball graces the intersection with Tahquitz Canyon Way.

Star-struck visitors could easily miss the **Village Green Heritage Center**, 219 S Palm Canyon Drive, a small brick plaza around a fountain and surrounded by a handful of buildings including the 1884 McCallum Adobe, "Miss Cornelia's Little House" (made of railroad ties), and the **Agua Caliente Cultural Museum** (June–Aug Fri–Sun 10am–4pm; Sept–April Wed–Sat 10am–5pm, Sun noon–5pm; free; Ⓦwww.accmuseum.org), with its collection of basketry and pottery.

Don't miss the **Palm Springs Art Museum**, 101 Museum Drive (Oct–May Tues, Wed & Fri–Sun 10am–5pm, Thurs noon–8pm; June–Sept Wed & Fri–Sun 10am–5pm, Thurs noon–8pm; $12.50, but free Thurs 4–8pm; Ⓣ760/322-4800, Ⓦwww.psmuseum.org), where the obvious wealth of its benefactors has been put to superb use in a striking Brutalist building complete with cactus-filled sculpture gardens. The focus is on both traditional and contemporary art, principally from California, though with wider-ranging Native American and Southwestern art. Galleries with diverting exhibits surround a large central space, dotted with works by major sculptors such as Henry Moore, Barbara Hepworth and Alexander Calder. The mezzanine is usually devoted to Mesoamerican artworks often contrasting Classic-period figurines with more modern works, perhaps by

Celebrity house tours

Knowing that they're in the thick of a megastar refugee camp, few can resist the opportunity to see the homes and country clubs of the international elite on a **celebrity tour**. As tacky as they are, these tours have some voyeuristic appeal, allowing you to spy on places like Bob Hope's enormous house and the star-studded area known as **Little Tuscany** – Palm Springs' prettiest quarter, where the famous keep their weekend homes. The tours only view the houses through the minibus window, but in the end it's not the homes that make the tours worthwhile but rather the fascinating trivia about the lives of those who live (or lived) in them. Most of the big names had their heyday over fifty years ago so you'll need to be well up with your classic movies to really appreciate the fine detail.

Best of the Best Tours (Ⓣ760/320-1365, Ⓦwww.bestofthebesttours.com) conduct entertaining two-hour jaunts around Palm Springs (daily; $25), driving past enough homes to satiate most people's celebrity craving. They pick up at the *Spa Hotel*, Downtown: call for times.

Of course, if you've got a car, you can do it yourself with a $5 *Map of the Stars' Homes* from the visitor centre (see p.222), but you'll miss the sharp anecdotal commentary that makes it such fun.

Palm Springs' popularity among the rich and famous during the Forties, Fifties and Sixties saw a massive building-boom. The more discerning newcomers employed young, Modernist architects such as Richard Neutra, who was "governed by the goal of building environmental harmony, functional efficiency, and human enhancement into the experience of everyday living." His work, and that of contemporaries Albert Frey and R.M. Schindler, became known as **Mid-Century Modern**, with its expression in these parts often dubbed Desert Modern or even Palm Springs Modern. After several decades in the architectural wilderness, Palm Springs has seen a surge of interest in its soaring rooflines, glass walls, unity of form and sympathy for the desert setting. The town's renewed cachet means long-ignored houses by the movement's luminaries are now highly sought after. Many can be viewed from the road by driving the route on the *Palm Springs Modern map* ($5) from the visitor centre, but you'll see a lot more (and learn fascinating details about the architects and their clients) by joining PS Modern Tours (☎760/318-6118, ✉PSmoderntours@aol.com). Their three-hour minivan tours ($75) visit the exteriors of assorted residential, commercial and civic buildings, including Richard Neutra's 1946 Kaufmann House (designed for Edgar Kaufmann, who commissioned Frank Lloyd Wright's Fallingwater in Pennsylvania); the 1968 Elrod Residence, with its spectacular living room used for scenes in the Bond flick *Diamonds are Forever*; and the 1962 House of Tomorrow, which later became Elvis and Priscilla's "Honeymoon Hideaway". Tours run all year on demand, but less frequently in summer.

If you're really keen, plan your visit around **Modernism Week** (🌐www.modernism week.com), in mid-to late February, when there are double-decker bus tours, talks, movie showings and cocktail parties in fabulous houses. Book events and accommodation months in advance.

twentieth-century Mexican muralists, Rivera, Orozco and Siqueiros. Spend a few minutes admiring the excellent contemporary **studio glass** collection with marvellous cast works such as Clifford Rainey's *Fragmented Shadow of Time* and Karen LaMonte's *Pianist's Dress Impression*. Look out, too, for Duane Hanson's unnervingly realistic *Old Couple on a Bench* – their watches even tell the time if the staff remember to change the batteries.

Once you've cooled off indoors, check out Downtown's most anarchic piece of landscape gardening at **Moorten Botanical Garden**, 1701 S Palm Canyon Drive (Mon, Tues & Thurs–Sat 9am–4.30pm, Sun 10am–4pm; $3; ☎760/327-6555), a bizarre and somewhat shambolic cornucopia of just about every desert plant – cacti, succulents, dwarf trees etc – lumped together in no particular order, but interesting for those who won't be venturing beyond town to see them in their natural habitat.

Out by the airport, the **Palm Springs Air Museum**, 745 N Gene Autry Trail (daily 10am–5pm; $12; 🌐www.palmspringsairmuseum.org), contains an impressive collection of World War II European and US fighters and bombers, along with associated material on the campaigns they flew in and their pilots. The museum is easily identified by the F-14 and F-16 "Top Gun" fighters proudly displayed outside.

Palm Springs Aerial Tramway and Mount San Jacinto State Park

When the desert heat becomes too much to bear, you can travel through five climatic zones from the arid desert floor to (sometimes) snow-covered alpine hiking trails atop Mount San Jacinto by riding the **Palm Springs Aerial Tramway** (Mon–Fri 10am–9.45pm, Sat & Sun 8am–10.30pm; $23, $31 with dinner at the *Pines*; ☎1-888/515-8726, 🌐www.pstramway.com), located on Tramway Road, four miles southwest of Hwy-111 on the northern edge of Palm Springs. Every thirty minutes a large cable car sets off up the rocky Chino Canyon, bound for the Mountain Station at 8516ft – a rise of almost six thousand feet. Each car is fitted with a rotating floor that makes two full revolutions on the twelve-minute journey, giving breathtaking 360-degree views outdone only by those from the top, which stretch 75 miles all the way to the Salton Sea. The temperature up here is a welcome 30°F cooler than in the valley, so bring something to keep warm or hide indoors, where you can watch a decent video on the tramway's construction or relax in the cafeteria-style *Pines* restaurant, bar, or fine-dining restaurant *Peaks*. Outside are viewing decks and access to a couple of forested **short trails**: the three-quarter-mile Discovery Trail loop and the mile-and-a-half Desert View Trail, with views down onto the Coachella Valley below. From November 15 until April 15, snow conditions permitting, the **Adventure Center** (Thurs, Fri & Mon 10am–4pm, Sat & Sun 9am–4pm) offers cross-country **skiing** ($21 a day) and **snowshoeing** ($18 a day).

To stray further into the surrounding wilderness of the 14,000-acre **Mount San Jacinto State Park**, you'll need a permit from the State Park Ranger Station just outside the Mountain Station. This gives prepared hikers the freedom to summit the nearby peak of 10,834-foot Mount San Jacinto (11 miles round-trip; 4–6hr; 2300 ft ascent), or explore a number of other forest trails. See the Idyllwild account on p.235 for more details.

Exploring the canyons

Desert enthusiasts visit Palm Springs for the **hiking** and **horseriding** opportunities in the canyons that incise the San Jacinto Mountains immediately west of town.

Indian Canyons

The best known and most accessible of the canyons are Palm Canyon, Andreas Canyon and Murray Canyon, known collectively as **Indian Canyons** (Oct–June daily 8am–5pm; July–Sept Fri–Sun 8am–5pm, call to check; $8; ☎760/323-6018, ⓦwww.indian-canyons.com), on part of the Agua Caliente Indian Reservation that lies to the south of Downtown. Centuries ago, ancestors of the Cahuilla tribe settled in the canyons and developed extensive communities, made possible by the good water supply and animal stock. They grew crops of melons, squash, beans and corn, hunted animals, and gathered plants and seeds for food and medicines. Evidence of this remains, and mountain sheep still roam the remoter areas despite the near extinction of some breeds. To reach the best of the remains, follow South Palm Canyon Drive about three miles south to the clearly signposted entrance, from where paved roads run to the entrances of each of the canyons.

The most popular is **Palm Canyon**, which comes choked with palms – some three thousand over seven miles – beside a seasonal stream along which runs the easy 1.5-mile Palm Canyon Trail. A one-mile loop visits the best of **Andreas Canyon**, noted for its rock formations and more popular than **Murray Canyon**, which is difficult to reach but offers a twelve-foot waterfall as a reward for those prepared to hike two miles. A tiny trading post at Palm Canyon sells hiking maps, refreshments and assorted native crafts, but to indulge in real Wild West fantasy you should see things on **horseback**. Smoke Tree Stables, 2500 Toledo Ave (☎760/327-1372, ⓦwww.smoketreestables.com), offers scheduled one-hour ($50) and two-hour ($90) riding tours of the canyons – well worth it, especially if you go in the early morning (tours start at 8am) to escape the midday heat. Longer rides are available by advance arrangement.

Tahquitz Canyon

After years of hippy colonization and subsequent abandonment, the local tribe has in recent years reopened **Tahquitz Canyon**, 500 W Mesquite Ave (Oct–June daily

8am–5pm; July–Sept Fri–Sun 8am–5pm; $12.50; ☎760/416-7044, ⓦwww
.tahquitzcanyon.com), where the visitor centre contains a small artefact-filled
museum and a theatre showing a video on the canyon's shamanic legend. Either
take a self-guided hike in the palmless canyon itself, or join one of the free guided
tours (at 8am, 10am, noon & 2pm), which spend around two and a half hours
hiking through beautiful country and past a sixty-foot waterfall.

Swimming and spas

If your hotel pool isn't large enough make straight for the **Olympic-sized pool** at
the Palm Springs Swim Center, Sunrise Way at Ramon Road (Mon–Fri 11am–5pm,
Sat & Sun 11am–3pm; $3.50; ☎760/323-8278). Lots more water gets used at the
16-acre **Knott's Soak City USA**, 1500 Gene Autry Trail (daily 10am–5pm or
6pm; $31, kids $20, parking $10; ☎760/327-0499, ⓦwww.knotts.com), where
you can surf on a one-acre wave pool and mess around on numerous waterslides.

For a substantially more relaxing experience, visit one of Palm Springs' day-spas,
particularly the elaborate Spa Resort Casino, 401 Amado Rd (daily 8am–7pm;
☎1-888/999-1995, ⓦwww.sparesortcasino.com), based around the **mineral
spring** that the Cahuilla discovered on the desert floor over a century ago. Here,
the basic "Taking of the Waters" ($40) gives you a sauna, spa, steam, eucalyptus
rooms, and as much time in the swimming pool and fitness centre as you desire.
You're encouraged, of course, to spend a lot more on massages (from $65) and
assorted skin and body care treatments (from $110), and at the on-site casino.

For something truly classy, head north to *Two Bunch Palms* (see p.231) or east to
The Well at the *Miramont Resort and Spa*, 45000 Indian Wells Lane (☎760/341-
2200, ⓦwww.miramontresort.com) in Indian Wells, one of the finest spas in the
country. An hour-long Mediterranean massage costs $130 ($145 at weekends) and
is apparently best preceded by a fifteen-minute hydrating "wine bath" ($45).

The other Coachella Valley towns

Palm Springs may have the prestige, but it is the other towns of the **Coachella
Valley** that now have the bulk of the swanky resorts, big-name shops and elegant
restaurants. On initial acquaintance, it is hard to tell one town from another as
they form an amorphous twenty-mile sprawl of gated communities, country clubs
and golf courses. Not all the boundaries between them are clearly marked, and on
their main drags they tend to share faceless low-slung architecture – but differences
become evident to those who have time to explore.

Hwy-111 runs the length of the valley through, or close to, most of the main
points of interest, but if you've got a specific destination in mind and want to avoid
endless stop lights, consider the faster **I-10** which runs parallel about four miles to
the north.

Cathedral City and Rancho Mirage

About five miles east of Palm Springs along Hwy-111, **Cathedral City** ("Cat
City") has no cathedral, but takes its name from the now-hidden Cathedral Canyon,
which apparently reminded early explorers of some medieval minster. It boomed
during Prohibition when the absence of a police force encouraged bawdy establishments to set up shop. You may well come here to drink or dine, or to tap into the
gay scene that's second only to the one in Palm Springs, but during the day there's
not a lot to see except for Jennifer Johnson's fabulous *Fountain of Life* sculpture,
complete with mosaic bighorn sheep, lizards and tortoises. Local Hispanic mothers
who spend their week tending the houses and swimming pools of the wealthy bring
their kids to play in the fountain here on Sunday afternoons.

Further east along the valley, the generally staid **Rancho Mirage** tends to attract dignitaries – and high-profile substance abusers. This so-called "Playground of the Presidents" was home to former President Gerald Ford until his death in 2006, and is also host to the upscale rehab clinic the **Betty Ford Center**. Frank Sinatra was the first of the stars to move to Rancho Mirage in 1956, and others soon followed. The city now recognizes its more illustrious associations in its street names: Frank, Gerald, Bob Hope and Dinah Shore all have drives named after them.

Palm Desert

Palm Desert, directly east along Hwy-111, is the safest place to witness the desert wildlife that flourishes in this inhospitable climate. Here, the ever-expanding **Living Desert**, 47900 Portola Ave (daily: June–Sept 8am–1.30pm; Oct–May 9am–5pm; $12.75; ⊕760/346-5694, ⓦwww.livingdesert.org), is the area's only essential sight, now encompassing over 1200 acres of irrigated and manicured sections of land. Basically a modern zoo, its various sections each represent a different desert region from around the world. Stroll among the cacti of the Mojave or the Chihuahua gardens, through an area specially designed to attract butterflies, or into a palm oasis. North American desert animals – coyotes, foxes, bighorn sheep, snakes and mountain lions – have now been supplemented by sections devoted to African species, such as wild dogs, gazelles, zebras, giraffes, cheetahs and warthogs. There are shady *palapas* and cooling "mist stations" every-where, but it is still best to arrive as the gates open for cool and fragrant morning air, particularly if you fancy the wilderness trail system, which penetrates the hill country behind the zoo. If you can't stand to walk around in the heat, hop on the shuttle ($6 all day), which makes frequent circuits of the park.

On nearby **El Paseo**, sometimes called the "Rodeo Drive of the Desert", you can glimpse a different species of local creature. The wealthy and the wishful thinkers flock to this mile-long strip of fashionable stores and galleries, which loops south off Hwy-111 and is one of the very few places in the whole Coachella Valley where you might leave your car and stroll. Come November (usually the first Sunday), the increasingly prevalent species *Homo golfus* turns out en masse for the nation's only **golf-cart parade** (⊕760/346-6111, ⓦwww.golfcartparade.com), with decorated buggies proceeding along El Paseo.

For more on local events and sights, call at the **Palm Desert Visitor Center**, 73470 El Paseo (daily 9am–5pm; ⊕1-800/873-2428, ⓦwww.palm-desert.org), in the heart of the swanky shops. For wilderness information, drive three miles south along Hwy-74 to the Santa Rosa and San Jacinto Mountains National Monument Visitor Center (daily: Oct–June 9am–4pm; July–Sept 8am–3pm).

Indian Wells and La Quinta

Adjoining Palm Desert, the city of **Indian Wells** has one of the highest per-capita incomes in the US, as well as the largest concentration of the Coachella Valley's grand **resorts**. It's known for its four-day New Year **Jazz Festival**, its high-profile **tennis tournaments** and its prestigious Desert Town Hall **lecture series** (see p.234).

Heading east, next comes **La Quinta**, named for the Valley's first exclusive resort – *Rancho La Quinta* – which was built in 1927 and thrived during the Depression, when Hollywood's escapist popularity rose as the country suffered. Director Frank Capra wrote the script for multiple-Oscar-winner *It Happened One Night* at the resort in 1934 and considered the place so lucky he kept coming back, bringing stars such as Greta Garbo in his wake. It's still so posh that it's not marked on the main road (take Washington Street south to Eisenhower to find it). The Santa Rosa Mountain backdrop is stunning, and the rich no longer get very dressed up, so you won't feel out of place if you come for a drink at the piano lounge.

Golf in the Coachella Valley

Look on Google Earth and the Coachella Valley seems to be all golf courses – a total of 130 of them. They smother Rancho Mirage, Palm Desert, Indian Wells and La Quinta where a home beside the fairway proclaims your arrival among the Coachella Valley elite. The top courses are among the finest anywhere, the barren mountains all around in spectacular contrast to the lush, green fairways and placid water traps. Of course, watering all those fairways is completely unsustainable, but no one seems too concerned about the gradually draining aquifer that underlies most of the valley, as long as places like Palm Desert's Bighorn and Indian Wells' Vintage Club Mountain Course continue to grace the pages of golfing magazines.

Many of the courses are **private**, with annual membership running up to $25,000 on top of a $350,000 initial joining fee. Semi-private and **public courses** are more accessible, though green fees can still be steep in winter: for bargains go in summer and play in the less fashionable afternoon or evening. One of the best public courses is the 36-hole Desert Willow Golf Resort, 38995 Desert Willow Drive, Palm Desert (℡760/346-7060, Ⓦwww.desertwillow.com), where morning green fees run $145 in the popular winter season but drop as low as $35 in summer. Alternatively, try one of the reservation agents such as Affordable Palm Springs Tee Times (℡760/324-5012, Ⓦwww.palmspringsteetimes.com), who book **tee times** at a range of courses up to two months in advance.

Indio

In stark contrast is neighbouring **Indio**, a low-key town whose agricultural roots show in its many date and citrus outlets. Approaching from behind *Rancho La Quinta* along 50th Avenue, you'll pass so many date groves you'll think you're in Saudi Arabia. Back on Hwy-111, stop in at the **Shields Date Gardens**, no. 80225 (daily 9am–5pm; free; ℡760/347-7768, Ⓦwww.shieldsdates.com), built in 1924 but renovated in the 1950s, for a date crystal shake ($3.75) at the original soda fountain. Wander out to see the date palms (all with ladders attached for harvesting), and don't miss the free film, *The Romance and Sex Life of the Date*, with its cheesy commentary partly recorded in the 1950s by Floyd Shields, who set up the town's huge February **Date Festival** which draws people from as far as LA to its wonderfully goofy camel and ostrich races.

Desert Hot Springs

Isolated on the north side of I-10, twelve miles north of Palm Springs, **Desert Hot Springs** was honoured in a 1999 competition for having the best-tasting water in the country. The underground wells for which the town is named supply water for the multitude of swimming pools as well as for drinking. A good jumping-off point for visiting Joshua Tree, it's somewhat more casual than the other Coachella Valley communities – except at **Two Bunch Palms** (℡1-800/472-4334, Ⓦwww.twobunchpalms.com; Ⓞ), a luxury resort nestled in between trailer parks and a favourite of celebrities from Los Angeles. Normal people are also welcome for day-spa treatments that start at about $120 per hour and spending your days soaking in the hot-springs pool with a book and a cocktail, with intermittent breaks for mud baths and massages, is not a bad way to pass the time.

Also be sure to check out **Cabot's Pueblo Museum**, 67616 E Desert View Ave (daily except Mon: May–Sept 9am–1pm; Oct–April 9am–4pm; $10; ℡760/329-7610, Ⓦwww.cabotsmuseum.org), in a four-storey Hopi-style structure built by one Cabot Yerxa over a twenty-year period. After a peripatetic adulthood in Alaska, Cuba and all over California, Cabot became Desert Hot Springs' first resident in 1913, then laboriously hand-dug the first well. He returned in his mid-50s in 1939 and began constructing what he intended to be both his house and a monument to the Indian people he had grown to love. Without formal plans and using home-made adobe bricks and any secondhand bits of wood he could get his hands on, he fashioned a wonderful, rambling, asymmetrical structure – adhering to the belief that symmetry retains evil spirits. Cabot died in 1965 having completed 35 rooms, several of which can now be visited on an entertaining 45-minute guided tour.

Eating

Palm Springs **restaurants** run the gamut from moneyed elegance to fast food, with some good ethnic options in between. If you come in the low season, the desert sun may squelch your appetite sufficiently that you go without eating most of the day and find yourself ravenous at dusk. Dedicated diners should also sample what's on offer in the rest of the Coachella Valley; our recommendations merely scrape the surface of the huge selection that's out there. Several of the best places shut up shop entirely in July and August, while those that stay open often offer substantial discounts – a good time to indulge. Only at the finest restaurants need you book in summer, but in winter places fill up quick and **reservations** are essential.

The nearest groceries are at Fresh & Easy Neighborhood Market, 102 S Sunrise Way (daily 8am–10pm), a mile east of Downtown Palm Springs along Tahquitz Canyon Way.

Palm Springs

Cheeky's 622 N Palm Canyon Drive. *The* place for breakfast, using seasonal, local and organic ingredients for the likes of goat's cheese and sun-dried tomato frittata ($10) perhaps with one of their half-dozen types of bacon – or even a bacon flight ($4). Also inventive lunches. Closed Tues & Wed.

Ignition 123 N Palm Canyon Drive. Small groups of slackers smoking hookahs ($15 apiece in dozens of flavours) on the front veranda distinguish this coffee house, which also has good espresso and free wi-fi.

Jake's Ready-To-Eat 664 N Palm Canyon Drive ☏760/327-4400. Dine on the lovely mist-cooled patio or in the main restaurant on beautifully constructed lunchtime sandwiches and salads (around $10), and dinners which might include pork chop with roasted garlic mash and grilled watermelon ($18). Full bar with happy hour 5–7pm nightly. Closed Sun evening and all day Mon.

Johannes 196 S Indian Canyon Drive ☏760/416-2244. The best of the modern, Downtown restaurants. Unpretentious but with superb-quality food ranging across international styles but with the occasional Austrian dish – schnitzel a speciality. Excellent lunch specials such as a cold seafood sampler ($15), and in summer they often have a low-cost tasting menu (3 courses for under $30), with everything in smaller portions – perfect for people who can't eat quite as much as Americans. Closed Mon lunch.

Koffi 555 N Palm Canyon Drive. The best espresso around (served in real cups if you wish), plus free wi-fi. Nice garden seating out back.

Las Casuelas Terraza 222 S Palm Canyon Drive ☏760/325-2794. *Las Casuelas* opened its original establishment in 1958 (still going strong at 368 N Palm Canyon Drive), but you can't beat this Spanish Colonial-style sister restaurant for its bustling atmosphere, stacks of mist-cooled outdoor seating centred on a palm-roofed bar, and usually some live entertainment. The food suffers from north-of-the-border blanding but is still tasty, and with combination plates for $11–17 and $6 margaritas it's not too expensive.

Le Vallauris 385 W Tahquitz Canyon Way ☏760/325-5059, ⊛www.levallauris.com. Landmark French-Mediterranean restaurant that regularly ranks as one of the very best in the area. Decor includes Flemish tapestries and Louis XV furniture but there's nothing stuffy about the impeccable service or superb food. Main courses are $15–20 at lunch, $35–45 at dinner, plus there's a *prix fixe* menu ($56) and Sunday brunch ($48). Closed July & Aug; reservations essential.

Melvyn's At the *Ingleside Inn* (see p.224). This classical Continental restaurant is old-fashioned in the best possible way – elegant, understated and serving beautifully prepared dishes such as their signature veal with avocado and *mousseline* sauce. Expect to part with $60 a head, a little less if you go for the four-course prix fixé dinner. Book in advance and leave time for a cocktail or two in the intimate bar beforehand. Piano accompaniment, dancing and celebrity-spotting are *de rigeur*.

Native Foods Café 1775 E Palm Canyon Drive in the Smoke Tree Village Mall. This totally vegan café puts a creative twist on traditional vegetarian fare. An eclectic menu, including tacos, pizzas, salads and a variety of veggie burgers, and modest prices ($8–10) make it a worthwhile spot. Lots of tofu, *tempeh* and *seitan*. Daily until 9pm.

Pomme Frite 256 S Palm Canyon Drive ⊤760/778-3727. Semi-casual French-Belgian joint that lends an air of Europe to Downtown. Kick off with artichoke hearts and calamari ($11), perhaps followed by a pot of steamed mussels in lemongrass broth ($22) or a California bouillabaisse ($24). Closed Tues.

Thai Smile 651 N Palm Canyon Drive. Mood lighting, Thai woodcuts and a fish tank create an appealing ambience for getting stuck into authentic Thai green curries and the occasional Szechwan dish for $11–15. Lunch specials are $9 and takeaway is available.

Tyler's Burgers 149 S Indian Canyon Drive. Awesome old-fashioned burgers, fries and classic coleslaw at modest prices, either inside or on the patio. Closed Mon.

The rest of the Coachella Valley

India Oven 35875 Date Palm Drive. The area's best curry restaurant is a modest affair, but the flavours are excellent. Drop in for a vegetarian or meaty lunchtime *thali* ($7), or something off the menu such as *bhindi masala* ($11) washed down with a mint *lassi* ($3.50).

Restorante Mamma Gina 73705 El Paseo ⊤760/568-9898. Long-standing Palm Desert favourite combining the freshest ingredients in original Florentine recipes such as *scaloppini piccata* or lobster meat and black-ink ravioli. Dinner mains $20–30.

Sammy's Woodfired Pizza 73595 El Paseo, in The Gardens mall. Local outlet of this California chain pizzeria, which does a great job offering whole-wheat and gluten-free crusts on concoctions such as prosciutto, arugula and pear, along with Neopolitan classics.

Shame on the Moon 69950 Frank Sinatra Drive at Hwy-111, Rancho Mirage ⊤760/324-5515. A loyal band of wealthy greyhairs and mature gay men frequent this dark, intimate restaurant/bar that's been here since the mid-1980s but feels very Sinatra 1960s. There's no cocktail menu, but Johnny and his team will whip up something fabulous to order, or stick around for the likes of sesame-crusted seared ahi tuna steak ($24). There are often three-course specials around $25 in summer; reservations a must in winter.

Nightlife and entertainment

The scattered nature of the Coachella Valley and the predominance of staid, moneyed residents does little to promote a thriving **nightlife**, though you might stop in at one of the resort **piano lounges**, where, if you shell out for an overpriced drink, you can sometimes catch surprisingly good jazz. Some of the casinos around the valley put on bands you might have wanted to see twenty or thirty years ago, when they were at their best – REO Speedwagon anyone? Pick up the monthly *Desert Guide* (ⓦwww.palmspringslife.com) for news on the current nightlife situation. Unless you hear of something that warrants the journey, you're best staying around Palm Springs, where nightlife tends to be on the retro side.

Palm Springs' main drag is particularly crowded on Thursday evenings, when the surprisingly funky **VillageFest street fair** (Oct–May 6–10pm; June–Sept 7–10pm) draws equal numbers of tourists and young locals. Traffic is temporarily barred from half a dozen blocks of North Palm Canyon Drive, which sprouts a kids' play-zone and booths selling everything from fresh-baked bread to tacky souvenirs and local crafts.

The **Annenberg Theater** (⊤760/325-4490), inside the Palm Springs Art Museum (see p.226), has a seasonal programme of shows, films and classical concerts, and there are a couple of other film and arts festivals worth seeking out.

Azul 369 N Palm Canyon Drive. The perfect spot for watching the action along Palm Canyon Drive is the *Azul*'s patio tables where the whole table-and-seats ensemble gently swings. Go easy on the cocktails as you tuck into their tapas-style small plates.

Fabulous Palm Springs Follies Plaza Theatre, 128 S Palm Canyon Drive ⊤760/327-0225, ⓦwww.psfollies.com. This historic theatre hosts a long-running and enormously popular professional vaudeville show, with artists aged between 56 and 86. Nov–May most days at 1.30 & 7pm. From $50.

Hunter's Video Bar 302 E Arenas Drive ☏760/323-0700. Large and lively gay venue that's the mainstay of the GBT scene with everything from trivia quizzes, pool table and all-day happy hour (until 7pm) to raunchy catwalk shows and dancing til 2am.

Toucans Tiki Lounge 2100 N Palm Canyon Drive ☏760/416-7584. The best gay dance-bar in town with a lively scene most nights – DJs, drag shows, 80s nights, etc – particularly on Tiki Fridays (weekly) when Hawaiian shirts are the go and all-comers are encouraged to get leid.

The Village Pub 266 S Palm Canyon Drive ☏760/323-3265. Worthwhile as a restaurant with lots of salads, pizzas and burgers at reasonable prices, but best for a few drinks and a little dancing. Live music nightly and no cover.

Zelda's 611 S Palm Canyon Drive ☏760/325-2375. There's not much of a cutting edge at Palm Springs' main nightclub, but the new venue is pretty flash and there's always a fun atmosphere with a broad-spectrum crowd dancing to Top 40, hip-hop, retro and whatever guest DJs put together. Dress up. Thurs–Sat 9pm–2am.

Festivals and events

If you're around in mid-January, don't miss out on the **Palm Springs International Film Festival** (ⓦ www.psfilmfest.org), which brings more nightlife to the city than the rest of the year combined, while in mid-March, the **La Quinta Arts Festival** (ⓦ www.la-quinta-arts-found.org) serves up fine art and entertainment.

Coachella Music and Arts ⓦ www.coachella .com. Mid-April. Massive three-day rock and alternative music festival packed with big-name artists. The 2010 event featured the Gorillaz, LCD Soundsystem, Jay Z and many more.

Country Music Festival ⓦ www.stagecoach festival.com. Late April. The Empire Polo Club in Indio draws many of the top names in country music – Keith Urban, Brooks & Dunn and Sugarland in 2010.

Desert Town Hall Lecture Series ⓦ www.desert townhall.org. Mid-Feb to mid-April. Indian Wells hosts four talks by high-profile speakers such as George W. Bush, Tony Blair, Malcolm Gladwell and Desmond Tutu. Tickets start at around $80 for a single lecture.

Dinah Shore Weekend ⓦ www.dinahshore weekend.com. Late March or early April. Major four-day lesbian fiesta which coincides with the Kraft Nabisco Championship golf tournament held at Mission Hills Country Club in Rancho Mirage on the Dinah Shore Tournament Course, named for her

contribution to the game. The tournament ranks second only to the US Women's Open, but golf often plays second fiddle to the numerous hotel pool parties at what has become the nation's hottest lesbian vacation event.

Palm Springs Pride ☏760/416-8711, ⓦ www .pspride.org. First weekend in Nov. Draws gay crowds for three days of entertainment, a street parade and more partying.

White Party ⓦ www.jeffreysanker.com. Mid-April. The single biggest event of the gay year, when over fifteen thousand gay men flock to Palm Springs for four days of hedonism centred on the *Renaissance Hotel*. It's been going since 1989 and has grown to the point where there are A-list celebrity shows (Lady Gaga in 2009) and nonstop parties throughout the four days (often in and around hotel pools). The biggest event, an all-nighter of epic proportions, is held Sat at the Palm Springs Convention Center. A three-day weekend pass giving access to the four major events goes for around $400.

Listings

Bank Bank of America, 588 S Palm Canyon Drive ☏760/340-1867.

Bookstore Barnes & Noble, 72840 Hwy-111, Palm Desert, or more conveniently at Just Fabulous, 515 N Palm Canyon Drive, which is particularly strong on Palm Springs architecture and style.

Hospital Desert Regional Medical Center, 1150 N Indian Canyon Drive ☏760/323-6511, ⓦ www .desertmedctr.com.

Internet The Palm Springs Public Library (see below) offers free internet access, plus there's free wi-fi at some of the cafés (see p.232).

Library Palm Springs Public Library, 300 S Sunrise Way (Tues 10am–7pm, Wed–Sat 10am–5pm; ☏760/322-7323, ⓦ www.palmspringslibrary.org).

Pharmacy Rite Aid Drug Store, 366 S Palm Canyon Drive; open 24/7.

Post office 333 E Amado Rd (Mon–Fri 8am–5pm, Sat 9am–3pm). Zip code 92262.

Around Palm Springs

As the largest desert community by far, the Coachella Valley towns, and Palm Springs in particular, make obvious bases for exploring the surrounding regions where urban comforts are often in short supply. Amenities can, however, be found in **Idyllwild**, a small mountain resort set among the pines high above Palm Springs that's ideal for weekend retreats from LA. The real desert starts to the north, where the **Morongo Basin** provides access to Joshua Tree National Park via the small roadside communities of **Yucca Valley**, **Joshua Tree** and **Twentynine Palms**.

Idyllwild

Five thousand feet up the slopes of Mount San Jacinto, **Idyllwild** is the perfect antidote to the in-your-face success of Palm Springs, fifty road-miles away. Pine-fresh, cool and snow-covered in winter, this small alpine town of about two thousand inhabitants has only a few chalet-style restaurants and hotels, but it's a great place to slow up the cash drain inevitably incurred on a visit to Palm Springs. Get here by heading twenty miles west along I-10 to Banning, then taking the exit for Hwy-243, which sweeps you up the mountain on a good but sharply curving road.

There's considerable temptation to set out on the magnificent trails of **Mount San Jacinto State Park** (which can be busy at weekends) or the surrounding wilderness areas. The permit rules are complicated and the best bet is to call first at the Forest Service's **Idyllwild Ranger Station**, 54270 Pine Crest (Mon–Fri 8am–3.30pm, Sat & Sun 8am–4.30pm; ☎909/382-2921), which has stacks of information about hiking and camping in the area. They'll sell you an **Adventure Pass** ($5 per day, $30 per year; America the Beautiful Annual Pass valid, see p.47; ⓦwww.fs.fed.us /r5/sanbernardino/ap), which allows you to park at the region's trailheads.

Hikes to consider include the **Deer Springs Trail** (six miles round-trip; 3–4hr; 1700-foot ascent), which leads up to Suicide Rock, one of two distinctive peaks rising a couple of thousand feet above the town. To get to the top of the Aerial Tramway (see p.227), follow the **Devil's Slide Trail** (sixteen miles round-trip; 7–9hr; 2300-foot ascent), for which permits are limited.

The library, 54185 Pine Crest (Mon & Fri 10am–6pm, Wed 11am–7pm, Sat 10am–4pm; ☎951/659-2300), has free **internet access**.

Accommodation

Places to stay are well scattered along the roads that fan out from Idyllwild's central shopping area. You can set up **camp** anywhere over two hundred feet away from trails and streams, or in designated Yellow Post Sites (Adventure Pass needed), which have fire rings but no water. There are also drive-in campgrounds run by the Forest Service (☎1-800/444-6777, ⓦwww.recreation.gov) and the county park (☎1-800/234-7275, ⓦwww.riversidecountyparks.org) at a cost of $10–28 per night.

Idyllwild campground Hwy-243. Woodsy campground in the heart of Idyllwild with spacious tent sites ($20), a couple with hookups ($45), and a nature trail.

Knotty Pine Cabins 54340 Pine Crest ☎951/659-2933, ⓦwww.knottypinecabinsidyllwild.com. Idyllwild's cheapest accommodation, with cosy, wood-panelled cabins fitted with quilts, fireplace and DVD player. ❷

Quiet Creek Inn 26345 Delano Drive ☎1-800/450-6110, ⓦwww.quietcreekinn.com. Beautifully appointed forest cabins set up for maximum relaxation. Most have a deck overlooking a creek and a fireplace with wood provided. Follow Tollgate Road off Hwy-243, a mile east of the centre. ❹

Strawberry Creek Bunkhouse 25525 Hwy-243, half a mile north of the ranger station ☎1-888/400-0071, ⓦwww.strawberry creekinn.com. About the best value around these parts, featuring wood-panelled rooms and catering to hikers, climbers and fishing folk. All have forest-view balconies and kitchenettes, and there's a range

of luxury cabins with spa tub and fireplace (⑤). A continental breakfast basket is included. ③
Strawberry Creek Inn 26370 Hwy-243 ☎0800/262-8969, ⊛www.strawberrycreekinn.com.

Pampered luxury in B&B style a few hundred yards south of the centre of town. Rooms are comfortable and well appointed, but vary in theme – Santa Fe, autumn, etc – so ask to see a few. ④

Eating

Café Aroma 54750 North Circle ☎951/659-5212. This upscale place does everything from coffee and scones early on to dinners such as scampi ravioli or *ossobuco* ($22–24). Most nights there is some form of live music.
Higher Grounds 54245 N Circle Drive. You can get your organic java fix and free wi-fi at this centrally located spot.

Red Kettle 54220 North Circle. For straightforward diner food, this is a locals' favourite serving fine all-day breakfasts, burgers and sandwiches, and dinner at weekends. They also sell a $10 packed lunch ideal for days on the trail.

The Morongo Basin

Driving from Palm Springs (or Los Angeles) to Joshua Tree National Park, the easiest access is through the vast tract of high desert known as the **MORONGO BASIN**, almost a thousand square miles of which is taken up by the massive Marine Corps Air Ground Combat Center (MCAGCC), just north of Twenty-nine Palms. Set aside a little time to visit the wildlife haven of the **Big Morongo Canyon Preserve**, the oddball **Desert Christ Park** and the Western charms of **Pioneertown**.

The Morongo Basin Transit Authority (☎1-800/794-6282, ⊛www.mbtabus .com) runs a regular **bus service** between Palm Springs and Yucca Valley, but it's too infrequent to be of much use.

Yucca Valley and around

Heading north off I-10 along Twentynine Palms Highway (Hwy-62), spend an hour or two at the **Big Morongo Canyon Preserve**, 11055 East Drive (daily 7.30am–sunset; donation; ⊛www.bigmorongo.org), a wildlife refuge with trails and boardwalks through the cottonwoods and willows of a vast oasis that's one of the largest bodies of natural surface water for miles around. It's a big hit with wildlife and keen birders, who might hope to spot vermilion and brown-crested flycatchers, Bell's vireo, summer tanager and a whole lot more – the preserve host keeps a list of recent sightings.

The Morongo Basin's largest settlement is **Yucca Valley**, an ugly string of highwayside malls around nine miles east. Follow Pioneertown Drive north off Hwy-62 and, after half a mile, turn right onto Sunnyslope Drive and continue half a mile to the **Desert Christ Park** (daily 7am–dusk; free; ⊛www.desertchristpark .org). Displayed here are 37 of local sculptor Antone Martin's massive, fifteen-foot-tall white concrete figures, erected in the 1950s and depicting tales from the Bible – a fittingly bizarre addition to the region. Return to Pioneertown Drive and continue 3.5 miles north to **Pioneertown**, an Old West town created in the 1940s for the filming of movies and TV series – a nice bit of synthetic cowboy country in case there isn't enough of the real thing around for you. There's even a bowling alley (Fri & Sat 2–10pm) that's little changed since it was built in 1947.

Tap into good **food** and a great atmosphere at *Pappy & Harriet's* (☎760/365-5956, ⊛www.pappyandharriets.com), a Tex-Mex and mesquite barbecue, where there's live music pretty much every night of the week. Indeed, this place has become the area's main venue for touring bands, occasionally attracting the odd internationally recognized artist. Local bands all come out for Sunday night.

It also has the area's most interesting **accommodation** in the form of the *Pioneertown Motel* (℡760/365-7001, Ⓦwww.pitowninn.com; ❷–❹), where clean but ageing rooms are made more appealing by a full kitchen and a variety of decor: cowboy, pioneer, seascape, etc.

Joshua Tree

Six miles east of Yucca Valley, the town of **Joshua Tree** centres on the intersection of Twentynine Palms Highway and Park Boulevard, which runs south to the national park's West Entrance. There's not much to the place, though it does attract a mixed bunch of artists who have opened some small, off-beat galleries, and musicians who run a couple of excellent **festivals**: the Joshua Tree Music Festival in mid-May and the Joshua Tree Roots Music Festival in mid-October (for both see Ⓦwww.joshuatreemusicfestival.com).

National Park information is best sought at the **visitor centre**, 6554 Park Blvd (see p.241), which also stocks books and has an attractive cactus garden outside. The cheapest **place to stay** is the basic, pool-equipped *High Desert Motel*, 61310 Twentynine Palms Hwy (℡1-888/367-3898; ❶). Opposite, the slightly run-down *Joshua Tree Inn*, 61259 Twentynine Palms Hwy (℡760/366-1188, Ⓦwww.joshuatreeinn .com; ❸), has comfortable rooms and suites with kitchens set around a pool but is mainly of interest to fans of Gram Parsons (see box, p.243) who died in Room 8. You can inscribe your thoughts in a little book known as the Sacred Heart Journal and add your guitar pick to the collection. There's considerably more comfort at 🎏*Spin and Margie's Desert Hideaway*, Sunkist Road, 3 miles east (℡760/366-9124, Ⓦwww .deserthideaway.com; ❹), with cool, tiled rooms vibrantly decorated in a desert style, some with full kitchen. You'll probably want to stay longer than the two-night minimum, relaxing in the cactus garden or playing petanque. For top-end luxury, book one of the two rooms at *Sacred Sands*, 63155 Quail Springs Rd (℡760/424-6407, Ⓦwww.sacredsands.com; ❽; two-night minimum), a gorgeous strawbale B&B just off the road into the national park, with sumptuous fittings including outdoor baths and even a sleeping platform under the stars.

Several reliable **places to eat** huddle within a block or so of each other along Twentynine Palms Highway at its junction with Park Boulevard. Try 🎏*Crossroads Café and Tavern*, no. 61715, for breakfasts, burgers, espresso, shakes and microbrews or tiny 🎏*Ricochet*, next door (℡760/366-1898) where most people just trust the chef, Rosa, to whip something up for them. They do have a short menu featuring breakfast, organic salads, wraps and Italian dinners (Mon–Wed only) and even sell vintage clothing. The unlikely-looking *Sam's Market*, 61380 Twentynine Palms Hwy is a good spot for a cheap curry.

Climbers and hikers needing to buy or **rent gear** should stop by Nomad Ventures, 61795 Twentynine Palms Hwy (℡760/366-4684), or nip across the road to Coyote Corner, 6535 Park Blvd (℡760/366-9683), where you can fill up your water jugs before heading into the park or have a **shower** ($4 for 7min) after several days of dust and sand.

The **library**, by the crossroads at 6465 Park Blvd (Mon–Fri 10am–6pm, Sat 10am–2pm; ℡760/366-8615), has free **internet access**.

Twentynine Palms

Fifteen miles east of the town of Joshua Tree and just two minutes' drive from the national park's North Entrance, the small highway-side desert town of **Twentynine Palms** (locally known as "two-nine") is a pleasant enough little place despite the occasional artillery booms from the nearby marine base.

The town runs for almost five miles along the highway and is divided into two sections separated by a small hill. The only sights to speak of are the national park's

Oasis Visitor Center (see p.241) on the eastern edge of town and the nearby Old Schoolhouse Museum, 6760 National Park Drive (June–Aug Sat & Sun 1–4pm; Oct–May Wed–Sun 1–4pm; free; ℡760/367-2366), whose partly restored schoolroom from 1927 has displays on the local mining industry, the military presence and desert wildlife.

Pick up **information** at the Twentynine Palms Chamber of Commerce, 73484 Twentynine Palms Hwy (Mon–Fri 9am–5pm, Sat & Sun 10am–4pm; ℡760/367-6197, ⓦwww.29chamber.org), and get **internet access** at the library, 6078 Adobe Road (Mon & Tues noon–8pm, Wed–Fri 10am–6pm, Sat 9am–5pm).

The best place in town to **stay** is the ☼ *Twentynine Palms Inn*, 73950 Inn Ave, off National Park Drive (℡760/367-3505, ⓦwww.29palmsinn.com; ❺), where an array of cosy adobe bungalows and wood-framed cabins is set around attractively arid grounds and gardens, and a central pool area contains a restaurant and bar. The inn was built in 1928 on the Oasis of Mara (see box, p.242), and has comfortable but fairly basic cabins. It's worth upgrading to a bungalow (❻) or even the lovely Irene's Historic Adobe (❾), which sleeps four.

It's a only a small step down to the welcoming *Circle C Lodge*, 6340 El Rey Ave, two miles west of town (℡1-800/545-9696, ⓦwww.circleclodge.com; ❺), where spacious and well-appointed rooms are ranged around a pool, spa and barbecue area. Among the cheaper options nearby is the large *Motel 6*, 72562 Twentynine Palms Hwy (℡760/367-2833; ❶), which has a pool.

The best **place to eat** is the *Twentynine Palms Inn*, with excellent lunches ($8–10) and dinners ($15–20), with many of the ingredients grown in the oasis gardens. For good espresso, bagels, breakfasts, wraps, smoothies and salads, try *WonderGarden Café*, 6257 Adobe Rd, where there's a shady patio out back.

Campers in need of a cleanup should head along to 29 Palms Family Fitness, 73782 Two Mile Rd at Adobe Road (℡760/361-8010), which has as-long-as-you-like **showers** with towels for $4.

Joshua Tree National Park

Spread over a transitional area where the high Mojave meets the lower Colorado Desert, **JOSHUA TREE NATIONAL PARK** is one of the most unusual and fascinating of California's national parks. Almost 1250 square miles have been set aside for the park's ragged and gnarled namesakes, which flourish in an otherwise sparsely vegetated landscape. If you're staying in Palm Springs, there's no excuse not to visit; if you've further to come, make the effort anyway.

The startling Joshua trees (see box, p.240) are only found in the northwestern quarter of the park, where they form a perfect counterpoint to surreal clusters of monzogranite boulders, great rock piles pushed up from the earth by the movements of the Pinto Mountain Fault running directly below. Often as tall as a hundred feet, their edges are rounded and smooth from thousands of years of flash floods and winds, but there are enough nodules, fissures and irregularities to make this superb **rock-climbing** territory.

Throughout, it's a mystical, even unearthly, landscape best appreciated at sunrise or sunset when the whole desert floor is bathed in red light. At noon it can feel like an alien and threatening furnace, with temperatures often reaching 125°F (52°C) in summer, though dropping to a more bearable 70°F (21°C) in winter. If you're visiting between May and October, you must stick to the higher elevations to enjoy Joshua Tree with any semblance of comfort. In the Low Desert part of the park, the Joshua trees thin out and the temperature rises as you descend below three thousand feet.

239

JOSHUA TREE NATIONAL PARK

MOJAVE DESERT

COLORADO DESERT

TRANSITION ZONE

OLD DALE MINING DISTRICT

PINTO MOUNTAINS

PINTO BASIN

Ocotillo Patch

Cholla Cactus Garden

HEXIE MOUNTAINS

Mastodon Peak

Cottonwood Spring Oasis

Lost Palms Oasis

BAJADA NATURE TRAIL

Cottonwood Visitor Center

COTTONWOOD MOUNTAINS

EAGLE MOUNTAINS

PINKHAM CANYON ROAD

BLACK EAGLE MINE ROAD

OLD DALE ROAD

PINTO BASIN ROAD

Twentynine Palms

Oasis Visitor Center

PARK BOULEVARD

Belle

White Tank

Skull Rock

Jumbo Rocks

GEOLOGY TOUR ROAD

BIG HORN PASS ROAD

Fortynine Palms

Indian Cove

BOX CANYON ROAD

Keys Ranch

QUEEN VALLEY

Ryan

Ryan Mountain

Lost Horse Mine

Barker Dam

Wonderland of Rocks Area

Hidden Valley

LOST HORSE VALLEY

Keys View

PARK BOULEVARD

COVINGTON FLATS

LITTLE SAN BERNARDINO MOUNTAINS

JOSHUA TREE NATIONAL PARK

MOJAVE DESERT

BOX S TRAIL

Joshua Tree

Black Rock Canyon

TRANSITION ZONE

see Palm Springs & The Coachella Valley map

COLORADO DESERT

Indio

Coachella

Palm Desert

Von's

Yucca Valley

Desert Christ Park

Pioneertown

Morongo Valley

Big Morongo Canyon Preserve

Desert Hot Springs

Palm Springs

EATING

Crossroads Café and Tavern	3
Pappy & Harriet's	1
Ricochet	3
Sam's Market	2
Twentynine Palms Inn	F
WonderGarden Café	4

ACCOMMODATION

Circle C Lodge	C
High Desert Motel	B
Joshua Tree Inn	D
Motel 6	C
Sacred Sands	A
Spin and Margie's Desert Hideaway	G
Twentynine Palms Inn	E
	F

Lake Havasu City (100 miles)

Phoenix (200 miles)

Amboy (30 miles)

Barstow (80 miles)

Los Angeles (95 miles)

Salton Sea (20 miles)

Anza-Borrego Desert (45 miles)

Rock Outcrops

Unpaved Road Surface

Suitable for 4WD only

0   5 miles

The Joshua tree

Unique to the Mojave Desert, the **Joshua tree** (*Yucca brevifolia*) is one of its oldest residents, with large examples probably over three hundred years old. The lack of growth rings makes their age difficult to determine. The Joshua tree isn't, in fact, a tree at all, but a type of yucca, itself a type of agave and therefore a giant member of the lily family.

Awkward-looking and ungainly, it got its unusual name from Mormons who travelled through the region in the 1850s and imagined the craggy branches to be the arms of Joshua leading them to the Promised Land. Of course, Native Americans had been familiar with Joshua trees for millennia, weaving the tough leaves into baskets and sandals, and eating the roasted seeds and flower buds. The trees became equally useful for homesteaders who arrived in the wake of the Mormons – the lack of better wood forced them to press the trunks of Joshua trees into use for fences and building material.

Joshua trees only grow at altitudes over **two thousand feet** and prefer extreme aridity and a bed of course sand and fine silt. By storing water in their spongy trunks, they can grow up to three inches a year, ultimately reaching heights of forty feet or more. To conserve energy, they only bloom when conditions are right, waiting for a crisp winter freeze, timely rains and the pollinating attentions of the yucca moth before erupting in a springtime display of creamy white-green flowers, which cluster on long stalks at the tips of the branches. Successful young saplings start life as a single shoot, but eventually a terminal bud dies or is injured and the plant splits to form two branches, which in turn divide over time, producing the Joshua trees' distinctive shapes.

Some history

"Joshua Tree" may be a familiar name today, thanks in part to U2's 1987 album of that name, but previously it was almost unknown. Unlike the vast bulk of the state, nobody, save a few Native Americans, prospectors and cowboys, had penetrated these remote environs. Despite receiving only around four inches of annual rainfall, the area is surprisingly lush, and it was grass that attracted the first significant pioneers. Forty-niners hurrying through on their way to the Sierra Nevada gold fields told tales of good pastures and early cattlemen were quick to follow, while rustlers discovered that the natural rocky corrals made perfect sites for branding their illegitimate herds before moving them out to the coast for sale. Ambushes and gunfights drove the rustlers to seek refuge in the mountains, where they discovered small traces of gold and sparked vigorous mining operations that continued until the 1940s. In recognition of the uniqueness of the area and the need for its preservation, the national park system took the land under its jurisdiction as a national monument in 1936 and has vigilantly maintained its beauty ever since. The park lost some of the original area to mining interests in the 1950s, but that was more than compensated for in 1994, when it was promoted to a **national park**, with the addition of 365 square miles.

Park practicalities

Less than an hour's drive northeast from Palm Springs, Joshua Tree National Park (always open; $15 per vehicle for 7 days, $5 per cyclist or hiker; Ⓦ www.nps.gov /jotr) is best approached through the Morongo Basin (see p.236) along Hwy-62, which branches off I-10. Besides camping (see opposite), there is neither lodging nor anywhere to eat or buy supplies within the park, so the Morongo Basin towns of Yucca Valley, Joshua Tree and Twentynine Palms are the main bases from which to explore. Visiting the park without your own **transport** is not really an option: at best, you're looking at a ten-mile desert walk to get to anything of interest.

You can enter the park via the West Entrance at the town of **Joshua Tree**, where there's a **visitor centre**, 6554 Park Blvd (daily 8am–5pm), or the North Entrance at **Twentynine Palms**, where you'll find the **Oasis Visitor Center** (daily 8am–5pm; ℡760/367-5500). Alternatively, if you're coming from the south, there's an entrance and the **Cottonwood Visitor Center** (generally daily 9am–3pm) seven miles north of I-10. It's worth stopping at one of the visitor centres to collect the free national park **map** and *Joshua Tree Guide*, which are fine for most purposes, though hikers will want a more **detailed map**, the best being Trails Illustrated's *Joshua Tree National Park* ($13).

Park staff run free, campground-based **ranger programmes** (generally mid-Feb to May and mid-Oct to mid-Dec, but also summer weekends), which might include campfire talks, discovery walks and geology hikes: check at the visitor centres for the current schedule.

Camping

Joshua Tree National Park has nine **campgrounds**, all concentrated in the northwest except for one at Cottonwood by the southern entrance. All have tables, fire rings (bring your own wood) and vault toilets, but only two (*Black Rock* and *Cottonwood*) have water supplies and flush toilets. The lack of showers and electrical and sewage hookups at any of the sites keeps the majority of RVs at bay, but in the popular winter months the place fills up quickly, especially at weekends. All campgrounds are good for up to six people and two vehicles and are first-come-first-served, though *Black Rock* and *Indian Cove* can be reserved from October to May. **Winter** nights can be very cold, and campers here between November and March should come with warm jackets and sleeping bags or head for the lower (and warmer) *Cottonwood* campground.

Over eighty percent of the park is designated wilderness where **backcountry camping** is permitted, provided you register before you head out. Twelve backcountry boards are dotted through the park at the start of most trails. Here you can self-register, leave your vehicle and study the regulations that include prohibition of camping within a mile of a road and five hundred feet of a trail.

The campgrounds are listed from northwest to southeast through the park.

Black Rock (100 sites; 4000ft) A large campground only accessible from outside the park. Reserve by calling ℡1-877/444-6777. Water available. $15.

Indian Cove (101 sites; 3200ft) Another large campground only accessible from outside the park. It's set among granite boulders and a trail from the eastern section of the campground road leads to Rattlesnake Canyon – its streams and waterfalls (depending on rainfall) breaking an otherwise eerie silence among the monoliths. Reservations on ℡1-877/444-6777. No water. $15.

Hidden Valley (39 sites; 4200ft) Popular campground that is almost entirely occupied by rock climbers in spring and fall. No water. $10.

Ryan (31 sites; 4300ft) Medium-sized campground amid some lovely rocks and trees. No water. $10.

Jumbo Rocks (124 sites; 4400ft) The highest and largest site in the park, often busy and with regular ranger programmes including a free one on Sat evenings (spring–fall). No water. $10.

Belle (18 sites; 3800ft) Small, quiet site amid some lovely rocks. No water. $10.

White Tank (15 sites; 3800ft) Relatively small and quiet site with a short nature trail to Arch Rock. No water. $10.

Cottonwood (62 sites; 3000ft) Being lower down, this is the pick for the cooler winter months. Water available. $15.

Exploring the park

The best way to enjoy the park is to be selective, especially in the hotter months when you'll find an ambitious schedule impossible. Casual observers will find a day-trip plenty, most likely a leisurely drive along **Park Boulevard** and **Pinto Basin Road** – the paved roads which run right through the park – perhaps joining a tour of Keys Ranch and driving up to Keys View. For desert-lovers a couple of

Nature trails and hikes in Joshua Tree National Park

To get a real feel for the majesty of the desert, you'll need to leave the main roads behind and hike, or at least follow one of the short (and mostly wheelchair-accessible) **nature trails** which have been set up throughout the park to help interpret something of desert ecology and plant life.

The more strenuous **hikes** outlined below are generally safe, but be sure to **stick to the trails**: Joshua Tree is full of abandoned gold mines, not all of them adequately fenced. Most of the listed trails are in the slightly cooler and higher Mojave Desert, but even on the easier trails allow around an hour per mile: there's very little shade and in summer you'll tire quickly. If you're experienced, well equipped and fancy heading out on anything more ambitious than the hikes described here (perhaps into the Pinto Basin), be sure to discuss your plans with a ranger; and anyone planning to stay out overnight in the wilderness must **register** at one of the trailhead backcountry boards. Finally, remember never to venture anywhere without a detailed map.

Nature trails

These are listed northwest to southeast through the park.

Oasis of Mara (800-yard loop) A series of explanatory panels around a significant fan-palm oasis right by the Oasis Visitor Center.

Cholla Cactus Garden (400-yard loop) A beautiful stroll among these superbly photogenic cacti.

Bajada (400-yard loop) Investigate the flora of a naturally sloping drainage half a mile north of the South Entrance.

Recommended hikes

These are listed northwest to southeast through the park.

49 Palms Oasis (3 miles; 2hr) Moderately strenuous, this leaves the badly signposted Canyon Road six miles west of the visitor centre at Twentynine Palms. A barren, rocky trail leads to this densely clustered and partly fire-blackened oasis, which continues to flourish on the seepage down the canyon. There's not enough water to swim in, nor are you allowed to camp (the oasis is officially closed 8pm–7am), but a late afternoon or evening visit presents the best wildlife rewards.

Lost Horse Mine (4 miles; 3hr) Starting a mile east of Keys View Road, this moderately difficult trail climbs 450ft to the mine, which made an average of $20,000 a week in the 1890s. The hike takes you through abandoned mining sites, with building foundations and equipment still intact, to the top of Lost Horse Mountain.

Ryan Mountain (3 miles; 2hr) Some of the best views in the park are from the top of Ryan Mountain (5461ft), seven hundred strenuous feet above the desert floor. Start at the parking area near the *Sheep Pass* campground and follow the trail past the Indian Cave, which contains bedrock mortars once used by the Cahuilla and Serrano.

Mastodon Peak (3 miles; 2hr) Another peak climb, less strenuous than Ryan Mountain but with good views, especially south to the Salton Sea. Start from the *Cottonwood* campground.

Lost Palms Oasis (8 miles; 5hr) This moderate trail, starting from the *Cottonwood* campground or nearby trailhead, leads across desert washes and past palo verde, cottonwood and ironwood trees to the largest stand of palms in the park. The trail offers a possible scrambling side-trip to Victory Palms. There's little surface water, but often enough to lure bighorn sheep.

nights camping out is a highlight that shouldn't be missed, and experienced hikers may want to take advantage of the park's excellent if strenuous trails and backcountry opportunities (see box above).

Many of the roads are unmarked, hard to negotiate and restricted to four-wheel-drive use. If a road is marked as such, don't even think about taking a normal car – you'll soon come to a grinding halt, and it could be quite a few panic-stricken hours before anybody finds you.

The northwest

Approaching from the township of Joshua Tree, you enter the park's northwestern corner and immediately find yourself in the **Wonderland of Rocks** area, comprising giant, rounded granite boulders that draw **rock climbers** from all over the world. The various clusters flank the road for about ten miles, giving plenty of opportunity to stop for a little bouldering, and also provide more adventurous routes for those suitably equipped and skilled.

A little further on, close to the *Hidden Valley* campground, a well-signposted one-mile nature trail loops into **Hidden Valley**, a near-complete natural circle of rock mounds where cattle rustlers used to hide out. To the north, a side road leads past the entrance to Keys Ranch (see below) to the rain-fed **Barker Dam**, Joshua Tree's crucial water supply, built around the turn of the twentieth century by cattlemen (and rustlers) to prevent their poor beasts from expiring halfway across the park. The route back from the dam passes a number of petroglyphs.

Keys Ranch

Just northeast of the *Hidden Valley* campground sits the **Keys Ranch**, only accessible by joining the informative and entertaining ranger-led **guided walking tour**

Safe at Home – Gram Parsons in Joshua Tree

A relatively minor star in his lifetime, **Gram Parsons**, the wild country outlaw of early Seventies rock, has since become one of the era's icons. His musical influence spreads wide, from ageing rockers such as his old friend Keith Richards to Evan Dando, Beck and the current breed of alt-country misfits, but his fame owes as much to his drug- and booze-fuelled life and the bizarre circumstances surrounding his death at the age of 27. It is a story embellished over the years by myth, fabrication and gossip. Joshua Tree was Gram's escape from the LA music pressure-cooker, and photos show him hanging out with Richards in pharmaceutically altered states, communing with nature, and scanning the night sky for UFOs. On his final visit, Gram and three friends spent September 18, 1973, consuming as much heroin, morphine, marijuana and Jack Daniels as possible, with Gram finally ODing that night in Room 8 at the *Joshua Tree Inn*.

Parsons' stepfather stood to benefit from Gram's estate if he could get the body back to Louisiana for burial. However, Gram and his friend and tour manager, Phil Kaufman, had already agreed "the survivor would take the other guy's body out to Joshua Tree, have a few drinks and burn it". Three days after Gram's death, Kaufman persuaded an airline employee to release Gram's casket, drove out to Joshua Tree, doused his body in gasoline and executed the wishes of his deceased friend. The body wasn't completely consumed, however, and Grams' remains now lie in a New Orleans cemetery. Kaufman was only charged with theft of a coffin and had to pay a $300 fine plus $708 for the coffin.

Fans come to stay at the *Joshua Tree Inn* (see p.237) and to visit a **makeshift shrine** near where his body was cremated. From the Cap Rock parking lot at the start of Keys View Road, follow a well-defined but unmarked trail around the west side of the rock to a point close to the road intersection. Here, a rock alcove is usually plastered with dedications, though the rangers consider it to be graffiti and periodically clean it off. For many years the spot was marked by a small concrete plinth daubed with "Gram – Safe at Home".

(Oct–May daily 10am & 1pm; June–Sept check at the visitor centres; $5; reservations recommended on ☏760/367-5555), which begins at the entrance to the ranch and takes around ninety minutes. You can buy tickets in advance at the Oasis Visitor Center, or just turn up and hope there is space. The ranch was once home to tough desert rat and indefatigable miner Bill Keys, a Russian by birth who lived here with his family from 1910 until his death (at age 89) in 1969 – long after less hardy men had abandoned the arid wasteland. He was briefly famous in 1943, when he was locked away for shooting one of his neighbours over a right-of-way argument, only to be bailed out by a friend, the mystery writer Erle Stanley Gardner. Keys and family made a spartan but surprisingly comfortable living from growing vegetables, mining, ranching and working as a farrier and general trader for just about everything a desert dweller could desire. The tour visits their ramshackle home, orchard site, workshop and even a schoolhouse that operated for seven years from 1935.

The centre and southeast

Bill Keys is further remembered at **Keys View**, eight miles south, a 5185-foot-high vista offering the best views in the whole park. On a good day, you can see as far as the Salton Sea and beyond into Mexico – a brilliant desert panorama of badlands and mountains. The trouble is, "good" days are rare since LA smog is funnelled between the mountains straight to Joshua Tree National Park, with the result that **air pollution** is a significant issue.

Continue along Park Boulevard past the start of the Ryan Mountain hike (see box, p.242) and the turnoff for **Geology Tour Road**, which leads down through

Biking and rock climbing in Joshua Tree National Park

While driving through Joshua Tree lessens your contact with the desert, and the need to carry all your water limits the scope for hiking, **biking** strikes a nice balance. With cyclists restricted to roads open to motor vehicles, you shouldn't come expecting genuine off-road action, but there's an increasing number of bikeable and challenging dirt roads. Armed with your own set of wheels (there is no bike rental anywhere near the park), consider heading out on popular fifteen- to twenty-mile routes like the Geology Tour Road, Covington Flats Road and Pinkham Canyon Road. These and more are listed in the *Joshua Tree Guide* (see p.241).

Since the 1970s, the fractured lumps of golden rock that pepper the northwestern corner of the park have become fabulously popular and world renowned for **rock climbing** and **bouldering**. Climbers keen to find a springtime training ground while the Sierra crags were still under snow began putting up routes which now see sticky-rubber traffic from October to May – the summer months are generally way too hot. In spring and fall, rock climbers sometimes base themselves here for weeks, usually at the *Hidden Valley* campground. Climbers should read the climbing ethics section of the park website and may want to call at the climbing shops in the township of Joshua Tree to obtain guidebooks; Coyote Corner lends guidebooks short term, but you'll probably want to buy one. The most comprehensive book is Randy Vogel's *Rock Climbing: Joshua Tree*, though his condensed and much cheaper *Joshua Tree National Park: Classic Rock Climbs* may suit short-term visitors. Boulderers will want *A Joshua Tree Bouldering* by Mary Ginery. Beginners, or those after instruction and guiding, should contact one of the climbing schools that operate here. Both Joshua Tree Rock Climbing School (☏1-800/890-4745, ⊛www.joshuatreerockclimbing.com) and Uprising (☏1-888/254-6266, ⊛www.uprising.com) offer a range of one-day courses for around $120 and improvers' weekends for around $225. Check the websites for course dates, or go for private guiding which costs around $315 a day for one person or $175 each for two.

the best of Joshua Tree's rock formations. A little further on, the *Jumbo Rocks* campground is the start of a hiking loop (1.7 miles) through boulders and desert washes to **Skull Rock**, which can also be easily seen from the road immediately east of the campground.

Moving along eastward, now on Pinto Basin Road, you'll pass *White Tank* campground (see p.241), which is worth a short stop for its trail through huge granite domes to a photogenic **rock arch**; the trail starts by site 9.

Almost at the transition zone between the Colorado and Mojave deserts and on the fringes of the Pinto Basin, the **Cholla Cactus Garden** is a quarter-mile loop through an astonishing concentration of the "jumping" **cholla** cactus (see box, p.48), as well as creosote bushes, jojoba and several other cactus species. It's a beautiful spot at any time, but come at dusk or dawn for the best chance of seeing the mainly nocturnal desert wood rat. Nearby, the almost barren desert at **Ocotillo Patch** comes stuffed with spindly ocotillo plants, most attractive in spring for their scarlet blooms.

The Imperial Valley and the Salton Sea

The patch of the Colorado Desert **south** of Joshua Tree and Palm Springs is one of the least friendly of all the California desert regions and its foreboding aspect discourages exploration. Frankly, there's little reason to head out this way unless you're heading for Anza-Borrego Desert State Park or the Mexican border.

Sandwiched between Hwy-111 and Hwy-86, which branch off I-10 soon after Palm Springs and the Coachella Valley, the area from the **Salton Sea** down to the migrant-worker towns of the agricultural **Imperial Valley** lies in the two-thousand-square-mile Salton Basin: the largest area of dry land below sea level in the western hemisphere.

Created accidentally in 1905 (see box, p.246), the Salton Sea and its shores were once extremely fashionable among the wealthy, attracting Frank Sinatra, Dean Martin and others to its yacht clubs; in its 1940s heyday, the lake was actually a bigger tourist draw than Yosemite National Park. A series of mid-1970s storms caused the lake to rise and swallow shoreline developments, but pollution was already having a detrimental impact on tourism. Nestled 235ft below sea level, the Salton Sea has no natural outlet and has been plagued over the years by agricultural runoff and toxic wastes carried in by two rivers from Mexico, making it excessively saline. Local promoters are desperate to point out that the problems are exaggerated, but people rarely swim and waterski here these days.

Still, the Salton Sea remains an important wintering area for shorebirds and waterfowl. Brown pelicans come by in summer, and terns and cormorants also nest here. The best place to see them is the **Sonny Bono Salton Sea National Wildlife Refuge** (daily dawn–dusk; free; Ⓦwww.fws.gov/saltonsea) at the lake's southern tip. There's a viewing platform by the informative **visitor centre** (April–Sept Mon–Fri 7am–3.30pm; Oct–March Mon–Fri 7am–3.30pm, Sat & Sun 8am–4.15pm; Ⓣ760/393-5278), or you can take the Rock Hill Trail for a closer look, a twenty-minute walk to the water's edge. To get to the refuge, take the poorly signposted backroads off Hwy-111 south of **Niland** or off Hwy-86 at **Westmorland**; both run past fields of alfalfa, cantaloupe, tomatoes and other crops, proof that just about anything will grow in this fertile land provided it is suitably irrigated.

If you've come this far, it's worth turning east along Niland's Main Street and travelling three miles to see **Salvation Mountain** (Ⓦwww.salvationmountain.us), a fantastic work of large-scale religious folk art that appeared in the 2007 movie

The accidental sea

At 35 miles long by 15 miles wide, the **Salton Sea** is California's largest lake, but one which only came into existence a century ago. Over the millennia, the shallow Salton Basin has repeatedly filled with floodwaters that spilled over from the Colorado River some fifty miles to the east, but each time the lake has dried up. When European Americans started pushing into the West, they recognized that the fertile Salton Basin and the surrounding Imperial Valley could be made super-productive by channelling water from the Colorado. In 1901, a development company did just that, but river silt soon blocked the channel and in 1905 almost the entire flow from the Colorado River was pouring into the Salton Basin. The deluge wasn't stanched for almost two years, by which time it had formed the Salton Sea – a huge freshwater lake up to fifty feet deep.

Into the Wild and built continuously since 1985 by friendly eccentric Leonard Knight, now pushing 80. He has devoted his later life to this wildly coloured mass of straw and adobe, liberally painted with extracts from the Bible and exhortations to "Repent" – there's even an abandoned motorboat used to represent Noah's Ark. Leonard adds to his structure – already thirty feet high and a hundred and fifty feet wide – each morning, but spends much of the day guiding the steady stream of visitors: a small donation is appreciated but never requested.

Agricultural work brings thousands of Mexicans north of the border, and the **restaurants** in these parts generally cater to them: practice your Spanish.

Anza-Borrego Desert State Park

Covering over 900 square miles, the **ANZA-BORREGO DESERT STATE PARK**, southwest of the Salton Sea, is the largest state park in the country outside Alaska and comes with a legend-strewn history spanning Native American tribes, the first white trailfinders and Gold Rush times. It boasts multifarious varieties of vegetation and geological quirks that can, with a little effort, be as rewarding as those of the better-known deserts to the north.

The park takes its double-barrelled name from Juan Bautista de Anza, a Spanish explorer who crossed the region in 1774, and the Spanish for the native bighorn sheep, borrego cimarron, which eats the brittlebush and agave found here. Some of Anza-Borrego can be covered by car (confidence on gravel roads is handy), although you'll need four-wheel drive for the more obscure – and most interesting – routes, and there are over five hundred miles of hiking trails and dirt roads.

During the fiercely hot summer months, the place is best left to the lizards, although most campgrounds and many hotels stay open all year. The most popular time to visit is the desert **blooming season** (typically a couple of weeks between late February and early April), though there's a fifty-percent chance in any given year that the wildflowers won't bloom at all. If you strike it lucky you'll be rewarded with scarlet ocotillo, orange poppies, white lilies, purple verbena and other intensely colourful – and fragrant – wildflowers. For the latest information call the 24-hour Wildflower Hotline (T760/767-4684). As well as taking the usual desert precautions (see box, p.219), you should read the comments on p.49 – this is mountain lion territory.

People also visit to look at the amazing, clear **starry skies** – Borrego Springs was recently designated as the country's second Dark Sky community, after Flagstaff, Arizona.

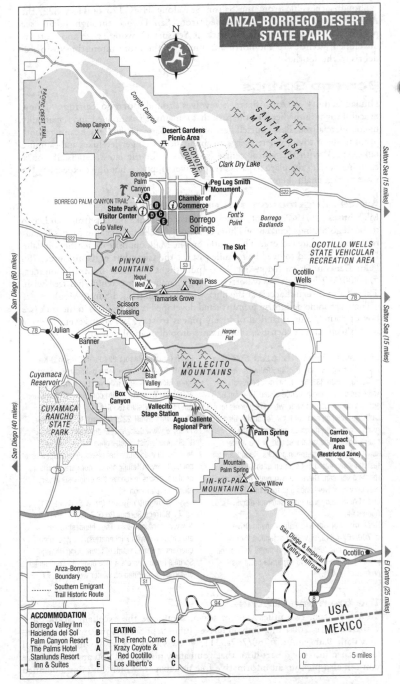

ANZA-BORREGO DESERT STATE PARK

N

PACIFIC CREST TRAIL

Coyote Canyon

Sheep Canyon

Desert Gardens Picnic Area

SANTA ROSA MOUNTAINS

COYOTE MOUNTAIN

Clark Dry Lake

Borrego Palm Canyon

Peg Leg Smith Monument

BORREGO PALM CANYON TRAIL

Chamber of Commerce

State Park Visitor Center

Borrego Springs

Font's Point

Borrego Badlands

Culp Valley

S22

The Slot

OCOTILLO WELLS STATE VEHICULAR RECREATION AREA

PINYON MOUNTAINS

S3

Yaqui Well

Yaqui Pass

Ocotillo Wells

Tamarisk Grove

S2

78

Salton Sea (15 miles)

Scissors Crossing

Harper Flat

78

Julian

Banner

VALLECITO MOUNTAINS

Cuyamaca Reservoir

Blair Valley

Box Canyon

CUYAMACA RANCHO STATE PARK

Vallecito Stage Station

Agua Caliente Regional Park

Palm Spring

Carrizo Impact Area (Restricted Zone)

79

S1

Mountain Palm Spring

IN-KO-PA MOUNTAINS

Bow Willow

S2

8

San Diego & Imperial Valley Railroad

Ocotillo

USA

MEXICO

S1

94

8

El Centro (25 miles)

Salton Sea (15 miles)

San Diego (60 miles)

San Diego (40 miles)

—— Anza-Borrego Boundary

-- - - Southern Emigrant Trail Historic Route

ACCOMMODATION
Borrego Valley Inn	C
Hacienda del Sol	B
Palm Canyon Resort	D
The Palms Hotel	A
Stanlunds Resort Inn & Suites	E

EATING
The French Corner	C
Krazy Coyote & Red Ocotillo	A
Los Jilberto's	C

0   5 miles

Though accessible from the Salton Sea along Hwy-178 or Hwy-S22, the Anza-Borrego is usually approached from San Diego, through Julian (see p.210). This way you'll hit the park at Scissors Crossing, with most of the developed facilities to the north and much of the more interesting historical debris to the south.

Borrego Springs

Human activity in Anza-Borrego revolves around **Borrego Springs**, a tiny, peaceful town in the heart of the park that remains self-contained and remarkably uncommercialized. Base yourself here or camp at *Borrego Palm Canyon* campground, just outside of town, where there's an abundance of ranger-led hikes and campfire talks: check with the visitor centre (see below) for the latest details. If you're camping out, it's the place to gather (expensive) supplies – but don't expect any big supermarket chains here.

Arrival, information and accommodation

MTS **buses** (☏ 619/231 1466, ⓦ www.sdmts.com) make the trip from San Diego to Borrego Springs (currently Thurs & Fri only). The bulk of the town's restaurants and shops are either in The Center or The Mall, opposite each other on Palm Drive. You'll need to head half a mile east for the **Chamber of Commerce**, 786 Palm Canyon Drive (Mon–Sat 9am–4pm, slightly shorter hours in summer; ☏ 1-800/559-5524, ⓦ www.borregospringschamber.com), which has free wi-fi. There's also **internet** access at the library by the Mall (closed Sun & Mon).

There are some delightful primitive and developed campgrounds in the park (see box opposite), plus a handful of lovely **places to stay**. In season, even the basic motels seem quite expensive, though rates drop dramatically in summer.

Hotels, motels and B&Bs

🏃 **Borrego Valley Inn** 405 Palm Canyon Drive ☏ 1-800/333-5810, ⓦ www.borrego valleyinn.com. A lovely adobe-styled 14-room B&B set in a cactus garden with two heated pools (one clothing-optional) and hot tubs. Terracotta-tiled a/c rooms come with fireplace and kitchenette, a hearty continental breakfast and, in the winter season, there are afternoon snacks. Rooms are all tastefully decorated but step up to the deluxe rooms if you can. There's a two-night minimum stay on winter weekends and from mid-Feb to the end of April, and multi-night summer discounts. Rooms ⑥

Hacienda del Sol 610 Palm Canyon Drive ☏ 760/767-5442, ⓦ www.haciendadelsol -borrego.com. Central, budget motel with some pricier kitchen units and separate cottages (winter only; ⑥). ❷

Palm Canyon Resort 221 Palm Canyon Drive ☏ 1-800/242-0044, ⓦ www.palmcanyonresort .com. Modern hotel a mile west of town done in ersatz Old West style, with comfortable rooms and full-hookup RV sites ($35). ❺

The Palms Hotel 2220 Hoberg Rd ☏ 760/767-7788, ⓦ www.thepalmsatindianhead.com. Stylish 1950s Modernist hotel – once the domain of Monroe, Brando and other celebrities – with a great pool, all very tastefully done. There are no phones or alarm clocks in rooms; the emphasis is very much on relaxation. ❻

🏃 **Stanlunds Resort Inn & Suites** 2771 Borrego Springs Rd ☏ 760/767-5501, ⓦ www.stanlunds.com. The cheapest rooms around (some with kitchenettes), located three quarters of a mile south of town along Borrego Springs Road. There's a nice pool and continental breakfast is provided on winter weekends. ❸

The town and around

Your first stop, two miles west of town, should be the excellent **State Park visitor centre**, 200 Palm Canyon Drive (June–Sept Sat & Sun 9am–5pm; Oct–May daily 9am–5pm; ☏ 760/767-5311, ⓦ www.parks.ca.gov), which is so well landscaped into the desert floor that you barely notice it as you approach. Here you can also pick up an informative free newspaper, which contains a detailed map of the park along with numerous suggestions for hikes. Outside, the half-mile **All-Access Nature Trail** allows you to weave across the desert and identify the flora.

A mile to the north, the main *Borrego Palm Canyon* campground marks the start of the **Borrego Palm Canyon Trail** (3 miles round-trip; 2hr; 600-foot ascent), the most popular trail in the park (day-use fee $8 per vehicle). It follows a detailed nature trail to one of the largest oases left in the US, with a quarter-mile of stream densely flanked by around a thousand mop-topped California fan palms (sometimes known as Washingtonia palms from their Latin name, *Washingtonia filifera*) – the only palms native to the western United States.

If you'd prefer to have the desert to yourself, consider one of the other hikes listed in the park's free annual newspaper: the Peña Spring Trail (0.6 miles round-trip) is good for spotting bird and wildlife, or try the tougher Hellhole Canyon/Maidenhair Falls Trail (6 miles round-trip), which involves some rock scrambling and ends at a canyon oasis.

Eating

The best **places to eat** often close in summer, but somewhere always stays open.

The French Corner 721 Avenida Sureste ☎760/767-5713. Informal French/Belgian-run crêperie and restaurant with French country decor that works surprisingly well in a Modernist desert building. A pair of savoury or sweet crêpes goes for $10–12, or go for the steak frites and salad ($18) followed by a delicious crème brûlée. French wines start at $20 a bottle. Closed Mon–Wed and from June to mid-Oct.

Krazy Coyote & Red Ocotillo At *The Palms Hotel* (see opposite). One restaurant with two menus makes this the most versatile of places around with patio dining overlooking the pool. The casual *Red Ocotillo* menu (all day) offers the likes of breakfast burrito ($7) or a Reuben sandwich ($9) while the *Krazy Coyote* dinner menu offers finer fare – perhaps sashimi ($13) followed by rack of lamb ($30). Closed June–Sept.

Los Jilberto's 655 Palm Canyon Drive The locals' favourite: a cheap but good Mexican – eat in or take away.

Camping in Anza-Borrego

Anza-Borrego Desert State Park manages two developed and nine primitive campgrounds, but this is one of the few parks that allows **open camping**, giving you the freedom to pitch a tent pretty much anywhere without a permit – although it's advisable to let someone know your plans. The few provisos are that you don't drive off-road, don't camp near water holes, camp away from developed campgrounds, light fires only in fire rings or metal containers, collect no firewood and leave the place as you found it, or cleaner.

The largest site and the only one with RV hookups, is the *Borrego Palm Canyon* campground a mile from the visitor centre (hookups $35, tents $25). *Tamarisk Grove*, thirteen miles south on Hwy-S3 ($25), is the only other developed site. Both charge $8 per vehicle for day-use of the facilities, which include water supply and coin-op **showers**. Both also organize **guided hikes** and have regular discussion and activity evenings led by a volunteer naturalist. Places can be reserved through ⓦwww .reserveamerica.com or at ☎1-800/444-7275 (essential for holidays and weekends, and in the March–April blooming season). The other primitive campgrounds fill on a first-come-first-served basis; those in the backcountry always have space. All are accessible by road vehicles and are free, except for *Bow Willow*, which charges $7 and is the only one with **drinking water**. Most sites are below 1500ft, which is fine in winter, but in the hotter months you might try *Culp Valley*, eight miles southwest of Borrego Springs, at a blissfully balmy 3400ft. In addition, there's a commercial campground at the Agua Caliente Regional Park (see p.250).

Anza-Borrego sights

Six miles east of Borrego Springs along Hwy-S22, there's a memorial marker to Peg Leg Smith, an infamous local spinner of yarns from Gold Rush days who is further celebrated by a festival of tall tales – the **Peg Leg Liars Contest** – which takes place at this spot on the first Saturday in April. Anybody can get up before the judges and fib their hearts out for five minutes, with the most outrageous stories earning a modest prize. Roughly four miles further on, a fairly tough dirt road (check with the State Park visitor centre or Chamber of Commerce for conditions) leads to **Font's Point** and a view over the **Borrego Badlands** – a long, sweeping plain devoid of vegetation, whose strange, stark charms are oddly inspiring. Sunset and sunrise are the best times to fully appreciate the layered alluvial banding.

If you want to be outside but shaded from the sun's fierce rays, make for **The Slot**, a narrow fifty-foot-deep canyon carved from the soft rock by infrequent flooding – though frequent enough that you definitely shouldn't venture here if there's any sign of rain in the vicinity. You can walk down into the canyon and follow it downstream for five minutes to a quarter-mile-long section where it's just wide enough for one person to squeeze through. To get here, travel 1.5 miles east from the junction of Borrego Springs Road and Hwy-78, then follow the very sandy Buttes Pass Road for 1.8 miles, keeping left at the only junction. The road is usually passable for ordinary cars but if you have any doubts about your or your vehicle's abilities, turn back.

At Scissors Crossing, Hwy-78 from Julian intersects Hwy-S2, which heads towards the park's southeast corner. It follows the line of the old **Butterfield Stage Route**, which began service in 1857 and was the first regular line of communication between the eastern states and the newly settled West. Along the way you pass through **Blair Valley**, with its primitive campground, to **Box Canyon**, where the Mormon Battalion of 1847, following what is now known as the **Southern Emigrant Trail Historic Route**, forced a passage along the desert wash. It isn't especially spectacular, but makes for some safe desert walking, never more than a couple of hundred yards from the road. Five miles further on, the **Vallecito Stage Station** (Sept–May 9am–sunset; June–Aug closed) is an old adobe stagecoach rest stop that gives a good indication of the comforts – or lack of them – of early desert travel. The building is in the grounds of a county-run **campground** ($19), which requires you to pay a day-use fee of $2 per vehicle to see it.

A further three miles south, the **Agua Caliente Regional Park** (Sept–May daily 9.30am–5pm; $5 per vehicle) contains a couple of naturally fed pools, one large outdoor affair kept at its natural 96°F and one smaller indoor pool at a more modest temperature, fitted with water jets. Most visitors stay at the **campground** (tents $15, hookups $20–25; reservations ℡858/565-3600), which surrounds the pools and gives you longer access for evening soaking.

South of here lies the least-visited portion of Anza-Borrego, good for isolated exploration and undisturbed views around Imperial Valley, where there's a vivid and spectacular clash as grey rock rises from the edges of the red desert floor, and a primitive **campground** close to the small oasis at *Mountain Palm Spring*.

Hiking, biking and other activities

Recreational opportunities in the park are strictly controlled to preserve the fragile ecosystem. **Hiking** is perhaps the most obvious pursuit, with the Borrego Palm Canyon Trail (see p.249) being the most popular. If you'd prefer to have the desert to yourself, consider one of the other hikes listed in the park's free annual newspaper: the Peña Spring Trail (0.6 miles round-trip) is good for spotting bird and wildlife, or try the tougher Hellhole Canyon/Maidenhair Falls Trail (6 miles round-trip), which involves some rock scrambling and ends at a canyon oasis.

Mountain bikers are not allowed on hiking trails, but provided you bring your own set of wheels (there are no local rentals available) you've free rein on almost 500 miles of dirt roads that cross the desert and mountains. If you'd rather have a larger saddle, try **desert horse trekking** with Smoketree Arabian Ranch (℡760/767-5850, ⓦwww.smoketreearabianranch.com), offering one-hour ($55) and two-hour ($95) rides, even in summer when they start at 7am.

The Western Mojave

The **western expanse** of the Mojave Desert spreads out on the north side of the San Gabriel Mountains, fifty miles from Los Angeles via Hwy-14. It's a barren plain that drivers have to cross in order to reach the alpine peaks of the eastern Sierra Nevada Mountains or Death Valley, at the Mojave's northern edge. The few towns that have taken root in this stretch of desert over the past few decades are populated by two sorts of people: retired couples who value the dry, clean air, and **aerospace** workers. The region's economy is wholly based on designing, building and testing airplanes, from B-1 bombers for the military to the *Voyager*, which made the first nonstop flight around the globe in 1987. The Post-World War II establishment of **Edwards Air Force Base**, on the desert and dry lakebeds east of the town of Mojave, has made the region the aerospace capital of the world, as well as one of the fastest-growing regions in California.

Lancaster, near Edwards Air Force Base, is the largest town and one of the few places to pick up supplies; **Mojave**, thirty miles north, is a desert crossroads that caters mainly to drive-by tourists. **Tehachapi**, twenty miles west and a few thousand feet higher, offers a cool retreat. Hwy-14 joins up with US-395 another forty miles north, just west of the huge naval air base at **China Lake** and the faceless town of **Ridgecrest**, useful mainly as a jumping-off point for some interesting attractions.

Palmdale, Lancaster and Mojave

Northbound travellers from Los Angeles hit the desert proper at the contiguous and equally soulless towns of **Palmdale** and **Lancaster**, the biggest places for miles. The nearby Edwards Air Force Base is the US military testing ground for experimental, high-speed and high-altitude aircraft (such as the *Blackbird*; see below), and incorporates NASA's **Dryden Flight Research Center** and a backup space-shuttle landing site. Even if you have no interest in military stuff, the region makes a reasonable base for exploring the desert hereabouts: Hwy-14 is the region's main artery and forays are best made from there. The area doesn't really warrant an overnight stop, but Lancaster and Palmdale have a full range of **chain hotels and motels**, and **Mojave** has a number of budget motels.

Palmdale

About the only thing of interest in **Palmdale** is the **Blackbird Airpark** (Fri–Sun 10am–5pm; free), three miles east of Hwy-14 along Avenue P. The two sinister-looking black planes standing by the roadside here are the fastest and highest-flying planes ever created. The YA-12 was designed in the 1950s as a prototype for the SR-71 – the *Blackbird* – a reconnaissance plane that could reach 2100 miles per hour at 85,000ft. Unless you strike one of the infrequent "open cockpit" days, all you can do is admire their sleek lines and astonishing statistics. If you visit when the park's closed, you still get to see the key planes from outside the fence, though you won't get access to the small visitor centre.

Lancaster: the poppy reserve and Saddleback Butte

Lancaster, seven miles north of Palmdale, was founded in 1876 when the Southern Pacific Railroad arrived. Turn west here along Avenue I and follow it fourteen miles to reach the **Antelope Valley California Poppy Reserve** (daily sunrise–sunset in poppy season; parking $8). You can stroll the easy desert trails at any time of year, but the main reason to come is to witness the place blanketed in the bright orange of California's state flower, the Golden Poppy. It is a temperamental and unpredictable plant, but given enough rain it usually blooms (perhaps two or three years in every five) between mid-March and late May; for details, call the Wildflower Hotline (Ⓣ661/724-1180). During the blooming season you can also visit the excellent **interpretive centre** (mid-March to mid-May daily 9am–5pm), which comes neatly embedded in the hillside and has displays of desert flora and fauna.

Saddleback Butte State Park, seventeen miles east of Lancaster at the junction of Avenue J and 170th Street (daily dawn–dusk; $6 per vehicle), centres on a smallish hill whose slopes are home to a splendid collection of Joshua trees. It's also a likely spot to catch a glimpse of the desert tortoise, for whom the park provides a refuge from the motorcyclists and ATV enthusiasts who tear around the region. There's a half-mile nature trail and a simple **campground** ($20), which is mostly underused but is popular for stargazing on summer weekends. Three miles southwest, the **Antelope Valley Indian Museum** on Avenue M (closed until Sept 2010; for hours contact Ⓣ661/946-3055 or Ⓦwww.avim.parks.ca.gov), housed in a mock Swiss chalet painted with Native American motifs, contains an extensive collection of ethnographic material from all over the state.

Mojave

MOJAVE, strung out along the highway thirty miles north of Lancaster, is a major junction on the interstate rail network, though it's used solely by freight trains. The town itself – largely a mile-long highway strip of gas stations, $40-a-night motels, and franchised 24-hour fast-food restaurants – is a good place to fill up on essentials before continuing north into Owens Valley or Death Valley.

Mojave hit the headlines in 2004 as the launch and landing site of **SpaceShipOne**, which became the first privately funded spaceship to achieve suborbital flight (around 62 miles above the earth) twice within fourteen days, thereby claiming the $10 million reward from the X Prize Foundation.

The same clear, dry conditions that favour space launching make the Mojave Air & Space Port (Ⓦwww.mojaveairport.com), a mile east of town, the perfect parking lot for mothballed airplanes. Surplus commercial airliners are pastured here, often for years, and you can see the rows of Airbus and 747 tailplanes still decked out in the livery of their owners. Flight fans set up base camp at the airport's daytime *Voyager Restaurant* diner where you can watch the activity of this working airport, listen in to the tower through radios at each table and access free wi-fi.

If you're heading north from here, consider a detour via the Desert Tortoise Natural Area (see p.254).

North of Mojave along Hwy-14

North from Mojave along Hwy-14 the desert is virtually uninhabited, the landscape marked only by the bald ridges of the foothills of the Sierra Nevada Mountains that rise to the west. Twenty-four miles north of Mojave, Hwy-14 passes through **Red Rock Canyon**, a brilliantly coloured, rocky badland of wonderfully eroded formations.

The highway passes right through the centre of the most impressive section, though if you walk just a hundred yards from the road you're more likely to see an eagle or coyote than another visitor. Better still, call at the **Red Rock Canyon State Park** (always open; $6 per vehicle), where the **visitor centre** (open spring & autumn Fri noon–7pm, Sat 9am–7pm, Sun 9am–3pm; closed summer and winter; ☎661/942-0662) can point you to a number of short trails. It also runs a weekend ranger programme of nature walks and campfire talks, ranging from guest lectures by Native Americans to discussions on movie-filming in the area. The adjacent *Ricardo* **campground** ($25) is fairly primitive but beautifully sited amid Joshua trees and colourful rocks.

Heading further north along US-395 brings you to the Owens Valley and the western entrance to Death Valley, regions covered in depth in Chapter Four.

Tehachapi

About twenty miles west from Mojave, Hwy-58 rises to **Tehachapi**, a pretty apple-growing centre at 4000ft that offers respite from the Mojave's heat plus a couple of minor sights. Some 4500 **wind generators** – built here since the early 1980s – make the Tehachapi Wind Resource Area, ranked along Cameron Ridge to the east, one of the world's most productive renewable-energy stations. They're very visible from Hwy-58, but there are few places to stop so you may prefer to follow Tehachapi Willow Springs Road, a minor route between Tehachapi and Mojave running just south of Hwy-58.

Train enthusiasts cross states to see groaning diesels hauling their mile-long string of boxcars around the **Tehachapi Loop**, eight miles west of town. Built in 1876 as the only means of scaling the steep slopes of the region, the tracks double back on themselves to make a complete 360° loop. It's an impressive sight to watch a train over 85 boxcars long twisting around a mountain, its front end 77ft above its tail. For the best view, follow the signs three miles from the Keene exit to a roadside plaque commemorating the loop's engineers.

Practicalities

For **information** about these and other local attractions, including pick-your-own-fruit orchards, antiques shops and ostrich farms, stop in at the **Chamber of Commerce**, 209 E Tehachapi Blvd (Mon–Fri 9am–5pm; ☎661/822-4180, Ⓦwww.tehachapi.com), right by the train tracks in the older section of town. Nearby you'll find **accommodation** at the basic *Santa Fe Motel*, 120 W Tehachapi Blvd (☎661/822-3184, Ⓕ822-7905; ❷), and the *Best Western Mountain Inn*, 418 W Tehachapi Blvd (☎661/822-5591; ❹). Eight miles southwest of town off Highline Road, there's **camping** (☎661/868-7000; $14) among the pines at a refreshing 6000ft in the *Tehachapi Mountain Park*, with toilets and water but no other facilities; it's sometimes snowbound in winter. Popular local **restaurants** include the daytime-only *Apple Shed*, 333 E Tehachapi Blvd, next to the visitor centre, good for country-style breakfasts, apple-pie breaks and espresso, and *Domingo's*, 20416 Valley Blvd (☎661/822-7611), a family-owned Mexican and seafood place in the newer section of town, a mile or so west.

Boron, the Rand Mining District and Ridgecrest

Busy Hwy-58 runs east from Mojave, skirting the northern side of Edwards Air Force Base for thirty miles to the Boron Road exit for the **Borax Visitor Center** (daily 9am–5pm; $3 per vehicle; Ⓦ www.borax.com/borax6.html), a modern complex on a hill overlooking a processing plant and the vast open-cast borax mine – the largest mine in California. Borax is sodium borate, a crystalline mineral which was originally used as a flux to improve the working properties of gold and silver, but more recently has found applications in everything from washing detergents to flat-screen TVs and fibreglass. The centre is primarily a promotional tool for the Borax Company, which owns the site, but call in if only to see the ten-minute video (complete with a 1960s snip of Ronald Reagan advertising hand cleaner), which finishes with curtains opening on a great view into the mile-wide, 650-foot-deep pit.

There's more on the history of boron extraction and the role of the twenty-mule teams, which hauled paired ten-tonne wagons of borax out of Death Valley and elsewhere, at the **Boron Twenty Mule Team Museum**, 26962 Twenty Mule Team Rd (daily 10am–4pm; donation; Ⓦ www.20muleteammuseum.com), in the one-street town of **BORON** three miles further east. The museum also has coverage of movies filmed here – parts of *Erin Brockovich*, for one – and has a display on the Solar Energy Generating Station (SEGS), whose shiny mirrors spread six miles across the desert around the junction of Hwy-58 and US-395.

The Desert Tortoise Natural Area

US-395 runs north from near Boron into the Rand Mining District, though you might fancy taking a detour to see California's state reptile at the **Desert Tortoise Natural Area** (8am–sunset, free; ☎951/683-3872, Ⓦ www.tortoise-tracks.org), a forty-square-mile area of protected habitat amid desert torn up by off-roaders. To get there, follow Hwy-58 eight miles west from Boron, then turn north on California City Boulevard towards California City. After ten miles, turn left onto the dirt Randsburg–Mojave Road, which runs four miles to the site. Here you'll find panels explaining the area's significance, and a network of easy desert trails which spur off the quarter-mile Main Loop Trail. Free leaflets provide guidance.

Randsburg

The near ghost town of **Randsburg**, thirty miles north of Boron along US-395, retains a certain Wild West charm on its 200-yard-long main street, with two bars, a dozen shops and the **Desert Museum**, 161 Butte Ave (Sat & Sun 10am–4pm; free), which has displays on the glory days of the 1890s, when upwards of three thousand people lived in the town, mining gold, silver and tungsten out of the arid, rocky hills. Scruffy-looking shacks surrounded by the detritus of ancient mines line the streets, which are very quiet midweek but pick up a little at weekends when off-roaders descend on the place and a couple of antique-cum-knick-knack shops open up.

The ⚒ **General Store**, 35 Butte Ave (☎760/374-2143), is a fascinating slice of history with its embossed tin ceiling, 1904 soda fountain (the super-thick chocolate shakes are locally celebrated), and a small restaurant surrounded by shelves of groceries and mining supplies. It's open daily, and is a good source of local **information**. Across the road, the *White House Saloon*, 168 Butte Ave (Fri–Sun 10am–4pm), looks like something straight out of a Western and sells burgers.

You're free to wander off and explore the nearby hills and old mine workings, but land-use conflict between off-roaders and the Bureau of Land Management, which is seeking to protect desert-tortoise habitat, means you should ask locally about areas which may be closed.

The only **accommodation** is *The Cottage Hotel*, 130 Butte Ave (☎760/374-2332, Ⓦ www.randsburg.com/arandsb.html; ❸), which provides four comfortable B&B rooms plus a separate cottage.

Ridgecrest

Twenty miles north of Randsburg, Hwy-178 cuts east towards Death Valley, reaching **Ridgecrest**, essentially a long string of malls along China Lake Boulevard, on the edge of the huge China Lake Naval Weapons Center. Jet fighters scream past overhead, taking target practice on land that's chock-full of ancient **petroglyphs** – the largest grouping in the western hemisphere. Though access to the sites is strictly controlled, you can get some idea of the native culture of the Mojave Desert by visiting the **Maturango Museum**, on the corner of China Lake Boulevard and East Las Flores Avenue (daily 10am–5pm; $5; ☎760/375-6900, ⓦwww.maturango.org). Aside from being a **visitor centre** (free), it has exhibits on both the natural and cultural history of the region, including examples of the rock-art figures pecked into dark basalt rocks. To get out and see the figures and designs in their natural surroundings, join a seasonal, full-day, volunteer-led **tour** (mid-Feb to mid-June & mid-Sept to mid-Dec most Sat and Sun; $35). The most concentrated collections of petroglyphs are on the military base, so foreigners are banned and US citizens must get access clearance at least ten days in advance: check the website and book weeks in advance.

It is less hassle straying four miles east of town to the BLM's **Wild Horse and Burro Corrals**, where dozens of animals are kept while waiting for adoption. Even if you're not prepared to take one home, you can make an appointment to visit (Mon–Fri 7.30am–4pm; free; ☎1-800/951-8720, ⓦwww.wildhorseand burro.blm.gov); for an enthusiastic reception, bring along some apples or carrots, though the burros are often too wild to approach.

Ridgecrest has an abundance of **accommodation**, the vast majority being chain motels and hotels. Try the basic *Budget Inn & Suite*, 831 N China Lake Blvd (☎760/375-1351; ❷), or the upscale *Carriage Inn*, 901 N China Lake Blvd (☎1-800/772-8527, ⓦwww.carriageinn.biz; ❹), which has poolside cabanas and a good restaurant. For something different, try the antique-furnished *BevLen Haus B&B*, 809 N Sanders St (☎760/375-1988, ⓦwww.bevlen.com; ❷), with en-suite rooms, outdoor hot tub and a hearty breakfast.

If you're not after one of the numerous franchise **restaurants**, seek out good espresso and free wi-fi at *Beanster's*, 1601 Triangle Drive, budget Vietnamese at *Pho Grand*, 634 S China Lake Blvd, or classy California cuisine at *Maddy's Cottage*, 411 S China Lake Blvd (☎760/375-0462; closed Sun & Mon), where the three-course *prix fixe* menu ($28) is a good bet.

Trona Pinnacles and Searles Valley

Hwy-178 runs northeast from Randsburg past the burro corrals and out into the dry and desolate **Searles Valley** bound for Death Valley National Park. Some sixteen miles northeast of Randsburg, a five-mile dirt road (passable except after rain) leads to the **Trona Pinnacles National Natural Landmark** (unrestricted access; free), where over five hundred tufa spires stretch up to 140ft. Mostly conical and grouped in clusters, these soft rock pinnacles were considered sufficiently extra terrestrial-looking to form a backdrop for parts of *Star Trek V* and are best viewed on the half-mile nature trail. There's free **camping** with a vault toilet but no water supply. You can find basic supplies six miles north on Hwy-178 at the industrial and substantially run-down borax-processing town of **Trona**.

Victorville, Barstow and around

The long desert drive from LA to Las Vegas takes you along I-15, part of which follows the original line of Route 66. You'll see little of the old road – or anything else of great interest – from the freeway, so you should take time out to explore a few minor attractions. **Victorville** warrants a brief detour to view the highway-side Americana in the Route 66 Museum, but **Barstow** is better for what lies nearby, particularly the coloured rocks of Rainbow Basin and the faux ghost town of Calico. Further east there are early human remains at the **Calico Dig**, and the etymological curiosity that is **Zzyzx**.

③ ## Victorville

I-15 heads north from the Los Angeles basin, slicing between the San Gabriel and San Bernardino mountains to reach the Mojave Desert. The first town of any size is **Victorville**, some eighty miles northeast of LA. It has all the motels, fast-food joints and gas stations you could ask for along the freeway, but it's worth ducking off into the old town centre for a quick look at the small **California Route 66 Museum**, 16825 D St at Fifth Street (Mon & Thurs–Sat 10am–4pm, Sun 11am–3pm; free; ☎760/951-0436, ⓦwww.califrt66 museum.org). Dedicated to American myth, it has devotional displays relating to the westernmost strip of the "Mother Road" (see box below). Relics from an old roadside attraction called "Hulaville" are the museum's most interesting feature, but there are also various old-time videos and a stack of nostalgic merchandise.

Route 66 in California

The advent of the interstates in the 1950s was the death knell for what John Steinbeck called **The Mother Road**. The umbilical cord between Chicago and Los Angeles, Route 66 was conceived in the 1920s when existing roads were stitched together to form a single 2400-mile route across eight states. It was just one of many such migration routes, but is the one that most captured the public imagination – not least through Nat King Cole's 1946 hit (*Get your kicks on*) *Route 66* – and became America's most famous highway. As freeways obliterated the old road and franchise hotels and restaurants populated their flanks, the old diners and mom-and-pop motels gradually disappeared, further enhancing its iconic status.

Large sections of the old route vanished long ago, but it was the realization that some of the last vestiges were about to disappear that kick-started a revival. Sections of the original route have since sprouted Route 66 signs, though these were promptly liberated by fans and you now tend to see "Historic Route 66" shields painted onto the asphalt. After considerable lobbying by Route 66 associations, Bill Clinton passed a National Preservation Bill benefiting the Route 66 Corridor in 1999, and the tourist machine now promotes the old road vigorously. Some 320 miles of the original route ran through California, and Kingman, Barstow and San Bernardino all get name-checked in the famous song, but the best-preserved section is in the Mojave Desert east of Barstow.

Fans will want to visit the small **museums** in Victorville (see above) and Barstow (see opposite), or even try to track down San Bernardino's classic *Wigwam Motel*, at 2728 W Foothill Blvd, Rialto (☎909/875-3005, ⓦwww.wigwammotel.com; ❷), but for most it's enough to drive the desert section that loops south off I-40 from Ludlow to Essex. One essential stop is **Amboy**, a place that seems instantly familiar from dozens of road-trip movies and car commercials principally because of the Modernist Atomic-Era sign for *Roy's* gas station and café. The whole minuscule town – including post office, abandoned church and dirt airstrip – was bought in 2005 by fast-food chicken magnate Albert Okura, who has reopened the gas station and sells snacks – the café and motel should follow in 2011 or 2012.

To delve deeper, check out websites such as ⓦwww.national66.com and www .historic66.com.

There's more Mother Road Americana two miles north at *Emma Jean's Holland-burger Café*, 17143 D St (Mon–Fri 5am–2.30pm, Sat 6am–12.30pm), a 1940s diner serving straightforward breakfasts and burgers in classic style.

Barstow and around

Almost thirty desert miles northeast of Victorville, **Barstow** is the crossroads of the Mojave and provides a welcome opportunity to stretch your legs, though for many months of the year, the relentless sun keeps people in their air-conditioned homes for a good part of the day. It's a small town, consisting of just one main road – part of the original **Route 66** (see box opposite) – lined with a selection of motels and restaurants that make a budget overnight stop possible.

Arrival, information and accommodation

Greyhound buses stop at 1611 E Main St where it crosses I-15, a mile east of Downtown, while **trains** drop you at the unstaffed Amtrak station in the Casa del Desierto (see below) on First Street. The **California Welcome Center** (daily 9am–6pm; ☎760/253-4782, ⓦwww.visitcwc.com), four miles west of Barstow in the Tanger Outlet Mall off I-15 at the Lenwood Road exit, has a good selection of maps of the surrounding area, lodging and restaurant guides, and various flyers on local attractions. Numerous **motels** line Main Street: rates start under $40.

Motels and campgrounds

Calico 7 miles east along I-15 ☎1-800/863-2542, ⓦwww.calicotown.com. Camping at a re-created ghost town (see p.258), with shaded canyons where you can pitch a tent for $25 or hook up campers for $28 per night.

Economy Inn 1243 E Main St ☎760/256-5601. A little frayed around the edges, but a decent motel with comfortable a/c rooms, pool, and free wi-fi. ❶

Owl Canyon campground Rainbow Basin, 11 miles north (see below). Simple camping with a vault toilet but no water. $6.

Ramada Inn 1511 E Main St ☎760/256-5673. Upscale, corporate-style motel offering comfortable rooms with cable TV, pool, free wi-fi and deluxe continental breakfast. Located 1.5 miles east of the centre near the East Main exit off I-15. ❸

Route 66 Motel 195 W Main St ☎760/256-7866. A genuine Route 66 motel, its yard dotted with hulks of 1940s and 1950s cars and decorated with old gas station signs. Rooms are old and a bit crummy, but some have round double beds. ❶

The town and around

Historical interest focuses on the grand 1911 **Harvey House**, also known as the Casa del Desierto (the "house of the desert"), built as a train station with associated restaurant and lodging. Trains still stop here and the building remains striking but is largely empty except for the **Western American Railroad Museum** (Fri–Sun 10am–4pm; donation suggested; ☎760/256-9276, ⓦwww.barstowrailmuseum .org) which is dedicated to preserving the history of Southwest railroading; and the **Route 66 "Mother Road" Museum**, 681 N First Ave (Fri–Sun 10am–4pm; free; ⓦwww.route66museum.org), which is full of highway Americana and some classic photos of yesteryear Barstow. For those with less specialized interests, there's the **Mojave River Valley Museum**, 270 E Virginia Way (daily 11am–4pm; free; ⓦwww.mojaververvalleymuseum.org), containing material on the social and natural history of the area, and a sizeable archeological collection including material from the Calico Dig (see p.258).

Around ten miles north of town, **Rainbow Basin** (unrestricted access), comprises rock formations cast in myriad shades, from vivid greens to deep reds, by thirty million years of wind erosion. The winding four-mile loop road around the canyon is best tackled around dawn or dusk. Camping is also available (see above).

Eight miles east on I-40, the hundred-acre field of mirrors is **SEGS II Solar Power Plant**, a surreal example of how California is putting its deserts to use. Anyone who has seen the film *Bagdad Café* (see p.709) will remember the light reflections the mirrors give off for miles around.

Eating and drinking

Mainstream **restaurants** sit snugly between the motels on Main Street: visit your favourite franchise or try one of our scattered recommendations.

Bagdad Café 46548 National Trails Hwy, Newberry Springs, 23 miles southeast. Basic diner that's become an iconic stop along Route 66 on the back of the 1988 film of the same name. Browse the scrapbook as you tuck into burgers, chicken-fried steak and seafood ($8–10), and take a look at the old Airstream trailer from the movie, which rots outside. Take the first Newberry Springs exit off I-40 and continue 3 miles east.

DiNapoli's Firehouse 1358 E Main St ☎760/256-1094. Rustic, regional Italian joint decorated with fire-fighting memorabilia and selling tasty hand-tossed pizza (from $13), hearty pasta dishes ($12–14) and seductive desserts. Closed Sun.

Idle Spurs Steak House 690 Old Hwy-58, ☎760/256-8888. This Barstow institution just north of town has been serving the best steaks around, washed down with microbrews or something from their extensive wine list, since the 1950s. Try filet mignon *brochette* ($18) or perhaps a prime rib and lobster tail combo ($40). To get there follow First Street 1.6 miles north, then left into Old Hwy-58.

Rosita's 540 W Main St ☎760/256-9218. Freshly made tortilla chips and excellent salsa set the tone for this cavernous and authentic Mexican place. There's a massive range of combination dishes ($10–12) plus lunch and early dinner specials ($7). Closed Mon.

Slash X Ranch Café 28040 Barstow Rd. Lively bar and café ten miles south of town on Hwy-247. A Barstow favourite since 1954 (and popular with dirt bikers, who tear up the desert nearby), it's great for burgers or just a few cold beers.

East of Barstow: along I-15

Attractively set in the colour-streaked Calico Hills seven miles northeast along I-15, then three miles north, the contrived **Calico Ghost Town** (daily 8am–dusk; $6, admission free with camping; ☎1-800/863-2542, ⊛www.calicotown.com) once produced millions of dollars of silver and borax and supported a population of almost four thousand. The town was quickly deserted when the silver ran out and has now been rather insensitively restored, with souvenir shops, hot-dog stands and a main thoroughfare lined with ersatz saloons, an old schoolhouse, a vaudeville playhouse and shops kitted out in period styles. However, should you so desire, there are miles of mining shafts and tunnels open to crawl around in.

There's a more highbrow appeal to the **Calico Early Man Site** (Wed 12.30–4.30pm, Thurs–Sun 9am–4.30pm; guided tours on request; entry $5, tours free; ⊛www.calicodig.com), at the Minneola Road exit off I-15, six miles northeast of the Calico exit, then 2.5 miles north. Since Louis Leakey excavated it in 1964 the "**Calico Dig**" has become one of the most important archeological sites in North America. Some of the old tools found here have been dated at around 20,000 years old, controversially establishing mankind's presence here several thousand years earlier than was previously thought – and the debate rages on. The self-guided tour of the dig isn't very instructive, so try to get on a guided tour, which makes it all come alive.

Afton Canyon, 23 miles further east and three miles off I-15, is only a couple of hundred feet deep but is striking nevertheless, with multicoloured strata formed by erosion from an extinct lake. This is one of the three places where the **Mojave River** flows above ground throughout the year, making this a marshy mecca for almost two hundred types of desert creatures, including rare bird species such as the vermillion flycatcher and summer tanager. There's **camping** here on a first-come-first-served basis ($6).

Some twenty miles further east, Zzyzx Road leads five miles south to the oasis of **Zzyzx** (pronounced "zie-zics"), on the edge of the usually arid Soda Dry Lake. From 1905 to 1940, the site was on the Tonopah & Tidewater Railroad, and when the company decamped the charismatic quack, preacher and LA radio personality **Curtis "Doc" Springer** set up a mineral springs resort. He renamed the spot Zzyzx, correctly surmising that the odd name would draw custom. Unfortunately, he never actually owned the land, and in 1974 he was evicted and the resort closed. Some dilapidated buildings continue to rot away, but most have been transformed into California State University's Desert Studies Center. You can just stroll around the artificial palm-fringed lake on what is effectively a nature trail, and search for evidence of the area's colourful history.

From the Zzyzx Road junction on I-15 it is six miles to Baker.

Baker and the Eastern Mojave

A couple of decent motels and restaurants and some fairly expensive gas stations just about sums up **Baker**. Death Valley lies immediately north, and it's in honour of the town's proximity to the country's hottest place that Baker has the world's tallest functioning **thermometer**, rising 134 feet to commemorate the highest temperature ever recorded in the US – 134°F in 1913. Baker is also a springboard for the Mojave National Preserve, so if you're not up for camping you may want to **stay** at the *Wills Fargo Motel* (T760/733-4477; ❷–❸), which has a heart-shaped pool and modest rooms. The supplies at the town's **general store** aren't cheap, but this is your last chance to stock up. Standing out from the franchise joints, the Mexican-run *Mad Greek* serves an eclectic and good-value range of choices, among them gyros, kebabs, burgers, Mexican dishes, espresso, pastries and delicious fresh strawberry shakes – more a sundae than a drink. Most dishes cost $7–9.

Mojave National Preserve

In 1994, 2500 square miles of undeveloped country wedged between I-15 and I-40 were set aside as the **MOJAVE NATIONAL PRESERVE**, a perfect spot to take a break from the freeway and maybe camp out a night or two to prepare for the excesses of Las Vegas, seventy miles ahead. It's a little higher than much of the desert hereabouts, making it a bit cooler in summer but also subject to winter snows.

The preserve's main roads all lead to the graceful Mission Revival-style **Kelso Depot**, built in 1924 for workers on the Union Pacific Railroad and now the main visitor centre (see p.260). There's no roofed accommodation in the park but several **campsites** are listed on p.260.

Preserve highlights

Approaching Kelso from Baker, Kelbaker Road shoots past a series of dramatic black-and-red **cinder cones**, created ten thousand years ago. Visible to the south of the Kelso Depot are the spectacular **Kelso Dunes**, a golden five-mile stretch of sand reaching seven hundred feet high. A sandy trail off Kelso Dunes Road wanders up to the dunes, where in half an hour you can be scrambling around and listening out for a faint booming sound caused by dry sand cascading down the steep upper slopes: apparently a rare phenomenon. There are free primitive camping spots nearby.

Fourteen miles northeast of Kelso, the small town of **Cima** (there's a little store here, but no gas) heralds **Cima Dome**, a perfectly formed batholith rising some 1500ft above the desert floor and cloaked in dense stands of Joshua trees. These are best explored on the **Teutonia Peak Trail** (4 miles round-trip).

Southeast of Cima, Mojave Road and Black Canyon Road provide access to the *Mid Hills* campground, from where the moderately difficult **Mid Hills to Hole-in-the-Wall Trail** (eight miles each way; 1200-foot ascent) winds through Wild Horse Canyon and ends up at the *Hole-in-the-Wall* campground. You can also drive to *Hole-in-the-Wall* campground, where there's a **visitor centre** (May–Sept Fri–Sun 9am–4pm; Oct–April daily 9am–4pm) and another great hike along the **Rings Trail** (half-mile round-trip), which involves a little scrambling and a descent into Banshee Canyon using metal rings anchored to the rock wall.

A further ten miles south, then six miles west, the vegetation at the 5900-acre **Providence Mountain State Recreation Area** changes from scrubby bushes at lower desert elevations to the piñon pines that grow along rocky Fountain Peak (6996ft) and Edgar Peak (7171ft). Some people come to camp, but most are here for the family-oriented hour-long tour of **Mitchell Caverns** (late May to early Sept Sat & Sun at 1.30pm; early Sept to late May daily at 1.30pm; $6; ☎760/928-2586), which were used for shelter by the Chemehuevi Indians and later by Oliver Stone for an acid-trip sequence in *The Doors* movie. Narrow in parts, it contains some moderately impressive stalactites, stalagmites, and rarer limestone formations.

Practicalities

Mojave is a big preserve (larger than Yosemite) so be sure to **go prepared**: fill up and buy supplies before entering, as there's no gas, just one tiny shop at Cima, and only camping for accommodation.

Information is best sought in the heart of the preserve at the **Kelso Depot Visitor Center** (daily 9am–5pm; ☎760/252-6108, ⓦwww.nps.gov/moja), where excellent displays focus on the region's geology, flora, fauna and social history. They've even re-created elements from the historic building's railroading heyday including a crew room and an old dinner-counter put to use as *The Beanery* (daily 9am–5pm) serving good sandwiches, salads and smoothies.

There are three formal **campgrounds**, all first-come-first-served and open year-round, and offering fire ring, table, toilets and water: the cool (sometimes snowy in winter) *Mid Hills* campground ($12) which is beautifully sited at 5600ft; the 4400ft *Hole-in-the-Wall* campground ($12), situated among striking volcanic rock formations and so named by Bob Hollimon, a member of the Butch Cassidy gang, because it reminded him of his former hideout in Wyoming; and the small, six-site *Providence Mountains State Recreation Area* located by Mitchell Caverns ($25). The authorities also allow limited, primitive, **roadside camping** at designated spots. Consult the park newspaper for full details, or head straight for Kelso Dunes Road, where there are numerous spots a mile beyond the hiking trailhead.

Travel details

Trains

Amtrak's Southwest Chief runs daily from LA to Chicago via Victorville (3hr), Barstow (4hr), and Flagstaff, Arizona, with daily LA departures at 6.55pm, returning at 8.15am.

The Sunset Limited plies the southern route from LA to New Orleans with stops in Palm Springs (2hr 30min) and Tucson, Arizona. It departs LA at 2.40pm on Sun, Wed, and Fri, and the return journey finishes in LA at 8.30am on the same days.

Buses

Unless otherwise stated, all buses are direct Greyhound services.

Barstow to: Las Vegas (7 daily; 2hr 40min); Los Angeles (7 daily; 3–4hr).

Borrego Springs to: San Diego (Metropolitan Transit System; 2 weekly; 2hr 50min).

Palm Springs to: Calexico (4 daily; 2hr 30min); Los Angeles (4 daily; 2hr 30min–3hr).

Death Valley, the Owens Valley and the Eastern Sierra

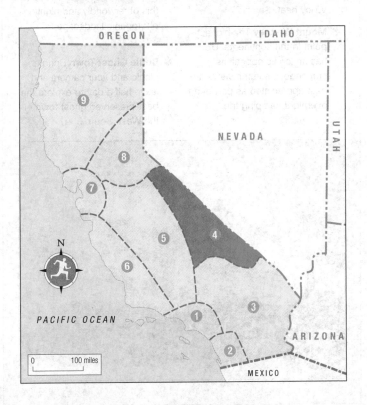

CHAPTER 4

Highlights

* **Rhyolite** Assorted Gold Rush ruins, a house made from bottles and a weird collection of fibreglass sculptures make this an essential stop on the fringes of Death Valley. See p.275

* **Scotty's Castle** The beautiful interiors of this Chicago millionaire's chateau make a cool respite from the Death Valley heat. See p.276

* **Mount Whitney** The highest point in the continental US has an iconic appeal; its stupendous summit views are best appreciated as part of an overnight camping trip. See p.282

* **Bristlecone Pine Forest** Visit the alpine forest atop the lofty and weathered White Mountains to see the gnarled and wizened forms of the world's most ancient living things – some nearly five millennia old. See p.285

* **Mono Lake** Paddle among the lakeside tufa towers on canoe or kayak trips through this otherworldly and highly photogenic landscape. See p.298

* **Bodie Ghost Town** Bring a picnic and your camera and leave half a day to explore the best-preserved ghost town in the West. See p.300

▲ Bodie Ghost Town

Death Valley, the Owens Valley and the Eastern Sierra

The far eastern edge of California, rising up from the Mojave Desert and cleaving to the border with Nevada, is a long narrow strip as scenically dramatic as anywhere else in the state, veering from blistering desert to ski country in the lee of the mighty Sierra Nevada mountains. It's a region devoid of interstates, scarcely populated, and, but for the scant reminders of gold-hungry pioneers, developed in only the most tentative way.

At the region's base, technically forming the Mojave's northern reach, is **Death Valley**. With the highest average summer temperatures on earth, and so remote that it's almost a region unto itself, this vast national park is a distillation of the classic desert landscape: an arid, otherworldly terrain of brilliantly coloured, bizarrely eroded rocks, mountains and sand dunes, all a hundred miles from the nearest town.

North of here, the towering **eastern** peaks of the **Sierra Nevada** are perfectly described by their Spanish name, which literally translates as "snowcapped saw." Virtually the entire range is preserved as wilderness, and hikers and mountaineers can get to higher altitudes quicker here than almost anywhere else in California: well-maintained roads lead to trailheads at over eight thousand feet, providing swift access to spires, glaciers and clear mountain lakes. **Mount Whitney**, the highest point in the continental US, marks the southernmost point of the chain, which continues north for an uninterrupted 150 miles to the backcountry of Yosemite National Park, and beyond.

At the foot of Mount Whitney, the five-mile-wide **Owens Valley** starts, hemmed in to the east by the **White Mountains**, nearly as high but drier and less hospitable than the High Sierra, and home to the ancient, gnarled **bristlecone pines**. In between the two mountain ranges, US-395 runs the length of the valley, which has few signs of settlement at all beyond the sporadic roadside towns and the larger **Bishop**. An hour's drive further north, **Mammoth Lakes** is the Eastern Sierra's busiest resort, thick with skiers in winter and fishers and mountain bikers in summer. Finally, at the point where many turn west for Yosemite, bizarre rock

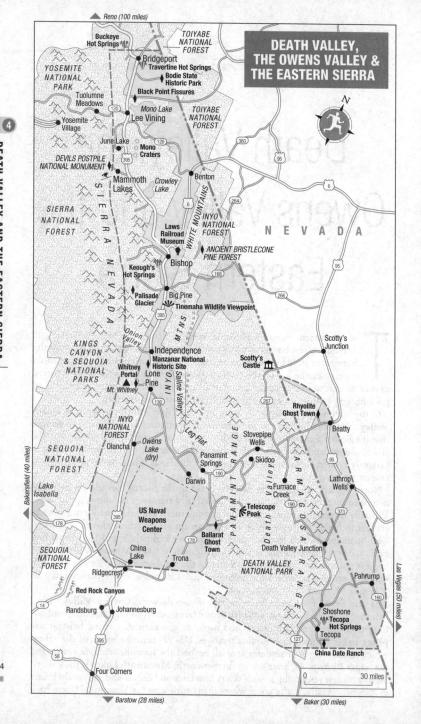

DEATH VALLEY,
THE OWENS VALLEY &
THE EASTERN SIERRA

▲ Reno (100 miles)

TOIYABE
NATIONAL
FOREST

Buckeye
Hot Springs

Bridgeport
Travertine Hot Springs
Bodie State
Historic Park
Black Point Fissures

YOSEMITE
NATIONAL
PARK

Tuolumne
Meadows

120

Mono Lake
Lee Vining

TOIYABE
NATIONAL
FOREST

Yosemite
Village

June Lake

Mono
Craters

120

360

95

DEVILS POSTPILE
NATIONAL MONUMENT

395

Crowley
Lake

Benton

264

6

Mammoth
Lakes

WHITE MOUNTAINS

6

NEVADA

SIERRA
NATIONAL
FOREST

Laws
Railroad
Museum

INYO
NATIONAL
FOREST

Ancient Bristlecone
Pine Forest

SIERRA NEVADA

Bishop

Keough's
Hot Springs

168

Palisade
Glacier

Big Pine

95

395

Tinemaha Wildlife Viewpoint

266

Onion
Valley

Independence

INYO MTNS

Saline Valley

Scotty's
Junction

KINGS
CANYON
& SEQUOIA
NATIONAL
PARKS

Whitney
Portal
Lone
Pine
Mt. Whitney

Manzanar National
Historic Site

Scotty's
Castle

267

136

Rhyolite
Ghost Town

Beatty

INYO
NATIONAL
FOREST

Owens
Lake
(dry)

Leg Flat

Stovepipe
Wells

ARMAGOSA RANGE

95

SEQUOIA
NATIONAL
FOREST

Olancha

Darwin

Panamint
Springs

Skidoo

190

Lathrop
Wells

Death Valley

Furnace
Creek

190

373

Bakersfield (40 miles)

Lake
Isabella

395

US Naval
Weapons
Center

178

Telescope
Peak

PANAMINT RANGE

Death Valley Junction

Las Vegas (50 miles)

SEQUOIA
NATIONAL
FOREST

China
Lake

Trona

Ballarat
Ghost
Town

DEATH VALLEY
NATIONAL PARK

AMARGOSA RANGE

Pahrump

160

178

Ridgecrest

Red Rock Canyon

14

Randsburg

Johannesburg

395

Shoshone
Tecopa
Hot Springs

Tecopa

127

58

Four Corners

China Date Ranch

0   30 miles

▼ Barstow (28 miles)   ▼ Baker (30 miles)

N

formations rise from the placid blue waters of primordial **Mono Lake**, set in a dramatic desert basin of volcanoes and steaming hot pools. Beyond, and far enough out of most people's way to deter the crowds, lies the wonderful ghost town of **Bodie**, which preserves a palpable sense of gold-town life eight thousand feet up in a parched, windswept valley.

Getting around

Getting around the region is best done by car, primarily using **US-395** – the lifeline of the Owens Valley and pretty much the only access to the area from within California. Once north of Mojave, where Hwy-58 branches west to Bakersfield, no road crosses the Sierra Nevada until Hwy-120, a route over the 10,000-foot Tioga Pass into Yosemite. Hwy-190, heading east from US-395 just south of Mount Whitney, cuts through the Panamint Range to Death Valley.

Neither Amtrak nor Greyhound run any services in the region, and the only long-distance **public transport** is the bus service by ESTA (℡1-800/922-1930, Ⓦeasternsierratransit.com), which travels along the Owens Valley linking Lancaster in the south (see p.251) and Reno, Nevada, in the north (see p.593). Both towns have onward connections, and buses generally have racks or space onboard to accommodate bikes.

A couple of small companies operate what are effectively taxi services up to mountain trailheads: visitor centres and outdoor gear shops are the best source of the latest info.

Death Valley National Park

Initially **Death Valley** seems an inhuman environment: burning hot, apparently lifeless and almost entirely without shade, much less water. If you just drive through in half a day, it can appear barren and monotonous, but longer acquaintance reveals multiple layers of interest. Death Valley itself is just the central portion (but very much the focal point) of the much larger **Death Valley National Park**, which extends a hundred miles from north to south and is almost as wide in some parts. Grand vistas sweep down from the subalpine slopes of the 11,000-foot **Telescope Peak** to **Badwater**, the lowest point in the western hemisphere at 282ft below sea level; sharply silhouetted hills are folded and eroded into deeply shadowed crevices, their exotic mineral content turning million-year-old mud flats into rainbows of sunlit phosphorescence; and stark hills harbour the bleached ruins of mining enterprises that briefly flourished against all odds.

It seems impossible that such a dry landscape could support any kind of life, yet it is home to a great variety of creatures, from snakes and giant eagles to tiny fish and bighorn sheep. What little vegetation there is can be fascinating both for its adaptation to the rigours of the environment and the almost sculptural effect it has on the landscape.

Most people – certainly most Americans – visit Death Valley in the **winter**, when daytime temperatures average around 70–80°F (21–27°C); at this time, visiting the sights is quite manageable and even lowland hikes are a pleasure. But the park is really known for its **summer air temperatures**, which average 112°F (44°C) and in 1913 peaked at 134°F (57°C), the highest temperature ever recorded in the US,

---

For advice on getting through the desert **safely**, see box, p.219. Flora and fauna dangers are covered on box, pp.48–49.

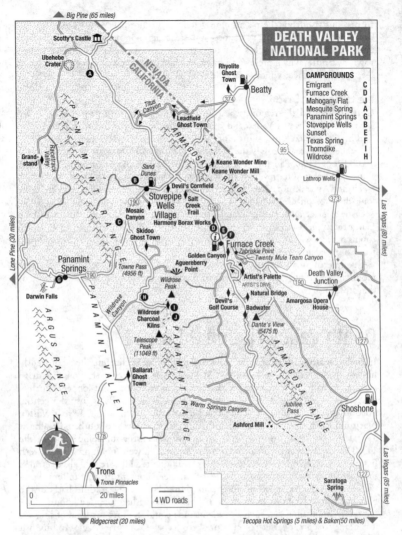

and only ever beaten by two degrees in Libya in 1922. There are frequent periods when the temperature tops 120°F (49°C) daily, and this is when many European visitors arrive, joining the car manufacturers who have been bringing their latest models out here for **extreme testing** ever since Dodge paved the way in 1913.

The best time to visit is spring, especially March and early April, when wildflowers may be in bloom (though many years they refuse to play ball) and daytime temperatures average a manageable 83°F (28°C), and nights are cool. At any time between October and May it's generally mild, with occasional rainfall on the surrounding mountains causing flash floods through otherwise bone-dry gullies and washes.

Throughout the park, roads and services are sparse, mostly concentrated in the central north–south valley for which the park is named. Hwy-190 runs the

What makes Death Valley so hot and dry

It's no surprise that **Death Valley** is **hot and dry** – it's part of the northern Mojave Desert, after all – but certain factors combine to make this small patch of land hotter than anywhere else on earth, based on a year-round average.

Perhaps the biggest contributor to its unforgiving heat is its location: Death Valley sits at sea level in the **rain shadow** of four mountain ranges, so it receives an average precipitation of only an inch and a half each year. Moisture in wind from the Pacific Ocean is lost as rainfall in the Coast Ranges, or as snowfall when the air struggles over the 14,000-foot Sierra Nevada. Very little moisture is left by the time the air gets east of the Sierra, and the last of it is squeezed out as it climbs over the Angus Range and the 11,000-foot Panamint Range.

As this very dry air descends from these heights it compresses, causing it to heat up until it finds itself trapped in a narrow basin where the beating sun, the lack of shade-giving plants and the low altitude allow the air temperature to reach unbearable levels. Even overnight the air doesn't get much chance to cool, as the surrounding mountains trap it to create strong, hot winds; at times it can feel like you're standing in front of a massive hairdryer.

length of the valley, linking **Furnace Creek** and **Stovepipe Wells**, the park's two main outposts for provisions and accommodation. Forays from these bases give access to extensive **sand dunes**, intriguing **ghost towns**, cool high-country camping in the **Panamint Range**, and the incongruous mansion known as **Scotty's Castle**.

Some history

The sculpted rock layers exposed in Death Valley, tinted by oxidized traces of various **mineral deposits**, comprise a nearly complete record of the earth's past. Relatively young **fossils** lie at the feet of 500-million-year-old mountains and the valley floors hold deposits left behind by Ice Age lakes, which covered most of the park's low-lying areas. There's also dramatic evidence of volcanic activity, particularly at the massive **Ubehebe Crater** on the north side of the park.

Humans have lived in and around Death Valley for ten thousand years, since a time when the region was still filled by a massive lake, the climate was quite mild and wildlife was more abundant. Later, wandering tribes of desert **Shoshone** wintered near perennial freshwater springs in the warm valley, spending the long, hot summers at cooler, higher elevations in the surrounding mountains. Some of their descendants, the Timbisha Shoshone, still live on a forty-acre patch of land at Furnace Creek. Displaced and then virtually ignored for decades, the tribe finally gained federal recognition in 1983, and in 2001 was granted seven thousand acres of park and nearby land. They keep largely to themselves.

The first non-natives passed through in 1849, looking for a shortcut to the Gold Rush towns on the other side of the Sierra Nevada; they ran out of food and water but most managed to survive, though the death of one of their number encouraged a survivor to dub the place Death Valley. For the next 75 years, the only people willing to brave the hardships of the desert were miners, who searched for and found deposits of gold, silver and copper. The most successful mining endeavours, though, were centred on **borates**, a harsh alkaline used in detergent soaps (and, eventually, in a variety of industries – everything from cosmetics to nuclear reactors). In the late nineteenth century, borate miners developed twenty-mule-team wagons to haul the borate ore across the deserts to the railroad line at Mojave.

In the 1920s, the first tourist facilities were developed, and in 1927 the *Inn at Furnace Creek* was built on the site of the former Furnace Creek mining camp. Six years later, the US government purchased the two million acres of Death Valley and its environs, to preserve the land as a national monument. In 1994, Congress accorded it national park status and added a further 1.3 million acres to its area, making Death Valley the largest national park in the country outside Alaska.

Approaching Death Valley: Tecopa Hot Springs, Shoshone and Death Valley Junction

Death Valley is a long way from anywhere, with **Las Vegas** being the nearest city, over 130 miles away. There's no scheduled **public transport** into the park. Be sure to top up your **gas** tank before you head in, as it is expensive in the park.

Hwy-127 branches off I-15 at Baker (see p.259) and cuts across desolate Mojave landscape into the Amargosa Valley before reaching any civilization. A couple of miles east of Hwy-127 and fifty-odd miles north of Baker, two dilapidated settlements of scrappy trailer homes (plus a one-horse town with an opera house) make unexpectedly decent places to stop off.

Tecopa Hot Springs

Tecopa Hot Springs has become a popular winter retreat, thanks to its natural **hot springs** (daily 9am–7pm; day-pass $7), experienced in separate men's and women's clothing-free concrete bathhouses. For a more intimate experience head for the nearby *Delight's Hot Springs Resort*, where you can soak in private, odour-free mineral pools ($10 per person all day).

Many people **stay** across the road from the hot springs at the bleak campground (tents $16, electric hookup $19), though you might prefer the old but well-kept cabins (with kitchenettes) at *Delight's Hot Springs Resort*, 368 Tecopa Hot Springs Road (℡1-800/928-8808, ⓦwww.delightshotspringsresort.com; ❸, RV hookups $39). Guests have free 24-hour access to private hot pools on site.

Three miles south, ⚑ *Cynthia's*, 2001 Old Spanish Trail (℡760/852-4580, ⓦwww.discovercynthias.com; tipis ❺, rooms ❹, hostel $22) offers a range of **accommodation** including a 13-bed hostel fashioned from an old trailer home with full kitchen and free wi-fi. Additional ageing trailer homes house private en-suite rooms (also with free wi-fi) with a real desert feel. For a prettier and more peaceful setting beside groves of date palms, go for *Cynthia's* three romantic tipis located four miles north at China Ranch Date Farm (see below). Tipis come with comfy beds, fresh linen, rugs on the ground, a fire grate for winter use and access to a kitchen, though most head up to the hostel where an excellent breakfast ($10 a head) is served. Cynthia is also promising to serve dinner by 2012, but in the meantime the only **restaurant** is *Pastels Bistro* (℡760/852-4420; often closed in summer), serving excellent dishes such as soba noodles with Asian greens and chicken breast ($15).

Even if you're not staying, it is worth making a detour to **China Ranch Date Farm**, China Ranch Road (daily 9am–5pm; ℡760/852-4415, ⓦwww.chinaranch.com), where you're free to wander among the mostly young groves, follow a shady streamside nature path, explore more widely along the Old Spanish Trail (a pack route between old mission stations) or repair to the cactus garden to enjoy a refreshing date shake and, of course, buy some dates. At cooler times of year, ask about the mile-long desert **trail** to a section of the Amargosa River, which though tiny, supports abundant birdlife and assorted invertebrates. There's even a small waterfall.

Shoshone

The dusty hamlet of **Shoshone**, eight miles north of Tecopa Hot Springs, wouldn't really rate a mention but for a gas station, a decent motel and a few date palms and tamarisk trees within striking distance of the park.

Spend a few minutes at the small **Shoshone Museum** (daily 9am–4pm, reduced hours in summer; ☏760/852-4524, ⓦwww.deathvalleychamber.org); ask them to direct you to **Doublin Gulch**, a series of hand-hewn cave homes once used by miners and so named because early in the twentieth century the area was so popular it kept "doublin" in size. The last resident only moved out in 1986.

Though you're still an hour south of Furnace Creek, consider **staying** at the simple but pleasant *Shoshone Inn* motel, Hwy-127 (☏760/852-4335; ❷), where you have access to the warm-spring-fed pool at the neighbouring *Shoshone RV Park*, Hwy-127 (☏760/852-4569; $25), which has electricity and water hookup.

For eating, the *Crowbar Café and Saloon* (☏760/852-4180) serves standard diner fare with antique photos around the walls, but don't miss the daytime 🍴 *C'est Si Bon* (closed Tues & Wed), the best **café** for miles around. Located in a former railroad building now tastefully decorated with artwork and photos, it has internet access and sells good espresso, Thai iced tea, smoothies, granola and yoghurt breakfasts, cheese platters, crêpes and home-made cakes. Much is organic and some produce is grown in the permaculture garden outside. The whole tiny town has free **wi-fi**.

The route into Death Valley continues north through Death Valley Junction (see below).

Death Valley Junction

Some 25 miles north of Shoshone you reach the tiny and virtually abandoned settlement of **Death Valley Junction**. It offers no fuel or supplies, but it does have the **Amargosa Opera House**, the creation of Marta Becket, a New York dancer and artist who settled here in 1967. The inside of the theatre is painted with trompe l'oeil balconies peopled by sixteenth-century Spanish nobles and revellers, apparently a confidence-building gesture for when audiences dwindled. For many years Ms Becket took almost all the roles in ballet-pantomimes, but she is now well into her 80s and her dancing days are over. She still puts on a 45-minute seated show discussing her life (typically Oct to early May Sun at 2pm only; $15; book a couple of months in advance on ☏760/852-4441, ⓦwww.amargosa-opera -house.com), which is followed by "If These Walls Could Talk", a performance in which **Sandy Scheller** brings the characters painted on the walls to life. Sandy also puts on her show on Saturday (Oct to early May; 7pm; $15). Alternatively, just stop by for the **tour** (all year except performance days, on request; $5).

The Opera House is part of the *Amargosa Hotel* (☏760/852-4441, ⓦwww .amargosa-opera-house.com; ❸), a pleasantly run-down adobe **hotel** built by the Pacific Coast Borax Company in 1924. It has no TVs or phones, but many of the rooms have been hand-painted by Marta. Ask to see a few before choosing – there's a trompe l'oeil wardrobe in the Jezebel room and cherubs in the Baroque. In the same building, the *Amargosa Café* does excellent **diner food** and great pies.

From Death Valley Junction it's an easy thirty-mile drive to **Furnace Creek**, passing Zabriskie Point and the junction for Dante's View (see p.274 for both) along the way.

Arrival and information

Entrance to the park (for seven days) is $20 per vehicle, or $10 per person if you are mad enough to walk or cycle (see box, p.274). You'll get an excellent map, the park newspaper with up-to-date details on campgrounds and visitor services and a glossy booklet on the national park. There are no staffed entrance stations, so pay at one of the self-serve machines near park entrances, or at one of the visitor centres and ranger stations.

Visitor facilities are concentrated in Furnace Creek and Stovepipe Wells, both just resorts with a motel, a restaurant or two, a gas station and a grocery store. The busier of the two, **Furnace Creek**, is right in the heart of the valley and has an excellent **visitor centre** (daily 8am–5pm; ☏760/786-3200, Ⓦwww.nps.gov /deva). The only other significant sources of information are the ranger stations at Stovepipe Wells and Scotty's Castle.

There are **no banks** in the park, but Furnace Creek and Stovepipe Wells both have ATMs. The park's only **mobile phone** coverage is around Furnace Creek (all major networks) and anywhere within direct line of sight of the repeater.

The best selection of **eating and drinking** places is at Furnace Creek, though there are restaurants at both Stovepipe Wells and Panamint Springs – all somewhat overpriced. Beatty offers a couple of inexpensive diners, though it's quite a long drive back to the park after dark. Expensive **grocery stores** with limited supplies are located at Furnace Creek and Stovepipe Wells.

Accommodation

While the main sights of Death Valley can be seen in a day, you really should try to stay the night. To get the full impact of a desert visit, **camping** is the most rewarding option. For most of the year you don't even need a tent – it isn't going to rain – though you'll need a sleeping bag, especially in winter, when nights can be cold. If camping isn't a possibility, you're limited to fairly expensive **hotels** and **motels** inside the park, or lower-cost choices in towns on the fringes such as Tecopa, Shoshone (for both see p.268) and Beatty (see p.276). These places are covered in the respective town accounts starting on p.268.

Hotels and motels

Within the park, only the *Inn at Furnace Creek* is worthy of special praise. Otherwise you have a choice of fairly overpriced **motel**-style accommodation at Furnace Creek, Stovepipe Wells and Panamint Springs. Beyond the park boundaries the range of options expands and prices come down, though you lose the chance to wake up with Death Valley all around you.

You should make reservations as early as possible, especially during peak winter holiday periods.

The Inn at Furnace Creek Furnace Creek ☏1-800/236-7916, Ⓦwww.furnacecreek resort.com. A beautiful Mission-style adobe hotel, built in the 1920s amid date palms and tended lawns, and *the* place to stay. Rooms are modern but tastefully done, many with great views across the valley to the Panamint Range. It's only open in the more fashionable cooler months when you can laze by the pool, which has bar service and is fed by naturally heated mineral springs. The on-site restaurant (see p.273) is the best around. Open early Oct to mid-May and especially busy mid-Feb to mid-April. Rooms & suites start around $330. ❾

Panamint Springs Resort Panamint Springs ☏775/482-7680, Ⓦwww.deathvalley.com. Ageing and pretty basic motel rooms (and no pool) 35 miles west of Stovepipe Wells, made more appealing by its restaurant and bar (see p.278) and free wi-fi. There's an adjacent campground (see p.271). ❸

The Ranch at Furnace Creek Furnace Creek ☏1-800/236-7916, Ⓦwww.furnacecreekresort .com. Functional, family-oriented and cheaper than the *Inn at Furnace Creek*, but lacking much of its atmosphere. The comfortable motel rooms are rather overpriced but at least you get free access to the chlorine-free mineral swimming pool. ❺

Stovepipe Wells Motel Stovepipe Wells ☏760/786-2387, Ⓦwww.stovepipewells.com. The cheapest option that's close to most of the park's main attractions, offering comfortable rooms, a mineral-water pool, a restaurant with buffet meals and a bar. Free wi-fi in guest lounge. Non-guests can use the pool for $4. ❸

Campgrounds and RV parks

Almost all the campgrounds in Death Valley National Park are operated by the National Park Service, most costing $12–14 a night, while sites without a water supply are free. The majority of National Park sites cannot be reserved and stays are limited to thirty days (so that people don't move in for the winter). Take note of the **altitude** listed for each, as this gives an idea of the temperatures you might expect, and remember that the only places with guaranteed shade are the canyons on the forested slopes of Telescope Peak, on the western edge of the park.

RV drivers will only find hookups inside the park at Furnace Creek, Stovepipe Wells and Panamint Springs, though most surrounding towns have facilities for RVs.

Free **backcountry camping** is allowed in most areas of the park, provided you keep two miles away from any roads (paved or otherwise) and two hundred yards from water sources. No permits are required, but voluntary backcountry **registration** is strongly recommended.

In the lowlands

Emigrant Open all year; 2100ft. Eight miles west of Stovepipe Wells, this is the only free lowland campground, and it's tent-only. Fires are not allowed but there are flush toilets and water. Free.

Furnace Creek ☎1-877/444-6777, ⊛www .recreation.gov. Open all year and reservable up to six months in advance in the winter months; -196ft. Though one of the largest campgrounds in the park, it still fills up very early on winter weekends. Comes equipped with water, flush toilets and a dump station. Mid-Oct to mid-April $18, mid-April to mid-Oct $12.

Mesquite Spring Open all year; 1800ft. Fairly small, pleasant and relatively shady site near Scotty's Castle on the north side of the park. Has water, flush toilets and a dump station. $12.

Panamint Springs Open all year; 1950ft ☎775/482-7680. Commercial campground with tent sites ($15), water and electric hookups ($30), plus $3 showers at *Panamint Springs Resort*.

Stovepipe Wells Campground Open mid-Oct to late April; sea level. Moderate-sized campground close to the Stovepipe Wells restaurant and pool. Comes with water, flush toilets and some fire pits. $12.

Stovepipe Wells RV Park Open all year; sea level. Run by the *Stovepipe Wells Motel* (see opposite), this bare lot has RV hookups for electricity, water and sewer. $30

Sunset Open Oct–April; -196ft. This enormous site, right in Furnace Creek, is virtually an RV parking lot. Fires are not allowed but there's water, flush toilets and a dump station. First-come-first-served. $12.

Texas Spring Open mid-Oct to late April; sea level. Furnace Creek's quietest site with water, flush toilets and fires permitted. First-come-first-served. $14.

In the hills

Mahogany Flat Open March–Nov; 8200ft. The remotest and coolest campground in the park; virtually identical to *Thorndike* (see below). Free.

Thorndike Open March–Nov; 7400ft. Small site in the pines which is usually only accessible in high-clearance or four-wheel-drive vehicles. There are pit toilets, but bring your own water. Free.

Wildrose Open all year; 4100ft. Expect moderate temperatures at this site on the way to the charcoal kilns. There are pit toilets and drinking water. Free.

Exploring Death Valley

You can get an unforgettable feel for Death Valley just by passing through, and you could quite easily see almost all the essential sights in a day. If you have the time, though, aim to spend at least a night here, if possible camped out somewhere far from the main centres of activity. Spend some time on foot, experiencing the huge, empty spaces and the unique landforms of Death Valley. Sunrise and sunset are the best times to experience the colour that's bleached out by the midday sun, and they're also the most likely times for seeing **wildlife**, mostly lizards, snakes and small rodents, which hide out through the heat of the day.

Most of the park's recognized sights lie south of Furnace Creek along the **Badwater road**, where colourful rocks line Artist's Drive and a small pond marks the lowest point in the western hemisphere. The hills immediately to the east offer a couple of great viewpoints – **Dante's View** and **Zabriskie Point** – but the bulk of visitors head swiftly north past the **Keane Wonder Mine** to the ever popular **Scotty's Castle**. It's out on a limb, so leave time to explore **Ubehebe Crater** and perhaps **Racetrack Valley** while you're up here. On Death Valley's western flank rises **Telescope Peak**, a much cooler place to go hiking or exploring the **Wildrose Charcoal Kilns**.

Furnace Creek

Furnace Creek is the hub of Death Valley, essentially an extended resort with the park's only significant **visitor centre** (see p.270), three campgrounds, the *Inn at Furnace Creek* and *Ranch* (for both, see p.270), several restaurants, a couple of bars, a general store, a post office and a **gas station** (gas available 24hr with a credit card). There's also a large **swimming pool** (guests free, others $5), which is constantly fed hot mineral water and kept at 82°F – a little warm for real swimming, but great for wallowing. **Internet** access is either through wi-fi (all over the resort) or a couple of computers in the general store – both charge $5 an hour.

Furnace Creek is home to the small **Borax Museum** (daily: May–Sept 9am–9pm; Oct–April 11am–7pm; free), located in an 1883 wooden building, the valley's oldest structure. The story of the mineral and its excavation is rather plodding, but don't overlook the fine collection of arrow points, some dating back two thousand years. Outside, heavy-wheeled borax wagons and an old steam locomotive are arranged around an 1880s *arrastre* used for grinding up gold ore. Armed with a little background knowledge, head two miles north to the old **Harmony Borax Works** (unrestricted entry), where a quarter-mile interpretive trail tells of the mine and processing plant.

The *Furnace Creek Ranch* is the only place in the national park offering organized **outdoor activities**. Palms and tamarisk trees line the fairways of the *Ranch*'s 18-hole **golf course** (℗760/786-3373) – the world's lowest grass course, at 214ft below sea level. It's open to anyone keen to pay the green fees (Oct–April $55, May–Sept $30, including cart; $15 for club rental). To check out the scenery and get a sense of how pioneers might have experienced Death Valley, join one of the walking-pace **horserides** offered at the *Ranch* (mid-Oct to early May; $45 for 1hr, $60 for 2hr; ℗760/786-3339). Even better, join one of the hour-long "full moon" rides ($45), which take place several nights a month.

The *Ranch* also has **bike rental** ($10 per hour, $49 for 24hr; ℗760/786-3372) and a range of suggested rides, all on asphalt or dirt roads. A great way to spend a few days exploring less visited locales is to **rent a jeep** from Farabee's Jeep Rentals (Sept–May only; $175 per 24hr day; ℗760/786-9872, ⓦwww.farabeesjeeprentals.com). You must be over 25 and should check rental insurance carefully. If you'd prefer someone else to do the driving, Pink Jeep (℗1-888/900-4480, ⓦwww.furnacecreekresort.com) will oblige with **tours** to Titus Canyon (3hr; $119), the Wildrose Charcoal Kilns (4hr; $129) and Racetrack Valley (6hr; $165).

Eating

Furnace creek has easily the widest **eating** options in Death Valley.

49er Café At *Furnace Creek Ranch*. Diner-style family restaurant with sandwiches and burgers ($12–14), pasta ($15), and steak and fish mains ($18–25). Open 7–9pm in winter, 11am–9pm in summer.

Corkscrew Saloon At *Furnace Creek Ranch*. After a day in the sun, join the few locals at this basic bar with Wii games, jukebox, draft beer, espresso, a limited selection of light meals and pizza to go (2–10pm only). Open until around midnight.

Inn at Furnace Creek Dining Room At the *Inn at Furnace Creek* ☎760/786-3385. Gourmet dining in a beautiful room almost unchanged since the 1920s. Soups, salads, sandwiches and pizza are available for lunch (when dress is casual), but at dinner expect the likes of chilled crab gazpacho ($10), mesquite-grilled quail ($12), followed by tortilla-crusted barramundi ($28), and be prepared to dress up; shorts and T-shirts are banned. It is also a great spot for afternoon tea or an evening cocktail. Open mid-Oct to mid-May; call ahead for dinner reservations.

Wrangler Buffet and Steakhouse At *Furnace Creek Ranch*. The *Ranch*'s main restaurant, serving buffet breakfast (6–9am or 10am; $11.25), buffet lunch (11am–2pm; $15) and dinners (5–10pm), including house salad ($6.50), chicken breast ($28) and assorted steaks ($28–38) served with vegetables and either a baked potato or fries.

The road to Badwater

Many of the park's most unusual sights are located south of Furnace Creek along the road to Badwater, which forks off Hwy-190 by the *Inn at Furnace Creek*. A good first stop, two miles along, is **Golden Canyon**. Periodic rainstorms over the centuries have washed a fifty-foot-deep, slot-shaped gully through the clay and silt here, revealing golden-hued walls that are particularly vibrant in the early evening. A three-quarter-mile-long interpretive trail winds into the U-shaped upper canyon, and a loop hike (see box, p.274) continues from there.

Five miles further on, signs point to **Artist's Drive**, a twisting one-way loop road. It's perhaps best left until the drive back, especially if this means catching the afternoon sun on the **Artist's Palette**, an evocatively eroded hillside covered in an intense mosaic of reds, golds, blacks and greens.

A couple of miles south, a dirt road heading west leads a mile to the **Devil's Golf Course**, a weird field of salt pinnacles and hummocks protruding a couple of feet from the desert floor. Capillary action draws saline solutions from below the surface, where alternating layers of salt and alluvial deposits from ancient lakes have been laid down over the millennia. As the occasional rainfall evaporates, the salt accretes to form a landscape as little like a golf course as you could imagine: small golf-hole-sized apertures in the mounds apparently give the place its name.

It's another five miles south to **Badwater**, an unpalatable but non-poisonous thirty-foot-wide pool of water, loaded with chloride and sulphates and the only home of the endangered, soft-shelled Badwater Snail. Notice how much hotter it feels in the humid air beside the water and take a look up on the hill behind where a sign marks sea level. From the pool, two rather uninteresting hikes, both around four miles long, lead across the hot, flat valley floor to the two **lowest points in the western hemisphere**, both at 282ft below sea level. Neither are marked and

---

Badwater Ultramarathon

Driving through Death Valley in mid-July can seem like madness even in an air-conditioned vehicle, but an international field of almost a hundred masochists choose this time of year to run the gruelling **Badwater Ultramarathon** (ⓦwww.badwater.com). Billed as "The World's Toughest Foot Race", it is undoubtedly one of the most demanding, extreme and prestigious in the world. Searing heat and draining dehydration are constant threats on this 135-mile road race, which kicks off 282ft below sea level at Badwater and, after a total elevation gain of around 14,000ft, finishes at the 8360-foot **Whitney Portal**, the trailhead for ascents of Mount Whitney. Around four fifths of the field typically finish, the slowest finishers taking around two days.

Al Arnold was the first to run the course in 1977, but the race didn't actually get under way until 1987; it has been run every year since. The current men's record, set in 2007 by Brazilian Valmir Nunes, is 22 hours 51 minutes, while the best female result is by American Jamie Donaldson, whose 2010 time was 26hr 16min.

there's little satisfaction in being just two feet lower than you were at the roadside, though it is worth wandering half a mile out to where the salt deposits form polygonal shapes on the valley floor.

Zabriskie Point and Dante's View

The badlands around **Zabriskie Point**, four miles south of Furnace Creek off Hwy-190 and overlooking Badwater and the Artist's Palette, were the inspiration for Antonioni's eponymous 1970 movie. Proximity to Furnace Creek makes this a popular sunrise destination, as photographers try to capture the early rays catching **Manly Beacon**, an eminence rising above the badlands.

Hiking and biking around Death Valley

In June, July and August you should restrict your hiking ambitions to the cooler trails around Telescope Peak and Wildrose Peak in the Panamint Range, but you still need to carry all your **water** with you and will want a wide-brimmed hat. In the cooler months lowland hikes become an appealing proposition.

You are prohibited from **mountain biking** along hiking trails within the national park, but that still leaves a great network of asphalt and dirt roads to explore. You'll probably want your own wheels; basic rentals are available in Furnace Creek (see p.272). The map provided with your entry ticket shows the major four-wheel-drive routes: Echo Canyon into the Funeral Mountains and the Inyo Mine, Cottonwood Canyon from Stovepipe Wells, and the Warm Springs Canyon/Butte Valley road in the south of the park are all worthwhile.

Whatever you do, always register your intended route at the visitor centre or any of the ranger stations, and for anything a little more adventurous than the walks listed here, get yourself a **topographic map** from the visitor centre.

Top hikes

Golden Canyon to Zabriskie Point (5 miles round-trip; 3hr; 500-foot ascent). An unmaintained, moderately strenuous trail along ridges and through badlands to Zabriskie Point. Done in reverse, it's all downhill.

Gower Gulch Loop (4 miles round-trip; 2–3hr; 200-foot ascent). Loop walk starting at Golden Canyon and following the interpretive trail to marker #10. From there follow a trail down Gower Gulch back to the start, including an easy scramble down a couple of dry falls. A leaflet on the hike is available from the visitor centre.

Mosaic Canyon (2 miles round-trip; 1hr; 100-foot ascent). A rough three-mile access road just west of Stovepipe Wells leads to the trailhead for a relatively easy hike through this narrow canyon, full of water-polished marble and mosaic-patterned walls. Beyond this most heavily trafficked section, the canyon carries on for another mile, with some scrambling at the upper end.

Telescope Peak (14 miles round-trip; 8hr; 3000-foot ascent). This easy-to-follow but moderately strenuous trail climbs from the trailhead by *Mahogany Flat* campground. It skirts a pair of 10,000-foot peaks and continues through bristlecone pines to the summit and its grand panorama of Death Valley, Mount Whitney and the eastern face of the Sierra Nevada. Sign the summit register while you admire the view. There's no water en route except for snowmelt (often well into June), which should be treated. Crampons and ice axes may be required in harsh winters and at all times you should self-register in the book a short way along the trail.

Wildrose Peak (8 miles round-trip; 5hr; 2000-foot ascent). If winter conditions or your own level of fitness rule out Telescope Peak, this hike makes a perfect, easier alternative. Start by the Charcoal Kilns on Wildrose Canyon Road and wind up through piñon pines and juniper to a stunning summit panorama.

The point's sculpted spires of banded rock are less interesting than **Dante's View**, a further 21 miles south off Hwy-190 and then ten miles on a very steep (and hot) road. From this point almost six thousand feet above the blinding white saltpan of Badwater, the valley floor does indeed look infernal. The view is best in the early morning, when the pink-and-gold Panamint Range across the valley is highlighted by the rising sun.

North from Furnace Creek

Twelve miles to the north, the **Keane Wonder Mine** and **Keane Wonder Mill** (unrestricted entry to both) were quite wonderful during their heyday. Between 1904, when the mine was discovered by Jack Keane, and 1916, gold and silver worth $1.1 million was extracted at the mountainside mine. The ore was then carried to the valley-floor mill using a three-quarter-mile-long aerial tramway, which is still more or less intact. From the parking lot by the remains of the mill, a very steep path climbs (an ascent of 1500ft) alongside the thirteen tramway towers to the lowest of the mineshafts. It's only a mile but seems a lot more in summer heat. Don't be tempted to seek shelter in the adits and shafts leading off the path; all are dangerous and most unfenced.

Just off Hwy-190, fourteen miles north of Furnace Creek, the **Salt Creek Interpretive Trail** comprises a half-mile boardwalk loop through a spring-fed wash. As usual, dawn and dusk offer your best chances of spotting the likes of bobcats, foxes, coyotes and great blue herons that come here to drink.

Just east of Stovepipe Wells and north of Hwy-190, the most extensive of the valley's **Mesquite Flat Dunes** spread out, fifteen rippled and contoured square miles of ever-changing sand dunes, some over a hundred feet high. Most people are happy to photograph them from the road (best in late afternoon), but while there are no formal trails, it is easy enough to pick a route out to the nearest of the dunes (about half a mile away) or even to the top of the highest dune (3–4 miles round-trip). On the opposite side of Hwy-190 stands the **Devil's Cornfield**, an expanse of tufted arrowweed grasses perched on mounds that make them look like corn shocks.

Stovepipe Wells, a couple of miles on from the dunes, is a good place to take a break with views of the dunes, and is handy for trips to **Mosaic Canyon** (see box opposite). The resort comprises just a ranger station, a grocery store, a campground (see p.271), a gas station and a motel (see p.270) with associated family **restaurant** and bar. The latter serves three à la carte meals a day in winter, then in summer has a buffet breakfast ($8) and an à la carte dinner but no lunch. Expect chicken taquitos ($8) and pork medallions ($18). The motel **pool** is open to the public ($4).

The northeast: Rhyolite, Beatty and Titus Canyon Road

Northeast of Stovepipe Wells, a side road heads just outside the park boundary to the appealing ghost town of **Rhyolite** (Ⓦ www.rhyolitesite.com), a former gold-town whose mines were prematurely closed in 1912, after just six boom years. Mismanagement and a lack of technological know-how were largely to blame, and the working Bullfrog Mine just outside the town attests to the area's continuing mineral wealth. By the time of its demise, the town had spread over the hillside (made of the town's namesake mineral) and had its own train station. The station is still the dominant structure, but the remains of other buildings, including a jail, schoolhouse and bank, still stand, as does Tom Kelly's **bottle house**, built of some thirty thousand beer and spirit bottles in 1906. A more recent attraction is the roadside Goldwell Open Air Museum (unrestricted access; Ⓦ www.goldwellmuseum.org), a distinctly oddball **sculpture garden** that was the brainchild of Belgian artist Albert Szukalski, who died in 2000 after getting other artists to contribute. It's filled with structures built from car parts and an arresting series of white fibreglass figures arranged in imitation of *The Last Supper*, and you can't help but notice the huge sheet-metal miner and similarly proportioned penguin that greet you as you enter town. Check the website for workshops and upcoming projects.

At nearby **Beatty**, Nevada, there's gas, a casino, the small **Chamber of Commerce** at 119 Main St (Tues–Sat 9am–3pm; ☎775/553-2424, ⊕www .beattynevada.org), and the folksy **Beatty Museum**, 417 Main St (daily 10am–3pm; free), which tells tales of the local Bullfrog Mining District.

You can **eat** good American breakfasts and cheap Mexican all day at *Ensenada Grill*, 600 2nd St, and if you want to **stay**, go for the new *Death Valley Inn & RV Park*, 651 S Hwy-95 (☎775/553-9400; RV hookups $25, rooms ❷), with clean, spacious rooms, a pool and a hot tub.

From Rhyolite and Beatty you can coast back down into the park on Hwy-374, watching Death Valley unfold from above. There's also the chance to explore the one-way **Titus Canyon Road** (high-clearance vehicles recommended), a three-hour, 26-mile epic which winds past a handful of rusty corrugated-iron shacks – all that's left of **Leadfield**, a 1926 mining boom town that never boomed. The highlight is **Titus Canyon** itself, a narrow defile where the road is forced to follow a dry riverbed between steep walls only thirty feet apart. The best of this can be seen from a parking area three miles east of the Scotty's Castle road.

Scotty's Castle

On the northern edge of the park, 45 miles from the visitor centre, stands **Scotty's Castle** (roughly hourly tours: Nov–April 9am–5pm, May–Oct 9.30am–4pm; $11). It's well out of the way of most other attractions but its popularity here is unsurpassed; hordes of tourists wait in long lines for the chance to wander through this surreal, unfinished, yet still luxurious mansion. Executed in extravagant Spanish Revival style, the castle was built during the 1920s – at a cost of $2 million – as the desert retreat of wealthy Chicago insurance broker Albert Johnson, and has been left pretty much as it was when Johnson died in 1948. He was seldom there, so local cowboy, prospector and publicity hound "Death Valley" Scotty claimed the house was his own, financed by his hidden gold mine – a fantasy Johnson was happy to indulge. The house features intricately carved wooden ceilings, waterfalls in the living room, beautifully crafted tiled floors and, most

Exploring the backcountry

The paved roads visit just a small fraction of what the park has to offer, and minor dirt roads (many not shown on the map the park provides on entry) thread into a backcountry full of abandoned mines and dramatic (if parched) scenery.

Going backcountry, however, involves increased **risk**. Even if you're only visiting established sights such as Racetrack Valley or driving Titus Canyon Road, the threat of sharp rocks causing flat tires is increased. While high-clearance vehicles with heavy-duty tires are recommended for these roads, ordinary cars can often get by quite happily, with care. That said, one flat is an inconvenience; two can mean a towing fee well into the hundreds of dollars, if not thousands.

If you're keen to do some real exploring, talk to the rangers at the visitor centre who will furnish you with the free *Death Valley Backcountry Roads* map, which shows all back roads and ranks them in five levels of difficulty. Most really do need a high-clearance **4X4**, and if you are renting, be sure to check that the insurance will cover you.

entertaining of all, a remote-controlled 1121-pipe organ. In winter, it's best to arrive as the doors open to avoid long waits for the fifty-minute **tours** (no reservations) of the opulently furnished house. Scotty himself lived here until 1954 and is buried on the hill just behind the house: a good place to wander while waiting for your tour.

To achieve city comforts in such an inhospitable environment, Johnson arranged for the latest conveniences to be installed: primitive air conditioning, a hydro-electric generating system and other minor marvels can be seen on the one-hour **Underground Tour** (Nov–April 4–8 tours daily; May–Sept only if staff are available; $11). There's also the **Lower Vine Ranch Tour** (generally winter weekends, see current activities schedule in the visitor centre; $15; reserve on ℡760/786-2392), which visits the wooden cabin that was Scotty's official home for twenty years.

Ubehebe Crater, Racetrack Valley and the Eureka Sand Dunes

Eight miles southwest of Scotty's Castle – though it might as well be five hundred miles for all the people who venture here – gapes the half-mile-wide, 500-foot-deep **Ubehebe Crater**, the rust-coloured result of a massive volcanic explosion some three thousand years ago. Half a mile south sits its thousand-year-old younger brother, **Little Hebe** and beyond the craters, the road (high-clearance vehicles recommended, but ordinary cars can usually cope; see box opposite) continues twenty dusty miles south to **Teakettle Junction**, where visitors hang teakettles, many of them elaborately decorated, on a signpost. From here it's a further seven miles to **Racetrack Valley**, a 2.5-mile-long mud flat punctuated by **The Grandstand**, a weird black-rock intrusion that breaks up the place's symmetry. Park two miles south of The Grandstand, then walk half a mile southeast for the best view of **The Racetrack**, where small boulders seem slowly to be racing, leaving faint trails in their wake. Scientists believe that the boulders are pushed along the sometimes icy surface by very high winds, though no one has ever seen them move. Two miles further on there's a very primitive, waterless **campsite**.

A high-clearance vehicle is also recommended to visit **Eureka Sand Dunes**, forty miles northwest of Scotty's Castle. Far more impressive than the Mesquite Flat Dunes around Stovepipe Wells, these stand up to seven hundred feet above the surrounding land, making them the highest dunes in California and a dramatic place to witness sunrise or sunset. While here, keep your eyes open for the Eureka Dunes grass and evening primrose, both indigenous to the area and federally protected.

Western Death Valley

West of Stovepipe Wells, Hwy-190 heads out of the park bound for Lone Pine with a sprinkling of minor sights along the way. Emigrant Canyon road provides an opportunity to escape the heat and dust of the desert floor and climb up into the mountainous, pine-clad backcountry on the western slopes of the **Panamint Range** – the coolest part of the park.

Aguereberry Point, Wildrose Charcoal Kilns and Telescope Peak

Ten miles up Emigrant Canyon Road, a nine-mile dirt track turns off to the very meagre remains of **Skidoo Ghost Town**, a 1915 gold-mining camp of seven hundred people that was watered by snowmelt from Telescope Peak, 23 miles away, and kept informed by telegraph from Rhyolite. There's very little to see, so a better side-trip is to **Aguereberry Point**, a wonderful viewpoint looking six thousand feet down into Death Valley and reached along a six-mile dirt road off Emigrant Canyon Road.

Further south, the *Wildrose* campground (see p.271) marks the start of a steep, five-mile road up Wildrose Canyon to the **Wildrose Charcoal Kilns**. This series of ten massive, beehive-shaped stone kilns, each some 25ft tall, was used in the 1880s to make charcoal from piñon and juniper logs for use in the smelters of local silver mines. Beyond here, the road deteriorates (high-clearance recommended) and climbs through juniper and pine forests past free campgrounds (see p.271) and the trailhead for the strenuous hike up the 11,049ft **Telescope Peak** (see box, p.274).

Panamint Springs, Lee Flat and Saline Valley

Sticking with Hwy-19 you pass **Panamint Springs**, twenty miles southwest of Stovepipe Wells, just a motel, campground (see p.270 & p.271) and the associated **restaurant** and bar serving breakfast to 11am ($8–13), daytime sandwiches and burgers ($11–13) and good pasta ($14–16), salad and steak dinners ($18–27). Eat either inside or out on the shady terrace, which is cool enough for outdoor summer dining or sipping a beer in the night air. A mile west, a two-mile dirt road south brings you to the start of a mile-long creekside trail to the thirty-foot, spring-fed **Darwin Falls**. It's hardly dramatic, but it does feed a welcome and shady cottonwood oasis, though because it supplies Panamint Springs with water, swimming is not allowed.

You might not expect to see Joshua trees in Death Valley, but **Lee Flat**, a dozen miles west of Panamint Springs, has a whole forest of them on its higher slopes. At this point most visitors continue west towards Lone Pine passing the dry bed of what, until the 1920s, used to be **Owens Lake**, which for part of the nineteenth century carried steamships loaded with gold bullion. The water that would naturally flow into the lake has been diverted to Los Angeles via the aqueduct that parallels US-395, leaving a pan of toxic alkali dust. Schemes are currently underway to control this by planting native vegetation and drip-feeding a quarter of the water flow back into the ecosystem.

Adventurous drivers with sturdy vehicles might fancy exploring the northwestern corner of the park. A dirt road leads north past more Joshua trees at Lower Lee Flat, then continues on a very rough and unsigned fifty-mile trek out to **Saline Valley** – get the *Death Valley Backcountry Roads* map (free from the visitor centre) and ask for local advice about road conditions. The highlights are the generally clothing-free **hot springs** at Saline Warm Spring and the adjacent Palm Hot Spring, both easily spotted by the palm trees. Other than hot water, vault toilets and a free, primitive campground there are no facilities, so take everything you might need. After a dip it's possible to continue north to meet US-395 at Big Pine.

The Owens Valley

Rising out of the northern reaches of the Mojave Desert, the Sierra Nevada mountains announce themselves with a bang. Two hundred miles north of Los Angeles, **Mount Whitney** is the highest point on a silver-grey knifelike ridge of pinnacles that forms an eleven-thousand-foot rampart of granite. It provides a wonderful backdrop to the **OWENS VALLEY**, a hot, dry and numinously thrilling stretch of desolate, semi-desert landscape, running north from **Lone Pine** to beyond **Bishop**.

The small towns along its length don't really amount to much and if you're intent on visiting California's more cultural sights, you could easily drive

Sierra pass and trailhead closures

After coming through the Mojave or Death Valley, it seems hard to imagine that many of the passes across the Sierra Nevada can remain closed well into June. The authorities try to open **Tioga Pass** (Hwy-120 from Mono Lake into Yosemite) by Memorial Day weekend (at the end of May), but harsh winters sometimes leave it closed until late June. Passes to the north of here, **Hwy-108** and **Hwy-4**, tend to open a couple of weeks earlier, in mid-May. All three close again with the first heavy snowfall, perhaps around late October or early November. **Hwy-88**, yet further north, stays open all year. For information on the state of the highways contact CalTrans (☎1-800/427-7623, ⊛www.dot.ca.gov).

Eastern Sierra **trailheads** are equally affected by snow, with most only accessible from May until early November. Even in June and early July the trails leading from the trailheads can be impassable without an ice axe and crampons.

through in half a day. However, for scenic beauty and access to a range of outdoor activities, the Owens Valley is hard to beat. Twisting mountain roads rise quickly from the hot valley floor to cool, 10,000-foot-high trailheads ideal for **hiking** among Sierra lakes and forests or setting out for the summit of Mount Whitney or other peaks.

The Owens Valley is billed as the deepest valley in the US, and with its floor averaging 4000ft of elevation and the mountains on either side topping out above 14,000ft, that seems completely believable. Its eastern wall is formed by the contiguous **Inyo Mountains** and **White Mountains**; rounded and weathered in comparison with the Sierra and less dramatic, they have their own beauty, especially around the wonderful **Ancient Bristlecone Pine Forest**, which contains the world's oldest trees.

US-395 runs the length of the Owens Valley, a vital lifeline through a region that's almost entirely unpopulated outside of a handful of small towns, though a few solitary souls live in old sheds and caravans off the many dirt roads and tracks that cross the valley floor. Naturally a semi-desert with only around five inches of rain a year, the region relies on Sierra snowmelt, which once made it a prime spot for growing apples and pears. Since 1913, though, its plentiful natural water supply has been drained away to fill the swimming pools of Los Angeles (see box, p.299).

Lone Pine, Mount Whitney and around

LONE PINE isn't much more than a single-street rural town strung with motels, gas stations and restaurants, but it's lent a more vibrant air by being at the crossroads of desert and mountains. Any night of the week, there'll be desert rats mixing with Mount Whitney wilderness hikers and tourists recovering from the rigours of Death Valley. It also makes a good base and supply post for exploring the area, particularly if you're not prepared to camp out.

Part of what really makes it special is the unparalleled access it provides to the 14,497-foot summit of **MOUNT WHITNEY** – the highest point in the US outside Alaska. The view of the sharply pointed High Sierra peaks which dominate the town – captured by photographer Ansel Adams in a much-reproduced shot of the full moon suspended above stark cliffs – is fantastic.

Arrival, information and accommodation

ESTA **buses** stop outside Statham Hall at 138 Jackson Street, not far from the **Chamber of Commerce**, 120 S Main Street (May–Sept Mon–Sat 8.30am–5pm;

Nov–April Mon–Fri 8.30am–4.30pm; ☎760-876-4444, ⊛www.lonepine chamber.org), which is fine for local information. For details of hiking and camping throughout eastern California, visit the excellent **Eastern Sierra InterAgency Visitor Center** (daily 8am–5pm, 6pm in summer; ☎760/876-6222, ⊛www.r5.fs.fed.us/inyo), two miles south of town on US-395 at the junction of Hwy-136, the Death Valley road. Most of the region is protected within the massive **Inyo National Forest** and covered by the very helpful *Inyo National Forest* **map** ($10), which covers everything between Mount Whitney and Yosemite National Park, including all hiking routes and campgrounds. The map clearly shows the extent of the City of Los Angeles's holdings in the Owens Valley – basically the entire valley floor, bought in the early years of the twentieth century to slake the thirst of the expanding city (see box, p.299). From mid-June to mid-September, the **swimming pool** at the high school on Muir Street south of town is open to visitors (Tues, Wed, Fri & Sat noon–5pm; $2).

Accommodation is limited to a few motel-style places in town and plenty of **campgrounds**, all off Whitney Portal Road, which heads west from town at the lights.

Motels and hostel

Budget Inn Motel 138 Willow St ☎1-877/283-4381. Simple budget motel with fridge, microwave and a/c, located in the centre of town, just off US-395. ❷

De La Cour Ranch 5000 Horseshoe Meadow Rd ☎760/264-3213, ⊛www.delacour-ranch.com. Located ten miles west of (and 2000 feet higher than) Lone Pine on a lavender and horse ranch, this delightful spot has just three cabins set in a fold in the hills with long views. All come with fully made-up beds, but lack electricity and two share an external bathroom. The third (❹) has indoor toilet and shower, propane wall lights and sleeps four relatively comfortably. It's a great getaway, so bring food and you won't need to leave for a couple of days. ❶

Dow Villa Motel 310 S Main St ☎1-800/824-9317, ⊛www.dowvillamotel.com. Large complex with an older section (the original Dow Hotel) built in 1923 to house movie-industry visitors (though John Wayne always requested Room 20 in the newer motel section). There's an impressive range of accommodation, from basic bathless rooms in the hotel, rooms with bath and plush motel units, some with big TV, VCR/DVD and whirlpool. ❶–❺

Whitney Portal Hostel 238 S Main St ☎760/876-0030, ⊛www.whitneyportalstore.com. Though it lacks any backpacker hostel feel, they do have 6-bed and 10-bed dorms (each with en-suite bathroom) and a host of en-suite rooms with 4 bunks. There's a communal fridge and microwave, free wi-fi, and non-guests can shower for $5. Bunks $23, rooms ❷

Campgrounds

Portagee Joe Campground Tuttle Creek Rd (all year; 3800ft). Handily sited just three quarters of a mile outside Lone Pine, with toilets, water and some shade. Follow Whitney Portal Road for half a mile, then turn left into Tuttle Creek Road. $10.

Tuttle Creek Campground (all year; 5100ft). Basic waterless campground three miles out on Horseshoe Meadow Road. $5.

Whitney Portal Campground 12 miles west of Lone Pine (late May to late Oct; 8100ft). Family-oriented site at the base of the Mount Whitney trail. Reservable on ☎1-877/444-6777, ⊛www.recreation.gov. $19.

Whitney Portal Trailhead Campground 12 miles west of Lone Pine (mid-May to late Oct; 8300ft). Hiker-oriented site perfect for the night before your Whitney ascent; maximum one-night stay. $10.

The town and the Alabama Hills

Lone Pine loves to celebrate its **movie heritage**. The Alabama Hills immediately west of town were used extensively as the backdrop for Westerns from the 1920s to the 1950s, then Western TV series in the 1960s, and more recently the occasional science-fiction movie and car commercial. You'll see photos of stars of yesteryear all over town, but the place to key into the scene is the **Museum of Lone Pine Film History** at the corner of US-395 and Hopalong Cassidy Lane at the southern end of town (Mon–Wed 10am–6pm, Thurs–Sat 10am–7pm, Sun

10am–4pm; $5; ⓦ www.lonepinefilmhistorymuseum.org). Watch the twelve-minute film, then browse the impressive collection of old movie posters, the 1937 Plymouth driven by Humphrey Bogart through the Alabama Hills in *High Sierra* and some fabulous suits by Nudie, the rodeo tailor. You can't miss his fabulous white 1975 Cadillac Eldorado convertible with its five-foot-wide bullhorns, silver dollar upholstery and mounted revolvers with mother-of-pearl grips. Look out for **screenings** of movies filmed in the area (Thurs & Fri evening and Sat afternoon) or visit during the **Lone Pine Film Festival** (ⓦ www.lonepinefilmfestival.org), held over Columbus Day weekend (the second weekend in October).

Between Lone Pine and the Sierra Nevada stand the **Alabama Hills**, a rugged expanse of brown, tan, orange and black granite and some metamorphic rock that's been sculpted into bizarre shapes over 160 million years. Some of the oddest formations are linked by the **Picture Rocks Circle**, a paved road that loops around from Whitney Portal Road, passing rocks apparently shaped like bullfrogs, walruses and baboons; it takes a degree of imagination and precise positioning to pick them all out, but it's an attractive drive nonetheless, especially at sunset. A map (free from the visitor centres; see opposite) details the best spots and marks the sites used as backdrops for many early Westerns, as well as the 1939 epic *Gunga Din*.

There's also plenty of scope for hiking and scrambling among the rocks. A couple of fairly unspectacular but photogenic natural **rock arches** act as a focus for your wanderings; dusk is particularly pleasant, with the scent of sagebrush in the air. The best of the arches is off Movie Road, just west of Lone Pine, where a ten-minute walk should find you at an eight-foot span.

Eating

There's an adequate range of **restaurants** for the night or two you're going to be here.

Bonanza 104 N Main St ☎760/876-4768. Authentic Mexican serving basic but filling dishes such as ranchero steak ($13), plus several vegetarian options.
The Espresso Parlor 123 N Main St. Good coffee and muffins plus internet access ($7/hr) and wi-fi (free).
Mt Whitney Restaurant 227 S Main St. Reliable diner that backs up its claim to serve "the best

burgers in town" with half a dozen types of patties – chicken, ostrich, venison, veggie – on which to build your creation.
Seasons 206 S Main St ☎760/876-8927. Lone Pine's best restaurant, serving excellent home-made pasta dishes ($19–21) and great steaks ($23–30), including elk. Dinner only.

Whitney Portal

Ten miles west of the Alabama Hills lies **Whitney Portal** (usually accessible May to early Nov), the 8000-foot-high trailhead for hiking up Mount Whitney. Even if a full-on slog to the summit is furthest from your mind, you might appreciate a refreshing break from the valley frazzle in the cool shade of the pines and hemlocks. What's more, there's a small fast-food counter and general store for when you need fortifying between strolls around the trout-stocked pond, along the cascading stream, or up the Mount Whitney Trail to Lone Pine Lake (five miles round-trip; no permit required).

Manzanar National Historic Site

Twelve miles north of Lone Pine, on the former site of the most productive of the Owens Valley apple and pear orchards, stand the concrete foundations of the **Manzanar National Historic Site** (daytime access; free; ☎760/878-2194, ⓦ www.nps.gov/manz), where more than ten thousand Americans of Japanese

Hiking up to the 14,497-foot **summit** of Mount Whitney is a real challenge: it's a very strenuous, 22-mile round-trip, made especially difficult by the lack of oxygen atop the highest point in all 48 contiguous states (see p.48 for advice on Acute Mountain Sickness). Vigorous hikers starting before dawn from the 8322-foot trailhead can be up and back before dark, but a couple of days spent acclimatizing up here is advisable, and the whole experience is enhanced by camping out at least one night along the route. The trail gains over a mile in elevation, cutting up past alpine lakes to boulder-strewn Trail Crest Pass – the southern end of the 211-mile John Muir Trail that heads north to Yosemite. From the pass it ascends along the cliff-tops, finally reaching the rounded hump of the summit itself, where there's a **stone cabin** – not a place you'd choose to be during a lightning storm. Water is available along the first half of the route but must be filtered or treated.

Ambitious hikers with experience in scrambling or technical rock climbing will enjoy the **"Mountaineers' Route"**, which follows the North Fork of Lone Pine Creek, taking a more direct and much steeper (though no quicker) route to the summit past the bases of the numerous rock climbs on the mountain's east face. Ropes aren't generally needed, but you'll need a head for heights and perhaps a helmet. Ask for directions and current advice at the ranger station and at the Whitney Portal store.

The **Inyo National Forest**, which manages Mount Whitney, also controls permits for various other sections of the 78,000-acre wilderness area detailed in this chapter. Except for the Whitney Trail and the North Fork of Lone Pine Creek (the Mountaineers' Route), day-use permits are not required, but a permit (free; reservations $5 per person) is needed if you want to spend the night; enquire at the Eastern Sierra Interagency Visitor Center (see p.280) for the ranger station nearest the region you'd like to hike. Sixty percent of permits can be reserved. Out of season (Nov–April), self-issue permits are available at local ranger stations and the Eastern Sierra Interagency Visitor Center.

descent were corralled during World War II. Considering them a threat to national security, the US government uprooted whole families, confiscated all their property and brought them here until the end of the war. Claims for compensation were only settled in 1988 when President Reagan finally offered the sixty thousand survivors of the state's internment camps an official apology and agreed to pay millions of dollars in damages. Ringed by barbed wire, the one-square-mile camp was filled with row upon row of wooden barracks but everything was razed when the camp was closed in 1945. Now only a couple of pagoda-like sentry posts, an auditorium, and a small cemetery remain among the sagebrush and scraggy cottonwoods. As the bronze plaque on the guardhouse says: "May the injustices and humiliation suffered here as a result of hysteria, racism and economic exploitation never emerge again." Oddly poignant, in times when it can seem that anyone of Arab descent is considered suspicious. Former internees return each year, on the last Saturday in April, leaving mementos on a kind of cenotaph in the cemetery, which is inscribed with Japanese characters meaning "soul-consoling tower".

The National Park Service has turned the auditorium into an excellent **Interpretive Center** (daily: April–Oct 9am–5.30pm; Nov–March 9am–4.30pm; free) where the moving 22-minute film *Remembering Manzanar* runs every half-hour. Pick up a leaflet for the three-mile **auto tour** past 27 points of interest around the camp, including remaining examples of Japanese gardens. Check the website for details of free, guided **walking tours** (30–90min).

4

Obtaining permits

Such is the popularity of Whitney that from May to October **overnight and day-hikers** must obtain a permit ($15 reservation fee) through the Whitney Zone **lottery**, which takes place in February. Dates in July, August and September (the only time the trail is generally totally free of snow) fill up fast, so May (when you may need an ice axe), June, and October (when there may be some snow on the ground) are better bets. The permit quota used for day-hikers is less competitive, though you should seriously consider your ability and fitness.

Apply for an overnight or day-use **wilderness permit** by fax or mail (not phone) through Inyo National Forest Wilderness Permit Office, 351 Pacu Lane, Suite 200, Bishop, CA 93514 (☏760/873-2483, Ⓕ873-2484, Ⓦwww.r5.fs.fed.us/inyo), making sure it is postmarked or dated in February. Application forms can be downloaded from the website. If you're not that organized (or miss out, as around half the applicants do), your best shot is to check the website for availability. Starting from mid-May you can apply for any spaces at least two days before your planned ascent (fax, mail or phone in this instance). Free **last-minute permits** can be obtained from the Eastern Sierra Interagency Visitor Center a day in advance of your planned ascent after 11am: avoid weekends when demand is highest.

There are no toilets beside the Whitney trails so all hikers are required to carry out all solid waste: special bags are issued with wilderness permits. Overnight hikers are also required to pack their food in a **bear-resistant food canister**, which can be rented from the ranger station ($2.50 per day; min $5), the Whitney Portal Store (rent $2 per day or buy for $50) and local sporting-goods stores. Once armed with a permit, drive to Whitney Portal, where you can park for the duration of your hike. The Chamber of Commerce can put you in touch with a shuttle service up to the trailhead, or you can hitch. Day-hikers will want to **camp** at the small, first-come-first-served *Whitney Portal Trailhead* campground ($10) and be ready for an early start. Overnight hikers have more leisure and can plan to hike to one of two designated campgrounds (both first-come-first-served and free): *Outpost Camp* at 3.8 miles and *Trail Camp* at 6.2 miles.

Independence and around

The sleepy town of **Independence**, six miles north of Manzanar, was founded on the Fourth of July, 1862, a fact celebrated annually with a parade down Edwards Street (US-395) followed by a mass barbecue and fireworks show in **Dehy Park**, along tree-shaded Independence Creek on the north side of town. The park is marked by a large steam locomotive, which once ran from here to Nevada on narrow-gauge tracks.

The main reason to stop is to visit the **Eastern California Museum** at 155 N Grant St (daily 10am–5pm; donation; ☏760/878-0258), three blocks west of the porticoed County Courthouse, which contains an evocative and affecting exhibit detailing the experiences of many of the young children who were held at Manzanar. The museum has reconstructed part of a family-sized barrack unit, and also holds an extensive collection of photos of camp life (not always on show) taken by Toyo Miyatake, who was interned at Manzanar and managed to smuggle in a lens and film holders.

The museum also has displays on native Paiute basketry and the natural environment of the Owens Valley, including the **California bighorn sheep**, a protected species which inhabits the mountains to the west of Independence. These nimble rock-climbers with massive curling horns now number only around a hundred and fifty, and efforts to establish new populations are thwarted by appreciative mountain lions, who promptly eat them.

Practicalities

Local information is available from the Independence **Chamber of Commerce**, 139 N Edwards St (Mon & Tues 9am–5pm, Fri 8am–4pm; ☏760/878-0084, ⓦwww.independence-ca.com). If you're in the anti-camping camp, Independence offers a few **places to stay** indoors. Try the inexpensive *Courthouse Motel*, at 157 N Edwards St (☏1-800/801-0703; ❷), or the 1927 *Winnedumah Hotel*, 211 N Edwards St (☏760/878-2040, ⓦwww.winnedumah.com; ❸), once a film-star haven that has retained its atmosphere, especially in the comfy lounge, which comes decorated with local paintings and native crafts. A good breakfast is included. There's also the *Independence Creek* campground ($10), half a mile west of town on Onion Valley Road.

The choice of **restaurants** is very limited, though the wonderful and eccentrically French-run ⚜ *Still Life Café*, 135 S Edwards St (daily except Tues & Wed 11am–2pm & 5.30–9pm; ☏760/878-2555), serves burgers and sandwiches for lunch and excels with its evening French menu, which might extend to *entrecôtes* of pork with caramelized onions ($23), or a delicious tuna-packed pasta *puttanesca* ($20). Wines are mostly French, many available by the glass.

Around Independence

West from Independence, the minor Onion Valley Road twists up the mountains to the pine-shrouded trailhead at **Onion Valley**, fifteen miles away. The *Onion Valley* **campground** (June–Sept; 9200ft; $16; ⓦwww.recreation.gov) marks the start of **hiking** trails across the Sierra Nevada into Kings Canyon National Park, a sixteen-mile journey over Kearsarge Pass to Cedar Grove (see p.334). This is the easiest and shortest route across the Sierra (wilderness permit required).

The **Tinemaha Wildlife Viewpoint**, thirty miles north of Independence, warrants a brief pause for spotting members of the five-hundred-strong herd of **tule elk**, now protected California natives which were nearly wiped out by the end of the nineteenth century. A few dozen were relocated here from the San Joaquin Valley in 1914 and they seem to be thriving.

Big Pine and around

There's not a great deal to **Big Pine**, 28 miles to the north of Independence, but it does act as a gateway to three of the most impressive natural phenomena in California: the **Palisade Glacier**, in the Sierra Nevada to the west of town; the Ancient Bristlecone Pine Forest, in the barren **White Mountains** to the east; and the northern reaches of Death Valley, in particular the Eureka Sand Dunes (see p.277) and the hot springs of the Saline Valley (see p.278).

There are three affordable **motels** along US-395 including *Starlight Motel*, 511 S Main St (☏760/938-2011; ❷), which has cable, free wi-fi and a shady barbecue deck. There's also the *Glacier View* **campground** (tents $12, hookup $17) half a mile north of town at the junction of Hwy-168, and several more camping spots up Glacier Lodge Road (see p.286). Good diner **food** is available at the *Country Kitchen*, 181 S Main St.

Just off US-395 seven miles north of Big Pine, there's a worthwhile diversion to **Keough's Hot Springs**, Keough's Hot Springs Road (daily except Tues 9am–7pm or later; $8; ☏760/872-4670, ⓦwww.keoughshotsprings.com), a mineral-water-fed swimming pool and hot soaking pool that was once the social centre of the region, now restored to something of its former glory. They have camping (tents $20, RV hookups $25) and a couple of wooden-floored tent cabins equipped with fully made-up beds (❷ including pool entry).

A couple of hundred yards before the springs' entrance a dirt road cuts north to some **natural hot springs**, where locals have created a couple of clothing-optional bathing pools, their idyllic setting only slightly marred by the overhead power wires and indiscriminate littering.

The White Mountains

Rising to the east of Big Pine, the intimidating **WHITE MOUNTAINS** are effectively an alpine desert: bald, dry and little visited, yet almost as high as the Sierra. The range is made up of some of the oldest, most fossil-filled rock in California, and geologically has more in common with the Great Basin to the east than the spiky Sierra, which came into being several hundred million years later. It looks like it, too: the scrubby, undulating high country appears more Scottish than Californian. The mountains are accessible via Hwy-168: be sure to fill up on gas and **drinking water**, both of which are unavailable east of US-395.

Snow renders the **Ancient Bristlecone Pine Forest** off-limits for all but three or four months in the summer. **Schulman Grove** ($2.50 per person or $5 per car) is the most accessible collection, some 23 miles from Big Pine along a paved road that twists up from Hwy-168. The grove is split up into three self-guided nature trails, all at 10,000ft and therefore tougher than their length would indicate. Best is the four-mile Methuselah Trail which loops around past the oldest tree, the 4700-year-old Methuselah, though you'll have to guess which of the trees it is since it is unmarked due to fears of vandalism. It links to the Bristlecone Cabin Trail (2 miles) which winds past cabins from an old Mexican mine. Trails start at the temporary **visitor center** (June–Sept daily 10am–5pm; late May & Oct call for hours; ☎760/873-2500), which will be replaced by a stylish eco-structure by late 2012. Inside, you'll be able to learn about the importance of the grove's namesake, Dr Edmund Schulman. An early practitioner of dendrochronology, he revealed the extreme age of these trees in the mid-1950s and applied the knowledge gained from core samples to correct a puzzling error in early carbon-dating techniques. Free ranger talks are scheduled frequently throughout July and August.

Bristlecone pines

Great Basin **bristlecone pines** (*Pinus longaeva*) are the oldest known living things on earth. Some of them have been alive for over 4700 years (1500 years more than any sequoia). The oldest examples cling to thin alkaline soils between 10,000 and 11,000 feet, where the low precipitation keeps the growing season to only 45 days a year. But such conditions, which limit the trees' girth expansion to an inch every hundred years, promotes the dense resin-rich and rot-resistant wood that lasts for millennia. Battered and beaten by the harsh environment into bizarrely beautiful shapes and forms, they look like nothing so much as twenty-foot lumps of driftwood. The most photogenic examples comprise mostly **dead wood**, the live section often sustained by a thin ribbon of bark. Even when dead, the wind-scoured trunks and twisted limbs hang on without decaying for upwards of another thousand years, slowly being eroded by wind-driven ice and sand.

Bristlecones thrive at lower altitudes and in richer soils than those in the White Mountains, growing tall and wide. But they seldom live as long as specimens subjected to the harsher conditions and, in fact, they're hardly recognizable as bristlecone pines – only the five-needle bundles and the egg-shaped, barbed cone which lends the tree its name, give the game away.

For more information, consult the Inyo Forest website at ⓦwww.r5.fs.fed.us/inyo or, better still, the excellent ⓦwww.sonic.net/bristlecone.

Patriarch Grove, twelve miles further on, along a dusty dirt road that gives spectacular views of the Sierra Nevada to the west and the Great Basin ranges of the deserts to the east, contains the Patriarch Tree, the largest of the bristlecone pines. Four miles beyond here, a research station (closed to the public) studies the physiology of high-altitude plant and animal life, which is in many ways similar to that of the arctic regions. From here you can hike to the summit of **White Mountain** (14 miles round-trip; 6–8hr; 2500-foot ascent), the highest point in the range and at 14,246ft the third highest in California.

There is **camping** (vault toilets but no water) at the 8600-foot *Grandview* campground (all year; $3 donation), two miles south of Schulman Grove. The ranger station in Bishop can provide details of backcountry camping in the surrounding forest and tell you which springs and small creeks (if any) are flowing.

The Palisade Glacier

The **Palisade Glacier** is the southernmost glacier in the US and the largest in California. It sits at the foot of the impressive Palisade Crest, centre of one of the greatest concentrations of enjoyable alpine climbing in the Eastern Sierra: Norman Clyde Peak in the south is named after California's most prolific early mountaineer; the immense bulk of Temple Crag offers a range of routes unparalleled outside of Yosemite Valley; and, to the north, Thunderbolt Peak and Mount Agassiz are highlights of the Inconsolable Range. The Palisade Glacier itself is an excellent introduction to snow and ice climbing.

Hikers not suitably equipped for technical climbing can still get a sense of this wondrous area by hiking from the trailhead at Big Pine Canyon, ten miles west of Big Pine at the end of Glacier Lodge Road; follow Crocker Street from Big Pine. July, August and September are generally snow-free and best for hiking along the trail to **First Lake** (9 miles round-trip; 5–7hr; 2300-foot ascent). From here a network of shorter trails diverges to six more lakes and to the base of the **Palisade Glacier** (18 miles round-trip from the parking lot; 10–12hr; 4600-foot ascent). Backcountry campers must obtain a **permit** (see box, p.283).

At the trailhead, you'll find three **campgrounds** (late April–Oct; $20) – *Sage Flat, Upper Sage Flat* and *Big Pine Creek* – all above seven thousand feet and with water and toilets; and the free *First Falls* walk-in site at 8300ft, a mile beyond the trailhead. *Glacier Lodge* (℡760/938-2837, 🌐www.jewelofthesierra.com; ➍), right at the end of the road, is a slightly more luxurious option, with cabins, RV parking ($35–50), overnight parking for hikers ($5), a limited general store and showers (10am–4pm only; $4).

Bishop

BISHOP, fifteen miles north of Big Pine, rivals Mammoth Lakes as the **outdoor pursuits** capital of the Eastern Sierra. It doesn't have downhill skiing on its doorstep, but its proximity to the wilderness makes it an excellent base from which to explore the surrounding mountains; if you want to try cross-country skiing, fly-fishing and especially rock climbing, there's no better place to be, with some of the world's best mountaineers offering their services through lessons and guided trips. With a population of 3500 it's the largest town in the Owens Valley, yet maintains a laidback ambience which makes it worth hanging about to enjoy.

Arrival, information and accommodation

Almost everything of interest lies along or just off Main Street (US-395), where you'll find the ESTA **bus stop** at 201 S Warren St and the main **visitor centre**, 690 N Main St (Mon–Fri 10am–5pm, Sat & Sun 10am–4pm; ℡1-888/395-3952,

@www.bishopvisitor.com). For specific information on **hiking** and **camping** in the area and permission to visit the local petroglyphs, contact the **Public Lands Information Center**, 798 N Main St (June–Sept daily 8am–5pm; Oct–May Mon–Fri 8.30am–4.30pm; ⊤760/873-2500), which also issues wilderness permits. There's a reasonable range of **accommodation**, for which booking in advance is advised on summer weekends (especially during **festivals**; see p.288). There is a **campground** in town (see below) and plenty of Inyo National Forest sites all around.

Hotels, motels and campgrounds

Best Western Creekside Inn 725 N Main St ⊤1-800/273-3550, @www.bishopcreekside.com. Modern, upscale hotel in the centre of town offering large rooms (some with kitchenette for $10–20 extra), complimentary breakfast, free wi-fi and an outdoor pool. ❺

Brown's Town Campground Schober Lane, off US-395, a mile south of town ⊤760/873-8522. Large Old West-themed RV and tent campground, with kids' play area and other facilities, costing $20 for tents and $25 for water and electric hookup.

Joseph House Inn 376 W Yaney St ⊤760-872-3389, @www.josephhouseinn.com.

Upscale five-room B&B in three acres of gardens, with nicely decorated rooms, outdoor hot tub, free wi-fi, wine and cheese on arrival, and a full gourmet breakfast served either inside or on the terrace. ❺

The Trees Motel 796 W Line St ⊤760/873-6391. Fairly basic family-owned motel with low rates in a quiet setting half a mile off the main street. ❷

The Village Motel 286 W Elm St ⊤1-888/668-5546, @www.bishopvillagemotel.com. Budget motel with renovated rooms, all with microwave and fridge (some with fully equipped kitchen), free wi-fi and access to the outdoor pool (heated in summer and fall). Peacefully sited off the busy main drag. Rooms ❷, kitchen suites ❹

The Town

Specific sights in town are few, though anyone interested in gorgeous images of the Sierra and beyond should visit the top-class Mountain Light Gallery, 106 S Main Street at Line Street (daily 10am–6pm; free; ⊤760/873-7700, @www .mountainlight.com), lined with photos by Galen Rowell, one of the world's foremost landscape photojournalists until his untimely death in a plane crash in 2002. Also a talented rock climber and mountaineer, Rowell photographed the region for over thirty years and extended his oeuvre to Patagonia, the Himalayas, northern Canada, Alaska, Antarctica and elsewhere. You'll have to part with well over $500 to obtain one of the large-scale framed photos that line the walls, but it is well worth half an hour's browsing.

Outdoor activities

Outdoor enthusiasts congregate in Bishop, their rigs laden with tents, sleeping bags, mountain bikes, rock-climbing gear, fishing tackle, crampons and ice axes.

All year round there is somewhere to **rock climb**, particularly the High Sierra peaks around Rock Creek, about twenty miles north of Bishop, and Tuolumne in Yosemite (see p.355). For more information, visit Wilson's Eastside Sports, 224 N Main St (⊤760/873-7520, @www.eastsidesports.com), an excellent mountaineering and sporting-goods supply shop with gear rental and a climbers' notice board.

Bishop also attracts brigades of **fishing** enthusiasts seeking the rainbow trout placed in the streams and lakes by the state government. The main trout season runs from late April to late October, heralded by the Blake Jones Trout Derby which takes place in mid-March at the Pleasant Valley Reservoir, six miles north along US-395. There's a huge assembly of fisherfolk on the last Saturday in April around **Crowley Lake**, an artificial reservoir built thirty miles north of town to hold water diverted from Mono Lake.

Eating and drinking

With a huge 24-hour Vons store at 1190 N Main St, as well as a number of good cafés and diners, Bishop is a good place to feast after a few days in the hills and to buy **food and supplies** for the next leg.

Black Sheep Espresso Bar 124 S Main St. They take their coffee seriously at this cosy café tucked in behind Spellbinder Books. There are all manner of intriguing roasts, typically organic, plus light meals, smoothies and free wi-fi.

Erick Schat's Bakkery 736 N Main St. Huge and bustling pseudo-Dutch bakery that's been making its "Original Sheepherder Bread" since early in the twentieth century. There are dozens of other varieties (such as multigrain and sourdough), and tables for tucking into their sandwiches ($8) and huge range of cakes and pastries.

Jack's Restaurant and Bakery 437 N Main St. Well-regarded diner that bakes its own bread, used in their extensive range of burgers and sandwiches. Leave space for a plate of their locally famous waffles or a slice of fruit pie. Open from 6am for breakfast.

Meadow Farms Smokehouse 2345 N Sierra Hwy. Located almost 2 miles north on US-395 this basic takeaway (with a few tables) makes the best sandwiches in town, many based around their mahogany-smoked bacon.

Whiskey Creek 524 N Main St ☎760/873-7174. Among Bishop's more upscale restaurants, with a sunny deck and an attached bar (where you can also eat) serving Whiskey Creek microbrews. Open for breakfast, lunch and dinner which might start with tempura shrimp ($12) and follow with ribs or halibut ($21–24) and a warm, apple bread pudding ($7).

Listings

Climbing and hiking guides For expert instruction or guided rock climbing, alpine climbing and ski mountaineering contact Sierra Mountain Center, 174 W Line St (☎760/873-8526, ⓦwww.sierra mountaincenter.com), or Sierra Mountaineering International, 236 N Main St (☎760/872-4929, ⓦwww.sierramountaineering.com).

Festivals Bishop comes alive over Memorial Day weekend for Mule Days (☎760/872-4263, ⓦwww.muledays.org), with a huge parade, mule-drawn chariot racing, a country hoedown, an arts and crafts fair and much more. The Tri-County Fair over Labor Day weekend includes a Wild West Rodeo.

Hospital Northern Inyo Hospital, 150 Pioneer Lane (☎760/873-5811), has 24-hour emergency and intensive care.

Internet Schat.net, 174 N Main St ($5/hr).

Library 210 Academy St (☎760/873-5115) has speedy internet access and is open Mon, Wed & Fri 10am–6pm, Tues & Thurs noon–8pm, Sat 10am–1pm.

Movies Bishop Twin Theatre, 237 N Main St, shows the latest Hollywood offerings.

Showers and laundry Showers and laundry at the Wash Tub, 236 Warren St (daily 7am–9pm; $5), or visit the Park Pool, 688 N Main St, behind the visitor centre ($5).

Around Bishop and north towards Mammoth

You may well stay and eat in Bishop, but the main attractions lie outside town, mostly along **South Lake Road** (Hwy-168), which climbs some fifteen miles to the west through aspens and cottonwoods to a cluster of alpine lakes and 10,000-foot trailheads, or north where the volcanic tablelands harbour **native petroglyphs**.

If you need a ride to the trailheads, contact Wilson's (see p.287) who always know the latest on shuttle operations.

West along Hwy-168

Roughly six miles west of Bishop the narrow, unpaved Buttermilk Road leads northwest off the highway into an arid land of lumpy hills and large, golden granite rocks known as the **Buttermilk Boulders**. Year-round, rock climbers from around the state pit themselves against an almost limitless selection of low-lying boulder problems in this beautiful setting. Visit Wilson's (see p.287) for details and guidebooks.

Hwy-168 ends at the dammed **Lake Sabrina**, where there's a restaurant that sells fishing tackle and rents boats. Nearby, **South Lake**, also nineteen miles from Bishop, is flanked by *Parchers Resort* (℡760/873-4177, Ⓦ www.parchersresort .net; ⑨), with a general store, fishing shop, horseriding, kayak rentals, cabins with varying degrees of luxury and $6 public showers. A number of **hiking routes** set off up into the High Sierra wilderness from trailheads at these lakes.

The trail from South Lake over Bishop Pass heads into Dusy Basin, where you can see the effects of centuries of glaciation in the bowl-like cirques and giant "erratic" boulders left by the receding masses of ice. Another path follows the northern fork of Bishop Creek under the rust-coloured cliffs of the Paiute Crags, before climbing over Paiute Pass into the Desolation Lakes area of the John Muir Wilderness. There are a number of **campgrounds** between 7500 and 9000 feet up – almost all with water and costing $21 a night. The shady *Sabrina* site, right by the lake of the same name, is one of the best.

Laws and the Red Rock Canyon petroglyphs

On the northern edge of Bishop, US-395 divides from US-6, which runs north and east into Nevada. Four miles along US-6 is the **Laws Railroad Museum** (daily 10am–4pm; donation; Ⓦ www.lawsmuseum.org), a handful of relocated old buildings and a slender black train known as the "Slim Princess" arranged in the restored old town of **Laws**. From 1883 to 1959 this was an important way station on the narrow-gauge line between Carson City and Owens Lake, just south of Lone Pine.

Northwest of Laws, a stark desert plateau harbours the **Red Rock Canyon Petroglyphs**, where ancient native peoples have carved numerous mysterious and beautiful designs – spirals, geometric forms, even spacey figures – onto the rocks. There are no permits, fees or gates to open, but visitors must sign in at the Public Lands Information Center in Bishop (see p.287) where they'll give you a map that pinpoints three petroglyph concentrations, the most interesting being at Chidago and Red Rock Canyon.

Mammoth Lakes and around

Forty miles north of Bishop you've climbed up to around 6500 feet into the **Mono Basin** heralded by the pine-shrouded town of **MAMMOTH LAKES** three miles west of US-395. Together with the associated skiing, snowboarding and mountain-biking hotspot of **Mammoth Mountain**, this is the Eastern Sierra's biggest resort and one that is challenged in California only by those around Lake Tahoe. Popular with weekenders from LA (just four hours away), it is rapidly joining the ranks of the winter-sports mega-resorts, such as Vail in the Rockies and Whistler/Blackcomb in Canada. A single company now owns the ski operation, large chunks of Mammoth real estate and the **Village at Mammoth** development, complete with pricey hotels, swanky stores and direct access to the mountain via the Village Gondola. The town's tiny airport now even has scheduled flights from San Jose, Portland, Seattle and Reno during the ski season. Although skiing and summer fishing are Mammoth's traditional attractions, the town is increasingly hyped for its accessible mountain-biking terrain and a number of on- and off-road bike races.

Residents are torn between enthusiasm for the new opportunities presented and nostalgia for the way things used to be, but for the moment Mammoth remains unbeatable for outdoor activities and is scenically as dramatic as just about

4

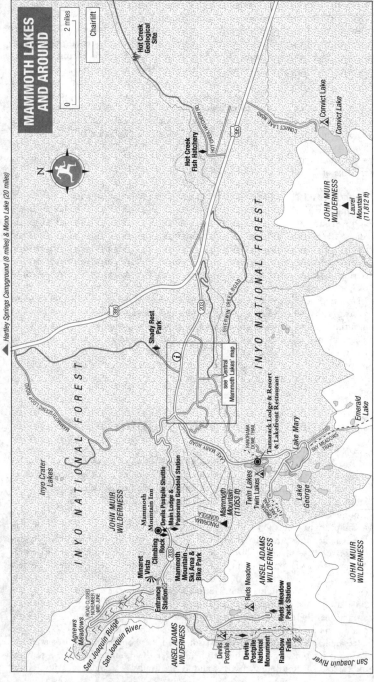

▲ Bishop (30 miles)

MAMMOTH LAKES AND AROUND

0 ——— 2 miles

—— Chairlift

◀ Hartley Springs Campground (8 miles) & Mono Lake (20 miles)

N

Hot Creek Geological Site

Hot Creek Fish Hatchery

HOT CREEK HATCHERY RD

395

Convict Lake
Convict Lake
CONVICT LAKE ROAD

JOHN MUIR WILDERNESS

Laurel Mountain (11,812 ft)

INYO NATIONAL FOREST

395

203

SHERWIN CREEK ROAD

Shady Rest Park

i

see 'Central Mammoth Lakes' map

INYO NATIONAL FOREST

MAMMOTH SCENIC LOOP ROAD

INYO NATIONAL FOREST

Inyo Crater Lakes

PANORAMA DOME TRAIL

Emerald Lake

LAKE MARY ROAD

Tamarack Lodge & Resort & Lakefront Restaurant

Lake Mary

SKY MEADOWS TRAIL

JOHN MUIR WILDERNESS

Mammoth Mountain Inn

Devils Postpile Shuttle

Main Lodge & Panorama Gondola Station

PANORAMA GONDOLA

Mammoth Mountain (11,053 ft)

Twin Lakes
Twin Lakes

Lake George

CRYSTAL LAKE TRAIL

Climbing Rock

203

Minaret Vista

Entrance Station

Mammoth Mountain Ski Area & Bike Park

ANSEL ADAMS WILDERNESS

Reds Meadow

ANSEL ADAMS WILDERNESS

JOHN MUIR WILDERNESS

Agnews Meadows

ROAD CLOSED NOVEMBER-JUNE

San Joaquin Ridge

San Joaquin River

Reds Meadow Pack Station

Devils Postpile

Devils Postpile National Monument

Rainbow Falls

San Joaquin River

anywhere in the Sierra. You may find the testosterone overload oppressive and the town overpriced, but it's easy to escape to the hills during the day and return each evening to good food, lively bars and even a couple of movie theatres.

Arrival and information

Hwy-203 runs three miles west from US-395 into the town of Mammoth Lakes, from where it continues six miles to the Main Lodge for Mammoth Mountain, then ascends the San Joaquin Ridge and drops down to the Devils Postpile National Monument.

Year-round **ESTA buses** (see p.265) stop four times a week in the *McDonald's* parking lot on Hwy-203. There's also a seasonal **YARTS service** to Tuolumne Meadows and Yosemite Valley (July & Aug once daily; June & Sept Sat & Sun only; ⓦwww.yarts.com), which departs from *Mammoth Mountain Inn*, opposite the Main Lodge, at 7am and returns that evening around 9pm.

The best source of practical information for the area is the combined US Forest Service and Mammoth Lakes **visitor centre** (daily 8am–5pm; ⓣ760/924-5500, ⓦwww.visitmammoth.com), on the main highway half a mile east of the town centre. Pick up a free town map which details the half-dozen **free bus routes** which go everywhere you'll want to. The most useful is the Town Trolley (daily 9am–10pm; every 20–30min). Alternatively, **rent a bike** (see p.296).

Accommodation

About every second building in Mammoth is a condo, but there are numerous other **accommodation** opportunities (including a hostel), so beds are at a premium only during ski-season weekends. Winter prices are highest, summer rates (quoted here) are still fairly high and some relative bargains can be found in the months in between. If you fancy staying in a **condo**, contact Mammoth Mountain Reservations (ⓣ1-800/223-3032, ⓦwww.mammothreservations.com).

There is also mile upon mile of backcountry in which to pitch a tent, and so many established sites that you'll be almost overwhelmed by choice. Some twenty **campgrounds** lie within a ten-mile radius of town, the two main concentrations being around Twin Lakes and along Minaret Road. Almost all come with water, cost $20–21 and are let on a first-come-first-served basis. The *Inyo National Forest Visitor Guide* (available free from the visitor centre) has full details along with rules for free dispersed camping on the surrounding national forest lands.

Motels, B&Bs and condos

Cinnamon Bear Inn 113 Center St ⓣ1-800/845-2873, ⓦwww.cinnamonbearinn.com. Reasonably priced, 22-room B&B inn done in New England colonial style, with comfortable rooms, all with TV and phone (and some with VCR or DVD), use of hot tub, wine-and-nibbles happy hour on arrival and a full breakfast. Some rooms have kitchenettes, one has a four-poster bed and there are four economy rooms (❷) which sleep two but ideally suit singles. Midweek ❺–❻

Davison Street Guest House 19 Davison St ⓣ760/924-2188, ⓦwww.mammoth-guest.com. Mammoth's only backpacker hostel is in a wooden A-frame chalet with mountain views from its deck.

There's a spacious lounge, good communal cooking facilities, bunks in fairly compact dorms (summer $28, winter weeknights $35, winter weekends $49), three-bed rooms (❶–❸) and one en-suite room for an extra $20.

The M Inn Mammoth 75 Joaquin Rd ⓣ760/934-2710, ⓦwww.themammothinn.com. Clean and functional small hotel with Minimalist styling in its ten rooms, all with private baths and some with jacuzzis. There are also a couple of cheaper rooms with shared bath. A self-serve breakfast is included. ❹–❻

Motel 6 3372 Main St ⓣ760/934-6660, ⓦwww.motel6.com. Basic motel close to the town centre, with all you really need at an affordable price. ❷

Sierra Nevada Lodge 164 Old Mammoth Rd ☎1-800/824-5132, ⓦwww.sierra nevadalodge.com. Recently renovated hotel with a nice lobby done with a kind of Southwestern hunting-lodge feel and with a massive open fire surrounded by comfy benches. Great-value rooms (some come with a wood burner) are comfortable and rates include continental breakfast (served in their restaurant), access to a pool and hot tub and even a mini-golf course. There are also several fully self-contained 3-bedroom chalets that are great for groups. ④

Tamarack Lodge & Resort Lake Mary Rd ☎1-800/626-6684, ⓦwww.tamaracklodge.com. Away from the town in a woodsy setting right by Twin Lake, on the edge of a cross-country-ski area, this luxurious lodge in rustic style offers lodge rooms in the main building (some with shared bath) plus fully self-contained cabins in the woods, some with wood-burning stoves. ⑥–⑨

Westin Monache Resort 50 Hillside Drive ☎888/716-8123, ⓦwww.westinmammoth.com /sierra. Mammoth's top hotel, right in the heart of the Village at Mammoth with beautifully decorated public areas, 230 lovely rooms, outdoor pool, hot tub and gym. There's easy access to loads of restaurants and bars and all sorts of internet packages and specials. ⑥

Camping and RVs

Convict Lake Late April to Oct; 7600ft. Wooded, lakeside national forest campground just west of US-395, around four miles south of the Mammoth turn-off, with the longest open season in the area. Showers are available at the nearby *Convict Lake Resort* (☎760/934-3800, ⓦwww.convictlake.com; $2 for two minutes). $20.

Devils Postpile Late June to mid-Oct; 7500ft. National Park Service campground along Minaret Road, half a mile from the rocks themselves and a good base for hikes to Rainbow Falls or along the John Muir Trail. $14.

Hartley Springs Early May–Oct; 8400ft. Just one of several primitive waterless campgrounds in the area, this one located 1.5 miles west of US-395 along Glass Flow Road, around eleven miles north of the Mammoth turn-off. Free.

Mammoth Mountain RV Park Hwy-203 ☎1-800/582-4603, ⓦwww.mammothrv.com. Year-round, all-mod-cons RV park right in town, opposite the visitor centre, with shady pool, hot tub, kids' play areas, free wi-fi, tent sites ($27) and a range of partial and full hookup sites ($42–47).

New Shady Rest Early May to mid-Oct; 7800ft. Large and busy campground close to town with flush toilets and a dump station. Several sites can be reserved on ☎1-877/444-6777 or ⓦwww .recreation.gov. $20.

Reds Meadow Mid-June to mid-Oct; 7600ft. National-forest campground along Minaret Road and within easy hiking distance of Devils Postpile, Rainbow Falls and a nice nature trail around Sotcher Lake. It also comes with a natural hot spring bathhouse open to all (donations appreciated). $20.

Twin Lakes Late May to Oct; 8700ft. The longest-open of five near-identical sites in this area of glacially scooped lakebeds, a mile southwest of Mammoth Lakes township. Lakeside setting among the pines and plenty of hiking trails nearby. $21.

The Town

Mammoth is all about getting **outdoors** and aside from eating, drinking and mooching around the sports shops and factory clothing outlets, you'll find little reason to spend much time in town. You can learn about Mammoth's gold-mining and timber-milling origins at the small **Mammoth Museum**, 5489 Sherwin Creek Road (June–Sept daily 10am–6pm; $2 donation), located in a 1920s log cabin. Winter sports fans will find more of interest in the **Mammoth Ski Museum**, 100 College Parkway (Wed–Sat noon–5pm; $5; ☎760/934-6592, ⓦwww.mammoth skimuseum.org), a small but well-presented collection of skiing-related paraphernalia, most of it amassed over sixty years by one Mason Beekley. Inside are the expected racks of old skis, a chair from the original Mammoth chairlift and a 450-year-old book by a Swedish monk which illustrates skiing, but the museum's strength is in the graphic arts: the walls come lined with vintage ski posters, photos (some by Ansel Adams) and even woodcuts.

Mammoth Mountain

There's more fun to be had four miles west of the centre, up on the slopes of the dormant volcano called **MAMMOTH MOUNTAIN**, where the **Panorama**

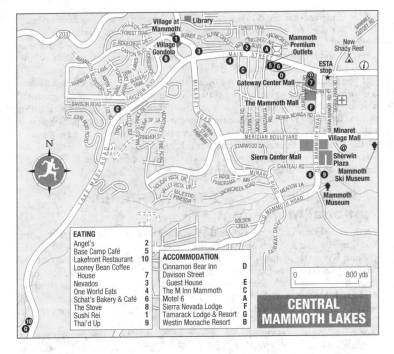

The map shows:

EATING

Angel's	2
Base Camp Café	5
Lakefront Restaurant	10
Looney Bean Coffee House	7
Nevados	3
One World Eats	4
Schat's Bakery & Café	6
The Stove	8
Sushi Rei	1
Thai'd Up	9

ACCOMMODATION

Cinnamon Bear Inn	D
Davison Street Guest House	E
The M Inn Mammoth	C
Motel 6	A
Sierra Nevada Lodge	F
Tamarack Lodge & Resort	G
Westin Monache Resort	B

0 — 800 yds

CENTRAL MAMMOTH LAKES

Gondola (all year except Oct to mid-Nov daily 9am–4.30pm; $21 round-trip, ride and lunch $25) will whisk you to the top in eight minutes. An interpretive centre here lets you enjoy the fine mountain views through telescopes.

If you'd rather work up a sweat, there are a number of ways to do just that: mountain biking, hiking (see box, p.294), plus stacks of people willing to get you **rock climbing** (see p.297).

Mountain biking

Once the ski runs have shed their winter snow, the slopes transform into the 3500-acre **Mammoth Mountain Bike Park** (late June to Sept daily 9am–4.30pm; ☏760/934-0706, ⓦwww.mammothmountain.com), with over eighty miles of groomed singletrack trails. Chairlifts quickly give you and your bike an altitude boost, allowing you to hurtle down the twisting sandy trails, brushing pines and negotiating small jumps and tree roots. The emphasis here is definitely on downhill, and when you're transported to the rarefied, eleven-thousand-foot air at the top of the chairlift, you very quickly appreciate the logic of this. The bike park produces a colour map of the mountain showing the lifts and trails in four grades of difficulty and indicates "X-Zones" of enhanced free-riding terrain for more aggressive riders. Beginners often take the **Downtown** run into Mammoth (from where a bike shuttle bus returns you to the bike park), while those with a little more skill or ambition might opt for the **Beach Cruiser**, which carves its way down the western side of the mountain from near the summit. Experts and those with a death wish can tackle the **Kamikaze**, scene of the ultimate downhill race which has traditionally formed the centrepiece of the annual World Cup racing weekend (usually around late Sept), when competitors hit speeds of sixty miles per hour.

The basic **park-use fee** ($10) gives you access to the trails and you can rent bikes for $45 a day. In addition, there's a complex selection of deals such as the Unlimited (one day $42, two days $75), which gives all-day access to the Panorama Gondola and the bike shuttle from town. Gondola and bike-rental combos include a two-hour package ($58) and a full-day unlimited deal ($87).

If you don't fancy forking out for use of the bike park, or just prefer something a little gentler, there's plenty more **trail riding** around the resort, made comfortable by mid-summer temperatures reliably in the seventies. Several bike stores around town will point you in the right direction and rent bikes (see p.296), which can also be taken to the bike park. Likely candidates include the relatively gentle Shady Rest Park, close to central Mammoth; the Lakes Basin area near *Tamarack Resort*; and Inyo and Mono craters. The visitor centre offers free trail maps and a brochure on route descriptions and trail ethics.

Along Minaret Road: Devils Postpile National Monument

From the ski area, the narrow and winding **Minaret Road** (typically open mid-June to mid-Oct) climbs briefly to a nine-thousand-foot pass in the San Joaquin Ridge, then plummets toward the headwaters of the Middle Fork of the San Joaquin River, ending some eight miles beyond at the Reds Meadow pack station. This is the only road access into the evocatively named **Devils Postpile National Monument** (free but see shuttle bus info; ⓦ www.nps.gov/depo), which centres on a collection of slender, blue-grey basalt columns ranged like

---

Hiking around Mammoth

Interwoven among the bike trails on Mammoth Mountain are a couple of **hiking paths** which top out at the summit. The views are stupendous but, as with many volcanoes, the hiking isn't the best and you're better off riding the gondola (see p.292) and saving your legs for hikes elsewhere.

Below are the best of the **short hikes** around Mammoth. No permits are required for these, though you'll need to obtain a free **wilderness permit** if you want to spend the night in the Ansel Adams or John Muir wilderness areas to the west. The number of overnight hikers allowed to set off from each trailhead is limited during the **quota season** from May to October. Visit ⓦ www.r5.fs.fed.us/inyo to reserve a permit ($5 reservation fee) up to six months in advance or at least two days in advance at the visitor centre after 11am on the day before you are going to head out.

Crystal Lake (3.5 miles round-trip; 2hr; 650-foot ascent). From the Lake George trailhead the path skirts high above Lake George, revealing increasingly dramatic views as you climb towards Crystal Lake, hunkered below Crystal Crag. Fit hikers can tack on the Mammoth Crest Trail (a further 2.5 miles round-trip; 2–3hr; 1000-foot ascent).

Panorama Dome Trail (1 mile round-trip; 30min; 100-foot ascent). Great views over the town and the Owens Valley reward hikers of this short sylvan trail, from Twin Lakes on Lake Mary Road (see map, p.290).

Rainbow Falls Trail (5 miles; 2hr; 300-foot ascent). Moderate hike that combines the two key features of the Devils Postpile National Monument. Start from the *Devils Postpile* campground and stroll to the monument itself, then continue to the top of Rainbow Falls.

Sky Meadows Trail (4 miles; 1hr 30min–2hr; 1200-foot ascent). Starting at the southern end of Lake Mary, this delightful hike along the wildflower-flanked Coldwater Creek passes Emerald Lake on its way to Sky Meadow, at the foot of the striking Blue Crag.

Skiing at Mammoth

With one of the longest ski seasons in California (from early November often until well into June), three thousand vertical feet of skiing and more than its fair share of deep, dreamy powder, **Mammoth Mountain** (daily 8.30am–4pm; ☏1-800/626-6684, ⓦwww.mammothmountain.com) ranks as one of California's premier ski mountains. It's well balanced, too, with roughly equal areas of beginner, intermediate and expert terrain, plus seven snow parks and three halfpipes. Add to that a cat's cradle of intersecting gondolas and chairlifts – seemingly being added to each year and now numbering over thirty – bundles of snowmaking equipment and a whole resort of bars and restaurants designed with après-ski in mind, and you can hardly go wrong.

Pick up **lift tickets** ($87) from the Main Lodge on Minaret Road, where you can also rent **equipment** ($34 for basic skis, boots and poles, or snowboard and boots), and book a one-day beginner package with lesson, gear rental and lift ticket ($149).

Off the mountain there are stacks of **cross-country skiing** trails; *Tamarack Lodge & Resort* (see p.292) offers ski packages, including instruction, tours and rentals, and charges $26 a day for access to the trails.

If you prefer a motorized approach to the white stuff, you can rent gear and clothing from DJ's Snowmobile Adventures (☏760/935-4480, ⓦwww.snowmobilemammoth .com), which has rentals from ninety minutes (single $98, double $128) to three hours ($180/240).

hundreds of pencils stood on end. Some are as tall as sixty feet while others are twisted, warped and broken to form a talus slope of shattered rubble. It was formed as lava from a vent near Mammoth Mountain cooled and fractured into multisided forms, a phenomenon best appreciated by skirting round to the top of the columns. The Postpile itself is a half-mile stroll from the *Devils Postpile* campground and its small **ranger station** (mid-June to mid-Oct daily 9am–4pm), where you can join daily ranger-led walks at 11am and free evening campfire programmes (twice weekly at 8pm).

The second highlight of the National Monument is **Rainbow Falls**, where the Middle Fork of the San Joaquin River plunges 101ft into a deep pool, the spray refracting to give the falls its name, especially at midday. It's two miles from the Postpile through Reds Meadow, reached on a pleasant hike (see box opposite).

Throughout the summer, Minaret Road is closed to private vehicles during the day and you must access Devils Postpile by **shuttle bus** (mid-June to early Sept daily 7.30am–7pm, last bus leaves the Postpile 7.45pm; day-pass $7 per person, three-day pass $14, America the Beautiful Senior and Annual passes not accepted), which leaves every 20 to 40 minutes from the Mammoth Mountain Main Lodge Adventure Center. Campers are allowed vehicular access at all times, and outside shuttle hours others can drive along Minaret Road; drive over before 7am and you can leave whenever you wish. In theory, drivers and their passengers still have to pay, but there is unlikely to be anyone to take your money.

During the day, the furthest you can drive without taking the shuttle bus is **Minaret Vista**, a parking lot high on the San Joaquin Ridge with wonderful views of the **Minaret Peaks**, a spiky volcanic ridge just south of pointed Mount Ritter – one of the Sierra's most enticing high peaks.

Eating, drinking and nightlife

Mammoth has easily the best and broadest selection of **restaurants**, **cafés** and **bars** (some with **live music**) on this side of the Sierra, many of them ranged around the central plaza at The Village at Mammoth. It's a welcome change after the relative austerity elsewhere in the mountains but the drain on your finances may come as a shock. Pick up **groceries** at Von's, in the Minaret Village mall, and healthy goodies at Sundance Earth Foods in The Gateway Center Mall on Old Mammoth Road.

Angel's 20 Sierra Blvd at Main St ☎760/934-7427. The menu has a Southwestern kick at this broadly appealing, family-friendly restaurant. The *Angel's* salad ($5) and jalapeño corn fritters ($7) are very good, and there's a decent selection of burgers ($8–11) and $10 mains, such as spinach and mushroom lasagne. The small bar serves a handful of microbrews.

Base Camp Café 3325 Main St. Great low-cost café usually bustling with the outdoors and active set, here for the hearty breakfasts (mostly $5–9), tasty wraps and sandwiches and bargain daily specials, organic espresso coffees and microbrews. Also open for dinner (Thurs–Sun to around 9pm).

Lakefront Restaurant *Tamarack Lodge* ☎760/934-2442. Superb lake views accompany equally outstanding dishes from a menu with French-Californian leanings, which might include wild mushroom strudel ($12), walnut-crusted chicken breast ($23) and a sumptuous selection of desserts and ports. No lunch in winter.

Looney Bean Coffee House The Mammoth Mall. The most vibrant of Mammoth's coffee bars, with good coffee, muffins and more, served up to dedicated regulars either inside (where there's a stack of magazines) or out front. Stays open late in the ski season and the free wi-fi is very popular.

Nevados Main St and Minaret Rd ☎760/934-4466. A favourite with the foodies, with an eclectic menu featuring anything from crisp, *nori*-wrapped shrimp with wasabi to hazelnut-crusted rack of lamb; there's also a $40 *prix fixe* deal for an appetizer, main and dessert.

One World Eats 3711 Main St ☎760/934-5600. Everything is freshly made at this casual Armenian-run place where the menu trawls the eastern Mediterranean for the likes of *tzatziki*, babaganoush, falafel, *gyros* and winter lentil or borscht soups (mostly under $10). Dinner might include a rustic rack of lamb ($25) followed by house-made *baklava* ($4.50).

Schat's Bakery & Café 3305 Main St. Easily the best range of baked goods in town, either to take away or to eat in with a coffee. The crisp Danishes, *baklava* and handmade chocolates are all toothsome, plus there are two dozen types of bread, deli sandwiches and freshly squeezed OJ.

The Stove 644 Old Mammoth Rd. Long-standing Mammoth favourite for its traditional country cooking, serving egg, waffle and pancake breakfasts (around $9), sandwiches, and full meals later on – all in massive portions.

Sushi Rei 6201 Minaret Rd ☎760/924-8140. The stylish spot to go for *teriyaki*, *udon*, *ramen* and, of course, pretty decent sushi for somewhere so far from the sea. Plenty of choice, and *nigiri* start at $6.

Thai'd Up 587 Old Mammoth Rd ☎760/934-7355. Terrible name, but tasty food is served in this diminutive Thai restaurant. Try summer rolls (served cold; $6) followed by Panang curry ($12). Lunch Wed–Sat, dinner daily except Tues.

Listings

Bookstores Booky Joint in the Minaret Village Mall (☎760/934-2176) has the best all-round selection.
Festivals During the annual Jazz Jubilee, held over four days around the second weekend in July (⊛www.mammothjazz.org), bars, restaurants and impromptu venues around town pack out with predominantly trad-jazz types. Blues fans should come later for the Festival of Beers and Bluesapalooza (⊛www.mammothbluesbrewsfest.com), held over the first weekend in Aug.
Film First-run Hollywood fare at the Minaret Cinema in the Minaret Village Mall (☎760/934-3131).
Fishing Rent gear, get fly and spinner advice and gather the latest news at Kittredge Sports, 3218 Main St (☎760/943-7566, ⊛www.kittredgesports .com). Mary Lake and Crowley Lake (see p.287)

are popular (sometimes crowded) spots, as is the trout-filled San Joaquin River near the Devils Postpile.
Internet The library (see below) has free internet and wi-fi. There's also access and wi-fi at the *Stellar Brew* coffee house, 3280 Main St (☎760/924-3559).
Laundry Aloha Sudz, beside *Looney Bean Coffee*.
Library 400 Sierra Park Rd (Mon–Fri 10am–7pm, Sat 9am–5.30pm).
Medical care Mammoth Hospital, 85 Sierra Park Rd ☎760/934-3311. Modern place with 24hr emergency care.
Mountain biking Footloose Sports, Main Street at Old Mammoth Road (☎760/934-2400, ⊛www .footloosesports.com), rents hardtail and

One of the pleasures of any extended visit to the Owens Valley is soaking your bones in one of the numerous **hot springs**. None is well signposted and most are primarily used by locals, who are welcoming enough if you are respectful. Springs tend to be tucked miles away down some rutted dirt road and often comprise little more than a ring of rocks or a hollowed-out tub into which people have diverted the waters to create pools of differing temperatures. Most are **clothing-optional**, but you'll stand out as a tourist if you don't strip off. We've mentioned several springs in the text – those in the Saline Valley (p.278), Keough's Hot Springs (p.284), Travertine Hot Springs and Buckeye Hot Springs (both p.301) – but the best idea is simply to ask around.

All the springs are the result of groundwater being heated by magma, which rises close to the surface in these parts. In fact, Mammoth Mountain stands on the edge of a geologically volatile region known as the **Long Valley Caldera**. A vast oval some eighteen miles by twelve, the Caldera was formed 760,000 years ago when a massive eruption spread ash as far away as Nebraska. Vulcanism has continued with the creation of Mammoth Mountain around 50,000 years ago, the Mono Craters and, most recently, **Paoha Island** in Mono Lake, only 300 years back. To get a brief taster, visit the **Hot Creek Geological Site** (daily dawn–dusk; free) three miles east of US-395, on Hot Creek Hatchery Road three miles south of the exit for Mammoth Lakes. Jets of boiling water mix with the otherwise chilly snowmelt water to form pools ranging from tepid to scalding. This was once a popular warm-bathing spot, but after a geyser erupted in the pool in 2006 the US Forest Service banned swimming. It's still worth a quick detour, though.

United States Geological Survey scientists monitor ground-temperature changes, land deformation and frequency and amplitude of quakes. An **eruption** is not likely in the near future, but you can keep up to date at ⓦvolcanoes .usgs.gov/lvo.

full-suspension bikes ($10–15 per hr, $30–45 per day), plus the latest demo models ($30/90) and organizes weekly group rides. Mammoth Sporting Goods, Sierra Center Mall (ⓣ760/934-3239, ⓦwww.mammothsportinggoods.com), offers slightly better rates for a similar range of machines and also runs assorted free group rides (mostly July & Aug) for all ability levels.

Rock and alpine climbing Mammoth Mountain runs family-oriented sessions on a 32-foot artificial climbing rock (late June to Sept daily 10am–5pm; single climb $12, or $25 an hour) in front of the *Mammoth Mountain Inn*. To get out on the real stuff, contact Southern Yosemite Mountain Guides (ⓣ1-800/231-4575, ⓦwww.symg.com), who offer all sorts of rock and alpine guiding service. The Bishop-based guide services (see p.288) also run trips in the Mammoth area.

Showers In Mammoth township try Mammoth Mountain RV Park (daily 10am–5pm; $5). In the Devils Postpile area, head for the natural hot-spring-fed bathhouse at the *Reds Meadow* campground (donations appreciated).

Mono Lake and around

North of Mammoth the landscapes become more open. The Sierra still provides the western backdrop, but as the White Mountains drop away to the south you enter the fringes of the Great Basin, which stretches away across Nevada towards Utah. Mostly sagebrush semi-desert, it's inhospitable territory but a fascinating area centred on the freakish **Mono Lake**. The few people who live hereabouts cluster in the lakeside **Lee Vining** or the peaceful town of **Bridgeport**, but a century ago the place to be was **Bodie**, now a fascinating ghost town.

> **Yosemite-bound?**
>
> Lee Vining is more than two hours by car from Yosemite Valley but makes an afford-
> able base for exploring the eastern reaches of **Yosemite National Park**, particularly
> the Tuolumne Meadows area, only about twenty miles distant.

Mono Lake and Lee Vining

The blue expanse of **MONO LAKE** sits in the middle of a volcanic desert
tableland, its sixty square miles reflecting the statuesque, snowcapped mass of the
Eastern Sierra Nevada. At over a million years old, it's an ancient lake with two
large volcanic islands – the light-coloured **Paoha** and the black **Negit** –
surrounded by salty, alkaline water. It resembles a science-fiction landscape, with
great towers and spires formed by mineral deposits ringing the shores; hot springs
surround the lake, and all around the basin are signs of lava flows and volcanic
activity, especially in the cones of the Mono Craters, just to the south.

The lake's most distinctive feature, the strange, sandcastle-like **tufa** formations,
were increasingly exposed from the early 1940s to the mid-1990s as the City of
Los Angeles drained away the waters that flow into the lake (see box opposite). The
towers of tufa were formed underwater, where calcium-bearing freshwater springs
well up through the carbonate-rich lake water; the calcium and carbonate combine
as limestone, slowly growing into the weird formations you can see today.

Lee Vining overlooking Mono Lake, is the only settlement anywhere nearby,
offering a basic range of visitor services but not a great deal more.

Arrival, information and accommodation

Before striking out for a close look at the lake and its tufa, call in at both of the
excellent visitor centres. In the heart of Lee Vining sits the town's **Mono Lake
Committee Information Center** (daily: July & Aug 8am–9pm; rest of year
9am–5pm; ☎760/647-6595, ⓦwww.leevining.com and www.monolake.org);
it's partly the showcase for the committee's battle for Mono Lake, featuring an
excellent twenty-minute video presentation, but also has helpful staff and an
excellent bookstore concentrating on the environment and the Eastern Sierra.
There's also a tasteful gift shop and **internet access**.

A mile north along US-395, the **Mono Basin Scenic Area Visitor Center**
(April–Nov daily 9am–4.30pm; Dec–March closed; ☎760/873-2408, ⓦwww
.r5.fs.fed.us/inyo) features lake-related exhibits, a good short film about geology
and ecology lectures by rangers.

Accommodation is concentrated in Lee Vining. There are a number of $14–19
Forest Service **campgrounds** along Lee Vining Creek off Tioga Pass Road,
Hwy-120, or you could consider the county-run *Lundy Canyon* campground ($8;
no water) on Lundy Lake Road, about eight miles north of Lee Vining off US-395.

Motels, B&Bs and campground

El Mono Motel US-395 ☎760/647-6310,
ⓦwww.elmonomotel.com. This cute motel is the
cheapest in town, lacks phones and TVs and has
rooms that are small but well kept and cheerfully
decorated. ❷

Hess House B&B 50 Lee Vining Ave ☎760/647-
6416, ⓦwww.hesshousebandb.com. Tucked
behind *El Mono Motel*, this welcoming homestay
has just two guest rooms sharing a bathroom and
guest lounge. The part-Paiute owner puts on a
good breakfast and knows a few local stories. ❹

Mono Vista RV Park US-395 ☎760/647-6401.
Central spot catering to RVs ($28–35) and tents
($20), and with showers for non-guests ($2.50 for
5min; daily 9am–6pm).

Murphey's Motel 51493 US-395 ☎1-800/334-
6316, ⓦwww.murpheysyosemite.com. Clean, well-
presented motel in the centre of town, with cable TV,
a/c, bathrooms with both shower and tub. Some units
have a kitchen at no extra cost. Good single rates. ❹

Mono Lake is one of the oldest on the continent and has survived several ice ages and all the volcanic activity that the area can throw at it, but the lake's biggest threat has been the City of Los Angeles, which owns the riparian rights to Mono Lake's catchment.

From 1892 to 1904, the fledgling city of Los Angeles experienced a twelve-year drought and started looking to the Owens River as a reliable source of water that could be easily channelled to the city. Under the auspices of the Los Angeles Department of Water and Power, the city bought up almost the entire Owens Valley, then diverted the river and its tributaries into a 223-mile, gravity-fed **aqueduct** to take this water to LA. Farms and orchards in the once-productive Owens Valley were rendered useless without water, and Owens Lake near Lone Pine was left to dry up entirely.

The aqueduct was completed in 1913, but the growing city demanded ever more water. Consequently, in 1941, LA diverted four of the five streams that fed Mono Lake through an eleven-mile tunnel into its Los Angeles Aqueduct, sparking a legal battle surrounding the depletion of the lake itself – long one of the biggest **environmental controversies** in California.

Over the next fifty years, the **water level** in Mono Lake dropped over forty feet, a disaster not only because of the lake's unique beauty, but also because Mono Lake is the primary nesting ground for **California gulls** and a critical resting point for hundreds of thousands of migratory eared **grebes** and **phalaropes**. The lake was down to roughly half its natural size and as the levels dropped, the islands in the middle of the lake where the gulls lay their eggs became peninsulas and consequently the colonies fell prey to coyotes and other mainland predators. As less fresh water reached the lake it became increasingly saline, threatening the unique local ecosystem – about all that will thrive in the harsh conditions are brine shrimp and alkali flies, both essential food sources for the birdlife. Humans, too, are affected by the changes the lake is experiencing: winds blowing across the saltpans left behind by the receding water create alkaline clouds containing selenium and arsenic, both contributors to lung disease.

Seemingly oblivious to the plight of the lake, the City of Los Angeles built a second aqueduct in 1970 and the water level dropped even faster, sometimes falling eighteen inches in a single year. Prompted by scientific reports of an impending ecological disaster, a small group of activists set up the **Mono Lake Committee** (Ⓦwww .monolake.org) in 1978, fighting for the preservation of this unique ecosystem partly through the courts and partly through publicity campaigns – "Save Mono Lake" bumper stickers were once de rigueur for concerned citizens. Though the California Supreme Court declared in 1983 that Mono Lake must be saved, it wasn't until 1994 that emergency action was taken. A target water height of 6377ft above sea level (later raised to 6392ft) was grudgingly agreed upon to make **Negit Island** safe for nesting birds. Streams dry for decades are now flowing again, and warm springs formerly located by lakeside interpretive trails are submerged. The target level – 18ft higher than its recorded minimum, but still 25ft below its pre-diversion level – won't be reached by the time the agreement is up for re-negotiation in 2014, something that concentrates the ongoing efforts of the Mono Lake Committee.

Exploring Mono Lake

Everyone's first stop is **South Tufa**, five miles east of US-395 via Hwy-120 ($3 a day), the single best place to admire the tufa spires. Boardwalks and trails lead you among these twenty-foot-high limestone cathedrals and along the lakeshore, where photo ops turn up around every corner. About a mile to the east lies **Navy Beach** (free), where there are a few more (less spectacular) spires, and you can float in water at least twice as buoyant as (and a thousand times more alkaline than) seawater. Even towards the end of summer the water is chilly, however, and some find that the salt stings. Look out too for the small but wonderfully intricate **sand tufas** nearby.

To add an educational component to your explorations, join one of the **guided walks** (July to early Sept daily 10am, 1pm & 6pm) around the tufa formations, run by the Mono Lake Basin Scenic Area Visitor Center. You can also sign up for one of the Mono Lake Committee's regular hour-long **canoe trips** (mid-June to early Sept Sat & Sun 8am, 9.30am & 11am; $24; reservations recommended ☎760/647-6595), on which you'll paddle around the tufa towers, learning about their formation, and hear details of migrating birdlife and the brine shrimp they feed on. You could also go by **kayak** with Mammoth Lakes-based Caldera Kayaks (reservations on ☎760/934-1691, ⊛www.calderakayak.com), which runs natural history tours on Mono Lake (3hr; $110 each for two, $75 each for groups of 3 or more).

Adjacent to the south shore of the lake stands **Panum Crater**, a 700-year-old volcano riddled with deep fissures and fifty-foot towers of lava, accessed by the short and fairly easy **Plug Trail** and **Rim Trail**. This is the most recent of the **Mono Craters**, a series of volcanic cones stretching twelve miles south from here towards Crowley Lake. It constitutes the youngest mountain range in North America, formed entirely over the last forty thousand years.

On the north shore of the lake, three miles along US-395, a side road leads to **Mono County Park**, where a guided boardwalk trail heads down to the lakefront and the best examples of mushroom-shaped tufa towers. A further five miles along this (mostly washboard gravel) side road is the trailhead for the **Black Point Fissures**, the result of a massive underwater eruption of molten lava some thirteen thousand years ago. As the lava cooled and contracted, cracks and fissures formed on the top, some only a few feet wide but as deep as fifty feet. You can explore their depths, but pick up a directions sheet from the visitor centre and be prepared for hot, dry and sandy conditions, and give yourself at least a couple of hours.

Eating

You'll find a small selection of **places to eat** in Lee Vining.

Latte Da On US-395 at *El Mono Motel*; see p.298. Organic espressos and free wi-fi.

Nicely's On US-395 in Lee Vining. Great Fifties vinyl palace serving up reliable diner food to tourists and dedicated locals. All your favourites are here, including a three-egg omelette ($9), jumbo burger and fries ($8) and breaded steak ($13), plus the obligatory slice of one of their many fruit pies ($4). Daily 6am–9pm, closed Tues & Wed in winter.

Whoa Nellie Deli Inside the Tioga Gas Mart, Hwy-120 East at US-395. The best quick food for miles around is served in the unlikely setting of the Mobil gas station, though in summer you can sit at tables outside. There's always a lively atmosphere and they dish up great tortilla soup, jambalaya ($13), fish tacos ($12), burgers and steaks, along with espresso, microbrews and margaritas. There's also pizza by the slice and often live music outside on Thursday and Sunday evenings in July and Aug. Closed Nov–March.

Bodie Ghost Town

In the 1880s, the gold-mining town of **Bodie**, eighteen miles north of Lee Vining and then thirteen miles (three of them dirt) east of US-395, boasted three breweries, some sixty saloons and dance halls and a population of nearly ten thousand. It also had a well-earned reputation as the raunchiest and most lawless mining camp in the West. Contemporary accounts describe a town that ended each day with a shootout on Main Street, while the firehouse bell, rung once for every year of a murdered man's life, seemed never to stop sounding. The town hit the headlines in 1877, when a rather unproductive mine collapsed and exposed an enormously rich vein. Within four years this was the second largest town in the state after San Francisco, even supporting its own Chinatown. By 1885, **gold and silver** currently valued at around $1.5 billion had been extracted, but a drop in the gold price made mining largely unprofitable. The town dwindled and then was virtually destroyed by two disastrous fires, the second in 1932. The school finally closed in 1942, but a few hardy souls stuck it out until the early 1960s, when the site was taken over by the State of California.

What remains has been turned into **Bodie State Historic Park** (daily: June to early Sept 9am–6pm; early Sept–May 10am–3pm; $7; ☎760/647-6445, ⓦwww .parks.ca.gov), where the lack of theme-park tampering gives the place an authentically eerie atmosphere absent from other US ghost towns. Bodie is almost 8400ft above sea level and, although the park is open throughout the year, snow often prevents vehicular access between December and April; call ahead for road conditions. If you can get in during that time, bundle up: Bodie is often cited on the national weather report as having the lowest temperature in the US. Whenever you go, remember to bring all you need, as there are no services at the site.

A good self-guided tour booklet leads you around many of the 150-odd wooden buildings – about six percent of the original town – surviving in a state of arrested decay around the intact town centre. Some buildings have been re-roofed and others supported in some way, but it is by and large a faithful preservation: even the dirty dishes are much as they were in the 1940s, little damaged by seventy years of weathering. The **Miner's Union Building** on Main Street was the centre of the town's social life; founded in 1877, the union was the first in California, organized by workers at the Standard and Midnight mines. The building now houses a small **museum** (daily: June–Aug 9am–6pm; May & Sept 9am–5pm; free), which paints a graphic picture of mining life. Various **tours** depart from here in the summer, though schedules are flexible and you should call ahead if you have specific interests. One visits the **Standard Consolidated Stamp Mill** (generally June–Aug daily, call for times; 50min duration; free) which is otherwise off limits, while another follows a ridge (weekends only at 10am; free) which offers some of the best views of Bodie. Other highlights of the town include the **Methodist church** with its intact pipe organ, the **general store** with its beautiful pressed-steel ceiling, the **saloon**, and the **cemetery** on the hill, where lie the remains of Bill Bodey, after whom the town was (sort of) named.

Bridgeport

Seven miles north of the Bodie road junction along US-395 is tiny **Bridgeport**, an isolated village in the middle of a mountain-girt plain that provided the new start in life for fugitive Robert Mitchum in the film-noir masterpiece *Out of the Past*. The gas station he owned in the film is long gone from the time-warped Main Street, though the place is otherwise little changed from a pretty high-country ranching community typically full of **fishermen** through the summer. If you want to join their ranks, head to Ken's Sporting Goods, 258 Main St (☎760/9332-7707, ⓦwww.kenssport.com), for local information and all the tackle you could desire.

Consider sticking around the region long enough to enjoy the local hot springs, one of the most popular ways to wind down after a day wrestling trout. The handiest are **Travertine Hot Springs**: follow US-395 half a mile south of town, turn left into Jack Sawyer Road, then fork left at the first junction and keep right for a mile. Many prefer the streamside setting of the lovely **Buckeye Hot Springs**, reached by following US-395 four miles north of Bridgeport, turning left for

Buckeye Campground and continuing 4.6 miles to where a rough track leads from a dirt parking area to three small pools beside the river.

With the lure of the springs, you may want to stay overnight, and **accommodation** options include the motel-style *Silver Maple Inn*, 310 Main St (☎760/932-7383, ⓦwww.silvermapleinn.com; closed Nov–May; ❹) and the associated *The Cain House*, 340 Main St (☎760/923-7383, ⓦwww.silvermapleinn.com; closed Nov–April; ❹), a beautifully furnished B&B. Across the street, the decrepit-looking *Bodie Victorian Hotel* (☎760/932-7020; closed Dec–May; ❶–❷) occupies a building which, like several in Bridgeport, is said to have been transported here from Bodie. Floors are far from level but all rooms have bathrooms and some come with bordello-chic decor.

For **eating**, there are excellent breakfasts and lunches at *Hays Street Café*, 21 Hays St, on the southern approach to town; espresso and free wi-fi at *1881 Café*, 362 Main St; and reasonably priced grills, sandwiches and speciality pizzas at *Rhino's Bar & Grill*, 226 Main St. A drive six miles south along US-395 is rewarded with reliable down-home Italian and American dining at *Virginia Creek Settlement* (☎760/932-7780, ⓦwww.virginiacrksettlement.com; closed Mon), renowned in the region for its fresh and tasty steaks (from $22), pasta dishes ($15–17) and pizzas (from $17).

From Bridgeport, US-395 continues north into Nevada, through the capital Carson City and the gambling hotspot of Reno, both described fully in Chapter Eight.

Travel details

Neither Greyhound buses nor Amtrak trains run any services within this region. The only long-distance bus services are the ESTA bus along the Owens Valley (see p.265) and the summer-only YARTS service from Mammoth Lakes to Yosemite (see p.291).

Buses

Big Pine to: Bishop (4 weekly; 15min); Ridgecrest (4 weekly; 2hr).

Bishop to: Big Pine (4 weekly; 15min); Bridgeport (4 weekly; 2hr); Independence (4 weekly; 1hr); Lancaster (3 weekly; 4hr 15min); Lee Vining (4 weekly; 1hr 25min); Lone Pine (4 weekly; 1hr 10min); Mammoth Lakes (4 weekly; 50min); Reno (4 weekly; 4hr 45min); Ridgecrest (4 weekly; 2hr 20min).

Bridgeport to: Bishop (4 weekly; 2hr); Reno (4 weekly; 2hr 50min).

Independence to: Ridgecrest (4 weekly; 1hr 35min).

Lee Vining to: Mammoth Lakes (4 weekly; 30min); Reno (4 weekly; 3hr 20min).

Lone Pine to: Ridgecrest (4 weekly; 1hr 20min).

Mammoth Lakes to: Bishop (4 weekly; 50min); Lee Vining (4 weekly; 30min); Reno (4 weekly; 4hr); Tuolumne Meadows (summer 2–7 weekly; 1hr); Yosemite Valley (summer 2–7 weekly; 3hr).

5

The San Joaquin Valley, Yosemite and the Western Sierra

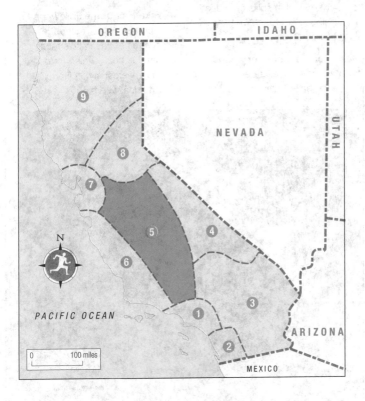

CHAPTER 5   # Highlights

* **Basque cuisine** Sample one of Bakersfield's Basque restaurants, notably the *Noriega Hotel*, where groaning dishes and jugs of wine are served at long, communal tables. See p.311

* **Kern River** Experience some of California's finest and most accessible whitewater rafting on the Kern, which spills off the lofty slopes of Mount Whitney. See p.312

* **Forestiere Underground Gardens** Delve below the baked hardpan into a labyrinth of rooms where an Italian subway-tunneller carved out his home and fruit orchard. See p.317

* **Giant Forest** The densest collection of the world's largest trees, the mighty sequoias, looms in this section of Sequoia National Park, accessible by a panoply of trails. See p.329

* **Hike Half Dome** Follow the wonderful Mist Trail to the summit of Yosemite's most famous peak, which forms the sheerest cliff in North America. See p.356

▲ Sequoias, Giant Forest

5

The San Joaquin Valley, Yosemite and the Western Sierra

The vast interior of California – stretching three hundred miles from the edges of the Mojave Desert in the south right up to the Gold Country and Northern California in the north – is covered by the wide floor of the agricultural **San Joaquin Valley**, flanked on the east by the massive Sierra Nevada mountains. It's a region of unparalleled beauty, yet the ninety percent of Californians who live on the coast are barely aware of the area, encountering it only while driving between LA and San Francisco on the admittedly tedious I-5, and consider it the height of hicksville.

The San Joaquin Valley is radically different from the rest of California. During the 1940s, this arid land was made super-fertile by a massive programme of aqueduct building, using water flowing from the mountains to irrigate the area. The valley, as flat as a pancake, now almost totally comprises farmland, periodically enlivened by scattered cities that offer a taste of ordinary California life away from the glitz of LA and San Francisco. More than anywhere else in the state, the abundance of low-paying agricultural jobs has encouraged decades of immigration from south of the border and there are now towns in the San Joaquin Valley where Spanish is the first language and **taquerías** outnumber burger joints. Sadly San Joaquin town planning dictates that everyone must drive everywhere, leading to a dense photochemical haze – trapped by mountains on both flanks – that is so thick the pristine peaks once visible throughout the year are now seldom seen.

Coastal Californians primarily pass through the San Joaquin Valley to reach the **national parks** that cover the foothills and upper reaches of the Sierra Nevada mountains. From the valley, a gentle ascent through rolling, grassy foothills takes you into dense forests of huge pine and fir trees, interspersed with tranquil lakes and cut by deep rocky canyons. The most impressive sections are protected within three national parks. **Sequoia** is home to the last few stands of giant sequoia trees that form the centrepiece of a rich natural landscape. **Kings Canyon** shares a common border with Sequoia – together they make up one huge park – and presents a similar, slightly wilder array of Sierra wonders. **Yosemite**, with its

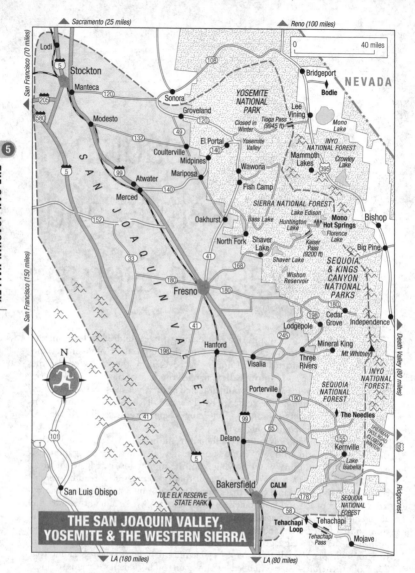

▲ Sacramento (25 miles)   ▲ Reno (100 miles)

Lodi

Stockton

Manteca

Sonora

Groveland

120

Modesto

49

132

Coulterville

El Portal

Midpines

Atwater

Mariposa

140

Merced

152

Oakhurst

North Fork

Shaver Lake

Fresno

Hanford

Visalia

Porterville

Delano

Bakersfield

San Luis Obispo

108

YOSEMITE
NATIONAL
PARK

Tioga Pass
(9945 ft)

Closed in
Winter

Yosemite
Valley

140

Wawona

Fish Camp

SIERRA NATIONAL FOREST

Bass Lake

Huntington
Lake

Shaver Lake

Kaiser
Pass
(9200 ft)

Wishon
Reservoir

180

168

245

198

Three
Rivers

190

65

99

155

155

CALM

178

58

TULE ELK RESERVE
STATE PARK

Tehachapi
Loop

Tehachapi
Pass

Bridgeport

Bodie

NEVADA

Lee
Vining

Mono
Lake

INYO
NATIONAL
FOREST

Mammoth
Lakes

Crowley
Lake

395

Lake Edison

Mono
Hot Springs

Florence
Lake

Bishop

Big Pine

SEQUOIA
& KINGS
CANYON
NATIONAL
PARKS

Cedar
Grove

Independence

Lodgepole

Mineral King

Mt Whitney

INYO
NATIONAL
FOREST

SEQUOIA
NATIONAL
FOREST

The Needles

Kernville

Lake
Isabella

SEQUOIA
NATIONAL
FOREST

Tehachapi

Mojave

0 ——— 40 miles

N

**THE SAN JOAQUIN VALLEY,
YOSEMITE & THE WESTERN SIERRA**

▼ LA (180 miles)   ▼ LA (80 miles)

towering walls of silvery granite artfully sculpted by Ice Age glaciers, is the most
famous of the parks and one of the absolute must-sees in California. While only a
few narrow, twisting roads penetrate the hundred miles of wilderness in between
these three parks, the entire region is crisscrossed by hiking trails leading up into
the pristine alpine backcountry of the **Sierra Nevada**, which contains the
glistening summits of some of the highest mountains in the country.

Getting around

Drivers who aren't particularly interested in exploring the wilds can simply barrel
through on I-5, an arrow-straight interstate through the western edge of the San

Joaquin Valley that's the quickest route between LA and San Francisco. Six daily **trains** and frequent Greyhound **buses** run through the valley, stopping at the larger cities and towns along Hwy-99 – Merced being the most useful with its bus connections to Yosemite. Otherwise, getting to the mountains is all but impossible without your own vehicle, though with a bit of advance planning you can join one of the many camping trips organized by the Sierra Club, the California-based environmentalist group (see p.46).

The San Joaquin Valley

The **SAN JOAQUIN VALLEY** grows more fruit and vegetables than any other agricultural region of its size in the world – a fact that touches the lives, in one way or another, of every one of its inhabitants. The area is much more conservative and Midwestern in feel than the rest of California, but even if the nightlife begins and ends with the local ice-cream parlour, it can all be refreshingly small-scale and enjoyable after visiting the big coastal cities. Admittedly, none of the towns has the energy to detain you long and, between the settlements, the drab hundred-mile vistas of almond groves and vineyards can be sheer torture. The weather, too, can be a challenge – summers in the San Joaquin are frequently scorching and winters bring the cold and thick tule fog, so aim to visit in spring or fall, particularly March, when the fruit trees are in full bloom.

Bakersfield, just across the rocky peaks north of Los Angeles, is hardly the most prepossessing destination, but its **country music** scene has long been the best in the state and, surprisingly enough, there are few better places on this side of the Atlantic to sample **Basque cuisine**. Bakersfield also offers a museum recording the beginnings of the local population and the chance to sample some of the state's finest **whitewater rafting** on the nearby Kern River. Further on lies likeable **Visalia** and the well-restored turn-of-the-twentieth-century town of **Hanford**. In many ways the region's linchpin, **Fresno** is the closest thing the valley has to a bustling urban centre. Though economically thriving, it's frequently cited as one of the least desirable places to live in the US. On arrival it's easy to see why, though you shouldn't pass up the opportunity to visit the bizarre labyrinth of **Forestiere Underground Gardens**.

Beyond Fresno, in the northern reaches of the valley, lie sedate **Merced** and slightly more boisterous **Modesto**, the inspiration for George Lucas's movie *American Graffiti*. At the top end of the valley, **Stockton** is scenically improved by the delta that connects the city to the sea, but is otherwise a place of few pleasures, though you may pass through on your way from San Francisco to the Gold Country or the national parks.

Bakersfield and around

BAKERSFIELD's flat and featureless look does nothing to suggest that this is California's liveliest country-music community, with a couple of venues where locally and nationally rated musicians perform. It also has the country's largest

▲ Visalia (70 miles)   ▲ Trouts (800 yds)

BAKERSFIELD

Kern County Museum

Buck Owens' Crystal Palace

Board of Trade

Greyhound Station

Bakersfield Museum of Art

Arena

Library

CVB Train Station

EATING & NIGHTLIFE
Buck Owens' Crystal Palace	1
Guthrie's Alley Cat	3
Mama Roomba	3
Manuel's Casa de Mariscos	4
Noriega Hotel	2
Padre Hotel	C

ACCOMMODATION
EZ-8	B
La Quinta	A
Padre Hotel	C

0   600 yds

▼ Los Angeles (110 miles)

community of Basque descent, making it *the* place to taste Basque cuisine, at its best in one of the specialist restaurants run by descendants of sheepherders who migrated to the San Joaquin Valley in the early twentieth century. Add in an increasingly **vibrant Downtown** area and this old oil town is less and less deserving of the disdain levelled at it by the rest of the state.

The town was founded in 1851 when Colonel Thomas Baker made his field available as a stagecoach rest stop. **Oil** was discovered in the region in 1899 and Bakersfield has since cemented its hold on the state's production – the surrounding Kern County produces ten percent of US output. For a quick taster, drive three miles northwest of Downtown to Panorama Drive from where you can gaze across the **Kern River Oil Field**, with over 9500 nodding-donkey pump jacks scattered across the parched hills. At night the blue locator lights on each one create a sparkling vista.

On the outskirts of town a progressive small **zoo** warrants a visit and if the hills are calling out, it's only an hour's drive east to **Kernville**, which provides the venue for a full range of springtime **whitewater rafting**.

Arrival, information and accommodation

Bakersfield is an important public transport hub and the Downtown area – half a dozen blocks each way from the junction of 19th Street and Chester Avenue – is home to both the **Greyhound station**, 1820 18th St (☎661/327-5617) and the **Amtrak station**, 601 Truxton Ave, the southern terminus of Amtrak's San Joaquin route from San Francisco (connections to LA via Thruway bus). Travelling by bus, you may need to change routes here – although overnight stops are rarely necessary. The best source of information is the **Convention and Visitors**

Bureau (CVB), 515 Truxton Ave (Mon–Fri 8am–5pm; ☎866/425-7353 and ☎661/852-7282, ⓦwww.bakersfieldcvb.org), right by the Amtrak station. There's also the **Kern County Board of Trade**, 2101 Oak St (Mon–Fri 8am–5pm; ☎1-800/500-5376, ⓦwww.visitkern.com), which has free wi-fi. Free internet access is likewise available at the **library**, 710 Truxton Ave (Tues–Thurs 11am–7pm, Fri & Sat 10am–6pm; ☎661/868-0701).

Bakersfield is dotted with clusters of mainstream **motels** and **hotels** (all excellent value), plus a superb boutique hotel.

Hotels, motels and campground

EZ-8 2604 Buck Owens Blvd ☎661/322-1901, ⓦwww.ez8motels.com. One of Bakersfield's cheapest motels, with a pool and handily placed a short stagger from *Buck Owens' Crystal Palace*. ❶

Kern River County Park 15 miles east of Downtown, ☎661/868-7000. On the shores of Lake Ming are Bakersfield's nearest tent sites, grassy and reasonably shaded but with no hookups. Mid-March to mid-Oct $22 per vehicle; mid-Oct to mid-March $11 per vehicle.

La Quinta 3232 Riverside Drive ☎1-800/753-3757 & 661-325-7400, ⓦwww.lq.com. Comfortable mid-range hotel close to *Buck Owens'*

Crystal Palace, with pool, free wi-fi and complimentary continental breakfast. ❷

Padre Hotel 1702 18th St ☎1888/443 3387, ⓦwww.thepadrehotel.com. Wonderful conversion of a classic eight-storey Downtown hotel from the 1920s, now given the boutique treatment. Top-quality linen, large flat-screen TVs and super-stylish bathrooms feature in the 100+ rooms and suites, which are very competitively priced. Icons of Bakersfield life are referenced in bespoke wallpaper featuring oil derricks and steer skulls – all very *There Will Be Blood*. There's also free wi-fi, iPod docking stations, valet parking, room service, and a pool is promised in the near future. Rooms ❹, suites ❼

The Town

Bakersfield owes its existence to the fertile soil around the Kern River and to the discovery of local oil and gas deposits. The **Kern County Museum**, a mile north of Downtown at 3801 Chester Ave (Mon–Sat 10am–5pm, Sun noon–5pm, last admission 3pm; $10; ⓦwww.kcmuseum.org), documents the town's petrochemical roots through "Black Gold: The Oil Experience", a modern science, technology and history exhibit complete with 1922 nodding-donkey pump, a moderately enlightening eighteen-minute movie, and an unconvincing mock-up "undersea journey" in a diving bell. Leave time to browse the fifty-plus (mostly) restored rail wagons and assorted buildings, many dating from the late nineteenth or early twentieth century. Visitors needing to get kids out of the heat will want to check out the hands-on science exhibits in the site's **Lori Brock Children's Discovery Center**.

For something a little more highbrow, visit the **Bakersfield Museum of Art**, 1930 R St (Tues–Fri 10am–4pm, Sat & Sun noon–4pm; $5; ⓦwww.bmoa .org), which usually has interesting touring exhibits, along with its own collection with works by Georgia O'Keeffe and Diego Rivera.

Wildlife fans will have to stray a little further out, where the greatest interest is at the **California Living Museum (CALM)**, 10500 Alfred Harrell Hwy (daily: March–Sept 9am–5pm; Oct–Feb 9am–4pm; $9; ⓦwww.calmzoo.org), some twelve miles east of town off the road to Kernville. It's effectively a small zoo, but one focusing solely on California's native species and only those animals that have been injured and cannot be returned to the wild. Stroll around the landscaped grounds past the golden and bald eagles, pause to admire the black bears and bobcats, then repair to the reptile house with its array of snakes and lizards. The animals tend to hide from the heat of the day, so come early.

Half an hour west of Bakersfield is the **Tule Elk Reserve State Park**, Morris Road (daily 8am–sunset; free), where around thirty of these beasts can be seen

The main reason to dally for more than a few hours in Bakersfield is to hear **country music**. The roots of Bakersfield's scene are with the dust-bowl Okies who arrived in the San Joaquin Valley during the Depression, bringing their hillbilly instruments and campfire songs with them. This rustic entertainment quickly broadened into more contemporary styles, developed in the bars and clubs where future legends such as Merle Haggard and Buck Owens cut their teeth. A failed attempt to turn Bakersfield into "Nashville West" during the 1960s left the town eager to promote the distinctive **"Bakersfield Sound"**, a far less slick and commercial affair than its Tennessee counterpart: check out the 1988 hit *Streets of Bakersfield*, a duet by Buck Owens and Dwight Yoakam.

One venue not to be missed – and the last of the genuine old honky-tonks – is *Trout's*, 805 N Chester Ave (☎661/399-6700, ⋓www.troutsblackboard.com), a slightly seedy country-music bar a couple of miles north of Downtown that's been in business since 1945. There's live music nightly on a couple of dancefloors and you can get up to speed with evening line-dance lessons (Tues–Fri). There's seldom a cover charge for someone spinning platters and only a small one for live sets (perhaps $5), usually entailing one band playing for four or five hours from around 8pm and taking a fifteen-minute break every hour. Stetson hats and Nudie shirts are the sartorial order of the day and audiences span generations.

Closer to town, the ersatz-Western *Buck Owens' Crystal Palace*, 2800 Buck Owens Blvd (☎661/328-7560, ⋓www.buckowens.com), is very much the showpiece for the Buck Owens empire, though the master himself died in 2006. It's a cabaret-style setup (Tues–Thurs free, Fri & Sat $5) with burgers and grills available while local and touring bands perform on Wednesday and Thursday; Tuesday is karaoke night. Buck's band, The Buckeroos (sometime fronted by his son Buddy), perform on Friday and Saturday nights at 7.30pm, playing numbers from Buck's back catalogue, classic country tunes and beyond.

Cases around the walls make up a small **museum** (Tues–Sat 11am–4pm; $5, but visible for nothing during any show) of knick-knacks Buck picked up over the years – promo photos, Buck Rogers bolo tie clasps, platinum records, red-white-and-blue guitars and a glittering display of rhinestone jackets.

from a viewing platform. Large herds used to roam hereabouts, but hunting and loss of habitat forced them to the brink of extinction early in the twentieth century; only projects like this and a major relocation to the Owens Valley (see p.284) have saved them. To get here, follow Stockdale Highway west for twenty miles, and then just after crossing I-5, follow the signs a mile or so south on Morris Road.

Eating and nightlife

Though there are plenty of other worthwhile options for **eating**, you shouldn't pass through without trying Basque food. **Nightlife** now extends beyond slide-guitar and torch songs, with a number of places Downtown offering local rock bands several nights a week, usually with no cover charge. Stroll 19th Street and see what turns up.

Buck Owens' Crystal Palace 2800 Buck Owens Drive ☎661/328-7560, ⋓www.buckowens.com. Eat a meal while you watch a show (see above) or come for the extensive Sunday brunch (9.30am–2pm; $22). Closed Sun evening & Mon.

Guthrie's Alley Cat 1525 Wall St. In an alley parallel to 19th St, this dim bar with pool table is a long-standing Bakersfield favourite.

Mama Roomba 1814 Eye St ☎661/322-6262. Cuban and Mexican touches add interest to this small tapas restaurant, where you might sample garlic octopus ($10), corn-and-cheese empanadas ($8) or a larger dish such as Havana-style pork chops with fried onions ($14). Wash it down with a jug of sangria or repair to the intimate bar. Closed Sun.

Manuel's Casa de Mariscos 515 Union Ave ☎661/325 8834. Excellent family-run Mexican seafood restaurant particularly noted for their shrimp dishes and weekday lunch specials. Closed Mon.

Noriega Hotel 525 Summer St ☎661/322-8419. The most authentic Basque place is this 1893 restaurant where louvered shutters and ceiling fans cool diners at long, communal tables. They serve an all-you-can-eat set menu of soup, salad, beans, pasta, a meat dish, and cheese to finish, along with jug wine to keep you going. There

are three sittings ($10 breakfast from 7–9am, $14 lunch at noon sharp and $20 dinner at 7pm), and reservations are recommended for dinner, which will include the Basque speciality of pickled tongue. Closed Mon.

Padre Hotel 1702 18th St. This revamped hotel is rapidly becoming the heart of the Downtown scene with something for everyone: a *Brimstones* sports and cocktail bar with great, solid food; *Farmacy* espresso bar, where images of farm animals observe you eating breakfast; the classy *Belvedere* with its 20-foot ceiling, fresh seasonal cooking (mains $20–25) and a wine list with plenty by the glass (mostly Californian with French and New World wines plugging the gaps); and *Prairie Fire*, a loungy, rooftop deck with smooth sounds, fire pit, a light menu and occasional live music, especially on Sangria Sundays.

Kernville and the Kern River

After a night spent in Bakersfield's honky-tonks, clear your head by driving fifty miles northeast to the small, appealing town of **KERNVILLE** clustered on the banks of the **Kern River**, which churns down from the slopes of Mount Whitney and spills into Lake Isabella, just downstream. It's a peaceful, retiree-dominated place, but come on a summer weekend, or anytime in July and August, and it's full of adrenalin junkies blasting mountain bikes along the local trails or negotiating the rapids in all manner of aquatic paraphernalia.

Arrival and information

For general information contact the central **Chamber of Commerce**, 11447 Kernville Rd (year-round Mon, Tues, Thurs & Fri 9am–4pm, Wed 9am–1pm, May–Aug also Sat 10am–2pm; ☎760/376-2629, ⓦwww.kernvillechamber.org); for details on the wooded country to the north, call in at the **Kernville Ranger Station**, 105 Whitney Rd (Mon–Fri 8am–4.30pm; ☎760/376-3781, ⓦwww .fs.fed.us/r5/sequoia), next to the museum.

Accommodation

Kernville is big enough to have a bank, ATM, post office and supermarket, but there isn't a very wide range of **accommodation**. Central motels start at around $90 and tent **campers** can stay in the various RV parks around town, but are better off in the string of riverside campgrounds to the north (see p.313).

Falling Waters River Resort 15729 Sierra Way, 3 miles north of town ☎1-888/376-2242, ⓦwww.chuckrichards.com. Low-key, child- and dog-friendly complex with a range of accommodation: simple lodge rooms, more spacious motel-style rooms and river-view cottages slightly marred by overenthusiastic decor. ❸–❺
Kern River Inn B&B 119 Kern River Drive ☎1-800/986-4382, ⓦwww.kernriverinn.com. Sumptuous B&B with individually decorated river-view rooms featuring whirlpool tub or fireplace. ❹–❺

The Kernville Inn 11042 Kernville Rd ☎1-877/393-7900, ⓦwww.kernvilleinn.com. The best-value motel, right in the centre and with a pool and comfortable rooms, including some pricier ones with kitchens. Rates increase $20 at weekends. ❹
Whispering Pines Lodge 13745 Sierra Way, a mile north of town ☎1-877/241-4100, ⓦwww .kernvalley.com/inns. Relaxed spot with luxurious cottages, many with balconies overlooking the river, plus a nice pool and a delicious breakfast served on the terrace. ❻–❼

The Town

Most people come to ride the Kern, which ranks as one of the steepest "navigable" rivers in the United States, dropping over 12,000ft in 150 miles and producing some truly exhilarating **whitewater** opportunities, especially along a forty-mile section around Kernville. The tougher stuff is generally left to the experts, but during the season, which usually runs from May until early August (longer after heavy winters), commercial rafting operators vie for custom (see box below). If you've got time to kill while friends raft, delve into the native, gold mining and lumbering history in the **Kern Valley Museum**, 49 Big Blue Rd (Thurs–Sun 10am–4pm; free), or take a look at their film room of movies shot in the area, mostly Westerns: John Wayne features prominently.

Eating and drinking

Big Blue Bear 101 Piute Drive ☏ 760/376-2442. Espresso haven with free wi-fi.

Ewings on the Kern 125 Buena Vista Drive ☏ 760/376-2411. Good-value mainstream dining – ribs, halibut etc – with great views over the river and mountains from the deck. Daily except Wed, from 4pm.

Johnny McNally's Sierra Way, 15 miles north of Kernville ☏ 760/376-2430. Great steaks in an unpretentious family-dining setting. The 40-ounce porterhouse ($45) will see you through the next day as well.

Kern River Brewing Co 13415 Sierra Way ☏ 760/376-2337, ⊛ www.kernriverbrewing.com.

Kern River adventures

Three main sections of the Kern River are regularly **rafted**: the **Lower Kern**, downstream of Lake Isabella (Class III–IV; generally June–Aug); the **Upper Kern**, immediately upstream of Kernville (Class III–IV; early May to June); and **The Forks**, fifteen miles upstream of Kernville (Class V; early May to June), which drops an impressive sixty feet per mile.

By far the most popular section is the Upper Kern, the site for the **Lickety-Split** rafting trip – one for families and first-timers, with some long, bouncy rapids. This one-hour excursion (including the bus ride to the put-in) costs around $30, and with over half a dozen operators running trips throughout the day, there is little need to book ahead. Other trips run less frequently and you should reserve in advance, though you've got a better chance midweek when crowds are thinner and prices a few dollars lower. The pick of these are the day-trips on the Upper Kern, which run close to the $160 mark ($180 at weekends), the two-day Lower Kern trip ($320, weekends $350) and the two- or three-day backcountry trips on The Forks, which range around $700–900. Wetsuits (essential early in the season and for the longer trips) usually cost extra. Within this basic framework there are any number of permutations, some involving inflatable kayaks: check with Sierra South, 11300 Kernville Rd (☏ 1-800/457-2082, ⊛ www.sierrasouth.com) or Whitewater Voyages (☏ 1-800/400-7238, ⊛ www.whitewatervoyages.com).

As you'd expect, **kayaking** is also big here, and Sierra South supplement their rafting operation with one of Southern California's top kayaking schools, offering Eskimo rolling sessions, instruction at all levels and guided multiday river trips, all generally costing around $170 a day. They also offer full-day beginner's **rock climbing** lessons ($125) on the nearby Kernville Slab, as do Mountain & River Adventures, 11113 Kernville Rd (☏ 1-800/861-6553, ⊛ www.mtnriver.com), who stretch up to intermediate grades and have their own outdoor climbing wall three miles north along Sierra Way.

Permits, available free from the Kernville Ranger Station and any of the area's other Forest Service offices, are necessary even if you have your own equipment for private rafting or kayaking expeditions.

Lively restaurant and bar serving burgers, salads and great fish'n'chips (all $9–11), plus four toothsome microbrews. It's all eased down with occasional live music (particularly on summer weekends).

That's Italian 9 Big Blue Rd ☎760/376-6020. Reliable restaurant by the central park serving northern-Italian cuisine. Closed Mon & weekday lunches.

Sequoia National Forest

Wedged between Lake Isabella and Sequoia National Park lies **SEQUOIA NATIONAL FOREST**, a vast canopy of pine trees punctuated by massive, glacier-polished domes and gleaming granite spires. Much of it is untouched wilderness that's barely less stunning than the national parks to the north and in recognition of this a large section was re-designated the **Giant Sequoia National Monument** (unrestricted access) as one of Bill Clinton's final gestures before leaving office. True to its name, it's packed with giant sequoias (in 38 small groves) and, as the forest is far less visited than the national parks, it's perfect for those seeking total solitude; hiking trails run virtually everywhere. Camping only requires a free permit for your stove or fire, available from the ranger stations dotted around the perimeter of the forest, which also have details of the scores of drive-in campsites – some free, others up to $18 a pitch.

There's **no public transport** through here, but the roads are in good shape, though subject to **snow closure** in winter (mid-Nov to mid-May). To find out about conditions and closures, visit Ⓦwww.dot.ca.gov/hq/roadinfo or call ☎1-800/427-7623.

Sierra Way and the Western Divide Highway

From Kernville, Sierra Way follows the Upper Kern River north past numerous basic camping sites (free) and half a dozen shaded, waterside campgrounds ($18; reserve for summer weekends on ☎1-877/444-6777), eventually reaching Johnsondale Bridge, twenty miles north of Kernville. From the bridge, hikers can follow the **River Trail** upstream, passing the numerous rapids of The Forks section of the Kern, great for spotting rafters and kayakers on weekend afternoons and even for camping at one of several free walk-in sites along the river; the first is about a ten-minute hike.

Beyond Johnsondale Bridge, follow Sierra Way west and start climbing to tiny Johnsondale – just a seasonal store and restaurant – where a trail access road cuts 23 miles north to the Jerkey Meadow trailhead. The access road gives great views of The Needles (see below) and abundant dispersed **camping**, best four miles along at *Camping Area 4*, where the stream has sculpted a lovely series of **bathing pools** and smooth rocks for sunning yourself. A few miles further along, the *Lower Peppermint* campground ($17) has toilets and water.

Continuing along Sierra Way, it's seven miles to a road junction where you join the twisting and narrow **Western Divide Highway** (Hwy-190) which, after a couple of miles, passes the **Trail of a Hundred Giants** ($5 per vehicle), an easy, shaded interpretive trail around a stand of huge sequoias. Among more giant trees across the road is the *Redwood Meadow* campground (early April to mid-Nov; $17; book at ☎1-877/444-6777 or Ⓦwww.recreation.gov).

Further north, you catch glimpses of magnificent Sierra vistas as the road climbs above the 7000-foot mark, but for the best views it's worth pressing on five miles to the 7200-foot exfoliated scalp of **Dome Rock**, just half a mile off the highway, or **The Needles**, a further three miles on. This series of tall pinnacles – the Magician, the Wizard and the Warlock, among others – presents some of America's most demanding crack climbs, and can be visited on the moderate, undulating hiking and biking **Needles Lookout Trail** (5 miles round-trip; 2hr), which starts three miles off the highway up a dirt road. The final switchback leads to a fire-lookout station (generally open to visitors Wed–Sun 9am–6pm during the June–Oct fire season), precariously perched atop the Magician with supreme views over the Kern Valley and across to Mount Whitney.

Nearby **accommodation** includes the *Quaking Aspen* campground (early April to mid-Nov; $18), half a mile to the north of The Needles; the woodsy *Mountain Top B&B*, half a mile to the south (☏ 1-888/867-4784, ⓦ www.mountaintopbnb .com; ⑤); and the adjacent *Ponderosa Lodge* (☏ 559/542-2579; ④), with pleasant motel rooms, a restaurant, bar, grocery store and expensive gas. From here onwards, the Western Divide Highway executes endless twists and turns forty miles down to the valley town of Porterville, where you can turn right for Sequoia and Kings Canyon national parks or continue straight to rejoin Hwy-99 and head north to Visalia.

Visalia

Seventy miles north of Bakersfield, the agricultural town of **VISALIA** makes a comfortable base for exploring Sequoia and Kings Canyon national parks, an hour's drive east along Hwy-198. It also has the only **bus service** into the parks.

Arrival, information and accommodation

Greyhound buses, along with KART buses from Hanford (☏ 559/584-0101) and the shuttle to Sequoia and Kings Canyon national parks (see p.322), arrive at the Downtown **transit centre**, 425 E Oak St (☏ 559/734-3507). The shuttle also stops outside the **CVB**, 303 N Acequia Ave (Mon–Fri 9am–5pm; ☏ 559/334-0141, ⓦ www.visitvisalia.org), three blocks to the southwest. **Accommodation** here is a bargain; if you're on a budget, this is a good place to splash out on a B&B.

Hotels, motels and B&Bs

Ben Maddox House B&B 601 N Encina St ☏ 1-800/401-9800, ⓦ www.benmaddoxhouse .com. Chatty, Irish-American Lucy is an attentive host in this large, pool-equipped redwood house built in 1876 for Ben Maddox, the man who brought hydroelectricity to the San Joaquin Valley. A few rough edges need attention but it can be good value, particularly with discounts for multi-night and midweek stays. ⑤–⑥

Comfort Suites 210 E Acequia Ave ☏ 1-800/4CHOICE or 559/738-1700, ⓦ www .visalialodging.com. Modern and central hotel with little character but good facilities including fitness centre and outdoor hot tub. ③

Econo Lodge 1400 S Mooney Blvd ☏ 1-877-424-6423 or 559/732-6641, ⓦ www.econolodge .com. The best of the town's budget motels, recently renovated, with pool, flat-screen TVs, free wi-fi and an included light breakfast. ①

Lamp Liter Inn 3300 W Mineral King Ave ☏ 1-800/662-6692, ⓦ www.lampliter.net. Pleasant 100-room hotel surrounded by lawns and featuring a very nice pool, sports bar and grill. ④

The Spalding House 631 N Encina ☏ 559/739-7877, ⓦ www.thespaldinghouse .com. Local lumberman W.R. Spalding built this fine Colonial Revival home, now a beautifully appointed B&B. Suites all have separate bathroom and sitting room and come with a gourmet breakfast. ③

The Town

The oak forests which initially lured the San Joaquin's first settlers have long gone, but Visalia remains a pretty place with a compact and leafy town centre that invites strolls in the relative cool of the evening. The **CVB** (see above) have a leaflet detailing a self-guided walking tour of the grand old houses in its older parts. Further out, **Mooney Grove Park**, three miles down South Mooney Boulevard (daily except Tues & Wed; nominally $6 per vehicle, though often free midweek), contains a huge slice of a giant sequoia which marks the **Tulare County Museum** (Thurs–Mon 10am–4pm; free), packed with intricate Yokuts basketry and a collection of buildings and agricultural equipment brought here from around the region. Close to the park's south entrance, a bronze replica of the *End of the Trail* statue portrays the defeat of Native Americans at the hands of advancing white settlers. It was made in 1915 and was intended to mark the closing of the western frontier.

Eating and drinking

Visalia has some of the best places to **eat** for miles around.

5

Brewbakers 219 E Main St ☎ 559/627-2739. Dine among the polished steel and brass tanks of this lively brewpub, which serves tempting burgers, salads and thick, chewy pizza, all for under $10. There's often live music to encourage you to sample their half-dozen brews.

Café 225 225 W Main St ☎ 559/733-2967. A modern bistro and tapas bar with an eclectic menu that features artichoke fritters ($5.50), steak frites ($17) and prosciutto and roasted garlic pizza ($12). Closed Sun.

Tazzaria 208 W Main St. Lively daytime spot for great lunches, cakes, good espresso and free wi-fi.

The Vintage Press 216 N Willis St ☎ 559/733-3033. Serving California continental cuisine, this fine restaurant has ranked as one of the best in the San Joaquin Valley for over four decades. Succumb to wild mushrooms in puff pastry with cognac, followed by red snapper with toasted almonds and capers and finally a dessert and coffee, all for around $55 a head – or much more if you explore the vast and wonderful wine list.

Hanford

Restful, small-town **HANFORD**, twenty miles west of Visalia on Hwy-198, was named after James Hanford, a paymaster on the Southern Pacific Railroad who became popular with his employees when he took to paying them in gold. The town formed part of a spur on the railroad and remains a stop on the Amtrak route between Los Angeles and San Francisco.

Hanford centres on Courthouse Square, once the core of local life at the beginning of the twentieth century. The honey-coloured **Courthouse** retains many of its Neoclassical features, including a magnificent staircase. Much less ostentatious are the rows of two-storey porched dwellings, four blocks east of the square (between 7th & 8th), marking the district that was home to most of the eight hundred or so Chinese families who came to Hanford to work on the railroad. At the centre of the community was the **Taoist Temple** on China Alley (open first Sat of the month noon–6pm or call ☎ 559/582-4508). Built in 1893, the temple served both a spiritual and a social function, providing free lodging to work-seeking Chinese immigrants, and was used as a Chinese school during the early 1920s. Everything inside is original, from the teak burl figurines to the marble chairs and it's a shame that entry is so restricted.

There's more to see six miles south of town at **The Clark Center for Japanese Art & Culture**, 15770 Tenth Ave (Tues–Sat 12.30–5pm, closed Aug; $5; ⓦwww .ccjac.org), incongruously located on the land of local cattle rancher Bill Clark. With the guidance of friends and mentors Ruth and Sherman Lee, Clark has been amassing Japanese scrolls, folding screens, lacquerware and sculpture since the 1970s and even designed the institute's Japanese-inspired building and his adjacent house and garden. Slip off your shoes and admire the dragon-in-clouds temple ceiling before entering the main room, where you can sit on tatami mats to view the works up close. Only a small portion of the collection is on show at any one time but there are always outstanding pieces, some dating back to the tenth century and many from the Edo Period (1615–1868). In particular, look out for two superb thirteenth-century sculptural pieces: the *Bodhisattva of the Wish-granting Jewel* and the *Daiitoko Myoo* – the institute's signature piece – with its multi-limbed figure astride a kneeling ox. Docent-led tours (Sat 1pm; free) are particularly illuminating.

Practicalities

KART **buses** (℡559/584-0101) run from Visalia (three daily Mon–Fri) and Fresno (two daily Mon, Wed & Fri) and arrive on Seventh Street near the town's **visitor centre** (Mon–Fri 9am–5pm; ℡559/582-5024, ⓦwww.visithanford .com), which is conveniently located inside the handsomely restored Amtrak depot at 200 Santa Fe Ave.

If you need to stay, try the central, mid-range *Comfort Inn*, 10 N Irwin St (℡559/584 9300; ❹), which offers free wi-fi, a heated outdoor pool and continental breakfast; while the *Irwin Street Inn*, 522 N Irwin (℡1-866/583-7378, ⓦwww.irwinstreetinn.net; ❷–❺), comprises four restored Victorian homes, furnished with antiques and with a restaurant on site.

Eating options are limited but adequate. Grab an espresso, sandwich or smoothie at *Art Works*, 120 W 6th St (℡559/583-8790), with free wi-fi and occasional live music or sample the rich creaminess of the made-on-the-premises ice cream at Hanford's classic 1920s diner, *Superior Dairy*, 325 N Douty St.

Fresno

FRESNO, with its population of 400,000, is the largest city between LA and San Francisco and an increasingly Hispanic one. In some ways it feels little more than an overgrown farming town but it's very much the hub of business in the San Joaquin Valley and is experiencing ongoing urban renewal. Witness such stridently modern buildings as the delta-winged, steel-and-glass **Fresno City Hall**, close to the Amtrak station and the stadium for Fresno's Minor League baseball team, the Grizzlies, Downtown. Still, there's an odd mix of civic pride and urban decay, the latter fuelling Fresno's status as one of the US's crime hotspots.

Arrival, information and accommodation

The **bus** and **train** terminals are Downtown – Greyhound at 1033 H St (℡559/268-1829) and Amtrak at 2650 Tulare St – both an easy walk from the **visitor centre**, on the corner of Fresno and O streets (Mon–Fri 10am–3pm, Sat 11am–2pm; ℡559/237-0988, ⓦwww.playfresno.org), housed in a distinctive, 1894 water tower. The nearby Fresno County Library, 2420 Mariposa St (Mon–Thurs 9am–9pm, Fri & Sat 9am–6pm, Sun 1–6pm; ℡559/488-3195), has free **internet access**.

Non-drivers can walk around Downtown or catch the Fresno Area Express **buses** ($1, exact change; ℡559/621-7433), if only to reach Forestiere Underground Gardens. Route #20, picked up Downtown on Van Ness (every 30–60min), comes within a mile of the gardens and you can transfer to the #9 for the last stretch. Routes #22 #26, and #28 travel between Van Ness and the Tower District.

There is little accommodation beyond **motels**, many clustered near the junction of Olive Avenue (the Tower District's main drag) and Hwy-99: avoid the marginal places charging rock-bottom rates. Downtown, make for *Super 8*, 2127 Inyo St at L St (℡1-800/800-8000, ⓦwww.super8.com; ❷), with a pool and free continental

FRESNO

0   800 yds

TOWER
DISTRICT

EATING & NIGHTLIFE	
Chicken Pie Shop	3
Java City	5
Roger Rocka's Dinner Theater	2
Sequoia Brewing Company	1
Veni Vidi Vici	4

ACCOMMODATION	
Days Inn	B
La Quinta Inn	A
Super 8	C

Roeding Park

Chaffee
Zoo

Farmers Market

Metropolita
Museum

Meux
Home
Museum

City
Hall

Train Station

Library

Fulton
Mall

City Airport

Greyhound
Station

THE SAN JOAQUIN VALLEY | Fresno

breakfast. To stay near the Tower District, opt for *Days Inn*, 1101 N Parkway Drive
(T1-800/329-7466, Wwww.daysinn.com; **●**), with free wi-fi and a pool, and
marginally nicer than the nearby *Motel 6* for not much more money. Alternatively,
step up to *La Quinta Inn*, 330 E Fir Ave T559/449-0928, Wwww.lq.com; **●**), with
comfy, well-appointed rooms, a gym and staff that really care about the place. It's
just off Hwy-41, six miles north of Downtown on the way to Yosemite.

The Town

Consider spending a night here visiting the fascinating **Forestiere Underground
Gardens**, a one-of-a-kind warren of rooms hewn out of the hardpan to protect
one man and his crops from the heat, and exploring the nightlife in the vibrant
Tower District. During the spring blooming season, allow an hour or two to
follow at least part of the 62-mile **Blossom Trail**, which weaves among fruit
orchards, citrus groves and the vineyards that make Fresno the world's raisin
capital. Late February to early March is best.

Forestiere Underground Gardens and Kearney
Mansion

The one place which turns Fresno into a destination in its own right is **Forestiere
Underground Gardens**, 5021 W Shaw Avenue (one-hour tours on the hour:
March & Nov Sat & Sun 11am–2pm; April, May, Sept & Oct Wed–Fri 11am–2pm,
Sat & Sun 10am–2pm; June–Aug Wed–Sun 10am–4pm; $12; T559/271-0734,
Wwww.undergroundgardens.com), seven miles northwest of the centre, a block
east of the Shaw Avenue exit off Hwy-99. A subterranean labyrinth of over fifty
rooms, the gardens were constructed by Sicilian émigré and former Boston and
New York subway tunneller Baldassare Forestiere, who came to Fresno in 1905.

In a fanatical attempt to stay cool and protect his crops, Forestiere put his digging know-how to work, building underground living quarters and skylit orchards with just a shovel and wheelbarrow using chunks of hardpan to create supporting arches. He gradually improved techniques for maximizing his yield but wasn't above playful twists like a glass-bottomed underground aquarium and a subterranean bathtub fed by water heated in the midday sun. He died in 1946, his forty years of work producing a vast earth honeycomb, part of which was destroyed by the construction of Hwy-99 next door, while another section awaits restoration. Wandering around the remainder of what he achieved is a fascinating way to pass an hour out of the heat of the day, enlivened by the tour guide's anecdotes.

With more time to spare, head seven miles west from Downtown along Kearney Boulevard, a long, straight, palm-lined avenue that was once the private driveway through the huge Kearney Park ($5 per vehicle; free with Mansion entry) to the **Kearney Mansion** (Fri–Sun tours at 1pm, 2pm & 3pm; $5). It was built between 1900 and 1903 for M. Theo Kearney, an English-born agricultural pioneer and raisin mogul, who maintained it in the opulent French Renaissance style to which he seemed addicted. He had even grander plans to grace Fresno with a French château, the mind-boggling designs for which are displayed here.

Downtown Fresno

Downtown sights are limited to a couple of fairly minor museums. The **Meux Home Museum**, 1007 R St at Tulare Street (guided tours Fri–Sun noon–3.30pm; $5; ☎559/233-8007, ⓦwww.meux.mus.ca.us), is Fresno's only surviving late nineteenth-century house, built for what was then the staggering sum of $12,000. This was the home of a doctor who arrived from the Deep South, bringing with him the novelty of a two-storey house and a plethora of trendy Victorian features – all quite out of sync with the Fresno that has sprawled up around it.

A couple of miles north of Downtown, the **Fresno Art Museum**, 2233 N 1st St in Radio Park (Thurs–Sun noon–4pm; $5, Sun free; ☎559/441-4221, ⓦwww.fresnoartmuseum.org), has a changing roster of high-quality modern art that's usually worth browsing. In addition to an attractive sculpture garden, there are rooms devoted to pre-Columbian Mexican art spanning Mesoamerican styles from 2500 years ago until the arrival of the Spanish in the early sixteenth century. There's also a relatively minor but beautiful 1926 Diego Rivera canvas, *El Dia de las Flores, Xochimilco*, along with an explanation of how it came to be here.

Eating and drinking

Downtown, grab a coffee, soup or bagel at Java City, 2134 Kern St; but the best dining territory is the **Tower District**, three miles north, once something of a hippy hangout due to its proximity to the City College campus. Today it has a well-scrubbed liberal feel, plus several blocks of antique shops, bookstores and eating places. For basic diner food visit the *Chicken Pie Shop*, 861 E Olive Ave, locally famed for its chicken (and excellent fruit) pies at bargain prices, or step up to the *Sequoia Brewing Company*, 777 E Olive Ave (☎559/264-5521), where eleven excellent tap beers are supplemented by live music (Wed, Fri & Sat; no cover) and good-value meals which extend to brick-oven pizzas, pasta dishes and salads. The fanciest evening dining is at *Veni Vidi Vici*, 1116 N Fulton St (☎559/266-5510; closed Mon), a dim and moody restaurant (with a patio for outdoor dining) with an eclectic range of dishes such as Vietnamese baby spinach salad ($8) and juniper-berry pork chop ($28). After 10pm it becomes a lively bar. For **entertainment**, visit *Roger Rocka's Dinner Theater*, 1226 N Wishon (☎559/266-9494, ⓦwww.rogerrockas.com), with Broadway-style shows in this 250-seat theatre preceded either by a sumptuous buffet (Wed, Thurs & Sun matinee; $45 all up) or a table-service meal (Fri & Sat; $48). Closed Mon & Tues.

Northern San Joaquin Valley

The towns of the northern San Joaquin Valley largely follow the pattern of those strung along Hwy-99 further south. Founded on agriculture, all had the hearts ripped out of them by suburban sprawl in the latter half of the twentieth century, leaving only winos, crazies and a lot of poor Mexican immigrants. But in recent years the town centres have rebounded. Enough of the old Downtown streets remain to evoke something out of an Edward Hopper painting, but the smartened-up cityscapes are all increasingly pleasant places to stroll, the ubiquitous taquerías now joined by java joints.

None of the three main towns warrant more than a few hours' exploration. You may spend the night in **Merced**, especially if Yosemite-bound; **Modesto** offers a couple of interesting sites and vestiges of the 1950s; and **Stockton** has a certain down-at-heel charm.

Merced and around

The best thing about sluggish **MERCED**, fifty miles north of Fresno, is its court-house, a gem of a building in the main square that's maintained as the **County Courthouse Museum**, N Street at W 20th Street (Wed–Sun 1–4pm; free; ⓦ www.mercedmuseum.org). This striking Italian Renaissance-style structure with columns, elaborately sculptured window frames and a cupola topped by a statue of the Goddess of Justice (minus her customary blindfold), was raised in 1875 when it completely dominated the few dozen shacks that comprised the town. Impressively restored in period style, the courtroom now contains local memorabilia – the most exotic item being an 1870s Taoist shrine, found by chance in a makeshift temple above a Chinese restaurant. A pleasant half-hour can also be spent in the mostly contemporary galleries in the **Merced Multicultural Arts Center**, 645 W Main St (Mon–Fri 9am–4.30pm, Sat 10am–2pm; free; ⓦ www.artsmerced.org).

Six miles north of Merced, close to the bedroom community of **Atwater** – and signposted off Hwy-99 – lies the **Castle Air Museum** (daily: May–Oct 9am–5pm; Nov–April 10am–4pm; $10; ⓦ www.castleairmuseum.org), home to fifty-odd military aircraft dating from World War II to Vietnam, mostly bulky bombers with a few fighters thrown in, including the world's fastest plane, the SR-71. Route #8 of Merced's transit system, "The Bus" (Mon–Sat only; ⓣ 1-800/345-3111), runs out here about every ninety minutes for $2 each way.

Practicalities

If none of these sights is much of a reason to visit Merced, the convenient **bus links to Yosemite** are. Greyhounds from Bakersfield, Sacramento and San Francisco stop Downtown at the **Transpo Center** on W 16th Street at N Street, where you'll find the **Merced California Welcome Center**, 710 W 16th St (8.30am–5pm; ⓣ 1-866/295-3757), which covers the region but has some local info (also found at ⓦ www.yosemite-gateway.org). The **Amtrak station** is somewhat isolated at 24th and K streets, about ten blocks away on the opposite side of the town centre: follow K Street off W 16th Street. Train and bus stations are both stops for the four daily **YARTS buses** (ⓣ 1-877/989-2787, ⓦ www.yarts .com) to Yosemite: see p.342 for more on getting to the national park.

Accommodation

If you're relying on public transport, the best **place to stay** by far is the reservations-only *HI–Merced Home Hostel*. Drivers in need of a motel should take the Mariposa/Yosemite exit from Hwy-99, where there are a couple of good options.

Comfort Inn 730 Motel Drive ☎1-877/424-6423 or 209/383-0333. Mid-range motel with all the expected facilities including pool, sauna and free wi-fi. ③

🏃 **HI–Merced Home Hostel** ☎209/725-0407, ✉merced@hiusa.org. Reservations-only 6-bed hostel that has limited check-in and access hours (7–9am & 5–10pm), but this is a small price to pay for a ride to and from the stations, an enthusiastic welcome, as much information as you can handle and a free dessert every evening. It's a great place to hook up with Yosemite-bound travellers, who frequently rent cars together (see p.342).

Dorms $15, non-members $18; room $42, non-members $48.
The Hooper House - Bear Creek Inn 575 W North Bear Creek Drive ☎209/723-3991, ⓦwww.hooperhouse.com. B&B in a lovely Colonial-style house furnished with polished floors, plain painted walls and an understated smattering of antique furnishings. It's all tastefully done and breakfast is served in a grand dining room. ⑥
Slumber Motel 1315 W 16th St ☎209/722-5783, ⓦwww.slumbermotel.com. The pick of a string of basic, budget motels half a mile west of the Transpo Center (left as you step out of the door), with a small pool, cable TV and free wi-fi. ①

Eating and drinking

There are several good **places to eat** Downtown and if you're looking to **rent a car** to head up to Yosemite, try Enterprise, 1334 W Main St (☎209/722-1600), which has vehicles from $40 a day and some great weekend deals.

🏃 **Café Cinema** 661 W Main St. Retro salt and pepper shakers behind the open kitchen match the lime-green counter stools in this quality breakfast and lunch diner with the usual range of burgers and sandwiches plus Mexican specials.
La Nita's 1327 18th St at T ☎209/723-2291. Authentic Mexican dining about ten blocks from the

bus station, offering all the expected south-of-the-border staples along with *menudo* (tripe and hominy soup) and *albondigas*, or Mexican meatballs (both $8). Lunch specials change daily and there are hearty combination plates for under $10. Closed Mon dinner.
Wired 450 W 18th St. Muffins plus good espresso (made from fair-trade organic beans) and fast internet access ($5 per hr). Closed Sat & Sun.

Modesto

Forty miles north of Merced along Hwy-99 you reach the town of **MODESTO**, which got its unusual name after prominent San Francisco banker William Ralston was too modest to accept the new town being named after him. Much later, it was the childhood home of movie director George Lucas, and became the inspiration (though not the location) for his movie *American Graffiti*, the classic portrayal of growing up in small-town America during the late 1950s. The movie contains a number of references to local people, particularly the teachers who rubbed Lucas up the wrong way in his formative years. Sadly, after several years of bad behaviour, local ordinances put an end to the fine art of **cruising**, though in recent years the American Graffiti Classic Car Show (middle weekend in June) has stepped in with hundreds of classic cars from all over the state and beyond, dusted off and cruised through the city. A more evocative celebration of the era is the 🏃**A&W Root Beer Drive-In**, 1404 G St, which has roller-skating "car-hop" waitresses serving root-beer floats ordered from illuminated car-side menus. Despite the cruising ban, you'll still see the better-kept rigs parked here on Friday and Saturday nights (until 10pm), when Elvis and Marilyn impersonators are often in evidence.

More imposingly, the Victorian **McHenry Mansion** at 906 15th St (Sun–Fri 12.30–4pm; donation; ⓦwww.mchenrymuseum.org) is jam-packed with fixtures,

5

fittings and the personal effects of a family whose fate was linked with Modesto's for years. Robert McHenry was a successful wheat rancher in the mid-nineteenth century who did much to bring about a general uplift in the agricultural wellbeing of the area. Docent-led tours enhance appreciation of the house, its history and restoration after being rented out as apartments until the early 1970s.

A block from the mansion, a fine Victorian building originally financed by the McHenry family as the fledgling city's library now operates as the **McHenry Museum**, 1402 I St (Tues–Sun noon–4pm; free; same contact info as mansion), which sports mock-ups of a blacksmith's shop, dentist's surgery and gathering of cattle brands, revealing something of bygone days, although lacking the period atmosphere of the mansion.

Practicalities

You can find out more about the town and pick up maps at Modesto's **visitor centre**, 1150 9th St at L Street (Mon–Fri 8am–5pm; ☏1-888/640-8467, Ⓦwww.visitmodesto.com). Greyhound **buses** stop Downtown at the Modesto Transport Center, 1001 9th St at J Street, handy for such **accommodation** as the huge, upscale *Doubletree Hotel*, 1150 9th St (☏1-800/222-8733; ❹), which includes a pool, sauna and exercise room. It's a step downmarket to the *Rodeway Inn*, 936 McHenry Ave, one mile north of Downtown (☏209/523-7701, Ⓦwww.hotel-modesto.com; ❶), which is basic but clean with an outdoor pool and free breakfast.

You'll find Downtown liberally supplied with decent **places to eat**. The 🍴 *Queen Bean*, 1126 14th St at K St (open 7am–10pm or midnight; ☏209/521-8000), serves breakfast, espresso, cakes and great sandwiches in a converted house, and often has bands playing at weekends; there's free **wi-fi**, too. Beer drinkers will want to seek out *St Stan's Brewery, Pub and Restaurant*, 821 L St (☏209/524-2337), where you've a choice of eight draught beers to wash down a burger or more substantial meal.

Stockton

The immediately striking thing about **STOCKTON**, perched at the far northern limit of the San Joaquin Valley some thirty miles north of Modesto, is the occasional sight of ocean-going freighters so far inland. The San Joaquin and Sacramento rivers converge here, creating a vast delta with thousands of inlets and bays, and a sixty-mile deep-water canal (built in the early 1930s) enables vessels to carry the produce of the valley's farms (especially Japan-bound bagged rice) past San Francisco and directly out to sea. But the geography that aided commerce also saddled Stockton with the image of a grim place to live and a tough city to work in. During the Gold Rush it was a supply stop en route to the mines, and it became a gigantic flophouse for broken and dispirited ex-miners who gave up their dreams of fortune and returned here to toil on the waterfront. Though valiant efforts have been made to shed this reputation and beautify the less attractive districts of this city of a quarter of a million, it's still primarily a hard-working, sleeves-rolled-up place.

A smattering of buildings Downtown evokes the early decades of the twentieth century and makes Stockton an oft-demanded film set. John Huston's downbeat boxing picture *Fat City*, for example, was shot here. Marginally more appealing are the blocks bordered by Harding Way and Park, El Dorado and California streets, a short way north of the centre. This area has been preserved as the **Magnolia Historical District**, with sixteen intriguing specimens of domestic architecture spanning seven decades from the 1860s.

Roughly a mile west of the Magnolia District, in Victory Park, Stockton gathers totems of its past in the varied and large stock of the **Haggin Museum**, 1201 N Pershing Ave (Wed–Fri 1.30–5pm Sat & Sun noon–5pm; $5; ☎209/940-6300, ⓦwww.hagginmuseum.org). Not surprisingly, much is given over to agriculture, including the city's finest moment: the invention by local farmers of a caterpillar tread to enable tractors to travel over muddy ground. In tremendous contrast, the museum also contains Yosemite oils by Albert Bierstadt and a batch of nineteenth-century French paintings, including works by Renoir and Gauguin, as well as Bouguereau's monumental 1878 painting of nymphs bathing, *The Nymphaeum*.

Practicalities

Stockton's **Greyhound station** is Downtown at 121 S Center St, a third of a mile east of the **Chamber of Commerce**, Waterfront Warehouse, 445 W Weber Ave (Mon–Fri 8am–noon & 1–5pm; ☎209/547-2770, ⓦwww.visitstockton.org), which has limited information but stocks a free leaflet on the Magnolia District. **Amtrak** has two stops: Downtown at 735 S San Joaquin St, and half a mile northeast at the corner of North Aurora and East Weber streets.

If you're forced to stay over, you can choose among the plentiful mid-range chain **hotels** and budget motels, mostly near the Waterloo Road exit off Hwy-99. Downtown, try the pool-equipped *Howard Johnson Express Inn*, 33 N Center St (☎1-800/446-4656, ⓦwww.hojo.com; ❷), close to the Greyhound station. The essential stop for **eating** near Downtown is the Chinese *On Lock Sam*, 333 S Sutter St (☎209/466-4561), standing here since 1898. Nearby *Yasoo Yani*, 326 E Main St (☎209/464-3108; closed Sat & Sun), does a fine *souvlaki*, salad and fries for about $9. There's more choice along the so-called **Miracle Mile**, a stretch of Pacific Avenue starting around a mile north of Downtown where, among the bookshops and restaurants you'll find the family-oriented *Valley Brewing Company*, 157 W Adams St, and *Ave On The Mile*, 2333 Pacific Ave, good for cocktails and gourmet panini.

Sequoia and Kings Canyon national parks

Separate parks but jointly run and with a long common border, **SEQUOIA AND KINGS CANYON NATIONAL PARKS** (see box, p.324) contain an immense variety of geology, flora and fauna. **Sequoia National Park**, as you might expect from its name, boasts the thickest concentration – and the biggest individual specimens – of giant sequoia trees to be found anywhere. These ancient trees tend to outshine (and certainly outgrow) the other features of the park – an assortment of meadows, peaks, canyons and caves swathed in pine and fir. **Kings Canyon National Park** doesn't have as many big trees but compensates with a gaping canyon gored out of the rock by the Kings River, which cascades in torrents down from the High Sierra during the spring snowmelt

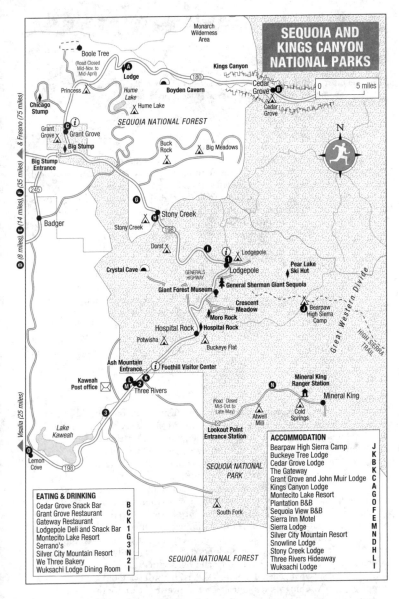

SEQUOIA AND KINGS CANYON NATIONAL PARKS

Monarch Wilderness Area

Kings Canyon

0   5 miles

Boole Tree
(Road Closed Mid-Nov. to Mid-April)
Lodge
Princess
Boyden Cavern
Cedar Grove
Cedar Grove
Hume Lake
Hume Lake
Chicago Stump
SEQUOIA NATIONAL FOREST
Grant Grove
Grant Grove
Big Stump
Big Stump Entrance
Buck Rock
Big Meadows
Badger
Stony Creek
Stony Creek
Dorst
Crystal Cave
Lodgepole
GENERALS HIGHWAY
Lodgepole
Pear Lake Ski Hut
Giant Forest Museum
General Sherman Giant Sequoia
Crescent Meadow
Moro Rock
Bearpaw High Sierra Camp
Hospital Rock
Hospital Rock
Potwisha
Buckeye Flat
Ash Mountain Entrance
Foothill Visitor Center
Kaweah Post office
Three Rivers
Mineral King Ranger Station
Mineral King
(Road Closed Mid-Oct to Late May)
Atwell Mill
Cold Springs
Lookout Point Entrance Station
Lake Kaweah
SEQUOIA NATIONAL PARK
Lemon Cove

Great Western Divide
HIGH SIERRA TRAIL

N

& Fresno (75 miles)
F (35 miles)
E (14 miles)
D (8 miles)
Visalia (25 miles)

THE SAN JOAQUIN VALLEY | Sequoia and Kings Canyon national parks

5

ACCOMMODATION

Bearpaw High Sierra Camp	J
Buckeye Tree Lodge	K
Cedar Grove Lodge	B
The Gateway	K
Grant Grove and John Muir Lodge	C
Kings Canyon Lodge	A
Montecito Lake Resort	G
Plantation B&B	O
Sequoia View B&B	F
Sierra Inn Motel	E
Sierra Lodge	M
Silver City Mountain Resort	N
Snowline Lodge	D
Stony Creek Lodge	H
Three Rivers Hideaway	L
Wuksachi Lodge	I

South Fork

SEQUOIA NATIONAL FOREST

EATING & DRINKING

Cedar Grove Snack Bar	B
Grant Grove Restaurant	C
Gateway Restaurant	K
Lodgepole Deli and Snack Bar	1
Montecito Lake Resort	G
Serrano's	3
Silver City Mountain Resort	N
We Three Bakery	2
Wuksachi Lodge Dining Room	I

period. There's less of a packaged tourism feel here than in Yosemite: the few established sights (principally the big trees) are near the main roads and concentrate the crowds, leaving the vast majority of the landscape untrammelled and unspoiled, but well within reach for willing hikers. Through it all runs the **Generals Highway**, actually a fairly slow and winding paved road which links two of the biggest sequoias hereabouts, the General Sherman Tree and the General Grant Tree.

Park, monument or forest?

With two national parks and the Giant Sequoia National Monument, all surrounded by the Sierra National Forest and the Sequoia National Forest, the Sequoia and Kings Canyon region has become a confusing patchwork of federally administered areas. For the most part, it won't matter which section you're in, though rules (particularly for hunting and camping) are more relaxed in the national forests.

Approaching from the south you twist your way up from Three Rivers to **Giant Forest**, site of the park's best museum, right in the heart of a massive grove of enormous trees. From here, **Crescent Meadow Road** spurs off southeast past the dramatic **Moro Rock** and under the **Tunnel Log** to **Crescent Meadow** and **Tharp's Cabin**, fashioned from a fallen sequoia. The Generals Highway continues to **Lodgepole**, base for some excellent trails through deep forests, the longer treks rising above the tree line to reveal the barren peaks and superb sights of the High Sierra. Further north, **Grant Grove** offers accommodation and dining, making this the main base for visiting sights such as the **General Grant Tree** and assorted sequoia graveyards – fields of massive severed stumps. Some 25 miles to the east, **Cedar Grove** huddles in the bottom of Kings Canyon at the start of most of the marked hikes. Access is along Hwy-180 (closed in winter; usually mid-Nov to mid-April) which spectacularly skirts the colossal canyon. The **best time to come** to the parks is in late summer and fall, when the days are still warm, the nights are getting chilly at altitude, the roads remain free of snow and most visitors have left. Bear in mind that although most roads are kept open through the winter, Hwy-180 into Kings Canyon is closed and snow blocks the road into Mineral King (see box opposite). May and June can also be good, especially in Kings Canyon, where snowmelt swells the Kings River dramatically and the canyon-side yuccas are in bloom.

Some history

The land now encompassed by the Sequoia and Kings Canyon national parks was once the domain of **Yokuts sub-tribes** – the Monache, Potwisha and Kaweah peoples – who made summer forays into the high country from their permanent settlements in the lowlands, especially along the Middle Fork of the Kaweah River. The first real European contact came with the 1849 California **Gold Rush**, when prospectors came in search of pasture and a direct route through the mountains. Word of abundant lumber soon got out and loggers came to stake their claims in the lowlands. The high country was widely ignored until, in 1858, local natives led **Hale Tharp**, a cattleman from Three Rivers, up to the sequoias around Moro Rock. Tharp spent the next thirty summers up there in his log home; John Muir visited him and wrote about the area, bringing it to the attention of the general public and the loggers. Before long, narrow-gauge railways and log flumes littered the area, mainly for clearing fir and pine rather than the sequoias, which tended to shatter when felled. Nonetheless, Visalia conservationist George Stewart campaigned in Washington for some degree of **preservation** for the big trees and, in 1890, four square miles around Grant Grove became Grant Grove National Park, the country's **third national park**. In 1940 this was incorporated into the newly formed Kings Canyon National Park.

Park practicalities

The national parks are accessible by public transport on the **Visalia to Giant Forest Shuttle** ($7.50 each way, including park entrance fee; ☎1-877/287-4453,

The high country of both parks is covered in a blanket of **snow**, usually from November until April or May, and while this limits a great deal of sightseeing and walking it also opens up opportunities for some superb cross-country skiing. With chains, **access** is seldom much of a problem. Both main roads into the parks are kept open all year. The Generals Highway is also ploughed after snowfall, but sometimes takes a few days to clear: it's best, then, to choose one section of the parks as a base. Kings Canyon's Cedar Grove is off limits to cars from mid-November to mid-April, but Grant Grove stays open all year. Facilities are restricted and camping is only available at snow-free lowland sites.

The big winter activities up here are **cross-country skiing** and **snowshoeing**. Hwy-180 gives access to two places at the hub of miles of marked trails: the Grant Grove Ski Touring Center at Grant Grove (Nov–April; call SKC on ☏559/335-5500), where there's ski and snowshoe rental, guided naturalist snowshoe walks at weekends, restaurants and accommodation; and the *Montecito Lake Resort* (see p.327), with its own groomed trails, also open to day-visitors for $25. Nearby, the mile-long Big Meadows Nordic Ski Trail is perfect beginner's terrain. To the south, *Wuksachi Lodge* (see p.327) has groomed trails and plenty of scope in the backcountry: skis ($24 a day) and snowshoes ($15) can both be rented. Unless you are staying at *Wuksachi Lodge* or are a super-hardy camper, you'll need to return to Three Rivers for somewhere to stay.

Ⓦwww.sequioashuttle.com), a two-and-a-half-hour run. Once in the parks, make use of three **free shuttles** (late May to early Sept daily 9am–6pm every 15min): the **Gray Route** links Giant Forest with Crescent Meadow via Moro Rock; the **Green Route** plies the Generals Highway between Giant Forest, the Sherman Tree, Lodgepole and Wuksachi; and the Purple Route continues north from Lodgepole and Wuksachi to the *Dorst* campground.

The twin parks are also easy to reach by **car**. The fastest approach is along Hwy-180 from Fresno, though it's slightly shorter following Hwy-198 from Visalia, a 55-mile drive including a tortuous 15-mile ascent. Consider looping in one entrance and out the other, and make sure you stock up in advance with **cash** and **gas**, though some of both is available (see p.334).

The parks are always open: **park entry** costs $20 per car, or $10 per hiker or biker, and is valid for seven days. Fees are collected at the entrance stations, where you'll be given an excellent map and a copy of the free quarterly newspaper with the latest listings of **ranger programmes** and general information on the parks.

For information, call at one of the five **visitor centres**: the park headquarters at **Foothills**, a mile north of the southern (Hwy-198) entrance (daily: June–Aug 8am–6pm; Sept–May 8am–4.30pm; ☏559/565-3341, Ⓦwww.nps.gov/seki); and others at Lodgepole, Giant Forest Museum, Grant Grove Village and Cedar Grove Village. There's also a useful **ranger station** at Mineral King; see the relevant accounts for opening hours.

You'll most likely **eat** close to where you are staying, so we've listed restaurants throughout the Guide. There are **food** markets and fairly basic summer-only cafeterias at Lodgepole (the most extensive), Stony Creek and Cedar Grove Village, though none of them are spectacular and prices will be higher than places outside the park, such as Three Rivers. Much the same applies to **restaurants**, with Three Rivers offering the best local selection at reasonable prices. In the restaurants inside the parks, diner fare prevails, with the exception of the restaurant at *Wuksachi Lodge*.

Except during public holidays, there's always plenty of **camping space** in the parks and the surrounding national forest. Below, we've picked the best of the campsites: all are first-come-first-served except for *Lodgepole*, *Princess* and *Hume* (reserve up to six months ahead on ☎1-877/444-6777, ⓦ www.recreation.gov). RV drivers won't find any hookups, but there are summer-only dump stations at *Potwisha*, *Lodgepole* and *Princess*. Collecting "dead and down" firewood is permitted in both the national park and the national forest, but for cooking you really want to bring along a portable stove. There are public **showers** at several locations (see p.335). For **backcountry** camping, see the box on p.332.

Campsites are listed south to north, and the night-time temperatures you can expect are indicated by the site's altitude. **Fees** are sometimes reduced or waived outside the main summer season and when piped water is disconnected, especially in winter.

Cold Springs Mineral King (late May to Oct; $12; 7500ft). Excellent shaded riverside site 25 miles west of Hwy-198, with some very quiet walk-in sites. Drinking water available.

Potwisha (all year; $18; 2100ft). Smallish, RV-dominated site close to Hwy-198, three miles northeast of the park's southern entrance and beside the Marble Fork of the Kaweah River. Water and flush toilets.

Buckeye Flat (late May to mid-Oct; $18; 2800ft). Peaceful, trailer-free site six miles east of Hwy-198, close to the park's southern entrance and beside the Middle Fork of the Kaweah River. Water and flush toilets.

Lodgepole (all year; $18, or $20 if reserved; 6700ft). Largest and busiest of the sites, four miles north of Giant Forest Village and close to the market, snack stand, laundry and showers. Reservations essential late May to late September, when pay showers, a camp store, water and flush toilets are all made available.

Buck Rock (late May to Oct; free; 7500ft). Excellent and under-utilized national forest site three miles east of the highway, midway between Lodgepole and Grant Grove Village. No water.

Sunset, **Azalea** and **Crystal Spring** Grant Grove Village ($18, $10 in winter; 6500ft). Comparable large sites all within a few hundred yards of the Grant Grove visitor centre.

Princess (mid-May to Sept; $18; 5900ft). National forest campground with water and toilets, handily sited on the way into Kings Canyon. Reserve through the Forest Service.

Hume Lake (late May to Oct; $20; 5200ft). Reservable national forest site with water, toilets, and lake swimming for the brave.

Sheep Creek, **Sentinel**, **Canyon View** and **Moraine** Cedar Grove Village (early May to mid-Oct; $18; 4600ft). Contiguous forest sites around the Cedar Grove visitor centre. *Canyon View* is tents-only. All have flush toilets.

Accommodation

Inside the parks, **accommodation** (ranging from rustic cabins to luxurious rooms) is managed by two concessionaires: Sequoia-Kings Canyon Park Services (SKC; ☎559/335-5500 or 1-866/522-6986, ⓦ www.sequoia-kingscanyon.com) operate in Cedar Grove, Grant Grove and Stony Creek; while Delaware North (DN; ☎1-888/252-5757, ⓦ www.visitsequoia.com) cover Lodgepole, Wuksachi and *Bearpaw High Sierra Camp*. You can pick up cancellations upon arrival, but space is at a premium during the summer, when booking a couple of months in advance is advisable. Rates quoted are for the summer season, but huge savings can be had outside peak times, especially at the pricier places.

Price and availability force many to stay just **outside the parks**. There is limited choice along Hwy-180, but Three Rivers, on Hwy-198, has a good selection: booking ahead is advised at **weekends** through the summer and holidays. Rates can also be up to one price code higher on Friday and Saturday nights, though this varies with demand.

Within the parks, we have included all available roofed accommodation below; just a selection of the best places to stay are listed otherwise. For **camping**, see box opposite.

In the parks and national forest

Bearpaw High Sierra Camp Mid-June to mid-Sept; call DN. Soft beds, fluffy towels, hot showers and hearty meals served up in magnificent wilderness are the trump cards for this cluster of six wooden-floored permanent tents at 7800ft, an 11-mile walk east of Giant Forest Village. There's no electricity, everything is helicoptered in for the season, and breakfast and dinner are included in the price. Most weekends and holidays are taken immediately after booking opens on Jan 2, though you've a reasonable chance of an on-spec place on weeknights in June and Sept. $175 per person based on two sharing; $75 for additional adult in tent.

Cedar Grove Mid-May to mid-Oct; call SKC. Cosy lodge with private bathroom and a/c, right by the Kings River and in the same block as the fast-food restaurant and shop. ➍–➏

Grant Grove and John Muir Lodge All year; call SKC. The parks' widest selection of ways to sleep under a roof, with most options accommodating up to four people. The most basic are the summer-only canvas-roofed cabins (early June to early Sept), with linen service but no electricity. Ageing, rustic cabins (late May to late Nov) have been nicely restored and modernized and come with cook stove and propane heater. For a private bath step up to the bath cabins (all year) or the swanky, modern *John Muir Lodge*, with very comfortable hotel rooms and wi-fi. ➋–➏

Kings Canyon Lodge Hwy-180; late April to Nov; ☎ 559/335-2405, ⓦ www.thekingscanyonlodge .com. Guarding the entrance to Kings Canyon with views of Spanish Mountain this quaint and rustic 1930s former hunting lodge has simple rooms and cabins, a pricier 2-bedroom cabin sleeping 8, with full kitchen and a straightforward café/bar with bear and mountain-lion skins on the ceiling. ➍

Montecito Lake Resort Generals Highway ☎ 1-800/227-9900, ⓦ www.mslodge.com. A large but low-key family resort, tastefully set next to an artificial lake with all manner of activities: canoeing, swimming, horseriding, wakeboarding and volleyball in summer; and snowshoeing,

skating and cross-country skiing in winter. It's booked in six-night blocks from mid-June to early Sept (though you can book Saturday night separately), but at other times you can almost always stay in rustic cabins ($99 per person, weekends $139) or lodge rooms with private bath ($129 per person, weekends $159). Rates include all meals (which are pretty good) and many of the activities.

Stony Creek Generals Hwy; early May to early Oct; call SKC. Plain, comfortable motel-style rooms with satellite TV and showers in a block with a good restaurant and a grocery store. A generous continental breakfast is included. Discounts in May, Sept and Oct. ➏

Wuksachi Lodge All year; call DN. Directly competing with the *John Muir Lodge* for the best rooms in the park, the *Wuksachi* consists of several blocks of rooms (ask for mountain views) widely scattered in the woods around an elegant central lounge and restaurant area. ➏

South of the parks: Lemon Cove, Three Rivers and Mineral King

Buckeye Tree Lodge 46000 Hwy-198, Three Rivers, just south of the park entrance ☎ 559/561-5900, ⓦ www.buckeyetree.com. Small and ageing but comfortable modern rooms with TV, private bathrooms and verandas overlooking the foaming river. Comes equipped with a nice pool and free wi-fi. They also run *Sequoia Village Inn* across the road, with some appealing, woodsy, self-contained cabins, each with barbecue area and some sleeping 12. ➏

The Gateway 45978 Hwy-198, Three Rivers, just south of the park entrance ☎ 559/561-4133, ⓦ www.gateway-sequoia.com. Old but clean and perfectly functional motel-style rooms with satellite TV, plus a honeymoon cabin with dry sauna and patio and a two-bedroom house sleeping eight with self-catering facilities ($265–325). It's located right beside the Kaweah River and the better rooms have a deck overlooking the water. ➏

Plantation B&B 33038 Hwy-198, Lemon Cove, 17 miles south of the park entrance ☎ 1-800/240-1466, ⓦ www.theplantation.net.

Luxurious *Gone With the Wind*-themed B&B with comfortable en-suite rooms and truly delicious breakfasts, located twenty minutes' drive from the park entrance. The Belle Watling room comes bordello-hued with a clawfoot tub. Outside there's a heated pool, hot tub and lawns dotted with palm trees. ⑤

Sierra Lodge 43175 Hwy-198, Three Rivers, 4 miles south of the park entrance ☏1-888/575-2555, ⓦwww.sierra-lodge.com. Usually the cheapest motel in the district, an old but spacious and clean lodge with pool and modernized en-suite rooms, many with decks and some featuring wood-burning fireplaces. Also suites, some of which have cooking facilities. Free internet and wi-fi. ③

🏃 **Silver City Mountain Resort** Mineral King, 20 miles east of Three Rivers ☏559/561-3223, ⓦwww.silvercityresort.com. A bucolic bolthole in the woods, which has been catering to committed regulars and casual visitors since the 1930s. The rustic cabins are gorgeous with potbelly stoves, kitchen and propane lighting, and some come with a toilet. The more modern chalets have full bathroom and electric lighting whenever the generator is running. Sheets and towels are provided for out-of-state guests (otherwise bring your own) and there's a two-night minimum stay. Bring food for self-catering, though there is a store with limited supplies, and the resort has a restaurant attached (see opposite). There's limited wi-fi for guests. Open late May–early Oct. ④–⑨

Three Rivers Hideaway 43365 Hwy-198, 3.7 miles south of the park entrance ☏559/561-4413, ⓦwww.threerivershideaway.com. Small RV and tent site with ageing but renovated cabins (some pricier ones with kitchens) at the lowest prices in the district. Tents $30, RV hookups $29–34, cabins ②

Along Hwy-180

Sequoia View B&B 1384 S Frankwood Ave, Sanger, just off Hwy-180 ☏1-866/738 6420, ⓦwww.svbnb.com. A small winery, 20 miles east of Fresno and 35 miles west of the park entrance, with three large and tastefully furnished luxury suites, two with king-sized sleigh beds and one with a balcony above the tasting room. A full country breakfast is served. ⑤

Snowline Lodge 44138 Hwy-180, eight miles west of the park entrance ☏559/336 2300, ⓦwww.cyndissnowlinelodge.com. Host Cyndi is rapidly revamping this once neglected lodge. Already, the simple en-suite rooms (some with a/c) have been smartened up and breakfast is served on the deck. A honeymoon suite and family room with kitchen are in the pipeline and a woodsy restaurant and bar should be up and running by the time you read this. There's also a rustic two-room cabin up behind (⑤). Everyone has access to the hot tub, there's internet access and you'll probably find your national flag flying from one of the flagpoles. ③

Three Rivers

Approaching the park from the south, you pass through **Three Rivers**, a lowland community strung out for seven miles along Hwy-198 and providing the greatest concentration of accommodation anywhere near the parks. As you approach the centre of town, six miles south of the park entrance, a sign directs you three miles west to the **Kaweah Post Office**, the smallest still operating in California, with its original brass-and-glass private boxes.

Three rivers has several good **places to eat**: *Serrano's*, 40869 Hwy-198, six miles south of the park entrance looks spartan but dishes up authentic, low-cost Mexican, best eaten outside on a balmy summer's evening with a Mexican beer; *We Three Bakery*, 43368 Hwy-198, 3.7 miles south of the park entrance, makes a great, friendly stop for breakfast or lunch either inside or out, or for their freshly baked cakes and pastries and free wi-fi; and the *Gateway Restaurant*, 45978 Hwy-198, just south of the park entrance (☏559/561-4133), superbly set with a shady deck hung out over the Kaweah River, is great for a lunch of chicken tostadas ($14) or salmon burgers ($14), the Sunday Champagne brunch ($26), or very good dinners (mains $25–39).

Mineral King

A couple of miles north of Three Rivers, the twisting, early 1880s Mineral King Road (open late May to Oct) branches 25 miles east into the southern section of the park to **Mineral King**, sitting in a scalloped bowl at 7800ft surrounded by snowy peaks and glacial lakes. This is the only part of the high country accessible by car (but not RVs, buses or trailers) and makes a superb hiking base. Eager prospectors built the thoroughfare hoping the area would yield silver. It didn't, the mines were abandoned and the region was left largely in peace until the mid-1960s, when Disney threatened to build a huge ski resort here. Thankfully the plan was defeated and the region was finally included in Sequoia National Park in 1978. Today there are just a few small stands of sequoias, a couple of basic campgrounds, one quaint resort and near-complete tranquillity. Having negotiated the seven-hundred-odd twists and turns from the highway, you can relax by the river before hiking up over steep Sawtooth Pass and into the alpine bowls of the glaciated basins beyond. There's also a gentler introduction to the flora and fauna of Mineral King by way of a short **nature trail** from the *Cold Springs* campground.

Pick up wilderness permits ($15 per group per trip) for overnight hikes at the **ranger station** (June to early Sept daily 8am–4pm; ☎559/565-3768) opposite the *Cold Springs* campground. They're in great demand in July and August: reservations can be made in advance from March 1, and some permits are offered on a first-come-first-served basis. From late May to mid-July, protect any vehicles left overnight against **marmot** attack: chicken wire can be rented or bought from *Silver City* (see opposite).

Unless you're committed to camping, the place to stay is the *Silver City Mountain Resort* (see opposite), five miles before the end of the road, which has a small, low-cost **restaurant**, fully open Thursday to Monday but only open for coffee and their excellent home-made fruit pies on Tuesday and Wednesday.

Giant Forest

Entering the park on **Hwy-180 from Visalia**, you pass the roadside **Hospital Rock**, impressively decorated with rock drawings from an ancient Monache settlement, whose evolution and culture is explained in the adjacent exhibit. The **Generals Highway** then twists rapidly uphill into **GIANT FOREST**, the world's greatest accessible concentration of giant sequoias. Until 1998, Giant Forest contained a small village which threatened the health of the sequoias. Now, you'd hardly know anything had been there but for the former shop, restaurant and gas station now operating as the **Giant Forest Museum** (daily: July & Aug 8am–6pm; June & Sept 8am–5pm; Oct–May 9am–4.30pm; free), which shows some great footage of sequoia-felling and early tourism. Outside, the fire-damaged Sentinel Tree is barricaded to allow seedlings a chance to get established.

Various short hikes fan out from here through the trees, including the **Beetle Rock Trail** (5min round-trip), which affords a view down to the San Joaquin Valley, and the **Big Trees Trail** (0.6-mile loop; 30min–1hr), which follows a well-formed boardwalk along the perimeter of Round Meadow.

Along Crescent Meadow Road

The densest concentration of sights is along **Crescent Meadow Road**, which spurs off the main highway just before the Giant Forest Museum. The first photo-op is the **Auto Log**, a fallen trunk originally chiselled flat enough for motorists to nose up onto it, though rot has now put an end to this practice. Beyond here, a side loop leads to **Moro Rock**, a granite monolith streaking wildly upward from the green hillside. On a clear day, views from its remarkably level top can stretch 150 miles across the San Joaquin Valley and, in the other direction, to the towering Sierra. Thanks to a concrete staircase, it's a comparatively easy climb to the summit, although at nearly 7000ft the nearly 400 steps can be a strain.

The life of the giant sequoia

Call it what you will – the sierra redwood, *Sequoiadendron giganteum*, or just "big tree" – the **giant sequoia** is the earth's most massive living thing. Some of these arboreal monsters weigh in at a whopping one thousand tonnes, courtesy of a thick trunk that barely tapers from base to crown. They're also among the oldest trees found anywhere, many reaching 2000 or even 3000 years of age.

Sequoias are only found in around 75 isolated groves on the western slopes of California's **Sierra Nevada** and grow naturally between elevations of 5000ft and 8500ft from just south of Sequoia National Park to just north of Yosemite National Park. Specimens planted all over the world during the nineteenth century seem to thrive but haven't yet reached the enormous dimensions seen here.

The cinnamon-coloured bark of young sequoias is easily confused with that of the incense cedar, but as they age, there's no mistaking the thick spongy outer layer that protects the sapwood from the fires that periodically sweep through the forests. **Fire** is, in fact, a critical element in the propagation of sequoias; the hen-egg-sized female cones pack hundreds of seeds but require intense heat to open them. Few seeds ever sprout as they need perfect conditions, usually where an old tree has fallen and left a hole in the canopy, allowing plenty of light to fall on rich mineral soil.

Young trees are conical, but as they mature the lower branches drop off to leave a top-heavy crown. A shallow, **wide root system** keeps them upright, but eventually heavy snowfall or high winds topple ageing trees. With its tannin-rich timber, a giant sequoia may lie where it fell for hundreds of years. John Muir discovered one still largely intact with a 380-year-old silver fir growing out of the depression it had created.

Back on the road, you pass under the **Tunnel Log**: a tree that fell across the road in 1937 and has since had a vehicle-sized hole cut through its lower half. Further on, **Crescent Meadow** is, like other grassy fields in the area, more accurately a marsh, and too wet for the sequoias that form an impressive boundary around it. Looking across the meadow gives the best opportunity to appreciate the changing shape of the ageing sequoia. The trail circling its perimeter (1.5 miles; 1hr; mainly flat) leads to **Log Meadow**, to which a farmer, Hale Tharp, searching for a summer grazing ground for his sheep, was led by local Native Americans in 1856. He became one of the first white men to see the giant sequoias, and the first to actually live in one – a hollowed-out specimen which still exists, remembered as **Tharp's Log**. Peer inside to appreciate the hewn-out shelves.

The General Sherman Tree and Crystal Cave

North of Crescent Meadow Road, the Generals Highway enters the thickest section of Giant Forest and the biggest sequoia of them all (reachable on foot by various connecting trails). The 3000-year-old **General Sherman Tree** is 275ft high and has a base diameter of 36ft. While it's certainly a thrill to be face-to-bark with what is widely held to be the largest living thing on earth, its extraordinary dimensions are hard to grasp in the midst of all the almost equally monstrous sequoias around – not to mention the other tremendous batch that can be seen on the **Congress Trail** (2 miles; 1–2hr; negligible ascent), which starts from the General Sherman Tree itself. Parking is several hundred yards from the General Sherman Tree, so consider catching the **free shuttle bus** from Giant Forest.

When you've had your fill of the magnificent trees, consider a trip nine miles from Giant Forest along a minor road to **Crystal Cave** (45-minute guided tours mid-May to Oct daily 11am–4pm; $13), which has a fairly diverting batch of stalagmites and stalactites. The early morning tours are not usually full, and whatever time you go, remember to take a jacket as the cave is at a constant 50°F. Those with a deeper interest in the cave's origins and features should join the ninety-minute **Discovery Tour** (mid-June to Aug Mon–Fri 4.15pm; $20), or even the **Historic Candle-light Tour** (mid-June to late Sept Thurs–Sun at 5.30pm; $20), which dwells on the cave's discovery, with candles adding atmosphere.

Tickets for cave trips cannot be bought at the caves themselves, but must be purchased at the Lodgepole or Foothills visitor centres at least a couple of hours beforehand.

Lodgepole, Wuksachi and Stony Creek

Whatever your plans, make sure you stop at **Lodgepole Village**, three miles north of the General Sherman Tree where the **visitor centre** (daily: July & Aug 8am–6pm; May, June & Sept 8am–5pm; ☏559/565-4436) shows the eight-minute *Saving Sequoias* movie on the restoration of the Giant Forest area in the late 1990s. With its grocery store, showers, laundry and campground, Lodgepole is very much at the centre of Sequoia's visitor activities, and its situation at one end of the Tokopah Valley, a glacially formed canyon (not unlike the much larger Yosemite Valley), makes it an ideal starting point to explore a number of hiking trails (see box, p.332). **Eating** is done at the *Lodgepole Deli and Snack Bar* (closed Nov–March), the best of the parks' budget eating places with respectable readymade sandwiches, salads and ice cream at the deli (daily 11am–6pm) and a selection of burgers, fries and drinks at the snack bar (daily 8am–7.45pm).

Beyond Lodgepole the Generals Highway turns west and runs four miles to **Wuksachi**, just a fancy modern lodge (p.327), and the *Wuksachi Lodge Dining Room* (☏559/565-4070), the **finest restaurant** in the twin parks, with Reuben sandwiches and the like ($10) at lunch and more formal dinners such as seared trout ($20) and steaks ($25) all served in a modern baronial-style room. There's also a full buffet breakfast (continental $8; full $13) and the bar is open daily until 11pm.

The road soon swings north again and passes into the Giant Sequoia National Monument – where **Stony Creek** offers accommodation (see p.327) and a fairly mainstream **diner/restaurant** (late May to Oct daily 11am–2pm & 4–7.30pm) serving decent pizza and calzone. There is also accommodation at *Montecito Lake Resort*, where the restaurant serves hearty buffet breakfasts (7.30–9am; $9), lunches (noon–1.30pm; $10) and dinners (5.30–7pm; $20) communally at large tables. There's a bar open until 10pm.

Grant Grove, the Big Stump Area and Hume Lake

A good base for exploring the northern sections of the parks, **Grant Grove** is set amid concentrated stands of sequoias, sugar pines, incense cedar, black oak and mountain dogwoods. Along with accommodation (see p.327), a post office and a small supermarket you'll find a **restaurant** with diner fare – burgers, sandwiches and breakfasts – plus fish, chicken and steak dinners for $15–20 and pizza to stay or go ($14 for a 14-inch plus $1.50 per topping; summer only). There's also an espresso kiosk with seating out on the umbrella-shaded terrace. The useful **visitor centre** (daily: June–Aug 8am–7pm; May & Sept 8am–5pm; Oct–April 9am–4.30pm; ☏559/565-4307) can supply all the background information you'll need, and contains a small **museum** (free entry) with old-time photos, a cross-section of a tree and a kids' Discovery Room where you can examine tree seeds under a microscope.

Exploring the Sequoia and Kings Canyon backcountry

The **trails** in Kings Canyon and Sequoia see far less traffic than those in Yosemite, but can still get busy in high summer. Almost all those leaving from Mineral King and Kings Canyon climb very steeply, so if you're looking for easy and moderate hikes, jump to the second subheading below.

There are **no restrictions** on day-walks, but a quota system (operational late May to late Sept) applies if you are planning to camp in the backcountry. A quarter of the places are offered on a first-come-first-served basis and, provided you are fairly flexible, you should be able to land something by turning up at the ranger station nearest to your proposed trailhead from 1pm on the day before you wish to start. Details for advance **wilderness permits** are given at ⓦwww.nps.gov/seki/planyourvisit/wilderness.htm, where you can download an application form. There is a one-off **wilderness camping fee** ($15 per group per trip), which entitles you to camp in the backcountry, preferably at an already impacted site. Reservations are accepted after March 1 and at least two weeks before your start date, and outside the quota period permits can be self-issued at trailheads. Park visitor centres sell an excellent 1:80,000 scale Trails Illustrated **topographical map** of the parks (#205; $12).

Remember that this is **bear country**: read the box on p.344. Bear canisters can be rented ($5 per trip) at Mineral King, Foothills, Lodgepole, Grant Grove and Cedar Grove, and bought ($66) at the Lodgepole store and most visitor centres.

From Mineral King

Eagle Lake Trail (7 miles round-trip; 4–6hr; 2200-foot ascent) Starting from the parking area a mile beyond the ranger station, this trail begins gently but gets tougher towards the lovely Eagle Lake. Highlights include the Eagle Sink Hole (where the river vanishes) and some fantastic views.

Mosquito Lakes No. 1 Trail (7 miles round-trip; 4–5hr; 1150-foot ascent) Follows the first half of the Eagle Lake Trail, then branches left to the lowest of the Mosquito Lakes at 9000ft.

Paradise Peak via Paradise Ridge Trail (9 miles round-trip; 9hr; 2800-foot ascent) Superb walk starting opposite the *Atwell Mill* campground and climbing steeply to Paradise Ridge, which affords views of Moro Rock. From there it's a fairly flat stroll to Paradise Peak (9300ft).

From Giant Forest, Wolverton and Lodgepole

Alta Peak and Alta Meadows Trail (14 miles round-trip; 8–10hr; 4000-foot ascent) Starting at the Wolverton trailhead, this strenuous but rewarding hike rises 4000ft

Grant Grove is home to a couple of trees that rival the General Sherman for bulk, the **Robert E. Lee Tree** and the **General Grant Tree**. The General Grant is the world's second largest tree and was proclaimed as "The Nation's Christmas Tree" by President Coolidge in 1926. Every year, on the second Sunday in December, the people of the nearby town of Sanger hold a yuletide celebration with carols sung under its snow-weighted boughs. A half-mile trail calls at the **Fallen Monarch**, which you can walk through, and the **Gamlin Cabin**, where Israel and Thomas Gamlin lived while exploiting their timber claim until 1878. The massive stump of one of the trees' scalps remains after a slice was shipped to the 1876 Centennial Exhibition in Philadelphia – an attempt to convince cynical easterners that such enormous trees really existed.

Two miles south of Grant Grove, the **Big Stump Area** unsurprisingly gets its name from the gargantuan stumps that litter the place – remnants from early logging of sequoias carried out during the 1880s. An easy trail (one to two miles over seven miles. Initially following the Lakes Trail (see below), it eventually starts on a daunting near-vertical hike to the stunning Alta Peak.

Little Baldy Trail (3.5 miles round-trip; 2–3hr; 700-foot ascent) Starting from Little Baldy Saddle, six miles north of Lodgepole, this loop trail leads to a rocky summit with spectacular views.

Tokopah Falls Trail (3 miles round-trip; 2–3hr; 500-foot ascent) Fairly easy valley walk beside the Marble Fork of the Kaweah River and leading to impressive granite cliffs and the Tokopah Falls, which cascade into a cool pool, perfect for a bracing dip. Start at the eastern end of the *Lodgepole* campground.

The Watchtower and Lakes Trail (13 miles round-trip; 6–8hr; 2300-foot ascent) A popular if fatiguing trail leading up from the Wolverton trailhead to the Watchtower (3–5hr round-trip), an exposed tower of granite overlooking Tokapah Falls far below. From there the path leads past three lakes in increasingly gorgeous and stark glacial cirques. The two furthest lakes, Emerald Lake (9200ft) and Pear Lake (9500ft), have campgrounds that, for the adventurous and experienced, make good starting points for self-guided trekking into the mountains.

From Kings Canyon

Cedar Grove Overlook Trail (5 miles round-trip; 3–4hr; 1200-foot ascent) Starting half a mile north of Cedar Grove Village on Pack Station Road, this trail switch-backs steeply through forest and chaparral to a viewpoint overlooking Kings Canyon.

Don Cecil Trail to Lookout Peak (13 miles round-trip; 7–9hr; 4000-foot ascent) Starting 400yd east of Cedar Grove Village, a strenuous trail that largely follows the pre-highway route into Kings Canyon. After two miles you reach the shady glen of Sheep Creek Cascade before pressing on up the canyon to the wonderfully panoramic summit.

Mist Falls Trail (9 miles round-trip; 3–5hr; 600-foot ascent). This easy, sandy trail starts from Road's End, eventually climbing steeply past numerous thundering cataracts to Mist Falls, one of the largest waterfalls in the twin parks.

Rae Lakes Loop (4–5 days round-trip) One of the best of the multiday hikes in these parts, following the Kings River up past Mist Falls and beyond, through Paradise Valley and Castle Domes Meadow to Woods Creek Crossing, where the route meets the John Muir Trail. It follows this for eight miles, passing Rae Lakes before returning to Kings Canyon along Bubbs Creek and the South Fork of the Kings River.

depending on how many sad stumps you can bear to see) leads through this scene of devastation to the **Mark Twain Stump**, the headstone of another monster killed to impress.

About eight miles north of Grant Grove, a minor road spurs off three miles to **Hume Lake**, actually a reservoir built in 1908 to provide water for logging flumes. Handily placed for local hiking trails, it's also a delightful spot to swim or launch your canoe and makes a good place to spend a night beside the lake at the comparatively large *Hume Lake* **campground** (see p.326). At the head of the lake, the facilities of the *Hume Lake Christian Camp* provide expensive gas, groceries, an ATM and a coffee shop.

Kings Canyon Highway

From Grant Grove, Hwy-180 heads into **Kings Canyon**, which some measurements make the deepest canyon in the US, at some 7900ft. Whatever the facts, its walls of granite and gleaming blue marble, and the white pockmarks of spectacularly blooming yucca plants (particularly in May and early June), are visually stunning. A vast area of the wilderness beyond is drained by the South Fork of the Kings River, a raging torrent during the springtime snowmelt spate, and perilous for wading at any time: people have been swept away even when paddling close to the bank in a seemingly placid section.

Consider a side trip past the sequoia graveyard of **Stump Meadow** to a trailhead for the **Boole Tree**, the world's fattest sequoia and one that towers above the forest where all other sequoias were felled. The loggers apparently appreciated its girth and spared it. It's seldom visited, perhaps on account of its position on a two-mile loop trail: take the gentler left-hand trail and you'll be there in around half an hour.

Near the foot of the canyon, the road passes the less compelling of the region's two show caves, the **Boyden Cavern** (45-minute tours on the hour daily: June–Aug 10am–5pm; late April to May & Sept to early Nov 11am–4pm; $13; ⓦwww.boydencavern.com), whose interior has a number of bizarre formations growing out of the 40,000-year-old rock, their impact intensified by the cave's cool, still interior.

Cedar Grove

Past Boyden Cavern, Kings Canyon sheds its V-shape and gains a floor. Among incense cedars at an altitude of 4600ft is **Cedar Grove**, the area's only settlement, comprising a lodge (see p.327), several campgrounds, a **visitor centre** (mid-May to early Sept daily 9am–5pm; ☏559/565-3793), a food store and a **snack bar** that serves barely adequate self-serve meals with paper plates. It is open for standard egg and pancake breakfasts (7–10.30am), burger and sandwich lunches (11am–2pm), plus a handful of steak and chicken dinners for around $15–20 (5–8pm).

Three miles east are the **Roaring River Falls** which, when in spate, undoubtedly merit their name. Apart from the obvious appeal of the scenery, the main things to see around here are the birdlife and **flowers** – leopard lilies, shooting stars, violets, Indian paintbrush, lupines and others – best seen on the **nature trail** around the edge of **Zumwalt Meadow** (1.5 miles; 1–2hr; flat; $1.50 trail booklet available in the parking lot). The meadow boasts a collection of big-leaf maple, cat's-tails and creek dogwood, and there's often a chance for an eyeful of animal life.

Just a mile further, Kings Canyon Road comes to an end at **Road's End**, from where a network of hiking trails penetrates the multitude of canyons and peaks that constitute the Kings River Sierra. Almost all are best enjoyed with a tent and some provisions. To obtain **wilderness permits** in this area, call at the Road's End Wilderness Permit Station (June to mid-Sept daily 7am–3pm) at the end of Hwy-180. The less ambitious only need to venture a hundred yards riverward to **Muir Rock** to see where John Muir (see box, p.340) conducted early meetings of the Sierra Club.

Listings

Banks There are no banks in either park, but credit cards and travellers' cheques are widely accepted. Lodgepole, Stony Creek, Grant Grove and Cedar Grove have ATMs.

Cycling Bikes are not permitted on trails within the parks, limiting you to park roads, many of which are very steep and have limited space for passing. A better bet is the network of trails in the surrounding national forest.

Gas There's no gas available in the parks, so drivers should fill up in Visalia or Fresno, or with slightly pricier stuff at Three Rivers. In desperation, you can get expensive gas at Stony Creek Village, the *Hume Lake Christian Camp* (see p.333) and at

Kings Canyon Lodge on Hwy-180, which claims to have the oldest pair of gravity-fed pumps in the country, dating back to the 1920s.

Horseriding Stables and pack stations exist in three locations throughout the national parks and surrounding forest, mostly open from mid- or late May to early September: the Horse Corral between Lodgepole and Grant Grove (☎ 559/565-3404, ⓦ www.horsecorralpackers.com), Grant Grove (☎ 559/335-9292) and Cedar Grove (☎ 559/565-3464). All offer anything from an hour in the saddle ($40) to multiday backcountry excursions.

Internet access There's free wi-fi at the restaurant in Grant Grove, at *Wuksachi Lodge* and at *We Three Bakery* in Three Rivers. Otherwise head for Three Rivers Library, 42052 Eggers Drive (Wed & Fri 10am–1pm & 2–6pm, Thurs noon–5pm & 6–8pm), five miles south of the park entrance.

Laundry Lodgepole, Cedar Grove Village and Stony Creek have coin-operated laundries open daily 8am–8pm in summer.

Phones There are public phones where people congregate. Mobile-phone coverage is patchy at best.

Post offices At Lodgepole (Mon–Fri 8am–1pm & 2–4pm) and at Grant Grove (Mon–Fri 9am–3.30pm, Sat 10–noon).

Rafting From mid-April to the end of June, Three Rivers-based Kaweah Whitewater Adventures (☎ 1-800/229-8658, ⓦ www.kaweah-whitewater .com) runs a series of rafting trips on the Kaweah River between Three Rivers and Lake Kaweah. Trips range from a relatively gentle two hours ($50) to serious Class IV full-day trips ($140).

Showers There are showers at Lodgepole (summer daily 8am–1pm & 3–8pm; coin-op, 12 quarters for 10min), Stony Creek (mid-May to Sept daily 8am–7.30pm; $4 token for 10min), Grant Grove Village (all year daily 11am–4pm; 4 quarters for 3min) and Cedar Grove Village (summer daily 7am–1pm & 3–7pm; $3.50 for 10min).

The Sierra National Forest

If you fancy exploring some gorgeous granite and cedar country without the clamour of the national parks to the north and south head straight for the **SIERRA NATIONAL FOREST**, a gaping tract of land between Kings Canyon and Yosemite. It's far less well known than Yosemite, Sequoia or Kings Canyon and lacks the environmental protection given to the parks – many of the rivers have been **dammed** as part of the "Big Creek" project that helped make the San Joaquin the agricultural heart of California. With only modest hyperbole, the Sierra meltwater in these parts is touted as "the hardest-working water in the world".

Much of the forest has been developed into resort areas that are better for fishing and boating than hiking. Residents of the San Joaquin Valley stream up here throughout the summer for weekend getaways. That said, there are any number of remote corners to explore, not least the rugged, unspoilt terrain of the vast **John Muir Wilderness** and the neighbouring **Ansel Adams Wilderness**, which contain some of the starkest peaks and lushest alpine meadows of the High Sierra. If you want to discover complete solitude and hike and camp in isolation, this is the place to do it, though you'll need a vehicle: public transport is virtually nonexistent. We haven't highlighted any walks in this area: there are hundreds of them and any of the **ranger stations** can suggest suitable hikes, supply free permits (necessary for any overnight hikes into most of the forest) and sell you the detailed *Sierra National Forest Map* ($10), useful even if you are only driving.

Mono Hot Springs and the John Muir Wilderness

A forty-mile drive from Fresno along Hwy-168 through a parched and knobbly landscape dotted with blue, live and scrub oak soon brings you to the Pineridge District, the best place for adventurous hiking. Around **Kaiser Pass**, which scrapes 9200ft, you'll find isolated alpine landscapes served by decent campgrounds, a couple of minor resorts and even some relaxing **hot springs**.

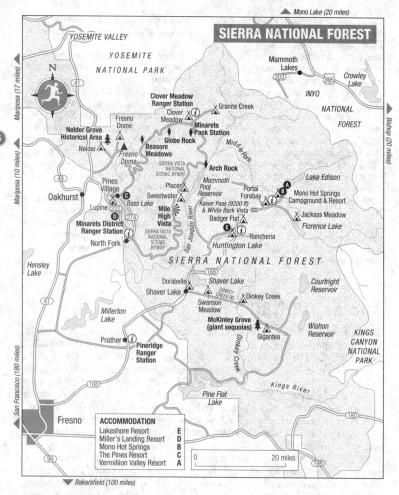

▲ Mono Lake (20 miles)

SIERRA NATIONAL FOREST

YOSEMITE VALLEY

YOSEMITE
NATIONAL PARK

Mammoth
Lakes

INYO

Crowley
Lake

NATIONAL

FOREST

Clover Meadow
Ranger Station

x Granite Creek

Clover
Meadow

Fresno
Dome

**Nelder Grove
Historical Area**

**Minarets
Pack Station**

Globe Rock

Nelder

Beasore
Meadows

Fresno
Dome

SIERRA VISTA
NATIONAL
SCENIC BYWAY

Arch Rock

Mammoth
Pool
Reservoir

Portal
Forebay

Lake Edison

A

B

Mono Hot Springs
Campground & Resort

Placer

Pines
Village

Oakhurst

Sweetwater

C

Bass Lake

**Mile
High
Vista**

Lupine

**Minarets District
Ranger Station**

D

North Fork

Kaiser Pass (9200 ft)
& White Bark Vista

Badger Flat

E

Jackass Meadow

Florence Lake

Rancheria

Huntington Lake

SIERRA
VISTA
NATIONAL
SCENIC
BYWAY

S I E R R A   N A T I O N A L   F O R E S T

Hensley
Lake

Mariposa (17 miles) ◄

Mariposa (10 miles) ◄

San Francisco (180 miles) ◄

Bishop (20 miles) ►

Dorabelle

Shaver Lake

Shaver Lake

DINKEY
CREEK RD

x Dinkey Creek

Courtright
Reservoir

Millerton
Lake

Prather

**Pineridge
Ranger
Station**

Swanson
Meadow

**McKinley Grove
(giant sequoias)**

Gigantea

Wishon
Reservoir

KINGS
CANYON
NATIONAL
PARK

Kings River

Fresno

Pine Flat
Lake

ACCOMMODATION

Lakeshore Resort	**E**
Miller's Landing Resort	**D**
Mono Hot Springs	**B**
The Pines Resort	**C**
Vermillion Valley Resort	**A**

0   20 miles

▼ Bakersfield (100 miles)

Hwy-168 penetrates seventy miles into the forest among the snow-capped peaks of the **JOHN MUIR WILDERNESS**. It's a drive of at least four hours, even in good weather – and this is an area prone to bad weather and road closure. The best source of information is the **High Sierra Ranger District** office (April–Nov daily 8am–4.30pm; Dec–March Mon–Fri 8am–4.30pm; ☏559/855-5355), located along Hwy-168 at Prather, five miles west of the forest entrance. There are also ranger stations near Rancheria Falls and Mono Hot Springs (see opposite).

From the ranger station, the good and fast Hwy-168 climbs rapidly over eighteen miles to **Shaver Lake**, a mile-high, pine-girt community, where half of Fresno comes to fish and jet-ski. Grab an espresso and breakfast with free wi-fi at *Bob's Blue Sky Café*, 41781 Hwy-168, stock up with supplies and keep going

Many campgrounds in the Sierra National Forest can be booked between Memorial Day and Labor Day through ⊛www.recreation.gov (☏1-877/444-6777).

twenty miles east to **Huntington Lake**, which feels more isolated. Just before the lake, the *Rancheria* campground (open all year; reservable; $20) marks the turn-off to **Rancheria Falls**. A side road, east off Hwy-168, leads a mile to the head of the mile-long **Rancheria Falls Trail** (350-foot ascent), which winds through broadleaf woods to the 150-foot falls. Continuing west around Huntington Lake, you soon hit the 1920s *Lakeshore Resort* (☎559/893-3193, ⓦwww.lakeshoreresort .com; RV parking $30; ③), with rustic, knotty pine **cabins**, most sleeping four or five. There's a great, woodsy **restaurant**, a lively log-built saloon, a gas station, post office and general store all a few yards from the lake, and from here on the lakeshore is almost entirely taken up by $20-a-night campsites.

Beyond Kaiser Pass: Mono Hot Springs and around

Just after Rancheria Falls, Hwy-162 veers off over Kaiser Pass (open June–Oct only) on a rapidly deteriorating road up to 9200ft and passing the *Badger Flat* campground ($18; no water) along the way. Over the pass is a vast basin, draining the south fork of the San Joaquin River. The lumpy single-lane road drops past the beautiful *Portal Forebay* campground ($16; lake water) to a fork in the road: north to Lake Edison, its approach marred by a huge earth dam, and west to Florence Lake.

Mono Hot Springs, two miles north of the junction on the road to Lake Edison, is the best thing about the region and a great place to relax and clean up after hikes. For the full hot-springs experience, head for the 🍴 *Mono Hot Springs Resort* (mid-May to Oct; ☎559/325-1710, ⓦwww.monohotsprings.com; cabins ②–④), where all cabin prices include free use of the therapeutic mineral pools and spa. Right on the banks of the San Joaquin River, the resort is a modest affair with individual mineral baths ($6 for non-guests; $10 for an all-day pass), showers ($5) and massages ($40 per half-hour). Outside, there's a chlorinated spa filled with spring water, costing $6 for an all-day pass. Accommodation ranges from simple cabins with communal ablutions and no linen to more commodious affairs with toilets and kitchen. Typically there's a three-night minimum but you may be able to slot into a shorter gap, especially at either end of the season.

The resort also has a small lunch-and-dinner restaurant, a limited general store, the *Mono Hot Springs* campground (early June to late Sept; ⓦwww.recreation .gov; $18) and a post office used for mail and food pickups by hikers on the nearby John Muir and Pacific Crest trails (the latter being an epic, 2650-mile trek from the Mexican border to the Canadian frontier, typically taking around five months). Across the river, follow a track 220yd downstream to a pair of five-foot-deep concrete **bathing tanks** (unrestricted access) that are perfect for soaking your bones while stargazing. This is just one of many pools on this side of the river; ask around.

Beyond Mono Hot Springs the wonderfully scenic road continues to **Lake Edison** and the *Vermillion Valley Resort* (☎559/259-4000, ⓦwww.edisonlake.com; tent cabins ①, motel units ③), mainly geared towards boaters and anglers but also useful for entry into the John Muir Wilderness, easily accessed by a small **ferry** across the lake (June–Sept twice daily; $10 each way).

Florence Lake is more immediately appealing than Lake Edison: there's a greater sense of being hemmed in by mountains, and it's reached through an unearthly landscape of wrinkled granite shattered over the centuries by contorted junipers. There's a small store, the *Jackass Meadow* campground (June–Sept; reservable; $18), located unnervingly below the dam, and another ferry across the lake (late May to late Sept; 5 daily; $11 each way; ⓦwww.florence-lake.com) which opens up multi-day hikes along the John Muir and Pacific Crest trails, and to the northern end of Kings Canyon National Park. If you can't face being totally self-sufficient, you can sometimes stay at the *Muir Trail Ranch* (June–Sept only; ☎209/966-3195, Ⓦwww.muirtrailranch.com), a cabin and tent retreat with hot pools and horses located in magical scenery four miles beyond the far end of Florence Lake. When not taken over by groups, it is open for short stays (usually the first three weeks in June and the last week in Sept) at $140 per person per night for tent cabin, breakfast, packed lunch, and dinner, but not including horses, charged at $60 per half-day. Access is by the cross-lake ferry, and then you either hike or arrange to be met with a horse.

⑤ Bass Lake

The northern reaches of the Sierra National Forest are most easily reached from **Oakhurst** (see p.345), the centre of the Mariposa District and just seven miles west of the biggest tourist attraction in the area – the pine-fringed **Bass Lake**. A stomping ground of Hell's Angels in the 1960s – the leather and licentiousness memorably described in Hunter S. Thompson's *Hell's Angels* – Bass Lake is nowadays a family resort, crowded with boaters and anglers in summer. For detailed campground and hiking information, consult the Bass Lake Ranger District office (see below).

Road 222 runs right around the lake, though not always within sight of it. At the main settlement, **Pines Village**, you can buy groceries, eat well and **spend the night** at the swanky *Pines Resort* (☎1-800/350-7463, Ⓦwww.basslake.com; ◐) in luxurious two-storey chalets with kitchens or even more palatial lakeside suites. By the southwestern tip of the lake, *Miller's Landing Resort*, 37976 Road 222 (☎1-866/657-4386, Ⓦwww.millerslanding.com; ◐), offers deluxe cabins sleeping six or more. *Miller's Landing* is also the best place to rent aquatic equipment – including fishing boats ($70 for 6hr) and jet skis ($100 an hour) – and they have public showers ($3) and laundry.

The western side of Bass Lake is slung with $25-a-night family **campgrounds**, most oriented towards long stays beside your camper. In summer, book well in advance (see box, p.336), though no-shows are sometimes available at the Bass Lake Recreation Area office, 39900 Road 222, on the southwest side of the lake (late May to early Sept daily 8am–6pm; ☎559/642-3212). For tent campers, the best site is *Lupine* ($25), just north of Miller's Landing.

Sierra Vista Scenic Byway

If Bass Lake is too commercial and overcrowded for you, the antidote starts immediately to the north. The peaceful **SIERRA VISTA SCENIC BYWAY** makes a ninety-mile circuit east of Hwy-41 accessing several basic campgrounds and trailheads for the magnificent **Ansel Adams Wilderness**. A straight circuit (snow-free July–Oct) takes five hours, and is especially slow going on the rough dirt roads of the north side. Stock up on supplies before you start: there are a couple of stores and gas stations dotted along the way, but they're not cheap and the range is limited. Accommodation on the circuit is largely limited to campgrounds, all (except three free sites) costing $16.

The best source of information on the circuit is the **Bass Lake Ranger District** office (Mon–Fri 8am–4.30pm; ☎559/877-2218), in the hamlet of North Fork at the southern end of Bass Lake, where you can pick up a **map** – important, as there are numerous confusing forestry roads and few signposts. Tackle the route in the direction described as route-finding is easier.

Before setting off, consider a **meal** at *La Cabaña*, 32762 Road 222 in North Fork (closed Sun & Mon), a nondescript shack serving excellent and authentic Mexican dishes and burgers, most for under $8.

The south side

Before setting out from North Fork, check out the **Sierra Mono Indian Museum** (Mon–Fri 10am–3pm; $5), with some good examples of local Native American basketry and beadwork, as well as a lot of stuffed animals in glass cases. Once on your way, the first point of interest is the **Jesse Ross Cabin**, fifteen miles along, an 1860s hewn-log original that has been restored and brought to the site, and left open so you can poke around inside. Ten miles later, **Mile High Vista** reveals endless views of muscle-bound mountain ranges and bursting granite domes stretching back to Mammoth Mountain (see p.292). Further on, an eight-mile side road cuts south to the dammed **Mammoth Pool**, where anglers boat on the lake and smoke their catch at one of the four lake- and streamside **campgrounds** (all $17).

Back on the Scenic Byway, you'll pass the rather disappointing **Arch Rock**, where the earth under a slab of granite has been undermined to leave a kind of bridge, and continue climbing to the *Minarets Pack Station* (mid-June to Sept; ☏559/868-3405, ⊛www.highsierrapackers.org/min.htm). Apart from a general store and reasonable meals, the station offers simple lodging ($13 a night) and **horseback trips** from $60. It's a great base for wilderness trips, many of which start by the **Clover Meadow Wilderness Ranger Station**, a couple of miles up a spur road (late June to mid-Sept daily 9am–5pm; permits available). Nearby are two wonderful free campgrounds, *Clover Meadow* and *Granite Creek*, both at 7000ft, the former with potable water.

The north side

The *Minarets Pack Station* marks the start of the descent from the backcountry and the end of the asphalt; for the next few miles you're on rough dirt, generally navigable in ordinary passenger vehicles when clear of snow. The hulking form of **Globe Rock** heralds the return to asphalt, which runs down to **Beasore Meadow**, where **Jones Store** (open mid-June to mid-Oct) has supplied groceries, gas and basic meals (8am–8pm) for the best part of a century, and offers showers to hikers. A short distance further on you reach Cold Springs Meadow, the junction with Sky Ranch Road (follow it left to continue the loop) and a spur to the wonderful *Fresno Dome* campground ($17; no water; 6400ft), a great base for a moderately strenuous walk to the top of the exfoliated granite namesake.

The Scenic Byway then passes several $16 campgrounds, most without running water, en route to the **Nelder Grove Historical Area** (unrestricted entry), a couple of miles north along a dirt road. Over a hundred giant sequoias are scattered through the forest here, though the overall impression is of devastation evidenced by the number of enormous stumps among the second-growth sugar pine, white fir and cedar. The mile-long "Shadow of the Giants" interpretive walk explains the logging activities that took place here in the 1880s and early 1890s and, with its low visitor count, offers a more serene communion with these majestic trees than in Yosemite. A second interpretive trail leads from the nearby wooded *Nelder Grove* campground (free; stream water; 3500ft) to **Bull Buck Tree**, which, with its base circumference of 99ft, was once a serious contender for the world's largest tree. Though slimmer in the base, Sequoia National Park's General Sherman Tree is taller and broader at the top and so takes the prize. From here it's seven twisting miles back to Hwy-41, reached at a point around four miles north of Oakhurst.

Yosemite National Park

No temple made with hands can compare with the Yosemite. Every rock in its walls seems to glow with life. Some lean back in majestic repose; others, absolutely sheer or nearly so for thousands of feet, advance beyond their companions in thoughtful attitudes, giving welcome to storms and calms alike, seemingly aware, yet heedless, of everything going on about them.

John Muir, *The Yosemite*

More gushing adjectives have been thrown at **YOSEMITE NATIONAL PARK** than at any other part of California. But however excessive the hyperbole may seem, once you enter the park and turn the corner that reveals Yosemite Valley – only a small part of the park but the one at which most of the verbiage is aimed – you realize it's actually an understatement. For many, **Yosemite Valley** is the single most dramatic piece of geology to be found anywhere in the world. Just seven miles long and one mile across at its widest point, the Valley is walled by nearly vertical, three-thousand-foot cliffs whose sides are streaked by cascading waterfalls and whose tops, a variety of domes and pinnacles, form a jagged silhouette against the sky. At ground level, too, the sights can be staggeringly impressive. Grassy meadows are framed by oak, cedar, maple and fir trees, with a variety of wildflowers and animals in attendance – deer, coyotes and even black

John Muir and the Sierra Club

John Muir was one of nature's most eloquent advocates, a champion of all things wild who spent ten years living in Yosemite Valley in the 1870s, and the rest of his life campaigning for its preservation. Born in Scotland in 1838, he grew up in Wisconsin, became a mechanical inventor and embarked on his first journey at the age of 27, noting in his diary, "All drawbacks overcome… joyful and free… I chose to become a tramp." After walking a thousand miles to Florida with little more than a volume of Keats' poems and a plant press for company, he ended up in California in 1868 and asked for "anywhere that is wild". Working in Yosemite Valley as a sheepherder, mill worker and hotel clerk, he spent every waking moment exploring the mountains and waterfalls, travelling light and usually going to sleep hungry under the stars.

He dubbed the Sierra Nevada the "**Range of Light**", and spent years developing his theory of how glaciers shaped the range. His articles gradually won him academic acceptance, and the general public was soon devouring his journal-based books, such as *My First Summer in the Sierra* and *The Yosemite*, which became classics.

Muir was desperate to protect his beloved landscape from the depredations of sheep grazing, timber cutting and homesteading, and through magazine articles and influential contacts goaded Congress into creating Yosemite National Park in 1890. Two years later, he set up the **Sierra Club**, an organization whose motto "Take only photographs; leave only footprints" has become a model for like-minded groups around the world. Despite his successes, in 1913 Muir failed to save the Hetch Hetchy Valley from being dammed (see p.355), a blow that undoubtedly hastened his death a year later.

The publicity Muir generated actually aided the formation of the present **National Park Service** in 1916, which promised – and has since provided – greater protection for Yosemite. This inspirational man is honoured in place-names throughout California, not least in the 211-mile John Muir Trail, which twists through his favourite scenery from Yosemite Valley south to Mount Whitney.

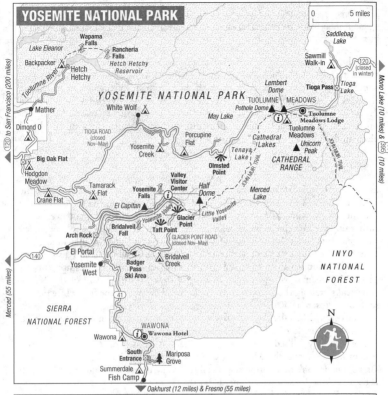

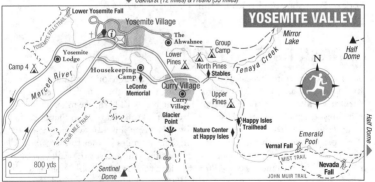

bears are not uncommon. As if that wasn't enough, in the southern reaches of the park near **Wawona**, sequoias grow almost as densely and to dimensions as vast as those in Sequoia National Park.

Understandably, you're not the first to appreciate Yosemite's appeal. Each year Yosemite has to cope with almost four million visitors, and if you're looking for peace it's advisable to avoid Yosemite Valley and Wawona on weekends and holidays. That said, the whole park is diverse and massive enough

Yosemite National Park is covered in further detail – along with the fifty best hikes – in the **Rough Guide to Yosemite, Sequoia and Kings Canyon**.

to endure the crowds: you can visit at any time of year, even in winter when the waterfalls turn to ice and the trails are blocked by snow, and out of high summer even the valley itself resists getting crammed. Further-flung reaches of the park, especially around the crisp alpine **Tuolumne Meadows** (pronounced "too-OL-uh-mee") and the completely wild backcountry beyond them, are much less busy all year round, providing just about the most peaceful and elemental settings you could imagine.

Some history

Yosemite Valley was created over thousands of years by glaciers gouging through and enlarging the canyon of the Merced River; the ice scraped away much of the softer portions of granite but only scarred the harder sections, which became the present cliffs. As the glaciers melted a lake formed, filling the valley and eventually silting up to create the present valley floor. The **Awahneechee** people occupied the area quite peaceably for some four thousand years until the mid-nineteenth century, when the increasingly threatening presence of white Gold Rush settlers in the San Joaquin Valley provoked the tribes to raid the nearest encampments. In 1851, Major James Savage led the **Mariposa Battalion** in pursuit of the Native Americans, trailing them beyond the foothills and becoming the first white men to set foot in Yosemite Valley. It wasn't long before the two groups clashed properly, and the original population was moved out to make way for farmers, foresters and, soon after, tourists (the first group of sightseers arrived in 1855). Appreciative visitors quickly rallied to conserve the natural beauty of the area: in 1864 Yosemite Valley and the Mariposa Grove were preserved as the Yosemite Land Grant, the nation's first region specifically set aside to protect wilderness. In 1890 it became America's third national park, thanks in great part to the campaigning work of Scottish naturalist **John Muir** (see box, p.340).

Approaching Yosemite

Getting to Yosemite by car is straightforward, though on summer weekends parking can be a problem. Three roads from the San Joaquin Valley end up at **Yosemite Valley**, roughly in the centre of the park's 1200 square miles and home to its most dramatic scenery: Hwy-120 from Stockton and the San Francisco Bay Area; Hwy-140 from Merced; and Hwy-41 from Fresno, which passes the **Mariposa Grove** and **Wawona**, from where it's 27 miles further to the valley. All these roads are generally kept open throughout the year as far as the valley, though in extreme circumstances Hwy-120 is the first to close. The only road into the eastern side of the park is Hwy-120, the 10,000-foot Tioga Road, which branches off US-395 close to Lee Vining – though this is usually closed from late October to early June and in bad weather.

In an effort to encourage visitors to arrive by **public transport**, the Park Service and local authorities maintain the YARTS bus system (☎1-877/989-2787, ⓦwww.yarts.com), running a useful service along Hwy-140 from Merced (see p.319), which has Amtrak and Greyhound connections. There are four departures daily picking up at both the Merced Transpo Center and the Amtrak station and arriving (after brief stops en route at all towns and significant accommodation) in the valley almost three hours later. A couple more services run into the valley from Mariposa along the same route and there's a limited summer service from Mammoth Lakes (see p.289) and Lee Vining over Tioga Pass and through Tuolumne Meadows to Yosemite Valley. **Timetables** are available on the YARTS website and from visitor centres in the area. **Tickets** can be bought on board, and the round-trip **fare** (which includes the park entrance fee) to Yosemite from Merced is $25, from Mariposa and Midpines $12 and from El Portal just $7.

Tours to Yosemite

Generally speaking, anything called a **sightseeing tour** that begins outside the park will take you on an unsatisfying race through the valley. An alternative to this trend is **Yosemite Bug Bus Tours** (℡1-866/826-7108, ⓦwww.yosemitebugbus .com), which offers a range of trips, usually with accommodation and meals just outside the park at the *Yosemite Bug* (see p.349). The most frequent trip is the Two-Day-Two-Night Tour (all-year Mon, Wed & Fri; dorm $245, en-suite room $590 for two) starting in San Francisco and spending both nights at the *Bug*. Visits to Mariposa Grove, Sentinel Dome, Yosemite Valley and the Mist Trail are supplemented by swimming, meals and campfires at the *Bug*. For something more adventurous, go for the Bug-based two-day Yosemite Backcountry Backpacking trips (June–Sept; $245–400), which involve exploring the high country and camping out in spectacular locations: see the website for details.

San Francisco-based tours in converted "communal" buses are run by **Green Tortoise** (℡1-800/867-8647, ⓦwww.greentortoise.com). These are geared towards active, outdoorsy types who enjoy camping out and pitching in. Their weekend trip (March–Sept; departs 9pm Fri returns 7am Mon; $141 plus $45 food fund) heads to the valley and the Mariposa Grove; a three-day trip (June–Sept; Mon evening departures; $209 plus $61 food fund) also allows half a day in Tuolumne Meadows and time around nearby Mono Lake. **Incredible Adventures** (℡1-800/777-8464, ⓦwww.incadventures.com), likewise San Francisco-based, offers another line of enjoyable minibus tours. The one-day trip ($149) includes a quick jaunt around the main Yosemite Valley sights and three hours to explore and hike. The more satisfying three-day-two-night camping tour ($240) includes high-country hiking around Tuolumne and visiting the sequoias.

The gateway towns

The heavy demand for accommodation within the park drives many to consider staying in one of the small, mostly former gold-mining towns along the main access roads. These are increasingly gearing themselves to park-bound tourists and do a reasonable job offering both lodging and food, though they are a poor substitute for actually staying in the park.

Approaching from the east: Lee Vining

From sometime around late May or early June until late October you can approach Yosemite from the east over the 10,000-foot Tioga Pass from US-395 and the town of **Lee Vining** (see p.298). You're almost two hours' drive from the Yosemite Valley heartland, but this area provides unparalleled access to the Tuolumne Meadows high country. Unless you want to stay in Lee Vining, or at the lodge or campground in Tuolumne Meadows (see p.348 & p.351 respectively), your best bet is to **camp** just outside the park at the *Sawmill Walk-in* campground or at *Lee Vining Creek* (see p.351).

Approaching from the west: Groveland and Mariposa

Better bets for bases outside of the park are the western towns, particularly tiny **Groveland**, forty miles from the valley on Hwy-120, which retains wooden sidewalks with verandas, exudes a liberal air and has several good places to stay (see p.348) and eat (see p.360). Stop in at the Mountain Sage shop, 18653 Hwy-120 (ⓦwww.mtnsage.com), for an espresso while you browse their fine stock of fair-trade crafts and natural history books plus an excellent photo gallery.

Further south, Hwy-140 runs through the bustling Gold Rush town of **Mariposa**, 45 miles from the valley, which boasts the oldest law-enforcement establishment west of the Mississippi still in continuous use: the **Mariposa County Courthouse**, on Jones Street at Tenth Street. Built without nails, the lumber was rough-cut from a nearby stand of white pine, and you can still see the saw marks on the hand-planed spectator benches. During business hours (Mon–Fri 8am–5pm) you can sit in during proceedings. The convicted were often sent down the street to the **Historic 1858 Jail**, corner of Bullion and Fifth streets, which may be open for informal tours of the austere interior: ask around.

The town's heritage is further celebrated at the **Museum and History Center**, on Jesse Street at 12th Street (daily 10am–4pm; $4; ☏209/966-2924, ⓦwww .mariposamuseum.com), mildly diverting for its mock-up of a Gold Rush-era store and the large-scale mining paraphernalia scattered outside. In truth, you're better off at the **California State Mining and Mineral Museum**, two miles south on Hwy-49 (Thurs–Sun: May–Sept 10am–5pm; Oct–April 10am–4pm; $4; ☏209/742-7625, ⓦwww.parks.ca.gov), which revels in the glory days of the mid-nineteenth century with realistic reconstructions of a mine and stamp mill plus a vault where, among the assorted treasures, lies the largest existing crystalline gold nugget uncovered in California, a thirteen-pound chunk valued at over $1 million.

You'll find all you need to know about Yosemite and its surroundings at the very helpful **Mariposa County Visitor Center**, 5158 Hwy-140 (daily: mid-May to mid-Oct 7am–8pm; mid-Oct to mid-May 8am–5pm; ☏209/966-7081, ⓦwww.mariposa.org). Free **internet access** is available at the library, beside the courthouse at Jones and Tenth streets (Mon & Sat 8.30am–4pm, Tues–Fri 8.30am–6pm).

Further east along Hwy-140, on the way to Yosemite, the small towns of **Midpines** and **El Portal** also offer affordable lodging outside of the park (see p.349).

Smarter than the average bear

Yosemite **bears** (see p.48 for more on these beasts) may not be smarter than their cousins outside the park, but their familiarity with humans makes them more determined to get a free meal. They're not deterred by tent walls or car doors, and safe **food storage** is now mandatory in the park. As they say, "a fed bear is a dead bear", so do them and yourself a favour by keeping all food and smelly items – deodorant, sunscreen, toothpaste – either inside your room or in the metal lockers at campgrounds, parking lots and trailheads. You can be fined up to $5000.

Out in the backcountry, campers must use portable plastic **bear canisters** to store food. Sows have taught their cubs to climb along slender branches, so the old method of hanging food in trees seldom works.

You are encouraged to **report bear-related problems** and sightings on ☏209/372-0322.

Approaching from the south: Oakhurst and Fish Camp

Yosemite visitors arriving from the south will come through **Oakhurst**, fifteen miles south of the southern park entrance, a small but booming sprawl of strip malls and sky-high signs for chain hotels and fast-food joints. Despite its lack of atmosphere, it makes a handy base for the southern section of the park and, with your own transport, day-trips into Yosemite Valley, fifty miles distant. The relocated buildings of the **Fresno Flats Historical Park**, almost a mile from the centre on Road 427 (unrestricted access), won't detain you for long, but armloads of information on Yosemite are available at the **Yosemite Sierra Visitors Bureau**, 41969 Hwy-41 (Mon–Sat 8.30am–5pm, Sun 9am–1pm; ☏559/683-4636, Ⓦwww.yosemite.travel).

The tiny huddle of hotels which makes up **Fish Camp** lies ten miles north of Oakhurst, handy for Wawona and the Mariposa Grove and good for keeping the kids quiet with the **Yosemite Mountain Sugar Pine Railroad**, 56001 Hwy-41 (mid-March to Oct 1–4 departures daily; $18; ☏559/683-7273, Ⓦwww.ymsprr.com), a two-mile track into the forest plied by an oil-burning steam locomotive that once carted hewn timber. In the height of summer, several trains run each day, giving you the option of spending some time at the picnic area in the woods at the far end.

Arrival and information

Yosemite National Park (general information ☏209/372-0200, Ⓦwww.nps.gov/yose) is always open: **park entry** costs $20 per vehicle including passengers, or $10 for each cyclist and hiker, and is valid for seven days. Pay at the ranger stations when you enter, or if they're closed, at the visitor centre in the valley or when you leave. To encourage use of public transport, bus passengers pay no entry fees.

On arrival at any of the park entrances, you'll be given an excellent map of the park, the glossy annual *Yosemite* booklet and the current *Yosemite Guide* listings paper, which comes out every few weeks and covers current events and the extensive range of (mostly free) ranger programmes. The **Valley Visitor Center** at **Yosemite Village** (daily: June–Sept 9am–7.30pm; Oct–May 9am–5pm or

---

Winter in Yosemite

From December to April, those prepared to cope with blocked roads – the Tioga Pass is always closed in winter – and below-freezing temperatures are amply rewarded at Yosemite; thick snow, frozen waterfalls and far fewer people make for almost unimaginable beauty and silence. **Accommodation** is cheaper at these times, too (check Ⓦwww.yosemitepark.com for special deals), and much easier to obtain, though weekends can still get pretty full. Many low-country **campgrounds** are open and restrictions on backcountry camping are eased – though you'll want a good sleeping bag and tent.

Much of Yosemite is fabulous **skiing** territory. Lessons, equipment rental, tows and 25 miles of groomed cross-country trails are available at the **Badger Pass Ski Area** (Ⓦwww.badgerpass.com) on the road to Glacier Point, accessible via the free bus from the valley. The overnight cross-country ski trips to Glacier Point ($350) are excellent. **Ice skating** is a popular pastime at the open-air Curry Village rink in Yosemite Valley (normally $8, plus $3 skate rental).

Be aware if driving into the park that **tire chains** are recommended from November to April and can be rented in towns approaching the park. Inside the park, they are only available for sale.

Rock climbing in Yosemite

Rock climbers around the world flock to Yosemite, drawn by the challenge of inching up 3000-foot walls of sheer granite that soar up towards the California sun. Acres of superb, clean rock, easily accessible world-class routes and reliable summer weather draw a vibrant climbing community bubbling over with campfire tales.

The best place to marvel at climbers' antics is from the roadside next to **El Cap Meadows**, always dotted with tourists training binoculars on the park's biggest slab of granite, **El Capitan**. The apparently featureless face hides hairline crack systems a thousand feet long and seemingly insurmountable overhangs whose scale is made apparent only by the flea-like figures of climbers.

The world's most famous climb, **The Nose**, traces a line up the prow of El Capitan. Climbers typically spend three to five nights on the route, but speed attempts have brought the record down to an astounding 2 hours, 43 minutes, 33 seconds. The **North American Wall** route lies to the right, passing directly through a massive stain on the rock that looks remarkably like a map of North America.

Some history

Technical rock climbing kicked off here in 1933, when four Bay Area climbers reached what is now known as the Lunch Ledge, 1000ft up Washington Column – the tower opposite Half Dome. With the aid of heavy steel **pitons** for driving into cracks, and equally weighty **karabiners** for attaching the ropes to the pitons, climbers began to knock off climbs such as the **Royal Arches** route, which weaves its way up the ledges and slabs behind *The Ahwahnee*.

After World War II, Swiss-born blacksmith **John Salathé** pushed standards to new levels by climbing **Lost Arrow Spire**, which rises to the right of Yosemite Falls and casts an afternoon shadow on the wall nearby. He even fashioned tough carbon-steel pitons from the axles of a Model A Ford.

For the next twenty years Salathé's mantle was assumed by classical purist **Royal Robbins** and goal-oriented **Warren Harding**. Little love was lost between them but when Robbins' team first scaled the face of **Half Dome** in 1957, Harding was on the summit to congratulate them. The climb ranked as the hardest in North America, and Yosemite became an international forcing ground for aid climbing. Now even the mighty El Cap seemed possible. **The Nose** refused to submit for seventeen months, even after Warren Harding used four massive pitons fashioned from stove legs scavenged from the Berkeley city dump and drove them into what are still known as the Stoveleg Cracks. Harding and two colleagues finally topped

6pm; ℡209/372-0299), supplies information and maps, including a topographic map ($12) essential for any adventurous hikes. The other main visitor centres are at **Tuolumne Meadows** (mid-June to Sept daily 9am–5pm or 6pm; ℡209/372-0263) and **Wawona** (mid-May to mid-Sept daily 8.30am–5pm; ℡209/375-9531). For **free** hiking permits and all the route-planning help you could ask for, visit the **Wilderness Center** (mid-May to June and early Sept to mid-Oct daily 8am–5pm; July to early Sept daily 8am–5pm; closed in winter; ℡209/372-0745) next door to the Valley Visitor Center.

Park transport

While having your own vehicle is a boon for exploring the wider park, traffic congestion spoils everyone's fun on the valley floor. If you're driving in just for the day, leave your vehicle in the day-use parking lots at Yosemite and Curry out in 1958 after a single thirteen-day push, the culmination of 47 days' work on the route.

The demands of ever harder climbs have pushed the development of an extensive **armoury** of bathooks, birdbeaks, bongs, bugaboos, circleheads, fifi hooks, lost arrows and RURPs, all employed either to grapple a ledge or wedge into cracks of different sizes. Climbers employ death-defying **pendulums**, and repeatedly sweep across the face to gain momentum until they can lunge out at a tiny flake or fingertip hold. They are forced to spend nights slung in a kind of lightweight camp bed known as a **portaledge** and haul food, gallons of water, sleeping bags, warm clothing and wet-weather gear. As Yosemite veteran John Long writes: "Climbing a wall can be a monumental pain in the ass. No one could pay you enough to do it. A thousand dollars would be too little by far. But you wouldn't sell the least of the memories for ten times that sum."

The 1960s became the **Golden Age** of climbing, when Yosemite Valley drew a motley collection of dropouts and misfits, many ranking among the world's finest climbers. Purists at the top of their sport became disenchanted with the artificiality of aid ascents and began to "free" pitches: not hauling up on all the hardware, but using it only for protection in case of a fall. The culmination of years of cutting-edge climbing and months of route-specific training was Lynn Hill's ground-breaking free ascent of The Nose in 1993, praised and admired by all, if ruefully by some in Yosemite's traditionally macho climbing community.

Practicalities

The **best months** for climbing in Yosemite Valley are April, May, September and October. In summer, the climbs on the domes around Tuolumne Meadows are cooler and usually considered a better bet. In the valley, everyone stays at the bohemian **Camp 4** (see p.350), where there's a great sense of camaraderie and an excellent **bulletin board** for teaming up with climbing partners, selling gear, organizing a ride or just meeting friends.

The best stock of climbing gear is the Mountain Shop in Curry Village (daily 8am–8pm), also home to the Yosemite Mountaineering School (℗209/372-8344, ⓦwww.yosemitemountaineering.com), which runs daily courses ranging from the one-day beginners' classes (from $120) through to various intermediate classes and private full-day guided climbs (one person $285, two people $210 each).

To catch something of the spirit of the scene, read *Camp 4: Recollections of a Yosemite Rockclimber* (The Mountaineers) by Steve Roper.

villages; you can then use the free and frequent **Yosemite Valley Shuttle Bus** that passes close to all the main points of interest, trailheads and accommodation areas. In high season, the service runs roughly every 10–20 minutes between 7am and 10pm to most sections of the valley, with slightly reduced hours at other times.

Although bicycles are not allowed off paved surfaces, **cycling** around the twelve miles of dedicated bike paths is an excellent way to get around the valley. *Yosemite Lodge* and *Curry Village* (April–Nov only) both rent city bikes for $9.50 per hour or $25.50 per day.

To stray further afield use the **hikers buses** (reservations ℗209/372-1240), which call at roadside trailheads on the way to Tuolumne Meadows and Glacier Point, and double as round-trip narrated tours for those on a tighter schedule. The **Tuolumne Meadows Tour and Hikers Bus** (mid-June to early Sept; $14.50 one way, $23 round-trip) makes a 2 hour 30 minutes run, leaving *Yosemite Lodge* at 8.20am and departing Tuolumne at 2pm, giving just over three hours at the meadows. The **Glacier Point Tour and Hikers Bus** (June–Oct

2–3 daily; $25 one way, $41 round-trip) runs up to Glacier Point, where it stays for around an hour.

There are always **guided tours** (☎209/372-1240, ⓦwww.yosemitepark.com), which range from the rather dull two-hour valley floor spin ($25), to the more satisfying all-day Mariposa and Glacier Point Grand Tour (June–Oct; $82); all are bookable through accommodation reception areas.

Accommodation

Once in the park, **accommodation** can be a problem; it's almost essential to book well in advance and anything other than camping can be expensive. Even canvas tents cost what you would pay for a reasonable motel elsewhere. All accommodation in the national park – the majority of it right in the valley – is operated by **DNC** (☎801/559-5000, ⓦwww.yosemitepark.com) and should be booked a few weeks ahead, even earlier for holiday weekends. Places generally reduce their rates in winter, though weekend prices remain close to high-season levels. One solution to the problem is to stay just outside the park (see below) and commute into it daily.

In the valley

The Ahwahnee A short distance from Yosemite Village at shuttle stop 3 (call DNC). Undoubtedly the finest place to stay in Yosemite, with rooms decorated in the hotel's Native American motif. Usually booked months in advance despite room rates starting close to $450, but worth visiting to view the wonderfully grand public areas, or for a drink or a meal. ❾

Curry Village A mile from Yosemite Village at shuttle stops 13b and 20 (call DNC). A large family-oriented area dotted mostly with canvas tent cabins fitted with beds on a wooden plinth. There are also cramped solid-walled cabins with their own bathroom and a few spacious motel-style rooms. Rooms ❻, cabins ❶–❹

Housekeeping Camp Half a mile from Yosemite Village at shuttle stop 12 (call DNC). Ranks of simple concrete-walled plastic-roofed cabins with beds on sleeping platforms and the use of a fire grate and picnic table. April to mid-Oct only. ❸

Yosemite Lodge Half a mile west of Yosemite Village at shuttle stop 8 (call DNC). Sprawling middle-market accommodation popular with tour groups, its proximity to restaurants, grocery stores and a pool making it perhaps the most convenient choice in the valley. Rooms are motel-style, all with private bath, TV and phone, but no a/c. ❼

Outside the valley

Tuolumne Meadows Lodge Tuolumne Meadows (call DNC). Seventy canvas tent cabins, each with four beds and a wood-burning stove but no electricity, located at nearly 9000ft and perfect for

the first or last night of a long hiking trip. Open July to mid-Sept only; meals and showers available. ❹

Wawona Hotel Wawona (call DNC; front desk ☎209/375-6556). An elegant New England-style hotel, parts of which date from 1879, with attractive public areas, distinctive wooden verandas and grounds that include a pool, tennis courts and a nine-hole golf course. Rooms all lack phone, TV and a/c, but have been gracefully restored with old-style furniture, Victorian patterned wallpaper and ceiling fans – though those in the main lodge are fairly small and lack bathrooms. ❺

White Wolf Lodge About halfway from the valley to Tuolumne Meadows (call DNC). Spacious four-berth tent cabins with wood-burning stove and candles, perfectly sited for day-hikes to Lukens and Harden lakes and the Grand Canyon of the Tuolumne River. Also four motel-style cabins. Open July to mid-Sept only. ❸–❹

Hwy-120: Groveland

Accommodation is listed by increasing distance from Yosemite.

Evergreen Lodge 33160 Evergreen Rd, Mather, a mile west of the Big Oak Flat Entrance then 7 miles north of Hwy-120 West; ☎1-800/935-6343, ⓦwww.evergreenlodge.com. More than just a place to rest your head, this resort amid the pines comprises 88 modernized cabins scattered around the main lodge and recreation building. So-called "Custom campers" are provided with tent, mattress and sleeping bag. There's a general store with espresso bar, good restaurant, bar (the only places you'll find TV) and nightly entertainment. You can even rent bikes and join a number of tours and activities. Custom camping ❷, cabins ❻

Yosemite Westgate Lodge 7633 Hwy-120, 13 miles from the Big Oak Flat Entrance ☎1-888/315-2378, ⓦwww.yosemitewestgate.com. The closest standard motel on Hwy-120, with the comforts of satellite TV, phone, pool and hot tub. There's a decent restaurant next door and two kids under 12 stay free with two adults; rates drop dramatically in winter. ❻

Groveland Motel & Indian Village 18933 Hwy-120, Groveland, 25 miles from the Big Oak Flat Entrance ☎1-888/849-3529, ⓦwww .grovelandmotel.net. Either pitch your own tent ($25), use one of their tents supplied with airbeds, or step up to some fairly basic a/c cabins with cable TV or even mobile homes with small kitchens. ❶–❹

🏃 **Hotel Charlotte** 18736 Hwy-120, Groveland, 25 miles from the Big Oak Flat Entrance ☎209/962-6455, ⓦwww.hotelcharlotte .com. This charming ten-room hotel, dating back to 1921, has been lovingly updated. Rooms are mostly small but all have beautiful old-fashioned bathrooms, individually controlled a/c, satellite TV and phones with free calls throughout the US. Rates include a good buffet breakfast and there's free wi-fi throughout the hotel. ❹

🏃 **Groveland Hotel** 18767 Hwy-120, Groveland, 25 miles from the Big Oak Flat Entrance ☎1-800/273-3314, ⓦwww.groveland .com. Gorgeous mining-era hotel with luxurious, individually styled, antique-filled rooms, most with deep baths. Suites feature spa tubs and real fires. ❺

Hwy-140: Mariposa, Midpines and El Portal

Accommodation is listed by increasing distance from Yosemite.

Yosemite Cedar Lodge 9966 Hwy-140, El Portal, 8 miles west of the Arch Rock Entrance ☎1-800/321-5261, ⓦwww.yosemiteresorts.us. Large hotel complex with indoor and outdoor pools, on-site restaurant and 200 rooms and suites. There's a fair chance of getting something here when everywhere else is full. ❺

Bear Creek Cabins 6993 Hwy-140, Midpines, 10 miles east of Mariposa, 23 miles west of the Arch Rock Entrance ☎1-888/303-6993, ⓦwww .yosemitecabins.com. Large, well-maintained log cabins divided into four: two sleep four and come with kitchenette, while the two very spacious suites come with a separate living room, gas fireplace and a full kitchen. All have satellite TV and access to a deck and barbecue area. ❹–❺

🏃 **Yosemite Bug Rustic Mountain Resort** 6979 Hwy-140, Midpines, 23 miles west of the Arch Rock Entrance ☎1-866/826-7108, ⓦwww.yosemitebug.com. Set in twenty acres of woodland, this low- to mid-range HI-USA hostel and lodge is the handiest budget accommodation near Yosemite. Basic self-catering facilities exist for those staying in dorms, but there's also the excellent, licensed *Café at the Bug* (see p.360). Comfortable mixed and single-sex dorms ($22, non-members $25) are supplemented by tent cabins, shared-bath private rooms and very cosy and distinctively decorated en-suite rooms with decks but no phone or TV. There's free internet and wi-fi, a lounge with books and games, access to a good summer swimming hole, hot tub, sauna, massage and yoga classes, and a YARTS bus stop outside. Reservations essential May–Sept. ❶–❹

Muir Lodge 6833 Hwy-140, Midpines, 8.6 miles east of Mariposa, 23.2 miles west of the Arch Rock Entrance ☎209/966-2468, ⓦwww.yosemitemuir lodge.com. Old and basic motel units that haven't been upgraded for many years but are at least clean and cheap. Also one three-bed dorm ($29 per person). ❷

River Rock Inn 4993 7th St ☎209/966-5793, ⓦwww.riverrockcafe.com. Peaceful, welcoming and good-value seven-room budget motel just off Mariposa's main drag with stylishly decorated smallish rooms (and a couple of larger suites) all equipped with a/c, fridge and coffee pot. Continental breakfast (included) is served in the adjacent *River Rock Deli*. ❸

Comfort Inn 4994 Bullion St, Mariposa, 35 miles from the Arch Rock Entrance ☎1-800/221-2222, ⓦwww.comfortinn.com. Modern mid-range motel with wi-fi and a/c in all rooms, access to an outdoor pool and hot tub, and a continental breakfast included. Some suites with cooking facilities. ❹

🏃 **Highland House B&B Inn** 3125 Wild Dove Lane, Mariposa, 35 miles from the Arch Rock Entrance ☎209/966-3737, ⓦwww.highland houseinn.com. It's worth the effort to reach this tranquil B&B, tucked away amid ponderosa pines and incense cedars around twelve miles northeast of Mariposa. The three attractively furnished rooms all have private bathroom with tub and shower, and the suite has a four-poster bed, fireplace and DVD player. Breakfasts are substantial, there's a full kitchen for guests' use and the common area even has a pool table. Located off Jerseydale Road, but call Michael for detailed directions. Reserve well ahead in summer. ❹

Hwy-41: Oakhurst and Fish Camp

Accommodation is listed by increasing distance from Yosemite.

White Chief Mountain Lodge 7776 White Chief Mountain Rd, Fish Camp ☎559/683-5444, ⓦwww.whitechiefmountainlodge.com; closed Nov to March. Choose from one of the ageing but well-equipped and clean motel rooms or one of the 4-berth cottages all in a peaceful setting. Good value, and there's a diner-style restaurant on-site. Rooms ❹, cottage ❻

🏃 **Narrow Gauge Inn** 48571 Hwy-41, Fish Camp ☎1-888/644-9050, ⓦwww.narrowgaugeinn.com. Attractive lodge with a wide selection of rooms, many with a balcony and views over the forest, and a fine on-site restaurant (see p.360). All rooms come with phone, TV and continental breakfast, and the inn has a pool and spa. ❺

Hounds Tooth Inn 42071 Hwy-41, 3 miles north of Oakhurst ☎1-888/642-6610, ⓦwww.houndstoothinn.com. Luxurious B&B with a dozen individually decorated rooms, most with either a fireplace or spa bath (or both) and all with a/c. The friendly hosts provide complimentary wine each evening and delicious buffet breakfasts. ❹

Days Inn 40662 Hwy-41, Oakhurst ☎1-800/329-7644, ⓦwww.daysinn.com. One of the cheapest of Oakhurst's franchise motels but still kept to a high standard, with comfortable rooms, a pool, HBO, free wi-fi and continental breakfast. ❺

🏃 **The Homestead** 41110 Rd 600, 2.5 miles off Hwy-49 in Ahwahnee, near Oakhurst ☎1-800/483-0495, ⓦwww.homesteadcottages.com. Just a handful of beautifully outfitted adobe cottages – a/c, TV, gas grill – each with full self-catering facilities, comfortable lounge area and a nice deck. Two-night minimum stay at weekends. Loft ❺, cottages ❼

Camping

As with any national park, **camping** is the best way to really feel part of your surroundings, though this is less true in the large and crowded campgrounds of Yosemite Valley. In summer it's almost essential to book beforehand (☎1-877/444-6777, ⓦwww.recreation.gov): reservations open in one-month chunks, four to five months in advance, so to book for the month beginning July 15 you should call from February 15 (from 7am Pacific time). Otherwise you'll need to show up at the Curry Village Reservations Office very early in the morning and hope for cancellations. Other than *Camp 4* (see below), all valley sites cost $20 and none have **showers** or **laundry** facilities (see p.361). Between May and mid-September you're only allowed to camp for one week in Yosemite Valley and a total of two weeks in the whole park; outside this summer season you can move in for up to a month. Camping outside recognized sites in the valley is strictly forbidden. **RV** campers can use all the main campgrounds: there are no hookups, but you'll find dump stations in Yosemite Valley, Wawona, and at Tuolumne Meadows (summer only).

In addition to the main campgrounds, there are **backpacker campgrounds** in Yosemite Valley, Tuolumne Meadows, White Wolf and Hetch Hetchy, designed for hikers about to start (or just finishing) a wilderness trip and costing $5 per night – you must have a wilderness permit to use these.

Finally, with enough time, you'll want to get out to one of several **primitive campgrounds** in the backcountry. Designed specifically for hikers, these have fire rings and some source of water, which must be treated. To use them, or to camp elsewhere in the backcountry, you must get a **free wilderness permit** (see box, p.357) – you must camp a mile from any road, four miles from a populated area and at least a hundred yards from water sources and trails. Camping on the summit of Half Dome is not permitted. Remember to carry a stove and fuel, as indiscriminate use of trees could jeopardize future visitors' freedom to camp in the backcountry.

In the valley

🏃 **Camp 4 Walk-in** (all year; $5 per person; 4000ft). First-come-first-served campground west of and away from the other valley sites, popular with dirtbag rock-climbers. It's a fairly

bohemian (some would say squalid) place, with six-person sites just a few yards from a dusty parking lot. It's often full by 9am, especially in spring and fall, so join the line early.

North Pines, Upper Pines, Lower Pines (March–Oct, *Upper Pines* all year; $20; 4000ft). Largely indistinguishable, pine-shrouded sites, all with toilets, water and fire rings. Popular with RV users. Reservations essential.

The rest of the park

Bridalveil Creek (July to early Sept; $14; 7200ft). High-country, first-come-first-served campground off Glacier Point Rd, with good access to wilderness trails.

Crane Flat (June–Sept; $20; 6200ft). Large campground northwest of the valley, at the start of Hwy-120 and close to a stand of sequoias. Reservations required.

Hodgdon Meadow (all year; $20; 4900ft). Relatively quiet campground right on the park's western boundary just off Hwy-120. Take Old Big Oak Flat Rd for half a mile. Reservations required May–Sept, first-come-first-served ($14) at other times.

Porcupine Flat (July to early Sept; $10; 8100ft). Attractive and small first-come-first-served campground near the road to Tuolumne Meadows, almost forty miles from the valley. Stream water available.

Tamarack Flat (June–Sept; $10; 6300ft). Small campground two miles off Hwy-120 Tioga Rd, 23 miles from the valley and with only limited RV access. Stream water available.

Tuolumne Meadows (July–Sept; $20; 8600ft). Large and popular streamside campground with flush toilets and piped water, set beside a sub-alpine meadow. Half the sites are available by advance reservation, half by same-day reservation.

Wawona (all year; $20; 4000ft). The only site in the southern sector of the park, approximately a mile north of the *Wawona Hotel*. Some walk-in sites are reserved for car-free campers. Reservations required May–Sept; rest of year $14.

White Wolf (July to mid-Sept; $14; 8000ft). First-come-first-served tent and RV site a mile north of Hwy-120, midway between the valley and Tuolumne Meadows.

Yosemite Creek (July to early Sept; $10; 7600ft). First-come-first-served tent-only site ideal for escaping the crowds, though it can fill up very quickly in the summer. Inconveniently sited five miles off Hwy-120, but almost equidistant between the valley and Tuolumne Meadows. Stream water available.

Outside the park

Dimond O Evergreen Rd, off Hwy-120 West (late April to mid-Oct; $21; 4400ft). Gorgeous national-forest campground one mile west of the Big Oak Flat Entrance, with tent and RV sites, piped water, pit toilets and a riverside setting. Some sites reservable through ⓦ recreation.gov.

Lee Vining Creek Off Hwy-120 East, nine miles west of the Tioga Pass Entrance (late April to Oct; $14–19; 7800ft). A series of almost identical, streamside national-forest campgrounds along Poole Power Plant Rd.

Sawmill Walk-in Mile 1.5 Saddlebag Lake Road, 3.7 miles east of the Tioga Pass Entrance (June to mid-Oct; $14; 9800ft). Primitive walk-in campground around 400yd from its parking lot, superbly sited amid jagged peaks that feel a world away from the glaciated domes around Tuolumne. No reservations.

Summerdale Hwy-41 (June–Oct; $20; 5000ft). National forest campground 1.5 miles south of the park's South Entrance and handy for both Wawona and the Mariposa Grove. Book through ⓦ recreation.gov.

Yosemite Valley

Even the most evocative photography can only hint at the pleasure of simply gazing at **YOSEMITE VALLEY**. From three-thousand-foot granite cliffs to the subtle colourings of wildflowers, the variations in the valley can be both enormous and discreet. Nowhere else in the world is there such an array of rock faces and cascades concentrated in such a small area – though a mild winter can cause many of these falls to dry up as early as July. Easy walks around the lush meadows to waterfalls and lakes prepare you for much tougher treks into the backcountry (see box, p.357).

If there is any drawback to the valley, it's that this is the busiest part of Yosemite, and you're rarely far from other visitors or the park's commercial trappings, notably in **Yosemite Village** and **Curry Village**, the two main concentrations of shops and restaurants. Most of the crowds can be easily left behind by taking any path which contains much of a slope, but a couple of days exploring the valley leaves you more than ready to press on to the park's less populated regions.

The big cliffs

However you approach the valley, your view will be partially blocked by **El Capitan**, a vast monolith jutting forward from the adjacent cliffs and looming 3593ft above the valley floor. One of the largest pieces of exposed granite in the world, "The Captain" is a full 320 acres of grey-tan granite, seemingly devoid of vegetation and almost vertical. Its enormous size draws rock climbers from all over the world (see p.346).

The grandeur of "the captain" is only matched by the stunning, 8842-foot **Half Dome**, which rises almost 5000ft from the valley floor. Its 2000-foot northwest face is only seven degrees off the vertical, making it the sheerest cliff in North America. Though stunning from the valley, the best views of Half Dome are from Glacier Point (see p.357), especially around sunset.

Ambitious day-hikers wanting to get up close and personal can make it to the dome's thirteen-acre summit, tackling the final four hundred feet by way of a steep steel-cable staircase (see box, p.356) hooked onto the rock's curving back. Once at the top, the brave can inch out towards the edge of the projecting lip for a vertiginous look straight down the face.

The major waterfalls

At 2425ft, **Yosemite Falls** is widely claimed to be the fifth highest waterfall in the world, and the highest in North America. It's a somewhat spurious assertion, since it is actually two falls separated by 675ft of churning rapids and chutes known as **Middle Cascade**. Nonetheless, the 1430-foot **Upper Yosemite Fall** and the 320-foot **Lower Yosemite Fall** are magnificent, especially in May and early June when runoff from melting snow turns them into a foaming torrent. The flow typically dries up by mid-August. A quarter-mile asphalt trail (from shuttle bus stop 6) leads towards the falls along an avenue of incense cedars and ponderosa pines, creating a perfect photo op. Perhaps the most sensual waterfall in the park is the 620-foot **Bridalveil Fall**, a slender ribbon at the valley's western end, which in Ahwahneechee goes by the name of *Pohono* or "spirit of the puffing wind". Winds often blow the cascade outward up to twenty feet away from its base, drawing the spray into a delicate lacy veil, particularly from April to June. The quarter-mile trail from the parking lot is four miles west of the village and not accessible by shuttle bus.

Two of the park's most striking falls are guaranteed to still be active year-round, but are sequestered away from the road up the Merced River canyon, near Happy Isles (see opposite). It's a relatively easy walk to get a glimpse of the distant 317-foot **Vernal Fall**, a curtain of water about eighty feet wide that casts bright rainbows as you walk along the wonderful Mist Trail (see box, p.356). It requires much more commitment to hike steeply upstream as far as the 594-foot **Nevada Fall**, but it's worth the effort for a close look at this sweeping cascade that free-falls for half its height, then fans out onto the apron below.

Yosemite Village

Very much the heart of the valley, **Yosemite Village** is not really a cohesive "village" at all, but a scattered settlement of low buildings where mule deer wander freely. You'll find yourself returning time and again to visit shops, restaurants, banking facilities, internet access points, the post office (see p.361 for the last three) and the **Valley Visitor Center** (see p.345 for hours). Here you can watch the 23-minute *Spirit of Yosemite* (every 30min), which has great footage of the park through the seasons. For more great images walk a few steps east to the **Ansel Adams Gallery** and its collection of fine-art prints, posters and postcards.

Immediately west of the visitor centre the **Yosemite Museum** (daily 9am–5pm; free) is home to a small selection of artefacts focusing on Native American heritage, specifically the local Ahwahneechee and the neighbouring Mono Lake Paiute, with whom they traded and intermarried. One of the few crafts to flourish after contact with whites was **basketwork**: fine examples on display include a superbly detailed 1930s Mono Lake Paiute basket almost three feet in diameter, and its even larger Miwok/Paiute equivalent, painstakingly created by famed basket-maker Lucy Telles. Basket-making demonstrations are given by Ahwahneechee practitioners throughout the day. A couple of **feather-trimmed dance capes** warrant a look, as does the buckskin dress worn by natives in the 1920s and 1930s during tourist demonstrations of basket-weaving and dance. Though completely alien to the Miwok tradition, the Plains-style buckskin clothing and feather headdresses fulfilled the expectations of the whites who came to watch. Outside, a self-guided trail weaves around the **Indian Village of Ahwahneechee** (always open; free), with its cluster of reconstructed Indian buildings.

Fifty yards west of the museum, the **Yosemite Cemetery** (always open; free) holds the graves of early white settlers including those of early orchardist **James Lamon** and park guardian **Galen Clark**.

One essential stop, even if you don't intend to stay or eat, is **The Ahwahnee** hotel (shuttle stop 3). It was built in grand style in 1927 from local rock and is decorated with Native American motifs and some wonderful oriental rugs and carpets. Originally intended to blend into its surroundings and attract the richer type of tourist, it still does both fairly effortlessly – pop in for a few minutes to sink into the deep sofas and view the collection of paintings of Yosemite's early days.

Curry Village and the eastern valley

At some point, almost everyone finds themselves at the eastern end of the valley, home to all the main campgrounds along with the permanent cabins of *Housekeeping Camp* and the tent cabin complex of **Curry Village**. This is a direct descendant of **Camp Curry**, started in 1899 by David and Jeannie Curry, who were keen to share their adopted home in the valley and charged just $12 a week for a "good bed, and a clean napkin every meal". It's now a rambling area of tent cabins and wooden chalets centred on a small complex of restaurants, shops, pay showers and an outdoor amphitheatre hosting ranger programmes and evening shows. There's also a winter ice rink, bike rental and a kiosk that rents rafts for use on the nearby Merced River.

The western end of *Curry Village* is marked by the **LeConte Memorial Lodge** (May–Sept Wed–Sun 10am–4pm; free; shuttle stop 12), a small, rough-hewn granite-block structure where the **Sierra Club** maintains displays on its history, runs a conservation library and has a fascinating relief map of the valley dating back to around 1885. The Lodge itself was built by the Sierra Club in 1903 to commemorate the eminent geologist and early supporter of John Muir, **Joseph LeConte** (1823–1901), and as the Sierra Club's Yosemite headquarters, it was managed for a couple of summers in the early 1920s by **Ansel Adams**. Their evening programmes (usually Fri–Sun; free) are a little more highbrow than those elsewhere in the park and might include a slide show or talk by some luminary; check the *Yosemite Guide* for details.

East of *Curry Village*, the **Nature Center at Happy Isles** (mid-May to mid-Sept daily 10am–4pm or later; free; shuttle stop 16) contains a family-friendly set of displays on flora and fauna, a hands-on exhibit allowing you to feel how hunks of rough granite get weathered down to sand and an exhibit on a year in the life of a bear. Check out the **rockfall exhibit**, at the rear of the Nature Center, where a number of explanatory panels highlight the pulverized rock and flattened trees that resulted from a massive rockfall in 1996.

Ansel Adams

Few photographers have stamped their vision on a place as unforgettably as **Ansel Adams** did with Yosemite Valley. While he worked all over the American West, Yosemite was Adams' home and the subject of his most celebrated works, icons of American landscape photography such as 1940's *Jeffrey Pine – Sentinel Dome*; *Clearing Winter Storm* from 1944; and *Moon and Half Dome* from 1960.

Born in 1902 into a moderately wealthy San Francisco family, Adams was given a Box Brownie when he was 14, on his first trip to Yosemite. He claimed that he knew his "destiny" on that first visit to Yosemite, and soon turned his attentions to the mountains.

He first made a mark in 1927 with *Monolith, The Face of Half Dome*, his first successful **visualization**: Adams believed that, before pressing the shutter, the photographer should have a clear idea of the final image and think through the entire photographic process, considering how lenses, filters, exposure, development and printing need to be used to achieve that visualization. This approach may seem obvious today, but compared to the hit-and-miss methods of the time, it was little short of revolutionary.

In the 1940s, there was still very little money in photography, and Adams took on commercial assignments, including shooting menu photos for *The Ahwahnee*. While still demanding the highest standard of reproduction, the artist had tempered his perfectionism by the 1950s and allowed his work to appear on postcards, calendars and posters. By now he was virtually a household name, and for the first time in his life he began making money to match his status as the grand old man of Western photography. His final triumph came in 1979, when MoMA, in New York, put on the huge "Yosemite and the Range of Light" exhibition. That same year, he was asked to make an official portrait of President Jimmy Carter – the first time a photographer had been assigned an official presidential portrait – and was subsequently awarded the nation's highest civilian honour, the Medal of Freedom.

Throughout his life, Adams was equally passionate about **conservation**. In 1932 he had a direct hand in creating Kings Canyon National Park, and two years later he became a director of the **Sierra Club**, overseeing several successful environmental campaigns until 1971. He never quit campaigning for conservation.

Adams died on April 22, 1984, aged 82, and posthumously lent his name to both Mount Ansel Adams and a huge chunk of the High Sierra south of Yosemite National Park, now known as the Ansel Adams Wilderness.

One of the most rewarding of the easy trails near Curry Village leads from shuttle stop 17 around the edge of the valley floor to **Mirror Lake** (2 miles; 1hr; 100-foot ascent). This compellingly calm lake (typically dry in late summer) lies beneath and reflects the great bulk of Half Dome; it's best seen in the early morning before too many others arrive. Most visitors to Mirror Lake follow the traffic-free paved road from the shuttle stop, but several smaller parallel paths (easily found to the left of the main track) will steer you clear of the asphalt and the crowds.

Northern Yosemite

From the valley, Big Oak Flat Road climbs rapidly to Crane Flat, where there's a store and the closest gas station to the valley. From here Hwy-120 West runs to the Big Oak Flat Entrance and **Hetch Hetchy**, once a scenic rival for Yosemite Valley, though now partially filled with a water supply for San Francisco.

East of Crane Flat, **Tioga Road** (Hwy-120 East) climbs through dense forests into the Yosemite high country around Tenaya Lake, Tuolumne Meadows and Tioga Pass – open grasslands pocked by polished granite domes and with a southern horizon delineated by the sawtooth crest of the **Cathedral Range**.

Hetch Hetchy

John Muir's passion for Yosemite Valley was matched by his desire to preserve the beauty of **Hetch Hetchy**, eighteen miles north of the valley. Once a near replica of Yosemite Valley, with grassy, oak-filled meadows and soaring granite walls, it's now largely under the dammed waters of the slender Hetch Hetchy reservoir. When it came under threat from power- and water-supply interests in San Francisco in 1901, Muir battled for twelve years, instigating the first environmental letter-writing campaign to Congress. Eventually, in 1913, the cause was lost. Now, only the view of granite domes and waterfalls from the path crossing the **O'Shaughnessey Dam** gives some sense of what it must have been like. All this is best seen on a short and mostly flat hike which initially crosses the dam, passes through a short tunnel and follows the north bank of the reservoir to **Wapama Falls** (five miles round-trip) and on to **Rancheria Falls** (a further four miles each way). Both falls are at their best in May and June and are dry by August.

Tioga Road and Tuolumne Meadows

From Crane Flat the eastbound **Tioga Road** soon passes a parking lot from where there's a mile-long walking trail to the **Tuolumne Grove** of giant sequoias, nowhere near as spectacular as the Mariposa Grove (see p.358), but easier to reach – and it's always an honour to be among these giants. Tioga Road then climbs steadily through deep pine forests past the *White Wolf* and *Porcupine* campgrounds, rising above 8000ft just before **Olmsted Point** – right up there with Glacier Point as one of Yosemite's finest roadside views – which looks down Tenaya Creek towards Half Dome.

The alpine area around **Tuolumne Meadows** (literally "meadow in the sky") has an atmosphere quite different from the valley, 55 miles (about a ninety-minute drive) away. The landscape here, at 8600ft, is much more open and the air always has a fresh, crisp bite. That said, there can still be good-sized blasts of carbon monoxide at peak times in the vicinity of the campground and *Tuolumne Meadows Lodge* (see p.348) – the only accommodation base in the area.

Being almost five thousand feet higher than Yosemite Valley makes Tuolumne Meadows a better starting point for **hiking** (see box, p.356) into the surrounding High Sierra wilderness. The meadows themselves are the largest in the entire Sierra: twelve miles long, between quarter and half a mile wide, and threaded by the meandering Tuolumne River. Snow usually lingers here until the end of June, forcing the **wildflowers** to contend with a short growing season. They respond with a glorious burst of colour in July, a wonderful time to wander.

The distinctively glaciated granite form of **Lembert Dome** squats at the eastern end of the meadows, gazing across the grasslands towards its western twin, **Pothole Dome**, which makes a great sunset destination. The mountain scenery is particularly striking to the south, where the **Cathedral Range** offers a horizon of slender spires and knife-blade ridges. Look out for the appropriately named **Unicorn Peak** and **Cathedral Peak**, a textbook example of a glaciated "Matter-horn", where glaciers have carved away the rock on all sides and left a sharp, pointed summit. Some of the best views are from the naturally carbonated **Soda Springs** (see box, p.356), described in 1863 as "pungent and delightful to the taste". And so it is, though the Park Service discourages drinking from it.

There are no restrictions on **day-hiking** in Yosemite, so for all the following hikes you need only equip yourself properly – map, raingear, food, etc – get to the trailhead, and set off. Unless otherwise noted, the following distances and times are for a round-trip.

Day-hikes from Yosemite Valley

Four-mile Trail to Glacier Point (10 miles; 5–6hr; 3200-foot ascent). Magnificent views of Yosemite Valley and Sentinel Rock from a steep asphalt path that is one of the valley's more popular day-walks. Generally open mid-May to Oct.

Half Dome (16 miles; 9–12hr; 4800-foot ascent). This is one of the valley's finest and most arduous walks, initially following the Mist Trail (see below) and continuing around the back of Half Dome. The final 400ft ascends over the huge, smooth, humped back, aided by a pair of steel cables and wooden steps (in place late-May to mid-Nov). In 2010 a reservation system was instituted for Fri, Sat & Sun ascents. These were booked up within minutes of going on sale and it seems likely that the reservation system will be extended to every day in the season: check ⓦ www.nps .gov/yose/planyourvisit/hdpermits.htm for the latest details and bookings. Once at the summit, anyone concerned about their outdoor credibility will want to edge out to the very lip of the abyss and peer down the sheer, 2000-foot northwest face. If you plan a one-day assault, you'll need to start at the crack of dawn.

Mist Trail to the top of Vernal Fall (3 miles; 2–3hr; 1100-foot ascent). If you only do one hike in Yosemite, this is it, especially during the spring snowmelt, when Vernal Fall is often framed by a rainbow and hikers get drenched in spray; bring a raincoat or plan to get wet. Start at shuttle stop 16 and head uphill, crossing a footbridge with great views of the Fall. Then follow the Mist Trail along a narrow path which, though hardly dangerous, demands sure footing and a head for heights. At the top of the Fall, either retrace your steps to the trailhead or return via the John Muir Trail.

Upper Yosemite Fall (7 miles; 4–7hr; 2700-foot ascent). This popular, energy-sapping hike climbs steeply to the north rim of the valley, with great views of Upper Yosemite Fall and the opportunity to sit virtually on the edge of the Fall, gazing down at the Lilliputian activity below in Yosemite Village. Its northern aspect keeps the trail open longer than most (April–Dec) but it's best done during the spring snowmelt: start before 7am to avoid the worst of the midday heat. The trailhead is just by *Camp 4* (shuttle stop 7).

Day-hikes from Tuolumne Meadows

Soda Springs and Parsons Lodge (4-mile loop; 2hr; negligible ascent). An easy meander around some of Tuolumne Meadows' best and most accessible features.

The Tuolumne Meadows Tour and Hikers Bus (see p.347) runs up here once a day from Yosemite Valley, stopping at trailheads along the journey and at various points around Tuolumne Meadows, including the **visitor centre** (see p.346). There's also a **free shuttle** service linking Tuolumne to Olmsted Point, just west of Tenaya Lake (June to mid-Sept daily 7am–6pm).

Southern Yosemite

The southern end of the park contains a broad swathe of sharply peaked mountains extending twenty miles from the foothills in the west to the Sierra crest in the east. In summer, visitors congregate at **Wawona**, where the hotel and campground

Cross the meadow from a trailhead 300yd east of the visitor centre to reach the Soda Springs and Parsons Lodge, then follow a broad trail to the base of Lembert Dome; either walk back along Tioga Road or use the shuttle bus.

Lembert Dome (3.7-mile loop; 2–3hr; 850-foot ascent). Great views from the top of the meadows' most prominent feature, plus examples of glacially polished rock and "erratic" boulders left behind by retreating glaciers. Start at the parking lot at the dome's base and follow signs for Dog Lake, then head right to ascend via the bare rock of the dome's northeast corner. Descend, then turn right to complete a loop around the dome.

Cathedral Lakes (8 miles; 4–6hr; 1000-foot ascent). A candidate for the best Tuolumne day-hike, this route follows several miles of the John Muir Trail as far as a pair of gorgeous tarns in open alpine country with long views to a serrated skyline. Hike from the trailhead just west of the Tuolumne Meadows visitor centre and enjoy the gradually improving views of the twin spires of Cathedral Peak. Near its base are Upper Cathedral Lake (with excellent camping) and Lower Cathedral Lake, a divine spot lodged in a cirque now partly filled with lush meadows, and split by a ridge of hard rock polished smooth by ancient glaciers.

Multiday hikes

Camping out overnight opens up the majority of Yosemite's eight hundred miles of backcountry trails. Choosing from the enormous range of paths is almost impossible, though some of the most popular are those running between Yosemite Valley and Tuolumne Meadows, a two-day hike for anyone with reasonable fitness. Further suggestions are outlined in the *Rough Guide to Yosemite, Sequoia and Kings Canyon*.

To camp out overnight you need a **wilderness permit**, available free from ranger stations – at Wawona, Big Oak Flat, Hetch Hetchy and Tuolumne – and the Wilderness Center in Yosemite Village. Numbers are limited by a quota system, but with a little flexibility you'll often find you can get a permit the day before you wish to start your hike. Large groups, people with tight schedules and anyone hiking at busy times should **reserve in advance** (details at Ⓦwww.nps.gov/yose/planyourvisit /wildpermits.htm; $5 per person).

When obtaining your permit you'll be instructed in **backcountry etiquette** (see p.47, especially water purification, waste disposal and proper use of the required **bear-resistant food canister** (rentals $5 per week). **Camping gear** (though not tents) can be rented quite reasonably from Yosemite Mountaineering School (see p.347).

provide most services, or at the nearby **Mariposa Grove**, the most impressive of the park's stands of giant sequoias. Roughly midway between Yosemite Valley and Wawona, Glacier Point Road carves its way to the park's **viewpoint** *par excellence* at **Glacier Point**, right on the rim of Yosemite Valley and on a level with the face of Half Dome.

Glacier Point, Sentinel Dome and Taft Point

The most spectacular views of Yosemite Valley are from **Glacier Point**, the top of an almost sheer, 3200-foot cliff, 32 miles by road (usually open mid-May to late Oct) from Yosemite Valley. The valley floor lies directly beneath the viewing point, and there are tremendous views across to Half Dome and to the distant snow-capped summits of the High Sierra. It's possible to get here on foot along the very steep Four-Mile Trail (see box, p.356), though you may prefer to use the **Glacier Point Tour and Hikers Bus** (see p.347) from the valley and then hike down.

The road to Glacier Point passes the **Badger Pass Ski Area** (generally open mid-Dec to early April; ℡209/372-1000, ⓦwww.badgerpass.com), which has a few short tows and a ski school that runs excellent **cross-country ski** trips eleven miles to the viewpoint. You'll also pass a number of signposted trailheads for easy and longer hikes. One of the best is to the 8122-foot summit of **Sentinel Dome** (two miles round-trip), a gleaming granite scalp topped by the rotting remains of a Jeffrey pine made famous by Ansel Adams' photos from the 1940s. From the Sentinel Dome parking lot, a second dusty trail leads west to **Taft Point** (two miles round-trip), where El Capitan and Yosemite Falls can be seen from a vertiginous viewpoint. Nearby, the granite edges of the valley rim have been deeply incised to form what are known as the **Taft Point Fissures**.

Wawona and the Mariposa Grove

There's a decidedly relaxed pace at **Wawona**, 27 miles (or an hour's drive) south of Yosemite Village on Hwy-41. Most people spend their time here strolling the grounds of the landmark *Wawona Hotel* (see p.348), surrounded by a nine-hole golf course where $40 will get you a full eighteen-hole round (plus $22.50 for club rental, if needed) on the Sierra's oldest course. Close by is the **Pioneer Yosemite History Center**, a collection of buildings culled from the early times of white habitation, which can be visited on a self-guided walking tour (free). The jail, homesteads and covered bridge are good for a scoot around, and through the summer months (particularly weekends) the buildings are open and interpreted by attendant rangers. Once away from the main road, the area makes a quiet spot for a picnic.

The **Mariposa Grove**, three miles east of Hwy-41 on a small road that cuts off just past the park's southern entrance, is the biggest and best of Yosemite's groves of giant sequoia trees. To get to the towering growths, walk the 2.5-mile loop trail from the parking lot at the end of the road, or take the narrated **Big Trees Tour** around the grove (June–Oct 9am–5pm; $25.50), which follows a paved road to the major sights. There's also a free shuttle to the parking area from Wawona.

Trails around the sequoia groves call first at the **Fallen Monarch**, familiar from the 1899 photo, widely reproduced on postcards, in which cavalry officers and their horses stand atop the prostrate tree. The most renowned of the grouping, well marked along the route, is the **Grizzly Giant**, thought to be 2700 years old and with a lower branch thicker than the trunk of any non-sequoia in the grove. Other highlights include the **Wawona Tunnel Tree**, through which people drove their cars until it fell in 1969, the similarly bored **California Tunnel Tree**, which you can walk through, and all manner of trees which have grown together, split apart, been struck by lightning or are simply staggeringly large. It's also worth dropping into the **Mariposa Grove Museum** (summer daily 10am–4.30pm; free), towards the top end of the trail, which has modest displays and photos of the mighty trees. For more on the life of the sequoia, see the box, on p.330.

Eating, drinking and entertainment

With a couple of notable exceptions, **eating** in Yosemite is more a function than a pleasure. Food, whether in restaurants or in the grocery stores around Yosemite Village (where there's a well-stocked supermarket), Curry Village, Wawona and Tuolumne Meadows, is at least twenty percent more expensive than outside the park. Restaurants serve beer and wine, plus there's a lively **bar** at *Yosemite Lodge*, a swankier affair at *The Ahwahnee* and a lounge with occasional piano entertainment at the *Wawona Hotel*. **Outside the park** the dining options are considerably better, with plenty of good restaurants and a smattering of bars in the gateway towns of Groveland, Mariposa and Oakhurst.

To help visitors interpret Yosemite, the Park Service and related organizations run a number of **ranger programmes** – nature hikes, photo walks, talks about bears, etc – most of which are free. In addition, there's **evening entertainment** in the form of ranger-led campfire talks at most of the campgrounds, occasional stargazing sessions, natural history slide shows and music shows. The *Yosemite Guide* newspaper carries a full catalogue of events, along with listings of the *Yosemite Theater* programme ($8), which presents three ninety-minute one-man shows featuring the talents of actor Lee Stetson, who has been impersonating John Muir since 1982.

In the valley

Ahwahnee Bar *The Ahwahnee* (7am–11pm). This morning espresso bar turns into an intimate piano bar perfect for indulging in something from their selection of Armagnacs, ports and classic martinis ($10–25), and perhaps an antipasto plate for two ($21). There's live music most Fri and Sat nights, usually something subdued.

Ahwahnee Dining Room *The Ahwahnee* ☎209/372-1489. One of the most beautiful restaurants in the US, built in baronial style with 34-foot-high ceilings of exposed beams, rustic iron chandeliers and floor-to-ceiling leaded windows. The food is by far the best in Yosemite: eggs Benedict ($18), smoked-duck Caesar salad ($15) and Kobe beef short-rib pot roast with mushrooms and baby fennel ($35). The Sunday brunch ($44) is stupendous. Casual dress is permitted during the day, but in the evening men need long trousers, collared shirt and closed shoes; women should be similarly smartly attired.

Degnan's Deli Yosemite Village. Some of the best takeaway food in the Valley with bowls of soup ($3–4) and chilli ($4–5), and massive made-on-the-spot sandwiches, burritos and salads for around $7. There's also a good selection of snacks and drinks, and the same building has a pizza restaurant and a café.

Pavilion Buffet *Curry Village*. Great-value all-you-can-eat breakfasts ($11.50) with plenty of fresh fruit, juices, eggs, bacon, hash browns, waffles, yoghurt and more. Dinner ($15) runs to salads, build-your-own tacos, chicken-fried steak, simple pasta dishes, cakes and sodas. Buy a beer or wine at the adjacent bar and carry it through.

Pizza Deck and Curry Bar *Curry Village*. Very much the place to repair to on balmy evenings after a hard day in the hills. Fight for an outdoor table while you wait for a pretty decent build-your-own pizza (from $22 for twelve slices) and maybe an elegant 23oz schooner of quality draft beer ($8) or a daiquiri, margarita or two ($7.60).

Yosemite Lodge Food Court *Yosemite Lodge*. Bright self-serve café/restaurant with a full range of cold and cooked breakfasts ($4–8), muffins, danishes and coffee, plus lunches and dinners that range from a grilled chicken sandwich, pizza or gyro platter (all $7) to pasta and meatballs ($9) or chicken, vegetables and rice ($9).

The rest of the park

Tuolumne Meadows Lodge ☎209/372-8413. Family-style breakfasts ($6–10) and burgers, steak, chicken and fish dinners ($15–30) served in a large tent beside the Tuolumne River.

Wawona Hotel Dining Room Semi-formal dining off white linen tablecloths, though the food is neither very expensive nor particularly special. Still, you can lunch on chicken-alfredo, ratatouille or a club sandwich ($10), then dress smart for dinner, such as pan-fried trout ($26) and an apple blueberry crisp ($8). There's also a Saturday barbecue (late May to early Sept 5–7pm; $20 a head).

White Wolf Lodge Just off Hwy-120 ☎209/252-4848. Standard breakfasts followed by large portions of good-value American food in rustic surroundings for $23 (fixed menu changes daily).

Hwy-120: Groveland

Café Charlotte 18959 Hwy-120, Groveland ☎209/962-6455. Excellent little restaurant where the casualness of the atmosphere belies a serious approach to the quality of the food. There's everything from pasta (including vegan and kids' dishes) to chicken Jerusalem (with artichokes and mushrooms) and succulent steaks (all $16–25), plus lip-smacking desserts. Licensed and BYO.

Cocina Michoacana 18370 Hwy-120, Groveland. Authentic and low-priced Mexican spot; $10 will get you either a great breakfast of scrambled eggs with strips of steak or one of the daily lunch specials, and later they serve a full range of favourites including great fajitas ($21–25 for two) and melt-in-your-mouth breaded shrimps.

Iron Door 18761 Main St, Groveland. Wonderfully atmospheric bar, reliably claimed to be the oldest saloon in California. It comes with pool table and all manner of paraphernalia on the walls, plus a live band most weekends and a decent restaurant next door.

Victorian Room *Groveland Hotel*, 18767 Hwy-120 ☎209/962-4000. The best restaurant in town, with a seasonally changing menu and nightly chef's specials – perhaps crab cakes with cilantro and caper sauce, or honey-glazed baby back pork ribs. Expect to pay $45–50 for three courses, including a glass or two from their massive wine list.

Hwy-140: Mariposa, Midpines and El Portal

Café at the Bug *Yosemite Bug Rustic Mountain Resort*, Midpines. Licensed café with quality food at a good price: wholesome breakfasts ($4.50–8), packed lunches ($6.50) and dinners ($8–18). If you don't mind the slightly frenetic hostel atmosphere, it's definitely worth the drive out for slow-roasted Cajun pork or baked trout fillet with butter pecan sauce. Good microbrews on tap as well, plus free wi-fi and internet.

Happy Burger 5120 Hwy-140 at 12th St. An enormous array of good, cheap diner food –

breakfast burrito ($5), tuna melt ($6), teriyaki chicken salad ($7) – to take away or eat in at Formica booths. There's a fine jukebox and the entire place is decorated with tragic Seventies album covers. Free wi-fi.

High Country Café Hwy-140 & Hwy-49, Mariposa. Daytime health-food café with sandwiches ($6–7), salads, burritos and fruit smoothies. There's also a health-food store next door offering good bread, organic fruit and goodies in bulk bins that are perfect for trail mix. Closed Sun.

Savoury's 5034 Hwy-140 ☎209/966-7677. The pick of Mariposa's restaurants, offering a relaxed atmosphere with a touch of class. Modern decor of bare concrete floors and painted block walls hung with striking Yosemite prints sets the tone for a delectable menu of dishes such as chipotle chicken ($17), roasted garlic cream scallops ($22) and spinach and pine-nut pasta ($16), perhaps followed by chocolate bread pudding ($5). Wine is available by the glass. Dinner only; closed Wed.

Sugar Pine Café 5038 Hwy-140. Red leatherette booths and diamond-tiled floors give a retro feel to this quality diner where everything is made from scratch, including great baked goods – apple turnovers, scones, blackberry pie and German chocolate cake. There's a short menu of breakfasts, burgers and a handful of dinner mains, served until 8pm. Closed Sun evening & Mon.

Hwy-41: Oakhurst and Fish Camp

The Grind 40879 Hwy-41, a mile north of Oakhurst. Relaxed java joint with mismatched chairs and newspapers, ideal for breakfast burritos, toothsome muffins, sandwiches, cakes and good espresso at modest prices. Also operates as a bar, often with live music at weekends.

The Narrow Gauge Inn 48571 Hwy-41, Fish Camp ☎559/683-6446. Fine dining in an old-world setting with candlelight and a warming fire. Start by dipping sourdough into a rich fondue and continue with charbroiled swordfish or filet mignon. Expect to pay $45 each, more with wine. Open mid-April to mid-Oct Wed–Sun 5.30–9pm.

West Coast sounds

An astonishing number of famous acts and trends have emerged from California. In the 1950s and 1960s it was known for the pop of the Platters and the Beach Boys, but after 1967's Monterey Pop Festival, the floodgates were open to any rock band with an electric flair. After mellowing in the 1970s with the Cocaine Cowboy sound of the Eagles and Jackson Browne, the California music scene reacted with the punk energy of X, the Dead Kennedys and Black Flag. Sunset Strip metal, West Coast rap and alternative bands followed, contributing to today's crazy quilt of sounds and styles.

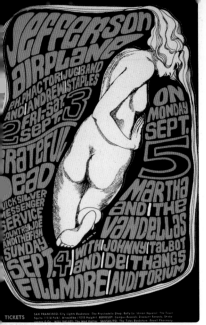

TICKETS

1960s festival poster ▲

Snoop Dogg ▼

The psychedelic scene

If Brian Wilson's soaring harmonies and the surf sounds of the Beach Boys were the prototypical California sound, the real revolution started in the mid-1960s with the hippy drug culture in San Francisco – epitomized by legends such as the Grateful Dead and Jefferson Airplane. Armed with flowers, LSD and instruments like sitars alongside their guitars were luminaries such as Quicksilver Messenger Service, It's a Beautiful Day, and Janis Joplin's Big Brother & the Holding Company. LA produced equally iconic acts like The Doors, Buffalo Springfield and Love.

Jazz, r'n'b and rap

LA once boasted an exemplary jazz scene, with legends like Charles Mingus playing for diverse audiences, and the Bay Area's Sly Stone was a DJ and producer before he helped develop the funk sound with his Family Stone. However, the most potent force in black popular music was West Coast hip-hop, whose angry "gangsta" attitudes were developed by Ice Cube and Eazy-E of NWA in the 1980s. Over the next decade, producer Dr Dre (another NWA alumnus) and collaborators like Snoop Dogg perfected the form, developing a genre of laidback beats and violent lyrics that portrayed the realities of inner-city life.

Country and latin

Not surprisingly for a state with a huge Latino population, Hispanic music is a constant element of the California playlist. While the music's home is still below the border, various local bands – East LA's Los Lobos among them – have contributed to its songbook. Bakersfield is country music's California outpost, far to the west of its original heartland. Country sounds influenced some of California's best-known 1970s rock acts, such as the Eagles and Gram Parsons, but the sound really hit the mark with legends such as Buck Owens and Merle Haggard and LA-bred Dwight Yoakam.

Punk and alternative

At the end of the 1970s, seminal bands like the Germs were followed by X, the Dead Kennedys, the Minutemen and Black Flag, who mixed aggression and black humour to go with the slam dancing. The lessons of the **punk and hardcore** scenes were absorbed by the **alternative** bands of the following era, from the Red Hot Chili Peppers and Jane's Addition to No Doubt, and current rockers like Silversun Pickups, Earlimart and Beck.

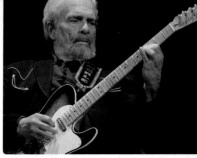

▲ Merle Haggard

▼ The Hollywood Bowl

▼ Red Hot Chili Peppers

Top 10 venues

▶▶ **924 Gilman** Berkeley. Underground hardcore and punk; p.523.

▶▶ **Boom Boom Room** San Francisco. Great blues and roots acts; p.490.

▶▶ **Buck Owens' Crystal Palace** Bakersfield. Prime spot for country and Western; p.310.

▶▶ **Casbah** San Diego. Top-shelf indie and alternative; p.198.

▶▶ **El Floridita** Los Angeles. Live latin music and dancing; p.151.

▶▶ **The Fillmore** San Francisco. Major rock headliners; p.490.

▶▶ **Great American Music Hall** San Francisco. Atmospheric rock venue; p.490.

▶▶ **The Hollywood Bowl** Hollywood. Open-air classical concerts; p.152.

▶▶ **Spaceland** Los Angeles. Independent punk and alternative; p.150.

▶▶ **Whisky-a-Go-Go** West Hollywood. Mainly hard rock and metal; p.150.

A California playlist

California Dreamin' The Mamas & the Papas (1966). Breezy gem about homesick hippies lost in the cold of an East Coast winter.

California Über Alles The Dead Kennedys (1980). Scathing attack on the pernicious state of affairs during Governor Jerry Brown's 1980s.

Californication Red Hot Chili Peppers (1999). A slice of melancholia lamenting the state's stereotype superficiality and pop-culture obsessions.

Fake Tales of California Arctic Monkeys (2005). Pithy dig at cultural pseuds, where a lad from Rotherham fakes Stateside credentials.

If You're Going to San Francisco Scott McKenzie (1967). Unashamed paean to the hippy generation and Sixties counterculture.

LA Neil Young (1973). Aggressive ode to that "city in the smog" where the Canadian troubadour made his home and fortune.

LA County Lyle Lovett (1988). A dark story of jealousy-fuelled murder, set to the tune of some of the loveliest country music you're likely to hear.

LA Woman The Doors (1971). This epic track offers the story of Jim's latest sexual indulgence (and an urban metaphor).

Saturday Afternoon Jefferson Airplane (1967). Psychedelic anthem exalting one of Golden Gate Park's massive 1967 "be-ins".

(Sittin' on) The Dock of the Bay Otis Redding (1968). Still-moving R&B tale of a Georgia exile who finds himself adrift and alone in the Bay Area.

Straight Outta Compton NWA (1989). Early gangsta-rap single that paints a terrifying portrait of street warfare in LA.

NWA ▲

The Doors ▼

Otis Redding ▼

Listings

Banks There are no banks in Yosemite, though there are several 24hr ATMs.

Books The Yosemite Bookstore, by the Valley Visitor Center, has a good selection of Yosemite-related books and maps; the Ansel Adams Gallery specializes in photography and nature publications; and the Mountain Shop at *Curry Village* stocks climbing guides.

Gas Unavailable in Yosemite Valley but sold at moderate prices at Crane Flat (all year), Wawona (all year) and Tuolumne Meadows (summer only).

Guided trips The Yosemite Mountaineering School (☎209/372-8344, ⓦwww.yosemit emountaineering.com) runs guided backpacking, rock-climbing and alpine trips from around $125 each per day for groups of four or more.

Horseriding Saddle trips accommodating riders of all standards are run from stables in Yosemite Valley (late April–Sept), Tuolumne Meadows (late June to Sept) and Wawona (May–Sept): scenic rides cost $60 for two hours, $119 for the day; ☎209/372-8348.

Internet One first-come-first-served 30-minute session per week at the Yosemite Village public library (see below). Also five feed-in-the-dollar-bills computers at *Degnan's Café* in Yosemite Village, free wi-fi at *Curry Village*, and wi-fi (free for guests) at *Yosemite Lodge* and *The Ahwahnee*.

Laundry There's a coin-op affair at *Housekeeping Camp* (8am–8pm).

Library The Yosemite Village public library (Mon 8.30–11.30am, Tues 10am–2pm, Wed 8.30am–12.30pm, Thurs 4–7pm) is located just west of the Yosemite Museum in a building signed "Girls Club".

Medical assistance Yosemite Medical Clinic, between Yosemite Village and *The Ahwahnee* (☎209/372-4637), has 24hr emergency care and drop-in and urgent care (daily 8am–7pm), and accepts appointments (Mon–Fri 8am–5pm). Dental treatment (☎209/372-4200) is also available.

Photography The Ansel Adams Gallery in Yosemite Village (ⓦwww.anseladams.com) runs assorted free photography walks (check *Yosemite Guide* for times) and more specialized courses.

Rafting Inside the park, *Curry Village* rents six-berth rafts ($26 per person; June & July only) allowing you to float gently along a placid section of the Merced River – the cost includes a return bus ride. Outside the park, from April to June, far more rugged (Class III–IV) one-day stretches are run in the traditional guided fashion by nonprofit ARTA River Trips (☎1-800/323-2782, ⓦwww .arta.org), Whitewater Voyages (☎1-800/400-7238, ⓦwww.whitewatervoyages.com), Zephyr Whitewater Expeditions (☎1-800/431-3636, ⓦwww.zrafting.com) and others, all charging around $140–150 midweek and $150–170 at weekends.

Showers The park's only public showers are in Yosemite Valley at *Curry Village* (24hr; $5), but outside the peak summer season there's often nobody to either provide a towel or take your money.

Swimming There are pools in the valley at *Yosemite Lodge* and *Curry Village* (both free to hotel guests and $5 for others), the *Wawona Hotel* and *The Ahwahnee* both have pools for guests, and there are numerous small river beaches throughout the valley and at Wawona.

Travel details

Trains

The San Joaquin service runs four times daily between Bakersfield and Emeryville, near Oakland, from where Amtrak Thruway buses run into San Francisco. Amtrak Thruway bus connections from San Diego, Orange County and Los Angeles link with the train at Bakersfield.

Bakersfield to: Emeryville (6hr); Fresno (2hr); Hanford (1hr 20min); Merced (3hr); San Francisco (3 daily; 7–8hr); Stockton (4hr).

Buses

All buses are Greyhound except for Visalia to San Luis Obispo, which is run by Orange Belt Stages (☎1-800/266-7433, ⓦwww.orangebelt .com). The company often uses Amtrak and Greyhound stations as hubs for their limited network.

Bakersfield to: Hanford (1 daily, 3hr); Los Angeles (11 daily; 2–3hr); Merced (7 daily; 3hr 30min–4hr); San Francisco (3 daily; 7–8hr).

Fresno to: Los Angeles (11 daily; 4hr 20min–5hr 50min); Merced (7 daily; 1hr 10min); Modesto (9 daily; 2hr); San Francisco (4 daily; 5hr); Stockton (6 daily; 3hr).

Hanford to: Bakersfield (1 daily; 3hr); San Luis Obispo (2 daily; 3hr); Visalia (2 daily; 30min).

Merced to: Bakersfield (7 daily; 3hr 30min–4hr); Fresno (7 daily; 1hr 10min); Los Angeles (7 daily; 6–7hr); Modesto (7 daily; 1hr); Sacramento (5 daily; 3hr); San Francisco (2 daily; 4hr); Stockton (5 daily; 1hr 30min); Yosemite (4–5 daily; 2hr 45min).

Modesto to: Fresno (9 daily; 2hr); Los Angeles (9 daily; 6–8hr); Merced (7 daily; 1hr); San Francisco (2 daily; 2hr 30min–3hr).

Stockton to: Fresno (6 daily; 3hr); Los Angeles (8 daily; 6hr–8hr 30min); Merced (5 daily; 1hr 30min); Sacramento (8 daily; 1hr); San Francisco (7 daily; 5–6hr).

Visalia to: Hanford (2 daily; 30min); Los Angeles (4 daily; 4–5hr); San Francisco (2 daily; 7hr); San Luis Obispo (2 daily; 4hr 30min).

6

The Central Coast

CHAPTER 6

Highlights

✳ **Channel Islands National Park** This beguiling chain of desert islands off the coast north of Los Angeles offers spectacular hiking and the chance to spot passing whales. See p.371

✳ **Hearst Castle** One of the most intriguing sights in America: a palatial monument to the life and ego of publishing magnate William Randolph Hearst. See p.393

✳ **Mission San Antonio de Padua** The best conserved of all the missions, and an evocative place to imagine the colonial California of two hundred years ago. See p.397

✳ **Big Sur** Boasting a strikingly rugged coastline and some of the state's most stunning waterfalls, this sparsely populated region continues to retain its wild character. See p.400

✳ **Monterey Bay Aquarium** The superb, enormous Outer Bay tank and ever-charming sea otters help make this sea-life museum a world-class destination. See p.412

✳ **Santa Cruz Boardwalk** A classic California seaside promenade where carnival food, an amusement arcade and a rickety wooden roller coaster all make for irresistible fun. See p.423

▲ Big Sur

The Central Coast

T he four hundred miles of the **CENTRAL COAST** between LA and San Francisco cover one of the most beautiful oceanside stretches anywhere in the world, a blend of sandy beaches and rocky cliffs, rural charm and urban energy. Sparsely populated outside a few medium-sized towns, much of the area is seemingly free from the pressures of modern life. Indeed, first-time visitors may be surprised to find just how much of the region survives in its natural state, despite nestling snugly between two of the world's largest and richest cities. The mountain ranges that separate the shore from the farms of the inland valleys are for the most part pristine wilderness, sometimes covered in thick forests of tall and slender redwood trees, while, in winter especially, fast-flowing rivers and streams course down valleys to the sea. All along the shore, sea otters and seals play in the waves, and endangered grey whales pass close by on their annual migration from Alaska to Mexico.

At **Big Sur**, the brooding Santa Lucia Mountains rise steeply out of the thundering Pacific surf, and **Point Lobos**, at the area's northern tip, is the best place to experience this untouched environment at its most dramatic. Nature aside, though, the Central Coast also marks the gradual transition from Southern to Northern California. The two largest towns here are **Santa Barbara**, a conservative, wealthy resort a hundred miles north of Los Angeles, and **Santa Cruz**, 75 miles south of San Francisco, where long hair and tie-dyes blend with yuppie refugees from the Bay Area. What the two towns have in common is miles of broad, clean **beaches**, with chilly waters but excellent surf, and a branch of the University of California energizing the local nightlife. In between, small **San Luis Obispo** provides a feasible base for the Central Coast's biggest tourist attraction, **Hearst Castle**, an opulent hilltop palace that was once the estate of publishing magnate William Randolph Hearst.

The Central Coast also contains the bulk and the best of the late eighteenth-century Spanish Colonial **missions** – the first European settlements on the West Coast, set up to convert the natives to Christianity while co-opting their labour. Almost all of the major towns that exist here today grew up around the adobe walls and red-tiled roofs of these Catholic military and religious outposts. Each was deliberately situated a long day's walk from the next and typically comprised a church and a cloistered monastery, enclosed within thick walls to prevent attack by native tribes. **Monterey**, a hundred miles south of San Francisco, was the capital of California under Spain, and later Mexico, and today retains more of its early nineteenth-century architecture than any other city in the state. It's also a good base for one of the most beautiful of the missions, which stands three miles south in the upper-crust seaside resort of **Carmel**.

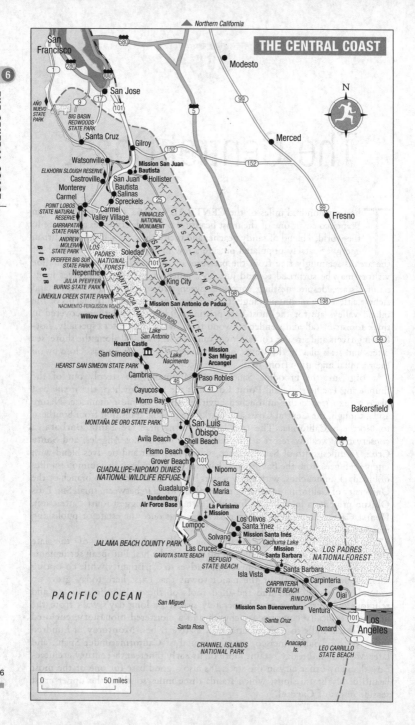

THE CENTRAL COAST

Northern California

Modesto

San Francisco

San Jose

AÑO NUEVO STATE PARK

BIG BASIN REDWOODS STATE PARK

Santa Cruz

Watsonville

Gilroy

Merced

ELKHORN SLOUGH RESERVE

Castroville

San Juan Bautista

Monterey

Salinas

Spreckels

Mission San Juan Bautista

Hollister

Carmel

Carmel Valley Village

POINT LOBOS STATE NATURAL RESERVE

PINNACLES NATIONAL MONUMENT

GARRAPATA STATE PARK

ANDREW MOLERA STATE PARK

LOS PADRES NATIONAL FOREST

Soledad

PFEIFFER BIG SUR STATE PARK

Nepenthe

JULIA PFEIFFER BURNS STATE PARK

LIMEKILN CREEK STATE PARK

NACIMIENTO-FERGUSSON ROAD

Willow Creek

King City

Fresno

Mission San Antonio de Padua

JOLON ROAD

Lake San Antonio

Hearst Castle

San Simeon

Lake Nacimiento

Mission San Miguel Arcangel

HEARST SAN SIMEON STATE PARK

Cambria

Paso Robles

Cayucos

Morro Bay

Bakersfield

MORRO BAY STATE PARK

MONTAÑA DE ORO STATE PARK

San Luis Obispo

Avila Beach

Shell Beach

Pismo Beach

Grover Beach

Nipomo

GUADALUPE-NIPOMO DUNES NATIONAL WILDLIFE REFUGE

Guadalupe

Santa Maria

Vandenberg Air Force Base

La Purisima Mission

Los Olivos

Santa Ynez

Lompoc

Solvang

Mission Santa Inés

Cachuma Lake

JALAMA BEACH COUNTY PARK

Las Cruces

Mission Santa Barbara

LOS PADRES NATIONAL FOREST

GAVIOTA STATE BEACH

REFUGIO STATE BEACH

Isla Vista

Santa Barbara

PACIFIC OCEAN

CARPINTERIA STATE BEACH

Carpinteria

Ojai

RINCON

San Miguel

Mission San Buenaventura

Ventura

Los Angeles

Santa Cruz

Oxnard

Santa Rosa

Anacapa Is.

CHANNEL ISLANDS NATIONAL PARK

LEO CARRILLO STATE BEACH

BIG SUR

SANTA LUCIA RANGE

SALINAS VALLEY

COASTAL RANGE

0   50 miles

Getting around the Central Coast is easy enough: some of the best views in the state can be had from Amtrak's daily Coast Starlight train, which runs right along the coast up to San Luis Obispo before cutting inland north to San Francisco. The Pacific Surfliner, by contrast, is a shorter jaunt along the southern coastal section, linking San Luis Obispo to LA and San Diego with three trains a day. Greyhound buses stop at most of the towns, particularly those along the main highway, US-101 – though the best route, if you've got a car, is the smaller Hwy-1, which follows the coast all the way but takes twice as long. **Places to stay** are relatively easy to find, at least outside summer weekends when otherwise quiet towns and beaches are packed solid with vacationers. Opportunities for **camping** are plentiful, too, in a string of state parks, beaches and forests.

Ventura

Beyond the northwestern fringes of the Los Angeles metroplex, **VENTURA** is an eye-catching little town on the Pacific that offers a few good reasons to stop, including buying fresh strawberries and other seasonal produce from the roadside stalls and catching a boat out to the offshore Channel Islands (see p.371) from the harbour, four miles southwest of town. There's also a scattering of relics from the Spanish, Mexican, and early American past – tour these and the town's selection of galleries and boutiques with the aid of brochures from the **visitor centre**, 101 S California St (T 1-800/333-2989, W www.ventura-usa.com). The town's namesake, along with its most historical sight, is just north of the US-101 and Hwy-1 intersection, where the **Mission San Buenaventura**, 211 E Main St (Mon–Fri 10am–5pm, Sat 9am–5pm, Sun 10am–4pm; $2; T 805/643-4318, W www.sanbuenaventuramission.org), was raised in 1782 as the ninth of the 21 California missions and the last founded by Junípero Serra (whose graceful bronze statue stands in front of the Neoclassical City Hall, at 501 Poli St). Although the mission has been repeatedly damaged by neglect or earthquakes and then restored, it still retains a quaint parochial charm that makes it a worthwhile stop for passers-by or more intrepid "mission tourists" – though if you're looking for truly inspired church architecture, this unassuming Spanish Colonial relic probably won't fit the bill. Nearby, the **Ortega Adobe**, 215 W Main St (daily summer 9am–4pm, rest of year Sat & Sun only; T 805/658-4726), is a modest, whitewashed Spanish-style dwelling from 1857 that's best known as the original site of a well-known chilli producer. It gives a hint of the style that used to dominate the town but has since given way to more modern construction.

Main Street is also home to two small but engaging museums. The **Albinger Archaeological Museum**, 113 E Main St (call for current hours; free; T 805/648-5823, W www.albingermuseum.org), has displays on 3500 years of local history, from ancient Native American cultures such as the Chumash, who were locally present as far back as 1500 BC, right up to the Spanish era – including parts of the nearby mission's original foundation, dating from the 1780s. Across the st, the **Ventura County Museum of History and Art**, 100 E Main St (Tues–Sun 11am–6pm; $4; T 805/653-0323, W www.venturamuseum.org), takes up where the former leaves off, with exhibits on local pioneer families and antique agricultural machinery, plus preserved old saddles, Catholic devotional paintings and more contemporary artefacts from native tribes.

Another glimpse of early life in California can be found at **Olivas Adobe Historical Park**, further out at 4200 Olivas Park Drive (grounds daily 10am–4pm, tours Sat & Sun 10am–4pm; donation; T 805/644-6542, W www.olivasadobe.org), where the titular adobe was once the centrepiece of land baron Jose Olivas's estate in the 1840s, before the Mexican–American War altered the balance of power in the region. Still, Olivas, his wife, and their 21 children lived out the century here, and today it's decorated in the rustic but elegant style appropriate for a major landowner of the mid-nineteenth century, with antique tools and furnishings and a family chapel on display, as well as rose and herb gardens.

Ventura is a fine spot for engaging in outdoor activities; start at the restored 1872 **San Buenaventura Pier**, located where California Street ends, for fishing or light snacks, then head a mile north along a beachside promenade to **Surfer's Point**, a thin strip of sand that's a prime location to put a surfboard or windsurfer in the waves. You can rent boards for $7 per hour or $30 per day (and wetsuits for half that price) at the Ventura Surf Shop, 88 E Thompson Blvd (☎805/643-1062).

Before you launch an expedition to the Channel Islands, visit the **Channel Islands National Park visitor centre**, 1901 Spinnaker Drive (daily 8.30am–5pm; ☎805/658-5730, ⓦwww.nps.gov/chis), next to the ferry landing in Ventura Harbor, which covers the geology and plant and animal life of these beautiful islands, including seals, sea lions, pelicans and giant kelp forests. It also has current information on arranging trips, and an **observation tower** from which, on fine days, you can view the islands. (For more on the national park, see p.371).

Practicalities

Amtrak **trains** (Pacific Surfliner only) pull in near Harbor Boulevard and Figueroa Street. However, Greyhound recently cut services to Ventura; instead, get off the bus in Oxnard at the transit centre at 201 E 4th St, then take the local **transport** service, Gold Coast Transit (tickets $1.35; ☎805/487-4222, ⓦwww.goldcoasttransit.org), to connect to Ventura, Ojai and other towns in the county. The **visitor centre** (see above) has local maps and lists of tour bus and shuttle operators.

Ventura is a clear choice for **accommodation** between LA and Santa Barbara. For something beyond the usual chain lodging, the *Bella Maggiore Inn*, 67 S California St (☎805/652-0277; ❾), is old-fashioned and a bit tatty in places, but has two dozen rooms that variously come with balconies, jacuzzis or fireplaces, in a fetching space with a courtyard and fountains. Alternatively, the best of the mainstream spots is the *Comfort Inn*, 2094 E Harbor Blvd (☎805/653-5000, ⓦwww.comfortinn.com; ❻), good value for its high-speed internet access, clean furnishings and free breakfast, and its suites which have kitchens, jacuzzis and fireplaces. For **eating**, the *Taj Café*, 574 E Main St (☎805/652-1521), has better Indian fare than you might expect, with an appealing array of masala and tandoori dishes and spicy chutneys, while *the* top spot for breakfast, for its hearty pancakes, waffles, hash, and biscuits and gravy, is *Allison's Country Café*, 3429 Telegraph Rd (☎805/644-9072).

Oxnard to Carpinteria

Ventura is the major point of interest between LA and Santa Barbara, but if you're intent on exploring the Central Coast in detail, you may find yourself just south in the military and agricultural burg of **Oxnard**, mainly useful as a transit stop for those on the way to Ventura (see p.367). There's not much to detain you for more than half a day, although **Heritage Square**, between A, B, 7th and 8th streets (guided tours leave from 715 South A St, Sat 10am–4pm, Sun 1–4pm; $3;

ⓣ805/483-7960, ⓦheritagesquareoxnard.com), does offer a re-sited collection of a dozen Victorian structures, highlighted by a stately water tower, the Queen Anne-styled Justin Petit Ranch House, and the Carpenter Gothic-flavoured Pfeiler Ranch House. Just as appealing, the **Carnegie Art Museum** is housed in a historic 1907 Neoclassical library at 424 South C St (Thurs–Sat 10am–5pm, Sun 1–5pm; $3; ⓣ805/385-8157, ⓦwww.carnegieam.org) and showcases the work of local artists in temporary exhibits. The copious holdings of the **Murphy Auto Museum**, 2230 Statham Blvd (Sat & Sun 10am–4pm; $9; ⓣ805/487-4333, ⓦwww.murphyautomuseum.org), on the other hand, are best suited to those interested in exploring classic cars, namely a decent selection of vintage Packards, a Model T, a Rolls, a Bentley and more. Contact the **visitor centre**, 1000 Town Center Rd, Suite 135 (ⓣ1-800/2-OXNARD, ⓦwww.visitoxnard.com), for more information on any of these sites, the town's many worthwhile fruit stands and the agreeable Downtown Farmers Market at Fifth and B Sts (Thurs 9am–1pm, ⓣ805/483-7960) where you can sample the region's copious produce.

Thirteen miles north of Ventura, the area's best surfers head to **Rincon Beach Park** (daily 8am–dusk), a legendary point off Hwy-101 on the Ventura County line where many LA surf gods have ventured to get away from the Malibu crowds. It's best surfed in the winter at low tide to take advantage of its killer reef-break.

Three miles west of here, **Carpinteria** is a beachside hamlet that's good for its laidback Southern-California beach vibe; a small but high-quality farmers' market at 800 Linden Ave (Thurs: summer 4–7pm, winter 3–6pm; ⓣ805/962-5354); an early October **avocado festival** (ⓦwww.avofest.com) that presents the subtropical fruit in all its glory; and several long, uncluttered **beaches** largely free from tourist traffic, with regular closures along part of the shoreline in the winter and spring to allow for bird and seal activity. The **Chamber of Commerce**, 1056-B Eugenia Place (ⓣ805/684-5479, ⓦwww.carpinteriachamber.org), has more information on surfing rentals and town listings. For a distinctive **stay** in town, camp at **Carpinteria State Beach** ($35; ⓣ1-800/444-7275, ⓦwww.reserveamerica .com), one of the better stretches of sand in these parts, with tidepools and wintertime views of whales and sea lions.

Ojai

Nestled in the hills above Ventura, the hamlet of **OJAI** (pronounced "O-hi") is a wealthy resort community frequented by weekend jet-setters and celebrities from LA, replete with exclusive spas and tennis clubs dotting the surrounding countryside. Consequently, perhaps, it's also a New Age hub that's the headquarters of the Krishnamurti Society, honouring the Indian Theosophist who, in the 1920s, lived and lectured in the Ojai Valley, which he considered "a vessel of comprehension, intelligence and truth". The Pine Cottage, the house where the philosopher once lived, is the setting for the **Krishnamurti Visitor Center and Library**, four miles northeast of town at 1098 McAndrew Road (Thurs & Fri 1–5pm, Sat & Sun 10am–5pm; free; ⓣ805/646-4948, ⓦwww.kfa.org), which details his progressive ideas on spirituality through books, DVDs and so on. The mellow **Pepper Retreat** in a classic ranch house, nearby at no. 1130 (ⓣ1-877/355-5986, ⓦwww.peppertreeretreat.com; ❹), offers eight modern rooms and lets you get further into the holistic spirit by taking nature walks in a shaded glade and enjoying vegetarian meals, all in a setting where Krishnamurti once hosted the likes of Aldous Huxley, Igor Stravinsky and The Beatles. From here you can also access the numerous hiking trails that lead up into the marvellous preserve of **Los Padres National Forest**, whose nearest ranger station is at 1190 E Ojai Avenue (Mon–Fri 8am–4.30pm; ℡805/646-4348, Ⓦwww.fs.fed.us/r5 /lospadres) and stocks maps, passes, camping information and other materials for exploring the outback of this two-million-acre expanse. The nearest campsite to Ojai, eight miles away off Hwy-33, is Wheeler Gorge (sites $20–40, day-use $10; ℡805/640-1977, Ⓦwww.rockymountainrec.com), sited among the majestic forest peaks, with plenty of options for fishing and hiking.

The town itself is adorned with the graceful Spanish Revival architecture that glassworks magnate Edward Drummond Libbey introduced here a century ago after a devastating fire, exemplified best by the post office's iconic **bell tower** and the adjoining, curvaceous **pergola** at Libbey Park, E Ojai Avenue at S Signal Street. The **Ojai Valley Museum**, 130 W Ojai Avenue (Thurs–Fri 1–4pm, Sat 10am–4pm, Sun noon–4pm; $4; ℡805/640-1390, Ⓦwww.ojaivalleymuseum .org), housed in a former Mission Revival church built in 1919, has engaging exhibits on history, agriculture, oil prospecting and art, highlighted by a Chumash garden that recalls the local peoples who predated the American settlers.

Numerous festivals and events – celebrating everything from film and music to wine and spirituality – take place throughout Ojai during the year (see visitor centre, below, for details), but the highlight is the mid-October **Ojai Day** (Ⓦwww.ojaiday.com), an annual street fair that features local food, music and craftworks as well as belly dancing, aromatherapy and poetry readings, culminating with the painting of a giant mandala.

Practicalities

You can reach Ojai from Ventura or Oxnard on Gold Coast Transit (line #16; tickets $1.35; ℡805/487-4222, Ⓦwww.goldcoasttransit.org). Near Libbey Park, the **visitor centre**, 201 S Signal St (℡805/646-8126, Ⓦwww.ojaichamber.org), is a good place for information on the town's historical architecture and numerous old-fashioned **inns and B&Bs**. On a country farm ten minutes from Downtown, the *Farm Hostel* (℡805/646-0311, Ⓦwww.hostelhandbook.com/farmhostel /default.htm) offers a bucolic setting for foreign visitors only, with free pickup from nearby Greyhound and Amtrak stations and dorm beds for $15, but you must have an international air-travel ticket or current visa (3- or 6-month period) to stay. For any kind of visitors, but particularly golfers, the cushy, Mission-flavoured *Ojai Valley Inn & Spa*, 905 Country Club Rd (℡1-800/422-6524, Ⓦwww .ojairesort.com; two-night weekend minimum; ❾), has a graceful design and numerous elegant rooms and suites for upwards of $400 a night; and the *Lavender Inn*, 210 E Matilija St (℡1-877/646-6635, Ⓦwww.lavenderinn.com; ❺–❽), is a tasteful B&B that, along with its flowery rooms and cottages, also has lovely gardens and a day-spa and offers cooking classes. Also appealing is the *Su Nido Inn*, 301 N Montgomery St (℡805/646-7080, Ⓦwww.sunidoinn.com; ❼), an attractive, Spanish Colonial-themed inn whose best suites boast fireplaces and large-screen TVs, some with balconies.

The top of the local **food** chain is *Suzanne's Cuisine*, 502 W Ojai Ave (℡805/640-1961), whose eclectic Cal-cuisine offerings include inexpensive lunchtime fare like calamari sandwiches, poached salmon and Reubens, while among the pricier dinners are rack of lamb, Cornish game hen, seafood and savoury pastas. The more affordable *Ojai Café Emporium*, 108 S Montgomery St, is good for its well-priced breakfasts of waffles and omelettes, and lunches of burgers, salads and a smattering of Mexican fare. Better on the latter count, though, is *Ruben's Burritos*, 104 N Signal St, which doles out the titular stuffed tortilla in a range of cheap, rib-stuffing varieties.

Channel Islands National Park

Stretching north from Santa Catalina Island off the coast of Los Angeles, a chain of fascinating desert islands is preserved as the 250,000-acre **CHANNEL ISLANDS NATIONAL PARK**, offering excellent hiking trails and splendid views of marine life, as well as fishing and scuba and skin diving through the many caves, coves and shipwrecks in the crystal-clear Pacific waters. Five of the eight islands are accessible as part of the park, though the closest, Anacapa, some fourteen miles south of Ventura, sees the most ecotourist traffic. The best time to visit is between February and April, when you can engage in **whale-watching**. Inland **hiking** requires a permit (☏805/658-5711, ⓦwww.nps.gov/chis) and **divers** can explore the two exposed wrecks on either side of the island.

Park practicalities

If you're considering visiting the Channel Islands, the best introduction to their unique geology, flora and fauna can be found in Ventura at the park's **visitor centre**, 1901 Spinnaker Drive (daily 8.30am–5pm; free; ☏805/658-5730), which also offers models, films and telescopes to view the islands at a distance. More information is available at the Outdoors Santa Barbara Visitor Center, in that town at 113 Harbor Way, 4th Floor (daily 10am–5pm; ☏805/884-1475, ⓦoutdoorsb .noaa.gov).

The Nature Conservancy acquired ninety percent of the islands in 1988 and has made them accessible to the public on **day-trip tours**. Nearly the only way to visit the park is by boat, through operators that run from Ventura Harbor. Anacapa is served by several tours run by Island Packers, 1691 Spinnaker Drive, three miles west of US-101 and a mile south of Ventura (☏805/642-7688 for 24-hour recorded information, ☏805/642-1393 for reservations 9am–5pm, ⓦwww .islandpackers.com). Packages include all-day trips with two to five hours on the given island ($45–75, depending on the island), two-day camping excursions ($58–108) and whale-watching outings that last about three hours and start at $32. The trip over takes ninety minutes to three hours each way (or four to five hours for San Miguel); boats don't run every day and often fill up so reserve ahead. Truth Aquatics, 301 W Cabrillo Blvd, Santa Barbara (☏805/962-1127, ⓦwww .truthaquatics.com), has alternative itineraries to all the islands on smaller vessels at higher prices, including two-day hiking, diving and kayaking excursions.

You can also reach Santa Rosa Island on a half-hour **flight** from Channel Islands Aviation (☏805/987-1301, ⓦwww.flycia.com), which runs half-day weekend excursions ($160) or overnight camping excursions ($300), both setting off from Camarillo Airport (off US-101, 20 miles south of Ventura). Santa Cruz Island is also the destination for kayak trips from Ventura and Santa Barbara (see p.372).

There are a number of free, primitive **campgrounds** (permits $15 per night; make reservations at ☏1-877/444-6777 or ⓦreservations.nps.gov) on each island if you want to rough it. Bring plenty of food and especially water, as none is available on the island.

The islands

One-mile-square **Anacapa** (Chumash for "mirage") is actually two islets. **West Anacapa** is largely a refuge for nesting brown pelicans, most of it off limits, except **Frenchy's Cove**, a pristine beach and good base for scuba or snorkeling expeditions. **East Anacapa** has a small visitor centre and a 1.5-mile nature trail, and is known for its signature **Arch Rock**, encompassing a thin rocky bridge over the waves. There are no beaches here, but swimming in the cove where the boats dock is allowed. Like the other islands, Anacapa is a volcanic outcrop whose cliffs and crags were carved by glaciers during the last Ice Age and its rocky headlands and steep promontories over the sea will give you pause before venturing off the trail. West of Anacapa, **Santa Cruz** is the largest and highest of the islands, rich in its fauna – from bald eagles and scrub jays to native foxes – and diverse landscapes that range from forbidding canyons to lovely green valleys. It's owned by the Nature Conservancy and throughout the island you can hike or even camp in the remote landscapes.

Almost as big as Santa Cruz, **Santa Rosa** has many grasslands, canyons and steep ravines, but overall contains gentler terrain – though it's still compelling for its hiking and kayaking opportunities. Especially interesting are its archeological sites, some of which date back 11,000 years and are still being investigated for their Chumash settlement relics. The most distant island – windswept **San Miguel**, fifty miles offshore – is alive with elephant seals and sea lions, and is thought to be the burial place of sixteenth-century Spanish explorer Juan Cabrillo. No grave has been found, but a monument has been erected at Cuyler Harbor on the island's eastern end. Seasoned hikers may also wish to make the rugged cross-island trip to Point Bennett to spy on the plentiful wildlife. However, the island is only for the most gung-ho nature explorers: it's frequently foggy and windy and its surrounding rocks make for a white-knuckle sailing trip (park-approved boat tours only).

South of the main islands lies the smallest of the Channel group, **Santa Barbara**, named by Sebastian Vizcaíno, who dropped by on St Barbara's Day, December 4, 1602. The island's appeal these days is largely due to its sea lions, kestrels, larks and meadowlarks, which can be seen on land gradually recovering its native flora after years of destruction by now-extinct rabbits.

Of the three other islands in the full chain, **San Clemente** (the furthest south) and **San Nicolas** are controlled by the US Navy, while the most urbanized, **Santa Catalina**, is a different sort of experience that constitutes its own weekend trip from LA (see p.123 for information).

Santa Barbara

The speedy US-101 that whips along the coast above Ventura slows to a more leisurely pace a hundred miles north of Los Angeles at **SANTA BARBARA**, a seaside resort beautifully situated on the gently sloping hills above the Pacific – and named after the patron saint of firefighters and artillerymen. The town's low-rise Spanish Colonial Revival buildings feature red-tiled roofs and white stucco walls, an evocative backdrop to the palm-lined **beaches** below, winding along a gently curving bay.

Once home to Ronald Reagan, and a weekend escape for much of the old money of Los Angeles, Santa Barbara has a traditional conservative side, but is largely a provincial place; for the most part, local culture is confined to playing volleyball, surfing, cycling, sipping coffee or cruising in expensive convertibles along the shore. After an essential visit to **Mission Santa Barbara** and a leisurely walk along the pier, most visitors will quickly get a sense of the place and move on, though there's more to the town and the area if you have the time to explore.

Arrival, information and transport

Greyhound **buses** arrive from LA and San Francisco every few hours, stopping Downtown at 34 W Carrillo St, while Amtrak **trains** stop at 209 State St, a block

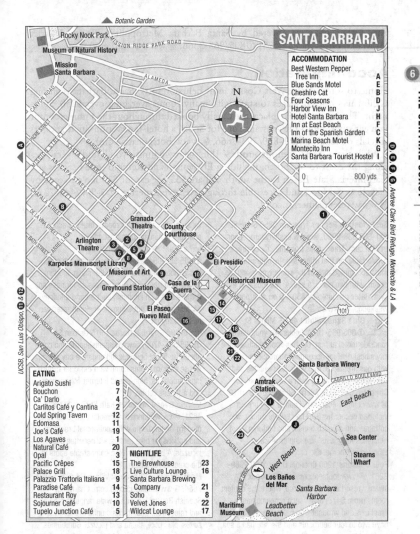

SANTA BARBARA

Botanic Garden

Rocky Nook Park
MISSION RIDGE PARK ROAD

Museum of Natural History

Mission
Santa Barbara

ALAMEDA

N

GARDEN STREET

CANYON ROAD

MISSION STREET

SANTA BARBARA STREET

LAGUNA STREET

GARDEN STREET

VICTORIA STREET

ANAPAMU STREET

GARCIA ROAD

SOLA STREET

ANAPAMU STREET

PEDREGOSA STREET

ARRELLAGA STREET

MICHELTORENA ST

ANACAPA STREET

STATE STREET

CHAPALA STREET

DE LA VINA STREET

BATH STREET

FIGUEROA STREET

CARRILLO STREET

ALTA VISTA STREET

SALSIPUEDES STREET

N. MILPAS STREET

CANON PERDIDO STREET

Granada
Theatre

County
Courthouse

El Presidio

Arlington
Theatre

Karpeles Manuscript Library

Museum of Art

Greyhound Station

Casa de la
Guerra

Historical Museum

El Paseo
Nuevo Mall

CASTILLO - ORTEGA STREET

DE LA GUERRA ST

COTA STREET

SANTA BARBARA STREET

GUTIERREZ STREET

MONTECITO STREET

101

HALEY STREET

Santa Barbara Winery

CARRILLO BOULEVARD

Amtrak
Station

SAN PASCUAL AVENUE

SAN ANDRES STREET

SAN PASCUAL STREET

CASTILLO ST

East Beach

Sea Center

West Beach

Stearns
Wharf

SHORELINE DRIVE

Los Baños
del Mar

Santa Barbara
Harbor

Maritime
Museum

Leadbetter
Beach

UCSB, San Luis Obispo ① & ②

① & ②

Andrée Clark Bird Refuge, Montecito & LA

ACCOMMODATION

Best Western Pepper Tree Inn	A
Blue Sands Motel	E
Cheshire Cat	B
Four Seasons	D
Harbor View Inn	J
Hotel Santa Barbara	H
Inn at East Beach	F
Inn of the Spanish Garden	C
Marina Beach Motel	K
Montecito Inn	G
Santa Barbara Tourist Hostel	I

0   800 yds

EATING

Arigato Sushi	6
Bouchon	7
Ca' Darlo	4
Carlitos Café y Cantina	2
Cold Spring Tavern	12
Edomasa	11
Joe's Café	19
Los Agaves	1
Natural Café	20
Opal	3
Pacific Crêpes	15
Palace Grill	18
Palazzio Trattoria Italiana	9
Paradise Café	14
Restaurant Roy	13
Sojourner Café	10
Tupelo Junction Café	5

NIGHTLIFE

The Brewhouse	23
Live Culture Lounge	16
Santa Barbara Brewing Company	21
Soho	8
Velvet Jones	22
Wildcat Lounge	17

west of US-101. Santa Barbara **airport** (☎805/683-4011, ⊛www.flysba.com), eight miles north of the town centre at 500 Fowler Rd (near UC Santa Barbara), has a limited and often expensive scheduled service to other cities in the Western US, hosting airlines such as American, United, Delta and Alaska.

For more information on Santa Barbara, or for help with finding a place to stay, contact the **visitor centre**, 1 Garden St (Mon–Sat 9am–5pm, Sun 10am–5pm; ☎805/965-3021, ⊛www.santabarbara.com). The US Forest Service office, 3505 Paradise Rd (Mon–Fri 8am–4.30pm; ☎805/967-3481, ⊛www.r5.fs.fed .us/lospadres), can provide information on **hiking** in the adjoining Los Padres National Forest, steering you toward the many trails accessible from town.

Getting around Santa Barbara mainly involves walking, though there's a 25¢ **shuttle** that loops between Downtown and the beach, and from the harbour to the zoo. Other areas are covered by Santa Barbara Metropolitan Transit District (SBMTD) **buses** (fares $1.75; ☎ 805/963-3366, ⓦ www.sbmtd.gov).

Accommodation

Home to some of the West Coast's most deluxe resorts, Santa Barbara is among California's priciest places to **stay**, with many rooms averaging over $250–300 a night. The less expensive places are usually booked throughout the summer, but if you get stuck, enlist the assistance of Hot Spots, a hotel-reservation site that offers specials on lodging (☎ 1-800/793-7666, ⓦ www.hotspotsusa.com).

While there are no **campgrounds** within the town limits, you'll find several sites along the coast to the north, including El Capitan and Refugio state beaches and Carpinteria State Beach to the south. All are $35 per car, or $10 if you come by bicycle or on foot, and accessible through Reserve America (☎ 1-800/444-7275, ⓦ www.reserveamerica.com).

Best Western Pepper Tree Inn 3850 State St ☎ 1-800/338-0030, ⓦ www.bestwesternpepper treeinn.com. Three miles from the city centre, a comfortable inn that offers slightly better rates than most accommodation of the same type along the beach, with two pools, a sauna, hot tubs and a gym. Rates can jump by $50–70 on summer weekends, otherwise ⑥

Blue Sands Motel 421 S Milpas St ☎ 805/965-1624. Looks like your average roadside motel at first, but this spot is actually the city's best deal for accommodation: clean rooms with gas fireplaces, free wi-fi, kitchenettes and flat-screen TVs – along with a heated pool. ⑤

Cheshire Cat 36 W Valerio St ☎ 805/569-1610, ⓦ www.cheshirecat.com. Loaded with precious Victorian decor, this B&B has twelve rooms, two cottages and a coach house, and features a hot tub, bikes for guests' use and an *Alice in Wonderland* theme. ⑦

Four Seasons 1260 Channel Drive ☎ 805/969-2261, ⓦ www.fourseasons.com. The apex of swanky resort style in the area, where the opulent rooms (from $475) boast such amenities as fireplaces and wrought-iron balconies, the suites have two to four bedrooms and the site has a spa, pool and fitness centre. ⑨

Harbor View Inn 28 W Cabrillo Blvd ☎ 1-800/755-0222, ⓦ www.harborviewinnsb.com. One of the more appealing luxury hotels around, offering on-site restaurant and bar, pool and jacuzzis and elegant rooms with patios or balconies. ⑧

Hotel Santa Barbara 533 State St ☎ 805/957-9300, ⓦ www.hotelsantabarbara.com. Considering its prime Downtown location, this spot offers good

value for its comfortable rooms, internet access and complimentary breakfast. ⑦

Inn at East Beach 1029 Orilla del Mar ☎ 805/965-0546, ⓦ www.innateastbeach.com. Has a motel-like appearance but clean, modern rooms with free wi-fi, microwaves and fridges and some suites with kitchens, built around a kidney-shaped pool. ⑥, but summer weekend rates can be $100 higher.

Inn of the Spanish Garden 915 Garden St ☎ 805/564-4700, ⓦ www.spanishgardeninn.com. About the finest boutique lodgings the city offers, whose elegant rooms come with designer furnish-ings, fireplaces, high-speed internet connections and a fitness centre. ⑨

Marina Beach Motel 21 Bath St ☎ 1-877/627-4621, ⓦ www.marinabeachmotel.com. Clean and modern motel rooms with continental breakfast and options for bike rentals, kitchenettes and jacuzzis. A bit cheaper than comparable spots in the area. ⑤, summer ⑦

Montecito Inn 1295 Coast Village Rd ☎ 805/969-7854, ⓦ www.montecitoinn.com. Charming, Spanish Revival inn with a wide range of rooms and rates, from quaint, basic units to elaborate suites, plus pool, sauna and jacuzzi. Sometimes has summer discounts of $100 or so. Otherwise ⑧

Santa Barbara Tourist Hostel 134 Chapala St ☎ 805/963-0154, ⓦ www.sbhostel.com. Centrally located hostel near the beach and State Street with bicycle and surfboard rentals, internet access and complimentary breakfast. Dorm rooms go for $22–35, with private rooms also available ($55–95), some with private bath (extra $4–10, depending on room).

The Town

Up until the 1920s, Santa Barbara was a fairly typical California beachside community, with Victorian and historic-revival styles mixed with a handful of

Santa Barbara County wineries

Wine fanatics shouldn't miss a visit to Santa Barbara County's copious vineyards, of which there are more than one hundred. Although it's not the Napa Valley per se, the area does offer plenty of **wineries** with the requisite tastings and merchandise for sale. Slightly beyond the town's centre, not far from US-101, the **Santa Barbara Winery**, 202 Anacapa St at Yanonali Street (daily 10am–5pm; $25 private tastings with advance notice at ☎805/963-3633, ⓦwww.sbwinery.com), is worth a stop to see one of the oldest commercial wineries in the county, built in 1962. You can get more information on this and other wineries by contacting the Santa Barbara Vintners' Association (☎805/688-0881, ⓦwww.sbcountywines.com) or the similar WineCountry site (☎707/265-1835, ⓦwww.santabarbara.winecountry.com), which also has information on winery-related lodging and restaurants throughout the state. True fanatics may enjoy a more extensive trip courtesy of **Cloud Climbers** (by reservation only at ☎805/646-3200, ⓦwww.ccjeeps.com), who for $120 will take you on a six-hour jeep tour of local wineries, with lunch and four tasting fees included.

Spanish Colonial cast-offs from the nineteenth century – with the Presidio and Mission among the more noteworthy relics. Somewhat ironically, Santa Barbara owes its current, heavily Spanish-flavoured atmosphere, with its attendant quaintness and historical "authenticity", to a devastating **earthquake** in 1925, after which the city authorities decided to rebuild virtually the entire town as an apocryphal Mission-era village – even the massive "historic" El Paseo shopping mall has a whitewashed adobe facade. This was surprisingly successful and Santa Barbara is now synonymous through California (and the nation) with genteel oceanside living in antique splendour. The square-mile **town centre**, squeezed between the south-facing **beaches** and the foothills of the Santa Ynez Mountains, has one of the region's liveliest street scenes. The main drag, **State Street**, is home to an assortment of diners, bookstores, coffee bars and nightclubs catering as much to the needs of locals – among them twenty thousand UC Santa Barbara students – as to visitors.

The historic centre

The **historic centre** of Santa Barbara lies mostly along State Street a few blocks inland from the highway, where the town's few genuine Mission-era structures are preserved as **El Presidio de Santa Barbara**, a collection of whitewashed adobe buildings two blocks east of State Street at 123 E Cañon Perdido St (daily 10.30am–4.30pm; $5; ⓦwww.sbthp.org/presidio.htm), built around the fourth and last of the Spanish military garrisons in the region – though only the living quarters of the soldiers who once guarded the site remain. One of these structures, the modest **El Cuartel**, is the second oldest building in California, dating from 1782, and now houses historical exhibits and a scale model of the small Spanish colony. A block away, at 136 E De la Guerra St, the **Santa Barbara Historical Museum** (Tues–Sat 10am–5pm, Sun noon–5pm; free; ☎805/966-1601, ⓦwww.santabarbaramuseum.com), built around an 1817 adobe, presents an array of middling local artworks and rotating exhibits on Spanish- and Mexican-era life and other aspects of the city's past, from Ice Age geology to artefacts from native settlements to modern photographs. Near the museum, where De la Guerra Street meets State Street, the **Casa de la Guerra** (Sat & Sun noon–4pm; $5; ☎805/965-0093, ⓦwww.sbthp.org/casa.htm) preserves what was, in the 1820s, one of the more upscale residences in town (though still built in the spartan Spanish Colonial style), home to one of the Presidio's commanders. These days, it holds spurs, saddles, toys and weapons, plus exhibits of antique tools, furniture and religious icons. After it survived the 1925 earthquake that otherwise obliterated much of Downtown, the Casa became a template for the type of Spanish Colonial style that, in its revival form, continues to dominate the town's design.

On the corner of State and Anapamu, at 1130 State St, the fine **Santa Barbara Museum of Art** (Tues–Sun 11am–5pm; $9; ☎805/963-4364, ☻www.sbmuseart .org) features some classical Greek and Egyptian statuary, a smattering of French Impressionists, an Asian collection of some note and interesting modern photography. There's an appealing if scattershot selection of European greats, from minor works of Bonnard and Matisse to more engaging pieces from Chagall, Kandinsky and Miró. Its main features, though, come from its **American collection**, which is particularly strong in nineteenth-century landscape painters such as Albert Bierstadt, realists such as George Bellows and Thomas Eakins and postwar Californian modernists such as Richard Diebenkorn. Just east, the still-functioning **County Courthouse**, 1100 Anacapa St (Mon–Fri 8am–5pm, Sat & Sun 10am–4.30pm; free; ☎805/962-6464, ☻www.santabarbaracourthouse.org), is a Spanish Revival gem, an idiosyncratic 1929 variation on the Mission theme that's widely known as one of the finest public buildings in the US, with striking murals, tilework and fountain. Enjoy a free tour (daily 2pm, also Mon, Tues & Fri 10.30am) or take a break in the sunken gardens, explore the quirky staircases, or climb the seventy-foot "**El Mirador**" clocktower for a nice view out over the town. From here you can get a fine perspective on how successful this little burg has been in transforming its California beach-town look into a homegrown version of early modern Spain.

Two blocks up State Street, at no. 1317, the landmark 1930s **Arlington Theatre** (☎805/963-4408, ☻www.thearlingtontheatre.com) is an intact and functional movie palace and performance venue, with a trompe l'oeil interior modelled after an atmospheric Spanish village plaza. The modest but respected Santa Barbara Symphony (tickets $30–75; ☎805/898-9386, ☻www.thesymphony.org) performs a block away at the 1924 Moorish-flavoured **Granada theatre**, 1216 State St, gloriously renovated to serve as the town's main performing arts centre (☎805/899-2222, ☻www.granadasb.org). Nearby, at 21 W Anapamu St, the beautifully decorated **Karpeles Manuscript Library** (Wed–Sun 10am–4pm; free; ☎805/962-5322, ☻www.rain.org/~karpeles) is home to a diverse array of original documents that show in temporary exhibitions and may include such notable items as the Constitution of the Confederate States of America, Napoleon's battle plans for his Russian invasion, handwritten orchestral scores, and the manuscripts of famous figures such as Mark Twain, Thomas Edison, John Locke and Jorge Luis Borges.

The beaches and around

Half a mile down State Street from the town centre, Cabrillo Boulevard runs along the south-facing shore, a long, clean strip stretching from the yacht and fishing harbour beyond palm-lined **West Beach** to the volleyball courts and golden sands of **East Beach**. At the foot of State Street, take a stroll among the pelicans on the 1872 **Stearns Wharf** (☻www.stearnswharf.org), the oldest wooden pier in the state. The victim of several earthquakes and fires, it was nearly destroyed most recently in November 1998 when a third of it was engulfed in flames, but it has since been restored to its former glory. The wharf is lined with knickknack shops, seafood restaurants, ice cream stands, and the **Ty Warner Sea Center** (daily 10am–5pm; $8; ☎805/962-2526), an annexe of the Museum of Natural History (see opposite), offering a tot-friendly selection of touch tanks, interactive exhibits, whale bones and tide pools.

Outdoor fun in Santa Barbara

Just west of the pier, athletes keep in shape in the fifty-metre Los Baños del Mar heated **swimming pool**, 401 Shoreline Drive (dawn–10pm; $5; ℡805/966-6110), an open-air, year-round facility. **Windsurfers** can be rented from beachfront stalls and **kayaks** are available from Paddle Sports, 117 Harbor Way (℡805/899-4925, ⓦwww .kayaksb.com), starting at $25 for two hours and $50 for a full day. This outfit can also arrange kayak trips to the Channel Islands for around $200 per person for an all-day journey. If you're interested in exploring the town by **bicycle**, Wheel Fun Rentals, 22 State St (℡805/966-2282, ⓦwww.wheelfunrentals.com), and 23 E Cabrillo Blvd (same contact info), has a variety of models from tandems to tricycles, with basic two-wheelers going for around $20–35 a day, plus canoes and paddleboats, and provides a map of Santa Barbara's extensive system of bike paths. Get good **hiking** information from Santa Barbara Hikes (ⓦwww.santabarbarahikes.com); the longest and most satisfying path leads west twelve miles along the bluffs to Isla Vista and UC Santa Barbara, passing a mile or so back from the rarely crowded, creekside Arroyo Burro Beach (locally known as "Hendry's"), four miles west of the wharf at the end of Las Positas Road. Alternatively, head along the beachfront bike path two miles east past the small but worthwhile Santa Barbara Zoo, 500 Niños Drive (daily 10am–5pm; $12; ℡805/962-6310, ⓦwww.santabarbarazoo.org) – notable for its sharks, stingrays and turtles, plus a handful of monkeys and excellent display of sea lions – and cycle around the Andree Clark Bird Refuge, 1400 E Cabrillo Blvd (daily dawn–10pm), a 42-acre saltwater marsh where you can see many interesting seabirds, including egrets, herons and cormorants.

Just west, the **Santa Barbara Maritime Museum**, 113 Harbor Way, Suite 190 (Thurs–Tues 10am–6pm; $7; ℡805/962-8404, ⓦwww.sbmm.org), occupies the site of the old Naval Reserve Center and showcases old-fashioned ship models and exhibits on the whaling and tallow trade, seal hunting, native Chumash canoes and the current nautical practices of recovering shipwrecks and communicating with shore. A few vessels are outside, including a bathyscaphe submersible for plumbing the deep.

Mission Santa Barbara and beyond

The mission from which the city takes its name, **Mission Santa Barbara** (daily 9am–4.30pm; $5; ℡805/682-4713, ⓦwww.sbmission.org), is located in the hills above town at 2201 Laguna St. Known as the "Queen of the Missions", its imposing twin-towered facade – facing out over a perfectly manicured garden towards the sea – combines Romanesque and Mission styles, giving it a formidable character lacking in some of the prettier outposts in the chain. The present structure, built to replace a series of three adobe churches that had been destroyed by earthquakes, was finished and dedicated in 1820 by Franciscan friars, but the huge 1925 earthquake damaged the mission and the ensuing restoration cost nearly $400,000. Today, a small **museum** displays artefacts from the mission archives, and the cemetery contains the remains of some four thousand Native Americans, many of whom helped build the original complex, which includes aqueducts, water-works, a grist mill and two reservoirs, with the old pottery kiln and tanning vats now in ruin. To get to the mission, take SBMTD bus #22 (daily 6.30am–5.30pm) from the Courthouse along Anapamu Street Downtown, or walk or drive the half mile from State Street up Mission Street and Mission Canyon.

Just beyond the mission at 2559 Puerta del Sol Road, the **Museum of Natural History** (daily 10am–5pm; $10; ℡805/682-4711, ⓦwww.sbnature.org)

showcases intriguing artefacts from Chumash culture, various dioramas of mammals, birds, reptiles and insects, a planetarium and actual skeletons of such extinct creatures as the pygmy mammoth, taken from Santa Rosa Island, off the Santa Barbara coast in Channel Islands National Park (see p.371). For a closer glimpse of nature, continue on into the hills from the mission until you come to the splendid **Botanic Garden**, 1212 Mission Canyon Rd (daily 9am–6pm, Nov– Feb closes 5pm; $8; ☎805/682-4726, ⓦwww.sbbg.org), whose 65 acres feature pleasant hiking trails amid endemic cacti, manzanita, trees and wildflowers – a relaxing respite among hillside meadows and glades.

Eating

Santa Barbara has a number of very good and very expensive **restaurants**, but it also has many more affordable options offering a range of cuisines. Since it's right on the Pacific, you'll find a lot of seafood and sushi; Mexican places are also numerous and the ever-popular local variety of California cuisine finds a place in many establishments.

Arigato Sushi 1225 State St ☎805/965-6074. The main draw for sushi in town, a boutique Japanese spot that's a bit on the pricey side, with the requisite modernist chic and hipster diners – but the fresh, delicious raw fish tends to justify the expense.

Bouchon 9 W Victoria St ☎805/730-1160. Among the town's top choices for elite dining, a California cuisine favourite that presents such rotating items as escargot, rack of lamb or venison, maple-glazed duck breast and a full selection of fresh seafood.

Ca' Darlo 37 E Victoria St ☎805/884-9419. Although there are a number of upscale Italian haunts in town, this is one of the few that lives up to its prices, with a fine set of cheeses and pastas and main dishes that may include roasted quail, veal chops, crêpes and fresh fish.

Carlitos Café y Cantina 1234 State St ☎805/962-7117. Good, affordable Mexican fare in a somewhat touristy spot, with the usual staples plus more enjoyable items like shrimp fajitas and empanadas, stuffed chillies, taquitos and grilled giant prawns.

Cold Spring Tavern 5995 Stagecoach Rd ☎805/967-0066. Tucked away in the hills, this is the place for fresh regional game presented in a clubby lodge setting, with favourites such as rabbit medallions, venison chilli, BBQ ribs and duck breast regularly on the menu. Dinner can be expensive, but lunch and breakfast are more affordable.

Edomasa 2710 De La Vina St ☎805/687-0210. Affordable, cosy sushi joint with a good menu and nice presentation – the salmon, marina and ginger shrimp rolls are top-notch. Frequented more by locals than tourist interlopers. Open until midnight, 1am on weekends.

Joe's Café 536 State St ☎805/966-4638. Long-established bar and grill, still a great place to stop off for a burger, chowder, steak sandwich or pot roast. More or less midway between the beach and the Downtown museums.

Los Agaves 600 N Milpas St ☎805/564-2626. Terrific *mole* dishes, quesadillas, chile poblano and sautéed shrimp – not to mention rib-stuffing burritos – make this inexpensive Mexican haunt a great stop and excellent value if you're hungry for good food.

Natural Café 508 State St. Good and cheap veggie meals – with pasta, sandwiches, salads, falafel and desserts – plus meat mains such as tacos and enchiladas, in a prime spot for people-watching. Part of a regional chain.

Opal 1325 State St ☎805-966-9676. Fresh and inventive California cuisine with dishes such as crab cakes, tiger prawns and a range of pizzas and pastas. Mostly mid-priced menu, though the duck and steak main courses are more toward the upper end.

Pacific Crêpes 705 Anacapa St. About as close to a decent crêpe as you're going to get between San Francisco and LA, in this case authentically prepared by real French cooks, who do an especially good job on the dessert crêpes.

Palace Grill 8 E Cota St ☎805/963-5000. Engaging mid-priced spot with strong cocktails and scrumptious Cajun cuisine, of which the likes of crawfish étouffée, jambalaya piquante, blackened redfish and a mean bread pudding will set your taste buds dancing.

Palazzio Trattoria Italiana 1026 State St ☎805/564-1985. One of the better Italian restaurants in town, with old-fashioned sauce-heavy cuisine, gut-buster-sized portions, moderate prices and one mean tiramisù.

Paradise Café 702 Anacapa St ☎ 805/962-4416. Stylish, mid-level indoor/outdoor grill with good steaks and steak sandwiches, fresh seafood, solid pies and burgers. Service can be marginal at times.
Restaurant Roy 7 W Carrillo St ☎ 805/966-5636. Tasty little restaurant whose pricey main dishes include savoury items like bacon-wrapped filet mignon, grilled ahi tuna, rack of lamb and home-made pastas. There's also a variety of art, cocktails and backgammon contests.
Sojourner Café 134 E Cañon Perdido St ☎ 805/965-7922. A range of affordable vegetarian food – pastas, salads, stews and a few Mexican and Indian-inspired items – in a friendly bohemian setting, with occasional art shows as well.
Tupelo Junction Café 1218 State St ☎ 805/899-3100. One of the town's best spots for breakfast, in this case heavily in the Southern vein, focusing on such rib-stuffing items as mushroom-and-truffle scrambles, crab cake and potato hash, vanilla French toast and Maine lobster chowder. Also with affordable lunches and more expensive dinners.

Nightlife

There are quite a few **bars** and **clubs** along State Street, especially Downtown; for the most up-to-date **nightlife** listings, check out a copy of the free weekly *Santa Barbara Independent* (ⓦ www.independent.com), available at area bookstores, record stores and convenience marts.

The Brewhouse 229 W Montecito St ☎ 805/884-4664. Enjoyable brewpub with around ten handcrafted beers, including some savoury Belgian-style ales, plus decent comfort food (meatloaf, burgers etc) and live music Wed–Sun.
Live Culture Lounge 11 W De la Guerra, in the Paseo Nuevo Mall ☎ 805/845-8800. Curious wine-bar-café-gallery that also presents handcrafted brews, eclectic live music, grilled sandwiches and frozen yoghurt. The food is enjoyable and affordable and the cocktails strong and inventive.
Santa Barbara Brewing Company 501 State St ☎ 805/730-1040. Serviceable American fare – burgers, seafood and sandwiches – with solid microbrewed beers and live music on weekends. The Rincon Red and State Street Stout are both worth a swig.

Soho 1221 State St ☎ 805/962-7776, ⓦ www.sohosb.com. Favourite local place to catch a jazz show, with nightly performances and the occasional big name. Mixes the vibe with frequent rock, acoustic and world-beat artists and bands.
Velvet Jones 423 State St ☎ 805/965-8676, ⓦ www.velvet-jones.com. Among the few good places in town to catch a show, typically of the indie variety, from Thurs–Sat, and the odd comedy and reggae show at other times.
Wildcat Lounge 15 W Ortega St ☎ 805/962-7970, ⓦ www.wildcatlounge.com. A good spot for seeing electronica DJs and various bands in a chic atmosphere with a mix of locals, students and out-of-towners.

On from Santa Barbara

Continuing north from Santa Barbara, you can either cut inland through the wine region of the Santa Ynez Valley or continue along the coast, where you'll pass **Goleta Beach** – popular with families – as well as the grubby town of **Isla Vista**, which borders the **University of California, Santa Barbara** campus. Isla Vista Beach has some good tide pools and, at its west end, a popular surfing area at **Coal Oil Point** ("Devereux Beach" to locals), named after the natural tar deposits that seep through its sand. The estuary nearby has been preserved as a botanical study centre and nature refuge, where birders will find much of interest on a walk around the perimeter of the reserve.

All along this part of the coast, the **beaches** face almost due south, making the surf quite lively and causing the sun to both rise and set over the Pacific in winter. Almost twenty miles outside Santa Barbara, **El Capitan State Beach** is a popular surfing spot, with some tide pools as well. **Refugio State Beach**, another three miles along US-101, is one of the prettiest in California – palm trees dotting the sands next to a small creek lend it a tropical feel. Inland on Refugio Road, up the canyon high in the hills, stands **Rancho El Cielo**, the one-time "Western White House" of Ronald Reagan, and now a centre for right-wing student activism. Wind-swept **Gaviota State Beach** is not as pretty as Refugio thirteen miles to the east, but there's a fishing pier and a large wooden railway viaduct that bridges the mouth of the canyon. Each of these state-managed beaches contain **campgrounds**, with reservations available through Reserve America (℡1-800/444-7275, ⊛www .reserveamerica.com; $35).

Half a mile off the highway in Gaviota State Park, but a world away from the speeding traffic, is the small **Las Cruces hot spring** (dawn–dusk), a pool of 100°F mineral water set in a shady, peaceful ravine. To get there, take the turn-off for Hwy-1, but stay on the east side of the highway and double back onto a small road, continuing quarter of a mile to the parking area at the end. Walk about three-quarters of a mile up the trail and look for Las Cruces's murky pools, where the soothing water feels better than it looks.

Santa Ynez Valley

An alternative to US-101's coastal route out of Santa Barbara is Hwy-154, which climbs steeply over **San Marcos Pass** and drops into **Santa Ynez Valley**. It's a pleasant route through a prime wine-growing region (see box, p.375) that's popular with motorcyclists and gung-ho bicyclists.

Three miles north of Santa Barbara, the walls of **Chumash Painted Cave State Historic Park** (dawn–dusk; ℡805/733-3713, ⊛www.parks.ca.gov), set on narrow Painted Caves Road off Hwy-154, are coloured with pre-conquest Native American art. You can't actually enter the sandstone cave – it's been closed off to protect against vandalism – but peering in will still give you a good look at the vivid, thousand-year-old paintings, the unique shapes of which offer a perspective of the natives' view of supernatural forces and the afterlife. Six miles further along Hwy-154, popular **Cachuma Lake Recreation Area** features a large **campground** (daily 8am–dusk; day-use $8, campsites $20–25; ℡805/686-5055, ⊛www .sbparks.org) complete with yurts ($60–70) and cabins ($135–210). Since it's a massive reservoir that holds the water supply for Santa Barbara, no swimming or paddling is allowed; however, opportunities abound for drier activities such as biking, fishing and horseriding.

Beyond the lake, Hwy-246 cuts off to Solvang, while Hwy-154 continues through the vineyards around the hamlet of **Los Olivos**. Although the town would prefer you to focus on wine, it's also known as the former site of Michael Jackson's 2800-acre **Neverland Ranch**, five miles north at 5225 Figueroa Mountain Road (though not visible from the roadside), where the late pop icon once resided along with Bubbles the Chimp in an amusement-park setting – Ferris wheel, hundreds of zoo animals, a museum devoted to himself, and all.

Solvang and around

Although it may be difficult to imagine anyone falling for the sham windmills and plastic storks that fill the saccharine-sweet town of **Solvang** ("sunny fields" in Danish), people come by the busload to visit the community, established in 1911 by expat Danish teachers from the Midwest looking for a place to found a Danish folk school. Today the town, three miles off US-101 on Hwy-246, exists as a sort of Scandinavian fantasyland, with locals dressing in "traditional costume" to entertain all comers.

Instead of staying in a nondescript, Danish-themed motel, consider splurging at the elegant *Inn at Petersen Village*, 1576 Mission Drive (℡1-800/321-8985,

Ⓦ www.peterseninn.com; Ⓘ), where basic **rooms** are pricey but include canopy beds (sans Victoriana); the inn's Tower Suite ($380) comprises three levels with a cosy fireplace and whirring hot tub. Otherwise, the best and most affordable local accommodation is *King Frederik Inn*, 1617 Copenhagen Drive (Ⓣ 1-800/549-9955, Ⓦ www.bwkingfrederik.com; Ⓘ), a clunky, ultra-basic "Old World" property with standard motel units, pool, hot tub and continental breakfast. When it comes time to **eat**, *Paula's Pancake House*, 1531 Mission Drive (Ⓣ 805/688-2867), is a reliable breakfast choice for its Danish apple pancakes, while *Café Angelica*, 490 1st St (Ⓣ 805/686-9970), is a solid spot for dinner, featuring serviceable pasta and seafood dishes and a mean, stuffed filet mignon, all $20 and under. For information about Solvang's raft of Danish-themed museums – such as the **Hans Christian Andersen Museum**, upstairs at 1680 Mission Drive (daily 10am–5pm; donation requested; Ⓣ 805/688-2052), which holds displays on the Danish writer's life and first editions of his works *Thumbelina* and *The Ugly Duckling* – try one of the **visitor information** kiosks operated by the local CVB (Ⓣ 1-800/468-6765, Ⓦ www.solvangusa.com).

Mission Santa Inés, at 1760 Mission Drive (daily 9am–4.30pm; $5; Ⓣ 805/688-4815, Ⓦ www.missionsantaines.org), is hidden away behind the rows of gingerbread buildings on the eastern edge of town. A century before the Danes tried to make the place look like home, Spanish men of faith erected the nineteenth mission in their chain here in 1804. Though the structure has undergone numerous restorations, the buildings are original, and the trompe l'oeil green-marble trim on the church's interior walls is one of the best surviving examples of mission-era decorative art. An excellent museum is also on the grounds, displaying furnishings, art, vestments and documents, including a set of plaques praising the Franciscan fathers for improving the lives of the native Chumash.

Six miles from Solvang off US-101, **Nojoqui** (pronounced No-ho-kee) **Falls County Park** (daily 8am–dusk; Ⓣ 805/934-6123, Ⓦ www.sbparks.org) offers a gentle, ten-minute walk that brings you to a 75-foot waterfall. The route to the park is gorgeous, winding along Alisal Road under thick garlands of Spanish moss that dangle from a canopy of oak trees.

Lompoc and around

Not far beyond Gaviota, Hwy-1 branches off from US-101 on a marvellous route through the inland valleys of the Santa Ynez Mountains. **LOMPOC** (pronounced lom-POKE), the only town for miles, calls itself the "flower seed-growing capital of the world" and claims to produce as much as three-quarters of the seeds sold on earth; in summer, you'll see a thick carpet of colour covering the surrounding, gently rolling countryside. For information detailing where particular flora have been planted this season, contact the **Lompoc Valley Chamber of Commerce**, 111 South I St (Mon–Fri 9am–5pm; Ⓣ 1-800/240-0999, Ⓦ www.lompoc.com), where you can also learn about the 75 folksy **murals** that have sprung up to add flavour in recent years to Lompoc's otherwise bland Downtown. There are a few oddball murals in the bunch, including one on the side of the Chamber of Commerce in fantastic praise of "Diatomaceous Mining"; meanwhile, the eerie "Patriotism" mural, at 140 South H St, was painted by inmates of the nearby federal prison and features a missile blasting off in front of a glowing American-flag horizon.

For tourist information at weekends, head to the free **Lompoc Museum**, 200 South H St (Tues–Fri 1–5pm, Sat & Sun 1–4pm; Ⓣ 805/736-3888, Ⓦ www .lompocmuseum.org), where the collection is strong on local archeology, with a number of Chumash and other Native American artefacts. It also has material on the town's **original mission site**, the scant remains of which can be found three blocks to the south on F Street, off Locust Avenue.

Nearby **Vandenberg Air Force Base**, which sprawls west of Lompoc and is where various new missiles and guidance systems get put through their paces over the Pacific Ocean, keeps interlopers from using most of its gorgeous beaches for gentler pursuits. The missiles' vapour trails are visible for miles, particularly at sunset, though the only way to see any of the action up close is by riding the Amtrak Coast Starlight train route (see p.33), which runs along the otherwise remote coast. The route was **Jack Kerouac**'s favourite rail journey – he worked for a while as a brakeman on the train and subsequently used the "Midnight Ghost" for a free ride between Los Angeles and the Bay Area. Aerospace enthusiasts who plan at least one week ahead can visit the air base's launch pads and missile silo on free three-hour **tours** (9.45am second Wed of month; ☎805/606-3595, ⓦwww.vandenberg.af.mil). Alternatively, you can head thirteen miles west of Lompoc through the base to the tall sand dunes at **Ocean Beach County Park** (daily 8am–sunset; free; ☎805/934-6123, ⓦwww.sbparks.org), a broad strand at the mouth of the Santa Ynez River, the nesting grounds of many seabirds.

Another accessible stretch of sand in the area, **Jalama Beach County Park**, at the end of twisting Jalama Road fourteen miles off Hwy-1 (☎805/736-3504, ⓦwww.sbparks.org; daily 8am–dusk; $8), spreads beneath coastal bluffs, where you can camp overnight ($20–25). If you'd rather sleep indoors, Lompoc's most reasonable **accommodation** can be found at *O'Cairns Inn*, 1020 E Ocean Drive (☎1-866/735-7770, ⓦwww.ocairnsinn.com; ❷), which features clean, modern rooms and continental breakfast. Lompoc may not be known for an abundance of quality **dining**, but *Sissy's Uptown Café*, 112 South I St, is one exception, good for its home-made soups, sandwiches, veggie options and, at dinner, steaks.

La Purísima Mission State Park

Four miles east of Lompoc and signposted off Hwy-246, **La Purísima Mission State Park** (daily 9am–5pm; $6 per vehicle; ☎805/733-3713, ⓦwww.lapurisima mission.org) is the most complete and authentic reconstruction of any of the 21 Spanish missions in California, and one of the best places to get an idea of what life might have been like in these early settlements. La Misión la Purísima Concepción de Maria Santísima was founded in 1787 on a site three miles north of here, and by 1804 had converted around 1500 Chumash, one-third of whom died in a smallpox epidemic over the next two years. In 1812, an earthquake destroyed all the buildings, and the Franciscan fathers decided to move to the present site. The new design was the only mission in the chain to be built in a linear fashion rather than in a defensive quadrangle, normally used both to confine Native Americans and to keep others out – an especially important detail as the number of able-bodied residents had been slashed by the epidemic. The complex did not last long, however, after the missions were secularized in 1834; like all the rest, it was soon abandoned and gradually fell into disrepair.

The buildings that stand here today were rebuilt on the ruins of the mission as part of a Depression-era work project. From 1933 to 1940, over two hundred men lived and worked on the site, studying the remaining ruins and rebuilding the church and outbuildings using period tools and methods. Workers made adobe bricks from straw and mud, shaped roof timbers with hand tools and even took the colours of their paints from native plants.

The heart of the mission is a narrow church, decorated as it would have been in the 1820s. On display in the nearby old wagon-house are small but engaging presentations of documents and artefacts from the mission era, as well as photographs of the mission's reconstruction; a brand-new **visitor centre** also contains a host of intriguing exhibits. Once a month in summer you might catch a "Purísima People's Day", when volunteers turn the calendar back to 1822 as docents dress as padres while natives hold a traditional Mass.

Santa Maria and Guadalupe

Most of the land along the Santa Maria River, 75 miles north of Santa Barbara, is given over to agriculture, and both Hwy-1 and US-101 pass through a number of farm towns and villages. **Santa Maria** is the largest and most developed, though it hardly merits a stop except to refuel or for a peek at the historic planes on display at the **Museum of Flight**, 3015 Airpark Drive (Fri–Sun 10am–4pm; $5; ☏805/922-8758, ⓦwww.smmof.org). Other towns in the area seem to have hardly changed since the 1930s, when thousands of Okies, as they were known, fled to the region from the Dust Bowl of the Midwest.

Some 25 miles north of Lompoc, Hwy-1 passes through the centre of **Guadalupe**, a small farming village where Spanish signs and advertisements far outnumber those in English, and ramshackle saloons, cafés and vegetable stalls line the dusty streets. Several miles west along the coast lies **Guadalupe-Nipomo Dunes National Wildlife Refuge** (☏805/343-9151; dawn–dusk; free), where you can look for whales out at sea or climb the 500ft sand dunes. The tallest along the California coast, the dunes surround wetlands that are habitat for endangered seabirds. More bizarrely, buried within these dunes is much of the movie set for Cecil B. DeMille's original 1924 silent epic, *The Ten Commandments* (later remade with Charlton Heston), when the sands stood in for ancient Egypt in the director's monumental re-creation of "The City of Pharaoh". Disinterred relics from the set, which was buried instead of taken apart to save money, are on view in the **visitor centre** operated by the non-profit Guadalupe-Nipomo Dunes Center back in Guadalupe, 1055 Guadalupe St (Tues–Sun 10am–4pm; ☏805/343-2455, ⓦwww.dunescenter.org).

Pismo Beach and Avila Beach

About ten miles further up the coast, the enormous sand dunes subside just south of the "Five Cities", of which **Pismo Beach** is by far the most desirable for visitors; it's here in the so-called Clam Capital of the World that Hwy-1 reconnects with US-101 for a dozen miles on its inland approach to San Luis Obispo. As you continue northbound from Pismo Beach, you can follow the Avila Road exit to the area's last outpost of Southern California-style beach life, **Avila Beach**, where the party atmosphere continues all summer long despite the awkward presence of the nuclear Diablo Canyon Power Plant straddling an earthquake fault a mere six miles up the coast.

Pismo Beach and Shell Beach

Sand is such a dominant element in this region that the portion of the dunes three miles south of **PISMO BEACH** is open to off-road vehicle enthusiasts, who tear over the sandpiles at **Oceano Dunes State Vehicular Recreation Area** (☏805/473-7220; day-use $5) in dune buggies and four-wheel-drives, motoring along the beach to reach them. This is California's only **drive-on beach**, with another portion of the dunes protected as a **nature reserve**.

Pismo State Beach (☏805/489-1869; camping reservations available at ☏1-800/444-7275 or ⓦwww.reserveamerica.com; $35) has hot showers and beach camping, and is a good place to see the black-and-orange monarch butter-flies that spend the winter here in eucalyptus trees within their own designated grove; for more information, visit ⓦwww.monarchbutterfly.org. However, the once-plentiful **Pismo clam** that gave the town its name (from the Chumash word *pismu*, or "blobs of tar" that the shells resemble) have been so depleted that any you might dig up nowadays are probably under the 4.5-inch legal minimum size. To try your luck at clamming, you'll need a California fishing licence from the Department of Fish and Game (Ⓣ916/928-6882, ⓦwww.dfg.ca.gov; one-day licence $13.40).

Most of the town's commercial activity happens near where Pomeroy Avenue crosses Hwy-1. If you have no interest in dune-riding or watersports, you're in the wrong place, as the glut of surf shops here will attest. Beach Cycle Rentals, 150 Hinds Ave (Ⓣ805/773-5518), one of several similar local dealers, offers **bicycle and surfboard rentals**; you can also walk out on the sizeable pier for overhead views of surfers riding the waves.

If you continue just north of town to **Shell Beach**, you'll come to the redoubtable **Dinosaur Caves Park** (dawn–dusk; free; Ⓣ805/773-4657), where craggy sea stacks dot the landscape and poke out in the waves, their various caves, coves, arches and passages making for a geologist's and kayaker's delight. All kinds of rock, from mica to serpentine, are mashed together in this dramatic, mottled seascape, with the best views available by paddling out into the protected inlet. Don't get your hopes up for seeing extinct reptiles, however – the place was named for a short-lived tourist attraction that took the form of a concrete dinosaur. You can also rent kayaks here, at Central Coast Kayaks, 1879 Shell Beach Rd ($19–25 per hour; Ⓣ805/773-3500, ⓦwww.centralcoastkayaks.com).

Practicalities

Pismo Beach's **visitor centre**, 581 Dolliver St (Mon–Sat 9am–5pm; Ⓣ1-800/443-7778, ⓦwww.classiccalifornia.com), can help with maps and accommodation. Locally you'll find a number of affordable **motels**, including the *Sea Gypsy*, 1020 Cypress St (Ⓣ1-800/592-5923, ⓦwww.seagypsymotel.com; ❸), which has clean, modern decor; for an additional premium, you can get a studio with kitchen and balcony. Right on the beach, the *Kon Tiki Inn*, 1621 Price St (Ⓣ1-888/566-8454, ⓦwww.kontikiinn.com; ❺), has a health club, decent restaurant and pool to go with its nice rooms, many featuring balconies and sea views.

Dining options in Pismo Beach are similarly attractive. People have been known to drive far distances for the clam chowder at the ⚡ *Cracked Crab*, 751 Price St (Ⓣ805/773-2722); the popular restaurant is also known for its excellent shrimp and a host of other crustaceans and fish including, of course, crab. *Rosa's*, 491 Price St (Ⓣ805/773-0551), serves up hearty and affordable pasta, pizza and seafood, or for a slightly more upscale experience, try *Giuseppe's*, 891 Price St (Ⓣ805/773-2870), an old-world-style Italian spot with a menu full of simple yet delicious items.

Avila Beach

North of Pismo Beach, the coastline becomes more rugged, with caves and tide pools lurking below ever-eroding bluffs, and sea lions in the many coves. The three-mile-long strand in front of the summer resort town of **AVILA BEACH** is finally recovering from a devastating ecological disaster caused by a 1990s spill from a nearby oil refinery. The ambitious clean-up and reconstruction project that began soon after the spill has helped restore much of the area to its original state.

Avila Beach contains numerous golf courses, resorts, tourist shops and **inns** with ocean views, the cheapest being the *Inn at Avila Beach*, 256 Front St (℡805/595-2300, ⓦwww.avilabeachca.com; ⓞ), which wears its faded beachfront style well. Nearby, the swanky *Avila Lighthouse Suites*, 550 Front St (℡805/627-1900, ⓦwww.avilalighthousesuites.com; ⓞ), has ocean-view units that variously come with fireplaces, parlours and wet bars. The *Olde Port Inn* (℡805/595-2515), dramatically perched out over Port San Luis on Pier 3, is *the* town's choice spot to **eat**; naturally, the menu primarily consists of seafood, so try the fish tacos for lunch or the spicy cioppino stew for dinner. Down on the beach, you'll find teenagers on the loose from families cruising the boardwalk, while almost everyone of drinking age takes refuge in the town's boisterous **bars**.

A scenic, unpaved route towards San Luis Obispo, **See Canyon Road**, cuts north from Avila Beach, gradually climbing up the narrow, overgrown canyon between sharply profiled volcanic cones, with terrific views over the Pacific. At the end of See Canyon Road, turn right on Prefumo Canyon Road to reach San Luis Obispo.

San Luis Obispo

The inviting community of **SAN LUIS OBISPO** (locally, "SLO") is an underappreciated gem – part agricultural, part collegiate and a pleasant place to dawdle and browse. The town boasts well-preserved architecture, from turreted Victorian residences along **Buchon Street**, south of the town centre, to the Art Deco Fremont Theater on Monterey Street. There are a number of good places to eat, some decent pubs and nightclubs, and – summer weekends notwithstanding – affordable accommodation, all set amid a vibrant community energized by Cal Poly San Luis Obispo's twenty thousand students.

Arrival and information

San Luis Obispo's Greyhound terminal is at 150 South St (℡805/543-2121), not far from its Downtown; there are regular **bus** connections with both Los Angeles and San Francisco. Amtrak **trains** stop several times each day at the end of Santa Rosa Street, half a mile south of the business district. This is the northern terminus of the Pacific Surfliner route, from which you can transfer to Coast Starlight trains covering the entire coast. You can **get around** for $1.50 on the local transit system, SLO Transit (℡805/541-2877), or the wider-ranging Regional Transit Authority ($1.50–4.50; ℡805/781-4472, ⓦwww.slorta.org), which links to Morro Bay and Pismo Beach, among other nearby destinations.

Pick up a free walking-tour map highlighting much of the town's best architecture from the **visitor centre** at 1039 Chorro St (Sun–Wed 10am–5pm, Thurs–Sat 10am–7pm; ℡805/781-2670, ⓦwww.visitslo.com), and to find out what's on and where, check out the free weekly *New Times* (ⓦwww.newtimesslo .com) or the "Ticket" supplement every Friday in the *San Luis Obispo Tribune* (ⓦwww.sanluisobispo.com).

Accommodation

Rates at San Luis Obispo **hotels and inns** are generally reasonable, if not outright low. If you're looking to rough it, the best **camping** nearby is south of town beyond Pismo Beach, or north up Hwy-1 near Morro Bay.

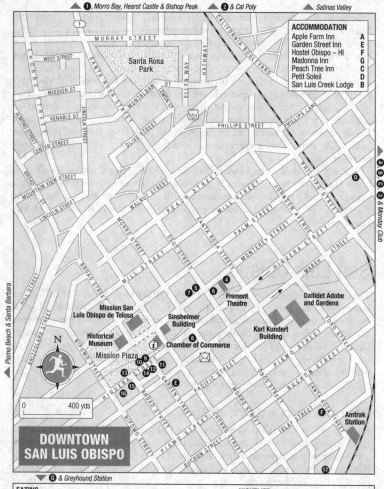

▲ **①**, *Morro Bay, Hearst Castle & Bishop Peak* ▲ **②** *& Cal Poly* ▲ *Salinas Valley*

ACCOMMODATION

Apple Farm Inn	A
Garden Street Inn	E
Hostel Obispo – HI	F
Madonna Inn	G
Peach Tree Inn	C
Petit Soleil	D
San Luis Creek Lodge	B

Ⓐ, Ⓑ, Ⓒ, Ⓖ *& Monday Club* ▶

Mission San Luis Obispo de Tolosa

Sinsheimer Building

Fremont Theatre

Dallidet Adobe and Gardens

Historical Museum

Karl Kundert Building

Mission Plaza

Chamber of Commerce

0 — 400 yds

DOWNTOWN SAN LUIS OBISPO

◀ *Pismo Beach & Santa Barbara*

▼ **G** *& Greyhound Station*

EATING				NIGHTLIFE	
Apple Farm Restaurant		Koberl at Blue	7	Boo Boo Records	5
& Bakery	3	Mondeo	8	Chrstopher Cohan Performing Arts Center	2
Big Sky Cafe	15	Mo's Smokehouse BBQ	6	Downtown Brewing Co	12
Buona Tavola	4	Novo	10	Frog and Peach	9
Café Roma	17	Oasis	16	Linnea's	11
F. McLintock's	13	Taj Palace	1	Mother's Tavern	14

Apple Farm Inn 2015 Monterey St ☎1-800/255-2040, ⊛www.applefarm.com. Agreeable inn where rooms include Victoriana furnishings, canopy beds and fireplaces; excellent B&B-style breakfasts are also on offer. Rates are lower in the Trellis Court building than the *Inn* proper. Ⓖ

Garden Street Inn 1212 Garden St ☎805/545-9802, ⊛www.gardenstreetinn.com. Very central B&B in a restored 1887 Victorian

with comfortable, mildly themed rooms and suites (Emerald Isle, Walden, etc). There's complimentary wine on arrival and gourmet cooked breakfasts. Ⓔ

Hostel Obispo-HI 1617 Santa Rosa St ☎805/544-4678, ⊛www.hostelobispo.com. Comfortable hostel with lounge, patio and bike rentals. Dorm beds ($24–27) and private rooms (starting at $45) available.

The world's first motel

The Milestone Mo-Tel opened in San Luis Obispo in 1925 at 2223 Monterey St, designed to take advantage of growing car ownership among Americans. Initially, enthusiastic Model T drivers had used automobile "campgrounds" for overnight stays, pitching tents alongside their cars, and since San Luis Obispo is about halfway between San Francisco and Los Angeles, it became an especially popular choice for overnight stops. Savvy architect **Arthur Heineman**, who'd recently overseen the development of residential bungalows, recognized the potential of adapting the bungalow concept for the travel industry, combining the convenience of a campground with the comfort and respectability (not to mention higher prices) of a hotel – a "motor hotel" which, because those words couldn't fit on the sign, became a "mo-tel".

Heineman and his brother Alfred opened the first motel in the auto nexus of San Luis Obispo, but envisioned a chain stretching from San Diego to Seattle, each one-day's journey from the next, much like the first European settlements along El Camino Real – hence the Mission-style architecture of the existing *Milestone Mo-Tel* building. Unfortunately, only one motel was built, and Heineman didn't even manage to copyright the word he'd coined. It entered the dictionary in 1950, long after hundreds of copycats had sprung up across America.

The *Milestone*, later the *Motel Inn*, closed in 1991 and, despite some promise of restoration from its new owners – the adjoining *Apple Farm Inn* (see opposite) – it continues to fall into decay, a faded relic from the glory days of California car culture.

Madonna Inn 100 Madonna Rd ☎1-800/543-9666, ⊛www.madonnainn.com. The standard "theme" rooms, cottages and suites – from fairy-tale cutesy to Stone Age caveman – at this kitsch monstrosity can be a disappointment at such inflated rates; the imposingly shocking-pink, chalet-style lobby may be enough to satiate your curiosity. Still, an essential landmark for many visitors. ⑥–⑨

Peach Tree Inn 2001 Monterey St ☎1-800/227-6396, ⊛www.peachtreeinn.com. One of the town's better budget offerings, with serviceable rooms and continental breakfast. ⑧

Petit Soleil 1473 Monterey St ☎805/549-0321, ⊛www.petitsoleilslo.com. Very stylish French-themed B&B offering modish decor in each uniquely designed room; there's also an even more elegant "Joie de Vivre" suite and exceptionally tasty continental breakfasts. ⑦

San Luis Creek Lodge 1941 Monterey St ☎805/541-1122, ⊛www.sanluiscreeklodge.com. Centrally located inn offering 25 smart rooms in three buildings, each in a vaguely Greek Revival, Tudor and Craftsman style. Some units have fireplaces, jacuzzis or balconies, and breakfast is included. ⑥

The Town

San Luis Obispo is eminently walkable, with a compact core built around the late eighteenth-century **Mission San Luis Obispo de Tolosa**, 751 Palm St (Mon & Wed–Fri 9am–5pm, Tue noon–5pm; free; ☎805/781-8220, ⊛www.mission sanluisobispo.org). A fairly plain church, it was the fifth structure in the mission trail and the prototype for the now-ubiquitous red-tiled roof – developed as a replacement for the original, flammable thatch, which caught fire here in 1776 during an attack by Native Americans. Wander through the garden and find a native Chumash oven, a statue of mission founder Padre Junípero Serra and grapevines of the sort used in the production of some of California's earliest wines. Between the mission and the visitor centre, **Mission Plaza**'s terraces step down along San Luis Creek. It's a leafy, restful spot adorned with endemic California trees and plants, crisscrossed by footpaths and bridges and overlooked by a number of stores and outdoor restaurants on the south bank – a delightful place to dawdle with a book.

Downstream and across a small park, you'll find the **San Luis Obispo County Historical Museum**, 696 Monterey St (Wed–Mon 10am–4pm; free; ☏805/543-0638, Ⓦwww.slochs.org), which holds a low-key collection of local, primarily domestic artefacts housed in a richly detailed 1904 Carnegie library. The main drag, **Higuera Street** (pronounced "hee-GEHR-ah"), a block south of Mission Plaza, springs to life for the town's weekly **Farmers' Market** (Thurs 5–9pm; free), when it's closed to cars and filled with food booths and musicians; all of SLO seems to come out to sample the food and entertainment of this weekly funfest. Less appetizing but just as interesting to some is **Bubble Gum Alley**, a narrow passage off Higuera Street near its intersection with Broad Street, where the walls are slathered in chewed pieces of the alley's namesake elastic candy, some over fifty years old.

Though a number of commercial buildings of minor architectural note are detailed on the Chamber of Commerce's **self-guided walking tour**, the only one not to be missed is the **Karl Kundert Building**, a doctor's surgery (no admittance except for patients) designed by Frank Lloyd Wright, at Santa Rosa and Pacific streets. Though built in 1956, it resembles a truncated chunk of Wright's much earlier Robie House in Chicago, with oddball window cutouts amid the red brick design. Close by, at the end of Pacific Street, stands the **Dallidet Adobe and Gardens**, at no. 1185 (☏805/543-6762; call for times and availability of tours; donation requested), one of San Luis Obispo County's oldest buildings. Constructed by a disillusioned French forty-niner who, eluded by fortune in the Mother Lode, ended up living in town, it's set among manicured grounds with two redwoods over 125ft tall. Also not to be missed, particularly if you're on your way to Julia Morgan's Hearst Castle (see p.393), is the architect's **Monday Club** at 1815 Monterey St, a private building exemplifying a more modest approach to the Mission Revival style with its tiled roof, stucco walls and tasteful geometry.

If you fancy a bit of exercise, you can **hike** up 1546ft **Bishop Peak**, which looms over SLO to the northwest and is the tallest point among a chain of peaks known as the Morros. Two paths, Bishop Peak Trail (4 miles; 1200ft ascent) and Felsman Loop (3 miles; 700ft ascent), wind through grassland and oak woodland up and around the mountain's rocky slopes, and are accessible via both Patricia Drive Trailhead and Highland Drive Trailhead. Visit Ⓦwww.santalucia.sierraclub.org for trailhead directions and further details.

Eating

Higuera Street Downtown and its cross streets are the places to **eat** in town – especially during the weekly Farmers' Market each Thursday evening, when barbecues and other food stalls are set up amid the crowd along Higuera.

Apple Farm Restaurant & Bakery 2015 Monterey St. Set inside the *Apple Farm Inn*, this casual family-style restaurant serves traditional American dishes, straight-up breakfasts of pancakes and French toast, plus pies galore.

Big Sky Café 1121 Broad St ☏805/545-5401. An airy, modern place with an emphasis on both vegetarian fare and seafood. It's popular for items such as *pozole* stew, yam risotto and ginger noodles, as well as carnivore-friendly choices like braised lamb shank and sirloin sandwiches.

Buona Tavola 1037 Monterey St ☏805/545-8000. Small and stylish bistro with a good range of moderately priced Northern-Italian wine and food, from *agnolotti di scampi* to *zuppa di pollo*.

Café Roma 1020 Railroad Ave ☏805/541-6800. Popular, family-owned Italian restaurant known for its excellent pasta dishes. Numerous seafood, steak and veal mains are also available, and everything's served in a pleasant, romantic setting.

F. McLintocks 686 Higuera St. Family-oriented restaurant with an Old West atmosphere, part of a local chainlet doling out solid burgers, pastas and sandwiches (try the gooey tri-tip French dip) for around $12 each. Steaks and chops also available.

Koberl at Blue 988 Monterey St ☏805/783-1135. Swanky lounge/bar/restaurant with bare brick walls, dark wood fixtures and a dressier crowd than most spots in town. Graze on snacks in the lounge or, in the restaurant, opt for dinner portions of coriander scallops, strip steak or rack of lamb.

Mondeo 893 Higuera St. Asian-fusion-inflected fast-food joint where everything on the inventive, made-to-order menu can be served as a wrap or bowl. Try an Americana with swordfish or meatloaf, or a Mediterraneo with basil scampi; the home-made ginger ale's also terrific.

Mo's Smokehouse BBQ 1005 Monterey St. Although no one will confuse SLO with Texas, the barbecue at this joint is as good as any you'll find on the Central Coast. Go for the tender pulled pork or ribs, and pair your wonderfully greasy meat with a side of beans, slaw or fried green tomatoes.

Novo 726 Higuera St ☎ 805/543-3986. Affordable fusion dining, where international dishes – from Moroccan quail salad to Singapore satay to duck *mole* – are mixed and matched with mostly successful results.

Oasis 675 Higuera St ☎ 805/543-1155. Delicious Mediterranean restaurant that features weekend belly-dancing. Try the chicken with sweet potatoes and raisins or any of the great-value lunches.

Taj Palace 795 E Foothill Blvd. SLO's main Indian choice is slightly pricier than you'd expect – particularly considering its university-adjacent location – but still worth it. The buffet lunch is the best option.

Nightlife

San Luis Obispo's sizeable student population supports more **nightlife** than you might expect for such a relatively small California town. You'll also find a couple of popular **bars** and **cafés** on and just off Higuera Street, around the Mission Plaza area.

Boo Boo Records 978 Monterey St ☎ 805/541-0657, ⓦ www.booboorecords.com. One of the true holdouts in the tradition of great independent record stores, with occasional live in-store performances.

Christopher Cohan Performing Arts Center On the Cal Poly campus, off Grand Ave ☎ 1-888/233-2787, ⓦ www.pacslo.org. A considerable concert hall presenting a wide variety of musical performances, including classical, opera, choral, dance and jazz.

Downtown Brewing Co 1119 Garden St ☎ 805/543-1843, ⓦ www.Downtownbrew.com. The major venue on the SLO nightlife scene, featuring two bars spread over two floors and hosting performances by local and touring bands.

Frog and Peach 728 Higuera St ☎ 805/595-3764. A popular local pub with cheap drinks and performers across a range of genres.

Linnaea's 1110 Garden St ☎ 805/541-5888, ⓦ www.linnaeas.com. Café serving good espresso and offering live music – from indie rock to folk to piano blues – on its small stage. Also hosts occasional movie nights.

Mother's Tavern 725 Higuera St ☎ 805/541-8733, ⓦ www.motherstavern.com. Bar and grill with drink specials and regular performances by DJs and local karaoke wizards.

Around San Luis Obispo

North of San Luis Obispo the highways diverge once again, with US-101 speeding up through Salinas Valley (see p.395) while Hwy-1 follows a spectacular coastal route. The first dozen miles of Hwy-1 follow a series of hills rising around the plugs of nine extinct volcanoes, dormant for twenty million years and ranging from 500 to over 1500ft high; the eighth volcano in the series, **Morro Rock**, is in the sea close to the coast, while the ninth is buried under the Pacific's churning waters. According to local lore, Morro Rock was named by the sixteenth-century explorer Juan Cabrillo, who thought it looked like the Moorish turbans in southern Spain; later road-builders thought it looked more like a quarry for gathering stone and altered its look for the worse. Nowadays, it's off limits to the public in order to protect the nesting areas of the endangered peregrine falcon.

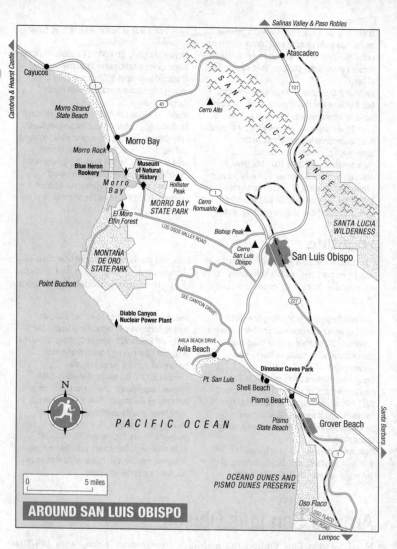

Salinas Valley & Paso Robles

Atascadero

Cambria & Hearst Castle

Cayucos

Morro Strand
State Beach

Cerro Alto

Morro Bay

Morro Rock

Blue Heron
Rookery

Museum
of Natural
History

Morro
Bay

Hollister
Peak

MORRO BAY
STATE PARK

Cerro
Romualdo

El Moro
Elfin Forest

LOS OSOS VALLEY ROAD

Bishop Peak

SANTA LUCIA
WILDERNESS

Cerro
San Luis
Obispo

San Luis Obispo

MONTAÑA
DE ORO
STATE PARK

Point Buchon

SEE CANYON DRIVE

Diablo Canyon
Nuclear Power Plant

AVILA BEACH DRIVE

Avila Beach

Dinosaur Caves Park

Pt. San Luis

Shell Beach

Pismo Beach

Grover Beach

PACIFIC OCEAN

Pismo
State Beach

Santa Barbara

N

0   5 miles

OCEANO DUNES AND
PISMO DUNES PRESERVE

Oso Flaco

LOSO FLACO
LAKE ROAD

AROUND SAN LUIS OBISPO

Lompoc

Morro Bay

Most impressive from a distance, Morro Rock dominates the fine harbour at the easy-paced town of **MORRO BAY**, near a collection of wetlands and mud flats (as well as a seawater inlet) where local fishing boats unload their catches to sell in the many fish markets along the waterfront. One of the best views of the rock and surrounding coastline is from atop **Cerro Alto**, a 2620ft volcanic cone with good hiking and camping ($18 per night), eight miles east of Morro Bay off Hwy-41. Closer in, providing another good view from a point above the bay a mile south of town at the end of Main Street, the **Museum of Natural History** (daily 10am–5pm; adults $2, kids free; ☎805/772-2694, ⓦwww.morrobaymuseum.org) is an excellent interactive ecology museum aimed squarely at curious kids, where the best display offers visitors the chance to build their own sand dune. North of the museum, paddling a kayak (see below) is the best way to see the **Blue Heron Rookery**, where eucalyptus trees attract great seabirds, as well as egrets and cormorants, though you're not allowed to land here since it's a protected reserve. Opposite the museum, there's **camping** for $35 a night in **Morro Bay State Park** (day-use $8; ☏805/772-2560, ⓦwww.parks.ca.gov; camping reservations available at ☏1-800/444-7275 or ⓦwww.reserveamerica.com), which also has a lagoon, marina and golf course, as well as opportunities for hiking, fishing and birding.

Across the bay, the thin sandy peninsula that protects the harbour is hard to reach except by boat – it's entirely undeveloped and about the only place where you stand a chance of still finding Pismo clams (see p.384). Another intriguing site, on the bay's southeastern shore, is the **El Moro Elfin Forest**, at the end of 16th Street in Los Osos (dawn–dusk; free), a 90-acre preserve of pygmy oak trees that offers good strolling over walkways and paths amid its copious sand dunes. To access many of these places you can rent **kayaks** or **canoes** from any number of Morro Bay outfitters; try Kayak Horizons, at 551 Embarcadero (☏805/772-6444, ⓦwww.kayakhorizons.com; $9–13 per hour and $24–32 per half-day for a kayak, $18 per hour and $42 per half-day for a canoe).

A few miles from the El Moro Elfin Forest near the southwest corner of the bay, **Montaña de Oro State Park** (daily dawn–dusk; day-use free; ☏805/772-7434, ⓦwww.parks.ca.gov), at the end of Los Osos Valley Road (which turns into Pecho Valley Road), is much more primitive than Morro Bay State Park and contains excellent tide pools as well as a good beach at Spooner's Cove. The windswept promontory stands solidly against the crashing sea, offering rugged hiking along the shore and through the sagebrush and eucalyptus trees of the upland hillsides, which in spring are covered in golden poppies – giving rise to the park's name, which is Spanish for "gold mountain". The dramatic landscape also makes an interesting and worthwhile spot for **camping** ($20–25; reserve at ☏1-800/444-7275 or ⓦwww.reserveamerica.com).

Practicalities

For **accommodation** closer to town, there's a handful of affordable chains in and around Morro Bay, though it's worth trying the more enjoyable *El Morro Masterpiece Motel*, 1206 Main St (☏805/772-5633, ⓦwww.masterpiecemotels .com; ❹), which has rooms with microwaves and fridges, some with balconies and fireplaces, and various classical artworks showcased on the walls – hence the name. If you want a fancier spot, *Ascot Suites*, 260 Morro Bay Blvd (☏805/772-4437, ⓦwww.ascotinn.com; ❺), will more than suffice with its elegant rooms and suites that offer hot tubs, fireplaces and, in some units, balconies. Both places follow Central Coast custom by raising rates considerably on summer weekends. For **food**, try *Hofbrau Der Albatross*, 901 Embarcadero, a deluxe burger joint with bratwurst and dipped sandwiches also on the menu, or *Lolo's*, 2848 Main St, for tasty Mexican staples. For additional local information, drop by Morro Bay's **visitor centre**, at 845 Embarcadero, Suite D (Mon–Sat 10am–6pm; ☏1-800/231-0592, ⓦwww.morrobay.org).

Cayucos

The next town north is **Cayucos**, six miles along Hwy-1, originally a small port built by Englishman James Cass in the 1870s and now a sleepy place ranged along sandy beaches with a nice pier – a pleasant enough pit-stop along a journey up the coast. The *Cypress Tree Motel*, 125 S Ocean Ave (☏805/995-3917, ⓦwww .cypresstreemotel.com; ❸), is just one block from the beach, with clean, old-fashioned rooms fitted with kitchenettes and loosely themed around birds, Route 66 and the Wild West, among other motifs. Also worthy if you don't mind twee decor is the oceanfront *Seaside Motel*, 42 S Ocean Ave (℡1-800/549-0900, ⓦwww.seasidemotel.com; ❹), with its clean and comfortable standard rooms and suites. For coffee, muffins and pastries, *Kelley's*, 155 N Ocean Ave, is a solid bet; if you're craving a square meal, head to *Hoppe's Garden Bistro*, 78 N Ocean Ave (℡805/995-1006), where a seasonal menu focuses on fresh ingredients to help create delicious California cuisine that pairs well with the region's estimable wines. Surprisingly, the town also has some of the area's best **nightlife**, with the terrific *Old Cayucos Tavern and Card Room*, 130 N Ocean Ave (℡805/995-3209), anchoring the two-block-long ramshackle town centre with live bands on weekends and late-night poker in the room. For more information, contact the Cayucos **Chamber of Commerce** (℡805/995-1200, ⓦwww.cayucoschamber.com).

Cambria

About sixteen miles up Hwy-1, **Cambria** is glutted with pricey amenities thanks in part to everything it's done to cash in on its proximity to Hearst Castle, less than ten miles further north. Hidden away in a wooded valley half a mile off Hwy-1, Cambria was an established town serving the local ranchers and fishermen long before Hearst Castle became the region's prime tourist attraction, and it maintains a certain allure since its residents have enacted ordinances that make any view-blocking development illegal. The older section of town, known as Main Village, is half a mile east of Hwy-1 on Main Street, while the newer part of town with most of the cheaper hotels is referred to as East Village.

Cambria holds one acknowledged oddity: **Nit Wit Ridge**, 881 Hillcrest Drive (tours by appointment; free; ℡805/927-2690). This patently weird slice of whimsy was the brainchild of one Art Beal, who came to Cambria from San Francisco in the 1920s and bought a plot of land where, over a fifty-year period, he built a Baroque castle out of trash, thus earning him the moniker "Captain Nit Wit". Recycling old toilet seats as picture frames or water pipes as handrails, this eccentric misfit's glorious folly lay abandoned for ten years after his death in 1992. These days, it's gradually being restored by new owners, who offer tours of this labyrinthine house that's an offbeat, low-rent counterpoint to the luxuries of nearby Hearst Castle.

Back across Hwy-1, seafront Moonstone Beach Drive offers plenty of **places to stay**, but you'll pay dearly for the views. One of the better pricey options is the *FogCatcher Inn*, 6400 Moonstone Beach Drive (℡1-800/425-4121, ⓦwww.fogcatcherinn.com; ❼), which has smart, modern rooms with gas fireplaces, mini-fridges, microwaves and ocean views in its better units. More affordable, though less dramatically sited, is the *Bluebird Inn*, 1880 Main St (℡1-800/552-5434, ⓦwww.bluebirdmotel.com; ❷–❼), offering standard units with basic decor and amenities, plus more elaborate creek-side rooms with balconies and fireplaces; en-suite units are also available. For more options, visit Cambria's **Chamber of Commerce**, 767 Main St (Mon–Fri 9am–5pm, Sat & Sun noon–4pm; ℡805/927-3624, ⓦwww.cambriachamber.org).

Camping is available at Hearst San Simeon State Park (℡1-800/444-7275 or ⓦwww.reserveamerica.com), two miles north along the coast. There are two campgrounds here: San Simeon Creek has facilities that include showers ($35), while Washburn is a primitive, pitch-only area ($20), a mile from the beach. If you plan to visit between March and September, reserve a spot well ahead.

When it's time to **eat**, the menu at *Robin's*, 4095 Burton Drive (℡805/927-5007), features clever main courses such as lobster enchiladas and spiced lamb

William Randolph Hearst: the real Citizen Kane

Born in 1863, **William Randolph Hearst** was the only son of a multimillionaire mining engineer. Throughout his life, he remained avidly devoted to his mother, Phoebe Apperson Hearst, one of California's most sincere and generous philanthropists – a founder of both the University of California and the Traveler's Aid Society. Hearst learned his trade in New York City working for the inventor of inflammatory **"yellow journalism"** Joseph Pulitzer, who had four rules for how to sell newspapers: emphasize the sensational, elaborate the facts, manufacture the news and use games and contests. When he published his own newspaper, Hearst took this advice to heart, his *Morning Journal* fanning the flames of American imperialism to help ignite the **Spanish–American War** of 1898. As he told his correspondents in Cuba: "You provide the pictures, and I'll provide the war." Hearst eventually controlled an empire that, at its peak during the 1930s, sold 25 percent of the newspapers in the entire country, including two other New York papers, the *Washington Times* and the *Detroit News* – as well as *Cosmopolitan* and *Good Housekeeping* magazines. In California, Hearst's power was even more pronounced, with his San Francisco and Los Angeles papers controlling over sixty percent of the total market. Besides his many newspapers, Hearst also owned eleven radio stations and two movie studios.

It was through his movie-studio proprietorship that he made his mistress **Marion Davies** a star. Davies' relationship with Hearst endured despite constant accusations of gold-digging and rumours swirling around a mysterious death onboard Hearst's boat (allegedly, Hearst murdered film-studio pioneer Thomas Ince and covered it up). When the Depression hit, Hearst was forced to sell off most of his holdings but remained a wealthy man; he continued to exert power and influence until his death, aged 88, at Davies' ranch in 1951. She stuck by him until the end, despite the private sniggers of his upper-crust cohorts; in explanation, Davies is said to have shrugged, "My mother raised me to be a gold-digger, but I fell in love."

rolls, as well as vegetarian fare; mains run from $15–26. *The Sow's Ear Café*, 2248 Main St (T 805/927-4865), is another local favourite for its range of mid-priced cuisine, including unique items like lobster pot pie.

Hearst Castle and San Simeon

Forty-five miles northwest of San Luis Obispo, **HEARST CASTLE** sits on a hilltop overlooking rolling ranchlands and the Pacific Ocean. Far and away the biggest attraction for miles, the former holiday home of **William Randolph Hearst** is one of the most opulent and extravagant houses in the world. Its interior combines walls, floors and ceilings torn from European churches and castles with Gothic fireplaces and Moorish tiles. Nearly every room is bursting with Greek vases and medieval tapestries, and even the many pools are lined with works of art. Ironically, the same financial power and lust for collecting that allowed Hearst to hoard these artefacts have made them viewable to more people than ever would have seen them had they remained in their respective lands. Though the castle was once a weekend retreat for the most famous politicians and movie stars of the 1920s and 1930s – Hearst's highly selective range of guests included Winston Churchill, Walt Disney and Charles Lindbergh, while the most frequent weekenders were Cary Grant and Charlie Chaplin – it now brings in more than a million visitors a year.

The castle

Hearst Castle, which Hearst himself referred to as "the ranch" (its official name is now "Hearst San Simeon State Historical Monument"), is the extravagant palace one would expect from the man whose grandstanding character and domination of the national media inspired Orson Welles's classic film *Citizen Kane*. The structure is actually more a complex of buildings than a "castle"; three guesthouses circle the hundred-room main **Casa Grande**, in which Hearst himself held court. What may come as a surprise is the harmony with which the many diverse art treasures he collected were brought together by his mother's favourite architect, **Julia Morgan** – herself a pioneer in the use of Spanish Mission elements in California architecture, from the Monday Club in San Luis Obispo (see p.388) to Los Angeles's landmark Herald-Examiner Building (Broadway and 11th Street). Here, Morgan designed each room and building in the spirit of the masterpieces destined to be housed inside – and received only $80,000 for her efforts, a paltry sum that nonetheless didn't keep her from acting as Hearst's personal architect for several more decades.

The ranchland had been in the family since 1865, bought by Hearst's father, mining magnate and senator George Hearst, and after the death of Hearst's mother Phoebe in 1919, construction began in earnest on his fantasies. This started on the southern edge of the 250,000-acre ranch, which became Hearst's own private, free-roaming zoo full of lions, tigers, zebras and bears. Though it kept on for another three decades, the work was never truly completed, since rooms would often be torn out as soon as they were finished in order to accommodate more acquired treasure. It's no wonder that the castle looks more like a church than a mansion: the main facade is a twin-towered copy of a Mudejar cathedral in Ronda, Spain, while the main door was pilfered from a convent there. Casa Grande stands at the top of steps that curve up from an expansive **Neptune Pool** (one of the most photographed in the world), which is filled with pure spring water and lined by a Greek colonnade and marble statues. Indoors, the **Roman Pool** is lined with blue Venetian glass and gold tiles, its soft lights reflecting in the water's steamy surface.

Highlights inside the castle include the **Refectory**, a stunning dining chamber lined with choir stalls removed from Spanish and Italian churches and bedecked pompously with heraldic flags; the **Library**, stuffed with thousands of rare and musty volumes; and the **Gothic Suite**, where Hearst conducted his daily business in medieval splendour, and whose grand, gloomy fireplace may have served as the inspiration for Kane's more colossal, jaw-like hearth. The **private cinema** is also not to be missed, where Hearst saw first-cuts of Hollywood films before they were released to the general public. The one disappointing element of the interior is its art collection: there are plenty of cherry-cheeked Madonnas and minor Old Masters, but not a single standout work – Hearst's taste was more decorative than artistic.

Outside the castle proper, the seventeen **Neptune Pool dressing rooms** are still hung with period swimwear and sports equipment. Also of note are the elaborate **guesthouses**, highlighted by the Eastern-themed **Casa del Mar** – which Marion Davies claimed to be Hearst's favourite spot on the whole estate – and **Casa del Monte**, a smaller guesthouse loaded with tapestries and overlooking the Santa Lucia Mountains. The estate's extensive Italian- and Spanish-influenced gardens, terraces and walkways merit a full tour in themselves as they feature hundreds of species of rare and imported flowers and trees.

Practicalities

To properly absorb Hearst Castle, it's recommended you take one of the guided **tours** (daily 8.20am–3.50pm; $24–30; ☎1-800/444-4445, outside US ☎1-916/414-8400 ext 4100, ⓦwww.hearstcastle.com), which depart from the state park's **visitor centre**, well-signed off Hwy-1 eight miles north of Cambria; a **self-guided tour** (March–Sept) entitled Gardens and Vistas is also available. **Tour 1**, the Experience Tour, which includes a lush film on the building's construction plus an introductory spin around the Casa del Sol guesthouse and the main rooms of Casa Grande, is usually recommended for the first visit. More worthwhile is **Tour 2**, which leads a smaller group around Casa Grande's upper floors. Docent narratives about Hearst are highly informative as you poke around the Gothic Suite, containing Hearst's library and office, and the Doge's Suite, his Venetian-flavoured bedroom, giving a more personal insight into the man than merely gawping at the staterooms seen on Tour 1; the main difference between the two tours is that you miss the film.

If you're fascinated enough to stay for the whole day, **Tour 3** is strictly for aficionados, concentrating as it does on the Casa del Monte guesthouse and the north wing of Casa Grande, while **Tour 4** (April–Oct) focuses on Casa del Mar and the gardens, including the estimable wine cellar. **Tour 5** (Oct–Dec; $30) runs on selected evenings, in which docents in period dress take visitors through the castle on a visit that combines elements of tours 1, 2 and 4, all while eerily speaking of Hearst in the present tense. The visit ends at the lamp-lit Neptune Pool with stories of the legendary figures who once frolicked there after dark. All tours include stops at the Neptune and Roman pools.

For each tour, budget around two hours (Tour 5 is slightly longer), including the trundling bus ride from the visitor centre to the hilltop. It's highly recommended you **book** as far in advance as possible; all tours leave from the same depot at the rear of the visitor centre, through the double doors past the ticket office. Make sure you collect your tickets before lining up for the tour. If you've arrived early, you can pass time in the mildly diverting **museum** (daily 9am–5pm; free) in the rear half of the visitor centre.

San Simeon and north

The old fishing pier at **San Simeon**, the remains of a harbour town along the coast just north of Hearst Castle, is where Hearst's considerable treasures were unloaded, along with the many tonnes of concrete and steel that went into the building of his palatial estate. Before the Hearsts bought up the land, San Simeon was a whaling and shipping port, of which all that remains is a one-room schoolhouse and the c.1852 *Sebastian's Store*, 442 San Simeon Rd (T 805/927-4217), a combination post office, café, history museum and souvenir shop. The peaceful and lovely **beach** near the pier is protected by San Simeon Point, which hooks out into the Pacific, making it safe for swimming. Along and near the highway three miles south, and still marked as part of San Simeon, are some basic **motels**; try the *Days Inn*, 9280 Castillo Drive (T 805/927-8659, W www.daysinn.com; ➌), which has a heated pool and rooms with balconies and fireplaces.

North of Hearst Castle, the region mostly consists of rolling grasslands and cattle ranches, still owned and run by the Hearst family, with scattered buildings on the distant hills. About three miles past San Simeon, at **Piedras Blancas**, a small strip of sand provides a resting point for a large colony of **elephant seals**; trails lead past a gate near the car park down to the beach, where you can watch the huge piles of furry blubber cuddle with one another and frolic in the waves. Beyond here, the highway seems to drop off in mid-air, marking the southern edge of Big Sur (see p.400), one of the most dramatic stretches of coastline in North America.

Paso Robles and Salinas Valley

If you don't have time to linger, US-101 – accessed from the coast via Hwy-46, five miles south of Cambria – heads north through **PASO ROBLES** and **Salinas Valley** and takes no more than four hours to cover the 230 miles between San Luis Obispo and San Francisco, compared to the full day it takes to drive the more scenic coast through Big Sur; unless you have your own wheels, you don't really have a choice, as both Greyhound and Amtrak follow the faster inland route. Four-lane US-101 closely follows the path of El Camino Real, the trail that linked the 21 Spanish **missions**, along the Salinas River. It runs through farmland that's so fertile, it's earned the nickname the "Salad Bowl of the World", thanks to the millions of lettuce heads (known as "green gold") it produces, largely picked by Mexican immigrants who populate the small towns that dot the valley.

Paso Robles and around

The small city of **Paso Robles** ("ROBE-ulls") is thirty miles north of San Luis Obispo and surrounded by horse ranches and nut farms. Despite a 6.5 magnitude earthquake in 2003 that collapsed a nineteenth-century clocktower Downtown, the town has rebounded quickly and there's little evidence of destruction.

The **visitor centre**, 1225 Park St (Mon–Fri 8.30am–5pm, Sat 10am–4pm; ☎805/238-0506, ⓦwww.pasorobleschamber.com), stocks a free map of the surrounding 150-odd **wineries**, many regarded as among the finest in the state; visit ⓦwww.pasowine.com for more information. Turley Wine Cellars, 2900 Vineyard Drive (☎805/434-1030, ⓦwww.turleywinecellars.com), makes superb Zinfandel from nearly century-old vines, while Tablas Creek Vineyard, 9339 Adelaida Rd (☎805/237-1231, ⓦwww.tablascreek.com), founded by the Perrin family of Châteauneuf-du-Pape fame, is another area favourite. If beer's more your speed, local powerhouse Firestone Walker, 1400 Ramada Drive (☎805/238-2556, ⓦwww.firestonewalker.com), offers free tours of its **brewery** at weekends or by appointment during the week.

Devotees of films such as *East of Eden* and *Rebel without a Cause* will want to drive about thirty miles east of Paso Robles on Hwy-46, past the junction of Hwy-41 near Cholame, where many come to pay respects at the stainless-steel monument near the site where **James Dean** fatally crashed in a silver Porsche 550 Spyder on September 30, 1955.

Central **accommodation** includes the *Paso Robles Inn*, on the town square at 1103 Spring St (☎1-800/676-1713, ⓦwww.pasoroblesinn.com; ❺–❼), which has comfortable rooms, some including two-person tubs on the balconies with water fed by local hot springs. A much cheaper nearby alternative is the austere but clean *Melody Ranch Motel*, 939 Spring St (☎805/238-3911; ❷). Out among the vines, try *Ann & George's Bed and Breakfast*, 1965 Niderer Rd (☎805/423-2760, ⓦwww.voladoresvineyard.com; ❻), offering bucolic and comfortable lodgings on the grounds of the Voladores Vineyard, five miles southwest of Paso Robles; discounts are offered for multiple-night stays.

Restaurants aplenty cluster around the town square; the best of the lot is *Lombardi's*, 836 11th St (☎805/237-7786), serving tasty pastas and gorgonzola-lashed pizzas in a casual setting.

Missions San Miguel Arcangel and San Antonio de Padua

Even if you're racing up the highway, set aside time for an essential peek at one of the most intact and authentic of California's Spanish missions, **Mission San Miguel Arcangel**, 775 Mission St (daily 10am–4.30pm; donation requested; ☎805/469-3256, ⓦwww.missionsanmiguel.org), just off US-101 in tiny **San Miguel**. Founded in 1797 as the sixteenth mission in the chain, the current building dates from 1816 and is the only one not to have undergone heavy-handed restoration. Following the missions' heyday but prior to falling into disrepair, it was used for a while as a saloon and dancehall; the chapel was left mostly unscathed, with colourful painted decoration and a marvellous sunburst reredos, complete with a striking Eye of God – all painted by Native Americans. The compound's other buildings are notable for their rough imprecision, with irregularly arched openings and unplastered walls forming a courtyard around a cactus garden. The mission was the most high-profile casualty of Paso Robles' 2003 earthquake; it didn't topple, but it sustained enough significant damage to be shuttered to the public for more than five years until a full retrofit made it safe.

If you're so inspired, you can venture about fifty miles northwest of Paso Robles to **Mission San Antonio de Padua** (daily 10am–4pm; grounds and church free, museum $5; ☏831/385-4478, ⓦwww.missionsanantonio.net), another fascinating, if remote, link along California's chain of Franciscan mission outposts. To reach it, drive north on US-101 to Bradley, the southernmost town in Salinas Valley, and follow Jolon Road (G18) twenty miles to the entrance of Fort Hunter Liggett Army base. After inspecting your driver's licence and vehicle registration, uniformed guards will grant passage five miles into the base, where the mission sits. This undervisited restoration of the 1771 original settlement is less sanitized than most other missions, and offers a clear glimpse into how life might have been for the missionaries and their converts. Third to be founded, San Antonio de Padua was among the most prosperous of all California's missions, and around the extensive grounds in a wide valley of oak trees and tall grasses, there's a monastic peace, especially around the inner courtyard and dim church with its flickering candles.

The large house across the valley from the mission used to belong to William Hearst, who sold it along with most of the land between here and Hearst Castle to the government in 1940 to help clear a $120-million debt. Today, the *Hacienda Guest Lodge* (☏831/386-2900; ●), as it's now called, offers rather ascetic **accommodation**.

Soledad and Pinnacles National Monument

To get back to US-101, retrace your route to the hamlet of Jolon, then follow Jolon Road north to nondescript **King City**; those headed to the eastern entrance of Pinnacles National Monument should follow road G13 from here to the northeast. Otherwise, follow US-101 twenty miles north of King City to **Soledad**, a quiet, predominantly Mexican farming town principally of interest for its proximity to Pinnacles' western entrance, as well as its *panaderías* offering cakes and fresh tortillas.

The inland region's major natural attraction, **Pinnacles National Monument** ($5; ☏831/389-4485, ⓦwww.nps.gov/pinn), is full of startling volcanic spires, cool caves and brilliant reds and golds, all set against blue sky. It's best visited in spring (especially March and April), when the air is still cool and the chaparral hillsides are lushly green and sprinkled with wildflowers. Also watch for legions of bees, as this park boasts the highest known bee diversity in the world – some four hundred species in all.

For most, the main attraction is a day or two spent **hiking** some of the 35 miles of lovely and well-maintained trails. Pinnacles is compact enough that it's quite possible to hike from one side to the other and back in one long day, as only three miles set apart the dead ends of its east and west roads. Note that shade is rare here, so avoid hiking in the middle of the day in summer and remember to carry plenty of water. Backcountry camping is not permitted.

One of the best hikes is the **Balconies Trail** (two-mile loop; 100ft ascent), most easily accessed from the west, which skirts the multicoloured, 600ft face of the Balconies outcrop, then returns via a series of talus **caves** (be sure to pack a flashlight or headlamp) formed by huge boulders now wedged between the walls of the narrow canyons. An excellent **park loop** (10 miles; 1600ft ascent) can be undertaken from either entrance, a trek that, by combining several trails (including the Balconies), takes in the best of the park's high and low country.

Park practicalities

The park has east and west entrances, but no road transects its steep spires; several trails allow you to explore Pinnacles' wonders from either entrance, however. Somewhat surprisingly, most of the park's facilities are centred around the more remote **eastern entrance** (open 24hr; accessed along G13 and Hwy-25), including the Bear Gulch Visitor Center (daily 9am–5pm) and the swimming pool-equipped *Pinnacles Campground* (☏831/444-6777, ⊛www.recreation.gov; $23). If you plan to **camp** here in the spring months, reservations are virtually essential.

Amenities at Pinnacles' **western entrance** (gates open 7.30am–8pm) consist of little more than a ranger station and toilets, with overnight stays not allowed. Still, its accessibility off Hwy-101 from Soledad, from where Hwy-146 runs eleven winding miles to the park, makes it the better option for day-visits.

For **accommodation** in Soledad itself, pull into the dull but serviceable *Soledad Motel 8*, 1013 Front St (☏831/678-3814; ❷) or, for something more upmarket, head to the swanky *Inn at the Pinnacles*, 32025 Stonewall Canyon Rd (☏831/678-2400, ⊛www.innatthepinnacles.com; ❻), on Hwy-146 just a mile short of the park's western entrance. There's a small handful of top-rate Mexican **restaurants** in Soledad, among which *La Fuente*, 101 Oak St (☏831/678-3130), stands out for its excellent main courses.

Salinas and around

The seat of Monterey County, **SALINAS**, about twenty-five miles north of Soledad, is a sprawling agricultural-based city of 150,000 inhabitants. Although it's perhaps best known these days for the **California Rodeo** (daily tickets $13–20; ☏1-800/771-8807, ⊛www.carodeo.com) held during the third week in July and the biggest in the state, it's also the 1902 birthplace of Nobel Prize-winning writer **John Steinbeck** (see box opposite); in fact, Salinas and its namesake agricultural valley to the south are often bracketed together as Steinbeck Country. Despite leaving in his mid-20s to live in Monterey and later New York, the region heavily nurtured his imagination, and many of his naturalistic stories and novels, including the epic *East of Eden*, were set in and around the valley.

The best introduction to both the man and the region is the large, modern **National Steinbeck Center**, 1 Main St (daily 10am–5pm; $10.95; ☏831/775-4721, ⊛www.steinbeck.org), which takes you on an engaging, interactive journey through the author's life and work. A fifteen-minute biographical film offers an informative and lively approach to Steinbeck and sets the tone for the rest of the museum, throughout which snippets of films and material from sound archives play prominent roles; it's all inspiring enough that you may well find yourself purchasing a novel or two from the centre's excellent store. A new wing is devoted to the **Agriculture Museum**, which explores the history of vegetable growing in the region as well as the arrival of Latinos during World War II when labour was short, all presented in both English and Spanish.

Further exploration of Steinbeck's Salinas connections is best done using the centre's free *Oldtown Walking Tour* **map**, which highlights locales in the surrounding area that were influential in the writer's life. An obvious highlight is the author's childhood home, the **Steinbeck House**, two blocks west of the museum at 132 Central Ave (Tues–Sat 11.30am–2pm; call or check website for tour availability; ☏831/424-2735, ⊛www.steinbeckhouse.com), which has been turned into an English-style tearoom. Before leaving Downtown, stroll the tree-lined Main Street with its prettified Victorian buildings, clothing boutiques and craft stores, as well as the 1921 Art Deco **Fox Theater** at no. 239.

Today, much as in Steinbeck's day, Salinas is a hotbed of labour disputes, with the gap between the low-paid manual labourers who pick the produce and the

The novels of John Steinbeck

John Steinbeck's novels and short stories are as remarkable for their historical content as for their narratives; he had a newspaperman's eye for the hardships of working-class life. *The Grapes of Wrath*, his best-known work, was made into a film starring Henry Fonda while still at the top of the bestseller lists, having captured the popular imagination for its portrayal of the Depression-era miseries of the Joad family on their migration to California from the Oklahoma Dust Bowl. *Cannery Row* followed in 1945, a nostalgic portrait of Monterey fisheries, which ironically went into steep decline the year the book was published. Steinbeck spent the next four years writing *East of Eden*, an allegorical retelling of the biblical story of Cain and Abel against the landscape of the Salinas Valley; in this book, which he saw as his masterpiece, Steinbeck expresses many of the values that underlie the rest of his works.

Much of Steinbeck's writing is concerned with the dignity of labour, as well as the inequalities of an economic system that "allows children to go hungry in the midst of rotting plenty". Although he was circumspect about his own political stance, there was a violent backlash against Steinbeck in Salinas for what were seen as his Communist sympathies once *The Grapes of Wrath* became a bestseller in 1939. Later, he was so wounded at the outcry over his worthiness for the Nobel Prize for Literature in 1962 that he never wrote another word. He died in New York City in 1968; today his ashes are buried in Salinas in the **Garden of Memories Cemetery**, 768 Abbott St.

wealthy owners of agribusiness empires who run the giant farms still unbridged. In the 1960s and early 1970s, the United Farm Workers union, under the leadership of **César Chávez** and Dolores Huerta, had great success in organizing and demanding better pay and working conditions for the almost exclusively Latino workforce, masterminding a very effective boycott of the valley's main product, lettuce. But workers are once again under siege, with wages far below what they were two decades ago amid increasing worries about the dangers of exposure to pesticides and agricultural chemicals.

If you're heading west towards Monterey on Hwy-68, call in briefly at **Spreckels**, a small town three miles beyond Salinas that was raised in 1898 for employees of the Spreckels sugar factory (whose scion was Adolph Spreckels, husband of the wild, art-loving beauty Alma – see p.462). Parts of the *East of Eden* film were shot here, including the famous scene in which James Dean – playing Cal – hurls blocks of ice down a chute to get his father's attention.

Practicalities

Greyhound **buses** between Los Angeles and San Francisco stop in the centre of Salinas roughly five times daily at 19 W Gabilan St (☏831/424-4418) near Salinas Street; Amtrak Coast Starlight **trains** leave once a day in each direction, two blocks away at 30 Railroad Ave.

The city's **Chamber of Commerce** at 119 E Alisal St (Mon, Wed & Fri 8am–5pm, Tues & Thurs 9.30am–5pm; ☏831/751-7725, ⓦwww.salinas chamber.com) can help with accommodation – often useful in summer when Monterey, twenty miles west, is booked solid. Monterey-Salinas Transit bus #20 makes the 55-minute trip to Monterey several times daily from the Transit Center at 110 Salinas St.

Hordes of franchise **motel** signs are visible from Hwy-101, with *Quality Inn*, 144 Kern St (☏831/758-8850, ⓦwww.salinasqualityinn.com; ❷), being the best of the lot, despite wildly fluctuating rates based on season. There are quite a few renowned Mexican **restaurants** around Salinas, the oldest and most central being

Rosita's Armory Café, 231 Salinas St, where you can settle into one of the big green booths and chow down on delicious mains such as cheese-stuffed enchiladas and chile colorado for about $10.

Big Sur

While not an official geographical designation, **BIG SUR** is the de facto regional name for the ninety miles of rocky cliffs and crashing seas along the California coast between San Simeon and the Monterey Peninsula; it extends inland about twenty miles, well into the Santa Lucia Mountains. Driving north on Hwy-1, you'll know you've reached it when the estuaries and beaches of the Central Coast give way to a jagged-edged coastline and dense tangles of redwoods, the southernmost groves in the trees' long coastal chain. Named by the Spanish *El Pais Grande del Sur* (the "big country to the south" of their colony at Monterey), it's still a wild and craggy region that's breathtakingly unspoiled.

Before Hwy-1 was completed in 1937, the few inhabitants of Big Sur had to be almost entirely self-sufficient by farming, raising cattle and trapping sea otters for their furs. The only connections with the rest of the world were via the infrequently used steamship line to Monterey, or a nearly impassable trail over the mountains to Salinas Valley. Despite improved transport links, fewer people live here today (about one thousand) than in 1900, and most of the land is still owned by a handful of families, many of whom are descendants of Big Sur's original pioneers. Locals have banded together to protect the land from obtrusive development, while also fighting government plans to allow offshore oil drilling; to their credit, their ornery determination has paid off.

Big Sur's coast is also the protected habitat of the **sea otter**, and **grey whales** pass by close to the shore on their annual winter migration. A visit in April or May will reveal vibrant **wildflowers** and lilac-coloured ceanothus bushes under increasingly foggy skies, though the sun generally shines unhindered during autumn months. Summer weekends see the roads and campgrounds packed to overflowing – and the wildness of the area dampened – by many eager visitors.

Resist the temptation to bust through Big Sur in a single day; the best way to enjoy its isolation and beauty is slowly. Leave the car behind as often as you can and wander through its numerous parks, where a mere ten-minute walk can completely remove you from any sign of the built environment.

Information and getting around

While narrow Hwy-1 is a perennial favourite with cyclists, most visitors will need a car to follow the dramatic route as it winds exhilaratingly through bedrock cliffs several hundred feet above the Pacific Ocean. The only **public transport** through Big Sur is Monterey-Salinas Transit (MST) bus #22 from Monterey Transit Plaza, which runs as far south as *Nepenthe* restaurant; its schedule varies throughout the year, so call ☎1-888/678-2871 or check ⊚www.mst.org.

The central section of Big Sur around Hwy-1 is the most developed and interesting for first-time visitors, with the region's three main inhabited areas all near **Pfeiffer Big Sur State Park** (see p.404): around the post office, two miles south of the park; at Fernwood, a mile north past the park's main entrance; and at an area called the Village, a further mile and a half north. Pfeiffer Big Sur is a great base for Big Sur exploration, where you can swim among giant boulders, hike up redwood canyons to a waterfall or sunbathe on a beautiful, sandy beach. Conveniently, its day-use fee ($10) is also valid at Julia Pfeiffer Burns and Andrew Molera state parks.

Facilities such as gas stations and grocery stores are scattered and surprisingly scarce here, and since you should expect those you do find to be premium-priced, it's best to fill your gas tank and go shopping before your visit. Note as well that **mobile-phone coverage** around Big Sur is patchy at best; as for **internet access**, it's available at most lodgings and at public terminals at the Henry Miller Library (see p.403). Pick up a free copy of the indispensable *Big Sur Guide* publication at park information offices or stores along the highway; otherwise, visit the **Chamber of Commerce** (Mon, Wed & Fri 9am–1pm; ☎ 831/667-2100, ⓦ www .bigsurcalifornia.org) or Big Sur Ranger Station near Pfeiffer Big Sur State Park headquarters (see p.404) for backcountry camping permits and plenty of local wisdom.

Accommodation

In keeping with Big Sur's backwoods qualities, most of the available **accommodation** is in rustic lodges, with scattered affordability. Note that the few rooms on offer are full most nights throughout the summer, especially on weekends; book well in advance.

Campgrounds are dotted all along the Big Sur coast and popular year-round, in addition to a few less developed ones in the **Santa Lucia Mountains** above; visit ⓦ www.campone .com for additional information. Unless otherwise stated, sites at all campgrounds listed below may be reserved by calling ☎ 1-800/444-7275 or visiting ⓦ www.reserve america.com.

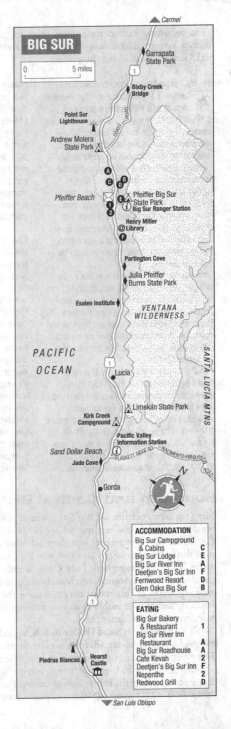

BIG SUR

0 — 5 miles

▲ Carmel

Garrapata State Park

Bixby Creek Bridge

COAST ROAD

Point Sur Lighthouse

Andrew Molera State Park

Pfeiffer Beach

A
B
C
D
E

Pfeiffer Big Sur State Park
Big Sur Ranger Station

1
2

Henry Miller @ Library

F

Partington Cove

Julia Pfeiffer Burns State Park

Esalen Institute

VENTANA WILDERNESS

PACIFIC OCEAN

Lucia

Limekiln State Park

SANTA LUCIA MTNS

Kirk Creek Campground

Pacific Valley Information Station

Sand Dollar Beach

Jade Cove

PLASKETT RIDGE RD

NACIMIENTO-FERGUSSON RD

Gorda

N

Piedras Blancas

Hearst Castle

▼ San Luis Obispo

ACCOMMODATION

Big Sur Campground & Cabins	C
Big Sur Lodge	E
Big Sur River Inn	A
Deetjen's Big Sur Inn	F
Fernwood Resort	D
Glen Oaks Big Sur	B

EATING

Big Sur Bakery & Restaurant	1
Big Sur River Inn Restaurant	A
Big Sur Roadhouse	A
Cafe Kevah	2
Deetjen's Big Sur Inn	F
Nepenthe	2
Redwood Grill	D

The following listings are ordered from south to north. Instead of using each location's street address along Hwy-1, approximate distances from Big Sur's major parks are instead used here as guides.

Inns, motels and cabins

Deetjen's Big Sur Inn Hwy-1, seven miles north of Julia Pfeiffer Burns State Park ☎831/667-2377, ⊛www.deetjens.com. Built by a Norwegian immigrant, this laid-back compound (with great restaurant and bar) offers comfortably rustic lodging. Ski lodgestyle log cabins feature fireplaces, rocking chairs, old-fashioned leaded windows and lots of wood panelling. ❷–❻

Big Sur Lodge In Pfeiffer Big Sur State Park ☎1-800/424-4787, ⊛www.bigsurlodge.com. Plushly furnished rooms, each with porch and enormous sit-down showers. Some rooms have fireplaces and all have access to a nice outdoor pool and restaurant. Rates include entrance fee to area state parks. ❻

Fernwood Resort Hwy-1, just over half a mile north of Pfeiffer Big Sur State Park ☎831/667-2422, ⊛www.fernwoodbigsur.com. Basic motel rooms are at least fairly cheap for these parts, though rooms fitted with hot tub and fireplace are much nicer. Down towards the river are wooded sites for tents ($40), plus austere but affordable tent cabins. ❶–❻

Glen Oaks Big Sur Hwy-1, one mile north of Pfeiffer Big Sur State Park ☎831/667-2105, ⊛www.glenoaksbigsur.com. Redwood posts and adobe bricks form the framework for classily remodelled rooms, each with modern gas fireplace; cabins and cottages are also available. ❼–❾

Big Sur Campgrounds & Cabins Hwy-1, one mile north of Pfeiffer Big Sur State Park ☎831/667-2322, ⊛www.bigsurcamp.com.

Inviting riverside campground with the area's best cabins: wooden tent affairs sleeping up to three (❹) and fancier places (❻–❾). Tent sites $45–55.

Big Sur River Inn Hwy-1, two and a half miles north of Pfeiffer Big Sur State Park ☎1-800/548-3610, ⊛www.bigsurriverinn.com. Woodsy lodge with a handful of fine riverside suites complete with down comforters and verandas; less expensive, basic motel-style rooms are situated across Hwy-1. There's a handy grocery store and charming restaurant (see p.405) on-site as well. ❻

Camping

Kirk Creek Campground ☎805/434-1996, ⊛www.campone.com. Set on an exposed bluff five miles north of Pacific Valley ranger station, this is the only campground in the area that's both right on the coast and has walk-in sites ($5). $22.

Limekiln State Park Two miles north of *Kirk Creek*, with hot showers and a developed trail to the limekilns, redwoods and a waterfall. $35.

Pfeiffer Big Sur State Park The most popular campground in the area, with spacious and well-shaded sites, many among the redwoods. Hot showers, a well-stocked store and even a launderette are all available, along with walk-in sites for $5. $35–50.

Andrew Molera State Park Just one-third of a mile from the parking lot and half a mile from the beach, this walk-in campground in a vast ten-acre meadow is first-come first-served, so arrive early. Camping fee also includes park day-use fee. $25.

Southern and Central Big Sur

The southern coastline of Big Sur is the region at its most gentle, with sandy beaches nestled below eroding yellow-ochre cliffs. Thirty miles north of Hearst Castle, the cliffs get steeper and the road more tortuous around the vista point at **Willow Creek**, where you can watch surfers and sea otters playing in the waves (albeit not together). **Jade Cove**, a mile north, takes its name from the translucent stones sometimes found here, mainly by scuba-divers offshore; crashing waves at this rocky cove reinforce the awesome power of the sea. To reach it, follow a brambly trail ten minutes from the highway, marked by a wooden stile in the cattle fence.

Half a mile north is **Sand Dollar Beach**, a good place to enjoy the surf or watch **hang-gliders**, which launch from sites in the mountains off Plaskett Ridge Road. This steep, one-lane route, which ends at Nacimiento–Fergusson Road several winding miles north, is great fun on a mountain bike and leads to a few isolated campgrounds along the ridge. Visit or call the **Pacific Valley information station** (☎805/927-4211; irregular hours) one mile north for details on the area.

The coastal **campground** at **Kirk Creek** (see opposite) sits at the foot of Nacimiento–Fergusson Road, which twists over the Santa Lucia Mountains to Salinas Valley via Mission San Antonio de Padua (see p.397). **Limekiln Creek**, two miles north of the junction, is named after the hundred-year-old kilns that survive in good condition along the creek behind the namesake state park's **campground**. In the 1880s, local limestone was burned in these kilns to extract lime powder for use as cement, then carried on a complex aerial tramway to be loaded onto ships at Rockland Landing. The ships that carried the lime to Monterey in turn brought in most of the supplies to isolated Big Sur.

Esalen to the Henry Miller Library

Esalen (ESS-uhlun), ten miles further north, is named for the Esselen band of local Native Americans who once frequented the healing waters of the natural **hot springs** here, located at the top of a cliff two hundred feet above the raging Pacific surf. Since the 1960s, when all sorts of people came to Big Sur to smoke dope and get back to nature, the springs have been owned and operated by the Esalen Institute (T 831/667-3000, W www.esalen.org) – the devotees of which tend to arrive in luxury vehicles for overnight stays, massage treatments, yoga workshops and seminars on "potentialities and values of human existence". Esalen's hot springs, however, are available nightly to non-guests for $20 between 1 and 3am; call T 831/667-3047 to reserve.

Julia Pfeiffer Burns State Park (daily dawn–dusk; $10; T 831/667-2315, W www.parks.ca.gov), three miles north of Esalen along McWay Creek, has some of the best day-hikes in the Big Sur area, the most spectacular of which is a ten-minute walk from the parking area, under the highway along the edge of the cliff and to an overlook of spectacular **McWay Falls**, which crashes onto a beach below Saddle Rock. A less-travelled path leads down from Hwy-1 two miles north of the waterfall (at milepost 37.85) through a 200ft-long tunnel to the wave-washed remains of a small wharf at **Partington Cove**, one of the few places in southern Big Sur where you can actually reach the seashore itself. Call ahead for trail conditions, as mudslides here are not uncommon.

About eight miles north of Julia Pfeiffer Burns State Park, stop in at the **Henry Miller Library** (Wed–Mon 11am–6pm; free; T 831/667-2574, W www .henrymiller.org) where the secluded front lawn is a pleasant place to grab a coffee or use the free wi-fi. There's little Millerabilia on display, but employees will happily show you plenty if you ask. Miller's own home, back near Partington Cove, is now a private residence; this house was owned by his old friend Emil White and now stands as a ramshackle bookshop-cum-monument to the *Tropic of Cancer* author's work.

Nepenthe to Pfeiffer Big Sur State Park

It's with Nepenthe that Big Sur's commercial development begins in earnest, however quietly. This dramatically sited complex, which consists of a café and restaurant (see p.405), gallery and bookstore full of Miller's works is named after the mythical drug that induces forgetfulness. Just over a mile north, you'll find the region's post office, as well as a **gas station**; nearby, unmarked Sycamore Canyon Road leads a mile west to Big Sur's best strand, **Pfeiffer Beach** (dawn–dusk; $5 per car; T 831/667-2315), a white-sand, sometimes windy stretch dominated by a charismatic hump of rock whose colour varies from brown to red to orange in the changing light. Park where you can at the end of the road and walk through an archway of cypress trees along the lagoon down to the sand.

Back on the highway, one mile north of the post office, the route drops behind a coastal ridge into the valley of the **Big Sur River**, where most accommodation and dining options are located. Stop at **Big Sur Ranger Station** (℡831/667-2315; hours vary seasonally), where helpful personnel distribute backcountry camping and campfire permits for Ventana Wilderness in the adjacent Santa Lucia Mountains, and are otherwise the region's finest repository of park information. A popular hike leads steeply up from the Pine Ridge trailhead behind the station and ten miles into the lush mountains to **Sykes Hot Springs** (unrestricted entry), just downstream from the free campground at *Sykes Camp* along the Big Sur River. This extraordinary amble is an overnight expedition and requires at least five hours of hiking each way.

Plumb in the middle of the river valley, **Pfeiffer Big Sur State Park** (daily dawn–dusk; $10; ℡831/667-2315, ⓦwww.parks.ca.gov) is one of the most beautiful and enjoyable parks in all of California, with miles of hiking trails and excellent swimming along the Big Sur River. In late spring and summer, the crystal-clear water in the river runs highest, creating deep swimming holes among the large boulders plunked along the bottom of its narrow, steep-walled gorge. Nude sunbathing is tolerated (except on national holidays, when the park tends to be overrun with swarms of screaming children) and, since the park is sheltered a mile or so inland, the weather is warmer and sunnier than elsewhere along this part of the coast. The park also holds the main **campground** (see p.402) in the Big Sur region.

The most popular hiking trail in the park leads to the sixty-foot **Pfeiffer Falls**, half a mile up a narrow canyon shaded by redwood trees; look for the trailhead opposite the park entrance. The bridges over the river here possess an understated grace, as does the nearby amphitheatre – built by the Civilian Conservation Corps during the Depression – where rangers give excellent campfire talks and slide shows about Big Sur during summer months.

Northern Big Sur

Andrew Molera State Park (daily dawn–dusk; $10; ℡831/667-2315, ⓦwww .parks.ca.gov), five miles north of Pfeiffer Big Sur State Park, is the largest park in Big Sur, with well over two miles of rocky oceanfront reached by a mile-long trail. It occupies the site of what was once the El Sur Ranch, one of the earliest and most successful Big Sur cattle ranches, initially run in the early nineteenth century by Juan Bautista Alvarado, who became California governor in 1836; it was later overseen by English sea captain Roger Cooper, whose cabin is preserved here. Although the cabin itself isn't open to the public, you can reach the site on some of the fifteen miles of hiking trails also used for a variety of guided **horseback rides** ($40–70; ℡1-800/942-5486, ⓦwww.molerahorsebacktours .com) that run from one to two and a half hours. The park also has a walk-in **campground** (see p.402).

Three miles north of the state park along Hwy-1, **Point Sur Lighthouse** (ⓦwww.pointsur.org) perches on a volcanic outcrop. It can only be visited by taking a volunteer-given walking **tour** ($8, moonlight tours $15; check website for schedule), which includes three hours exploring the lighthouse and its ancillary buildings. Five miles further north, **Bixby Creek Bridge** was ranked as the longest single-span concrete bridge in the world when its construction was completed in 1932. It's the most impressive (and photogenic) engineering feat of the entire Coast Road project, a local construction programme sponsored by the Works Progress Administration during the Depression.

An alternative route from Andrew Molera State Park begins opposite the park's entrance, where **Coast Road** takes off inland from Hwy-1 up steep hills to offer panoramic views over miles of wave-lashed Pacific coastline. The partly paved, roughly ten-mile road winds over wide-open ranchlands and through deep, slender canyons until it rejoins the main highway at Bixby Creek Bridge.

The northernmost stop along Big Sur's coast, and about ten miles before Hwy-1 drops into Carmel, is wildflower-rich **Garrapata State Park** (daily dawn–dusk; free; T831/624-4909, W www.parks.ca.gov). A mile-long trail leads from the highway out to the tip of **Soberanes Point**, a beautiful spot from which you can watch for sea otters and grey whales.

Eating

A number of places to **eat and drink** in Big Sur are attached to the inns listed on p.402; many are fairly basic burger-and-beer joints, but there are a few special ones worth searching out, some for their good food and others for their views of the Pacific. Because of Big Sur's isolation, prices here are around 25 percent higher than you'll pay in a proper town.

As with Big Sur's accommodation listings, these are ordered from south to north, with approximate distances from major parks and landmarks used as guides.

Deetjen's Big Sur Inn Hwy-1, seven miles north of Julia Pfeiffer Burns State Park T831/667-2377. Excellent, unhurried breakfasts (under $10) and a variety of top-quality fish and vegetarian dinners ($13–25) served in a snug, redwood-panelled room.

Nepenthe T831/667-2345. Definitely not for the thrifty, this high-profile steak-and-seafood restaurant boasts a warm amber mood, unforgettable views (sunset whale-watching is possible in season) and an après-ski-like atmosphere. Mains $25–37.

Cafe Kevah Nepenthe. Set directly below upmarket *Nepenthe*, this relaxed outdoor terrace café serves tasty baked goods and brunch, as well as salads and panini ($10–15) each morning and afternoon. Closed Jan.

Big Sur Bakery & Restaurant One and a half miles north of Nepenthe T831/667-0520. Far from simply churning out cakes and pastries, this moderately priced café has an on-site rotisserie in which it cooks all its meats. The lunch menu features terrific pizzas and sandwiches, while the

dinner menu leans on meats and seafood, with vegetarian main courses also available. Mains $18–32.

Redwood Grill Hwy-1, just over half a mile north of Pfeiffer Big Sur State Park. Budget diner (all things relative) at *Fernwood Resort* serving good salads and sandwiches for around $15. Ribs are available at dinner for $18, and there's a breakfast buffet for $11.

Big Sur River Inn Restaurant The Village, Hwy-1, two and a half miles north of Pfeiffer Big Sur State Park T831/667-2700. Century-old, yet upscale restaurant serving a creative range of seafood and meat dishes in a spacious, redwood-log dining room, complete with toasty fireplace. Mains $18–38.

Big Sur Roadhouse The Village, Hwy-1, two and a half miles north of Pfeiffer Big Sur State Park T831/667-2264. California / Latin American cuisine such as stuffed pasilla peppers and adobo-marinated steaks served in a cosy, flower-filled cottage. Don't miss the chunky guacamole. Mains $16–26.

Monterey Peninsula

Immediately north of Big Sur, the rocky promontory and gnarled cypress trees of the **MONTEREY PENINSULA** amplify the collision between cliffs and thundering sea. Though the manicured towns here now thrive thanks to a regular flow of tourists, each manages to retain its individual character. Secluded **Carmel** is by far the poshest, although its star-struck election of Clint Eastwood as mayor in 1986 somewhat dispelled its sniffy reputation for a time. Around the peninsula and to the northwest, the resolutely upscale village of **Pebble Beach** is primarily known for its golf courses (it hosted the US Open in 2010), while **Pacific Grove** stands at the peninsula's tip with spectacular views over the sea – a pleasant, if

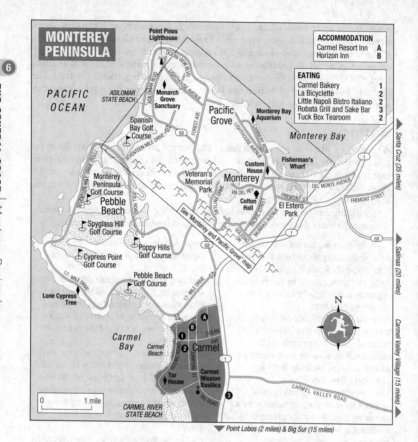

Point Lobos (2 miles) & Big Sur (15 miles)

rather sleepy, place best known for butterflies and Victorian architecture. The largest town, and the most convenient and practical base from which to explore the peninsula, is **Monterey** itself; it was the capital of California under both the Spanish and the Mexicans, and today it retains many old adobe houses and places of genuine historic appeal. Monterey's local population is also a little younger than those of the other towns, which helps lend it the area's liveliest nightlife and restaurant scenes.

Arrival, information and getting around

The Monterey Peninsula juts out into the Pacific to form Monterey Bay, one hundred miles south of San Francisco. Hwy-1 cuts across its neck, while Hwy-68 links up with US-101 to the east in Salinas, twenty miles inland. Greyhound **buses** and Amtrak **trains** stop in Salinas and connect with Monterey-Salinas Transit (MST) buses several times daily (see opposite).

Drop by the **Monterey CVB's visitor centre**, set in the History & Maritime Museum at 5 Custom House Plaza (daily 9am–5pm; ☎1-877/666-8373, ⓦwww .seemonterey.com), where staff can share plenty of knowledge on local accommodations and attractions. The **Pacific Grove Chamber of Commerce**, 584 Central Ave at Forest (Mon–Fri 9.30am–5pm, Sat 10am–3pm; ☎1-800/656-6650,

ⓦ www.pacificgrove.org), across from the Museum of Natural History, has walking-tour maps of local historic buildings and can help find you a room in town. The best guide to what's on in the area is the widely available freebie *Monterey County Weekly* (ⓦ www.montereycountyweekly.com), which contains listings of movies, live music, art galleries and such.

Wi-fi and **internet**-ready computer terminals are available free of charge at the Monterey Public Library, 625 Pacific St (Mon 1–9pm, Tues & Wed 10am–9pm, Thurs & Fri 10am–6pm, Sat & Sun 1–5pm; ⓣ 831/646-3932, ⓦ www.monterey .org/library). Monterey's main **post office** is located at 565 Hartnell St (Mon–Fri 8.30am–5pm, Sat 10am–2pm; ⓣ 831/372-4063).

Getting around the area is surprisingly easy. MST buses (ⓣ 1-888/678-2871, ⓦ www.mst.org) run between 7am and 6pm (11pm on some routes), radiating out from Transit Plaza in the historic core of Monterey and ranging as far afield as Nepenthe in Big Sur and even San Jose. Journeys within the Monterey Peninsula cost $2.50; call or check MST's website for additional fare information. Particularly useful routes are #4 and #5, which link Monterey with Carmel; #20, which runs between Monterey and both Amtrak and Greyhound in Salinas; and #1, which runs along Lighthouse Avenue past the main sights and out to Pacific Grove. There's also a **free trolley** running regularly from Downtown Monterey to the Monterey Bay Aquarium via Fisherman's Wharf (summer only; daily 10am–7pm).

Alternately, you can rent a **bike** to get around the area, if you so desire. Try one of Adventures by the Sea's several locations around the peninsula, including 201 Alvarado St ($7 per hour, $25 per day; ⓣ 831/372-1807, ⓦ www .adventuresbythesea.com).

Accommodation

The Monterey Peninsula is among the most exclusive and expensive vacation destinations in California, with nightly **hotel** and **bed-and-breakfast** room rates averaging well over $100. This may tempt you to stay elsewhere – in Santa Cruz or Salinas, perhaps – and simply come here for the day; the other budget option is to check in at one of the many **motels** lining North Fremont Street or Munras Avenue, about one mile from the city centre. You can expect big crowds all summer, especially on **weekends**, even though that's when room rates shoot up massively (summer weekend **prices** are quoted below) and there's often a two-night minimum stay (particularly at B&Bs). Try to visit in spring or autumn, when the peninsula is quieter, lodging is cheaper and the coastal weather is sunnier.

The Monterey Peninsula's only local **campground** is at Veteran's Memorial Park ($27, walk-in sites $5; ⓣ 831/646-3865, ⓦ www.monterey.org/rec), on Jefferson Street one mile west of Downtown Monterey in the hills above town. It's the picturesque site of Steinbeck's fictional Tortilla Flat and is set among trees with picnic tables and fire rings at all 40 sites, available on a first-come, first-served basis.

Monterey

America's Best Value Presidents Inn 1150 Munras Ave ⓣ 1-877/922-1150, ⓦ www.americas bestvaluecypressgardensinnmunras.com. One of the better motels along Munras Avenue, with a leafy garden, large pool, jacuzzi, gym and free continental breakfast. ⑤

Mariposa Inn & Suites 1386 Munras Ave ⓣ 1-800/824-2295, ⓦ www.mariposamonterey .com. Rambling complex offering cosy rooms with fireplaces and full amenities, including balconies

and a heated pool. Townhouse suites also available. ⑥

Monterey Hostel - HI 778 Hawthorne St ⓣ 831/649-0375, ⓦ www.montereyhostel.org. Well-managed hostel with a spacious common room and pleasant dorms, near Cannery Row. HI members $22.50, non-members $25.50; private rooms (②), not available to single travellers.

Monterey Plaza Hotel & Spa 400 Cannery Row ⓣ 831/646-1700, ⓦ www.montereyplazahotel.com. Sited amid Cannery Row's action – it's three blocks from Monterey Bay Aquarium – this four-star water-front hotel boasts plush rooms, outstanding views and *Schooners Bistro on the Bay* (see p.416). ❼

Pacific Grove

🏃 **Anton Inn** 1095 Lighthouse Ave
☎1-888/242-6866, ⓦwww.antoninn.com. The clean lines and understated modern decor at this classy inn mark a refreshing change from the overabundance of Victoriana in Pacific Grove. All rooms have electric fireplaces, while some feature hot tubs. ❽

Bide-a-Wee Inn & Cottages 221 Asilomar Blvd
☎831/372-2330, ⓦwww.bideaweeinn.com. Nicely spruced-up, reasonably priced rooms with modern, homely furnishings, including mini-fridges and microwaves; cottages with kitchenettes also on offer. Rooms ❺, cottages ❺–❻

Green Gables Inn 301 Ocean View Blvd
☎1-800/722-1774, ⓦwww.greengablesinnpg .com. Lush lodging in one of the prettiest houses in a town full of them, on the waterfront just a few blocks from Monterey Bay Aquarium. Evening wine and buffet breakfast are served in the ocean-view lounge with fireplace. ❺

Pacific Grove Inn 581 Pine Ave ☎831/375-2825, ⓦwww.pacificgroveinn.com. Five blocks from the shore, this thoughtfully modernized 1904 mansion has well over a dozen spacious rooms, some with sea views. Continental breakfast is included. ❼

🏃 **Rosedale Inn** 775 Asilomar Blvd
☎1-800/822-5606, ⓦwww.rosedaleinn .com. These log-cabin-style rooms are refreshingly modern, with ceiling fans and pine furniture, as well as fireplaces and jacuzzi baths. The real standout, though, is the affable staff. ❻

Carmel

Carmel Resort Inn Carpenter Ave between First and Second aves ☎1-800/454-3700, ⓦwww .carmelresortinn.com. Motel-style cottage rooms include microwaves, mini-fridges and fireplaces; continental breakfast is also served. Surprisingly inexpensive for Carmel. ❻

Horizon Inn Junipero Ave and 3rd St
☎1-800/350-7723, ⓦwww.horizoninncarmel.com. Another relatively affordable place with cosy rooms, a breakfast basket delivered to your door and access to an outdoor hot tub. ❺

Monterey

The city of **MONTEREY** rests in a quiet niche along the bay formed by the forested Monterey Peninsula; it proudly proclaims itself the most historic city in California – a boast that, for once, may be true. Its compact centre features some of the best vernacular **buildings** of California's Spanish and Mexican colonial past, most of which stand unassumingly within a few blocks of the tourist-thronged waterfront. The single best stop – and one of the unmissable highlights of the entire Central Coast – is the **Monterey Bay Aquarium**, a mile west of Downtown along Cannery Row.

Monterey was named by Spanish merchant and explorer Sebastian Vizcaíno, who landed in 1602 after a seven-month voyage from Mexico to find an abundant supply of fresh water and wild game. Despite his enthusiasm for the site, the area was not colonized until 1770, when the second mission in the chain – the headquarters of the whole operation – was built in Monterey before being moved to its permanent site in Carmel. During the era of Spanish rule, the Presidio de Monterey was also the military headquarters for the whole of Alta California, and thereafter Monterey continued to be the leading administrative and commercial centre of a truly enormous, albeit sparsely populated, territory that extended east to the Rocky Mountains and north to Canada.

American interest in Monterey was purely commercial until 1842, when an American naval commodore received a false report that the US and Mexico were at war, and that the English were poised to take California. Commodore Catesby Jones anchored at Monterey and demanded the peaceful surrender of the port; two days later, the American flag was raised. The armed but cordial US occupation lasted only until Jones examined the official documents closely and realized he'd gotten a few critical details wrong; his exuberance ultimately cost him his job. When the Mexican–American War began in earnest in 1846, the United States took possession of Monterey without resistance. The discovery of gold in the Sierra Nevada foothills soon focused attention upon San Francisco, and Monterey

Robert Louis Stevenson and Monterey

The Gold Rush of 1849 bypassed Monterey for San Francisco, leaving the community little more than a somnolent Mexican fishing village – which was pretty much how the town looked in the fall of 1879, when a feverishly ill 29-year-old Scotsman arrived by stagecoach, flat broke and desperately in love with a married woman. **Robert Louis Stevenson** came to Monterey for fresh air and to see **Fanny Osbourne**, whom he had met while travelling in France two years before. He stayed here three months, writing occasional articles for the local newspaper and telling stories in exchange for his meals at a saloon-restaurant run by Frenchman Jules Simoneau. It's said that Stevenson started *Treasure Island* here and used Point Lobos (see p.415) as his inspiration for Spyglass Hill.

Stevenson witnessed Monterey – no longer politically crucial, but not yet a tourism hotspot – in transition, something he addressed in his essay *The Old and New Pacific Capitals*. He foresaw that the lifestyle that had endured since the Mexican era was no match for the "Yankee craft" of the "millionaire vulgarians of the Big Bonanza" – Charles Crocker, for one. One of San Francisco's "Big Four" railroad barons (see box, p.558), Crocker made Stevenson sound positively prescient by opening his lavish Hotel Del Monte in 1880, which helped turn the sleepy town into a seaside resort of international renown practically overnight.

became something of a backwater, barely affected by the waves of immigration that soon flowed into California.

The waterfront and Old Monterey

In the late nineteenth century, when Monterey first tried to pass itself off to wealthy visitors from San Francisco and beyond as an upscale resort, there was a great deal of local doubt as to whether demand would ever match supply. Those worries have long since been neatly put to bed along with the visiting mass that stays here nightly; tourism is now Monterey's main livelihood.

Old Monterey extends half a mile inland from the waterfront, but many of its most interesting buildings are concentrated along tacky **Fisherman's Wharf**, where the catch of the day is more likely to be families from San Jose than the formerly abundant sardines. Most of the commercial fishermen moved out long ago, leaving the old wharves and canneries as relics of a once-prosperous industry. Scores of chubby **sea lions** have persevered, however, and continue to float by under the piers.

The most prominent building near the wharf, at 5 Custom House Plaza, is the **Monterey History & Maritime Museum** (T 831/372-2608, W www.monterey history.org; call or check website for hours), scheduled to reopen in 2011 after an extensive renovation. It holds a well-displayed but essentially mundane collection of ships in glass cases, enlivened by interesting background on the town's defunct sardine industry.

Many of Monterey's historic adobe buildings have survived in pristine condition; to get inside several of them, join one of the free, 45-minute guided **walking tours** along the **Path of History** (T 831/649-7118; call for current schedule), which leave from the Pacific House Museum, on the east side of the plaza near the History & Maritime Museum. This roughly 1.5-mile trail, marked with small yellow tiles at regular intervals on the sidewalk, connects 37 sites scattered throughout the quarter-mile square of the modern city, an area designated as **Monterey State Historic Park** (T 831/649-7118, W www.parks.ca.gov). Alternatively, you can download a podcast tour of the trail at W www.historic monterey.org – a good idea, since drastic state budget cuts have put the guided walking tours' availability in peril (see box, p.412).

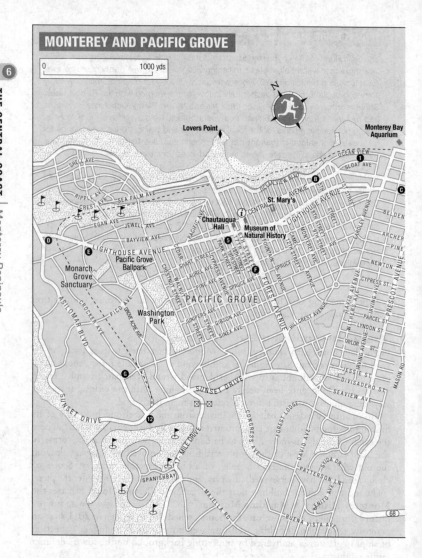

MONTEREY AND PACIFIC GROVE

At various intervals since its 1847 construction, the **Pacific House Museum** has been a courthouse, rooming house and dancehall. Today, it's the best of the local **museums**, with displays on Monterey history and a fair collection of Native American artefacts; its lobby acts as an informal information centre for Monterey State Historic Park. While in the area, be sure to wander by the **Custom House**, the oldest governmental building on the West Coast, portions of which were built by Spain in 1814, Mexico in 1827 and the US in 1846. The balconied building has been restored and now displays 150-year-old crates of coffee and liquor in a small museum inside.

The best place to get a feel for life in Old Monterey is the **Larkin House**, on Jefferson Street a block south of Alvarado, former home of successful entrepreneur

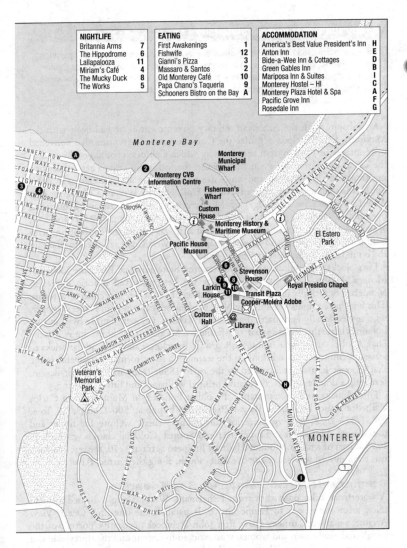

Thomas Larkin, the first and only American Consul to California. The New England-born Larkin, the wealthy owner of a general store and redwood lumber business, was one of the most important and influential figures in early California, actively involved in efforts to attract American settlers here and lobbying Californians to turn toward the increasingly powerful United States and away from the erratic government of Mexico. Through his designs for his own house and the Custom House near Fisherman's Wharf, Larkin is credited with developing the now-familiar Monterey style of architecture, which combines local adobe walls and the balconies of Southern plantation homes with a puritan Yankee's taste in ornament. Larkin House, the first two-storey adobe in California, is filled with many millions of dollars of antiques and is surrounded by lush gardens.

California's beleaguered state parks

Be sure to call ☏831/649-7118 or check ⓦ www.parks.ca.gov for hours of operation for the Pacific, Custom and Larkin houses and the Cooper-Molera Adobe, as California's budget woes have desperately slashed funding for Monterey State Historic Park, as well as that of several other parks across the state.

As unhappy with the American military government as he had been with the Mexicans, Larkin helped organize the Constitutional Convention that convened in Monterey in 1849 to draft the terms by which California could be admitted to the US as the 31st state – which happened the following year. These watershed meetings were held in the grand white stone building just down the street from his house, the then newly completed **Colton Hall**, built by William Colton, the first American *alcalde* (mayor-judge) of Monterey. It's now an engaging **museum** operated by the city of Monterey (daily 10am–4pm; free; ☏831/646-5648, ⓦ www.monterey.org/museum), furnished as it was during the convention, with quill pens on the tables and an early map of the West Coast, all used to draw up the boundaries of the nascent Golden State.

Two blocks east and also part of Monterey State Historic Park, the **Cooper-Molera Adobe**, 525 Polk St, is one of the best preserved historic homes in Monterey, beautifully illustrating the evolution of Monterey in architectural terms. This housing complex was built by New England sea captain John Rogers Cooper, who settled locally and married a Mexican woman. Cooper's family lived in two buildings here: the first is a squat, old-fashioned Mexican-style house, known as the Diaz Adobe, with simple, whitewashed walls, no closets and thick adobe bricks to serve as primitive air-conditioning; the second is a more formal, fashionable home that Cooper himself constructed in the early 1850s from an East Coast design, featuring a double parlour, decorative printed wallpaper and fitted carpeting.

Three blocks further east stands the oldest building in Monterey, San Carlos Cathedral, also known as **Royal Presidio Chapel** at 500 Church St (free; ☏831/373-2628, ⓦ www.sancarloscathedral.net; check website for hours and tour times). This small and much-restored Spanish Colonial church was built in 1795 as part of a mission founded here by Junípero Serra in 1770, the rest of which was soon moved to a better site five miles south, along the Carmel River.

Cannery Row and Monterey Bay Aquarium

A waterfront **bike path** runs from Fisherman's Wharf along a disused railroad track a few miles out to Pacific Grove. It parallels the one-time Ocean View Avenue, renamed **Cannery Row** after John Steinbeck's evocative portrait of the rough-and-ready men and women who worked in and around the thirty-odd fish canneries here. During World War II, Monterey was the sardine capital of the western world, catching and canning some 200,000 tonnes each year. However, overfishing ensured that by 1945 the sardines were more or less all gone, and the canneries were abandoned, falling into disrepair until the 1970s, when they were rebuilt, redecorated and converted into shopping malls and flashy restaurants, many with names adopted from Steinbeck's stories.

Ride, walk or take the free trolley from a mile west of Fisherman's Wharf to visit the magnificent **Monterey Bay Aquarium** (hours vary seasonally; $29.95; ☏831/648-4800, ⓦ www.montereybayaquarium.org), set at the western end of Cannery Row, one of the largest, most stunning displays of underwater life in the world. The place can be very busy in summer, but reserving online beforehand can save you from waiting in line. The space is built upon the foundations of an old sardine cannery and housed in industrial-style buildings that blend a sense of adventure with pleasant promenades along the bay.

The aquarium's eastern end is largely devoted to the **Outer Bay** section, an enormous tank with vast windows providing matchless views of the species that populate the deep waters just beyond the bay. Lazy hammerhead sharks glide among foul-tempered tuna, while barracuda dart past and massive sunfish make their stately circuit of the tank's perimeter.

Towards the middle of the building, the **sea otters** always draw a crowd, particularly at feeding time (10.30am, 1.30pm & 3.30pm). These playful critters are now relatively common out in the bay, but were once hunted nearly to extinction for their uncommonly soft fur. At the western end of the aquarium, habitats close to shore are presented in the **kelp forest**, where mesmerizing, ever-circling schools of silver anchovies avoid the sharks.

The complex also opens directly onto the bay, allowing you to step out and peer into **wild tide pools** after observing the captive tanks.

Pacific Grove and 17-Mile Drive

PACIFIC GROVE – or "Butterfly Town USA", as it likes to call itself – stands curiously apart from the rest of the peninsula, less known but more impressively situated than its famous neighbours. The town began as a campground and Methodist retreat in 1875, a summertime tent city for revivalist Christians in which strong drink, naked flesh and reading the Sunday papers were firmly prohibited. The Methodists have long since moved on, but otherwise the town is little changed. Its quiet streets, lined by pine trees and grand old Victorian wooden homes, are enlivened by hundreds of thousands of orange-and-black **monarch butterflies**, which arrive here each winter from all over the western US and Canada. In fact, the migration of these butterflies is so crucial to the local economy that they're protected by local law: there's a $1000 fine for "molesting a butterfly in any way".

Downtown Pacific Grove is centred upon the intersection of Forest Avenue and Lighthouse Avenue, two miles northwest of central Monterey. A block down Forest Avenue at no. 165, the **Pacific Grove Museum of Natural History** (Tues–Sun 10am–5pm; $3 donation; ☎831/648-5716, ⓦwww.pgmuseum.org) has an informative collection of local wildlife, including lots of butterflies, over four hundred stuffed birds, a relief model of the Monterey Peninsula and Big Sur, and exhibits on the ways of life of the native Costanoan and Salinan peoples. Nearby, about the only reminder of the Methodist camp meetings are the tiny, intricately detailed wooden cottages along 16th and 17th streets which date from the revival days; in some cases wooden boards were simply nailed over the frames of canvas tents to make them habitable year-round.

A block west of the Museum of Natural History, **Chautauqua Hall** was, in the 1880s, the focus of town life as the West Coast headquarters of the instructional and populist Chautauqua Movement, a left-leaning, travelling university that reached thousands of Americans before accessible higher education existed. Nowadays, the plain white building is used as a dancehall every Saturday at 7pm (ⓦwww.pgdance.org; $10–15), where on any given weekend you'll find music and dancing encompassing styles as diverse as tango, swing, fox trot and merengue.

Ocean View Boulevard circles the town along the coast, passing the headland of **Lovers Point** – originally called Lovers of Jesus Point – where preachers used to hold sunrise services. Surrounded in early summer by colourful red-and-purple blankets of blooming ice plants, it's one of the peninsula's finest beaches, where you can lounge and swim along the intimate, protected strand. Ocean View Boulevard runs another mile along the coast out to the tip of the peninsula, where the 1855 **Point Pinos Lighthouse**, Asilomar Boulevard (Thurs–Mon 1–4pm; $2 donation; ℡831/648-5716, Ⓦwww.pgmuseum.org), is the oldest continuously operating lighthouse on the California coast.

Duck a couple of blocks inland here to visit the **Monarch Grove Sanctuary**, Ridge Road off Lighthouse Avenue (dawn–dusk; free), where between early November and late February you can spot giant brown clumps of monarchs discreetly congregating high in the eucalyptus treetops. Ocean View Boulevard continues from Point Pinos Lighthouse, but changes its name to Sunset Drive as it leads to **Asilomar State Beach** (dawn–dusk; free; ℡831/646-6442, Ⓦwww .parks.ca.gov), a wild strand lashed by dramatic surf. It's too dangerous for swimming, though the rocky shore provides homes for all sorts of tide-pool life.

At this point, it's logical to continue your explorations along **17-MILE DRIVE**, a privately owned, scenic toll road ($9.50 per car) which loops from Pacific Grove along the coast south to Carmel, swooping past the golf courses and country clubs of Pebble Beach along the way. Don't miss the trussed-up figure of the **Lone Cypress** halfway along the route, the subject of many a postcard; there are enough beautiful vistas of the rugged coastline to almost make it worth braving the hordes that pack the route on most weekends.

Carmel and around

Set on gently rising headlands above a sculpted and largely untouched rocky shore, the village of **CARMEL** fans out from a few neat rows of just-so shops along Ocean Avenue to reveal assorted posh mansions. Besides all the rampant cuteness, Carmel's only real crime is its ridiculously inflated price scale; think of it as the West Coast's middle-aged answer to New York's Hamptons.

The town's reputation as a rich resort belies its origins, for there was nothing much here until the San Francisco earthquake and fire of 1906 led a number of artists and writers from the city to take refuge in the area, forming a bohemian colony on the wild and uninhabited slopes that soon became infamous throughout the state for its free-spirited excess. The figurehead of the group was poet George Sterling; part-time members included Jack London, Mary Austin and the young Sinclair Lewis. It was a short-lived alliance, however, and by the 1920s the group had parted ways, inviting an influx of wealthy San Franciscans to soon put Carmel well on its way to becoming the exclusive corner it is today.

Despite the continued growth of tourism in the area, Carmel – its official name is Carmel-by-the-Sea – still seems the epitome of parochial snobbishness, with an array of laws enacted to stringently maintain the gingerbread charm of the town's central district (parking meters and street addresses are prohibited, for instance). One long-term byproduct of this bizarre rebellion against street numbers was that all mail had to be picked up in person from the post office – at least until recently, when a local resident sued for home delivery and was rewarded with the chance to pay a premium to have mail delivered.

The village and beaches

Carmel's central business district is largely designer-shopping territory: Carmel Plaza Mall at Ocean Avenue and Mission Street holds branches of Tiffany and Louis Vuitton, and a number of tacky, overpriced art **galleries** are strung along Dolores Street. One exception is the Weston Gallery on Sixth Street between Dolores and Lincoln streets (Tues–Sat 10.30am–5.30pm; ℡831/624-4453, Ⓦwww.westongallery.com), worth a look for its regular shows of top contemporary photographers and permanent display of works by Fox Talbot, Ansel Adams and Edward Weston, who lived in Carmel most of his life.

The town's best feature, however, is the largely untouched coastline nearby, among the most beautiful in California. City-managed **Carmel Beach** (free), at the foot of Ocean Avenue, is a tranquil cove of emerald blue water bordered by soft white sand and cypress-covered cliffs; its tides are deceptively strong and dangerous, though, so be careful if you chance a swim.

A mile south from Carmel Beach along Carmel Bay sits **Tor House**, which, when built in 1919, was the only building on the then-treeless headland. Poet Robinson Jeffers (whose very long, starkly tragic narrative poems were far more popular in his time than they are today) built the small cottage and adjacent tower on his own from granite boulders he hauled from the cove below. There are hourly guided tours of the house and surrounding gardens (Fri & Sat 10am–3pm; $7; T831/624-1813, W www.torhouse.org), and though they saddle visitors with an obsequious account of the now-obscure writer's life and work, the house itself is worth the overload. Each tour takes only six people, so reserve well in advance. Note that the entrance is at 26304 Ocean View Ave, one block from the cliff-top; also be sure to allow ample time for parking as there are very few street spaces in this residential neighbourhood.

Another quarter of a mile along Scenic Road, around the tip of Carmel Point, you'll find the idyllic, mile-long **Carmel River State Beach** (T831/649-2836, W www.parks.ca.gov). It's less visited than the city beach and includes a bird sanctuary on a freshwater lagoon. Again, if you brave the frigid ocean waves, beware of strong tides and currents, especially at the south end of the beach, where the sand falls away at a very steep angle to cause potentially hazardous surf.

Carmel Mission

Half a mile or so up the Carmel River from the beach, also reachable by following Junípero Avenue from Downtown, **Carmel Mission Basilica** at 3080 Rio Rd (Mon–Sat 9.30am–5pm, Sun 10.30am–5pm; $6.50; T831/624-1271, W www.carmelmission.org), was founded in Monterey in 1770 by Junípero Serra as the second of the California missions and the headquarters of the chain; it was later moved to Carmel. Father Serra never got to see the finished church – he died before its completion and is buried under the floor in front of the altar. Finally completed in 1797, the sandstone church has undergone one of the most painstakingly authentic restorations in the entire mission chain, a process well detailed in one of the three fine **museums** set in the compound. By 1937, when reconstruction began, the facility had lain derelict for more than eighty years and was little more than its foundations and a few feet of wall; today the whimsically ornate structure stands firmly as the most romantic mission in the entire chain.

Point Lobos State Natural Reserve

Two miles south of the mission along Hwy-1, **Point Lobos State Natural Reserve** (daily 8am–sunset; $10; T831/624-4909, W www.parks.ca.gov) boasts plenty of justification to support its humble claim of being "the greatest meeting of land and water in the world". There are over 250 bird and animal species that pepper its **hiking trails**, while the sea here is one of the richest underwater habitats in California.

Because Point Lobos itself juts so far out into the ocean, it contains some of the earth's most undisturbed views of the sea, as craggy granite pinnacles – landforms that helped inspire Robert Louis Stevenson's *Treasure Island* – reach out of jagged blue coves. Sea lions and otters frolic in the crashing surf, just below the many vantage points along the park's coastal trail. Grey whales are often seen as close as one hundred yards away on their southerly migration route in January before returning with young calves in April and May. The spectacular park, named after *lobos marinos* – the noisy, barking sea lions that group on the rocks off the reserve's tip – also protects some of the few remaining Monterey cypress trees on its knife-edged headland, despite being buffeted by tireless coastal gusts.

Finally, the park's Whalers and Bluefish coves are excellent **diving** spots for anyone with proper certification. Call ⓣ831/624-8413 for information and reservations.

Carmel Valley

About fifteen miles inland, east along route G16, lies **Carmel Valley Village**, where the weather is warmer and more predictable than the coast – one of the reasons this country hamlet can bill itself as the epicentre of Monterey County's wine country. In the valley that surrounds the village, you'll find a number of vineyards in a pastoral setting where the quietude comes as a big breath of relief after tourist-cramped Carmel. Contact the Monterey County Vintners & Growers Association (ⓣ831/375-9400, ⓦwww.montereywines.org) for a wealth of information on area **wineries**; one of the most pleasant is Joullian, which operates a tasting room at 2 Village Drive (daily 11am–5pm; ⓣ831/659-8100, ⓦwww.joullian.com), and where the friendly staff is happy to share the region's wine-making history.

Eating

The Monterey area has many excellent places to **eat**, and though prices tend to float near resort level, competition for tourist dollars ensures quality. If you're on a tight budget, check restaurants on Monterey's north side along North Fremont Street, on and around Lighthouse Avenue (just south of Cannery Row) and in the shopping centres along Hwy-1 south of Carmel.

Monterey

Gianni's Pizza 725 Lighthouse Ave. Lively pizza and pasta joint where you order at the counter, grab a beer at the bar, seat yourself and wait for tasty, no-nonsense dishes such as veggie lasagna, linguini and clams or a twelve-inch pizza. Mains $9–15.

Massaro & Santos Coast Guard Pier ⓣ831/649-6700. Dine here for views across the bay and the fish-crammed bouillabaisse; loads of daily specials are also available. Mains $14–25.

Miriam's Café 615 Lighthouse Ave, Monterey. Cosy, homespun nook a few blocks from Cannery Row where Miriam herself often brews delicious lattes and other café staples.

Old Monterey Café 489 Alvarado St, Monterey. Often bustling, this longtime favourite serves reasonably priced breakfasts (generally under $8) and excellent sandwiches. Breakfast and lunch only.

Papa Chano's Taqueria 462 Alvarado St. One of the few great bargain eateries in town, where authentic Mexican specialities fill the menu. In true California taquería style, everything's under $10.

Schooners Bistro on the Bay In the *Monterey Plaza Hotel & Spa*, 400 Cannery Row ⓣ831/646-1706. Colourful, upscale bistro in a historic hotel with great views over the bay. Try a grilled, local Castroville artichoke served with herb mayonnaise followed by seafood pasta. Mains $15–28.

Pacific Grove

First Awakenings 125 Oceanview Blvd. Located inside the American Tin Cannery building, this is an excellent spot for hearty breakfasts, salads and sandwiches, served inside or out on the terrace.

Fishwife 1996 Sunset Drive ⓣ831/375-7107. Long-standing local favourite adjacent to Asilomar Beach, serving peerless Caribbean-tinged California cuisine at reasonable prices amid cosy, unpretentious surroundings. Try the king prawns sautéed in red onions, chillies and lime juice. Mains $15–25.

Carmel

Carmel Bakery Ocean Ave and Lincoln Lane, Carmel. Refreshing, low-key café on the village's main drag, serving old-fashioned gooey cakes and coffee to browsing locals.

La Bicyclette Dolores and 7th sts ⓣ831/622-9899. Wooden tables and ceiling-hung copper pots help set a suitably rustic tone for this delightful, dinner-only French country restaurant. Mains $25 and up.

Little Napoli Bistro Italiano Dolores and 7th sts ⓣ831/626-6335. Among the village's many mid-range Italian restaurants, this tiny, charming spot stands out for its oversized portions of fresh pasta dishes made with original sauces. Mains $16–28.

Robata Grill and Sake Bar 3658 The Barnyard ☎831/624-2643. Tasty sushi and tempura served in a warm, wood-panelled setting; there's also a heated patio. Certainly not cheap, but likeably unpretentious considering its surroundings.

Tuck Box Tearoom Dolores St between Ocean and 7th, Carmel. Breakfast, lunch and afternoon tea are available at this half-timbered, mock-Tudor Olde England cottage. Costly and kitschy, but fun.

Nightlife

The Monterey area has always been better known as a sleepy, romantic getaway than a hub of hip coffee culture and nightlife. That said, the peninsula's best selection of bars is in Monterey itself and the **Monterey Jazz Festival** each September (ⓦ www.montereyjazzfestival.org) is the oldest continuous festival in the world, drawing crowds from afar. Check the widely available *Monterey County Weekly* (ⓦ www.montereycountyweekly.com) for current entertainment listings.

Britannia Arms 444 Alvarado St, Monterey. Authentic enough British pub that's oddly incongruous in the heart of tourist Monterey, filled as it is with a largely local crowd. Greasy pub grub ($10–15) dominates the menu, as do over two dozen beers on tap, including several English favourites.
The Hippodrome 321 Alvarado St, Monterey ☎831/646-9244, ⓦ www.hippclub.com. Lively Downtown club with three dancefloors, a youngish crowd and occasional live hip-hop performances; more fun than hip.
Lallapalooza 474 Alvarado St, Monterey ☎831/645-9036. Smooth martini bar (with

reasonable restaurant attached) featuring olive-themed art on the walls, a small sidewalk terrace and a stylish oval bar – the dressiest place in town to imbibe.
The Mucky Duck 479 Alvarado St, Monterey ☎831/655-3031. With frequent DJ dancing and occasional live music on the back patio, this friendly and popular Tudor-style bar/restaurant is a strong bet for a fun night out.
The Works 667 Lighthouse Ave, Pacific Grove ☎831/372-2242, ⓦ www.theworkspg.com. A Pacific Grove hangout, this relaxed bookstore and café also hosts live music most weekend evenings.

North from Monterey

The landscape around **Monterey Bay**, between the peninsula and the beach town of Santa Cruz, 45 miles north, is almost entirely given over to agriculture. **Castroville**, ten miles north along Hwy-1, has two claims to fame, one far more glamorous than the other. Today, surrounded by farmland, it produces more than 85 percent of the nation's artichokes – try them deep-fried in one of the local cafés. Of more interest may be the fact that in 1947, the first woman to be crowned Artichoke Queen was one Norma Jean Baker, later known as Marilyn Monroe. The wide **Pajaro Valley**, five miles further north, is covered with apple orchards rife with white blossoms each spring. At the mouths of the Pajaro and Salinas rivers, the marshlands that ring the bay are habitats for many of California's endangered species of coastal wildlife and migratory birds.

Four miles northwest of Castroville, **Moss Landing** is an excellent place to stop for seafood – try *Phil's Fish Market*, 7600 Sandholdt Rd (daily 8.30am–9pm, ☎831/633-2152), dramatically poised on a small island linked by a short bridge to the mainland, where you can pick from the catch of the day, then fish a bottle of white wine from the cooler. At the nearby **Elkhorn Slough National Estuarine Research Reserve** (Wed–Sun 9am–5pm, free guided tours Sat & Sun 10am & 1pm; $2.50; ☎831/728-2822, ⓦ www.elkhornslough.org) you may spot a falcon or eagle among the 340 bird species that call the slough home. Guided **boat tours** can be booked through Elkhorn Slough Safari on the harbour ($32; ☎831/633-5555, ⓦ www.elkhornslough.com) but an even better way to cosy up to the harbour's sea otters is to rent a **kayak**, available through Kayak Connection ($35–50; ☎831/724-5692, ⓦ www.kayakconnection.com), which also offers shuttle service ($15) if you wish to paddle with the tide rather than against it.

The **beaches** along the bay to Santa Cruz are often windy and not very exciting, though they're lined by sand dunes that can provide hours of exploration. Four miles inland, **Watsonville** is really only of use to travellers as a transfer point where the Monterey and Santa Cruz **bus** systems connect.

San Juan Bautista

Inland from Monterey Bay, a few miles east of US-101 between Salinas and San Francisco, tiny **San Juan Bautista** is an old Mexican town that, but for a modest smattering of collectibles shops, has hardly changed since it was bypassed by the railroad in 1876. The early nineteenth-century **Mission San Juan Bautista** (daily 9.30am–4.30pm; $4; ☎831/623-4528, ⓦwww.oldmissionsjb.org), the largest of the California missions – and still the parish church of San Juan Bautista – stands on the north side of the town's central plaza, its original bells still ringing out. The arcaded monastery wing that stretches out to the left of the church contains relics and historical exhibits, including a vast collection of ceremonial robes. If it all looks a bit familiar, you may have seen it before – the climactic stairway chase scene in Alfred Hitchcock's *Vertigo* was filmed here.

The town that grew up around the mission was once the largest in central California and has been preserved as **San Juan Bautista State Historic Park** (daily 10am–4.30pm; $3; ☎831/623-4881, ⓦwww.parks.ca.gov), with exhibits around the spacious central square interpreting all the restored buildings. On the west side of the plaza, the two-storey, balconied adobe Plaza Hotel was a popular stopping place on the stagecoach route between San Francisco and Los Angeles. Next door, the 1840 **Castro-Breen Adobe**, once the administrative headquarters of Mexican California, eventually belonged to the Breen family – survivors of the ill-fated Donner Party (see box, p.593) who made a small fortune in the Gold Rush.

Across from the mission, the large **Plaza Hall** was built to serve as the seat of the emergent county government, but when the county seat was awarded instead to Hollister – a small farming community eight miles east, and the scene of a motorcycle gang's rampage that inspired the movie *The Wild One* – the building was turned into a dancehall and saloon. The adjacent stables display a range of old stagecoaches and wagons, and explain how to decipher an array of cattle brands, from "lazy H" to "rockin' double B".

The commercial centre of San Juan Bautista, a block south of the plaza, lines Third Street in a row of evocatively decaying facades. If you're hungry, the best of the half-dozen **places to eat** is *Jardines de San Juan*, 115 3rd St (☎831/632-4466), a high-quality Mexican restaurant with champion margaritas and shaded seating under an attractive arbour. Alternatively, try the unfussy and friendly *Mission Café*, on the corner at 300 3rd St (☎831/623-2220), which serves tasty breakfasts and lunches, or pull up a chair at *Joan & Peter's German Restaurant*, 322 3rd St (☎831/623-4521), for hearty bratwurst lunches ($10) and *wurstteller* mains ($19.50).

San Juan Bautista is definitely short on **lodging**, but if you need a room, there's the no-frills *San Juan Inn*, 410 The Alameda (☎831/623-4380, ⓦwww.sanjuan innca.com; ❷). For more local **information**, contact the Chamber of Commerce, 209 3rd St (☎831/623-2454, ⓦwww.sjbchamber.com; call for variable hours).

Santa Cruz

Seventy-five miles south of San Francisco, the edgy – and maddening – city of **SANTA CRUZ** is a difficult place to pin down. In many ways it's the quintessential California coastal town, with miles of beaches for sunning and superb surfing, thousands of acres of mountainside forests for hiking and a historic seaside amusement

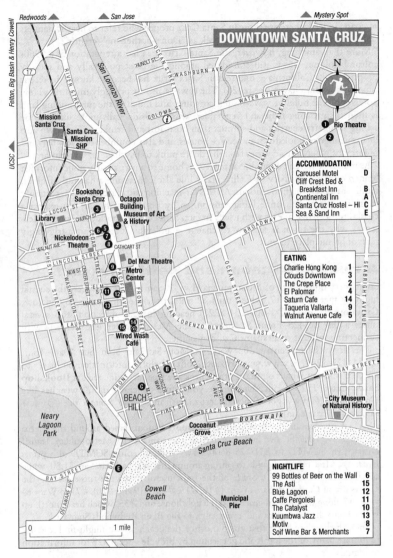

park complete with a vintage wooden rollercoaster. It's also home to eagerly displayed wealth, as well as a great number of homeless who benefit from the town's generous civic resources, joining with its hippie past to bring out the crustier side of local life.

Santa Cruz enjoyed – or, rather, endured – a growth spurt in the late 1990s, when it was commandeered as a dormitory suburb for Silicon Valley during the dot-com boom. This era pushed property prices up significantly and drove some long-term locals away; the boom has long since stabilized, but prices haven't dropped much. Even so, some of Santa Cruz's outlying communities, particularly in the wooded mountains to the immediate north, maintain an almost redneck feel more akin to far Northern California than this otherwise languid, laid-back stretch of coast; indeed, there are those in Santa Cruz proper who refer to nearby hamlets such as Ben Lomond and Boulder Creek as "Don't-bother-me' territory".

More than anything, however, the Santa Cruz area has a reputation as a 1960s cultural holdout and is still considered among the most politically and socially progressive in California – one reason Santa Cruz has become known in recent times as a **lesbian** haven (see p.428). The town is also surprisingly untouristy: few hotels spoil the miles of wave-beaten coastline, and much of the surrounding land is used for growing fruit and vegetables, with roadside stalls more likely to be selling fresh strawberries and sprouts than postcards and trinkets. The town also boasts a range of bookstores and coffee houses, and also a number of lively bars and nightclubs where music varies from hardcore punk to psychedelic surf-guitar.

As if all that weren't enough, Santa Cruz is home to a particularly nonconformist branch of the University of California, while also containing a handful of quiet, family-oriented neighbourhoods. All this far-reaching cultural diversity is certainly cause for the town's underlying tension, so by no means should you expect a coastal resort town at ease with itself. In fact, Santa Cruz's motley mixture under-scores why the town is so slow to change – and why it's such an intriguingly schizophrenic place to visit.

Arrival, information and getting around

Some forty miles north of Monterey via Hwy-1, Santa Cruz sits where the coastal highway meets Hwy-17, which runs 32 miles over the mountains to San Jose. **Greyhound buses** (℡1-800/231-2222) heading in each direction stop several times a day at 425 Front St, opposite the Metro Center (see below), with connecting services to all major California cities.

The city's **visitor centre**, 303 Water St (Mon–Sat 9am–5pm, Sun 10am–4pm; ℡831/425-1234, ⓦwww.santacruz.org), offers helpful information on places to stay. To find out what's on in the area, check the free magazine rack at **Bookshop Santa Cruz**, 1520 Pacific Ave, where you'll find generally useful weeklies like *Good Times* (ⓦwww.goodtimessantacruz.com) and *Metro Santa Cruz* (ⓦwww.metrosantacruz.com).

Santa Cruz has an excellent **public transport** system, based around the Metro Center at 920 Pacific Ave and operated by the Santa Cruz Metropolitan Transit District, or SCMTD (℡831/425-8600, ⓦwww.scmtd.com). SCMTD also prints *Headways*, a free bilingual guide to getting around the area; basic fares are $1.50, while an all-day pass costs $4.50. Some of the most useful routes are those serving the University of California, Santa Cruz (#10, #15, #16, #19 and #20), #71 to Watson-ville, #7 along the western beaches to the lighthouse and #35, which heads north up Hwy-9 into the mountains and, eventually, to Big Basin Redwoods State Park.

Though there are buses that go to most of the beaches, you might find it easier to imitate many of the locals and get around by **bicycle** – see p.428 for information on rentals.

Accommodation

Compared to most California beach resorts, **accommodation** in the Santa Cruz area can be moderately priced and easy to come by, especially during the week or outside of summer. Still, you should expect wildly varying seasonal rates, as a room that goes for $50 midweek in winter can easily cost three times that amount on a July or August weekend (summer weekend prices are quoted below). Also keep in mind that most of the following establishments may offer weekly rates, and there's a clump of inexpensive motels along Ocean Street. As well, **camping** opportunities around Santa Cruz are abundant and varied, from beaches to forests.

If you're **heading north**, or just want to base yourself out of town, consider Davenport (see below), *Costanoa* (see p.525) or the wonderful hostel at Pigeon Point (for the latter pair, see p.526), all situated along coastal Hwy-1 on the way to Half Moon Bay and San Francisco.

Hotels, motels, B&Bs and hostels

Capitola Venetian Hotel 1500 Wharf Rd, Capitola ☎1-800/332-2780, ⓦwww.capitolavenetian.com. Quirky, ageing beachfront hotel just across the bridge from Capitola's lively esplanade. All rooms have kitchens with gas stoves; some are two-bedroom suites. ❼

Carousel Motel 110 Riverside Ave, Santa Cruz ☎831/425-7090, ⓦwww.santacruzmotels.com. A sparklingly clean bargain, with simple rooms fitted with blond wood furniture and loud, 1980s-inspired bedcovers. All rooms have microwaves and there's free continental breakfast included. Even better, it's directly across from the boardwalk. ❻

Cliff Crest Bed & Breakfast Inn 407 Cliff St, Santa Cruz ☎831/427-2609, ⓦwww.cliffcrestinn.com. Eclectically furnished Queen Anne-style Victorian home (c.1887) with five guestrooms and a self-contained carriage house, all set among lovely gardens atop Beach Hill. It's within walking distance of Downtown and the boardwalk, and rates include a full breakfast served in the solarium. ❻

Continental Inn 414 Ocean St, Santa Cruz ☎1-800/343-6941, ⓦwww.continentalinnsantacruz.com. Comfortable, if basic, accommodation within easy walking distance of the boardwalk and Downtown. ❻

Davenport Roadhouse 1 Davenport Ave, Davenport ☎831/426-8801, ⓦwww.davenportroadhouse.com. Boutique, reasonably priced inn eleven miles northwest of Santa Cruz along Hwy-1. Rooms are small, but tastefully decorated; many feature ocean views. There's also a terrific downstairs restaurant (see p.427). ❺

Historic Sand Rock Farm 6901 Freedom Blvd, Aptos ☎831/688-8005, ⓦwww.sandrockfarm.com. This secluded five-room guesthouse, eleven miles east of Downtown Santa Cruz, has been lovingly restored and filled with arts-and-crafts antiques; multi-course, made-to-order breakfasts are lavish and delicious. ❻

Pleasure Point Inn 23665 E Cliff Drive, Santa Cruz ☎831/475-4657, ⓦwww.pleasurepointinn.com. A well-designed, hip inn with cliff-top views, a roof sundeck and a hot tub; rooms have built-in stereos and jacuzzi baths. Highly recommended for anyone averse to chintz. ❼

Santa Cruz Hostel-HI 321 Main St ☎831/423-8304, ⓦwww.hi-santacruz.org. Well-situated hostel with an informal atmosphere set in a series of 1870s cottages just a couple blocks from the beach. The place is closed during the day (10am–5pm) and often booked up well in advance. Members $25, nonmembers $28, private rooms ❷

Sea & Sand Inn 201 W Cliff Drive, Santa Cruz ☎831/427-3400, ⓦwww.santacruzmotels.com. This small, upscale motel boasts fine sea views, while flowerboxes burst with colour under every window. Larger groups can opt for one of the individual cottages (❽) with private patio and outdoor jacuzzi. Complimentary breakfast included. ❼

Campgrounds

Big Basin Redwoods State Park Nine miles west of Boulder Creek on Hwy-236, ☎831/338-8860, ⓦwww.santacruzstateparks.org; reservations ☎1-800/444-7275, ⓦwww.reserveamerica.com. Lush, enormous park in the Santa Cruz Mountains with both drive-in ($35) and walk-in ($8) sites, 23 miles north of Santa Cruz.

Henry Cowell Redwoods State Park Felton ☎831/335-7077, ⓦwww.santacruzstateparks.org; reservations ☎1-800/444-7275, ⓦwww.reserveamerica.com. Located just above UC Santa Cruz in a redwood grove along the San Lorenzo River. Closed in winter. $35; bike-in sites $7.

New Brighton State Beach Capitola ☎831/464-6330, ⓦwww.santacruzstateparks.org; reservations ☎1-800/444-7275, ⓦwww.reserveamerica.com. Seven miles east of Santa Cruz on the edge of the beachfront village of Capitola, this campground is set on bluffs above a lengthy strand. Reservations essential. $35–50.

The Town

Santa Cruz provides a sharp contrast to the upscale resort sophistication of Monterey Peninsula across the bay. The community of 55,000 residents (plus 15,000 students) spreads out at the foot of thickly wooded mountains along a clean, sandy shore that's within a twenty-minute walk of most areas of town.

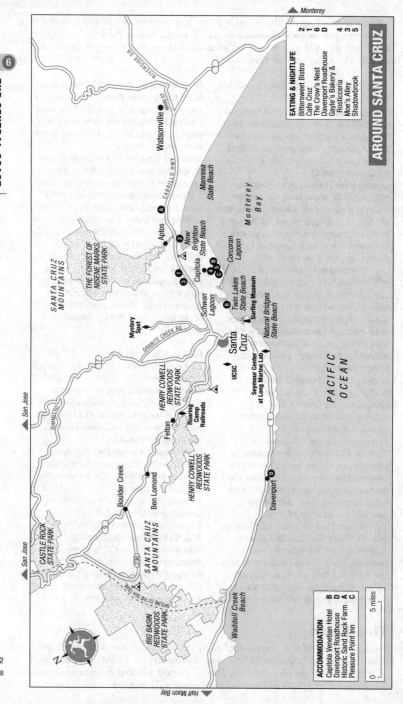

EATING & NIGHTLIFE

Bittersweet Bistro	2
Cafe Cruz	1
The Crow's Nest	6
Davenport Roadhouse	D
Gayle's Bakery & Rosticceria	4
Moe's Alley	3
Shadowbrook	5

AROUND SANTA CRUZ

Monterey Bay

PACIFIC OCEAN

SANTA CRUZ MOUNTAINS

THE FOREST OF NISENE MARKS STATE PARK

Watsonville

Aptos

New Brighton State Beach

Capitola

Manresa State Beach

Corcoran Lagoon

Schwan Lagoon

Twin Lakes State Beach

Surfing Museum

Natural Bridges State Beach

Mystery Spot

GRANITE CREEK RD

HENRY COWELL REDWOODS STATE PARK

Roaring Camp Railroads

Felton

Santa Cruz

UCSC

Seymour Center at Long Marine Lab

▲ San Jose

SUMMIT RD

Boulder Creek

Ben Lomond

CASTLE ROCK STATE PARK

▲ San Jose

236

SANTA CRUZ MOUNTAINS

SKYLINE TO THE SEA TRAIL

BIG BASIN REDWOODS STATE PARK

Waddell Creek Beach

Davenport

CABRILLO HWY

MAIN ST

RIVERSIDE DR

ACCOMMODATION

Capitola Venetian Hotel	B
Davenport Roadhouse	D
Historic Sand Rock Farm	A
Pleasure Point Inn	C

0   5 miles

N

▲ Half Moon Bay

The sluggish San Lorenzo River wraps around the town centre, two blocks east of **Pacific Avenue**, a landscaped and pedestrianized stretch that's Santa Cruz's principal business street, lined with bookstores, beachwear shops and cafés. Disheveled hippies wander ceaselessly along here, brushing shoulders with well-heeled shoppers dodging into clothing and furniture stores. The homeless (and the practically homeless) cluster around park benches in the area, playing musical instruments, distributing literature or simply dozing off.

The devastating Loma Prieta Earthquake of 1989 – the epicentre of which was only about ten miles northeast of here in the mountains (see box, p.426) – damaged a large portion of Downtown Santa Cruz, but one place that survived intact is the ornate brick-and-stone **Octagon Building**, 118 Cooper St, at the north end of Pacific Avenue. Completed in 1882 as the Santa Cruz Hall of Records, it now houses a café. Adjacent is the **Museum of Art & History**, 705 Front St (Tues–Sun 11am–5pm; $5, free first Fri of month; ℡831/429-1964, Ⓦwww.santacruzmah.org), with spirited displays on the region's history; its grounds include a sculpture garden, as well as a rooftop gallery with excellent views of town.

Several blocks away, past the clocktower fountain on Pacific Avenue and up Mission Street, **Santa Cruz Mission State Historic Park** (or **SHP**), 144 School St (Thurs–Sat 10am–4pm; free; ℡831/426-5686, Ⓦwww.parks.ca.gov), displays fragments dating from the region's earlier Spanish colonial days in a restored army barracks. The complex includes a half-scale replica of **Mission Santa Cruz**, a replacement that dates from the twentieth century; the original adobe church was destroyed by an earthquake in 1857.

Beach Hill rises at the foot of Pacific Avenue, its slopes lined with some of Santa Cruz's finest turn-of-the-century homes. Look for the striking Queen Anne-style house at 417 Cliff St and the slightly odd structure around the corner at 912 3rd St, constructed from the remains of a shipwreck.

The Beach Boardwalk and around

The main local beach, known simply as **Santa Cruz Beach**, is wide and sandy, with lots of volleyball courts and water that's safe and warm enough for swimming in summer. Not surprisingly, it can get crowded and rowdy, so for a bit more peace and quiet, or to catch the largest waves, simply follow the coastline east or west of town to one of the smaller beaches hidden away at the foot of the cliffs; most are undeveloped and fairly accessible.

The main beach area is dominated by the **Santa Cruz Beach Boardwalk** (hours vary seasonally; all-day unlimited rides $29.95, individual rides $3–5; ℡831/423-5590, Ⓦwww.beachboardwalk.com), which stretches half a mile along the sands. Full of bumper cars, shooting galleries, corndog stands, log flume rides, roller coasters, Ferris wheels and a 1911 vintage carousel, this is the best surviving beachfront amusement park on the West Coast; it's packed solid on summer days with day-tripping area families and teenagers on the prowl. While the latest thrill is the Double Shot – which shoots riders from the ground to the top of its 125ft tower in seconds – the star attraction will always be the aged **Giant Dipper**, a wild wooden rollercoaster that's jolted the bones of close to fifty million people and is listed on the National Register of Historic Places; you may recognize it from films such as *Sudden Impact* or *The Lost Boys*. The boardwalk first opened in 1907, and its oldest surviving structure, the elegant **Cocoanut Grove** at its west end, recently underwent a multimillion-dollar restoration.

Just west of the boardwalk, the century-old wooden **Municipal Pier** juts half a mile out into the bay, crammed with fresh-fish shops, seafood grills and gift stores. You don't need a licence to join the crab fishermen at the end of the pier – simply rent tackle from one of the many bait shops close at hand. Just east of the boardwalk, across the river, the small **Santa Cruz City Museum of Natural History**, 1305 E Cliff Drive (summer Wed–Sun 10am–5pm, rest of year Tues–Sat 10am–5pm; $2.50, free first Thurs of month; ℡831/420-6115, ⓦwww.santacruz museums.org), marked by a concrete whale, has concise displays describing local animals and sea creatures, as well as a brief description of the local Native American culture, near which you can try your hand at grinding acorns in a mortar and pestle.

Steamer Lane, Natural Bridges and around

The beaches west of the Santa Cruz Boardwalk, along **West Cliff Drive**, are pounded daily by some of the state's biggest waves, not least at Cowell Beach's **Steamer Lane**, off the tip of Lighthouse Point beyond the Municipal Pier. Santa Cruz surfers have a reputation for being less than welcoming to non-locals, but if you want to get in the water and give it a shot, Club Ed (℡831/464-0177, ⓦwww.club-ed.com), in the beach car park, will rent boards and wetsuits and also assist with lessons.

Ghosts of surfers past are animated at the evocative **Santa Cruz Surfing Museum** (summer Wed–Mon 10am–5pm, rest of year Thurs–Mon noon–4pm; free, but donation requested; ℡831/420-6289, ⓦwww.santacruzsurfingmuseum .org), in the old red-brick lighthouse building at Point Santa Cruz, above Cowell Beach. The tiny museum holds surfboards ranging from twelve-foot redwood planks used by the sport's local pioneers to modern, multi-finned cutters.

Both a cliff-side bicycle path and West Cliff Drive run two miles from here to **Natural Bridges State Beach** (8am–sunset; $10; ℡831/423-4609, ⓦwww .santacruzstateparks.org). Near the sands, waves have cut holes through coastal cliffs to form delicate arches in the remaining stone; three of the four bridges after which the park was named have since collapsed, however, leaving large stacks of stone protruding from the surf. The park is also famous for its annual gathering of monarch butterflies, thousands of which arrive each winter.

A mile further on, the cliff-top **Seymour Center at Long Marine Lab** (summer daily 10am–5pm, rest of year Tues–Sat 10am–5pm and Sun noon–5pm; $6, check website for free days; ℡831/459-3800, ⓦseymourcenter.ucsc.edu), 100 Shaffer Road at the end of Delaware Avenue, is a working laboratory that offers kid-friendly insights into the region's undersea life through informative displays, windows into labs and touch tanks packed with sea stars and anemones. Free, hour-long **tours** (hourly 1–3pm) go behind the scenes, and the 87ft-long blue whale skeleton outside never fails to impress.

Lagoons and Capitola

East of Downtown Santa Cruz, **East Cliff Drive** winds along the top of the bluffs past many coves and estuaries. The nearest of the two coastal lagoons that border the volleyball courts at **Twin Lakes State Beach**, half a mile east at Seventh Avenue (free; ℡831/427-4868, ⓦwww.santacruzstateparks.org), was dredged and converted into a marina in the 1960s; **Schwan Lagoon**, about quarter of a mile on, remains intact, its marshy wetlands serving as a refuge for seabirds and migrating waterfowl. Twin Lakes Beach is often a little warmer than the surrounding area, thanks to its proximity to Schwan Lagoon. Beyond here, good tide pools can be found half a mile further east at **Corcoran Lagoon**.

East Cliff Drive continues past popular surfing spots off rocky **Pleasure Point** to the beachfront burg of **Capitola**; its relatively conservative mood provides a counterpoint to that of Santa Cruz. The small town began as a fishing village where residents lived off the giant tuna that populated Monterey Bay. In time it became popular as a holiday spot with its own rail line, and although the large wooden railroad trestle hasn't been in use for decades, it still dominates what is now a moneyed town, rising over the soft and peaceful sands surrounding the old wharf. Capitola is especially attractive in late summer, when hundreds of begonias – the town's main produce – are in bloom; at any time of year, it's a relaxing escape from the crazier Santa Cruz crowd. The local **Chamber of Commerce**, 716-G Capitola Ave (ⓣ831/475-6522, ⓦwww.capitolachamber.com), has all the usual information.

UCSC and the Santa Cruz Mountains

The **University of California, Santa Cruz (UCSC)**, on the hills above the town, is very much a product of the 1960s. Until the early 2000s, students didn't take exams or get grades, until the demands of graduate schools elsewhere forced change; still, its academic programmes continue to stress individual exploration of topics rather than rote learning. Whereas other University of California branches have adopted a fierce and proud bear as school mascot, it's a telltale sign that UCSC's is a Plato-reading banana slug. Its campus design is even a deliberate attempt to stand apart from traditional schools, with its heavily wooded two thousand acres divided into small, autonomous colleges where deer stroll among the redwood trees overlooking Monterey Bay. Free guided tours start from the **visitor centre** at the foot of campus (ⓣ831/459-4118, reservations required), but if you don't have time for a full look, pop by the **UCSC Arboretum** (daily 9am–5pm; $5; ⓣ831/427-2998, ⓦarboretum.ucsc.edu), famous for its experimental cultivation techniques and collections of plants from New Zealand, South Africa, Australia and South America, all landscaped as they would be in their original habitats.

About three miles up Branciforte Drive from Downtown Santa Cruz, there's a point within the woods where normal laws of gravity no longer apply. Here, trees grow at odd angles, pendulums swing counterclockwise and balls roll uphill – all thanks to the **Mystery Spot** (hours vary seasonally; frequent 45-minute tours, reservations suggested on weekends and holidays; $5 per person plus $5 parking; ⓣ831/423-8897, ⓦwww.mysteryspot.com). Tours of this freaky, inexplicable place are hokey yet amusing, during which guides lead groups up, down and every which way via a small shed that teeters on the edge of the hill, demonstrating in seven different ways how the laws of physics seem to not apply here. Much of the amusement is more reliant on canny perspective tricks than metaphysical skullduggery, but even so, it's a diverting treat as guides posit various theories about what caused the Mystery Spot's seeming taunts of gravity, including everything from extraterrestrial interference to excess carbon dioxide seeping up from the earth.

High in the mountains that separate Santa Cruz from the San Francisco Bay Area, you'll find the village of **Felton**, seven miles north of Santa Cruz on Hwy-9, home to **Roaring Camp Railroads** (parking $8; ⓣ831/335-4484, ⓦwww.roaring camp.com), based around buildings dating back to the 1880s. **Roaring Camp & Big Trees Narrow Gauge Railroad** ($21.50) departs from here and steams over trestle bridges on a six-mile run among the massive redwoods that cover the slopes of Bear Mountain, taking a little over an hour. From the same station, the diesel-hauled, standard-gauge **Big Trees & Pacific Beach Train** ($23.50) powers down to the Santa Cruz Beach Boardwalk and back in three hours.

Further exploration into the Santa Cruz Mountains beyond Felton reveals divine **Big Basin Redwoods State Park** ($10; ⓣ831/338-8860, ⓦwww.santa cruzstateparks.org), about twenty winding miles northwest of Santa Cruz. Here at California's oldest state park, over eighty miles of **hiking trails** (see box, p.426) lead in every direction: into dense wilderness through scores of 300ft redwood trees; up ridges affording views across the bay to Monterey; and down to the Pacific Ocean at Waddell Beach, about twenty miles along Hwy-1 from Santa Cruz, and a favourite spot for watching windsurfers and kiteboarders negotiate the foamy currents. Camping is also available in the park (see p.421).

Hiking near Santa Cruz

Helping form the backbone of California's Coast Range, the redwood-studded **Santa Cruz Mountains** reach nearly 4000ft, stretch almost as far north as San Francisco and provide extraordinary hiking opportunities at a trio of state parks close to Santa Cruz. **The Forest of Nisene Marks State Park** (dawn–dusk; $8; ☎831/763-7062, ⓦwww.santacruzstateparks.org), nine miles due east of Downtown Santa Cruz, holds the epicentre of the 1989 Loma Prieta Earthquake. To reach it from the Mary Easton Picnic Area just beyond the main entrance, follow the main road past the site of a former mill to the Aptos Creek Trail, off which a simple sign marks the spot; it's a gentle climb (about 200ft) over less than three miles. The rest of the park is laced with trails, with backcountry camping available six miles into the interior.

Larger and more developed than Nisene Marks, **Big Basin Redwoods State Park** (see p.425) is another forested hiking paradise. Its signature amble is the Skyline to the Sea Trail, a thirty-mile route that begins in nearby Castle Rock State Park before winding its way through Big Basin Redwoods all the way to the Pacific. Its final eleven miles – the trail's easiest section – begin near Big Basin Redwoods' visitor centre and pass by stunning Berry Creek Falls en route to Waddell Beach. If you're staying in Santa Cruz, you can complete this hike one-way by riding SCMTD bus #35 from Santa Cruz to the trailhead; once you reach the trail's end, hop aboard bus #40 at Waddell Beach back to Santa Cruz. Check ⓦwww.scmtd.com for exact timetables.

Only a little more than five miles north of Downtown Santa Cruz along Hwy-9, **Henry Cowell Redwoods State Park** is the best pick of the lot for a quick visit and a short hike; camping is available if you wish to extend your stay (see p.421). The mostly flat, wheelchair-accessible Redwood Grove Loop Trail (about one mile in length), just past the entrance at the northern end of the park, is ideal for a slow stroll, on which you can expect to continually crane your neck as you contemplate the 1500-year-old trees that tower overhead.

Eating

Restaurants in and around Santa Cruz are surprisingly diverse, encompassing vegetarian cafés, all-American burger joints, fine dining and a number of worthwhile seafood establishments on the wharf. The Wednesday-afternoon **Farmers' Market** at the corner of Cedar and Lincoln streets, near Downtown, is immensely popular with locals and a good place to pick up fresh produce.

Bittersweet Bistro 787 Rio Del Mar Blvd, Aptos ☎831/662-9799. Delicately prepared gourmet fish and pasta dishes for $19–30; save room for the sumptuously presented desserts. Nine miles east of Downtown Santa Cruz along Hwy-1.

Café Cruz 2621 41st Ave, Soquel ☎831/476-3801. Delicious, reasonably priced Italian food in a Tuscan-inspired (if inauspiciously located) courtyard setting. Located five miles east of central Santa Cruz.

Charlie Hong Kong 1141 Soquel Ave, Santa Cruz. Innocent-looking hut with a small amount of outdoor seating, where organic, mostly vegetarian noodle dishes – green curry chicken, spicy noodle beef – cost $6–11. Vietnamese sandwiches also available.

Clouds Downtown 110 Church St, Santa Cruz ☎831/429-2000. Well-seasoned meats, Cal-Italian

dishes and an extensive choice of cocktails, all served in a pleasantly vibrant environment. The stuffed portobello mushrooms are especially good. Mains go for $16–25.

The Crêpe Place 1134 Soquel Ave, Santa Cruz. Longtime local favourite dishing out bargain stuffed crêpes with savoury and sweet fillings; try the Crêpe Gatsby, stuffed with pesto, mushrooms, spinach, chicken and three kinds of cheese. The flower-filled back garden is a charming place to lounge on a warm summer evening.

The Crow's Nest 2218 E Cliff Drive, Santa Cruz ☎831/476-4560. The modern American, fish-dominated menu here contains a number of tasty mains ($19–29), but the real reason to visit this harbour spot is for its spectacular views across the water, particularly at sunset. There's also a pub upstairs.

Davenport Roadhouse 1 Davenport Ave, Davenport ☎831/426-8801. A fifteen-minute drive up Hwy-1 from Santa Cruz, well worth it for unique organic dishes such as artichoke leek lasagna and wood-grilled salmon; wood-fired pizzas, pasta, burgers and chowder are also on offer.

El Palomar 1336 Pacific Ave, Santa Cruz ☎831/425-7575. Don't be put off by this restaurant's location – it's on the ground floor of a historic building that now houses government-subsidized apartments – for its Mexican dishes are likely the best in town. All the usuals (enchiladas, fajitas) are done well, along with several seafood specialities. Mains $12–21.

Gayle's Bakery & Rosticceria 504 Bay Ave, Capitola. Ever-popular bakery and deli five miles east of Downtown Santa Cruz where you can sit inside or out while tucking into freshly made sandwiches and wraps ($7) or a huge range of salads (priced by weight). Don't pass by the delicious cakes.

Saturn Café 145 Laurel St, Santa Cruz. Wacky vegetarian diner set in a round building and decorated with red vinyl banquettes and Formica tables. The menu ranges from burgers and sandwiches to vegan breakfasts, and almost everything's $10 and under. One of the few late-night dining options in town – it's open until 3am.

Shadowbrook 1750 Wharf Rd, Capitola ☎831/475-1511. A lush venue for a romantic dinner, this upscale destination has a variety of mains (including steak, seafood and vegan options) for $21–34, served on terraces which step down to the banks of Soquel Creek. Beware of dodgy singers performing Gordon Lightfoot classics at weekends.

Taquería Vallarta 1101A Pacific Ave, Santa Cruz. It may look like a fast-food joint, but this taquería cranks out hefty portions of authentic Cal-Mex dishes – get yourself full on a super burrito and a tangy agua fresca for about $10. Ask for extra tortilla chips to take advantage of the self-service salsa bar.

Walnut Avenue Café 106 Walnut Ave, Santa Cruz. This diner is a local favourite, dishing out massive breakfasts and lunches for generally under $10, and only a block off Pacific Avenue.

Nightlife

Santa Cruz has the Central Coast's best and most varied **nightlife**, ranging from coffee houses to bars and nightclubs where music varies from surf-thrash to reggae to hard rock. For simply hanging out, your best choices are the espresso bars and coffee houses lining Pacific Avenue; if you have your heart set on seeing a show or film, check *Good Times* and *Metro Santa Cruz* for current listings.

The Rio Theatre, 1205 Soquel Ave (☎831/423-8209, ⓦwww.riotheatre.com), is a performance venue that focuses on an eclectic selection of live bands; for first-run foreign and indie films, head to the co-managed Del Mar, 1124 Pacific Ave (☎831/469-3220, ⓦwww.thenick.com), or Nickelodeon movie theatres, 210 Lincoln St (☎831/426-7500, ⓦwww.thenick.com).

All places listed are within Santa Cruz proper.

99 Bottles of Beer on the Wall 110 Walnut Ave ☎831/459-9999. This airy pub offers over forty beers on tap; the crowd's friendly and a bit more mainstream than in many other local watering-holes. Great California burgers along with quiz, karaoke and music nights.

The Asti 715 Pacific Ave. Divey old-timers' cocktail lounge that now also attracts postmodern artsy types who quietly revel in its retro grittiness.

Blue Lagoon 923 Pacific Ave ☎831/423-7117, ⓦwww.thebluelagoon.com. Lively bar and nightclub where DJs spin anything from Top 40 to industrial – check the website for nightly details. Live bands frequently hold court as well. Come early for drink specials.

Caffe Pergolesi 418 Cedar St ☎831/426-1775. Fun, friendly coffee house often full of students hunched over laptops; it's attractively set in an old wooden villa with a garden. Open until 11pm nightly, with occasional live music.

The Catalyst 1011 Pacific Ave ☎831/423-1338, ⓦwww.catalystclub.com. The main venue in town for big-name touring artists, this medium-sized club has something happening almost nightly. Cover charges vary wildly, depending on the headliner, and the staff can be brusque.

Kuumbwa Jazz 320 Cedar St ☎831/427-2227, ⓦwww.kuumbwajazz.org. The city's showcase for traditional and modern jazz, in a friendly and intimate garden setting tucked down a small alley. Mon and Thurs nights often see big names (such as Chick Corea and Lee Ritenour). Cover charges vary between $10–30.

Moe's Alley 1535 Commercial Way ☎831/479-1854, ⓦwww.moesalley.com. Reggae and blues are mainstays at this amiable venue six nights a week,

Gay and lesbian Santa Cruz

Over the last few decades, Santa Cruz has established itself as one of the country's hippest **lesbian** hangouts; it also boasts an increasingly sizeable gay population, so much so that some local wags have taken to calling it Santa Cruise. Most local **accommodation** is gay-friendly, though there are currently no exclusively gay inns. Open until the wee hours, *Saturn Café* (see p.427) is an especially popular gay and lesbian hangout.

For more information, contact or stop by the well-connected Diversity Center Of Santa Cruz, 1117 Soquel Ave (T831/425-5422, Wwww.diversitycenter.org).

but you can also expect salsa, jam rock and world music on any given night. Cover usually $10–25. **Motiv** 1209 Pacific Ave T831/429-8070. Hit-and-miss dance club frequented by local hipsters and UCSC students, with a modern vibe and DJs spinning house music. Try the inviting upstairs bar. Open until 2am.

Soif Wine Bar & Merchants 105 Walnut Ave T831/423-2020. Popular with young sophisticates, this hotspot is bathed in warm light with varnished wooden tables; the menu features small plates along with more than fifty wines by the glass. Live jazz on Mon and Tues.

Listings

Bike rental Electric Sierra Cycles, 302 Pacific Ave, Santa Cruz (T1-877/372-8773, Wwww.electricrec bikes.com), charges $35 a day for mountain or cruiser bikes; alternatively, try Family Cycling Center, 914 41st Ave, Santa Cruz (T831/475-3883, Wwww.familycycling.com), where cruisers are less ($25 a day) but mountain bikes are more ($50).
Internet Visit *Caffe Pergolesi* (see p.427) or any of the Santa Cruz Public Library system's several branches (see below) for free wireless internet access.
Kayak rental Venture Quest, on the wharf at 110 Beach St, Santa Cruz (T831/427-2267,

Wwww.kayaksantacruz.com), rents open-top kayaks for $30 for 3hr, or $50 all day.
Laundry Head to Surf City Suds, 228 Cardiff Place, Santa Cruz (T831/334-8098), a green-certified Laundromat located a couple miles west of Downtown and adjacent to UCSC.
Library 224 Church St (T831/420-5700, Wwww .santacruzpl.org; Fri closed, Sat 11am–5pm, Sun 1–5pm, Mon 1–7pm, Tues–Thurs 11am–7pm). Nine other branches in the Santa Cruz area.
Post office 850 Front St (Mon–Fri 9am–5pm, Sat & Sun closed); ZIP code is 93940. Four other branches in the Santa Cruz area.

Travel details

Trains

Amtrak's Coast Starlight leaves Los Angeles at 10.15am daily for Oakland (1 daily; 11hr), stopping at Santa Barbara (2hr 30min), San Luis Obispo (5hr 20min), Salinas (8hr 15min), San Jose (10hr 15min), and connecting to San Francisco via shuttle bus. It then continues from Oakland on through Sacramento, Chico, Redding and Oregon to Seattle. One train a day leaves Oakland at 8.50am on the return route (12hr).

Buses

All buses operated by Greyhound unless otherwise noted.
Salinas to: Los Angeles (5 daily; 8hr), San Francisco (6 daily; 2–4hr).
San Luis Obispo to: Los Angeles (6 daily; 4–5hr); San Francisco (4 daily; 7hr).
Santa Barbara to: Los Angeles (7 daily; 3hr); San Francisco (4 daily; 10hr).
Santa Cruz to: Los Angeles (5 daily; 9–10hr); Oakland (3 daily; 2hr); San Francisco (4 daily; 2hr 45min); San Jose (4 daily; 1hr).

San Francisco and the Bay Area

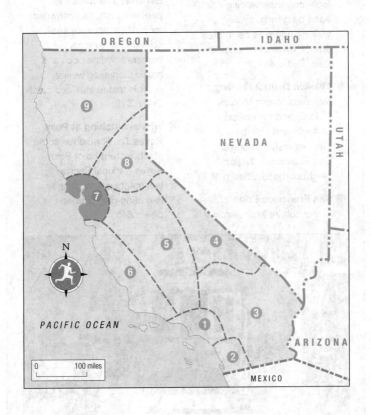

CHAPTER 7 **Highlights**

❋ **Cable cars** These glorious trolleys rattle and clang their way up and over some of the city's steepest grades in time-honoured style. See p.447

❋ **Golden Gate Bridge** San Francisco's signature sight is gorgeous in any light – or fog – and experiencing it first-hand by driving, cycling or walking under its celebrated orange towers is a singular thrill. See p.461

❋ **Mission District** Bustling taquerías, iconic Mission Dolores and the collision of Anglo and Latino cultures make for one of San Francisco's liveliest neighbourhoods. See p.467

❋ **San Francisco Pride** Queer culture exuberantly takes over much of the city on a late June weekend, with boisterous parades, outlandish costumes and the colours of the rainbow flag all taking centre stage. See p.495

❋ **University of California, Berkeley** This attractive, park-like campus, renowned for political activism and scientific innovation, is bordered by fine book and music stores, as well as notable restaurants and cafés. See p.512

❋ **Whale-watching at Point Reyes** The lighthouse at the southwestern tip of Point Reyes National Seashore is a great spot to glimpse migrating grey whales. See p.545

▲ San Francisco cable cars

San Francisco and the Bay Area

One of America's most stunningly sited cities – and one whose locals usually won't hesitate to make that claim – **SAN FRANCISCO** sits poised on the northern tip of a long peninsula at the western edge of North America. Indeed, the city has much to gloat about, not least the breathtaking natural beauty that surrounds it: rugged ocean coastline and churning bay waters, dense fog banks and air that's refreshingly cool year-round. Along the streets of this eminently walkable city rest a cluster of distinct neighbourhoods, by turn precious and hip, lined by rows of restored Victorian homes and sparkling residential lofts, just-so boutiques and dusty secondhand bookstores.

San Franciscans like to think of their city as Northern California's cultured, idealistic counterpart to the mass entertainment capital of Los Angeles in the south, and to an extent they're right: this is where the United Nations originated, and the city's indissoluble connections to the Beat, hippie and gay rights movements have become almost as synonymous with the international view of San Francisco as the Golden Gate Bridge and its famed cable cars. Still, despite its attempt to stand apart from the rest of the state (and often, the nation), it's still an undeniably Californian place – after all, blue jeans, topless waitressing and oversize burritos all got their start here.

San Francisco's self-awareness – some would say narcissism, given certain locals' tendency to refer to it as simply "The City" to non-residents – is rooted in the sheer physical aspect of the place. Streets all over town lean on impossibly steep gradients to reveal stunning views and few other cities in the world can boast San Francisco's romantic climate once blanket fogs roll in on a moment's notice to surreally envelop trees, buildings and hilltops in thick mist. Autumn is the best time for sunny days, with warm temperatures and cloudless skies often filling the days of September and October.

The city proper may occupy a mere 48 square miles, but the metropolitan **BAY AREA** sprawls far beyond those narrow confines, its nine counties home to over seven million residents and growing; even seemingly finite San Francisco itself – the second-densest city in the US – is in the midst of a growth spurt, albeit largely upward via high-rises rather than outward. In the East Bay, over one of two great bridges that connect San Francisco with the rest of the region, sits blue-collar **Oakland** and the university locus of **Berkeley**, each offering their own unique antidote to the limelit city across the water. Overland to the immediate

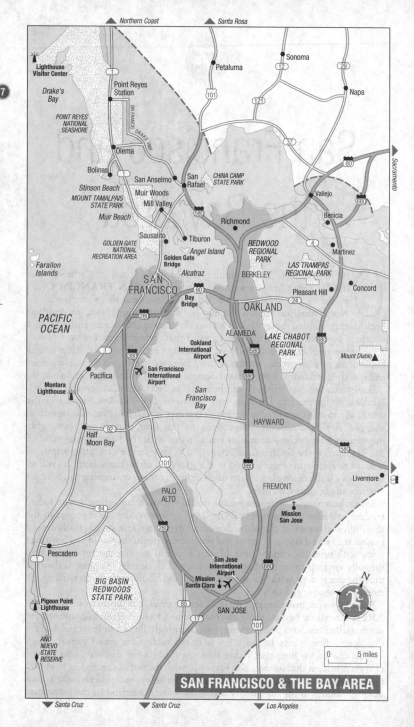

SAN FRANCISCO & THE BAY AREA

south of San Francisco lay the quietly affluent and self-assured suburbs of the **Peninsula**; further down is the San Jose-centred **South Bay**, where the lucrative computer and technology industries of Silicon Valley have made it the economic powerhouse of the entire Bay Area. Across the Golden Gate Bridge to the north, provincial **Marin County** contains some of the Bay Area's wealthiest residential enclaves, its wooded landscape and rugged coastline presenting a bucolic harbinger of the delights of California's earthy northern coast. Finally, well inland from the coast, redwoods give way to the vine-slathered hills of the brand-name **Wine Country** that have made Sonoma and Napa counties prime visitor destinations since the 1980s.

San Francisco

A compact city of some four dozen or so hills by its namesake bay, San Francisco is one of the few US cities where you can survive comfortably without a car. Indeed, given how expensive and time-consuming parking can be – not to mention how agreeable the city's freeze-free climate is – walking is the ideal daytime mode for taking in the renowned museums, stately Victorian homes, sophisticated and historic neighbourhoods and stirring hilltop vistas. After dark, San Francisco is quite safe for visitors exercising reasonable caution; it's best known to many for its astonishing assortment of restaurants and bars.

Some history

The original inhabitants of San Francisco were the **Ohlone people**, who lived in roughly 35 villages spread out around the bay. In 1776, **Mission Dolores**, the sixth in the chain of Spanish Catholic missions that ran the length of California, was established; harsh mission life, combined with the spread of European diseases, killed off the natives within a few generations. Mexicans took over from the Spanish in the early 1820s, but their hold was tenuous, and the area finally came under American rule after the **Bear Flag Revolt** of 1846, which took place north of San Francisco in Sonoma. The bloodless coup was supported by local land-owning *alcaldes* (a hybrid of judge and mayor), who recognized the land's huge economic potential. The coup brought US Marines, sailing on the USS *Portsmouth*, into the San Francisco Bay that year, prompting one soldier, John Fremont, to christen its spectacular entrance the "**Golden Gate**". The Marines docked their boat at the tiny town plaza founded the previous decade by British sailor William Richardson and renamed it **Portsmouth Square**, raising an American flag and claiming the city for the United States. The following year, the hamlet known as Yerba Buena was rechristened San Francisco, honouring the dying wish of Father Junípero Serra, the Franciscan founder of California's missions.

In 1848, San Francisco's population exploded when pioneer Sam Brannan bounded across Portsmouth Square waving bottles of gold dust he claimed came from the Sierra foothills, thereby igniting the **Gold Rush**. Within a year, fifty thousand pioneers had arrived from all over the country as well as overseas (especially China), turning San Francisco from a muddy village and wasteland of

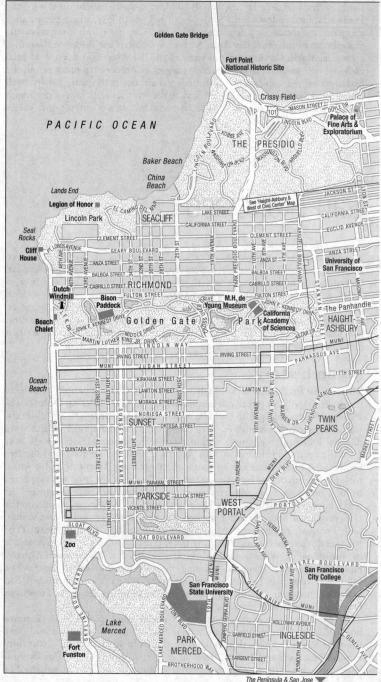

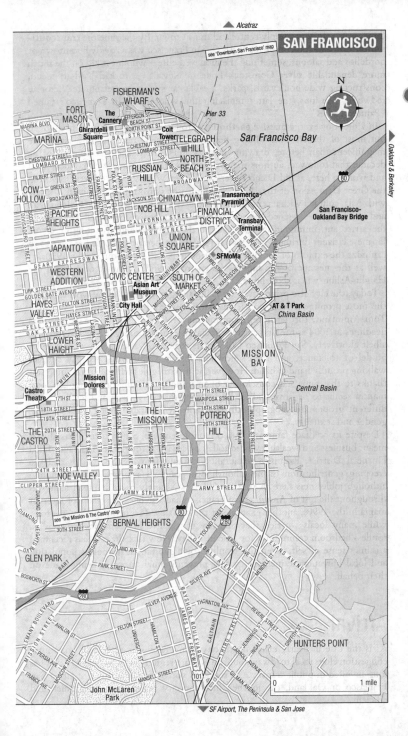

7

SAN FRANCISCO

▲ Alcatraz

see 'Downtown San Francisco' map

N

San Francisco Bay

Pier 33

FISHERMAN'S WHARF

FORT MASON

The Cannery

Ghirardelli Square

MARINA

MARINA BLVD

Colt Tower

JEFFERSON ST

BEACH ST

NORTH POINT STREET

BAY STREET

TELEGRAPH HILL

NORTH BEACH

CHESTNUT STREET

LOMBARD STREET

RUSSIAN HILL

COLUMBUS AVE

BROADWAY

CHESTNUT STREET

LOMBARD STREET

COW HOLLOW

GREEN ST

GREEN STREET

FILBERT STREET

UNION STREET

BROADWAY

PACIFIC HEIGHTS

JACKSON ST

NOB HILL

CHINATOWN

Transamerica Pyramid

FINANCIAL DISTRICT

CALIFORNIA STREET

PINE STREET

BUSH STREET

Transbay Terminal

THE EMBARCADERO

San Francisco–Oakland Bay Bridge

▶ Oakland & Berkeley

80

JAPANTOWN

GEARY EXPRESSWAY

WESTERN ADDITION

UNION SQUARE

SFMoMa

TURK STREET

GOLDEN GATE AVENUE

FULTON STREET

CIVIC CENTER

Asian Art Museum

City Hall

SOUTH OF MARKET

AT & T Park

China Basin

HAYES VALLEY

HAYES STREET

FELL STREET

OAK STREET

LOWER HAIGHT

MISSION BAY

Central Basin

Castro Theatre

17TH ST

Mission Dolores

16TH STREET

17TH STREET

MARIPOSA STREET

POTRERO HILL

20TH STREET

THE CASTRO

18TH STREET

19TH STREET

20TH STREET

THE MISSION

NOE VALLEY

24TH STREET

CLIPPER STREET

ARMY STREET

ARMY STREET

see 'The Mission & The Castro' map

BERNAL HEIGHTS

30TH STREET

80

280

GLEN PARK

CORTLAND AVE

PARK STREET

JERROLD AVE

EVANS AVENUE

BOSWORTH ST

280

SILVER AVE

HUNTERS POINT

THORNTON AVE

REVERE STREET

BAYSHORE BOULEVARD

JAMES LICK FREEWAY

John McLaren Park

MANSELL STREET

101

0 ——— 1 mile

▼ SF Airport, The Peninsula & San Jose

dunes into a thriving supply centre and transit town. By the time the **transcontinental railroad** was completed in 1869, San Francisco was a rowdy boomtown of bordellos and saloons, something the moneyed elite – who hit it big on the much more dependable silver Comstock Lode in Nevada – worked hard to mend, constructing wide boulevards, parks, a cable car system and elaborate Victorian redwood mansions, the latter replacing the whores as San Francisco's famed "Painted Ladies".

In 1906, however, a massive **earthquake**, followed by three days of fire, wiped out most of the city. Rebuilding began immediately, resulting in a city more magnificent than before, drawing anew writers, artists and free spirits. In the decades that followed, authors such as Dashiell Hammett and Jack London lived and worked here, as did Diego Rivera and other WPA-sponsored artists. During the Great Depression of the 1930s, San Francisco's position as the nexus of trade with Asia, coupled with its engineering projects – including both the Golden Gate and Bay bridges – lessened the agonies of the Depression for its residents. While the strict anti-immigration laws against the Chinese and the internment of Japanese citizens during World War II remains in memory, people here prefer to canonize the exploits of the Beat Generation in North Beach during the 1950s, as well as the message of the hippies drawn from 1967's Summer of Love in the Haight-Ashbury neighbourhood.

Today, the city also prides itself on being the **gay capital** of the world: one of the most prominent local politicians is openly gay former stand-up comedian Tom Ammiano; furthermore, longtime mayor Gavin Newsom made national headlines in 2004 as the first elected official in America to legalize gay weddings, albeit abortively. San Francisco basks in its reputation as a liberal enclave and a model of tolerance, and there's nowhere in town you won't see gay couples walking proudly hand in hand. However, it also struggles with a certain smugness thanks to that same self-consciously open-minded attitude; one unspoken local mantra seems to be "live and let live" rather than "live *with* and let live", and different groups are geographically and tribally separated along lines of race, gender and sexuality.

Despite its boldface fame as a hub of counterculture, San Francisco has always meant business and wealth, evinced today by a walk through the skyscraper-filled Financial District. Exquisite restaurants, art museums, designer malls and the creeping gentrification of neighbourhoods point to a strong local economy, although joblessness here in the late 2000s was nearly as widespread as it was throughout the rest of America. San Francisco had also been the cradle of internet mania in the 1990s, another example of the city's eye for the main chance – for a while many locals worried that one day they'd live in "SanFrancisco.com", a soulless bedroom community for Silicon Valley. Now that the city has reclaimed a calmer sense of self, it remains troubled by a substantial **homeless** population and local bureaucratic inefficiency that prevents much progress being made on their behalf.

Arrival

As is the case in nearly every major city, San Francisco's rush-hour commuter congestion clogs local roadways, but this is a rare region in the western US that has long invested in public transit. As a result, if you're touching down at either San Francisco or Oakland, the journey into the city proper is usually quick and efficient.

By plane

All international and most domestic flights arrive at **San Francisco International Airport**, or SFO (☎1-800/435-9736, ⓦwww.flysfo.com), located about fifteen miles south of the city. There are several ways of getting into the central city from here, each of which is clearly signed at the baggage-reclaim areas. The best option is BART (ⓦwww.bart.gov), whose electric **trains** whisk you from the airport to the heart of Downtown for $8.10 in thirty minutes, with regular departures. San Mateo County Transit (SamTrans) **buses** (☎1-800/660-4287, ⓦwww.samtrans.org) leave every hour from the lower level of the airport; the KX express ($5) takes around twenty-five minutes to reach the Transbay Terminal Downtown. A number of private **minibus shuttles** depart every five to ten minutes from the lower level of the circular road and take passengers to any San Francisco destination; try SuperShuttle (☎1-800/258-3826, ⓦwww.supershuttle.com), which charges $17 per person but only $10 for each additional person in your party. **Taxis** from the airport cost $35–50 (plus tip) for any Downtown location, more for the East Bay and Marin County – only worth considering if you can split the charges with others. If you're planning to drive, the usual **car rental** agencies operate free shuttle buses from the upper level to their car lots.

Several domestic airlines fly into smaller **Oakland International Airport** (OAK; see p.501 for details), across the bay. It's efficiently connected with San Francisco via the $3 AirBART shuttle bus, which drops you at the Coliseum/Oakland Airport BART station; once there, board BART ($3.80) for San Francisco. The entire journey typically takes less than forty-five minutes.

By bus, train and car

All of San Francisco's **Greyhound** services (☎1-800/231-2222, ⓦwww.greyhound.com) use the new temporary **Transbay Terminal**, bound by Main, Folsom, Beale and Howard streets, two blocks south of Market Street; the new Terminal is scheduled to open a few blocks away by 2015. **Amtrak** trains stop

---

Festivals in San Francisco

San Francisco hosts a huge range of special festivals – the biggest of which are detailed below. (For gay and lesbian-geared events, see box, p.495).

Chinese New Year ☎415/986-1370, ⓦwww.chineseparade.com. Late Jan or early Feb. A massive, week-long celebration around the lunar New Year. Its main event is the Golden Dragon Parade, headed by the namesake 75-foot-long dragon.

Cherry Blossom Festival ☎415/563-2313, ⓦwww.nccbf.org. Late April. Otherwise-sedate Japantown is riotously transformed with a wide assortment of activities (including a beauty pageant) over two consecutive weekends; the festival culminates in a parade from Civic Center.

Bay to Breakers ☎415/359-2800, ⓦwww.baytobreakers.com. Third Sun in May. This legendarily campy event – disguised as a cross-town, 12-kilometre fun run – is an excuse for locals to don a costume; or in the case of some, no costume at all. Recent attempts to curtail drinking and debauchery along the race route have met with limited success.

Hardly Strictly Bluegrass ⓦwww.strictlybluegrass.com. First weekend in Oct. Three-day music festival in Golden Gate Park featuring small- and big-name performers performing acoustically – and for free – on multiple stages. Hugely popular, so arrive early to stake out space.

across the bay in **Richmond** (the most efficient BART transfer point) and continue to **Emeryville**, from where free shuttle buses run across the Bay Bridge to Downtown San Francisco.

From the east, the only route **by car** into San Francisco is across the Bay Bridge ($5 toll) on I-80, which traces a path clear across the US via Sacramento, Chicago and New York. If you're approaching from San Jose in the south, workaday US-101 or verdant I-280 will be your bridgeless (and free) points of entry; the sole gateway along the city's north shore is US-101's Golden Gate Bridge ($6 toll) from neighbouring Marin County.

Information

The **San Francisco Visitor Information Center**, on the lower level of Hallidie Plaza, adjacent to the end of the cable car line at 900 Market St at Powell (Mon–Fri 9am–5pm, Sat & Sun 9am–3pm, Nov–April closed Sun; ☎415/391-2000, ⓦwww.onlyinsanfrancisco.com) has free maps of the city and the Bay Area, and can help with lodging and travel plans. Its free **San Francisco Book** provides detailed, if selective, information about accommodation, entertainment, exhibitions and stores. The good-value **City Pass** ($59; ⓦwww.citypass.com), which pays for entry into a host of museums, a bay cruise, free Muni rides and other discounts for nine days, is also available here.

The city's main **newspaper** is the *San Francisco Chronicle* (ⓦwww.sfgate.com), rarely considered one of the better US dailies but still handy for getting up to speed on life in the Bay Area; for comprehensive arts and food listings, check *96Hours,* a four-day weekend entertainment guide available in each Thursday's edition, as well as the Sunday edition's pink-coloured *Datebook,* which contains previews and reviews for the coming week. The city's alternative press picks up the slack the more conservative *Chronicle* leaves behind, resulting in two fine free weekly papers, the *San Francisco Bay Guardian* (ⓦwww.sfbg.com) and *SF Weekly* (ⓦwww.sfweekly.com), available in sidewalk boxes all around town. Both offer in-depth features on local life and full music and club listings.

City transport

San Francisco's **public transport** may often be maligned by locals for its unpredictable schedule, but it covers every neighbourhood relatively inexpensively. **Cycling** is also an option, though you'll need to be continually alert for wayward drivers and have strong legs to tackle the city's brutal hills. If you can budget the time, **walking** is often your best bet, with each turn revealing surprises.

For a wealth of information on all forms of Bay Area transport, including real-time traffic maps, visit ⓦwww.511.org.

Muni

San Francisco's public transport is its beleaguered **Muni** (☎415/673-6864, ⓦwww.sfmta.com), which operates a comprehensive network of buses, streetcars and cable cars that trundle up and around (and tunnel through) the city's hills. The flat **fare** is $2 on buses and trains (exact change only), with a possible increase on the horizon; with each ticket you buy, make sure you get a **free transfer** – good on all lines (except cable cars) for at least ninety minutes from the time you receive

Main Muni routes

Useful bus routes

5-Fulton Begins Downtown; heads near Haight-Ashbury and alongside Golden Gate Park; terminates near Ocean Beach.

12-Folsom Begins in the Mission; heads through South of Market and along Embarcadero; terminates in Russian Hill.

22-Fillmore Begins in Potrero Hill; heads through the Mission, Western Addition and Pacific Heights; terminates in the Marina.

28-19th Avenue Begins in the Marina; heads through Presidio to Golden Gate Bridge, and through the Richmond and Sunset; terminates at Daly City BART.

30-Stockton Begins Downtown; heads through Chinatown and North Beach; terminates in the Marina.

38-Geary Begins Downtown; heads through the Tenderloin, Western Addition and the Richmond; terminates near Ocean Beach.

47-Van Ness Begins at Caltrain Depot; heads through Civic Center; terminates at Fisherman's Wharf.

Useful streetcar lines

F-Market Restored vintage trolleys from around the world begin in the Castro, head Downtown, and terminate at Fisherman's Wharf. Always has an interesting dynamic for its popularity with local commuters and visitors alike.

J-Church Begins in Downtown subway; heads along edge of the Castro and Mission; terminates at Balboa Park.

L-Taraval Begins in Downtown subway; heads to the Castro and West Portal; terminates near San Francisco Zoo.

N-Judah Begins near Caltrain Depot; heads through Downtown subway, along edge of the Castro and Haight-Ashbury and through Cole Valley and the Sunset; terminates at Ocean Beach.

Cable car routes

California Street Begins Downtown at foot of California St at Market St; heads up and over Nob Hill; terminates at California St and Van Ness Ave. Scheduled for closure until June 2011 due to maintenance.

Powell-Mason Begins Downtown at foot of Powell St at Market St; heads along edge of North Beach; terminates at Mason St and Bay St near Fisherman's Wharf.

Powell-Hyde Begins Downtown at foot of Powell St at Market St; heads through Union Square and Russian Hill; terminates at end of Hyde St at Jefferson St near Fisherman's Wharf.

it. Muni streetcars run until about 1am nightly; after that, owl **buses** run sporadically between 1am–5am. A single **cable car** fare is as steep as the hills the vessels climb: $5, with no free transfers.

If you're staying a few days, the Muni **Passport** is available in one-day, three-day and seven-day denominations ($13, $20 & $26, respectively) and is valid for unlimited travel on both Muni and BART within San Francisco. A **Fast Pass** costs $70 for a full calendar month and is also accepted by both Muni and BART within city limits; a Muni-only monthly pass ($60) is also available. Buy passes in baggage claim areas at SFO or at select locations around the city – visit Ⓦ www.sfmta.com for more information. You can also purchase a handy Muni map ($3) from the Visitor Information Center.

Walking tours

A great way to get to know the quieter, historical side of San Francisco is to take a **walking tour**. The better ones keep group size small and are run by locals who know their subject matter backward and forward. Some, like those sponsored by the library, are free; reservations are recommended for all walks.

City Guides ℡415/557-4266, ⓦwww.sfcityguides.org. A terrific series sponsored by the library and covering every San Francisco neighbourhood, also offering themed walks on topics ranging from the Gold Rush to the Beat Generation. Its wide-ranging subject matter means you'll often trek alongside locals instead of fellow tourists. Free, but small donations solicited.

Cruisin' the Castro ℡415/255-1821, ⓦwww.cruisinthecastro.com. Founded by the grand dame of San Francisco walks, Ms Trevor Hailey, this tour explains how and why San Francisco became the gay capital of the world. It's as much a history lesson as a sightseeing stroll. $35–45.

Haight-Ashbury Flower Power Walking Tour ℡415/863-1621, ⓦwww.hippygourmet.com. Quite thorough rundown of the Human Be-in, Grateful Dead, the Summer of Love and the Haight's distant past as a Victorian resort destination. $20.

HobNob Tours ℡650/814-6303, ⓦwww.hobnobtours.com. Terrific, information-packed ramble around the haunts of Silver Kings and Robber Barons, mostly in and around Grace Cathedral. Recommended. $30.

Mission Mural Walk ℡415/285-2287, ⓦwww.precitaeyes.org. Two-hour stroll hosted by mural artists that leads around the Mission's famed outdoor wall paintings. $12–15.

Victorian Home Walk ℡415/252-9485, ⓦwww.victorianwalk.com. Leisurely tour through Pacific Heights, where you'll learn to tell the difference between a Queen Anne, Italianate and Stick-Style Vic. $25.

Wok Wiz Tours ℡650/355-9657, ⓦwww.wokwiz.com. A walk through Chinatown run by chef-writer Shirley Fong-Torres and her team. Plenty of anecdotes but a little thin on historical information. $35, or $45 for tour and dim sum lunch.

BART and Caltrain

BART – short for Bay Area Rapid Transit (℡415/989-2278, ⓦwww.bart.gov) – is the region's electric rail transport system. Although access is limited within San Francisco to Market and Mission streets and a few neighbourhoods in the southern part of the city, it does a good job of connecting San Francisco with myriad Easy Bay communities and airports on both sides of the bay. Tickets aren't cheap ($1.75–5.95 one way, depending how far you ride), but the system features five routes with clean and comfortable trains that follow a fixed schedule and arrive about every ten minutes. Tickets can be purchased on the station concourse; save your ticket after entering the station, as you'll also need it when exiting your destination station. Note that the system shuts down for maintenance each night between about 1and 5am.

With its depot at Fourth and Townsend in South of Market, **Caltrain** (℡1-800/660-4287, ⓦwww.caltrain.com) links San Francisco with Peninsula and South Bay communities and is a good option if you're travelling beyond the final Peninsula BART stop at Millbrae.

Taxis and car rental

Taxis ply the streets, although they can be quite expensive and difficult to find outside of Downtown, especially on weekends. If you're phoning ahead, try Veterans Cab (℡415/552-1300) or Yellow Cab (℡415/333-3333). Fares within the city are roughly $5 for the first mile, plus a customary fifteen-percent tip.

The only reason to **rent a car** in San Francisco is if you plan to explore the outlying Bay Area, Wine Country or north or south along the coast. Driving among San Francisco's tangle of transit vehicles, cyclists and pedestrians – to say nothing of its hair-raising hills – can be a real headache for first-timers, while looking for available parking often requires a monk's patience. Still, if you accept the challenge, pay attention to posted speed limits (usually no more than 35mph), don't speed through yellow lights and always yield to pedestrians waiting at a crosswalk. Take equal care to observe the city's law of curbing wheels – turn wheels into the curb if the car points downhill, away from the curb if uphill; violators are subject to citation and fines.

Ferries

A picturesque – if not particularly quick or cheap – way of touring the bay is by boat. Two companies operate regular **ferry** services from San Francisco: Golden Gate Ferry (ⓣ511 toll-free or 415/455-2000, ⓦwww.goldengate.org), running commuter hours to Sausalito and Larkspur in Marin County, calls in at the Ferry Building along the Embarcadero near the end of Market Street; Blue & Gold Fleet (ⓣ415/705-8200, ⓦwww.blueandgoldfleet.com) operates boats to Angel Island, Oakland and Alameda, Sausalito, Tiburon and Vallejo from Pier 39 at Fisherman's Wharf. For information on Alcatraz ferries, see box, p.459.

Cycling

Cycling is a great way to experience San Francisco. Golden Gate Park, the Marina, the Presidio and Ocean Beach all have excellent paved trails and some off-road routes. Throughout the city, marked bike routes with dedicated lanes direct riders to all major points of interest – just keep in mind that these routes were chosen for their relative lack of car traffic and not the flatness of their gradients.

The handiest option for rentals is Blazing Saddles (ⓣ415/202-8888, ⓦwww.blazingsaddles.com), with several locations – two of the most convenient are at 1095 Columbus Ave at Francisco Street in North Beach, and Pier 41 at Fisherman's Wharf. Rates for a standard bike are $28 per day, but check the company's website for coupons. For a tranquil trek through undeveloped nature, head north over the Golden Gate Bridge – the western side is reserved solely for bikes – into the Marin Headlands for trails that follow seaside cliffs into verdant valleys (see p.539); alternatively, ride across the bridge to Sausalito (see p.540) and catch a ferry back to the city.

Finally, **bikes** are allowed on Muni buses equipped with bicycle racks (on the front of the bus) and on BART, except during peak hours.

Tours

One way to orientate yourself is by booking an **organized tour**. Gray Line Tour ($41; ⓣ1-888/428-6937, ⓦwww.graylinesanfrancisco.com) buses putter around town for a somewhat tedious three and a half hours. If you want to get off solid ground for an hour, Blue & Gold Fleet (ⓣ415/705-8200, ⓦwww.blueandgoldfleet.com) operates **bay cruises** from Pier 39, though be warned that everything may be shrouded in fog, making the price ($24; online bookings $19) less than worth it. Undoubtedly, the most exciting – and expensive – tours are aerial: the best local operator is San Francisco Helicopter Tours (ⓣ1-800/400-2404, ⓦwww.sfhelicoptertours.com), which offers a variety of spectacular options over the Bay Area beginning at $160 per passenger for a twenty-minute flight.

Accommodation

San Francisco residents complain frequently about skyrocketing rents, and it's no different for visitors. Expect accommodation to cost around $120 per night in a reasonable hotel or motel, slightly less out of season; to get the best deal, be sure to reserve well in advance, especially for summer and early autumn visits.

The **Visitor Information Center** (see p.438) will provide the latest accommodation options, while **San Francisco Reservations** (Mon–Fri 6am–11pm, Sat & Sun 8am–11pm; ☎1-800/677-1500, ⓦwww.hotelres.com) can help find you the best rates on rooms. For **B&Bs**, contact **Bed and Breakfast San Francisco** (Mon–Fri 9am–5.30pm; ☎415/899-0060, ⓦwww.bbsf.com). If funds are particularly tight, look into one of the many excellent **hostels** (see p.445), where lodging rates start around $25. Specific **gay and lesbian** accommodation is listed on p.495. Bear in mind that all quoted room rates are subject to a fourteen-percent local occupancy tax.

Finally, other than a group-only campground in the Presidio, there's nowhere legal to **camp** in San Francisco itself, so if you're determined to sleep underneath the stars, head to any number of parks in the East Bay, down the Peninsula or in Marin County.

Hotels, motels and B&Bs

Union Square and around

See map on pp.448–449.

Clift Hotel 495 Geary St at Taylor, Theater District ☎1-800/697-1791, ⓦwww.morganshotelgroup .com. the old-school *Clift Hotel* is yet another postmodern Ian Schrager–Philippe Starck conversion. Expensive rooms are vaguely oriental and feature quirky touches like sleigh beds and Louis XIV-style chairs with mirrors on the seat and back. ⓽

Golden Gate Hotel 775 Bush St at Mason, Union Square ☎1-800/835-1118, ⓦwww .goldengatehotel.com. Friendly, European-style B&B with warmly furnished rooms, some with shared baths. Beautiful, original iron elevator and Edwardian interior. ⓽

Grant Hotel 753 Bush St at Mason, Union Square ☎1-800/522-0979, ⓦwww.granthotel.net. A good deal for its location, this hotel has small but clean rooms, overpowered a little by the relentlessly maroon carpets. Basic but convenient. ⓷

Hotel Adagio 550 Geary St at Jones, Union Square ☎415/775-5000, ⓦwww.jdvhotels.com. The decor at this pricey hotel echoes its ornate Spanish Revival facade with deep reds and ochres. Rooms are spacious and exude a calming feng shui vibe. ⓽

Hotel Diva 440 Geary St at Mason, Theater District ☎1-800/553-1900, ⓦwww .hoteldiva.com. Trendy, modern art hotel with spacious rooms, as well as sleek metal and leather furniture. Particularly well positioned if you're planning to see theatre, with A.C.T. and the Curran directly across the street. ⓻

Hotel Monaco 501 Geary St at Taylor, Theater District ☎1-866/622-5284, ⓦwww.monaco-sf .com. Quirky boutique hotel housed in a historic Beaux Arts building. There are canopied beds in each room, and the rest of the decor's equally riotous, colourful and a little over the top. Ask about the complimentary goldfish. ⓻

Hotel Triton 342 Grant Ave at Bush, Union Square ☎1-800/800-1299, ⓦwww.hotel-tritonsf.com. Trippy, ecofriendly hotel that offers modern amenities such as a 24hr gym and video game systems, as well as more unusual services like nightly tarot-card readings and a round-the-clock yoga channel. The rooms themselves are stylish but gaudy, painted in rich, clashing colours and plenty of gold. Weeknight ⓹, weekend ⓻

InterContinental Mark Hopkins One Nob Hill Circle, Nob Hill ☎415/392-3434, ⓦwww .intercontinentalmarkhopkins.com. Grand, castle-like hotel that was once the chic choice of writers and movie stars: it's more corporate these days in both clientele and design, although its rates are surprisingly reasonable. All rooms are identical, but room prices rise as the floors do. It's also known for its *Top of the Mark* rooftop bar (see p.486). ⓹–⓺

Orchard Hotel 665 Bush St at Powell, Union Square ☎1-888/717-2881, ⓦwww.theorchard hotel.com. A little-known gem, this hotel's rates are lower than its ample amenities would suggest. Every room has a DVD player (with free movies on loan) and is surprisingly spacious, decorated like a clubby study in dark teak woods and striped fabrics. ⓺

Phoenix Hotel 601 Eddy St at Larkin, Tenderloin ⊤1-800/248-9466, ⓦwww.jdvhotels.com. A favourite with touring bands, this raucous retro motel conversion feels more Los Angeles than San Francisco and features a small pool. Its 44 rooms are eclectically decorated in tropical colours with changing local artwork on the walls. ❺

Renoir Hotel 45 McAllister St at Seventh, Tenderloin ⊤1-800/576-3388, ⓦwww.renoirhotel .com. The superior rooms at this wedge-shaped landmark are about $25 extra, but worth it if you can snag one of the oddly shaped large ones at the building's apex. It's especially popular during Pride weekend for its Market Street views along the parade route. ❺

Sir Francis Drake 450 Powell St at Sutter, Union Square ⊤1-800/795-7129, ⓦwww.sirfrancis drake.com. The lobby here's a hallucinogenic evocation of all things heraldic, crammed with faux British memorabilia, chandeliers and drippingly ornate gold plasterwork. Thankfully, the rooms are calmer, with a gentle apple-green colour scheme and full facilities. The hotel's known for its classic bar, *Harry Denton's Starlight Room*. ❻

Westin St Francis 335 Powell St at Sutter, Union Square ⊤1-866/500-0338, ⓦwww .westinstfrancis.com. This historic hotel has a sumptuous lobby, four restaurants and lounges, a fitness centre and a spa. The rooms in the historic main building, which dates to the early 1900s, have high ceilings and chandeliers, while those in the newer tower are contemporary, with views across the city. ❻

South of Market

See map on pp.448–449.

Four Seasons 757 Market St at Third ⊤415/633-3000, ⓦwww.fourseasons.com. Sparkling hotel with spectacular views across the city, where plush rooms ($400 and up) are the ultimate indulgence, from the soft, luxurious comforters to the stand-alone two-person shower stocked with Bulgari beauty products. The place to stay if someone else is paying. ❾

Good Hotel 112 7th St at Mission ⊤415/621-7001, ⓦwwwjdvhotels.com. Fun, eco-aware hotel within walking distance of several museums, featuring pet-friendly accommodation and free bicycle rental for all guests. ❺

Hotel Griffon 155 Steuart St at Mission ⊤1-800/321-2201, ⓦwww.hotelgriffon.com. Secluded hotel close to the waterfront. Rooms are elegant and understated, with exposed brick walls and window seats. Weeknight ❼, weekend ❽

Hotel Vitale 8 Mission St, ⊤1-888/890-8688, ⓦwww.hotelvitale.com. Steps from the Ferry

Building, this luxury boutique hotel boasts 199 elegant contemporary rooms (many with bay views) and an on-site spa with rooftop soaking tubs. The bar at the ground-level *Americano* restaurant is a happy-hour favourite of the Downtown crowd, with patio seating along the Embarcadero. ❾

The Mosser 54 4th St at Market ⊤1-800/227-3804, ⓦwww.themosser .com. This hotel is a funky conversion fusing Victorian touches with mod leather sofas. The chocolate-and-olive rooms may be tiny, but the place is one of the best-value in town, especially given its central location. Shared bath ❸, en suite ❺

Palace Hotel 2 New Montgomery St at Market ⊤415/512-1111, ⓦwww.sfpalace.com. Hushed, opulent landmark known for its fabulous *Garden Court* tearoom and the fact that US President Warren Harding died here in 1923. The grand lobby and corridors are mismatched with small rooms decorated in lush golds and greens like an English country house. ❻

North Beach, Chinatown and Fisherman's Wharf
See map on p.448–449.

Argonaut Hotel 495 Jefferson St at Hyde, Fisherman's Wharf ⊤1-866/415-0704, ⓦwww .argonauthotel.com. This nautical-themed hotel in the Cannery complex has large, lush rooms set in pleasant blue and gold colours. Amenities and impressive views abound, and it's surprisingly quiet for its location. ❽

Baldwin Hotel 321 Grant Ave at Bush, Chinatown ⊤1-800/622-5394, ⓦwww.baldwinhotel.com. Given its hub location on the edge of Chinatown, the *Baldwin*'s oatmeal-and-taupe rooms – outfitted in neutral colours with simple furnishings and ceiling fans – offer relief from the noisy streets. Weeknight ❸, weekend ❹

Hotel Astoria 510 Bush St at Grant, Chinatown ⊤1-800/666-6696, ⓦwww.hotelastoria-sf.com. Located right next to the arch at the entrance to Chinatown, the decor here is friskier than at many other budget hotels, with TV and full in-room amenities. Continental breakfast is included in the rate and there's discounted parking nearby. Shared bath ❶, en suite ❷

Hotel Boheme 444 Columbus Ave at Vallejo, North Beach ⊤415/433-9111, ⓦwww.hotelboheme .com. Set amid North Beach's heartland, this small, fifteen-room hotel has tiny but dramatic rooms done in rich, dark colours, with Art Deco-ish bathrooms and free wi-fi. Columbus Avenue can be noisy, so if you're a light sleeper, ask for a room at the back. ❻

San Remo 2237 Mason St at Chestnut, North Beach ☎1-800/352-7366, ⊛www.sanremohotel.com. Quirky option close to Fisherman's Wharf. Rooms in this warren-like converted house are cosy and chintzy – all share spotless bathrooms and only a few have sinks. There are no phones or TVs in the rooms and no elevator. ❸

SW Hotel 615 Broadway at Grant, North Beach ☎415/362-2999, ⊛www.swhotel.com. Elegant boutique hotel with large rooms full of modern Asian decor, including carved armoires and headboards and bright yellow bedspreads. ❹

Washington Square Inn 1660 Stockton St at Union, North Beach ☎1-800/388-0220, ⊛www.wsisf.com. This B&B-style hotel overlooking Washington Square has large, airy rooms decorated in modern shades of taupe and cream; staff is friendly and amenable. ❻

Cow Hollow and around

Best Western Hotel Tomo 1800 Sutter St at Buchanan, Japantown ☎1-888/822-8666, ⊛www.jdvhotels.com. Ripped straight from the pages of a Japanese comic book, the 125 rooms at this fun hotel feature anime murals, beanbag chairs and contemporary Japanese decor; some boast private balconies. Across the street from the Japan Center and convenient to Fillmore Street's boutiques and restaurants. See map on p.471. ❺

Cow Hollow Motor Inn 2190 Lombard St at Steiner, Cow Hollow ☎415/921-5800, ⊛www.cowhollowmotorinn.com. Swiss chalet-style inn, with plentiful parking and charmingly dated common areas. The rooms, though, are bland, if enormous. ❺

Hotel Del Sol 3100 Webster St at Lombard, Cow Hollow ☎415/921-5520, ⊛www.jdvhotels.com. Funky, offbeat motor lodge with a tropical theme, plus a swimming pool. The colour scheme combines zesty walls with chunky mosaics and palm trees wrapped in fairy lights. ❻

Laurel Inn 444 Presidio Ave at California, Laurel Heights ☎1-800/552-8735, ⊛www.thelaurelinn.com. Located one block from Sacramento Street's antique shops and eight blocks west of Fillmore Street's bustling strip of cafés and retailers. Decor is a stylish update of 1950s Americana, with muted graphic prints and simple fixtures. See map on p.471. ❻

Queen Anne Hotel 1590 Sutter St at Octavia, Pacific Heights ☎1-800/227-3970, ⊛www.queenanne.com. Gloriously restored Victorian building enjoying its second life as a boutique B&B. Each room is stuffed with gold-accented Rococo furniture and bunches of silk flowers; the parlour (where afternoon tea and sherry is served) is stuffed with museum-quality period furniture. See map on p.471. Weeknight ❹, weekend ❺

Surf Motel 2265 Lombard St at Pierce, Cow Hollow ☎415/922-1950, ⊛www.surfmotorinn.com. Old-school budget motel offering two tiers of bright, simple rooms that are sparklingly clean. Ask for a room at the back, since busy Lombard Street roars past the main entrance. Weeknight ❷, weekend ❸

The Mission and the Castro
See map on p.468.

Beck's Motor Lodge 2222 Market St at Sanchez, Castro ☎1-800/227-4360, ⊛www.becksmotorlodgesf.com. The clientele at this old-fashioned drive-in motel is more mixed than you'd expect from its location, and the soft, bluish rooms are plusher than the gaudy yellow exterior might suggest. If you're a light sleeper, ask for a room well away from hectic Market Street. One of only a few non-B&B accommodation options in the area. ❹

The Inn San Francisco 943 S Van Ness at 20th, Mission ☎1-800/359-0913, ⊛www.innsf.com. Superb, sprawling B&B in two adjoining historic Victorians. The 1872 mansion has fifteen dark and stylish rooms; the 1904 extension next door holds six more. Breakfast buffet, redwood hot tub, on-site parking and the rooftop sun deck with stunning views are all major plusses. Shared bath ❹, en suite ❻

Hayes Valley and west
See map on p.471.

Carl Hotel 198 Carl St at Stanyan, Cole Valley ☎415/661-5679, ⊛www.carlhotel.ypguides.net. Plainer than many of the surrounding B&Bs, this hotel is a bargain for its Golden Gate Park-adjacent location. Rooms are small but floral, with microwaves and refrigerators; the six with shared bath are especially well priced. Shared bath ❸, en suite ❹

The Chateau Tivoli 1057 Steiner St at Fulton, Alamo Square ☎1-800/228-1647, ⊛www.chateautivoli.com. History figures prominently here, whether in the furniture (one of the beds was owned by Charles de Gaulle), the rooms named for Jack London and Isadora Duncan (among others) or the building itself (built for an early local lumber baron). It's grand and quite serious accommodation, but a luxurious alternative to many of the cosy B&Bs elsewhere in town. Weeknight shared bath ❸, weekend shared bath ❹, weeknight en suite ❻, weekend en suite ❻

Hayes Valley Inn 417 Gough St at Hayes, Hayes Valley ☎1-800/930-7999, ⊛www.hayesvalleyinn .com. Homely rooms at this semi-secluded neighbourhood inn include minimal furnishings, and baths are shared. The well-stocked kitchen/ breakfast room, however, is a major plus. Weeknight ❷, weekend ❺

Ocean Park Motel 2690 46th Ave at Wawona, Parkside ☎415/566-7020, ⊛www.ocean parkmotel.com. Fully across the city from Downtown, San Francisco's oldest Art Deco motel is convenient for the coast and the zoo. The outdoor hot tub and pleasant garden courtyard are nice touches. ❺

The Red Victorian Bed, Breakfast & Art 1665 Haight St at Cole, Haight-Ashbury ☎415/864- 1978, ⊛www.redvic.com. Quirky B&B decorated with the owner's ethnic arts, where the TV-free rooms vary from simple to opulent. Breakfast's a lavish, highly communal affair. Look for the goldfish-filled toilet cistern in one of the shared bathrooms. Shared bath ❸, en suite ❺

Stanyan Park Hotel 750 Stanyan St at Waller, Haight-Ashbury ☎415/751-1000, ⊛www.stanyan park.com. Across from Golden Gate Park, this small hotel has 35 sumptuous rooms busily decorated in country florals, with heavy drapes and junior four- poster beds. ❼

Hostels

See maps on pp.448–449 and p.468.

Adelaide Hostel 51 Isadora Duncan Lane off Taylor St at Geary, Theater District ☎877/359-1915, ⊛www.adelaidehostel.com. 100-bed hostel that includes both multi-person dorms ($25) and private rooms ($60). There's a big, sofa-filled lounge, backyard deck, clean kitchen and free wi-fi. Also hefty continental breakfasts and cheap laundry. Open 24hr.

City Center Hostel - HI 685 Ellis St at Larkin, Tenderloin ☎415/474-5721, ⊛www.sfhostels .com. Spiffy hostel with 272 beds divided into four-person dorms, each with en-suite bath. With plenty of activities laid on (such as nightly movies and communal pancake breakfasts), it's good for meeting other travellers; its only downside is the location in a dodgy part of the Tenderloin, so women in particular should exercise caution after dark. There's no curfew, and overall it's friendly and funky. Dorms $25–30, private rooms ❸

Downtown Hostel - HI 312 Mason St at Geary, Theater District ☎415/788-5604, ⊛www .sfhostels.com. With almost 300 beds, this Downtown hostel still fills up quickly in peak season. Its four-person dorms are spotless, sharing bathroom facilities among eight people. There's a kitchen with microwave and vending machines, a small reading room and internet access, all available 24hr. Dorms $27–30, private rooms ❷

Elements Hotel 2524 Mission St, Mission ☎1-866/327-8407, ⊛www.elementssf .com. One of the only places to stay in the heart of the Mission, this fresh-looking hostel calls itself a hotel and features en-suite rooms ($30, Julu & Aug ❷) that are light-filled and modern; women-only, men-only and mixed dorm rooms ($25) are also available. Free internet access, complimentary continental breakfast and stunning city views from the rooftop bar, *Medjool* (see p.488).

Fisherman's Wharf Hostel - HI Building 240, Fort Mason ☎415/771-7277, ⊛www.sfhostels .com. High above the waterfront between the Golden Gate Bridge and Fisherman's Wharf, this is a choice option for the outdoorsy traveller, mostly thanks to its location in a rolling park. Be aware that although public transport connects the hostel with the city's main sights, it's nonetheless a little out of the way. Dorms $24–30, private rooms ❷

Green Tortoise 494 Broadway at Kearny, North Beach ☎1-800/867-8647, ⊛www.greentortoise .com. Laidback destination with dorm beds for $25–30 and private rooms (with shared bath) for $60. Both options include free internet and luggage storage, complimentary breakfast daily (and dinner three nights a week) and use of the small sauna. No curfew. Dorm and private rooms both available. Green Tortoise also runs popular bus trips around the state – see p.34.

Pacific Tradewinds 680 Sacramento St at Kearny, Chinatown ☎1-888/734-6783, ⊛www .pactradewinds.com. Small hostel (less than forty beds) offering free internet access, a clean kitchen and a large communal dining table that makes meeting fellow travellers easy. It's certainly an international hub – house rules are posted in almost forty languages, including Afrikaans and Catalan. Book well ahead in high season. $29.50.

USA Hostel 711 Post St at Jones, Tenderloin ☎415/440-5600, ⊛www.usahostels.com. A friendly and fun place on a safe edge of the gritty Tenderloin. There's a 45-seat movie theatre (with complimentary popcorn) on site, along with free all-you-can-make pancakes and oatmeal in the morning. Large lockers and wi-fi included. Dorms go for $40, private rooms for $85.

The first thing that strikes visitors about San Francisco is that it is a city of hills and diverse neighbourhoods. Here, as a general rule, geographical elevation is a stout indicator of wealth – the higher you live, the better off you are. Commercial square-footage is surprisingly small and mostly confined to the Downtown area, and the rest of the city is composed primarily of residential districts with street-level shopping, easily explored on foot. Armed with a good map and strong legs, you could plough through much of the city in a couple of days, but the best way to get to know San Francisco is to dawdle, unbound by itineraries; its most interesting neighbourhoods merit – at the very least – half a day each of simply hanging out.

Most of the hills that rise above the town serve as geographic barriers between neighbourhoods. The flattest stretch of land, created by landfill and bulldozing, is the bay-adjacent section of **Downtown**, which itself includes the far northeast corner of the Peninsula as bordered by I-80 to the south, US-101 (Van Ness Avenue) to the west, and the water. The city centre is bisected by the wide, diagonal thoroughfare of **Market Street**, a main reference point for many of your wanderings. Lined with stores and office buildings, Market begins across from the water's edge of the **Embarcadero** and runs southwest, brushing against the corporate high-rises of the **Financial District**, the shopping quarter of **Union Square**, the scruffy **Tenderloin** and chic **Hayes Valley,** before finally reaching the primarily gay district of the **Castro**. It then spirals around **Twin Peaks**, the most prominent of San Francisco's considerable heights.

South and east of Market Street stands the **South of Market (SoMa)** district, which used to be one of the city centre's few industrial enclaves until the artsy, nightclubbing crowd discovered it. Development poured in during the flush 1990s, funding the **San Francisco Museum of Modern Art** and the glorious waterfalls at **Yerba Buena Gardens**, but the neighbourhood suffered after the bursting of the internet bubble; its recovery has been slow but steady in the years since. Adjacent to South of Market near the waterfront, long-neglected **Mission Bay** has been re-zoned for housing and businesses, and is now anchored by **AT&T Park**, the lovely waterfront baseball park built for the San Francisco Giants.

Southwest from there sits one of San Francisco's most vibrant neighbourhoods, the **Mission**. Built around the wedding cake-like Mission Dolores and, thanks to fog-blocking hills, often sunnier than other parts of the city, the largely Latino neighbourhood offers enough food, cinema, nightclubs and shops to fill a separate vacation – or at least a day away from the well-trodden tourist path elsewhere in the city.

North and west of Market Street, the land rises dramatically, and with it property values, as evinced by the stunning mansions atop **Nob Hill**, the city's one-time province of railroad barons. Beside this posh residential quarter and a short cable-car ride or walk down the hill rests cluttered **Chinatown**, a thriving neighbourhood of apartments, restaurants, temples and shops fanning out from **Portsmouth Square**. Most of the land east of the square, towards the bay, used to be entirely water before hundreds of sailors heading for the Gold Rush abandoned their ships, resulting in an unnatural extension of the waterfront. The beached boats rapidly piled up along the shore until merchants began using the dry-docked vessels as hotels, bars and shops. Now it's filled by the towering Transamerica Pyramid, which shadows the **Jackson Square** historical district, full of restored businesses. The diagonal artery **Columbus Avenue**, which separates Portsmouth and Jackson squares, is the spine of the Italian enclave of **North Beach**, much loved by Beat writers, espresso drinkers and weekend revellers. North Beach

Cable cars

San Francisco's **cable cars** first appeared in 1873, the brainchild of Andrew Hallidie, an enterprising engineer with a taste for moneymaking schemes. The Scotland-born Hallidie is said to have been inspired to find an alternative to horse-drawn carriages when he saw a team of horses badly injured while trying to pull a dray up a steep hill in the rain. More than equine welfare was under threat – his father had patented a strong wire rope that had been extensively used in the mines of eastern California, but once the Gold Rush slowed, Hallidie needed a new application for his family's signature product, and a privately owned transit system reliant upon strong cable seemed the ideal solution.

The cable car **pulley system** was dubbed "Hallidie's Folly" by unconvinced San Franciscans, but doubters were soon proved wrong as lofted neighbourhoods such as Nob Hill became accessible; businesses and homes were suddenly constructed along cable-car routes. At their peak, just before the 1906 earthquake, more than six hundred cable cars plied eight lines and 112 miles of track throughout the city, travelling at a maximum of 9.5mph.

Unfortunately, the system was hit hard by a pair of obstacles: the devastation wrought by the 1906 earthquake – which wrecked large chunks of track – and the eventual onset of the automobile. However, when it was rumoured in 1947 that the ailing system would be phased out altogether, a local activist named Frieda Klussman organized a citizens' committee to save the cable cars. Protests worked, and seventeen years later the beloved cars were placed on the National Register of Historic Places, at which time the remaining few miles of track were saved. Today there are 44 cars in use – each unique – and about 23 miles of moving cable underground. Since the mid-1980s, Muni has been rebuilding the cars by hand on an ongoing basis, requiring as much as 3000 hours and $275,000 per car.

extends to the northernmost tip of the city, the tourist-trap waterfront known as **Fisherman's Wharf**, but not before passing the peaks of **Russian Hill** – home to famously curvy Lombard Street – and **Telegraph Hill**, perch of celebrated Coit Tower.

Paved trails along the northern waterfront lead west towards **Golden Gate Bridge**, passing the expansive green parklands of **Fort Mason** and **Crissy Field** and through the ritzy **Marina** district, home to the Palace of Fine Arts. High above to the south, the mansions and Victorians of **Pacific Heights** snuggle up against neighbourhood restaurants and designer boutiques, along with spectacular views of the bridges and bay from hilltop parks. Pacific Heights then slopes down south to nondescript **Japantown** and the residential, but increasingly fun, **Western Addition**. Directly west of here, you'll come to **Haight–Ashbury**, once San Francisco's Victorian resort quarter before flower children took over in the 1960s. Today it's a ragtag collection of used-clothing stores and hippies squeezing as much money as they can from their fading past; abutting **Golden Gate Park**, the neighbourhood also suffers from a highly visible homeless population.

The western and southern areas of San Francisco are resolutely residential, but still hold scattered attractions and charms. **Geary Boulevard**, the main east–west passage through the city's northern sector, begins in the Financial District and ends at the Pacific Ocean in the **Richmond** district. Geary is lined with some of the city's best Asian and Russian restaurants, while a block north, the Clement Street area just east of Park Presidio Boulevard is known more and more as **"New Chinatown"** for its collection of Chinese groceries, hot-pot restaurants and dim sum cafeterias. The Richmond is hugged by nature on three sides: the coastline

DOWNTOWN SAN FRANCISCO

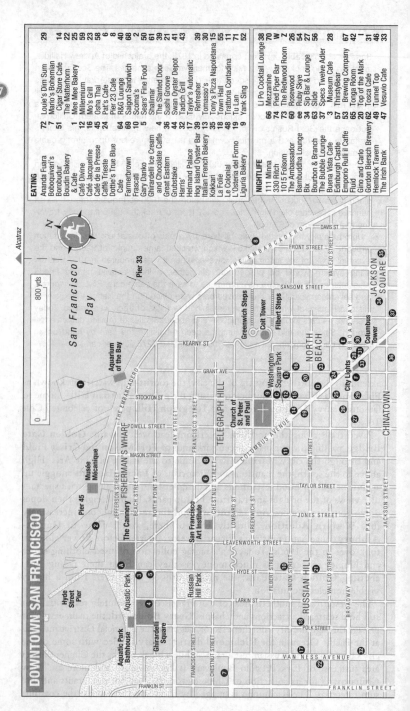

EATING	
Ananda Fuara	29
Boboquivari's	7
Borobudur	51
Boudin Bakery & Cafe	1
Café Divine	12
Café Jacqueline	16
Café de la Presse	45
Caffè Trieste	24
Dottie's True Blue Cafe	
Frascati	64
Gary Danko	69
Ghirardelli Ice Cream and Chocolate Caffe	4
Great Eastern	36
Grubstake	44
Harris	32
Helmand Palace	17
Hog Island Oyster Bar	39
Italian French Bakery	13
Kokkari	35
La Folie	18
Le Colonial	48
L'Osteria del Forno	19
Liguria Bakery	9
Louie's Dim Sum	72
Mario's Bohemian Cigar Store Cafe	51
The Matterhorn	1
Mee Mee Bakery	12
Millennium	59
Mo's Grill	23
Osha Thai	58
Pat's Café	6
Pier 23 Cafe	8
R&G Lounge	40
Saigon Sandwich	2
Scoma's	50
Sears' Fine Food	61
Shalimar	39
The Slanted Door	21
Sushi Groove	41
Swan Oyster Depot	43
Tadich Grill	
Taylor's Automatic Refresher	39
Tomasso's	30
Tony's Pizza Napoletana	15
Town Hall	55
Trattoria Contadina	11
Tu Lan	71
Yank Sing	52

NIGHTLIFE	
111 Minna	66
330 Ritch	70
1015 Folsom	74
The Ambassador	73
Bambuddha Lounge	60
Bix	ee
Bourbon & Branch	34
The Bubble Lounge	63
Buena Vista Cafe	37
Edinburgh Castle	57
Emporio Rulli il Caffe	3
Fluid	53
Gino and Carlo	65
Gordon Biersch Brewery	62
Hemlock Tavern	49
The Irish Bank	47
Li Po Cocktail Lounge	38
Mezzanine	70
Pied Piper Bar	W
The Redwood Room	2
Rosewood	26
Ruby Skye	54
Sip Bar & Lounge	27
Slide	56
Specs Twelve Adler Museum Cafe	28
ThirstyBear Brewing Company	67
Tonga Room	42
Top of the Mark	1
Tosca Cafe	31
Tunnel Top	46
Vesuvio Cafe	33

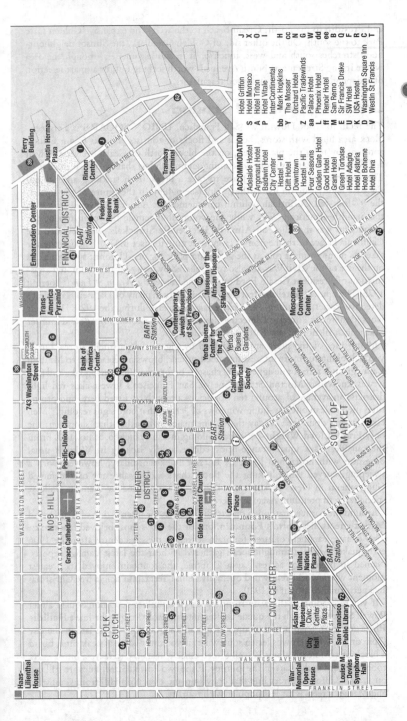

ACCOMMODATION			
Adelaide Hostel	J	Hotel Griffon	H
Argonaut Hotel	S	Hotel Monaco	X
Baldwin Hotel	A	Hotel Triton	O
City Center	P	Hotel Vitale	I
Hostel – HI		InterContinental	
Clift Hotel	bb	Mark Hopkins	cc
Downtown	Y	The Mosser	N
Hostel – HI		Orchard Hotel	G
Four Seasons	Z	Pacific Tradewinds	W
Golden Gate Hotel	aa	Palace Hotel	dd
Good Hotel	L	Phoenix Hotel	ee
Grant Hotel	ff	Renoir Hotel	B
Green Tortoise	M	San Remo	Q
Hotel Adagio	E	Sir Francis Drake	F
Hotel Astoria	U	SW Hotel	R
Hotel Bohème	D	USA Hostel	C
Hotel Diva	V	Washington Square Inn	T
		Westin St Francis	

and **Presidio** to the north; Ocean Beach to the west; and expansive Golden Gate Park to the south. On the other side of Golden Gate Park, the **Sunset** neighbourhood stretches south and west, much of it in subtle sameness, though the area where Irving Street meets Ninth Avenue is worth seeking out for a smart selection of independent boutiques and good restaurants.

Union Square and around

The retail focus of Downtown San Francisco, **UNION SQUARE** is a sixteen-block area filled with stores, hotels and flocks of tourists. Thanks to a gruelling and lengthy refit, the plaza itself, on the block north of Geary between Powell and Stockton streets, is more welcoming and much less shabby than it once was. The benches here are a good place to take a break from trekking around and there's a handy café on its northeast rim (see p.485). In the centre of the square, the 97-foot-tall Corinthian column commemorates Admiral Dewey's success in the Spanish–American War, while the voluptuous female figure on top of the monument was modelled on **Alma de Bretteville Spreckels**, who founded the California Palace of the Legion of Honor art museum (see p.476). Though the site takes its name from its role as the gathering place for pro-Unionist speechmakers on the eve of the Civil War, it's also remembered by many for the attempted assassination of President Gerald Ford outside the bordering *Westin St Francis* hotel in 1975. The opulent hotel also featured prominently in many of Dashiell Hammett's detective stories, including *The Maltese Falcon* – in fact, during the 1920s Hammett worked there as a Pinkerton detective, investigating the notorious rape and murder case against silent film star Fatty Arbuckle.

Many sides of the plaza are dominated by gigantic department stores, but if you're looking for more interesting, albeit pricier, browsing, head east to **Maiden Lane**, ground zero for designer-label chasers. Before the 1906 earthquake and fire, it was known as Morton Street, one of San Francisco's lowest-class red-light districts; an average of around ten homicides a month occurred here, and prostitutes used to lean out low-hung windows of "cribs" that bore signs reading, "Men taken in and done for". Today there's one major sight other than shopping: the only **Frank Lloyd Wright**-designed building in San Francisco, at no. 140. From the outside, it's a squat orange-brick edifice, oddly lacking in Wright's usual obsession with horizontal lines; its interior is extraordinary, however, with a sweeping, curved ramp linking the floors that's a clear ancestor of the famed Guggenheim in New York. The building's now occupied by Xanadu Gallery, specializing in premium Asian art pieces.

Around the corner, marooned on a traffic island at the intersection of Kearny and Market streets, lies **Lotta's Fountain**, one of the city's most beloved landmarks. This ornate, caramel-coloured fountain served as message centre after the 1906 earthquake, where distraught locals gathered to hear the latest damage reports. Named in honour of actress Lotta Crabtree, the fountain enjoyed its greatest moment when world-renowned opera diva Luisa Tetrazinni sang a free Christmas Eve performance atop it in 1910.

If you're heading to the waterfront, **cable cars** run beside Union Square along Powell Street, although the queue is often interminably long at the line's **Hallidie Plaza** southern terminus. A couple of queue-dodging tips: come late in the day (7pm or so), when crowds lessen somewhat; if you must come at peak time, board a block or two north along Powell Street, since drivers try to leave a bit of extra room onboard at the start of the journey. If the two Powell Street lines are still too busy, the California Street line that crawls up and over Nob Hill from California and Market streets is far less popular with tourists.

The Theater District

The area between Union Square and the gritty Tenderloin is known as the **Theater District**, although most of the playhouses lack the grandeur of many old theatres in New York or London; two exceptions are noted below. Despite its proximity to a number of tourist attractions, this neighbourhood is a convenient bolthole from Union Square's madding crowds and a secluded place to stay within the city centre.

The Theater District is anchored by two theatres along Geary Street: **American Conservatory Theater**'s remarkable eponymous performance venue at no. 415 and the **Curran Theatre** at no. 445. Taking design cues from a Napoleonic palace, A.C.T.'s grand, colonnaded Neoclassical building opened in 1910 and was originally known as the Geary Theater. It sustained significant structural damage in the 1989 Loma Prieta earthquake and did not reopen until seven years later; it was renamed in 2006, and today the theatre's namesake company usually performs major plays five nights a week. The Curran, immediately next door, dates from 1922 and first operated as a vaudeville stage; these days, it hosts crowd-pleasing productions such as *A Chorus Line* and *Hairspray*. For performance details on both theatres, see p.492.

Nob Hill

The posh hotels and Masonic institutions of **Nob Hill**, south of Russian Hill and west of Chinatown, exemplify San Francisco's old money, for it was here that the four men who transformed California through railroads all built their houses. Once you've made the stiff climb (or taken the California line cable car) up, there are very few real sights as such, apart from the astounding views over the city and beyond.

Originally called California Street Hill, the 376ft knoll was once scrubland occupied by sheep. The invention of the cable car in the late nineteenth century (see box, p.447) made it more accessible to Gold Rush millionaires, and the area soon became known as Nob Hill (from "nabob", a Moghul prince or "snob"; or, "knob" as in rounded hill) after the **Big Four** – Leland Stanford, Collis P. Huntington, Mark Hopkins and Charles Crocker – came to the area to construct the Central Pacific Railroad and, eventually, build their mansions here.

Ostentatious designs built out of Marin County redwood were the fashion, but unfortunately, after the earthquake and fire of 1906, almost all the mansions on Nob Hill had burned to the ground. The single exception can be viewed at 1000 California St, at the corner of Mason Street, where James C. Flood bucked local fashions and instead emulated the brownstone style popular in New York; the **Flood Mansion**, constructed in 1886 at the cost of a cool $1 million, is now home to the private **Pacific-Union Club**, an exclusive fraternal organization. Across California Street, you'll find another jaw-dropping view – and even more startling prices – at San Francisco's most famous vista-bar, the *Top of the Mark* (see p.486), in the **InterContinental Mark Hopkins**.

Overlooking Huntington Park, the manicured green space at the summit of Nob Hill, is one of the biggest hunks of sham-Gothic architecture in the US, **Grace Cathedral**, 1100 California St (Sun–Fri 7am–6pm, Sat 8am–6pm; ☏415/749-6300, ⓦwww.gracecathedral.org). Although this pale copy of Paris's Notre Dame was begun after the 1906 fire on land donated by the Crocker family, it took until the early 1960s to finish – and it suffers from a hotchpotch of styles as a result. The building offers an impression of unloved hugeness, despite florid (if hopelessly out of place) touches like the faithful replicas of Ghiberti's Renaissance doors from the Florence Baptistry adorning the main entrance. Inside, the AIDS Interfaith Chapel to the right of the main entrance features a cast-bronze altar as centrepiece, picked out in gold and silver leaf and designed by the late pop artist Keith Haring.

Chinatown

CHINATOWN's twenty-four square blocks make up one of the largest Chinese communities in the world outside Asia; it's also the oldest such enclave in America. Its roots lie in the migration of Chinese labourers to the city after the completion of the transcontinental railroad, and the arrival of Chinese sailors keen to benefit from the Gold Rush. San Francisco is still known in China as "Old Gold Mountain", its storied moniker from the nineteenth century, but the city didn't extend much of a welcome; rather, Chinese immigrants were met not only by a tide of vicious racial attacks, but also the unapologetically racist **1882 Chinese Exclusion Act**, a US federal law that banned new immigration and forbade thousands of single Chinese men from both dating local women and bringing wives from China. A rip-roaring prostitution and gambling quarter thus developed, controlled by gangs known as *tongs*. However, with the loosening of immigration laws due to China's partnership with the US during World War II, and decades of hard work by its residents, Chinatown has grown into a self-made success.

Many visitors and even locals assume that the neighbourhood remains autonomous, cut off from San Francisco by language and cultural barriers; however, the district actually boasts one of the city's highest voter turnouts on election days. Today's population, descendants of Cantonese- and Fujianese-speaking southern mainlanders, as well as Taiwanese, has been joined by Mandarin-speaking northerners, Vietnamese, Koreans, Thais and Laotians, turning the area into a virtual **Asiatown**. Though sleepy by night, during the day the area bustles with activity. Overcrowding is compounded by a brisk tourist trade, although sadly, Chinatown – and Grant Avenue in particular – contains some of the city's tackiest stores and facades, more evocative of a cheesy part of Hong Kong than Beijing or Shanghai. Indeed, Chinese visitors are often disappointed by the neighbourhood's disorder and pandering to tourists; for a truer sense of everyday Chinese life in San Francisco, you're better off heading to the Richmond (see p.476), or at least diverting over to far less touristy Stockton Street.

Chinatown streets

The best way to approach Chinatown is through the dramatic **Chinatown Gate**, on the southern end of Grant Avenue at Bush Street. Facing south, per *feng shui* precepts, it's a large dragon-clad arch, given to the city by the People's Republic of China in 1969, and adorned with a four-character inscription that translates to "The reason to exist is to serve the public good". It's hard to see how that idea is carried out on the blocks ahead, however, as Grant's sidewalks are paved with plastic Buddhas, cloisonné "health balls", noisemakers and chirping mechanical crickets that assault the ear and eye from many doorways.

One of the oldest thoroughfares in the city, **Grant Avenue** – originally called Dupont Street – was once a wicked ensemble of opium dens, bordellos and gambling huts policed, if not terrorized, by *tong* hatchet-men. After the 1906 fire, the city decided to rename it in honour of president and Civil War hero Ulysses S. Grant and in the process helped to excise the seedy excesses for which it had become infamous. Note the two pagoda-topped buildings on the corner of Grant Avenue and California Street, the Sing Fat and Sing Chong – important because they were the first to be constructed after the 1906 fire, signalling Chinese resolve to remain on their much-coveted land.

Running parallel to Grant Avenue one city block west, **Stockton Street** is a commercial artery for Chinatown locals, packed with grocery stores and dim sum shops, as well as herbalists and fishmongers. Between Stockton Street and Grant Avenue, narrow **Waverly Place** also runs north–south and holds two opulent but skilfully hidden temples: **Norras**, on the third floor of no. 109, and **Tien Hou** (pronounced "TEE-en how") on the fourth floor of no. 125. The latter is especially impressive, a Taoist temple dedicated to the Goddess of Heaven, its ornate interior splashed with gold and vermilion and its ceiling dripping with tassels and red lanterns. Both temples are still in use and open to visitors (daily 10am–5pm); if you visit, note the pyramids of oranges, considered lucky because the Cantonese pronunciation of "orange" sounds similar to the word for wealth. Although the temples don't charge admission, it's respectful to leave a donation and not use cameras inside. Note, too, a number of tiny octagonal mirrors fastened to the balcony of 829 Sacramento St at the southern end of Waverly Place – they're intended to ward off evil spirits.

Portsmouth Square and around

Set between Washington, Clay and Kearny streets, **Portsmouth Square** was San Francisco's original city centre and its first port of entry. The plaza has since become, for all intents and purposes, Chinatown's living room, and today it's primarily worth visiting to simply absorb everyday neighbourhood life, with spirited card games played atop cardboard boxes and other makeshift tables as children let off steam in the adjacent playground. Indeed, it's hard to imagine the city springing up from this once-dusty patch of land, but it was here that Englishman William Richardson received permission from Mexican rulers to begin a trading post on the edge of San Francisco Bay. When John Montgomery came ashore in 1846 to claim the land for the United States, he raised his flag here and named the square after his ship; the spot where he first planted the Stars and Stripes is marked by the one often flying in the square today.

There are a few points of interest in Portsmouth Square, although nothing especially outstanding. Near Montgomery's flagpole is a replica of the galleon *Hispaniola* from the novel *Treasure Island*, a monument to writer **Robert Louis Stevenson** who spent much time observing the locals in Portsmouth Square during his brief sojourn in San Francisco and the Monterey Peninsula in the late 1870s. The most recent addition to the square is the already weathered bronze *Goddess of Democracy* statue near the playground, a replica of a sculpture in Beijing's Tiananmen Square.

Just outside Portsmouth Square, at **743 Washington Street**, stands a small red pagoda-like structure built in 1909 for the Chinese American Telephone Exchange – it's set on the original site of the office of Sam Brannan's *California Star* newspaper, which carried the news of the earliest ore discoveries back to the East Coast in 1848, and thus played a major role in the Gold Rush. A team of telephone operators worked here throughout the first half of the 1900s, routing calls solely by memory since no Chinatown phone listings existed; it was restored in 1960 by a bank and remains a financial institution today. Note how the roof curves out and then back on itself, keeping evil spirits at bay since they're said to travel in a straight line.

Financial District

Stretching along Market Street between Chinatown, Union Square and the water-front, San Francisco's **Financial District** is the city's business hub; to experience it at its liveliest, wander through on a weekday around lunchtime. The area is home to San Francisco's two signature skyscrapers, each of which arose towards the end of the Brutalist era. The first, the 779ft-tall **Bank of America Center**, 555 California St, is a broad-shouldered monolith of dark granite – depending on natural lighting and your vantage point, it can look either brown or vaguely reddish – that dominates the skyline and has divided the city into fans and those who would like to see it razed at once; the latter doubtlessly cheered when it was used for exterior shots in the 1974 disaster film *The Towering Inferno*. A few blocks away stands the city's most recognizable high-rise, the **Transamerica Pyramid**, 600 Montgomery St, still one of the hundred tallest buildings in the world. The off-white, once-controversial structure – which more resembles a squared-off rocket than an actual pyramid – opened to business tenants in 1972, a mere three years after the opening of the rust-hued Bank of America Center, which it immediately upstaged.

Jackson Square

Confusingly, there's no plaza in **Jackson Square**. The area bordered by Washington, Columbus, Pacific and Battery streets wasn't known by its current name until the 1960s, when interior designers who'd recently opened showrooms here decided on a suitably artsy yet old-fashioned tag to replace the notorious **Barbary Coast**, San Francisco's district of vice during the nineteenth century. In its earlier rough-and-tumble era, a constant stream of sailors provided unrivalled demand for illicit entertainment; the area was nicknamed "Baghdad by the Bay" for its unsavoury reputation as a nexus for shanghai'ing, which involved hapless young males being given Mickey Finns and, once unconscious, dragged aboard sailing ships into involuntary servitude. Though buildings here remarkably survived the 1906 disaster, raunchy local businesses were hugely affected as nearby residential areas were levelled. The double whammy of fire and fury (chiefly, the relentless campaigning from William Randolph Hearst's *Examiner* newspaper against the district) soon put an end to the Barbary Coast's heyday.

Remains of San Francisco's earliest days can be seen today in the restored red-brick structures of Jackson Square's **historical district**. Of particular note is the **Hotaling Building**, at nos. 451–455, a distillery that was saved by a savvy manager at the height of the 1906 fire. Afterward, local wags came up with the doggerel: "If as they say God spanked the town for being so over frisky, why did he burn the churches down and spare Hotaling's whiskey?"

Montgomery Street, near Jackson Square's western flank, in particular has retained much of its historic character. No. 732 was the home of San Francisco's first literary magazine, the *Golden Era*, founded in the 1850s; it helped launch the careers of Bret Harte and Mark Twain. Later, John Steinbeck and William Saroyan spent many a night drinking in the long-vanished Black Cat Café down the street.

As the district merges with North Beach and Chinatown, at the intersection of Jackson Street and Columbus Avenue stands the distinctive green-copper siding of the **Columbus Tower**, 916 Kearny St. It's now owned by director and Bay Area resident Francis Ford Coppola, and houses on its ground floor *Café Zoetrope* (named for Coppola's production company, American Zoetrope), decorated with mementos from Coppola's career and Italian paraphernalia.

North Beach

Sandwiched by Chinatown to the south and Fisherman's Wharf to the north, inland **NORTH BEACH** has always been a gateway for immigrants. Italian immigration to San Francisco was ignited, unsurprisingly, by the Gold Rush, although it gained momentum at the end of the nineteenth century, when this area began to develop the characteristics – *focaccia* bakeries, salami grocers – of a true *Piccola Italia*. The freewheeling European flavour here, coupled with robust nightlife and wide availability of housing, attracted rebel writers like Lawrence Ferlinghetti, Allen Ginsberg and Jack Kerouac in the 1950s, making North Beach the nexus of the **Beat movement** (see box opposite).

The main route through North Beach is **Columbus Avenue**, proudly tagged by the colours of the Italian flag painted on each lamppost and now one of San Francisco's liveliest nocturnal drags. At its southern end at the crossroads of

The Beats in North Beach

Beat literature didn't begin in San Francisco; rather, it emerged in 1940s New York, where bohemian **Jack Kerouac** had joined with Ivy League-educated **Allen Ginsberg**, as well as **William Burroughs**, to bemoan the conservative political climate there. The group soon moved out West, most of them settling in North Beach and securing jobs at the docks to help longshoremen unload fishing boats. The initial rumblings of interest in the movement were signalled by the 1953 opening of the first bookstore in America dedicated solely to paperbacks: **Lawrence Ferlinghetti**'s City Lights bookstore (see below) drew attention to the area as the latest literary capital of California.

But it wasn't until the publication four years later of Ginsberg's pornographic protest poem *Howl* – originally written simply for his own pleasure rather than for printing – that mainstream America took notice. Police moved in on City Lights to prevent the sale of the book, inadvertently catapulting the Beats to national notoriety – assisted by press hysteria over their hedonistic antics, including heavy drinking and an immense fondness for pot – that matched the fame earned by the literary merits of their work. Ginsberg's case went all the way to the Supreme Court, which eventually ruled that so long as a work has "redeeming social value" it could not be considered pornographic. Within six months, Jack Kerouac's *On the Road*, inspired by his friend Neal Cassady's benzedrine monologues and several cross-country trips, had shot to the top of the bestseller lists, cementing the Beats' fame.

It's said that the word Beatnik was jokily coined by legendary San Francisco newspaper columnist Herb Caen, who noted that the writers were as far out as the recently launched Soviet rocket, Sputnik. Soon, North Beach was synonymous across America with a wild and subversive lifestyle, an image that drove away the original artsy intelligentsia, many of whom ended up in **Haight-Ashbury**. In their place, heat-seeking libertines swamped the area, accompanied by tourists on "Beatnik Tours" who were promised sidewalks clogged with black-bereted, goateed trendsetters banging bongos. (The more enterprising fringes of bohemia responded in kind with "The Squaresville Tour" of the neighbouring Financial District, dressed in Bermuda shorts and carrying plaques that read "Hi, Squares".) Soon enough, of course, the Italians who'd once dominated North Beach reclaimed it from the dwindling Beat movement.

The legend of the Beats, though, has yet to die. It's been significantly aided by Ferlinghetti's successful campaign to rename certain smaller North Beach streets after local literary figures – the alley next to City Lights, for example, is now known as Jack Kerouac Alley.

Columbus and Broadway, you'll find the former site of many old bars and comedy clubs from the 1950s, where politically conscious comedians like Mort Sahl and Lenny Bruce performed. Many of the venues are now adult entertainment establishments, which took over spaces here during the death throes of the Beat movement. In fact, one of the city's legacies is the topless waitress phenomenon: it was at the *Condor Club*, 300 Columbus Ave, one night in 1964 that Carol "44 Inches" Doda slipped out of her top and into the history books.

Still, the biggest draw near the intersection of Columbus and Broadway is **City Lights**, 261 Columbus Ave (daily 10am–midnight; ℡415/362-8193, ⓦwww .citylights.com), a bookstore that's a beacon of San Francisco culture. Opened in 1953 by Lawrence Ferlinghetti, and still owned by him today, it soldiers on despite the encroachment of big-name chains. The best reason to drop in is the upstairs poetry room, where you'll find everything from $1 mini-books and poster-size poems by Beatnik legends to various collections and anthologies, including titles from City Lights' own imprint.

The area grows more Italian as you head north from Broadway – expect plenty of delis, cafés and restaurants selling cured meats, strong coffee and plates of tagliatelle, respectively. One exception is the section of **Grant Avenue** north of Vallejo, where you'll find one of the best emerging shopping streets in the city, lined with clothing stores and other various boutiques. Grant Avenue is also the site of two neighbourhood landmarks: San Francisco's oldest bar, *The Saloon*, at no. 1232 (see p.491), a rare North Beach survivor of the 1906 fire that persists as a lively dive bursting with nightly blues acts; and, *Caffè Trieste*, at the corner of Grant and Vallejo Street (see p.485), where the jukebox plays opera classics and, on certain Saturdays, you can catch performances by mandolin players or operatic vocalists.

The soul of North Beach is **Washington Square Park**, a grassy gathering spot and public backyard that plays host to dozens of older, local Chinese each morning practicing tai chi. On the north side of the park, the white lacy spires of the **Church of St Peter and Paul** look like a pair of fairytale castles rising from the North Beach flats. Although it's seen as the spiritual home of the local Italian community, the church also offers masses in Cantonese along with the expected English and Italian. The interior is a vast nineteenth-century confection, underlit even on sunny days.

Russian Hill

West of North Beach, elegant **Russian Hill**, named for six unknown Russian sailors who died on an expedition here in the early 1800s and were buried on its southeastern flank, has the odd point of interest. The modest high-rises at the top of the hill were fiercely contested when they were first built in the 1920s, prompting many of San Francisco's stringent zoning laws. Most people, though, come here for the white-knuckle drive down **Lombard Street** (see box below), a terracotta-tiled waterchute for cars. Its tight, narrow curves swoop down one block, and there's a 5mph speed limit here – not that you'll be able to drive much faster given the usual queue. The best time to enjoy it is early morning or, better still, late at night when the city lights twinkle below and most of the tourists have gone.

It's easy to get your bearings in the neighbourhood, as the cable car tracks along **Hyde Street** neatly divide the district in two. Two blocks east down the hill, the

---

San Francisco's steepest (and twistiest) streets

Though no San Francisco street can match **Lombard** for its fabled curves, there's another, lesser-known auto twistathon in town, adjacent to the US-101 freeway in the Potrero Hill neighbourhood: **Vermont Street** between 20th and 22nd. Its scenery may not be as picturesque as its Russian Hill counterpart, but it's virtually guaranteed that you won't have to wait in a queue to trundle down its one-way turns.

Another uniquely San Francisco thrill – provided your car's brakes and clutch are up to snuff – is to plummet down (or in certain cases when the streets aren't one-way, slog up) any of the city's **steepest streets**. Much pride among locals hinges on a driver's ability to negotiate San Francisco's most precipitous climbs and drops, particularly with a manual transmission vehicle.

Here's a quick rundown of the sharpest drivable grades in town, including degree of steepness.

- Filbert Street between Leavenworth and Hyde, Russian Hill (31.5°)
- 22nd Street between Church and Vicksburg, Noe Valley (31.5°)
- Jones Street between Filbert and Union, Russian Hill (29.0°)
- Duboce Street between Alpine and Buena Vista Ave East, Roosevelt Terrace (27.9°)
- Jones Street between Union and Green, Russian Hill (26.0°)

low-rise Mission-style building of the **San Francisco Art Institute**, 800 Chestnut St at Leavenworth (daily 9am–8pm; free; ☎415/771-7020, ⓦwww.sfai.edu) clings to the side of a steep incline. It's easy to miss this place, which is in fact the oldest art school in the West; Jerry Garcia and Lawrence Ferlinghetti passed through the school's open studios and Ansel Adams started its photography department. Its one unmissable sight is the **Diego Rivera Gallery** and its outstanding mural, *The Making of a Fresco Showing the Building of a City*. Executed by the Mexican painter at the height of his fame in 1931, the fresco cleverly includes Rivera himself sitting with his back to the viewer in the centre of the painting – find the chubby figure looking on as others construct a giant human being in front of him.

Telegraph Hill

Due east of North Beach and dominated by Coit Tower, **Telegraph Hill** is a quiet cluster of slope-hugging homes. The most direct path up its slope is Filbert Street, but be aware that the gradient east of Grant Avenue is very steep; since there are few parking spots up at the tower, non-walkers are better off waiting for the 39-Coit Muni bus to the top. Once you reach the summit, it's easy to see why the peak was used as a signal tower for ships entering the Golden Gate: standing where the statue of Christopher Columbus is today, a watchman on the hill would identify the boat's origin and name by the flags flying on the mast and relay the information via telegraph to the docks along Fisherman's Wharf.

The Columbus statue stands in **Pioneer Park**, which was donated to the city by private citizens in 1875 and has a lovely green space on its south side ideal for sitting and picking out the sights below. Directly above looms **Coit Tower** (daily 10am–6pm; lobby free, $5 for elevator to top; ☎415/362-0808), a 210ft-tall pillar built in 1933 with a chunk of firefighter-benefactor Lillie Coit's money after her death. Provided there isn't too long a line for the cramped elevator, the trip to the open-air viewing platform is well worth it – a stunning panorama with unimpeded vistas in every direction.

While waiting to ascend to the top, take some time to admire the **frescoes** at the interior's base. These were an early project overseen by the Public Works of Art Authority, a predecessor of the better-known Works Progress Administration that employed artists to decorate public and government buildings during the Depression. Those chosen for this project were students of **Diego Rivera**, who was both artistically and politically influenced by Russian Communism. As in his work, the figures are typically muscular and somber, emphasizing the glory of labour, although there's a wide variation in style and quality between panels, despite their thematic cohesion. The San Francisco City Guides organization (☎415/557-4266, ⓦwww.sfcityguides.org) leads a free **tour** of the murals every Saturday at 11am – meet at the tower's main entrance.

Coit Tower may be Telegraph Hill's most visible (and visited) attraction, but it's along the pair of canopied **pedestrian paths** clinging to its eastern flank that the true identity of this urban peak comes into focus. These steep walkways pass between oversized bungalows and gardens both wild and manicured. The brick **Greenwich steps** drop from the east side of the small Pioneer Park parking lot (look for the street sign) down to a hillside block of Montgomery Street; at no. 1440 Montgomery, the steps continue down the sharp slope to Sansome Street. As you descend to the east, look for the cleared area to the left of the paved path with a bench and, for comic measure, an uprooted parking meter replanted next to it. Also look and listen for the famed flock of parrots – 200 strong, and counting – that now calls this side of Telegraph Hill home. The birds' green plumage sometimes makes them difficult to spot in the tall trees, but you can't miss their squawking.

A block south of Greenwich, the **Filbert steps** trace an even steeper path up and down Telegraph Hill, with the lengthy stretch of the footpath between Sansome and Montgomery still laid with wooden planks. There's also boardwalk on the route's most florid offshoot, Napier Lane, which overflows with foliage and is exhilaratingly fragrant with honeysuckle and roses in spring. The cottage at 224 Filbert dates from the 1860s and was thoroughly restored in the late 1970s, while many of the other small homes in the immediate area are equally charming.

Along the Embarcadero

The thin, long waterfront district known as **THE EMBARCADERO** is centred on the **Ferry Building** and extends from Mission Bay up to Fisherman's Wharf. Cut off from the rest of San Francisco for three decades by a double-decker highway – fatally damaged in the 1989 earthquake and demolished a few years later – the graceful building, at the foot of Market Street, was modelled on the Giralda in Seville, Spain; it's now listed as a National Historic Landmark. Before the bridges were built in the 1930s, it was the arrival point for fifty thousand daily cross-bay commuters; following a long period of neglect beginning in the 1940s, it's once again a working ferry terminus for an increasingly revitalized commuter service. In 2003, following a multi-million-dollar facelift, its grand nave reopened as a gourmet food marketplace (see p.478), now one of the city's premier attractions for locals and visitors alike.

The best time to stop by is during the **Ferry Plaza Farmers Market** (year-round Sat 8am–2pm, Tues 10am–2pm; April–Nov also Thurs 4–8pm; ☎415/291-3276, ⓦwww.ferryplazafarmersmarket.com), with local produce sold from numerous stalls set up around the building. Thousands of local foodies flock here to sample snacks and there are also regular recipe demonstrations from local name-brand chefs. Many farmers only sell on one of the four different days, so it's worth checking back more than once.

Across the multi-lane thoroughfare, it's perhaps fitting that **Justin Herman Plaza** – named in honour of San Francisco's father of urban renewal who, in the name of progress, bulldozed acres of historic buildings in the Western Addition after World War II – should be home to San Francisco's least revered modernist work of art. French-Canadian artist Armand Vaillancourt's 1971 *Quebec Libre!*, known locally as simply the **Vaillancourt Fountain**, is a tangled mass of square concrete tubing that looks as if it were inspired by air-conditioning ducts. (One particularly sour local columnist lambasted it as the product of a giant dog with square bowels.) In fact, the visually jumbled statement on provincial sovereignty attempted to echo the overhead highway that rimmed the plaza back when the fountain was built; today, with the freeway thankfully gone, there's a movement to have the fountain done away with as well.

Fisherman's Wharf

If the districts of San Francisco are a family, then **Fisherman's Wharf** is the boisterous uncle who showed up at the reunion in a ghastly shirt, put a lampshade on his head and never left. This city doesn't go dramatically out of its way to court and fleece tourists, but the Wharf is a grand exception, its scores of tacky souvenir shops and overpriced restaurants exposing this area's mission of raking in disposable tourist dollars. The area flourished as a serious fishing port well into the twentieth century, although these days, the few fishermen that can afford the exorbitant mooring charges have usually finished their trawling by early morning and are gone by the time most visitors arrive.

Alcatraz

Before the rocky islet of **Alcatraz** became America's most dreaded high-security prison in 1934, it had already served as a fortress and military jail. Surrounded by the bone-chilling water of San Francisco Bay, it made an ideal place to hold the nation's most wanted criminals, including Al Capone and Machine Gun Kelly. Conditions were inhumane: inmates were kept in solitary confinement, in cells no larger than nine by five feet, most without light; they were not allowed to eat together, read newspapers, play cards or even talk; relatives could visit for only two hours each month. Escape really was impossible: nine men managed to get off "The Roc," but none gained his freedom, and the only two to reach the mainland (using a jacket stuffed with inflated surgical rings as a raft) were soon apprehended.

Due to its massive running costs, the prison finally closed in 1963. The island remained abandoned until 1969, when a group of **Native Americans** staged an occupation as part of a peaceful attempt to claim the island for their people, citing treaties that designated all federal land not in use as automatically reverting to their ownership. Using all the bureaucratic trickery it could muster, the US government finally ousted them two years later, claiming the operative lighthouse qualified it as active.

Alcatraz got its name as a result of poor map-reading and questionable diction. An early Spanish explorer christened one island in San Francisco Bay Isla de Alcatraces ("Island of Pelicans") in honour of the hundreds of birds living on it; however, the island he was referring to is not the one known today as Alcatraz. The pelicans' old home is now called Yerba Buena Island because a clumsy English sea captain became confused when mapping the bay in 1826. He wrongly assumed that the tiny, rocky islet – set between the mainland and Angel Island, and pelted with guano – must be the birds' home, so he marked it down in mangled Spanglish as "Alcatraz", then assigned the name Yerba Buena to the other island that is today's halfway point of the Bay Bridge.

At least 750,000 tourists each year take the excellent hour-long, self-guided audio tour of the abandoned prison, which includes sharp anecdotal commentary as well as re-enactments of prison life featuring improvised voices of the likes of Capone and Kelly. **Ferries** to Alcatraz leave from Pier 33 (frequent departures from 9am–3.55pm, last ferry returns at 6.15pm; night tour departs at 5.55pm and 6.45pm; day tour $26, night tour $33; ☎415/981-7625, ⓦwww.alcatrazcruises.com); allow at least three hours for a visit, including cruise time. Advance **reservations** are essential – in peak season, it's nearly impossible to snag a ticket for a same-day visit.

Aside from embarking on a bay cruise from Pier 39 (see p.441) and a few worthwhile seafood restaurants (see p.478), the most endearing attraction here is the large colony of barking **sea lions** that often take over a number of floating platforms between piers 39 and 41. However, one recent winter saw them head north to the Oregon coast for more abundant food, so if the packs of charmingly noisy pinnipeds have gone missing during your visit, a sure bet for viewing aquatic life is the **Aquarium of the Bay** at Pier 39 (June–Aug daily 9am–8pm; Sept–May Mon–Thurs 10am–6pm, Fri–Sun 10am–7pm; $14.95; ☎888/732-3483, ⓦwww .aquariumofthebay.com). Exhibits here are standard fare for sea-life museums, although the petting pool with leopard sharks and bat rays is a nice diversion. The top attraction is "Under the Bay", where you're treated to spectacular close-ups of fish and crustaceans as you trundle slowly through a 300ft viewing tunnel – assuming you can ignore the cloying muzak overhead. Another entertaining pick nearby is the **Musée Mécanique** on Pier 45 (Mon–Fri 10am–7pm, Sat & Sun 10am–8pm; free; ☎415/346-2000, ⓦwww.museemechanique.org) which houses an extensive collection of vintage arcade machines and 1980s video games.

Aquatic Park

West of the Wharf, the pandering tourist trade recedes, although pockets persist next to **Aquatic Park** in the form of caricature portrait artists and dull, occasionally nettlesome street musicians. This area's best asset is **San Francisco Maritime National Historic Park**, a low-key complex that includes restored sailing vessels, curving jetties, impressive nautical architecture and a sandy spit. Drop into the fine visitor centre, 499 Jefferson St at Hyde (summer 9.30am–6pm; rest of year 9.30am–5pm; ⊤415/447-5000, ⓦwww.nps.gov/safr), which offers an extensive display of local maritime history. Nearby, the **Hyde Street Pier**, in its working heyday, served numerous ferries that shuttled passengers (and in later years, their cars) between San Francisco and Sausalito, Tiburon and Berkeley before the 1937 opening of the Golden Gate Bridge quickly rendered these services useless. Today, there's no charge to wander down the wooden slats perched over the bay and peruse the exhibits, and free ranger tours meet regularly throughout the day at the foot of the pier. However, to board one of the painstakingly preserved ships, you'll need to pick up a ticket at the visitor centre.

Aquatic Park itself lies at the end of Jefferson Street, established in the 1930s by the Dolphin Club and the South End Club, longstanding private swimming and rowing organizations still based on Jefferson today. Plenty of benches and grass here make this a pleasant spot for a picnic if the weather's agreeable, while the park's southeast corner is the terminus for the Powell-Hyde cable car line, the city's steepest.

The Streamline Moderne-styled **Aquatic Park Bathhouse**, 900 Beach St at Polk (daily 10am–4pm; free), commands attention directly behind Aquatic Park. Originally opened in 1939, near the tail end of the Art Deco era, its gently sloping corners and clean lines emulate the sleek ocean-liners of the day; throughout the ensuing decades, it served as a public bathhouse, World War II troop centre and, most recently, a maritime museum. After having undergone an extensive refit for its 70th birthday, it's now essentially empty, all the better to step inside to absorb its extensive murals portraying real and mythical sea creatures.

The Marina and around

West of Fisherman's Wharf, the **MARINA** is one of the city's greenest neighbourhoods and enjoys a prime location along a stretch of waterfront that boasts the Golden Gate Bridge and Marin Headlands as a photogenic backdrop. The neighbourhood itself is homogeneously young, white, professional and straight, and its swanky yacht clubs and jogger-laden paths prompt consistent derision from artier locals. Although it was built specifically to celebrate the rebirth of the city after the massive earthquake of 1906, the Marina was the worst casualty of the earthquake in 1989 when tremors tore through fragile landfill and caused extensive damage. The district's commercial centre runs along Chestnut Street between Broderick and Fillmore, with many amenities geared to swinging singles with disposable income.

Just east of the Marina and uphill from Fisherman's Wharf, **Fort Mason** (⊤415/345-7500, ⓦwww.fortmason.org) was a Civil War defence installation whose old buildings in its lower, waterfront section are now occupied by around fifty nonprofit groups, including theatres, galleries and museums. Its more bucolic upper section is rich with the scent of eucalyptus trees and boasts an enormous meadow, hidden picnic areas, excellent bay views and even a hostel housed in a converted barracks (see p.445).

San Francisco's most theatrical piece of architecture lies about a mile west at Marina Boulevard and Baker Street: the **Palace of Fine Arts**, 3301 Lyon St, is not the museum its name suggests, but a huge, freely interpreted classical ruin

Golden Gate Bridge

The orange towers of the **Golden Gate Bridge** – likely the most photographed bridge in the world – are visible from almost every point of elevation in San Francisco. As much an architectural feat as an engineering one, construction on the Golden Gate was begun in January 1933 and completed in May 1937, at which point it rendered the hitherto essential ferry crossing redundant.

Overseen by Chicago-born Joseph Strauss, the final design was in fact the brainchild of his local-born assistant, Irving Morrow. The first massive suspension bridge in the world, with a span of 4200ft, it ranked until 1959 as the world's longest; it was designed to withstand winds of up to a hundred miles an hour and swing as much as 27 feet (and sag as many as ten) in high winds. It's only been closed for weather three times, most recently one day in 1983 when 75mph gusts blew through the channel.

Handsome on a clear day, the bridge takes on an eerie quality when the thick white fogs pour in and hide it almost completely. Interestingly, its ruddy colour was originally intended as a temporary undercoat before the grey topcoat was applied; locals liked it so much, however, that the bridge has remained swathed in "international orange" ever since – and it takes more than five thousand gallons of paint annually to keep it that way.

You can either drive, bike or walk across; the **toll** is collected from southbound drivers only and is $6 per car. The walk across its 1.7-mile span, however gusty, offers the best opportunity to take in the bridge's enormous size and absorb the views of the city in one direction and the Marin Headlands in the other.

designed by Bernard Maybeck that anyone can wander around. It was erected for the Panama Pacific International Exhibition in 1915; when all the other buildings were torn down, the palace was saved simply because locals thought it too beautiful to destroy. Unfortunately, since it was built of wood, plaster and burlap, it crumbled with dignity until the late 1950s when a wealthy resident put up money for the structure to be recast in reinforced concrete. To a modern eye, the palace is a moody and mournfully sentimental piece of Victoriana, complete with weeping figures on the colonnade by sculptor Ulric Ellerhusen, said to represent the melancholy of life without art. Next door, the **Exploratorium**, 3601 Lyon St at Baker, is the best kids' museum in San Francisco (Tues–Sun 10am–5pm; $15, kids $10–12, free first Wed of month; ℡415/561-0360, ⓦwww.exploratorium .edu), with hundreds of hands-on exhibits, including the excellent Tactile Dome (reservations essential; $20 includes museum admission; ℡415/561-0362) – a complete sensory-deprivation space explored on hands and knees that's huge fun for anyone not claustrophobic.

From here, the waterfront stretches west along **Crissy Field**, a former military airfield now popular with picnickers who come to enjoy some of the city's best views of the Golden Gate Bridge (see box above); along with the Embarcadero and Golden Gate Park, it's one of the most pleasant places in the city for a stroll or run. At the field's western edge is the **Warming Hut** (℡415/561-3040; daily 9am–5pm), an old army shed turned café and bookstore where you can recharge with a coffee and a sandwich before pressing on to the base of the Golden Gate Bridge. Here you'll find **Fort Point National Historic Site** (Thurs–Mon 10am–5pm; free; ℡415/556-1693, ⓦwww.nps.gov/fopo), a brick fortress built in the 1850s on the initial landing place of the city's first Spanish settlers. It was to have been demolished to make way for the Golden Gate, but the clever design of the bridge's southern approach – note the additional arch overhead – left it intact. It's a dramatic site with surf pounding away beneath the great span of the bridge high above, a view made famous by Kim Novak's near-fatal leap into the bay in Alfred Hitchcock's *Vertigo*.

Cow Hollow

A few blocks inland from the Marina, south of Lombard Street, **Cow Hollow** was originally a small valley of pastures and dairies in the post-Gold Rush years. The area languished until the 1950s, when problems with open sewage and complaints from neighbours on prestigious Pacific Heights about the smell of the cows allowed enterprising merchants to transform the area. The gorgeous old Victorian houses have since been refitted, especially around Filbert and Green streets, and the stretch of Union Street between Van Ness Avenue and Divisadero Street now holds one of the city's densest concentrations of upmarket boutiques. The district is constantly alive with neighbourhood shoppers and its leafy streets and dearth of tourist sights is what keeps it appealing.

Pacific Heights and around

Perched between Cow Hollow and Japantown, wealthy **PACIFIC HEIGHTS** is home to some of the city's most monumental Victorian piles and stone mansions – a millionaires' ghetto poised around two windswept parks. The lavishly proportioned houses that cling atop these hills today are the chosen domains of local business magnates and the odd bestselling novelist, such as Danielle Steel, who lives in one of the largest houses in the city.

Pacific Heights is neatly divided by north–south **Fillmore Street**, another upscale shopping and dining corridor in the vein of Cow Hollow's Union Street. To its west lies **Alta Plaza Park**, at Clay and Steiner streets, where local dog-walkers earn their keep by exercising pampered pooches; here you'll also see many of the large dwellings that have earned the neighbourhood its reputation as a moneyed enclave. East of Fillmore are swanky Art Deco apartment buildings and, facing the cypress-dotted peak of **Lafayette Park**, several more outsize homes, the most notable of which is the **Spreckels Mansion**, 2080 Washington St at Octavia. This gaudily decadent white-stone palace was constructed for sugar magnate Adolph Spreckels and his wayward wife, Alma, a former nude model who posed for the statue at the centre of Union Square (see p.450); these days, she's mainly remembered for being Auguste Rodin's first US patron and filling the local art museum she built, the California Palace of the Legion of Honor (see p.476), with her spectacular collection of his work. The home she shared with her husband is now owned by romance pulpist Steel, who pumped a fortune into the structure's restoration and upkeep.

For admission to a Pacific Heights home, however, you'll have to head two blocks east to the ornate **Haas–Lilienthal House** at 2007 Franklin St at Washington (tours every 20–30min, Wed & Sat noon–3pm, Sun 11am–4pm; $8; ⓣ415/441-3004, ⓦwww.sfheritage.org). This double-sized Queen Anne Victorian was built by wealthy merchant William Haas and the talky, one-hour

---

Victorian architecture

Constructed from redwood culled from the Marin Headlands across the Golden Gate, San Francisco's **Victorians** enjoyed their greatest popularity in the late nineteenth century, preferred by homeowners who could use "signature details" in crafting the facade to differentiate their house from others. This ostentation came at a price: unlike many of the stone-built homes, the earthquake and fire of 1906 easily destroyed most of the city's grandest Victorians, and the axe-ravaged hillsides of Marin County made replacing them difficult. Also, the trend after 1906 eschewed embellishment, instead ushering in an era of muted stone or stucco designs still seen around town today.

tours are more illuminating about his family's day-to-day life than the architecture of the building. Even so, the place is a grand symbol of old wealth, with intricate wooden towers outside and Tiffany art-glass and stencilled leather panelling inside.

Japantown

Those looking to satisfy a craving for a steaming bowl of ramen or Hello Kitty contraband can push south along Fillmore and into **Japantown**, a once-thriving neighbourhood that never recovered from World War II, when its entire community was hauled off to internment camps. Although a small handful of the district's shops have roots in the early 1900s, the Japantown of today is essentially an unattractive, c.1968 indoor shopping complex with an eastern flavour – the Japan Center – around which only a small percentage of San Francisco's Japanese-Americans now live. Its one notable sight is the 100ft-tall **Peace Pagoda**, standing in the central plaza like a stack of poured-concrete space-age mushrooms. Nearby is the excellent **Kabuki Hot Springs**, 1750 Geary Blvd at Fillmore (daily 10am–9.45pm; $22 weekdays, $25 weekends; ☎415/922-6000, ⓦwww.kabukisprings.com), an island of respite where the communal baths, saunas and steam rooms alternate days for men and women, with Tuesday set aside for co-ed bathing.

South of Market, the Tenderloin and Civic Center

While San Francisco neighbourhoods such as Cow Hollow can seem like an urban utopia, the city's central districts, the adjoining **Tenderloin** and **Civic Center**, reveal harsher realities. Particularly in the Tenderloin, the homeless and disaffected are very much in evidence, their constant presence in the shadow of City Hall a reminder of societal and governmental failures. In contrast, once-derelict **South of Market** has taken a surprising upswing in the last two decades, thanks in part to internet start-up companies attracted to the district's lower rents. When the dot-com crash came in the early 2000s, the techies fled and the neighbourhood backslid into griminess, although these days it's reviving once more – at night it booms with the muffled reverberations of dance clubs and slick wine bars. As well, **Yerba Buena Gardens**, a museum and entertainment complex nearer to Downtown, draws plenty of visitors, as does the baseball park along the shore to the east, beautifully integrated as it is into the city's waterfront.

South of Market

The distinctly urban district **SOMA** – **S**outh **o**f **Ma**rket Street – stretches diagonally from the Mission in the southwest to the waterfront in the northeast. While the western sections have traditionally been working-class, it's ironic, given the area's gritty era up until the early 1990s, that waterfront **Rincon Hill** and South Park were home to the first of the city's banking elite. By the 1870s, they were drawn away to Nob Hill by the newly invented cable car and within thirty years South of Market had been turned over to industrial development and warehouses. The poorer community that remained was largely driven out by fires following the 1906 earthquake and Rincon Hill was eventually flattened to make way for the new Bay Bridge in the 1930s. Despite the neighbourhood's new affluence – evinced by scores of high-rise residences – there are still areas that are downright dangerous, the most notorious being Sixth Street between Market and Mission.

A block inland from the waterfront is the **Rincon Center**, located at 101 Spear St and Mission. Constructed in 1939 as a postal centre, its smooth and imposing lines, outer simplicity and ornamented interior make it a fine example of Depression Moderne architecture. Its lobby is lavishly decorated with murals about California history, the largest commission ever by the WPA, painted by Russian expat artist Anton Refregier in 1941. Another noteworthy nearby attraction is the **California Historical Society**, 678 Mission St at Second (Wed–Sat noon–4.30pm; $3; ℡415/357-1848, ⓦwww.californiahistoricalsociety.org), a tiny, offbeat gem that showcases ephemera, maps and photographs from the state's history; its collection is especially strong on the cultural and political fallout from early Spanish settlement.

Yerba Buena Gardens and surrounding museums

An indication of how hard San Francisco has tried to spiff up the neighbourhood, **Yerba Buena Gardens** (daily dawn–10pm; free; ⓦwww.yerbabuenagardens.org) boasts inviting lawns and benches that are often packed with office workers during lunchtime on warm weekdays. Look for the 50ft granite waterfall memorial to Martin Luther King Jr, inscribed with extracts from his speeches, and on the terrace above it, the Sister Cities garden which features flora from each of the thirteen cities worldwide that are twinned with San Francisco – look for camellias from Shanghai and cyclamen from Haifa, among others.

Just east of the Gardens but on the same block stands **Yerba Buena Center for the Arts**, 701 Mission St at Third (galleries Thurs & Fri 2–8pm, Sat noon–8pm, Sun noon–6pm; $7, free first Tues of month; ℡415/978-2700, ⓦwww.ybca.org), initially conceived as a forum for community art projects but now expanded to host international touring exhibitions and performances in its two main spaces. The small second-floor screening room shows works by local experimental filmmakers, as well as themed programmes of cult and underground films – check the website for a schedule of upcoming screenings.

Opposite Yerba Buena across Third Street is one of the Bay Area's landmark museums: the **SF Museum of Modern Art** (SFMoMA) at 151 3rd St (Thurs 10am–8.45pm, Fri–Tues 10am–5.45pm, closed Wed; $18.00, free first Tues of every month, half-price Thurs 6–8.45pm; ℡415/357-4000, ⓦwww.sfmoma.org). A striking structure designed by Swiss architect Mario Botta, SFMoMA vies to be the West Coast's premier exhibition space, regularly hosting touring shows from New York and Europe while steadily assembling a collection worthy of its superlative housing; a sizeable expansion is expected to be completed by 2016. Head to the upper floors for temporary exhibits, and make sure to stop by the fine outdoor sculpture garden on the fourth floor. The best permanent holdings are of the **California school**, with works by Richard Diebenkorn and others, plus a notable collection of **abstract expressionist** works by Mark Rothko, Jackson Pollock and Robert Rauschenberg. Whatever the quality of work within, the building itself threatens to steal the show with a huge central skylight and a slatted, vertigo-inducing metal catwalk connecting the upper galleries.

Also nearby is the **Museum of the African Diaspora**, 685 Mission St at Third (Wed–Sat 11am–6pm, closed Sun–Tues; $10; ℡415/358-7200, ⓦwww.moadsf.org), which spotlights traditional African art, work inspired by the horrors of slavery and modern pieces in a range of media. One block away, you'll see a striking, askew blue cube: the atrium gallery attached to the **Contemporary Jewish Museum of San Francisco**, 736 Mission St (Thurs 1–8pm, Fri–Tues 11am–5pm, closed Wed; $10; ℡415/655-7800, ⓦwww.thecjm.org). The museum has no permanent collection; instead, it hosts smartly curated exhibitions spanning Jewish history and culture, such as retrospectives of Gertrude Stein and *Shrek* creator William Steig.

South Park and around

Walking further south along unscenic Third Street might not seem to promise much, but hidden between Bryant and Brannan streets is the surprising sanctuary of **South Park**, a picturesque European-style common. The park is a nexus of the city's multimedia community, and locals have been able to gauge the health of the industry by the number of office workers eating lunch in the park. Its shops and cafés can be on the pricey side, but it's still an extremely pleasant place to get a meal or lounge for the afternoon.

Its name may not be pretty, but **AT&T Park**, the San Francisco Giants' baseball park south of South Park, is one of the finest venues of its kind in the country. Brilliantly sited along the water in one of the sunniest parts of town, its outfield opens onto the bay, with concession stands featuring local microbrews and the ballpark's signature garlic fries. The Giants' season stretches from April to September (and occasionally into October); for information on catching a game, see p.45.

If you just want to see the ballpark, terrific **tours** leave from the Giants Dugout Store on the Third Street side of the ballpark (daily, except when day games are scheduled, 10.30am & 12.30pm; $12.50; ☏415/972-2400, ⓦwww.sfgiants.com). You'll not only get to sit in the padded dugout and wander on the turf, but you'll also be able to avail yourself of superb views out across the city to the Bay Bridge from the ballpark's upper level.

The Tenderloin

The **TENDERLOIN**, sandwiched on the north side of Market Street between Civic Center and heavily touristed Union Square, is one of the poorest and most notorious areas in San Francisco. This gritty, uninviting area remains a blemish on the heart of the city, though you should be safe as long as you keep your wits about you, exercise extra caution after dark and don't mind vagrants asking you for money.

The area's **oddball name** has never been definitively explained. One tale is that nineteenth-century police were rewarded with choice cuts of steak for serving a particularly perilous tour of duty here. A less flattering version is that, thanks to the constant bribes they collected from the gambling houses and brothels, those same policemen were able to dine in the city's finest restaurants. Yet others say that the name is based on the district's shank shape or even its notoriety for flesh-flashing brothels; whatever the answer, it's always been the seediest part of town.

Recent waves of South and Southeast Asian immigrants have begun transforming the neighbourhood, establishing numerous spots for a cheap bowl of curry or Vietnamese *pho*. If you're not too busy hurrying to your destination, there are a few sights worth seeing tucked into its corners, the best of which is **Glide Memorial Church** at 330 Ellis St at Taylor (☏415/674-6000, ⓦwww.glide.org). The church provides a wide range of social services for the neighbourhood's downtrodden, but it's best known for its rollicking, ninety-minute Sunday services, which attract a gloriously diverse crowd ranging from pious locals to drag queens (Sun 9am & 11am). Be sure to arrive at least an hour ahead if you want a seat in the main church – the overflow usually has to make do with watching the proceedings via closed-captioned television in a separate room nearby.

Along the western edge of the Tenderloin, on Polk Street between O'Farrell and California streets, lies **Polk Gulch**, a dodgy corridor packed with lively bars that's also a congregating point for the city's transgender community and a hub for the flesh trade. The intersection of O'Farrell and Polk is home to a neighbourhood landmark of sorts, the raunchy strip club known as **Mitchell Brothers O'Farrell Theatre** (Mon–Thurs 12.30pm–1.30am, Fri & Sat 12.30pm–2.30am, Sun 6.30pm–1.30am; $20 before 7pm and all hours Sun, $40 after 7pm;

415/776-6686, ⓦwww.ofarrell.com). The Mitchell boys achieved considerable notoriety in the 1970s when they persuaded a young Ivory Snow soap model named Marilyn Chambers to star in their porn film *Behind the Green Door*, which they debuted at the Cannes Film Festival. Just as the pair eventually slipped back into obscurity, they made a tragic return to tabloid fame when Jim Mitchell shot and killed his brother Artie in 1991.

Civic Center and around

To the immediate southwest of the grubby Tenderloin stands San Francisco's grandest architectural gesture: the complex of Beaux Arts buildings known as the **CIVIC CENTER**. This cluster was the brainchild of brilliant urban planner Daniel Burnham – even before the calamities of 1906, he proposed levelling San Francisco and building a grand civic plaza, extensive subways and boulevard-like traffic arteries fanning out like spokes across the city. Unfortunately, after the earthquake, the city was choked in bureaucracy and his plan was heavily diluted until only the civic plaza was approved. Even then, it wasn't finished until several years after his death. Despite Burnham's beliefs that grand architectural answers would help remedy social inequities, certain locals think today's Civic Center is simply an extension of the Tenderloin with bigger, more attractive buildings.

Most people arrive via the Civic Center Muni and BART station at the corner of Market and Leavenworth streets, where they're immediately disgorged into mostly unappealing **United Nations Plaza**, built to commemorate the founding of the UN here in 1945 – look for the UN Charter etched on a black stone shard. The space is filled with fountains, homeless and little else, so unless it's filled with vendors participating in the **Heart of the City Farmers' Market** (Sun 7am–5pm, Wed 7am–5.30pm; ⓦwww.hocfarmersmarket.org), there's not much reason to dawdle here.

The first building you're likely to see is the **San Francisco Public Library**, 100 Larkin St at Grove (Mon & Sat 10am–6pm, Tues–Thurs 9am–8pm, Fri noon–6pm, Sun noon–5pm; free; ☎415/557-4400, ⓦwww.sfpl.org), which moved to this airy, custom-built space fifteen years ago from its original site across the street, now the Asian Art Museum (see below). The inviting building contains the James C. Hormel Gay and Lesbian Center (named in honour of the gay activist and meat magnate), the first of its kind in the nation, topped by a dome with a mural depicting leading figures in gay rights and literary movements.

Adjacent stands the **Asian Art Museum**, 200 Larkin St at McAllister (Tues, Wed, Fri–Sun 10am–5pm, Thurs 10am–9pm; $12, $5 after 5pm Thurs, free first Tues of month; ☎415/581-3500, ⓦwww.asianart.org), relocated from its original, earthquake-crippled quarters next to the M.H. de Young Museum in Golden Gate Park (see p.473). The building conversion was masterminded by Gae Aulenti, the same woman who shored up the fabulous Musée d'Orsay in Paris from a dingy old train station; here, Aulenti opened the musty, bookstack-crammed interior and created a welcoming space ideal for the massive collection on show. With more than ten thousand paintings, sculptures, ceramics and textiles from all over Asia, this museum is almost overwhelming in its size, so it's worth picking up an audio guide to navigate the highlights. The museum's most precious holding is undoubtedly the oldest known Chinese Buddha image, dating back to 338 AD; there's also a superb, well-priced café accessible to both visitors and passers-by.

The spacious, green central plaza in front of these buildings is usually dotted with political protesters, homeless and passers-through; unmissably grand **City Hall** (Mon–Fri 8am–8pm; ☎415/554-4933, ⓦwww.ci.sf.ca.us/cityhall) stands on the other side. After San Francisco's first city hall was destroyed in 1906, a contest with a prize of $25,000 was announced for local architectural firms to design a new building. The winning design was by Bakewell and Brown, former students of the École des Beaux Arts in Paris, who wanted to create a structure inspired by the haughty, gilded dome of Les Invalides there. City Hall cost an astonishing $3.5 million to build, and includes more than ten acres of marble that was shipped west from New England and Italy. It was here in 1978 that conservative ex-Supervisor Dan White crawled through an open window on the mammoth building's north side and assassinated Mayor George Moscone and gay City Supervisor Harvey Milk (see box, p.470). The best way to see City Hall's grand interior is on one of the free **tours** (℡415/554-6139; Mon–Fri 10am, noon & 2pm) – simply show up at the Docent Tour kiosk on the rear side of the main building facing Van Ness Avenue.

Directly behind City Hall on Van Ness are San Francisco's cultural mainstays, the most elegant of which is the **War Memorial Opera House**, where the United Nations Charter was signed in 1945. Today, it's home to both the San Francisco Opera and Ballet and its understated grandeur is in sharp contrast to the giant modernist fishbowl of the **Louise M. Davies Symphony Hall** one block down. Opened in 1980, the latter has some fans in the progressive architecture camp, though the general consensus is that it's an aberration of the otherwise tastefully harmonious scheme of the Civic Center. Both buildings enjoy a healthy patronage and San Francisco's elite gather here regularly; unfortunately, few performances are subsidized, so don't expect budget ticket prices. (For schedule details, see p.492).

Be sure to detour west from here to reach **Hayes Valley**, reborn when the earthquake-damaged freeway that once overshadowed it was demolished in the 1990s. It's much more racially integrated than many of the city's older neighbourhoods; here, sleek boutiques sit alongside earthier remnants of the area's past, although a number of the former seem to encroach with each passing year. Lined with shady trees and cafés, as well as some of the funkiest homeware and clothing stores around, the district's main business strip, Hayes Street, is a fun place to wander aimlessly and browse.

The Mission

San Franciscans often speak of today's **MISSION** district as a "neighbourhood in transition", but the phrase could easily be applied throughout much of its history – the longest of any San Francisco burgh. After California's annexation, the area became home to succeeding waves of immigrants: first Scandinavians, followed by a significant Irish influx, then a sizeable Latin American settlement. Though long heavily Latino, this melting pot is now a destination for local Anglos who head to trendy bars and restaurants – notably along Valencia Street – which jostle for space with old taquerias and grocery stores; rising rents have engendered a certain amount of ill will towards newcomers. Still, at various points in its history, the Mission has been one of the city's richest neighbourhoods and one of its poorest, making this latest transformation another in a long line of facelifts. What doesn't change is the Mission's generally pleasant weather: the mass of Twin Peaks acts as a giant windbreak, and when much of the rest of the city is shrouded in spring and summer fog, the Mission can be bright and (relatively) warm.

The area gets its name from the oldest building in the city, **Misión San Francisco de Asis**, more commonly known as **Mission Dolores**, 3321 16th St at Dolores ($5 donation requested; ℡415/621-8203, ⓦwww.missiondolores.org). Its moniker dates back to the first European camp here, for the Spanish arrived on the Friday before Palm Sunday – the Friday of Sorrows – and finding an ample freshwater supply, decided to pitch their tents here, naming the site *Laguna de los Dolores*. The first mass celebrated at Mission Dolores on June 29, 1776 marks the

THE MISSION &
THE CASTRO

Levi Strauss
Building

Mission
Dolores

Castro
Theater

THE
CASTRO

Dolores
Park

THE
MISSION

Women's
Building

EATING

Bagdad Café	9
Bi-Rite Creamery	16
Bissap Baobab	22
Boogaloos	30
Delfina	18
Dosa	25
El Trébol	34
Foreign Cinema	27
Goood Frikin Chicken	38
Herbivore	24
La Taqueria	36
Luna Park	15
Mitchell's Ice Cream	37
Papalote	35
Ritual Coffee Roasters	26
Samovar Tea Lounge	17
Taqueria Can-cún	20
Tartine	19
Ti Couz	8
Truly Mediterranean	11

ACCOMMODATION

24 Henry	A
Beck's Motor Lodge	B
Elements Hotel	F
Inn on Castro	C
The Inn San Francisco	E
The Parker Guest House	D

NIGHTLIFE

Amnesia	21
The Attic	33
Bruno's	23
Butter	3
The Café	13
Dalva	10
DNA Lounge	2
Doc's Clock	28
The Eagle Tavern	5
Esta Noche	12
Laszlo	27
Latin American Club	30
Lexington Club	20
The Lone Palm	29
Lucky 13	6
Make-Out Room	32
Martuni's	1
Medjool	F
Pilsner Inn	7
Revolution Café	31
Skylark	12
Twin Peaks Tavern	14
Zeitgeist	4

NOE VALLEY

Bernal Heights Park

0   300 yds

official founding of the city, though the community was then known as Yerba Buena. The evolution of San Francisco is reflected in the mission's architecture: the original building, dating from 1782, is squat and relatively spare, while the more prominent basilica next door, built in 1913, is a riot of ornate design. Aside from periodic tour-bus herds, the building can be quite serene, with a stained-glass-lit interior offering a pleasant opportunity to gaze into the city's long-erased past. The backyard cemetery (made famous in Hitchcock's *Vertigo*) holds the graves of the mission's founders, as well as hundreds of "converted" Native Americans. Far removed from the plastic gimmickry of Fisherman's Wharf, this is one of the city's best historical icons.

A short walk from the mission down stately, palm-tree-lined Dolores Street, one of the most attractive stretches of asphalt in the city, brings you to the sunbather-covered slopes of **Dolores Park**. An immensely popular gathering spot for all walks of neighbourhood life, its southwest corner transforms on weekends into "Dolores Beach", where members of the Castro gay community come to bronze their gym-toned muscles (if the sun's out). As you head east into the heart of the neighbourhood, you'll hit **Valencia Street**, among the city's best shopping and dining strips, packed with boutiques, thrift stores, chic restaurants and, of course, several taquerías; browsing and eating your way through this strip between 16th and 24th streets can be one of San Francisco's finest delights. At its northern end is the original **Levi Strauss factory building**, 250 Valencia St (now a school), a huge lemon-yellow structure set back from the road. While the jeans Levi's makes today bear only a remote resemblance to the original rugged item invented during the Gold Rush, they have outlasted countless trends and the company's flagship store is now a fixture of Union Square.

If Valencia Street is the hipster heart of the Mission, then **Mission Street**, one city block east, is the commercial hub of the **Latino community**, lined with numerous produce and meat markets, as well as retailers selling a virtually identical stock of clothing and kitschy religious items; there's certainly no shortage of taquerías here, either. It's mostly untouched by the gentrification that has bled into other areas of the district – while there are a few relatively new bars and restaurants scattered throughout, this strip still primarily caters to the needs of local Latino families.

The hundreds of **murals** around the Mission underscore a strong sense of community pride and Hispanic heritage. The greatest concentration of work can be found on **Balmy Alley**, an unassuming back way between Treat and Harrison streets in the neighbourhood's southern section, where's there barely an inch of wall unadorned. The murals here are painted on wooden fences, rather than stucco walls, and are regularly refreshed and replaced. The project began during a small community-organizing event in the 1970s, but the tiny street has become the spiritual centre of a burgeoning Latino arts movement that has grown out of both the US civil rights struggle and pro-democracy movements in South America. Frankly, many of the murals are more heartfelt than they are either skilled or beautiful; it's worth stopping by for a peek, although the heavy-handed political imagery can be wearying. For an informed tour of the artwork, contact **Precita Eyes Mural Arts and Visitors Center**, 2981 24th St at Harrison (tours Sat & Sun 11am and 1.30pm; $12–15; ⊤415/285-2287, ⊛www.precitaeyes.org), which has sponsored most of the paintings since its founding in 1971; the organization also sells maps of the neighbourhood's murals ($5).

The Castro and Twin Peaks

Directly west of the Mission, and gentrified by the city's gay community during the 1970s as a primarily residential quarter, the **CASTRO** was ground zero for the bacchanalian atmosphere that prevailed in San Francisco's gay culture during that decade. However, the assassination of gay City Supervisor Harvey Milk in 1978 (see box, p.470) and the onset of the AIDS epidemic motivated many in the community to focus their energies on political organizing instead of the wild life. As a result, the community now finds itself increasingly wealthy, politically influential and mellowed, adopting the self-consciously enlightened demeanour of what is probably the world's most prominent gay community. But with this

The assassination of Harvey Milk

In 1977, eight years after New York's Stonewall riots brought gay political activism into the spotlight, Castro camera-shop owner **Harvey Milk** won election as San Francisco's first openly gay supervisor (or councillor), and quickly became one of the most prominent gay officials in the country. Milk was a celebrated figure for the city's gay community, nicknamed the "Mayor of Castro Street", so it came as a horrifying shock when, just the following year, former Supervisor **Dan White** snuck into City Hall and shot both Milk and Mayor George Moscone dead.

White was an ex-cop who had resigned from the board, claiming he couldn't live on the small salary. In fact, he was angered that the liberal policies of Moscone and Milk didn't accord with his conservative views; a staunch Catholic, White saw himself as a spokesman for San Francisco's many blue-collar Irish families and, as an ex-policeman, the defender of the family values he believed gay rights were damaging. During his 1979 trial, White's attorneys claimed that harmful additives in his junk food-laden diet had driven him temporarily insane – a plea which came to be known as the infamous **"Twinkie defense"** (Twinkies being synthetic-cream cakes) – and was sentenced to five years' imprisonment for manslaughter. The gay community exploded when the news of White's light sentence was announced, and the "White Night" riots that followed were among the most violent San Francisco has ever witnessed, as protesters stormed City Hall, turning over and burning police cars as they went. White was released from prison in 1985 and moved to Los Angeles, where he committed suicide shortly after. In a happier coda, current State Assemblyman Tom Ammiano, a former stand-up comedian who has said that he found the courage to publicly come out as gay through Milk's activism, has figured prominently in the city's political climate since the 1990s, narrowly missing a mayoral victory in 1999.

comfort has come a certain conservatism, and while activists argue that residents must still lead the fight on human-rights issues such as AIDS funding and legal recognition of gay couples, many in the area seem increasingly concerned about more immediate quality-of-life issues such as keeping chain stores out.

The best way to while away an afternoon or evening here is to simply wander its sloping streets. The heart of the district, along **Castro Street**, is filled with stores, restaurants and bars all proudly flying the rainbow flag, and it's usually packed with people whatever the time of day; it's especially vibrant on a Sunday afternoon, full of men strolling, cruising and sipping coffee on the sidewalk. If you're lucky, you might spot one of the **Sisters of Perpetual Indulgence**, volunteers who dress as white-faced nuns to promote safe-sex and HIV awareness in a camp parody of Catholic pageantry. If the crowds of people are too much, head for the neighbourhood's side streets, scrupulously manicured and lined with neat rows of brightly painted Victorians.

Back on the main drag, the **Castro Theatre**, 429 Castro St (℡415/621-6120, Ⓦwww.thecastrotheatre.com), with its lovely Art Deco neon sign rising high above the street, is a landmark that shines brightly in a neighbourhood where people, not places, are the star attractions. Screening a well-curated schedule of classic film revivals and unusual premieres, the unofficial "Castro Cathedral" manages to find quality cinema that's more than a match for the theatre itself, a stunning example of the Mediterranean Revival style. Its foamy balconies, wall-mounted busts of heroic figures and massive ceiling ornamentation lend an air of affirmed glamour, though you'll have to come for a movie showing to get in.

After leaving the Castro, make an effort to ascend **TWIN PEAKS**, about a mile and a half uphill along Market Street from its intersection with Castro Street. The highest point in the city, Twin Peaks offers a terrific view of the San Francisco

Peninsula; during the day, busloads of tourists arrive to point their cameras, while in summer crowds often build up waiting (often futilely) for the fog to lift. Instead, try visiting on a clear night to pick out landmarks along either side of the shimmering artery of Market Street.

Haight-Ashbury

Two miles west of the city's Downtown, **HAIGHT–ASHBURY** lent its name to an entire era, receiving in return a fame on which it has traded mercilessly ever since. Originally part of the Western Addition (see p.473), the neighbourhood was unofficially carved off following the widespread publication of a picture of the Grateful Dead posing at the sign denoting the intersection of Haight and Ashbury

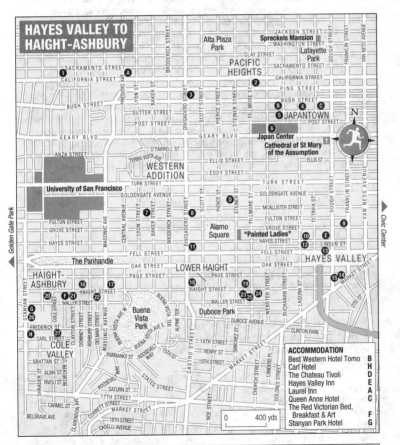

EATING				NIGHTLIFE			
Askew Grill	21	Jardinière	9	Mifune	6	The Alembic	20	Place Pigalle	10
Benkyodo	5	Kate's Kitchen	24	Nopa	11	Aub Zam Zam	F	Toronado	23
Blue Bottle Coffee	13	Kiss Sushi	4	Rosamunde		Hotel Biron	15	Trax	22
Burgermeister	27	The Little Chihuahua	18	Sausage Grill	23	Kezar Pub	26		
Frankie's Bohemian Café	3	Little Star Pizza	8	Royal Ground Coffee	2	Mad Dog in			
Frjtz	12	Magnolia Gastropub		Sociale	1	the Fog	19		
Green Chile Kitchen	7	and Brewery	17	Thep Phanom	25	Noc Noc	23		
		Massawa	16	Zuni	14				

ACCOMMODATION

Best Western Hotel Tomo	B
Carl Hotel	H
The Chateau Tivoli	D
Hayes Valley Inn	E
Laurel Inn	A
Queen Anne Hotel	C
The Red Victorian Bed, Breakfast & Art	F
Stanyan Park Hotel	G

Hippies

The first **hippies** were an offshoot of the Beats, many of whom had moved out of their increasingly expensive North Beach flats to take advantage of the low rents and large spaces in the Victorian houses in what became known as the Haight-Ashbury. The post-Beat bohemia that subsequently began to develop here in the early 1960s was initially a small affair, involving drug use and the embrace of Eastern religion and philosophy, together with a marked anti-American political stance and a desire for world peace. Where Beat philosophy had emphasized self-indulgence, the hippies, on the face of it at least, attempted to be more embracing, focusing on self-coined concepts such as "universal truth" and "cosmic awareness". Naturally it took a few big names to get the ball rolling, and characters like **Ken Kesey** and his Merry Prank-sters soon set a precedent of wild living, challenging authority and dropping out (as they saw it) of the established norms of society. Drugs were particularly important, and considered an integral part of the movement. **LSD** especially, the affects of which were just being discovered and which at the time was not actually illegal, was claimed as an avant-garde art form. It was pumped out in private laboratories and distributed by Timothy Leary and his network of supporters with a prescription – "Turn on, tune in, drop out" – that galvanized a generation into inactivity.

Before long, life in the Haight began to take on a theatrical quality: Pop Art found mass appeal, light shows became legion, fashion turned colourfully flamboyant, and the Grateful Dead, Jefferson Airplane and Janis Joplin all made international names for themselves. Backed by the business weight of irascible local promoter Bill Graham, San Francisco's **psychedelic music** scene became a genuine force nation-wide and it wasn't long before kids from all over America started turning up in Haight-Ashbury for the free food, free drugs and free love. In no time, "money" became a dirty word, the hip became "heads" and the rest of the world were "straights".

Among other illustrious tenants of the Haight in the 1960s, writer Kenneth Rexroth (see p.473) hosted a popular radio show and wrote for the San Francisco Examiner. Hunter S. Thompson, too, spent time here researching and writing his book *Hell's Angels*, becoming instantly unpopular with neighbours for inviting his biker subjects round his apartment on Parnassus Street for noisy, long and occasionally dangerous drinking and drug-taking sessions.

Things inevitably turned sour towards the end of the decade, but during the heady days of the massive "be-in" in Golden Gate Park in 1966 and the so-called **Summer of Love** the following year, the area became home to no less than 75,000 transitory pilgrims who saw it as the headquarters of alternative culture.

streets. Despite the ardent nostalgia of some locals, "the Haight" (as locals invariably call it) has changed dramatically since it emerged in the 1960s as the focus of that decade's countercultural scene; even with its attractive strips of Edwardian and Victorian buildings, today's version feels like a tie-dyed theme park of sorts, full of young and itinerant homeless, shops offering hippie-themed souvenirs and secondhand vintage clothes, and a confrontational vibe hanging in the air that sullies the district's love-is-all sloganeering. It's not an area completely without charms, however: the neighbourhood claims some excellent restaurants and fun bars (see p.482), as well as one of the finest independent music retailers in the US, massive **Amoeba Music** (see p.498), housed in an old bowling alley.

Divisadero Street divides the district in half, with the **Upper Haight** stretching west to Golden Gate Park and the **Lower Haight** running east to Buchanan Street. Long an African-American neighbourhood, the Lower Haight was transformed in the 1990s into a centre of the city's DJ culture, and though the Mission has stolen much of the Lower Haight's trend-hopping spotlight since, the neighbourhood remains torn between its older and newer identities – a conflict that has occasionally led to tensions. It's best to exercise caution at night, particularly in the vicinity of Webster Street.

In much the same way that the Lower Haight tends to be overshadowed by its internationally known sibling up the hill, former resident **Kenneth Rexroth** (1905–82) has largely been overshadowed by the writers he inspired. As a poet, novelist and translator of Chinese literature, Rexroth lived a wildly adventurous life that served as an inspiration for Jack Kerouac and crew. While not open to the public, you can take a walk past Rexroth's old apartment at 250 Scott St, a place where several of the early Beats crashed upon first arriving in San Francisco.

Continuing uphill back towards the Upper Haight will bring you to **Buena Vista Park**, a mountainous forest full of Monterey pines and other local foliage. Enjoyed by dog walkers in the daylight hours, come nightfall the park plays host to much sex-in-the-shrubbery, so keep your wits about you should you pass through after dark. Continuing westward as you navigate the increasing numbers of panhandlers along Haight Street, the **Grateful Dead's former house**, 710 Ashbury at Haight, was once ground zero for the counterculture. A 1967 drug bust only added to the band's myth, which survived countless tours and a rotating cast of keyboard players; even the 1995 death of guitarist Jerry Garcia has done little to quell fans' devotion.

The Panhandle and Western Addition

Two blocks north of Haight Street, the **PANHANDLE** is a rivulet of greenery that drifts like a tributary into Golden Gate Park to the west. Though its grass is noticeably scraggly these days, this was once a ritzy thoroughfare catering to horse-drawn carriages, and the lovely houses flanking it speak of wealthier times; the area north of the Panhandle now even boasts a trendy nickname, **NoPa** (**No**rth of **Pa**nhandle).

Spreading north and east of the Haight, the sizeable **WESTERN ADDITION** is one of the central city's few predominantly black neighbourhoods – somewhat dangerous near its public housing and, but for one standout sight, certainly not tourist territory. The nadir for the neighbourhood came in the wake of World War II, when the dual forces of urban renewal and blunderheaded civic planner **Justin Herman** – honoured with a public park along the Embarcadero (see p.458) – led to the demolishing of a chunk of the area's precious Victorian housing, eventually replaced with acres of monolithic concrete apartment blocks; sadly, few vestiges of the Western Addition's history or character remain.

One truly grand exception is a small area around **Alamo Square**, a hilltop park surrounded by Hayes, Scott, Fulton and Steiner streets, just uphill from the Lower Haight. A staple of every tour-bus company in town, the park's southeast slope is home to small flocks of amateur photographers eager to snap a picture of the **"Painted Ladies"**. These seven Victorian houses, originally built in 1894 and colourfully and attractively restored, have been postcard subjects for years; the largest of the lot, on the corner of Steiner and Grove streets, was placed on the market for $4 million in 2010. Even if you're without a camera, it's still worth a visit for picnicking opportunities and brilliant eastward **views** that, on a clear day, stretch across the city, the bay and beyond.

Golden Gate Park

Unlike most American cities, San Francisco is not short on green space, and **GOLDEN GATE PARK** is its largest, a civic treasure simultaneously rich with museums and quiet natural environments that would require days to fully explore. The 1017-acre park offers welcome respite to city residents, who flood its meadows, forests, lakesides and plazas at every opportunity.

Spreading three miles west from the Haight as far as the shore of the Pacific, Golden Gate Park was designed in 1871 by Park Commissioner William Hall in the style of Frederick Law Olmsted, the man behind Central Park in New York; it was ultimately constructed – on what was then an area of wild sand dunes buffeted by the sea's spray – with the help of a dike to protect the western side from the sea. Inconveniently, the area's famous fog fails to stick to any sort of daily schedule or pattern and a late morning gripped in the clutch of grey skies can turn into a sunny afternoon by lunchtime – and vice versa – so be sure to dress in layers. Although the original planners intended to keep the park free of buildings, that proved impossible and its eastern half is now dotted with striking structures holding must-see sights such as the California Academy of Sciences and the Conservatory of Flowers. Most date from the 1894 California Midwinter Exposition, the first World's Fair held in California, which was designed as a recession-busting sideshow by local newspaperman M.H. de Young; it was so successful that de Young was honoured with a permanent museum in his name (see below).

The park's newest star attraction is the hugely popular **California Academy of Sciences** (Mon–Sat 9.30am–5pm, Sun 11am–5pm; $24.95, free third Wed of month; ☎415/379-8000, ⊛www.calacademy.org), whose grass-roofed structure is a high-profile nod towards sustainable building practices. Inside the grand entrance, you'll be immediately struck by the glass-encased **tropical rainforest** consisting of four spherical storeys of humidity-enhanced life, including bat caves and butterflies galore as well as a host of rainforest foliage. Also on-site, the **Steinhart Aquarium** is home to nearly forty thousand water-dependent animals, from African penguins and giant Pacific octopus to stingrays and piranhas, while the **Morrison Planetarium**, housed in a gigantic dome, presents two lively shows on its 75ft projection screen – check the website for times. Also be sure to take the lift up to the **Living Roof**, which includes a variety of native wildflowers and seven grassy hillocks that pay homage to San Francisco's seven major hills.

Across the tree-lined plaza known as the Music Concourse, the **M.H. de Young Museum** (Tues–Thurs, Sat & Sun 9.30am–5.15pm, Fri 9.30am–8.45pm; $10, free first Tues of each month; ☎415/750-3600, ⊛www.thinker.org) was, like the California Academy of Sciences, flashily rebuilt from the ground up in the last decade. It lends almost as much space to major touring shows as to its own varied collection, which wanders through sub-Saharan Africa and the Americas and includes some four hundred works of art from New Guinea. The de Young's acknowledged highlights are its **American paintings** – with more than a thousand on display, they make up one of the best collections of its kind, and include works by Georgia O'Keeffe, Edward Hopper, Thomas Eakins and George Caleb Bingham. But like SFMoMA across town, its structure vies for equal attention, with some locals joking that the angular copper-clad building landed in evergreen Golden Gate Park right out of a sci-fi B-movie. Spend some time here, though, and the interplay between modernist behemoth and outdoor public space becomes apparent, with interior courts filled with the park's trademark ferns. The museum deserves an entire morning, capped by lunch in the excellent *de Young Café*, which has outdoor seating next to a sculpture garden. Finally, don't leave without visiting the ninth-floor observation tower (free) for sweeping views across the park and city.

Next door to the de Young, the equally popular **Japanese Tea Garden** (daily: March–Oct 9am–6pm; Nov–Feb 9am–4.45pm; $5, free daily before 10am; ☎415/666-3232, ⊛www.japaneseteagardensf.com) is a holdout from 1894 and beautifully landscaped by the Hagiwara family, who were also responsible for the invention of the fortune cookie during the Pan-Pacific Exposition of 1915 (despite the prevailing belief that fortune cookies are Chinese). The Hagiwaras looked after the garden until World War II, when, along with all other Japanese-Americans, they were sent to internment camps. The best way to enjoy the garden is to arrive right when it opens for tea and fortune cookies in the teahouse; then, wander among the bridges, statues (including a massive bronze Buddha), footpaths, pools filled with shiny oversized carp, and bonsai and cherry trees before the usual busloads of tourists descend later in the morning.

A ten-minute walk from the museums and Japanese Tea Garden, the whitewashed wooden frame of the delightful **Conservatory of Flowers** (Tues–Sun 10am–4.30pm; $7; ☏415/831-2090, ⓦwww.conservatoryofflowers.org) resembles a Victorian greenhouse. It was manufactured in Ireland for San Jose millionaire James Lick, who died before he could take possession of it; the building was eventually donated and shipped piecemeal to San Francisco in the 1870s. The attractive space is divided into several sections, including a temporary exhibition space, a room filled with Victorian-style potted plants, lowland and highland tropics areas (in the latter, look for the spindly orchids from the Andes) and, best of all, a cool, aquatic-plant room boasting tractor-wheel-sized Victoria water lilies.

Wander south back through the Music Concourse to the **San Francisco Botanical Garden at Strybing Arboretum** (April–Oct 9am–6pm; Nov–March 10am–5pm; $7; ☏415/661-1316, ⓦwww.sfbotanicalgarden.org), with entrances across from the Tea Garden or near Ninth Avenue and Lincoln Way. This 75-acre hideaway is home to more than seven thousand varieties of plants, with miniature gardens focusing on specimens from regions ranging from desert to tropical; especially appealing is the headily scented garden of fragrance, as well as the towering grove of redwoods towards the garden's west end. For a free tour, stop by the bookstore inside the main gate (weekdays 1.30pm, weekends 10.30am & 1.30pm) or the Ninth Avenue entrance (Wed, Fri & Sun 2pm).

Adjacent to the Arboretum's north entrance is the tiny, hedged green space known as the **Shakespeare Garden** (dawn–dusk; free). Centred on an old-fashioned sundial and dotted with benches, it showcases every flower and plant mentioned in Shakespeare's plays and poems, with a metal plaque full of the relevant quotations on a brick wall at the edge of the lawn.

Perhaps the most unusual sight in Golden Gate Park is its **Bison Paddock** (free), where a small herd of the stately, tonne-weighing beasts roam a field north of JFK Drive near 38th Avenue, far from their native land over one thousand miles east of San Francisco. They're fenced in with hefty metal railings and the closest you can get to the grunting giants is in their feeding area at the far west end. At the edge of the park across the Great Highway from Ocean Beach, passing a lush tulip garden below the charming, if oddly incongruous **Windmill** near the park's northwest corner, you'll find the **Beach Chalet** (☏415/386-8439, ⓦwww .beachchalet.com). This two-storey, white-pillared building was designed by Willis Polk and houses a series of 1930s frescoes in its lobby depicting the growth of San Francisco as a city and the creation of Golden Gate Park. It also holds a small visitor centre that provides information about the park's numerous guided walking tours, as well as a pair of lively restaurants that are terrific for late weekend brunches or, on a sunny afternoon, chilling out in the back garden with beers from the on-site brewery.

The Richmond, the Sunset and Ocean Beach

Golden Gate Park is hemmed in by two large, primarily residential neighbour-hoods: the **RICHMOND** to the north and the **SUNSET** to the south. As late as the 1920s, much of what now makes up these two districts remained mile after mile of sand dunes, stretching to the ocean. And while residents of the city's more intensely urban districts might turn up their noses and say that, in terms of liveliness, not much has changed in the decades since, the truth is that both neighbourhoods – the multiethnic Richmond in particular – offer several rewarding oases of activity. More than the tourist-saturated Downtown neighbourhoods, this area is a window into a less-seen side of San Francisco: a comfortable, if at times lethargic, blend of cultures set near the coastline along the city's western edge.

Stretching towards the city's southern border, buffeted by sea breezes and fog, **OCEAN BEACH** seems constantly on the brink of being either washed out or blown into locals' backyards. Aside from a small community of particularly hearty surfers (most notably twang-rock crooner Chris Isaak), the strand is the near-exclusive territory of joggers and dog walkers. Perched precipitously above the northern end of the beach, the original **Cliff House**, 1090 Point Lobos Road (T 415/386-3300, W www.cliffhouse.com), was built in 1863 and became a popular seaside resort for the city's wealthiest families. Twice destroyed by fire, the complex – today primarily restaurants – underwent a radical renovation in the early 2000s to upgrade its rather faded interior. On the lower landing is the **Camera Obscura** (11am–sunset, weather permitting; $2; T 415/750-0415), which uses a rotating mirror – and a trick of light – to give entrants a panoramic view of the surrounding area, which mostly includes epic surf crashing on nearby rocks. Just north of the Cliff House complex and down by the water, you'll find the remains of another bygone amusement: the **Sutro Baths**. This collection of opulent recreational pools, gardens and elegant sculptures, all covered with one hundred thousand feet of stained glass, was sadly destroyed by fire in the 1960s.

The Legion of Honor

The stately **Legion of Honor** (Tues–Sun 9.30am–5.15pm; $10, free first Tues of each month; T 415/750-3600, W www.legionofhonor.org) is one of the most intriguing museums in San Francisco. The building itself, built in 1920 by local patron Alma de Bretteville Spreckels (see p.462), is no less staggering than its hilltop setting far above the Golden Gate. The museum's Rodin holdings are breathtaking in their depth and range, all the way down to a cast of *The Thinker* set dramatically on a pedestal in the centre of the front courtyard; with over eighty pieces on display, it's one of the best collections of its kind in the world. Sadly, the otherwise fine museum is somewhat let down by its lacklustre collection of Old Masters – many of the artworks, including those by Giambologna, Cellini and Cranach, are "attributed to" or from "the workshop of", rather than bona fide masterpieces.

Eating

With an abundance of nearby farms showering the city's farmers' markets with fresh produce, a culture that increasingly emphasizes sustainable food practices and a local population with a sharp proclivity for eating out, it's little wonder that San Francisco is one of the world's elite **restaurant** cities. Its dining scene may be remarkably convivial, but this is a city where people take few things more seriously than food.

Restaurants

San Francisco has long been known for its **fine-dining** restaurant experiences, and more recently for its wealth of low-end marvels such as **taquerias**, **dim sum eateries** and **curry houses**. Indeed, the greatest asset of San Francisco's restaurants is their staggering variety, not only in terms of types of cuisine, but also in price

Late-night eating

While certainly not a late-night eating town like Paris or New York, San Francisco nonetheless possesses a number of restaurants and cafés that cater to nocturnal stomach grumblings. The following establishments are the best of the bunch serving food after 11pm, with neighbourhood and type of food noted.

Bagdad Café Castro, American. See p.481.

Great Eastern Chinatown, Chinese. See p.479.

Grubstake Polk Gulch, American and Portuguese. See p.477.

Magnolia Gastropub and Brewery Haight-Ashbury, California / New American. See p.483.

Osha Thai Tenderloin, Thai. See p.478.

Taqueria Can-cún Mission, Mexican. See p.482.

ranges and overall experiences. Adding to all this is a recent explosion of mobile vendors – chefs behind the wheel of catering trucks serving so-called **street food**, encompassing crepes to barbecue to waffles – that's having a huge effect on how the city eats out, with locals following day-to-day locations and hours of operation of their favourites via websites and Twitter feeds. Check Ⓦ www.sfcartproject .com for further details.

The local slant of cooking, dubbed **California cuisine**, is a development of French nouvelle cooking, preserving the focus on a wide mix of fresh, locally available foods, but widening the scope of influences considerably. The California style's range of dishes is seemingly endless and could include something as light as a cracker-crusted pizza with shrimp and arugula, or a heavier selection like herb-crusted rack of lamb with root-vegetable hash and watercress; many local California-style restaurants also often incorporate a pan-Asian edge to many recipes.

Downtown and around

See map on pp.448–449.

Ananda Fuara 1298 Market St at Larkin, Civic Center ☎415/621-1994. This affordable and popular vegetarian restaurant casts a wide net – a group of four could easily sample meatless dishes spanning the culinary styles of Mexico, the Middle East, the American South and South Asia.

Borobudur 700 Post St at Jones, Tenderloin ☎415/775-1512. Indonesian powerhouse that fuses Indian and Thai influences with often extraordinary results. Don't pass up the *roti prata* (grilled, flaky bread) and curry dipping sauce appetizer. Mains about $10.

Dottie's True Blue Café 522 Jones St at O'Farrell, Tenderloin. An intimate, inexpensive spot that's become immensely popular with locals and visitors. The oversize pastries and breads (don't leave without trying the chilli cornbread), as well as generous platters of breakfast favourites, make it worth your patience. Breakfast and lunch only.

Farmerbrown 25 Mason St at Turk, Tenderloin ☎415/409-3276. Excellent corner spot that uses organic ingredients from California African-American farmers to deliver on its promise of "farm-fresh soul food". All-you-can-eat weekend brunches ($16.50) full of Southern staples pack in crowds, while dinner is a lively affair as well.

Grubstake 1525 Pine St at Polk, Polk Gulch. Its dining counter set in an old railcar, this classic diner dishes out all the American basics (and breakfast all night!); what really sets it apart, however, are all the Portuguese specialities on the menu, including *caldo verde* soup. Open 5pm–4am. Mains $8–15.

Kokkari 200 Jackson St at Front, Jackson Square ☎415/981-0983. This bustling restaurant's Greek influence runs deep, relying as it does on Hellenic staples such as lamb and aubergine. Its huge open fireplace heats two bedazzling dining rooms decorated with oriental rugs and goatskin lampshades. Mains $20–30.

Le Colonial 20 Cosmo Place at Taylor, Union Square ☎415/931-3600. Upscale Vietnamese restaurant with a quiet French influence, boasting lush, 1920s-themed dining quarters decked out with tile floors, palm fronds and ceiling fans. Mains over $30; dinner only.

Millennium *Hotel California*, 580 Geary St at Jones, Theater District ☎415/345-3900. Surprisingly pricey vegetarian standby that takes kitchen creativity to meat-free heights by using obscure ingredients such as *sambal, huitlacoche* and *papazul*. The menu changes frequently, so one night's semolina griddle-cake could be maple-glazed smoked tempeh the next. Mains around $25; dinner only.

Osha Thai 696 Geary St at Jones, Tenderloin. One of several local branches, this stylish Thai noodle shop does the basics right and stays open late (Sun–Thurs until 1am, Fri & Sat until 3am). Almost everything is under $14.

Saigon Sandwich 560 Larkin St at Eddy, Tenderloin. Cupboard-sized, lunch-only shop selling sizeable, made-to-order *banh mi* (Vietnamese sandwiches) for no more than $3.25; ask the hardworking ladies behind the counter to add lashings of fresh carrot and bundles of cilantro. Expect a line out the door every afternoon. Cash only.

Sears' Fine Food 439 Powell St at Post, Union Square. Local old-timers claim *Sears'* signature breakfast dish – 18 little Swedish pancakes for $9.50, eleven thousand of which are made daily – hasn't changed at all over the decades. Amber chairs and tiled flooring add to the ambience.

Shalimar 532 Jones St at O'Farrell, Tenderloin. The chicken tikka masala is the main attraction at this austere South Asian joint, although the lamb saag is just as exceptional (and generous in its portion). Afterwards, expect to smell as if you yourself have been doused in spices and baked in the tandoor oven. Mains under $10.

Tadich Grill 240 California St at Front, Financial District ☏415/391-1849. Specializing in seafood, this Downtown classic has been in business since the Gold Rush; today it's half-diner, half-gentleman's club, with a seasoned group of waiters nearly as stiff as their white jackets. Mains $20 and up.

Embarcadero and Fisherman's Wharf

See map on pp.448–449.

Boudin Bakery & Café Pier 39, Fisherman's Wharf. Café serving some of the finest sourdough around, made using yeast descended from the first batch from Gold Rush times. A variety of cheap salads, sandwiches and sourdough pizzas are available, in addition to the inevitable chowder in a bread bowl.

Gary Danko 800 North Point St at Hyde, Fisher-man's Wharf ☏415/749-2060. Don't let the location put you off – this understated oasis regularly vies for the title of best restaurant in food-obsessed San Francisco. Granted, it's performance food served with a flourish, but it's utterly splurge-worthy. Reserve well ahead. *Prix fixe* menus $68–102; dinner only.

Ghirardelli Ice Cream and Chocolate Caffé 900 North Point St at Larkin, Fisherman's Wharf. This perennially popular, old-fashioned ice-cream parlour is the ideal setting to sample a decadent range of desserts. The sprawling Earthquake Sundae ($19.06, fittingly) is especially gooey – plan to share it with several friends.

Hog Island Oyster Bar 1 Ferry Building, Embarcadero ☏415/391-7117. This outpost of the Tomales Bay (Marin County) farm hosts mollusc devotees who sit elbow to elbow at the wrap-around granite bar; the lists of available oysters, wines and beers are equally impressive. It's $15–17 for six oysters, $50–56 for two dozen. The creamy oyster stew is a perennial hit.

Pier 23 Café Pier 23, Embarcadero ☏415/362-5125. Sit on this roadhouse's heated deck and enjoy casual seafood and sandwiches along with immediate bay views. There's live music most nights, ranging from jazz to reggae and salsa.

Scoma's Pier 47, Fisherman's Wharf ☏415/929-1730. If you can't resist the allure of the tourist-targeting seafood palaces that crowd the Wharf, *Scoma's* is likely your safest choice. Just steel yourself for sky-high prices and be sure to make a reservation, as this is reportedly the highest-volume restaurant west of the Mississippi.

The Slanted Door 1 Ferry Building, Embarcadero ☏415/861-8032. The daily-changing menu at this gorgeously sited, continually buzzing restaurant is light French-Vietnamese. There's a raw bar and several deliciously fragrant chicken dishes available, and the tea list is remarkably diverse. Mains cost around $18–36, and you'd be well advised to either book in advance or find an off-peak time to drop in.

Taylor's Automatic Refresher 1 Ferry Building, Embarcadero. Fancified, yet inexpensive burger stand with an immense alfresco dining area off the Embarcadero pedestrian path that's a major draw on sunny afternoons. Touted burgers, sweet-potato fries and super-thick milkshakes are all made from fresh ingredients.

South of Market

See map on pp.448–449.

Coco500 500 Brannan St at Fourth ☏415/543-2222. Deeply flavourful California-Mediterranean cuisine presented in a chic setting warmed by caramel-and-blue walls adorned with local artwork. Mains $15 and up.

Primo Patio 214 Townsend St at Third. A terrific choice for a unique, budget lunch, where sandwiches, burgers and similarly simple dishes are spiced with a subtle Caribbean twist – try the jerk chicken or blackened snapper. The backyard patio offers a pleasant escape from the industrial surroundings. Lunch only.

Town Hall 342 Howard St at Fremont ☏415/908-3900. An old ship-engine-manufacturing building hosts this roomy, vibrant restaurant, where New Orleans-inspired dishes such as grilled gulf shrimp are tempered by California cuisine's lighter influence. Mains $16–20.

Tu Lan 8 6th St at Market. Cheap, flavourful Vietnamese in a cramped and dingy space on one of the seediest blocks in town – and completely worth the adventure. Should you sit at the sticky counter, you'll be nearly singed by the flames from the stove; just try to avoid looking up at the grubby ceiling.

Yank Sing 49 Stevenson St at First ☏415/541-4949. One of the better (if more expensive) places for dim sum in the city. Though it's routinely packed, the staff can almost always find a spot for you; come early to select from leftfield varieties like snow-pea-shoot dumplings that populate the circulating carts. Brunch/lunch only.

North Beach and Chinatown

See map on pp.448–449.

Café Divine 1600 Stockton St at Union, North Beach ☏415/986-3414. Across from Washington Square, this airy, bistro-inspired café does all three meals. Its menu is casual and often light, and the six varieties of pizzetta ($11–14) are the most popular items here. Inviting outdoor tables line the sidewalks around the corner space.

Café Jacqueline 1454 Grant Ave at Union, North Beach ☏415/981-5565. A romantic, candlelit gourmet experience in an airy dining room that feels like a French country cottage. The menu here is entirely made up of soufflés (all over $20), both savoury and sweet; since every dish is made to order, plan on making an evening of it. Dinner only.

Great Eastern 649 Jackson St at Kearny, Chinatown ☏415/986-2500. Elegant and traditional restaurant serving favourites such as sautéed squab with Chinese broccoli. Open late; mains over $20.

Italian French Bakery 1501 Grant Ave at Union, North Beach. This tiny bakery wafts the enticing smell of freshly baked bread up and down the block. Grab a slice of focaccia, a pastry or a flavoured baguette (rosemary, whole wheat) and enjoy it at one of the window counter stools.

L'Osteria del Forno 519 Columbus Ave at Green, North Beach. This postage-stamp-sized nook is a humble refuge from the gaudy tourist traps right across Columbus Ave. The menu's short and

driven by whatever's freshest at the market, although the eight or so *foccacine* sandwiches (well under $10) are a standby. Reservations aren't taken, so a wait may be inevitable even at off-peak times. Cash only.

Liguria Bakery 1700 Stockton St at Filbert, North Beach. Marvellous old-world bakery with vintage scales and cash registers in its front display windows. Fresh focaccia is the smart order here, and there's no shortage of choices: onion, garlic, rosemary and mushroom, among others. It's best to arrive earlier than later, as it simply closes when the day's goods are sold out. Cash only.

Louie's Dim Sum 1236 Stockton St at Pacific, Chinatown. This tiny shop has glistening, pearly dumplings arranged in vast metal trays and although the variety's limited, they're all cheap and delicious.

Mario's Bohemian Cigar Store Café 566 Columbus Ave at Union, North Beach. Stogies haven't been sold on these premises for ages, but the chunky, home-made focaccia sandwiches and corner location make this area institution a terrific place to grab a cheap bite and absorb the neighbourhood scene – its bar is a great spot for an unpretentious nightcap.

Mee Mee Bakery 1328 Stockton St at Broadway, Chinatown. A little-known Chinatown gem with an on-site fortune-cookie bakery that fills the space with a hot, sweet smell. Closed evenings.

Mo's Grill 1322 Grant Ave at Vallejo, North Beach. This no-frills shop cooks beef over a volcanic rock grill to produce some of San Francisco's best (and chunkiest) hamburgers – for under $10. The house fries are also noteworthy, and good breakfasts are available until mid-afternoon each day.

Pat's Café 2330 Taylor St at Chestnut, North Beach. Eminently inviting breakfast/lunch spot right along the Powell-Mason cable car line. It's bright and airy, but the charming decor can't overshadow the delicious, affordable and occasionally rich food – the peppery home fries and banana granola pancakes are especially recommended.

R&G Lounge 631 Kearny St at Commercial, Chinatown ☏415/982-7877. Behind frosted windows looms this enormous Hong Kong-style restaurant that draws a diverse crowd. The fairly priced dishes (most under $18) are presented family-style and there's a heavy slant towards seafood.

Tommaso's 1042 Kearny St at Pacific, North Beach ☏415/398-9696. Claiming to be the West Coast birthplace of the wood-fired pizza oven, this neighbourhood stalwart hasn't lost a step in popularity since opening in 1935 as Lupo's. And for good reason: the thin-crust pizzas ($20–26 for a

15-inch large) are terrific, while the seven-layer lasagne is wonderfully gooey.

🏃 **Tony's Pizza Napoletana** 1570 Stockton St at Union, North Beach ☎415/835-9888. World Pizza Cup champion Tony Gemignani's corner pizzeria bakes up to six hundred pizzas in several styles daily, from his prized, gossamer-thin-crusted Margherita ($19; only 73 made each day) to an extra-saucy New Jersey version. Service is remarkably attentive, and it's best to sit near the brick oven to watch the chefs in action.

🏃 **Trattoria Contadina** 1800 Mason St at Union, North Beach ☎415/982-5728. Family-owned, warm and charming, with white cloth-swathed tables and photograph-covered walls. The rigatoni with aubergine and smoked mozzarella is a top option and the Powell-Mason cable car will drop you off steps from the front door. Mains under $20.

The Marina, Cow Hollow and Russian Hill

See map on pp.448–449.

Baker Street Bistro 2953 Baker St at Lombard, Cow Hollow ☎415/931-1475. A cramped but charming café with a handful of outdoor tables, where a neighbourhood crowd enjoys simple food served by French staff. The $16.50 *prix fixe* dinner on weeknights (and weekends before 7pm) is a remarkable bargain.

Betelnut 2030 Union St at Buchanan, Cow Hollow ☎415/929-8855. This sceney, jam-packed standby offers well-executed tastes on small plates from a number of Asian cultures. Choose from Malaysian curries, Indonesian chicken, Japanese udon noodles, Singapore prawns, Sri Lankan fish and more; you should be able to get in and out for under $30.

Boboquivari's 1450 Lombard St at Van Ness, Marina ☎415/441-8880. Disregarding the black-and-red striped awnings and the restaurant's namesake, creepy jester over the door, "Bobo's" serves one of San Francisco's most desired cuts of beef, its bone-in filet mignon ($39). If you're thinking of investing, call ahead to ensure the cut will be available. Dinner only.

🏃 **Frascati** 1901 Hyde St at Green, Russian Hill ☎415/928-1406. Vividly romantic, bi-level bistro on a prime corner. Uniquely paired California dishes such as maple-leaf duck breast with herb and huckleberry sauce retain a level of comfort, and the wine list is extensive. Dinner only; mains $20–30.

Greens Building A, Fort Mason Center ☎415/771-6222. San Francisco's original vegetarian restaurant remains popular thanks to its continually inventive menu, picturesque pier setting and airy interior. It's surprisingly casual, given the quality and price of the food. Mains over $20.

Harris' 2100 Van Ness Ave at Pacific, Russian Hill ☎415/673-1888. Proudly old-fashioned and one of the premier steakhouses in the city, with padded chairs, comfy leather booths and thick velvet curtains. There's practically every cut of beef imaginable on the menu – from filet mignon to Kobe ribeye – and all are buttery-sweet and tender. Just be sure to pack your credit card, as steak dinners begin at $39. Dinner only.

Helmand Palace 2424 Van Ness Ave at Green, Russian Hill ☎415/345-0072. The menu at this popular Afghani restaurant is filled with tangy and spicy staples – try the *kaddo* (caramelized pumpkin on a bed of yoghurt) or the *chapandaz* (grilled beef tenderloin). Plenty of vegetarian items are also available. Mains top out around $15; dinner only.

La Folie 2316 Polk St at Green, Russian Hill ☎415/776-5577. Magnificent Provençal food served *sans* attitude or pretension. There are typically several five-course *prix fixe* options ($75–105) to choose from – make a reservation if you fancy a gourmet treat. Dinner only.

Mamacita 2317 Chestnut St at Scott, Marina ☎415/346-8494. Beautifully presented, reasonably priced dishes with an emphasis on fresh, local ingredients. The ranchero-decorated dining room can get quite loud, but the kitchen's signature mains ($11–18) might be worth losing a bit of hearing for. Dinner only.

The Matterhorn 2323 Van Ness Ave at Vallejo, Russian Hill ☎415/885-6116. Lurking in a nondescript apartment building, this restaurant is known for cheese, beef and chocolate fondues; its ski-lodge decor was shipped in pieces from the Swiss motherland and reassembled on site. Beef fondues for two are $46; cheese fondues for two, $38.50.

Sushi Groove 1916 Hyde St at Green, Russian Hill ☎415/440-1905. Self-consciously stylish restaurant serving inventive and original *maki* rolls, a sprinkling of Pan-Asian fusion dishes and furiously strong sake martinis. The two downsides are the sometimes sloppy service and the tiny size of the place, which can translate into long waits for seating. $20–30 for a full meal.

Swan Oyster Depot 1517 Polk St at California, Russian Hill. Expect no frills at this legendary seafood joint with its huge marble countertop and tiled walls. Endure the inevitable wait, grab a stool and hang onto it, and suck down some cheap shellfish or a bowl of chowder. Breakfast and lunch only.

San Francisco's super burrito

Philadelphia has its cheesesteaks, New York its pastrami sandwiches and Texas its barbecue. In San Francisco, the **super burrito** is not only the premier bargain food, but truly a local phenomenon. The city is home to well over 150 **taquerias** – informal Mexican restaurants specializing in tacos, quesadillas, tortas and, of course, burritos – and locals are often heard debating their favourites effusively.

San Francisco's take on the burrito differs from its Southern California cousin not only in its comparatively gargantuan size, but also in its ingredient list. Whereas a San Diego-style burrito can be an austere meal of meat, cheese and salsa scattered about a standard-size tortilla, the San Francisco version stuffs a jumbo tortilla with any number of grilled or barbecued meats, Spanish rice, beans (choices include whole pinto, black or refried), melted cheese, *pico de gallo* (a splashy mix of diced tomato, onion, jalapeño and cilantro), guacamole or slices of avocado, a splatter of salsa and even sour cream. And with its emphasis on vegetables, grains and legumes, the burrito also easily lends itself to vegetarian and vegan variants.

Most San Francisco taquerias wrap their goods in aluminium foil for easy handling, as the majority of locals eat burritos by hand. Expect to pay $5–8 for a super burrito and to not have much of an appetite for hours afterward. Forego the utensils, order a Mexican beer or non-alcoholic *agua fresca* (fruit drink) with your foiled meal and you'll fit right in.

The Mission, the Castro and around

See map on p.468.

Bagdad Café 2295 Market St at 16th, Castro. Specializing in comfort food, this longtime corner diner is the best 24hr option in the neighbourhood; everything's around $10–12.

Bi-Rite Creamery 3692 18th St at Dolores, Mission. Tiny ice-cream shop that hits all the right notes with its artisanal flavours. Usual suspects like mint chip and chocolate share freezer space with unique concoctions such as toasted coconut and honey lavender.

Bissap Baobab 2323 Mission St at 19th, Mission ℡415/826-9287. This bustling West African spot attracts a diverse crowd of Mission hipsters and African expats, and its vegetarian-friendly menu features vegetable and peanut *mafe* stew from Mali, as well as meatier choices including Senegalese *dibi* (grilled meat with onion sauce). Mains $9–13.

Boogaloos 3296 22nd St at Valencia, Mission. Breakfast is the big draw here: black beans and chorizo feature heavily on the Latinized versions of American diner classics, while the Temple o' Spuds ($6.50) is an orgy of potatoes, melted cheese, sour cream and green onions. Breakfast and lunch only.

Delfina 3621 18th St at Guerrero, Mission ℡415/552-4055. Continually buzzing, dinner-only restaurant that attracts nearly every sort of San Franciscan. The light, Cal-Ital dishes rarely miss the mark, while its pizzeria next door (open for lunch and dinner) is just as terrific. Mains over $20.

Dosa 995 Valencia St at 21st St, Mission ℡415/642-3672. Dosa's crêpe-like namesake item – and its close cousin, the thicker *uttapam* – dominate its South Indian menu, while the terracotta dining room is welcoming and not too noisy. Dinner only; mains $10–20.

El Trébol 3324 24th St at Mission, Mission. Run by a husband-and-wife team, this café serves excellent versions of Nicaraguan standards such as *churrasco* (grilled beef) and *chancho con yucca* (fried pork) in a haphazard atmosphere washed with Latin music. Most dishes cost well under $10.

Foreign Cinema 2534 Mission St at 21st, Mission ℡415/648-7600. The "dinner and a movie" concept is redefined at this upscale, expensive restaurant, where films are projected onto a large outdoor wall. The menu's as noteworthy as the offbeat concept, with the exhaustive oyster-heavy raw bar ($2.50–3 per oyster) making for showy opening credits. Mains $16–30.

Goood Frikin Chicken 10 29th St at Mission, Mission. Superbly seasoned poultry that warrants the extra 'o' in this airy restaurant's goofy name. The dining room is cast in various earth tones, with the ceiling and walls covered in soothing landscape murals. Mains under $10.

Herbivore 983 Valencia St at 21st, Mission ℡415/826-5657. There's no meat or dairy in sight at this all-vegan restaurant, boasting popular dishes like lentil loaf with mashed potatoes or giant bowls of coconut noodle soup. Everything's generally under $12, with breakfast available daily.

Just for You 732 22nd St at Third, Potrero Hill ☏ 415/647-3033. This out-of-the-way gem produces some of the fluffiest (and largest!) *beignets* outside of New Orleans. All breads are house-made (try the raisin cinnamon toast), while the enormous pancakes are the stuff of legend. In addition to breakfast and lunch daily, it's also open for dinner on weeknights. Mains about $10.

La Taqueria 2889 Mission St at 25th, Mission. Pass on the often sloppy, poorly constructed burritos at this Mission stalwart and head straight for the menu's true strength: the super taco (about $6, including guacamole).

Le P'tit Laurent 699 Chenery St at Diamond, Glen Park ☏ 415/334-3235. Carnivores won't want to miss the meaty cassoulet (complete with full leg of duck) and memorable desserts here; the service and overall vibe are equally warm. Conveniently, it's steps from the Glen Park BART station. Dinner only; mains over $20.

Luna Park 694 Valencia St at 18th, Mission ☏ 415/553-8584. This darkly lit neighbourhood staple is decked out like a lush bordello, with deep red walls, ornamental chandeliers and menus in the shape of little black books. Most dishes, such as a tuna salad niçoise or breaded pork chop stuffed with mushrooms and gruyere, hover around $15.

Papalote 3409 24th St at Valencia, Mission ☏ 415/970-8815. Peerless Cal-Mex cuisine – there's nary a poor menu choice to be made, from the top-grade nachos to anything that includes the perfectly grilled *carne asada*. The warm chips and otherworldly salsa make for a double *coup de grâce*. Everything's under $10.

Mitchell's Ice Cream 688 San Jose Ave at 29th, Mission. Local legend that produces its extensive selection of flavours on-site, from the mainstream (French vanilla, strawberry) to the far leftfield (avocado, sweet bean).

Taqueria Can-cún 2288 Mission St at 19th, Mission. Standby taqueria featuring a rose-strewn shrine to Our Lady of Guadalupe and some of the finest grilled tortillas in the Mission. Go for a terrific, budget-priced super burrito (about $6), or for a belt-busting eye-opener, drop in for breakfast. Open late nightly.

Taqueria San Francisco 2794 24th St at York, Mission. The quintessential San Francisco taqueria (look no further than its name), where burritos are weighty and characterized by flaky grilled tortillas and rustic meats like *al pastor* (rotisserie-grilled pork). Expect bouncy tuba-pop from the jukebox. Cash only; burritos and plate meals under $10.

Tartine 600 Guerrero St at 18th, Mission. Quite possibly San Francisco's most popular bakery, and with good reason: this *boulangerie*'s pies, pastries, hot-pressed sandwiches and fresh breads are some of the finest around, and consequently, lines often twist out the door.

Ti Couz 3108 16th St at Valencia, Mission. This enduringly popular *crêperie* was one of the pioneers of the now-bustling Mission scene on Valencia Street. It still holds its place as one of the finer inexpensive restaurants in town, serving savoury buckwheat pancakes for under $10, along with flat, plate-served dessert crêpes.

Truly Mediterranean 3109 16th St at Valencia, Mission. *Truly Med*'s inexpensive shawarmas are wrapped in thin, crispy *lavash* bread – though there's barely anywhere to sit and enjoy them in the tiny windowfront restaurant that's open late most nights. The busy staff's spontaneous singing and dancing is a bonus.

Walzwerk 381 S Van Ness Ave at 15th, Mission ☏ 415/551-7181. Cramped spot serving hearty Deutsch comfort food such as pork *schnitzel* with seasonal vegetables ($16) or *bratwurst* with mashed potatoes and sauerkraut ($15). Framed East German pop records and large portraits of twentieth-century Eastern Bloc industry evoke past eras behind the Iron Curtain. Dinner only.

Hayes Valley to Haight-Ashbury

See map on p.471.

Asqew Grill 1607 Haight St at Clayton, Haight-Ashbury ☏ 415/701-9301. A refreshing option specializing in more than a dozen different kinds of grilled skewers – from pork, apple and pear to shrimp, tomato and squash.

Burgermeister 86 Carl St at Cole, Cole Valley. Increasingly popular spot that broils excellent gourmet half-pound burgers. All the mainstream choices are available, as well as a handful of unusual options (such as the mango burger) for the adventurous. Burgers under $10.

Frankie's Bohemian Café 1862 Divisadero St at Pine, Western Addition ☏ 415/921-4725. Amber wood-lined bar-restaurant where the house speciality is a burly Czech mess called *brambory*, which piles meat and/or veggies atop a pan-fried bed of potato and zucchini. Burgers, salads and 20-oz beers fill out the menu. Mains $10–15.

Frjtz 581 Hayes St at Laguna, Hayes Valley. Often-packed spot serving cones of thick and crunchy Belgian-style fries with dips such as creamy wasabi mayo and spicy yoghurt-peanut. Sandwiches and crêpes are also available for about $10.

Green Chile Kitchen 1801 McAllister St at Baker, Western Addition ☏ 415/440-9411.

Extraordinarily flavourful cuisine from the state of New Mexico, further enhanced by robust chillies – request "Christmas" sauce for a dollar extra, and you'll get both red and green chillies on (or in) your meal.

Jardinière 300 Grove St at Franklin, Hayes Valley ☏ 415/861-5555. This two-storey brick space makes for an indulgent splurge, but it's worth it for every impeccable plate passed your way. Most of the menu changes regularly (although thankfully, the aged-cheese platter is a constant), but you can expect innovative dishes like Alaskan halibut with morel mushrooms ($37). Dinner only.

Kate's Kitchen 471 Haight St at Fillmore, Lower Haight. When you first stare down at the monstrous plates of budget breakfast fare served here, it's a little hard to think about saving room for extras. But treat yourself to six hush puppies ($3.75) to take away – deep-fried lumps of corn meal served with honey-touched "pooh butter".

🏃 **The Little Chihuahua** 292 Divisadero St at Page, Lower Haight. Not your garden variety taqueria at all – look for unique menu items such as Mexican French toast and fried plantain burritos alongside standard favourites like tortilla soup and enchiladas. Everything's under $10.

Little Star Pizza 846 Divisadero St at McAllister, Western Addition ☏ 415/441-1118. One of San Francisco's top pizzerias, dimly lit and packed nightly with hipsters enjoying its lively bar and jukebox blasting American and British indie rock. The kitchen bakes deep-dish and thin-crust pizzas ($15–23) with equal aplomb. Dinner only.

Magnolia Gastropub and Brewery 1398 Haight St at Masonic, Haight-Ashbury ☏ 415/864-7468. The menu at this popular corner spot goes beyond standard pub food – although there's a good burger and plenty of sausages to choose from – to include pan-roasted sea bass ($24) and smoked duck breast ($23). An on-site brewery produces American riffs on classic British ales, and food's usually served until midnight.

Massawa 1538 Haight St at Ashbury, Haight-Ashbury ☏ 415/621-4129. Terrific East African eatery where you shouldn't expect to keep your hands clean as you stab at saucily delicious items with spongy *injera* bread, all presented together family-style on a gigantic platter. Mains $10–15.

🏃 **Nopa** 560 Divisadero St at Hayes, Western Addition ☏ 415/864-8643. Buzzing, impossibly popular hotspot which leans on a number of cuisine styles, from New American (country pork chop, rotisserie herbed chicken) to further afield (Moroccan vegetable *tagine*, baked pastas). Dinner only; mains under $20.

Rosamunde Sausage Grill 545 Haight St at Fillmore, Lower Haight. Tiny storefront serving terrific, inexpensive grilled sausages on sesame rolls. Savvy customers place their order, head next door to *Toronado* (see p.489) and await their sausage's delivery over a beer.

Thep Phanom 400 Waller St at Fillmore, Lower Haight ☏ 415/431-2526. This corner Thai spot pulls in diners from all over town – and often, beyond – for its fragrant curries ($10–15). The spinach with peanut sauce is sweet and sharp, while the Three's Company seafood medley in coconut sauce is equally divine. Dinner only.

Zuni 1658 Market St at Gough, Hayes Valley ☏ 415/552-2522. Once nouveau, now a staple, this airy and triangular restaurant boasts the most famous Caesar salad in town – made with home-cured anchovies – and an equally legendary focaccia hamburger. If you decide on the custom-roasted chicken ($48), be sure you enjoy the company you're with – you're likely to wait an hour for it to emerge from the kitchen.

Pacific Heights and Japantown

See map on p.471.

Benkyodo 1747 Buchanan St at Sutter, Japantown. Selling hundreds of confectionary snacks daily, this popular Japanese bakery is inexpensive, so it's easy to fill up on dessert for a small sum.

Kiss Sushi 1700 Laguna St at Sutter, Japantown ☏ 415/474-2866. You'll need to phone ahead for a reservation at this signless, blink-and-you'll-miss-it spot with a mere dozen seats available; it's also quite expensive, with a full meal often running upwards of $65 per person. Once in the door, expect as many as eight courses if you order the *omakase* course (chef's choice).

Mifune 1737 Post St at Fillmore, Japantown. More elegant than most of its drab neighbours inside the Japan Center, this noodle house features a large array of soup toppings and a small selection of sushi.

🏃 **Sociale** 3665 Sacramento St at Spruce, Pacific Heights ☏ 415/921-3200. Intimate Italian bistro worth seeking out at the end of its verdant pedestrian lane. Go for the heated dining courtyard, cosy atmosphere and fontina cheese-crammed fried olives appetizer. Mains $20–30.

The Richmond and the Sunset

Arizmendi 1331 Ninth Ave at Irving, Sunset. The artisanal breads and pastries are reason enough to head to this small, earthy and inexpensive bakery, but its regular rotation of gourmet pizza is the true surprise treat. Baked goods and pizzas vary daily.

Aziza 5800 Geary Blvd at 22nd, Richmond ☎415/752-2222. Moroccan fine-dining destination with opulent decor, a superb wine list and fun touches like a rose-water-filled pewter basin presented for pre-meal handwashing. The menu's packed with California-accented North African specialities. Dinner only; mains $20–30.

Brothers Korean BBQ 4128 Geary Blvd at Sixth, Richmond. The decor here is nothing to get excited about, but the moderately priced feasts of marinated meats and myriad, pungent side-dishes are worth the visit. Certain tables have sunken *hibachis* on which you can cook your own meats. Mains $12–20.

Chapeau! 126 Clement St at Second, Richmond ☎415/750-9787. Exceptional, Provençal-inspired meats and seafood served amid the neighbourhood's raft of Asian restaurants; there's a terrific three-course *prix fixe* for $38. Dinner only.

Gordo Taqueria 1233 Ninth Ave at Lincoln, Sunset. Efficient burrito shop that lives up to its name (which translates to "fat" in English) by specializing in hefty, stumpy slabs on a par with any in town. The menu's as simple as can be, including only tacos, burritos and quesadillas, and everything's under $6. Cash only.

Mandalay 4348 California St at Sixth, Richmond. The go-to appetizer here is *balada*, a crispy pancake tailormade for dipping in its accompanying curry sauce. Although the menu features chow mein and Singapore-style noodles, overall the choices here are Burmese – a delectable, saucy melange of Thai, Indian and Chinese cuisines. Mains top out at $12.

🏃 **Park Chow** 1240 Ninth Ave at Lincoln, Sunset ☎415/665-9912. Surprisingly huge space with a menu that's all over the globe, from salads, American comfort food, pizzas and pastas, to artisan cheese plates and even a handful of Asian noodle dishes. Mains $10–15.

Pizzetta 211 211 23rd Ave at California, Richmond ☎415/379-9880. Expect inventive and unusual organic thin-crust pizza at this miniscule (only four tables) nook on a quiet residential street. There's a different menu each week, offering whatever's fresh and seasonal. Cash only; pizzas are under $15.

Pluto's 627 Irving St at Seventh, Sunset. Custom salads are the big draw here, as they're among the biggest, best and cheapest anywhere; elsewhere on the menu, the turkey and stuffing is a soul-warming option any day of the year. Mains under $10.

Q 225 Clement St at Third, Inner Richmond. This hopping spot along Clement Street's restaurant row is an over-the-top diner, sporting funky features such as a booth where a tree grows through the table. Portions are generous, and the menu's mostly comfort food such as meatloaf on mashed potatoes and beer-battered catfish; meatless choices are also available. Mains $13–17; brunch on weekends.

Spices! 294 Eighth Ave at Clement, Richmond. This inexpensive, humbly sized Taiwanese–Szechuan upstart is known for brazen dishes like beef tendon and hot and sour intestine noodle soup, although rest assured that plenty of less eyebrow-raising options exist on the menu. As you'd expect from the restaurant's name, numbing spice can be added to nearly every dish upon request. Expect crowds of young Asian hipsters, giggly teen servers and MTV Asia burbling on the overhead television. Cash only.

🏃 **Thanh Long** 4101 Judah St at 46th Ave, Sunset ☎415/665-1146. An unlikely destination restaurant far from San Francisco's core, *Thanh Long* was San Francisco's first Vietnamese restaurant in the early 1970s (during the Vietnam War, no less); it's become increasingly French-inspired and upscale in the years since. Its soothing dining room's bedecked in blonde wood panelling and earth tones. Dinner only; mains $18 and up.

Cafés

A coffee-loving city like few others, San Francisco is liberally dotted with excellent **cafés** serving first-rate blends, along with other assorted beverages (often including beer and wine). More social than utilitarian, people hang out in these generally lively venues as much to pass time as to refresh themselves, although an increasing number of wi-fi cafés cater to industrious laptop users.

See maps on pp.448–449, p.468 and p.471.

🏃 **Blue Bottle Coffee** 315 Linden St at Gough, Hayes Valley. Located down an alley off a main thoroughfare, this quirky spot – little more than a kiosk, really – offers

own-roasted coffee that has taken San Francisco by storm. Cold brews make a surprising appearance on the menu, as do a few milk-based beverages. Closes at 6pm.

Café de la Presse 352 Grant Ave at Bush, Union Square. Parisian-inspired café with a good selection of European magazines and newspapers.
Caffé Trieste 601 Vallejo St at Grant, North Beach. This local institution is where espresso made its West Coast debut in 1956. Today, it's known almost as much for its mandolin sessions and opera recitals as for its own-roasted, thick-bodied coffee.
Crossroads Café 699 Delancey St at Brannan, South of Market. The sprawling, inexpensive menu here covers all three meals and ranges from fruit smoothies and egg sandwiches to creative salads and tapas dishes. What's more, the relaxed, waterfront-adjacent setting encourages lingering – you could easily spend the better part of a morning or afternoon enjoying the sunny courtyard along the Embarcadero.
Emporio Rulli il Caffé Stockton St at Post St, Union Square. A popular shopping pitstop with mandolin-drenched Italian ballads spilling out of its speakers, this café in Union Square itself serves bracingly strong coffee, as well as breakfast and lunch panini starting around $6. There are tables outside on the square if you want to lounge.

Ritual Coffee Roasters 1026 Valencia St at 21st, Mission. The impossibly hipster-chic clientele at this vaunted café can't overshadow the outstanding coffee, roasted on-premise using the company's own beans. Try the intense espresso, which boasts flavours of hazelnut and caramel.
Royal Ground Coffee 2060 Fillmore St at California, Pacific Heights. Situated among the boutiques and restaurants along Fillmore, this branch of a low-key local chain has pleasant sidewalk seating, great for people-watching.
Samovar Tea Lounge 498 Sanchez St at 18th, Castro. Earthy, cushion-filled café that serves more than a hundred varieties of tea, as well as tasty Asian snacks such as baked tofu with miso chutney. The overstuffed wicker chairs are a great place to curl up with a book for an afternoon.
Trouble Coffee 4033 Judah St at 45th Ave, Sunset. A few blocks in from the coastline sits this pint-sized powerhouse, operated by young eccentrics remarkably passionate about their trade. The menu's simple: coffee, coconut, toast.

Nightlife

While suitably famous for its restaurants, San Francisco is also a great drinking town, with a huge number of **bars** ranging from comfortably scruffy jukebox joints to chic lounges and clubby watering holes; and although its **clubs** aren't world-class, they can nonetheless make for a fun night of dancing and carousing.

San Francisco beers

While its surrounding countryside may be internationally known for wine making, the city of San Francisco is renowned for its **craft beers**. The best-known local product is so-called **steam** beer, a lager-bitter hybrid invented when early local brewers, finding the ice needed for lager production too expensive, instead fermented their yeast at room temperature like an ale. The result was a beer with the lower ABV of lager but the hearty flavour of bitter. (The precise origin of the odd name, unfortunately, has never been established.) To find out more, take one of the engaging, free tours at **Anchor Steam Brewery**, 1705 Mariposa St at Carolina, Potrero Hill (weekday afternoons only; reservations essential ☏415/863-8350, Ⓦwww.anchorbrewing.com), whose namesake product is a local treasure and universally available at bars and stores.

The pick of San Francisco brewpubs:

21st Amendment Brewery South of Market. See p.487.

Beach Chalet Brewery and Restaurant Golden Gate Park. See p.475.

Gordon Biersch Brewery South of Market. See p.535.

Magnolia Gastropub and Brewery Haight-Ashbury. See p.483.

ThirstyBear Brewing Company South of Market. See p.487.

Bars

Though spread fairly evenly over the city, happening **bars** are particularly numerous in the Mission and the area between Hayes Valley and Haight-Ashbury, where they seem to line up one after the other. Some charmingly seedy dark horses are found in the Tenderloin; at the opposite end of the spectrum, young-sophisticate cruising spots populate the Marina and slick lounges speckle Downtown and South of Market. Of course, the city has many specifically **gay and lesbian bars** (see p.495), most plentifully in the Castro and South of Market, with a few scattered in the Mission. According to California law, there's **no smoking** allowed in any bar unless its sole employees are the owners; to assuage all concerned parties, a clever handful of San Francisco taverns have constructed enclosed spaces expressly built for puffing.

Downtown and around

See map on pp.448–449.

The Ambassador 673 Geary St at Jones, Tenderloin ☎415/563-8192. Crystal chandeliers, a marble bar and red carpeting give this Tenderloin cocktail lounge an air of old Vegas cool, while nightly DJs root the scene firmly in the present. Reserve ahead for one of the high-backed black leather booths, which feature rotary phones to dial up the bar.

Bambuddha Lounge Phoenix Hotel, 601 Eddy St at Larkin, Tenderloin ☎415/885-5088. Skip the overly sleek, South Pacific-inspired cocktail lounge here and head outside by the pool. DJs and strong drinks make it a regular favourite for locals.

Bix 56 Gold St at Montgomery, Jackson Square. Hidden on a tiny side-street, this bar-restaurant's decor maintains a touch of 1940s glamour. It's often packed after work with a somewhat formal Downtown crowd enjoying the bar's famed gin Martinis.

Bourbon & Branch 501 Jones St at O'Farrell, Tenderloin ⊛ www.bourbonandbranch.com. A reservations-only bar (book online) that's garnered plenty of buzz for its re-creation of a Prohibition-era speakeasy; indeed, this fiercely retro spot is nowhere to order a vodka and Red Bull. Give the password at the unmarked door and you'll be whisked into a dimly lit space with wooden booths, burgundy velvet wallpaper and a pressed-tin ceiling.

The Bubble Lounge 714 Montgomery St at Columbus, Jackson Square. Champagne bar that lures a young, gussied-up crowd onto its squishy sofas. There's a vast selection of fizz (divided between light, medium and full-bodied), as well as classic cocktails such as Bellinis and Chambords.

Edinburgh Castle 950 Geary St at Polk, Tenderloin ☎415/885-4074. Evocative Scottish bar filled with Highland memorabilia. The room upstairs regularly hosts live performances, while the pub grub comes straight from co-owned chippie The Old Chelsea, right around the corner. Arrive early on Tuesday for trivia night.

Hemlock Tavern 1131 Polk St at Post, Tenderloin ☎415/923-0923. Fun hipster bar with a free jukebox heavy on punk, fresh peanut shells on the floor, live music in its back room (see p.491) and a handy, enclosed patio where smokers can puff and sip in peace.

The Irish Bank 10 Mark Lane at Bush, Union Square. An appealing respite from the nearby shopping district, with plenty of alfresco alley seating, pub fare and all the requisite Irish artefacts.

The Redwood Room Clift Hotel, 495 Geary St at Taylor, Theater District. This clubby landmark bar was made over to include lightboxes on the walls that display shifting, fading paintings. It's fun and swank – just don't choke on the comically high drink prices.

Slide 430 Mason St at Geary, Theater District. Access to this underground homage to the 1920s is via a serpentine slide, which leads to a swish cocktail lounge.

Tonga Room Fairmont Hotel, 950 Mason St at California, Nob Hill ☎415/772-5278. Ultra-campy bar styled like a Polynesian village, complete with pond, simulated rainstorms and grass-skirted band strangling jazz and pop covers to death upon a floating raft. Cocktails are outrageously overpriced, but the happy hour buffet (under $10) helps make up for it.

Top of the Mark InterContinental Mark Hopkins, One Nob Hill Circle, Nob Hill ☎415/616-6916. Panoramic views of the city make the pricey cocktails here worthwhile. There's a $5–15 cover when there's live jazz (Tues–Sat).

Tunnel Top 601 Bush St at Stockton, Union Square ☎415/722-6620. Fun spot atop the Stockton Tunnel which boasts stiff drinks, a terrific balcony and DJs.

South of Market and around

See maps on pp.448–449 and p.434.

21st Amendment Brewery 563 2nd St at Brannan, South of Market. This bright, lively brewpub, across from South Park two blocks from the ballpark, turns out a dozen or so tasty micro-brews, which it serves alongside decent burgers and other pub fare to a down-to-earth crowd.

Butter 354 11th St at Folsom, South of Market. Fun, stylized "white trash" bar that's nonetheless a hopeless case of forced irony in this warehouse-and-lofts neighbourhood. It's full of imitation trailer-park decor – look no further than the bar covered in shingles – and has a food window that serves only microwaveable junk food (think tater tots and the like).

District 216 Townsend St at Third, South of Market. Rekindling the exuberant spirit of the dot-com days, this wine bar has high ceilings and exposed brick walls and draws a young, well-heeled crowd. There's an eclectic selection of more than thirty wines by the glass, plus small plates such as pizzettas ($10–14) and *salumi* ($12).

Gordon Biersch Brewery 2 Harrison St at Embarcadero, South of Market. Bayfront outpost of the successful Peninsula microbrewery, housed in a converted coffee warehouse with a lovely view of the Bay Bridge. Its patio has heat lamps, so it's habitable even on a chilly evening.

Pied Piper Bar *Palace Hotel*, 2 New Montgomery St at Market, South of Market. Named for the mural hovering behind its bar, this mahogany-panelled room is a secluded, elegant place for a Martini.

The Ramp 855 Terry Francois St at Illinois, Mission Bay. Way out on the old docks, it's worth the trek here from Downtown to sit on the patio and sip beverages while overlooking the evocative disused piers and boatyards.

ThirstyBear Brewing Company 661 Howard St at Second, South of Market. A combination brewpub and tapas bar, packed in the evenings with local workers; the food's well priced ($7–12 a plate) and tasty (try the fried calamari).

North Beach and Chinatown

See map on pp.448–449.

Gino and Carlo 548 Green St at Grant, North Beach. Neighbourhood watering-hole once popular with pressmen, now with longtime regulars. A welcoming place overall, with pinball and pool available.

Li Po Cocktail Lounge 916 Grant Ave at Jackson, Chinatown. Named after the Chinese poet, charmingly grotty *Li Po* is one of the few places to drink in Chinatown. Enter through the false cavern front and grab a drink among the regulars, some of whom are local literary luminaries.

Rosewood 732 Broadway at Stockton, North Beach. Best visited on weeknights, this deliberately hidden bolthole doesn't even have a sign outside. The retro interior is complemented by great lounge-core DJs; downsides include the pricey drinks and loads of out-of-towners who pour in at weekends.

Sip Bar & Lounge 787 Broadway at Powell, North Beach ☎415/699-6545. Adding a splash of style to the North Beach scene, this friendly lounge has nightly DJs spinning everything from hip-hop to pop after 10pm.

Specs Twelve Adler Museum Café 12 Saroyan Place at Columbus, North Beach. Known locally as simply "Specs", this friendly dive set just off North Beach's main drag is known for its chatty barstaff and is decked out with loads of oddities from the high seas. Its regulars may be older eccentrics, but it's popular with just about everybody.

Tosca Café 242 Columbus Ave at Pacific, North Beach. A bar so classic it feels like a Hollywood set: bartenders in white waistcoats, arias (or perhaps Sinatra) wafting out of the jukebox and a long line of cocktail glasses along the bar filled with the house drink, a brandy-laced cappuccino. Even the average tee-totalling San Franciscan has been here at least once.

Vesuvio Café 255 Columbus Ave at Jack Kerouac Alley, North Beach. Even if it weren't once the regular hangout of Kerouac and company, North Beach's most famous bar would still merit a visit for at least one drink for its inviting atmosphere.

The Marina, Cow Hollow and Fisherman's Wharf

Balboa Café 3199 Fillmore St at Greenwich, Cow Hollow. This dark-wood bar, with high ceilings and an excellent wine list, is packed most nights of the week with Marina singles on the prowl. The bartenders whip up a superb Bloody Mary, and the burger, served on a baguette, is patently unique.

Buena Vista Café 2765 Hyde St at Beach, Fisherman's Wharf. Ever crowded with tourists (and a few locals), this San Francisco landmark has been churning out its famed concoction, Irish coffee, since 1952. See map on pp.448–449.

Liverpool Lil's 2942 Lyon St at Greenwich, Cow Hollow. This old-fashioned Brit pub is a refreshing spot for pints of Bass ale and steak-and-kidney pie; the kitchen's open until 1am.

Nectar Wine Lounge 3330 Steiner St at Chestnut, Marina. Upscale oenophile haven with a late-night, loungey vibe. Expect a sophisticated-looking crowd, an eclectic and extensive wine list and a menu full of salads and small cheese-and-*salumi* plates.

The Mission and around

See map on p.468.

Amnesia 853 Valencia St at 19th, Mission ☎415/970-0012, ⓦwww.amnesiathebar.com. Small, red-lit bar serving wine, craft beers and *soju* cocktails. Entertainment can be far-reaching from night to night: bluegrass bands and hip-hop DJs to karaoke and politically charged puppet shows. Cover charges range from free to $10.

The Attic 3336 24th St at Mission, Mission. Beloved dive that's so dark, it takes your eyes time to adjust to the low lighting. Sure enough, the decor is clearly inspired by a vintage attic, with oddball antiques set in random places.

Dalva 3121 16th St at Valencia, Mission. Wonderfully divey and dark, but easy to miss along 16th Street's glut of bars, this wafer-thin space brings in a diverse crowd to chat and drink.

Doc's Clock 2575 Mission St at 21st, Mission. Deco-styled bar, easy to spot thanks to the hot-pink neon sign blazing out front; consistently popular with Missionites.

🏃 **Latin American Club** 3286 22nd St at Valencia, Mission. Cosy place with a neighbourhood feel, great for an early chat over drinks before the crowds arrive later in the evening. The loft space above the entrance is full of piñatas, Mexican streamers and assorted trinkets.

Laszlo 2526 Mission St at 21st, Mission ☎415/401-0810. This industrial-chic bar, attached to film-themed *Foreign Cinema* (see p.481) next door, is itself unsurprisingly named in homage to the movies (Jean-Paul Belmondo's character in *À Bout de Souffle*). DJs spin nightly, while the cocktails – especially the mojitos – are outstanding.

The Lone Palm 3394 22nd St at Guerrero, Mission. Like some forgotten Vegas revue bar from the 1950s, this candlelit cocktail lounge – less than a block off the well-trod Valencia corridor – is a gem. White cloths cover the raised tables and a TV above the bar plays classic American movies.

🏃 **Lucky 13** 2140 Market St at Church, Castro. Straight bar on the outskirts of the Castro with an extensive selection of international beers. It's filled with pool-players chomping on free popcorn; there's a loud jukebox inside and a humble patio out back.

Make-Out Room 3225 22nd St at Mission, Mission ☎415/647-2888, ⓦwww.makeoutroom.com. Yet another terrific Mission watering-hole, with curved vinyl booths, streamers aplenty dangling

from the ceiling and nightly entertainment – typically soul DJs or local indie bands. Covers rarely exceed $7.

Medjool 2522 Mission St at 21st, Mission. This multi-level Mediterranean restaurant-lounge boasts a rare rooftop perch from which to enjoy wraparound city views. The catch is that there can be lots of posing to contend with, and you'll be hard-pressed to find a Mission resident here.

Revolution Café 3248 22nd St at Valencia, Mission ☎415/642-0474. This hybrid bar and café boasts alfresco drinking, ginger lattes, an upright piano available to any and all comers, and nightly live music that includes (but isn't limited to) jazz, Brazilian and classical. Despite constant throngs packing the small space, its atmosphere is laidback and resolutely bohemian.

Zeitgeist 199 Valencia St at Duboce, Mission. This friendly cyclist bar is a Mission institution, with an enormous outdoor beer garden that's wildly popular on sunny afternoons. Come for punk tunes, tattooed bartenders, afternoon cookouts at weekends and hordes of beers on tap.

Hayes Valley to Haight-Ashbury

See map on p.471.

🏃 **The Alembic** 1725 Haight St at Cole, Haight-Ashbury. Offering a refreshing break from the dog-eared Haight scene, this small, stylish spot is serious about its liquor, with a wide selection of small-batch bourbons, ryes and gins poured by knowledgeable, friendly bartenders. There's also a short menu of ethnic comfort food (think Moroccan spiced lamb burgers) along with beers from nearby brewery *Magnolia* (see p.483).

Aub Zam Zam 1663 Haight St at Clayton, Haight-Ashbury. Bar regulars purchased this Casbah-style cocktail lounge after the death of its ornery owner, Bruno, and have just about managed to retain its alternately surly/warm vibe. There's a great jazz jukebox to boot.

Hotel Biron 45 Rose St at Gough, Hayes Valley. Tucked away down an alley, this intimate wine bar – it's only a hotel in name – has a quality selection of California and European wines, as well as a small menu of cheeses and olives. Revolving exhibitions of local art adorn the walls.

Kezar Pub 770 Stanyan St at Beulah, Haight-Ashbury ☎415/386-9292. Lively neighbourhood pub with pool, darts and all kinds of sports shown on a slew of overhead TVs.

Mad Dog in the Fog 530 Haight St at Fillmore, Lower Haight ☎415/626-7279. Aptly named tavern that's one of the Lower Haight's most loyally patronized bars, with darts, English beer, footie on TV and a trivia night each Thursday.

Noc Noc 557 Haight St at Steiner, Lower Haight. Dark, super-groovy spot with bizarre decor befitting a post-apocalyptic tribal cave. The bar doesn't have a licence to sell hard alcohol, but it does make sake cocktails and boasts a solid range of beers.

Place Pigalle 520 Hayes St at Gough, Hayes Valley. Decorated in plush, deep reds, this friendly lounge boasts rotating art on the walls and the neighbourhood's most popular pool table.

Toronado 547 Haight St at Fillmore, Lower Haight. Renowned for its vast selection of international beers, this cacophonous tavern should be the first stop on any beer aficionado's itinerary.

The Richmond and the Sunset

Abbey Tavern 4100 Geary Blvd at Fifth, Richmond ☏415/221-7767. Quintessentially Irish, this sports pub is friendly and upscale, often hosting live Irish folk music when there isn't a can't-miss game on TV.

Trad'r Sam 6150 Geary Blvd at 26th Ave, Outer Richmond. San Francisco's original tiki bar is a bit of a trek from the central neighbourhoods, but go for the enormous and colourful – and occasionally flaming – cocktails such as the $14 Scorpion Bowl.

Yancy's Saloon 734 Irving St at Ninth, Sunset. One of San Francisco's only bars with a collegiate vibe, this mellow and plant-festooned place has free darts and cheap drinks.

Clubs

A night out in San Francisco is more of a party than a feverish pose, so while the city's collection of **clubs** will never be confused with more celebrated scenes in Miami or New York, there are a few upsides to its humbler scope: namely that you'll be hard-pressed to encounter high cover charges, ridiculously priced drinks or long lines. By far the greatest concentration of nightspots is found among the wide boulevards and warehouses in South of Market (including several with addresses doubling as names), although the Mission also has a small handful of places that get hopping on weekends; North Beach, too, is home to a couple of lounges that veer into club terrain later at night.

Unlike most other major cities, where the action never gets going until after midnight, most San Francisco clubs close at 2am, so you can usually be sure of finding things well under way around 10pm. Note that some operate dress codes, with jeans, T-shirts and team gear barred – call or check venue websites for details.

See maps on pp.448–449, p.468 and p.495 for details on dedicated gay and lesbian clubs.

111 Minna 111 Minna St at 2nd St, South of Market ☏415/974-1719. Combination bar, art gallery and DJ venue set a short way down an alley. It gets busier, noisier and more raucous as the evening wears on. Free–$8.

330 Ritch 330 Ritch St at Townsend, South of Market ☏415/541-9574, ⓦwww.330ritch.com. The only constant at this small, out-of-the-way club is its location. Different nights attract wildly varied crowds, but it's best known for its Thursday night Popscene party, ground zero for lovers of British indie rock and 1980s alternative. $5–15.

1015 Folsom 1015 Folsom St at Sixth, South of Market ☏415/431-1200, ⓦwww.1015.com. Multi-level megaclub that's popular across the board for late-night dancing. The music's largely house and trance with big names often spinning on the main floor; Saturdays see a Latin music night. $15–20.

Bruno's 2389 Mission St at 20th, Mission ☏415/643-5200, ⓦwww.brunossf.com. Like something from a Scorsese film, this retro dance venue is filled with 1960s-style furniture. If it's

danceable – hip-hop, R&B, soul, funk – you'll hear it here at some point. Open Fri and Sat. $10.

Club Cocomo 650 Indiana St at Mariposa, Potrero Hill ☏415/824-6910, ⓦwww.cafe cocomo.com. The spot to hit if salsa's your thing. There's an outdoor patio for cooling off, plus salsa lessons (included in cover) several nights a week. $5–15.

DNA Lounge 375 11th St at Harrison, South of Market ☏415/626-1409, ⓦwww.dnalounge.com. Longtime club that changes its music style nightly but consistently draws a young, mixed gay/straight crowd. Downstairs is a large dancefloor, while the mezzanine is a sofa-packed lounge ideal for chilling. $15–20.

The End Up 401 6th St at Harrison, South of Market ☏415/646-0999, ⓦwww .theendup.com. Best known as the home of Sunday's all-day T-Dance party (6am–8pm), this stalwart club attracts a mixed bag of hardcore clubbers for after-hours dancing on the cramped dancefloor; if you need a break from the beat assault, there's an outdoor patio with plenty of seating. $5–10.

Fluid 662 Mission St at Third, South of Market ☏415/615-6888, ⓦwww.fluidsf.com. Dressy "ultra lounge" playing mostly hip-hop and mainstream house. The large first room is the lounge, its mirrored walls illuminated by the neon, flashing floor; the rear room is home to a tiny dancefloor.

Mezzanine 444 Jessie St at Fifth, South of Market ☏415/625-8880, ⓦwww.mezzaninesf.com. Massive megaclub featuring mainstream, brand-name DJs, as well as gigs by indie rock, reggae and hip-hop acts, although the space's acoustics benefit DJs rather than live bands. Cover varies wildly depending on headliner.

Mighty 119 Utah St at 15th, Potrero Hill ☏415/762-0151, ⓦwww.mighty119.com. Huddled close to the freeway, this converted warehouse space is a combination art gallery, performance venue, club and lounge (check out the frozen vodka bar). As for the music, it's mostly live funk or DJs spinning old-school classic house. Open Thurs–Sat. $5 and up.

Ruby Skye 420 Mason St at Geary, Union Square ☏415/693-0777, ⓦwww.rubyskye.com. The biggest mainstream DJs tend to stop through this gorgeous, spacious Victorian dancehall, where programming skews towards trance, house, drum'n'bass and techno. $15 and up.

Skylark 3089 16th St at Valencia, Mission ☏415/621-9294, ⓦwww.skylarkbar.com. Popular for its intimate vibe, low lighting, strong drinks and varied DJs, this spot makes for an inexpensive night out. No cover.

Live music

San Francisco's **music scene** reflects the character of the city as a whole: progressive and ever-evolving, but also a little bit nostalgic. It's never recaptured its crucial 1960s role, though since the 1990s the city has helped launch acid (or beat-heavy) jazz, a classic swing revival and the East Bay punk-pop sound championed by Green Day and Rancid. Options abound here for catching live rock, and young underground bands frequently emerge to make waves beyond the Bay Area. The city is also a prime stop for touring **jazz, blues** and **international** acts; as for **Latin music**, there's little chance of catching authentic performers other than at *Roccapulco* (see opposite) – a surprising development given the city's thriving Latino community.

Major venues

Bimbo's 365 Club 1025 Columbus at Chestnut, North Beach ☏415/474-0365, ⓦwww .bimbos365club.com. Dating back to the 1930s, this elegant, intimate club schedules underground European acts, kitschy tribute bands and big-name rock acts in equal proportion.

🏃 **The Fillmore** 1805 Geary St at Fillmore, Western Addition ☏415/346-6000, ⓦwww .thefillmore.com. This storied ballroom auditorium was at the heart of 1960s counterculture, masterminded by legendary local promoter Bill Graham. It's still a terrific spot for catching up-and-comers and longtime favourites alike – the sort of place bands love to perform.

🏃 **Great American Music Hall** 859 O'Farrell St at Polk, Tenderloin ☏415/885-0750, ⓦwww.musichallsf.com. A former bordello converted long ago into a beloved venue for rock, blues and international acts. The ornately moulded balcony offers seats with terrific views for those who arrive early.

The Warfield 982 Market St at Sixth, Tenderloin ☏415/775-7722, ⓦwww.thewarfieldtheatre.com.

In many ways a counterpart to the iconic, smaller Fillmore across town, this theatre offers a grand setting for enjoying top-tier touring artists. There's reserved balcony seating, as well as general admission tickets that put you close to the stage.

Yoshi's 1330 Fillmore St at Eddy, Western Addition ☏415/655-5600, ⓦwww.yoshis.com. With a balcony, sizeable dancefloor, round stage and supreme sound system, Oakland's long-fabled jazz club has expanded across the bay to draw big names across a variety of genres. $12–32.

Clubs and smaller venues

🏃 **Boom Boom Room** 1601 Fillmore St at Geary, Western Addition ☏415/673-8000, ⓦwww.boomboomblues.com. Once owned by late blues legend John Lee Hooker, this small, intimate bar with a chequerboard floor delivers blues and roots acts nightly. $7–20.

🏃 **Bottom of the Hill** 1233 17th St at Missouri, Potrero Hill ☏415/621-4455, ⓦwww.bottom ofthehill.com. Well off the beaten path, San Francisco's celebrated indie-rock stronghold draws crowds nightly for local and nationally touring acts. $8–15.

Café du Nord 2170 Market St at Sanchez, Castro ☎ 415/861-5016, ⊛ www.cafedu nord.com. This old subterranean speakeasy is a terrific place to enjoy touring or local rock bands, with the occasional swing and folk act booked for good measure. The amber-walled Swedish American Hall upstairs also regularly features shows. $10–20.

Elbo Room 647 Valencia St at 17th St, Mission ☎ 415/552-7788, ⊛ www.elbo.com. A local cradle of acid jazz in the early 1990s, this neighbourhood spot now hosts a smorgasbord of bands and DJs, from rock to reggae to soul. $6–10.

Hemlock Tavern 1131 Polk St at Hemlock, Polk Gulch ☎ 415/923-0923, ⊛ www.hemlocktavern .com. All types of hipster-approved music is performed in the shoebox-sized room at the back of this popular bar, from underground pop to arty noise to electro-punk-disco to ukulele country. Free–$8.

The Independent 628 Divisadero St at Hayes, Western Addition ☎ 415/771-1421, ⊛ www .theindependentsf.com. This mid-sized club with disarmingly friendly staff and exceptional sound specializes in booking acts from near (Rogue Wave) and far (Vieux Farka Toure). $10–20.

The Plough and Stars 116 Clement St at Second, Richmond ☎ 415/751-1122, ⊛ www .theploughandstars.com. Local Irish expats cram into this terrific pub for pints and live folk, bluegrass and Americana music at 9pm nightly. Small cover on weekends, no cover on weeknights.

Rickshaw Stop 155 Fell St at Van Ness, Hayes Valley ☎ 415/861-2011. Hayes Valley bar-club known for live indie-rock shows, as well as its monthly bhangra DJ night and queer "Cockblock" dance party on alternating Saturdays. Wed–Sat. $7–15.

Roccapulco Supper Club 3140 Mission St at Cesar Chavez, Mission ☎ 415/648-6611, ⊛ www .roccapulco.com. Sizeable, welcoming club (with serviceable Mexican restaurant) that books salsa and Tejano music, including performers rarely heard in the US. Salsa lessons happen every Friday and Saturday night at 8.30pm, and there's a dress code. $12–20.

The Saloon 1232 Grant Ave at Vallejo, North Beach ☎ 415/989-7666, ⊛ www.sfblues.net/saloon. Lively, low-brow hardcore blues venue, wonderfully anachronistic among the encroaching boutiques along upper Grant's shopping and dining strip.

Slim's 333 11th St at Folsom, South of Market ☎ 415/255-0333, ⊛ www.slims-sf.com. Owned by local 1970s hitmaker Boz Scaggs, this cavernous brick space is a prime venue to catch an array of punk, alternative and international music. $10–30.

Performing arts and film

San Francisco has a great reputation for **opera and classical music**; its symphony orchestra and ballet companies are considered world-class, and its opera is among the most highly regarded in the US. **Theatre** here is accessible and much less costly than elsewhere, but most of the mainstream Downtown venues – barring a couple of exceptions – are mediocre, forever staging Broadway reruns; you'd do better to explore the more interesting fringe circuit.

While the city's **comedy** scene can be lively at times, it's **film** that's almost as big an obsession as dining out in San Francisco – historic neighbourhood theatres and modern multiplexes thrive equally.

Ballet, opera and symphony

In addition to the listings below, the **Stern Grove Festival** puts on free, open-air performances by the local symphony orchestra, opera and ballet companies every Sunday at 2pm during the summer months at its namesake park at 19th Avenue and Sloat Boulevard, in the city's outlying Parkside district. Arrive early to secure a spot on the lawn; public transport (Muni lines #K, L, M, 23 and 28) is recommended.

San Francisco Ballet War Memorial Opera House, 301 Van Ness Ave at Grove, Civic Center ☎ 415/865-2000, ⊛ www.sfballet.org. The city's ballet company, the oldest and one of the largest in the US, puts on an ambitious annual programme (Jan–May) of both classical and contemporary dance. Founded in 1933, the ballet was the first American company to stage full-length productions of *Swan Lake* and *The Nutcracker* (still performed annually at Christmas). Tickets begin at $30, while

7

standing-room tickets are sometimes sold two hours before performances for $10–12.

San Francisco Opera War Memorial Opera House, 301 Van Ness Ave at Grove, Civic Center ⊤415/864-3330, ⍵www.sfopera.org. The War Memorial makes an opulent venue for the San Francisco Opera, which has been performing here since the building opened in 1932 and today shares the venue with the Ballet. A typical season for this internationally regarded company offers a mixture of avant-garde stagings by composers such as John Adams or André Previn, along with acclaimed productions of perennial favourites by Wagner or Puccini. The season runs Sept–Dec, with a short summer season in June and July. Tickets are $25–200.

San Francisco Symphony Louise M. Davies Symphony Hall, 201 Van Ness Ave at Hayes, Civic Center ⊤415/864-6000, ⍵www.sfsymphony.org. Since the 1995 arrival of conductor Michael Tilson Thomas, this once-musty institution has catapulted to the first rank of American symphony orchestras. Though Thomas's relentless self-promotion can be off-putting, his emphasis on the works of twentieth-century composers has added considerable vibrancy to the company's programming. The season runs Sept–May; depending on the performance, tickets range from $35–125, with day-of-performance rush tickets available for $20.

Theatre

The majority of the city's **theatres** congregate just west of Union Square; most aren't especially innovative, but tickets are reasonably affordable, and there's usually good availability. A handful of more inventive theatre companies are scattered around town, and each September the **San Francisco Fringe Festival** (⊤415/931-1094, ⍵www.sffringe.org), featuring over 250 experimental performances, is held at several venues – the Exit Theatre (see below) is often a primary location. Tickets are usually priced at $8–15.

Consult *San Francisco Chronicle*'s "96 Hours" supplement each Thursday, or check ⍵www.sfgate.com and the local weeklies to learn about the latest productions in town. Tickets for the city's major houses can be purchased either through the individual theatre's box offices or through **Ticketmaster** (⊤415/421-8497, ⍵www.ticketmaster.com). For last-minute bargains, try the **Tix Bay Area** booth (Tues–Fri 11am–6pm, Sat 10am–6pm, Sun 10am–3pm; ⊤415/430-1140, ⍵www.theatrebayarea.org) located on the west side of Union Square opposite the *Westin St Francis* hotel. Each day's bargains are listed at 11am on the website.

Major theatres

American Conservatory Theater (A.C.T.) 415 Geary St at Taylor, Theater District ⊤415/749-2228, ⍵www.act-sf.org. Leading resident group that mixes newly commissioned works and innovative renditions of the classics, with inventive set design and staging. $17–67, although preview shows can cost as little as $10.

Curran Theatre 445 Geary St at Mason, Theater District ⊤415/551-2000, ⍵www.shnsf.com. Former vaudeville theatre that now presents both hit Broadway plays and musicals. Pre-Broadway tryouts are common here: Tony magnet *Wicked* was workshopped for several weeks at the Curran before hitting New York. Tickets $30–90.

Yerba Buena Center for the Arts 701 Mission St at Third, South of Market ⊤415/978-2787, ⍵www.ybca.org. This modern, 750-seat performance space showcases local talents in programmes like the Hip-Hop Theater Festival, as well as touring shows. Tickets $15–50.

Smaller theatres

BATS Improv Bayfront Theater, Fort Mason Center ⊤415/474-6776, ⍵www.improv.org. Celebrated long-form improv company (its titular acronym stands for Bay Area Theatresports) that stages shows such as *Improvised Elvis: The Musical* year-round. Tickets $17–20.

Beach Blanket Babylon *Club Fugazi*, 678 Green St at Powell, North Beach ⊤415/421-4222, ⍵www.beachblanketbabylon.com. This legendary musical revue has been running continuously since 1974, though it regularly incorporates new spoofs of current events. Expect celebrity impersonations and towering hats, and be sure to reserve in advance. Tickets $25–56.

Exit Theatre 156 Eddy St at Taylor, Tenderloin ⊤415/673-3847, ⍵www.theexit.org. One of the best spots in town for cutting-edge theatre, known for women-centric plays and performances. Tickets $10–30.

Magic Theatre Fort Mason Center, Building D
℡ 415/441-8822, ⊚ www.magictheatre.org. The
busiest and largest local company after A.C.T.
specializes in the works of contemporary
playwrights, as well as those by emerging new
talents. Tickets $25–55.
The Marsh 1062 Valencia St at 22nd, Mission
℡ 1-800/838-3006, ⊚ www.themarsh.org. This
long-standing alternative space hosts fine solo
shows, many with an offbeat bent; Mondays are

test nights for works in progress. Tickets often on a
sliding scale between $15–30.
Theatre Rhinoceros Roving locations
℡ 1-800/838-3006, ⊚ www.therhino.org. The
city's top queer theatre company presents
productions that range from heartfelt political
drama to raunchy cabaret acts. It's currently in
search of a new permanent home, so check the
website for performance locations. $15–25.

Comedy

Thanks largely to an active club scene, comedy in San Francisco is regaining an
audience, with local punters turning up in increasing numbers for laugh nights
staged at bars, music venues and tiny theatres in the city. Check ⊚ www.sfstandup
.com for an extensive list of comedy shows in and around San Francisco, including
headliners appearing at the major clubs listed below. Also sniff through listings for
"open mic" nights, when unknowns and audience members get onstage and have
a go; there's rarely a cover charge for these evenings, and even if the acts are
ghastly, it can make for a fun time.

Clubhouse Comedy 414 Mason St at Post, Union
Square ⊚ www.clubhousecomedy.com. This
offshoot of San Francisco Comedy College puts on
popular shows at weekends and the bring-your-
own-alcohol policy ensures a convivial scene.
Tickets are typically $5–10.
Cobb's Comedy Club 915 Columbus Ave at
Lombard, North Beach ℡ 415/928-4320, ⊚ www
.cobbscomedy.com. A 400-seat room not far from
Fisherman's Wharf that consistently hosts mid-profile
touring comedians. Tickets can cost $30 for weekend
performances, plus a two-drink minimum.
The Punch Line 444 Battery St at Clay, Financial
District ℡ 415/397-7573, ⊚ www.punchline
comedyclub.com. Frontrunner in name cachet

among San Francisco's few full-scale comedy
venues, this strangely located cabaret books
nightly shows featuring well-known headliners.
Tickets usually start at $15, with a two-drink
minimum.
Purple Onion 140 Columbus St at Jackson,
North Beach ℡ 415/956-1653, ⊚ www
.caffemacaroni.com. Once a stage for Lenny
Bruce, Woody Allen and Phyllis Diller in the 1950s
and 1960s, this 80-seat cellar venue has been
revived as a comedy venue under the ownership
of adjacent restaurant *Caffè Macaroni*. Check the
website for upcoming acts, as bookings can be
inconsistent. Tickets $8–20.

Film

San Francisco **film** buffs enjoy a great assortment of local cinemas, from old-time
single-screen movie houses showing independent releases to enormous multiplexes projecting the latest major studio blockbusters. A strong community of
underground filmgoers also ensures a slate of truly alternative programming at a
few leftfield venues around town, and the **San Francisco International Film
Festival** (℡ 415/931-3456, ⊚ www.sfiff.org) in late April and early May offers an
eclectic and oddball selection, mainly at the Castro Theatre and Sundance Kabuki.
Tickets can go quickly and you'll need to book well in advance for all but the most
obscure selections.

Castro Theatre 429 Castro St at 17th,
Castro ℡ 415/621-6120, ⊚ www.thecastro
theatre.com. San Francisco's signature, c.1922
movie palace offers foreign films, classic revivals,
seating for over 1400 and the most enthusiastic
audience in town. Arrive early at evening

screenings to listen to the Wurlitzer organ and gaze
up at the spectacular chandelier.
Lumiere Theatre 1572 California St at Polk,
Russian Hill, Polk Gulch ℡ 415/267-4893, ⊚ www
.landmarktheatres.com. Located right on the
California cable-car line, this neighbourhood

cinema offers a mix of short-run rarities and new-release foreign films.

Embarcadero Center Cinema 1 Embarcadero Center, Financial District ☏415/267-4893, ⓦwww .landmarktheatres.com. Popular Downtown complex showing both first-run independents and Oscar contenders.

The Red Vic 1727 Haight St at Cole, Haight-Ashbury ☏415/668-3994, ⓦwww.redvicmovie house.com. Grab a wooden bowl full of popcorn and kick your feet up on the natty chairs and couches at this friendly collective, where the calendar is peppered with cult hits, surf movies and directors' cuts of legendary movies such as *Apocalypse Now*.

The Roxie 3117 16th St at Valencia, Mission ☏415/863-1087, ⓦwww.roxie.com. Venerable, pugnacious indie moviehouse that's always been willing to take a risk on documentaries and little-known foreign directors – although it's not above screening old Cheech & Chong favourites.

Sundance Kabuki 1881 Post St at Fillmore, Japantown ☏415/346-3243, ⓦwww.sundance cinemas.com. With advance reserved seating, sustainable details like "spudware" utensils and three eating/drinking destinations inside, this facility is like few other cinemas in the US. Programming varies from mainstream fare to eclectica.

Gay and lesbian San Francisco

San Francisco's reputation as a city of gay celebration is not new – in fact, it may be a bit outdated. Though still considered by most to be the gay capital of the world, its **gay and lesbian community** has made a definite move from the outrageous to the mainstream – a measure of its political success. The exuberant energy that went into the parading of the 1970s has taken on a much more sober, down-to-business attitude, and these days you'll find more political activists organizing conferences than drag queens throwing parties. Nowadays San Franciscans appreciate and recognize the huge economic and cultural impact of gays on the city, and openly gay politicians or businesspeople are not as much of an issue to locals as they would be anywhere else in the US, making it easy to forget that things were not always this way.

San Francisco's **gay scene** has also mellowed socially, though gay parties, parades and street fairs here still swing better than most. Like any well-organized section of society, the gay scene definitely has its social season – see opposite for highlights. Though **lesbian culture** flowered here in the 1980s and women's club nights still exist, the scene is more in evidence in bookstores than bars. Many lesbians have claimed Oakland for their own, though Bernal Heights and some areas of the Mission continue to be particularly girl-friendly.

Details of gay accommodation, bars and clubs appear on p.495 and gay-oriented theatre venues and bookstores are listed under the relevant headings throughout this chapter.

Information and resources

Located along the Castro district's main artery, the **Charles M. Holmes Campus at the Center**, 1800 Market St at Octavia, Hayes Valley (Mon–Thurs noon–10pm, Fri noon–6pm, Sat 9am–6pm; ☏415/865-5555, ⓦwww.sfcenter .org), is San Francisco's leading gay and lesbian community resource, with knowledgeable staff and plenty of information available at its first-floor information desk. Further Downtown, the **GLBT Historical Society Museum**, 657 Mission St at New Montgomery, Suite 300 (exhibit galleries Tues–Sat 1–5pm; archives and reading room Sat 1–5pm; ☏415/777-5455, ⓦwww.glbthistory.org) includes historical exhibits, programmes and art showings, as well as extensive resource archives and a reading room. For **news, information and event listings**, visit the online homes of the *Bay Times* (ⓦwww.sfbaytimes.com) and *Bay Area Reporter* (ⓦwww.ebar.com); regular print editions are also available in the Castro and other neighbourhoods.

Gay and lesbian events

AIDS Candlelight Memorial ℡415/863-4676, ℮www.candlelightmemorial.org. May. Procession from the Castro to Civic Center, commemorating all those who have died of AIDS.

Frameline ℡415/703-8650, ℮www.frameline.org. June. Short films and features from amateurs and auteurs, generally shown at the Castro Theatre, as well as the Roxie and Victoria theatres in the Mission. The oldest and largest event of its kind in the world.

San Francisco Pride ℡415/864-0831, ℮www.sfpride.org. June. One of the largest Pride festivals in the world, with an all-day parade to match. The Saturday night Dyke March is more homespun than the increasingly corporate Pride parade the following afternoon, but the whole weekend is one giant celebration of queer culture.

Up Your Alley Fair ℡415/777-3247, ℮www.folsomstreetfair.com/alley. July. The hardcore brother of Folsom Street Fair (see below) takes place on nearby Dore Alley; it's a more sex-driven event, with fewer onlookers and plenty of S&M.

Folsom Street Fair ℡415/777-3247, ℮www.folsomstreetfair.com. September. Legendary leather street-fair that seems to get more and more popular with curious voyeurs every year. Nevertheless, it's a friendly event full of unwholesome fun, held at the peak of San Francisco's good-weather season.

Castro Street Fair ℡415/841-1824, ℮www.castrostreetfair.org. October. Food and craft stalls, as well as entertainment, take over the Castro for a day.

Accommodation

Choose almost any hotel in San Francisco and a same-sex couple won't raise an eyebrow at check-in; some, like the *Queen Anne* and *Renoir* hotels (see p.444 & p.443), attract equal numbers of gay and straight visitors. Listed below are a few places that cater especially to gay and lesbian travellers. See map on p.468.

24 Henry 24 Henry St at Sanchez, Castro ℡1-800/900-5686, ℮www.24henry.com. Tucked away on a leafy residential street north of Market, this guesthouse contains five simple rooms (one with private bath) and makes a friendly retreat from the cruisey Castro scene nearby. ❸

Elaine's Hidden Haven 4005 Folsom St at Tompkins, Bernal Heights ℡1-800/446-9050, ℮www.sfhiddenhaven.com. Sequestered on a quiet, sloped street with parking, this private, lesbian-operated suite is attached to the owners' home. There's a hammock and burbling fountain in the back garden and a kitchen if you'd rather cook your own meals. ❸

Inn on Castro 321 Castro St at Market, Castro ℡415/861-0321, ℮www.innoncastro.com. This luxurious B&B is spread across two nearby houses, with eight rooms and three apartments available – all of which are brightly decorated in individual styles and have private baths. There's also a funky lounge where you can meet other guests. ❺

The Parker Guest House 520 Church St at 18th, Castro ℡1-888/520-7275, ℮www .parkerguesthouse.com. This 21-room converted mansion is set in beautiful gardens and features ample common areas, a sunny breakfast room and a sauna. ❺

Bars and clubs

San Francisco's **gay bars** are many and varied, ranging from cosy cocktail lounges to no-holds-barred leather-and-chain hangouts. The city doesn't have nearly the number of **lesbian bars** it once did, but a small handful of good ones still exist around town, particularly in Bernal Heights, up the hill from the Mission.

Many of the bars below may crank up the music later in the evening and transform into mini-clubs; among those listed here, however, only the *Café* and the *Stud* are true gay **dance clubs**. It's a good idea to check local listings for information, as new venues seem to come and go all the time. See maps on pp.448–449 and p.468.

The Café 2369 Market St at 17th, Castro ☏415/861-3846, ⊛www.cafesf.com. With its mainstream Hi-NRG/house DJs, cheap cover and nightly happy hour until 9pm, this longtime staple of the Castro club scene remains a crowd-pleaser. It's classic out-and-proud Castro, from the thumping beats to the rainbow-coloured socks strategically placed on male dancers.

The Eagle Tavern 398 12th St at Harrison, South of Market ☏415/626-0880. Mostly popular with thirty-somethings and older, although the Sunday beer specials bring in a slightly more diverse crowd. There's a great outdoor patio, live music on Thursdays and the odd mud-wrestling night.

Esta Noche 3079 16th St at Valencia, Mission ☏415/861-5757. A fun, if dingy and smelly Latino drag bar that attracts a youngish, racially mixed clientele. There's a raucous drag revue every Friday and Saturday night and drink specials until 9pm nightly. Expect to hear Ricky Martin.

Lexington Club 3464 19th St at Lexington, Mission. One of the few places in the city where the girls outnumber the boys – men must be accompanied by a woman to enter – this bustling lesbian bar attracts all sorts with its no-nonsense decor, friendly atmosphere and excellent jukebox.

Martuni's 4 Valencia St at Market, Mission. This two-room piano bar serving kitschy drinks on the edge of the Mission, Castro and Hayes Valley attracts a well-heeled, diverse crowd, with many keen to sing along to classics from Judy, Liza and Edith.

Pilsner Inn 225 Church St at Market, Castro. Mature neighbourhood bar that fills nightly with a diverse crowd playing pool and darts. There's a large patio out back, and a generally welcoming, open vibe.

Powerhouse 1347 Folsom St at Dore Alley, South of Market ☏415/552-8689. One of the prime pick-up joints in the city, this cruisey bar boasts a patio and plenty of convenient dark corners inside. Every Thursday evening sees a "wet undie" contest.

Stray Bar 309 Cortland Ave at Bennington, Bernal Heights. This welcoming neighbourhood tavern attracts a remarkably mixed crowd, although it's biggest with Bernal Heights lesbians. You may be asked to make room at the stool next to you for a customer's dog.

The Stud 399 Folsom St at Ninth, South of Market ☏415/863-6623, ⊛www.studsf.com. Legendary club that's been on the scene since the mid-1960s. It's still as popular as ever, attracting a diverse, energetic and uninhibited crowd. Don't miss the fabulously freaky drag-queen cabaret at Tranny-shack every Tuesday.

Trax 1437 Haight St at Masonic, Haight-Ashbury. The Haight's only gay bar is a bit of a dive, though it's been spiffed up slightly from its grungy yesteryear. There's a mix of gays and straights, so it's much less cruisey than other bars.

Twin Peaks Tavern 410 Castro St at Market, Castro. This corner saloon is famous for being the first gay bar in America to install transparent picture windows rather than blacked-out barriers. These days, it's laidback and filled with middle-class, older white men; a great spot for watching the lively Castro sidewalk scene.

🏃 **Wild Side West** 424 Cortland Ave at Andover, Bernal Heights. Unpretentious and friendly tavern at the centre of the Bernal Heights lesbian scene, with plenty of kitsch Americana to gaze at. There's a lovely garden out back, but without heat lamps, you'd be well advised to stay inside on a cold evening.

Shopping

Aside from the retail palaces around **Union Square** (including Macy's, Saks and practically every major designer label), San Francisco's shopping scene is refreshingly edgy, peppered with stylish homeware stores and one-off boutiques selling locally designed clothes. There's also a brilliantly varied selection of **independent booksellers** and **music stores,** and you can also expect to find a number of top **food retailers** in this gastronomically obsessed town.

It's worth remembering that, unlike many other American cities, stores in San Francisco close relatively early – 6pm Monday to Saturday and 5pm on Sunday isn't unusual – so start your major shopping expeditions early.

Shopping neighbourhoods

San Francisco's prime **shopping streets**, arranged by neighbourhood and detailed below, are sure to provide a heaping (and potentially costly) dose of retail therapy to even the most inveterate shopaholics.

The Castro Castro St between 17th and 19th streets; Market Street between Castro and Church. Gay-oriented boutiques, clubwear and shoes.

Cow Hollow Union St between Steiner and Gough. Sweet – if rather conservative – women-geared boutiques, shoe stores and homeware retailers.

Haight-Ashbury Haight Street between Stanyan and Masonic. Clothing, especially vintage and secondhand.

Hayes Valley Hayes St between Franklin and Laguna. Trendy but upscale, with edgy boutiques for men and women, as well as jewellery galleries and other high-end goodies.

The Marina Chestnut St between Broderick and Fillmore. Heavily yuppified strip of health-food stores, wine shops and women's clothing boutiques.

The Mission Valencia St between 16th and 21st. The best choice for urban hipsters, with lots of used furniture and clothing stores, bookshops and even the odd ironic pirate-gear retailer.

North Beach Grant Ave between Filbert and Vallejo. Inviting boutiques, homeware retailers and shops specializing in rare maps; also one of the newest and freshest places to find cool clothes.

Bookstores

Unsurprisingly, for a city with such a rich literary history, San Francisco excels in terrific **speciality bookstores**, from the legendary City Lights in North Beach to the new literary hub in the Mission, home to some of the city's most energized – and politicized – bookstores. As for **secondhand booksellers**, there's a fine selection in the city, but rabid old-book buyers should head to Oakland and Berkeley for even richer pickings. Most bookstores tend to be open daily from roughly 10am to 8pm, though City Lights is open daily until midnight.

General

The Booksmith 1644 Haight St at Cole, Haight-Ashbury. Solid neighbourhood shop stocking mainstream as well as countercultural titles; notable for high-profile author readings.

City Lights 261 Columbus Ave at Broadway, North Beach. Internationally storied bookstore with oddball sections such as "Stolen Continents" and "Muckraking" scattered about, and an excellent poetry room upstairs.

Green Apple Books 506 Clement St at Sixth Ave, Richmond. Wonderfully browsable store with deftly amusing touches like the regular section called "Books That Will Never Be Oprah's Picks". There's a smaller, less impressive music annexe a few doors down.

Specialist and secondhand

Argonaut Book Shop 786 Sutter St at Jones, Tenderloin. The best bookshop by far for local history, specializing in volumes on California and the West, from the Gold Rush to contemporary times. The knowledgeable staff is another major plus.

A Different Light Bookstore 489 Castro St at 18th, Castro ☎415/431-0891. Well-stocked shop featuring gay and lesbian titles, with an especially strong fiction section. Author events, including readings, are held regularly.

Dog Eared Books 900 Valencia St at 20th, Mission. Corner bookstore along Valencia's shopping strip with a sharp selection of budget-priced remainders, as well as an eclectic range of secondhand titles, most in terrific condition.

Get Lost Travel Books 1825 Market St at Guerrero, Mission. Triangular, uniquely designed speciality shop filled with unusual titles, along with standard guidebooks and travel-related gear.

Kayo Books 814 Post St at Leavenworth, Tenderloin. Glorious vintage paperback store full of bargain classics, from pulpy mysteries and sci-fi to campy 1950s sleaze fiction. Thurs–Sat only.

Modern Times Bookstore 888 Valencia St at 20th, Mission ☎415/282-9246. Hefty stock of Latin American literature and progressive political publications, as well as a small but well-chosen selection of gay and lesbian literature and radical feminist magazines. Stages regular readings of authors' works.

Record stores

Despite the predicted extinction of brick-and-mortar music retailers, several excellent speciality **record stores** soldier on in San Francisco, including shops wholly devoted to specific genres such as old-school soul and punk.

Amoeba Music 1855 Haight St at Stanyan, Haight-Ashbury. Enormously housed in a former bowling alley, this renowned emporium is one of the largest independent music retailers in the US. Its encyclopedic selection of modern music is a treasure-trove for all stripes of music fans, where ploughing through the stacks of new and used vinyl, CDs, DVDs and assorted memorabilia can while away a full afternoon.

Aquarius Records 1055 Valencia St at 21st, Mission. Aggressively indie shop with hip staff and an emphasis on all kinds of underground styles, from noise-rock to experimental and electronic.

Force of Habit Records 3565 20th St at Lexington, Mission ☏415/255-PUNK. The selection here is heavy on punk – expect to find everything from original Clash vinyl to the latest Green Day smash.

Recycled Records 1377 Haight St at Masonic, Haight-Ashbury. While mediocre for CDs, this longtime neighbourhood favourite shines best with its extensive vinyl selection, from old film soundtracks to good-condition Stones and Dylan records. Everything's secondhand, and prices are often negotiable.

Rooky Ricardo's 448 Haight St at Webster, Lower Haight. It's all soul, all the time, at this somewhat dusty but well-meaning shop in one of San Francisco's oldest African-American neighbourhoods.

Food and drink

Be sure to try **local specialities** such as Boudin's sourdough bread (see p.478), Gallo salami and Anchor Steam beer (see p.485) – all of which are true San Francisco treats. The Ferry Building, along the Embarcadero, offers an easy way to graze goods from some of northern California's best speciality food producers, with everything from bread and cheese to wine and tea on offer; its outside plaza is also home to the area's biggest farmers' market (see p.458).

If you're looking for everyday essentials, loads of **supermarkets** exist all across the city, including several branches of affordable speciality retailer Trader Joe's – its outposts on Bryant Street in South of Market and Bay Street along North Beach's northern edge are often the most convenient for visitors. California **alcohol** laws are fairly liberal: most stores carrying food also sell booze, provided you're at least 21 years of age with photo identification.

Andronico's 1200 Irving St at Funston, Sunset. The Bay Area's gourmet answer to Safeway, this pricey supermarket sells gorgeous produce and also has microbrews, good wine, craft breads, fancy cheeses, an olive bar and a terrific deli.

Cowgirl Creamery's Artisan Cheese Shop 1 Ferry Building, Embarcadero. Top-notch cheese shop featuring selections from small producers around the world, as well as the Point Reyes Station creamery's own award-winning concoctions, such as crème fraîche.

Golden Gate Meat Company 1 Ferry Building, Embarcadero. Butcher shop and charcuterie carving organic meats daily, from the usual suspects (beef, poultry) all the way to exotic game and offal. Exceptional, reasonably priced sandwiches are also available to go.

Haig's Delicacies 642 Clement St at Seventh Ave, Richmond. One of the city's oldest international food shops, *Haig's* shelves are stocked with hard-to-find food imports from around the globe, from Indian chutneys to Mediterranean meze.

The Jug Shop 1567 Pacific Ave at Polk, Russian Hill. Large wine retailer best known for its inexpensive California varietals and interesting range of New World vintages; it also has more than two hundred varieties of similarly well priced beers.

Molinari Delicatessen 373 Columbus Ave at Vallejo, North Beach. Rich with the singular aroma of cured meats, this bustling North Beach staple is jammed with Italian goodies, both familiar and exotic. Pick the bread of your choice and order a sandwich to go.

PlumpJack Wines 3201 Fillmore St at Greenwich, Cow Hollow. If you're looking to surprise the oenophile in your life with an obscure California vintage, this is your first stop – it boasts an exhaustive selection of wines from across the state.

The Real Food Company 3060 Fillmore St at Filbert, Cow Hollow. Smallish, artsy grocery store with an excellent gourmet meat counter and delicious whole-wheat pastries; it also carries

potions, vitamins and myriad health-foods. Also at 2140 Polk St, Russian Hill.

Scharffen Berger Chocolate Maker 1 Ferry Building, Embarcadero. A truly mouth-watering array of chocolate bars, sauces and other goodies from this famed Berkeley chocolate-maker.

Speciality stores and local labels

Flight 001 525 Hayes St at Octavia, Hayes Valley. This sleek, futuristic travel store sells books, funky accessories (think chunky, Day-Glo luggage tags and all-in-one shaving kits) and dapper carry-on bags. The place to stock up if you only travel first-class – or want to act like it.

Good Vibrations 603 Valencia St at 17th, Mission. Gloriously erotic store that's a co-op run by men and women; its mission is to destigmatize sex shops and make browsing fun and comfortable. It's packed with every imaginable sex toy, plus racks of erotica and candy-store-style jars of condoms. There's another branch at 1620 Polk St at Sacramento, Polk Gulch.

Jeremys 2 South Park at Second, SoMa. Local designer discount boutique where you just might find last spring's Prada dress at a fraction of the original price.

Levi's 300 Post St at Stockton, Union Square. Four levels of jeans, tops and jackets that serve as the iconic label's flagship store. Offers the company's Original Spin service, by which customers can order customized denim.

Paolo Shoes 524 Hayes St at Laguna, Hayes Valley. Local gem where designer Paolo Iantorno makes available his edgy, yet wearable limited-edition men's and women's shoe designs, which are otherwise sold in Italy. Be sure to bring your credit card, as prices hover between $200–300.

Retro Fit 910 Valencia St at 20th, Mission. Poppy, sometimes kitschy selection of smart vintage clothes; don't expect bargains, but it's well worth a visit for a chance to fish out that spot-on shirt or just-right jacket. You can also pick a style of blank T-shirt, then choose custom artwork to be transferred onto it.

Wasteland 1660 Haight St at Belvedere, Haight-Ashbury. Smart, high-end apparel sorted by style and colour. You'll pay for the ease of browsing, but it's one of the best places to find top-condition, fashionable vintage wear.

Worn Out West 582 Castro St at 19th, Castro. Shop devoted to gay fetish gear, all secondhand. Browse through Western wear, leather-studded collars, cuffs and even bow ties, plus a smattering of sex toys.

Listings

American Express Travel 455 Market St at First, Financial District (☎415/536-2600; Mon–Fri 9am–5.30pm, Sat 10am–2pm).

Car rental All major firms have branches at SFO, as well as within the city itself. Alamo: 750 Bush St at Powell, Union Square ☎1-888/826-6893; Avis: 675 Post St at Jones, Union Square ☎415/929-2555; Budget: 321 Mason St at O'Farrell, Union Square ☎415/928-7864; Dollar: 364 O'Farrell St at Taylor, Union Square ☎415/771-0836; Enterprise: 222 Mason St at Ellis, Union Square ☎415/831-1700; Hertz: 550 O'Farrell St at Jones, Tenderloin ☎415/771-2200.

Consulates Australia: 575 Market St at Second, Financial District ☎415/644-3620; Canada: 580 California St at Kearny, Financial District ☎415/834-3180; Ireland: 44 Montgomery at Post, Financial District ☎415/392-4214; UK: 1 Sansome St at Market, Financial District ☎415/617-1300.

Dental treatment For a free referral, call the San Francisco Dental Society (☎415/928-7337) or visit the California Dental Association's website (⊛www.cda.org/finddentist).

Disabled access Steep hills aside, the Bay Area is generally considered one of the most barrier-free regions around. Most public buildings have been built (or modified) for disabled access, all BART stations are accessible and most buses have lowering platforms for wheelchairs – and, usually, understanding drivers. For more information, visit ⊛www.accessnca.com.

Hospitals California Pacific Medical Center's Davies Campus, Castro and Duboce streets, Castro (☎415/600-6000), is in the geographic centre of the city and has 24hr emergency care and a doctors' referral service.

Internet Wi-fi is now a citywide standard in San Francisco and most travellers with laptops will be able to find a café with free or low-cost access in any neighbourhood, if not at their hotel or hostel.

Legal advice Contact the Bar Association of San Francisco for its Lawyer Referral & Information Service (☎ 415/989-1616, ⓦ www.sfbar.org).

Library Main Library: 100 Larkin St at Grove, Civic Center ☎ 415/557-4400, ⓦ www.sfpl.org; see p.466 for hours. Numerous branch locations in neighbourhoods around the city.

Passport and visa US Bureau of Citizenship and Immigration Services, 630 Sansome St at Washington, Financial District ☎ 415/844-5110, ⓦ www.uscis.gov.

Pharmacies Walgreens 24hr pharmacies: 498 Castro St at 18th, Castro ☎ 415/861-3136; 3201 Divisadero St at Lombard, Marina ☎ 415/931-6417; 459 Powell St at Sutter, Union Square ☎ 415/984-0790.

Post offices Bring photo identification to collect general delivery mail at one of three locations:

101 Hyde St at Fulton, Civic Center (Mon–Fri 9am–5pm); 150 Sutter St at Montgomery, Financial District (Mon–Fri 8am–5pm); 180 Steuart St at Mission, Embarcadero (Mon–Fri 7am–6pm, Sat 9am–2pm). Packages will only be held for ten days before being returned to sender ☎ 1-800/275-8777, ⓦ www.usps.com.

Religious services Grace Cathedral, 1100 California St at Taylor, Nob Hill (☎ 415/749-6300, ⓦ www.gracecathedral.org), is San Francisco's main Episcopalian (Anglican) congregation. Catholics can worship at the Cathedral of St Mary of the Assumption, 1111 Gough St at Geary, Pacific Heights (☎ 415/567-2020, ⓦ www.stmarycathedralsf.org). The city's grandest synagogue is Congregation Emanu-El, 2 Lake St at Arguello, Richmond (☎ 415/751-2535, ⓦ www.emanuelsf.org).

Sales tax A 9.5 percent tax is added to virtually all non-food items bought in a store, making prices slightly higher here than in the rest of California.

The Bay Area

Of the nearly seven million people who make their home in the San Francisco **Bay Area**, barely more than one in ten lives in the actual city of San Francisco. Everyone else is spread around one of the many less-renowned cities and suburbs that ring the bay, either down the Peninsula or across one of the two impressively engineered bridges that span the chilly waters of the world's most exquisite natural harbour. There's no doubt about the supporting role these places play in relation to San Francisco – always "the city" – but each has a distinctive character and contributes to the range of people and landscapes that makes the Bay Area one of the most desirable places in the US to live or visit.

Across the steel Bay Bridge, eight miles from Downtown San Francisco, the **East Bay** is home to the lively, left-leaning cities of **Oakland** and **Berkeley**, which together have some of the best bookstores and restaurants in the greater Bay Area, as well as a good proportion of the live music venues. The weather's generally much sunnier and warmer here too and it's easy to reach by way of the BART trains that race under the bay. The remainder of the East Bay is contained in Contra Costa County, which includes the short-lived early state capital of California, **Benicia**, as well as some leafy valleys and lofty **Mount Diablo**.

South of the city, the **Peninsula** holds some of San Francisco's oldest and most upscale suburbs, spreading down through the computer-rich **Silicon Valley** and into **San Jose** – now America's tenth largest city, which easily surpasses San Francisco in both square mileage and population, though apart from a few excellent museums there's not a lot to see. The **beaches** and seaside towns such as **Half Moon Bay** to the west, however, are excellent – sandy, clean and uncrowded – and a couple of youth hostels in old lighthouses perch on the edge of the Pacific.

For some of the most beautiful land- and seascapes in California, cross the Golden Gate Bridge or ride a ferry to **Marin County**, a mountainous peninsula that's half wealthy suburbia and half unspoiled hiking country, with **redwood forests** rising sheer out of the thundering Pacific Ocean. A range of 2500-foot peaks, crowned by **Mount Tamalpais**, divides the county down the middle, separating the yacht clubs and plush bay-view houses of **Sausalito** and **Tiburon** from the nearly untouched wilderness that runs along the Pacific Coast, culminating in the **Point Reyes National Seashore**.

The East Bay

The largest and most travelled bridge in California, connecting Downtown San Francisco to the **East Bay**, the **Bay Bridge** is part graceful suspension bridge and part heavy-duty steel truss. Built in 1933 as an economic booster during the Depression, the bridge is made from enough steel cable to wrap around the earth three times. Completed just seven months before the more famous Golden Gate, it works a lot harder for a lot less respect: a hundred million vehicles cross it each year. Local scribe Herb Caen dubbed it "the car-strangled spanner", a reflection of its often-clogged lanes. Indeed, the bridge's only claim to fame – apart from the much-broadcast videotape of its partial collapse during the 1989 earthquake – is that **Treasure Island**, where the two halves of the bridge meet, hosted the 1939 World's Fair. During World War II the island became a Navy base, but since the end of the Cold War it has been undergoing a gradual transfer to the City of San Francisco.

The Bay Bridge eventually empties into **Oakland**, a hard-working, blue-collar city at the heart of the East Bay. The city traditionally earned its livelihood from shipping and transport services, as evidenced by the enormous cranes in the massive Port of Oakland, but has undergone something of a renaissance by attracting businesses and workers from the information technology industry. Oakland spreads north along wooded foothills to **Berkeley**, an image-conscious university town that looks out to the Golden Gate and collects a mixed bag of earnest young students, much-pierced dropouts, aging 1960s radicals and Nobel Prize-winning nuclear physicists in its Cafés and bookstores.

Berkeley and Oakland blend together so much as to be virtually the same city and the hills above them are topped by a twenty-mile string of **regional parks**, providing much-needed fresh air and quick relief from the populated grids below. Spreading east and north of the hills is Contra Costa County, a huge area that contains some intriguing, historically important waterfront towns – well worth a stop if you're passing through on the way to the Wine Country – as well as some of the Bay Area's most inward-looking suburban sprawl. Across the narrow Carquinez Strait, further around the **North Bay** from the oil-refinery landscape of Richmond, lies the sleepy and little-visited former state capital of **Benicia**, vitally important during California's first twenty years of existence after the 1849 Gold Rush. In contrast, standing out from the soulless dormitory communities that fill the often baking-hot **inland valleys** are the preserved homes of an unlikely pair of influential writers: the naturalist John Muir, who, when not out hiking around Yosemite and the High Sierra, lived most of his life near **Martinez**, and the playwright Eugene O'Neill, who wrote many of his angst-ridden works at the foot of **Mount Diablo**, the Bay Area's most significant peak.

Arrival

Even if you are staying in San Francisco during your visit to the Bay Area, it's just as convenient and sometimes better value to fly direct to **Oakland International Airport** (☎510/577-4015, automated flight info ☎1-800/992-7433,

Ⓦwww.oaklandairport.com), particularly if you're coming from elsewhere in the US. Most major domestic airlines serve the facility, which is less crowded and more accessible than its San Francisco counterpart. It's an easy trip from the airport into town: the **AirBART** shuttle van (every 15min; $3; Ⓣ510/569-8310) runs to the Coliseum BART station, from where you can hop on **BART** to Berkeley, Oakland or San Francisco. Numerous door-to-door **shuttle buses** run from the airport to East Bay stops and into the city, such as A1 American (Ⓣ1-877/378-3596, Ⓦwww.a1americanshuttle.com) – expect to pay around $20 to Downtown Oakland, $30–40 to San Francisco. **Taxis** charge about $25 into Oakland and $45 into Downtown San Francisco.

The **Greyhound** station is in an insalubrious part of northern Oakland, alongside the I-980 freeway at 2103 San Pablo Ave (Ⓣ510/832-4730). **Amtrak** terminates at Second Street near Jack London Square, where a free Thruway shuttle bus heads across the Bay Bridge to the Transbay Terminal. A better option for heading into San Francisco, though, is to get off at Richmond and change onto the nearby BART trains. The most enjoyable way to arrive in the East Bay is aboard an Alameda–Oakland **ferry** ($6.25 one way; Ⓣ510/522-3300, Ⓦwww.eastbayferry.com), which sails every hour or two from San Francisco's Ferry Building and Pier 41 to Oakland's Jack London Square. The fleet also runs a service to Angel Island via Pier 41, departing from Oakland (mid-May to late Oct Sat & Sun 9am, returns 3.10pm; $14.50 round-trip, including park admission).

Information

The **Oakland CVB**, next to the enormous *Marriott Hotel* at 463 11th St (Mon–Fri 8.30am–5pm; Ⓣ510/839-9000, Ⓦwww.oaklandcvb.com), is the best source for maps, brochures and information on lodging and activities in the metropolitan area. In Berkeley, check in at the **Visit Berkeley office**, 2030 Addison St (Mon–Fri 9am–noon & 2–5pm; Ⓣ510/549-7040, Ⓦwww.visitberkeley.com). The **University of California's Visitor Services**, 101 Sproul Hall (Mon–Fri 8.30am–4.30pm; Ⓣ510/642-5215, Ⓦwww.berkeley.edu/visitors), on Sproul Plaza, has plenty of information about the Berkeley campus, hands out free self-guided tour brochures and conducts ninety-minute tours (see p.513). For information on hiking or horseriding in the many parks that top the Oakland and Berkeley hills, contact the **East Bay Regional Parks District**, 2950 Peralta Oaks Court, Oakland (Ⓣ510/562-7275, Ⓦwww.ebparks.org). The widely available *East Bay Express* (issued every Wed; free) has the most comprehensive listings of what's on in the vibrant East Bay music and arts scene and the daily *Oakland Tribune* (75¢) is also worth a look for its coverage of local politics and sporting events.

Getting around

The East Bay is linked to San Francisco (including the airport) via the underground BART Transbay **subway** (see p.440). Four lines run underneath the bay, while a fifth line operates its entire length in the East Bay between Richmond and Fremont. To phone BART from the East Bay call Ⓣ510/465-2278, or check Ⓦwww.bart.gov. From East Bay BART stations, pick up a **free transfer**, saving you 25¢ on the $2 fares of the efficient AC Transit (Ⓣ510/817-1717 ext 1111, Ⓦwww.actransit.org) **bus service**, which covers the entire East Bay. AC Transit also runs buses on a number of routes to Oakland and Berkeley from the Transbay Terminal in San Francisco. These operate all night and are the only way of getting across the bay by public transport once BART has shut down. A smaller-scale bus company that also proves useful is the Contra Costa County Connection

(☎925/676-7500, ⓦwww.cccta.org), running buses to most of the inland areas, including the John Muir and Eugene O'Neill historic houses.

One of the best ways to get around the East Bay is by **bike**. A fine cycle route follows Skyline and Grizzly Peak boulevards along the wooded crest of the hills between Berkeley and Lake Chabot. Within Berkeley itself, the Ohlone Greenway makes for a pleasant cycling or walking route up through North Berkeley to El Cerrito. Not many places rent bikes in the East Bay but one exception is Solano Avenue Cyclery, 1554 Solano Ave, Berkeley (☎510/524-1094, ⓦwww .solanoavenuecyclery.com), whose rates are $35 for a day or $140 per week for a standard bike, more for a fancy sports or mountain model. For those interested in **walking tours**, the City of Oakland sponsors free "discovery tours" (May–Oct Wed & Sat 10am; ☎510/238-3234) of various neighbourhoods.

If you're **driving**, allow yourself plenty of time to get anywhere: the East Bay has some of California's worst traffic, with the Bay Bridge and I-80 in particular jam-packed sixteen hours a day. Car-pool lanes are becoming increasingly popular, so having three or more people in your vehicle can speed things up, at least slightly.

Accommodation

The East Bay's **motels** and **hotels** are barely any better value than their San Francisco equivalents, although Berkeley in particular offers a convenient but quieter base. **Bed and breakfasts** often represent the best deals, tucked away as they are in Berkeley's leafy hills. Check with the Berkeley & Oakland Bed and Breakfast Network (☎510/547-6380, ⓦwww.bbonline.com/ca/berkeley -oakland) for a complete list. A few **campgrounds** and **dorm beds** are available in summertime, such as the summer-only student rooms in Stern Hall through the Summer Visitor Housing agency at 2601 Warring St, Berkeley (☎510/642-4444, ⓦconferenceservices.berkeley.edu).

Oakland

Jack London Inn 444 Embarcadero West, Oakland ☎1-800/549-8780, ⓦwww.jacklondoninn.com. Remodelled hotel/motel with a 1950s feel, located next to Jack London Square, providing one of the East Bay's best deals. ❶

Waterfront Plaza Hotel Jack London Square, Oakland ☎1-800/729-3638, ⓦwww.jdvhotels .com. Plush, modern hotel located on the best stretch of the Oakland waterfront, right among the square's amenities. ❻

Berkeley

Bancroft Hotel 2680 Bancroft Way, Berkeley ☎1-800/549-1002, ⓦwww.bancrofthotel.com. Small hotel with 22 rooms with queen beds, a good location right by the UC campus and fine service. Breakfast included. ❺

Berkeley City Club 2315 Durant Ave, Berkeley ☎510/848-7800, ⓦwww.berkeleyhistoricalhotel .com. Two blocks from the UC campus, this B&B was designed by Hearst Castle architect Julia Morgan, with an indoor swimming pool and exercise room. Each of the spacious rooms has a private bath. ❺

Berkeley YMCA 2001 Allston Way ☎510/848-6400, ⓦwww.baymca.org. Berkeley's best bargain accommodation, a block from BART; rates, starting at $45 for a single, include use of gym and pool. No dorms. ❷

Claremont Resort & Spa 41 Tunnel Rd, Berkeley ☎1-800/551-7266, ⓦwww .claremontresort.com. Built in 1915, The *Claremont* is the lap of luxury among Berkeley hotels. Lavish rooms come with data ports for your laptop, hairdryers, cable TV and big windows, some overlooking the large outdoor pool; spa sessions begin around $100 per hour for facials or massages. ❽

French Hotel 1538 Shattuck Ave, North Berkeley ☎510/548-9930, ⓦwww.french-hotel.com. Small and comfortable hotel with 18 standard rooms in the heart of Berkeley's Gourmet Ghetto. ❹

Golden Bear Inn 1620 San Pablo Ave, West Berkeley ☎1-800/525-6770, ⓦwww.golden bearinn.com. The most pleasant of the many motels in the "flatlands" of West Berkeley, whose decent rooms have smart furnishings. ❷

Nash Hotel 2045 University Ave, Berkeley ☎510/841-1163, ⓦwww.nashhotel.com. Recently refurbished Chinese-owned hotel; the rooms are now clean and decently furnished, though on the small side. ❷

Rose Garden Inn 2740 Telegraph Ave, Berkeley
℡1-800/992-9005, ⓦwww.rosegardeninn.com.
All 40 rooms are stylishly decorated with fireplaces
in this attractive mock-Tudor mansion half a mile
south of UC Berkeley. ❹

Further out
East Brother Light Station 117 Park Place,
Point Richmond ℡510/233-2385, ⓦebls.org.
Five rooms in a converted lighthouse, on an
island in the straits linking the San Francisco and
San Pablo bays. Not a handy base for seeing the
sights; this is an adventurous retreat for an
evening. Prices include highly rated gourmet
dinners with wine as well as breakfast. Thursday
to Sunday nights only. ❽

Union Hotel and Gardens 401 1st St, Benicia
℡707/746-0100, ⓦwww.unionhotelbenicia.com.
Historic hotel and once a bordello, now converted
into a classy bed and breakfast with twelve rooms,
all featuring a jacuzzi. ❸

Campgrounds
Chabot Family Campground Off I-580 in East
Oakland ℡1-888/327-2757, ⓦwww.ebparks.org.
Year-round tent-only places, with hot showers and
lots of good hiking nearby. Reservations wise in
summer; $20 per site.
Mount Diablo State Park 20 miles east of
Oakland off I-680 in Contra Costa County
℡510/837-2525, ⓦwww.parks.ca.gov. RV and
tent places in three separate sites; $30.

Oakland

What was the use of me having come from Oakland, it was not natural for me to
have come from there yes write about it if I like or anything if I like but not there,
there is no there there.

Gertrude Stein, *Everybody's Autobiography*

As the workhorse of the Bay Area, **OAKLAND** is commonly known as a place of
little or no play. One of the busiest ports on the West Coast and the western
terminal of the country's rail network, it's also the spawning ground of some of
America's most unabashedly revolutionary **political movements**, such as the
militant **Black Panthers**, who gave a radical voice to the African-American
population, and the **Symbionese Liberation Army**, who demanded a ransom for
kidnapped heiress Patty Hearst in the form of free food distribution to the poor.

The city is also the birthplace of literary legends **Gertrude Stein** and **Jack
London**, who grew up here at approximately the same time, though in entirely
different circumstances – Stein was a stockbroker's daughter, while London was an
orphaned delinquent. Most of the waterfront where London used to steal oysters
and lobsters is now named in his memory, while Stein, who was actually born in
East Oakland, is all but ignored here, not surprising given her famously unflattering quote about the place.

Indeed it is only in recent years that the city has begun to shake off its negative
image through recent efforts to revitalize (some say gentrify) the town and slash its
infamous crime rate. These were initiated by former Mayor **Jerry "Moonbeam"
Brown**, who drew in thousands of new residents by advertising the city's lower
rents and consistently sunny climate, and were continued in less flamboyant style
by his successor, Ronald V. Dellums. Rents in the increasingly popular **Rockridge**
and **Lake Merritt** districts now rival San Francisco prices. The city has also
attracted a significant number of lesbians, who've left San Francisco's Castro and
Mission, as well as a great number of artists pushed from their SoMa lofts by
sky-high rents into the warehouses of West Oakland.

Downtown Oakland

Coming by BART from San Francisco, get off at the Twelfth Street–Civic Center
station and you'll find yourself at the open-air shopping and office space of **City
Center** in the heart of **DOWNTOWN OAKLAND**. Bustling on weekdays with
the nine-to-five contingent, the area can seem eerily deserted outside at other
times. Downtown's compact district of spruced-up Victorian storefronts,

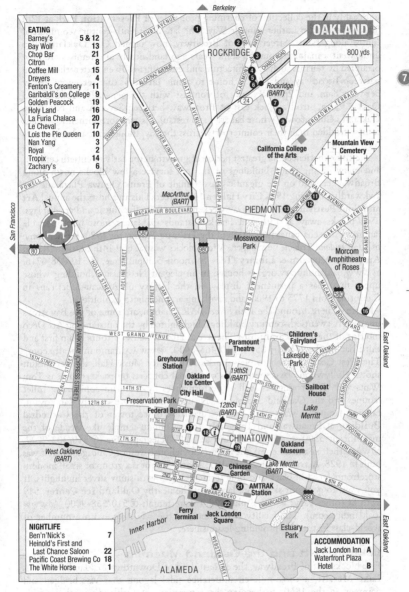

OAKLAND

▲ *Berkeley*

ASHBY AVENUE

0   800 yds

ROCKRIDGE

Rockridge (BART)

BROADWAY TERRACE

EATING

Barney's	5 & 12
Bay Wolf	13
Chop Bar	21
Citron	8
Coffee Mill	15
Dreyers	4
Fenton's Creamery	11
Garibaldi's on College	9
Golden Peacock	19
Holy Land	16
La Furia Chalaca	20
Le Cheval	17
Lois the Pie Queen	10
Nan Yang	3
Royal	2
Tropix	14
Zachary's	6

ALCATRAZ AVENUE

SHATTUCK AVENUE

CLAREMONT AVENUE

COLLEGE AVENUE

CHABOT ROAD

24

Mountain View Cemetery

California College of the Arts

PLEASANT VALLEY AVENUE

POWELL ST.

San Francisco

80

N

STANFORD AVE.

MARTIN LUTHER KING JR WAY

MacArthur (BART)

TELEGRAPH AVENUE

W MACARTHUR BOULEVARD

PIEDMONT

PIEDMONT AVE.

BROADWAY

OAKLAND AVENUE

GRAND AVENUE

24

Mosswood Park

980

580

HOLLIS STREET

ADELINE STREET

MARKET STREET

SAN PABLO AVENUE

BROADWAY

Morcom Amphitheatre of Roses

MACARTHUR BOULEVARD

580

East Bay

MANDELA PARKWAY (CYPRESS STREET)

PERALTA STREET

16TH STREET

WEST GRAND AVENUE

Paramount Theatre

Children's Fairyland

BELLEVUE AVENUE

Lakeside Park

LAKESHORE AVENUE

East Bay

Greyhound Station

19thSt (BART)

19TH STREET

WEBSTER STREET

HARRISON STREET

Sailboat House

Lake Merritt

14TH ST

12TH STREET

Oakland Ice Center
City Hall

Preservation Park
Federal Building

12thSt (BART)

11TH ST

9TH ST

7TH ST

LAKESIDE DRIVE

PARK BLVD

FOOTHILL BLVD

West Oakland (BART)

4TH ST

2ND ST

WASHINGTON

CHINATOWN

7TH ST

Lake Merritt (BART)

Oakland Museum

E 14TH STREET

E 8TH STREET

EMBARCADERO

Chinese Garden

AMTRAK Station

880

East Oakland

NIGHTLIFE

Ben'n'Nick's	7
Heinold's First and Last Chance Saloon	22
Pacific Coast Brewing Co	18
The White Horse	1

Inner Harbor

Ferry Terminal

Jack London Square

EMBARCADERO

Estuary Park

WEBSTER STREET

ALAMEDA

ACCOMMODATION

Jack London Inn	A
Waterfront Plaza Hotel	B

overlooked by modern hotels and office buildings, has undergone an ambitious programme of restoration and redevelopment for well over a decade. Fraught with allegations of illegal dealings and incompetent planning, the initiative has not been an unqualified success. One of the more controversial projects was the moat-like I-980 freeway, the main route through Oakland since the collapse of the Cypress Freeway in the 1989 earthquake; to make room, entire blocks were cleared of houses. Yet there were efforts to maintain the city's architectural heritage, most noticeably in the collection of charming properties of **Preservation Park** at 12th Street and Martin Luther King Jr Way. The late nineteenth-century commercial centre along Ninth Street west of Broadway, now tagged **Old Oakland**, also underwent a major restoration some years ago, and nearly all premises are now occupied by tenants such as architecture and design firms. Even better, the section between Broadway and Clay is home to a fine **farmers' market** every Friday between 8am and 2pm. By way of contrast with the generally subdued Old Oakland area, stroll a block east of Broadway, between Seventh and Ninth, to Oakland's **Chinatown**, whose bakeries and restaurants are more authentic and less tourist-trodden than their counterparts across the bay, though not as lively nor as picturesque.

The city experienced its greatest period of growth in the early twentieth century, and many of the grand buildings of this era survive a few blocks north along Broadway, centred on the gigantic grass triangle of **Frank Ogawa Plaza** and the awkwardly imposing 1914 **City Hall** on 14th Street. This area hosts the annual **Art and Soul Festival** over Labor Day weekend, featuring live music and art displays. Two blocks away at 13th and Franklin stands Oakland's most unmistakeable landmark, the chateauesque lantern of the **Tribune Tower**, the 1920s former home of the *Oakland Tribune* newspaper. A few blocks west at 659 14th St, the **African American Museum & Library** (Tues–Sat noon–5.30pm; free; ℡ 510/238-6716, ⓦ www.oaklandlibrary.org) is housed in an elegant Neoclassical building whose upper floor has a permanent display on the history of African-Americans in California from 1775 to 1900, and revolving art and photo exhibitions.

North of here, around the 19th Street BART station, are some of the Bay Area's finest early twentieth-century buildings, highlighted by the outstanding Art Deco interior of the 1931 **Paramount Theatre** at 2025 Broadway (tours 10am first and third Sat of the month; $5; ℡ 510/465-6400, ⓦ www.paramounttheatre.com). The West Coast's answer to New York's Radio City Music Hall, the Paramount shows Hollywood classics and hosts occasional concerts by rockers such as Tom Waits and Neil Young, as well as performances by stand-up comedians, ballet troupes and the Oakland Symphony. Nearby buildings are equally flamboyant, ranging from the wafer-thin Gothic "flatiron" office tower of the **Cathedral Building** at Broadway and Telegraph, to the Hindu-temple-like facade of the magnificent 3500-seat **Fox Oakland** at 1807 Telegraph Ave (℡ 510/302-2277, ⓦ www.thefoxoakland.com), the largest moviehouse west of Chicago when it was built in 1928. Across the street, the 1931 **Floral Depot** is a group of small modern storefronts faced in black-and-blue terracotta tiles with shiny silver highlights. If you want to get your skates on, lace up at the nearby **Oakland Ice Center**, 519 18th St (times vary; $5.50–8 plus $2.50 skate rental; ℡ 510/268-9000, ⓦ www .oaklandice.com). The facility is the finest in the Bay Area, with a number of world-class instructors providing lessons here.

Lake Merritt and the Oakland Museum

Five blocks east of Broadway, the eastern third of Downtown Oakland comprises **Lake Merritt**, a three-mile-circumference tidal lagoon that was bridged and dammed in the 1860s to become the centrepiece of Oakland's most desirable neighbourhood. All that remains of the many fine houses that once circled the lake is the elegant **Camron-Stanford House**, on the southwest shore at 1418 Lakeside Drive, a graceful Italianate mansion whose sumptuous interior is open for visits (3rd Wed of the month 1–4pm; $5; ℡ 510/444-1876, ⓦ www.cshouse.org). The lake is also the nation's oldest wildlife refuge, with migrating flocks of ducks, geese and herons breaking their journeys here. **Lakeside Park** lines the north shore, where you can rent canoes, rowboats, kayaks, pedal boats, sailboats and catamarans

($10–18 per hour, $10–20 deposit) from the **Sailboat House** (March–May Mon–Fri 10.30am–6pm, Sat & Sun 10.30am–5pm; summer Mon–Fri 9am–6pm, Sat & Sun 10am–6pm; ⊤510/238-2196, ⊛www.sailoakland.com). If you don't want to steer yourself, you can be serenaded on the overpriced but romantic Gondola Servizio (from $40 for 30min; ⊤1-866/737-8494, ⊛www.gondolaservizio.com).

Kids will like the puppet shows and pony rides at the **Children's Fairyland** (summer Mon–Fri 10am–4pm, Sat & Sun 10am–5pm; times vary through rest of year; $7; ⊤510/452-2259, ⊛www.fairyland.org), along Grand Avenue on the northwest edge of the park. At night, the lake is lit up by the "Necklace of Lights", an elegant source of local pride. Once you reach the north side of the lake, be sure to stroll under the MacArthur Freeway to soak up the relaxed atmosphere of the cafés and shops along Grand and Lakeshore avenues. Note the huge Art Deco-cum-mock-Classical facade of the still-functioning **Grand Lake Movie Theater**, a bastion of subversive political films.

Two blocks south of the lake, only a block up from the Lake Merritt BART station, the **Oakland Museum**, 1000 Oak St (Wed, Sat & Sun 11am–5pm, Thurs & Fri 11am–8pm; $12, free first Sun of the month; ⊤510/238-2200, ⊛www.museumca.org), is undoubtedly Oakland's most worthwhile stop, not only for the exhibits but also for the superb modern building in which they are housed, topped by a terraced rooftop sculpture garden that gives great views out over the lake and the city. The museum covers many diverse areas: displays on the **ecology** of California, including a simulated walk from the seaside through various natural habitats up to the 14,000-foot summits of the Sierra Nevada mountains; state history, ranging from old mining equipment to the guitar that Berkeley-born Country Joe MacDonald played at the Woodstock Festival in 1969; and a broad survey of works by California artists and craftspeople, highlights of which include turn-of-the-twentieth-century **furniture**. There's also an excellent collection of **photography** by Eadweard Muybridge, Dorothea Lange, Imogen Cunningham and many others, as well as a collector's gallery that rents and sells works by California artists.

Jack London Square

Half a mile south of Downtown Oakland at the foot of Broadway, waterfront **Jack London Square** is Oakland's sole concession to the tourist trade. Also accessible by direct ferry from San Francisco (see p.441), this somewhat sterile complex of boutiques and restaurants was named after the self-taught writer who grew up pirating shellfish around here but is about as distant from the spirit of the man as it's possible to get. Jack London's best story, *The Call of the Wild*, was written about his adventures in the Alaskan Yukon, where he carved his initials in a small cabin that has been reconstructed here. The one sight worth stopping at is **Heinold's First and Last Chance Saloon** (see p.522), built in 1883 from the hull of a whaling ship. Jack London really did drink here, and the collection of yellowed portraits of him on the wall are the only genuine thing about the writer you'll find on the square.

Aside from London memorabilia, there are a few other interesting things to do here. At the western end of the square you can visit a couple of **historical vessels**; dockside tours are available for both the *Light Ship Relief* (Sat & Sun 11am–4pm; $5; ⊤510/272-0544) and the USS *Potomac* (Wed, Fri & Sun 11am–3pm; $10; ⊤510/627-1215, ⊛www.usspotomac.org), Franklin D. Roosevelt's famous "floating White House". On Sunday, the square bustles with the weekly farmers' market or there's a good **Produce Market**, a few short blocks inland along Third and Fourth streets. This bustling warehouse district has fruit and vegetables by the forklift-load, and is at its liveliest early in the morning, from about 5am.

East Oakland

The bulk of Oakland spreads along foothills and flatlands to the east of Downtown, in neighbourhoods running down the main thoroughfares of Foothill and MacArthur boulevards. Gertrude Stein grew up here, though her childhood home was long ago torn down and replaced by a dozen Craftsman-style bungalows – the simple 1920s wooden houses that cover most of **East Oakland**, each fronted by a patch of lawn and divided from its neighbour by a narrow concrete driveway. The main artery through the area is East 14th Street, whose string of cheap Mexican restaurants and Latino shops sums up its ethnic ambience.

A quick way out from the gridded streets and sidewalks of the city is to take AC Transit bus #64 from Downtown east up into the hills to **Joaquin Miller Park**, the most easily accessible of Oakland's hilltop open spaces. It stands on the former grounds of "The Hights", the misspelled home of the "Poet of the Sierras", Joaquin Miller, who made his name playing the eccentric frontier American in the literary salons of 1870s London. Renowned more for his outrageous behaviour than his literary prowess, he became famous by wearing bizarre clothes and biting debutantes on the ankle. For years, Japanese poet Yone Noguchi also lived here, working the sprinkler as Miller impressed lady visitors with a rain dance he claimed to have learned from Native Americans.

Perched in the hills at the foot of the park, the pointed towers of the **Mormon Temple**, 4766 Lincoln Ave, look like missile-launchers designed by the Wizard of Oz – unmissable by day or floodlit night. In December, speakers hidden in the landscaping make it seem as if the plants are singing Christmas carols. Though you can't go inside the main temple unless you're a confirmed Mormon, there are great views from its courtyard out over the entire Bay Area, and a small museum explains the tenets of the faith (daily 9am–9pm; free); expect to be greeted and offered a free personalized tour of the museum by one of the faithful upon entering. Several miles up in the hills behind the temple, the gigantic **Chabot Space & Science Center**, 10000 Skyline Blvd (Wed & Thurs 10am–5pm, Fri & Sat 10am–10pm, Sun 11am–5pm; summer also Tues 10am–5pm; $14.95; ⓣ510/336-7300, ⓦwww.chabotspace.org), is a state-of-the-art museum with permanent interactive displays, temporary exhibitions, working telescopes and a fine **planetarium** – daytime shows are included in the admission but special evening events cost extra. The museum can be reached on AC Transit bus #53 from the Fruitvale BART station.

Out past the airport in the suburb of San Leandro, the **Oakland Zoo** (summer Mon–Fri 10am–4pm, Sat & Sun 10am–5.30pm; winter daily 10am–4pm; $12.50; ⓣ510/632-9525, ⓦwww.oaklandzoo.org) is home to over three hundred species of animals, comfortably nestled in the rolling hills of 525-acre Knowland Park; AC Transit bus #56 heads out here from Oakland, while it costs $7 to park a car. The only other place of interest out in this direction is in **Fremont**, at the end of the BART line, where the peaceful and leafy **Mission San Jose de Guadalupe** (daily 10am–5pm; donation), which was completely rebuilt some years ago, stands on Mission Boulevard south of the I-680 freeway.

North Oakland and Rockridge

The high-priced hills of **North Oakland**, which lost three thousand homes and 26 people in a horrific fire in 1991, are still lush and green, though the thick foliage that made the area so attractive has never been allowed to grow back fully in order to prevent more fires. These bay-view homes, some of the area's most valuable real estate, look out across some of its poorest – the neglected flatlands below, which in the 1960s were the proving grounds of Black Panthers Bobby Seale and Huey Newton.

Broadway is the dividing line between the two halves of North Oakland, and also gives access (via the handy AC Transit #51 bus) to most sights and activities. East of Broadway, **Piedmont Avenue**, one of Oakland's most neighbourly streets, is lined by a number of small bookstores and cafés. At the north end of Piedmont Avenue, the **Mountain View Cemetery** was laid out in 1863 by Frederick Law Olmsted (designer of New York's Central Park) and holds the elaborate dynastic tombs of San Francisco's most powerful families – the Crockers, the Bechtels and the Ghirardellis. Next door, the columbarium, known as the **Chapel of the Chimes**, 4499 Piedmont Ave (daily 9am–5pm; free; ☏510/654-0123), was designed by Julia Morgan of Hearst Castle fame during her decade-long involvement with the chapel, beginning in 1921. The structure is remarkable for its seemingly endless series of urn-filled rooms, grouped together around sky-lit courtyards, bubbling fountains and intimate sanctuaries – all connected by ornate staircases of every conceivable length. Morgan wanted the space to sing of life, not death, and she's succeeded – there's no better place in Oakland to wander about in peace, or even plop down with a book. Try to visit during one of the regular concerts held here for a completely unique – and distinctly Californian – experience.

Back on Broadway, just past College Avenue, Broadway Terrace climbs up along the edge of the fire area to small **Lake Temescal**, where you can swim in summer, then continues on up to the forested ridge at the **Robert Sibley Regional Preserve**. This includes the 1761-foot volcanic cone of Round Top Peak and offers panoramas of the entire Bay Area. The peak has been dubbed the "Volcanic Witch Project" by the local media due to the five mysterious mazes, carved into the dirt and lined with stones, located in the canyons around the crater. Nobody knows where they came from, but navigating the designs leads to their centre, where visitors add to the pile of diverse offerings. Skyline Boulevard runs through the park, connecting to Lake Chabot twelve miles south and Grizzly Peak Boulevard, which winds five miles north through the Berkeley Hills to Tilden Park.

The majority of the Broadway traffic, including the AC Transit #51 bus, cuts off onto College Avenue through Oakland's most upscale shopping district, **Rockridge**, whose upper reaches merge into Berkeley. Spreading for half a mile on either side of the Rockridge BART station, the quirky stores and restaurants here, despite their undeniable yuppie overtones, surpass Piedmont's in variety and volume.

Berkeley

This Berkeley was like no somnolent Siwash out of her own past at all, but more akin to those Far Eastern or Latin American universities you read about, those autonomous culture media where the most beloved of folklores may be brought into doubt, cataclysmic of dissents voiced, suicidal of commitments chosen – the sort that bring governments down.

Thomas Pynchon, *The Crying of Lot 49*

More than any other American city, **BERKELEY** conjures up an image of 1960s student dissent. When college campuses across the nation were **protesting** the Vietnam War, it was the students of the University of California, Berkeley, who led the charge – gaining a name as the vanguard of what was increasingly seen as a challenge to the authority of the state. Full-scale battles were fought almost daily here at one point, on the campus and its surrounding streets, and there were times when Berkeley looked almost on the brink of revolution itself: students (and others) throwing stones and gas bombs were met with tear-gas volleys and

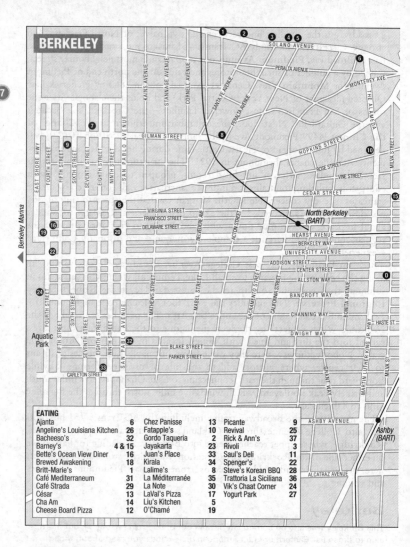

BERKELEY

North Berkeley (BART)

Aquatic Park

Ashby (BART)

EATING

Ajanta	6	Chez Panisse	13	Picante	9
Angeline's Louisiana Kitchen	26	Fatapple's	10	Revival	25
Bacheeso's	32	Gordo Taqueria	2	Rick & Ann's	37
Barney's	4 & 15	Jayakarta	23	Rivoli	3
Bette's Ocean View Diner	16	Juan's Place	33	Saul's Deli	11
Brewed Awakening	18	Kirala	34	Spenger's	22
Britt-Marie's	1	Lalime's	8	Steve's Korean BBQ	28
Café Mediterraneum	31	La Méditerranée	35	Trattoria La Siciliana	36
Café Strada	29	La Note	30	Vik's Chaat Corner	24
César	13	LaVal's Pizza	17	Yogurt Park	27
Cha Am	14	Liu's Kitchen	5		
Cheese Board Pizza	12	O'Chamé	19		

truncheons by National Guard troops under the nominal command of then-Governor Ronald Reagan.

Such action was inspired by the mood of the time and continued well into the 1970s, although during the conservative 1980s and Clinton-dominated 1990s, Berkeley politics became far less confrontational. Yet despite an influx of more conformist students, a surge in the number of exclusive restaurants and the dismantling of the city's rent-control programme, the progressive legacy has remained in the city's independent **bookstores** (see box, p.512) and at sporadic political demonstrations. Even though such an obvious target for bile as George W. Bush is no longer in power, Berkeley remains a bastion of the **antiwar movement** and streets like Telegraph Avenue are festooned with posters, stickers, badges and T-shirts questioning the occupation of Iraq and the war in Afghanistan.

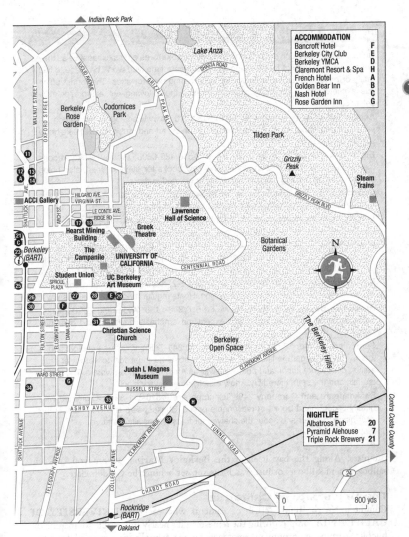

ACCOMMODATION

Bancroft Hotel	F
Berkeley City Club	E
Berkeley YMCA	D
Claremont Resort & Spa	H
French Hotel	A
Golden Bear Inn	B
Nash Hotel	C
Rose Garden Inn	G

NIGHTLIFE

Albatross Pub	20
Pyramid Alehouse	7
Triple Rock Brewery	21

The **University of California**, right in the centre of town, completely dominates Berkeley and makes a logical starting point for a visit. Its many grand buildings and over 30,000 students give off a definite energy, which spills down the raucous stretch of Telegraph Avenue that runs south from the campus and holds most of the student hangouts, including a dozen or so lively cafés, as well as a number of fine bookstores. Older students, and a good percentage of the faculty, congregate in the **Northside** area, the part of **North Berkeley** just above the campus, popping down from their woodsy hillside homes to partake of goodies from the **Gourmet Ghetto**, a stretch of Shattuck Avenue crammed with restaurants, delis and bakeries. Of quite distinct character are the flatlands that spread through **West Berkeley** down to the bay, a poorer but increasingly gentrified district that mixes old Victorian houses with builders' yards and light-industrial

Berkeley's bookstores

Unsurprisingly for a university town, Berkeley's **bookstores** are as exhaustive as they are exhausting. Perfect for browsing and taking your time, you won't be made to feel guilty or obliged to buy a book you've been poring over for ages. The tourist office has a useful list of over fifty shops, of which the following are a representative selection:

Analog Books 1816 Euclid Ave ☎510/843-1816, ⍟www.analogbookstore.com. A variety of quality books to choose from on graphics, art and music, as well as a good stock of magazines.

Black Oak Books 2618 San Pablo Ave ☎510/486-0698, ⍟www.blackoakbooks .com. Huge selection of secondhand and new books for every interest; also holds regular evening readings by internationally acclaimed authors.

Comic Relief 2026 Shattuck Ave ☎510/843-5002, ⍟www.comicrelief.net. All the mainstream stuff, plus self-published mini-comics by locals.

Lewin's Metaphysical Books 2644 Ashby Ave ☎510/843-4491. The place to come for the best selection on spirituality, religion, astrology and other arcane subjects.

Moe's Books 2476 Telegraph Ave ☎510/849-2087, ⍟www.moesbooks.com. An enormous selection of new and used books on four floors, with esoteric surprises in every field of study; perfect for academics, book collectors and browsers.

Mrs Dalloway's 2904 College Ave ☎510/704-8222, ⍟www.mrsdalloways.com. New store specializing in literature and gardening. Hosts regular readings and slideshows.

Revolution Books 2425 Channing Way ☎510/848-1196. Wide range of books on political themes with, as you might expect, an emphasis on leftist and anarchist thought.

Serendipity Books 1201 University Ave ☎510/841-7455, ⍟www.serendipitybooks .com. This vast, garage-like bookstore is an absolute must for collectors of first-edition or obscure fiction and poetry, as well as African- American writers. The prices are fair, and the staff, incredibly, know exactly where everything is.

Shakespeare and Company 2499 Telegraph Ave ☎510/841-8916. Crammed with quality secondhand books at reasonable prices, Shakespeare and Company is the best place to linger and scour the shelves for finds, especially literature.

premises. Along the bay itself is the **Berkeley Marina**, where you can rent sailboards and sailboats or just watch the sun set behind the Golden Gate.

The University of California

Caught up in the frantic crush of students who pack the **UNIVERSITY OF CALIFORNIA** campus during the semesters, it's nearly impossible to imagine the bucolic learning environment envisaged by the school's high-minded founders. When the Reverend Henry Durant and other East Coast academics decided to set up shop here in the 1860s, these rolling foothills were still largely given over to dairy herds and wheatfields. In 1866, while surveying the land, a trustee recited "Westward the course of the empire takes its way", from a poem by George Berkeley. Moved by the moment, all assembled agreed to name their school after the bishop. Construction work on the two campus buildings – imaginatively named North Hall and South Hall – was still going on when the first 200 students, including 22 women, moved here from Oakland in 1873. Since then an increasing number of buildings have been squeezed into the half-mile-square main campus, and the state-funded university has become one of America's most prestigious, with so many Nobel laureates on the faculty that it's said you have to win one just to get a parking permit. University physicists built the first cyclotron and plutonium was discovered here in 1941, along with thirteen other synthetic elements (including berkelium and californium). As such, sketches for the first atomic bomb began here. Nuclear weaponry and overcrowding aside, the beautifully landscaped campus, stepping down from the eucalyptus-covered Berkeley Hills toward the Golden Gate, is eminently strollable. With maps posted everywhere, you'd have to try hard to get lost – though enthusiastic students will show you around on a free ninety-minute **tour** (Mon–Sat 10am, Sun 1pm; ℡510/642-5215), explaining the campus's history, architecture and flavour. Be sure to take one if you want a fuller picture of Berkeley beyond looking at facades and the faces of passing students. Tours begin from the University's Visitor Services (see p.502), except at weekends, when they start at the Campanile (see below).

A number of footpaths climb the hill from the Berkeley BART station on Shattuck Avenue, but the best way to get a feel for the place is to follow Strawberry Creek from the top of Center Street across the southeast corner of the campus, emerging from the groves of redwood and eucalyptus trees at **Sproul Plaza**. The largest public space on campus, it's often enlivened by street musicians playing for change on the steps of the **Student Union** building. Sather Gate, which bridges Strawberry Creek at the north end of Sproul Plaza, marks the entrance to the older part of the campus. Up the hill, past the imposing facade of Wheeler Hall, the 1914 landmark **Campanile** (Mon–Fri 10am–4pm; $2) is modelled after the one in the Piazza San Marco in Venice; take an elevator to the top for a great view of the campus and the entire Bay Area. At the foot of the tower stands the redbrick **South Hall**, the sole survivor of the original pair of buildings.

Higher up in the hills, above the 80,000-seat Memorial Stadium, the lushly landscaped **Botanical Garden** (daily 9am–5pm, closed first Tues of month; $9, free on first Thurs of month; ℡510/643-2755) defeats on-campus claustrophobia with its thirty acres of plants and cacti. Near the crest of the hills, with great views out over the bay, a full-sized fibreglass sculpture of a whale stretches out in front of the space-age **Lawrence Hall of Science** (daily 10am–5pm; $12; ℡510/642-5132, ⓦwww.lawrencehallofscience.org), an excellent museum and learning centre that features earthquake simulations, model dinosaurs and a planetarium, plus hands-on exhibits for kids in the Wizard's Lab. Both the gardens and the Lawrence Hall of Science are accessible on weekdays via the free UC Berkeley Shuttle bus from the campus or the Berkeley BART station.

In the southeast corner of the campus, the **Phoebe Hearst Museum of Anthropology** in Kroeber Hall (Wed–Sat 10am–4.30pm, Sun noon–4pm; free; ℡510/642-3682, ⓦwww.hearstmuseum.berkeley.edu) holds a variety of changing exhibits as well as an intriguing display of artefacts made by Ishi, the last surviving Yahi Indian who was found near Mount Lassen in Northern California in 1911. Anthropologist (and father of writer Ursula Le Guin) Alfred Kroeber brought Ishi to the museum, then located on the UC San Francisco campus, where he lived under the scrutiny of scientists and journalists – in effect, in a state of captivity – until his death from tuberculosis a few years later.

The brutally modern, angular concrete of the **Berkeley Art Museum** at 2626 Bancroft Way (Wed & Fri–Sun 11am–5pm, Thurs 11am–7pm; $10, free on first Thurs; ℡510/642-0808, ⓦwww.bampfa.berkeley.edu) is a stark contrast to the campus's older buildings. Its sky-lit, open-plan galleries hold works by Picasso, Cézanne, Rubens and other notables, although the star of the show is the collection of 1950s American painter Hans Hofmann's energetic and colourful abstract paintings on the top floor. The museum is renowned for its cutting-edge, changing exhibitions: the main space hosts a range of major shows – such as Robert Mapplethorpe's controversial photographs – while the Matrix Gallery focuses on lesser-known, generally local artists. The **Pacific Film Archive**, diagonally opposite at 2575 Bancroft, features nightly showings of classics and obscurities, while other artistic fare can be enjoyed at **Zellerbach Hall** (see p.523).

Telegraph Avenue

Downtown Berkeley – basically two department stores, a few banks, a post office and the City Hall building – lies west of the university campus around the Berkeley BART station on Shattuck Avenue, but the real activity centres on **Telegraph Avenue**, which runs south of the university from Sproul Plaza. This thoroughfare saw some of the worst of the 1960s riots and is still a frenetic bustle, especially the four short blocks closest to the university, which are packed with cafés and secondhand bookstores. Sidewalk vendors selling jewellery and subversive souvenirs are not as ubiquitous as they used to be but down-and-outs still hustle for spare change and spout psychotic poetry. At no. 2455 the original Amoeba Records (☎510/549-1125), whose vast younger sister is across the bay in Haight-Ashbury, still houses the East Bay's widest selection of used and new music.

People's Park, now a slightly seedy and partly overgrown plot of land half a block up behind Amoeba, was another battleground in the late 1960s, when organized and spirited resistance to the university's plans to develop the site into dormitories brought out the troops, who shot dead an onlooker by mistake. To many, the fact that the park is still a community-controlled open space (and outdoor flophouse for Berkeley's legions of pushers and homeless) symbolizes a small victory in the battle against the Establishment, though it's not a pleasant or particularly safe place to hang about, at least after dark. Though its message is rather undermined by its insalubrious surroundings, a mural along Haste Street recalls some of the reasons why the battles were fought, in the words of student leader Mario Savio: "There's a time when the operation of the machine becomes so odious, makes you so sick at heart, that you can't take part, you can't even tacitly take part. And you've got to put your bodies upon the gears and upon the wheels, upon the levers, upon all the apparatus, and you've got to make it stop."

Directly across Bowditch Street from People's Park stands one of the finest buildings in the Bay Area, Bernard Maybeck's **Christian Science Church**. Built in 1910, it's an eclectic and thoroughly modern structure, laid out in a simple Greek-cross floor plan and spanned by a massive redwood truss with carved Gothic tracery and Byzantine painted decoration. The interior is only open on Sundays for worship and for tours at 11am, but the outside is worth lingering over, its cascade of gently pitched roofs and porticoes carrying the eye from one handcrafted detail to another.

North Berkeley

North Berkeley is a subdued neighbourhood of professors and postgraduate students, spreading from the flat leafy blocks around the BART lines to the steep, twisting streets that climb up the lushly overgrown hills north of the campus. At the foot of the hills, some of the Bay Area's finest **restaurants** and **delis** – most famously *Chez Panisse* (see p.520) – have sprung up along **Shattuck Avenue** to form the so-called Gourmet Ghetto. There are also a few **galleries**, most notably ACCI, 1652 Shattuck Ave (Tues–Thurs 11am–6pm, Fri 11am–7pm, Sat 10am–6pm, Sun noon–5pm; free; ☎510/843-2527), an arts-and-crafts co-operative designed to exhibit and sell the work of local artists. Over a mile further northwest, where Berkeley meets Albany, **Solano Avenue** is fast catching up as a trendy shopping and dining area with a dazzling array of outlets, such as Tibetan craft shops, draped along its curved length.

Euclid Avenue, off Hearst and next to the north gate of the university, is a sort of antidote to Telegraph Avenue, a quiet grove of coffee joints and pizza parlours frequented by grad students and the focal point of the largely academic enclave known as Northside. Above Euclid (if you want to avoid the fairly steep walk, take the daily #65 bus or the weekdays-only #8) there are few more pleasant places for a picnic than the Berkeley Rose Garden at the corner of Euclid Avenue and Bayview Place (daily dawn–dusk; free), a terraced amphitheatre filled with some three thousand varieties of rose and looking out across the bay to San Francisco. Built as part of a WPA job-creation scheme during the Depression, a wooden pergola rings the top, stepping down to a small spring.

Tucked among the ridges of Berkeley Hills, a number of enticing parks give great views over the flatlands and the bay. The largest and highest of them, Tilden Park, spreads along the crest of the hills, encompassing over two thousand acres of near wilderness. Kids can enjoy a ride on the carved wooden horses of the carousel or through the redwood trees on the 1950s mini steam train. In the warmer months, don't miss a swim in soothing Lake Anza (lifeguard on duty May–Sept daily, some weekends in April & Oct 11am–6pm; $3.50).

Nearer to town, between the north end of Shattuck Avenue and the east end of Solano Avenue, the grey basalt knob of Indian Rock stands out from the foothills, challenging rock climbers who hone their skills on its forty-foot vertical faces. Carved into similarly hard volcanic stone across the street are the mortar holes used by the Ohlone to grind acorns into flour. Those who just want to appreciate the extraordinary view from the rock can take the steps around its back.

West Berkeley

From Downtown Berkeley and the UC campus, University Avenue runs in an almost imperceptible gradient downhill toward the bay, lined by increasingly shabby frontages of motels and massage parlours. The liveliest part of this West Berkeley area is around the intersection of University and San Pablo avenues, where a community of recent immigrants from India and Pakistan have set up stores and restaurants that serve some of the best of the Bay Area's curries.

The area between San Pablo Avenue and the bay is the oldest part of Berkeley and a handful of hundred-year-old houses and churches – such as the two white-spired Gothic Revival structures on Hearst Avenue – survive from the time when this district was a separate city, known as Ocean View. The neighbourhood also holds remnants of Berkeley's industrial past and many of the old warehouses and factory premises have been converted into living and working spaces for artists, craftspeople and software companies. The newly polished and yuppified stretch of Fourth Street between Gilman and University features upscale furniture outlets and quaint gourmet delis, as well as some outstanding restaurants (see p.519). Just to the south of here at 708 Addison St, you can take a tour of the huge Takara Sake USA Inc. brewery, whose tasting room and museum grant the opportunity to sample the company's products in elegant Japanese surroundings and learn about the process of sake-making (daily noon–6pm; free; ☎510/540-8250).

The North Bay and inland valleys

Compared to the urbanized bayfront cities of Oakland and Berkeley, the rest of the East Bay is sparsely populated, and places of interest are few and far between. The North Bay is home to some of the Bay Area's heaviest industry – oil refineries and chemical plants dominate the landscape – but also holds a few remarkably unchanged waterfront towns that merit a side trip if you're passing by. Away from the bay, the inland valleys are a whole other world of dry rolling hills dominated by the towering peak of **Mount Diablo**. Dozens of tract-home developments have made commuter suburbs out of what were once cattle ranches and farms but so far the region has been able to absorb the numbers and still feels rural, despite having doubled in population in the past thirty years.

The North Bay

North of Berkeley there's not a whole lot to see or do. Off the Eastshore Freeway in mostly mundane **Albany**, Golden Gate Fields has **horse racing** from October to June, and beyond it, the **Albany Mud Flats** are a fascinating place to stroll; impromptu works of art made from discarded materials vie with wild irises to attract the passer-by's eye in this reclaimed landfill jutting out into the bay. About a mile from Albany, **El Cerrito**'s main contribution to world culture was the band Creedence Clearwater Revival, who staged most of their *Born on the Bayou* publicity photographs in the wilds of Tilden Park in the hills above. The town is still home to one of the best record stores in California, Down Home Music, at 10341 San Pablo Ave (℡510/525-2129), which stocks an eclectic array of blues, gospel, Cajun, Tex-Mex, old time, jazz, world and rock.

Rough and depressing **Richmond**, at the top of the bay, was once a boomtown, whose Kaiser Shipyards built ships during World War II and employed 100,000 workers between 1940 and its closure in 1945. Now it's the proud home of the gigantic Standard Oil refinery, which you drive through before crossing the **Richmond–San Rafael Bridge** ($5) to Marin County. About the only reason to stop in Richmond is that it marks the north end of the BART line, and the adjacent Amtrak station is a better changing point for journeys to and from San Francisco than the terminal in West Oakland.

Benicia

On the north side of the Carquinez Straits, connected by the Carquinez Bridge ($5) and hard to get to without a car (turn right onto I-780 after the bridge), **Benicia** is the most substantial of the historic waterfront towns, but one that has definitely seen better days. Founded in 1847, it initially rivalled San Francisco as the major Bay Area port and was even the state capital for a time. Despite Benicia's better weather and fine deep-water harbour, San Francisco, which is closer to the ocean, eventually became the main transport point for the fortunes of the Gold Rush and the town very nearly faded away altogether. Examples of Benicia's efforts to become a major city stand poignantly around the very compact Downtown area, most conspicuously the 1852 Greek Revival structure that was used as the **first State Capitol** for just thirteen months. The building has been restored as a **museum** (Wed–Sun 10am–5pm; $3; ℡707/745-3385), furnished in the legislative style of the time, complete with top hats on the tables and shining spittoons every few feet.

A walking-tour map of Benicia's many intact Victorian houses and churches is available from the **Chamber of Commerce**, 601 1st St (Mon–Fri 8.30am–5pm, Sat & Sun 11am–3pm; ℡707/745-2120, ⓦwww.beniciachamber.com). Included on the itinerary are the steeply pitched roofs and gingerbread eaves of the **Frisbie-Walsh house** at 235 East L St, a prefabricated Gothic Revival building shipped here in pieces from Boston in 1849. Across the City Hall park, the arched ceiling beams of **St Paul's Episcopal Church** look like an upturned ship's hull; it was built by shipwrights from the Pacific Mail Steamship Company, one of Benicia's many successful nineteenth-century shipyards.

Since the early 1990s, Benicia has attracted a number of artists and crafts-people and you can watch glassblowers and furniture makers at work in the **Benicia Glass Studios** at 675 East H St (Mon–Sat 10am–4pm, Sun in summer noon–5pm; free).

Ceramic artist Judy Chicago and sculptor Robert Arneson are among those who have worked in the converted studios and modern light-industrial parks around the sprawling fortifications of the old **Benicia Arsenal**, whose thickly walled sandstone buildings east of the Downtown area formed the main army storage facility for weapons and ammunition from 1851 until the Korean Conflict.

One of the oddest parts of the complex is the **Camel Barn** in the **Benicia Historical Museum** (Wed–Sun 1–4pm; free; ☎707/745-5435, ⓦwww.benicia historicalmuseum.org): the structure used to house camels that the army imported in 1856 to transport supplies across the deserts of the southwestern US. The experiment failed and the camels were kept here until they were sold off in 1864.

The inland valleys

BART tunnels from Oakland through the Berkeley Hills to the leafy-green stock-broker settlement of **Orinda**, continuing east through the increasingly hot and dry landscape to **Concord**, site of a controversial nuclear-weapons depot. In the mid-Nineties, a civilly disobedient blockade here ended in protester Brian Wilson losing his legs under the wheels of a slow-moving munitions train. The event raised public awareness of the atomic activities and earned Wilson a place in the Lawrence Ferlinghetti poem *A Buddha in the Woodpile*. These days, however, it's business as usual at the depot.

From the Pleasant Hill BART station, one stop before the end of the line, Contra Costa County Connection buses leave every thirty minutes for **Martinez**, the seat of county government and a major Amtrak hub, passing the preserved home of naturalist **John Muir**, at 4202 Alhambra Ave (Wed–Sun 10am–5pm; $3; ☎925/228-8860, ⓦwww.nps.gov/jomu), just off Hwy-4 two miles south of Martinez. Muir, an articulate, persuasive Scot whose writings

---

Nemesis at Altamont

Uncannily timed at the dying embers of the Sixties and often referred to as "the nemesis of the Woodstock generation", the concert headlined by the **Rolling Stones** at the **Altamont Speedway**, fifteen miles southeast of Mount Diablo, on December 6, 1969, ended in total disaster. The free event was conceived to be a sort of second Woodstock, staged in order to counter allegations that the Stones had ripped off their fans during a long US tour. The band, however, inadvisably hired a chapter of Hell's Angels instead of professional security to maintain order and the result, predictably enough, was chaos. Three people ended up dead, one kicked and stabbed to death by the Hell's Angels themselves.

The whole sorry tale was remarkably captured on film by brothers David and Albert Maysles (plus co-director Charlotte Zerwin) and released the following year as their documentary *Gimme Shelter*. The footage of the concert clearly shows the deteriorating mood and growing menace in the crowd, exemplified by the scene when Jefferson Airplane vocalist Marty Balin jumped down into the fray to break up a fight, earning himself a broken jaw. By the time the Stones came on stage matters were patently out of hand, and after several interruptions and pleas for sanity by Mick Jagger, all hell broke loose during, ironically, *Sympathy for the Devil*. Jagger, Richards and company are later shown watching footage of the incident with numb looks on their faces as the glint of a knife signals the fatal stabbing during the following number.

Those interested in NASCAR can still attend races at the site, now known as the Altamont Motorsports Park (☎925/423-3272, ⓦwww.altamontmotorsportspark .com), while counterculture historians may find a pilgrimage to the scene of the crime oddly rewarding.

and political activism were of vital importance in the preservation of America's wilderness, spent much of his life exploring and writing about the majestic Sierra Nevada, particularly Yosemite. He was also one of the founders of the **Sierra Club** – a wilderness lobby and education organization that retains a strong presence today (see p.46). Anyone familiar with the image of this thin, bearded man wandering the mountains with his knapsack, notebook and packet of tea might be surprised to see his very conventional, upper-class Victorian home, now restored to its appearance when Muir died in 1914. The bulk of Muir's personal belongings and artefacts are displayed in his study on the upper floor and in the adjacent room an exhibition documents the history of the Sierra Club and Muir's battles to protect America's wilderness. Also included in the modest fee is entry to the still-productive orchard and the 1849 **Martinez Adobe**, homestead of the original Spanish land-grant settlers and now a small **museum** of Mexican colonial culture.

At the foot of Mount Diablo, fifteen miles south, playwright **Eugene O'Neill** used the money he received for winning the Nobel Prize for Literature in 1936 to build a home and sanctuary for himself, which he named **Tao House**. It was here, before 1944 when he was struck down with Parkinson's disease, that he wrote many of his best-known plays: *The Iceman Cometh*, *A Moon for the Misbegotten* and *Long Day's Journey into Night*. Readings and performances of his works are sometimes given in the house, which is open to visitors, though you must reserve a place on one of the free guided **tours** (Wed–Sun 10am & 12.30pm; ℡925/838-0249, Ⓦwww.nps.gov/euon). As it's now protected National Park Service land, there's no parking on site, so the tours pick you up in the ritzy town of **Danville**, at a location given when you book. Danville's richest neighborhood, Blackhawk, is the home of the **Blackhawk Automotive Museum**, 3700 Blackhawk Plaza Circle (Wed–Sun 10am–5pm; $10; ℡925/736-2277, Ⓦwww.blackhawkmuseum.org), where you'll find an impressive collection of classic cars from Britain, Germany, Italy and the US, along with artwork inspired by them.

Mount Diablo

Majestic **Mount Diablo** rises up from the rolling ranchlands at its foot to a height of nearly four thousand feet, its summit and flanks preserved within **Mount Diablo State Park** (daily 8am–sunset; $10 per vehicle). North Gate, the main road through the park, comes within three hundred feet of the top, so it's a popular place for an outing and you're unlikely to be alone to enjoy the marvellous view: on a clear day you can see over two hundred miles in every direction. There's no public transport, though the Sierra Club sometimes organizes day-trips (see p.46).

Two main entrances lead into the park, both well marked off I-680. The one from the southwest by way of Danville passes by the **ranger station**, where you can pick up a trail map ($5) listing the best day-hikes. The other runs from the northwest by way of Walnut Creek, and the routes join together five miles from the summit, beside which the attractive **visitor centre** (daily 10am–4pm; ℡925/837-6119) contains a free interpretive museum and observation deck. March and April, when the wildflowers are out, are the best months to come and since mornings are ideal for getting the clearest view, you should drive to the top first and then head back down to a trailhead for a hike, or to one of the many picnic spots for a leisurely lunch. In summer it can get desperately hot and dry, with parts of the park closed due to fire danger.

Eating

Home to **California cuisine** and some of the best restaurants in the state, Berkeley is an upmarket diner's paradise. But it's also a college town, so you can eat cheaply and well, especially around the campus and along Telegraph Avenue. The rest of the East Bay is less remarkable, except when it comes to plain **American food** such as barbecued ribs, grilled steaks or deli sandwiches, for which it's unbeatable.

One of the best things about visiting the East Bay is the opportunity to enjoy its many **cafés**. Concentrated most densely around the UC Berkeley campus, they're on a par with the best of San Francisco's North Beach for bohemian atmosphere. If you're not after a caffeine fix, you can generally also get a glass of beer, wine, or fresh fruit juice, though for serious drinking you'll be better off in one of the many bars (see p.522).

Oakland

Barney's 4162 Piedmont Ave, North Oakland; 5819 College Ave, Rockridge; 1600 Shattuck Ave, Berkeley; and 1591 Solano Ave, Berkeley. The East Bay's most popular burgers – including meatless ones – smothered in dozens of different toppings.

Bay Wolf 3853 Piedmont Ave, North Oakland ☏510/655-6004. Comfortable restaurant serving an ever-changing, expensive menu with items such as duck-liver flan, slow-cooked coriander-scented pork roast and sardines *escabeche* with spinach.

Chop Bar 247 4th St, Oakland ☏510/834-2467. Smart new restaurant in a converted warehouse, whose curved bar also serves fine ales. Main dishes such as Yucatan chicken with *jicama* salad and black beans are a snip at $15.

Citron 5484 College Ave, Rockridge ☏510/653-5484. Neighbourhood gem of a bistro that rivals San Francisco's best restaurants. Warm, unpretentious service and exquisite French-influenced food, with main courses such as lamb and pork ribs, costing around $25.

Dreyers 5925 College Ave, Rockridge. Oakland's own rich ice cream, which is distributed throughout California, is served at this small, slightly dull Rockridge café.

Fenton's Creamery 4226 Piedmont Ave, North Oakland. A brightly lit, 1950s ice cream and sandwich shop open until 11pm on weeknights, midnight on weekends.

Garibaldi's on College 5356 College Ave, Rockridge ☏510/595-4000. Quality upmarket Italian in remodelled premises, serving delicious pasta dishes with an emphasis on fine wines. Some of the sauces have a spicy Arabic and Middle Eastern element.

Golden Peacock 825 Webster St, Oakland. One of the most popular places in Chinatown, famous for its wonton soups, clay pot and *mu shu* dishes. Most items well under $10.

Holy Land 677 Rand Ave, North Oakland ☏510/272-0535. Casual diner-style kosher restaurant just beyond the freeway north of Lake Merritt, serving moderately priced Israeli food, including excellent falafel.

La Furia Chalaca 310 Broadway, Oakland ☏510/451-4206. Impressive range of seafood with pasta and various Peruvian sauces, as well as some meat dishes such as the excellent braised pork.

Le Cheval 1007 Clay St, Oakland ☏510/763-8495. Serving ample portions of exquisite Vietnamese at reasonable prices in chic, spacious surroundings – try the lemon-grass beef. There's a new smaller location *Le Petit Cheval* in Berkeley at 2600A Bancroft Way ☏510/704-8018.

Lois the Pie Queen 851 60th St at Adeline, North Oakland. Famous around the bay for its southern-style sweet potato and fresh fruit pies, this cosy diner also serves massive breakfasts and Sunday dinners, all for $10 or less.

Nan Yang 6048 College Ave, Rockridge ☏510/655-3298. Burmese food served in colourful, large, palate-exciting portions. The political refugee owner/chef is willing to discuss all his esoteric delicacies.

Tropix 3814 Piedmont Ave, North Oakland ☏510/653-2444. Large portions of fruity Caribbean delicacies at reasonable prices, with authentic jerk sauce and thirst-quenching mango juice.

Zachary's 5801 College Ave, Rockridge ☏510/655-6385 and 1853 Solano Ave, North Berkeley ☏510/525-5950. Zealously defended as the best pizza in the Bay Area, *Zachary's* is also one of the only places offering the rich, deep-dish Chicago-style pies.

Berkeley

Ajanta 1888 Solano Ave, North Berkeley ☏510/526-4373. Pretty upmarket curry house featuring an interesting array of dishes from different parts of India and Pakistan not found in many other establishments, such as duck curry Kerala and Dhaniwal *murg korma*.

Angeline's Louisiana Kitchen 2261 Shattuck Ave, Berkeley ✆510/548-6900. Classic New Orleans cuisine such as voodoo shrimp and fried catfish are rustled up for around $14 in this lively new place that also has great sounds.

Bette's Ocean View Diner 1807 4th St, West Berkeley. Named after the neighbourhood, not after the vista, but serving up some of the Bay Area's best breakfasts and lunches. Very popular on weekends, when you may have to wait an hour for a table.

Britt-Marie's 1369 Solano Ave, Albany ✆510/527-1314. Along with a fine selection of mostly California wines by the glass, this place serves well-priced eclectic home-cooking such as goat's cheese tart, plus outstanding chocolate cake.

César 1515 Shattuck Ave, North Berkeley ✆510/883-0222. Perpetually crowded tapas bar serving small portions overflowing with taste. The combination of quality and a relaxed atmosphere has made it a cultish destination for locals, though be mindful that prices for the small dishes can add up.

Cha Am 1543 Shattuck Ave, North Berkeley. Climb the stairs up to this unlikely, always crowded, small restaurant for deliciously spicy Thai food at moderate prices. The adjacent *Dara's* is similar, with Laotian food as well.

Cheese Board Pizza 1512 Shattuck Ave, North Berkeley. Tiny storefront selling some of the world's most delicious and unique pizza at very reasonable prices. Well worth searching out but keeps irregular hours: usually Tues–Sat 11.30am–2pm & 4.30–7pm.

🏃 **Chez Panisse** 1517 Shattuck Ave, North Berkeley ✆510/548-5525. The California restaurant to which all others are compared, its chef Alice Waters is widely credited for inventing California cuisine with delights like Wolfe Ranch quail with sweet onion marmalade or grilled Sonoma liberty duck breast with olive sauce and niçoise stuffed vegetables. The set menu starts at $65 per head on Mon, rising to $95 at weekends, although the café section is somewhat less expensive. Reservations essential.

Fatapple's 1346 Martin Luther King Jr Way, North Berkeley. Crowded but pleasant family-oriented restaurant with excellent, cheap American breakfasts and an assortment of sandwiches and burgers for lunch or dinner.

Gordo Taqueria 1423 Solano Ave, Albany. Right on the north Berkeley border, this great little takeaway does a huge turnover in superb burritos and tacos with all the trimmings for as little as $4–6. Eat your choice with a pint in *Pub* opposite (see p.522).

Jayakarta 2026 University Ave, Berkeley. Very inexpensive Indonesian joint offering no frills but extremely tasty dishes such as *nasi padang*, a mixture of boiled egg, chicken hearts, pork and stinky beans in chilli.

Juan's Place 941 Carleton St, West Berkeley ✆510/845-6904. One of Berkeley's oldest Mexican restaurants, serving heaps of great food to an interesting mix of people at moderate prices – meat dishes cost around $10.

Kirala 2100 Ward St, Berkeley ✆510/549-3486. Many argue that *Kirala* serves the best sushi in the Bay Area; others argue that it's simply the best in the world. Moderate pricing, too – expect to pay around $20 to get your fill.

Lalime's 1329 Gilman St, North Berkeley ✆510/527-9838. A typically upmarket yet casual venue for wealthy academics to feast on the likes of Alaskan sockeye salmon or veal sweetbreads. Main courses go for around $25.

La Méditerranée 2936 College Ave, Berkeley ✆510/540-7773. This Ashby area restaurant has good Greek and Middle Eastern dishes, such as Levantine meat tart or various kebabs for $10 or less, served indoors or on the large patio.

La Note 2377 Shattuck Ave, Berkeley ✆510/843-1535. The appropriately sunny, light cuisine of Provence isn't the only flavour you'll find in this petite dining room: students and teachers from the Jazzschool (sic) next door routinely stop in for casual jam sessions.

LaVal's Pizza 1834 Euclid Ave, Berkeley ✆510/843-5617. Lively graduate-student hangout near the North Gate of campus. Pool table, wide-screen TV broadcasting sports, wide selection of microbrews and great pizza. Lunch specials often a feature.

Liu's Kitchen 1593 Solano Ave, North Berkeley. Huge helpings of tasty Chinese fare at very low prices – the filling pot-stickers are a meal in themselves.

O'Chamé 1830 4th St, West Berkeley ✆510/841-8783. Highly rated Japanese restaurant, with beautifully prepared sashimi and sushi as well as a full range of authentic Japanese specialities such as teriyaki salmon. A treat in the $20–25 range.

Picante 1328 6th St, West Berkeley ✆510/525-3121. Fine and very reasonably priced tacos with fresh salsa, plus live jazz on weekends. Nicely decorated, with an outdoor patio for fine weather.

Revival 2102 Shattuck Ave, Berkeley ✆510/549-9950. This new string to Berkeley's culinary bow serves the likes of *zatar*-braised McCormick ranch goat and roasted Sonoma duck breast in snazzily understated surroundings. Main courses in the $20–25 range.

Rick & Ann's 2922 Domingo Ave, Berkeley. Even in Berkeley folks sometimes want meatloaf and mashed potatoes instead of arugula, and to get their fill of both the crowds line up outside this neighbourhood diner every weekend.

Rivoli 1539 Solano Ave, North Berkeley ☎510/526-2542. Delivers all that's wonderful about Berkeley dining: first-rate fresh food based on Italian and French cuisine, courteous service and a casual, friendly atmosphere. Main dishes such as lobster mousse and Dungeness crab ravioli cost over $20.

Saul's Deli 1475 Shattuck Ave, North Berkeley. For pastrami, corned beef, *kreplach* or *knishes*, this is the place. Great sandwiches and picnic fixings to take away, plus a full range of sit-down evening meals.

Spenger's 1919 4th St, West Berkeley. With a spacious sit-down restaurant and cheap takeaway counter, this is a local institution. As one of the largest chains in the Bay Area, *Spenger's* serves up literally tonnes of simple but well-cooked seafood dishes to thousands of customers daily.

Steve's Korean BBQ In the Durant Center, 2521 Durant Ave, Berkeley. Excellent, low-priced Korean food (*kimchee* to die for). Other cafés in this small mall sell Mexican food, sushi, healthy sandwiches, deep-fried doughnuts and slices of pizza, plus bargain pitchers of beer.

Trattoria La Siciliana 2993 College Ave, Berkeley ☎510/704-1474. Intimate, family-run Italian place with a wide range of antipasti, pastas, risotti and specialities such as stuffed beef roll for under $20.

Vik's Chaat Corner 2390 4th St, West Berkeley. Now in new saffron-coloured premises, this institution (expect long queues at weekends) offers a wide array of South Indian delights such as *masala dosa* or *bhel puri*, as well as daily specials. Open until 6pm.

Yogurt Park 2433A Durant Ave, Berkeley. Frozen yoghurt is the speciality here; open until midnight for the student throngs.

Cafés

Bacheeso's 2501 San Pablo Ave, West Berkeley ☎510/644-2035. A good range of quality coffees and chais, as well as good breakfasts, are brewed in this brightly coloured spot. Occasional live music in the evenings.

Brewed Awakening 1807 Euclid Ave, North Berkeley. Spacious coffee and teahouse near the North Gate of campus, frequented by professors and grad students. Friendly staff, plenty of seating and lovely artwork on the redbrick walls explain why this is annually rated the "Best Café to Study In" by the student press.

Café Mediterraneum 2475 Telegraph Ave, Berkeley. Berkeley's oldest café featuring sidewalk seating. Straight out of the Beat archives: beards and berets optional, battered paperbacks de rigueur.

Café Strada 2300 College Ave, Berkeley. Spacious, open-air café where art and architecture students cross paths with would-be lawyers and chess wizards.

Coffee Mill 3363 Grand Ave, North Oakland ☎510/465-4224. Elongated room that doubles as an art gallery and often hosts poetry readings. Also a great bakery.

Royal 6255 College Ave, Rockridge. Bright, modern and relaxing spot in the Rockridge area, with outdoor seating. Perfect for a leisurely afternoon with the newspaper.

Food shops and markets

Berkeley Bowl 2020 Oregon St, Berkeley. Only in Berkeley would such an enormous produce, bulk and health-food market take over premises from Safeway. The least expensive grocery in town, with the largest selection of fresh food.

Cheese Board 1504 Shattuck Ave, North Berkeley. Collectively owned and operated since 1967, this was one of the first outposts in Berkeley's Gourmet Ghetto, offering over 200 varieties of cheese and a range of delicious breads.

Epicurious Garden 1511 Shattuck Ave, North Berkeley. This new indoor mall of top-notch produce and takeaway snacks includes half a dozen independent outlets, such as Alegio chocolate and Picoso Mexican, as well as a Japanese tea garden at the back.

Monterey Foods 1550 Hopkins St, North Berkeley. The main supplier of exotic produce to Berkeley's gourmet restaurants, this boisterous market also has the highest-quality fresh fruit and vegetables available.

Vintage Berkeley 2113 Vine St, North Berkeley. Excellent outlet for quality domestic and imported wines, mostly under $20, housed in a cute old pump station. The highly knowledgeable staff will match a wine with any meal.

Nightlife and entertainment

The East Bay's **bars**, particularly in rough-hewn Oakland, are grittier versions of what you'd find in San Francisco; they're mostly blue-collar, convivial and invariably cheaper, while unsurprisingly, Berkeley's bars are brimming with students and academics. **Nightlife** is where the East Bay really comes into its own. Dancing to canned music and paying high prices for flashy decor is not a popular pastime here, although more venues have at least one dance/trance night these days, often Thursday. On the other hand, there are still dozens of **live music** venues, particularly in Oakland, covering a range of musical tastes and styles – from small, unpretentious jazz clubs to buzzing R&B venues. Berkeley's clubs tend more towards folk and world music, with other places dedicated to underground rock, and the university itself holds two of the best medium-sized venues in the entire Bay Area. **Tickets** for most venues are available at their box office or, for a service charge, through BASS (☎510/762-2277).

Though not bad by US standards, the East Bay **theatre** scene isn't exactly thriving, and shows tend to be politically inspired rather than dramatically innovative. By contrast, the range of **films** (tickets $8–10) is first-class, with over a dozen cinemas showing new releases and Berkeley's revamped Pacific Film Archive, one of the world's finest film libraries, filling its screens with obscure but brilliant art flicks. Check the free *East Bay Express* (ⓦ www.eastbayexpress.com) or the *SF Weekly* (ⓦ www.sfweekly.com) for details of what's on.

Bars

Albatross Pub 1822 San Pablo Ave, West Berkeley ☎510/843-2473. Popular student super-bar, replete with darts, pool, board games and fireplace. Serves a large selection of ales from around the world. Live jazz, flamenco and blues music on weekends (free–$5).

Ben'n'Nick's 5612 College Ave, Rockridge. Lively bar with good recorded rock music and tasty food.

Heinold's First and Last Chance Saloon 56 Jack London Square, Oakland. Authentic waterfront bar that's hardly changed since the turn of the century, when Jack London was a regular. They still haven't bothered to fix the slanted floor caused by the 1906 earthquake.

Pacific Coast Brewing Co 906 Washington St, Oakland. Oakland's only real microbrewery, which conjures up a range of decent brews and offers quite an extensive menu too. Attracts Downtown office workers as well as a younger crowd later on.

Pub (Schmidt's Tobacco & Trading Co) 1492 Solano Ave, Albany. Just past the official Berkeley limit, this small, relaxed bar lures a mixture of bookworms and game players with a good selection of beers. They even get away with a semi-open smoking area out back, perhaps because their other speciality is selling the evil weed. You can even eat takeaway food here.

Pyramid Alehouse 901 Gilman St, West Berkeley ☎510/528-9880. This huge, postindustrial space makes a surprisingly casual spot to sip the suds.

Outdoor film screenings on weekend nights during summer.

Triple Rock Brewery 1920 Shattuck Ave, Berkeley. Buzzing, all-American microbrewery with decent food: the decor is Edward Hopper-era retro, and as well as their own nitrogenated beers at weekends they have a couple of fine cask-conditioned ales.

The White Horse 6560 Telegraph Ave at 66th St, Oakland. Oakland's oldest gay bar – a smallish, friendly place, with mixed nightly dancing for men and women.

Major performance venues

Berkeley Community Theatre 1930 Allston Way, Berkeley ☎510/845-2308. Jimi Hendrix played here and the 3500-seat theatre still hosts major rock concerts and community events. Tickets through the usual agents.

Center for Contemporary Music Mills College, 5000 MacArthur Blvd, Oakland ☎510/430-2191, ⓦ www.mills.edu. One of the prime centres in the world for experimental music.

Oakland Coliseum 7000 Coliseum Way, near the airport ☎510/639-7700, ⓦ www.coliseum.com. Mostly stadium shows here, inside the 18,000-seat Oracle Arena or outdoors in the adjacent 55,000-seat coliseum. Used to be a favourite gig of the Grateful Dead's.

Paramount Theatre 2025 Broadway, Downtown Oakland ☎510/465-6400, ⓦ www.paramount theatre.com. Beautifully restored Art Deco masterpiece, hosting classical concerts, big-name crooners, ballets, operas and a growing roster of rap and rock shows. Ticket office Tues–Sat noon–5pm; $25–100. Some nights they play old Hollywood classics for $5.

Zellerbach Hall and the outdoor **Greek Theatre** on the UC Berkeley campus ☎510/642-9988, ⓦwww.calperfs.berkeley.edu. Two of the top spots for catching big names touring the Bay Area during the academic year. Zellerbach showcases drama, classical and world music and dance, while the Greek welcomes more popular acts. Tickets $20–100.

Live music venues

924 Gilman 924 Gilman St, West Berkeley ☎510/525-9926, ⓦwww.924gilman.org. Part social project, part outer edge of the hardcore punk scene in a bare, squat-like old warehouse. Weekends only; cover $5–10.

The Alley 3325 Grand Ave, North Oakland ☎510/444-8505. Ramshackle black-timber piano bar, decorated with business cards and with live old-time blues merchants on the keyboards. No cover.

Ashkenaz 1317 San Pablo Ave, West Berkeley ☎510/525-5054, ⓦwww.ashkenaz.com. World-music and dance café. Acts range from modern Afrobeat to the best of the Balkans. Kids and under-21s welcome. Cover $10–20.

Blakes on Telegraph 2367 Telegraph Ave, Berkeley ☎510/848-0886, ⓦwww.blakeson telegraph.com. Student-patronized saloon with a varied roster of live music most nights of the week and DJs the rest. Latin, funk, soul, hip-hop, roots, rock, reggae, blues and more. $5–15.

Freight & Salvage 2020 Addison St, Berkeley ☎510/644-2020, ⓦwww.freightandsalvage.org. Since this nonprofit organization relocated to this pleasant performance space with a great sound system, it has re-established its name for showcasing up-and-coming acts. $5–25.

La Peña Cultural Center 3105 Shattuck Ave, Berkeley, near Ashby BART ☎510/849-2568, ⓦwww.lapena.org. More folk than rock, and some Latin, often politically charged – the website encourages cultural activism for social change. $8–20.

Yoshi's World Class Jazz House 510 Embarcadero West, Oakland ☎510/238-9200, ⓦwww.yoshis.com. The West Coast's premier jazz club near Jack London Square attracts an impressive roster of performers nightly. The place is almost always full. Most shows $10–20, more for big names.

Film

Berkeley Oaks Theater 1875 Solano Ave, Berkeley ☎510/526-1836, ⓦwww.berkeleyoaks .com. A mixture of mainstream and political films are shown at this cosy, renovated Art Deco cinema, built in 1925.

California Theatre 2113 Kittredge St, Berkeley ☎510/464-5980, ⓦwww.landmarktheatres.com. This renovated cinema near the campus shows a mixture of big releases and more off-beat films. Landmark also operates the Shattuck Cinemas around the corner.

Grand Lake Theater 3200 Grand Ave, Oakland ☎510/452-3556, ⓦwww.renaissancerialto.com. The *grande dame* of East Bay picture palaces, just above Lake Merritt, showing the best of the current major releases, with special emphasis on politically alternative works.

Pacific Film Archive 2575 Bancroft at Bowditch St, Berkeley ☎510/642-5249, ⓦwww.bampfa .berkeley.edu. The archive's splendid new digs plays the West Coast's best selection of cinema. It features nightly showings of classics, third world and experimental films, plus revivals of otherwise forgotten favorites. Call for listings or pick up a free monthly calendar around campus. Two films a night.

Theatre

Berkeley Repertory Theater 2025 Addison St, Berkeley ☎510/845-4700, ⓦwww.berkeleyrep .org. One of the West Coast's most highly respected theatre companies, presenting updated classics and contemporary plays in an intimate modern theatre. Tickets $29–73; fifty percent discounts for students and under-30s with advance booking.

Black Repertory Group 3201 Adeline St, Berkeley ☎510/652-2120, ⓦwww.blackrepertorygroup .com. After years of struggling, this politically conscious company moved into its own specially built home near Ashby BART in 1987; since then they've encouraged new talent with great success. Tickets $15–30.

California Shakespeare Festival Siesta Valley, Orinda ☎510/548-9666, ⓦwww.calshakes.org. This annual, summer-long festival has a gorgeous open-air home in the wooded East Bay Hills. Tickets $34–65.

Julia Morgan Center for the Arts 2640 College Ave, Berkeley ☎510/845-8542, ⓦwww .juliamorgan.org. A variety of touring shows stop off in this cunningly converted old church. Tickets usually $15–30, but some "pay what you can" shows.

The Peninsula

The city of San Francisco sits at the tip of a five-mile-wide neck of land commonly referred to as **the Peninsula**. Home to old money and new technology, the Peninsula stretches along the bay for fifty miles of relentless suburbia south from San Francisco, ending up in the futuristic roadside landscape of the **"Silicon Valley"** around **San Jose**, the fastest-growing city in California and now tenth-largest in the US.

There was a time when the region was largely agricultural, but the computer boom – spurred by Stanford University in **Palo Alto** – has replaced orange groves and fig trees with office complexes and parking lots. Surprisingly, however, most of the land along the **coast** – separated from the bayfront sprawl by a spur of redwood-covered ridges – remains rural and largely undeveloped; it also contains some excellent **beaches** and a couple of affably down-to-earth communities, all well-served by public transport.

Information

The **Palo Alto Chamber of Commerce**, 122 Hamilton Ave (Mon–Fri 9am–5pm; ☎650/324-3121, ⓦwww.paloaltochamber.com), has lists of local restaurants and cycle routes. For information on Stanford University, contact its visitor centre (Mon–Fri 8am–5pm, Sat & Sun 9am–5pm; ☎650/723-2560, ⓦwww.stanford .edu) in the Memorial Auditorium opposite Hoover Tower, or get a copy of the free *Stanford Daily*, published weekdays. To find out what's on in the area and where, pick up a free copy of the *Palo Alto Weekly* (ⓦwww.paloaltoonline.com), available at most local shops.

At the southern end of the bay, the **San Jose CVB** is at 408 S Almaden (Mon–Fri 8am–5pm, Sat & Sun 11am–5pm; ☎1-800/726-5673, ⓦwww.sanjose.org), in a back corner of the massive Convention Center. For an idea of local news and events, pick up a copy of the excellent *San Jose Mercury* daily newspaper (ⓦwww .mercurynews.com) or the free weekly *Metro* (ⓦwww.metroactive.com), although the latter usually lists as many events for San Francisco as it does for the South Bay. The website ⓦwww.siliconvalley.citysearch.com also holds a cache of reviews and features on the area.

Along the coast, the **Chamber of Commerce** in **Pacifica**, 225 Rockaway Beach Ave (Mon–Fri 9am–5pm, Sat & Sun 10am–4.30pm; ☎650/355-4122, ⓦwww .pacificachamber.com), is the nearest to San Francisco on the Peninsula. Further south, the **Half Moon Bay Chamber of Commerce**, at 235 Main St(Mon–Fri 9am–5pm, Sat & Sun 10am–3pm; ☎650/726-8380, ⓦwww.halfmoonbay chamber.org), gives out walking-tour maps and information on accommodation. Another way of finding out what's happening is to log on to ⓦwww.visithalf moonbay.org.

Getting around

BART only travels down the Peninsula as far as Millbrae but you can connect onto SamTrans (☎1-800/660-4287, ⓦwww.samtrans.com) **buses** south to Palo Alto or along the coast to Half Moon Bay. For longer distances, **CalTrain** (☎1-800/660-4287, ⓦwww.caltrain.com) offers a rail service at least every half an hour from its terminal at Fourth and King streets in Downtown San Francisco, stopping at most bayside towns between the city and Gilroy ($2.50–11.25) via San Jose ($7.75); Greyhound runs regular buses along US-101 to and from its San Jose terminal at 70 S Almaden. Santa Clara Valley Transit Authority (VTA; $2, day-pass $6; ☎408/321-2300, ⓦwww.vta.org) runs buses and modern trolleys around metropolitan San Jose. Most major domestic airlines fly direct into **Norman J. Mineta San Jose International Airport** (☎408/501-7600, ⓦwww.sjc.org), very close to Downtown San Jose; the VTA SJC Airport Flyer bus runs to Downtown San Jose and Santa Clara for $4, plus there's the usual choice of taxis, limos and shuttles for fancier rides to your destination.

Accommodation

Budget-conscious visitors to San Francisco often choose to stay on the Peninsula rather than in the city. Dozens of $60-a-night motels line Hwy-82 – "El Camino Real", the old main highway – and can save you a lot of money. If you're arriving late or departing on an early flight from SFO you might even want to avail yourself of one of the many airport hotels. There are also two low-priced, pleasant **hostels**, housed on the premises of old lighthouses right on the Pacific Coast. On the other hand, San Jose's **hotels** are largely overpriced, catering more to the conventioneering corporate world than the tourist or traveller, though they offer decent deals at weekends.

Hotels and motels

Bay Landing Hotel 1550 Bayshore Hwy, Burlingame ☎650/259-9000, ⓦwww.baylandinghotel.com. One of the best options at the north end of the Peninsula, with views of the bay and planes taking off from SFO. Refreshingly, it's a family-owned place with quality rooms and service. ⑤

Beach House 4100 N Cabrillo Hwy, 3 miles north of Half Moon Bay ☎1-800/315-9366, ⓦwww.beach-house.com. Large, modern resort hotel with fully equipped loft-suites, all with balconies, overlooking Pillar Point Harbor and the ocean. Excellent value for this price range. ⑥

Cardinal Hotel 235 Hamilton Ave, Palo Alto ☎650/323-5101, ⓦwww.cardinalhotel.com. Reasonably comfortable hotel in the heart of Downtown Palo Alto. En-suite rooms cost almost double those with shared baths. ③

Costanoa 2001 Rossi Rd at Hwy-1, 3 miles north of Año Nuevo ☎650/879-1100, ⓦwww.costanoa.com. Unique and relaxed resort with an emphasis on communing with nature and spa treatments. Offers camping and RV sites (from $50), as well as top-notch canvas-walled tent bungalows and swish lodges that cost over $300. ③

Fairmont Hotel 170 S Market St, San Jose ☎1-800/441-1414, ⓦwww.fairmont.com. San Jose's finest hotel, part of the luxury chain which began in San Francisco, is located in the heart of Downtown on the plaza. All the expected amenities, such as room service, swimming pool and lounge, plus sparkling rooms; discounts at weekends. ⑦

Garden Court Hotel 520 Cowper St, Palo Alto ☎650/322-9000, ⓦwww.gardencourt.com. Very upmarket place, built in attractive Mission style, in a handy Downtown location. All rooms boast full facilities and balconies. Suites go for nearly $700. ⑨

Hotel De Anza 233 W Santa Clara St, San Jose ☎1-800/843-3700, ⓦwww.hoteldeanza.com. Smart business- and conference-oriented hotel with full amenities in one of the livelier sections of town. Special weekend rates and packages. ④

Howard Johnson Express 1215 S 1st St, San Jose ☎1-800/509-7666, ⓦwww.hojo.com. Adequate if charmless rooms Downtown, within walking distance of the city's main nightspots. ③

Landis Shores Oceanfront Inn 211 Mirada Rd, 2 miles north of Half Moon Bay ☎650/726-6644, ⓦwww.landisshores.com. With rooms overlooking the Pacific waves, this smart modern hotel offers all the friendly touches of a B&B along with state-of-the-art amenities. Afternoon wine from the owner's huge cellar is on the house. ⑧

Pacifica Motor Inn 200 Rockaway Beach Ave, Pacifica ☎1-800/522-3772, ⓦwww.pacifica motorinn.com. Large rooms just a block off the beach in a hamlet alongside Hwy-1. ②

B&Bs

Farallone Inn 1410 Main St, Montara ☎1-800/818-7316, ⓦwww.faralloneinn.com. Restored mansion whose rooms vary in size from extremely cosy to penthouse suites – but all have jacuzzis. ②

Old Thyme Inn 779 Main St, Half Moon Bay ☎1-800/720-4277, ⓦwww.oldthymeinn.com. Seven incredibly quaint rooms, each with a private tub, in a lovely Victorian house surrounded by luxuriant herb and flower gardens and with paintings by the owner. ⑤

Pillar Point B&B 380 Capistrano Rd, Princeton-by-the-Sea ☎1-800/400-8281, ⓦwww.pillarpointinn.com. Pretty house with lovely rooms, a library, outdoor deck and topiary garden. Close to Pillar Point Harbor and a range of restaurants. ⑤

San Benito House 356 Main St, Half Moon Bay
☎650/726-3425, ⓦwww.sanbenitohouse.com.
Twelve restful B&B rooms in a 100-year-old
building, just a mile from the beach. Excellent
restaurant downstairs. ❸

Hostels

🏃 HI–Pigeon Point Lighthouse Hwy-1, just
south of Pescadero ☎650/879-0633,
ⓦwww.norcalhostels.org. Worth planning a trip
around, this beautiful hostel, fifty miles south of
San Francisco, is ideally placed for exploring the
nearby redwood forests or Año Nuevo State
Reserve. Office hours 7.30–10pm; check-in from
3.30pm. Members $23–25 per night, non-members
$26–28; reservations essential in summer. Private
rooms from $59 to $111 family room.

HI–Point Montara Lighthouse 16th St/Hwy-1,
Montara ☎650/728-7177, ⓦwww.norcalhostels
.org. Rooms are in the converted outhouses of an
1875 lighthouse, 25 miles south of San Francisco;
take SamTrans bus #294 from Pacifica. Office
hours 7.30am–10pm. Members $23–25 per night,
non-members $26–28; reservations essential in
summer. Private rooms $66–76.

Campgrounds

Butano State Park Pescadero ☎650/879-2040. RV
and tent spaces in a beautiful redwood forest; book
on ☎1-800/444-7275 or ⓦwww.parks.ca.gov. $35.
Half Moon Bay State Beach Half Moon Bay
☎650/726-8820. Tent sites in the woods behind
the beach; book on ☎1-800/444-7275, ⓦwww
.parks.ca.gov. $35–50, plus hike/bike-in $7.

South along the bay

US-101 runs south from San Francisco along the bay to San Jose, through over
fifty miles of unmitigated sprawl lined by light-industrial estates and shopping
malls. There's one place along the freeway in **San Mateo** worth a visit: the **Coyote
Point Museum**, 1651 Coyote Point Drive (Tues–Sat 10am–5pm, Sun noon–5pm;
$8; ☎650/342-7755, ⓦwww.coyoteptmuseum.org), four miles south of the
airport off Poplar Avenue. Surrounded by a large bayfront park, the museum
showcases examples of the natural life of the San Francisco Bay, from tidal insects
to birds of prey, all exhibited in engaging and informative displays and enhanced
by interactive computers and documentary films.

Six-lane freeways don't usually qualify as scenic routes, but an exception is
I-280, one of the newest and most expensive freeways in California. It runs
parallel to US-101 but avoids the worst of the bayside mess by cutting through
wooded valleys down the centre of the Peninsula. Just beyond the San Francisco
city limits the road passes through **Colma**, a unique place filled with cemeteries,
which, other than the military burial grounds in the Presidio, are prohibited
within San Francisco. Besides the expected roll-call of deceased San Francisco
luminaries, including Levi Strauss and William Hearst, are a few surprises, such as
Wild West gunman Wyatt Earp.

Further south, beyond the vast Crystal Springs Reservoir, just off I-280 on
Canada Road near the well-heeled town of **Woodside**, luscious gardens
surround the palatial **Filoli Estate** (mid-Feb to late Oct Tues–Sat 10am–3.30pm,
Sun 11am–3.30pm, last admission 2.30pm; tours by reservation only; $12;
☎650/364-8300 ext 507, ⓦwww.filoli.org). The 45-room mansion, designed
in 1915 in neo-Palladian style by architect Willis Polk, may look familiar – it
was used in the TV series *Dynasty* as the Denver home of the Carrington clan.
The gardens, however, are the real draw, especially in the spring when everything's in bloom.

Palo Alto and Stanford University

PALO ALTO, just south and three miles east of Woodside between I-280 and
US-101, is a small, leafy community which, despite its proximity to Stanford,
exudes little of the college-town vigour of its northern rival, Berkeley. In
recent years, Palo Alto has become something of a social centre for Silicon
Valley's nouveau riche, as evidenced by the trendy cafés and chic new

restaurants that have popped up along its main drag, **University Avenue**. The computer-industry-boom job market made more than a few people rich and small houses in the quaint neighbourhoods surrounding Downtown can cost up to a million dollars.

In terms of sights, the town doesn't have a lot to offer other than Spanish Colonial homes, but it's a great place for a lazy stroll and a gourmet meal. Monthly historic tours of Palo Alto's neighbourhoods take place during summer (T650/299-8878), and otherwise the best of the city's designs can be seen along **Ramona Street**. Be aware, however, that **East Palo Alto**, on the bay side of US-101, has a well-deserved reputation for gang- and drug-related violence. This is ironic as the area was founded in the 1920s as the utopian Runnymeade Colony, an agricultural, poultry-raising co-operative. These days Grateful Dead guitarist Jerry Garcia's hometown is about as far as you can get off the San Francisco tourist trail.

STANFORD UNIVERSITY, spreading out from the west end of University Avenue, is by contrast one of the tamest places you could imagine. The university is among the top – and most expensive – in the US, though when it opened in 1891, founded by railroad magnate Leland Stanford in memory of his dead son, it offered free tuition. Stanford's reputation as an arch-conservative think-tank was enhanced by Ronald Reagan's offer to donate his video library to the school (though Stanford politely declined) but it hasn't always been an entirely boring place. Ken Kesey came here from Oregon in 1958 on a writing fellowship, working nights as an orderly on the psychiatric ward of one local hospital, and getting paid $75 a day to test experimental drugs such as LSD in another. Drawing on both experiences, Kesey wrote *One Flew Over the Cuckoo's Nest* in 1960 and quickly became a counterculture hero. The period is admirably chronicled by Tom Wolfe in *The Electric Kool-aid Acid Test*. In keeping with that spirit, Stanford is now the home of the Center for the Explanation of Consciousness, which conducts various experiments in human consciousness and is bridging the gap between the physical and metaphysical.

Approaching from the Palo Alto CalTrain and SamTrans bus station, which acts as a buffer between the town and the university, you enter the campus via a half-mile-long, palm-tree-lined boulevard which deposits you at its heart, the **Quadrangle**, bordered by the colourful gold-leaf mosaics of the **Memorial Church** and the phallic **Hoover Tower**, whose observation platform (daily 10am–4pm; $2) is worth ascending for the view. Free hour-long walking tours of the campus leave from here daily at 11am and 3.15pm, though it's fairly big and best seen by car or bike. Indeed, driving tours in a golf cart are offered daily at 1pm during term and some of the holidays ($5) from Memorial Auditorium.

While you're here, don't miss one of the finest museums in the Bay Area. The **Iris and B. Gerald Cantor Center for Visual Arts** comprises 27 galleries (spread over 120,000 square feet) of treasures from six continents, dating from 500 BC to the present (Wed–Sun 11am–5pm, Thurs 11am–8pm; free; T650/723-4177, Wwww.museum.stanford.edu). Housed in the old Stanford Museum of Art at the intersection of Lomita Drive and Museum Way, the Cantor Center incorporates the former structure, damaged in the 1989 earthquake, with a new wing, including a bookshop and café. One of the finest pieces in the permanent collection is the stunning *Plum Garden, Kameido*, by Japanese artist Hiroshige. Be sure to have a look at the distinguished collection of over two hundred **Rodin sculptures**, including a *Gates of Hell* flanked by a shamed *Adam and Eve*, displayed in an attractive outdoor setting on the museum's south side. There's a version of *The Thinker* here as well, forming a sort of Bay Area bookend with the rendition that fronts the Palace of the Legion of Honor Museum in San Francisco.

San Jose

Burt Bacharach wouldn't need to ask the way to **SAN JOSE** today – heading south from San Francisco, it should take under an hour (avoiding peak times) to reach the heart of the heat and smog that collects below the bay. Sitting at the southern end of the Peninsula, San Jose has in the past thirty years emerged as the civic heart of Silicon Valley, spurred by the growth of local behemoths Apple, Cisco, Intel and Hewlett-Packard. San Jose's priority of late has been the development of a culture beyond that of geeks, so new museums, shopping centres, restaurants, clubs and performing arts companies have mushroomed throughout the compact Downtown area. While the nightlife and cultural scene here can't begin to compete with San Francisco, there are enough attractions around the city's clean and sunny streets to warrant a short stay.

Downtown San Jose

Though now rooted in the modern high-tech world, San Jose's 1777 founding actually makes it one of the oldest settlements – and the oldest city – in California. The only sign of that **Downtown** is the 1797 **Peralta Adobe**, at 184 W St John St (tours by arrangement, minimum 5 people; $6; ℡408/287-2290, ⊛www .historysanjose.org), notable more for having survived the encroaching suburbia than for anything on display in its sparse, whitewashed interior. Admission includes a tour of the **Fallon House**, a Victorian mansion across the street, built by the city's seventh mayor in 1855, a one-time frontiersman in the Fremont expedition.

The two blocks of San Pedro Street that run south of the adobe form a restaurant row known as **San Pedro Square**. There's no central plaza as such, just a collection of some of San Jose's best eateries (see p.533). Further south, down Market Street, lies the pleasant and palm-dotted **Plaza de César Chávez**. The plaza is San Jose's town square and there's no better place to lounge on the grass, read on one of the many wooden benches or play in the unique **fountain** whose shooting spumes are a favourite hangout for kids.

A block north of the plaza, the **Cathedral Basilica of St Joseph** stands on the site of the first Catholic parish in California, circa 1803. The present building was dedicated in 1997 and you should duck inside to see its painted cupola, stained-glass windows and Stations of the Cross. Masses are held daily, often in Spanish. Next door to the church at 110 S Market, the fantastic **San Jose Museum of Art** (Tues–Sun 11am–5pm; $8; ℡408/294-2787, ⊛www.sjmusart.org) is set in the old post office building built in 1892, to which a new wing was added in 1991. The museum contains more than one thousand twentieth-century works, with the spotlight falling on post-1980 Bay Area artists. A relationship with New York's Whitney Museum of American Art allows the museum to exhibit works from the Whitney's vast permanent collection. The sweeping, open galleries are flooded with light, as is the attached café, including its outdoor patio with a plaza view.

Facing the southwest corner of the plaza, Downtown's biggest draw is the **Tech Museum of Innovation**, at 201 S Market St (daily 10am–5pm; $10; ℡408/294-8324, ⊛www.thetech.org), with its hands-on displays of high-tech engineering. There are three floors of exhibits, as well as the inevitable IMAX theatre (one show included in entry; extra show $5). Highlights include a programme that allows you to design a virtual rollercoaster, regular demonstrations of state-of-the-art surgical instruments and the chance to communicate with interactive robots. Unfortunately, the queues to access many of the best exhibits can seem like a virtual hell, and, unless you're a computer junkie, you may leave the museum feeling more like you've attempted to read an impervious software manual than visited a popular museum.

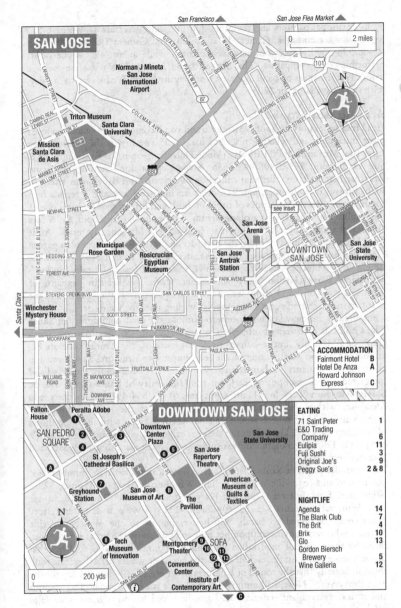

SAN JOSE

San Francisco ▲   San Jose Flea Market ▲

0   2 miles

Norman J Mineta
San Jose
International
Airport

Triton Museum
Santa Clara
University

Mission
Santa Clara
de Asis

Municipal
Rose Garden

Rosicrucian
Egyptian
Museum

San Jose
Arena

San Jose
Amtrak
Station

DOWNTOWN
SAN JOSE

San Jose
State
University

see inset

Winchester
Mystery House

ACCOMMODATION
Fairmont Hotel   **B**
Hotel De Anza   **A**
Howard Johnson
   Express   **C**

DOWNTOWN SAN JOSE

Fallon
House

Peralta Adobe

SAN PEDRO
SQUARE

Downtown
Center
Plaza

San Jose
State University

St Joseph's
Cathedral Basilica

San Jose
Repertory
Theatre

Greyhound
Station

San Jose
Museum of Art

The
Pavilion

American
Museum of
Quilts &
Textiles

Tech
Museum
of Innovation

Montgomery
Theater

SOFA

Convention
Center

Institute of
Contemporary Art

0   200 yds

EATING
71 Saint Peter   1
E&O Trading
   Company   6
Eulipia   11
Fuji Sushi   3
Original Joe's   9
Peggy Sue's   2 & 8

NIGHTLIFE
Agenda   14
The Blank Club   7
The Brit   4
Brix   10
Glo   13
Gordon Biersch
   Brewery   5
Wine Galleria   12

Aside from the attractions around the plaza, San Jose's other area worth walking through is the buzzing **"SoFA"** entertainment district, short for South First Street. The heart of San Jose's nightlife, it has half a dozen clubs and discos along with a popular wine bar (see p.534). There's plenty to see during the day as well, including the **Institute of Contemporary Art** (Tues–Fri 10am–5pm, Sat noon–5pm; free; ☏408/283-8155, ⓦwww.sjica.org) at 451 S 1st St. The ICA's large, sunny space exhibits modern art, mainly Bay Area artists, but also work by international painters and sculptors. On the same street are Downtown San Jose's twin **art cinemas**, Camera 12 at no. 201 and Camera 3 at no. 288 (both ☎408/998-3300, ⓦwww.cameracinemas.com), while at no. 490 is one of its performing arts companies, **The Stage** (☎408/283-7142, ⓦwww.sanjosestage.com). Performances of contemporary work regularly run Wednesday to Sunday, with tickets available for $20–50.

Around San Jose

Head four miles northwest of Downtown and you'll come across two of San Jose's more intriguing and relaxing places to hang out. The first is the **Rosicrucian Egyptian Museum**, 1600 Park Ave (Mon–Thurs 9am–5pm, Fri 9am–8pm, Sat & Sun 11am–6pm; $9; ☎408/947-3636, ⓦwww.egyptianmuseum.org), a grand structure that contains a brilliant collection of Assyrian and Babylonian artefacts, with displays of mummies, amulets, other ancient jewellery and a replica of a tomb. Don't miss the mummies of baboons, birds and fish on the left-hand side of the tomb wing. There's also a **planetarium**, whose shows (daily 2pm, Sat & Sun also 3.30pm; free) cover such esoteric subjects as "The Mithraic Mysteries". Aside from fascinating exhibits within, the best part about the Rosicrucian is its garden grounds, featuring a replica of the Akhenaten Temple from Luxor. Across the street and two blocks west of the museum is the second peaceful locale, San Jose's **Municipal Rose Garden** (daily 8am–sunset; free). This beautiful expanse of green and rows of wonderfully scented rose bushes is perfect for a picnic and the fountain in the garden's centre is a popular wading pool for youngsters.

Engulfed in the sprawl of northwestern San Jose, the small community of **Santa Clara** holds its own area of interest. The late eighteenth-century **Mission Santa Clara de Asis** (daily sunrise–sunset; free), just south of The Alameda (Route 82) at 500 El Camino Real, is one of the least impressive structures in the mission chain but its remnants – it burned in a 1926 fire – have been subtly preserved and integrated into the campus of the Jesuit-run **University of Santa Clara**. The **de Saisset Museum** (Tues–Sun 11am–4pm; free; ☎408/554-4528, ⓦwww.scu.edu /desaisset) within the complex traces the history of the mission through a permanent display of objects recovered from its ruins, along with changing shows of contemporary art. The bell in the belfry is original, a gift from King Carlos IV of Spain in 1798. Overall, the university is a green, quiet place to stroll around and pass an afternoon.

A few miles south of Santa Clara is a true American tourist trap, unmissable if you're into such over-the-top yarns. The **Winchester Mystery House**, 525 S Winchester Blvd, just off I-280 near Hwy-17 (daily summer 9am–7pm, winter 9am–5pm; various tours $25–33; ☎408/247-1313, ⓦwww.winchestermystery house.com), belonged to Sarah Winchester, heiress to the Winchester rifle fortune, who was convinced upon her husband's death in 1884 that he had been taken by the spirits of men killed with his weapons. The ghosts told her that unless a room was built for each of them, the same fate would befall her. She took them so literally that the sound of hammers never ceased – 24 hours a day for the next thirty years. Now, still unfinished, the house is a hotchpotch of extensions and styles: extravagant staircases lead nowhere and windows open onto solid brick walls.

The coast

The largely undeveloped **coastline** of the Peninsula south of San Francisco is worlds away from the inland valleys. A few small towns, countless beaches and salty prides of sea lions trace the way 75 miles south to the mellow summer fun of Santa Cruz and Capitola. Bluffs protect the many **nudist beaches** from prying eyes and make a popular launching pad for hang-glider pilots, particularly at **Fort Funston**, a mile south of the San Francisco Zoo, which is also the point where the earthquake-causing San Andreas Fault enters the sea, not to surface again until Point Reyes. **Skyline Boulevard** follows the coast from here past the repetitious tracts of proverbial ticky-tacky houses that make up Daly City, before heading inland towards Woodside at its intersection with Hwy-1, which continues south along the coast. Driving **Hwy-1** can be a relaxing jaunt providing jaw-dropping views of the ocean, as long as you avoid the summer-weekend traffic jams. Try hitting the road at sunrise if you can manage it and, provided the fog isn't obscuring everything, expect a magical ride.

Pacifica and around

San Pedro Point, a popular surfing beach fifteen miles south of San Francisco proper, and the town of **Pacifica** mark the southern extent of the city's suburban sprawl. Pacifica is a pleasant stopover for lunch and wave-gazing around Rockaway Beach. Visit the friendly **Chamber of Commerce** (see p.524) for free maps of the area, including trail guides for **Sweeney Ridge**, from where Spanish explorer Gaspar de Portola discovered the San Francisco Bay in 1769. Pacifica's old **Ocean Shore Railroad Depot** here, now a private residence, is one of the few surviving remnants of an ill-advised train line between San Francisco and Santa Cruz. Wiped out during the 1906 earthquake, the line was in any case never more than a third complete. Its few patrons had to transfer back and forth by ferry to connect the stretches of track that were built, the traces of which you can still see scarring the face of the bluffs. The continually eroding cliffs make construction of any route along the coast difficult, as evidenced a mile south by the **Devil's Slide**, which has required constant repairs over the decades but will finally close in 2012 when a new tunnel opens. The slide area was also a popular dumping spot for corpses of those who fell foul of rum-runners during Prohibition and is featured under various names in many of Dashiell Hammett's detective stories.

Just south of the Devil's Slide, the sands of **Gray Whale Cove State Beach** (daily 8am–sunset; free) are clothing-optional. Despite the name, it's not an especially great place to look for migrating grey whales but the stairway at the bus stop does lead down to a fine strand. Two miles south and a good half-mile off Hwy-1, the red-roofed buildings of the 1875 **Montara Lighthouse**, set among the windswept Monterey pine trees at the top of a steep cliff, have been converted into a youth hostel (see p.526). Just south of the turn to the lighthouse, at the end of California Street, the **Fitzgerald Marine Reserve** (T 650/728-3584, W www.fitzgeraldreserve.org) has three miles of diverse oceanic habitat, peaceful trails and, at low tide, the best tide pools in the Bay Area. The ranger often gives free interpretive walks through the reserve at low tide, the best time to explore, so call ahead or ask at one of the coast's tourist offices for low-tide times. At the south end of the reserve, Pillar Point juts out into the Pacific; just to the east, fishing boats dock at Pillar Point Harbor.

Captured in all its raging glory in the surfing documentary *Riding Giants*, **Mavericks Beach**, just off Pillar Point beyond the enormous communications dish, boasts the largest waves in North America and attracts some of the world's best (and craziest) surfers when conditions are right. Just watching them can be an exhilarating way to spend an hour or so and hundreds of people do just that every day. There's a long breakwater you can walk out on, too, but remember never to turn your back to the ocean – rogue waves have crashed in and swept unsuspecting tourists to their deaths. The surrounding villages of **Princeton-by-the-Sea**, whose main drag beside the marina has become extremely trendy, and **El Grenada** both have good restaurants serving freshly caught fish and seafood. Further along, surfers also frequent the waters just offshore from the splendid long stretch of **Miramar Beach**. After a day in the water or on the beach, the place to head is the beachfront *Douglas Beach House* (see p.535), an informal jazz club and beer bar that faces the sands.

Half Moon Bay

Half Moon Bay, twenty miles south of the city and the only town of any size along the coast between San Francisco and Santa Cruz, takes its name from the crescent-shaped bay formed by Pillar Point. It was originally called Spanishtown as it was founded when Spanish settlers forced the native Costonoa off the land in the 1840s and is thus the oldest European settlement in San Mateo County. Lined by miles of sandy beaches, the town is surprisingly rural considering its proximity to San Francisco and Silicon Valley and sports a number of ornate Victorian wooden houses clustered around its centre. The oldest of these, at the north end of Main Street, was built in 1849 just across a little stone bridge over Pillarcitos Creek. The **Chamber of Commerce** (see p.524) has free walking-tour maps of the town and information on the two annual festivals for which the place is well known. The first is the **Holy Ghost and Pentecost Festival**, a parade and barbecue held on the seventh Sunday after Easter; the other is the **Pumpkin Festival,** which celebrates the harvest of the area's many pumpkin farms just in time for Halloween, when the fields around town are full of families searching for the perfect jack-o'-lantern to greet the hordes of trick-or-treaters. If you fancy an **equestrian** experience, the combined Sea Horse and Friendly Acres ranches, one mile north of town at 2150 N Cabrillo Hwy (daily 8am–5.30pm; ☏650/726-9903, Ⓦwww.horserentals.com/seahorse.html), have trail **rides** for $55 per hour and ninety-minute beach rides for $65. **Half Moon Bay State Park** (daily 8am–sunset; $10 parking), half a mile west of the town, has a great stretch of beach and good camping (see p.526).

The Butano redwoods and Pescadero

If you've got a car and it's not a great day for the beach, head up into the hills above the coast, where the thousands of acres of the **Butano Redwood Forest** feel at their most ancient and primeval in the greyest, gloomiest weather. About half of the land between San Jose and the coast is protected from development in a variety of state and county parks, all of which are virtually deserted despite being within a thirty-minute drive of the Silicon Valley sprawl. Any one of a dozen roads heads through endless stands of untouched forest and even the briefest of walks will take you seemingly miles from any sign of civilization. Hwy-84 climbs up from San Gregorio through the Sam McDonald County Park to the hamlet of **La Honda**, where Ken Kesey had his ranch during the Sixties and once notoriously invited the Hell's Angels to a party. From here, you can continue on to Palo Alto or loop back to the coast via Pescadero Road.

A mile before you reach the quaint town of **Pescadero**, Cloverdale Road heads south to **Butano State Park**, where you can hike and camp overlooking the Pacific. Tiny Pescadero itself has one of the best places to eat on the Peninsula – *Duarte's* (see p.534) – as well as a gas station, just about the last place to fill up north of Santa Cruz. Just north of the turnoff to the village from Hwy-1, Pescadero State Beach is yet another fine spot for a dip, with no time restrictions or parking fee. The marsh between the beach and the town is a great place for watching waterfowl, especially at high tide. Pescadero, which was founded by Portuguese fishermen, celebrates the same **Holy Ghost Festival** as Half Moon Bay but a week earlier, on the sixth Sunday after Easter. The festival is also known by its Portuguese name of Chamarita.

Five miles south of Pescadero, you can stay the night in the old lighthouse-keeper's quarters and soak your bones in a marvellous hot tub at the *HI-Pigeon Point Lighthouse Hostel* (see p.526). The grounds of the light station are open to visitors (daily 8am–sunset; free; ☏650/879-2120) but the structure itself is closed. The calmest, most pleasant beach for wading is **Bean Hollow State Beach**, a mile north of the hostel; it's free but has very limited parking.

The Año Nuevo State Reserve

If you're here between mid-December and the end of March continue south another five miles to the **Año Nuevo State Reserve** for a chance to see one of nature's most bizarre spectacles – the mating rituals of **northern elephant seals**. These massive, ungainly creatures, fifteen feet long and weighing up to three tonnes, were once found all along the coast, though they were nearly hunted to extinction by whalers in the nineteenth century. During the mating season, the beach is literally a seething mass of blubbery bodies, with the trunk-nosed males fighting it out for the right to sire as many as fifty pups in a season. At any time of the year, you're likely to see half a dozen or so dozing in the sands. The reserve is also good for birding, and in March you might even catch sight of migrating grey whales.

The slowly resurgent Año Nuevo elephant seal population is still carefully protected and during the breeding season the obligatory guided tours – designed to protect spectators as much as to give the seals some privacy – begin booking in October (hourly 8am–4pm; $7 per person, $10 parking; ☏1-800/444-4445, Ⓦwww.parks.ca.gov). Otherwise tickets are usually made available to people staying at the *Pigeon Point Lighthouse Hostel*, and from April to November you can get a free permit from the park entrance to visit the point.

Eating

The **restaurants** on the Peninsula, particularly in pseudo-ritzy Palo Alto, are increasingly on a par with their San Franciscan counterparts. Many, filled with wealthy young computer executives, require dinner reservations every night of the week. In San Jose, consider dining around San Pedro Square for a good choice of cuisine. The coastal towns, especially Half Moon Bay, also boast some top-quality places.

71 Saint Peter 71 N San Pedro St, San Jose ☏408/971-8523. Patio dining and oyster bar centred on a menu of filet mignon, pork loin, chicken and salads, with most main courses just over $20. Extremely hot with the in-crowd. Lunch Mon–Fri, dinner nightly.

Barbara's Fish Trap 281 Capistrano Rd off Hwy-1, Princeton-by-the-Sea ☏650/728-7049. Oceanfront seafood restaurant with good-value fish dinners and an unbeatable view.

Bistro Elan 448 S California Ave, Palo Alto ☏650/327-0284. Serving spiffy Cal cuisine such as duck confit and pan-seared Maine scallops, to the cyber-elite. Prices are rather steep at over $20 per dinner entrée, so consider a lunchtime visit when dishes are around $15. Closed Sun & Mon.

Café Capistrano 480 Capistrano Rd off Hwy-1, Princeton-by-the-Sea ☏650/728-7699. Inexpensive and authentic Mayan fare such as slow-roasted pork is on offer at this unpretentious place.

Café Gibraltar 425 Ave Alhambra, El Granada ☏650/560-9039. Set back from Hwy-1 but with ocean views, this classy establishment boasts fine decor and finer Mediterranean cuisine made from local organic produce. Delights such as *arni fricasse* (Greek-style lamb) cost around $25.

Caffè del Doge 419 University Ave, Palo Alto ☏650/323-3600. Relaxing, colourful hangout for Palo Alto's intellectual crowd; a branch of the Venice original.

Cetrella 845 Main St, Half Moon Bay ☏650/726-4090. Classy Italian/Mediterranean restaurant with a huge dining room, serving delights such as Australian lamb sirloin in kalamata olive tapenade. Dinner main courses are around $25 but there's a cheaper café/bar section too.

Coconuts 642 Ramona St, Palo Alto ☏650/329-9533. This colourful Caribbean restaurant and bar rustles up all the West Indian favourites such as curried goat and jerk chicken for $10–15, as well as great cocktails.

Duarte's 202 Stage Rd, Pescadero. Platefuls of traditional American food (especially fish) for around $10 are served in this down-home find, connected to a bar full of locals in cowboy hats. Famous for their artichoke soup.

E&O Trading Company 96 S 1st St, San Jose ☏ 408/938-4100. Upscale Southeast Asian grill featuring shaking beef, Shiso pepper grilled salmon and other Vietnamese/Indonesian fare. Main courses around $20.

Eulipia 374 S 1st St, San Jose ☏ 408/280-6161. Stylish dinner spot boasting well-prepared versions of California-cuisine staples such as grilled fish and fresh pastas. Main courses $15–30. Closed Mon.

Evvia 420 Emerson St, Palo Alto ☏ 650/326-0983. Rather pricey Greek lamb and goat dishes such as *paidakia arnisia* and *katsiki yiouvetsi*, as well as baked fish and other Hellenic faves, served in a cosy yet elegant dining room. Full bar.

Fuji Sushi 56 W Santa Clara St, San Jose ☏ 408/298-3854. Snazzy Japanese restaurant offering a bewildering array of sushi rolls, sashimi, bento boxes and main dishes such as teriyaki and BBQ eel for little over $10.

Hookah Nites Café 371 S 1st St, San Jose. Avant-garde art is showcased in this spacious and trendy venue, which serves fresh coffee and pastries.

Hyderabad House 448 University Ave, Palo Alto. Inexpensive Indian restaurant combining dishes from both north and south, with subtle touches of ginger and coconut.

Krung Siam 423 University Ave, Palo Alto ☏ 650/322-5900. Classy but not too expensive restaurant serving beautifully presented traditional Thai fare. Try the *pad kae* (pan-fried lamb) or the green curry.

La Cheminée 530 Bryant St, Palo Alto ☏ 650/329-0695. Quality fare, such as lavender-encrusted halibut or pork Dijon, are among the delights at this French bistro. Mostly under $20 per entrée.

La Costanera 8150 Cabrillo Hwy (Hwy-1), between Pacifica and Montara ☏ 650/728-1600. One of the newest and most highly-rated coastal restaurants, serving traditional Peruvian recipes in a California-style dining space overlooking the ocean. There's a range of *ceviche* and delights such as duck-leg stew in dark beer sauce for $20.

Nick's Seashore Restaurant 101 Rockaway Beach, Pacifica. Beloved enough to reel folks in from the city regularly, this all-purpose joint attached to a motel provides cheap brekky, moderate pasta and pricier steak/seafood dishes.

Original Joe's 301 S 1st St, San Jose. Grab a stool at the counter or settle into one of the comfy vinyl booths and enjoy a burger and fries or a plate of pasta at this San Jose institution, where $10 still goes a long way. Open until 1am.

Pasta Moon 315 Main St, Half Moon Bay ☏ 650/726-5125. Elegant but unpretentious Italian place that serves excellent pizza, pasta and mouth-watering dishes such as seafood *spiedini*. Main courses $21–28.

Peggy Sue's 29 N San Pedro St, San Jose. Inexpensive milkshakes, burgers and fries served in a 1950s setting. Also has a vegetarian and kids' menu. There's a second location a few blocks away at 185 Park Ave.

Rock'n'Rob's 450 Dundee Way, Rockaway Beach, Pacifica. This famous modern diner decorated in the old style churns out tonnes of burgers and fries all day, but no breakfast.

Sam's Chowder House 4210 Cabrillo Hwy (Hwy-1), 3 miles north of Half Moon Bay ☏ 650/712-0245. Large, modern restaurant with wonderful ocean views, serving generous portions of seafood, fish and steak at around $20 a pop.

St Michael's Alley 806 Emerson St, Palo Alto ☏ 650/326-2530. This former student hangout has become one of Palo Alto's hottest bistros, serving "casual California" cuisine. A fine wine list and weekend brunch ($10–18) keeps guests coming back for more.

Nightlife

For a serious night out on the town, you're better off heading up to San Francisco, though there are a number of good **bars** and **clubs** on the Peninsula – particularly in San Jose's SoFA district, but also in the studenty environs of Palo Alto.

Agenda 399 S 1st St, San Jose ☏ 408/287-3991. A bar/restaurant/lounge in SoFA that heralded the arrival of nightlife in San Jose. DJ, dancing and live jazz nightly.

The Blank Club 44 S Almaden, San Jose ☏ 408/292-5265. Live shows most nights and the only regular space for indie, punk and alternative sounds.

Blue Chalk Café 630 Ramona St, Palo Alto ☏ 650/326-1020. Students and techies have been flocking to this wildly successful bar/pool-hall/restaurant ever since it opened in 1993. Regular live music.

The Brit 173 W Santa Clara St, San Jose ☏ 408/266-0550. Popular British-themed pub with fish'n'chips, real ale, footie (meaning soccer) on TV and a trivia quiz night.

Brix 349 S 1st St, San Jose ☎ 408/947-1975. The city's premier gay nightclub, featuring go-go boys and girls, video jockeys and the latest dance hits. Great cocktails if you'd rather just sip than gyrate.

Cameron's Inn 1410 Cabrillo Hwy, 1 mile south of Half Moon Bay ☎ 650/726-5705. The other main UK-style joint on the Peninsula, with imported ales, pub grub and games, as well as two London double-deckers outside, one for smoking and one for kids' videos.

Douglas Beach House Miramar Beach, 2.5 miles north of Half Moon Bay on Hwy-1, then west down Medio Ave ☎ 650/726-4143, ⓦ www.bachddsoc.org. Two-storey country beach house with fireplace and outside deck; international jazz performers are frequently hosted by the Bach Dancing & Dynamite Society. The quieter *Ebb Tide Café* below is open Thurs–Sun.

Glo 394 S 1st St, San Jose ☎ 408/280-1977. Dance music from light hip-hop to heavy disco is featured at this club, which imports top DJs from SF, LA and Vegas on Sat nights.

Gordon Biersch Brewery 640 Emerson St, Palo Alto ☎ 650/323-7723. Among the first and best of the Bay Area's microbrewery-cum-restaurants. Also in San Francisco (see p.487) and in Downtown San Jose at 33 E San Fernando St.

Half Moon Bay Brewing Co. 390 Capistrano Rd, Princeton-by-the-Sea ☎ 650/728-2739. Lively watering hole with a rock soundtrack, where you can get your kisser round a range of decent brews from blonde through amber to brown ale. Also has a popular restaurant serving California and American cuisine.

Moss Beach Distillery Beach and Ocean, Moss Beach ☎ 650/728-0220. If you don't feel like paying out $20 per entrée at this popular restaurant, snuggle up under a wool blanket, order a drink and an appetizer and watch the sunset from the patio overlooking the ocean.

Wine Galleria 377 S 1st St, San Jose. Large wine bar with plush sofas and a huge array of vintages for sale by the glass, with specials such as five glasses for $20.

Marin County

Across the Golden Gate from San Francisco, **Marin County** (pronounced "Ma-RINN") is an unabashed introduction to California self-indulgence: an elitist pleasure zone of conspicuous luxury and abundant natural beauty, with sunshine, high mountains, thick redwood forests and sandy if often fog-bound beaches. Often ranked as the wealthiest county in the US, Marin has attracted a sizeable contingent of Northern California's rich young professionals, many of whom grew up during the Flower Power years of the 1960s and lend the place its New Age feel and reputation. Though many of the cocaine-and-hot-tub devotees who seemed to populate the swanky waterside towns in the 1970s have traded in their drug habits for mountain bikes – which were invented here – life in Marin still centres on personal pleasure and the throngs you see hiking and cycling at weekends, not to mention the hundreds of esoteric self-help practitioners (rolfing, rebirthing and soul-travel therapists fill up the classified ads of the local papers) prove that residents of Marin work hard to maintain their easy air of physical and mental wellbeing.

Flashy modern ferries, appointed with fully stocked bars, sail across the bay from San Francisco and present a marvellous initial view of the county. As you head past desolate Alcatraz Island, curvaceous **Mount Tamalpais** looms larger until you land near its foot in one of the chic bayside settlements of **Sausalito** or **Tiburon**. **Angel Island**, in the middle of the bay but most easily accessed from Tiburon, provides relief from the excessive style-consciousness of both towns, retaining a wild, untouched feeling among the eerie ruins of derelict military fortifications.

Sausalito and Tiburon (and their associated lifestyles) are only a small part of Marin. The bulk of the county rests on the slopes of the ridge of peaks that divides the Peninsula down the middle, separating the sophisticated harbourside towns in the east from the untrammelled wilderness of the Pacific Coast in the west. The **Marin Headlands**, just across the Golden Gate Bridge from San Francisco, hold

535

time-warped old battlements and gun emplacements that once protected San Francisco's harbour from would-be invaders, and now overlook hikers and cyclists enjoying the acres of open space and wildlife. Along the coastline that spreads north, the broad shore of **Stinson Beach** is the Bay Area's finest and widest stretch of sand, beyond which Hwy-1 clings to the coast past the counterculture village of **Bolinas** to seascapes around **Point Reyes**, where it's thought Sir Francis Drake may have landed in 1579. Whale-and seal-watchers congregate here year-round for glimpses of migrations and matings.

Inland, the heights of Mount Tamalpais, and specifically **Muir Woods**, are a magnet to sightseers and nature lovers, who come to wander through one of the county's few surviving stands of the native coastal redwood trees. Such trees covered most of Marin before they were chopped down to build and rebuild the wooden houses of San Francisco. The long-vanished lumber mills of the rustic town of **Mill Valley**, overlooking the bay from the slopes of Mount Tam, as it's locally known, bear the guilt for much of this destruction; the oldest town in Marin County is now home to an eclectic bunch of art galleries and cafés. Further north, Marin's largest town, **San Rafael**, is rather bland, though its outskirts contain two of the most unusual attractions in the county: **Frank Lloyd Wright**'s peculiar Civic Center complex and the preserved remnants of an old Chinese fishing village in **China Camp State Park**.

Arrival

Just getting to Marin County can be a great start to a day out from San Francisco. Golden Gate Transit **ferries** (☎415/923-2000 in San Francisco, ☎415/455-2000 in Marin, ⓦwww.goldengate.org) leave from the Ferry Building on the Embarcadero, crossing the bay past Alcatraz Island to **Sausalito** (Mon–Fri 7.40am–7.55pm, Sat & Sun 10.40am–6.30pm) and **Larkspur** (Mon–Fri 6.25am–9.40pm, Sat & Sun 12.40–7.15pm); they run every thirty to forty minutes during the rush hour, roughly hourly during the rest of the day, and about every ninety minutes to two hours on weekends and holidays. Tickets cost $8.25 one way to either destination and refreshments are sold on board. The slightly more expensive and less frequent Blue and Gold Fleet ($10 one way; ☎415/773-1188, ⓦwww.blueandgoldfleet .com) sails from Pier 41 at Fisherman's Wharf to Sausalito (Mon–Fri 11.15am– 5.10pm, Sat & Sun 11am–7.05pm) and **Tiburon** (Mon–Fri 10.50am–7.15pm, Sat & Sun 9.40am–7.05pm) – from where the Angel Island ferry (times vary; $13.50 round-trip, including state park entry fee; $1 per bicycle; ☎415/435-2131, ⓦwww.angelislandferry.com) nips back and forth to **Angel Island State Park** daily in summer, weekends-only in the winter. Blue and Gold Fleet provides additional weekday rush-hour crossings to Tiburon from the Ferry Building and a daily excursion service direct to Angel Island ($16 round-trip) from Pier 41 and the Ferry Building. Note that the ferry timetables change quarterly, so it's best to check in advance.

Information

Three main on-the-spot sources can provide further information on Marin County: the inconveniently located **Marin County Visitors Bureau**, signposted off US-101 at 1 Mitchell Blvd, San Rafael (Mon–Fri 9am–5pm; ☎1-866/925-2060, ⓦwww.visitmarin.org); the **Sausalito Visitor Center**, occupying a modest hut at 780 Bridgeway Ave (Tues–Sun 11.30am–4pm; ☎415/332-0505, ⓦwww .sausalito.org); and the **Mill Valley Chamber of Commerce**, 85 Throckmorton Ave (Mon–Fri 10am–noon & 1–4pm; ☎415/388-9700, ⓦwww.millvalley.org), in the centre of the town. Note that the latter two open rather erratically.

For information on hiking and camping in the wilderness and beach areas, depending on where you're heading, contact the **Golden Gate National Recreation Area**, Building 201, Fort Mason Center, San Francisco (Mon–Fri 9.30am–4.30pm; T 415/561-3000), or the **Marin Headlands Visitor Center** (daily 9.30am–4.30pm; T 415/331-1540, W www.nps.gov/goga); other outlets are the **Mount Tamalpais State Park Visitor Center**, 801 Panoramic Hwy, Mill Valley (daily 8am–5.30pm; T 415/388-2070, W www.mttam.net), and the Point Reyes National Seashore's **Bear Valley Visitors Center**, Point Reyes (Mon–Fri 9am–5pm, Sat & Sun 8am–5pm; T 415/464-5100, W www.nps.gov/pore). Information on what's on in Marin can be found in the widely available local freesheets, such as the down-to-earth *Coastal Post* (W www.coastal-post.com) or the New-Agey *Pacific Sun* (W www.pacificsun.com).

Getting around

Golden Gate Transit runs a comprehensive **bus service** around Marin County and across the Golden Gate Bridge from the Transbay Terminal in San Francisco (same contacts as ferries, see p.441), and publishes a helpful and free system map and timetable, including all ferry services. Bus fares range from $2 to $6.15, with routes running every thirty minutes throughout the day, and once an hour late at night. Some areas can only be reached by GGT commuter services, which run during the morning and evening rush hours (call ahead to check schedules). On Sundays only, San Francisco's MUNI bus #76 runs hourly from San Francisco direct to the Marin Headlands. Golden Gate Transit route #40/42, the only service available between Marin County and the East Bay, runs from the San Rafael Transit Center to the Del Norte BART station in El Cerrito ($4.15 each way).

If you'd rather avoid the hassle of bus connections, Gray Line (T 415/558-9400, W www.grayline.com) offers guided **bus tours** of varying duration from the Transbay Terminal in San Francisco, taking in Sausalito and Muir Woods (daily year-round 9am, check for increased services in summer; $49–68); the Blue and Gold Fleet ferry also has a bus trip to Muir Woods (daily 9.15am & 2.15pm; 3hr 30min; $55) with an option to return by ferry from Tiburon to Pier 41 in the city.

One of the best ways to get around Marin is by **bike**, particularly using a mountain bike to cruise the many trails that crisscross the county, especially in the Marin Headlands. If you want to ride on the road, Sir Francis Drake Highway – from Larkspur to Point Reyes – makes a good route, though it's best to avoid weekends, when the roads can get clogged up with cars. All ferry services to Marin allow bicycles.

Accommodation

You might prefer simply to dip into Marin County using San Francisco as a base, and if you've got a car or manage to time the bus connections right it's certainly possible, at least for the southernmost parts of the county. However, it can be nicer to take a more leisurely look at Marin, staying over for a couple of nights in some well-chosen spots. Sadly, there are few **hotels**, and those that there are often charge well in excess of $100 a night; **motels** are hardly ubiquitous, though there are a couple of attractively faded ones along the coast. If you want to stay in a B&B, contact Marin Bed and Breakfast (T 415/485-1971, W www.marinbedand breakfast.com), which can fix you up with rooms in comfortable private homes all over Marin County from $70 a night for two, ranging from courtyard hideaways on the beach in Tiburon to houseboats in Sausalito. The best bet for budget accommodation is a dorm bed in either of the beautifully situated **hostels** along the western beaches.

Hotels and motels

Casa Madrona 801 Bridgeway Ave, Sausalito ☎1-800/288-0502, ⊛www.casamadrona.com. Deluxe, European-style hotel with a new extension spreading up the hill above the bay. Spa facilities available and the *Mikayla* restaurant is highly rated. ❼

Colonial Motel 1735 Lincoln Ave, San Rafael ☎1-888/785-2111, ⊛www.colonialinnmarin.com. Quiet, well-furnished and friendly motel in a residential neighbourhood, with very low rates. ❶

Grand Hotel 15 Brighton Ave, Bolinas ☎415/868-1757. Just two budget rooms in a funky, run-down old hotel above a secondhand shop. Sometimes only operates at weekends. ❷

Hotel Sausalito 16 El Portal, Sausalito ☎1-888/442-0700, ⊛www.hotelsausalito.com. This boutique hotel has sixteen stylish rooms with views across the park and harbour. Owned and run by an entertaining Scot. ❺

The Lodge At Tiburon 1651 Tiburon Blvd, Tiburon ☎415/435-3133, ⊛www.larkspurhotels.com. Smart modern hotel with a rustic feel. Comfortable rooms, all with CD/DVD players, some with jacuzzis. Rather inept staff. ❻

Mill Valley Inn 165 Throckmorton Ave, Mill Valley ☎1-800/595-2100, ⊛www.jdvhotels.com. By far the best hotel in Marin County, this gorgeous European-style inn boasts elegant rooms, two private cottages and a central location. Complimentary breakfast and wine hour. ❻

Ocean Court Motel 18 Arenal St, Stinson Beach ☎415/868-0212, ⊛www.oceancourt.ws. Large, simple rooms with kitchens, just a block from the beach and west of Hwy-1; you pay for the location though. ❹

Stinson Beach Motel 3416 Shoreline Hwy, Stinson Beach ☎415/868-1712, ⊛www.stinson beachmotel.com. Average, slightly overpriced roadside motel right on Hwy-1, with tiny rooms. Five minutes' walk to the beach. ❸

B&Bs

Blue Heron Inn 11 Wharf Rd, Bolinas ☎415/868-1102. Lovely double rooms in an unbeatable locale with ocean view. A friendly welcome and its own restaurant serving good seafood and steaks help make this an excellent choice. ❹

Lindisfarne Guest House Green Gulch Farm Zen Center, Muir Beach ☎415/383-3134, ⊛www.sfzc.org. Restful rooms in a meditation retreat set in a secluded valley above Muir Beach. Price includes three excellent vegetarian buffet meals. ❸

Mountain Home Inn 810 Panoramic Hwy, Mill Valley ☎1-877/381-9001, ⊛www.mtnhomeinn.com. Romantically located near Mount Tamalpais' crest, this B&B offers great views and endless hiking opportunities. Some rooms with hot tubs. ❻

Olema Inn 10,000 Sir Francis Drake Blvd, Olema ☎1-800/532-9252, ⊛www.theolemainn.com. Wonderful little B&B with comfy rooms near the entrance to Point Reyes National Seashore, on a site that's been a hotel since 1876. Features a gourmet restaurant serving seafood and a full bar with heady wine list. Ideal for a break from the city. ❻

Pelican Inn 10 Pacific Way, Muir Beach ☎415/383-6000, ⊛www.pelicaninn.com. Very comfortable rooms in a romantic pseudo-English country inn, with good bar and restaurant downstairs, serving full English breakfast and fine ales. A ten-minute walk from beautiful Muir Beach. ❻

Ten Inverness Way 10 Inverness Way, Inverness ☎415/669-1648, ⊛www.teninvernessway.com. Quiet and restful, with a hot tub and complimentary evening wine, in a small village of good restaurants and bakeries on the fringes of Point Reyes. ❺

Hostels

HI–Marin Headlands Building 941, Fort Barry, Marin Headlands ☎1-800/909-4776, ⊛www.norcalhostels.org. Hard to get to without a car – it's near Rodeo Lagoon just off Bunker Road, five miles west of Sausalito – but worth the effort for its setting, in a cosy old army barracks near the ocean. On Sundays and holidays only, MUNI bus #76 from San Francisco stops right outside. Closed 10am–3.30pm, except for registration. Dorm beds from $22 a night; private rooms from $72.

HI–Point Reyes In Point Reyes National Seashore ☎415/663-8811, ⊛www.norcalhostels.org. Also hard to reach without your own transport: just off Limantour Road six miles west of the visitor centre and two miles from the beach, it's located in an old ranch house and surrounded by meadows and forests. Closed 10am–4.30pm. Dorm beds from $22 a night; private rooms from $64.

Campgrounds

Angel Island State Park Angel Island ☎415/435-5390, ⊛www.angelisland.org. Nine primitive walk-in sites (and one group kayak-in site) with great views of San Francisco, which explains why they cost as much per night as more developed sites elsewhere ($30). In summer it's essential to book.

China Camp State Park Off N San Pedro Rd, north of San Rafael ☎415/456-0766. Walk-in plots (just 600ft from the parking lot) overlooking a lovely meadow. First-come-first-camped for $35 a night. April–Oct reserve on ☎1-800/444-7275, ⊛www.parks.ca.gov.

Marin Headlands Just across the Golden Gate Bridge ☎ 415/561-4304, ⊛ www.nps.gov/goga. Five campgrounds, the best of which is very popular *Kirby Cove* (open April–Oct only), at the northern foot of the Golden Gate Bridge (reservations ☎ 1-877/444-6777, ⊛ www.recreation.gov; $25). Of the remaining sites, one is a group camp ($35), and the other three are free.

Mount Tamalpais State Park Above Mill Valley ☎ 415/388-2070. Two separate campgrounds ($25) for backpackers, one on the slopes of the mountain and the other towards the coast at Steep Ravine, which also has a few rustic cabins ($75 a night). Reserve on ☎ 1-800/444-7275, ⊛ www.parks.ca.gov.

Point Reyes National Seashore 40 miles northwest of San Francisco ☎ 415/663-1092. A wide range of hike-in sites for backpackers, near the beach or in the forest. Reserve sites up to two months in advance (weekdays 9am–2pm; $15; ☎ 415/663-8054).

Samuel P. Taylor State Park On Sir Francis Drake Blvd, 15 miles west of San Rafael ☎ 415/488-9897. Deluxe, car-accessible plots with hot showers, spread along a river for $35 a night; basic hiker/biker sites for $5. Don't miss the swimming hole or bat caves. In summer, reserve on ☎ 1-800/444-7275, ⊛ www.parks.ca.gov.

Across the Golden Gate: the Marin Headlands and Sausalito

The largely undeveloped **MARIN HEADLANDS** of the Golden Gate National Recreation Area, across the Golden Gate Bridge from San Francisco, afford some of the most impressive views of the bridge and the city behind. As the regular fog rolls in, the breathtaking image of the bridge's stanchions tantalizingly drifting in and out of sight and the fleeting glimpses of Downtown skyscrapers will abide long in the memory. Take the first turn as you exit the bridge (Alexander Avenue) and follow the sign back to San Francisco – the one-way circle trip back to the bridge heads first to the west along Conzelman Road and up a steep hill. You'll pass through a largely undeveloped land, dotted with the concrete remains of old forts and gun emplacements standing guard over the entrance to the bay, dating from as far back as the Civil War and as recent as World War II. The coastline here is much more rugged than it is on the San Francisco side, making it a great place for an aimless cliff-top hike or a stroll along one of the beaches at the bottom of treacherous footpaths.

The first installation as you climb the steep hill up the headlands is **Battery Wallace**, the largest and most impressive of the artillery sites along the rocky coast here, cut through a hillside above the southwestern tip of the Peninsula. The angular military geometry survives, framing views of the Pacific Ocean and the Golden Gate Bridge. Otherwise, continue along Conzelman for incredible views of the city from any of the many turnouts. For birdwatching, walk from the Battery Wallace parking lot through tunnels that lead five hundred yards to the opposite bluff, overlooking **Point Bonita Lighthouse** far below, where various sea birds and birds of prey can be seen in large numbers. To reach Point Bonita by vehicle, drive down the one-way lane that Conzelman becomes and keep winding down to the lighthouse. It stands sentry at the very end of the headlands and is open for tours (Sat–Mon 12.30–3.30pm; free). Conzelman comes to a "T" in the road; turn left and park your car on the side of the road or at the parking lot three hundred yards west, at the end of the drive. To reach the lighthouse, you have to walk the half-mile pathway down, a beautiful stroll that takes you through a tunnel cut into the cliff, and across a precarious suspension bridge.

Looping back around, you'll be heading northeast on Bunker Road. If you really want to relive holocaustic Cold War nightmares, you can visit the **Nike Missiles Site** (first Sun only 12.30–3.30pm; ⊛ www.atomictourist.com/nike.htm) at **Fort Barry** and take a free guided tour of an abandoned 1950s ballistic-missile launchpad, complete with disarmed nuclear missiles. If you're after a more pacifistic pastime, stop off at the **Marin Headlands Visitor Center** (see p.537) alongside

Rodeo Lagoon for free maps of popular hiking trails in the area. Across the road and a bit further along, one of the largest of Fort Barry's old residential buildings has been converted into the spacious but homely *HI–Marin Headlands* hostel (see p.538), an excellent base for more extended explorations of the inland ridges and valleys.

Turn off to the left where Bunker Road snakes down to wide, sandy **Rodeo Beach** (#76 MUNI bus from San Francisco: Sun & holidays only). The beach separates the chilly ocean from the marshy warm water of **Rodeo Lagoon**, where swimming is prohibited to protect nesting sea birds. North of the lagoon, you can visit the **Marine Mammal Center** (daily 10am–5pm; free; ☎415/289-7355, ⓦwww.marinemammalcenter.org), which rescues and rehabilitates injured and orphaned sea creatures, including dolphins and sea otters.

Sausalito

SAUSALITO, fronting the bay below US-101, is a picturesque, snug little town of exclusive restaurants and pricey boutiques along a pretty waterfront promenade. Expensive, quirkily designed houses climb the overgrown cliffs above **Bridgeway Avenue**, the main route through town. Sausalito used to be a fairly gritty community of fishermen and sea-traders, full of bars and bordellos, and despite its upscale modern face it still makes a fun day out from San Francisco by ferry, the boats arriving next to the Sausalito Yacht Club in the centre of town. Hang out in one of the waterfront bars and watch the crowds strolling along the esplanade or climb the stairways above Bridgeway Avenue and amble around the leafy hills. A more energetic diversion is sea-kayaking, and Sea Trek (☎415/488-1000, ⓦwww.seatrekkayak.com) rents single or double sea-kayaks beginning at $20/35 for one hour's worth of superb paddling around the bay. They offer sit-on-top kayaks, lessons and safe routes for first-timers, or closed kayaks and directions around Angel Island for the more experienced.

The old working wharves and warehouses that made Sausalito a haven for smugglers and Prohibition-era rum-runners are long gone; most have been taken over by dull strip-malls. However, some stretches of it have, for the moment at least, survived the tourist onslaught. A mile north of the town centre along Bridgeway Avenue, an ad hoc community of exotic **barges** and **houseboats**, some of which have been moored here since the 1950s, are still staving off eviction to make room for yet another luxury marina. In the meantime, many of the boats – one looks like a South Pacific island, another like the Taj Mahal – can be viewed at Waldo Point, half a mile beyond the cavernous concrete **Bay Model Visitor Center**, 2100 Bridgeway Ave (June–Aug Tues–Fri 9am–4pm, Sat & Sun 10am–5pm; Sept–May Tues–Sat 9am–4pm; free; ☎415/332-3871, ⓦwww.spn .usace.army.mil/bmvc). Inside the huge building, elevated walkways lead you around a scale model of the bay and its surrounding deltas and aquatic inhabitants, offering insight on the enormity and diversity of this area.

Back towards the Golden Gate Bridge at 557 McReynolds Road is the **Bay Area Discovery Museum** (Tues–Fri 9am–4pm, Sat & Sun 10am–5pm; $10, kids $8, free every first Wed; ☎415/339-3900, ⓦwww.baykidsmuseum.org). Within the remodelled barracks of **Fort Baker**, it holds a series of activities and workshops for youngsters up to 10 or so, including art and media rooms as well as the outdoor Lookout Cove area. Here kids can play in a mini-tide pool, on a shipwreck or on the model of the Golden Gate Bridge as it was during construction – pretty cool, as the real one is visible in the distance if it's clear.

The Marin County Coast to Bolinas

The **Shoreline Highway**, Hwy-1, cuts off west from US-101 just north of Sausalito, following the old main highway towards Mill Valley (see p.542). The first turn on the left, Tennessee Valley Road, leads up to the less-visited northern expanses of the Golden Gate National Recreation Area. You can take a beautiful three-mile hike from the parking lot at the end of the road, heading down along the secluded and lushly green **Tennessee Valley** to a small beach along a rocky cove, or you can take a trail-ride lesson on horseback from Miwok Livery at 701 Tennessee Valley Rd ($75 for 90min; ☏415/383-8048, ⊛www.miwokstables.com).

Hwy-1 twists up the canyon to a crest, where **Panoramic Highway** spears off to the right, following the ridge north to Muir Woods and Mount Tamalpais; Golden Gate Transit bus #63 to Stinson Beach follows this route every hour on weekends and holidays only. Be warned, however, that the hillsides are usually choked with fog until 11am and most of the day in summer, making the approach from San Francisco to Stinson Beach/Bolinas via Hwy-1 both dangerous and uninteresting. Two miles before you reach the crest, a small paved lane cuts off to the left, dropping down to the bottom of the broad canyon to the **Green Gulch Farm Zen Center** (☏415/383-3134, ⊛www.sfzc.org), an organic farm and Buddhist retreat with an authentic Japanese teahouse and a simple but refined prayer hall. On Sunday mornings the centre is open from 8.15am for a public meditation period and an informal lecture on Zen Buddhism at 10.15am (suggested donation $5), after which you can stroll down to Muir Beach or stay for lunch ($8). If you're interested in learning more about Zen, inquire about the centre's Guest Student Program, which enables initiates to stay from five days to several weeks at a time for $20 a night. Residents rise well before dawn for meditation and prayer, then work much of the day in the gardens, tending the vegetables that are eventually served in many of the Bay Area's finest restaurants (notably *Greens* in San Francisco – see p.480). If you just want a weekend retreat, you can also stay overnight in the far more upmarket *Lindisfarne Guest House* (see p.538) on the grounds.

Beyond the Zen Center, the road down from Muir Woods rejoins Hwy-1 at **Muir Beach**, usually uncrowded and beautifully secluded in a semicircular cove. Three miles north, **Steep Ravine** drops sharply down the cliffs to a small beach, past very rustic cabins and a campground, bookable through Mount Tamalpais State Park (see p.542). A mile on is the small and lovely **Red Rocks** nudist beach, down a steep trail from a parking area along the highway. **Stinson Beach**, which is bigger, and more popular despite the rather cold water, is a mile further. It gets packed at weekends in summer, when the traffic can be nightmarish but at least there's a huge, free car park behind the dunes.

Bolinas and southern Point Reyes

At the tip of the headland, due west from Stinson Beach, is the laidback village of **Bolinas**, though you may have a hard time finding it – road signs marking the turnoff from Hwy-1 are removed as soon as they're put up by locals hoping to keep the place to themselves. The campaign may have backfired, though, since press coverage of the "sign war" has done more to publicize the town than any road sign ever did. To get there, take the first left beyond the estuary and follow the road to the end. Bolinas is completely surrounded by federal property – the Golden Gate National Recreation Area and Point Reyes National Seashore – and even the lagoon has been declared a National Bird Sanctuary. Known for its leftist hippy culture, the village itself has been home at different times to Grace Slick and Paul Kantner, a regular colony of artists, bearded handymen, writers (the late trout-fishing author Richard Brautigan and basketball diarist Jim Carroll among them), and stray dogs. There's not a lot to see apart from the small **Bolinas Museum**, 48 Wharf Rd (Fri 1–5pm, Sat & Sun noon–5pm; free; ☏415/868-0330, ⊛www.bolinasmuseum.org), which has a few historical displays and works by local artists in a set of converted cottages around a courtyard. Mostly, it's just a case of people-watching and taking in the relaxed atmosphere.

Beyond Bolinas, there's a rocky beach at the end of Wharf Road west of the village and, half a mile west at the end of Elm Road, **Duxbury Reef Nature Reserve** lures visitors to its tide pools, full of sea stars, crabs and sea anemones. Otherwise, Mesa Road heads north from Bolinas past the **Point Reyes Bird Observatory** (℡415/868-1221, ⊛www.prbo.org) – open for informal tours all day, though best visited in the morning. The first bird observatory in the US, this is still an important research and study centre and if you time it right you may be able to watch, or even help, the staff as they put coloured bands on the birds, such as cormorants and sandpipers, to keep track of them. Beyond here, the unpaved road leads on to the **Palomarin Trailhead**, the southern access into the Point Reyes National Seashore (see p.545). The best of the many beautiful hikes around the area takes you past a number of small lakes and meadows for three miles to **Alamere Falls**, which throughout the winter and spring cascade down the cliffs onto Wildcat Beach. **Bass Lake**, the first along the trail, is a great spot for a swim and is best entered from one of the two rope-swings that hang above its shore.

At the junction of Bolinas Road and Hwy-1, cross the highway and head due east. If the road is open (landslides cause frequent closures), continue up this route, the **Bolinas–Fairfax Road**, for a superb, winding drive through redwoods and grassy hillsides. When you reach the "T" in the road, turn left to get to Fairfax, or right to scale Mount Tamalpais.

Mount Tamalpais and Muir Woods National Monument

Mount Tamalpais, fondly known as Mount Tam, dominates the skyline of Marin County, hulking over the cool canyons of the rest of the county and dividing it into two distinct parts: the wild western slopes above the Pacific Coast and the increasingly suburban communities along the calmer bay frontage. Panoramic Highway branches off from Hwy-1 along the crest through the center of **Mount Tamalpais State Park** (℡415/388-2070, ⊛www.mttam.net), which has some thirty miles of hiking trails and many campgrounds, though most of the redwoods which once covered its slopes have long since been chopped down to form the posts and beams of San Francisco's Victorian houses. One grove of these towering trees does remain, however, protected as the **Muir Woods National Monument** (daily 8am–sunset; $5; ℡415/388-2595, ⊛www.nps.gov/muwo), a mile down Muir Woods Road from Panoramic Highway. It's a tranquil and majestic spot, with sunlight filtering through the 300-foot trees down to the laurel- and fern-covered canyon below. The canyon's steep sides are what saved it from Mill Valley's lumbermen, and today it's one of the few first-growth redwood groves between San Francisco and the fantastic forests of Redwood National Park (see p.645), up the coast towards the Oregon border.

One way to avoid the crowds that descend here at weekends, and the only way to get here on public transport, is to enter the woods from the top by way of a two-mile hike from the **Pan Toll Ranger Station** (℡415/388-2070) on Panoramic Highway – which is a stop on the Golden Gate Transit #63 bus route. As the state park headquarters, the station has maps and information on hiking and camping, and rangers can suggest hikes to suit your mood and interests. From here the **Pan Toll Road** turns off to the right along the ridge to within a hundred yards of the 2571-foot summit of Mount Tamalpais, where red-necked turkey vultures listlessly circle against breathtaking views of the distant Sierra Nevada.

Mill Valley

From the east peak of Mount Tamalpais, a quick two-mile hike downhill follows the **Temelpa Trail** through velvety shrubs of chaparral to **Mill Valley**, the oldest and most enticing of Marin County's inland towns – also accessible every thirty minutes by Golden Gate Transit bus #10 from San Francisco and Sausalito. Originally a logging centre, it was from here that the destruction of the surrounding redwoods was organized, though for many years the town has made a healthy living out of tourism. You can still follow the route of the defunct **Mill Valley and Mount Tamalpais Scenic Railroad** from the end of Summit Avenue in Mill Valley, a popular trip with daredevils on mountain bikes, which were, incidentally, invented here.

Though much of Mill Valley's attraction lies in its easy access to hiking and mountain-bike trails up Mount Tam, its compact yet relaxed centre has a number of cafés and some good shops and galleries. The *Depot Bookstore and Café* (Mon–Sat 7am–10pm, Sun 8am–10pm; ☎415/383-2665) is a popular bookshop, café and meeting place at 87 Throckmorton Ave, next door to the Chamber of Commerce (see p.536), which has free maps of Mount Tam and area hiking trails. Across the street, the **Pleasure Principle** is a reminder of the Northern California eclecticism hidden beneath a posh surface – the store, the self-declared UFO headquarters of Mill Valley, is also the proud purveyor of a large vintage porn collection. If you're in the area in early October, don't miss the **Mill Valley Film Festival**, a world-class event that draws a host of up-and-coming directors, as well as Bay Area stars such as Robin Williams and Sharon Stone; for programme information, call ☎415/383-5346, or check ⓦwww.mvff.com.

Tiburon

Tiburon, at the tip of a narrow peninsula three miles east of US-101 and five miles from Mill Valley, is, like Sausalito, a ritzy harbourside village to which hundreds of people come each weekend, many of them via direct Blue and Gold Fleet **ferries** from San Francisco's Fisherman's Wharf. It's a relaxed place, less touristy than Sausalito, and if you're in the mood to take it easy and watch the boats sail across the bay, sitting out on the sunny deck of one of the many cafés and bars can be idyllic. There are few specific sights to look out for here, but it's pleasant enough to simply wander around, browsing the galleries and antique shops. The best of these are grouped together in **Ark Row**, at the west end of Main Street, where the quirky buildings are actually old houseboats that were beached here early in the century. Further along, you can get a taste of the Wine Country at the Windsor Vineyards tasting room, 72 Main St (daily 10am–6pm; ☎415/435-3113, ⓦwww.windsorvineyards.com). On a hill above the town stands **Old St Hilary's Church** (April–Oct Wed–Sun 1–4pm; ☎415/789-0066), a Carpenter Gothic beauty best seen in the spring, when the surrounding fields are covered with multi-colored buckwheat, flax and paintbrush.

Cyclists can cruise around the many plush houses of **Belvedere Island**, just across the Beach Road Bridge from the west end of Main Street, enjoying the fine views of the bay and Golden Gate Bridge. More ambitious bikers can continue along the waterfront bike path, which winds from the bijou shops and galleries three miles west along undeveloped Richardson Bay frontage to a bird sanctuary at **Greenwood Cove**. The pristine Victorian house here is now the western headquarters of the National Audubon Society and open for tours on Sundays (10am–4pm; free; ☎415/388-2524, ⓦwww.audubon.org); a small interpretive centre has displays on local and migratory birds and wildlife.

Angel Island

However appealing, the pleasures of Tiburon are soon exhausted, and you'd be well advised to take the Angel Island Ferry (see p.536) a mile offshore to the largest island in the San Francisco Bay, ten times the size of Alcatraz. **Angel Island** is officially a state park but over the years it has served a variety of purposes, everything from a home for Miwok Native Americans to a World War II prisoner-of-war camp. It's full of ghostly ruins of old military installations, but it's the nature that lures people to Angel Island nowadays, with its oak and eucalyptus trees and sagebrush covering the hills above rocky coves and sandy beaches, giving the island a feel quite apart from the mainland. It offers some pleasant biking opportunities as well: a five-mile road rings the island, and an unpaved track, along with a number of hiking trails, leads up to the 800-foot hump of **Mount Livermore**, with panoramic views of the Bay Area.

The ferry arrives at **Ayala Cove**, where a small snack bar selling hot dogs and cold drinks provides the only sustenance available on the island – bring a picnic if you plan to spend the day here. The nearby **visitor centre** (daily 9am–4pm; ☎415/435-1915), in an old building that was built as a quarantine facility for soldiers returning from the Philippines after the Spanish–American War, has displays on the island's history. Around the point on the northwest corner of the island the **North Garrison**, built in 1905, was the site of a prisoner-of-war camp during World War II; while the larger **East Garrison**, on the bay half a mile beyond, was the major transfer point for soldiers bound for the South Pacific.

Quarry Beach around the point is the best on the island, a clean sandy shore that's protected from the winds blowing in through the Golden Gate; it's also a popular landing spot for kayakers and canoeists who paddle across the bay from Berkeley. **Camping** on Angel Island (see p.538) is well worth considering for the views of San Francisco and the East Bay at night; the nine sites fill up fast, so make reservations well ahead. For **tours** of Angel Island, contact Angel Island TramTours (☎415/897-0715, ⓦwww.angelisland.com), which gives one-hour tours ($13.50) and rents mountain bikes ($10 per hour, $35 per day).

Sir Francis Drake Boulevard and Central Marin County

The quickest route to the wilds of the Point Reyes National Seashore and the only way to get there on public transport is by way of **Sir Francis Drake Boulevard**, which cuts across central Marin County through the inland towns of **San Anselmo** and **Fairfax**, reaching the coast thirty miles west at a crescent-shaped bay where, in 1579, Drake supposedly landed and claimed all of what he called Nova Albion for England. The route makes an excellent day-long cycling tour, with the reward of good beaches, a youth hostel and some tasty restaurants at the end of the road.

The Larkspur Golden Gate Transit **ferry**, which leaves from the Ferry Building in San Francisco, is the longest of the bay crossings. Primarily a commuter route, it docks at the modern space-frame terminal at Larkspur Landing. The monolithic, red-tile-roofed complex you see on the bayfront a mile east is the maximum-security **San Quentin State Prison**, which houses the state's most violent and notorious criminals. It was of here that Johnny Cash sang so resonantly "I hate every stone of you." If you arrive by car over the Richmond–San Rafael Bridge, follow road signs off Hwy-101 for the **San Quentin Prison Museum**, Building 106, Dolores Way (Mon–Fri 10am–4pm, Sat 11.45am–3.15pm; $2; ☎415/454-8808).

San Anselmo and Point Reyes Station

San Anselmo, set in a broad valley two miles north of Mount Tam, calls itself "the antiques capital of Northern California" and sports a tiny centre of speciality shops, furniture stores and cafés that draw many San Francisco shoppers on weekends. The ivy-covered **San Francisco Theological Seminary** off Bolinas

Avenue, which dominates the town from the hill above, is worth a quick peek for the view and mission-styled architecture. At serene **Robson-Harrington Park** on Crescent Avenue you can picnic among well-tended gardens, while the very green and leafy **Creek Park** follows the creek that winds through the town centre. Otherwise there's not a lot to do except stop in at a restaurant or café or browse through fine bookstores, such as Oliver's Books, 645 San Anselmo Ave (☎415/454-4421).

Ten miles beyond fairly nondescript Fairfax, which San Anselmo merges into, Sir Francis Drake Boulevard winds through gentle and increasingly pastoral hills, passing **Samuel P. Taylor State Park**, which has excellent camping (see p.539). Five miles more brings you to the coastal Hwy-1 and the hamlet of **Olema**, which has good food and lodging. A mile north of Olema sits the tourist town of **POINT REYES STATION**, another good place to stop off. Have a bite to eat or pick up picnic supplies on the quaint main street before heading off to enjoy the wide open spaces of the Point Reyes National Seashore just beyond.

The Point Reyes National Seashore

From Point Reyes Station, Sir Francis Drake Boulevard heads out to the westernmost tip of Marin County at Point Reyes through the **POINT REYES NATIONAL SEASHORE**, a near-island of wilderness surrounded on three sides by more than fifty miles of isolated coastline – pine forests and sunny meadows bordered by rocky cliffs and sandy, windswept beaches. This wing-shaped landmass, something of an aberration along the generally straight coastline north of San Francisco, is in fact a rogue piece of the earth's crust that has been drifting slowly and steadily northward along the San Andreas Fault, having started some six million years ago as a suburb of Los Angeles. When the great earthquake of 1906 shattered San Francisco, the land here – the quake's epicentre – shifted over sixteen feet in an instant, though damage was confined to a few skewed cattle fences.

The park's **visitor centre** (see p.537), two miles southwest of Point Reyes Station near Olema, just off Hwy-1 on Bear Valley Road, holds engaging displays on the geology and natural history of the region. Rangers dish out excellent hiking and cycling itineraries, and have up-to-date information on the weather, which can change quickly and be cold and windy along the coast even when it's hot and sunny here, three miles inland. They also handle permits and reservations for the various hike-in **campgrounds** within the park. Nearby, a replica of a native Miwok village has an authentic religious **roundhouse**, and a popular hike follows the Bear Valley Trail along Coast Creek four miles to **Arch Rock**, a large tunnel in the seaside cliffs that you can walk through at low tide.

North of the visitor centre, Limantour Road heads west six miles to the *HI–Point Reyes Hostel* (see p.538), continuing on another two miles to the coast at **Limantour Beach**, one of the best protected swimming beaches and a good place to watch the sea birds in the adjacent estuary. Bear Valley Road rejoins Sir Francis Drake Boulevard just past Limantour Road, leading north along Tomales Bay through the village of **Inverness**, so named because the landscape reminded an early settler of his home in the Scottish Highlands. Eight miles west of Inverness, a turn leads down past **Drake's Bay Oyster Farm** (daily 8am–4.30pm; ☎415/669-1149) – which sells the bivalves for around $10 a dozen, less than half the price you'd pay in San Francisco – to **Drake's Beach**, the presumed landing spot of Sir Francis in 1579 (his voyage journal makes the exact location unclear). Appropriately, the coastline here resembles the southern coast of England, often cold, wet and windy, with chalk-white cliffs rising above the wide, sandy beach. The road continues southwest another four miles to the very tip of Point Reyes. A precarious-looking **lighthouse** (Thurs–Sun 10am–4.30pm; free) stands firm against the crashing surf and the bluffs are excellent for watching migrating **grey whales** from mid-March to April and late December to early February. Just over a mile back from the lighthouse a narrow road leads to **Chimney Rock**, where you can often see basking **elephant seals** or **sea lions** from the overlook. Keep in mind the distance and slow speeds it takes to reach these spots, which is hard to judge on a map. From the visitor centre, it's 15 miles to Drakes Beach and 23 miles to the lighthouse. Check with the rangers on weather conditions before setting out. From late December through April a shuttle bus (9.30am–5.30pm; $5) runs roughly every twenty minutes on weekends and holidays out to the lighthouse and Chimney Rock, and the roads are closed to private vehicles to avoid congestion.

The northern tip of the Point Reyes National Seashore, **Tomales Point**, is accessible via Pierce Point Road, which turns off Sir Francis Drake Boulevard two miles north of Inverness. Jutting out into Tomales Bay, it's the least-visited section of the park and a refuge for hefty **tule elk**; it's also a great place to admire the lupins, poppies and other wildflowers that appear in the spring. The best swimming (or rather least freezing water) is at **Heart's Desire Beach**, just before the end of the road. Down the bluffs from where the road comes to a dead end, there are excellent tidal pools at rocky **McClure's Beach**. North of Point Reyes Station, Hwy-1 continues past the famed oyster beds of Tomales Bay north along the crashing surf and up the Northern California coast.

San Rafael and around

You may pass through **San Rafael** on your way north from San Francisco on US-101 but there's little to detain you. The county seat and the only sizeable city in Marin County, it has none of the woodsy qualities that make the other towns special, though you'll come across a couple of good restaurants and bars along Fourth Street, the main drag. Its lone attraction is the old **Mission San Rafael Arcangel** (daily 11am–4pm; free), in fact a 1949 replica that was built near the site of the 1817 original on Fifth Avenue at A Street. The real point of interest, however, is well on the northern outskirts in the shape of the Marin County Civic Center.

The **Marin County Civic Center** (Mon–Fri 9am–5pm; tours Wed 10.30am; $5; ☎415/499-6646), spanning the hills just east of US-101 a mile north of central San Rafael, is a strange, otherworldly complex of administrative offices, plus an excellent performance space that resembles a giant viaduct capped by a bright-blue-tiled roof. These buildings were architect **Frank Lloyd Wright**'s one and only government project, and although the huge circus tents and amusement park at the core of the designer's conception were never built, it does have some interesting touches, such as the atrium lobbies that open directly to the outdoors.

Six miles north of San Rafael, the **Lucas Valley Road** turns off west, twisting across Marin to Point Reyes. Although he lives and works here, it was not named after *Star Wars* filmmaker George Lucas, whose sprawling **Skywalker Ranch** studios are well hidden off the road. Hwy-37 cuts off east, eight miles north of San Rafael, heading around the top of the bay into the Wine Country of the Sonoma and Napa valleys (see p.606).

Eating

Marin's **restaurants** are as varied in personality as the people who inhabit the county – homely neighbourhood **cafés** dish out nutritious portions to healthy mountain-bikers, well-appointed waterside restaurants cater to tourists and gourmet establishments serve delicate concoctions to affluent executives.

Avatar's Punjabi Burritos 15 Madrona St, Mill Valley. A dastardly simple cross-cultural innovation: inexpensive burritos stuffed with delicious spicy curries. Does a brisk takeaway trade, as there are only two tables inside.

Bridgeway Café 633 Bridgeway, Sausalito. A good place to relax over a coffee or grab a gourmet egg breakfast at reasonable prices by local standards.

Broken Drum 1132 4th St, San Rafael. Lively brewery/grill with pavement seating, where you can tuck into cheapish fish tacos with mango salsa or mesquite-grilled ribs, and drink fine ale.

Bubba's Diner 566 San Anselmo Ave, San Anselmo. Hip little diner with a friendly and casual atmosphere, combining old-fashioned looks with a contemporary use of mostly organic produce.

Depot Bookstore and Café 87 Throckmorton Ave, Mill Valley ☎415/383-2665. Lively café in an old train station, sharing space with a bookstore and newsstand. Weekly readings from local and nationally recognized authors.

Dipsea Café 200 Shoreline Hwy, Mill Valley. Hearty pancakes, omelettes, sandwiches and salads, especially good before a day out hiking on Mount Tamalpais. Breakfast and lunch only.

Dish 507 Miller Ave, Mill Valley. Typical of Marin, this new diner serves a mixture of down-home and more exotic recipes at affordable prices, while using organic and sustainably farmed produce. Try preceding your burger with Thai soup.

Farmhouse Grill 10005 Hwy-1, Olema. The farm-fresh ingredients that go into the down-home cooking make this a good stop for mostly meaty lunches or dinners. Also a friendly bar.

Fish 350 Harbor Drive, Sausalito ☎415/331-3474. This place makes a point of serving sustainable fish and seafood in undoubted style. Follow the Portuguese red chowder with a fish taco plate for only $13.

Guaymas 5 Main St, Tiburon ☎415/435-6300. Some of the most unique, inventive Cal-Mex cuisine in the Bay Area, paired with a spectacular view of the city. Main courses in the $15–30 range.

Java Rama 546 San Anselmo Ave, San Anselmo. Speciality coffees and pastries, along with modern rock on the stereo, attracts a young crowd.

Le Garage 85 Liberty Ship Way, Sausalito ☎415/332-5625. Set in a modern complex on a quiet part of the waterfront, this bistro serves excellent French dishes such as monkfish ragout and duck confit in the $15–25 range.

Mountain Home Inn 810 Panoramic Hwy, above Mill Valley ☎415/381-9000. A place that's as good for the view of the surrounding valleys as for the food, with broiled meat and fish dishes served up in a rustic lodge on the slopes of Mount Tamalpais. Fixed evening menu for $38.

Orchid 726 San Anselmo Ave, San Anselmo ☎415/457-9470. Family restaurant dishing up spicy Thai fare, including a fine range of curries and zesty salads, including the *nua sun* with beef.

Sam's Anchor Café 27 Main St, Tiburon. This rough-hewn, amiable waterfront café and bar has been around for more than 75 years. Good burgers, sandwiches and very popular Sunday brunches are best enjoyed on the outdoor deck.

Sartaj India Cafe 43 Caledonia St, Sausalito. Great, inexpensive Indian place that does a selection of meat and veggie dishes, including *thalis*, and, oddly enough, bagels for those who can't stomach a spicy breakfast.

Station House Café 11180 Hwy-1 (Main St), Point Reyes Station ☎415/663-1515. Serving three meals daily, this friendly local favourite entices diners from miles around to sample their grilled seafood and top-notch steaks.

Stinson Beach Grill 3465 Shoreline Hwy, Stinson Beach ☎415/868-2002. Somewhat pricey, but relaxed, with outdoor dining – look out for the bright-blue building right in the heart of town. Mainly steaks and seafood, but leave room for the glorious puddings.

Sweden House 35 Main St, Tiburon. Great coffee and marvellous pastries on a jetty overlooking the yacht harbour, all for surprisingly reasonable prices.

Sweet Ginger 400 Caledonia St, Sausalito ☎415/332-1683. Moderately priced, small Japanese restaurant that serves sushi, sashimi and main courses such as tempura and teriyaki.

The Tavern at Lark Creek 234 Magnolia Ave, Larkspur ☎415/924-7766. One of the county's best finds. The contemporary American food at this classy restored Victorian is surprisingly reasonable with main courses mostly under $20: the food, such as blue-cheese soufflé and BBQ bacon meatloaf, is exquisite, the service first-rate and the atmosphere charming.

Tommy's Wok 3001 Bridgeway, Sausalito ☎415/332-5818. This Chinese joint specializes in organic vegetables, free-range meats and fresh seafood, cooked in Mandarin, Hunan and Szechuan recipes.

Vladimir's Czech Restaurant 12785 Sir Francis Drake Blvd, Inverness ☎415/669-1021. This relic of rural Bohemia in the far West has been serving up tasty items such as Moravian cabbage roll, roast duckling and apple strudel since 1960.

Nightlife

While Marin County **nightlife** is never as charged as it gets in San Francisco, almost every town has any number of welcoming saloon-like **bars**. In addition, since most of the honchos of the Bay Area music scene and dozens of lesser-known but no less brilliant session musicians and songwriters live here, Marin's nightclubs are unsurpassed for catching big names in intimate locales.

Fourth Street Tavern 711 4th St, San Rafael ☎415/454-4044. Gutsy, no-frills beer bar with free, bluesy music most nights.

Marin Brewing Company 1809 Larkspur Landing, Larkspur. Lively pub opposite the Larkspur ferry terminal, with half a dozen tasty ales – try the Mt Tam pale ale or the Point Reyes porter – all brewed on the premises. Good bar food too.

Mill Valley Beerworks 173 Throckmorton Ave, Mill Valley. Run by two brothers, this sleek modern bar would look more at home in the big city. Still the handcrafted draught beers and bottled imports are worth investigating.

No Name Bar 757 Bridgeway Ave, Sausalito ☎415/332-1392. An ex-haunt of the Beats, hosting live jazz several times per week beginning at 8pm and on Sun from 3–7pm.

Smiley's Schooner Saloon 41 Wharf Rd, Bolinas. The bartender calls the customers by name here at one of the oldest continually operating bars in the state, just about to celebrate its 150th birthday.

The Woods 19 Corte Madeira Ave, Mill Valley ☎415/389-6637. The converted old Masonic cinema sporadically hosts shows of a wide range of genres from jazz to indie rock.

Travel details

Trains

Free Amtrak shuttle buses depart San Francisco from the Ferry Building (where there's a full service ticket office 6am–11pm), as well as six other points Downtown and in SoMa, to the Emeryville depot, from where the Coast Starlight train departs daily at 10.12pm north to Sacramento, Portland and Seattle, and 8.20am south to San Jose, Salinas, San Luis Obispo, Santa Barbara, Los Angeles and San Diego. The California Zephyr leaves daily at 9.50am for Sacramento, Truckee, Reno and all the way to Chicago. The San Joaquin route operates six times daily to Stockton, Fresno and Bakersfield, where there are Amtrak Thruway bus connections to Los Angeles. Amtrak's Capitol Corridor route links Oakland with San Jose.

San Francisco–San Jose commuters rely more on CalTrain (see p.440). About fifty trains make the trip each way daily, taking 1hr on the Baby Bullet or 1hr 30min or longer on the local. The main San Francisco station is at Fourth and King st.

Oakland/Emeryville to: Bakersfield (6 daily; 6hr 10min–6hr 45min); Fresno (6 daily; 4hr 5min–4hr 40min); Los Angeles (1 daily; 12hr 40min); Portland (1 daily; 18hr); Reno (1 daily; 7hr); Sacramento (12–17 daily; 2–3hr); Salinas (1 daily; 2hr 45min); San Diego (1 daily; 16hr); San Jose (7 daily; 1hr);

San Luis Obispo (1 daily; 5hr 40min); Santa Barbara (1 daily; 9hr 30min); Seattle (1 daily; 23hr); Stockton (6 daily; 1hr 45min–2hr 20min); Truckee (1 daily; 5hr 50min).

Buses

These are the major long-distance Greyhound services. Note the number of services can vary during the course of the year. Destinations nearer to San Francisco such as San Rafael and Santa Rosa are also served by local companies, as outlined in the "Getting around" sections of the relevant chapters.

Oakland/Emeryville to: Santa Cruz (3 daily; 2hr).

San Francisco to: Eureka (1 daily; 6hr 45min); Los Angeles (12 daily; 7hr 25min–11hr 50min, also one Green Tortoise per week in each direction along the coast); Redding (4 daily; 5hr 45min–9hr 50min); Reno (6 daily; 5hr 10min–6hr 35min); Sacramento (9 daily; 2hr–2hr 40min); Salinas (6 daily; 2–4hr); San Diego (6 daily; 10hr 30min–12hr 45min); San Jose (9 daily; 1hr–1hr 45min); San Rafael (1 daily; 1hr); Santa Barbara (3 daily; 8hr 40min–9hr 20min); San Luis Obispo (4 daily; 7hr);Santa Cruz (3 daily; 2hr 50min); Santa Rosa (1 daily; 1hr 45min).

San Jose to: Santa Cruz (4 daily; 1hr).

The Gold Country and
Lake Tahoe

CHAPTER 8 **Highlights**

✳ **Sacramento Capitol building** This elegant Classical Revival structure has some spectacular architectural detailing and the comprehensive tours provide a glimpse into California's government. See p.558

✳ **Indian Grinding Rock** In this state historic park nine miles from Jackson, the Miwok Indians once carved hundreds of small cups into the limestone, still visible today. See p.567

✳ **Jamestown's Railtown 1897 State Historic Park** Even if you're not a trainspotter, it's worth stopping by to see the old engines, thanks to the enthusiastic, endlessly knowledgeable docents. See p.572

✳ **The Empire Mine State Park** Now retired among thick stands of pine, the impressive array of mining equipment here is a contemplative reflection on California's Gold Rush heyday. See p.576

✳ **Lake Tahoe** This region guarantees beautiful scenery at any time of year, whether you're skiing the slopes or paddling on the lake itself. See p.582

✳ **Virginia City, Nevada** This mining town exudes a more tangible Wild West atmosphere than most of its California counterparts. See p.599

▲ Lake Tahoe

The Gold Country and Lake Tahoe

The gold of California is a touchstone which has betrayed the rottenness, the baseness, of mankind. Satan, from one of his elevations, showed mankind the kingdom of California, and they entered into a compact with him at once.

Henry David Thoreau, *Journal*, February 1, 1852

About 150 years before techies from all over the world rushed to California in search of Silicon Valley gold, the rough-and-ready forty-niners invaded the **GOLD COUNTRY** of the Sierra Nevada to pan for the real thing. The first prospectors on the scene – about 150 miles northeast of San Francisco – sometimes found large nuggets of solid gold sitting along the riverbanks. They worked all day in the hot sun, wading through fast-flowing, ice-cold rivers to recover trace amounts of the precious metal that had been eroded out of the hard-rock veins of the **Mother Lode** – the name miners gave to the rich sources of gold at the heart of the mining district.

The region ranges from the foothills near Yosemite National Park to the deep gorge of the Yuba River, two hundred miles north. In many parts throughout this area, little seems to have changed since the argonauts began their digging and even in the air-conditioned comfort of your rental car – without one it's nearly impossible to navigate the area – distances from one town to the next may seem exponentially greater than they appear on the map: count on plenty of hairpin bends and steep climbs.

The **Mother Lode** was first discovered in 1848 at Sutter's Mill in **Coloma**, forty miles east of **Sacramento**, the largest city in the Gold Country and the state capital. Once a tiny military outpost and farming community that boomed as a supply town for miners, Sacramento lies between two distinct mining areas to the north and south. The **northern mines**, around the twin towns of **Grass Valley** and **Nevada City**, were the richest fields and today retain most of their Gold Rush buildings in an unspoiled, near-alpine setting halfway up the towering peaks of the Sierra Nevada. The hot and dusty **southern mines**, on the other hand, became depopulated faster than their northern neighbours. These towns were the rowdiest and wildest of all and it's not too hard to imagine that many of the abandoned towns sprinkled over the area once supported upwards of fifty saloons and gambling parlours, each with its own cast of cardsharps and thieves, as immortalized by writers like Bret Harte and Mark Twain.

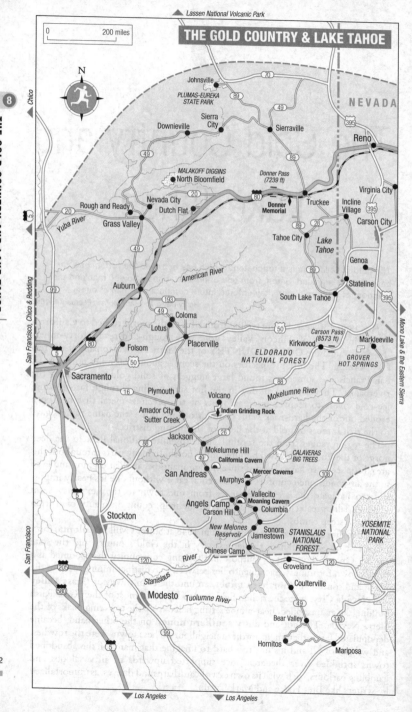

THE GOLD COUNTRY & LAKE TAHOE

0   200 miles

N

Lassen National Volcanic Park

NEVADA

Johnsville
PLUMAS-EUREKA
STATE PARK

Downieville   Sierra
City   Sierraville

Reno

MALAKOFF DIGGINS
North Bloomfield

Donner Pass
(7239 ft)

Virginia City

Rough and Ready   Nevada City
Dutch Flat

Donner
Memorial   Truckee   Incline
Village

Grass Valley
Yuba River

Carson City

Tahoe City   Lake
Tahoe

Auburn   American River

Genoa

South Lake Tahoe   Stateline

Coloma

Lotus

Carson Pass
(8573 ft)   Markleeville

Folsom   Placerville   Kirkwood
ELDORADO
NATIONAL FOREST   GROVER
HOT SPRINGS

Sacramento

Plymouth   Mokelumne River

Volcano

Amador City   Indian Grinding Rock
Sutter Creek

Jackson

Mokelumne Hill   CALAVERAS
BIG TREES

California Cavern

San Andreas   Mercer Caverns

Murphys

Angels Camp   Vallecito   Moaning Cavern
Carson Hill   Columbia

Stockton   New Melones   Sonora   STANISLAUS
Reservoir   Jamestown   NATIONAL
FOREST

YOSEMITE
NATIONAL
PARK

Chinese Camp

River

Groveland

Stanislaus

Coulterville

Modesto   Tuolumne River

Bear Valley

Hornitos   Mariposa

Los Angeles   Los Angeles

Most of the mountainous forest along the Sierra crest is preserved as near-pristine wilderness, with excellent hiking, camping and backpacking. There's great skiing in winter around the mountainous rim of **Lake Tahoe** on the border between California and Nevada, aglow under the bright lights of the casinos that line its southeastern shore. East of the mountains, in the dry Nevada desert, sit the highway towns of **Reno**, famed for low-budget weddings and speedy divorces and **Carson City**, the Nevada state capital and one-time boomtown of the Comstock silver mines.

Getting around

Hwy-49 runs north to south, linking most of the sights of the Gold Country; two main highways, US-50 and I-80, along with the transcontinental **railroad**, cross the Sierra Nevada through the heart of the region and there is frequent Greyhound **bus** service to some of the major towns. To get a real feel for the Gold Country, however, and to reach the most evocative ghost towns, you'll need a **car**. Also, though it's all very scenic, **cycling** throughout the region is not a viable option: the distances between the sights are long and the roads are far too hilly and narrow for comfort.

Sacramento and the Central Mother Lode

Roughly midway between San Francisco and the crest of the Sierra Nevada and well connected by Greyhound, Amtrak and the arterial I-5 highway, **Sacramento** is likely to be your first stop in the Gold Country. It's the quintessential American state capital, with sleepy tree-lined streets fanning out from the elegant State Capitol building. The city's waterfront quarter, restored to the style of Pony Express days, contains the region's largest collection of Gold Rush-era buildings. From Sacramento, two main routes climb east through the gentle foothills of the Mother Lode: US-50 passes through the old supply town of **Placerville** on its way to Lake Tahoe, while I-80 zooms by **Auburn** over the Donner Pass into Nevada. Both towns have retained enough of their Gold Rush past to merit at least a brief look if you're passing through and both make good bases for the more picturesque towns of the southern and northern mines respectively.

Sacramento

Until recently, **SACRAMENTO** had the reputation of being decidedly dull, a suburban enclave of politicians and bureaucrats surrounded by miles of marshes and farmland. The government has long loomed large over the city, filling its streets on weekdays and emptying the centre at weekends; but in recent years residential neighbourhoods have reawakened, especially around the Midtown area,

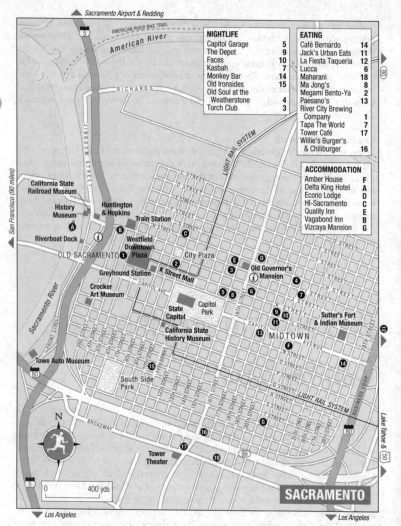

NIGHTLIFE

Capitol Garage	5
The Depot	9
Faces	10
Kasbah	7
Monkey Bar	14
Old Ironsides	15
Old Soul at the Weatherstone	4
Torch Club	3

EATING

Café Bernardo	14
Jack's Urban Eats	11
La Fiesta Taqueria	12
Lucca	6
Maharani	18
Ma Jong's	8
Megami Bento-Ya	2
Paesano's	13
River City Brewing Company	1
Tapa The World	7
Tower Café	17
Willie's Burger's & Chiliburger	16

ACCOMMODATION

Amber House	F
Delta King Hotel	A
Econo Lodge	D
HI-Sacramento	C
Quality Inn	E
Vagabond Inn	B
Vizcaya Mansion	G

SACRAMENTO

thanks to the cafés and restaurants that have mushroomed on many of the leafier blocks. The election of Arnold "the Governator" Schwarzenegger in a 2003 election didn't hurt either: his dash of Hollywood pizzazz (and Kennedy-grade connections courtesy of his wife, TV anchor Maria Shriver) energized the city and he was generally viewed as a moderate governor; his second term drew to a close in late 2010. Schwarzenegger aside, there's increasing local pride in the city's Gold Rush history, which has led to important historic preservation and restoration projects, injecting some much-needed tourist dollars into the local economy during the ongoing recession.

Some history

Before gold was discovered in 1848, the area around Sacramento belonged entirely to one man, **John Sutter**. He came here from Switzerland in 1839 to farm the flat, marshy lands at the foot of the Sierra Nevada, which were then within Mexican California. Sacramento, the prosperous community he founded, became a main stopping place for the few trappers and travellers who made their way inland or across the range of peaks. Yet it was after the discovery of flakes of **gold** in the foothills forty miles east that things really took off and the small trading post was transformed.

Sutter's 50,000-acre settlement, set at the confluence of the Sacramento and American rivers in the flatlands of the northern San Joaquin Valley, was granted to him by the Mexican government and he worked hard to build the colony into a busy trading centre and cattle ranch. He was poised to become a wealthy man when his hopes were thwarted by the discovery of gold at a nearby sawmill. His workers quit their jobs to go prospecting and many thousands more flocked to the goldfields, trampling over Sutter's land. The small colony was soon overrun: since ships could sail upriver from the San Francisco Bay, Sacramento quickly became the main supply point for miners bound for the isolated camps in the foothills above. The city prospered, and in 1854 Sacramento snagged the title of **California state capital**, thanks to its equidistance between the gold mines, the rich farmlands of the San Joaquin Valley and the financial centre of San Francisco. As the Gold Rush faded, Sacramento remained important as a transportation hub, first as the western terminus of the Pony Express and later as the western headquarters of the transcontinental railroad. Although its administrative role saved the city when mining dollars dwindled, it also smothered much of its rough, pioneer edges and it has taken a long time to develop a distinct, urban personality.

Arrival, information and city transport

At the intersection of the I-5, I-80, US-50 and Hwy-99 freeways, Sacramento is the hub for many long-distance transport networks. Sacramento International **airport** (☎916/874-0700, ⓦwww.sacairports.org), twelve miles northwest of Downtown, is served by most major domestic airlines. SuperShuttle Sacramento vans (☎1-800/258-3826, ⓦwww.supershuttle.com) can take you directly to any Downtown destination for $14. Thanks to the city's status as a governmental hub, public transport links are plentiful. There are up to sixteen daily **trains** (☎1-800/872-7245, ⓦwww.amtrak.com) connecting Sacramento with the Bay Area and further afield; these stop at the Amtrak station at 4th and I streets, near Old Sacramento. An almost continuous stream of Greyhound **buses** pulls into the bus depot at 715 L St, a block from the K Street Mall (☎1-800/231-2222).

There are two **visitor centres**: one in the heart of tourist-clogged Old Sacramento at 1002 2nd St (daily 10am–5pm; ☎916/442-7644, ⓦwww.old sacramento.com) and another not far from the State Capitol at 1608 I St (Mon– Fri 8am–5pm; ☎916/808-7777, ⓦwww.sacramento365.com). Pick up a copy of the handy *Sacramento Visitors' Guide* at these offices or almost everywhere tourists congregate; you can also get an informative self-guided walking tour of Sacramento's historic architecture. For further information on **events and entertainment**, check out the free *Sacramento News & Review* (ⓦwww.news review.com). Otherwise, there's *Ticket*, the Friday supplement to the *Sacramento Bee* newspaper (50¢; ⓦwww.sacbee.com), or the free music listings publication *Alive & Kicking* (ⓦwww.alivenkicking.com). The city's gay and lesbian scene is lively enough to spawn two freesheets, *MGW* (ⓦwww.momguesswhat.com) and *Outword* (ⓦwww.outwordmagazine.com).

The city is compact, flat and largely **walkable**, though many locals get around by **bike** – the best deals are at Bikes and Bites, 1013 12th St (☎916/705-0452, ⓦwww.bikesandbites.com), which rents out cruisers from $10 for two hours. The city centre is crisscrossed with an extensive **bus and light rail** network

– timetables and maps are available from the visitor centres and the Regional Transit office, 1225 R St (Mon–Fri 9am–5.30pm; ℡916/321-2877, ⓦwww .sacrt.com). The service (flat fare $2.50, day-pass $6) you're most likely to use is #30, connecting the Amtrak station, K Street Mall, the State Capitol and Old Sacramento. The **riverboat tours** leaving from the L Street landing in Old Sacramento are popular if corny: the paddle-wheel steamboats *Matthew McKinley* and *Spirit of Sacramento* offer varied trips along the Sacramento River ($18–45; ℡1-800/433-0263).

Accommodation

Sacramento has plenty of reasonably priced places to stay, all within easy walking distance of the centre. Most **motels** and **hotels** cluster around **Downtown**, the trendy **Midtown** area, where much of the city's nightlife is centred, with some in the outskirts. Choices are limited primarily to unexciting chains with a few B&Bs thrown in, with weekend rates often steeply discounted. The only **campground** within easy reach is KOA's RV-heavy *Sacramento West/Old Town* site, 3951 Lake Rd (℡1-800/562-2747, ⓦwww.sacramentokoa.com), four miles west of Downtown, which has some cabins (❷).

Amber House Bed & Breakfast Inn 1315 22nd St at N, Midtown ℡1-800/755-6526, ⓦwww .amberhouse.com. The pick of the city's B&Bs, with luxurious rooms, including marble baths, and sumptuous breakfasts. A worthwhile treat to avoid the endless chain motels nearby. ❻
Delta King Hotel 1000 Front St, Old Sacramento ℡1-800/825-5464, ⓦwww.deltaking.com. A 1926 paddle-wheel riverboat now permanently moored on the waterfront. Although the rooms fail to justify their "stateroom" advertising, the vessel makes an enjoyably unusual place to stay. Be aware the area is usually throbbing with visitors at weekends, and prices rise accordingly. ❹
Econo Lodge 711 16th St at H, Downtown ℡1-800/553-2666, ⓦwww.econolodge.com. A good budget option, with basic but comfortable rooms. ❶
HI–Sacramento 925 H St at 10th, Downtown ℡916/443-1691, ⓦwww.norcalhostels.org. This

hostel is housed in a rambling 1885 mansion with all the usual facilities, plus free bike rental, but there's a daytime lockout and 11pm curfew. Dorm beds $28–31, rooms ❶
Quality Inn 818 15th St at I, Downtown ℡1-800/228-5151, ⓦwww.qualityinn.com. Refurbished rooms near the old Governor's Mansion in a standard chain hotel equipped with a pool. Best deal in town. ❶
Vagabond Inn 909 3rd St at J, Old Town ℡1-800/522-1555, ⓦwww.vagabondinn.com. Motor lodge-style accommodation near the river and Old Sacramento: there's a pool and free shuttle to public transport hubs. ❷
Vizcaya Mansion 2019 21st St at T, Midtown ℡916/448-1300, ⓦwww.sterlinghotel sacramento.com. A lavish, historic property with elegantly furnished rooms and marble-tiled bathrooms. ❻

The Town

Most of the local attractions in Sacramento are close together, in one of the three main areas that together comprise the city centre: the I-5 highway quarantines **Old Sacramento** from the commercial hub of **Downtown**, centred on K Street Mall, as well as the funkier, residential **Midtown** district further east.

Old Sacramento and the riverfront

Sacramento grew up **along the riverfront**, where the wharves, warehouses, saloons and stores of the city's historic core have been restored and converted into the novelty shops and theme restaurants of **OLD SACRAMENTO**. It's a shame that such a large collection of authentic Gold Rush-era architecture should be choked with such relentless fakery: costumed sales staff hawking souvenirs and tourist-chasing bars dressed up as faux Wild West saloons. In fact, although most of the buildings are original, some stood elsewhere until they were forcibly relocated here in the 1960s to make way for the massive I-5 highway that carves this area off from the rest of the city centre. To avoid the stampede of tourists in search of tacky souvenirs, it's best to avoid Old Sacramento completely at weekends, since that's when the place seems most inauthentic, its streets more like a Hollywood backlot than the real thing.

The area's three main historical attractions stand in a row along **I Street**: the smallest is **Huntington & Hopkins Hardware**, a store-turned-museum at no. 113 (Tues–Sun 10am–5pm; free). Here, the **Big Four** – Leland Stanford, Mark Hopkins, Collis P. Huntington and Charles Crocker – held their first meeting to mastermind the Central Pacific and later Southern Pacific railroads (see box, p.558). It's now decked out as a spartan 1840s supply store, highlighting the humble beginnings of the ruthless Huntington and the henpecked Hopkins. Upstairs there's a low-key homage to the men, with a re-creation of their boardroom and an archive of rail history.

More railway history is chronicled next door at the **California State Railroad Museum** at 111 I St (daily 10am–5pm; $9), which boasts a range of lavishly restored 1860s locomotives with "cow-catcher" front grilles and huge bulbous smokestacks. Perhaps due to its exhaustive exhibits on early railroad technology, it's more suited to dedicated trainspotters than casual tourists. The best part is the old passenger station and freight depot a block south, which is also part of the museum. From here you can take a seven-mile, 45-minute **ride** beside the river on a vintage train (April–Sept Sat & Sun hourly 11am–5pm; $9).

For a broader view of the area's past, the **Sacramento History Museum** at 101 I St (daily 10am–5pm; $5) features a hands-on display about the early newspapers in California (including the *Sacramento Bee*, founded in 1857), as well as coverage of more recent history, like the Depression-era diner run by the pioneering African-American Dunlap family.

Pass over the highway to reach the nearby **Crocker Art Museum** at 216 O St between 2nd and 3rd (check for hours and admission on ☏916/264-5423, ⓦwww.newcrocker.org). Housing paintings collected by Supreme Court judge Edwin Crocker, brother of railroad baron Charles, the gallery was about to open after refurbishment at the time of writing. Expect a few pictures of early California life amid the works by mainly European artists, including drawings by Dürer, Rembrandt, Boucher and Fragonard. More appropriate to its setting, in the shadow of the massive I-5 and I-80 interchange at 2200 Front St, the **Towe Auto Museum** (daily 10am–6pm; $8; ☏916/442-6802, ⓦwww.toweautomuseum .org) offers an impressive collection of antique cars and trucks, from Model Ts and As to classic '57 T-birds and "woody" station wagons.

Downtown

Running east from the riverfront and Old Sacramento, past the Greyhound and Amtrak stations, the **K Street Mall** is the commercial heart of **DOWNTOWN SACRAMENTO**, with the end of the light rail network running through the centre of a pedestrianized shopping precinct. While its western reaches are rather drab, the street grows livelier the closer it gets to the massive, open-air **Westfield Downtown Plaza** shopping complex. Every major retail name is here, along with a food court and an enormous cinema; at its western end is a tunnel that takes pedestrians under the highway to connect with Old Sacramento.

Northeast of the mall, at 16th and H, stands the old **Governor's Mansion** (tours daily on the hour 10am–4pm; $5; ⓦwww.parks.ca.gov). Although built in 1877 as a private home, this enormous and elaborate Victorian house was home to California's governors for more than sixty years until 1967, when then-governor Ronald Reagan abandoned its high ceilings and narrow staircases in favour of a

The Big Four and California's early railroads

Starting in 1861, the **Central Pacific** and **Southern Pacific railroads** monopolized transportation and dominated the economy and politics of California and the western US for over twenty years. These companies were the creation of just four men – Leland Stanford, Mark Hopkins, Collis P. Huntington and Charles Crocker – known collectively as the **Big Four**.

For an initial investment of $15,000, the four financiers, along with the railroad designer and engineer Theodore Judah who died before its completion in 1883, received federal subsidies of $50,000 per mile of track laid – twice what it actually cost. On top of this, they were granted half the land in a forty-mile strip bordering the railroad: as the network expanded, the Southern Pacific became the largest landowner in California, owning over twenty percent of the state. This unregulated monopoly – caricatured in the liberal press as a grasping **octopus** – had the power to make or break farmers and manufacturers dependent upon it for the transportation of goods. In the cities, particularly Oakland and Los Angeles, it was able to demand massive concessions from local government as an inducement for rail connections. By the end of the nineteenth century, the Big Four had extracted and extorted a fortune worth over $200 million each and ran a network that stretched across the country to New Orleans.

Although the Big Four all built fabulous mansions on San Francisco's swanky Nob Hill (see p.451), those palaces were destroyed by the 1906 earthquake and fire soon after the men's deaths. The four's most enduring monument is arguably the prestigious university that vain Leland Stanford endowed in honour of his namesake and only son after the boy's early death.

ranch-style house on the outskirts of town. Today, the meringue-like mansion has been restored to its former glory and is a perfect place to begin a self-guided **walking tour** of Sacramento's historic architecture with one of the detailed free brochures published by the Sacramento visitor centre.

The city's most imposing edifice is the **State Capitol**, with its Classical Revival dome, built in the 1860s, although there have been several significant, if insensitive, additions since then. It was restored to nineteenth-century opulence in 1976 in what was then the largest such project in US history; it underwent another heavy restoration following a bizarre incident in early 2001 when a mentally unstable truck driver ploughed his milk tanker into the southern facade and caused almost $15 million in damage. Now, in the post 9-11 and milk truck world, you need photo ID to enter the building: once inside, you're free to ramble around the main floor using the self-guided leaflets on offer in the rotunda. You'll see more, though, if you take one of the free **tours** (Mon–Fri 8am–5pm, Sat & Sun 9am–5pm, last tour 4pm; ℡916/324-0333, Ⓦwww.capitolmuseum.ca.gov) that leave hourly from Room B-27 on the lower ground floor. The tours will take you through administrative rooms set up as if it were April 1906, when the devastating San Francisco earthquake occurred. You'll also visit the salmon-pink Senate Gallery and lush green Assembly Room; in the latter, note the gargoyle's face in the egg-and-dart ceiling moulding, sticking its tongue out at whoever's at the podium. Outside, the popular park around the Capitol is delightful, filled with dazzling flowerbeds, enormous trees and a plague of friendly squirrels.

The **California State History Museum**, 1020 O St (Mon–Sat 10am–5pm, Sun noon–5pm; $8.50), is an enormous, cutting-edge facility that focuses on both the state's physical history and the development of the often lampooned, laidback world view of its inhabitants. The layout is rather confusing, since each exhibit bleeds into the next, but don't miss the eye-catching re-creation of an early

Chinese herbalist store or the perky TV montage showing Californians' often amusing reflections on their home state.

Midtown

Sacramento's trendiest district is **Midtown**, a pleasant area for a leisurely, leafy stroll; city planners planted trees on almost every street, so there's ample shade from the relentless sunshine. Here, although there are few actual attractions, you'll find dozens of funky restaurants and cafés (see below) dotted among the old Victorian mansions, especially along Capitol Avenue, not to mention one of the city's best sights, **Sutter's Fort State Historic Park** (daily 10am–5pm; $5). This re-creation of Sacramento's original settlement stands at 27th and L streets: the main entrance is on the south side. Inside, motion-triggered audio commentary describes each room, like the blacksmith's and the bakery, and an adobe house exhibits relics from the Gold Rush; its quiet atmosphere gives a vivid sense of early European life in California.

One block north, the small **California State Indian Museum** at 2618 K St (daily 10am–5pm; $3) displays a scant and poorly laid out collection of tools, handicrafts and ceremonial objects of the Native Americans of the Central Valley and the Sierra Nevada. It also recounts the story of Ishi, the last of the Yahi Indians, who was paraded around towns as a curiosity in the early twentieth century.

Eating

Dozens of fast-food stands, ice-cream shops and overpriced Western-themed **restaurants** fill Old Sacramento but you'd do better to steer clear of these and search out the places listed below. Many Downtown restaurants cater primarily to office workers and are therefore closed in the evening; for dinner, it's better to stroll over to Midtown, around 20th Street and Capitol Avenue.

Café Bernardo 2726 Capitol Ave, Midtown ☏916/443-1180. Large refectory-style restaurant where you can order huge portions of cheap, healthy food from the counter and eat in a Tuscan-style dining room. The menu's mainly Italian, with pastas, salads and small pizzas, although breakfast is more classic American. Also branches at 1415 L St and 1431 R St.

Jack's Urban Eats 1230 20th St, Midtown ☏916/444-0307. Bargain rotisserie, serving slab-like sandwiches of juicy herbed chicken or steak for $6–7 and great urban-style fries, with blue cheese and spicy chilli oil. Chic ambience and a few canvases by local artists on the walls.

La Fiesta Taqueria 1105 Alhambra Blvd, Midtown ☏916/454-5616. Near Sutter's Fort, this authentic and very inexpensive place bashes out marvellous super-burritos and tacos with some unusual meat selections like *lengue*. Good help-yourself salsa-and-chips bar too.

Lucca 1615 J St, Downtown ☏916/669-5300. The space here is low-key – bare brick walls, no tablecloths – as is the rustic, Tuscan food, which goes for $10–20. Try the pan-roasted salmon or chicken *saltimbocca*.

Maharani 1812 Broadway, Downtown ☏916/441-2172. Slightly pricey California-style Indian that's light on oil, but still heavy on all the traditional spices – try the tandoori chicken for $12.

Ma Jong's 1116 15th St, Downtown ☏916/442-7555. Great value pan-Asian diner set in the modern Park Downtown complex. You can get a choice of meat, prawns or veg in different styles such as Thai basil special or Mongolian, all under $10.

Megami Bento-Ya 1010 10th St, Downtown ☏916/448-4512. A bargain Japanese restaurant with many entrées like sesame chicken under $10. Also good-value sushi plates. Mon–Fri only.

Old Soul at the Weatherstone 812 21st St, Midtown. Sacramento's standout café, with a large interior space and huge courtyard, serving great coffee and pastries. There's free wi-fi too.

Paesano's 1806 Capitol Ave, Midtown ☏916/447-8646. Brick-walled pizzeria serving hearty portions of pasta and oven-baked sandwiches at reasonable prices.

River City Brewing Company 545 Downtown Plaza ☏916/447-2745. This slick, modern brewpub at the west end of the K Street Mall serves standard American food at regular prices, enhanced by tasty beers (some brewed on site).

🏃 **Tapa the World** 2115 J St, Midtown ☏916/442-4353. Choose from twenty different tapas such as *chorizo con papas*, all $4–8, or enjoy a full meal of paella, lamb or fresh fish, while being serenaded by flamenco guitar.

Tower Café 1518 Broadway, Downtown ☏916/441-0222. The furnishings at this casual restaurant are as eclectic as the food, with walls covered in masks and tapestries. The menu features dishes from all over the world such as Kingston chicken, Florentine ravioli and Thai green curry, all around $15.

Willie's Burgers and Chiliburger 2415 16th St, Downtown ☏916/444-2006. Old-school burger joint serving up sloppy, unmissable cooked-to-order burgers and fries, as well as tamales and hot, sweet *beignets* at breakfast time.

Nightlife

Sacramento's **nightlife** can be rather flat, especially in the centre of the city once the office workers have headed home to the suburbs. Still, there are some lively **bars**, mostly in Midtown. If you fancy a flick, the Crest Theatre at 1013 K St (☏916/442-7378, ⊛www.thecrest.com) shows a mixture of mainstream and indie releases.

Capitol Garage 1427 L St, Downtown ☏916/444-3633, ⊛www.capitolgarage.com. A restaurant-cum-club, featuring occasional local bands and regular karaoke and dub/reggae nights. Nominal cover.

The Depot 2001 K St, Midtown ☏916/441-6823. Friendly, gay video bar, with comedy, quiz, pool and theme nights.

Faces 200 K St, Downtown ☏916/448-7798. The city's largest and predominantly gay nightclub with three dancefloors, four patios and nine bars; cover $5–10.

Kasbah 2115 J St, Midtown ☏916/442-4288. The latest venture by the brother-and-sister team who own *Tapa the World* next door (see above), this unique bar draped in exotic soft furnishings is a fun place to sip a top-drawer cocktail while watching the nightly belly-dancers.

Monkey Bar 2730 Capitol Ave, Midtown ☏916/442-8490. Hip joint with mosaic details and a mixed preppy-indie crowd, this is the best place to drink locally and serves bargain cocktails for under $5.

Old Ironsides 1901 10th St, Downtown ☏916/443-9751, ⊛www.theoldironsides.com. A good spot for offbeat live music, mostly indie rock. Also has open-mic and dance-club nights, plus there's decent food. Most nights entry is free, though a few events cost $5–7.

Torch Club 904 15th St, Downtown ☏916/443-2797, ⊛www.torchclub.net. The town's oldest blues haunt, featuring local and national acts for $10 or less. Closed Mon.

The Central Mother Lode

From Sacramento, US-50 and I-80 head east through the heart of the Gold Country, up and over the mountains past Lake Tahoe and into the state of Nevada. The roads closely follow the old stagecoach routes over the Donner Pass, named in honour of the gruesomely tragic exploration (see box, p.593). In the mid-1860s, local citizens, seeking to improve dwindling fortunes after the Gold Rush subsided, joined forces with railroad engineer Theodore Judah to finance and build the first railroad crossing of the Sierra Nevada over much the same route – even along much of the same track – that Amtrak uses today. The area's less touristed than the northern or southern mines: either **Placerville** or **Auburn** make good bases, with affordable accommodation and some local points of interest in each. Placerville's especially handy if you want to sample some of the vintages produced locally in the El Dorado wine country. And while they may not be nearly as postcard-perfect as the towns elsewhere in the region, **Folsom** and **Coloma**, in between the two highways on the American River, are both worth exploring for their less-touristy Gold Rush feel.

Folsom

Apart from an unfortunate incident when Folsom Dam on the American River broke and caused flooding twenty miles downstream, most people know of **Folsom** thanks to the Johnny Cash song about being "stuck in Folsom Prison" after having "shot a man in Reno, just to watch him die". The stone-faced **Folsom State Prison**, two miles north of town on Green Valley Road, has an arts-and-crafts gallery (daily 8am–5pm) selling works by prisoners, who get the proceeds when released. It's more interesting stopping at the small **Folsom Prison Museum** across the road (daily 10am–4pm; $2), which is filled with grisly photographs, the medical records of murderers and thieves who were hanged for their crimes, and a whole arsenal of handmade escape tools recovered from prisoners over the years.

Folsom itself is attractive enough, with a single main street, Sutter Street, of restored homes and buildings that date from the days of the Pony Express. A reconstruction of the 1860 Wells Fargo office makes an imposing setting for the **Folsom History Museum**, at no. 823 (Tues–Sun 11am–4pm; $4), whose prized possessions include a working scale-model of a steam-powered gold dredge, artefacts from the Chinese community that settled here in the 1850s and a huge mural depicting the area's main native people, the Maidu.

El Dorado wine country

In the 1860s, when the now-famous and over-commercialized Napa and Sonoma valleys were growing potatoes, **vineyards** flourished in El Dorado County. However, the fields were neglected after the Gold Rush and killed off by phylloxera, a nasty yellow aphid that gorges itself on vine roots; it wasn't until 1972 that vineyards were systematically re-established. Since then, however, the **wineries** in El Dorado County, especially around Placerville, have rapidly gained a reputation that belies their diminutive size. Most are low-key affairs where no charge is levied for tasting or tours and you're encouraged to enjoy a bottle out on the veranda. At quiet times, you may even be shown around by the wine maker.

The differences in altitude and soil types throughout the region lend themselves to a broad range of grape varieties and the producers here are often criticized for being unfocused; regardless, in recent years local wineries have regularly snagged awards. Zinfandel and Sauvignon Blanc are big, but it's the Syrah/Merlot blends that attract the attention and the Barbera (from a Piedmontese grape) is said to be one of the best in the world.

If you're out for a relaxed day's tasting, avoid the two consecutive **Passport Weekends** ($75; ℡1-800/306-3956, ⊛www.eldoradowines.org), usually the last weekend in March and the first in April and booked out months in advance, although the purchase of this passport does entitle you to all manner of foodie extravagances to complement the tastings. Better to pick up the **El Dorado Wine Country Tour** leaflet from the El Dorado Chamber of Commerce in Placerville (see p.562) and make your way to the Boeger Vineyard, 1709 Carson Rd (daily 10am–5pm; ℡530/622-8094, ⊛www.boegerwinery.com), less than a mile from the Greyhound stop (see p.562), where you can sit in an arbour of apples and pears. Also try the Lava Cap Vineyard, 2221 Fruitridge Rd (daily 11am–5pm; ℡530/621-0175, ⊛www.lavacap.com), which in recent years has produced some excellent Chardonnay and Muscat Canelli.

The quality of the local produce – not only grapes, but also apples, pears, peaches, cherries and various berries – is widely celebrated around the district, especially during the **Apple Hill Festival** (℡530/644-7692, ⊛www.applehill.com) in October, when a shuttle bus runs from Placerville to the majority of the orchards and wineries situated in the Apple Hill region. At other times, you'll have to make your own way along the winding country roads just north of I-50 and east of town.

In town, the Folsom **Chamber of Commerce**, 200 Wool St (Mon–Fri 9am–5pm, Sat 11am–4pm; T1-800/377-1414, Wwww.folsomchamber.com), has the usual brochures. There are plenty of chain **restaurants** around town but a superior choice is the *Balcony Bistro*, 801 Sutter St (T916/985-2605), where you can enjoy some fine French food and a view of the historic Downtown. For **accommodation**, the best bet is the *Lake Natoma Inn*, 702 Gold Lake Drive (T1-800/808-5253, Wwww.lakenatomainn.com; ❹), which has huge rooms, plus a restaurant and a spa.

Placerville

PLACERVILLE, twenty miles east of Folsom, takes a perverse delight in having been known originally as Hangtown for its practice of lynching alleged criminals in pairs and stringing them up from a tree in the centre of town. Despite these gruesome beginnings, Placerville has always been more of a market than a mining town and is now a major crossroads, halfway between Sacramento and Lake Tahoe at the junction of US-50 and Hwy-49. For a time in the mid-1850s it was the third largest city in California and many of the state's most powerful historical figures got their start here: railroad magnates Mark Hopkins and Collis P. Huntington were local merchants, while car mogul John Studebaker made wheelbarrows for the miners.

The modern town spreads out along the highways in a string of fast-food restaurants, gas stations and motels. The old Main Street, running parallel to US-50, retains some of the Gold Rush architecture, with an effigy dangling by the neck in front of the *Hangman's Tree* bar, built over the site where the town's infamous tree once grew. At 441 Main St is the oldest continuously operating hardware store west of the Mississippi, and you'll see many fine old houses scattered among the pine trees in the steep valleys to the north and south of the centre. Nearby, one of the best of the Gold Country museums is in the sprawling El Dorado County Fairgrounds, just north of US-50. This, the **El Dorado County Historical Museum**, 104 Placerville Drive (Wed–Sat 10am–4pm, Sun noon–4pm; free), gives a broad historical overview of the county from the Miwok to the modern day, including logging trains and a mock-up of a general store, plus pioneer wagons and Native American handicrafts. For more on the days of the argonauts, head across US-50 to the **Gold Bug Mine Park** on Bedford Avenue (April–Oct daily 10am–4pm; Nov–March Sat & Sun noon–4pm; $5); admission includes an audio tour of this typical Mother Lode mine, including a hard-rock mining site and a stamp mill showing the ore extraction process. If you want to try your luck hunting for gold, you can rent a pan for $2 an hour – though don't expect to find anything.

Practicalities

The only long-distance **bus** connection is the daily Amtrak Thruway service #20A, which leaves Sacramento at 10.05am and drops you on Main Street an hour later. El Dorado Transit buses provide local transport ($1.50–2.75; T530/642-5383, Wwww.eldoradotransit.com). There are a number of **accommodation** choices, such as the *Mother Lode Motel*, 1940 Broadway (T530/622-0895, Wwww.place rvillemotherlodemotel.com; ❶), and *National 9 Inn*, 1500 Broadway (T1-877/747-8713, Wwww.magnusonhotels.com; ❷), with slightly larger, newer rooms. For a pricier but more romantic stay, try *The Albert Shafsky House*, 2942 Coloma St (T530/642-2776, Wwww.shafsky.com; ❺), a historic B&B with period furnishings and gourmet breakfasts, reached by turning north off US-50 onto Hwy-49 at the traffic lights in town. The El Dorado County **Chamber of Commerce** office, 542 Main St (Mon–Sat: June–Oct 10am–2pm; Nov–May 11am–3pm; T530/621-5885, Wwww.eldoradocounty.org), has local information and can help set up **river-rafting** trips in Coloma (see box opposite).

As for **eating** options, try the local concoction, "the Hangtown Fry", an omelette-like scramble of bacon, eggs and breaded oysters. It's said to have been whipped up using ingredients that were scarce at the height of the Gold Rush for a wealthy miner who wanted the priciest dish on the menu: try one at *Chuck's Pancake House*, 1318 Broadway. *Sweetie Pie's*, at 577 Main St, serves great breakfasts and excellent cinnamon rolls. Grab an organic coffee or an authentic chai at *Cozmic Café*, housed inside the remnants of an actual gold mine, 594 Main St. If none of these appeal, *Heyday Café*, 325 Main St (℡530/626-9700), dishes up fine, affordable Italian food, with Mediterranean and Californian touches.

Coloma

Sights along Hwy-49 north of Placerville are few and far between but it was here that gold fever began on January 24, 1848, when James Marshall discovered flakes of gold in the tailrace of a mill he was building for John Sutter along the south fork of the American River at **Coloma**. By the summer of that year, thousands had flocked to the area, and by the following year Coloma was a town of ten thousand – though most left quickly following news of richer strikes elsewhere in the region and the town all but disappeared within a few years. The few surviving buildings, including two Chinese stores and the cabin where Marshall lived, have been preserved as the **Marshall Gold Discovery State Historic Park** (daily 8am–sunset, museum daily 10am–4.30pm; $6 entry; $8 parking). A reconstruction of **Sutter's Mill** stands along the river within the park and working demonstrations are held on most weekends at 10am and 1pm. There's a small historical museum across the road, and on a hill overlooking the town a statue marks the spot where Marshall is buried. Marshall never profited from his discovery and he spent most of his later years in poverty, claiming supernatural powers had helped him to find gold.

Whether or not you believe in ghosts, Coloma certainly has one attraction that will still turn your knuckles white: it's the best place to begin a **whitewater rafting** journey on the American River (see box below). If you decide to stay in town for the night, the choicest **accommodation** is the *Coloma Country Inn*, 345 High St (℡530/622-6919, ⓦwww.colomacountryinn.com; ❹), adjacent to the state park, with antique-crammed rooms and 2.5 acres of gardens. Barely a mile west of Coloma, on the main road through tiny **Lotus** at 1006 Lotus Rd, is the unexpected location for one of the region's finest restaurants: ⅈ *Café Mahjaic*, where you can savour delights like chocolate chipotle prawns and *coulotte espanole* steak for around $20 (℡530/622-9587; closed Sun & Mon).

> ### River rafting in the Gold Country
>
> Although plenty of people come through the area to see the Gold Rush sights, at least as many come to enjoy the thrills and spills of **whitewater rafting** and **kayaking** on the various forks of the American, Stanislaus, Tuolumne and Merced rivers, which wind down through the region from the Sierra crest. Whether you just want to float in a leisurely manner downstream or fancy careening through five-foot walls of water, contact one of the local river-trip operators, many of which are based around Coloma on the American River. Among the best are American River Recreation (℡1-800-333-7238, ⓦwww.arrafting.com), Beyond Limits Adventures (℡1-800/234-7238, ⓦwww.rivertrip.com), CBOC Whitewater Raft Adventures (℡1-800/356-2262, ⓦwww.cbocwhitewater.com), O.A.R.S. (℡1-800/346-6277, ⓦwww.oars.com) and Tributary Whitewater Tours (℡1-800/672-3846, ⓦwww.whitewatertours.com). Trips run from late spring through early autumn and start at about $90 per person per day midweek.

Auburn

Heading north thirty miles or so, the town of **Auburn**, built into a hillside on three levels, manages to preserve its Gold Rush-era charm, even though it's right at the crossroads of Hwy-49 and I-80. Greyhound **buses** plying between Sacramento and Reno stop at 246 Palm Ave and Amtrak **trains** depart from the unmanned station at 277 Nevada St. The outskirts are sprawling and modern but the Old Town, on Auburn's lowest level just off Hwy-49, is one of the best preserved and most picturesque of the Gold Rush sights, with antique stores and saloons clustered around a Spanish-style plaza. You'll also find California's oldest post office, in continuous use since 1848, and the unmissable red-and-white tower of the 1891 **firehouse**. There are also a number of undervisited museums like the **Gold Country Museum** at 1273 High St (Tues–Sun 11am–4pm; free), with an authentic tunnel on site and a replica of a miners' camp. More offbeat and unusual is the **Bernhard Museum Complex** at 291 Auburn-Folsom Rd (Tues–Sun 11am–4pm; free), mostly since its former owner was looking for liquid, rather than nugget, gold: come here for guided tours of an amateur viticulturist's 1851 home, as well as his carriage barn and modest winery.

For a free map and information on places to stay, stop by the **California Welcome Center**, north of town at 13411 Lincoln Way (Mon–Sat 9.30am–4.30pm, Sun 11am–4.30pm; T 530/887-2111, W www.visitplacer.com). Affordable **accommodation** is available at the no-frills *Super 8 Motel* at 140 E Hillcrest Drive in Auburn (T 1-800/800-8000, W www.super8.com; ①). For a good **meal**, try either *Bootlegger's Old Town Tavern and Grill*, 210 Washington St (T 530/889-2229), where anything from hamburgers to escargots is served in a stately brick building, or *Latitudes*, 130 Maple St (T 530/885-9535; closed Mon & Tues), for Californian interpretations of dishes like East Indian curried tofu or teriyaki tempeh.

The southern mines

South from Placerville, Hwy-49 passes through **Jackson**, which makes a convenient, if unattractive, base for exploring the many dainty villages scattered around the wine-growing countryside of **Amador County**; then the highway continues on through the mining towns of **Calaveras County**. The centre of **Tuolumne County** and the southern mining district is **Sonora**, a small, prosperous town of ornate Victorian houses set on ridges above steep gorges. Once an arch rival but now a ghost town, neighbouring **Columbia** has a carefully restored Gold Rush-era Main Street. The gold-mining district actually extended as far south as **Mariposa** but little remains to make it worth the trip unless you are passing through en route to Yosemite National Park (see p.340).

You'll need your own **transport** to see the southern Gold Country. Drivers be warned – **speed traps** are rampant around the southern mines, particularly in Amador County and on any roads leading to Yosemite, where the speed limits tend to be a bit unrealistic and regional traffic police await to rake in tourist revenue.

Panning, gambling and gunfighting

Though never as rich or successful as the diggings further north, the camps of the **southern mines** had a reputation for being the liveliest and most uproarious of all the Gold Rush settlements and inspired most of the popular images of the era: Wild West towns full of gambling halls, saloons and gunfights in the streets. Certainly the southern settlements were more ethnically varied than those to the north, even if most groups firmly stuck together. The mining methods here were also very different from those used to the north. Instead of digging out gold-bearing ore from deep underground, claims here were more often worked by itinerant, roving prospectors searching for bits of gold washed out of rocks by rivers and streams, known as **placer** gold (from the Spanish word meaning both "sand bar", where much of the gold was found, and – appropriately – "pleasure"). Nuggets were sometimes found sitting on the riverbanks, though most of the gold had to be laboriously separated from mud and gravel using handheld pans or larger sluices.

Mining wasn't a particularly lucrative existence: freelance miners roamed the countryside until they found a likely spot, then quickly blew most of their earnings, either in celebration or on the expensive supplies needed to carry on digging. Unsurprisingly, the boom towns that sprang up around the richest deposits were abandoned as soon as the gold ran out but a few slowly decaying ghost towns have managed to survive more or less intact to the present day, hidden among the forests and rolling ranchland that in spring are covered in fresh green grasses and brightly coloured wildflowers. Other sites were buried under the many **reservoirs** – built in the 1960s to provide a stable source of water for the agricultural San Joaquin Valley – that cover much of the lower elevations.

Amador County

South from Placerville and US-50, the old mining landscape of **AMADOR COUNTY** has been given over to the vineyards of one of California's up-and-coming **wine-growing** regions, best known for its robust Zinfandel, a full-flavoured vintage that thrives in the sun-baked soil. Most of the wineries are located above Hwy-49 in the Shenandoah Valley, near **Plymouth** on the north edge of the county. For a detailed map to all the local establishments, contact Amador Vintners in **Plymouth** (℡1-888/655-8614, ⊛www.amadorwine.com), where you can also **eat** at ☂ *Taste*, 9402 Main St (℡209/245-3463; dinner Thurs–Mon, lunch Sat only), one of the best restaurants in all of Gold Country, serving delights such as Hawaiian tombo tuna and grilled guinea hen. You can also **stay** near here at the secluded *Rancho Cicada Retreat*, 10001 Bell Rd (℡1-877/553-9481, ⊛www.ranchocicadaretreat.com; May–Oct; tents ❸, cabins ❹), which offers nature walks and group activities.

Amador City and Sutter Creek

About thirty miles east of Sacramento, Hwy-16 joins Hwy-49 at **Amador City**, whose short strip of antique shops gives it a cutesy Old West look. **Sutter Creek**, two miles south, is much larger than Amador City, but still little more than a row of tidy antique shops and restaurants catering to tourists along Hwy-49. Though there are a number of surprisingly large Victorian wooden homes – many styled after Puritan New England farmhouses – the town lacks the dishevelled spontaneity that animates many of the other Gold Rush towns, perhaps because its livelihood was never based on independent prospectors panning for placer gold but on hired hands working underground in the more organized and capital-intensive hard-rock mines. It was a lucrative business for the mine owners. The **Eureka Mine** operated until 1958: it was owned by one Hetty Green, the Warren Buffet of her day and at one time the richest woman in the world; at her death in 1916, her estate was worth $100 million. She, however, was notorious for her cheapness, wearing old shabby clothes and giving nothing to charity. Hetty earned her nickname "The Witch of Wall Street" from fellow investors who envied her savvy ruthlessness. Leland Stanford was more generous with the money he made from the **Lincoln Mine**, if no more personally endearing: he become a railroad magnate and governor of California, but used a chunk of his fortune to endow Stanford University (for more on Stanford and his cronies, see the box on p.558).

Practicalities

In Amador City, the landmark *Imperial Hotel* at the northern edge dominates the town, its four-foot-thick brick walls standing at a sharp bend in Hwy-49 and enclosing sunny double **rooms** (℡209/267-9172, ⓦwww.imperialamador .com; ❹). A great place to grab a snack or tasty picnic food is *Andrae's Bakery & Cheese Shop*, 14141 Hwy-49, which does gourmet sandwiches and cakes.

Sutter Creek holds the bulk of Amador County's **accommodation** and eating choices, with two central and very comfortable **B&Bs**: *The Foxes*, 77 Main St (℡1-800/987-3344, ⓦwww.foxesinn.com; ❺), with well-appointed rooms and claw-foot baths; and the larger *Sutter Creek Inn*, 75 Main St (℡209/267-5606, ⓦwww.suttercreekinn.com; ❸), with no TVs or phones but a nice garden with hammocks and a welcoming atmosphere. The *American Exchange Hotel*, 53 Main St (℡1-800/892-2276, ⓦwww.americanexchangehotel.com; ❹), has an attractive wooden facade, and the *Twisted Fork* **restaurant** below (℡209/267-5211) serves medium-priced steaks, pasta and salads. *Susan's Place*, in the Eureka Street Courtyard, a half-block east of Hwy-49 (lunch Thurs–Sun, also open for dinner Fri & Sat; ℡209/267-0945), serves good Mediterranean cuisine under a shaded gazebo and, across the street, the *Sutter Creek Coffee Roasting Co.* serves the best coffee in

Black Bart

The mysterious man known as **Black Bart** made an unlikely highwayman: Charles E. Bowles – sometimes Bolton – was a prominent and respectable San Francisco citizen in his 50s who claimed to be a wealthy mining engineer. In fact, Charles's background was rather more chequered: born to a farmer father in England, he'd emigrated to America as a child and moved to California to try his luck in the Gold Rush. His luck failed and, now married with children, Bowles enlisted in the Union Army, fighting through the Civil War.

Unsurprisingly, it left him a changed man. Once discharged, he drifted around the West Coast, losing contact with his family and trying his hand at silver mining. Finally, in 1875, Charlie turned to crime: over the next eight years, he commited almost thirty **stagecoach robberies**, which yielded a then-staggering income of $6000 a year. But what set Bart apart wasn't his money but his manners. No brutal thug, he instead always addressed his victims as "Sir" and "Madam", never shot them, and in a waggish touch, sometimes recited fragments of poetry before escaping with the loot. His name, incidentally, was pinched from a fictional story published in a local paper that mythologized a merciless criminal known as Black Bart.

But Bart's luck only held so long: he was finally discovered after dropping a handkerchief at the scene of a hold-up, the police nabbing him by tracing the laundry mark back to a San Francisco laundry and from there to Bowles. He spent four years of a six-year sentence in **San Quentin**. Of course, it was commuted for good behaviour and, after his release, he disappeared without trace.

town. For dessert, don't miss the *Sutter Creek Ice Cream Emporium*, 51 Main St, where the friendly owner may well play Scott Joplin tunes on the piano while you sip a milkshake. The helpful **visitor centre** is at 71A Main St (Thurs–Sat 10am–5pm, Sun 11am–2pm; ⓣ1-800/400-0305, ⓦwww.suttercreek.org).

Jackson

After Sutter Creek, the town of **Jackson**, four miles south, can seem distinctly blue-collar, mainly because of the huge Georgia Pacific lumber mill that serves as its northern gateway. Nevertheless, it's a more affordable base for exploring the surrounding countryside. Most of the well-preserved buildings in the small historic Downtown area were erected after a large fire in 1862 but today seem a bit lost amidst the encroaching modern businesses. Note the lovely, if architecturally inappropriate, 1939 Art Deco front on the **County Courthouse** at the top of the hill, while further along the crest, the **Amador County Museum**, 225 Church St (Wed–Sun 10am–4pm; donation), has displays of all the usual Gold Rush artefacts, but is worth a look most of all for its detailed models of the local hard-rock mines – with shafts over a mile deep – that were in use up until World War II. The headframes and some of the mining machinery are still standing a mile north of the museum on Jackson Gate Road, where two sixty-foot-diameter **tailing wheels** (8am–dusk; free), which carried away the waste from the Kennedy Mine, are accessible by way of short trails that lead up from a well-signposted parking area. The headframe of the 6000-foot shaft, the deepest in North America, stands out at the top of the slope, along Hwy-49. The other major mine in Jackson, the **Argonaut Mine** (of which nothing remains), was the scene of a tragedy in 1922, when 47 men were killed in an underground fire.

The **Amador County Chamber of Commerce**, 125 Peek St (Mon–Fri 8am–5pm; ⓣ1-800/726-4667, ⓦwww.amadorcountychamber.com), is rather awkwardly situated at the junction of Hwy-49 and Hwy-88, but offers a *Visitor's Guide to Amador County*, full of the usual maps and historical information. **Accommodation** options include the *Amador Motel* (ⓣ209/223-0970; ➋) and the *Jackson Lodge* (ⓣ1-888/333-0486, ⓦwww.thejacksonlodge.com; ➊), both on Hwy-49 north of town. *Mel and Faye's Diner*, 211 Mountain View Drive, on Hwy-49 near the town centre, is open all day for **breakfasts and burgers**, while *Café Max Swiss Bakery*, 140 Main St, serves pastries and a mean cup of coffee until 6pm Monday to Saturday. For **drinking**, the *Fargo Club*, 2 Main St, is the modern equivalent of a Wild West saloon, with cheap beers and all-night poker games.

Indian Grinding Rock and Volcano

Hwy-88 heads east from Jackson up the Sierra crest, through hills that contain one of the most fitting memorials to the Native Americans who lived here for thousands of years before the Gold Rush all but wiped them out. Nine miles from Jackson, off Hwy-88, a side road passes by the **Indian Grinding Rock State Historic Park** (daily dawn–dusk; $8 per car; ⓣ209/296-7488, ⓦwww.parks.ca.gov), where eleven hundred small cups – *Chaw' Se* in Miwok – were carved into the marbleized limestone outcropping to be used as mortars for grinding acorns into flour. It's the largest collection of bedrock mortars in North America and if you arrive near dawn or dusk and look closely from the small elevated platform next to the biggest of the flat rocks, you can just detect the faint outline of some of the 360 **petroglyphs** here. The state has developed the site into an interpretive centre and has, with the close participation of tribal elders and community leaders, constructed replicas of Miwok dwellings and religious buildings. Descendants of the Miwok gather here during the weekend following the fourth Friday in September for **Big Time**, a celebration of the survival of their culture with traditional arts, crafts and games. At the entrance to the site, the **Chaw'Se Regional Indian Museum** (Mon, Thurs & Fri 11am–2.30pm, Sat & Sun 10am–3.30pm) explores the past and present state of the ten Sierra Nevada native groups in a building said to simulate a Miwok roundhouse. The full process of producing acorn flour is covered but the lack of information on modern Miwok life is a sad testament to the extent of the devastation done to the culture. If you'd like to spend the night, a **campground** in the surrounding woods costs $25 per pitch; space is not reservable and is on a first-come-first-served basis. Note that the campground is closed for Native American gatherings on the third weekend in May, third weekend in June, and last weekend in September.

Named after the crater-like bowl in which it sits, **VOLCANO**, a tiny village a mile and a half north, once boasted over thirty saloons and dancehalls. Today, it claims nearly as many historic sites as Jackson but has been mercifully bypassed by all the latter's development and traffic. The densely forested countryside around the village makes it well worth a visit, especially during mid-March to mid-April, when **Daffodil Hill**, three miles north of Volcano, is carpeted with more than 300,000 of the bobbing yellow heads. Its other notable attraction is the creaky cannon known as "Old Abe": locals threatened to fire it at a rebellious band of confederate sympathizers during the Civil War – the sole threat of aggression to take place in California, even though not a single shot was actually exchanged. For such a small place, there are two good **accommodation** options: the friendly *St George Hotel* at 16104 Main St (℡209/296-4458, ⓦwww.stgeorgehotel .com; ❸), a B&B whose cheaper rooms have shared bathrooms; and the better-value *Union Pub & Inn*, round the corner at 21375 Consolation St (℡209/296-4458, ⓦwww.volcanounion.com; ❸), whose fine **restaurant** (Fri–Mon) is the sister to *Taste* in Plymouth (see p.565).

Calaveras County

CALAVERAS COUNTY lies across the Mokelumne River, eight miles south of Jackson, and is best known for being the setting of Mark Twain's first published story, *The Celebrated Jumping Frog of Calaveras County*. Today, precious few sights of historic interest remain, though there are plenty of options in the county for rugged outdoor recreation. The most northerly town in the county, **Mokelumne Hill**, or "Moke Hill", was as action-packed in its time as any of the southern Gold Rush towns but tourism has been slower to take hold here and today the town is just an all-but-abandoned cluster of ruined and half-restored buildings, not without a certain melancholy appeal. The **Mokelumne Hill Library & History Center** on Main Street (Tues & Wed 10am–5pm, Thurs 1–5pm, Fri 10am–2pm; free) has a modest exhibit on the history of the immediate area, once home to almost ten thousand people. The range of names and languages on the headstones of the **Protestant Cemetery**, on a hill a hundred yards west of town, gives a good idea of the mix of people who came from all over the world to the California mines.

San Andreas

Eight miles south, **San Andreas** hardly seems to warrant a second look: the biggest town for miles, it's now the Calaveras County seat, and has sacrificed historic character for commercial sprawl. The Calaveras County **Chamber of Commerce** publishes a handy map to the county that includes recreational

Limestone caverns in the Gold Country

Limestone caverns abound in the southern Gold Country: three have been developed expressly for public tours, the largest of which is the **Moaning Cavern** in Vallecito, just south of Hwy-4 and five miles east of Angels Camp off Parrots Ferry Road (mid-May to mid-Sept daily 9am–6pm; rest of year Mon–Fri 10–5pm, Sat & Sun 9am–5pm; $14.75 walking tour, $65 abseiling tour; ℡1-866/732-2837, ⓦwww .caverntours.com). Although discovered by gold miners in 1851, bones have been found here dating back 13,000 years. It didn't take long for locals to recognize the lucrative potential of the eerie, lacy rock formations and the caves were opened as a tourist attraction in 1919. The owners first inserted a 234-step spiral staircase to facilitate access and then corked the cavern's opening by building a gift shop on top of it: ironically, these renovations wrecked the cave's natural acoustics and muted the moaning sounds after which it's named.

The same company oversees **California Cavern** in Calaveras (mid-May to mid-Sept daily 10am–5pm; rest of year Sat & Sun 11am–4pm, Mon–Fri by appointment; $14.75; contact details above), a horizontal network of caves that's a better choice for vertigo sufferers unwilling to brave the precipitous stairs at Moaning Cavern. Here, you can even take a four-hour Middle Earth Expedition ($148; reservations essential), whereby you don coveralls and a lighted helmet and follow a professional guide through miles of craggy recesses.

The last of the local commercially developed sites, **Mercer Caverns**, a mile north of Murphys on Sheep Ranch Road, is known for the spectacular stalagmite and stalactite formations in its 800-foot-long gallery, resembling swooping angels' wings and giant flowers (Memorial Day to Labor Day Sun–Thurs 9am–5pm, Fri & Sat 9am–6pm; rest of year daily 10am–4.30pm; $12; ℡209/728-2101, ⓦwww .mercercaverns.com).

activities in the area; it's available from the visitor centre in Angels Camp (see below). What remains of old San Andreas survives along narrow Main Street, on a steep hill just east of the highway, where the 1893 granite-and-brick County Courthouse has been restored and now houses an interesting collection of Gold Rush memorabilia in the **Calaveras County Museum**, 30 N Main St (daily 10am–4pm; $2). There's a diverse collection of gold nuggets and miners' tools, such as sluice boxes and baskets, as well as Miwok artefacts and a replica of an 1880s general store. Local **nightlife** revolves around the *Black Bart Inn*, opposite at 35 N Main St (℡209/754-3808, ⓦwww.blackbartinn.net; ❷), which hosts bands on weekends and also offers inexpensive **accommodation**. It's named after the gentleman stagecoach robber who was captured and convicted here (see box, p.566).

Angels Camp and Carson Hill

The mining camps of southern Calaveras County were some of the richest in this part of Gold Country, both for the size of their nuggets and for the imaginations of their residents. The author Bret Harte spent an unhappy few years teaching in and around the mines in the mid-1850s and based his short story, *The Luck of Roaring Camp*, on his stay in **Angels Camp**, thirty miles south of Jackson. There isn't much to see here these days, though the Downtown feels mildly authentic. The county's main **visitor centre**, at 1192 S Main St (Mon– Fri 9am–5pm, Sat 10am–5pm, Sun 11am–3pm; ℡1-800/225-3764, ⓦwww .visitcalaveras.org), has information on the surrounding area as well as copious frog-related memorabilia in honour of **Mark Twain**. The saloon in the *Angels Hotel* on Main Street is where 29-year-old Twain heard a tale that inspired him to write his famous story, *The Celebrated Jumping Frog of Calaveras County*, about a frog-jumping competition (the saloon is now a discount tire store). Aside from the relentless onslaught of frog-themed souvenirs, the most unfortunate legacy of Twain's story is the **Jumping Frog Jubilee**; it's held with the local state fair on the third weekend in May each year and inexplicably attended by thousands of people who come to watch as pet amphibians compete to see who can jump furthest. On the north side of town, the **Angels Camp Museum**, 753 Main St (summer Thurs–Mon 10am–4pm; winter Sat & Sun 10am–4pm; $2), presents a cornucopia of gold-excavating equipment and memorabilia, as well as a carriage barn filled with historic horse-drawn vehicles. Unsurprisingly, the **place to stay** is called the *Jumping Frog Motel* (T 1-888/850-3764; ●), at 330 Murphy's Grade Rd.

Carson Hill, now a ghost town along Hwy-49 four miles south of Angels Camp, boasted the largest single nugget ever unearthed in California: 195 pounds of solid gold fifteen inches long and six inches thick, worth $43,000 when it was discovered in 1854 and well over a million dollars today. Nearby, **New Melones Reservoir** is the third largest reservoir in California and has all the camping ($14 tent-only, $18 RV and tent site; T 1-877/444-6777, W www.reserveusa.com), swimming, hiking, boating and other recreational possibilities you could hope for, not to mention spectacular, if man-made, views. It's seldom visited by the throngs who fly through the Gold Country on their way to pricier recreational areas: for more information, stop at the **visitor centre** (daily 10am–4pm; T 209/536-9094 ext. 22), just past Carson Hill on Hwy-49.

Murphys

Nine miles northeast of Angels Camp, up the fairly steep Hwy-4, **Murphys'** one and only street is shaded by locust trees and graced by rows of decaying monumental buildings. One of the Gold Country's few surviving wooden water flumes still stands on the town's northern edge, while the oldest structure here, at 470 Main St, now houses the **Old Timer's Museum** (Fri–Sun 11am–4pm, also Mon in summer; donation), a small gathering of documents with a wall-full of rifles. You can take a free one-hour walking tour from here at 10am on Sundays. If you want to **stay** in town, head across the street to the old *Murphys Hotel*, 457 Main St (T 1-800/532-7684, W www.murphyshotel.com; ●), which offers rustic double rooms. The **Calaveras Big Trees State Park** (visitor centre open daily 11am–3pm; winter Sat & Sun 11am–3pm; park dawn–dusk; $8 per car; T 209/795-3840, W www.parks.ca.gov), fifteen miles east, covers six thousand acres of gigantic sequoia trees, threaded with trails. It makes for fine ski-touring in winter, with **hiking** and **camping** (no reservations; $20–35) the rest of the year. Murphys is also a mini gourmet paradise with a smattering of **wine-tasting** rooms and a disproportionate number of **restaurants** for a town of its size. Try the swordfish, steaks or pasta at slightly upmarket *Grounds*, 402 Main St (T 209/728-8663), or the imaginative but pricey mostly vegetarian fare at *Mineral*, opposite at no. 419 (T 209/728-9743).

Tuolomne County

The mountains get a little taller, the ravines sharper and the scenery even more picturesque as Hwy-49 presses on south through **TUOLOMNE COUNTY**, which contains several more fascinating towns from the gold heyday.

Sonora

Sonora, fifteen miles southeast of Angels Camp, is the centre of the southern mining district: it was the site of the **Bonanza Mine**, one of the most lucrative Gold Rush digs. Now a logging town set on steep ravines, it makes a good base for exploring the southern region: there are two settlement clusters, Historic Sonora and the commercial district known as East Sonora. There's little to see beyond the false-fronted buildings and Victorian houses on the main **Washington Street** and the Gothic **St James Episcopal Church** at its far end, but it's a friendly, animated place. The small **Tuolumne County Museum**, in the old County Jail at 158 W Bradford Ave (daily 11am–2pm; free) is worth a look for the restored cellblock more than the collection of old clothes and photographs. There's also the superb Sonora Used Books at 21 S Washington St, with a vast selection of cheap paperbacks in good condition. Pick up architectural and historical walking-tour **maps** ($1) from the **Tuolumne County Visitors Bureau**, 542 W Stockton St (April–Sept Mon–Fri 9am–7pm, Sat 10am–6pm, Sun 10am–5pm; Oct–March Mon–Fri 9am–6pm, Sat 10am–6pm; ☏1-800/446-1333, ⓦwww.thegreatunfenced.com).

Two **hotel** options on Sonora's main strip, South Washington Street, are the old adobe *Gunn House* at no. 286 (☏209/532-3421, ⓦwww.gunnhousehotel .com; ❷), which has large, slightly dark rooms, and the *Sonora Days Inn* at no. 106 (☏209/532-2400, ⓦwww.daysinn.com; ❷), which offers a little more comfort but less character.

For **food**, try *Sonora Thai* at no. 51 (☏209/532-2355; closed Sun), or treat yourself to a delicious ice cream or smoothie in the classic parlour within Legends Books & Antiques at no. 131 (☏209/532-8120). After dark, there are several good options: *The Diamondback Grill* at no. 93 (☏209/532-6661) is a reliable option for hefty portions of meat for around $15. Of several **bars** on Washington, the retro *Zane Iron Horse Lounge* at no. 97 (☏209/532-4482) is the best place to find a hint of the Wild West and drink with the locals.

Columbia

Sonora's one-time arch rival, tourist-loving **Columbia**, three miles north on Parrots Ferry Road, now passes itself off as a ghost town with a carefully restored Main Street that gives an excellent – if contrived – idea of what Gold Rush life might have been like, complete with period costumed staff in the local hotels and restaurants. The town experienced a brief burst of riches after Dr Thaddeus Hildreth and his party picked up thirty pounds of gold in just two days in March 1850. Within a month, over five thousand miners were working claims limited by local law to ten square feet, and by 1854 Columbia was California's second largest city, with fifteen thousand inhabitants supporting some forty saloons, eight hotels and one school. Legend has it the town missed becoming the state capital by two votes – just as well, since by 1870 the gold had run out and Columbia was almost totally abandoned, but only after over two and a half million ounces of gold (worth nearly a billion dollars at today's prices) had been taken out of the surrounding area.

Thanks to agitation from locals, the entire town of Columbia is now preserved as a **State Historic Park** (daily 9am–5pm; free; ☏209/532-0150, ⓦwww.parks .ca.gov), though it's also a genuine town with an active Main Street and year-round residents. Most of the surviving buildings date from the late 1850s, rebuilt in brick after fire destroyed the town a second time. Roughly half of them house historical exhibits – including a dramatized visit to the frontier dentist's office, complete with a 200-proof anesthetic and tape-recorded screams. The rest have been converted into shops, restaurants and saloons, where you can sip a sarsaparilla or munch on a hot dog. Two notable structures are the **Claverie Mason Building**, once the heart of Columbia's Chinatown, and the atmospheric ruins of the **Bixel Brewery**, a mile or so north along Main Street from Downtown: although there's little to see now, it's an evocative change from the staged Victoriana in the centre. As you might imagine, the park/town can be nightmarishly crowded, especially on **Living History Days** (early June), when volunteers dress up and act out scenes from old times. If you want to escape the crowds, the corny but fun stagecoach ride (April–Sept Tues–Sun 10am–4.45pm, Oct–March Fri–Sun same hours; $5–6) leaves hourly from the Wells Fargo Building and zips along the old mining trails around the town. Alternatively, take a trip to the **Matelot Gulch gold mine**, where nuggets are still occasionally found: ninety-minute tours (hours vary; $12; ☎209/532-9693) start from the shack at the south end of Main Street and are hosted by amusingly crabby former miners. The modest **museum** (daily 10am–4pm; free) on Main Street also houses the local **visitor centre** (☎209/536-1672, ⓦwww.columbiacalifornia.com).

If you want to **stay**, the *Columbia City Hotel* at 22768 Main St (☎1-800/532-1479, ⓦwww.briggshospitalityllc.com; ④) is luxurious and central with a gourmet restaurant, while the *Columbia Inn Motel*, 22646 Broadway (☎209/533-0446, ⓦwww.columbiainnmotel.net; ❶), is basic but spotless, with a small pool and cheery staff. The best **food** in town is served up at *Bart's Black Skillet*, 22738 Main St (☎209/588-9300; lunch daily, dinner Thurs–Sat), where hearty portions of meat are the order of the day.

Jamestown

Three miles south of Sonora on Hwy-49, **Jamestown** serves as the southern gateway to the Gold Country for drivers entering on Hwy-120 from the San Francisco Bay Area. Before 1966, when much of Jamestown burned down in a fire, it was used as a location for many well-known Westerns: the classic TV series *Little House on the Prairie* spent several seasons filming in town and Clint Eastwood shot scenes for his Oscar-winning *Unforgiven* here. The train from that movie – also used forty years earlier in *High Noon*, starring Gary Cooper – can be found among many other steam giants in the **Railtown 1897 State Historic Park**, Jamestown's biggest attraction, five blocks east of Main Street at Fifth and Reservoir (daily: April–Oct 9.30am–4.30pm; Nov–March 10am–3pm; $5). At weekends from April to October, you can ride one of the vintage trains for an additional fee (hourly 11am–3pm; $13). Along with its train collection, Jamestown is one of the few Gold Country towns that still has a **working mine** – the huge open-pit Sonora Mining Corporation west of town on Hwy-49 – and a number of outfits take visitors on gold-mining expeditions. Among them, Gold Prospecting Expeditions, 18170 Main St (from $25 per hr; ☎1-800/596-0009, ⓦwww.goldprospecting.com), gives brief instruction in the arts of panning, sluicing and sniping, allowing you to scrape what miniscule traces you can from its local stream.

Main Street is the town's central thoroughfare, with a few **accommodation** choices: the *National Hotel*, 77 Main St (☎1-800/894-3446, ⓦwww.national-hotel.com; ④), has nine rooms and a casually elegant restaurant with a small bar. Nearby is the plush and historic ⚜ *Victorian Gold B&B* at 10382 Willow St (☎1-888/551-1849, ⓦwww.victoriangoldbb.com; ④): its antiquey rooms are a riot of Victoriana, most with claw-footed tubs and stained-glass windows. Otherwise, try the *Miner's Motel* (☎1-800/451-4176, ⓦwww.sonoraminersmotel.com; ❷) out at 18740 Hwy-108, almost halfway back towards Sonora.

For places to **eat** on Main Street, try the popular diner, *Mother Lode Coffee Shop*, at no. 18169, which is open for breakfast or lunch, or grab a gooey sundae at the old-fashioned *Here's the Scoop* ice-cream parlour, no. 18242. Nearby is the *Smoke Café* (T 209/984-3733), which serves tasty Southwestern-style Mexican food and huge margaritas in a touristy atmosphere; lunch specials hover around $7 and there's live music most nights.

Chinese Camp

Hwy-49 winds south from Sonora through some sixty miles of the sparsely populated, rolling foothills of **Mariposa County**, but first it passes the scant remains of the town of **Chinese Camp**. It was here that the worst of the Tong Wars between rival factions of Chinese miners took place in 1856, after the Chinese had been excluded from other mining camps in the area by white miners. Prejudice against all foreigners was rampant in the southern Gold Country, which accounts for its most enduring legend, that of the so-called Robin Hood of the Mother Lode, **Joaquin Murieta**. Though it's unlikely he ever existed, Murieta was an archetype representing the dispossessed Mexican miners driven to banditry by racist abuse at the hands of newly arrived white Americans. Today, amid the run-down shacks and trailers, there's little evidence of Chinese Camp's violent past, other than a historic marker on the main road.

The northern mines

The **northern section** of the Gold Country includes some of the most spectacularly beautiful scenery in California. Fast-flowing rivers cascade through steeply walled canyons whose slopes are covered in autumn with the flaming reds and golds of poplars and sugar maples, highlighted against an evergreen background of pine and fir trees. Unlike the freelance placer mines of the south, where wandering prospectors picked nuggets of gold out of the streams and rivers, the gold here was (and is) buried deep underground and had, therefore, to be pounded out of hard-rock ore. In spite of that, the **northern mines** were the most profitable, more than half of California's gold originating in the mines of **Nevada County** and most of that from **Grass Valley**'s Empire Mine (see p.576). Just north, the quaint Victorian houses of **Nevada City** make it the most alluring Gold Rush town.

A few miles away, at the end of a steep and twisting back road, the scarred yet curiously beautiful landforms of the **Malakoff Diggins** stand as an exotic reminder of the destruction wrought by overzealous miners. Hwy-49 winds further up into the mountains from Nevada City, along the Yuba River to the High Sierra hamlet of **Downieville**, at the foot of the towering Sierra Buttes, and even smaller **Sierra City**. From here you're within striking distance of the northernmost Gold Rush ghost town of **Johnsville**, which stands in an evocative state of arrested decay in the middle of the forests of **Plumas-Eureka State Park**, on the crest of the Sierra Nevada.

You need a **car** to get to any of the outlying sights, among which you'll find a few inexpensive motels and a handful of B&Bs; **camping** is an option too, often in unspoiled sites amid gorgeous mountain scenery.

Grass Valley and Nevada City

Twenty-five miles north of Auburn and I-80, the neighbouring towns of **Grass Valley** and **Nevada City** were the most prosperous and substantial of the gold-mining towns and are still thriving communities, four miles apart in beautiful surroundings in the lower reaches of the Sierra Nevada. Together they make one of the better Gold Country destinations, with museums that successfully conjure up the era and elaborately detailed, balconied buildings staggering up hills.

Gold was the lifeblood of the area as recently as the mid-1950s, and both towns look largely unchanged since the Gold Rush. The locals have retained some of the fiery determination of their rough-and-ready ancestors, as evidenced by the booming Downtown businesses that combine the Old West with big-city sophistication. Since the 1960s, a number of artists and craftspeople have also settled in the area, tempering the rugged regional culture with a vaguely alternative feel that's reflected in the free weekly *Community Endeavor* newspaper, the noncommercial community radio station KVMR (99.3FM) and the disproportionate number of bookshops. For a detailed rundown on the whole of Nevada County, including the mines, check out ⓦ www.ncgold.com.

Arrival and accommodation

Both towns are very compact and connected every thirty minutes by the Gold Country Stage **minibus** (Mon–Fri 7am–6pm, Sat 10am–5pm; $1.50, $4.50 for a day-pass; ⓣ 1-888/660-7433, ⓦ www.goldcountrystage.com), which follows the same stretch of road that burro trains and stagecoaches frequented in the twin towns' heyday, when it was the busiest four-mile route in California.

As for **accommodation**, there's a smattering of cheapish motels around but if you can fork out more for a **B&B** Nevada City in particular has some excellent options. Otherwise there are a couple of revamped Gold Rush **hotels**. See the box on p.579 for **camping** options. The hotels below are marked on the **maps** on p.575 and p.577.

Grass Valley

Coach N Four Motel 628 S Auburn St, Grass Valley ⓣ 530/273-8009, ⓦ www.grassvalley camotels.com. Handy for Empire State Park, this clean and comfortable motel offers the best rates around. ❶

Holbrooke Hotel 212 W Main St, Grass Valley ⓣ 1-800/933-7077, ⓦ www.holbrooke.com. Right in the centre of town, this historic hotel, where Mark Twain once stayed, has great rooms and an opulent bar-cum-restaurant. ❹

Holiday Lodge 1221 E Main St, Grass Valley ⓣ 1-800/742-7125, ⓦ www.holidaylodge.biz. Comfortable, no-frills rooms in a lodge featuring a swimming pool and free local calls. ❷

Swan-Levine House 328 S Church St, Grass Valley ⓣ 530/272-1873, ⓦ www.swanlevinehouse .com. Attractively decorated, sunny en-suite rooms in an old Victorian hospital. There's original artwork on display and the friendly owners give print-making lessons. ❹

Nevada City

Flume's End 317 S Pine St, Nevada City ⓣ 530/265-9665, ⓦ www.flumesend.com. A small inn across the Pine Creek Bridge from the centre of town, overlooking a pretty waterfall and featuring lovely gardens ranged along Deer Creek. ❺

National Hotel 211 Broad St, Nevada City ⓣ 530/265-4551, ⓦ www.thenationalhotel .com. The oldest continuously operated hotel in the West and a state historic landmark, with plenty of Gold Rush charm in the rooms and lobby, which boasts original photographs, musty wallpaper and a grand staircase. ❹

Northern Queen Inn 400 Railroad Ave, Nevada City ⓣ 1-800/226-3090, ⓦ www.northernqueeninn .com. Well-priced hotel with a heated pool. Attractive woodland cottages and chalets, along with simpler rooms in another building. Its *Trolley Junction* restaurant is good too. ❸

Outside Inn 575 E Broad St, Nevada City ⓣ 530/265-2233, ⓦ www.outsideinn.com. Quiet

1940s motel with a wide range of rooms and a swimming pool, only a ten-minute walk from the centre of town. **②**
Piety Hill Cottages 523 Sacramento St, Nevada City ☏1-800/443-2245,

Ⓦ www.pietyhillcottages.com. Cottages with kitchenettes, decorated in period furnishings in a garden setting; the smaller ones are an especially good deal. Gazebo-covered spa open April–Nov. **④**

Grass Valley

There's nothing Gold Country folk love better than telling a long tale about their town's toughest days, making it virtually impossible to pass through **GRASS VALLEY** without getting at least one rendition of the **Lola Montez** story. This Irish dancer and entertainer – the former mistress of Ludwig of Bavaria and friend of Victor Hugo and Franz Liszt – embarked on a highly successful tour of America in the 1850s, playing to packed houses from New York to San Francisco. Her provocative "Spider Dance", in which she wriggled about the stage shaking cork spiders out of her dress, didn't much impress the miners, but she liked the wild lifestyle of the town, gave up dancing, and retired to Grass Valley with her pet grizzly bear, which she kept tied up in the front yard.

A few mementos of Lola's life, such as clothes and accessories, are displayed in the **Grass Valley Museum**, in the Old St Mary's Academy at 410 South Church St (Tues–Fri 12.30–3.30pm; donation). The town's **tourist office** (Mon–Fri 9am–5pm, Sat 10am–3pm; ☏1-800/655-4667, Ⓦ www.grassvalleychamber.com) is housed in a replica of her home, on the south side of town at 248 Mill St. It also has reams of historical information, lists of accommodation and a walking-tour map of the town.

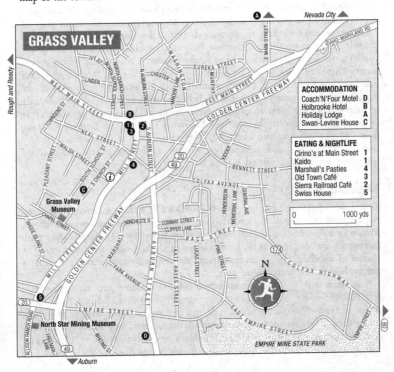

The North Star Powerhouse

The **North Star Powerhouse & Pelton Wheel Mining Exhibit**, to give it its full title, stands at the south end of Mill Street (early May to mid-Oct daily 10am–5pm; donation). It is one of the most evocative Gold Country museums, with enthusiastic guides and interesting exhibits illustrating Grass Valley's glory days. Housed in what used to be the power station for the North Star Mine, the centrepiece is the giant **Pelton wheel**. Patented in 1878 and resembling nothing so much as a thirty-foot-diameter bicycle wheel, the wheel became one of the most important inventions to come out of the Gold Country. Many Pelton wheels were used to generate electricity, though the one here drove an air compressor that powered the drills and hoists of the mine.

A series of dioramas in the museum describes the day-to-day working life of the miners, three-quarters of whom had emigrated here from the depressed tin mines of Cornwall in England. Besides their expertise at working deep underground, the "Cousin Jacks", as they were called by the non-Cornish miners, introduced the **Cornish pump** (not to mention the Cornish pasty, a traditional savoury pie) to the mines. You can see a mock-up of one of these mammoth beasts, which were designed to extract water from underground, as well as a scaled-down version of a noisy stamp mill, used for pulverizing gold-bearing quartz ore.

The Empire Mine State Park

The largest and richest gold mine in the state was the **Empire Mine**, now preserved as a state park a mile southeast of Grass Valley, just off Hwy-174 at the top of Empire Street. The 800-acre **park** (daily: July & Aug 9am–6pm; Sept–June 10am–5pm; $5) is surrounded by pines, among which are vast quantities of mining equipment and machinery. Standing among the machines, it's easy to imagine the din that shook the ground 24 hours a day or the skips of fifty men descending the now-desolate shaft into the 350 miles of underground tunnels. After more than six million ounces of gold had been recovered, the cost of getting the gold out of the ground exceeded $35 an ounce – the government-controlled price at the time – and production ceased. Most of the mine has been dismantled but there's a small, very informative **museum** at the entrance with a superb model of the whole underground system, built secretly to help predict the location of lucrative veins of gold. You can get some sense of the mine's prosperity by visiting the owner's house, the **Empire Cottage** (tours 1pm, June–Aug also 11am; $2), at the north end of the park – a vaguely English stone-and-brick manor house with a glowing, redwood-panelled interior overlooking a formal garden.

Nevada City

Towns don't get much quainter than **NEVADA CITY**, four miles north of Grass Valley, with its crooked rows of elaborate Victorian homes set on the winding, narrow, maple-tree-lined streets, which rise up from Hwy-49. It gets away with its cuteness by being one of the least changed of all the Gold Country towns. The cluster of excellent shops and restaurants in the town centre make it a good, if pricey, base for the surrounding area.

A smart first stop is the **tourist office** (Mon–Fri 9am–5pm, Sat 11am–4pm; ☏1-800/655-6569, ⊛www.nevadacitychamber.com) at 132 Main St, a block north of Hwy-49, where you can pick up a free walking-tour **map** of the town. There aren't many set-piece sights other than the restored, lacy-balconied and bell-towered **Firehouse Museum #1**, 214 Main St (daily: May–Oct 11am–4pm; Nov–April Fri–Sun noon–3pm; donation), which describes the social history of

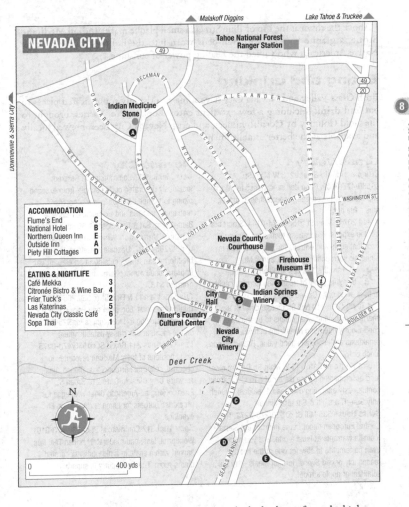

NEVADA CITY

Tahoe National Forest
Ranger Station

Indian Medicine
Stone

ACCOMMODATION

Flume's End	C
National Hotel	B
Northern Queen Inn	E
Outside Inn	A
Piety Hill Cottages	D

EATING & NIGHTLIFE

Café Mekka	3
Citronée Bistro & Wine Bar	4
Friar Tuck's	2
Las Katerinas	5
Nevada City Classic Café	6
Sopa Thai	1

Nevada County
Courthouse

Firehouse
Museum #1

City
Hall

Indian Springs
Winery

Miner's Foundry
Cultural Center

Nevada
City
Winery

Deer Creek

N

0   400 yds

the region. The heart of town is Broad Street, which climbs up from the highway past the imposing 1854 **National Hotel** (see p.574) and a number of antique shops and restaurants, all decked out in Gold Country balconies and wooden awnings. Almost the only exception to the rule of picturesque nostalgia is the Art Deco 1937 **City Hall**.

The **Miner's Foundry Cultural Center** (Mon–Fri 10am–3pm; free), close to the Deer Creek Canyon at 325 Spring St, is an old tool foundry converted into a cultural centre, art gallery, performance space and the KVMR radio studios. Immediately next door stands the **Nevada City Winery**, 321 Spring St (Sun–Thurs noon–5pm, Fri & Sat noon–6pm), where you can taste the produce of one of the state's oldest vineyards. If you'd like to sample some more, stop by the **Indian Springs Winery**, which has its tasting room at 303 Broad St (Sun–Thurs 11.30am–5pm, Fri & Sat 11.30am–6pm; ☎1-800/375-9311, ⓦwww .indianspringswines.com). Both wineries sell their product at very modest prices in comparison to those of the Wine Country.

Above the town at the top of Pine Street, a small plaque marks **Indian Medicine Stone**, a granite boulder with sun-beds worn into the hollows of the rock by Native Americans who valued the healing power of sunshine.

Eating and drinking

Both Grass Valley and Nevada City have some surprisingly sophisticated places to **eat and drink**, including a few excellent **cafés**. Look out for pasties, brought to the Gold Country by Cornish miners, and crisp Nevada City beer, brewed locally and available at the better establishments.

Grass Valley

Cirino's at Main Street 213 W Main St ☎530/477-6000. Good deli sandwiches for lunch and modestly priced Italian specialities at dinner, plus a full bar.

Kaido 207 W Main St ☎530/274-0144. Smart but not too expensive Japanese restaurant serving excellent sushi and entrées for just under $20 in authentic surroundings. Closed Sun & Mon.

Marshall's Pasties 203 Mill St. Mind-boggling array of fresh filled Cornish pasties, to take away only. Closed Sun.

Old Town Café 110 Mill St. Classic diner in a sharp renovation of what claims to be the oldest continuously operating restaurant in town. The breakfasts are especially good value. Breakfast and lunch only.

Sierra Railroad Café 111 W Main St. Decent diner food accompanied by the clatter of a model railroad continuously operating overhead. Breakfast & lunch only Sun–Thurs, Fri & Sat also dinner.

Swiss House 535 Mill St ☎530/273-8272. The Central European decor in the heart of the Sierra foothills warrants at least a grin, and you might even be tempted to stay for one of the hearty, reasonably priced Swiss-German meals – try the schnitzel or apple strudel.

Nevada City

Café Mekka 237 Commercial St. Relaxed, fabulously decorated coffee shop – from exposed piping to trompe l'oeil wallpaper – popular with teenagers, trendies and ex-hippies. Daily 8am–11pm, Sat & Sun closes 1.30am.

Citronée Bistro and Wine Bar 320 Broad St ☎530/265-5697. Upscale American-Mediterranean fusion cuisine in an elegant yet unpretentious atmosphere. The *coq au vin* is great at $18.

Friar Tuck's 111 N Pine St ☎530/265-9093. Quality American, European and Pacific Rim cuisine, including fondue dinners for $25–30, are on the menu at this classy establishment.

Las Katerinas 311 Broad St ☎530/478-0275. Huge portions of tasty Mexican favourites in cheerful, colourful surroundings. Closed Tues.

Nevada City Classic Café 216 Broad St. Plain-looking all-American diner with eggs for breakfast, burgers for lunch and tapas on Fri evenings.

Sopa Thai 312 Commercial St ☎530/470-0101. Wonderful, tasty and moderately priced Thai fare, served with a smile in a pleasantly decorated dining room. The green curry is superb.

Nevada County

The rest of the **NEVADA COUNTY** foothills are as attractive now as they were productive in the gold heyday. Before the deep, hard-rock mines were established in the late 1860s, there were mining camps spread all over the northern Gold Country, with evocative names like "Red Dog" and "You Bet", that disappeared as soon as the easily recovered surface deposits gave out. **Rough and Ready**, five miles west of Grass Valley, survives on the tourist trade alone – visitors come to take a look at the only mining town ever to secede from the United States, which Rough and Ready did in 1850. The band of veterans who founded the town, fresh from the Mexican–American War, opted to quit the Union in protest against unfair taxation by the federal government and although they declared their renewed allegiance in time for that summer's Fourth of July celebrations, the conflict was not officially resolved

Camping in Nevada County

One of the easiest ways to get a feel for the day-to-day life of the miners is to "rough it" yourself, **camping** out in one of the many accessible campgrounds in the surrounding hills, which you can only reach by car. On Hwy-20, just east of Nevada City, *Gene's Pineaire Campground*, at 31041 Relief Hill Rd, Washington (☏530/265-2832), and *Scott's Flat Lake*, on Scott's Flat Road (☏530/265-5302), are privately operated and have the best facilities; seven miles on, *White Cloud* is more remote – for details, contact the ranger station (☏530/265-4531) in Nevada City on Coyote Street, a quarter of a mile north past the tourist office. Rates at all sites start at around $20 but can be more in the high season.

until 1948. Now the handful of ramshackle buildings, including a gas station and a general store, only warrants the briefest of visits.

Six miles northwest of Rough and Ready, off the winding Bitney Springs Road in the **South Yuba River State Park**, stands the **Bridgeport covered bridge**, the longest single-span, wood-truss covered bridge in the world, spanning the Yuba River. The swimming spot underneath offers some relief from a hot summer's day, and the nearby visitor centre (hours vary; ☏530/432-2546) has plenty of information on the area's hiking trails, guided wildflower, history and birding tours, and the inevitable gold-panning demonstrations.

Malakoff Diggins State Park

The waters of the Yuba River are now crisp and clear, but when the Bridgeport Bridge was completed in 1862 they were being choked with mud and residue from the many **hydraulic mining** – or "hydraulicking" – operations upstream. Hydraulic mining was used here in the late 1850s to get at the trace deposits of gold that weren't worth recovering by orthodox methods. It was an unsophisticated technique: giant nozzles or monitors sprayed powerful jets of water against the gold-bearing hillsides, washing away tonnes of gravel, mud and trees just to recover a few ounces of gold. It also required an elaborate system of flumes and canals – some still used to supply water to local communities – to collect the water, which was sprayed at a rate of over thirty thousand gallons a minute. Worst of all, apart from the obvious destruction of the landscape, was the waste it caused, silting up rivers, causing floods, impairing navigation and eventually turning the San Francisco Bay, nearly 150 miles away, a muddy brown.

Site of the worst offense, whose excesses caused hydraulic mining to be outlawed in 1884, was the **Malakoff Diggins**, sixteen miles up steep and winding North Bloomfield Road from Nevada City (or accessible via the sixteen-mile Tyler Foote Crossing Road, which turns off Hwy-49 twelve miles northwest of Nevada City). Here, a canyon more than a mile long, half a mile wide and over six hundred feet deep was carved out of the red-and-gold earthen slopes. Natural erosion has softened the scars somewhat, sculpting pinnacles and towers into a miniature Grand Canyon, now preserved as a 3000-acre **state park** (summer daily sunrise–sunset; winter Sat & Sun sunrise–sunset; parking $8; ☏530/265-2740). While the park may seem just a short detour from Hwy-49 on your map, its interminable unmarked gravel roads and snaking bends may give you an eerie feeling. Old buildings from ghost towns around the Gold Country have been moved to the restored settlement of **North Bloomfield**, inside the park, where a small museum (June–Aug daily 10am–4pm; Sept–May Sat & Sun only, hours vary; free) shows a twenty-minute film on hydraulicking; there's a **campground** near the spooky

579

cliffs (☎1-800/444-7275, ⓦwww.parks.ca.gov; $35). While in the area, those interested in yoga and spirituality mustn't miss **Ananda's Retreat Center** (☎1-800/346-5350, ⓦwww.expandinglight.org), which occupies expansive mountainside grounds en route to the park at 14618 Tyler-Foote Road. Most of the grounds, shrines and the visitor centre are open to the public and regular courses are scheduled.

The High Sierra towns

From Nevada City, Hwy-49 climbs up along the Yuba River Gorge into some of the highest and most marvellous scenery in the Gold Country, where waterfalls tumble over sharp, black rocks bordered by tall pines and maple trees. In the middle of this wilderness, an hour's drive from Nevada City, **Downieville**, the most picturesque of the Gold Rush towns, spreads out along both banks of the river, crisscrossed by an assortment of narrow bridges. Still further up in the hills, **Sierra City** is another attractive town that deserves a look, but you are only likely to encounter tiny **Sierraville** if you're heading up into Plumas County (see p.654), a route that will take you close to the fascinating ghost town of **Johnsville**.

Downieville

Hwy-49 runs right through the centre of **DOWNIEVILLE**, slowing to a near-stop to negotiate tight curves that have not been widened since stagecoaches passed through. Thick stone buildings, some enhanced with delicate wooden balconies and porches, others with heavy iron doors and shutters, face raised wooden sidewalks, as their backs dangle precipitously over the steep banks of the river.

For what is now a peaceful and quiet little hamlet of three hundred people, Downieville seems strangely proud of its fairly nasty history. It has the distinction of being the only mining camp ever to have hanged a woman, Juanita, "a fiery Mexican dancehall girl" who stabbed a miner in self-defense. A restored wooden gallows, last used in 1885, still stands next to the County Jail on the south bank of the river to mark this ghastly heritage. Across the river and two blocks north, at the end of a row of 1850s storefronts, the **Downieville Museum** (May–Oct daily 11am–4pm; donation) is packed full of odd bits and historical artefacts, including a set of snowshoes for horses and a scaled-down model of the local stamp mill. You can pick up a walking-tour map of the town from the erratically opening **tourist kiosk** (May–Sept Sat & Sun only), on a prime grassy spot by the river.

For such a diminutive town there are several very decent **accommodation** options, including the *Riverside Inn* (☎1-888/883-5100, ⓦwww.downieville .us; ❸) and the nicely refurbished *Carriage House Inn* (☎1-800/296-2289, ⓦwww.downievillecarriagehouse.com; ❸), on opposite sides of the Yuba River where Hwy-49 crosses it. The *Sierra Shangri-La* (☎530/289-3455, ⓦwww.sierrashangrila.com; ❸), 2.5 miles further northeast in thick woods above the river, has B&B rooms and fully furnished cottages, the latter available by the week in summer.

Eating and drinking options can be found on Main Street, with the family-style *C & J's Downieville Diner* at no. 322, the inexpensive *Riverview Pizzeria* (☎530/289-3540) on the corner of Nevada Street and the *Gallows Café* at no. 118, where you can get a fine coffee.

Sierra City and Sierraville

Delightful **SIERRA CITY** does not offer much in the way of sights but oozes old-time Gold Country charm. The full-sized model of the original stamp mill is maintained in working order at the **Kentucky Mine Museum** (summer Wed–Sun 10am–4pm; $3), a mile east of town further up Hwy-49, where a guided tour (11am & 2pm; $5) takes you inside a reconstructed miner's cabin and down a mineshaft to give you a look at various pieces of equipment used for retrieving gold-bearing ore. Until the mine was shut down during World War II, the ore was dug out from tunnels under the massive **Sierra Buttes**, the craggy granite peaks that dominate the surrounding landscape. The museum hosts concerts during the summer.

Sierra City can be a useful base for visiting the surrounding area. Adequate **accommodation** is available year-round at *The Yuba River Inn* (☎530/862-1122, ⓦwww.yubariverinn.com; ❷), a rustic, cabin-like spot east on Hwy-49 by the river, and in town at the *Old Sierra City Hotel*, 212 Main St (☎530/862-1300, ⓔoschotel@inreach.com; ❷). Seasonal places include the plush but good-value *Busch & Heringlake Country Inn*, 231 Main St (☎530/862-1501; ❸), and the more down-to-earth *Herrington's Sierra Pines* resort (☎1-800/682-9848, ⓦwww .herringtonssierrapines.com; ❷), a little west of town. In the area you'll also find some of the most remote and attractive **campgrounds** in the Gold Country, including the *Sierra Campground*, seven miles beyond Sierra City, and *Chapman Creek*, another mile upstream on the Yuba River. All sites are $20 and can be reserved by calling High Sierra Campgrounds (☎530/993-1410). The best **place to eat** is the English-run *Red Moose Inn*, 224 Main St (☎530/862-1990), which serves fish'n'chips and filling sandwiches.

Hwy-49 continues east through the **Tahoe National Forest**, passing over the 6700-foot **Yuba Pass** on its way to join forces with Hwy-89 just north of Sattley at Bassett Junction. From here Hwy-89 heads north to Johnsville and south to Truckee and the Lake Tahoe area. Five miles south of the junction, there are basic facilities at **SIERRAVILLE**: at a pinch you could stay at the *Globe Hotel* (☎530/994-3773; ❸) or stop for a quick meal or drink at *Los Dos Hermanos* (☎530/994-1058; closed Mon), both by the T-junction where the two highways separate again in the middle of the tiny town.

Johnsville

Founded in 1870, **Johnsville** is, after Bodie (see p.300), the best preserved and most isolated old mining town in California. Located 25 miles north of Bassett Junction and five miles off Hwy-89, the ghost town is surrounded by over seven thousand acres of pine forest and magnificent scenery and lies at the centre of the **Plumas-Eureka State Park** – which has $35 campsites (☎1-800/444-7275, ⓦwww.parks.ca.gov) and miles of **hiking** trails. Johnsville's huge stamp mill and mine buildings are being restored; in the meantime, a small **museum** (June–Sept daily 9am–4pm; donation) describes the difficult task of digging for gold in the High Sierra winters. If you're looking for a bite to **eat**, the *Iron Door* (☎530/836-2376), right in the centre of the town's main road, serves up multinational cuisine, with an emphasis on steaks, schnitzel and pasta, in the premises of the old general store. Back towards Hwy-89 at 1228 Johnsville Road, the *Mohawk Café* offers quality bar food and snacks. For the rest of Plumas County and the Hwy-89 route northwest to Lassen Volcanic National Park, see p.657.

The Lake Tahoe circuit

High above the Gold Country, just east of the Sierra ridge, **Lake Tahoe** sits placidly in a dramatic alpine bowl, surrounded by high granite peaks and miles of thickly wooded forest. Its name means "lake of the sky" in the native Washoe language. Now it's a major tourist area; the sandy beaches and surrounding pine-tree wilderness are overrun with thousands of fun-lovers (predominantly families) throughout the summer and in winter the snow-covered slopes of the nearby peaks are packed with skiers. The eastern third of the lake lies in Nevada, where gambling is legal, and therefore glows with light from the neon signs of the inevitable **Stateline casinos**.

Little visited beyond an influx of winter skiers, **Truckee**, fifteen miles north of Lake Tahoe, ranges along the Truckee River, which flows out of Lake Tahoe down into the desert of Nevada's Great Basin. **Donner Pass**, just west of town, was named in memory of the pioneer Donner family, many of whom lost their lives when trapped here by heavy winter snows.

Across the border in **Nevada**, **Reno**, at the eastern foot of the Sierra Nevada, is a downmarket version of Las Vegas, popular with slot-machine junkies and elderly gamblers; others come to take advantage of Nevada's lax marriage and divorce laws. Though far smaller than Reno, **Carson City**, thirty miles south, is the Nevada state capital, with a couple of engaging museums that recount the town's frontier history. Heading a little deeper into Nevada, and up into the arid mountains to the east, the silver mines of the **Comstock Lode**, whose wealth paid for the building of much of San Francisco, are buried deep below the evocative, if touristy, **Virginia City**.

Lake Tahoe

Fault-formed **LAKE TAHOE** is one of the highest, deepest, cleanest, coldest and most beautiful lakes in the world. More than sixteen hundred feet deep, it is allegedly so cold that cowboys who drowned over a century ago have been recovered from its depths in perfectly preserved condition, gun holsters and all. The lake's position, straddling the border between California and Nevada, lends it a schizophrenic air, the dichotomy most evident at **South Lake Tahoe**, the lakeside's largest community, where ranks of restaurants, modest motels and pine-bound cottages stand cheek by jowl with the high-rise gambling dens of **Stateline**, just across the border. **Tahoe City**, the hub of the lake's north-western shore, does not escape the tourists but manages to retain a more relaxed, if somewhat exclusive, attitude. Expensive vacation homes and shabby family-oriented mini-resorts line much of the remainder of the lake. Tahoe is never truly off-season, luring weekenders from the Bay Area and beyond with clear, cool waters in the summer, snow-covered slopes in the winter, and gambling all year round. On holiday weekends, expect traffic to reach maddening levels; convoys of cars and trucks spilling over with ski equipment or mountain bikes stretch throughout the area. To take advantage of the natural resources and still avoid at least some of the crowds, you might consider staying south of Tahoe near **Kirkwood**, though during peak times even this area can fill up quickly.

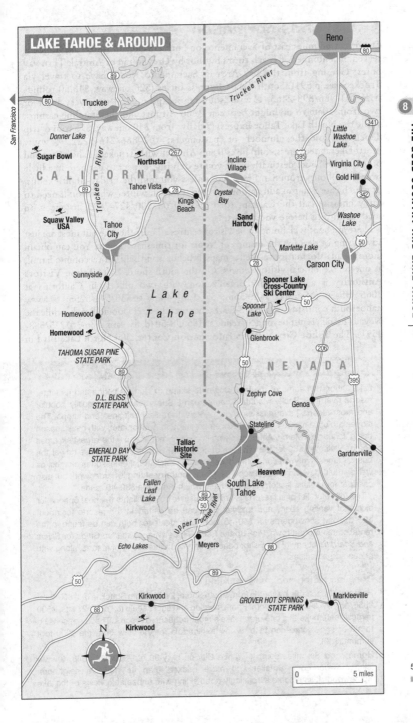

LAKE TAHOE & AROUND

San Francisco

Reno

Truckee River

Truckee

Donner Lake

Sugar Bowl

C A L I F O R N I A

Northstar

Little
Washoe
Lake

Virginia City

Gold Hill

Incline
Village

Tahoe Vista

Kings
Beach

Crystal
Bay

**Sand
Harbor**

Washoe
Lake

**Squaw Valley
USA**

Tahoe City

Marlette Lake

Sunnyside

L a k e
T a h o e

Carson City

**Spooner Lake
Cross-Country
Ski Center**

Homewood

Homewood

Spooner
Lake

*TAHOMA SUGAR PINE
STATE PARK*

Glenbrook

N E V A D A

*D.L. BLISS
STATE PARK*

Zephyr Cove

Genoa

*EMERALD BAY
STATE PARK*

**Tallac
Historic
Site**

Stateline

Gardnerville

Heavenly

Fallen
Leaf
Lake

South Lake
Tahoe

Upper Truckee River

Echo Lakes

Meyers

Kirkwood

*GROVER HOT SPRINGS
STATE PARK*

Markleeville

Kirkwood

N

0   5 miles

Arrival and information

One hundred miles east of Sacramento on both US-50 and I-80, Lake Tahoe is served by a number of coach **tours** but not by Greyhound or Amtrak Thruway buses. Coming from the Bay Area or Sacramento, you'll have to travel via Truckee (see p.591). South Tahoe Express **buses** ($26 oneway, $46.50 round-trip; ☎1-866/898-2463, ⓦwww.southtahoeexpress.com) run every hour or two from 10am to midnight between Reno Airport and the Stateline casinos, while the North Lake Tahoe Express (7 daily; from $40 oneway, $75 round-trip depending on the number of passengers; ☎1-866/216-5222, ⓦwww.northlaketahoeexpress.com) links Reno Airport with Truckee, Tahoe City and other North Shore destinations. If you're **driving**, expect to get here in a little over three hours from San Francisco, unless you join the Friday-night exodus, in which case you can add an hour or two, more in winter when you'll need to carry **chains**; call the Caltrans road phone (☎1-800/427-7623) to check on road conditions before you depart.

There are booths claiming to be visitor centres all over the lake but most are just advertising outlets for the casinos or fronts for timeshare agents. You can obtain more useful **information**, as well as maps, brochures and help with accommodation, at one of the official visitor centres. On the south shore, **Lake Tahoe Visitors Authority** is a cross-border organization with two offices: in California at 3066 US-50 (Mon–Fri 9am–5pm, Sat 9am–4pm; ☎530/541-5255, ⓦwww.tahoesouth.com), just before US-50 reaches the lake at El Dorado Beach, while the Nevada branch is just beyond Stateline at 195 US-50 (daily 9am–5pm; ☎775/588-4591). The **Tahoe City Visitors Information Center**, 380 North Lake Blvd in

Tahoe skiing and snowboarding

Lake Tahoe has some of the best **downhill skiing** in North America and its larger resorts rival their Rocky Mountain counterparts. **Snowboarding** is equally popular and most resorts have massive snow parks with radical halfpipes and jumps. The slopes are usually open from mid-November through April or later, with peak season being January to March. Although skiing is certainly not cheap – the largest ski areas charge well over $50 for the privilege of using their mountain for a single day at the busiest times – many resorts offer decent-value rental/lift ticket/lesson packages, as well as multi-day and online discounts. **Cross-country skiing** is harder work but also cheaper for rentals, lessons and trail fees, which are in the $30–40 range.

The following list of ski resorts is not exhaustive, but highlights the best options for skiers of varying ability and budget. Skis can be rented at the resorts for about $30–35, and snowboards for $40–45, but better deals for both can be found in the rental stores around town. Pick up the *Reno–Tahoe Winter Vacation Guide for Skiers and Boarders* at any of the visitor centres for a complete listing of resorts, along with prices and amenities.

Downhill skiing and snowboarding

Heavenly Reachable by shuttle from South Shore, 2 miles from Stateline ☎1-800/243-2836, ⓦwww.skiheavenly.com. Prime location and sheer scale (82 runs, 27 lifts, 3500 vertical feet) make this one of the lake's most frequented resorts. Those not seeking to ski or snowboard can take the aerial Gondola for the view from the 8200-foot summit ($30).

Homewood Six miles south of Tahoe City on Hwy-89 ☎1-800/824-6348, ⓦwww.skihomewood.com. Smaller and more relaxed than its massive neighbors, Homewood boasts some surprisingly good skiing with unbeatable views of the lake

Tahoe City (daily 9am–5pm; ☏1-888/824-6348, ⊛www.gotahoenorth.com), is the best bet for information on the North Shore region. Finally, the **Incline Village/Crystal Bay Visitors Bureau**, 969 Tahoe Blvd (Mon–Fri 8am–5pm, Sat & Sun 10am–4pm; ☏1-800/468-2463, ⊛www.gotahoenorth.com), is on the Nevada side of the north lake.

Getting around

BlueGo **buses** (☏530/541-7149, ⊛www.bluego.org) run 24 hours a day all over the South Lake Tahoe area, and will take you anywhere within a ten-mile radius for a flat $2 fare ($5 buys you an all-day pass); the company runs trolleys for the same fares in summer. In the north, TART buses (roughly 6am–6pm; $1.75 flat fare, $3.50 all-day pass; ☏1-800/736-6365, ⊛www.laketahoetransit.com) run between Sugar Pine Point and Incline Village, with a branch route from Tahoe City up to Truckee. In addition, the Tahoe Trolley (same contacts and fares as TART) runs between Tahoe City and Crystal Bay (6am–6pm), and also between Sugar Pine Point and Emerald Bay (9am–6pm); on summer evenings there's a free service between Squaw Valley and Incline Village (6pm–midnight), with a short extra route between Sunnyside and Crystal Bay (7–10.30pm).

Car rental, starting at about $30 a day, is available through the Stateline outlets of most national chains (see p.32). You could also **rent a bicycle** for around $25–40 a day from any of over a dozen lakeside shops in South Lake Tahoe – some of them offering a full range of **sports equipment rentals** – such as the Mountain Sports Center, Hwy-89 near the "Y" junction, Lakeview Sports, 3131 S Lake Blvd, or the welter of outlets lining Ski Run Boulevard on the way to Heavenly.

and reasonable prices. Offers good beginner packages which include equipment rental, a lesson and lift ticket.

Kirkwood Ski Resort South of Lake Tahoe on Hwy-88 ☏1-877/547-5966, ⊛www .kirkwood.com. Kirkwood manages to escape the overdeveloped feel of many of the Tahoe resorts while still providing some amazing skiing.

Squaw Valley USA Squaw Valley Road, between Truckee and Tahoe City ☏1-800/403-0206, ⊛www.squaw.com. Thirty-one lifts service over 4000 acres of unbeatable terrain at the site of the 1960 Winter Olympics. Non-skiers can take the cable car ($24) and use the ice-skating/swimming pool complex for minimal extra cost.

Sugar Bowl Ten miles west of Truckee at the Soda Springs–Norden exit ☏530/426-9000, ⊛www.sugarbowl.com. The closest ski area to San Francisco has ten lifts and newly expanded terrain. Inexplicably, this excellent mountain is often less crowded than others in the area.

Cross-country skiing

Kirkwood Cross Country Center South of Lake Tahoe on Hwy-88 ☏209/258-7248, ⊛www.kirkwood.com. More than fifty miles of groomed track and skating lanes for cross-country enthusiasts.

Royal Gorge Soda Springs, 10 miles west of Truckee ☏1-800/500-3871, ⊛www .royalgorge.com. The largest and best of Tahoe's cross-country resorts has 204 miles of groomed trails. Good midweek discounts.

Spooner Lake In Nevada at the intersection of US-50 and Hwy-28 ☏775/749-5349, ⊛www.spoonerlake.com. The closest cross-country resort to South Lake Tahoe has lake views and over 50 miles of groomed trails.

Hiking, biking and camping around Lake Tahoe

Of the many wonderful hikes in the Lake Tahoe area, only one – the 150-mile **Tahoe Rim Trail** – makes the circuit of the lake, some of it on the **Pacific Crest Trail**, which follows the Sierra ridge from Canada to the Mexican border. Most people tackle only a tiny section of it, such as **Kingsbury Grade** to **Big Meadows** (22 miles), starting off Hwy-207 northwest of South Lake Tahoe and finishing on US-50, south of the lake.

Along the western side of the lake, the Tahoe Rim Trail follows the Pacific Crest Trail through the glaciated valleys and granite peaks of the **Desolation Wilderness**. Here, **wilderness permits** ($5) are required by all users, though for day-users these are self-issued. For overnighters, a quota system operates in summer: fifty percent of these are first-come-first-served on the day of entry from the Forest Service visitor centre; the remainder can be reserved up to ninety days in advance (℡530/644-6048). Among the most strenuous trails here is the five-mile Bayview Trail to Fontanillis Lake. The other wilderness areas around Tahoe – Granite Chief to the northwest and Mount Rose to the northeast – are used much less and consequently no wilderness permits are needed, though campfire permits are.

There are also many **mountain-biking** trails around the lake: **Meiss County**, between Hwy-89 and Hwy-88 twenty miles south of South Lake Tahoe, is a favoured area, where several beautiful lakes that escape most tourist itineraries are located. **Fallen Leaf Lake**, **Echo Lakes**, and **Angora Lake** are all pleasant, somewhat remote alternatives to the big T. Biking trails near the south shore include the three-mile loop of the **Pope-Baldwin Trail**, and you can pick up the popular **Marlett Lake/Flume Trail** in the Nevada State Park.

Ask at the **US Forest Service Visitor Center**, 870 Emerald Bay Rd (summer daily 8am–5.30pm; ℡530/543-2674, ⓦwww.fs.fed.us/r5), three miles northwest of the junction where Hwy-89 and US-50 separate to the west and east of the lake, for recommendations, free maps and brochures on the entire area.

Camping

For overall range and quality of facilities, Lake Tahoe's best **campground** is *Campground by the Lake*, on the lakeshore three miles west of Stateline (℡530/542-6096; $26–36). Other South Shore sites include *Fallen Leaf* (℡530/544-0426, reserve through NRRS ℡1-877/444-6777, ⓦwww.reserveusa.com; $28) and *Eagle Point* (℡530/541-3030, reserve on ℡1-800/444-7275, ⓦwww.parks.ca.gov; $25), which is in Emerald Bay State Park. Details for sites at the *Camp Richardson* and *Zephyr Cove* resorts can be found in the accommodation listings on opposite. North Shore has several sites within striking distance of Tahoe City, including the nicely located *Tahoe State Recreation Area* (℡530/583-3074, reserve on ℡1-800/444-7275, ⓦwww.parks.ca.gov; $35), right in the centre and just as crowded as you would expect. A mile and a half east, *Lake Forest* (℡530/583-3796; $15) is cheaper, though further from the beach and cannot be reserved, and two miles southwest along Hwy-89 there's the large *William Kent* site (℡530/583-3642, reserve through NRRS ℡1-877/444-6777; $23). Halfway down the west shore, *Sugar Pine Point* (℡530/525-7982, reserve on ℡1-800/444-7275, ⓦwww.parks.ca.gov; $25) has lovely sites in thick pine forest.

On North Lake Boulevard in Tahoe City, try Olympic Bike Shop, no. 620, or The Back Country, no. 255.

Accommodation

Most of the hundred or so **motels** that circle the lake are collected together along US-50 in South Lake Tahoe. During the week, except in summer, many have bargain rates, from around $45 for a double; however, these rates can more than double on weekends or in summer. Bear in mind the price codes below are based on the lowest high-season rates. Don't expect great deals at the **casinos**; there are fewer than in Las Vegas or Reno, and the casino hotels charge whatever the busy market will bear. If you're having trouble finding a room, try the tourist offices listed on p.584.

Tahoe City lacks the range and competition of its southerly neighbour, South Lake Tahoe, so you can expect to pay slightly more for a room there, although the reprieve from the bustle may just make the extra cost worth it if you're looking for peace and quiet. There are also a few other pleasant options dotted around the lake. **Camping** (see box, p.586) is only an option during summer.

South Shore

Big Pines Mountain House 4083 Cedar Ave, South Lake Tahoe ☎1-800/288-4083, ⓦwww.thebig pines.com. Only a few blocks from the beach and Heavenly Village, this pleasant wooded hotel offers 70 comfortable rooms and a swimming pool. ❶

Camp Richardson Resort Hwy-89 between Emerald Bay and South Lake Tahoe ☎1-800/544-1801, ⓦwww.camprichardson.com. Hotel-style rooms and comfortable cabins with full kitchens on a 150-acre resort that also has campsites from $35. In summer, cabins are available by the week only. ❸

Harveys Lake Tahoe US-50, Stateline, Nevada ☎1-800/648-3353, ⓦwww.harrahs.com. Deluxe casino and resort; the best rooms overlook the lake. Packages include buffet brunches and spa discounts. ❻

Inn by the Lake 3300 Lake Tahoe Blvd, South Lake Tahoe ☎1-800/877-1466, ⓦwww.innbythel ake.com. Nicely furnished rooms, a heated swimming pool and jacuzzi and use of bicycles render this relaxing spot good value for money. Free shuttle bus to the casinos. ❺

Paradice Motel 953 Park Ave, South Lake Tahoe ☎530/544-6800, ⓦwww.paradicemoteltahoe .com. The play on words in the name of this "boutique" motel indicates its proximity to the Stateline casinos, yet the street is quiet and the rooms a cut above the usual. There are four larger suites too. ❹

Pine Cone Acre 735 Emerald Bay Rd, between Emerald Bay and South Lake Tahoe ☎530/541-0375. Set in wooded grounds with a quieter location than most, the pleasant Pine Cone Acre offers a fridge and microwave in each room. ❸

Sorensen's 14255 Hwy-88, Hope Valley ☎1-800/423-9949, ⓦwww.sorensensresort .com. Enveloped by the aspens of Hope Valley, about a half-hour drive away from South Shore on the west fork of the Carson River, Sorensen's features kitsch and cozy cabins with a Bavarian ski-lodge theme. ❹

Zephyr Cove Resort 760 US-50, Zephyr Cove, Nevada ☎1-800/238-2463, ⓦwww.zephyrcove .com. Run by the same management as the MS Dixie II (see p.588), its deluxe lodge rooms and lakeside cabins are away from the hubbub in a quiet, pine-clad nook. Also has expensive (around $60) RV sites. ❼

North Shore

Ferrari's Crown Motel 8200 N Lake Blvd, Kings Beach ☎1-800/645-2260, ⓦwww.tahoecrown .com. Relatively smart budget motel right by the lake, though you'll pay double for a room with a view. ❸

Lake of the Sky Motor Inn 955 N Lake Blvd, Tahoe City ☎530/583-3305, ⓦwww .lakeoftheskyinn.com. Better value than the slightly more expensive Tahoe City Inn opposite, with greater comfort and more pleasant decor. ❹

Parkside Inn at Incline 1003 Tahoe Blvd, Incline Village ☎1-800/824-6391, ⓦwww.innatincline .com. Nestled in a secluded forest setting, with private beach access, indoor pool, spa and sauna. ❸

Pepper Tree Inn 645 N Lake Blvd, Tahoe City ☎1-800/624-8580, ⓦwww.peppertreetahoe.com. Heated pool and standard hotel accommodation in an otherwise rather characterless high-rise. ❸

Resort at Squaw Creek 400 Squaw Creek Rd, Olympic Valley ☎1-800/327-3353, ⓦwww .squawcreek.com. The area's most lavish resort with sweeping mountain views and luxurious accommodations, though rather a stilted atmosphere. There's a golf course, private ski-lift and shopping mall thrown in too. ❽

River Ranch Lodge Hwy-89 at Alpine Meadows Road, Alpine Meadows ☎1-800/535-9900, ⓦwww.riverranchlodge.com. Historic and casual lodge on the Truckee River with one of the lake's best restaurants (see p.591); the cheapest rooms are right above the dining room. ❸

Sunnyside 1850 W Lake Blvd, 1 mile south of Tahoe City ☎1-800/822-2754, ⓦwww .sunnysideresort.com. Large, comfortable mountain lodge right on the lakeshore. Unbeatable views of the lake from many rooms and a popular restaurant and cocktail deck on the ground floor. ⑤

Tahoma Meadows Cottages 6821 W Lake Blvd, Tahoma ☎1-866/525-1553, ⓦwww.tahoma meadows.com. Well-furnished and homely cottages in a lovely setting on the west shore, seven miles south of Tahoe City. ③

Tamarack Lodge 2311 N Lake Blvd, 1 mile northeast of Tahoe City ☎1-888/824-6323, ⓦwww.tamarackattahoe.com. Nestled on a pleasant wooded knoll, you'll get more for your money at this comfortable and clean lodging than almost anywhere else on the lake. Some larger cabins too. ②

South Lake Tahoe and Stateline

Almost all of Tahoe's lakeshore is developed in some way or another, but nowhere is it as concentrated and overbearing as at the contiguous settlements of **South Lake Tahoe** and **Stateline**. The latter is compact, a clutch of gambling houses huddled, as you might expect, along the Nevada–California border. The half-dozen or so casinos compete for the attentions of tourists, almost all of whom base themselves in the much larger South Lake Tahoe on the California side. This is the best place to organize one of the many **outdoor activities** the lake has to offer. Power-boating, waterskiing, surfing, parasailing, scuba diving, canoeing and mountain biking are just a few of the options on the menus of local equipment-rental offices (see p.585). If you happen to lose your holiday allowance at the tables and slot machines, you can always explore the beautiful hiking trails, parks and beaches that adorn the surrounding area.

Though many stretches of the route around Lake Tahoe are stunning, the entire 72-mile **drive** is perhaps not the most beautiful in America, as at least one locally produced brochure touts. Another way to see the lake is to take a paddlewheel **boat cruise** on the MS *Dixie II* from Zephyr Cove, reached on a free shuttle from South Lake Tahoe, or *Tahoe Queen* from Ski Run Marina in South Lake Tahoe itself (timetable varies; $39–75; ☎775/589-4906, ⓦwww.zephyrcove.com); the more expensive cruises include dinner. Even more impressive is the view of the lake from above, in one of the neighbouring ski resort's **aerial trams**; the most convenient and popular is the Gondola at Heavenly (see p.584), which runs from a smart terminal only a couple of blocks from Stateline. Finally, in bad weather you can always visit the modest **Lake Tahoe Historical Museum**, next to the visitor centre at 3058 US-50 (summer Wed–Mon 11am–3pm; winter Fri & Sat 11am–3pm; free; ☎530/541-5458, ⓦwww.laketahoemuseum.org), which has a small collection of local artefacts and historical displays.

West around the lake

In summer, many enjoyable music and arts events take place at the **Tallac Historic Site** (mid-June to mid-Sept daily dawn–dusk; prices vary; ☎530/544-7383, ⓦwww.tahoeheritage.org), beside Hwy-89 on the western side of the lake just northwest of the "Y" (where Hwy-89 and US-50 separate to the west and east). Even when there's nothing special going on, the site's sumptuous wooden homes – constructed by wealthy San Franciscans as lakeside vacation retreats in the late 1800s – are well worth a look. You can also see the remains of the lavish casino-hotel erected by Elias "Lucky" Baldwin, which brought the rich and famous to Lake Tahoe's shores until it was destroyed by fire in 1914. Inside the former Baldwin house, the **Tallac Museum** (daily 10am–4pm; free) records the family's impact on the region.

The prettiest part of the lake, however, is along the southwest shore, where **Emerald Bay State Park**, ten miles from South Lake Tahoe (daily 8am–dusk; $7–8 per vehicle), surrounds a narrow, rock-strewn inlet. In the park, at the end of a steep, mile-long trail from the parking lot, is **Vikingsholm**, an authentic reproduction of a Viking castle built as a summer home in 1929 and open for half-hourly **tours** (summer daily 10am–4pm; $5). A short way out in the bay, diminutive **Fanette**, Lake Tahoe's only island, pokes pine-clad above the water. Its only structure is the defunct 1929 teahouse built by Vikingsholm's original owner, Lara Knight. From Vikingsholm, the stunning **Rubicon Trail** runs two miles north along the lakeside to **Rubicon Bay**, flanked by other grand old mansions dating from the days when Lake Tahoe was accessible only to the most well-heeled of travellers. You can also drive here on Hwy-89 and enter through the **D.L. Bliss State Park** (daily 8am–dusk; very limited parking $8), just to the north. Less than five miles further north, thickly pined **Ed Z'berg Sugar Pine Point State Park** (daily 8am–dusk; $8 per vehicle) offers more lakeside relaxation and has one of only two year-round campgrounds (see box, p.586) in the area. It also attracts crowds to see the vast **Hellman-Ehrman Mansion** (guided tours daily 10am–3pm on the hour; $5), decorated in a happy blend of 1930s opulence and backcountry rustic, and surrounded by extensive lakefront grounds.

Kirkwood and Grover Hot Springs State Park

About two dozen miles southwest of Tahoe, a dozen west of where Hwy-89 joins Hwy-88, **Kirkwood** is home to a popular ski resort (see box, p.585) and is a destination in its own right, with plenty of **outdoor recreation** possibilities without all the Tahoe hype. Stop by the adventure centre in Kirkwood Village (Mon–Fri 9am–5pm, Sat & Sun 9am–6pm; ℗209/258-6000) for information on accommodation, equipment rental and hiking in the surrounding area, which holds nearly a dozen lakes, such as Winnemucca and Woods. For **accommodation**, try the *Lodge at Kirkwood* in the village (℗1-800/967-7500, Ⓦwww.kirkwood.com; ❹).

A dozen miles southeast from the junction of Hwy-89 and Hwy-88 is **Markleeville**, a town of two hundred people on the Sierra crest. The major attraction here is the **Grover Hot Springs State Park**, four miles west (May to mid-Sept daily 9am–9pm; closed last two weeks in Sept; reduced hours in winter; $8 per vehicle, $5 pool use), with two concrete, spring-filled tubs – one hot, one tepid – in which the water appears yellow-green due to mineral deposits on the pool bottom. There's a **campground** on site for $35 per night (℗1-800/444-7275, Ⓦwww.parks.ca.gov).

Tahoe City and around

TAHOE CITY, on the north end of the lake, is less developed and more compact than South Lake Tahoe, and a close-knit population of permanent residents coupled with a family-oriented atmosphere give it a more relaxed, peaceful disposition. Still, you're never far from the tourist crowds who flock here all year long.

At the western end of town, Hwy-89 meets Hwy-28 at Fanny Bridge, named for the body part (posterior rather than anterior in American English) that greets drivers as people lean over the edge to view the giant trout in the **Truckee River**. Flow-regulating sluice gates at the mouth of the river are remotely controlled from Reno, but were once operated by a gatekeeper who lived in what is now the **Gatekeeper's Museum** (May to late Sept daily 11am–5pm; $3), containing a well-presented hotchpotch of artefacts from the nineteenth century, and a good collection of native basketware. Nearby, the **Truckee River Bike Trail** begins its three-mile waterside meander west to the *River Ranch Lodge* (see p.587), which is also the end of a popular river-rafting route. **Rafting** down the Truckee is the thing to do on warm summer days, though it's really more of a relaxing social affair than a serious or challenging adventure. Stop at one of the boat-rental stands along the river across from the Chevron station, or call Tahoe Whitewater Tours (half-day trip $68; ☎1-800/442-7238, Ⓦwww.gowhitewater.com) to book. On the lake itself, an even more relaxed excursion is a **cruise** with the *Tahoe Gal* ($28–35; ☎1-800/218-2464, Ⓦwww.tahoegal.com), leaving from the jetty at 850 N Lake Blvd.

A couple of miles south along Hwy-89, five hundred yards past the Kaspian picnic grounds, it's well worth **hiking** ten minutes up the unmarked trail to the top of **Eagle Rock** (see box, p.586, for more ambitious hiking suggestions). The amazing panoramic views that surround you as you look down on the expansive royal-blue lake make this one of the world's greatest picnic spots. Several miles further south along Hwy-89 is **Chamber's Beach**, a popular spot for sunning and **swimming** in summer.

You could also visit **Squaw Valley**, the site of the 1960 Winter Olympics, five miles west of Tahoe City off Hwy-89, although the original facilities (except the flame and the Olympic rings) are now swamped by the rampant development that has made this California's largest ski resort (see box, p.585). In the valley below, **hiking**, **horseriding** and **mountain biking** are all popular summertime activities.

East from Tahoe City are some unremarkable settlements but decent stretches of beach at **Tahoe Vista** and **King's Beach** on Carnelian Bay. As soon as you cross the Nevada state line from King's Beach into **Incline Village**, you're greeted by the predictable huddle of **casinos**, though they're not as numerous or in-your-face as at the south end of the lake. Consequently, the casual visitor might find having a flutter at the *Crystal Bay* or *Cal-Neva* somewhat less sordid and garish. Unfortunately the beaches here only open to guests at the casino hotels, but better swimming options are close at hand. Once you leave the buildings behind at the northeast corner of the lake and bear south, you enter one of the most appealing and quietest stretches. **Lake Tahoe Nevada State Park** boasts a great beach at **Sand Harbor** – though the water is always prohibitively cold – and has trails winding up through the backcountry to the Tahoe Rim Trail. Just south, **Secret Harbor** is an appropriate location for an idyllic nudist beach, where gawkers are not tolerated.

Eating and drinking

South Lake Tahoe has few exceptional **restaurants**; average burger-and-steak places, rustic in decor with raging fireplaces, are commonplace. Far better are the **buffets** at the Nevada **casinos** – *Harrah's*, for example, serves a wonderful, all-you-can-eat spread – though they're not as cheap as in Reno or Vegas. The casinos are also good places to **drink** and hold most of the region's **entertainment** options: low-budget Vegas-style revues, by and large. For its size, Tahoe City has a fair range of moderately priced restaurants as well as a couple of happening **bars**, all within a few minutes of each other.

South Shore

The Brewery at Lake Tahoe 3542 Lake Tahoe Blvd, South Lake Tahoe ☎530/544-2739. Microbrewery with decent ales ranging from pale to porter, including their signature Bad Ass, and food specials such as beer-steamed shrimp and quality steaks.

Dory's Oar and The Tudor Pub 1041 Fremont Ave, South Lake Tahoe ☎530/541-6603. Interesting combo establishment which offers international cuisine – burgers, tapas, Italian and British pub food – to suit all budgets, plus proper beer, of course.
El Papagayo Grill 3132 Lake Tahoe Blvd, South Lake Tahoe ☎530/577-3344. Inexpensive but

good-quality Mexican that includes some unusual vegetarian and even vegan items on the menu. Fine views from the upstairs deck.

Nephele's 1169 Ski Run Blvd, South Lake Tahoe ☎530/544-8130. Long-standing restaurant at the foot of the Heavenly ski resort, with a great selection of California cuisine: grilled meat, fish and pasta dishes cost $18–30.

Scusa! 1142 Ski Run Blvd ☎530/542-0100. Tastefully colourful decor and good service complement the fine seafood, meat and pasta at this well-respected Italian restaurant. Entrees $16–25.

Sprouts 3123 US-50 near Alameda Ave, South Lake Tahoe ☎530/541-6969. Almost, but not completely vegetarian, with excellent organic sandwiches, burritos and smoothies.

Taj Mahal 3838 Lake Tahoe Blvd, South Lake Tahoe ☎530/541-6495. Inexpensive North-Indian joint with a cheap daily eleven-item lunch buffet. Its lamb specialities for around $10 are the best choice.

Tep's Villa Roma 3450 Lake Tahoe Blvd, South Lake Tahoe ☎530/541-8227. South Shore institution serving up generous portions of hearty Italian food, including several simple yet superb vegetarian pasta dishes for about $10.

Womack's Texas Style Bar-B-Q 4041 Lake Tahoe Blvd, South Lake Tahoe ☎530/544-2268. The best place for finger-lickin' ribs, steaks and other southwestern favourites for $15–25. Decent bar too.

North Shore

Bridgetender Bar & Grill 30 W Lake Blvd, Tahoe City ☎530/583-3342. Friendly, rustic bar with good music, a fine range of beers and huge portions of ribs, burgers and more for $9–15.

Corkscrew's Wine & Cheese Bar 760 N Lake Blvd, Tahoe City. Hidden in Cobblestone Mall, this sleek little wine bar is an equally popular spot for summer evening or après-ski drinks.

Hacienda del Lago 760 N Lake Blvd, Tahoe City ☎530/583-0358. Tasty Mexican fare at moderate prices on the upper level of the Boatworks Mall; great lake views from the open deck. Margaritas and Latin or jazz music on many evenings.

Jasons' Beachside Grille 8338 N Lake Blvd, Kings Beach ☎530/546-3315. Classic American fare such as gourmet burgers for around $10, plus pricier seafood, pasta, a salad bar and great desserts. Outside deck with lake views.

Lakehouse Pizza & Eggschange 120 Grove St, Tahoe City ☎530/583-2222. In the Lakehouse Mall, Tahoe's best place for pizza is also a popular spot for cocktails on the lake at sundown. The second part of the name refers to the fine brekkies.

River Ranch Hwy-89 and Alpine Meadows Rd, Tahoe City ☎530/583-4264. Great curved dining room to maximize the Truckee River views and a deck in summer. A filet mignon will set you back $30 but the quality of the cuisine is a cut above the Tahoe average.

Soule Domain 9983 Cove Ave, King's Beach ☎530/546-7529. Typical Tahoe rustic elegance in unexpected surroundings. Lots of seafood and ethnic dishes, such as curried cashew chicken, plus other seafood and meaty delights for $20–30.

Spindleshanks 6873 N Lake Blvd, Tahoe Vista ☎530/546-2191. American bistro and wine bar, serving imaginative dishes like pan-roasted artichokes and chipotle lime-marinated brick chicken at reasonable prices.

Tahoe House Bakery 625 West Lake Blvd, Tahoe City. Family-style bakery with lots of deli items for picnics, such as gourmet salads and sauces. Popular with locals.

Yama Sushi and Robata Grill 950 North Lake Blvd, Tahoe City ☎530/583-9262. An excellent range of tempura, sushi and grilled *robata* dishes, all expertly prepared, makes this Lake Tahoe's top Japanese restaurant. Many items under $10.

Za's 395 North Lake Blvd, Tahoe City ☎530/583-1812. At the back of the friendly *Pete and Peter's* bar, this pizzeria also has a wide variety of pasta dishes.

Truckee and around

Just off I-80 along the main transcontinental Amtrak route, **TRUCKEE**, fifteen miles north of Lake Tahoe, makes a refreshing change from the tourist-dependent towns around the lake. A small town mostly lining the north bank of the Truckee River, it retains a fair amount of its late nineteenth-century wooden architecture along the main section of Donner Pass Road, which many locals still refer to as Commercial Row; some of it appeared as backdrop in Charlie Chaplin's *The Gold Rush*. Truckee is usually viewed as more of a stopover than a destination in its own right, with a livelihood dependent on the logging industry and the railroad. However, the town's rough, lively edge makes it as good a base as any from which to see the Lake Tahoe area.

Practicalities

Greyhound **buses** to and from San Francisco stop twice a day in Truckee, from where up to eleven daily TART buses (see p.585) continue on to Tahoe City. There's one daily Amtrak **train** in each direction from the station on Commercial Row in the middle of town. The **California Welcome Center** is at 10065 Donner Pass Rd (daily 9am–5.30pm; ℡530/587-2757, Ⓦwww.truckee.com), has all the usual brochures and maps, as well as friendly staff. In addition, where Hwy-89 branches north off I-80, an easy-to-miss **Forest Service Ranger Station** (Mon–Fri 8am–4.30pm; ℡530/587-3558) offers details of camping and hiking in the surrounding countryside.

Truckee's best **accommodation** deal is the *Truckee Hotel*, close to the train station at 10007 Bridge St (℡1-800/659-6921, Ⓦwww.truckeehotel.com; ❶), decked out in Victorian B&B style, with a fine restaurant; or the *River Street Inn*, a quaint brick-and-wood building at 10009 E River St (℡530/550-9290, Ⓦwww.riverstreetinntruckee.com; ❸). At the top of the range is the splendid alpine-style ⚡ *Cedar House Sport Hotel*, a few minutes' drive from Downtown at 10918 Brockway Rd (℡530/582-5655, Ⓦwww.cedarhousesporthotel.com; ❻). Several **campgrounds** with varying amenities line the Truckee River between the town and Lake Tahoe, off Hwy-89: the closest and largest is *Granite Flat* ($19–40), three miles from Truckee; others are *Goose Meadows* ($17–19), and *Silver Creek* ($17–19) five and nine miles south respectively (all three locations ℡530/587-3558).

Commercial Row has a number of good **eating** options, especially the diner-style *Coffee And...* at 10106 Donner Pass Rd, which is only open until 2pm. For cheap all-day meals, try *The Truckee Diner*, on the other side of the tracks at 10144 W River St, or *El Toro Bravo*, a decent taquería at 10186 Donner Pass Rd (℡530/587-3557). *Dragonfly*, 10118 Donner Pass Rd (℡530/587-0557), is a refreshingly modern place providing a mixture of slightly upmarket Pacific Rim, Southeast Asian and American cuisine on its rooftop terrace. For chocolate so good that you might consider hibernating here through a brutal Truckee winter, try the award-winning cappuccino truffles at Sweets, 10118 Donner Pass Rd. Though the old bucket-of-blood saloons of frontier lore are long gone, there are a few good places to stop for a **drink**, including the *Bar of America* (℡530/587-3110), at 10042 Donner Pass Rd, which has free live music most nights, or the *Past Time Club*, 10096 Donner Pass Rd (℡530/582-9219), the best spot for great live blues and jazz.

Donner Lake

Two miles west of Truckee, surrounded by alpine cliffs of silver-grey granite, **Donner Lake** was the site of one of the most gruesome and notorious tragedies of early California, when pioneers trapped by winter snows were forced to eat the bodies of their dead companions (see box opposite).

The horrific tale of the Donner party is recounted in some detail in the small **Emigrant Trail Museum** (daily: summer 9am–5pm; rest of year 9am–4pm; donation; ℡530/582-7892) – just off Donner Pass Road, three miles west of Truckee in **Donner Memorial State Park** (8am–sunset; $8 per vehicle) – which shows a re-enactment of the events in the hourly, 26-minute video that's so over-the-top most viewers will have a hard time choking back their chuckles. Outside, the **Pioneer Monument** stands on a plinth as high as the snow was deep that

The Donner party

The 91-member **Donner party**, named after one of the pioneer families among the group, set off for California in April 1846 from Illinois across the Great Plains, following a shortcut recommended by the first traveller's guide to the West Coast (the 1845 *Emigrant's Guide to California and Oregon*), which actually took three weeks longer than the established route. By October, they had reached what is now Reno and decided to rest a week to regain their strength for the arduous crossing of the Sierra Nevada mountains – a delay that proved fatal. When at last they set off, early snowfall blocked their route beyond Donner Lake, and the group was forced to stop and build crude shelters, hoping that the snow would melt and allow them to complete their crossing; it didn't, and they were stuck.

Within a month, the pioneers were running out of provisions, and a party of fifteen set out across the mountains to try to reach **Sutter's Fort** in Sacramento. They struggled through yet another storm and, a month later, two men and five women stumbled into the fort, having survived by eating the bodies of the men who had died. A rescue party set off from Sutter's Fort immediately, only to find more of the same: thirty or so half-crazed survivors, living off the meat of their fellow travellers.

fateful winter of 1846 – 22ft. From the museum, an easy nature trail winds through the forest past a memorial plaque marking the site where the majority of the Donner party built its simple cabins. Nearby, on the southeastern shore of the lake, there's a summer-only **campground** ($35; ☎1-800/444-7275, ⓦwww .parks.ca.gov). A number of more comfortable places to stay are strung along the northern side of the lake, most notably the luxurious ✦ *Donner Lake Village Resort*, 15695 Donner Pass Rd (☎1-800/979-0402, ⓦwww.donnerlakevillage.com; ❹), which has its own little marina and stretch of beach.

Above Donner Lake, the Southern Pacific Railroad tracks climb west over the **Donner Pass** through tunnels built by Chinese labourers during the nineteenth century – still one of the main rail routes across the Sierra Nevada. For much of the way, the tracks are protected from the usually heavy winter snow by a series of wooden sheds, which you can see from across the valley, where Donner Pass Road snakes up the steep cliffs. On well-signposted Hwy-40, there's a scenic overlook where you can get that prize-winning photo of Donner Lake and possibly a glimpse beyond to Tahoe. Further on, rock climbers from the nearby Alpine Skills Institute (☎530/426-9108, ⓦwww .alpineskills.com) can often be seen honing their talents on the 200-foot granite faces; the institute offers a variety of climbing and mountaineering courses and trips. At the crest, the road passes the Soda Springs, Sugar Bowl and Royal Gorge **ski areas** before rejoining I-80.

Into Nevada: Reno and around

On I-80 at the foot of the Sierra Nevada, thirty miles east of Truckee, **RENO, NEVADA** has plenty of bargain places to stay and eat, making it a reasonable stop-off, especially if you enjoy gambling. The town itself, apart from the stream of blazing casino neon, is not much to look at, having sprung up out of nowhere in the middle of the desert on the hopes that the gambling industry alone could sustain its existence. Nevertheless, its setting – with the snowcapped Sierra peaks as a distant backdrop and the Truckee River winding through – is nice enough and,

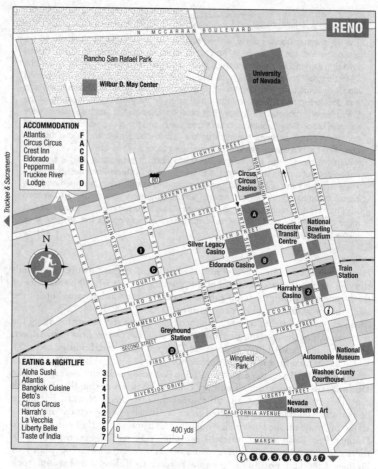

RENO

ACCOMMODATION
Atlantis	**F**
Circus Circus	**A**
Crest Inn	**C**
Eldorado	**B**
Peppermill	**E**
Truckee River Lodge	**D**

EATING & NIGHTLIFE
Aloha Sushi	**3**
Atlantis	**F**
Bangkok Cuisine	**4**
Beto's	**1**
Circus Circus	**A**
Harrah's	**2**
La Vecchia	**5**
Liberty Belle	**6**
Taste of India	**7**

0   400 yds

unlike Las Vegas, Reno maintains a small-town feel that residents are proud of. As the locals love to say – over and over again – Reno is the "biggest little town in the world". Even if you don't like to gamble, you can still pass a pleasant afternoon here ambling in the dry desert heat or visiting one of the mildly diverting museums. Reno also makes a decent base from which to visit Lake Tahoe, as well as the evocative mining towns of **Carson City** and **Virginia City**.

Arrival and information

Reno's Cannon International **Airport** (☎775/328-6400, Ⓦwww.renoairport .com) is served by most major domestic carriers. RTC bus #13 (6am–1am; $2 flat fare, $5 day-pass; ☎775/348-0480, Ⓦwww.rtcwashoe.com) makes the twenty-minute journey from the terminals to Reno's Downtown Citicenter transit centre, where you can connect to many of the company's other routes. Greyhound **buses** from San Francisco, via Sacramento and Truckee, and from LA, via the Owens Valley, use the terminal at 155 Stevenson St, also used by KT Services (☎775/945-2282), which operates a daily bus to Las Vegas and Phoenix.

The Amtrak *California Zephyr* **train** from Chicago stops in the centre of town at 135 Commercial Row.

The shiny modern **visitor centre** is located inside the Reno Town Mall at 4001 S Virginia St (Mon–Fri 8am–5pm; ☎1-800/367-7366, ⊛www.visitrenotahoe .com). On the sixteenth floor of 1 E 1st St, the **Chamber of Commerce** (Mon–Fri 9am–5pm; ☎775/337-3030, ⊛www.reno-sparkschamber.org) can also dish out advice and brochures.

Accommodation

Rock-bottom **accommodation** prices are plentiful midweek, at least outside the peak summer season, but if you arrive on a weekend you should book ahead and be prepared for rates to quadruple. This especially applies to the **casinos**, which often impose a two-night minimum weekend stay. You can also call the **Reno-Sparks Visitor and Convention Association**'s toll-free information and reservation line (☎1-800/367-7366) for help with finding a place to stay. **Camping** is an RV experience in Reno; for tent sites, head west to the numerous campgrounds around Lake Tahoe (see p.586).

Atlantis 3800 S Virginia St ☎1-800/723-6500, ⊛www.atlantiscasino.com. One of the newer casinos on the scene, it offers plusher amenities for the same rates as the older casinos in the centre of town, especially in its motor-lodge rooms. ❶

Circus Circus 500 N Sierra St ☎1-800/648-5010, ⊛www.circuscircusreno.com. One of the largest and tackiest casinos, with over 1600 popular rooms – check online for very low rates at slow times. ❶

Crest Inn 525 W 4th St ☎775/329-0808, ⓔcrestinn@aol.com. Simple, Downtown motel with few trimmings and rock-bottom prices. ❶

Eldorado 345 N Virginia St ☎1-800/777-5325, ⊛www.eldoradoreno.com. The nicer rooms are on the upper floors, while those lower down are cheaper in this bustling Downtown casino. Lots of online specials. ❶

Peppermill 2707 S Virginia St ☎1-866/821-9996, ⊛www.peppermillreno.com. Another large casino, slightly outside the centre of town; cushier than most, with special rates offered frequently. ❶

Truckee River Lodge 501 W 1st St ☎1-800/635-8950, ⊛www.truckeeriverlodge .com. Nonsmoking hotel near the river with an emphasis on recreation; it has its own fitness centre. ❷

The Town

It may lack the glitz and the glamour that make Vegas a global draw, but **Reno** is northern Nevada's number one **gambling** spot, offering a 24-hour diet of slot machines, blackjack, craps, keno, roulette and many more ways to win and lose a bundle. Gaming was only legalized in Nevada in 1931, but silver miners in Virginia City and Gold Hill regularly tried their hands at fortune's wheel back in the mid-nineteenth century, when a deck of cards was an almost mandatory part of a miner's kit. This tradition was revived with a vengeance when Reno came into being the following century.

The casinos

While nowhere near as grand as the Vegas gambling institutions, most of Reno's **casinos** still warrant a quick tour. If you can only handle visiting a couple, the best of the lot are: **Circus Circus**, 500 N Sierra St, where a small circus performs every half-hour, giving patrons a reason to look up from their dwindling savings; it runs seamlessly into **Silver Legacy**, whose main entrance is around the corner at 407 N Virginia St, revealing a planetarium-style dome with a makeshift 120-foot mining derrick underneath, appearing to draw silver ore out of the ground and spilling cascades of coins in the process. This is joined in turn with **Eldorado** and you can quite unwittingly wander between all three; the other main attraction for punters is **Harrah's**, a few blocks south at 219 N Center St, the classiest casino Downtown with row upon row of high-stakes slot machines and the occasional famous entertainer. If you want to compare these with one of the newer establishments further out, head south towards the brash opulence of **Peppermill** at 2707 S Virginia St. In order to learn more than you can glean from a solo jaunt through the casinos, contact the Reno–Tahoe Gaming Academy, 1313 S Virginia St (☎775/329-5665), for an overview of some of the rules of the major games followed by a behind-the-scenes **tour** of Reno's major gambling dens (hours vary; $10) – lessons are also available from $5.

The museums

Once you're ready to cash in all the casino clatter and any remaining chips for some peace and quiet, take refuge in one of Reno's many **museums**. The largest and most significant is the **National Automobile Museum** (The Harrah Collection), at Mill and Lake streets (Mon–Sat 9.30am–5.30pm, Sun 10am–4pm; $10), which holds the most comprehensive public display of automobiles in the western hemisphere. The sheer scale of the collection, with more than two hundred vintage and classic cars, some artfully arranged along re-created city streets of bygone decades, can't help but impress. The one time it's guaranteed to get crowded is during the Hot August Nites classic cars festival, when famous twentieth-century automobiles go on show. Those more into motifs than motors should take a look at the inventive contemporary exhibitions at the **Nevada Museum of Art**, 160 W Liberty St (Wed–Sun 10am–5pm, until 8pm on Thurs; $10).

You'll find Reno's most curious trove, however, at the **Wilbur D. May Center** (hours and prices vary; ☎775/785-5961, ⓦwww.maycenter.com), which sits on the edge of **Rancho San Rafael Park**, a mile north of Downtown Reno off North Sierra Street. The collection outlines the eventful life of Wilbur May (1898–1982) – a traveller, hunter, military aviator, cattle-breeder and heir to the May department store fortunes – with several rooms of furnishings, mounted animal heads and plunder from his trips to Africa and South America; the museum also houses temporary exhibitions. In summer only, the complex opens its **Great Basin Adventure** (hours vary; $8–12; ☎775/785-4319), where kids can pet animals, ride on ponies, shoot down a flume, and learn about Native Americans and dinosaurs.

Getting married (and divorced) in Reno

Many people come to Reno to get **married**, as it's so easy and inexpensive. If you decide to get hitched, you and your intended must be at least 18 years old and able to prove it, swear that you're not already married and appear before a judge at the **Washoe County Court** (daily 8am–midnight; ☎775/328-3275), south of the main casino district at South Virginia and Court streets, to obtain a **marriage licence** ($60). There is no waiting period or blood test required. Civil services are performed for an additional $50 at the **Commissioner for Civil Marriages**, 350 S Center Street (☎775/328-3461). If you want something a bit more special, however, **wedding chapels** all around the city will help you tie the knot, although they tend to be on the kitsch side. Arch of Reno at 155 N Virginia St (from $89; ☎775/786-6882, ⓦwww .archofreno.com) and the Silver Bells Wedding Chapel, further up at 628 N Virginia St (from $75; ☎1-800/221-9336, ⓦwww.silverbellsweddingchap.com), are two such places where you can get spliced with minimum fuss and cost. If it doesn't work out, you'll have to stay in Nevada for another six weeks before you can get a **divorce**.

On the other side of US-395, the **University of Nevada** campus hosts the **Nevada Historical Society**, 1650 N Virginia St (Wed–Sat 10am–5pm; $4), a museum full of items of local interest, especially Native American artefacts. Next door is the **Fleischmann Planetarium** (Mon & Tues 11am–5pm, Fri 11am–9pm, Sat 10am–9pm, Sun 10am–5pm; $10; ☎775/784-4811, ⓦwww.planetarium .unr.edu), where, among the telescopes and solar system galleries, OMNIMAX-style films (2–4 shows daily; $6) are projected onto a huge dome; the museum contains all four meteorites recovered in Nevada and impressive six-foot globes of Earth and the moon.

Eating and nightlife

All-you-can-eat casino buffets are the order of the day for tourists in Reno and seemingly everyone goes out and stuffs themselves to bursting. The buffets can be fun and of surprisingly good quality; the best are listed here along with locals' favourite alternatives, most of which are awkwardly spread over the south of the city. Tourists tend to stick to the shows in the casinos for **nightlife** but occasionally the city holds an art or music festival and the Pioneer Center for the Performing Arts at 100 S Virginia St (☎775/686-6610) is the regular spot for highbrow culture. Check Reno's free independent weekly *Reno News and Review* (ⓦwww.newsreview.com) for other listings. There are a number of **gay and lesbian bars** in town, including the popular *Patio Bar* at 600 W 5th St (☎775/323-6565).

Buffets

Atlantis 3800 S Virginia St ☎775/825-4700. Consistently and justifiably voted Best Buffet in Town by locals – well worth the extra couple of bucks. The casino also boasts the moderately priced *Café Alfresco* and more upscale *Seafood Steakhouse*, which has exceptional food, wine list and service.

Circus Circus 500 N Sierra St ☎1-800/648-5010. The place to go for a buffet meal if your budget is of greater concern than your stomach, with all-you-can-eat dinners for little over $10.

Harrah's 219 N Center St ☎775/786-3232. The most lavish Downtown casino buffet includes multiple entrees such as prime rib, crab legs, shrimp and a fine Asian section for around $15 most days. Their à la carte *Café Napa* is also recommended.

Restaurants

Aloha Sushi In the Mervyns shopping centre at 3338 Kietzke Lane ☎775/828-9611. A bit of a jump southeast from casino central, but reasonably priced and good. Try their speciality "Mountain" roll.

Bangkok Cuisine 55 Mt Rose St ☎775/322-0299. Cosy Thai family restaurant offering spicy dinners and filling lunch specials for around $7.

Beto's 575 W 5th St. Excellent and authentic self-service Mexican canteen, one of the best-value Downtown eateries outside of the casinos.

La Vecchia 3501 S Virginia St ☎775/322-7486. Relocated from its humble Downtown beginnings, this gourmet Italian restaurant offers several vegetarian choices as well as all the meaty favourites.

Liberty Belle Saloon & Restaurant 4250 S Virginia St ☎775/825-1776. Reasonably priced place famed for its prime rib with spinach salad and other meaty dishes. Established in 1958, it also houses a slot-machine collection and other memorabilia.

Taste of India 315 E Moana Lane ☎775/825-3008. Fresh, primarily Northern Indian specialities such as tandoori chicken and *palak* (spinach), plus a daily $8 lunch buffet.

Carson City

US-395 heads south from Reno along the jagged spires of the High Sierra past Mono Lake, Mount Whitney and Death Valley (see Chapter Four). Just thirty miles south of Reno, it briefly becomes Carson Street as it passes through **CARSON CITY**, the state capital of Nevada. It's small compared to Reno and despite the sprawling mess of fast-food joints, strip malls and car dealerships that surround its centre, it's well worth a visit, especially if you're interested in the history of mining. The city has a number of elegant buildings, excellent historical museums and a few world-weary casinos, populated mainly by old ladies.

Named, somewhat indirectly, after frontier explorer Kit Carson in 1858, Carson City is still redolent with Wild West history: you'll get a good introduction at the **Nevada State Museum & Mint** at 600 N Carson St (Wed–Sat 8.30am–4.30pm; $8). Housed in a sandstone structure built during the Civil War as the Carson Mint, the museum's exhibits deal with the geology and natural history of the Great Basin desert region, from prehistoric days up through the heyday of the 1860s, when the silver mines of the nearby Comstock Lode were at their peak. Amid the many guns and artefacts, the two best features of the museum are the reconstructed **Ghost Town** and a full-scale model of an **underground mine**, connected to the former by a tunnel and giving some sense of the cramped conditions in which miners worked. The **North Building** is home to the **Under One Sky** exhibition, featuring material about cowboys and Indians, natural history and children's interactive displays.

Four blocks from the museum, on the other side of Carson Street, the impressively restored **State Capitol**, 101 N Carson St (daily 8am–5pm; free), dating from 1871, merits a look for its stylish Neoclassical architecture and artefacts relating to Nevada's past, housed in an upper-storey room.

The **Nevada State Railway Museum**, 2180 S Carson St (Fri–Mon 8.30am–4.30pm; $5), a stone's throw from the visitor centre (see below), displays carefully restored locomotives and carriages, several of them from the long since defunct but fondly remembered Virginia & Truckee Railroad, founded in the nineteenth century.

Practicalities

Greyhound **buses** stop outside the Frontier Motel on North Carson Street. Amtrak Thruway services from Sacramento and South Lake Tahoe stop outside the Nugget casino at the junction of Robinson and Carson streets. For transport between Carson City and Reno airport, make an advance reservation with No Stress Express (around $40 one way; T1-800/426-5644, Wwww.nostressexpress.com). The **Convention and Visitors Bureau** is on the south side of town at 1900 S Carson St (Mon–Sat 9am–4pm, summer also Sun 9am–3pm; T1-800/638-2321, Wwww.visitcarson city.com); it sells the *Kit Carson Trail Map* ($2.50), a leaflet detailing a **walking tour** of the town, taking in the main museums, the state capitol and many of the fine 1870s Victorian wooden houses and churches on the west side.

There are a number of reasonably priced **motels** in town, among them the *Nugget Motel & Inn* at 651 N Stewart St (T1–800/933-5715, Wwww.nugget motel.com; ●), behind the Nugget casino, and the more colourful *Plaza Hotel*,

Mark Twain in Virginia City

A young writer named Samuel Clemens made his way to Virginia City in the 1860s with his older brother, who'd been appointed acting secretary to the governor of the Nevada Territory, to see what all the fuss was about. His descriptions of the wild life of the mining camp and of the desperately hard work men put in to get at the valuable ore were published years later under his adopted pseudonym, **Mark Twain**. Twain also spent some time in the declining Gold Rush towns of California's Mother Lode on the other side of the Sierra but his accounts of Virginia City life, collected in *Roughing It*, offer a hilarious eyewitness account of the hard-drinking life of the frontier miners.

801 S Carson St (℡1-888/227-1499, ⓦwww.carsoncityplaza.com; ❶), not far from the capitol building. A little further out is the plusher *Gold Dust West Casino* at 2171 US-50 (℡775/885-9000, ⓦwww.gdwcasino.com; ❷); as in Reno, prices rise at weekends but not by anything as much. If exploring Carson City gives you an appetite, **food choices** in town include *Heidi's Family Restaurant*, 1020 N Carson St, which serves generous American breakfasts and lunches, the basic *Howlin' Good BBQ & Grill*, 1701 N Carson St, or the rather more ambient *Firkin & Fox*, 310 S Carson St, which trades on its British pub style.

Virginia City

Much of the wealth on which Carson City – and indeed San Francisco – was built came from the silver mines of the Comstock Lode, a solid seam of pure silver discovered in 1859 underneath Mount Hamilton, fourteen miles east of Carson City off US-50. **VIRGINIA CITY** grew up on the steep slopes above the mines – the hard life of its miners was documented by a young Mark Twain (see box opposite) – and the town still exploits a rich vein, one which taps the pockets of tour parties bussed up here from Reno. But despite the camera-clicking throngs, there's a sense of authenticity to Virginia City missing from even the most evocative of the California mining towns. Perhaps it's the town's location, encircled by the barren Nevada Desert that so sharply contrasts with the diverse countryside of California's Gold Country, or perhaps it's the colourful advertisements that lure tourists to the many quirky museums. Whatever the reason, it's hard not to get caught up in the infectious Wild West atmosphere and stay longer than you'd intended. Still, not everyone who floods into town is here for the Gold Rush nostalgia – many visitors are here to frequent the **legal brothels**, another reminder of the town's frontier days.

Historic highlights include the **Mackay Mansion Museum**, 129 South D St (daily 10am–6pm; $5), a painstakingly preserved 1860s residence, and the **Nevada Gambling Museum**, 50 South C St (daily: April–Sept 10.30am–5pm; Oct–March 10.30am–4pm; $2), with its historic roulette wheel and other period game-room accessories. You can also poke your head into the **Bucket of Blood Saloon** at 1 South C St, which is delightfully crowded with period fixtures and crooked old furnishings. The mood of the era and current desire to cash in on it is summed up in **The Way It Was Museum**, 113 North C St (daily 10am–6pm; $3), with its collection of mining equipment, rare photos and maps, and fully stocked gift shop.

Practicalities

You can pick up a self-guided walking-tour map at the **Chamber of Commerce**, in the disused premises of the old *Crystal Bar Saloon* on the corner of Taylor and North C streets (daily 10am–5pm; ℡775/847-0311, ⓦwww.virginiacity-nv .org), or you can just as easily wander around and see the sights in your own time.

If you'd like to **stay in town**, there are a few decent options but no Reno-style resorts. The *Silver Queen*, at 28 North C St (℡775/847-0440; ❶), and *Comstock Lodge*, at 875 South C St (℡775/847-0233, ⓦwww.thecomstocklodge .com; ❶), are reasonable, if basic, options for spending the night on the main drag of an old boomtown. A 35-minute train ride on the **Virginia & Truckee Railroad** (late May to late Oct 10.30am–5pm; round-trip $9 diesel or $10 steam; ℡775/847-0380, ⓦwww.virginiatruckee.com) will take you from the depot at 370 F St a little over a mile up to the all-but-extinct town of **Gold Hill**, which consists primarily of the 🍴 *Gold Hill* hotel, restaurant and tavern (℡775/847-0111, ⓦwww.goldhillhotel.net; ❶). Nevada's oldest hotel, with good rates and atmosphere, it also lets out five more expensive lodges in ex-miners' houses around the tiny town. The railroad company also runs a ninety-minute route down to Carson City (round-trip $29 diesel, $48 steam).

Decent **dining** options include good Chinese cuisine at *Mandarin Garden*, 30 North B St (℡775/847-9288), whose outside deck affords great views, and cheaper bar food at the *Old Washoe Club*, 112 South C St, which claims to be the town's oldest saloon.

Genoa

South of Carson City in the Carson Valley lies another evocative Wild West scene, **GENOA**, the oldest town in Nevada. A good deal less stampeded by tourists than Virginia City, the main draw here is the curious **Mormon Station State Historic Park**, 2295 Main St (daily mid-May to mid-Oct 10am–4pm; $1), a replica of the original trading post and fort built on the site in 1851. To learn about walking tours in town, stop by the information counter in the **Genoa Courthouse Museum** at 2304 Main St (daily May–Oct 10am–4.30pm; $3; ℡775/782-4325). You can **stay** in comfort at the refurbished *Genoa Country Inn*, 2292 Main St (℡775/782-4500, ⓦwww.genoacountryinn.com; ➋), part of a complex mercifully built to blend in with the old architecture. Locals still congregate at the ⚥ *Genoa Bar & Saloon*, 2282 Main St, an atmospheric joint which claims to be Nevada's oldest continuously operating watering-hole, open for business since 1853.

Travel details

Trains

Reno to: Oakland/Emeryville (1 daily; 6hr 35min); Sacramento (1 daily; 5hr 40min); Truckee (1 daily; 1hr).
Sacramento to: Oakland/Emeryville (12–17 daily; 1hr 55min–3hr); Reno (1 daily; 5hr); Truckee (1 daily; 3hr 30min).

Buses

All buses are Greyhound unless otherwise stated.
Reno to: Las Vegas (2 daily; 18–20hr); Los Angeles (5 daily; 13–15hr); Sacramento

(5 daily; 2hr 40min–3hr 25min); San Francisco (5 daily; 5hr–6hr 45min).
Reno airport to: Stateline (10 daily South Tahoe Express; 1hr 30min).
Sacramento to: Los Angeles (8 daily; 7hr 20min–9hr 55min); Reno (5 daily; 2hr 40min–3hr 30min); San Francisco (7 daily; 2hr–2hr 45min); Truckee (2 daily; 2hr–2hr 40min).
South Lake Tahoe/Stateline to: Reno airport (10 daily South Tahoe Express; 1hr 30min).

Epicurean California

The rich diversity of California's food and wine holds many contradictions. Los Angeles is the land of protein bars, salads and the faddy diets of wannabe actresses but it's also known for its burgers and the innovative pizza of Wolfgang Puck. In the north, the San Francisco Bay Area spawned the state's signature California cuisine, a style of cooking that emphasizes the use of local, seasonal ingredients that is now the standard for fine dining in the US; it's also the birthplace of the modern-day burrito.

California cuisine

California cuisine got its start in Berkeley in the 1970s, when Alice Waters began preparing French recipes using the best local ingredients, adjusting the menu of her restaurant, *Chez Panisse* (see p.520), according to the seasons. LA's **Wolfgang Puck**, of the *Spago* restaurants and glitzy post-Oscar celebrity bashes, helped popularize the cuisine, and nowadays if you scan the day's menu at any fine California restaurant you might think you're reading a culinary sonnet to the state's myriad farms, as chefs colourfully chronicle the provenance of every morsel of pork and each artichoke leaf. Other celebrated California chefs include Michael Mina and Gary Danko (see p.478), both of whom have eponymous eateries in San Francisco, and Thomas Keller, whose *French Laundry* in Napa (see p.619) is widely considered the best restaurant in the country.

Spago, Beverly Hills ▲

Mel's Drive-In ▼

Burgers and fast food

What the Bay Area did for fine dining, Southern California did for the **hamburger**. The rise of this quintessentially American food is tied to the birth of car culture in 1940s LA, where the love of the automobile spawned a new type of restaurant, the **drive-in**. The world's most famous fast-food chain began in San Bernardino as a drive-in run by the McDonald brothers. Other California-born chains with roots in this era include *Jack in the Box*, *Taco Bell* and **In-N-Out**, the latter perhaps the most loved by Californians, who queue up to order fast food made from fresh ingredients – there are no microwaves or freezers, and you can watch nattily clad employees turn potatoes into fries right before your eyes.

The iconic *In-N-Out* ▼

A dash of spice

The burger aside, traditional California food draws inspiration from Latin America and Asia, hardly surprising considering the region's diverse population. The state also has its own style of Mexican cuisine, sometimes called **Cal-Mex**, which is lighter than the more commonly known Tex-Mex and incorporates plenty of veggies and seafood. In San Francisco, Cal-Mex is exemplified by large Mission-district burritos – bulging tortillas stuffed with rice, beans, zesty salsa and meat – whose style has become the norm at burrito chains across the US. In the south, the influence from Baja California is more prevalent, showing itself in fish tacos and crispy tostadas.

Excellent Asian restaurants, too, are dotted throughout LA and the Bay Area. LA boasts the country's best sushi and a surfeit of top-notch Korean, Thai and Vietnamese joints. The Bay Area also features delicious Chinese, Thai and Vietnamese, the latter particularly in San Jose, while South Asian restaurants continue to proliferate.

▲ Fish tacos

▼ Restaurant sign in LA's Chintatown

Seven of the best

▶▶ **A&W Root Beer Drive-in** A truly Californian experience; p.320.

▶▶ **Chez Panisse** Simply put, the home of California cuisine; p.520.

▶▶ **Iron Door Saloon** Classic Gold Rush-era bar; p.360.

▶▶ **The Little Chihuahua** Authentic and inexpensive Mexican; p.483.

▶▶ **Lost Coast Brewery** Superb microbrews, excellent food; p.642.

▶▶ **Pacific Dining Car** Classy, unique steakhouse; p.138.

▶▶ **Point Loma Seafoods** Marine delights beside the Pacific; p.195.

佳餚

Fruits of the vine

California is by far the largest and most famous wine-producing state in the US and its vintners were the first among those of the New World to prove that great wine can be produced outside of Europe. In contrast to those of Europe, California wines are often bold and fruity, a natural result of the climate.

Napa is the state's best-known wine region, but it only represents about four percent of the state's wine production; regions like Sonoma, Santa Barbara and Santa Cruz have won reputations for their superb wines as well.

The grape harvest ▲

Napa Valley vineyard ▼

Major wine regions

▶▶ **Central Valley** Three quarters of California's grapes come from the state's flat, hot agricultural heartland, although most of these are produced by the world's two biggest wine concerns – Gallo and Constellation. The best grapes are grown near Lodi and Clarksburg, with the former known for its Zinfandel, the latter its Chenin Blanc.

▶▶ **Napa** To avoid the crowds, skip the big-name wineries on Rte-29 and cruise the leafy Silverado Trail, or head to cooler Carneros, an area known for its Pinot Noir and Chardonnay; p.606.

▶▶ **Sonoma** Sprawling Sonoma's Russian River Valley produces some of the state's finest Pinot Noir, while nearby Dry Creek Valley is known for its Sauvignon Blanc and Zinfandel; p.624.

▶▶ **South Central Coast** Santa Barbara's grapes were romanced in the popular wine flick *Sideways* and rightly so – Santa Maria and Santa Ynez produce delicious Pinot Noirs; p.375.

▶▶ **North Central Coast** Highlights are found among the smaller wineries in the Santa Cruz Mountains, where the most notable wines are Chardonnays and Cabernets.

9

Northern California

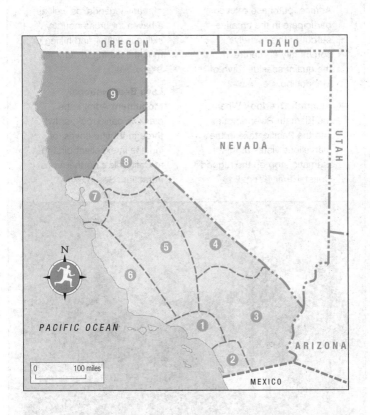

CHAPTER 9

Highlights

✳ **Russian River Valley wineries** Opportunities for leisurely wine-tasting against a glorious backdrop of vineyards and redwoods abound in this less commercialized part of Wine Country. See p.624

✳ **Mendocino Art Center** Admire, purchase or even participate in the creative output of this friendly community art centre in the quaint seaside town of Mendocino. See p.632

✳ **Klamath Overlook** Where the Klamath River empties into the Pacific, take in the marvellous vistas at this dramatic stop on the rugged Coastal Trail. See p.648

✳ **Lassen Volcanic National Park** Visit this top wilderness area to enjoy steaming geysers, high-altitude lakes, bracing walks and exhilarating campsites. See p.657

✳ **Mount Shasta** This huge volcanic peak is the subject of many legends, as well as a haven for cross-country skiing in winter and hiking or mountaineering in summer. See p.668

✳ **Lava Beds National Monument** Admire the black volcanic rock, crawl through tubular caves, or indulge in excellent birding at California's northernmost attraction. See p.675

▲ Mount Shasta

Northern California

The northern coast and interior of California covers around a third of the state, a gigantic area over three hundred and fifty miles long and two hundred wide, with a rugged rural landscape and an ethic far removed from the urban lifestyles to the south. It's a schizophrenic region of a schizophrenic state, coupling volcanoes with vineyards, fog-shrouded redwoods with scorched olive trees, loggers with environmentalists and legends of Bigfoot with movies of Ewoks. Northern Californians are tied to the land, and agriculture dominates the economy as well as the vistas. Deep-rooted forestry, fishing and cattle industries are also ever-present (even though the first two are in decline), along with the wild, crashing Pacific Coast and steady rain that supports a marijuana-growing region called the Emerald Triangle. Add only two major highways and the lack of a metropolis in favour of small, Main Street towns, and you have a region that has more in common with Oregon and Washington than Los Angeles or San Francisco. In that regard, Northern Californians have long rumbled about forming a state of their own. Indeed, in 1941 there was a proposal to form a state called Jefferson near Mount Shasta, an event that could have gained steam were it not for Japan's bombing of Pearl Harbor two days later, channelling collective energies into the war.

Immediately north of the Bay Area, the **Wine Country** might be your first – indeed your only – taste of Northern California, though it's by no means typical. The two valleys of **Napa** and **Sonoma** unfold along thirty miles of rolling hills and premium real estate, home to the California wine barons and San Franciscan weekenders wanting to escape in style. Napa is the reigning king of indulgence and high-calibre vintages, while Sonoma caters to a funkier set, with its interesting history and outdoor tours. The northwest corner of Sonoma County is the Wine Country's other "grape escape", an area of six varieties and resorts clustered around the **Russian River** and its tributaries. Further north and towards the coast, the **Anderson Valley** in Mendocino County holds another haven for vineyards. **Clear Lake**, to the north of the Wine Country, can also be included in a longer itinerary.

It's the **northern coast** which provides the most appealing, and slowest, route through the region, beginning just north of Marin County and continuing for three hundred miles on Hwy-1 and US-101 along rugged bluffs and through dense forests as far as the Oregon border. The landscape varies little at first, but given time reveals tangible shifts from the flat oyster beds of **Sonoma County**, to the seal and surfer breeding grounds around the coastal elegance of **Mendocino**, and to the big logging country further north in **Humboldt**. Trees are the main attraction up here: some thousands of years old and hundreds of feet high, dominating a very sparsely populated landscape swathed in swirling mists. In

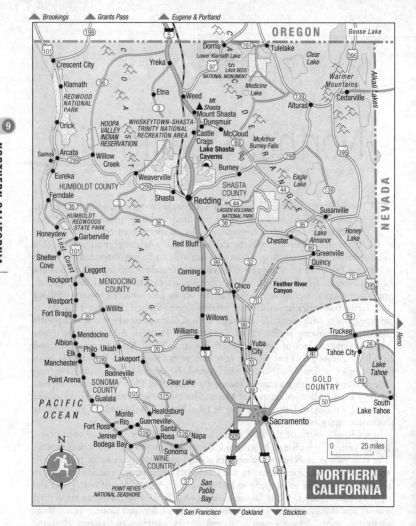

NORTHERN
CALIFORNIA

summer, areas like **Redwood National Park**, stretching into the most northerly **Del Norte County**, teem with campers and hikers but out of season they can provide idyllic experiences and an opportunity to coexist with the area's woodland creatures – including, legend has it, Bigfoot. Although the nightlife is rarely swinging in these parts, **Eureka**, the coast's largest urban area, and neighbouring college town of **Arcata**, towards the top end of the northern coast, make lively refuges when the great outdoors begins to pall.

The **interior** is more remote still, an enchanting land whose mystery and sheer physical enormity can't help but leave a lasting impression. I-5 neatly divides the region, cutting through the forgettable Sacramento Valley north to the **Shasta Cascades**, a mountainous area of isolated towns, massive lakes and a forbidding climate. In winter, much of this corner of the state is completely impassable, and the region's commercial activities are centred on the lower, warmer climes of the largest town and transport hub of **Redding**. Now boasting an excellent museum and iconic new bridge, Redding is a major crossroads serving **Whiskeytown-Shasta-Trinity National Recreation Area**, **Lassen Volcanic National Park**, **McArthur-Burney Falls State Park** and, northward, the railroad towns in the shadows of towering **Mount Shasta**. Up at the top of the interior, the eerie, moonlike terrain of the **Lava Beds National Monument** rewards those who make the effort to get there, and the wetlands of the **Klamath Basin**, which straddles the Oregon border, are a must for birders. In the very northeast corner of the state, rugged **Modoc County** is another paradise for admirers of natural beauty.

Unlike the Wine Country and the coast, locals all over the Shasta Cascades are actually glad to see tourists, and visitor centres take the time to explain the many outdoor recreational options. Food and lodging costs are cheap by California standards and the efficient network of highways – by-products of the logging industry – makes travel easy. Parts of the region fill up in summer but given the sheer enormity of the forests and the plethora of lakes, waterfalls, parks and bird sanctuaries, escaping the masses and finding peace is easy enough. Out of season, you may feel like you're the only one here at all.

Some history

As with elsewhere in California, the first inhabitants of the north were **Native Americans**, whose past has been all but erased, leaving only the odd desolate reservation or crafts museum. Much later, the **Russians** figured briefly in the region's history, when they had a modest nineteenth-century settlement at Fort Ross on the coast, ostensibly to protect their interests in otter hunting and fur trading, though more likely to promote territorial claims. **Mexican** explorers and maintenance costs that exceeded revenues prevented them from extending their hunting activities further south and in the 1840s they sold the fort to the **Americans**. It was the discovery of **gold** just to the south in 1848 that really helped put the north on the map. Not a lot has happened since, although in the 1980s New Ageism triggered a kind of future for the region, with low land prices pulling more and more devotees up here to sample the delights of a landscape they see as rich in rural symbolism. Hollywood has also been drawn to the region, using the north as a cost-effective way to travel to another place and time. *Robin Hood*, *Gone With the Wind*, *The Birds*, *The Return of the Jedi* and *Jurassic Park: The Lost World* are just a few examples of movies filmed amid the frozen-in-time beauty. Over the last two decades the spiralling rise in Bay Area property prices

Getting around Northern California

While many people see the Wine Country as an isolated trip from San Francisco, it's also feasible to take in the area en route to the less manicured territory further north. **Public transport** is sparse all over Northern California and to enjoy the region you'll need to be independently mobile. Infrequent Greyhound **buses** run from San Francisco and Sacramento up and down I-5, stopping in Chico, Redding and Mount Shasta, and US-101, with halts in Garberville, Eureka and Arcata. The complication is that none of these routes solves the problem of actually getting around once you've arrived, making a **driving tour** the only sensible option. The Wine Country can be seen pretty comprehensively in a long weekend, while the rest of Northern California requires a week for just the sketchiest impression. Only the largest of the region's towns have any local bus service, although for some of the remoter spots you could, perhaps, consider an organized trip, notably Green Tortoise's one-week tours (see p.34).

has led to a small but steady movement of more mainstream folk and retirees into some areas, searching for better value for money or a spacious second home. Many diehard locals are fearful of this influx spoiling the coast, in particular, and property prices have been creeping up as far north as Mendocino, though the Coastal Commission tightly controls development and farmers have so far resisted selling out on a large scale.

The Wine Country

"The coldest winter I ever spent was summer in San Francisco," quipped Mark Twain. Like Twain, many visitors to San Francisco can't get over the daily fog and winds that chill even the most promising August day. For this reason, heading into the golden, arid and balmy **Napa and Sonoma valleys**, less than an hour's drive north of San Francisco, can feel like entering another country. Here, around thirty thousand acres of vineyards, feeding hundreds of wineries and their upscale patrons, make the area the heart of the American wine industry in reputation, if not in volume. In truth, less than five percent of California's wine comes from the region, but what it does produce is some of America's best.

Predictably, the region is also one of America's wealthiest and most provincial, a fact that draws – and repels – a steady stream of tourists. There seems to be a bed and breakfast or spa for every grape on the vine, and tourism is gaining on wine production as the Wine Country's leading industry. Expect clogged highways and full hotels during much of peak season (May–Oct), especially at weekends, as well as packed tastings in the more popular wineries.

However, there are two sides to the Napa and Sonoma valleys. One, of course, is its prominence for serious, quality **wine** experiences. Almost all of the region's many wineries offer tours and tastings, usually for a small charge (typically $5–15); this sometimes includes the wineglass and usually a credit towards the purchase of a bottle. Aside from the type and flavour of the drink, wineries all differ in what they offer visitors. Some delight oenologists by explaining the process of growing grapes, some excite kids with tractor rides through the vineyard and some please thirsty patrons with generous samples. The other side to the Wine Country is its **natural landscape**. Separated by the Mayacamas Mountains, the Napa and Sonoma valleys feature some of the most gently beautiful geography in the state, from the Valley of the Moon to Mount St Helena. Once you've tired of sipping, check out ballooning, biking, horseriding, hiking and myriad historical sights, including Spanish missions and Jack London's homestead.

Nothing comes cheap around **Napa** and the town itself can be quickly done with unless you want to board the over-hyped Wine Train. But many small towns further up the valley, particularly **St Helena**, have retained enough of their early twentieth-century-homestead character to be a welcome relief. **Calistoga**, at the top of the valley, is famous for its hot springs, massages and spas. On the western side of the dividing Mayacamas Mountains, the smaller backroad wineries of the Sonoma Valley reflect the down-to-earth nature of the place, which is more beautiful and less crowded than its easterly neighbour. The town of **Sonoma** itself

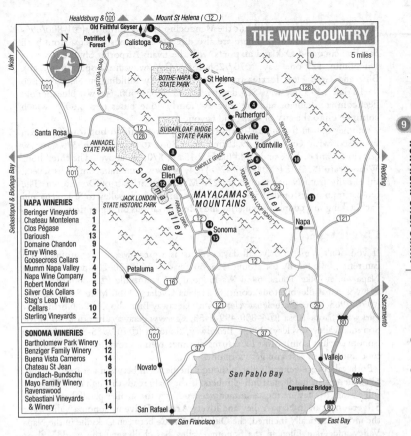

is by far the prettiest of the Wine Country communities, retaining a number of fine Mission-era structures around its gracious central plaza. **Santa Rosa**, at the north end of the valley, is the region's sole urban centre, handy for budget lodgings but otherwise unremarkable.

Arrival and getting around

The Wine Country region spreads north from the top of the San Francisco Bay in two parallel, thirty-mile-long valleys, **Napa and Sonoma**. As the Wine Country's attractions are spread over a fairly broad area, a **car** is pretty much essential. If you avoid the rush-hour traffic, it's about an hour's drive from San Francisco. Good highways ring the region, and a loop of the two valleys is conceivable in a day or so. Consider working against the flow of traffic by taking in Sonoma and Glen Ellen first, before crossing the Mayacamas by way of Santa Rosa and dropping into Calistoga, St Helena and Napa.

There are limited public **bus** options from Golden Gate Transit (☎707/541-2000, ⓦwww.goldengate.org), Greyhound (☎1-800/231-2222, ⓦwww.greyhound.com), Sonoma County Transit (☎1-800/345-7433, ⓦwww.sctransit.com), Napa Valley's Vine bus system (Mon–Sat; ☎1-800/696-6443,

Ⓦwww.nctpa.net/vine.cfm), and the Mendocino Transit Authority (Ⓣ1-800/696-4682, Ⓦwww.4mta.org). There are also direct connections to Napa from both San Francisco and Oakland **airports** with the Evans Airporter Shuttle (6 daily; 1hr 30min; $29 one way; Ⓣ707/255-1559, Ⓦwww.evanstransportation.com). Blue and Gold Fleet **ferries** travel from the Ferry Building in San Francisco (8–12 daily; $13 one way, $24 day-pass; Ⓣ415/705-5500, Ⓦwww.blueandgold fleet.com) to Vallejo, and are met by hourly Vine buses (see p.607), which continue on to the city of Napa and beyond.

Another option for the car-less is to sign up for a **guided bus tour** from San Francisco with Gray Line (9.15am; 9hr; $66; Ⓣ1-888/428-6937, Ⓦwww.grayline.com) or Blue and Gold (daily 9.15am; $70; see above). The three-hour **Wine Train** ($35–184; Ⓣ1-800/427-4124, Ⓦwww.winetrain.com) runs several times daily from Napa's station at 1275 McKinstry St, east of Downtown. The ten-car train of restored 1950s Pullman cars chugs up the valley to St Helena and back, taking in a couple of wineries and offering various dining options.

Cycling

If you don't want to drive all day, **cycling** is a great way to get around. You can rent a bike locally for around $25–60 per day and $120–200 per week from Napa Valley Bike Tours, 6488 Washington St, Yountville (Ⓣ1-800/707-2453, Ⓦwww.napavalleybiketours.com); St Helena Cyclery, 1156 Main St, St Helena (Ⓣ707/963-7736, Ⓦsthelenacyclery.com); Getaway Bike Shop, 2228 North Point Parkway, Santa Rosa (Ⓣ1-800/499-2453, Ⓦwww.getawayadventures.com); or Sonoma Valley Cyclery, 20091 Broadway, Sonoma (Ⓣ707/935-3377, Ⓦwww.sonomacyclery.com). Most local firms organize **tours**, providing bikes, helmets, food and vans in case you get worn out.

Both valleys are generally flat, although the peaks in between are steep enough to challenge the hardiest of hill-climbers. If the main roads through the valleys are full of cars, as they are most summer weekends, try the smaller parallel routes: the **Silverado Trail** in Napa Valley and lovely **Arnold Drive** in Sonoma Valley. For the more athletically inclined, the **Oakville Grade** between Oakville in the Napa Valley and Glen Ellen in the Sonoma Valley has challenged the world's finest riders. Check with the Santa Rosa Cycling Club (Ⓣ707/544-4803, Ⓦwww.srcc.com) for itineraries.

A bird's-eye view of the Wine Country

The most exciting way to see the region is on one of the widely touted **hot-air balloon rides**. These usually lift off at dawn and last sixty to ninety magical minutes, winding up with a champagne brunch. The most established of the operators is Napa Valley Balloons (Ⓣ1-800/253-2224, Ⓦnapavalleyballoons.com), who fly out of Yountville. Other options in Napa include the slightly cheaper Balloons Above the Valley (Ⓣ1-800/464-6824, Ⓦwww.balloonrides.com). The crunch comes when you realize the price – in the region of $200 a head whichever company you use – but it really is worth every cent. Make reservations a week in advance, especially in summer, though with the increasing number of balloon companies, same-day drop-bys are a possibility.

If it's thrills you're looking for, consider taking to the air in a World War II propeller **biplane**. Vintage Aircraft Company, 23982 Arnold Drive, Sonoma (Ⓣ707/938-2444, Ⓦwww.vintageaircraft.com), operates one- or two-person flights that take in both valleys. The basic choice is between the twenty-minute Scenic Flight ($175) and various forty-minute Explorer Flights ($295): add $50 to either for the extra thrill of some aerobatics.

Information

Not surprisingly for such a tourist-dependent area, the Wine Country has a well-developed network of **tourist information** outlets, though the rivalry between the two valleys makes it next to impossible to find out anything about Sonoma when you're in Napa, and vice versa. Both the **Napa Valley Visitors Bureau**, 1310 Napa Town Center off First Street in Downtown Napa (daily 9am–5pm; ☎707/226-7459, ⊛www.napavalley.com), and the **Sonoma Valley Visitors Bureau**, 453 1st St E at the centre of Sonoma Plaza (Mon–Sat 9am–5pm, Sun 10am–5pm; ☎707/996-1090, ⊛www.sonomavalley.com), should be able to tell you all you need to know about their respective areas; the smaller towns usually have a tourist office, too. If you're keen on touring the wineries, both the above places hand out basic free **maps** and sell more detailed ones ($3–5) giving the lowdown on the hundreds of producers.

Accommodation

Pricey **hotels** and **bed-and-breakfast inns** provide the bulk of the area's accommodation options, although there are some inexpensive **motels** in the more urban areas. During summer weekends, places are at a premium and prices can rise as much as fifty percent, so call ahead; from November to March, on the other hand, rates drop considerably, often by as much as half. In summer, the Sonoma Valley Visitors Bureau posts a daily list of available rooms in front of their Downtown office, and the Napa Valley Visitors Bureau can also help out (see above for both). Among the many other **accommodation services** are Bed and Breakfast Inns of Napa Valley (☎707/944-4444, ⊛www.bbinv.com), Napa Valley Reservations Unlimited (☎1-800/251-6272, ⊛www.napavalleyreservations .com) and the Bed and Breakfast Association of Sonoma Valley (☎1-800/969-4667, ⊛www.sonomabb.com).

Campers can find a pitch eight miles north of Sonoma at the Sugarloaf, Ridge State Park, 2605 Adobe Canyon Rd ($20; ☎707/833-5712), or outside Santa Rosa at the Spring Lake Regional Park, 391 Violetti Drive (May–Sept daily; Oct–April Sat & Sun; $19; ☎707/565-2267).

Napa Valley

Ambrose Bierce House 1515 Main St, St Helena ☎707/963-3003, ⊛www.ambrose biercehouse.com. Luxury accommodation in the 1872 house once inhabited by the misanthropic ghost-story writer after whom it is named. Breakfast is washed down with complimentary champagne. ❻

Calistoga Inn 1250 Lincoln Ave, Calistoga ☎707/942-4101, ⊛www.calistogainn.com. Comfortable double rooms (no twins), all with shared bathrooms, in a landmark building right on the main street, with its own restaurant and microbrewery. Good online midweek deals. ❷

Candlelight Inn 1045 Easum Drive, Napa ☎1-800/624-0395, ⊛www.candlelightinn.com. Spacious mock-Tudor mansion with a pool in its lovely grounds and luxurious interior, with rooms of varying sizes. Friendly and informal atmosphere, with free drinks and snacks. ❻

Discovery Inn 500 Silverado Trail, Napa ☎707/253-0892, ⊛www.napadiscoveryinn.com. This small motel-style place has adequately furnished modern rooms and is well placed a short drive south of Napa and the Silverado Trail wineries. ❷

Dr Wilkinson's Hot Springs 1507 Lincoln Ave, Calistoga ☎707/942-4102, ⊛www.drwilkinson .com. Legendary health spa and hotel Downtown. Choose from a variety of spacious, well-lit rooms with sparse furnishings, facing the courtyard or pool patio. TV and a/c. ❺

El Bonita Motel 195 Main St, St Helena ☎1-800/541-3284, ⊛www.elbonita.com. Old roadside motel lavishly done up in Art Deco style to suit its upmarket location, with a pool and hot tub.

Surrounded by a 2.5-acre garden, the rooms here contain microwaves and refrigerators. ❹

Garnett Creek Inn 1139 Lincoln Ave, Calistoga ☎707/942-9797, ⓦwww.garnettcreekinn.com. Gaily decorated old house at the Hwy-29 end of the main street, recently converted into a B&B and one of the best deals in this price code. Friendly and knowledgeable innkeeper. ❻

Harvest Inn 1 Main St, St Helena ☎1-800/950-8466, ⓦwww.harvestinn.com. English Tudor cottages at the edge of a vineyard. The place to stay if you can afford it, as the rooms ($329 and up) are huge and loaded with perks like a down-feather bed, fireplace and private terrace overlooking the garden or 14-acre vineyard. Also two outdoor heated pools, whirlpool spas and jogging/biking trails on site. ❾

Mount View Hotel and Spa 1457 Lincoln Ave, Calistoga ☎1-800/816-6877, ⓦwww.mountview hotel.com. Lively Art Deco-style hotel with spacious rooms and stylish cottages, featuring nightly jazz and a Cajun restaurant, *Catahoula*, on the ground floor. There's also a cottage with patio and hot tub from $329. ❻

🏃 **Oleander House** 7433 St Helena Hwy (Hwy-29), Yountville ☎1-800/788-0357, ⓦwww.oleander.com. Cosy and friendly B&B in a handy mid-valley location. Quiet enough despite being on the main road, which also keeps prices a tad lower. ❻

St Helena 1309 Main St, St Helena ☎707/963-4388, ⓦwww.hotelsthelena.net. Slightly claustrophobic (or cosy, depending on your mood) country-style hotel Downtown. European breakfast included. ❺

Travelodge Hotel & Suites 853 Coombs St, Napa ☎1-800/578-7878, ⓦwww.travelodge.com. Standard motel chain with several fancier suites featuring jacuzzis. Not especially great value but as cheap as it gets in Downtown Napa. ❸

Vintage Inn 6541 Washington St, Yountville ☎1-800/351-1133, ⓦwww.vintageinn.com. Huge luxury rooms from $340 in a modern hotel complex – all with fireplaces – plus swimming pool and free bike rental. Handy for Yountville's many fine restaurants, and great for romantic getaways, though drastically overpriced. ❾

The Wine Country Inn 1152 Lodi Lane, St Helena ☎707/963-7077, ⓦwww.winecountryinn.com. Patios, strolling gardens and a vineyard-side swimming pool distinguish this inn. The rooms are tasteful, uncluttered and furnished with antiques, and most come with fireplaces and start at $300. ❾

Sonoma Valley

Astro Motel 323 Santa Rosa Ave, Santa Rosa ☎707/545-8555, ⓦwww.sterba.com/astro. No frills at this Downtown Santa Rosa motel but some of the cheapest Wine Country rooms available. ❶

Cottage Inn & Spa 302 1st St E, Sonoma ☎1-800/944-1490, ⓦwww.cottageinnandspa.com. Owned by two interior designers, this tranquil, Downtown B&B comprises one room and six pricier suites, ranged around a relaxing courtyard with hot tub. ❼

Gaige House Inn 13540 Arnold Drive, Glen Ellen ☎1-800/935-0237, ⓦwww.jdvhotels.com. Beautifully restored Queen Anne farmhouse in a quiet and contemporary country setting. Unique, egg-shaped stone baths. ❼

Jack London Lodge 13740 Arnold Drive, Glen Ellen ☎707/938-8510, ⓦwww.jacklondonlodge.com. Modern motel near the Jack London State Park, with a good restaurant and pool. A smart place to try if Sonoma hotels are booked, or if you want a truly rural setting and fine stargazing. ❹

Kenwood Inn & Spa 10400 Sonoma Hwy, Kenwood ☎1-800/353-6966, ⓦwww.kenwoodinn.com. Deluxe, beautiful and secluded Italian-villa-style B&B with a fireplace in all suites – rooms range from $720 to over $1000 in high season. ❾

Swiss Hotel 18 W Spain St, Sonoma ☎707/938-2884, ⓦwww.swisshotelsonoma.com. A 90-year-old landmark building right on Sonoma's plaza, with a fine restaurant. The five rather small rooms have a view of either the garden patio or the plaza, and each comes with a four-poster queen-sized bed.

🏃 **Thistle Dew Inn** 171 W Spain St, Sonoma ☎1-800/382-7895, ⓦwww.thistledew.com. Sonoma's most raved-about B&B. Near Sonoma Plaza, it features five elegantly restored rooms, an amazing full breakfast and free bike rental. Some rooms come with a fireplace, private hot tub and patio. ❻

Napa Valley

A thirty-mile strip of gently landscaped corridors and lush hillsides, **NAPA VALLEY** looks more like southern France than a near-neighbour of the Pacific Ocean. In spring, the valley floor is covered with brilliant wildflowers that mellow into autumnal shades by grape-harvest time. Local Native Americans named the fish-rich river that flows through the valley "Napa", meaning "plenty"; the name was adopted by Spanish missionaries in the early nineteenth century but the natives themselves were soon wiped out. The few ranches the Spanish and Mexicans managed to establish were in turn taken over by Yankee traders, and by the 1850s, with California part of the US, the town of Napa was soon swallowed by the Gold Rush. Its location also made it a thriving river port, sending agricultural goods to San Francisco and serving as a supply point for farmers and ranchers. The opening of White Sulphur Springs in 1852, California's first mineral-springs resort, made Napa the vacation choice for San Francisco's elite. Settlers came, too, including Jacob Beringer in 1870. The rocky, well-drained soil he saw resembled that of his hometown of Mainz, Germany, and by 1875 he and his brother had established Beringer Vineyards, today America's oldest continually operating winery. Before long, Napa was bypassed by the railroads and unable to compete with other deepwater Bay Area ports, but the area's fine climate saved it from oblivion. The main route through the valley is Hwy-29, along which all the towns described here are strung, but for a quieter alternative route between Napa and Calistoga, the **Silverado Trail** to the east is highly recommended.

Napa, Yountville and Oakville

The town of **Napa** itself, at the southern end of the valley, is the anomaly of the region. The highway sprawl that greets travellers is fair warning to what the rest of this city of 60,000 has to offer: but for a proud courthouse and some intriguingly decrepit old warehouses along the Napa River, it's rather lacking in character. That said, Napa is worth a quick stop to visit the **Napa Valley Visitors Bureau** (see p.609). It's the most helpful in the whole valley and a good place to load up on free maps and brochures. Across the street, the Napa County Historical Society has free, informative materials on the region's pre-wine era. The only other minor attraction is the **Napa Firefighters Museum** at 1201 Main St (Wed–Sat 11am–4pm; free), which features an array of firefighting paraphernalia, or you might want to take in some culture at the attractive **Opera House** at 1030 Main St (T707/226-7372, Wnvoh.org).

Yountville, nine miles north on Hwy-29, is anchored by Vintage 1870, 6525 Washington St (daily 10.30am–5.30pm), a shopping complex in a converted winery that contains a range of touristic emporia. Aside from antique shops and a few restaurants, nothing in town exerts enough pull to merit a long stop, so push on three miles to tiny **Oakville**, further north along Hwy-29. Dominated by the massive Robert Mondavi winery (see box, p.613), Oakville features a dozen top-rated wineries, and almost all of them require an appointment and charge a tasting fee, ranging from around $10 to a whopping $25 for Opus One. Besides its high-calibre wines, Oakville is known for the wonderful Oakville Grocery at 7856 St Helena Hwy, an excellent deli packed with the finest local and imported foods.

St Helena

Eighteen miles from Napa and far more appealing, **St Helena** is the largest of all the antique-shop-filled villages you'll encounter heading north. Its main street, Hwy-29, is lined by some of the Wine Country's finest old buildings, many in pristine condition, and the town itself boasts some unlikely literary attractions. St Helena is also at the heart of a large concentration of wineries and this combination of history and location make it the de facto tourism capital of Napa Valley, home to a large concentration of luxurious lodgings and chic restaurants.

If you're driving through, at least stop off to see the quaint Craftsman-style homes that line residential **Oak Avenue**, and also to see remnants of two

Almost all of Napa Valley's **wineries** offer tastings, though not all have tours. There are more than three hundred wineries in all, producing wines of a very high standard, so your taste should ultimately determine the ones you visit. The following selections are some long-standing favourites, plus a few lesser-known hopefuls. Keep in mind that the intention is for you to get a sense of a winery's product, and perhaps buy some, rather than get tipsy, so don't expect more than a sip or two of any one sort – though some wineries do sell wines by the glass. If you want to buy a bottle, particularly from the larger producers, you can usually get it cheaper in supermarkets than at the wineries themselves, unless you ship in bulk.

Beringer Vineyards 2000 Main St, St Helena ℡707/963-7115, ⓦ www.beringer.com. Napa Valley's most famous piece of architecture, the gothic "Rhine House", modelled on the ancestral Rhine Valley home of Jacob Beringer, graces the cover of many a wine magazine. Expansive lawns and a grand tasting room, heavy on dark wood, make for a regal experience. Daily summer 10am–6pm, winter 10am–5pm. Tasting $15, tours $15–35.

Chateau Montelena 1429 Tubbs Lane, 2 miles north of Calistoga ℡707/942-9105, ⓦ www.montelena.com. Smaller but highly rated winery, nestled below Mount St Helena. The Cabernet Sauvignon in particular is acquiring a fine reputation. Daily 9.30am–4pm. Tasting $20.

Clos Pégase 1060 Dunaweal Lane, Calistoga ℡707/942-4981, ⓦ www.clospegase.com. A flamboyant upstart at the north end of the valley, this high-profile winery amalgamates fine wine and fine art, with a sculpture garden around buildings designed by postmodern architect Michael Graves. Daily 10.30am–5pm; free tours at 11.30am and 2pm. Tasting $10.

Darioush 4240 Silverado Trail, northeast of Napa ℡707/257-2345, ⓦ www.darioush.com. Grandiose new winery modelled on Persepolis and constructed with stone blocks imported by the owner from his native Iran. Cabernet Sauvignon and Shiraz are the signature wines. Daily 10.30am–5pm. Tasting $12–25, tours by appointment ($150–300).

Domaine Chandon 1 California Drive, Yountville ℡707/944-2280, ⓦ www.chandon.com. Sparkling wines from this progeny of France's Moët & Chandon can challenge the authentic French champagnes. Vast and modern, this winery and gallery is popular with connoisseurs and features a top-notch restaurant. Daily 10am–6pm; tours at 11.30am & 3pm. Tasting $18–25, tours $12.

Envy Wines 1170 Tubbs Lane, north of Calistoga ℡707/942-4677, ⓦ www.envywines.com. This friendly newcomer, a co-creation of veteran wine-maker Nils Venge and long-time wine collector Mark Carter of Eureka's *Carter House Inns* (see p.640), first bottled its produce as recently as 2007 but has already received awards. Sun–Thurs 10.30am–4.30pm, Fri & Sat 11am–5.30pm. Tasting $10 (waived with purchase).

unlikely past residents: Robert Louis Stevenson and Ambrose Bierce, both of whom lived in St Helena back in its days as a resort. The **Silverado Museum** (Tues–Sat noon–4pm; free), just off Main Street at 1490 Library Lane, has a collection of over eight thousand articles relating to Stevenson, who spent just under a year in the area, honeymooning and recovering from an illness (see p.615). It's claimed to be the second most extensive collection of Stevenson artefacts in the US, though the only thing of interest to any but the most obsessed fan is a scribbled-on manuscript of *Dr Jekyll and Mr Hyde*. The other half of the building is taken up by the **Napa Valley Wine Library** (same hours), a briefly entertaining barrage of photos and clippings relating to the development of local viticulture.

Goosecross Cellars 1119 State Lane, east of Yountville ℡1-800/276-9210, ⓦwww.goosecross.com. It's well worth taking time to locate this friendly family-run winery, tucked away off Yountville Cross Rd. Crush-time is fun and their Chardonnay especially good. Daily 10am–4.30pm. Tasting $5–10, tours by appointment ($20).

Mumm Napa Valley 8445 Silverado Trail, Rutherford ℡1-800/686-6272, ⓦwww.mummnapa.com. Opened in 1986 by G.H. Mumm, France's renowned champagne house, and Seagrams, the sparkling wines from this beautifully situated winery are good but superseded by sweeping views of the surrounding valleys. The tours are particularly engaging and fun, led by witty and informative guides. Daily 10am–4.45pm; free hourly tours 10am–3pm, on the hour. Tasting $6–25.

Napa Wine Company 7830-40 St Helena Hwy, Oakville ℡1-800/848-9630, ⓦwww.napawineco.com. Modelled on the co-operative wineries of France, the Napa Wine Company offers 25 small-vineyard owners access to state-of-the-art crushing and fermentation machinery, and also acts as a sales outlet for their vintages. Their tasting room is one of the best – and certainly the broadest – in Wine Country. Daily 10am–3.30pm. Tasting $10–25.

Robert Mondavi 7801 St Helena Hwy, Oakville ℡1-888/766-6328, ⓦwww.robertmondavi.com. Long the standard-bearer for Napa Valley wines ("Bob Red" and "Bob White" are house wines at many California restaurants), they have one of the most informative and least hard-sell tours. Tours and tasting daily 10am–5pm, reservations recommended. Tasting from $25, tours from $15.

Silver Oak Cellars 915 Oakville Cross Rd, Oakville ℡1-800/273-8809, ⓦwww.silveroak.com. Lovers of Cabernet Sauvignon mustn't miss a stop at Silver Oak, the crème de la crème of the heady red that costs over $100 a bottle in some San Francisco restaurants. Sadly, though, the original winery building burnt down in 2006. Mon–Sat 9am–5pm, Sun 11am–5pm; tours Mon–Sat 10am & 1pm, Sun 11am & 1pm. Tasting $20–40, tours $20.

Stag's Leap Wine Cellars 5766 Silverado Trail, east of Yountville ℡1-866/422-7523, ⓦwww.cask23.com. The winery that put Napa Valley on the international map by beating a bottle of Château Lafitte-Rothschild at a Paris tasting in 1976. Still quite highly rated. Daily 10am–4.30pm; tours by appointment 10.30am & 2pm. Tasting $15–30, tours $40.

Sterling Vineyards 1111 Dunaweal Lane, Calistoga ℡1-800/726-6136, ⓦwww.sterlingvineyards.com. Famous for the aerial tram ride that brings visitors up the 300-foot knoll to the tasting room, with a gorgeous view of Napa Valley. The extravagant white mansion, modelled after a monastery on the Greek island of Mykonos, is Napa's most recognizable. Tasting their wide selection of wines on the View Terrace is a memorable experience. Daily 10.30am–4.30pm; aerial tram, tasting, self-guided tour $25–40.

Calistoga and around

Beyond St Helena, towards the far northern end of the valley, the wineries become prettier and the traffic a little thinner. At the very tip of the valley, nestling at the foot of Mount St Helena, **CALISTOGA** is easily the most enjoyable Napa community, featuring around twenty wineries and some fancy bistros. The town, though, is better known for its mud baths and hot springs – and the mineral water that adorns every California supermarket shelf. Sam Brannan, a young Mormon entrepreneur who made a mint out of the Gold Rush, established a resort community here in 1860. In his groundbreaking speech he attempted to assert his desire to create the "Saratoga of California", modelled upon the Adirondack gem, but in the event got tongue-tied and coined the town's unique name.

Calistoga's main attraction, then as now, is the opportunity to soak in the soothing hot water that bubbles up here from deep in the earth. A multitude of **spas** and volcanic **mud baths**, together with a homely and health-conscious atmosphere, beckon city dwellers and tourists alike. The extravagant might enjoy *Dr Wilkinson's Hot Springs*, 1507 Lincoln Ave (baths from $77, treatments from $99; ☎707/942-4102, ⓦwww.drwilkinson.com), a legendary health spa and hotel whose heated mineral water and volcanic ash tension-relieving treatments have been overseen by the same family for almost fifty years. A number of slightly more down-to-earth establishments are spread along and off the mile-long main drag, Lincoln Avenue. *Golden Haven Hot Springs Spa and Resort*, 1713 Lake St (☎707/942-6793, ⓦwww.goldenhaven.com), for example, offers internet special one-hour mud baths from $49, $98 with a half-hour massage, making it a little cheaper than *Calistoga Spa*, 1006 Washington St (☎1-866/822-5772, ⓦwww.calistogaspa.com). If that's still too expensive, ask a local resident to spray you down with their garden hose – although even that might cost a few bucks given Calistoga water's restorative reputation.

Calistoga has one standard tourist attraction in the shape of the **Sharpsteen Museum and Sam Brannan Cottage**, 1113 Washington Street (daily 11am–4pm; $3 donation). Founded by long-serving Disney producer Ben Sharpsteen, the quaint little museum contains some of his personal effects, including his Oscar for the pearl-diving film *Ama Girls*, as well as a model of the original resort and lots of biographical material on Sam Brannan, plus a full-size re-creation of his cottage. In the same building you'll find the friendly **Chamber of Commerce** (Sun–Thurs 9am–5pm, Fri & Sat 9am–6pm; ☎1-866/306-5588, ⓦwww.calistogachamber.com).

Around Calistoga

Heading northwest out of town on Hwy-128 takes you up the ridge of the **Mayacamas**, a picturesque and steep drive that winds to the summit and spirals southwest, depositing you in Santa Rosa. More evidence of Calistoga's lively underground activity can be seen on this side of town at the **Old Faithful Geyser** (daily: summer 9am–6pm; winter 9am–5pm; $10), two miles north of town at 1299 Tubbs Lane, which spurts boiling water sixty feet into the air at nine- to forty-minute intervals, depending on the time of year. The water source was discovered during oil-drilling here in the 1920s, when search equipment struck a force estimated to be up to a thousand pounds per square foot; the equipment was blown away and, despite heroic efforts to control it, the geyser has continued to go off like clockwork ever since. Just south of the geyser, stylish Venetian artist Carlo Marchiori conducts weekly guided tours of his imaginatively decorated house, **Villa Ca'Toga** (May–Oct Sat 11am; $25). The Palladian villa is full of delicate whimsy – one room is painted as if you are a bird in a cage, another is adorned with painted cows – and the grounds secrete mock ruined temples, a Buddhist corner, and a shell-encrusted cave. An idea of his art can be gleaned, and tours arranged, through his gallery at 1206 Cedar St (☎707/942-3900, ⓦwww.catoga.com).

The **Petrified Forest** (daily: summer 9am–6pm; winter 9am–5pm; $10), five miles west of Calistoga, is a popular local tourist trap, but there's little worth stopping here for unless you're a geologist or really into hardened wood. After an entire redwood grove was toppled during an eruption of Mount St Helena some three million years ago, the forest here was petrified by the action of the silica-laden volcanic ash as it gradually seeped into the decomposing fibres of the uprooted trees. On Saturday at 11am, the docent-led Meadow Walk ($16) includes admission and a 75-minute tour.

Mount St Helena

The clearest sign of the local volcanic unrest is the massive conical mountain that marks the north end of the Napa Valley, **Mount St Helena**, some eight miles north of Calistoga. The 4343-foot summit is worth a climb for its great views – on a very clear day you can see Point Reyes and the Pacific Coast to the west, San Francisco to the south, the towering Sierra Nevada to the east and impressive Mount Shasta to the north. It is, however, a long steep climb (ten miles round-trip) and you need to set off early in the morning to enjoy it, well equipped with water and snacks.

The mountain and most of the surrounding land is protected and preserved as the **Robert Louis Stevenson Park** (daily 8am–sunset; free), though the connection is fairly weak: Stevenson spent his honeymoon here in 1880 in a bunkhouse with Fanny Osborne, recuperating from tuberculosis and exploring the valley – a plaque marks the spot where his bunkhouse once stood. Little else about the park's winding roads and dense shrub growth evokes its former notoriety, though it's a pretty enough place to take a break from the wineries and have a picnic. In Stevenson's novel, *Silverado Squatters*, he describes the highlight of the honeymoon as the day he managed to taste eighteen of local wine baron Jacob Schram's champagnes in one sitting. Quite an extravagance, especially considering that Schramsberg champagne is held in such high esteem that Richard Nixon took a few bottles with him when he went to visit Chairman Mao.

Sonoma Valley

On looks alone, the crescent-shaped **SONOMA VALLEY** beats Napa Valley hands down. This smaller, altogether more rustic stretch of land curves between oak-covered mountain ranges from the small town of **Sonoma** a few miles north along Hwy-12 to the hamlet of **Glen Ellen** and **Jack London State Park**, ending at the booming bedroom community of **Santa Rosa**. The area is known as the "Valley of the Moon", a label that's mined by tour operators for its connection to former resident Jack London, whose book of the same name retold a Native American legend about how, as you move through the valley, the moon seems to rise several times from behind the various peaks. The area has long been a favourite with visitors: Spain, England, Russia and Mexico have all raised their flags in Sonoma, proclaiming it their own. The US took over in 1846 during the Bear Flag Revolt against Mexico in Sonoma's central plaza and annexed all of California.

Sonoma Valley's **wineries** are generally smaller and more casual than their Napa counterparts, even though the Sonoma Valley fathered the wine industry from which Napa derives its fame. Colonel Agostin Haraszthy first started planting grapes here in the 1850s, and his Buena Vista Winery in Sonoma still operates today.

Sonoma

Behind a layer of somewhat touristy stores and restaurants, **Sonoma** retains a good deal of its Spanish and Mexican architecture. The town's charm emanates from the grassy square that acts as Downtown's centrepiece, where visitors and locals alike linger over newspapers or lazy picnics. This is indicative of the town's welcoming and relaxed feel, although as a popular retirement spot with a median age of about fifty, it's not exactly bubbling with action.

Nearly fifty **wineries** are scattered across the Sonoma Valley but there's a good concentration in a well-signposted group a mile east of Sonoma Plaza, down East Napa Street. Some are within walking distance but often along quirky back roads, so take a winery map from the tourist office and follow the signs closely. If you're tired of driving around, visit the handy Wine Exchange of Sonoma, 452 1st St E (daily 10am–5.30pm; ☎707/938-1794), a commercial tasting room where, for a small fee, you can sample the best wines from all over California. There's also a selection of 300 beers.

Bartholomew Park Winery 1000 Vineyard Lane ☎707/935-9511, ⓦwww.bartpark .com. This lavish Spanish Colonial building is surrounded by some great topiary in the gardens and extensive vineyards. The wines are relatively inexpensive vintages that appeal to the pocket and palate alike. There's a good little regional history museum, too, that also provides an introduction to local viticulture. Self-guided tours and tasting daily 11am–4.30pm. Tasting $10.

Benziger Family Winery 1883 London Ranch Rd, Glen Ellen ☎1-888/490-2739, ⓦwww.benziger.com. Beautiful vineyard perched on the side of an extinct volcano next to Jack London State Park. There are five or six daily tram tours through the fields ($15) with an emphasis on viticulture, or a self-guided tour introducing trellis techniques. Daily 10am–5pm. Tasting $10–15.

Buena Vista Carneros 18000 Old Winery Rd ☎1-800/926-1266, ⓦwww.buenavista carneros.com. Oldest and grandest of the wineries, founded in 1857, whose wine has re-established a good reputation after some slim years. The tasting room, a restored state historical landmark, features a small art gallery. Daily 10am–5pm. Tasting $10 including glass, self-guided tours free.

Chateau St Jean 8555 Sonoma Hwy, Kenwood ☎1-800/543-7572, ⓦwww .chateaustjean.com. Attractive estate with an overwhelming aroma of wine throughout the buildings. Quirky tower to climb from where you can admire the view of the surrounding countryside. Daily 10am–5pm; tours 11am & 2pm. Tasting $10–25, tours $50.

Gundlach-Bundschu 2000 Denmark St, Sonoma ☎707/939-3015, ⓦwww .gunbun.com. Set back about a mile away from the main cluster, Gun-Bun, as it's known to locals, is highly regarded, having stealthily crept up from the lower ranks of the wine league. The winery also hosts various theatrical, cinematic and musical events throughout the summer. Daily 11am–4.30pm. Tasting $10–20, tours by appointment ($20–40).

Mayo Family Winery 13101 Arnold Drive, Glen Ellen ☎707/938-9401, ⓦwww .mayofamilywinery.com. Relatively new winery with a cosy feel and a friendly welcome, matching the small-time production of under 5000 cases annually. It also has two other tasting rooms in the valley. Daily 10.30am–6.30pm; barrel tasting tours Fri–Sun 2pm & 4pm. Tasting free.

Ravenswood 18701 Gehricke Rd, Sonoma ☎707/933-2332 or 1-888/669-4679, ⓦwww.ravenswood-wine.com. Noted for their "gutsy, unapologetic" Zinfandel and advertising a "no wimpy" approach to the wine business, the staff at this unpretentious winery is particularly friendly and easy-going. Well-known to locals for its summer BBQs. Daily 10.30am–4.30pm, tours at 10.30am. Tasting $10–15, tour $15.

Sebastiani Vineyards & Winery 389 4th St E, Sonoma ☎1-800/888-5532, ⓦwww .sebastiani.com. One of California's oldest family wineries, only four blocks from central Sonoma, it boasts a smart hospitality centre, while the rest of the estate is slowly being returned to its original appearance. There's another tasting room on the central square at 103 W Napa St (☎707/933-3291). Daily 10am–5pm; free historical tours at 11am, 1pm & 3pm. Tasting $10–20.

Today, a number of historic buildings and relics stand in the sprawling **Sonoma State Historic Park** ($3 combined entry to all sites; all daily 10am–5pm). The restored **Mission San Francisco Solano de Sonoma** was the last and northernmost of the California missions, established by nervous Mexican rulers fearful of expansionist Russian fur-traders. Half a mile west stands the **General Vallejo Home**, the leader's ornate former residence, dominated by decorated, filigreed eaves and slender, Gothic-Revival arched windows. The chalet-style storehouse next door has been turned into a **museum** of artefacts from the general's reign.

There's more to Sonoma than historic buildings, however, and relaxing cafés, great restaurants, rare-book stores and a 1930s-era moviehouse ring the plaza, making Sonoma a nice town to come back to after a day in the vineyards.

Jack London State Park

Continuing north on Hwy-12, beautiful winding roads lead to the cosy hamlet of **Glen Ellen**, five miles from Sonoma, and more interestingly, **Jack London State Park** (daily: summer 9.30am–7pm; winter 10am–5pm; $8 per car; T707/938-5216, W www.jacklondonpark.com). Half a mile up London Ranch Road past the Benziger Family winery, the state park sits on the 140 acres of ranchland the famed author of *The Call of the Wild* owned with his wife Charmian. A one-mile walk through the woods leads to the ruins of the **Wolf House**, which was to be the London ancestral home: "My house will be standing, act of God permitting, for a thousand years," wrote the author. But in 1913, a month before they were to move in, the house burned to the ground, sparing only the boulder frame. Mounted blueprints point out the splendour that was to be: the mansion contained a manuscript room, sleeping tower, gun room and indoor reflecting pool. Nearby lies the final resting place of London – a red boulder from the house's ruins under which his wife sprinkled his ashes. Just off the parking lot, the **House of Happy Walls** (daily 10am–5pm; free) is a jewel of a London museum, housing an

The Bear Flag Revolt

Sonoma Plaza was the site of the **Bear Flag Revolt**, the 1846 event that propelled California into independence from Mexico and then statehood. In this much-romanticized episode, American settlers in the region, who had long lived in uneasy peace under the Spanish and, later, Mexican rulers, were threatened with expulsion from California along with all other non-Mexican immigrants. In response, a band of thirty armed settlers – including the infamous John Fremont and Kit Carson – descended upon the disused and unguarded presidio at Sonoma, taking the retired and much-respected commander, Colonel Mariano Guadalupe Vallejo, as their prisoner. Ironically, Vallejo had long advocated the American annexation of California and supported the aims of his rebel captors, but he was nonetheless bundled off to Sutter's Fort in Sacramento and held there while the militant settlers declared California an independent republic. The **Bear Flag**, which served as the model for the current state flag, was fashioned from a "feminine undergarment and muslin petticoat" and painted with a grizzly bear and single star. Raised on Sonoma Plaza, where a small plaque marks the spot today, the Bear Flag flew over the Republic of California for a short time. Three weeks later, the US declared war on Mexico and, without firing a shot, took possession of the entire Pacific Coast. While far from a frontier town now, Sonoma once had a much wilder side and in fact gave the English language a slang word for prostitutes. Not long after the Bear Flag revolt, General Lee Hooker arrived, bringing along a group of ladies employed to cheer up the troops. The ladies soon became known as "Hooker's girls", and then simply, "hookers".

interesting collection of souvenirs he picked up travelling the globe. Manuscripts, rejection letters (over six hundred before he was published for the first time), and the note explaining his and Charmian's resignation from the Socialist Party are among the exhibits. A nearby trail leads past a picnic ground to **London's Cottage** (Sat & Sun 10am–4pm; free), where he died.

Santa Rosa

Sixty miles due north of San Francisco on US-101 and about twenty miles from Sonoma on Hwy-12, **Santa Rosa**, the largest town in Sonoma County, sits at the top end of the valley and is more or less the hub of this part of the Wine Country. It's a very different world from the indulgence of other Wine Country towns, however; much of it is given over to shopping centres and strip malls. In an attempt to form a central pedestrian-only hub, **Historic Railroad Square** – a row of red-brick-facade boutiques – was created, but it lacks genuine character. With real estate prices higher than ever in the Bay Area, Santa Rosa is exploding with growth, making it both a bedroom community for San Francisco and site of the Wine Country's cheapest lodging, with major hotel and motel chains located around town. It also has a decent selection of restaurants and bars. Full listings of what the town has to offer can be found at the **CVB**, 9 4th St (Mon–Sat 9am–5pm, Sun 10am–5pm; ☎1-800/404-7673, ⓦwww.visitsantarosa.com), by Railroad Square.

You can kill an hour or two at the **Luther Burbank Home and Gardens**, at 204 Santa Rosa Ave (gardens daily 8am–dusk; free; guided tours Tues–Sun every half-hour 10am–3.30pm; $5), where California's best-known horticulturist lived; the splendid gardens showcase some of his most unusual hybrids. The **Redwood Empire Ice Arena**, 1667 W Steele Lane (☎707/546-7147, ⓦwww .snoopyshomeice.com), was built by *Peanuts* creator Charles Schulz as a gift to the community. The arena actually comprises two buildings: the ice-skating rink and the Charles M. Schulz Museum (Mon–Fri 11am–5pm, Sat & Sun 10am–5pm, closed Tues in winter; $10), a paean to all things *Peanuts*.

One enterprise few people would expect to find tucked away in the Wine Country is a full-blown **wildlife refuge**, yet spreading over four hundred acres of the pristine hills between the two valleys, five miles northeast of Santa Rosa, is **Safari West**, 3115 Porter Creek Rd (☎1-800/616-2695, ⓦwww.safariwest .com). Set up in 1989 by Peter Lang, son of *Daktari* producer Otto, the refuge runs breeding programmes for hundreds of rare mammal and bird species. Three-hour African-style **jeep tours** (daily: summer 9am, 1pm & 4pm; winter 10am & 2pm; $68) take you through vast open compounds of herd animals, and you can wander at leisure past large cages of cheetah and primates or the leafy aviary, while expert guides supply detailed background on the inhabitants. You can even feed the giraffe, if you're lucky. Accommodation in genuine African luxury tents, hung on stilted wooden decks, is available for a princely $225 per unit and filling buffet meals are served in the mess tent.

Eating and drinking

Culinary satisfaction looms around every corner in the Wine Country. California cuisine is ubiquitous in both valleys, with freshness and innovative presentation the order of the day. **Yountville**, in particular, is little more than a string of high-style restaurants, any of which is up there with the best in San Francisco in terms of quality and price. **St Helena** and **Calistoga**, though more low-key, are both gourmet paradises. **Sonoma**, too, has its share and is strong on Italian food, while the size of **Santa Rosa** allows for a good deal of diversity. **Bars** are mostly locals' or immigrant Hispanic workers' hangouts; more diverse entertainment is nearly nonexistent.

Napa Valley cafés and restaurants

All Seasons Bistro 1400 Lincoln Ave, Calistoga ☏707/942-9111. Exquisite main courses such as seared striped bass and marinated pork loin hover around $20 in this upscale but relaxed bistro.

Armadillo's 1304 Main St, St Helena. Good-value Mexican cuisine, such as fine quesadillas and burritos for well under $10, in a brightly painted dining room.

Bosko's Trattoria 1364 Lincoln Ave, Calistoga. Standard Italian restaurant preparing moderately priced, fresh pasta dishes and pizza for around $15. Cheerful and popular with families.

Bouchon 6534 Washington St, Yountville ☏707/944-8037. Parisian chic and haute cuisine at high prices – the *terrine de fois gras de canard* goes for $48.50, but most main courses average $30.

Brannan's 1374 Lincoln Ave, Calistoga ☏707/942-2233. Pecan-stuffed quail, fresh steamed oysters, and a wonderful wooden interior make this rather expensive, high-profile eatery worth a visit. Main courses $25–30.

Café Sarafornia 1413 Lincoln Ave, Calistoga. Famous for delicious and enormous all-day breakfasts and lunches, costing around $10. There are often long queues at weekends.

Cole's Chop House 1122 Main St, Napa ☏707/224-6328. The spot for huge chunks of well-prepared red meat but you'll pay at least $35 for a steak. Very spacious inside and top service, but with a somewhat stilted atmosphere.

The Model Bakery 1357 Main St, St Helena. Local hangout serving the best bread in Napa Valley, as well as sandwiches and pizza.

Mustards Grill 7399 St Helena Hwy (Hwy-29), Yountville ☏707/944-2424. Huge range of starters and main dishes, like "famous Mongolian pork chop", for around $25. Also does a range of gourmet sandwiches for around $12.

Neela's 975 Clinton St, Napa. Slightly upmarket place, right in the heart of Downtown Napa, serving cuisine from different parts of India, such as lamb vindaloo and various vegetarian dishes. Main courses $15–20. Closed Mon.

Rutherford Grill 1180 Rutherford Rd, Rutherford ☏707/963-1920. Large portions of classic yet classy contemporary American food – the mashed potatoes should not be missed – served in a sociable dining room, also popular for its martinis.

Tra Vigne 1050 Charter Oak Ave, St Helena ☏707/963-4444. This place feels as if you've been transported to Tuscany. Excellent food and fine wines served up in a lovely vine-covered courtyard or elegant dining room – but you pay for the privilege. Try the smoked and braised beef short ribs for $28. They also have a small deli.

Wine Spectator Greystone Restaurant 2555 Main St, St Helena ☏707/967-1010. California/Mediterranean cuisine served in an elegant ivy-walled mansion just outside of town, with a tastefully wacky Art Deco interior. Students from the respected culinary school serve up delicious, large portions of chicken, duck, fish and venison for $20–30.

Sonoma Valley cafés and restaurants

Café Citti 9049 Sonoma Hwy, Kenwood. Small, inexpensive trattoria with great Italian food and an intimate yet casual atmosphere. Gourmet salads such as marinated calamari for $10–12.

Café La Haye 140 E Napa St, Sonoma ☏707/935-5994. Only eleven tables, and always packed for its lovely, lively interior and tasty Italian/California cuisine. Main courses like chipotle-glazed pork chop cost around $20.

Coffee Garden Café 421 1st St W, Sonoma. Fresh sandwiches are served on the back patio of this 150-year-old adobe, which was converted into a café with small gift shop.

Cucina Viansa 400 E 1st St, Sonoma. Very reasonably priced at $10–15, considering the small but creative and delicious selection of Italian specialities on offer.

French Laundry 6640 Washington St, Yountville ☏707/944-2380. The classy ambience and superb presentation of dishes such as Moulard duck *foie gras en terrine* or Devil's Gulch Ranch rabbit make this a memorable dining experience. Chef Thomas Keller's tasting menu costs a cool $250.

Gary Chu's 611 Fifth Ave, Santa Rosa. Large helpings of high-quality, award-winning Chinese food, like orange-peel beef for $12 or honey walnut prawns for $13.50. Closed Mon.

The Girl & The Fig 110 W Spain St, Sonoma ☏707/938-3634. On the ground floor of the *Sonoma Hotel*, this well-known restaurant offers French dinners and weekend brunch from a menu as eclectic as its name. Main courses mainly a little over $20.

Glen Ellen Inn 13670 Arnold Drive, Glen Ellen
☎707/996-6409. A husband-and-wife
team cook and serve gourmet dishes, mostly
over $20, in an intimate, romantic dining room
with half a dozen tables. Specializes in oysters
and Martinis.

La Casa 121 E Spain St, Sonoma. Friendly,
festive and inexpensive Mexican restaurant just
across from the Sonoma Mission. Enjoy an
enchilada or refreshing margarita on the sunny
outdoor patio.

Rins Thai 139 E Napa St, Sonoma. Good range of
spicy curries and other Thai favourites such as
nuer prig king available for around $10 at this
modest restaurant, right on the main square.

Saffron Restaurant 13648 Arnold Drive, Glen
Ellen ☎707/938-4844. The food has a Hispanic
touch in this new establishment, which also stocks
fine wines from Spain. The delicious lentil soup is
indeed laced generously with saffron. Main
courses $13–25.

The Schellville Grill 22900 Broadway, Sonoma.
Popular local haunt, serving inexpensive breakfasts
and lunches daily and classic American dinners like
Memphis-style pulled pork Thurs–Sun. Live music
Sat eve and Sun lunch.

Bars

Amigos Grill and Cantina 19315 Sonoma Hwy,
Sonoma. Award-winning margaritas made from
your choice of one of 20 tequilas and a
home-made mix.

Ana's Cantina 1205 Main St, St Helena. Long-
standing, down-to-earth saloon and Mexican
restaurant with billiards and darts tournaments.

Compadres Bar and Grill 6539 Washington St,
Yountville. Outdoor patio seating and amazing
Martinis and margaritas, with free salsa and chips.

Downtown Joe's 902 Main St at Second, Napa.
One of Napa's most popular and lively bars, serving
sandwiches, ribs and pasta, with outdoor dining by
the river and beer brewed on the premises. About
the only place in town open until midnight and a
good spot to meet locals.

Murphy's Irish Pub 464 1st St E, Sonoma. Small
bar with an eclectic interior and a few outdoor
tables serving basic pub grub and European beers.
Live music most nights.

Third Street Aleworks 610 3rd St, Santa Rosa
☎707/523-3060. Frequent live music and hearty
American grub like burgers and pizza, washed
down with microbrewed ale, are the order of the
day at this lively joint.

The northern coast

The fog-bound towns and windswept, craggy beaches of the **NORTHERN
COAST** couldn't be further removed from Southern California's sandy, sunny
strip of ocean. Stretching north of San Francisco to the Oregon border, the
northern coast is better suited for hiking than sunbathing, with a climate of cool
temperatures year-round and a huge network of national, state and regional **parks**
preserving magnificent redwood trees. **Wildlife** thrives here and is always in view,
from seals lounging on rocks around Goat Rock Beach in the south to elk
chomping on berry bushes in the north, all against a backdrop of spectacular
scenery. Far rarer fauna has been spotted up here as well: the legendary Bigfoot
supposedly leaves footprints through the forest and Ewoks once battled the
Galactic Empire under the direction of *Star Wars* creator George Lucas, who used
areas north of Orick as the set for *The Return of the Jedi*.

The only way to see the coast properly is on the painfully slow but visually
magnificent Hwy-1, which hugs the coast for a hundred and fifty miles through
the wild counties of **Sonoma** and **Mendocino**, before turning sharply inland
at Legget to join US-101 and **Humboldt County**. The hundred miles of wild
coastline Hwy-1 never reaches has become known, appropriately, as the **Lost
Coast**, a virgin territory of campgrounds and trails. If you're heading for the
coast from the Wine Country, a pleasant route is via the quieter wineries of the
Russian River Valley, or you can take US-101 and detour inland further north

to placid **Clear Lake**, before cutting across to Mendocino. North of here, the redwoods take over, blanketing the landscape all the way to Oregon, doubling as raw material for the huge logging industries (the prime source of employment in the area) and the region's prime tourist attraction, most notably in the **Redwood National Park**. **Eureka**, the coast's largest city, is neighboured by lively **Arcata**, home to **Humboldt State University** and thousands of dreadlocked youngsters. The last stretch of redwood coast before the Oregon state line lies in **Del Norte County**, whose functional seat of **Crescent City** offers little to detain the visitor for long.

You'll need to be fairly independent to **get around** this region: only two Amtrak Thruway and two Greyhound buses a day travel via US-101, which parallels the coastal highway, but they don't link up with the coast until Eureka and terminate just north of there. Consequently most visitors travel by car and should, in summertime, expect legions of slow-moving campers trying to negotiate the two-lane roads' hairpin curves.

The Sonoma coast and Russian River Valley

Hwy-1 twists and winds along the edge of the **SONOMA COAST** through persistent fog that, once burned off by the sun, reveals oyster beds, seal breeding grounds and twenty-foot-high rhododendrons. A spectacular introduction to the northern coast, Sonoma County's western rim is never short on visitors due to its proximity to San Francisco. But tourist activity is confined to a few narrow corridors at the height of summer, leaving behind a network of north-coast villages and backwater wineries that for most of the year are all but asleep. The coast is colder and lonelier than the villages along the valley, and at some point most people head inland for a new scene and a break from the pervasive fog. What both areas have in common, though, is a reluctance to change. As wealthy San Franciscans cast their eyes towards the north for potential second-home sites, the California Coastal Commission's policy of beach access for all keeps the architects at bay, making the Sonoma coast one of the few remaining undeveloped coastal areas in California; the southern third of the coast is almost entirely state beach.

At the tiny town of Jenner, Hwy-116 heads inland along the Russian River, leading to the **Russian River Valley**, an affluent summer recreation area popular for its canoeing, swimming, wineries and gay resorts. This part of Sonoma County is also the centre of the Farm Trails ecotourism effort – check out Ⓦwww.farmtrails.org for more details.

The Sonoma coast

Bodega Bay, about 65 miles north of San Francisco, is the first Sonoma County village you reach on Hwy-1. Pomo and Miwok Indians populated the area peacefully for centuries, until Captain Lt Juan Francisco de la Bodega y Quadra Mollineda anchored his ship in the bay and "discovered" it in 1775. Hitchcock filmed the waterside scenes for *The Birds* here; an unsettling number of his cast's descendants can still be found squawking down by the harbour. Not so long ago, a depleted fishing industry, a couple of restaurants and some isolated seaside cottages were all there was to Bodega Bay, but since San Franciscans got wind of its appeal, holiday homes and modern retail developments now crowd the waterside.

If you're travelling the whole coast, Bodega Bay makes a tolerable first stop, although better beaches, weather and services exist in Jenner, fourteen miles north. Of several **places to stay**, the *Bodega Harbor Inn*, 1345 Bodega Ave (℡707/875-3594, ⓦwww.bodegaharborinn.com; ⑨), is the best value in town, while the extremely comfortable *Bodega Coast Inn*, 521 Hwy-1 (℡1-800/346-6999, ⓦwww.bodegacoastinn.com; ④), has beautifully refurbished rooms with fireplaces. If you don't have a reservation during peak times, the **Sonoma Coast Visitor Center**, 850 Hwy-1 (Mon–Thurs 10am–6pm, Fri & Sat 10am–8pm, Sun 10am–7pm; ℡707/875-3866, ⓦwww.bodegabay.com), has information on availability throughout the area. **Campgrounds** are available at *Bodega Dunes* in **Sonoma Coast State Beach** (℡707/875-3483, reserve on ℡1-800/444-7275, ⓦwww.parks.ca.gov; $25), two miles north of the village on Hwy-1 at the base of a windy peninsula known as **Bodega Head**. There are **hiking** and **horseriding** trails around the dunes behind the beach, although they get crowded in summer.

If you're looking for a **restaurant**, *Brisas del Mar*, 2001 Hwy-1, does inexpensive pastas and Mexican dishes, as well as seafood, while *Lucas Wharf*, 595 Hwy-1, specializes in crab (mid-Nov to June) and salmon (mid-May to Sept) dishes at around $20. As part of the upscale *Inn at the Tides*, the equally pricey *Tides Wharf & Restaurant*, 835 Hwy-1 (℡707/875-3652), gives a good viewpoint to watch fishing boats unload their catch, while hearty breakfasts, sandwiches and full meals can be enjoyed at the *Sandpiper Restaurant*, 1410 Bay Flat Rd. Bodega Bay Surf Shack in Pelican Plaza, 1400 Hwy-1 (℡707/875-3944, ⓦwww.bodegabaysurf .com), rents out bikes ($5 per hour), kayaks ($45 for 4hr) and surfing equipment ($12.95 per day).

North of Bodega Bay to Jenner

North of Bodega Bay, the coastline coarsens and the trails become more dramatic. It's a wonderful stretch to hike, although the shale formations are often unstable and you must stick to the trails, which are actually quite demanding. Of Sonoma's thirteen miles of beaches, the finest are surfer-friendly **Salmon Creek Beach**, a couple of miles north of Bodega Bay and site of the park headquarters, and **Goat Rock Beach**, at the top of the coast. The latter offers the chance to get close to harbour seals. For **horseriding**, *Chanslor Guest Ranch*, 2660 Hwy-1 (℡707/875-2721, ⓦwww.chanslorranch.com), offers a selection of rides, which range from a thirty-five-minute wetlands jaunt ($30–50 per person) to ninety-minute rides along Salmon Creek ($75–100).

Campgrounds are dotted along the coast (call ℡707/875-3483 for information), but the best **places to stay** are in the tiny seaside village of **Jenner**, which marks the turn-off for the Russian River Valley – a small, friendly place where you can stay in the salubrious rooms, cabins and cottages of *The Jenner Inn*, 10400 Hwy-1 (℡1-800/732-2377, ⓦwww.jennerinn.com; ④), or the quaint cabins of *River's End Resort* (℡707/865-2484, ⓦwww.ilovesunsets.com; ④). The **Russian River** joins the ocean in Jenner and a massive sand spit at its mouth provides a breeding ground for harbour seals from March to June. The *Seagull Deli*, 10439 Hwy-1, sells wonderful clam chowder on a deck along the river mouth to accompany your viewing.

Fort Ross and beyond

North of Jenner, the population evaporates and Hwy-1 turns into a slalom course of hairpin bends and steep inclines for twelve miles as far as **Fort Ross State Historic Park** (daily 8am–sunset; $8 per car), which houses the **Fort Compound** (daily 10am–4.30pm; free). At the start of the nineteenth century,

San Francisco was still the northernmost limit of Spanish occupation in Alta California and from 1812 to 1841 Russian fur traders quietly settled this part of the coast, clubbing the California sea otter almost to extinction, building a fort to use as a trading outpost and growing crops for the Russian stations in Alaska. Officially they posed no territorial claims but, by the time the Spanish had gauged the extent of the settlement, the fort was heavily armed and vigilantly manned with a view to continued eastward expansion. The Russians traded here for thirty years until over-hunting and the failure of their shipbuilding efforts led them to pull out of the region. Among the empty bunkers and storage halls, the most interesting buildings are the Russian Orthodox chapel and the commandant's house, with its fine library and wine cellar. At the entrance, a potting shed, which labours under the delusion that it is a **museum**, provides cursory details on the history of the fort, with a few maps and diagrams.

Fort Ross has a small beach and picnicking facilities, and you can **camp** just south of the park entrance at *Reef Campground* (☎707/847-3286; $18) or in **Salt Point State Park** (☎707/847-3221, reserve on ☎1-800/444-7275, ⓦwww .parks.ca.gov; $6–35), six miles north on Hwy-1. Two reasonable **hotel** options exist close to the two parks. *Fort Ross Lodge*, fifteen miles north of Jenner at 20705 Hwy-1 (☎707/847-3333, ⓦwww.fortrosslodge.com; ④), provides well-equipped rooms, each of which has a private patio and barbecue, and some much pricier suites with hot tubs. A little further north, the *Timber Cove Inn*, 21780 Hwy-1 (☎1-800/987-8319, ⓦwww.timbercoveinn.com; ⑤), is a step up in luxury, with splendid ocean views from the costlier rooms and an intimate **restaurant**. The restaurant at the *Salt Point Lodge*, 23255 Hwy-1 (☎707/847-3234), also serves fine seafood and steak dinners for $15–20.

One of Sonoma County's most accessible and beautiful beaches, part of Salt Point State Park, is at **Gerstle Cove** (daily 8am–sunset; $8 per car), which includes a paved, wheelchair-accessible path from the cove to Salt Point, past kelp beds, wave-battered rocks and lounging harbour seals. The park's rainfall and habitat make mushrooms thrive, and Gerstle Cove is a popular place for **mushroom gatherers** to park their cars and begin foraging, which the park permits. Ask the ranger for the sheet of guidelines when you enter the lot. Just north of Salt Point and a little inland, the **Kruse Rhododendron State Reserve** is a sanctuary for twenty-foot-high rhododendrons, indigenous to this part of the coast and in bloom from April to June. The beaches on this last stretch of the Sonoma coastline are usually deserted, save for a few abalone fishermen, driftwood and the seal pups who rest here. As usual, they're good for hiking and beachcombing but stick to the trails. From here you pass tiny and inconsequential Stewart's Point before entering the Mendocino coast (see p.630).

The Russian River Valley

Hwy-116 begins at Jenner and turns sharply inland, leaving behind the cool fogs of the coast and marking the western entrance to a relatively warm and pastoral area known as the **RUSSIAN RIVER VALLEY**. The tree-lined highway follows the river's course through twenty miles of what appear to be lazy backwater resorts but in fact are the major stomping grounds for partying weekend visitors from San Francisco. The valley's seat, **Guerneville**, has the most nightlife and lodging, while **Healdsburg** serves as the gatekeeper for the **wine area**, bordering US-101 and the Dry Creek and Alexander valleys.

The road that snakes through the valley is dotted with campgrounds every few miles, most with sites for the asking, although during the first weekend after Labor

The Guerneville Chamber of Commerce (see opposite) issues an excellent *Russian River Wine Road* map, which lists all the **wineries** spread along the entire course of the Russian River – now numbering nearly a hundred. Unlike their counterparts in Napa and Sonoma, few of the wineries here either organize guided tours or charge for wine-tasting. You can usually wander around at ease, guzzling as many and as much of the wines as you please. Some of the wines are of remarkably good quality, if not as well known as their Wine Country rivals. By car, you could easily travel up from the Sonoma coast and check out a couple of Russian River wineries in a day, although the infectiously slow pace may well detain you longer.

Dry Creek Vineyard 3770 Lambert Bridge Rd, 4 miles northwest of Healdsburg at Dry Creek Rd ☎1-800/864-9463, ⓦwww.drycreekvineyard.com. This family-owned operation is well known for its consistently top-class wines – particularly the Cabernet Sauvignon and Chardonnay. Picnic facilities. Daily 10.30am–4.30pm. Tasting $5–10.

Ferrari Carano 8761 Dry Creek Rd, 6 miles northwest of Healdsburg ☎1-800/831-0381, ⓦwww.ferrari-carano.com. One of the smartest wineries in the region, Ferrari is housed in a Neoclassical mansion with beautiful landscaped grounds. They specialize in Italian-style wines. Daily 10am–5pm. Tasting $5 (waived with purchase), tours by appointment.

Hop Kiln 6050 Westside Rd, over 5 miles south of Healdsburg ☎707/433-6491, ⓦwww.hopkilnwinery.com. Recently established, rustic winery with a traditional atmosphere but not a snobbish attitude. Ironically, a plaque marks the spot where kilns used to dry the hops when this was beer country. Picnic area. Daily 10am–5pm.

Korbel Champagne Cellars 13250 River Rd, 2 miles east of Guerneville ☎707/824-7000, ⓦwww.korbel.com. The bubbly itself – America's best-selling premium champagne – can be found anywhere but the wine and brandy are sold only from the cellars and are of notable quality. The estate where they are produced is lovely, surrounded by hillside gardens covered in blossoming violets, coral bells and hundreds of varieties of rose – perfect for quiet picnics. A microbrewery and upscale deli are also on the premises. Daily: summer 9am–5pm; winter 9am–4.30pm; tours 11am & 3pm.

Lake Sonoma 9990 Dry Creek Rd, Geyserville ☎707/473-2999, ⓦwww.lakesonomawinery.net. In a fine elevated setting at the far end of Dry Creek Valley from Healdsburg, Lake Sonoma makes a good range of wines and a particularly fine port and has a microbrewery on the premises. Daily 10am–4.30pm.

Porter Creek 8735 Westside Rd, over 5 miles east of Guerneville ☎707/433-6321, ⓦwww.portercreekvineyards.com. Small winery with a cottagey feel, producing all organic wines; Pinot Noir a speciality. Daily 10.30am–4.30pm.

Russian River Vineyards 5700 Gravenstein Hwy, Forestville, 5 miles from Guerneville along Hwy-116 ☎1-800/867-6567, ⓦwww.russianrivervineyards.com. One of the Russian River Valley's most accessible wineries, specializing in Zinfandels. The popular on-site restaurant *Stella's* (☎707/887-1562) serves Greek-inspired California dishes – dine on the patio and feast your eyes on the wildflower gardens. Daily 11am–5pm. Tasting $5 (waived with purchase), tours by appointment.

Day, when the region hosts the combined **Jazz on the River and Russian River Blues festivals**, things can get a bit tight. Bands set up on Johnson's Beach by the river and in the woods for impromptu jam sessions as well as regular scheduled events. Both events are run by the same promoters in the East Bay (☎510/655-9471, ⓦwww.omegaevents.com). Gourmets will enjoy the **Russian River Food and Wine Festival** on the last Sunday in September.

Sonoma County Transit (☏1-800/345-7433, ⊛www.sctransit.com) runs a fairly good weekday bus service (though patchy on weekends) between the Russian River resorts and Santa Rosa in the Wine Country, although to see much of the valley, you really need a car.

Guerneville

The main town of the Russian River Valley, **GUERNEVILLE**, came out some time ago. No longer disguised by the tourist office as a place where "a mixture of people respect each other's lifestyles", it's quite clearly a **gay resort** and has been for over twenty years: a lively retreat popular with tired city-dwellers who come here to unwind. Gay men predominate during the summer, except during two **Women's Weekends** (☏707/869-9000) – in early May and late September – when many of the hotels take only women.

If you don't fancy venturing along the valley, there's plenty to keep you busy without leaving town. Weekend visitors flock here for the canoeing, swimming and sunbathing that comprise the bulk of local activities. **Johnson's Beach**, on a placid reach of the river in the centre of town, is the prime spot, with canoes, pedal boats and tubes for rent at reasonable rates. But Guerneville's biggest natural asset is the magnificent **Armstrong Redwoods State Reserve** (☏707/869-2015; $8 per vehicle), two miles north at the top of Armstrong Woods Road – seven hundred acres of massive redwood trees, hiking and riding trails and primitive campsites. The visitor centre (daily 11am–3pm) can provide trail maps: take food and water and don't stray off the trails, as the densely forested central grove is quite forbidding and very easy to get lost in. One of the best ways to see it is on horseback; Horseback Adventures (☏707/887-2939, ⊛www.redwoodhorses.com) offers guided horseback tours that range from a half-day trail ride ($80) to overnight pack trips ($250 per horse per day). A natural amphitheatre provides the setting for the Redwood Forest Theater, once used for dramatic and musical productions during the summer but now simply a fine spot for rustic contemplation.

Practicalities

The **Chamber of Commerce & Visitor Center**, 16209 1st St (Mon–Sat 10am–5pm, Sun 10am–3pm; 24-hour info line ☏1-877/644-9001, ⊛www.russianriver.com), is welcoming and has good free maps of the area plus **accommodation** listings. As with most of the valley, B&Bs are the staple; two choices are the comfortable *Creekside Inn and Resort*, 16180 Neely Rd (☏1-800/776-6586, ⊛www.creeksideinn.com; ❸), and more luxurious *Applewood Inn & Restaurant*, 13555 Hwy-116 (☏707/869-9093, ⊛www.applewoodinn.com; ❻), which also features a highly acclaimed gourmet restaurant. Lower rates can be found at the gay-friendly *New Dynamic Inn*, 14030 Mill St (☏707/869-5082, ⊛www.newdynamicinn.com; ❹), a relaxed New Age establishment where "cosmic energies unite with you", while the *Highlands Resort*, 14000 Woodland Rd (☏707/869-0333, ⊛www.highlandsresort.com; ❷), also caters primarily to the gay community, and you can camp from $20. **Camping** is an easy option elsewhere, too: the *Austin Creek State Recreation Area*, Armstrong Woods Road (☏707/865-2391, ⊛www.parks.ca.gov; $25), is RV-free, while *Johnson's Beach and Resort*, 16241 1st St, also has cabins and rooms available ($20 per vehicle plus one person, extra people $5 each; ☏707/869-2022, ⊛www.johnsonsbeach.com; ❷).

Guerneville has a generous selection of reasonably priced, reliable **restaurants**, among them *Wild Jane's*, 16440 Main St (☏707/869-3600), which serves classic American/California cuisine and hosts live music. *Taqueria la Tapatia*, on the west side of town at 16632 Hwy-116, is an excellent, authentic and cheap Mexican joint. Really, though, it's the **nightlife** that makes Guerneville a worthwhile stop. *Main St Station*, 16280 Main St (☎707/869-0501), slings pizzas and offers nightly live jazz, while gay hangout *Rainbow Cattle Co*, 16220 Main St, gets livelier as the night draws on. Both the *Russian River Resort* ("*Triple R*"), 16390 4th St, and *Liquid Sky*, 16225 Main St, serve alcohol and food and are also popular with the gay crowd.

Monte Rio

The small town of **Monte Rio**, four miles west along the river from Guerneville, is definitely worth a look: a lovely old resort with big Victorian houses that are constantly being refurbished. For years it has been the entrance to the 2500-acre **Bohemian Grove**, a private park that plays host to the San Francisco-based Bohemian Club. A grown-up summer camp, its membership includes a very rich and very powerful male elite – ex-presidents, financiers, politicians and their peers. Every year in July they descend for "Bohemian Week" – the greatest men's party on earth, noted for its hijinks and high-priced hookers, away from prying cameras in the seclusion of the woods.

The most reasonable of Monte Rio's pricey **places to stay** is the expertly restored 🦌 *Highland Dell Resort*, 21050 River Blvd (☎707/865-2300, ⓦwww .highlanddell.com; ④), whose gourmet restaurant is highly praised, followed by the lovely *Rio Villa Beach Resort*, 20292 Hwy-116 (☎707/865-1143, ⓦwww .riovilla.com; ⑤), and *Village Inn*, 20822 River Blvd (☎707/865-2304, ⓦwww .villageinn-ca.com; ⑥), all in beautiful spots on opposite banks of the Russian River. Fill your belly at *Northwood Restaurant*, 19400 Hwy-116 (☎707/865-2454), serving up tasty, high-priced California cuisine.

The lonely, narrow **Cazadero Highway** just to the west makes a nice drive from here, curving north through the wooded valley and leading back to Fort Ross on the coast. At the north end of the bridge over the Russian River in Monte Rio, **cyclists** can begin the world-renowned King Ridge–Meyers Grade ride, a 55-mile loop (and 4500ft of climb) that heads along the Cazadero Highway and into the hills, finally descending to the coast and Hwy-1. Contact the Santa Rosa Cycling Club (☎707/544-4803, ⓦwww.srcc.com) for a complete itinerary.

Healdsburg

The peaceful modern town of **Healdsburg** straddles the invisible border between the Wine Country and the Russian River Valley and in a quiet way manages to get the best of both worlds. While **Veterans Memorial Beach**, a mile south of the pleasant plaza along the banks of the Russian River, is a popular spot for swimming, picnicking and canoeing in the summertime, there are also several dozen wineries, most of them family owned, within a few miles of the town centre. The only cultural diversion in town is the **Healdsburg Museum**, 221 Matheson St (Tues–Sun 11am–4pm; free), which displays local history through a decent collection of Pomo Indian basketry, nineteenth-century tools and crafts and eight thousand original photos. Romantic B&Bs have sprung up all over the area, including in the neighbouring village of **Geyserville**, and although the town's economic wellbeing is almost exclusively dependent on tourism, it still manages to maintain a relaxed, backcountry feel. The Healdsburg Area **Chamber of Commerce**, 217 Healdsburg Ave (Mon–Fri 9am–5pm, Sat 9am–3pm, Sun 10am–2pm; ☎1-800/648-9922, ⓦwww.healdsburg.com), provides winery and lodging information.

If you have the money to spend it's hard to beat the *Madrona Manor*, 1001 Westside Rd (☎1-800/258-4003, ⓦwww.madronamanor.com; ⑧), a luxurious

B&B in a Victorian-style mansion crowning a hilltop, with meticulously maintained gardens and a gourmet restaurant. A more economic, if less distinctive, option is the *Best Western Dry Creek Inn*, 198 Dry Creek Rd (T 1-800/222-5784, W www.drycreekinn.com; ❸).

Of several fine **restaurants** that circle the green, wooded plaza, ⚒ *Bistro Ralph*, 109 Plaza St (T 707/433-1380; brunch only on Sun), with sparse modern decor and well-crafted French/California cuisine dishes such as chicken *paillard* for around $20 a pop, is your best bet. For a cheaper meal accompanied by fine local ale, look no further than *Bear Republic Brewing Co*, 345 Healdsburg Ave. *Flying Goat Coffee Roastery and Café*, just off the main plaza at 324 Center St, is a great place to unwind with a newspaper.

Lake County and Clear Lake

An alternative route to the northern coast along Hwy-29 from the Wine Country or via Hwy-20, if coming from the I-5 north of Sacramento, is through often-neglected **LAKE COUNTY** and its centrepiece, **Clear Lake**, the largest natural freshwater lake in California. With a basin that was lifted above sea level some fifty million years ago by the collision of the Pacific and North American crustal plates, it is also one of the most ancient lakes on the continent, possibly even the oldest. The earliest inhabitants of its shores were the Pomo Indians, attracted by the mild climate and abundance of fish, who traded peacefully with other tribes and remained here undisturbed until they were displaced by white settlers; now they number just two percent of the population. With a surface area of sixty-four square miles and over a hundred miles of shoreline, the lake is renowned among anglers as the best **bass-fishing** territory in the country. Mostly surrounded by rolling hills, the lake is dominated by the green twin cone of **Mount Konocti**, a 4500-foot dormant volcano, which looms above its south shore. The largest city, conveniently named **Clearlake**, which occupies the southeast corner of the lake, has plenty of tourist facilities but is rather modern and faceless, so you're better off concentrating on the lakefront areas around **Lakeport** to the west and along the **North Shore**.

Clear Lake

A popular playground for vacationing middle classes up until World War II, **CLEAR LAKE** has been trying to reinvent itself as a holiday destination after several slim decades, during which it gained an unflattering reputation among many Californians as "white trash central". Evidence of this period can still be found in the rather dowdy motels that line parts of the lakeshore, some of which have been turned into recovery houses. However, the locals are once again trying to harness the lake's undoubted natural beauty, sunny climate and its location – a little over two hours from San Francisco – to make it an attractive destination. This effort is bolstered by promoting its suitability for all sorts of **water activities**: windsurfing, waterskiing, boating and fishing facilities are available all around the lake. Southeast of Lakeport, the adjacent attractions of **Clear Lake State Park** and **Soda Bay** provide ample opportunities to play or simply unwind, as does the string of small resorts on the lake's **North Shore**. As the revitalization process is still in its early stages, the visitor can easily find great deals on accommodation, dining and entertainment. It is also, by Northern California standards, relatively easy to spend time here without your own vehicle, thanks to decent **public transport** connections

once you arrive: the efficient Lake Transit service (☎707/263-3334, ⓦwww
.laketransit.org) runs frequent buses all around the lake every day except
Sunday and also has connections (Mon–Sat 4 daily) to Ukiah for Greyhound
and Amtrak Thruway services.

Lakeport

The county seat of **LAKEPORT** is the older and more picturesque of Clear
Lake's two towns, dating from the latter part of the nineteenth century, when
settlers moved into the picturesque area as gold fever began to wane. Although
the suburban sprawl along the lakefront gives the impression of a larger town,
it's home to fewer than five thousand people. If you arrive by Hwy-29, the first
point of call is the smart **Lakeport Regional Chamber of Commerce**, perched
on a green knoll right by the highway exit ramp at 875 Lakeport Blvd (Mon–Fri
9am–5pm, Sat 10am–2pm; ☎1-800/525-3743, ⓦwww.lakeportchamber.com).
As well as providing the usual brochures, maps and information, it affords a
splendid view across the lake. Downtown Lakeport still retains a good deal of
Victorian charm, with the original 1871 brick courthouse standing imperiously
on the gentle slopes of the grassy main square right in the heart of town. The
building now houses the **Lake County Museum**, 255 N Main St (Wed–Sat
10am–4pm, Sun noon–4pm; $2). Exhibits concentrate on the area's native
heritage, with a full-sized Pomo village diorama and large collection of baskets,
arrowheads and tools.

The dozen or so blocks of Main Street on either side of the square and the
roads leading down from it to the waterfront contain most of the town's
facilities. For **accommodation**, it's hard to beat *Mallard House Inn*, 970 N Main
St (☎707/262-1601, ⓦwww.mallardhouse.com; ❷), a friendly English-style
inn, while the posher *Lakeport English Inn*, 675 N Main St (☎707/263-4317,
ⓦwww.lakeportenglishinn.com; ❺), is the best of the B&Bs around here. A
little further north, *Skylark Shores*, 1120 N Main St (☎707/263-6151, ⓦwww
.skylarkshoreshotel.com; ❹), is typical of the resort motels to be found in the
vicinity, fairly uninspiring but in exquisite surroundings. Downtown **eating**
options include *Park Place*, 50 3rd St (☎707/263-0444), which serves filling
pasta, burgers and steaks, and the inexpensive Chinese food at *Chopstick*, 185 N
Main St. To stock up on **fishing** gear, stop at The King Connection, 2470
Reeves Lane (☎707/263-8856), and for boat or jet-ski rental contact Disney's
Water Sports, 401 S Main St (from $40 per half-hour; ☎707/263-0969,
ⓦwww.disneyswatersports.com).

Clear Lake State Park and Soda Bay

About six miles southeast of Lakeport, two adjacent areas are worthy of
exploration. The first is **Clear Lake State Park** (daily 8am–sunset; $8 per
vehicle; ☎707/279-4293), whose erratically opening visitor centre houses
displays on the lake's cultural and natural history, as well as a 700-gallon
aquarium of indigenous fish. The park also offers forest trails, a swimming
beach and four developed campgrounds (☎1-800/444-7275, ⓦwww.parks
.ca.gov; $20–35). Right below Mount Konocti, in the protected waters
between the park and Buckingham Peninsula, which almost spans the lake,
Soda Bay is another haven for swimming and watersports. The eastern shore
of the bay is blessed with soda springs, hence the name, which bubble up from
shafts over a hundred feet deep. Indian legend claims that the bubbling waters
mark the spot where Chief Konocti's daughter Lupiyoma threw herself into the
lake after her father and lover were killed in battle. A number of **places to stay**
line the bay, such as *Edgewater Resort*, 6420 Soda Bay Rd (☎1-800/396-6224,

@ www.edgewaterresort.net; @), which offers tent and RV sites from $35, as well as a few spacious family cabins. Almost next door, ☆ *The Lakeside Inn*, 6330 Soda Bay Rd (closed Mon–Wed), is a cosy English boozer serving meat pies and good ale; in fact it's an exact replica of its namesake in Southport, Lancashire, recorded in the *Guinness Book of Records* as the smallest pub in England.

Mount Konocti

Majestic **Mount Konocti**, clearly visible from just about anywhere on Clear Lake's circumference, is a multiple volcano, estimated to have first erupted some 600,000 years ago but inactive for the last several thousand years. Indeed, geologists have declared large parts of it officially extinct. Its name comes from the Pomo Indian words "kno" and "hatai", meaning "mountain" and "woman" respectively. Unfortunately, most of the mountain is under private ownership and visitor access is prohibited until a delayed public trail is completed. The nearest amenities can be found at **Kelseyville** on the lower southern reaches. These include the biggest resort in the region, *Konocti Harbor Resort & Spa*, 8727 Soda Bay Rd (℡1-800/660-5253, @ www.konoctiharbor.com; @), with accommodation ranging from motel-style rooms to beach cottages to a VIP suite that nudges $800 on special event weekends, as well as a spa, marina, sports facilities, restaurants and a concert hall.

North Shore

Some five miles north of Clearlake, Hwy-53 ends at Hwy-20, which continues northwest along the lake's **North Shore** past a series of small resorts under the shade of white oak and pepperwood trees. The first place you come to once the road hits the lake is Clearlake Oaks, which doesn't really merit a stop, so it's best to press on towards **Glenhaven**. A mile or so before the town are the rustic cabins of *Blue Fish Cove*, 10573 E Hwy-20 (℡707/998-1769, @ www.blue fishcove.com; @). At Glenhaven itself the *Sea Breeze Resort*, 9595 Harbor Drive (℡707/998-3327, @ www.seabreezeresort.net; @), has quaint, nicely decorated cottages; if you're seeking a **campground**, try *Glenhaven Beach* at 9625 E Hwy-20 (℡707/998-3406), where sites cost from $20. Inexpensive boat rental is also available here.

There's more going on, however, up towards the lake's northwest corner, which also boasts the longest stretches of beach. Five miles beyond Glenhaven in the larger settlement of **Lucerne**, the *Lakeview Inn*, 5960 E Hwy-20 (℡707/274-5515, @ www.lakeviewinnlucerne.com; @), offers some of the best-value rooms on the lake. The best dining option is *Taylors Bar & Grill*, 6034 E Hwy-20. Lucerne is also home to the informative **Lake County Visitor Center** (summer Mon–Sat 9am–6pm & Sun 10am–5pm; winter Mon–Sat 9am–5pm & Sun noon–4pm; ℡1-800/525-3743, @ www.lakecounty.com) at 6110 E Hwy-20.

Several miles further on, where Hwy-20 prepares to leave the lake behind as the shoreline dips south towards Lakeport, the pleasant town of **Nice** is the best base on the North Shore. Apart from more cheap cabins, there are a couple of attractive **B&Bs**: the unique railway-themed *Featherbed Railroad Company*, 2870 Lakeshore Blvd (℡1-800/966-6322, @ www.featherbedrailroad.com; @), where all the rooms are fashioned out of disused cabooses; and the more conventional *Gingerbread Cottages*, 4057 E Hwy-20 (℡707/274-0200, @ www.gingerbread cottages.com; @). Nice is also the most fruitful part of North Shore for **eating**: try the delicious and inexpensive American classics served all day at *The Marina Grill*, 3707 E Hwy-20; the fresh seafood, steaks and pasta at the *Harbor Bar & Grill*, 4561 E Hwy-20; or the well-prepared fish and barbecued meat at *The Boathouse*, 2685 Lakeshore Blvd.

The Mendocino coast

The coast of **Mendocino County**, 150 miles north of San Francisco, is a dramatic extension of the Sonoma coastline – the headlands a bit sharper, the surf a bit rougher, but otherwise more of the same. Sea stacks form a dotted line off the coast and there's an abundance of tide pools, making the area a prime spot for exploring the secrets of the ocean, either on foot or in diving gear. Surfers love it, too, for the waves and sandy beaches to be found between **Gualala** and **Albion**, and March brings out droves of people to watch migrating **whales**. Tourists tend to mass in charming **Mendocino** and gritty **Fort Bragg**, leaving the other small former logging towns along Hwy-1 preserved in the salt air and welcoming to visitors. The county also thrives as a location spot for the movie industry, having featured in such illustrious titles as *East of Eden*, *Frenchman's Creek*, *Same Time Next Year* and *The Fog*.

If you're already on the coast, you can continue to hug Hwy-1 all the way to Rockport when it turns east to join US-101, the last thirty miles constituting one of only two true wildernesses left on California's rim. The most direct route to Mendocino from the south, however, is to travel the length of the peaceful **Anderson Valley** by taking Hwy-128 north from US-101. The main coastal towns of Mendocino and Fort Bragg are connected to each other and the interior towns of **Willits** and **Ukiah** (both on US-101 and served by Greyhound) by the local **bus** operator Mendocino Transit Authority (℡1-800/696-4682, ⓦwww.4mta.org), which has additional routes south to Gualala and Santa Rosa.

The coast from Gualala to Albion

The first oceanside stop of note, once you leave Sonoma County on Hwy-1, is **Gualala**, which has developed into quite an artistic community, as well as a spot for holidaymakers due to its fine stretch of sand. A handy brochure locating the dozen or so **galleries** can be found at any one of them – try the central Dolphin Gallery (℡707/884-3896, ⓦwww.gualalaarts.org) in Sundstrom Mall, directly off Hwy-1. If you decide **to stay** here, look no further than the old *Gualala Hotel*, on the corner of Hwy-1 and the main plaza (℡707/884-3444; ❷), whose cheaper rooms have shared baths and which runs a good restaurant and old-style saloon. A pricier option is the *Surf Motel at Gualala* (℡1-888/451-7873, ⓦwww.surfinngualala.com; ❸), opposite the far corner of the plaza. Steak, seafood and pasta fills the menu at *Meza Grille*, up the hill at 39080 Hwy-1.

Beyond Gualala the route is very appealing, as Hwy-1 climbs up through increasingly wooded hillsides that afford tantalizing glimpses of the crashing waves at the frequent bends. Eventually the road straightens out somewhat as it turns inland to become the main street of nondescript **Point Arena**, fifteen miles or so north. A turn on the north side of town leads two miles to the impressive **Point Arena Lighthouse** (hours vary; $5; ℡1-877/725-4448, ⓦwww.pointarenalighthouse.com). Built in 1870 and rebuilt after the San Francisco earthquake of 1906, the landmark contains a small museum and the 115-foot tower is a great vantage point for viewing birds, whales and other ocean life.

Hwy-1 continues north through a mixture of coastal scrub and grazing land, rejoining the ocean around **Manchester Beach State Park** (daily 8am–sunset; free); its cheap campground ($15) is about half a mile inland from the largely deserted strand. Further on you reach the pretty village of **Elk**, which boasts an excellent driftwood-strewn beach and a couple of quaint but fairly pricey **places to stay**: the *Greenwood Pier Inn* at 5928 S Hwy-1 (℡1-800/807-3423, ⓦwww.greenwoodpierinn.com; ❻) has a wide range of rooms and deluxe cabins made entirely of redwood, as well as a multi-cuisine restaurant; while the *Griffin House Inn*, almost next door at no 5910 (℡707/877-3422, ⓦwww.griffinhouseinn.com; ⑤), is co-run with the adjoining, hearty *Bridget Dolan's Pub & Dinner House*. The road winds on through an extremely scenic stretch of cliffs counterpointed by sea stacks and crashing waves until it reaches **Albion**, a couple of miles north of the junction with Hwy-128. The small fishing village is only six miles south of Mendocino itself and has a couple of romantic **places to stay**: *Fensalden B&B Inn*, 33810 Navarro Ridge Rd (℡1-800/959-3850, ⓦwww.fensalden.com; ⑤), offers comfortable rural surroundings and distant sea views; while the *Albion River Inn*, 3790 N Hwy-1 (℡1-800/479-7944, ⓦwww.albionriverinn.com; ⑥), perches on the edge of a cliff and all the rooms except one face the ocean. The inn also has a first-class **restaurant**, serving superb California cuisine with a spectacular wine list and top service.

Mendocino

Continuing north, Hwy-1 passes the offshore kelp forests of Van Damme State Park before you reach the coast's most lauded stop, the decidedly touristy **MENDOCINO**. The quaint town sits on a broad-shouldered bluff with waves crashing on three sides; it's hard to find a spot here where you can't see the ocean sparkling in the distance. New England-style architecture is abundant, lending Mendo, as the locals call it, a down-home, almost cutesy air. Its appearance on the National Register of Historic Places and reputation as an artists' colony draw the curious up the coastal highway, and a fairly extensive network of B&Bs, restaurants and bars are more than happy to cater to their every need.

Accommodation

Room rates are high in and around Mendocino but there are good-value deals to be found, especially at a couple of the lovely oceanfront B&Bs to the south around Little River. Mendocino Coast Accommodations (℡1-800/262-7801, ⓦwww.mendocinovacations.com) can book rooms and holiday homes for free. There's $55 **camping** at Russian Gulch State Park and Van Damme State Park (book both at ℡1-800/444-7275, ⓦwww.parks.ca.gov), though both have a few $5 hike/bike sites.

The Inn at Schoolhouse Creek 7051 N Hwy-1, Little River ℡1-800/731-5525, ⓦwww.schoolhousecreek.com. Delightful B&B with a selection of differently designed cottages, set back from the ocean a couple of miles south of Mendo. Also has a unique massage yurt and outdoor hot tub. ⑤

Joshua Grindle Inn 44800 Little Lake Rd ℡1-800/474-6353, ⓦwww.joshgrin.com. Luxurious but intimate and friendly B&B, offering five standard and five deluxe rooms and serving excellent gourmet breakfasts. ⑤

Jughandle Creek Farm 3 miles north on Hwy-1, just beyond Caspar ℡707/964-4630, ⓦwww.jughandle.creekfarm.org. Funky place with rooms ($35 per person), cabins ($40) and tent sites ($12); there's a $5 discount if you're willing to donate an hour's work, and special youth and student rates. You can explore the trails in the woods and participate in nature-study programmes too. ❸

Little River Inn 2 miles south on Hwy-1 at Little River ℡1-888/466-5683, ⓦwww.littleriverinn.com. Wonderful spot with views over a bay full of sea stacks. Accommodations range from cosy rooms to spacious seafront cottages. The restaurant/bar is excellent, too. ❹

MacCallum House Inn 45020 Albion St ℡1-800/609-0492, ⓦwww.maccallumhouse.com. The largest B&B in town, with a range of smart rooms in the main house, as well as luxury suites, cottages, and two off-site properties. ⑥

Mendocino Hotel 45080 Main St ℡1-800/548-0513, ⓦwww.mendocinohotel.com. Luxurious, antique-filled rooms, the cheaper ones with shared baths, lend an air of class to this popular hotel. ❹

Sea Gull Inn 44960 Albion St ℡1-888/937-5204, ⓦwww.seagullbb.com. The best of the more affordable B&Bs right in the centre of town, with pastel-decorated rooms. ❹

The Town

Like other small settlements along the coast, Mendocino was originally a mill site and shipping port, established in 1852 by merchants from Maine who thought the proximity to the redwoods and exposed location made it a good site for sawmill operations. The industry has now vanished but the large community of artists has spawned craftsy commerce in the form of art galleries, gift shops and boutique delicatessens. This preservation didn't come about by accident. The state of California traded a block of old-growth forest with the Boise–Cascade logging company in exchange for the headlands surrounding the town. The headlands became a state park and Mendocino in turn became a living museum, with strict local ordinances mandating architectural design and upkeep.

The **visitor centre**, 735 Main St (daily 11am–4pm; ☏707/937-5397, ⊛www.visitmendocino.com), is located in **Ford House**, one of many mansions built by the Maine lumbermen in the style of their home state. The **Kelley House Museum**, 45007 Albion St (Fri–Mon 11am–3pm; $2 donation), has exhibits detailing the town's role as a centre for shipping redwood lumber to the miners during the Gold Rush, and conducts **walking tours** of the town on Saturday mornings at 11am – though you could do it yourself in under an hour. Chief among the numerous galleries is the **Mendocino Art Center**, 45200 Little Lake St (daily 10am–5pm; ☏1-800/653-3328, ⊛www.mendocinoart center.org), which has a revolving gallery for mainly Mendocino-based artists and runs workshops in ceramics, weaving, jewellery and metal sculpture. The **Mendocino Theatre Company** (☏707/937-4477, ⊛www.mendocino theatre.org) on the same premises puts on regular performances of both avant-garde and classic works.

There's plenty more to occupy you around town, with a long stroll along the headlands topping the list. **Hiking** and **cycling** are popular, with bikes available for around $40 a day from Catch a Canoe & Bicycles, Too (☏707/937-0273, ⊛www.catchacanoe.com), just south of Mendocino at the corner of Hwy-1 and Compche–Ukiah Road. They also rent outriggers and kayaks. At the west end of Main Street, hiking trails lead out into the **Mendocino Headlands**, where you can explore the grassy cliffs and make your way down to the tide pools next to the breaking waves. The **Russian Gulch State Park** ($8 per car; ☏707/937-5804), two miles north of town, has bike trails, beautiful fern glens and waterfalls. Just south of town, hiking and cycling trails weave through the unusual **Van Damme State Park** ($8 per car; ☏707/937-5804), which has a **Pygmy Forest** of ancient trees, stunted to waist-height because of poor drainage and soil chemicals. The coast of the park is punctuated with sea stacks and caves, carved by the pounding surf; two-hour sea-cave tours are available through Lost Coast Kayaking (daily 9am, 11.30am & 2pm; $50; ☏707/937-2434, ⊛www.lostcoastkayaking.com).

Abalone diving is extremely popular along the coast here, particularly just south of town in the small cove beside Van Damme State Park. In an attempt to thwart poaching, the practice is strictly regulated – the delectable gastropods are not available commercially, and you can only have three in your possession at any given time or collect a total of 24 in one season. To catch your own, visit Sub-Surface Progression Dive Center, 18600 Hwy-1 in Fort Bragg (☏707/964-3793, ⊛www.subsurfaceprogression.com), which leads all-inclusive, half-day diving expeditions.

Eating, drinking and entertainment

Mendocino is renowned for some gourmet **restaurants**, some of which are in the accommodations listed above, but there are also a few cheaper **cafés**, as well as a couple of down-to-earth **bars**.

The first weekend in March brings the **Mendocino Whale Festival** (☎1-800/726-2780), a celebration of food and headland views of whales returning to the Arctic. Moviegoers will enjoy the **Film Festival** every May (☎707/937-0171, ⓦwww.mendocinofilmfestival.com), and music-lovers the two-week **Mendocino Music Festival** (☎1-800/937-2044, ⓦwww.mendocinomusic.com) in the middle of July; although the emphasis is largely on classical music and opera, some blues and jazz bands from all over the state also perform.

Cafés, restaurants and bars

955 Ukiah Street 955 Ukiah St ☎707/937-1955. High-quality main courses such as rosemary-scented lamb stew ($25) follow equally delicious starters like duck and chickpea wontons in the elegant dining room. Closed Mon & Tues.

Café Beaujolais 961 Ukiah St ☎707/937-5614. The town's premier restaurant, whose founder wrote a book on organic California cuisine and which serves up a frequently changing menu of innovative main courses such as pan-roasted sturgeon fillet for around $20–35.

Dick's Place 45070 Main St. Mendocino's oldest bar, with all the robust conviviality you'd expect from a spit-and-sawdust saloon.

Mendocino Café 10451 Lansing St. This homely little place serves a surprisingly eclectic and inexpensive mix of salads, pastas and sandwiches.

Moosse Café 390 Kasten St ☎707/937-2611. A good choice for a filling lunch, as dinner main courses like North-Coast cioppino of prawns cost around double at $24–30.

Patterson's Pub 10485 Lansing St. Another friendly local joint with a range of fine ales, cocktails and a fairly buzzing atmosphere.

Fort Bragg and around

FORT BRAGG, a mere nine miles north of Mendocino, is very much the blue-collar flipside to its comfortable neighbour, although some of its trendier aspects have rubbed off. Still, for the most part, where Mendocino exists on wholefood, art and peaceful ocean walks, Fort Bragg brings you the rib shack and tattoo parlour. Until not long ago the town sat beneath the perpetual cloud of steam choked out from the lumbermills of the massive Georgia Pacific Corporation, which used to monopolize California's logging industry and provide much of the town's employment. There was once a fort here, but it was only used for ten years until the 1860s, when it was abandoned and the land sold off cheaply. The otherwise attractive **Noyo Harbor** (south of town on Hwy-1) is these days crammed with an equal number of pleasure boats and diminishing commercial-fishing craft, as the town attempts to cash in on Mendocino's tourist trade. Indeed, its proximity to the more isolated reaches of the Mendocino coast, an abundance of budget accommodation, and a bevy of inexpensive restaurants make it a good alternative to Mendocino.

Information and accommodation

Fort Bragg's **Chamber of Commerce** (Mon–Fri 9am–5pm, Sat & Sun 10am–3pm; ☎1-800/726-2780, ⓦwww.mendocinocoast.com) is at 217 S Main St. Most of the **motels** cluster along Hwy-1 close to the centre of town; **B&Bs** are more upscale, of course, but cheaper than those in Mendocino. There's **camping** among six miles of coastal pines and sandy beach at **MacKerricher State Park** ($5–35; reserve on ☎1-800/444-7275, ⓦwww.parks.ca.gov), three miles north of Fort Bragg.

Accommodation

Chelsea Inn 763 N Main St ☎707/964-4787 or 1-800/253-9972. The cheapest of the town's motels is in a renovated inn. No frills but comfortable enough. ❶

Grey Whale Inn B&B 615 N Main St ☎1-800/382-7244, ⓦwww.greywhaleinn.com. This quaint building covered in redwood clapboard has lovely, homely rooms with great views, as well as colourful grounds. ❸

Old Coast Hotel 101 N Franklin ☎1-888/468-3550, ⓦ www.oldcoasthotel.com. Comfortable rooms in a restored 1892 building, with a steak-and-seafood restaurant attached. ④

Surf Motel 1220 S Main St ☎1-800/339-5361, ⓦ www.surfmotelfortbragg.com. Slightly smarter than the *Chelsea Inn*, with better furnished and more attractive rooms. ①

The town and around

As for things to do, you could take a quick look at the historical exhibits of the **Guest House Museum** (Tues–Sun 10.30am–2.30pm; $2), in front of the train station at 343 Main St. Spend a worthwhile hour or two rummaging on **Glass Beach**, a ten-minute walk north of Downtown at the end of Elm Street, below an attractive overgrown headland. Used as the town's dump until the 1960s, the disposed articles have been smoothed by the ocean into a kaleidoscopic beachcomber's paradise of broken glassware and crockery fragments. You can take an amusing day-trip on the **Skunk Trains** operated by the Californian Western Railroad ($47 round-trip; ☎1-800/777-5865, ⓦ www.skunktrain.com), which run twice daily during the summer months and once in the shoulder seasons from the terminus on Laurel Street, forty miles inland to the tiny halt at **Northspur** and back. It's good fun to ride in the open observation car as it tunnels through mountains and rumbles across a series of high bridges on its route through the towering redwoods, taking almost three and a half hours to complete the trip. At Northspur you can connect with the tour from **Willits** (local depot ☎707/459-5248), on US-101 forty miles inland, which has interstate bus connections.

If you'd like to get out on the ocean, All Aboard Adventures, down by the water at 32400 N Harbor Drive (☎707/964-1881, ⓦ www.allaboardadventures.com), does fishing and crabbing trips for $80 and whale-watching expeditions from $35 per person.

A short drive or bus ride south of Fort Bragg will take you to the **Mendocino Coast Botanical Gardens**, 18220 N Hwy-1 (daily: March–Oct 9am–5pm; Nov–Feb 9am–4pm; $10), where you can see more or less every wildflower under the sun spread across 47 acres of prime coastal territory. It's particularly renowned for the many varieties of **rhododendron** that bloom in April and May. Heading north, the next stretch of Hwy-1 is the slowest, continuing for another twenty miles of road and windswept beach before leaving the coastline to turn inland and head over the mountains to meet US-101 at **Leggett**. Redwood country begins in earnest here: there's even a tree you can drive through (summer 8.30am–8pm; $5), though the best forests are further north. If you're peckish, stop for a filling all-American snack or meal at *Redwood Diner*. Further on, just before you cross the Humboldt County line, you can pause briefly at **Confusion Hill** to see the "world's largest chainsaw sculpture", hewn from redwood.

Eating and drinking

Fort Bragg's myriad **restaurants** tend to cater to the ravenous carnivore, although there are one or two places with more variety, as well as some good cafés.

Cafés, restaurants and bars

Egghead's 326 N Main St. A good place for a big breakfast, *Egghead's* lists 41 different omelettes on their menu. Daily 7am–2pm.

Headlands Coffeehouse 120 E Laurel St ☎707/964-1987. Vegetarians can take refuge in the hearty Italian offerings at this café, which also has live music and art exhibitions.

Jenny's Giant Burger 940 N Main St. Usually full of earthy locals scoffing large chunks of red meat, in an old-style place reminiscent of the Fifties.

🏃 **Mendo Bistro** 301 N Main St ☎707/964-4974. This genteel option, upstairs in the converted old Union Lumber Store complex, serves excellent, imaginative international cuisine, including gourmet pasta dishes, at moderate prices.

North Coast Brewing Company 444 N Main St.
If you're feeling thirsty, stop in for one of the
"handmade ales" at the award-winning *North*

Coast Brewing Company. Free tours of the brewery
itself, on the opposite side of Main Street, are
conducted at 12.30pm on Saturday.

The Anderson Valley

Running diagonally northwest for nearly twenty miles, from just south of its
small main town of **Boonville** to within a few miles of the coast, is the fertile
ANDERSON VALLEY, an amalgam of sunny rolling hills shaded by oaks and
madrones that merge into dark redwood forest. Hwy-128, connecting US-101
near Cloverdale to the coast at Albion, is the sole artery through the valley, which
has a long-standing reputation as a magnet for mavericks. The original settlers
were sheep farmers who saw so few outsiders between the 1880s and 1920s that
they developed their own language, **boontling**, snippets of which still survive
today. A good sixth of this odd dialect was known as "nonch harpin's", meaning
"objectionable talk", and largely referred to the then taboo subjects of sexual
activity and bodily functions. You can see examples of boontling in the names of
local beers and establishments, but if you want to know the full story, track down
a copy of *Boontling, An American Lingo* in local stores. During the twentieth
century, sheep farming gradually gave way to the cultivation of apples but, though
many orchards still exist, they are fast being replaced by more lucrative vineyards,
as the craze for California wine means this area is becoming a northern annexe of
the Wine Country, along with the **Yorkville Highlands**, the southeastern
extension of the valley. Most of the Anderson Valley's existing wineries line
Hwy-128 between the tiny settlements of **Philo** and **Navarro**. The area is also
famous for the excellent beer produced at the Anderson Valley Brewing Co, 17700
Hwy-253 (daily 11am–6pm, 7pm in summer; tours daily 1.30 & 3pm, except
Tues in winter; tasting $5; ☎1-800/207-2337, ⓦwww.avbc.com), just east of the
junction with Hwy-128 on the south side of Boonville. Their Hop Ottin' IPA (an
example of boontling) and rich amber ales are especially delicious.

Boonville and Philo

Despite having a population of little over seven hundred, **Boonville** still easily
manages to be the largest town in the Anderson Valley. Strung along its widened
half-mile section of Hwy-128 are some quaint shops, a hotel and a few places to
find sustenance. In terms of **accommodation**, the only choice in town is the
grand nineteenth-century *Boonville Hotel*, Hwy-128 at Lambert Lane (☎707/895-
2210, ⓦwww.boonvillehotel.com; ❹), whose rooms vary considerably in price
and luxury; the $350 Casita is worth splashing out on. Apart from the hotel's spicy
Mexican-influenced California **cuisine**, a fine range of Californian, Italian and
Mexican food is to be had at *Lauren's*, 14211 Hwy-128 (☎707/895-3857). You can
get quality bar food and **drink** your way through the entire range of Boonville
beers at the *Buckhorn Saloon*, 14081 Hwy-128, owned by the Anderson Valley
Brewing Co.

Six miles northwest of Boonville, the village of **Philo** has alternative venues to
spend the night or have a meal, although it's all rather cutesy. *The Philo Pottery Inn*,
8550 Hwy-128 (☎707/895-3069; ❹), is a plush **B&B** right in the village but the
best deal is at the nearby *Anderson Valley Inn*, 8480 Hwy-128 (☎707/895-3325,
ⓦwww.avinn.com; ❸). *Libby's Restaurant*, 8651 Hwy-128, serves up excellent,
inexpensive Mexican **food**, or you can grab a sandwich or picnic ingredients from
Lemon's Market, just down the road.

A great place to take your picnic is three miles northwest to **Hendy Woods
State Park** (☎707/895-3141; $8 per car), clearly signposted off Hwy-128. The
park features hiking trails through two sizeable redwood groves, fishing on the

There are now around thirty **wineries** dotted along the Anderson Valley and the number increases year by year. The cooler temperatures, especially at the northwest end, which sees the coastal fogs roll in, are better suited mostly to white varieties such as Gewürtzraminer, Chardonnay and Riesling, but the hardy Pinot Noir fares equally well. For further details you can contact the Mendocino Winegrowers Alliance in Ukiah (℡707/468-9886, Ⓦwww.truemendocinowine.com). About a dozen of the wineries have **open tastings** and there's rarely a fee, as they remain for the time being far less commercialized than their cousins further south. Here are a handful that would repay a visit.

Foursight 14475 Hwy-128, just south of Boonville ℡707/895-2889, Ⓦwww.foursight wines.com. Small family winery that produces particularly excellent Sauvignon Blanc and Pinot Noir, as well as a mean Gewürtzraminer. Fri–Mon 10am–4.30pm.

Goldeneye Winery 9200 Hwy-128, just south of Philo ℡707/895-3202, Ⓦwww .goldeneyewinery.com. This offshoot of Napa's Duckhorn produces wines from the Pinot Noir variety exclusively, including an excellent rosé. Daily 11am–4pm. Tasting $5–10.

Handley 3155 Hwy-128, about 2 miles south of Navarro ℡1-800/733-3151, Ⓦwww .handleycellars.com. A fine range of white wines – dry, sweet and sparkling – are produced at this family winery. The tasting room also has a nice little collection of oriental art. Daily: May–Oct 10am–6pm; Nov–April 10am–5pm.

Husch Vineyards 4400 Hwy-128, almost 3 miles south of Navarro ℡1-800/554-8724, Ⓦwww.huschvineyards.com. Founded in 1971, this small family winery is the oldest in the valley, and you're assured of a warm welcome at its rustic tasting room. Produces no less than 21 wines. Daily: summer 10am–6pm; winter 10am–5pm. Free tours Mon, Wed & Thurs 1pm & 3pm.

Navarro Vineyards 5601 Hwy-128, 3 miles north of Philo ℡1-800/537-9463, Ⓦwww .navarrowine.com. This small winery specializes in Alsatian-style wines, which it only sells directly to the consumer and select restaurants. It also concocts a wicked grape juice, so even the kids can enjoy a free sip or two here. Daily: summer 10am–6pm; winter 11am–5pm. Tours 10.30am & 3pm.

Roederer Estate 4501 Hwy-128, about 3 miles south of Navarro ℡707/895-2288, Ⓦwww.roedererestate.com. One of the higher-profile Mendocino wineries, specializing in sparkling vintages. Daily 10am–5pm. Tasting $5.

Navarro River, and **camping** for $5–35 (reserve on ℡1-800/444-7275, Ⓦwww .reserveamerica.com) or six-person cabins for $50. A mile or so beyond the park entrance, another signposted left turn leads four miles up through more redwood-clad ridges to *Highland Ranch* (℡707/895-3600, Ⓦwww.highlandranch.com; Ⓞ). The $295-per-person overnight charge ($245 off-season) at this friendly guest ranch, set amid a stunning three hundred acres, includes a luxury detached cabin, three meals, plus all drinks and most activities on offer, principally horseback riding and clay-pigeon shooting.

The Humboldt coast

Of the northern coastal counties, **HUMBOLDT** is by far the most beautiful and also the one most at odds with development: the good folk of Eureka famously voted to bar chainstore-behemoth WalMart from erecting a huge waterfront outlet in 1999. This is logging land, and the drive up US-101 gives a tour of giant sawmills fenced in by stacks of felled trees. Yet Humboldt County also contains the largest preserves of giant redwoods in the world in **Humboldt Redwoods State Park** and, north, **Redwood National Park**. Both are peaceful, other-worldly experiences not to be missed, though the absence of sunlight within the groves and the mossy surfaces can be eerie.

Locals worry that as more people discover the area, the rugged serve-yourself mentality here could quickly turn into a service economy. They still welcome outsiders but, beyond the few more touristic spots, do so on their own terms. The coastal highway's inability to trace Humboldt's southern coast formerly guaranteed isolation and earned the region the name of the **Lost Coast**. The area, while still isolated, is not quite as "lost" any more thanks to the construction of an airstrip in Shelter Cove and an infusion of hotels, restaurants and new homes.

Humboldt is perhaps most renowned for its "Emerald Triangle", which produces the majority of California's largest cash crop, **marijuana**. As the Humboldt coast's fishing and logging industries slide, more and more people have been turning to growing the stuff and new hydroponic techniques ensure that the potency of the ultra-thick buds is extremely high. The occasional bouts of aggressive law enforcement and a steady stream of crop-poaching have been met with defiant, booby-trapped and frequently armed protection of crops, so production continues apace. Apart from considerable areas of this alternative agriculture, the county is almost entirely forestland. The highway rejoins the coast at **Eureka** and **Arcata**, Humboldt's two major towns and both jumping-off points for the redwoods. These "ambassadors from another time", as John Steinbeck dubbed them, are at their 300-foot best in the **Redwood National Park**, which contains three state parks and covers some 106,000 acres of skyscraping forest.

As usual in this part of the state, **getting around** is going to be your biggest problem. Although Greyhound and Amtrak Thruway buses run as far as Arcata along US-101, they're hardly a satisfactory way to see the trees, and you'll need a car to make the trip worthwhile. **Hitchhiking** still goes on up here, and gaggles of locals gather at the gas stations and freeway entrances begging for rides. This is partly a throwback to the kinder decades when hitching was a normal practice on American roads but normal discretion should be exercised and remember that it is illegal on the freeway itself. For information on **what's on** in Humboldt, the free weekly *North Coast Journal* (Ⓦwww.northcoastjournal.com) details where to go and what to do in the area, as does the county website Ⓦwww.redwoods.info.

Southern Humboldt and the Lost Coast

The inaccessibility of the Humboldt's beautiful **LOST COAST** in the south of the county is ensured by the **Kings Range**, an area of impassable cliffs that shoots up several thousand feet from the ocean, so that even a road as sinuous as Hwy-1 can't negotiate a passage through. To get there you have to travel US-101 through deep redwood territory as far as tiny **Garberville**.

Garberville

A one-street town with a few good bars and hotels, **Garberville** is the centre of the cannabis industry and a lively break from the freeway. Each week, the local paper runs a "bust-barometer" which charts the week's pot raids, and every July, the town hosts the massive two-day **Reggae on the River** festival. Tickets cost over $100; contact ☎707/923-4583 or Ⓦwww.reggaeontheriver.com by early May to reserve them.

The town has bus connections with Eureka on HTA (see p.640) and the train line at Martinez, with the twice-daily Amtrak Thruway service. The town's **Chamber of Commerce** (summer daily, winter Mon–Fri 10am–4pm; ☎707/923-2613,

Ⓦwww.garberville.org) is located in the Redwood Drive Center at 782 Redwood Drive. For what you get, much of the town's **accommodation** is a bit overpriced. The *Benbow Inn*, several miles south of town at 445 Lake Benbow Drive (Ⓣ1-800/355-3301, Ⓦwww.benbowinn.com; ❸), is a flash place for such a rural location but has a couple of reasonably priced rooms; the smart *Humboldt House Inn*, 701 Redwood Drive (Ⓣ1-800/780-7234, Ⓦwww.humboldthouse inn.com; ❹), and the more basic *Sherwood Forest Motel*, 814 Redwood Drive (Ⓣ707/923-2721, Ⓦwww.sherwoodforestmotel.com; ❷), are decent alternatives. The closest **campground** is seven miles south at **Benbow State Recreation Area** ($35; Ⓣ707/923-3238), while five miles further south on US-101 **Richardson Grove State Park** in Piercy ($35; Ⓣ1-800/444-7275, Ⓦwww.parks.ca.gov) spreads over 1400 acres along the Eel River.

Even if you don't intend to stay in Garberville, at least stop off to sample some of the town's **restaurants** and **bars**, which turn out some of the best live bluegrass you're likely to hear in the state. Redwood Drive is lined with bars, cafés and restaurants: the *Woodrose Café* at no. 911 serves organic lunches, while *Treats Café* at no. 764 offers snacks, drinks and internet access. All the town bars tend to whoop it up in the evening; the noisiest of the lot is the *Branding Iron Saloon*, at no. 744 (Ⓣ707/923-2562), with a small cover for its live music at weekends. Subversive gifts and more innocent by-products of the region's industry can be obtained at The Hemp Connection, 412 Maple Lane, on the corner of Redwood Drive.

Shelter Cove

From Garberville, via the adjoining village of **Redway**, where you can enjoy a gourmet meal of delights such as pork chops with mushroom sauce at the *Mateel Café*, 3342 Redwood Drive (Ⓣ707/923-3020), the Briceland and Shelter Cove roads wind 23 miles through territory populated by old hippies and New Agers beetling around in battered vehicles. You eventually emerge on the **Lost Coast** at **Shelter Cove**, set in a tiny bay neatly folded between sea cliffs and headlands. First settled in the 1850s when gold was struck inland, its isolated position at the far end of the **Kings Range** kept the village small until recent years. Now, thanks to a new airstrip, weekenders arrive in their hordes and modern houses are indiscriminately dotted across the headland. It's the closest real settlement to the **hiking** and **wildlife** explorations of the surrounding wilderness, which remains inhabited only by deer, river otter, mink, black bear, bald eagles and falcons. Many travellers use either *Mario's Marina Motel*, 461 Machi Road (Ⓣ707/986-7595; ❸), or the *Beachcomber Inn*, 412 Machi Road (Ⓣ707/986-7551 or 1-800/718-4789; ❸), as a **base**; the former establishment has a good restaurant with a sea view from its extensive grounds and rents out various seafaring equipment.

Another fine spot to admire the ocean is from the **Cape Mendocino Lighthouse**, on Upper Pacific Drive (late May to late Sept daily 10.30am–3.30pm; free), which was reopened to the public in 1998 after being relocated from 25 miles further north, near Ferndale. To the north the 24-mile **Lost Coast Trail** runs along cliff-tops dotted with half a dozen primitive **campgrounds** ($8), most near streams and with access to black-sand beaches. Bring a tide book, as some points of the trail are impassable at high tide. Another trail takes you to the top of **Kings Peak**, which, at 4086ft, is the highest point on the continental US shoreline. Cape Mendocino can also lay claim to being the **westernmost point** of the lower 48 states.

Humboldt Redwoods State Park

The heart of redwood country begins in earnest a few miles north of Garberville, along US-101, when you enter the **Humboldt Redwoods State Park** (unrestricted entry; ☏707/946-2409, ⓦwww.humboldtredwoods.org): over 53,000 acres of predominantly virgin timber, protected from lumber companies, make this the largest of the redwood parks – though it is the least used. Thanks to the Save-the-Redwoods League, which has been acquiring land privately for the park, it continues to slowly expand year after year. At the Phillipsville exit, the serpentine **Avenue of the Giants** follows an old stagecoach road, weaving for 32 miles through trees that block all but a few strands of sunlight. This is the habitat of *Sequoia sempervirens*, the coast redwood, with ancestors dating back to the days of the dinosaur.

The Avenue parallels US-101, adding at least thirty minutes to your travel time, but there are several exits to the freeway if you're in a hurry. Pick up a free **Auto Tour** guide at the southern or northern entrances and, better still, stop at the **visitor centre** (daily: summer 9am–5pm; winter 10am–4pm; ☏707/946-2263), halfway along at **Burlington**, a mile south of Weott, which has fascinating inter-pretive exhibits on the redwoods, other flora and fauna, logging history and a catastrophic flood in 1964. At sporadic points along the Avenue, small stalls selling lumber products and refreshments dot the course of the highway. There's also another **Drive-Thru Tree** towards the southern end of the Avenue at Myers Flat ($3). Three developed **campgrounds** ($35–45; ☏1-800/444-7275, ⓦwww .parks.ca.gov), a simpler environmental one ($20) and a couple of hike/bike ones ($5), comprise your accommodation options within the park. *The Riverwood Inn* (☏707/943-3333, ⓦwww.riverwoodinn.info; ❷), in **Phillipsville** itself, is a good rustic place to stay; the bar/restaurant occasionally showcases live bluegrass and other styles of music and serves decent Mexican food, plus you're assured a friendly welcome from the locals.

The Avenue follows the south fork of the Eel River, eventually rejoining US-101 at **Pepperwood**. Ten miles before this junction, Mattole Road peels off to the left and provides the best **backcountry** access to the towering trees, which most visitors neglect, as well as further access to the Lost Coast.

Ferndale

Around fifteen miles north of Pepperwood, you should definitely detour a few miles west to **Ferndale**, unquestionably the Lost Coast's most attractive town, although with enough time on your hands an even better route is the stunningly scenic Lost Coast loop via Honeydew and Cape Mendocino. Promoting itself unabashedly as "California's best-preserved Victorian village", Ferndale certainly has its charms – for once the appealing architecture is not just confined to one quaint street but continues for blocks on either side of Main Street in a picturesque townscape of nineteenth-century houses and churches. Indeed, the entire town, founded in 1852, has been designated a State Historical Landmark. You can learn more about its history at the **Ferndale Museum**, 515 Shaw St (Feb–May & Oct–Dec Wed–Sat 11am–4pm, Sun 1–4pm; June–Sept Tues–Sat 11am–4pm, Sun 1–4pm; $2), by perusing the old newspaper cuttings, documents, photos and equipment that was once used in bygone occupations. The much more contemporary **Kinetic Sculpture Race Museum**, 581 Main St (daily 10am–5pm), within the Ferndale Art and Cultural Center, contains vehicles from the peculiar annual competition that takes place between Arcata and Ferndale (see p.643). Ferndale supports an active artistic community, so there are a disproportionate number of galleries and antique shops to browse through.

As you might expect, most of Ferndale's **accommodation** comes in the shape of stylish hotels and B&Bs, though the remote location keeps prices very reasonable. The *Victorian Inn*, 400 Ocean Ave (☏1-888/589-1808, ⓦwww.victorian villageinn.com; ❹), has comfortable rooms above its classy, carpeted lobby and lounge. Almost directly opposite at 315 Main St, *The Ivanhoe* (☎707/786-9000, ⓦwww.ivanhoe-hotel.com; ❸), claims to be the oldest hotel in town and the westernmost in the country; it also has a decent restaurant. Further along, the *Francis Creek Inn*, 577 Main St (☎707/786-9611, ⓦwww.franciscreekinn .com; ❸), is comfortable and slightly cheaper. *VI*, inside the *Victorian Inn*, serves quality California **cuisine** plus sandwiches and cocktails, while *Poppa Joe's*, 409 Main St, dishes up down-home breakfasts and lunches. The *Candystick Fountain & Grill*, 361 Main St, is the spot for an even cheaper snack or a whopping ice cream. The **entertainment** scene is appropriately low-key but you can drink in one of the hotel bars or catch a performance of the renowned Ferndale Repertory Theatre at 477 Main St (☎707/786-5483, ⓦwww.ferndale-rep.org).

Eureka

"Eureka", as is well known from the story of Archimedes, means "I have found it!" and, being the largest coastal settlement north of San Francisco, this expanding town would certainly displace a fair amount of water if dropped into the Pacific. Near the top of the north coast of California between the Arcata and Humboldt bays, **EUREKA** feels at first like an industrial, gritty and often foggy lumbermill town, though its **fishing industry** carries the most economic weight, providing ninety percent of the state's catch of Pacific Ocean shrimp and Dungeness crab, as well as two-thirds of its oysters. It may initially strike you as somewhere just to pass through but once you penetrate the typical strip malls that line US-101 on each side of town, you will discover an appealing centre, dotted with rather attractive Victorian mansions and cutesy B&Bs, an increasing number of galleries and restaurants and a number of worthwhile sights.

Arrival and information

Eureka has fairly limited **transport** links: Greyhound, 1603 4th St, connects Eureka to San Francisco once a day but only goes as far north as nearby Arcata. For getting around town or up the coast as far as Trinidad and south as far as Garberville, Humboldt Transit Authority, 133 V St (☎707/443-0826, ⓦwww .hta.org), operates **buses** every day except Sunday. The Eureka **visitor centre** is on the southern approach to town at 2112 Broadway (Mon–Fri 8.30am–5pm; ☎1-800/356-6381, ⓦwww.eurekachamber.com).

Accommodation

The collection of **motels** that punctuate the town's busiest streets make Eureka a reasonably economical base for exploring the redwoods to the north and south, although there is an increasing number of far classier **hotels** and **B&Bs** where you can be pampered. **Campgrounds** line US-101 between Eureka and Arcata; the best is the *KOA* (☎1-800/562-3136, ⓦwww.koa.com; from $26 per tent, RV hookups from $40, cabins $60), a large site with copious amenities four miles north of town at 4050 N US-101.

Abigail's Elegant Victorian Mansion 1406 C St ☎707/444-3144, ⓦwww.eureka-california.com. As the name suggests, this stylish B&B re-creates the opulence and splendour of a past era and even offers $20 vintage car rides round the old town. ❹

Carter House Inns 301 L St ☎1-800/404-1390, ⓦwww.carterhouse.com. All rooms are top quality within this enclave of four Victorian buildings arranged around a quiet junction,
including the private $625-a-night Carter Cottage and a superb restaurant (see p.642). Gourmet breakfast included. ❻

Eureka Inn 518 7th St ☎1-877/552-3985. Occupying an entire block, this huge landmark hotel, which reopened in 2010, has been completely refurbished. The rooms are simply furnished and the massive lobby area remains a time warp in deep red. ❸

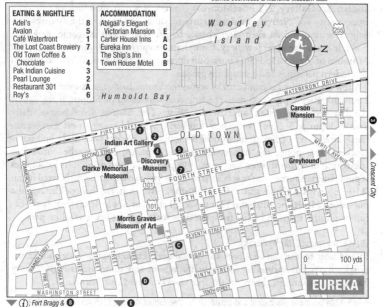

Inside the map:

EATING & NIGHTLIFE
Adel's 8
Avalon 5
Café Waterfront 1
The Lost Coast Brewery 7
Old Town Coffee & Chocolate 4
Pak Indian Cuisine 3
Pearl Lounge 2
Restaurant 301 A
Roy's 6

ACCOMMODATION
Abigail's Elegant Victorian Mansion E
Carter House Inns A
Eureka Inn C
The Ship's Inn D
Town House Motel B

Woodley Island

Humboldt Bay

Carson Mansion

OLD TOWN

Indian Art Gallery

Clarke Memorial Museum

Discovery Museum

Greyhound

Morris Graves Museum of Art

EUREKA

0 100 yds

Crescent City

(i), Fort Bragg & ⑧

The Ship's Inn 821 D St ☎1-877/443-7583, ⓦwww.shipsinn.net. There are only three rooms at this charming B&B, the warmly decorated Captain's Quarters and two cheaper pastel-shaded rooms. Excellent breakfasts. ④

Town House Motel 933 4th St ☎1-800/445-6888. The cleanest of the cluster of cheap motels heading north on US-101. Ideal budget base. ①

The City

Downtown Eureka is quite a mixed bag of neon-lit motels and chain restaurants, backing onto workaday rail- and shipyards, yet interspersed with some delightful Victorian architecture. Some colourful murals have also brightened things up and the pretty, compact **Old Town**, bounded by C, G, First and Third streets, at the edge of the bay, does its best to support a fledgling tourist economy. This area boasts an increasing number of lively restaurants, bars that would not look out of place in San Francisco and galleries. The area is at its liveliest on the first Saturday of each month, when the galleries and boutiques throw their doors open for **Arts Alive!** night, when there are various live musical performances.

The town's most iconic sight is the **Carson Mansion**, 143 M St at Second, an opulent Gothic pile built in the 1880s by William Carson, who made and lost fortunes in both timber and oil. Unfortunately, it is now a private club and can only be enjoyed from the street. **Fort Humboldt State Historic Park**, 3431 Fort Ave (daily 9am–5pm; free), gives a look at a restored army fort and not much else, disappointing given that the army general and future president Ulysses S. Grant used it for a headquarters in 1853. Visitors with children might be rewarded by dropping in at the **Discovery Museum**, 501 3rd St (Tues–Sat 10am–4pm, Sun noon–4pm; $4; ☎707/443-9694), which has rotating hands-on art and science displays for youngsters.

The collection of Native American art at the **Clarke Memorial Museum**, Third and E streets (Wed–Sat 11am–4pm; free), can't hold a candle to the stuff at the

Indian Art Gallery, 241 F St (Mon–Sat 10am–4.30pm; free), which affords a rare opportunity for Native American artists to show and market their works in a gallery setting and an even rarer chance to get your hands on some incredibly good, inexpensive silver jewellery. Completing an artistic trio, the **Morris Graves Museum of Art** at 636 F St (Thurs–Sun noon–5pm; $3 donation) has six galleries of modern paintings and a sculpture garden.

A few minutes by car from Eureka across the Samoa Bridge, squashed against the Louisiana–Pacific plywood mill, the tiny company town of **Samoa** is the site of the last remaining cookhouse in the West. The **Samoa Cookhouse** (daily 7am–3.30pm & 5–9pm) was where lumbermen would come to eat gargantuan meals after a day of felling redwoods. Although the oilskin tablecloths and burly workers have gone, the lumber-camp style remains, making the cookhouse something of an institution. Eating massive portions of red meat at its long tables is pure entertainment; you're served as much as you can eat of the daily fixed menu ($10–15) with a smile and a bit of history. Adjacent to the cookhouse, the one-room **Maritime Museum** (Tues, Wed, Fri & Sat noon–4pm; free) is chock-full of photos, maps and relics from the days when Eureka was a whaling port.

Eating and drinking

In addition to the *Samoa Cookhouse* (see above), **eating** options are numerous. Eureka has a fair sprinkling of **nightlife** venues and some increasingly trendy **bars**. For full listings, check out the free weekly *North Coast Journal*.

Adel's 1724 Broadway. Basic meat-and-potato meals and salads for about $10 make this local hangout on the south side of town a good option.

Avalon 239 G St ☎707/445-0500. Parisian meets California cuisine – at a price. The bacon-wrapped filet mignon costs $30 but a quality burger is half that. Dinner only, closed Mon.

Café Waterfront 102 F St. A very reliable choice for delicious seafood and burgers, where the fancier main courses cost around $15.

Lost Coast Brewery and Café 617 4th St. Serves large, hearty meat and fish dishes to a rambunctious crowd of discerning microbrew drinkers and sports fans.

Old Town Coffee & Chocolates 211 F St ☎707/445-8600. Ranks as the coast's finest coffee shop, with its beautiful red-brick interior and top-notch roasts. It's open until around 11pm and has fun open-mic nights.

Pak Indian Cuisine 1735 4th St. Good, simple curry house with a range of mild and spicy favourites from both sides of the border, mostly under $10.

The Pearl Lounge 507 2nd St ☎707/444-2017. The best example of old Eureka's new persona, this extremely chic joint, with sleek metal-and-glass bar and high-tech projection screen, is the spot to be seen with a cocktail. Live entertainment on Fri & Sat.

Restaurant 301 301 L St ☎707/444-8062. The *Carter House Inns'* classy dining room serves sumptuous set menus and à la carte dishes for around $25–30. The cuisine is mostly California with a French touch, and you can choose from one of the most extensive wine lists in the country.

Roy's 218 D St ☎707/442-4574. The place to head if you want to try one of the Old-Town Italian restaurants, with main courses costing around $20.

Arcata

ARCATA, only seven miles up the coast from Eureka, is far more immediately appealing, centred on a grassy central plaza that flies an Earth flag under those of the US and California. Beards and Birkenstocks are the norm in this small college town, with a large community of rat-race refugees and Sixties throwbacks, whose presence is manifest in some lively bars and the town's earthy, mellow pace. The beaches north of town are some of the best on the north coast, white-sanded, windswept and known for their easy hikeability and random parties. But think twice about diving headlong into the surf without a wetsuit, as the ocean in these parts is cold throughout the year.

The main square is the focal point of the town's shops and bars, with everything you're likely to want to see and do within easy walking distance. In the middle of the square rests a statue of President McKinley. Originally intended for nearby McKinleyville, it fell off the train on the way and stayed put in Arcata. Just east of the town centre, **Humboldt State University**, with its nationally known environmental education and natural resource management programmes, attracts a decidedly liberal student body, which contributes considerably to Arcata's leftist feel. If you're interested in the college's history and programmes, take one of the free student-led tours, which begin at the Plaza Avenue entrance on weekdays at 10am and 2pm and on Saturday at noon. Call ☎707/826-4402 for information.

At the foot of I Street, the **Arcata Marsh and Wildlife Sanctuary**, a restored former dump on 150 acres of wetland, is a peaceful place where you can lie on the boardwalk in the sun and listen to the birds. The Interpretive Center at 569 South G St (daily 9am–5pm; ☎707/826-2359) runs **guided wildlife walks** (Sat 2pm), as does the northwest chapter of the Audubon Society (Ⓦwww.rras.org), which meets at the very end of I Street at 8.30am every Saturday morning. Those who don't have time to explore the Redwood National Park can visit Arcata's own second-growth **community forest**, a beautiful 575-acre spot with manageable trails and ideal picnic areas, accessible by going east on 14th Street to Redwood Park Drive.

If you're around over Memorial Day weekend, don't miss the three-day **Kinetic Sculpture Race** (☎707/786-9259, Ⓦwww.kineticsculpturerace.org), a spectacular event in which competitors use human-powered contraptions of their own devising to propel themselves over land, water, dunes and marsh from Arcata to Ferndale.

Practicalities

Greyhound **buses** only head south from the station at 925 E St; there's also a Humboldt Transit Authority link with Eureka every day except Sunday. Going north, Redwood Coast Transit (☎707/464-6400, Ⓦwww.redwoodcoasttransit .org) runs a twice-daily service for $20 to Crescent City and on to Smith River. The **California Welcome Center**, over a mile north of town just off US-101 at 1635 Heindon Rd (daily 9am–5pm; ☎707/822-3619, Ⓦwww.arcatachamber .com), has free maps, brochures and displays from all over the state, plus lists of local accommodation and services.

Motels just out of town on US-101 are cheaper than the increasingly popular **B&Bs**, if a little less inviting, but still cost up to $60 per night. The best of these is the *Fairwinds Motel*, 1674 G St (☎1-866/352-5518, Ⓦwww.fairwindsmotel arcata.com; ❷). Of the central establishments, the *Hotel Arcata*, 708 9th St on the town's main square (☎1-800/344-1221, Ⓦwww.hotelarcata.com; ❸), is pretty stylish, while among the B&Bs, *The Lady Anne*, between the plaza and the college at 902 14th St (☎707/822-2797, Ⓦwww.ladyanneinn.com; ❹), has been an Arcata favourite for years. There are several **campgrounds** north of Arcata along the coast, but none within easy reach of town unless you've got a car. The nearest and cheapest is at **Clam Beach County Park** (☎707/445-765), eight miles north of town on US-101, where showerless sites cost $12 per car or $5 per walk-in, making it quite a party venue for dishevelled youngsters staying long-term. See p.644 for more distant options with better facilities.

Dotted around the plaza and tangential streets, Arcata's **bars** and **cafés** set the town apart. The best of the bunch, ⚡*Jambalaya* at 915 H St (☎707/822-4766), is actually more of a restaurant with a saucy Cajun touch and an additional nightly diet of R&B, jazz and rock bands. *Humboldt Brews*, 856 Tenth St, offers good ale and low-priced meals, and hosts regular gigs. There's also the relaxed *Café Mokka* at the *Finnish Country Sauna and Tubs* (☎707/822-2228), 495 J St, with live acoustic sets at the weekend and hot tubs in the garden for $17 an hour ($9 for 30min). On the corner of the plaza at 791 G St, *Café Brio* is the spot to enjoy a fine coffee, cake or snack. Good **restaurants** also abound – the vegetarian *Wildflower Café and Bakery*, 1604 G St, turns out first-rate, cheap organic meals, while *Abruzzi*, 780 H St, serves top-quality Italian dinners at moderate prices and *Sushi Spot*, 670 9th St, does hot Japanese favourites as well as sushi.

Around Arcata

If you've got a car, take time to explore the coastline just north of Arcata along US-101. On the way, make a short detour east of the highway through the modern strip-mall town of **McKinleyville**, near Clam Beach, in order to see the world's tallest **totem pole**. The gaily decorated, 160-foot ex-redwood stands proudly at the back of the McKinleyville Shopping Center, halfway along Central Avenue near the junction with City Center Road. If you're peckish, you can't beat the gourmet sandwiches on the other side of the main road at *Tastebuds*, 2011 Central Ave.

Moonstone Beach, about twelve miles north of town, is a vast, sandy strip that, save for the odd beachcomber, remains empty during the day but by night heats up with guitar-strumming student parties that rage for as long as the bracing climate allows. **Trinidad Harbor**, a few miles further on, is a good place to eat or drink, nose around the small shops or just sit down by the sea wall and watch the fishing boats being tossed about. Locals rave about the harbour's *Seascape Pier Restaurant* (T707/677-3762), whose menu of fresh fish, steaks and pasta tastes all the more delicious given its waterfront location. You'll find similar grub at more moderate prices back up in town at the *Trinidad Bay Eatery*, on the corner of Parker and Trinity streets. There are several good **accommodation** options a little to the north: the *Trinidad Inn*, 1170 Patrick's Point Drive (T707/677-3349, Wwww .trinidadinn.com; ❷), is a lovely motel in a quiet location, while the *Emerald Forest*, 733 Patrick's Point Drive (T707/677-3554, Wwww.cabinsintheredwoods .com; ❺), offers secluded cabins and tent sites for $30. If money is no object, then one of the most romantic retreats along the entire coast is the *Lost Whale Inn*, 3452 Patrick's Point Drive (T1-800/677-7849, Wlostwhaleinn.com; ❽); this luxurious and friendly B&B has an outdoor hot tub and access to a secluded little beach where seals frolic. **Patrick's Point State Park**, five miles north of Trinidad, sports an agate beach below rocky coastal bluffs and tours of a re-created Yurok village are conducted by appointment (T707/677-3570), although you can wander alone at will. The park also offers reasonably secluded **camping** for $35 (reserve on T1-800/444-7275, Wwww.parks.ca.gov). Several miles further on, **Big Lagoon County Park** (T707/445-7651; day-use $2) has tent spaces for $18 with a vehicle or $5 walk-in. The lagoon is also a great place for **kayaking**: Kayak Zak's (T707/498-1130, Wwww.kayakzak.com) rent single kayaks for $20 per hour, doubles for $25.

The legend of Bigfoot

Reports of giant 350- to 800-pound humanoids wandering the forests of north-western California have circulated since the late nineteenth century, fuelled by long-established Indian legends, though they weren't taken seriously until 1958, when a road maintenance crew found giant footprints in a remote area near Willow Creek. Photos were taken and the **Bigfoot** story went worldwide. Since then there have been more than fifty separate sightings of Bigfoot prints. At the crossroads in Willow Creek stands a huge wooden replica of the prehistoric-looking apeman, who in recent years has added kidnapping to his list of alleged activities.

Hoopa Valley Indian Reservation and around

A more adventurous destination is **Hoopa Valley Indian Reservation**, sixty miles inland, the largest in California. The often violent confrontations that until not many years ago took place here between Native Americans and whites over fishing territory have been consigned to history, yet few take the time to check out the valley. Although some of the youth still hang around listlessly, the local casino provides income and the atmosphere is friendly enough. If you're here in the last week in July you should make an effort to catch the All Indian Rodeo, held southwest of the village. Otherwise it's enough to visit the **Hoopa Tribal Museum**, located in the Hoopa Shopping Center on Hwy-96 (Tues–Fri 8am–5pm; summer also Sat 10am–4pm; free) – full of crafts, baskets and jewellery of the Hoopa (aka Natinixwe) and Yurok tribes.

To get to the reservation, take Hwy-299 east out of Arcata for forty miles until you hit **Willow Creek** – self-proclaimed gateway to **"Bigfoot Country"** – then take Hwy-96, the "Bigfoot Scenic Byway", north. Beside the Hwy-299/Hwy-96 junction, a statue of Bigfoot marks the entrance to the small **Willow Creek–China Flat Museum** (mid-April to Oct Wed–Sun 10am–4pm, rest of year by appointment; free; ☎530/629-2653), which displays a modest collection of Indian quilts and settlers' possessions, plus the obligatory Bigfoot curios. Next door, a small **Chamber of Commerce** hut (summer only daily 9am–5pm; ☎530/629-2693, ⊛www.willowcreekchamber.com) has details of Bigfoot's escapades, and information on **whitewater rafting** on the Smith, Klamath and Trinity rivers near here. Among the numerous rafting companies in the area, Bigfoot Rafting Company (☎1-800/722-2223, ⊛www.bigfootrafting.com) offers guided trips from $65. Otherwise, the town comprises a handful of grocery stores, diners and cheap **motels**, such as the inevitable *Bigfoot Motel*, 39116 Hwy-299 (☎530/629-2142, ⊛www.bigfootmotel.com; ❷). Of the **places to eat**, *Cinnabar Sam's*, 19 Willow Way, is the best bet for filling breakfast, sandwiches and Mexican or American meals. Just north of town, the Lower Trinity Ranger Station (summer Mon–Sat 9am–4.30pm; rest of year Mon–Fri 9am–4.30pm; ☎530/629-2118) handles camping and wilderness permits for the immediate surroundings. Continue east on Hwy-299 and you'll arrive in the Weaverville/Shasta area (see p.666), where you can join the super-speedy I-5 freeway.

The Redwood National and State parks

Way up in the top left-hand corner of California, the landscape is almost too spectacular for words and the long drive up here is rewarded with a couple of tiny towns and thick, dense redwood forests perfect for hiking and camping. Some thirty miles north of Arcata, **Orick** marks the southernmost end of this landscape, a contiguous strip of forest jointly managed as the **REDWOOD NATIONAL AND STATE PARKS** (unrestricted access; free), a massive area that stretches up into Del Norte County at the very northernmost point of California, ending at the rather dull town of **Crescent City**. The fragmented Redwood National Park and the three state parks which plug the gaps – Prairie Creek Redwood, Del Norte Coast Redwood, and Jedediah Smith Redwood – together contain some of the tallest trees in the world: the pride of California's forestland, especially between June and September when every school in the state seems to organize its summer camp here. One word of caution: **bears** and **mountain lions** inhabit this area, and you should heed the warnings on p.48.

Park practicalities

The parks' 58,000 acres divide into distinct areas: **Redwood National Park**, southwest of the Orick area; the **Prairie Creek Redwood State Park**, south of the riverside town of **Klamath**; and the area in the far north around the **Del Norte Coast Redwood** and **Jedediah Smith Redwood** state parks, in the environs of Crescent City in Del Norte County. The park **headquarters** are in Crescent City, at 1111 2nd St (daily summer 9am–6pm; winter 9am–4pm; ☎707/464-6101, ⓦwww.nps.gov /redw), but the **visitor centres** and **ranger stations** throughout the parks are far better for maps and information, including up-to-date hiking conditions and the weather forecast. Most useful is the **Thomas B. Kuchel Visitor Center** (daily: summer 9am–6pm; winter 9am–5pm; ☎707/465-7765), right by the southern entrance to Redwood National Park, before you get to Orick.

The two daily Redwood Coast Transit **buses** that run along US-101 to Crescent City and Smith River will, if asked, stop along forested stretches of the highway; if you're lucky, you can even flag them down. Still, unless you want to single out a specific area and stay there, which is hardly the best way to see the parks, you'll be stuck without a **car**.

As for accommodation, **camping** is your best bet. You can choose from the many developed, environmental, hiker/biker and primitive campgrounds spread throughout the parks, some of which are mentioned in the text below. There are also a few **motel/B&B** recommendations in the scenic areas and, if all else fails, a host of motels around Crescent City.

Orick and Tall Trees Grove

As the southernmost and most used entrance to the **Redwood National Park**, the Orick area is always busy. Its major attraction is **Tall Trees Grove**, home of one of the world's tallest trees – a mightily impressive specimen that stands at some 367ft. Incidentally, the tallest tree in the world, recently measured at 379ft, stands in an undisclosed location, inaccessible to the public. The easiest way to get to the Tall Trees Grove, with the least amount of trampling through thick undergrowth, is to drive yourself, although you'll need to get a free access permit (limited to fifty cars per day – only occasionally a problem even in high summer) at the visitor centre. Here you can also pick up a free trail guide that explains why some redwood cutting is being done to balance the damages inflicted on old growth in the past. When you reach the parking lot, it takes about half an hour to hike down the steep trail to the grove itself. The best view of the tallest redwood and its companions is from the mostly dry riverbed nearby. Some people prefer to hike the 8.5-mile **Redwood Creek Trail** (permit needed if staying overnight in the backcountry) from near Orick: take a right off US-101 onto Bald Hills Road, then, six hundred yards along, fork off to the picnic area where the trail starts. The bridge, 1.5 miles down the trail, is passable in summer only. A bit further east another trail turns north off Bald Hills Road and winds for half a mile to **Lady Bird Johnson Grove** – a collection of trees dedicated to former US President LBJ's wife, a big lover of flora and fauna right up to her death in 2007. A mile-long self-guided trail winds through the grove of these giant patriarchs. On the western side of US-101, across from the entrance to the Redwood Creek Trail, begins the **Coastal Trail**, which follows the coastline and takes backpackers up the entire length of all three state parks.

Practicalities

In **ORICK** itself, which actually lies two miles north of the entrance and ranger station, a few handy **facilities** string alongside US-101. Of the two **motels**, only the *Palm Motel & Café* (☎707/488-3381; ❷), which has adequate rooms and serves cheap burgers and sandwiches, is worth considering. You might also stop next door at the *Lumberjack* (aka *Hawgwild*) for a game of pool, an ice-cold beer and a wild game dinner, or cross the road for a delicious and inexpensive Mexican **meal** at *La Hacienda*. Three miles north of Orick, the beautifully situated *Redwood Adventures & Cabins* (☎1-866/733-9637, ⓦwww.redwoodadventures.com; ❻) offer superb ecofriendly cabins and a host of activities such as salmon fishing, horseriding, kayaking and guided hikes. Nearby, the narrow, gravel Davison Road turns coastwards for a bumpy eight miles to **Gold Bluffs Beach**, where you can **camp** for $20–35 in the stomping grounds of elk. The $8-per-vehicle fee also covers Fern Canyon, visited on an easy three-quarter-mile trail, its 45-foot walls slippery with moss, fern and lichen.

Prairie Creek Redwood State Park

Of the three state parks within the Redwood National Park area, **Prairie Creek** is the most varied and popular. Bear and elk often roam in plain sight, and you can take a ranger-led **tour** of the wild, dense redwood forest. Check with the **park office visitor centre** (daily: summer 9am–6pm; winter 9am–4pm; ☎707/465-7354) for details and informative displays. Whether you choose to go independently or opt for a tour, the main features of the park include the meadows of **Elk Prairie** in front of the ranger station, where herds of Roosevelt elk – massive beasts who can tip the scales over one thousand pounds – wander freely, protected from poachers. Remember that elk, like all wildlife, are unpredictable and should not be approached. Day-use of the park is $8 per vehicle but you can leave your car beside the road and wander at will; if you're pressed for time, there are some car-accessible routes through the woods. Overnighters can stay at a **campground** ($5–35) on the edge of Elk Prairie, at the hub of a network of hiking trails. Just south of the ranger station, on the east side of US-101, is the entrance to **Lost Man Creek**, an unpaved, 1.5-mile round-trip drive into an otherworldly grove of old-growth trees that passes by a cascade. To enter Prairie Creek Redwoods State Park, take the **Newton B. Drury Scenic Byway** off US-101 north of Lost Man Creek. A mile north of the ranger station, the magnificent **Big Tree Wayside** redwood, more than 300ft tall and, at over 21ft in diameter, one of the fattest of the coastal redwoods, overlooks the road. North of the Big Tree Wayside and before the byway rejoins US-101, the rough, gravel Coastal Drive branches off to the west following the Coastal Trail for 7.5 miles, leading to **High Bluff Overlook** and camping (free; no water) at **Flint Ridge**.

Klamath and around

KLAMATH, in Del Norte County, isn't technically part of the Redwood area nor, by most definitions, does it qualify as a town, as most of the buildings were washed away when the nearby Klamath River flooded in 1964. Nonetheless, there are spectacular coastal views from trails where the Klamath River meets the ocean, famed salmon and steelhead fishing in the river itself, a few decent accommodation options and, for a bit of fun, the **Trees of Mystery** (daily: summer 8am–7pm; winter 9am–5pm; $14) on US-101, where you cannot miss two huge wooden sculptures of Paul Bunyan and Babe, his blue ox. Taped stories of Bunyan's adventures emanate periodically from within the redwood stands and ethereal choral music greets you at the most impressive specimen of all, the **Cathedral Tree**, where nine trees have grown from one root structure to form a spooky circle. Enterprising Californians hold wedding services here throughout the year. The steep entry fee is somewhat justified by an aerial tram, which takes you from the top of the foot trail over the forest canopy to 750-foot **Ted's Ridge**. Here you're provided with binoculars to enhance your enjoyment of the ocean views to the west and tree-clad ridges and valleys to the east – from March to October, look out for the active osprey nest atop one distant redwood. Back down in the gift shop, the free **End of the Trail Museum** highlights artwork from a number of the region's Indian tribes. For some river activity, Klamath River Jet Boat Tours, 17635 Hwy-101 S (℡1-800/887-5387, ⓦwww.jetboattours.com), runs two-hour tours for $38 and can arrange guided fishing trips.

Further south, where Hwy-169 peels off from US-101, the 725-year-old living **Tour Thru Tree** on Terwer Valley Road (daylight hours; $5) provides a cute photo opportunity. The most spectacular scenery in Klamath, however, is not the trees but the ocean: take Requa Road about three quarters of a mile up above the estuary, to a point known as the **Klamath Overlook**, from where, once the fog has burnt off, there's an awe-inspiring view of the estuary meeting the sea and the rugged coastline to the south. From here you can pick up the Coastal Trail on foot, which leads north for ten miles along some of California's most remote beaches, ending at Endert's Beach in Crescent City.

Practicalities

The *Historic ReQua Inn*, 451 Requa Road (℡1-866/800-8777, ⓦwww.requainn .com; ❸), offers some of the best **accommodation** around. There are simple cabins at *Woodland Villa*, a mile and a half north of Requa (℡1-888/866-2466, ⓦwww.klamathusa.com; ❷) and small cottages with kitchenettes at *Camp Marigold* (℡1-800/621-8513, ⓔcampmar@tlk.net; ❷), just over one mile south of the Trees of Mystery. Three miles southeast of Klamath down Hwy-275, the *Rhode's End*, 115 Trobitz Road, Klamath Glen (℡707/482-1654, ⓦwww.rhodes -end.com; ❹), offers B&B accommodation along the Klamath River. Around five miles north of Trees of Mystery is the free, primitive *DeMartin* campground and two miles west of US-101 on Klamath Beach Road, *Riverwoods Campground* (℡707/482-5591) has shady tent sites for $20 on the south bank of the Klamath River, towards the river mouth.

Pickings are slim in the **eating** department around Klamath, especially in the evening, but the *Sweet Street Café*, 164 Klamath Blvd (℡707/482-3125), serves American standards throughout the day.

Crescent City

The northernmost outposts of the Redwood National Park, the Del Norte and Jedediah Smith state parks sit on either side of **Crescent City**, a rather forlorn place whose most attractive buildings were wiped out by a tsunami in 1964, leaving little to recommend it other than its budget accommodation and proximity to the parks. That said, the city is the halfway point on US-101 between San Francisco and Portland, Oregon, around 350 miles in each direction, and is therefore often used as a stopover. Redwood Coast Transit (℡707/464-6400, ⓦwww.redwoodcoasttransit.org) runs **buses** twice a day to Smith River, further inland, for $1.50 and down the coast to Arcata for $20. The **visitor centre** is at 1001 Front St (summer Mon–Sat 9am–5pm, Sun 10am–4pm; winter Mon–Fri 10am–4pm; ℡1-800/343-8300, ⓦexploredelnorte.com).

Crescent City's most popular tourist attraction is **Ocean World** (daily: summer 8am–dusk; winter 9am–dusk; $9.95), an unmissably large complex on US-101 south of town, which has a limited range of fish and other sea creatures. The guided tours that run every fifteen minutes are informative and give you the opportunity to handle many of the inmates – if you fancy picking up a starfish or stroking a shark or sea lion, this is the place for you. Take an hour to visit the **Battery Point Lighthouse** (April–Sept Wed–Sun 10am–4pm; tours sporadically during low tide; $3), reached by a causeway from the western end of town. The oldest working lighthouse on the West Coast, it houses a collection of artefacts from the *Brother Jonathan*, wrecked off Point St George in the 1870s. Because of this loss, the St George Lighthouse, the tallest and most expensive in the US, was built six miles north of Crescent City. The local history society maintains both this and the old-fashioned **Main Museum**, 577 H St (May–Sept Mon–Sat 10am–3pm; $3), whose dusty interior contains some Indian artefacts, quilts, old musical instruments, a lens from the St George Lighthouse, historical displays and, most interesting of all, original cells from the building's earlier incarnation as the county jail.

Practicalities

Among the several passable **motels**, try the pleasant *Crescent Beach Motel*, on the beach two miles south of town at 1455 US-101 S (☎707/464-5436, ⓦwww.crescentbeachmotel.com; ②), or the much cheaper *Gardenia Motel*, 119 L St (☎707/464-2181; ①), which offers no frills but is in a more central location. For a posher stay, try *Cottage By The Sea*, 205 South A St (☎1-877/642-2254, ⓦwww.waterfrontvacationrental.com; ④), a smart B&B perched on a bluff overlooking the ocean – you might even spot a migrating whale from your room. **Eating** options include the upmarket *Bistro Gardens*, 110 Anchor Way, for great pasta and vegetarian dishes, or the excellent, moderately priced seafood at *Fisherman's Restaurant*, 700 Hwy-101 S. Other fine ethnic choices are the Thai and Vietnamese cuisine at *Thai House*, 105 N St or *Los Compadres*, a cheap Mexican diner opposite the marina at 457 Hwy-101 S.

Del Norte and Jedediah Smith state parks

Del Norte State Park (☎707/465-2146), seven miles south of Crescent City, is worth visiting less for its redwood forests than its fantastic beach area and hiking trails, most of which are an easy two miles or so along the coastal ridge where the redwoods meet the sea. From May to July, wild rhododendrons and azaleas shoot up everywhere, laying a floral blanket across the park's floor. The Mill Creek **campground** (reserve on ☎1-800/444-7275 or ⓦwww.parks.ca.gov; $5–35) here sits next to a lovely stream through the woods. **Jedediah Smith State Park** (☎707/465-2144), nine miles east of Crescent City, is named after the European explorer who was the first white man to trek overland from the Mississippi to the Pacific in 1828, before being killed by Comanche tribes in Kansas in 1831. Not surprisingly, his name is everywhere: no less than eighteen separate redwood groves are dedicated to his memory. Sitting on the south fork of the Smith River, the park attracts many people who canoe downstream or simply sit on the riverbank and fish. Of the hiking trails, the **Stout Grove Trail** is the most popular, a flat, one-hour walk leading down to a most imposing Goliath – a 345-foot-tall, 20-foot-diameter redwood.

If you're heading further east and are in no hurry, you could opt for the painfully slow but scenic six-mile route that follows Howland Hill Road from Crescent City through the forest to the **Hiouchi Information Center** (mid-June to mid-Sept 9am–6pm; ☎707/458-3294) on Hwy-199. Branching off this are several blissfully short and easy trails (roughly half a mile each) that are quieter than the routes through the major parts of the park. The **Little Bald Hills Trail** east of Hiouchi traces a strenuous ten-mile hike that should take about eight hours. At the end of the Howland Hill Road you'll find the *Jedediah Smith Redwoods* campground (reserve on ☎1-800/444-7275, ⓦwww.parks.ca.gov; $5–35) and picnicking facilities. Back on the main road at 2097 Hwy-199, the *Hiouchi Motel* (☎1-888/881-0819, ⓦwww.hiouchimotel.com; ❷) has basic but adequate rooms, and about ten miles further on, shortly before you leave the redwoods of the **Six Rivers National Forest** behind, the *Patrick Creek Lodge & Historical Inn*, 13950 Hwy-199 (☎707/457-3323, ⓦwww.patrickcreeklodge.net; ❸), is the last place to stay in California on this route; there are good single rates on the stylish rooms, plus rustic cabins and an excellent but slightly pricey restaurant. The apparent detour into Oregon on Hwy-199 to connect with I-5 back south is actually by far the quickest way to reach the interior of Northern California from the extreme north coast.

The northern interior

As big as Ohio, yet with a population of only 250,000, the **NORTHERN INTERIOR** of California is about as remote as the state gets. Cut off from the coast by the **Shasta Cascade** range, it's a region dominated by forests, lakes, some fair-sized mountains and two thirds of the state's precipitation. It's largely uninhabited, and, for the most part, infrequently visited, which makes a spin up here all the more worthwhile. Locals take the time to chat and point out areas to explore, and the region's efficient network of hiking trails and roads usually remains empty of congestion.

I-5 leads through the very middle of this near wilderness, forging straight up the **Sacramento Valley** through acres of olive and nut trees, past the college towns of **Chico** to **Redding**, which makes a useful and inexpensive base for venturing out on loop trips a day or so at a time. Most accessible, immediately west and north of Redding, the **Whiskeytown–Shasta–Trinity National Recreation Area** is a series of three lakes and forests set aside for public use, especially in summer, when it's hard to avoid the camper vans, windsurfers, jet-skiers and packs of happy holidaymakers. A better bet lies east at **Lassen Volcanic National Park**, a stunning alpine landscape of sulphur springs and peaks, or in the scenic environs of **Plumas County** to the southeast, between Lassen and Lake Tahoe. Travelling on state highways through national forests north of Lassen reveals numerous roadside surprises, including towering **Burney Falls** and access points to the **Pacific Crest Trail**, the 1200-mile path from Canada to Mexico.

Further north, the crowds swell a bit in the shadows of **Mount Shasta**, a 14,000-foot volcano whose reputation as both spiritual convergence point and climbing challenge brings together an interesting cast of characters in the small town of the same name. Train buffs should stop in the historical railroad town of **Dunsmuir**, just south of Shasta, and anglers will find trout streams filled to the gills all around the area. North of Shasta, the mountains and pines give way to cattle and caves; the latter are part of the stunning lava fields of **Lava Beds National Monument**, the site of one of the saddest Indian wars in US history. Next to this desolate plain, migrating birds rest up in the gigantic sanctuary of the **Klamath Basin** before resuming their journeys on the **Pacific Flyway**. To the east, the scrubby volcanic landscape gradually transforms into the heavily wooded and mountainous terrain of **Modoc County**, where outdoor activities predominate.

It's the usual story with sparse **public transport**: reasonably frequent Greyhound buses connect San Francisco and Sacramento to Portland via I-5, stopping off at the Sacramento Valley towns and Redding on the way, while trains from Oakland stop in Redding, Chico and Dunsmuir. However, neither route provides anything close to comprehensive access to the area: anything worth seeing lies at least five miles from the nearest bus stop, even where there is one, and the area is just too big and the towns too far apart for bus travel, so you really need a **car**.

The Sacramento Valley

The **SACRAMENTO VALLEY** lays fair claim to being California's most uninteresting region: a flat, largely agricultural corridor of small, sleepy towns and endless vistas of wheat fields and fruit trees. By far the best thing to do is pass straight through on I-5, which cuts an almost two-hundred-mile-long swathe through the region, enabling you to forge right ahead to the more enticing far north quite painlessly in half a day. If you're coming from San Francisco, save time by taking the I-505 byway around Sacramento. The most worthwhile place to halt is **Chico**, while **Red Bluff** and **Corning** also have a couple of things in their favour.

Chico and around

Charming little **CHICO**, about midway between Sacramento and Redding and some twenty miles east of I-5 from the Orland exit, is a good stop off if you don't want to attempt to cover the whole valley from top to bottom in one day, or if you're here to visit Lassen Volcanic National Park (see p.657) and want choice of accommodation. It's home to **Chico State University**, a grassy institution of sandal-wearing students renowned more for their devotion to partying than academic pursuits. Chico was once the grounds surrounding the mansion of General John Bidwell, one of the first men to cash in on the Gold Rush. As such, the city's traditional layout around a plaza, numerous college eateries, and surrounding expanse of parkland make it something of an oasis compared to the dusty fields and sleepy towns beyond, although the detour east to the **Butte Creek Canyon** is worth the effort.

Arrival, information and getting around

Chico is right on Hwy-99. **Trains** stop at the unattended station at Fifth and Orange, as do Greyhound **buses**, which serve cities north and south along I-5 twice a day. The Coast Starlight train, from Los Angeles to Seattle, stops here once daily, though in the middle of the night in each direction. Most places are within walking distance of the town centre but the trails in Bidwell Park need to be biked to be appreciated. You can rent a bike for $35 per day from Campus Bicycles, right off the plaza at 330 Main St (℡530/345-2081, ⓦcampusbicycles.com); the shop also provides free maps for cyclists.

Chico's **Chamber of Commerce**, 300 Salem St (Mon–Fri 10am–4pm, Sat 11am–2pm; ℡1-800/852-8570, ⓦwww.chicochamber.com), has a terrific supply of information, from pamphlets outlining a historical walking tour through Downtown to mountain-bike trails and swimming-hole locations nearby. They also have updated accommodation lists. To find out what's on, consult the free *Chico News & Review* (ⓦwww.newsreview.com), published every Thursday.

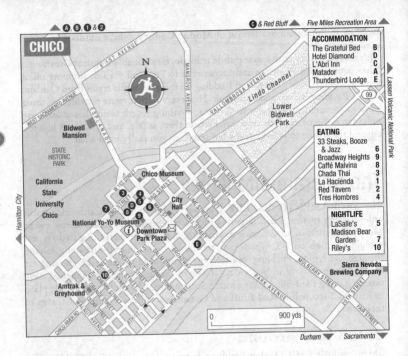

Accommodation

Chico has much more in the way of **accommodation** than it does in sights, though for **camping** you'll need to head to the Plumas National Forest to the east or Lassen Volcanic National Park. Motels are everywhere in town, particularly in the Main Street and Broadway area, and there are a couple of good B&Bs.

The Grateful Bed 1462 Arcadian Ave
ⓣ530/342-2464, ⓦwww.thegratefulbed.net. No tie-dye linen but a laidback atmosphere at this plush and friendly B&B, two blocks west of The Esplanade. ❹

Hotel Diamond 220 W 4th St ⓣ1-866/993-3100, ⓦwww.hoteldiamondchico.com. Imposing edifice with a range of swish rooms and suites, as well as an elegant lobby, restaurant and bar. ❺

L'Abri Inn 4350 Hwy-99 ⓣ1-800/489-3319, ⓦwww.labribandb.com. Five miles north of town, this place comprises three rooms in a ranch-style home with a serene country atmosphere. Enjoy a

sumptuous breakfast, then go out and pet the barnyard animals. ❹

The Matador Motel 1934 The Esplanade ⓣ530/342-7543. A pretty Spanish Revival building ten blocks north of the plaza; the tasteful rooms have individual tiling. Set around a courtyard, with palms shading one of Chico's largest pools, this is among Northern California's best deals. ❶

Thunderbird Lodge 715 Main St ⓣ530/343-7911. Decent motel two blocks from the plaza. Some of the simple rooms have fridges and all have coffee-makers. ❶

The Town

Chico doesn't have much by way of sights but strolling the leafy streets, college campus and shady riverside can be a relief after the monotonous drive up I-5. The 1904 **Chico Museum**, housed in the former Carnegie Library at the corner of Second and Main streets (mid-April to mid-Dec Wed–Sun noon–4pm; free; ⓣ530/891-4336, ⓦwww.chicomuseum.org), contains three distinct parts: a permanent historical section, a reconstruction of a Taoist temple altar and a gallery for rotating shows. You might also try the three-storey **Bidwell Mansion State**

Historic Park at 525 The Esplanade, the continuation of Main Street (Mon–Wed noon–5pm, Sat & Sun 11am–5pm; tours on the hour until 4pm; $6). Built in 1868, it's an attractive Italian country villa filled with family paraphernalia, visited on 45-minute anecdotal tours, though Bidwell Park (daylight hours; free) is a more pleasurable place to spend your time. Extending from the centre of the town for ten miles to the northeast, this semi-wilderness and oak parkland is where the first Robin Hood film, starring Errol Flynn, was made. Students frequent the **swimming holes** on Big Chico Creek in the Upper Park, accessed by taking Vallombrosa Avenue all the way east, turning left into Manzanita Avenue, then right on Wildwood Avenue and on past the golf course.

Back Downtown, you can visit the **Sierra Nevada Brewing Company**, 1075 E 20th St (free self-guided tours daily 10am–6pm); there is no official tasting, but you can sample the ten or so brews on tap for around $5 at the brewery's bar. Finally, those nostalgic for the innocent days of childhood will enjoy the **National Yo-Yo Museum**, 320 Broadway (Mon–Sat 10am–5.30pm, Sun 11am–4pm; free), where enthusiasts enjoy showing visitors around the thousands of exhibits and photos.

Eating and drinking

Chico does itself proud when it comes to **food** and the listings here are just a sample of what is on offer. If you're in town on the second Sunday in September look out for the **Taste of Chico festival**. Being a California State University town, there are many excellent places aimed at the younger customer, as well as a handful of lively **bars**, featuring live music by national acts. It's noticeably quieter when school's out, but on Friday evenings in summer, **free concerts** by talented locals draw the crowds to the Downtown Park Plaza, beginning at 7pm.

Restaurants

33 Steaks, Booze & Jazz 305 Main St ☎530/893-1903. Main courses such as the eponymous steaks cost around $20–30 in this smart restaurant/bar, which specializes in Martinis and hosts live jazz every evening. Closed Mon.

Broadway Heights 300 Broadway ☎530/899-8075. This modern upstairs establishment dishes up moderate California cuisine – dishes such as artichoke rosemary salmon go for around $15.

Caffè Malvina 234 W 3rd St. Italian restaurant with reasonably priced pasta and fish, plus some cheaper specials.

Chada Thai Downstairs at 117b W 2nd St. Authentic and predominantly vegetarian Thai cuisine at very affordable prices, especially at lunchtime. Closed Sun.

La Hacienda 2635 The Esplanade. *Bon Appetit* and *Gourmet* magazines have done features on this Mexican restaurant's special pink sauce, known to locals as "Heroin Sauce" for its addictive, sweet flavour. Try it on a tostada.

Red Tavern 1250 The Esplanade ☎530/894-3463. Quality California dishes such as chilled golden beet soup and caper-crusted sole are available for around $20 at this fairly upscale restaurant.

Tres Hombres 100 Broadway. Large restaurant popular with students for the wide selection of margaritas, as well as reasonably priced burritos, quesadillas, tostadas and tacos in a fun environment. Dinner until 10pm every night, drinks until 2am on weekends. Live jazz Sunday afternoons.

Bars

LaSalles 229 Broadway ☎530/893-1891. The place in Chico to down large quantities of inexpensive beer, play pool and listen to live rock bands.

Madison Bear Garden 316 W 2nd St. Popular with beer-swigging students from the nearby campus. Burgers, buffalo wings and other bar food is served.

Riley's 702 W 5th St. Catch the ball game on one of the many TV screens and hang out with the enthusiastic students at the most popular sports bar in Chico.

Around Chico

Ten miles outside Chico, south on Hwy-99 then east on Skyway to Humburg–Honey Run Road, the **Honey Run Covered Bridge** is one of the few remaining covered bridges in California. You can't drive on it, but its position in rugged Butte Creek Canyon over a riffling river leads to peaceful walking and swimming opportunities. Further east, the apple orchards of **Paradise** were used as a location for *Gone With the Wind*. You'll find the town's name quite apt if you **stay** at the unique ⚐ *Chapelle de l'Artiste*, 215 Wayland Road (☎530/228-0941, ⓦwww .chapelledelartiste.com; ⓞ), a superb mansion in opulent grounds with a pool and llama pastures. A gourmet dinner, usually in the company of the hosts, is included in the price.

Red Bluff and Corning

The largest town in Tehama County is **Red Bluff**, 45 miles north of Chico on Hwy-99. Despite its favourable location on the Sacramento River, the town is better known as a gas-and-lodging stop before the fifty-mile drive into Lassen along Hwy-36 or the push north to Redding and Mount Shasta on I-5. The Greyhound **bus** stops in front of the Salt Creek Deli at the junction of Hwy-36 and Antelope Road (Hwy-99) but there is no public transport on into Lassen. You may consider visiting the **Kelly-Griggs House Museum**, 311 Washington St (Thurs–Sun 1–4pm; donation), where there's an exhibit on Ishi, "the last wild Indian". There are a number of antique shops to browse in, as well as Gaumer's, on the I-5 side of the bridge at 78 Belle Mill Rd (Mon–Fri 9am–5pm; free), a jeweller's with an on-site **gemology museum**, displaying hundreds of precious stones, mining equipment, a lapidary workshop and a collection of corals and ammonites. The star exhibit is a sparkly four-foot-tall amethyst geode from Brazil.

If you decide to stay, there's a reasonable selection of ultra-cheap **motels** along Main Street – among them the *Crystal Motel*, 333 S Main St (☎530/527-1021, ⓦredbluffmotel.com; ❶), and the *M Star Hotel*, 210 S Main St (☎530/527-1150, ⓦwww.mstarhotelredbluff.com; ❷) – and a handful of diners and burger joints around town. The one classier **restaurant** is the *Riverside Bar & Grille*, 500 Riverside Way (☎530/528-0370), which serves great grilled steak and ribs on its patio overlooking the river by the bridge into town. For any further information, visit the **Chamber of Commerce**, 100 Main St (Mon–Fri 8.30am–5pm; ☎1-800/655-6225, ⓦwww.redbluffchamber.com).

If you bypass Chico and enter Tehama County from the south on I-5, an alternative stop for gas and provisions is **Corning**, home of the celebrated **Olive Pit**, 2156 Solano St, just east off the interstate. This only-in-America store and restaurant sells jars of olives, olive oil, garlic, almonds and pickles, while serving good grills and ice-cream as well. Martini-lovers can get bottles of olive-juice mixer, and a free tasting bar allows a trip around the world via olives – from Brine Greek wholes to Napa Valley Wine queens to French pitted and Sicilian cracked. The anchovy-stuffed greens are a must, and pint jars of all varieties go for around $4–8.

Plumas County

Many visitors travelling between Lake Tahoe and the Lassen/Mount Shasta region bypass the Sacramento Valley altogether by using Hwy-89, which winds its way through sparsely populated and scenically exquisite **PLUMAS COUNTY**. Although it boasts no major set-piece attraction, with only three traffic lights and constant vistas of pine-clad ridges, grassy valleys, sparkling lakes and trout-rich rivers, the county is rural California at its best. Geographically, it's significant as the meeting point of the lofty Sierra Nevada and volcanic Cascade mountain ranges. The area was home to the hunter-gatherer **Maidu Indians** before white settlers flooded into the valleys when gold frenzy took hold in the mid-nineteenth century, followed by a substantial number of Chinese. The veins of the precious metal were never as rich as those to the south, however, so the prospectors left and the **timber** industry soon took over as the prime economy. That too has since gone into decline, leaving farming as the main source of income for the few inhabitants, along with a smattering of tourism.

Coming from the south, you pass through the golfing and retirement paradise of Graeagle before Hwy-89 combines with Hwy-70 to form part of the **Feather River National Scenic Byway**; this leads to the county seat and commercial hub of **Quincy**, whose Old Town merits a wander. Further north, Hwy-89 continues solo through the cattle-grazing land of the **Indian Valley**, past the lazy town of **Greenville** to the recreational area of **Lake Almanor**, within easy striking distance of Lassen Volcanic National Park, whose snowcapped peaks are visible in the distance.

Quincy

Nestled on the lower western slopes of the northernmost reaches of the Sierra Nevada mountains, **Quincy** is a pleasant town divided by a hill into two distinct halves. Modern and functional East Quincy is not especially appealing but the blocks surrounding West Main Street in Quincy proper present some fine examples of Victorian architecture and are worth stopping at to look around. Behind the grand old Neoclassical **Courthouse**, which stands proudly near the junction where the highway through town veers from West Main Street into Crescent Street, you can visit the **Plumas County Museum**, 500 Jackson St (Tues–Sat 9am–4.30pm; $2). Inside you'll find informative displays on the area's Indian culture, the story of its settlement, and natural history, while the grounds contain an old buggy and an authentic 1890s gold-miner's cabin.

The best place to pick up info, maps and brochures is the very helpful **Plumas County Visitors Bureau** on the northern edge of town at 550 Crescent St (Mon–Sat 8am–5.30pm; ☎1-800/326-2247, ⓦwww.plumascounty.org). Of several **motels** around town, the best mix of location and economy is the *Gold Pan Motel*, 200 Crescent St (☎1-800/804-6541; ❶), while among the **B&Bs** in the old town *The Feather Bed*, 542 Jackson St (☎1-800/696-8624, ⓦwww.featherbed-inn .com; ❹), and *Ada's Place*, 562 Jackson St (☎530/283-1954, ⓦwww.adasplace .com; ❸), are both comfortable and suitably atmospheric. *Greenhorn Creek Guest Ranch*, twelve miles east of town and a mile and a half from the highway at 2116 Greenhorn Ranch Rd (☎1-800/334-6939, ⓦwww.greenhornranch.com; ❸), is the place to go for a Wild West experience – they specialize in packages including all meals and activities such as horseriding, fishing and hiking, but if it's not too busy you can stay on a room-only basis too. Though **eating** choices aren't spectacular in Quincy, you can grab a filling breakfast or lunch at the *Courthouse Café*, 525 W Main St, bang opposite – you guessed it – the courthouse, or enjoy a meaty or vegetarian meal, washed down by a microbrew, nearby at *Pangaea Café & Pub*, 461 Main St (closed Sat & Sun). East Quincy offers a few cheap and cheerful joints such as *Champions Pizza & Wings*, 60 E Main St, and *Mi Casita*, 875 E Main St, which serves copious quantities of authentic Mexican food.

Northern Plumas County

Leaving Quincy behind, Hwy-70 soon peels off to the left and continues to follow the middle fork of the Feather River southwest, while Hwy-89 meanders in a northerly direction through the rich grassy meadows, ranches and farms of the **Indian Valley** towards the old mining town of **Greenville**, 23 miles on from Quincy. A further nine miles brings you close to the western shore of **Lake Almanor**, an increasingly popular destination for boaters and families, with its main settlement of **Chester** at the northern end.

Greenville

Although it now depends more on cattle ranching and the felling of Christmas trees, sleepy **Greenville** still celebrates its mining heritage every summer with the **Gold Digger Days** festival on the third weekend of July. For the rest of the year it remains in its slumbers but its quietude and idyllic countryside setting still make a pleasant spot to break your journey. Though there's not much to see, just wandering along Main Street can give you a sense of the town's workaday past. If you stop for a bite to **eat**, the seafood, steaks and pasta at the *Main Street Dinner House* (closed Mon & Tues), opposite the fire station on Ann Street (Hwy-89), are inexpensive and filling, as are the burgers and pizza at *Mountain Valley Pizza*, 116 Ann St. To use the town as an overnight base for some hiking in the surrounding picturesque **Indian Valley**, the most distinctive option is the English-literature-themed *Yorkshire House B&B*, 421 Main St (☎530/284-1794, ⓦwww.yorkshire housebb.com; ❹).

Lake Almanor

Lake Almanor, created in 1914 by the Great Western Power Company's damming of the north fork of the Feather River, stands at an elevation of 4500ft and covers fifty-two square miles, making it the largest of Plumas County's many lakes. This is also where the Cascades and the Sierras truly meet. The lake's clear blue waters reach a comfortable seventy-five degrees in summer, rendering it ideal for **watersports**. Numerous resorts ring the pine-forested shoreline and most rent equipment for water-based activities, from high-speed waterskiing to leisurely fishing, and provide a range of **accommodation**. Several such enterprises are, in counterclockwise order around the lake: *Plumas Pines Resort*, on the west shore at 3000 Almanor Drive W, Canyon Dam (☎530/259-4343, ⓦwww.plumaspinesresort.com; ❷), with motel-style rooms, cabins and RV slots ($30), as well as decent food at its own *Boathouse Grill*; the shady *Lake Haven Resort*, on the east shore at 4379 Hwy-147 (☎530/596-3249, ⓦwww.lakehavenresort.com; ❸), which offers great sunset views from its cabins of varying size; and on the peninsula that juts out from the north shore, *Knotty Pine Resort*, 430 Peninsula Drive (☎530/596-3348, ⓦwww.knottypine.net; ❻), whose half-dozen two-bedroom cabins are ideal for groups of four or five. For **campers** there are simple sites all over the lake that are usually let on a first-come-first-served basis, though some can be booked through the US Forest Service (☎1-800/280-2267, ⓦwww.recreation .gov). Of the reasonable **restaurants** dotted round the lake, *Carol's Café & West Shore Deli*, 2392 Almanor Drive W, offers meat and fish main courses for under $20, while the *Gamboni's Peninsula Grill*, 401 Peninsula Drive, does tasty steaks and seafood, including sushi.

Chester

At the northwest corner of the lake, the only town on its shores, **Chester**, is a relaxed place with a splendid setting and a selection of amenities. You can get information on the whole region at the **Chamber of Commerce**, 529 Main St (summer Mon–Fri 9am–4pm, Sat 10am–2pm; winter Mon–Fri 10am–4pm; ☎1-800/350-4838, ⓦwww.chester-lakealmanor.com). The town's small museum, showcasing local history and Maidu Indian basketry, is inside the library at 210 First Ave (Mon–Wed & Fri 10am–1pm & 1.30pm–5.30pm, Thurs noon–5pm & 6–8pm, Sat 10am–2pm; free). Among the dozen places to **stay**, the simple rooms at the *Antlers Motel*, 268 Main St (T530/258-2722, Wwww.antlersmotel.com; ❷), are still as fresh as a daisy, while the cosy *Cinnamon Teal B&B*, 227 Feather River Drive (T530/258-3993, Wcinnamontealinn.net; ❷), provides somewhat more ambience and equally good value. For a step up in comfort, *Bidwell House*, 1 Main St (T530/258-3338, Wwww.bidwellhouse.com; ❸), has a range of delightful rooms. Two miles east of town on Hwy-36, *North Shore Campground* (T530/258-3376, Wwww.northshorecampground.com) is the biggest **campground** on the lake, with tent spaces for $35 and RV sites from $38. Once you've worked up an appetite on the lake, the *Ranch House*, 669 Main St (closed Mon), serves hearty down-home dinners, while the *Red Onion Grill*, 384 Main St, fires up quality steaks and pasta, and *Happy Garden*, 605 Main St, provides huge portions of Chinese standards.

Lassen Volcanic National Park

About fifty miles over gently sloping plains east from Red Bluff on Hwy-36, the 106,000 acres that make up the pine forests, crystal-green lakes and boiling thermal pools of the **LASSEN VOLCANIC NATIONAL PARK** are one of the most unearthly parts of California. A forbidding climate, which brings up to fifty feet of snowfall each year, keeps the area pretty much uninhabited, with the roads all blocked by snow and, apart from a brief June-to-October season, completely deserted. It lies at the southerly limit of the Cascades, a low, broad range which stretches six hundred miles north to Mount Garibaldi in British Columbia and is characterized by high volcanoes forming part of the Pacific Circle of Fire. Dominating the park at over 10,000ft is a fine example, **Mount Lassen** itself, which – although quiet in recent years – erupted in 1914, beginning a cycle of outbursts that climaxed in 1915, when the peak blew an enormous mushroom cloud some seven miles skyward, tearing the summit into chunks that landed as far away as Reno. Although nearly a hundred years of geothermal inactivity have since made the mountain a safe and fascinating place, scientists predict that of all the Californian volcanoes, Lassen is the likeliest to erupt again.

Arrival and information

Lassen is always open ($10 per vehicle for seven days, $5 per hiker or biker) but you'll have a big job ahead of you if planning to get in or around without a car. During the winter, when the roads in the park are almost always shut down due to snow, a car won't do you much good either – snowshoes and cross-country skis take over as popular modes of transportation.

The brand-new **Kohm Yah-mah-nee Visitor Center** (daily summer 9am–6pm, winter 9am–5pm; T530/595-4480, Wwww.nps.gov/lavo) is just beyond the southwest entrance, six miles north of where Hwy-89 peels off towards Lassen from Hwy-36. Park rangers hand out free maps, offer detailed advice and issue backcountry permits. There is also a fine display on Lassen's natural wonders, a good café, a giftshop and a bookstore. The older visitor centre (late May–Oct daily 9am–5pm; T530/595-4444 ext 5180) is at Manzanita Lake, just inside the north entrance, and incorporates the Loomis Museum (see p.660). The nearby Camper Store is the only place for provisions and gas within the park.

Camping in and around Lassen

During the few months of the year when conditions are suitable for camping, this is by far the best accommodation option. All **developed campgrounds** in the park are listed here and it points out those that can be reserved in advance (℡1-877/444-6777 ⓦwww.recreation.gov). Most remain open from June to October and cost $12–18. Remember that Lassen is **bear country**; follow the posted precautions for food and waste storage and make your presence known when hiking.

Primitive camping requires a free **wilderness permit** obtainable in advance from the park visitor centres and entrance stations. There is no self-registration and chosen sites must be a mile from developed campgrounds and a quarter of a mile from most specific sites of interest. In the surrounding **Lassen National Forest**, camping is permitted anywhere, though you'll need a free permit to operate a cooking stove or to light a fire; these are sometimes refused in the dry summer months. In addition, there are a couple of dozen private developed sites strung along the highways within thirty miles of Lassen, most charging between $15 and $25.

Butte Lake 6100ft. In the far northeast corner of the park, accessed by Hwy-44. Can accommodate trailers and has a boat launch. Reservable.

Juniper Lake 6800ft. In the far southeastern corner of the park, with good hiking trails nearby and swimming in the lake. Drinking water must be boiled or treated.

Manzanita Lake 5900ft. By far the largest of the Lassen campgrounds and the only one with a camp store (8am–8pm), firewood for sale, 24-hour showers (bring quarters) and a laundry. Trailers allowed and boat launch facilities available. Rangers run interpretive programmes from here. Open late May to snow closure. Reservable.

Southwest 6700ft. Small tent-only campground by the southwest entrance on Hwy-89 with walk-in sites, water and fire rings. Open year-round if you're equipped to brave it.

Summit Lake 6700ft. The pick of the Hwy-89 campgrounds, right in the centre of the park and at the hub of numerous hiking trails. It's divided into two sections: the northern half can take trailers and is equipped with flush toilets, the southern half only holes. There's swimming in the lake for the steel-skinned. Reservable.

Warner Valley 5700ft. Off Hwy-89 in the south of the park, this is a beautiful site but its distance from the road makes it only worth heading for if you're planning extended hiking in the region.

Accommodation

Apart from some cabins scheduled to be opened by the Manzanita Lake Camper Store in 2011 (call for details on ℡530/335-7557), the only way to **stay** inside Lassen is to **camp** (see box above) but even in August night temperatures can hover around freezing and many people prefer to stay in one of the resorts and lodges that pepper the surrounding forest. To be sure of a room in the popular summer months, it pays to book well ahead.

Childs Meadow Hwy-36, 9 miles southeast of southwest entrance ℡1-888/595-3383, ⓦwww.childsmeadowresort.com. One of the few choices on this side of the park, scenic and friendly *Childs Meadow* offers basic motel accommodation, more comfortable chalet rooms, tent sites for $20 and an on-site café. ❷

Hat Creek Resort Hwy-89, Old Station, 11 miles northeast of the north entrance ℡1-800/568-0109, ⓦwww.hatcreekresortrv.com. A complex of motel units and fancier cabins with kitchens (two-day minimum stay), plus tent sites from $21, RV sites from $30 and a deli. Closed mid-Nov to mid-March. ❷

Lassen Mineral Lodge Hwy-36, Mineral, 9 miles southwest of the southwest entrance on Hwy-36 ℡530/595-4422, ⓦwww.minerallodge.com. Unspectacular base-rate rooms and considerably

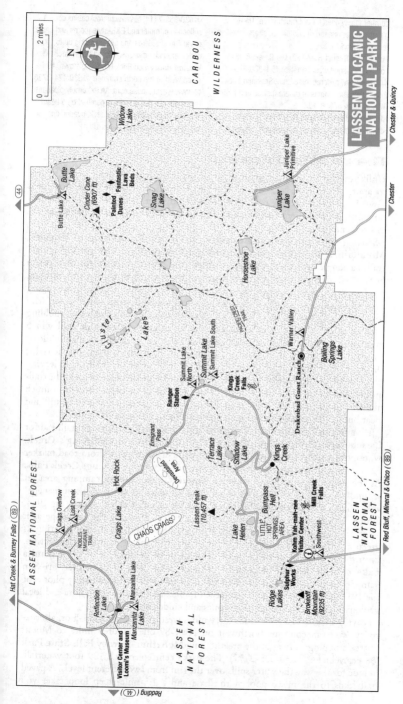

LASSEN VOLCANIC
NATIONAL PARK

9

N

0   2 miles

CARIBOU
WILDERNESS

Widow
Lake

Butte
Lake

Butte Lake

Cinder Cone
(6907 ft)

Painted   Fantastic
Dunes   Lava
            Beds

Snag
Lake

Juniper
Lake

Juniper Lake
Primitive

Horseshoe
Lake

Cluster

Lakes

PACIFIC CREST TRAIL

Summit Lake
North

Summit Lake

Summit Lake South

Ranger
Station

Kings Creek
Falls

Warner Valley

Drakesbad Guest Ranch

Boiling
Springs
Lake

Emigrant
Pass

Hot Rock

Dupont
Area

Crags Overflow

Lost Creek

NOBLES EMIGRANT TRAIL

Crags Lake

CHAOS CRAGS

Lassen Peak
(10,457 ft)

Terrace
Lake

Shadow
Lake

Kings Creek

Bumpass
Hell

LITTLE
HOT
SPRINGS
AREA

Kohm Yah-mah-nee
Visitor Center

Mill Creek
Falls

Southwest

Lake
Helen

Sulphur
Works

Ridge
Lakes

Brokeoff
Mountain
(9235 ft)

LASSEN
NATIONAL
FOREST

Reflection
Lake

Manzanita
Lake

Manzanita Lake

Visitor Center and
Loomis Museum

LASSEN
NATIONAL
FOREST

LASSEN NATIONAL FOREST

Hat Creek & Burney Falls (89)

44

Redding (44)

Red Bluff, Mineral & Chico (89)

Chester

Chester & Quincy

659

comfier family ones for not much more. There's a general store, restaurant and bar on site, as well as tent sites for $20. ❷

Mill Creek Resort Hwy-172, Mill Creek, 8 miles south of the southwest entrance ⊺1-888/595-4449, ⓦwww.millcreekresort.net. Set amid thick forest, there are cabins of different sizes and tent/RV spaces from $16. ❷

Rim Rock Ranch Resort 13275 Hwy-89, Old Station, 11 miles northeast of the north entrance ⊺530/335-7114, ⓦwww.rimrockcabins.com. A collection of motel and B&B-style rooms and cabins of varying standards, the best sleeping up to six, dotted around a meadow. Closed Nov–March. ❶

Weston House Red Rock Rd, Shingletown, 19 miles west of the north entrance ⊺530/474-3738, ⓦwww.westonhouse.com. An extremely pleasant B&B, with six elegant rooms perched on a beautiful volcanic ridge with pool and deck, overlooking the Ishi National Wilderness Area. ❹

The park and around

Unlike most other wilderness areas, you don't actually need to get out of the car to appreciate Lassen, as some of the best features are visible from the paved Hwy-89 that traverses the park. A thorough tour should take no more than a few hours. Pick up a copy of the *Road Guide: Lassen Volcanic National Park* ($5) at the visitor centres.

Starting from the southwest entrance, you'll pass the trailhead to **Brokeoff Mountain**, a six-mile round-trip hike through wildflowers. The first self-guided trail is a couple of miles further up – follow your nose and the **Sulfur Works** can be reached via a 200-foot boardwalk around its steaming fumaroles and burbling mud pots. The winding road climbs along the side of Diamond Peak before edging **Emerald Lake** and Lassen's show-stealer, **Bumpass Hell**, named after a man who lost a leg trying to cross it. This steaming valley of active pools and vents, bubbling away at a low rumble, can be reached on an undulating two-mile trail which eventually descends to a system of boardwalks that put you right in the middle of the stinky action. Recall the fate of Mr Bumpass, however, and stay on the trails; the crusts over the thermal features are brittle and easy to break through, leaving you, literally, in hot water. Across the road from Bumpass Hell's car park, the trails around the glassy surface of Emerald Lake are also spectacular, though in much quieter fashion; the lake itself resembles a sheet of green ice, perfectly still and clear but for the snow-covered rock mound which rises from its centre.

Just north of here, the road reaches its highest point (8511ft) at the trailhead for **Lassen Peak**. It then winds down to the flat meadows around **King's Creek**, whose trails along the winding water are popular for picnics. From road marker 32, a three-mile round-trip walk leads to the seventy-foot-tall **Kings Creek Falls**. At the halfway point you'll come to **Summit Lake**, a busy camping area set around a beautiful icy lake, from where you can start on the park's most manageable hiking trails. Press on further to the **Devastated Area**, where, in 1914, molten lava from Lassen poured down the valley, denuding the landscape as it went, ripping out every tree and patch of grass. Slowly the earth is recovering its green mantle but the most vivid impression is still one of complete destruction. From here it's a gauntlet of pines to the northern entrance, site of **Manzanita Lake** and the **Loomis Museum** (summer daily 9am–5pm; winter Fri–Sun 9am–5pm; free), a memorial to Benjamin Loomis, whose documentary photos of the 1914 eruption form the centrepiece of an exhibition strong on flora and local geology – plug domes, composite cones and cinder cones.

Leaving Lassen, Hwy-44 heads forty miles west to Redding and I-5 or, alternatively, you can continue northwest on Hwy-89 one hundred miles to Mount Shasta, stopping halfway at the breathtaking **McArthur–Burney Falls State Park** ($8 per vehicle; ⊺530/335-2777). The park's centrepiece is a 129-foot waterfall, unique for the way the water spills over the rim from two different levels. A paved trail leads to the misty pool at the base and a 1.5-mile steep loop takes you

For a volcanic landscape, a surprisingly large proportion of the walking trails in the park are predominantly flat, and the heavily glaciated terrain to the east of the main volcanic massif is pleasingly gentle. Rangers will point you toward the **hiking routes** best suited to your ability – the park's generally high elevations will leave all but the most experienced walker short of breath, and you should stick to the shorter trails at least until you're acclimatized. For anything but the most tentative explorations, pick up a copy of the full-colour *Hiking Trails of Lassen* ($19.95), which describes the most popular hikes.

Chaos Crags Lake (3.5 miles round-trip; 2–3hr; 800-foot ascent). From the Manzanita Lake campground access road, the path leads gently up through pine and fir forest to the peaceful lake. An adventurous extension climbs a ridge of loose rock to the top of Chaos Crags, affording a view of the whole park.

Cinder Cone (13 miles round-trip; 1 day; 800-foot ascent). Check with the rangers for the best seasonal starting point for this, Lassen's most spectacular hike, through the Painted Dunes and Fantastic Lava Beds before reaching Snag Lake. Can also be done as a 4-hour hike from Butte Lake.

Lassen Peak (5 miles round-trip; 4hr; 2000-foot ascent). A fairly strenuous hike from road marker 22 to the highest point in the park. Come prepared with water and warm clothing.

Manzanita Lake (1.5 miles; 1hr; flat). Easy trails on level ground make this one of the most popular short walks in the park.

Nobles Emigrant Trail (2.5 miles; 1–2hr; 200-foot ascent). The most accessible and one of the more interesting sections of a trail forged in 1850 starts opposite the Manzanita Lake entrance station and meets Hwy-89 at marker 60. It isn't maintained but is heavily compacted and easy going.

Paradise Meadows (3 miles round-trip; 3hr; 800-foot ascent). Starting either at the Hat Creek parking area (marker 42) or marker 27, and passing Terrace Lake on the way, this hike winds up at Paradise Meadows, ablaze with wildflowers in the summer and a marvellous spot to pass an afternoon.

downstream and then back up the other side of the pool to a bridge over the falls' headwater. The Pacific Crest Trail passes alongside nearby **Lake Briton**, and paddleboats, canoes and rowboats can be rented at the park entrance. Plentiful **camping** among the black oaks is available for $5–30 a night.

Eating

You don't have an awful lot to choose from in Lassen Volcanic National Park in terms of **food**. Apart from the Manzanita Lake Camper Store and visitor centre café, you'll have to go outside the park and even then it's slim pickings. Some of the accommodation options listed on p.658 have food; otherwise, *JJ's Café* (℗ 530/335-7225) in tiny Old Station, eleven miles northeast of the park, does filling breakfasts, lunches and pizza, or BBQ dinners.

Redding and around

At the heart of northern interior California, the sizeable modern town of **Redding** is often viewed simply as a hub for the region, without much to merit more than refuelling, grabbing a bite or changing transportation. It does, however, hold a certain degree of interest, especially its revitalized central stretch on the Sacramento River. Its diminutive neighbour **Shasta**, a once-lively gold-mining town just to the west, provides a historical counterpoint and seems a world away from the urban sprawl nearby.

Redding

With a spreading expanse of strip malls along I-5 that have made its central shopping complex virtually obsolete, **REDDING** first appears to be a bit of an anomaly amid the natural splendour of the northern interior. The region's largest city, with over 70,000 people, it's been a northern nexus since the late nineteenth century, when the Central Pacific Railroad came through. Today it remains a crossroads, bulging with cookie-cutter motels and diners that service traffic heading east to Lassen, west to Whiskeytown-Shasta-Trinity National Recreation Area, north to Mount Shasta, and south to San Francisco. In recent years, however, the opening of a major museum and iconic new bridge across the central stretch of the Sacramento River have done more to detain passers-through. The one annual event that has long attracted substantial crowds is the **Kool April Nites** classic-car meeting (℡1-800/874-7562, ⓦwww.koolapril nites.com) on the second or third weekend of April, the only time you're likely to encounter problems finding a room.

Though fiercely hot in summer, the temperature drops forbiddingly in some of the surrounding areas in winter. Bear in mind that what looks like a mild day in Redding could turn out to be blizzard conditions at higher elevations only a few miles away.

Arrival, getting around and information

Considering its position at the crossroads of Northern California, **public transport** in Redding is woefully inadequate, though at least the various modes of ground transport available all stop within easy walking distance of each other Downtown. The Greyhound station is at 1321 Butte St (℡530/241-2070, ⓦwww.greyhound.com), while the local RABA **bus** system depot (℡530/241-2877, ⓦwww.rabaride.com) is on California Street on the other side of the deserted shopping centre, with the Amtrak station right beside it. If you're in a hurry to reach Northern California from elsewhere on the West Coast, there are four United Express (℡1-800/241-6522, ⓦwww.united.com) **flight** connections daily from SFO to **Redding Municipal Airport** (℡530/224-4321), plus one or two daily from LA with Alaskan Airlines (℡1-800/547-9308, ⓦwww.alaskaair .com). There's no public transport from the airport (though some hotels have shuttles) and once here, you're not going to see much without a **car** anyway.

The town **visitor centre** (℡1-800/874-7562, ⓦwww.visitredding.org) is within and keeps the same hours as the Turtle Bay Exploration Park (see p.664). For broader information on the surrounding area and the whole of the northern interior and beyond, the **California Welcome Center**, just off I-5 nine miles south of Redding at 1699 Hwy-273, Anderson (Mon–Fri 9am–5pm, Sat & Sun 10am–4pm; ℡1-800/474-2782, ⓦwww.shastacascade.com), has a huge collection of maps, information and displays, and is staffed by helpful outdoors experts.

Accommodation

Motels are concentrated along Redding's old main strip, Market Street (Hwy-273), and Pine Street, while the smarter chain **hotels** tend to be along Hilltop Drive, Redding's newer service area east of I-5. A few **B&Bs** dotted around town round out the options.

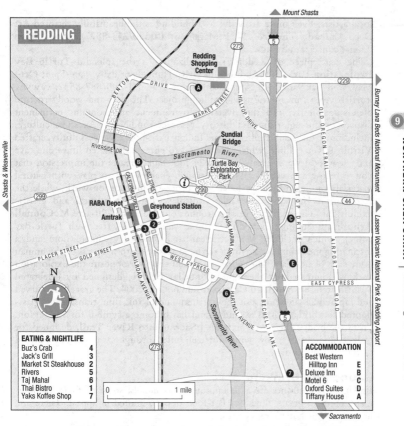

EATING & NIGHTLIFE

Buz's Crab	4
Jack's Grill	3
Market St Steakhouse	2
Rivers	5
Taj Mahal	6
Thai Bistro	1
Yaks Koffee Shop	7

ACCOMMODATION

Best Western Hilltop Inn	E
Deluxe Inn	B
Motel 6	C
Oxford Suites	D
Tiffany House	A

Best Western Hilltop Inn 2300 Hilltop Drive ☎1-800/336-4880, ⓦwww.bestwestern.com. This comfortable franchise – with its pool, sauna, buffet breakfasts and convivial grill – makes you feel you're staying somewhere more personal than your average chain. Specials available most of the year. ④

Deluxe Inn 1135 Market St ☎530/243-5141. This ultra-cheapie is fine for a night but hardly lives up to its name, with rather poky rooms. ①

Motel 6 1640 Hilltop Drive ☎1-800/466-8356, ⓦwww.motel6.com. The most central of three outlets in the Redding area, this one is basic but clean and efficient. ②

Oxford Suites 1967 Hilltop Drive ☎1-800/762-0133, ⓦwww.oxfordsuites.com. This West Coast chain offers smart and comfy suites at good rates. You can drink your two free happy-hour beverages in peace by the pool. ④

Tiffany House 1510 Barbara Rd ☎530/244-3225, ⓦwww.tiffanyhousebb.com. Just over a mile north of Downtown, the *Tiffany* is a plush yet good-value B&B in a converted Victorian house, with a pricier detached cottage behind. ④

The Town

Redding has worked hard to improve its image in order to tempt visitors to spend a day or two in its leafy urban environment before sampling the surrounding natural delights. Tourists are encouraged to stay in the newer areas near the freeway rather than in the dowdy old **Downtown** area, which has still not received the proposed injection of cash to spruce it up. One place to stop is the **Old City Hall Arts Center**, 1313 Market St (Tues–Fri 9am–5pm, Sat 11am–3pm; free; ☎530/241-7320), which has rotating displays of works by local artists. Even more attractive as a building is the beautifully restored Art Deco **Cascade Theatre**, 1731 Market St (℡530/243-8877), which hosts drama, concerts and films.

The centrepiece of Redding's revitalization is the splendid **Turtle Bay Exploration Park**, 800 Auditorium Drive (June–Sept daily 9am–5pm; Oct–May Wed–Sat 9am–5pm, Sun 10am–4pm; $14; ℡1-800/887-8532, ⓦwww.turtlebay.org), an ambitious $64 million project. The glass-and-wood structure blends seamlessly into the riverside environment and contains permanent displays on the region's natural history, resources, and Native American culture, including a full-scale replica of an Indian bark-house. The skilfully crafted **Visible River** exhibit, which allows you to enter a simulated limestone cave and view local water-creatures in a 24-foot tank, creates the impression that you're below a riverbank. The River Lab enables you to play with natural materials and learn by experience how processes like erosion work, while the Exploration Hall and Art Gallery display changing cultural and artistic exhibitions. The highlight of the grounds outside is the 220-acre **McConnell Arboretum** (summer 7am–dusk; winter 9am–5pm; $7, free with Turtle Bay entry), which includes Mediterranean and other dry-climate flora and a fascinating medicinal herb garden arranged according to the parts of the human body each plant treats. The central stretch of the river opposite the Exploration Park is dominated by the unique **Sundial Bridge**, designed by celebrated Spanish architect **Santiago Calatrava** and built in 2004. The gracefully curved and tapered 218-foot mast at the northern end of this slim, translucent, glass-floored footbridge forms a sundial and has become a symbol for the region. From the bridge the newly extended **Sacramento River Trail**, designed for walkers and cyclists, now winds thirteen miles through savannah and wetland sections to Shasta dam.

Eating and drinking

Redding's **restaurants** are as ubiquitous as its motels, some of them 24-hour, many of them greasy diners or fast-food outlets, limited in appeal. There are, however, some notable exceptions.

Buz's Crab 2159 East St. Just south of Downtown, this local institution rustles up a vast range of fish and seafood delights at very moderate prices.
Jack's Grill 1743 California St ℡530/241-9705. Popular restaurant that prepares fine grilled steak and shrimp and chicken dishes for $10–15. Reservations not accepted, and though you'll probably have to wait for a table, it's well worth it. Closed Sun.
Market St Steakhouse 1777 Market St ℡530/241-1777. As the name suggests, succulent steaks costing $18–32 are the speciality here, and the bar is a buzzing meeting-place in its own right.
Rivers 202 Hemsted Drive ℡530/222-1307. Steak, seafood and pasta are on the moderate

menu, as well as sumptuous desserts, and there is live music twice weekly.
Taj Mahal 40 Hartnell Ave ℡530/221-4655. Authentic North-Indian cuisine in a modern dining room; main courses are quite pricey at dinner, but there's a great lunch buffet seven days a week.
Thai Bistro 1270 Yuba St ℡530/244-4666. Small, brightly-lit dining room, serving well-prepared spicy Thai fare at slightly inflated prices.
Yaks Koffee Shop 3274 Bechelli Lane ℡530/223-9999. Massive, colourful place with a full range of coffees, smoothies, savoury snacks and sweet pastries. Several other branches have now popped up around town.

Shasta

Huddling four miles west of Redding, the ghost town of **Shasta** – not to be confused with Mount Shasta (see p.668) – is about the area's only option for historic entertainment, and it's a slim option at that. A booming gold-mining town when Redding was an insignificant dot on the map, Shasta's fortunes changed when the railroad tracks were laid to Redding in the late nineteenth century. Abandoned since then, it remains today a row of half-ruined brick buildings that were once part of a runaway prosperity and literally the end of the road for prospectors. All roads from San Francisco, Sacramento and other southerly points terminated at Shasta; beyond, rough and poorly marked trails made it almost impossible to find gold diggings along the Trinity, Salmon and Upper Sacramento rivers, so diggers contented themselves with the rich pickings in the surrounding area, pushing out the local Native Americans in a brutal territorial quest for good mining land.

The **Courthouse**, on the east side of Main Street, has been turned into a museum (Thurs–Sun 10am–5pm; $3), full of mining paraphernalia and paintings of past heroes, though best are the gallows at the back and the prison cells below – a grim reminder of the daily executions that went on here. The miners were a largely unruly lot and in the main room of the Courthouse a charter lays down some basic rules of conduct:

IV Thou shalt neither remember what thy friends do at home on the Sabbath day, lest the remembrance may not compare favorably with what thou doest here.
VII Thou shalt not kill the body by working in the rain, even though thou shalt make enough money to buy psychic attendance. Neither shalt thou destroy thyself by "tight" nor "slewed" nor "high" nor "corned" nor "three sheets to the wind," by drinking smoothly down brandy slings, gin cocktails, whiskey punches, rum toddies and egg nogs.

From *The Miners' Ten Commandments*

The **Shasta State Historic Park** (unrestricted entry) straddles two blocks of Main Street, and is less grand than it sounds, though it's a good place to stretch your legs before moving further west. Indistinguishable ruins of brick buildings are identified by plaques as stores and hotels, and the central area, not much bigger than the average garden, features miscellaneous mining machinery and a picnic area, along with a trail that loops around the back.

Whiskeytown-Shasta-Trinity National Recreation Area

To the west and north of Redding lies the **WHISKEYTOWN-SHASTA-TRINITY NATIONAL RECREATION AREA**. Assuming the roads are open – they're often blocked due to bad weather in winter – this huge chunk of land is open for public use daily, year-round. Its series of three impounded **lakes** – Whiskeytown, Trinity and Shasta – have artificial beaches, forests and camping facilities designed to meet the needs of anyone who has ever fancied themselves as a water skier, sailor or wilderness hiker. Sadly, during summer the area becomes completely congested, as windsurfers, motorboats, jet-skis and RVs block the narrow routes that serve the lakes. But in the low season, especially during the week, it can be supremely untouched, at least on the surface. In fact, there's an extensive system of tunnels, dams and aqueducts directing the plentiful waters of the Sacramento River to California's Central Valley to irrigate cash crops for the huge agribusinesses. The lakes are pretty enough, but residents complain they're not a patch on the wild waters that used to flow from the mountains before the Central Valley Project came along in the 1960s.

Whiskeytown Lake

Of the three, **Whiskeytown Lake**, just beyond Shasta, is the smallest, easiest to get to and inevitably the most popular. It's open all the time but day-use parking costs $5. Ideal for watersports, it hums with the sound of jet-skis and powerboats ripping across the still waters. The best place for **camping** and **hiking** is in the **Brandy Creek** area – a hairy five-mile drive along the narrow J.F. Kennedy Memorial Drive from the main entrance and **Whiskeytown Visitor Information Center** on Hwy-299 (daily: summer 9am–6pm; winter 10am–4pm; ☎530/246-1225, ⓦwww.nps.gov/whis), where you can pick up permits for primitive camping sites ($10) around the lake. There's a small store at the water's edge in Brandy Creek and three more developed campgrounds (summer $16–18) about a mile behind in the woods. One surprising feature is the **free kayak tours** run in the summer (call ☎530/242-3462).

Trinity Lake and Weaverville

After Hwy-299 has climbed over the wooded, 3213-foot Buckhorn Summit, you can turn northeast on Hwy-3 around forty miles west of Whiskeytown to **Trinity Lake**, officially called Clair Engle Lake, but not locally referred to as such. This is much quieter, used by fewer in summer, and in winter primarily a picturesque stop off for skiers on their way to the **Trinity Alps** area beyond, which in turn lead to the extensive **Salmon Mountains** range. There are several places to **stay** and enjoy the peaceful lapping waters. Of these, *Pinewood Cove*, 45110 Hwy-3 (☎1-800/988-5253, ⓦwww.pinewoodcove.com; ④), rents out boats of various sizes, and has campsites ($27.50) and luxury cabins for four, as do *Trinity Lake Resorts*, further north at 45810 Hwy-3 (☎1-800/255-5561, ⓦwww.trinitylakeresort.com; ⑤); they also have houseboats (minimum stay three nights) and a full restaurant. At its southern end, Lake Trinity squeezes through a narrow bottleneck to form the much slimmer and smaller Lewiston Lake, which can be reached by the back road that cuts the corner between Hwy-299 and Hwy-3. Camp for free on the grassy banks of the lake or stay in greater comfort at the *Old Lewiston Inn* (☎1-800/286-4441, ⓦwww.theoldlewistoninn.com; ④) in the diminutive old mining town of Lewiston itself, on the same road.

Weaverville

Sadly, many people don't bother to stop in the small Gold Rush town of **Weaverville**, 43 miles west of Redding, where Hwy-3 branches north to Trinity Lake, while Hwy-299 continues a further one hundred miles west to Eureka (see p.640) and the coast. The town's distinctive brick buildings, fitted with exterior spiral staircases, were built to withstand fires – indeed, the fire station itself is particularly noteworthy. The main draw, though, is the **Joss House** on Main Street (Thurs–Sun 10am–5pm; $4), a small Taoist temple built in 1874 by indentured Chinese mine-workers. A beautiful shrine still in use today, it features a three-thousand-year-old altar and can be visited on a sadly uninspiring guided tour (last tour 4pm). Next door, the **J.J. Jake Jackson Museum** (Jan–March Tues & Sat noon–4pm; April daily noon–4pm; May–Oct daily 10am–5pm; Nov & Dec Wed–Sat noon–4pm; $2) exhibits artefacts from the Gold Rush. On the opposite side of the road look out for California's oldest still-functioning pharmacy, which stocks a brilliant selection of remedies in glass jars within original glass-and-wood cabinets.

You can **stay** in some style at the refurbished 1861 *Weaverville Hotel*, 481 Main St (☎530/623-2222, ⓦwww.weavervillehotel.com; ⑤). Alternatives include the renovated *49er Gold Country Inn*, 880 Main St (☎530/623-4937,

ⓦwww.goldcountryinn.com; ❷), or the friendly *Motel Trinity* (☎1-877/623-5454, ⓦwww.moteltrinity.com; ❶), south of Hwy-3 at 1270 Main St, which has some rooms with jacuzzis for twice the price of basic ones.

For **food**, try the pizza, sandwiches and ice cream at the cosy *Christopher Robin's*, 227 Main St, or delicious Chinese cuisine in the dark-red interior of the *Red Dragon*, 625 Main St, across from the Joss House, appropriately enough. The *New York Saloon*, 225 Main St (☎530/623-3492), is a great place to mingle with the friendly locals over a pint of beer. For more information, consult the **Chamber of Commerce**, 501 Main St (Mon–Sat 9am–5pm; ☎1-800/487-4648, ⓦwww.trinitycounty.com), though it's not always open due to lack of volunteers.

Shasta Lake

East of the other two lakes and eight miles north of Redding is **Shasta Lake**. The biggest of the three lakes – larger than the San Francisco Bay in fact – it's marred by the unsightly and enormous **Shasta Dam**, 465ft high and over half a mile long, bang in the middle. Twice the mass of the Hoover Dam, it's the second largest dam in America, made of enough concrete to send a foot-square strip round the planet several times. Built between 1938 and 1945 as part of the enormous Central Valley irrigation project, the dam backs up the Sacramento, McCloud and Pit rivers to form the lake, the project's northern outpost. From the **visitor centre** (daily 8am–5pm; ☎530/275-4463), off I-5 on US-151, you can take one of the free **tours** (normally 9am, 11am, 1pm & 3pm but times and access can vary) of the **powerhouse** and into the dam, though security is tight and you cannot take cameras or mobile phones with you. Still, it's an entertaining 45 minutes, and the close-up views of the millions of gallons of water gushing down the face of the giant structure are memorable.

On the north side of the lake, the massive limestone formations of the **Shasta Caverns** (daily 2-hour tours: June–Aug every 30min 9am–4pm; April, May & Sept hourly 9am–3pm; winter 10am, noon & 2pm; $22) are the largest in California, jutting above ground and clearly visible from the freeway. The interior, however, conceals a fairly standard series of caves and tunnels in which stalactite and stalagmite formations are studded with crystals, flowstone deposits and miniature waterfalls. The admission price covers the short ferry journey from the ticket booth across an arm of Shasta Lake and the bus transfer on the other side.

If you turn west instead of east at the exit to the caverns, within a couple of miles you reach two great **places to stay**. First, in the small hillside settlement of **O'Brien**, the 🔥 *O'Brien Mountain Inn* (☎1-888/799-8026, ⓦwww.obrienmountaininn.com; ❺) is a welcoming country B&B whose star room is the detached Luke's Tree House Suite on stilts over the forest ($300). A little further on, the *Bridge Bay Resort*, 10300 Bridge Bay Rd (☎1-800/752-9669, ⓦwww.sevencrown.com; ❹), provides the only roofed accommodation right on the lake in the shape of motel rooms, suites, cabins and houseboats; you can also dine with a view of the water at the resort's *Tail of the Whale* restaurant. Seven miles north, off the first Lakehead exit, the *Lakeshore East Campground* on Lakeshore Drive (☎530/275-8113, ⓦwww.shastalakecamping.com) has tent sites from $16 and huge sturdy yurts, which can sleep five and are a snip at $45. From Lake Shasta, I-5 crosses the world's highest double-decker bridge and races up towards Mount Shasta, an impressive drive against a staggering backdrop of mountains and lakes.

Mount Shasta and Mount Shasta City

> When I first caught sight of it over the braided folds of the Sacramento Valley I was
> fifty miles away and afoot, alone and weary. Yet my blood turned to wine, and I
> have not been weary since.
>
> John Muir, about Mount Shasta

The lone peak of the 14,179-foot **MOUNT SHASTA** dominates the landscape
for a hundred miles all around, almost permanently snow-covered and hypnotically
beautiful, but menacing in its potential for destruction: it last erupted over two
hundred years ago but is still considered an active volcano. Summing up its isolated
magnificence, Joaquin Miller once described it as "lonely as God and as white as a

Climbing Mount Shasta

Even if you're only passing through the region, you'll be tempted to tackle Mount
Shasta. Ambling among the pines of the lower slopes is rewarding enough but the
assault on the summit is the main challenge – and it can be done in a day with basic
equipment and some determination.

Still, it's not a climb to be taken lightly, and every year several deaths occur and
numerous injuries are sustained through inexperience and overambition. The wise
stick to the routes prescribed by the **Mount Shasta Ranger District Office**, 204 W
Alma St (June–Aug daily 8am–4.30pm; Sept–May Mon–Fri 8am–4.30pm; ☏530/926-
4511), which insists that you obtain a **summit pass** (also self-issued outside the
office when closed and at the trailhead; $20) and enter your name in the **climbers'
register** before and after your ascent. Those not planning to go above 10,000ft only
require a free **wilderness permit**.

The mountain's isolation creates its own **weather**, which can change with alarming
rapidity. In early summer, when most novice attempts are made, the snow cover is
complete, making crampons and an ice axe a requirement to get a good grip; later
during the season, as the snow melts, patches of loose ash and cinder appear,
making the going more difficult and the chance of falling rock greater. Only at the
end of summer, with most of the snow melted, is there a chance of climbing safely
without **equipment**. There are countless equipment rental agencies in town, such
as The Fifth Season, 300 N Mount Shasta Blvd (☏530/926-3606, ⊛www.thefifth
season.com), which has the following rental prices for trips up to three days: boots
($30), crampons and ice axe ($24), mountain tent ($75), and sleeping bag ($30). They
also provide a mountain weather forecast on ☏530/926-5555 and are the meeting
place for Shasta Mountain Guides (☏530/926-3117, ⊛www.shastaguides.com), who
arrange jeep trips up the mountain and conduct rock and ice-climbing courses for all
levels, as well as backcountry skiing trips, from around $100 per day.

To be prepared for **storms** on the mountain, you'll want to bring extra food, stove
fuel, a good wind-resistant shelter and plenty of warm clothing. Even for fit, acclimatized climbers, **the ascent**, from 7000ft to over 14,000ft, takes eight to ten utterly
exhausting hours. The easiest, safest and most popular way up is via **Avalanche
Gulch** – just follow the footprints of the person in front of you. Drive up the mountain
on the Everitt Memorial Highway to the **Bunny Flat** trailhead at 7000ft. A gentle
hour's walk brings you to **Horse Camp** (7900ft), a good place to acclimatize and
spend the night before your ascent – there's drinking water, toilet facilities and a
knowledgeable caretaker who can offer good advice about your impending climb.
The return trip is done in four or five hours, depending on the recklessness of your
descent: Mount Shasta is a renowned spot for **glissading** – careering down the
slopes on a jacket or strong plastic sheet – a sport best left to those proficient in
ice-axe arrests, but wonderfully exhilarating nonetheless.

winter moon". Local lore is rich with tales of Lemurians – tall, barefoot men dressed in white robes – living inside the mountain, alongside their legendary neighbours the Yaktavians, who are said to be excellent bell-makers. Such tales have lent the mountain a bit of a *Twilight Zone* reputation and numerous UFO sightings and otherworldly experiences have made Mount Shasta a centre of the American **spiritualism** movement. This prominence was heightened in 1987 when five thousand people arrived to take part in the good vibes of the Harmonic Convergence, an attempt to channel the energies of sacred power spots into peace and harmony. Not all is peaceful on the mountain, however, as hundreds of climbers annually attempt to ascend its icy heights, an activity that has resulted in deaths, usually from falls or the ever-changing weather.

Just below the shadow of the behemoth sits the historic railroad town of **Dunsmuir** and, right up against the mountain, pleasant **Mount Shasta City**, a small town of shops, outfitters, spiritual bookstores and some wonderful restaurants. To the southeast, also commanding stunning views of the mountain, is pretty little **McCloud**, while on the northern flank of the peak rests **Weed**, another tiny town that offers some of the clearest views of Mount Shasta in summertime and access to Lava Beds National Monument. Further north towards the Oregon border, **Yreka** is more useful as an I-5 service stop than as a place to visit in its own right.

Arrival and information

Merely getting to Mount Shasta City without a car is a complex but rewarding journey: the nearest Greyhound **buses** will bring you is Weed (see p.673), seven miles north, while Amtrak **trains** stop six miles south in Dunsmuir, unfortunately in the middle of the night; from both towns, half a dozen or so daily STAGE buses (☎1-800/247-8243) run to the Mount Shasta Shopping Center next to the *Black Bear Diner*, although you'll have to wait at least three hours for the first bus from Dunsmuir. STAGE also operates five daily services to McCloud. The **Chamber of Commerce**, 300 Pine St (May–Sept Mon–Sat 9am–5.30pm, Sun 9am–4.30pm; Oct–April daily 10am–4pm; ☎1-800/926-4865, ⓦwww .mtshastachamber.com), has a rather limited selection of brochures; you can obtain more comprehensive information on the entire county from the **Siskiyou County Visitor Bureau** (☎1-877/847-8777, ⓦwww.visitsiskiyou.org), although there is no office to visit here.

Accommodation

Mount Shasta City has no shortage of **accommodation** and reservations should only be necessary on weekends in the height of summer. The suitably New Age organization of spiritual author Amorah Quan Yin (☎530/926-1122, ⓦwww .amorahquanyin.com) offers contacts for local lodging, as well as a fascinating insight into the Mount Shasta way of thinking.

Campgrounds abound in the surrounding area, but few have full amenities and hot showers are fairly essential when the mercury drops. More primitive sites tend to be free if there's no piped drinking water, though creek water is often available.

Hotels, motels and B&Bs

Alpenrose Cottage Guesthouse 204 E Hinckley St ☎530/926-6724, ⓦwww.snowcrest.net /alpenrose. A top-quality and friendly hostel-style guesthouse with a relaxed atmosphere and a great deck for watching the sunset over Mount Shasta, immediately behind. Follow the KOA signs a mile north on N Mount Shasta Blvd. ❷

Best Western Tree House 111 Morgan Way ☎1-800/545-7164, ⓦwww.bestwestern.com. One

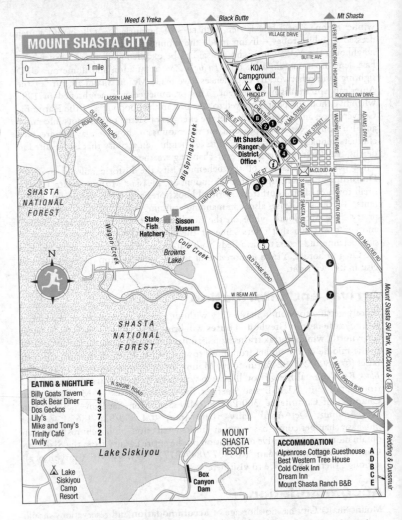

MOUNT SHASTA CITY

0   1 mile

EATING & NIGHTLIFE

Billy Goats Tavern	4
Black Bear Diner	5
Dos Geckos	3
Lily's	7
Mike and Tony's	6
Trinity Café	2
Vivify	1

ACCOMMODATION

Alpenrose Cottage Guesthouse	A
Best Western Tree House	D
Cold Creek Inn	B
Dream Inn	C
Mount Shasta Ranch B&B	E

of the more attractive and intimate members of the international chain, with all the usual amenities. Close to Downtown, too. ❹

Cold Creek Inn 724 N Mount Shasta Blvd ☎1-800/292-9421, ⓦwww.coldcreekinn.com. Nicely refurbished motel, an easily walkable few blocks to Downtown. Good internet specials. ❷

Dream Inn 326 Chestnut St ☎1-877/375-4744, ⓦwww.dreaminnmtshastacity.com. Very central and reasonably priced B&B, a block east of Mount Shasta Blvd, in a Victorian house with all the usual trappings. ❷

Mount Shasta Ranch B&B 1008 W. A. Barr Rd ☎530/926-3870, ⓦwww.stayinshasta.com. A stylish ranch house with spacious rooms, a

self-contained cottage, a hot spring and a great view of Mount Shasta. The cheaper rooms have shared bathrooms. ❶

Campgrounds

KOA 900 N Mount Shasta Blvd ☎1-800/736-3617, ⓦwww.koa.com. This fully equipped campground is a few blocks from Downtown. From $23 per tent; basic cabins from $53.

Lake Siskiyou Camp Resort Four miles southwest of town on Lake Siskiyou ☎1-888/926-2618. The most picturesque campground in the area is this woodland option, where you can picnic, bathe, and go boating. April–Oct; $22.

McBride Springs Everitt Memorial Hwy. Being lower down the same road as *Panther Meadows* (at 5000ft), this site tends to be open for longer. $10.

Panther Meadows At the end of the Everitt Memorial Hwy. The most useful of the primitive sites is the walk-in *Panther Meadows*, high up on the mountain (7400ft). Closed in winter. Free.

The town and around

Quite rightly, few people come to Mount Shasta for its museums, but in bad weather you might visit the otherwise missable **Sisson Museum**, 1 N Old Stage Road (April & May daily 1–4pm; June–Sept daily 10am–4pm; Oct–Dec Fri–Sun 1–4pm; donation), with a few examples of native basketware, a fair bit on pioneering life in the region, and some more diverting material on the mountain itself. The brown, rainbow and eastern brook trout in the **fish hatchery** outside (daily 8am–sunset; free) can be fed on food from a vending machine.

A couple of New Age **bookstores** and **gift shops** long North Mount Shasta Boulevard provide the key to some of the town's more offbeat activities. Book Nook at no. 331, for example, has a bulletin board and stacks of publications exhorting you to visit a sweat lodge or get in touch with the ascended masters. Shasta Vortex Adventures, 400 Chestnut St (℡530/926-4326, ⓦwww.shastavortex.com), is an interesting outfit whose primary business is providing personalized spiritual tours of the mountain, but they also offer other esoteric services. For a bit of **culture**, the Stage Door, 414 N Mount Shasta Blvd (℡530/555-1212, ⓦwww.stagedoorcabaret .com), is a small theatre showcasing drama and music at the back of a relaxed coffee shop. An increasing number of galleries is sprouting up, too.

Mainly, though, Mount Shasta is full of outfits hoping to help you into the **outdoors**, from trout fishing through dog sledding to, of course, mountain climbing. Competition keeps prices reasonable and the options wide open. Details on climbing Mount Shasta and other activities on its slopes are covered in the box on p.668. For aquatic thrills, whitewater-rafting trips on the churning Upper Sacramento are offered by Turtle River Rafting (℡1-800/726-3223, ⓦwww .turtleriver.com) and River Dancers (℡1-800/926-5002, ⓦwww.riverdancers .com), both starting at about $90 a day.

Eating and drinking

Aside from a rash of fast-food outlets towards I-5, Mount Shasta's **eating** options are largely health-conscious, with vegetarian dishes featured on almost every menu. Hardy mountain types are amply catered for, too, with plenty of opportunities to stoke up on hearty fare before hitting the mountain heights. You can gather picnic supplies with the handcrafted loaves from The Oven Bakery at 214 N Mount Shasta Blvd. Nightlife is low-key but there are a couple of established **bars**.

Billy Goats Tavern 107 Chestnut St. Friendly bar, good for drinking a pint with the locals but less inspired in the food department. Closed Sun & Mon.
Black Bear Diner 401 W Lake St. Wholesome family diner, a great place for heaped breakfasts or classic American dinners.
Dos Geckos 401 N Mt Shasta Blvd. Excellent build-your-own-burrito joint, with stunning views of the mountain from the patio.
Lily's 1013 S Mt Shasta Blvd. Moderately priced and consistently good restaurant serving California cuisine, vegetarian and Mexican dishes. Main courses cost around $17–22, sandwiches $8–10.

Mike and Tony's 501 S Mt Shasta Blvd. It may not look like much but this excellent Italian place specializes in home-made ravioli. Great Martinis, too. Dinner only; closed Tues & Wed.
Trinity Café 622 N Mt Shasta Blvd ℡530/926-6200. The best place for quality international cuisine made from local produce. The menu changes weekly and fine microbrewed ales are available on tap. Most main courses are over $20. Closed Sun & Mon.
Vivify 531 Chestnut St ℡530/926-1345. Stylish Japanese restaurant serving totally organic sushi and main meals at reasonable prices.

Around Mount Shasta

Apart from Mount Shasta itself and the surrounding towns covered here, there are several other natural delights to explore, which you'll certainly find less well-trodden in season than the main body of the mountain. Five miles north of town, the largely treeless cone of **Black Butte** (2.5 miles; 2–3hr; 1800-foot ascent) offers a more modest alternative to climbing Mount Shasta. The switchback trail to this 6325-foot volcanic plug dome is hard to find without the leaflet available from the ranger station or visitor centre.

If you have time, you'd also be well advised to explore the beautiful trails that climb four thousand feet up to the 225-million-year-old, glacier-polished granite crags at the aptly named **Castle Crags State Park** (daily 8am–dusk; $8 per car; ℡530/235-2684), thirteen miles south of Mount Shasta along I-5. Campgrounds with full amenities are available for $25 per night (℡1-800/444-7275, ⓦwww.parks.ca.gov) and primitive ones for $5–15 in the often deserted, 6200-acre forested park.

Mount Shasta Ski Park (℡1-800/754-7478, ⓦwww.skipark.com), near McCloud on Hwy-89, has yet to establish itself on the ski circuit, so its lift tickets (Mon–Thurs $29, Fri–Sun $39) and rental charges for skis ($23) and snowboards ($30) are quite reasonable. On the lower slopes, keep your eyes peeled for the inedible **watermelon snow**, its bright red appearance caused by a microbe which flourishes here – think Frank Zappa, just change the colour.

After a day or two trudging around or up Mount Shasta, **Stewart Mineral Springs** (Mon–Thurs & Sun 10am–6pm, Fri & Sat 10am–8pm; ℡530/938-2222, ⓦwww.stewartmineralsprings.com; ❷) at 4617 Stewart Springs Rd off I-5 just north of Weed, provides welcome relief. Individual bathing rooms in a cedar and pine forest glade soothe your aches away for $28, less if you stay in the very affordable cabins, teepees ($45) or campground ($35) here. Just before you reach the springs, you can take Parks Creek Road to the top of the ridge, from where it's a ninety-minute hike along the **Pacific Coast Trail** to tranquil Dead Fall Lakes.

Dunsmuir

One example of how the Shasta area looked in the past can be seen in the hamlet of **Dunsmuir**, even quainter than Mount Shasta City. Situated ten miles south of Mount Shasta on a steep hill sloping down from I-5, Dunsmuir's Downtown was bypassed by the freeway, essentially freezing the community in time. Now it makes its living as a historic railroad town and the main drag, **Dunsmuir Avenue**, is lined with restored hotels and shops, many of them taking the train theme a bit too far; expect to see shopkeepers dressed as train engineers and business names like Billy Puffer Suites. Amtrak **trains** stop at the usually deserted railway station, its last California halt before continuing north to Oregon. The **Visitors Bureau**, at Suite 100, 5915 Dunsmuir Ave (summer Wed–Sat 9.30am–noon & 1–5pm; ℡1-800/386-7684, ⓦwww.dunsmuir.com), has updated train and STAGE bus schedules, though opening hours are erratic.

Dunsmuir used to bill itself as a day-trip from Shasta, but now realizes that it has quietude and natural wonders of its own. Foremost among these are the Mossbrae and Hedge Creek **waterfalls**, along the Sacramento River Canyon, beautiful spots for walks and picnics. To reach **Mossbrae**, drive north on Dunsmuir Avenue to Scarlet Way, crossing the bridge and railroad tracks to the parking area. Follow the walking trail along the train tracks for one mile until you get to the railroad bridge. Don't cross, but continue along the tracks through the trees and you'll see the falls ahead. **Hedge Creek Falls** are accessible via the parking area at the North Dunsmuir exit on I-5.

If you plan **to stay**, the most central of the B&Bs in town is *The Dunsmuir Inn*, 5423 Dunsmuir Ave (☎530/1-888/386-7684; ❸). Under a mile south, the *Dunsmuir Lodge*, 6604 Dunsmuir Ave (☎1-877/235-2884, ⓦwww.dunsmuir lodge.net; ❷), is a little cheaper, while on the north side of town *Cave Springs*, 4727 Dunsmuir Ave (☎530/235-2721, ⓦwww.cavesprings.com; ❷), has a wide range of motel rooms and cabins, a couple of which have outdoor hot tubs overlooking the river. The most unique lodging in the area is the ⚘ *Railroad Park Resort* (☎530/235-0420, ⓦwww.rrpark.com; ❹), nearly three miles south at 100 Railroad Park Rd; most of the accommodations are fashioned out of old railway cabooses, though there are also some cabins and RV sites. Dunsmuir has become quite a gourmet paradise of late, with the appearance of several upscale **restaurants**. The *Cornerstone Bakery Café*, 5759 Dunsmuir Ave (☎530/235-2620; closed Tues), serves upmarket California-style breakfasts and lunches, while equally pricey is *Sengthong's*, 5855 Dunsmuir Ave, the place for quality Southeast Asian cuisine. Tasty Mediterranean evening meals are on the menu at *Café Maddalena*, 5801 Sacramento Ave (Thurs–Sun only). Two places for a cheaper meal on Dunsmuir Avenue are *Gary's Pizza Factory*, no. 5804, and *Las Gringas Taqueria*, no. 5740.

McCloud

McCloud, a delightful little town with stunning views of Mount Shasta, can make another good base for the area, especially if you plan to spend much time in the Ski Park (see opposite). The only cultural diversion is the small **Heritage Junction Museum** at 320 Main St (May–Oct Mon–Sat 11am–3pm, Sun 1–3pm; donation), loaded with a haphazard collection of bric-a-brac, memorabilia and woodcutters' gear. As for **accommodation**, the *McCloud Hotel*, right in town at 408 Main St (☎1-800/964-2823, ⓦwww.mccloudhotel.com; ❹), has smart rooms in a classy restored building and a fine restaurant, while an excellent B&B option just up the road is *Stoney Brook Inn*, 309 W Colombero Drive (☎1-800/369-6118, ⓦwww.stoneybrookinn.com; ❷), with some shared bathrooms and particularly good single rates. The only motel in the vicinity is the *McCloud Timber Inn*, 153 Squaw Valley Rd (☎530/964-2893; ❶), which boasts an attractive location and roomier-than-average lodgings. For a **meal**, try the tasty barbecue dishes at the *McCloud River Grille & Bar*, on the south side of Hwy-89 at 140 Squaw Valley Rd, which is also the town's main watering-hole. Grab a daytime snack at *Floyd's Frosty*, 125 Broadway, a Fifties-style joint offering hefty burgers, thick shakes and ice cream.

There's not much to do in the town itself, but the nearby **McCloud River Falls**, five miles east on Hwy-89, is a great spot for a picnic or gentle stroll. The falls, set amid thick woods, are divided into three distinct sections, each about one mile from the next and connected by a riverside walking trail but also accessible by road. If you're short of time, head for the more dramatic Middle Falls; at *Fowlers Camp*, near the Lower Falls, there's **camping**, often free because of the intermittent water supply, while the Upper Falls boast a lovely picnic area. Continuing southeast on Hwy-89, you'll eventually come to the more renowned and spectacular Burney Falls and, still further, Lassen Volcanic National Park (see p.657).

Weed

A gateway town to Klamath Falls, Oregon, and the Lava Beds National Monument, **Weed** can't compete with Mount Shasta City's hip charm. But, perhaps in a form of karmic justice, it gets the better view of the peak during the summertime. Too bad the tourism board couldn't leave it at that, instead of dressing up the place as a "historic lumber town" with the groaner of a slogan, "Weed love to see you". Those responsible can be found at the **Chamber of Commerce**, 34 Main St (summer daily 9am–5pm; winter Mon–Fri 10am–4pm; ☎1-877/938-4624, ⍟www.weedchamber.com), and will supply further information on the area as penance. Just off Main Street at 303 Gilman Ave, **Weed Historic Lumber Town Museum** (summer daily 10am–5pm; winter by appointment; donation; ☎530/938-0550) occupies the former courthouse and outlines local history, primarily that of the lumber industry; it also contains a couple of fine old vehicles.

The Greyhound **bus** office is at 628 S Weed Blvd (Mon–Sat 8.30am–4pm; ☎530/938-4454) and is also the nearest stop to Mount Shasta City. In town, the *Hi Lo Motel & Café*, 88 S Weed Blvd (☎530/938-2731; ❶), has decent rooms and a café that serves hash and eggs. On the northern end of Weed Boulevard, at no. 466, the *Motel 6* branch includes a nice outdoor pool and stunning sunrise views of Mount Shasta (☎1-800/466-8356, ⍟www.motel6.com; ❶). The best place for a meal is *Hungry Moose*, an excellent all-day diner located at 86 N Weed Blvd, or you can chill out with a healthier snack at *Buddha Belly Kitchen*, 51 Main St, which has a very loungeable lounge. *Papa's Place*, 203 Main Street, is a friendly bar for drinking beer with the locals and getting a basic bite to eat, but the best ales can be tasted and tours arranged at the Mt Shasta Brewing Company, 360 College Ave (Thurs–Sun 2–6pm; ☎530/938-2394, ⍟www.mtshastabrewingcompany.com).

Five miles outside of town, north on US-97 on the way to Oregon and Lava Beds, the **Living Memorial Sculpture Garden** (unrestricted entry; donation) is an intriguing remembrance of the Vietnam War. Artist Dennis Smith has created ten metal sculptures illustrating different aspects of an American soldier's experience in the war. Surrounding the art are about 53,000 pine trees, one for every American killed in Vietnam. The trees, art, silence and position under Mount Shasta add up to a very moving experience.

Yreka

There's little to justify more than an hour or two in quiet, leafy **Yreka** (pronounced "why-REE-ka"), twenty-five miles north of Weed on I-5, but it makes a pleasant break. The reason most people used to come here was to ride the Yreka Western Railroad, better known as the **Blue Goose**, but it has been suspended since 2008 due to economic constraints (check the situation on ☎1-800/973-5277, ⍟www.yrekawesternrr.com). The **Siskiyou County Museum**, 910 S Main St (Tues–Thurs 9am–3pm, Sat 10am–4pm; $3; ☎530/842-3836), deserves some attention, particularly the outdoor section (May–Oct same days 10am–3.30pm) with its historic buildings – church, houses and shops – transported here from around the county. Finally, there's a valuable collection of gold nuggets in the **County Courthouse**, 311 4th St (Mon–Fri 8am–5pm; free).

Yreka can be reached by STAGE **bus** from Mount Shasta, Dunsmuir and McCloud. The **Chamber of Commerce**, 117 W Miner St (summer daily 9am–5pm; winter Mon–Fri 9am–5pm; ☎530/842-1649, ⍟www.yrekachamber.com), issues maps for a self-guided Historic Walking Tour around Yreka's numerous Victorian homes. It can also help you find **accommodation** – not that it's hard to find, with plenty of chain motels such as the *Econolodge*, 526 S Main St (☎530/842-4404, ⍟www.econolodge.com; ❶), and independent ones like the *Klamath Motor Lodge*, 1111 S Main St (☎1-800/551-7255, ⍟www.klamathmotorlodge.net; ❷). Smarter accommodations can be found for almost the same price at the town's only B&B, the *Yreka Third Street Inn*, 326 3rd St (☎530/841-1120, ⍟www.yrekabedandbreakfast.com; ❸). Good eating options along S Main Street include *Nature's Kitchen*, a decent diner at no. 412 (closed Sun), *Natalee*, a simple Thai joint at no. 1225, and *China Dragon*, no. 520 (☎530/842 3444), where you can get inexpensive Chinese and American food. For a more romantic setting, try the excellent Italian cuisine at *Angelini's*, 322 W Miner St (☎530/842-5000).

A worthwhile twenty-mile detour south of Yreka along Hwy-3 takes you to charming, turn-of-the-century **Etna**. Its main claim to fame is the Etna Brewing Company, 131 Callahan St (Wed–Sun 11am–6pm; ☎530/467-5277), a tiny microbrewery which has gradually been gaining a fine reputation as its brews begin to be distributed more widely. Four or five of the malty real ales are usually available to taste, along with other beers, each and every one a drinker's dream, and you can usually take an impromptu tour; tasty bar food is also available. While here, check out the 1950s soda fountain in the Scott Valley Drugstore at the top of Main Street. And if you're really struck by the place, you can **camp** for free in the town park on Diggles Street or **stay** at the basic but comfortable *Etna Motel*, 317 Collier Way (☎530/467-5388; ●).

Lava Beds National Monument and around

After seeing Mount Shasta, you really should push on to the **LAVA BEDS NATIONAL MONUMENT**, which commemorates a war between the US and Modoc Indians on the far northern border of the state. Carved out of the huge **Modoc National Forest**, it's actually a series of volcanic caves you can explore and huge black lava flows with a history as violent as the natural forces that created them.

Lava Beds is one of the most remote, forgotten and beautiful of California's parks, with pungent yellow rabbit-brush blooming around the burnt rocks in autumn. It's in the heart of Modoc country, a desolate outback where cowboys still ride the range, and where, as the territory of one of the last major battles with the Native Americans, there's still a suspicious relationship between the settlers and the native peoples.

Today the Lava Beds region is inhabited only by wild deer and three million migrating ducks, which easily outnumber the trickle of tourists that make it this far. To the west and north, the **Klamath Basin National Wildlife Refuge** spreads over the border into Oregon. This stop on the Pacific Flyway draws birders

The land of the Modoc

Until the 1850s Gold Rush, the area which now defines the Lava Beds National Monument was home to the **Modoc tribe** but after their repeated and bloody confrontations with the miners, the government ordered them into a reservation with the Klamath, their traditional enemy. After only a few months, the Modoc drifted back to their homeland in the Lava Beds and in 1872 the army was sent in to return them by force to the reservation. It was driven back by 52 Modoc warriors under the leadership of one **Kientpoos**, better known as "Captain Jack", who held back an army of US regulars and volunteers twenty times the size of his for five months, from a stronghold at the northern tip of the park (see p.679). Eventually Captain Jack was betrayed by a member of his tribe, captured and hanged, while what remained of the tribe was sent off to a reservation in Oklahoma, where most of them died of malaria.

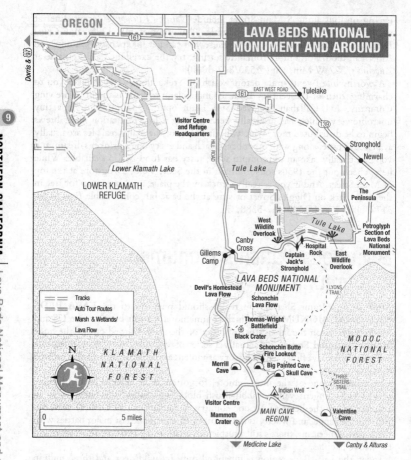

OREGON

161

EAST WEST ROAD   Tulelake

161

139

Visitor Centre
and Refuge
Headquarters

Stronghold

Newell

HILL ROAD

Lower Klamath Lake

Tule Lake

The
Peninsula

LOWER KLAMATH
REFUGE

Tule Lake

West
Wildlife
Overlook

Petroglyph
Section of
Lava Beds
National
Monument

Canby
Cross

Hospital
Rock

East
Wildlife
Overlook

Gillems
Camp

Captain
Jack's
Stronghold

LAVA BEDS
MONUMENT

LYONS
TRAIL

Devil's Homestead
Lava Flow

Schonchin
Lava Flow

Thomas-Wright
Battlefield

Black Crater

MODOC
NATIONAL
FOREST

N

KLAMATH
NATIONAL
FOREST

Schonchin Butte
Fire Lookout

Merrill
Cave

Big Painted Cave

Skull Cave

THREE
SISTERS
TRAIL

Indian Well

Tracks
Auto Tour Routes
Marsh & Wetlands/
Lava Flow

Visitor Centre

Mammoth
Crater

MAIN CAVE
REGION

Valentine
Cave

0   5 miles

Medicine Lake   Canby & Alturas

and hunters alike, hoping to catch sight of a rare eagle among the millions of migratory guests.

Park practicalities

Lava Beds National Monument ($10 per vehicle for seven days) is 160 miles northeast of Redding and inaccessible without a **car**. It's a day-trip from Mount Shasta, one and a half hours away, but can be combined with camping, spelunking and birding for a much longer stay. The most tortuous but undoubtedly scenic route follows Hwy-89 to Bartle, then passes Medicine Lake (see p.679); the approach via Hwy-139 is easier, but the best and fastest is from Weed, following US-97 through Dorris and then via Hwy-161 through the Klamath Basin National Wildlife Refuge (see p.679).

Pick up an excellent **map** of the monument from the **visitor centre**, just inside the southwestern entrance (daily: summer 8am–6pm; winter 8am–5pm; ☎530/667-8113, ⊛www.nps.gov/labe). Close by, at Indian Wells, is the park's one **campground** ($10). All **wilderness camping** throughout the monument is free and no permits are necessary but campers must pitch at least a quarter of a mile from any road, trail or camping area and fifty yards from any cave. Be warned, though, that elevation throughout the park ranges from 4000 to 5700 feet, so there's snow and freezing nights for much of the year, which can make camping uncomfortable.

Tulelake

The only **accommodation** near the park, and the one place to pick up supplies (the monument can only muster a drinks machine), is at **Tulelake**, fourteen miles north, which incidentally prides itself on being "the horseradish capital of the world". The near-deserted Main Street holds the extremely friendly and good-value *Fe's Bed & Breakfast*, no. 660 (℡1-877/478-0184, ⓦwww.fesbandb .com; ❷), while the only other option around town, the basic *Ellis Motel* (℡530/667-5342; ❶), is half a mile north on Hwy-139 but not much cheaper and should only be used as a stand-by. If birding is your main concern and you want to stay near the Lower Klamath Refuge (see p.680), then the *Winema Lodge* (℡530/667-5158, ⓦwww.winemalodge.com; ❷) is your best bet – it also serves meals on request.

The town has a couple of places to **eat**: *Mike and Wanda's*, just off Main Street at 423 Modoc Ave, has filling meals in the café and bar sections and a more expensive menu in the dining room in between. The area's top restaurant, however, is *Captain Jack's Stronghold* (℡530/664-5566), seven miles south on Hwy-139, which does excellent soups, steaks and home-made pies. Nearby is the **Modoc Ranger Station** (Mon–Fri 8am–4.30pm; ℡530/667-2246, ⓦwww.fs.fed.us/r5/modoc) with general information on the Modoc National Forest. Meanwhile, the town's **visitor information** office is in City Hall, 590 Main St (Mon–Fri 8am–5pm; ℡530/667-5522)

The one tourist attraction in town is the **Tulelake-Butte Valley Fair Museum of Local History** (Mon–Fri 9am–5pm, also Sat 9am–5pm in summer; $3), in the expansive fairgrounds at 800 S Main St. This complex contains excellent displays on geological features, wildlife, history (especially the Indian wars and World War II internment), Native American culture and current issues. The entry fee includes a one-hour interpretive **audio tour** to enhance your visit. The fairgrounds host an enormous annual **fair** during the week following Labor Day in September and you can camp on the grounds for $15 at any time.

The Monument

A day spent in the **Lava Beds** is akin to exploring the innards of a volcano, scampering down hollow tubes through which molten lava once coursed. The youngest of them were formed 30,000 years ago when volcanic upwellings sent molten, basaltic magma careering across the Modoc Plateau. As the magma came into contact with cool air, it solidified, leaving a flowing molten core feeding the expanding lava field downhill. In time, the magma flow stopped and the molten lava drained out, leaving the world's largest concentration of such hollow tubes – there were 746 at the last count in 2007. Most remain unexplored, but where the casing has collapsed, access is possible and you're free to scramble through. Some of the caves are so small that you have to crawl along on all fours, while others are an enormous 75ft in diameter. Some contain Native American **petroglyphs** – not to be confused with the names painted on the cave walls by J.D. Howard, one of the first white men to explore and name the caves.

You can borrow torches from the visitor centre and begin your explorations of the caves just outside. Initially, though, entering the darkness alone can be an unnerving experience, so many people prefer to take the **free guided ranger**

Exploring the Lava Beds

Most of the interest in Lava Beds lies around the visitor centre, where the largest concentration of caves can be visited on the short **Cave Loop** access road. For a confidence-building handle on your location in the twenty-five "developed" caves – less than a tenth of the known total – pick up the *Lava Caves Map* ($5.50) from the visitor centre. New ones are discovered all the time, so the possibilities are almost endless, but for the moment, the tried and tested caves below should satisfy.

Catacombs Cave At over a mile long, this is the longest open tube in the monument, though you need perseverance, a slim body and a cool head to get anywhere near the end. The profusion of interconnecting passageways makes it one of the most confusing; keep track of whether you are heading up- or downhill. On Cave Loop.

Golden Dome Cave The startling golden hues of the moist mossy roof lend the cave both its name and an otherworldly appearance. On Cave Loop.

Labyrinth Cave Striking geological features – lava pillars and lavacicles – and evidence of Native American habitation. At the entrance to Cave Loop.

Mushpot Cave Right by the visitor centre near the start of Cave Loop, this is the most developed of the caves. It provides a good introduction, is lit during centre opening hours and has interpretive panels highlighting key features.

Skull Cave Named after bighorn skulls found when the cave was discovered by early explorer E.L. Hopkins, this has the largest entrance of any of the lava tubes and contains ice all year round. About two miles north of Cave Loop.

Symbol Bridge and **Big Painted Cave** (1.5-mile round-trip; almost flat) Two very worthwhile caves adjacent to each other on a trail north of the visitor centre. No torch is needed, though one could come in handy. Some of the best examples of pictographs in the monument – tentatively dated between 1000 AD and 1500 AD – show up as different angles of sunlight catch the rocks beside the entrance. Respecting Modoc sensibilities, make two clockwise turns before descending into a large cave, open at both ends (hence the "bridge" name), in which zigzags, squiggles, sunbursts and human figures are depicted in grease and charcoal on a pumice-washed background. Make a single counterclockwise turn on departure for Big Painted Cave, where the pictographs are less impressive. In the mid-1920s, J.D. Howard excavated a small tunnel at the very back of the cave to reveal an ice flow in a cavity 15ft down: with a torch you can scramble down there. Two miles north of Cave Loop.

Valentine Cave Interesting because it combines various characteristic cave features, such as stalactites and catacombs. The ridges at the base of the walls leading down into the deep and wide chamber almost appear to be man-made, so even are their lines. About two miles southeast of Cave Loop.

walks (daily Memorial Day to Labor Day). Two-to-three-hour morning walks (9am) leave from the visitor centre and explore little-known sections of the monument; afternoon tours (usually 2pm) concentrate on ninety-minute guided cave trips; and in the evening (around 8.30–9pm) rangers lead hour-long campfire talks and slideshows, which shift to Mushpot Cave in bad weather.

If you do go independently, you must abide by a few **rules**. Don't go alone, wear decent shoes and take at least two torches. Borrowed torches must be returned by nightfall to ensure no one goes missing. For night explorations (the caves remain open), you'll need your own light source. Hard hats are strongly advised and can be purchased for $4 at the visitor centre.

If caves don't do it for you, the other attraction of Lava Beds is its well-documented history. Begin at the visitor centre for an exhibit on the Modoc War, including photos of its chief participants, including Modoc leader Captain Jack (see box, p.675), and scathing editorials from national papers condemning the US

Army over its mission. In the northern reaches of the park, around **Captain Jack's Stronghold**, a natural fortress of craggy lava flows and shallow caves on the shores of Old Tule Lake. When you arrive, pick up a trail book (50¢) from the car park and enjoy one of two well-narrated **self-guided trails** (one half a mile, the other 1.5 miles) through a war that in many ways typified the conquest of the West. When you get here you'll see how the Modoc managed to hide and move around through the passageways of the hills. Two miles west, **Canby Cross** marks a turning point in the war, when Captain Jack, coerced by the man who would later betray him, drew a gun during a council and murdered US General Canby and a pastor. Just northeast of Captain Jack's Stronghold, the shallow lava bowl of **Hospital Rock** marks the point where one Lt Sherwood, wounded by the Modoc, was unsuccessfully tended in a makeshift field hospital towards the end of the siege on the stronghold.

Around the monument

Small volcanic craters, buttes, spatter cones and chimneys dot Lava Beds but the flows which produced most of the lava tubes came from **Mammoth Crater** on the southern perimeter of the monument, where a short path leads to a viewpoint overlooking the deep conical crater.

Underlying the most recent of Lava Beds' fabulous creations is a bed of basalt, the product of a huge shield volcano with a profile so flat it's barely noticeable. Its core is now filled by the subalpine **Medicine Lake**, ten miles southwest of Mammoth Crater. Formerly a Modoc healing centre, the only therapies on offer today are fishing and swimming from the $10 campsites along the north shore. It's accessible via an unpaved road closed November to mid-May.

More volcanic spectacle lies just west at **Glass Mountain**, made almost entirely of glassy, black obsidian – source of Modoc arrowheads – but covered in fluffy, white pumice quarried for stonewashing jeans. A short and fairly easy trail leads in from the road. Just beyond the monument's northeast corner, a small outlier known as the Petroglyph Section contains **Petroglyph Point**, a 300-yard-long cliff face made of "tuff", volcanic rock formed when lava flows hit Old Tule Lake. The soft rock offers some fine, but cryptic, examples of ancient art: shields, female figures and a series of small circles thought to represent travel. The crevices are home to various bird species, especially horned owls. Pick up an interpretive leaflet at the visitor centre.

East of the Petroglyph Section, the road continues to Hwy-139 and the town of **Newell**, site of the **Tule Lake Camp**, where 110,000 people of Japanese descent, many of them American citizens, were interned without charge or trial between 1942 and 1946. There were as many as 18,000 inmates at any given time. Many of the camp buildings have been sold off to local farmers but the wood-sided police and military barracks remain and a simple plaque commemorates the disgraceful chapter and prays it will never be repeated. Nearby there was also a less well known camp for internees of German and Italian origin.

The most rewarding excursion from the monument, though, is to the **Klamath Basin National Wildlife Refuge** (open daylight hours), just to the north along Hill Road (Hwy-161), leading to US-97 and spreading into Oregon. One of the last **wetlands** in California, with swathes of open water and emerging vegetation on the shoreline, it attracts an estimated eighty percent of birds following the Pacific Flyway, the major migration routes from Alaska and northern Canada to Baja California in Mexico. In spring and autumn, almost a hundred species are present and the population tops a million. Bald eagles appear from December to January, bringing out hundreds of photographers trying to navigate the snowy road. Spring is the best time for migratory birds and autumn for waterfowl. The most accessible reaches of the reserve are the **Lower Klamath Refuge** and **Tule Lake**, an open body of water surrounded by reeds (*tule* in Modoc). At the northwestern corner of the latter on Hill Road, the **visitor centre** (Mon–Fri 8am–4.30pm, Sat & Sun 10am–4pm; ℡530/667-2231) contains some informative displays. Surprisingly, the best way of spotting the wildlife is by driving along designated routes: getting out of the car and walking scares the birds off.

Heading south back towards Mount Shasta on US-97, your car will be stopped in otherwise droll **Dorris** by agriculture agents checking to see if you're transporting fruit or vegetables from out of state. Say "No" nicely and they might give you a colour map to welcome you to California.

Modoc County

Occupying the far northeastern corner of California, wild and rugged **MODOC COUNTY** is bordered by equally thinly populated areas of Oregon and Nevada and is about as remote as it gets. Despite covering an immense area, the total population is only ten thousand, the majority of whom reside in the county seat of **Alturas**. Outside of that modest settlement, the mostly high-desert region is home to a lot more wildlife – bobcats, mule deer, antelope, elk, mountain lions, wolves and birds such as sandhill cranes and bald eagles – than people, many of whom rely on cattle ranging and alfalfa cultivation for their livelihood. On the eastern side, the imposing **Warner Mountains** divide the rest of the county from **Surprise Valley**, home to several small communities within spitting distance of the Nevada state line.

Historically the area belonged to three native tribes – the Modoc, the Paiute and the Pit River Indians. The creation of the Emigrant Trail in the late 1840s, the main east–west route into Northern California, brought white settlers to the region in increasing numbers and into all-too-common confrontation with indigenous people. For the next six decades, a series of violent conflicts earned the region the title of **Bloody Ground of the Pacific**. The settlers gradually took over, though the area's control was successively bounced around between Utah Territory, Nevada Territory and California's Shasta and Siskiyou counties before Modoc County was created in 1874. It retains a frontier feel to this day and has the highest per-capita gun ownership in the state, so it's no surprise that most locals and many of those who find their way here tend to occupy themselves with outdoor pursuits like hunting.

Alturas and around

Out-of-the-way **ALTURAS** is about sixty miles southeast of Tulelake via Hwy-137 and then Hwy-299, which you can also take all the way up from the Burney Falls area. Coming from Lava Beds, the black craggy rocks gradually give way to the increasingly pine-forested hills of the **Modoc National Forest**, which surround the town on three sides. The Modoc National Forest Service headquarters at 800 W 12th St (Mon–Fri 7.30am–4.30pm; ℡530/233-5811, ⓦwww.fs.fed.us/r5/modoc) provides a wealth of information on all the hiking, hunting, fishing and camping possibilities in the region, as well as some useful maps. For more info on the town itself, visit the **Chamber of Commerce**, 522 S Main St (Mon–Fri 9am–12.30pm & 1.30–4pm; ℡530/233-4434, ⓦwww.alturaschamber.org), though it's not always staffed. A glimpse into the region's turbulent past can be gained at the modest **Modoc County Historical Museum** (May–Oct

Mon–Sat 10am–4pm; $2), which occupies a modern building by the park at 600 S Main St; the displays concentrate on settler and Indian artefacts, as well as some of the county's natural history.

Though much of its dozen blocks are modern, Alturas, with its position by the mountains and the clear relation of the people to the land, manages to exude a Wild West atmosphere. The most obvious **places to stay** are the basic central motels such as the *Frontier Motel* at 1033 N Main St (T530/233-3383; ●), although the *Rim Rock Motel*, out of town at 22760 Hwy-395 N (T530/233-5455, Wwww.rimrockmotelalturas.com; ●) exudes a more fitting rustic air. Among the **eating** options, *Nipa's*, 1001 N Main St, dishes up a delightful combination of Thai and California cuisines in a laid-back setting; *Antonio's*, 220 S Main Street, is a slightly smarter Italian restaurant serving filling pasta, pizza and sandwiches; and *Norma's Taqueria*, 204 W 12th St, is the place for inexpensive and tasty Mexican grub.

Spreading out over thousands of acres south of Alturas, the **Modoc National Wildlife Refuge** (7am–sunset; free) is composed largely of unspoilt grasslands, incorporating some wetlands, and is home to many avian species, among them sandhill cranes, tundra swans, teal, pintail ducks and warblers, as well as migratory visitors such as white-fronted geese, pelicans, cormorants and egrets. The refuge starts only a couple of miles southeast of town – take the road between the Chamber of Commerce and the museum and turn right at the first main junction, after about half a mile, which takes you right there. Around twenty miles north of town, the **Devil's Garden** is a very different type of terrain, a densely forested plateau with more wetlands and a community of some four hundred wild horses – there are trails through the excellent hiking country but you should take a good map and be careful not to stray from the paths. A little further northeast, reachable by US-395, lies **Goose Lake**, which straddles the Oregon state line. Good for fishing and other recreational activities, its largest settlement, on the east shore, is **New Pine Creek**, nearly all of whose facilities lie on the Oregon side – making it a good place to head to for cheaper gas. Finally, nearby **Davis Creek**, just off US-395 towards the lake, is the site of numerous obsidian mines, and bucketfuls of the jagged black rocks can be carried away if you obtain a free permit from the Forest Service headquarters in Alturas.

The Warner Mountains and Surprise Valley

Providing a dramatic backdrop to Alturas, the proud ridges of the **Warner Mountains**, snowcapped for two thirds of the year and prone to snowfall in any month, exert a magnetic pull on the few outsiders who venture this far. The range is divided into north and south by the valley that carries Hwy-299 east through the mountains. This road passes by the **Cedar Pass Snowpark** (T530/233-3323), where you can ski during winter weekends – all-day rope tow and T-bar tickets range from $5 to $15, and ski and snowboard rental is very cheap at $10–15 per day. It is, however, nearby **South Warner Wilderness**, part of the extensive Modoc National Forest, which presents the most fruitful territory for exploration. Here seventy-seven miles of trails spread over more than seventy thousand acres of slopes, steeper on the east side than the west, offer excellent hiking opportunities. Get maps and details from the Forest Service headquarters in Alturas but make sure to carry provisions and all-weather gear. In the north, unpaved Route 9 ascends over the North Warners from US-395 near Goose Lake and climbs up over **Fandango Pass**, where the old Applegate Trail and Lassen forty-niner route converge. It's passable with care in a regular car and makes for a scenic alternative route east, with arresting views of Surprise Valley along the way.

On the sunrise side of the mountains, secretive **Surprise Valley** marks the border with Nevada and is hemmed in by more barren ridges to the east. Indeed, the fiercely independent types who live over here are said to feel more allegiance to the Silver State than the Golden State. Hwy-299 from Alturas ends in the pleasant small town of **Cedarville**, the largest in the valley, a modest claim though that may be. The only noteworthy sight is the re-created **pioneer village** of Louieville (unrestricted access; free) in the county fairgrounds, a couple of blocks east of Main Street. Among the venerable timber buildings are a church, a slaughterhouse and – here's the Wild West for you – two jails.

The **Chamber of Commerce** is in Warner Realty at 517 Main St (Tues & Thurs 9–11am; ☎530/279-2101), and a few brochures are available in the entrance to no. 519. Reasonable **accommodation** choices include the cutesy *J H Metzker House B&B*, 520 Main St (☎530/279-2650; ❸), and rustic *JnR Hotel*, opposite at 581 Main St (☎530/279-2423, ⓦwww.jnrhotel.com; ❶). The finest place to stay, however, is a real hidden gem, five miles due east: *Surprise Valley Hot Springs* (☎1-877/927-6426, ⓦwww.surprisevalleyhotsprings.com; ❹), whose splendid themed suites each have a naturally heated outdoor tub and would cost double if the location was not so remote. If you're hungry, the *Surprise Café*, 540 Main St, serves up classic home-style breakfasts and lunches, while *Country Hearth*, opposite at no. 551, also serves dinners.

From Cedarville you can branch south to even quieter Eagleville or, better yet, head north past a couple of white alkali lakes to pay a brief visit to **Fort Bidwell**, home to a thriving community of 150 Paiute Indians. Here you can pop into their modern community centre (flexible hours) to see a collection of rocks, trophies and an original peace-pipe.

Travel details

Trains

Oakland to: Chico (1 daily; 4hr 10min); Dunsmuir (1 daily; 7hr 20min); Redding (1 daily; 5hr 30min).
Redding to: Chico (1 daily; 1hr 30min); Dunsmuir (1 daily; 1hr 50min); Oakland (1 daily; 6hr 15min).

Buses

Schedules listed below are mostly Greyhound, with some county services where applicable. Some routes require a transfer. See individual town accounts for additional connecting local services.
Arcata to: Crescent City (2 daily; 2hr); Eureka (10–16 Mon–Sat, 1 Sun; 10–15min); San Francisco (1 daily; 7hr 30min); Santa Rosa (1 daily; 5hr 15min).
Chico to: Red Bluff (2 daily; 50min); Redding (2 daily; 1hr 30min); Sacramento (2 daily; 2hr 15min); San Francisco (2 daily; 6hr 30min–7hr 15min); Weed (1 daily; 3hr 20min).
Eureka to: Arcata (10–16 Mon–Sat, 1 Sun; 10–15min); San Francisco (1 daily; 7hr 20min); Santa Rosa (1 daily; 5hr 5min).
Redding to: Chico (2 daily; 1hr 30min); Red Bluff (2 daily; 40min); Sacramento (4 daily; 2hr 40min–3hr 50min); San Francisco (4 daily; 8hr 5min–9hr 55min).
San Francisco to: Arcata (1 daily; 7hr 5min); Chico (2 daily; 5hr–8hr 15min); Eureka (1 daily; 6hr 45min); Redding (4 daily; 6hr 30min–9hr 50min); Santa Rosa (hourly; 1hr 45min–2hr 25min); Weed (2 daily; 8hr 50min–11hr 40min).
Santa Rosa to: Arcata (1 daily; 5hr 10min); Eureka (1 daily; 5hr 10min); San Francisco (hourly; 2hr–2hr 15min).

Contexts

Contexts

History

T
o many people, California seems one of the least historic places on the planet. Unburdened by the past, it's a land where anything is possible, whose inhabitants live carefree lives, wholly in and for the present moment. Its very name, appropriately for all its idealized images, is a work of fiction, free of any historical significance. The word first appeared in a popular Spanish picaresque novel of the early 1500s, *Las Sergas de Esplandián* by García de Montalvo, as the name of an island, located "very near to the terrestrial paradise" and inhabited entirely by Amazons "without any men among them".

Native peoples

For thousands of years before the arrival of Europeans, the **aboriginal peoples** of California flourished in the naturally abundant land, living fairly peacefully in tribes along the coast and in the deserts and the forested mountains. Anthropologists estimate that nearly half the native population then living within the boundaries of the present-day US were spread throughout what's now California, in small, tribal villages of a few hundred people, each with a clearly defined territory and often its own distinct language. Since there was no political or social organization beyond the tribe, it was not difficult for the colonizing Spaniards to divide and conquer, effectively wiping the natives out – though admittedly more died of epidemics than outright genocide.

Very little remains to mark the existence of California's Native Americans: they had no form of written language, relatively undeveloped craft skills and built next to nothing that would last beyond the change of seasons. About the only signs of the coastal tribes are the piles of seashells and discarded arrowheads that have been found, from which anthropologists have deduced a bit about their cultures. Also, a few examples of **rock art** survive, as at the Chumash Painted Cave, near Santa Barbara on the Central Coast (see p.372). Similar sorts of petroglyph figures were drawn by the Paiute Native Americans, who lived in the deserts near Death Valley, and by the Miwok of the Sierra Nevada foothills.

Discovery and early exploration

The first Europeans to set foot in California were Spanish explorers, intent on extending their colony of New Spain, which, under the 1494 Treaty of Tordesillas, included all the New World lands west of Brazil and all of North America west of the Rocky Mountains. In 1535, **Hernán Cortés**, fresh from decimating the Aztecs, headed westward in search of a shortcut to Asia, which he believed to be adjacent to Mexico. Though he never reached what's now California, he set up a small colony at the southern tip of the Baja (or lower) California peninsula. Thinking it was an island, he named it Santa Cruz, writing in his journals that he soon expected to find the imagined island of the Amazons.

The first explorer to use the name California, and to reach what's now the US state, was **Juan Cabrillo**, who sighted San Diego harbour in 1542, and continued north along the coast to the Channel Islands off Santa Barbara. He died there six months later, persistent headwinds having made it impossible to sail any further north. His crew later made it as far as what is now the state of Oregon but were unable to find any safe anchorage and returned home starving and half-dead from scurvy. It was fifty years before another Spaniard braved the difficult journey: **Juan de Fuca**'s 1592 voyage caused great excitement when he claimed to have discovered the Northwest Passage, a potentially lucrative trade route across North America. It has long since turned out that there is really no such thing (de Fuca may have discovered the Puget Sound, outside Seattle), but Europeans continued to search for it for the next two hundred years.

The English explorer **Sir Francis Drake** arrived in the *Golden Hind* in 1579, taking a break from his piracy of Spanish vessels in order to make repairs. His landing spot, now called Drake's Bay, near Point Reyes north of San Francisco, had "white bancks and cliffes" that reminded him of Dover. Upon landing, he was met by a band of native Miwoks, who feted him with food and drink, and placed a feathered crown upon his head; in return, he claimed all of their lands – which he called Nova Albion (New England) – for Queen Elizabeth, supposedly leaving behind a brass plaque now on display in the Bancroft Library at the University of California.

Setting sail from Acapulco in 1602, **Sebastian Vizcaíno**, a Portuguese explorer under contract to Spain, made a more lasting impact than his predecessors, undertaking the most extensive exploration of the coast and bestowing most of the place names that survive. In order to impress his superiors he exaggerated the value of his discoveries, describing a perfect, sheltered harbour, which he named **Monterey** in honour of his patron in Mexico. Subsequent colonizers based their efforts on these fraudulent claims and the headquarters of the missions and military and administrative centre of the Spanish government remained at Monterey, one hundred miles south of San Francisco, for the next 75 years.

Colonization: the Spanish and the Russians

The Spanish occupation of California began in earnest in 1769, with a combination of military expediency (to prevent other powers from gaining a foothold) and Catholic missionary zeal (to convert the Native Americans). Father **Junípero Serra** and a company of three hundred soldiers and clergy set off from Mexico for Monterey, half of them by ship, the other half overland. In June 1770, after establishing a small mission and presidio (fort) at San Diego, the expedition arrived at Monterey, where another mission and small presidio were constructed; see the box on opposite for more. During this time the first towns, called **pueblos**, were established in order to attract settlers to what was still a distant and undesirable territory. The first was laid out in 1777 at San Jose, south of the new mission at San Francisco. Los Angeles, the second pueblo, was established in 1781, though neither had more than a hundred inhabitants until well into the nineteenth century.

One reason for Spain's military presence in California – which consisted of four presidios all told, with twelve cannon and only two hundred soldiers – was to prevent the expansion of the small **Russian** colony based in Alaska, mostly trappers collecting beaver and otter pelts in the northwestern states of Washington and Oregon. The two countries were at peace and relations friendly and in any case the Spanish presidios were in no position to enforce their territorial claims. In fact, they were so short of supplies and ammunition that they had to borrow the

California missions

Among the oldest European settlements in California, the state's 21 **missions**, established by the Spanish in the late eighteenth century, were built all along the coast, ostensibly to Catholicize the Native Americans, which they did with inquisitional fervour. In truth, each mission was accompanied by a pueblo, or secular settlement, and, most importantly, a presidio, or military fortress. Though masterminded by Franciscan Father **Junípero Serra**, most of the mission structures that survive today were built to the designs of Serra's successor, Father **Férmin de Lasuén**, who was in charge of the missions during the period of their greatest growth. By the time of his death in 1804, a chain of 21 missions, each a long day's walk from its neighbours and linked by the dirt path of **El Camino Real** ("The Royal Road"), ran from San Diego to Solano, north of San Francisco, ensuring that every mission was one day's ride or hard walk from the next. This proximity enabled easy commerce and communication along the chain. The missions flourished for more than a hundred years, converting and killing thousands of locals through a combination of forced evangelism and smallpox.

The complexes were broadly similar, with a church and cloistered residential structure surrounded by irrigated fields, vineyards and more extensive ranchlands. The labour of the Native American converts was co-opted: they were put to work making soap and candles, were often beaten and never educated. Objective accounts of the missionaries' treatment of the indigenous peoples are rare, though mission registries record twice as many deaths as they do births and their cemeteries are packed with Native American dead. Not all of the Native Americans gave up without a fight: many missions suffered from raid, and the now-ubiquitous red-tiled roofs were originally a replacement for the earlier thatch to better resist arson attacks.

Eventually, when the missions were secularized under Mexican rule in 1834, much of the land was given not to the indigenous peoples, but to the Spanish-speaking *Californio* ranchers. The missions' chequered reputation lasted at least until the later Victorian era, when sentimentalist writer **Helen Hunt Jackson** gave them an idyllic gloss in her bestselling potboiler *Ramona* – a hugely influential book responsible for the current image of missions as charming outposts of quiet spirituality and quaintly austere architecture.

The largest and most populous settlement was San Luis Rey de Francia (p.206) – its huge lavandería, or washing area, is now an impressive sunken garden – while arguably the most famous is San Juan Capistrano (p.113), which welcomes migrating swallows every March. Visitors will find the most evocative, if not necessarily authentic, sense of early settler life at the restorations at San Antonio de Padua (p.396) and La Purísima (p.382).

gunpowder to fire welcoming salutes whenever the two forces came into contact. Well aware of the Spanish weakness, the Russians established the outpost of **Fort Ross** in 1812, sixty miles north of San Francisco. This further undermined Spanish sovereignty over the region, though the Russians abandoned the fort in 1841, selling it to John Sutter (who features prominently in later California history; see p.689).

The Mexican era

While Spain, France and England were engaged in the bitter struggles of the Napoleonic Wars, the colonies of New Spain rebelled against imperial neglect, with Mexico finally gaining independence in 1821. The Mexican Republic, or the

United States of Mexico as the new country called itself, governed California as a territory. However, the fifteen distinct administrations it set up lacked the money to pay for improvements and the soldiers needed to enforce the laws, so they were unable to exercise any degree of authority.

The most important effect of the Mexican era was the final **secularization** in 1834, after years of gradual diminution, of the Franciscan missions. As most of the missionaries were Spanish, under Mexican rule they had seen their position steadily eroded by the increasingly wealthy, close-knit families of the Californios – Mexican immigrants who'd been granted vast tracts of ranchland. The government's intention was that half of the missions' extensive lands should go to the Indian converts but this was never carried out and the few powerful families divided most of it up among themselves.

In many ways this was the most lawless and wantonly wasteful period of California's history, an era described by **Richard Henry Dana** – scion of a distinguished Boston family, who dropped out of Harvard to sail to California – in his 1840 book *Two Years Before the Mast*. Most of the agriculture and cottage industries that had developed under the missionaries disappeared, and it was a point of pride among the Californios not to do any work that couldn't be done from horseback. Dana's Puritan values led him to heap scorn upon the "idle and thriftless people" who made nothing for themselves. For example, the large herds of cattle that lived on the mission lands were slaughtered for their hides and sold to Yankee traders, who turned the hides into leather which they sold back to the Californios at a tidy profit. "In the hands of an enterprising people", he wrote, "what a country this might be."

The first Americans

Throughout the Mexican and Spanish eras, foreigners were legally banned from settling, and the few who showed up, mostly sick or injured sailors dropped off to regain their health, were often jailed until they proved themselves useful, either as craftsmen or as traders able to supply needed goods. In the late 1820s, the first **Americans**, without exception males, began to make their way to California, tending to fit in with the existing Mexican culture, often marrying into established families, and converting to the Catholic faith. The American presence grew slowly but surely as more and more people emigrated, still mostly by way of a three-month sea voyage around Cape Horn. Among these was **Thomas Larkin**, a New England merchant who, in 1832, set up shop in Monterey, and later was instrumental in pointing the disgruntled Californios towards the more accommodating US; Larkin's wife Rachel was the first American woman on the West Coast.

The first people to make the four-month journey to California overland – in a covered wagon, just as in so many Hollywood Westerns – arrived in 1841, having forged a trail over the Sierra Nevada mountains via Truckee Pass, just north of Lake Tahoe. Soon after, hundreds of people each year were following in their tracks. In 1846, however, forty migrants, collectively known as the **Donner party**, died when they were trapped in the mountains by early winter snowfall (see box, p.593). The immense difficulties involved in reaching California, over land and by sea, kept population levels at a minimum, and by 1846 just seven thousand people, not counting Native Americans but including all the Spanish and Mexicans, lived in the entire region.

The Mexican–American War

From the 1830s onwards – inspired by **Manifest Destiny**, the popular, almost religious, belief that the United States was meant to cover the continent from coast to coast – US government policy regarding California was to buy all of Mexico's land north of the Rio Grande, the river that now divides the US and Mexico. President Andrew Jackson was highly suspicious of British designs on the West Coast – he himself had been held as a (14-year-old) prisoner of war during the Revolutionary War of 1776 – and various diplomatic overtures were made to the Mexican Republic, all of which backfired. In April 1846, Jackson's protégé, President James Polk, offered forty million dollars for all of New Mexico and the California territory but his simultaneous annexation of the newly independent Republic of Texas – which Mexico still claimed – resulted in the outbreak of war.

Almost all the fighting of the **Mexican–American War** took place in Texas; only one real battle was ever fought on California soil, at San Pasqual, northeast of San Diego, where a roving US battalion was surprised by a band of pro-Mexican Californios, who killed 22 soldiers and wounded another 15 before withdrawing south into Mexico. Monterey, still the territorial capital, was captured by the US Navy without a shot being fired and in January 1847, when the rebel Californios surrendered to the US forces at Cahuenga, near Los Angeles, the Americans controlled the entire West Coast.

Just before the war began, California had made a brief foray into the field of self-government: the short-lived **Bear Flag Republic**, whose only lasting effect was to create what's still the state flag, a prowling grizzly bear with the words "California Republic" written below. In June 1846, American settlers in the Sonoma Valley took over the local presidio – long abandoned by the Mexicans – and declared California independent, which lasted for all of three weeks until the US forces took command.

The Gold Rush

As part of the Treaty of Guadalupe Hidalgo, which formally ended the war in 1848, Mexico ceded all of the Alta California territory to the US. Nine days before the signing of the accord, in the distant foothills of the Sierra Nevada mountains, flakes of **gold** were discovered by workmen building a sawmill along the American River at Coloma, though it was months before this momentous conjunction of events became known.

At the time, California's non-Native American population was mostly concentrated in the few small towns along the coastal strip. Early rumours of gold attracted a trickle of prospectors, and, following news of their subsequent success, by the middle of 1849 – eighteen months after the initial find – men were flooding into California from all over, in the most madcap migration in world history. **Sutter's Fort**, a small agricultural community, trading post and stage stop which had been established six years earlier by **John Sutter** on the banks of the American River, was overrun by miners, who headed up into the nearby foothills to make their fortune. Some did, most didn't, but in any case, within fifteen years most of the gold had been picked clean. The miners moved on or went home and their camps vanished, prompting Mark Twain to write that "in no other land, in modern times, have towns so absolutely died and disappeared as in the old mining regions of California".

Statehood

C

CONTEXTS | History

Following the US takeover after the defeat of Mexico, a **Constitutional Convention** was held at Monterey in the autumn of 1849. The men who attended were not the miners – most of whom were more interested in searching for gold – but those who had been in California for some time (about three years on average). At the time, the Territory of California extended all the way east to Utah, so the main topic of discussion was where to place the eastern boundary of the intended state. The drawing up of a state constitution was also important, since it was the basis on which California applied for admission to the US. This constitution contained a couple of noteworthy inclusions – to protect the dignity of the manually labouring miners, **slavery** was prohibited; and to attract well-heeled **women** from the East Coast, California was the first state to recognize in legal terms the separate property of a married woman. In 1850, California was admitted to the US as the 31st state.

The Indian Wars

Though the US Civil War had little effect on California, throughout the 1850s and 1860s white settlers and US troops fought many bloody battles against the various Native American tribes whose lands the immigrants wanted. At first the government tried to move willing tribes to fairly large reservations but, as more settlers moved in, the tribes were pushed onto smaller and smaller tracts. The most powerful resistance to the well-armed invaders came in the mountainous northeast of California, where a band of **Modoc** fought a long-running guerrilla war, using their superior knowledge of the terrain to evade the US troops (see box, p.675).

Owing to a combination of disease and lack of food, as well as deliberate acts of violence, the Native American population was drastically reduced, and by 1870 almost ninety percent had been wiped out. The survivors were concentrated in small, relatively valueless reservations, where their descendants still live: the Cahuila near Palm Springs, the Paiute/Shoshone in the Owens Valley, and the Hupa on the northwest coast. All are naturally quite protective of their privacy.

The boom years: 1870–1900

After the Gold Rush, **San Francisco** boomed into a boisterous frontier town, exploding in population from five hundred to fifty thousand within five years. Though far removed from the mines themselves, the city was the main landing spot for ship-borne argonauts (as the prospectors were called), and the main supply town. Moreover, it was the place where successful miners went to blow their hard-earned cash on the whisky and women of the **Barbary Coast**, then the raunchiest waterfront in the world, full of brothels, saloons and opium dens. Ten years later, San Francisco enjoyed an even bigger boom as a result of the silver mines of the Comstock Lode in Nevada, owned mainly by San Franciscans, who displayed their wealth by building grand palaces and mansions on Nob Hill – still the city's most exclusive address (see p.451).

The completion in 1869 of the **transcontinental railroad**, built using imported Chinese labourers, was a major turning point in the settlement of California.

Whereas the trip across the country by stagecoach took at least a month and was subject to scorching hot weather and attacks by hostile natives, the crossing could now be completed in just five days.

In 1875, when the Santa Fe Railroad reached Los Angeles (the railroad company having extracted huge bribes from local officials to ensure the budding city wasn't bypassed), there were just ten thousand people living in the whole of **Southern California**, divided equally between San Diego and Los Angeles. A fare war developed between the two rival railroads, and ticket costs dropped to as little as $1 for a one-way ticket from New York. Land speculators placed advertisements in East Coast and European papers, offering cheap land for homesteaders in towns and suburbs all over the West Coast that, as often as not, existed only on paper. By the end of the nineteenth century, thousands of people, ranging from Midwestern farmers to the East Coast elite, had moved to California to take advantage of the fertile land and mild climate.

Hollywood, the war and after

The greatest boost to California's fortunes was, of course, the infant **film industry**, which moved here from the East Coast in 1911, attracted by the temperate climate, in which directors could shoot outdoors year-round, and by the incredibly cheap land, on which large indoor studios could be built at comparatively little cost. Within three years, movies like D.W. Griffith's *Birth of a Nation* – most of which was filmed along the dry banks of the Los Angeles River – were being cranked out by the hundreds.

Hollywood, a suburb of Los Angeles that was the site of many of the early studios, and which has ever since been the buzzword for the entire entertainment industry, has done more to promote the mystique of California as a pleasure garden than any other medium, disseminating images of its glamorous lifestyles around the globe. Los Angeles has since become established as an international centre for the music business as well.

This widespread, idealized image had a magnetic effect during the **Great Depression** of the 1930s, when thousands of people from all over the country descended upon California, which was perceived to be – and for the most part was – immune to the economic downturn that crippled the rest of the US. From the Dust Bowl Midwest, entire families, who came to be known as **Okies**, packed up everything they owned and set off for the farms of the Central Valley, an epic journey captured by John Steinbeck's bestselling novel *The Grapes of Wrath*, in the photographs of Dorothea Lange, and in the baleful tunes of folksinger Woody Guthrie. Some Californians who feared losing their jobs to the incoming Okies formed vigilante groups and, with the complicity of local and state police, set up roadblocks along the main highways to prevent unemployed outsiders from entering the state.

One Depression-era initiative to alleviate the poverty, and to get the economy moving again, were the government-sponsored **Works Progress Administration (WPA)** construction projects, ranging from restoring the California missions to building trails and park facilities, and commissioning artworks like the marvellous Social Realist murals in San Francisco's Coit Tower.

Things turned around when **World War II** brought heavy industry to California, as shipyards and aeroplane factories sprang up, providing well-paid employment in wartime factories. After the war, most stayed on, and today California companies – McDonnell Douglas, Lockheed, Rockwell and General

Dynamics, for example – still make up the roll call of suppliers to the US military and space programmes.

After the war, many of the soldiers who'd passed through on their way to the battlegrounds of the South Pacific came back to California and decided to stay on. There was plenty of well-paid work, and the US government subsidized house purchases for war veterans and, most importantly, constructed the **freeways** and interstate highways that enabled land speculators to build new commuter suburbs on land that had been used for farms and citrus orchards.

The **1950s** brought prosperity to the bulk of middle-class America (typified by President Dwight Eisenhower's goal of "two cars in every garage and a chicken in every pot"), and California, particularly San Francisco, became a nexus for alternative artists and writers, spurring an immigration of intellectuals that by the end of the decade had become manifest as the **Beat generation** – pegged "Beatniks" by San Francisco columnist Herb Caen, in honour of Sputnik, the Soviet space satellite.

The 1960s and 1970s

California remained at the forefront of youth and **social upheavals** into and throughout the **1960s**. In a series of drug tests carried out at Stanford University – paid for by the CIA, which was interested in developing a "truth drug" for interrogation purposes – unwitting students were dosed with **LSD**. One of the guinea pigs was the writer Ken Kesey, author of the highly acclaimed novel *One Flew Over the Cuckoo's Nest*. Kesey quite liked the experience and soon secured a personal supply of the drug (which was still legal) and toured the West Coast to spread the word of "acid". In and around San Francisco, Kesey and his crew, the Merry Pranksters, turned on huge crowds at **Electric Kool-Aid Acid Tests** – in which LSD was diluted into bowls of the soft drink Kool-Aid – complete with psychedelic light shows and music by the Grateful Dead. The acid craze reached its height during the **Summer of Love** in 1967, when the entire Haight-Ashbury district of San Francisco seemed populated by barefoot and drugged flower children.

Within a year the superficial peace of Flower Power was shattered, as protests mounted against US involvement in the **Vietnam War**; Martin Luther King Jr and Bobby Kennedy, heroes of left-leaning youth, were both gunned down – Kennedy in Los Angeles after winning the California primary of the 1968 presidential election. The militant **Black Panthers**, a group of black radical activists based in Oakland, terrorized a white population that had earlier been supporters of the civil rights movement. By the end of the 60s the "system", in California especially, seemed to be at breaking point, and the atrocities committed by **Charles Manson** and his "Family" seemed to signify a general collapse.

The antiwar protests, concentrated at the University of California campus in Berkeley, continued through the early **1970s**. Emerging from the milieu of revolutionary and radical groups, the Symbionese Liberation Army (SLA), a small, well-armed and stridently revolutionary group, set about the overthrow of the US, attracting media (and FBI) attention by murdering civil servants, robbing banks and, most famously, kidnapping 19-year-old heiress **Patty Hearst**. Amid much media attention, Hearst converted to the SLA's cause, changing her name to Tanya and, for the next two years – until her capture in 1977 – she went underground and participated in the group's activities, provoking national debate about her motives and beliefs.

California **politics**, after Watergate and the end of American involvement in Vietnam, seemed to lose whatever idealistic fervour it might once have had, and popular culture withdrew into self-satisfaction, typified by the smug harmonies of musicians like the Eagles and Jackson Browne. While the 60s upheavals were overseen by California Governor Ronald Reagan, who was ready and willing to fight the long-haired hippies, the 70s saw the reign of "Governor Moonbeam" **Jerry Brown**, under whose leadership California enacted some of the most stringent **antipollution** measures in the world. The state also actively encouraged the development of renewable forms of energy, such as solar and wind power, and protected the entire coastline from despoliation and development. The possession of under an ounce of **marijuana** was decriminalized (though it remains an offence to sell it), and the harvesting of marijuana continues to account for over $1 billion each year, making it the number-one cash crop in the number-one agricultural region in the US.

The 1980s and 1990s

The easy money of **1980s** Reaganomics and the trickle-down economy, which unsurprisingly never quite trickled down to the state's poorest, ended in a messy downturn. Many saw this as a disgraceful but fitting finale to a decade when greed was elevated to a virtue. LA junk-bond king Michael Milkin was convicted of multibillion-dollar fraud, and the Savings and Loan banking scandals enmeshed such high-ranking politicos as California Senator Alan Cranston. Consequently, the **1990s** kicked off with a stagnant property market and rising unemployment.

In **Los Angeles**, the videotaped beating of black motorist Rodney King by officers of the LA Police Department, and the subsequent acquittal of those officers, sparked off **rioting** in April 1992. State and federal authorities, forced into taking notice of LA's endemic poverty and violence, promised all sorts of new initiatives but achieved few concrete results. Race also dominated the year-long trial of black former football star **O.J. Simpson** – accused and finally acquitted of murdering his white ex-wife and her male friend – splitting public opinion into directly opposed camps of black and white.

All these factors combined to make the first five years of the 1990s perhaps the bleakest since the Great Depression, and **natural calamities** – regional flooding, Malibu fires and mudslides and two dramatic earthquakes – only added to the general malaise. Mike Davis's *City of Quartz*, despite flaws and inaccuracies, served as a secular bible for the time, an artfully written work based on the inevitable doom LA was facing. And with LA's chronic interethnic hatred, natural disasters, bureaucratic inaction and general public pessimism, it seemed that Davis was probably right.

The latter half of the decade saw **Richard Riordan**, a multimillionaire technocrat who served as LA mayor from 1992 to 2000, preside over a major **revival** in the city's fortunes and a restructuring of its economic base – aerospace and automotive giving way to tourism, real estate and, as always, Hollywood. New property developments attempted to revitalize deprived areas and even crime and violence tailed off marginally. However, these improvements probably owed more to the national economic upswing during the Clinton years than to purely local initiatives.

San Francisco also suffered in the early 90s; on top of AIDS-related illnesses stretching health services, the area was hit by a series of natural disasters. An **earthquake** in October 1989 devastated much of the San Francisco Bay Area, followed two years later by a massive **fire** in the Oakland Hills, which burned over two thousand homes and killed two dozen people – the third worst fire in US history.

But even more so than LA, San Francisco's economic upswing turned the city around, replacing pre-millennium jitters with Information Age optimism. The **Silicon Valley** industries boomed, with companies scrambling to find high-paid workers to fill their constantly growing rosters. San Jose, San Francisco's southern neighbour, surpassed the Golden Gate city in population, and even Oakland, the gritty East Bay port-town, started to receive a much-needed facelift. Still, not everyone in the Bay Area was happy with the apparent prosperity. **Gentrification** threatened to turn San Francisco from a province of activism into a playground for Silicon Valley's rich young things. Housing prices rocketed and with tenancy at 99 percent, forced out not only the city's poor but the lower middle class as well.

Contemporary California

The optimism that had overridden many concerns at the tail end of the old millennium soon took a pummelling once the new one started. The world's computers may not have gone belly-up at zero hour on Y2K but the high-tech industry became the biggest victim of a nationwide economic **recession** – the cause of it, in fact, according to many analysts. This immediately affected the Silicon Valley companies, which saw billions wiped off their stock values and had to offload employees faster than they had hired them, though there was some recovery in the middle of the decade. On the other hand, the Bay Area's notoriously inflated **property prices**, which originally slowed for the first time in a decade with the high-tech bust, have continued to cool off, though still not as badly as elsewhere in the nation, where the market is in severe crisis.

After a series of embarrassing Third World-type **power cuts** in 2001, the state was forced to fork out vast sums to import some of its shortfall in energy from other states. This and other areas of gross mismanagement led to widespread disaffection and a rare **recall** election (a vote of confidence, in effect) in October 2003, when Democrat Governer Gray Davis was replaced by Republican **Arnold Schwarzenegger**, the Hollywood actor. His main remit was to balance the ailing **state budget** and he set about it with a series of conservative measures to raise revenue, including hikes of day-use and camping fees in state parks, as well as cuts in welfare programmes and even the funding of tourism.

With the power crisis in mind, however, and environmentalists maintaining that there will not be a proper solution until serious money is invested in **renewable energy** sources, the "Governator" (as he became known thanks to one of his high-profile film roles) broke with broader Republican policy and passed a series of green measures towards this end, making protection of the environment another centrepiece of his administration. Such measures, combined with the advantage of being married to a member of the Kennedy clan and a relatively liberal social platform, although he stopped short of supporting gay marriage, resulted in him being re-elected in 2006. His second term, however, was beset by continuing difficulties in controlling the state budget, which, compounded by the **recession** that started in 2008, has reached a staggering projected deficit of almost $20 billion in the fiscal year 2010–11. As a result, and against the national trend towards the Republicans, **Jerry Brown** won a fiercely contested race against Meg Whitman to become Governor again in November 2010, almost three decades since his first stint.

California indeed remained a staunch **Democrat stronghold** against the swing back towards the right in the 2010 midterm elections. Having voted overwhelmingly for Barack Obama in the 2008 presidential elections, the state returned Barbara Boxer to the Senate and Nancy Pelosi, despite losing her position as the first female Speaker of the House, was among the Californian representatives who at least held their seats. Meanwhile, back in San Francisco and Berkeley, grassroots political **activism**, which underwent a renaissance in opposing George W. Bush's hardline domestic and international policies, continues to voice the conscience of the nation, as the **Peace Movement** protests against the continuing US mission in Afghanistan.

The other burning issue of recent years has been the ongoing battle over **gay marriage**. In November 2008, fifty-two percent of voters perhaps surprisingly passed **Proposition 8** (the California Marriage Protection Act), which banned same-sex marriage by means of a constitutional amendment. The state's gay population and liberal sympathizers were outraged and campaigned vigorously for the act to be **overturned**, which it eventually was by US district judge Vaughn Walker in August 2010. Christian Conservatives immediately lodged an **appeal**, and it seems likely that the final decision will be taken by the US Supreme Court, probably not before 2012.

In local politics, the most interesting developments have been at the southern end of the state. In 2005, Democrat and former union leader **Antonio Villaraigosa** was elected as LA's first Latino mayor in 133 years and his popularity led to re-election in 2009. Set against a background of rising national concern about illegal immigration, principally from Mexico, his success in two elections has emphasized the changing demographics of America and the power of the legal **Hispanic vote**. In this more conducive climate, the state's growing number of legitimate immigrant workers have also been leading the way in **union organization**, which some believe could energize the national labour movement.

California has also been on the receiving end of extreme weather conditions, most likely attributable to climate change. These have mainly taken the form of **wildfires**, which have ravaged many different parts of the state in recent years, destroying hundreds of thousands of acres of forest and property and even causing considerable numbers of casualties. There have also been disastrous spates of **flooding** in certain areas. Yet, despite all these setbacks, California still manages to cling to its aura as a Promised Land. Barring its complete destruction by the **Big One** (the earthquake that's destined one day to drop half of the state into the Pacific and wipe out the rest under massive tidal waves), California seems set to continue much as it is, acting as the pot of gold at the end of the West's mythical rainbow and as the place where America forever reinvents itself.

Wildlife and the environment

Though popularly imagined as little more than palm trees and golden sand beaches, California is hard to beat for sheer range of landscape. With glaciated alpine peaks and meadows, desolate desert sand dunes, and flat, fertile agricultural plains, it's no wonder that Hollywood filmmakers have so often and successfully used California locations to simulate distant and exotic scenes. These diverse environments also support an immense variety of plant and animal life, much of which – due to the protection offered by the various state and national parks, forests, and wilderness areas – is both easily accessible and unspoiled by encroaching civilization.

Background: geology, earthquakes and ecosystems

California's landscape has been formed over millions of years through the interaction of all the main geological processes: Ice Age glaciation, erosion, earthquakes and volcanic eruptions. The most impressive results can be seen in **Yosemite National Park**, east of San Francisco, where solid walls of granite have been sliced and chiselled into unforgettable cliffs and chasms. In contrast, the sand dunes of **Death Valley** are being constantly shaped and reshaped by the dry desert winds, surrounded by foothills tinted by oxidized mineral deposits into every colour of the spectrum.

Earthquakes – which earned Los Angeles the truck driver's nickname "Shakeytown" – are the most powerful expression of the volatile unrest underlying the placid surface. California sits on the Pacific "Ring of Fire", at the junction of two tectonic plates. Besides the occasional earthquake – like the 1906 one which flattened San Francisco, or the 1994 tremor which collapsed many of LA's freeways – this instability is also the cause of California's many volcanoes. Distinguished by their symmetrical, conical shape, almost all of them are now dormant, though Mount Lassen, in Northern California, did erupt in 1914 and 1915, destroying much of the surrounding forest. Along with the boiling mud pools that accompany even the dormant volcanoes, the most attractive features of volcanic regions are the bubbling **hot springs** – pools of water that flow up from underground, heated to a sybaritically soothing temperature. Hot springs occur naturally all over the state, and though some have now been developed into luxurious health spas, most remain in their natural condition, where you can soak your bones *au naturel* surrounded by mountain meadows or wide-open deserts. The best of these are listed throughout the Guide.

The major **ecosystems** of California are detailed below. The accounts are inevitably brief, as the area encompasses almost 320,000 square miles, ranging from moist coastal forests and the snowcapped Sierra Nevada peaks to Death Valley, 282ft below sea level and with an annual rainfall of two inches. These ecosystems are inhabited by a multitude of species. Native to California are 54 species of cactus, 135 species of amphibian and reptile, over 400 species of bird, and around 28,000 species of insect.

Some of the most fantastic **wildlife** is now extinct in its natural habitat: neither the grizzly bear (which still adorns the California state flag) nor the California condor (one of the world's largest birds, with a wingspan of over eight feet) have been seen in the California wilds for over half a century. But plenty of other creatures are still alive and thriving, like the otters, elephant seals and grey whales seen all along the coast, and the chubby marmots – shy mammals often found sunning themselves on rocks in higher reaches of the mountains. Plant life is equally varied, from the brilliant but short-lived desert wildflowers to the timeless bristlecone pine trees, which live for thousands of years on the arid peaks of the Great Basin desert.

The ocean

The **Pacific Ocean** determines California's climate, keeping the coastal temperatures moderate all year round. During the spring and summer, cold, nutrient-rich waters rise up to produce cooling banks of fog and abundant crops of phytoplankton (microscopic algae). The algae nourishes creatures such as krill (small shrimp), which in their turn provide sustenance for juvenile fish. This food chain offers fodder for millions of nesting **seabirds**, as well as harbour and elephant **seals**, California **sea lions**, and whales. **Grey whales**, the most common whale species spotted from land, were once almost hunted to the point of extinction, but have returned to the coast in large numbers. During their southward migration to their breeding grounds off Mexico, from December to January, it's easy to spy them from prominent headlands all along the coast, and most harbours have charter services offering whale-watching tours. On their way back to the Arctic Ocean, in February and March, the newborn whale pups can sometimes be seen playfully leaping out of the water, or "breaching". Look for the whale's white-plumed spout – once at the surface, it will usually blow several times in succession.

Tide pools

California's shoreline is composed of three primary ecosystems: tide pools, sandy beaches and estuaries. To explore the **tide pools**, first check to see when the low tides (two daily) will occur. Be careful of waves, don't be out too far from the shore when the tide returns, and watch your step – there are many small lives underfoot. Miles of tide pool-strewn beaches line the coast, some of the best at Pacific Grove near Monterey. Here you'll find **sea anemones** (they look like green zinnias), hermit crabs, purple and green shore crabs, red sponges, purple sea urchins, starfish ranging from the size of a dime to the size of a hubcap, mussels, abalone and Chinese-hat limpets – to name a few. You may also see black **oystercatchers**, their squawking easily heard over the surf, foraging for an unwary, lips-agape mussel. Gulls and black turnstones are also common, and during the summer brown pelicans dive for fish just offshore.

The life of the tide-pool party is the **hermit crab**, who protects its soft and vulnerable hindquarters with scavenged shells, usually those of the aptly named black turban snail. Hermit crabs scurry busily around in search of a detritus snack, or scuffle with other hermit crabs over the proprietorship of vacant snail shells.

Pacific Grove is also home to large populations of **sea otters**. Unlike most marine mammals, sea otters keep themselves warm with a thick, soft fur coat rather than blubber. The trade in sea otter pelts brought entrepreneurial Russian and British hunters to the West Coast, and by the mid-nineteenth century the otters were virtually extinct. In 1938, a small population was discovered along the Big Sur coast, and with careful protection otters have re-established themselves in the southern part of their range. They are charming creatures with big rubbery noses and Groucho Marx moustaches. With binoculars, it's easy to spot them among the bobbing kelp, where they lie on their backs opening sea urchins with a rock, or sleep entwined within a seat belt of kelp, which keeps them from floating away. The bulk of the population resides between Monterey Bay and the Channel Islands, but – aside from Pacific Grove – the best places to see them are Point Lobos State Park, Seventeen-Mile Drive and Monterey's Fisherman's Wharf, where, along with sea lions, they often come to beg for fish.

Many of the **seaweeds** you see growing from the rocks are edible. As one would expect from a Pacific beachfront, there are also palms – **sea palms**, with four-inch-long rubbery stems and flagella-like fronds. Their thick, root-like holdfasts provide shelter for small crabs. You'll also find giant **kelp** washed up on shore – harvested commercially for use in thickening ice cream.

Sand beaches

The long, golden **sandy beaches** for which California is so famous may look sterile from a distance. However, observe the margin of sand exposed as a gentle wave recedes, and you will see jet streams of small bubbles emerge from the holes of numerous clams and mole crabs. Small shorebirds called **sanderlings** race among the waves in search of these morsels, and sand dollars are often easy to find along the high-tide line.

The most unusual sandy-shore bathing beauties are the **northern elephant seals**, which will tolerate rocky beaches but favour soft sand mattresses for their rotund torsos. The males, or bulls, can reach lengths of over six metres and weigh upwards of four tonnes; the females, or cows, are petite by comparison – four metres long, and averaging a mere two thousand pounds in weight. They have large eyes, adapted for spotting fish in deep or murky waters; indeed, elephant seals are the deepest diving mammals, capable of staying underwater for twenty minutes at a time, reaching depths of over four thousand feet, where the pressure is over a hundred times that at the surface. They have to dive so deeply in order to avoid the attentions of the great white sharks who lurk offshore, for whom they are a favourite meal.

Elephant seals were decimated by commercial whalers in the mid-nineteenth century for their blubber and hides. By the turn of the twentieth century fewer than a hundred remained, but careful protection has partially restored the California population, which is concentrated on the Channel and Farallon islands, at Piedras Blancas just north of San Simeon, and at Año Nuevo State Park.

Elephant seals only emerge from the ocean to breed or moult; their name comes from the male's long, trunk-like proboscis, through which it produces a resonant pinging sound that biologists call "trumpeting", which is how it attracts a mate. The Año Nuevo beach is the best place to observe this ritual. In December and January, the bulls haul themselves out of the water and battle for dominance. The dominant alpha male will do most of the mating, siring as many as fifty young pups, one per mating, in a season. Other males fight it out at the fringes, each managing one or two couplings with the hapless, defenceless females. During this time, the beach is a seething mass of tonne upon tonne of blubbery seals – flopping sand over their backs to keep cool, and squabbling with their neighbours while making rude snoring and belching sounds. The adults depart in March but the weaned pups hang around until May.

Different age groups of elephant seals continue to use the beach at different times throughout the summer for moulting. Elephant seals are completely unafraid of people, but are huge enough to hurt or even kill you if you get in their way. Still, you're allowed to get close, except during mating season, when entry into the park is restricted to ranger-guided tours.

Estuaries

Throughout California, many **estuarine** or river-mouth habitats have been filled, diked, drained, "improved" with marinas, or contaminated by pollutants. Those that survive intact consist of a mixture of mud flats, exposed only at low tide, and salt marsh, together forming a critical wildlife area that provides nurseries for many kinds of invertebrates and fish, and nesting and wintering grounds for countless birds. Cord grass, a dominant wetlands plant, produces five to ten times as much oxygen and nutrients per acre as wheat.

Many interesting creatures live in the thick organic ooze, including the fat **innkeeper** (a revolting-looking pink hot-dog of a worm that sociably shares its burrow with a small crab and a fish), polychaete worms, clams and other goodies. Most prominent of estuary birds are the **great blue herons** and **great egrets**. Estuaries are the best place to see wintering shorebirds such as dunlin, dowitchers, eastern and western sandpipers, and yellowlegs, and peregrine falcons and osprey are also found here.

Important California estuaries include Elkhorn Slough, near Monterey, San Francisco Bay, and Bolinas Lagoon, some fifteen miles north.

Coastal meadows, hills and canyons

Along the shore, **coastal meadows** are bright with pink and yellow sand verbena, lupines, sea rocket, sea fig and the bright orange **California poppy**, the state flower. Slightly inland, hills are covered with coastal scrub, which consists largely of coyote brush. Coastal canyons contain broadleaf trees such as California laurel, alder, buckeye and oak – and a tangle of sword ferns, horsetail and cow parsnip.

Common rainy-season canyon inhabitants include four-inch-long banana slugs and rough-skinned newts. In winter, orange-and-black **Monarch butterflies** gather in large roosts in a few discreet locales, such as Bolinas, Santa Cruz and Pacific Grove. Coastal thickets also provide homes to weasels, bobcats, grey fox, raccoons, black-tailed deer, California quail and garter snakes. **Tule elk**, a once common member of the deer family, have also been reintroduced to the wild; good places to view them are on Tomales Point at the Point Reyes National Seashore (see p.545), and inland at reserves near Bakersfield (p.309) and in the Owens Valley (p.284).

River valleys

Like most fertile **river valleys**, the Sacramento and San Joaquin valleys – jointly known as the Central Valley – have both been greatly affected by agriculture. Riparian (streamside) vegetation has been logged, wetlands drained, and streams contaminated by agricultural runoff. Despite this, the habitat that does remain is a haven for wildlife. Wood ducks, kingfishers, swallows and warblers are common, as are grey foxes, raccoons and striped skunks. Regular winter migrants include snow and Canada geese, green-winged and cinnamon teals,

CONTEXTS | Wildlife and the environment

pintail, shovelers and widgeon. The refuges where many of these creatures live are well worth a visit, but don't be alarmed by large numbers of duck hunters – the term "refuge" is a misnomer. However, most have tour routes where hunting is prohibited.

Vernal pools are a valley community unique to California. Here, hardpan soils prevent the infiltration of winter rains, creating seasonal ponds. As these ponds slowly evaporate in April and May, sharply defined concentric floral rings come into bloom. The white is meadowfoam, the blue is the violet-like downingia and the yellow is goldfields. Swallows, meadowlarks, yellowlegs and stilts can also be found here.

Forests

One of the most notable indigenous features of California's forests are the wide expanses of **redwood** (*Sequoia sempervirens*) and **sequoia** (*Sequoiadendron giganteum*) **trees**, both exhibiting the same fibrous, reddish-brown bark. Redwoods are the world's tallest trees, while sequoias have the greatest base circumference and are the largest single organisms on earth; for more on the latter, see the box on p.330. Both species can live for over two thousand years, and recent research now indicates a maximum age of 3500 years for the sequoia. Their longevity is partially due to their bark: rich in tannin, it protects the tree from fungal and insect attack and inhibits fire damage. In fact, fire is beneficial to these trees and necessary for their germination; prescribed fires are set and controlled around them. The wood of the redwood in particular is much sought after both for its resistance to decay and its beauty – near any coastal forest you'll see signs advertising redwood burl furniture.

Redwoods and sequoias are the only surviving members of a family of perhaps forty species of tree which, fossil records show, grew worldwide 175 million years ago. **Redwoods** are a relict species, meaning they flourished in a moister climate during the Arcto-Tertiary (just after the golden age of the dinosaurs), and, as weather patterns change, have retreated to their current near-coastal haunts. Today they are found in a few pockets from the border with Oregon to just south of Monterey, and a tremendous battle between environmentalists and loggers is being waged over the remaining acres. These **virgin forests** provide homes to unique creatures, such as the spotted owl and marbled murrelet.

The floor of the redwood forest is a hushed place with little sunlight, the air suffused with a rufous glow from the bark, which gives the trees its name. One of the most common ground covers in the redwood forest is the redwood sorrel, or oxalis, with its shamrock leaves and tubular pink flowers; ferns are also numerous. Birds are usually high in the canopy and hard to see, but you might hear the double-whistled song of the varied thrush, or the "chickadee" call from the bird of that name. Roosevelt elk, larger than the tule elk, also inhabit the humid northwest forests. Prairie Creek Redwoods State Park, near the Oregon border, has a large herd.

Sequoias are found on the western slopes of the Sierra Nevada, most notably in Yosemite, Sequoia and Kings Canyon national parks – though trees from saplings given as state gifts can be found growing all over the world. Juvenile sequoias – say up to a thousand years old – exhibit a slender conical shape which, as the lower branches fall away, ages to the classic heavy-crowned figure, with its columnar trunk. For its bulk, its cones are astonishingly small, no bigger than a hen's egg, but they live on the tree for up to thirty years before falling.

The Sierra Nevada

In the late nineteenth century, the environmental movement was founded when John Muir fell in love with the **Sierra Nevada mountains**, which he called the Range of Light. Muir fought a losing battle to save Hetch Hetchy, a valley said to be as beautiful as Yosemite, but in the process the **Sierra Club** (see p.340) was born and the battle to save America's remaining wilderness began.

The Sierra Nevada, which runs almost the entire length of the state, has a sharp, craggy, freshly glaciated look. Many of the same conifers can be found as in the forests further west, but ponderosa and lodgepole pines are two of the dominants, and the forests tend to be drier and more open. Lower-elevation forests contain incense cedar, sugar pine (whose eighteen-inch cones are the longest in the world), and black oak. The oaks, along with dogwood and willows, produce spectacular autumnal colour. The east side of the range is drier and has large groves of aspen, a beautiful white-barked tree with small round leaves that tremble in the wind. **Wildflowers** flourish for a few short months here – shooting star, elephant's head and wild onions in early spring, asters and yarrow later in the season.

The dominant campground scoundrels are two sorts of noisy, squawking bird: Steller's jay and Clark's nutcracker. Black bears, who may make a raid on your camp, pose more danger to iceboxes than humans, but nonetheless you should treat them with caution. The friendly twenty-pound pot-bellied rodents that lounge around at the fringes of your encampment are **marmots**, who probably do more damage than bears: some specialize in chewing on radiator hoses of parked cars. For tips on dealing with wildlife safely and respectfully, see p.48.

Other common birds include mountain chickadees, yellow-rumped warblers, white-crowned sparrows and juncos, and among the mammals, deer, golden-mantled ground squirrels and chipmunks are plentiful.

The Great Basin

The little-known **Great Basin** stretches from the northernmost section of the state down almost to Death Valley, encompassing all of Nevada and parts of all the other bordering states. It's a land of many shrubs and few streams, and what streams do exist drain into saline lakes rather than the ocean.

Mono Lake, reflecting the 13,000-foot peaks of Yosemite National Park, is a spectacular example. Its salty waters support no fish but lots of algae, brine shrimp and brine flies, the latter two providing a smorgasbord for nesting gulls (the term "seagull" isn't strictly correct – many gulls nest inland) and migrating phalaropes and grebes. Like many Great Basin lakes, Mono Lake has been damaged through diversion of its freshwater feeder streams, in this case to provide water for the swimming pools of Los Angeles.

Great Basin plants tolerate hot summers, cold winters and little rain. The dominant Great Basin plant is **sagebrush**, whose dusky green leaves are wonderfully aromatic, especially after a summer thunderstorm. Other common plants include bitterbrush, desert peach, juniper and piñon pine. Piñon cones contain tasty nuts that were a mainstay of the Paiute diet.

The **sage grouse** is one of the most distinctive Great Basin birds. These turkey-like fowl feed on sage during the winter and depend on it for nesting and courtship habitat. In March and April, males gather at dancing grounds called leks, where they puff out small pink balloons on their necks, make soft drum-banging calls, and in general succeed in looking and sounding rather silly. The hens coyly scout out the talent by feigning greater interest in imaginary seeds.

Pronghorns are beautiful tawny-gold antelope seen in many locales in the Great Basin. Watch for their twinkling white rumps as you drive. Other Great Basin denizens include golden eagles, piñon jays, black-billed magpies, coyotes, feral horses and burros, black-tailed jackrabbits and western rattlesnakes. Large concentrations of waterfowl gather at Tule Lake in northeastern California, part of the Klamath Basin National Wildlife Refuge (see p.679), where hundreds of wintering **bald eagles** congregate in November before the cold really sets in.

The Mojave Desert

The **Mojave Desert** lies in the southeast corner of the state, near Death Valley. Like the Great Basin, the vegetation here consists primarily of drought-adapted shrubs, one of the commonest of which is creosote, with its olive-green leaves and puffy yellow flowers. Death Valley is renowned for its early spring wildflower shows. The alluvial fans are covered with desert trumpet, gravel ghost and pebble pincushion. The quantity and timing of rainfall determines when the floral display peaks, but it's usually some time between mid-February and mid-April in the lower elevations, late April to early June higher up. Besides shrubs, the Mojave has many interesting kinds of **cactus**. These include barrel, cottontop, cholla and beavertail cactus, and many members of the yucca family. Yuccas have stiff, lance-like leaves with sharp tips, a conspicuous representative being the **Joshua tree** (see p.240), whose twisting, arm-like branches are covered with shaggy, upward-pointing leaf fronds, which can reach to thirty feet high.

Many Mojave Desert animals conserve body moisture by foraging at night, including the kit fox, wood rat and various kinds of mice. The **kangaroo rat**, an appealing animal that hops rather than runs, has specially adapted kidneys that enable it to survive without drinking water. If you're lucky you might catch sight of the **bighorn sheep**, usually found in secluded canyons and on high ridges; the **desert fox**, a regular sight among the sand dunes; and the **coyote**, which frequently keeps cool in the shade. Other desert animals include birds like the roadrunner, ash-throated flycatcher, ladder-backed woodpecker, verdin and Lucy's warbler, and reptiles like the Mojave rattlesnake, sidewinder and chuckwalla.

California on film

I n the early 1910s, attracted by the sunshine, cheap labour, low taxes and rich variety of California landscapes, a handful of independent movie producers left the East Coast and the stranglehold monopoly of Thomas Edison's Motion Picture Patents Company, and set up shop in the small Los Angeles suburb of Hollywood. Within a decade Edison's company was defunct and Hollywood had become the movie capital of the world, with Southern California the setting for everything from Keystone Kops car chases to Tom Mix Westerns, not to mention the odd Biblical epic or historic romance.

Not surprisingly, since then the list of **movies** set in California, and especially LA, has become almost endless. What follows are those that make the most original use of California locations, and reflect the state's navel-gazing fascination with itself.

Hollywood does Hollywood

The Bad and the Beautiful (Vincente Minnelli, 1952). Bitter tale of the rise and fall of a ruthless Hollywood producer (Kirk Douglas), told in flashbacks by the star, writer and director he launched and subsequently lost.

Barton Fink (Joel Coen, 1991). Tinseltown in the 1940s is depicted by the Coen brothers as a dark world of greedy movie bosses, belligerent screenwriters and murderers disguised as travelling salesmen. Allegedly based on the experience of playwright Clifford Odets.

Ed Wood (Tim Burton, 1994). Loving tribute to the much-derided 1950s "auteur" of *Plan 9 from Outer Space* and *Glen or Glenda*. Gorgeously shot in black and white, with a magnificent performance by Martin Landau as an ailing Bela Lugosi.

Gods and Monsters (Bill Condon, 1998). An interesting tale of the final days of 1930s horror-film director James Whale (Ian McKellen), ignored by the Hollywood elite and slowly dying of malaise by his poolside. The title refers to a memorable Ernest Thesiger line from Whale's classic *Bride of Frankenstein*.

Good Morning, Babylon (Paolo and Vittorio Taviani, 1987). Two restorers of European cathedrals find themselves in 1910s Hollywood, working to build the monstrous Babylonian set for D.W. Griffith's *Intolerance*, in this story of the immigrant contribution to early Tinseltown.

In a Lonely Place (Nicholas Ray, 1950). A glamourless Hollywood peopled with alcoholic former matinee idols, star-struck hat-check girls and desperate agents forms the cynical background for this doomed romance between Humphrey Bogart's hot-tempered screenwriter and his elegant neighbour Gloria Grahame.

The Player (Robert Altman, 1992). Tim Robbins is a studio shark who thinks a disgruntled screenwriter is out to get him; he kills the writer (at South Pasadena's Rialto Theater), steals his girlfriend, and waits for the cops to unravel the mystery. A wickedly sharp satire about contemporary Hollywood, with some great celebrity cameos.

Singin' in the Rain (Stanley Donen & Gene Kelly, 1952). A merry trip through Hollywood set during the birth of the sound era. Gene Kelly, Donald O'Connor and Debbie Reynolds sing and dance to many classic tunes, including *Good Morning*, *Moses*, *Broadway Melody* and countless others.

A Star Is Born (George Cukor, 1954). The story of the rise of a starlet mirroring the demise of her Svengali. Janet Gaynor and Fredric March star in the early version (1937), Judy Garland and James Mason in the later. Both are worthwhile, while a 1976 remake with Barbra Streisand and Kris Kristofferson runs a distant third.

Sullivan's Travels (Preston Sturges, 1941). A high-spirited comedy about a director who wants to stop making schlock pictures and instead create gritty portrayals of what he thinks real life to be. The first two-thirds are great, the last third ends in mawkish fashion.

Sunset Boulevard (Billy Wilder, 1950). Award-winning film about a screenwriter falling into the clutches of a long-faded silent-movie star. William Holden was near the beginning of his career, Gloria Swanson well past the end of hers. Erich von Stroheim nicely fills in as Swanson's butler, and even Cecil B. DeMille makes a cameo.

Who Framed Roger Rabbit? (Robert Zemeckis, 1988). Despite being a live-action/cartoon hybrid, this is a revealing film about 1940s LA, where cartoon characters suffer abuse like everyone else and the big corporations seek to destroy the Red Car transit system.

LA noir

Chinatown (Roman Polanski, 1974). One of the essential films about the city. Jack Nicholson hunts down corruption in this dark criticism of the forces that animate the town: venal politicians, black-hearted land barons, crooked cops and a morally neutered populace. Great use of locations, from Echo Park to the San Fernando Valley.

Devil in a Blue Dress (Carl Franklin, 1995). Terrific modern noir, in which South Central detective Easy Rawlins (Denzel Washington) navigates the ethical squalor of elite 1940s white LA and discovers a few ugly truths about city leaders – most of which he already suspected.

Double Indemnity (Billy Wilder, 1944). The prototypical film noir. Greedy insurance salesman Fred MacMurray collaborates with harpy wife Barbara Stanwyck to murder her husband and cash in on the settlement. Edward G. Robinson lurks on the sidelines as MacMurray's boss.

Heat (Michael Mann, 1995). Stars big names like De Niro and Pacino, but this crime drama, which does include some stunning set pieces (eg a Downtown LA shootout), is ultimately less than the sum of its parts.

Jackie Brown (Quentin Tarantino, 1997). A glorious return to form for Pam Grier who, as a tough airline stewardess, plays the perfect foil for Samuel Jackson's smooth gangster. LA provides the gritty backdrop.

The Killing of a Chinese Bookie (John Cassavetes, 1976). Perfectly evoking the sleazy charms of the Sunset Strip, Cassavetes' behavioural crime story about a club owner (Ben Gazzara) in hock to the Mob is just one of his many great LA-based character studies.

LA Confidential (Curtis Hanson, 1997). Easily the best of all the contemporary noir films, a perfectly realized adaptation of James Ellroy's novel about brutal cops, victimized prostitutes and scheming politicians in 1950s LA.

The Long Goodbye (Robert Altman, 1973). Altman intentionally mangles noir conventions in this Chandler adaptation, which has Elliott Gould play Marlowe as a droning schlep who wanders across a desaturated landscape of casual corruption and bizarre characters.

One False Move (Carl Franklin, 1991). A disturbing early role for Billy Bob Thornton, as a murderous hick who kills some people in an LA bungalow with his girlfriend and psychotic, nerdy colleague Pluto, then gets pursued by the LAPD and a small-town Arkansas sheriff.

The Postman Always Rings Twice (Tay Garnett, 1946). Lana Turner and John Garfield star in this seamy – and excellent – adaptation of the James M. Cain novel, first brought to the screen as *Ossessione*, an Italian adaptation by Luchino Visconti.

🏃 **Touch of Evil** (Orson Welles, 1958). Supposedly set at a Mexican border town, this noir classic was actually shot in a seedy, decrepit Venice. A bizarre, baroque masterpiece with Charlton Heston playing a Mexican official, Janet Leigh as his beleaguered wife, and Welles himself as a bloated, corrupt cop addicted to candy bars.

True Romance (Tony Scott, 1993). With a Quentin Tarantino plot to guide them, Patricia Arquette and Christian Slater battle creeps and gangsters amid wonderful LA locations, from cruddy motels to *Rae's Diner* in Santa Monica.

Apocalyptic LA

🏃 **Blade Runner** (Ridley Scott, 1982). While the first theatrical version flopped (thanks to a slapped-on happy ending and annoying voiceover narration), the recut director's version establishes the film as a sci-fi classic, involving a dystopic future LA where "replicants" roam the streets and soulless corporations rule from pyramidal towers.

Earthquake (Mark Robson, 1974). Watch the Lake Hollywood dam collapse, people run for their lives, and chaos hold sway in the City of Angels. Originally presented in "Sensurround!"

Escape from LA (John Carpenter, 1996). LA is cut off from the mainland by an earthquake and declared so "ravaged by crime and immorality" that it's been turned into a dead zone for undesirables. Sent in to stop the insurrection, Kurt Russell battles psychotic plastic surgeons in Beverly Hills and surfs a tsunami to a showdown in a netherworld Disneyland.

Falling Down (Joel Schumacher, 1993). Fired defence-worker Michael Douglas tires of the traffic jams on the freeways and goes nuts in some of the city's poorer minority neighbourhoods. A fitting reflection of the bleak attitudes of riot-era LA.

Kiss Me Deadly (Robert Aldrich, 1955). Perhaps the bleakest of all noirs, starring Ralph Meeker as brutal detective Mike Hammer, who tramples on friends and enemies alike in his search for the great "whatsit" – a mysterious and deadly suitcase.

Mulholland Drive (David Lynch, 2001). A frightening take on the city by director Lynch, who uses nonlinear storytelling to present a tale of love, death, glamour and doom – in which elfin cowboys mutter cryptic threats, elegant chanteuses lip-sync to phantom melodies, and a blue key can unlock a shocking double identity.

The Terminator (James Cameron, 1984). Modern sci-fi classic, with Arnold Schwarzenegger as a robot from the future sent to kill the mother of an unborn rebel leader. Bravura special effects and amazing set pieces here were successfully followed up with the director's 1989 sequel, *T2: Judgment Day*, with Arnold as a good robot.

Modern LA

Boyz N the Hood (John Singleton, 1991). An excellent period piece that cemented the LA stereotype as a land of gangs and guns, starring Cuba Gooding Jr in his first big role, and Lawrence Fishburne as his dad.

Dogtown and Z-Boys (Stacy Peralta, 2002). Even if you have no interest in skateboarding, this is a fun, high-spirited look at the glory times of the sport in the mid-1970s, when a daring group of LA kids took to using the empty swimming pools of the elite as their own private skate-parks.

The Limey (Steven Soderbergh, 1999). Gangster Terence Stamp wanders into a morally adrift LA looking for his daughter's killer, and finds the burned-out husk of former hippy Peter Fonda.

Magnolia (Paul Thomas Anderson, 1999). A gut-wrenching travelogue of human misery. The San Fernando Valley serves as an emotional inferno of abusive parents, victimized children, haunted memories, plaintive songs, and a curious plague of frogs.

Mayor of the Sunset Strip (George Hickenlooper, 2003). Great, disturbing documentary about the titular character, a former stand-in for one of the Monkees, legendary DJ, lounge denizen, and apparent man-child who can't seem to get his life together, despite being pals with people like David Bowie.

Pulp Fiction (Quentin Tarantino, 1994). A successful collection of underworld stories presented in nonlinear fashion and set against a down-at-heel backdrop of LA streets, bars, diners and would-be torture chambers.

Short Cuts (Robert Altman, 1993). Vaguely linked vignettes tracing the lives of LA suburbanites, from a trailer-park couple in Downey to an elite doctor in the Santa Monica Mountains. Strong ensemble cast bolsters the intentionally fractured narrative.

Slums of Beverly Hills (Tamara Jenkins, 1998). Troubled teen Natasha Lyonne deals with growing pains in a less glamorous section of town, far from Rodeo Drive, where a pill-popping cousin, manic uncle, weird neighbours and her own expanding bustline are but a few of her worries.

Swingers (Doug Liman, 1996). Cocktail culture gets skewered in this flick about a couple of dudes who flit from club to club to eye "beautiful babies" and kibbitz like Rat Pack-era Sinatras. Many LA locales are shown, such as the *Dresden Room* and *The Derby*.

To Sleep with Anger (Charles Burnett, 1990). An interesting view of LA's overlooked, black middle class, directed with polish by a very under-rated African-American filmmaker.

Tupac and Biggie (Nick Broomfield, 2002). Eye-opening documentary about the murders of rappers Tupac Shakur and Notorious B.I.G., both of whom the director suggests may have been the victims of hip-hop producer Suge Knight, along with rogue elements of the LAPD.

If you're going to San Francisco

Bullitt (Peter Yates, 1968). The classic portrait of San Francisco, presented at breakneck speed in cinema's most famous car chase, ripping up and down the city's steep hills at a frenetic, still-amazing pace. No modern special effects for this legendary sequence, either.

The Conversation (Francis Ford Coppola, 1974). Opening with a mesmerizing sequence of high-tech eavesdropping in Union Square, Coppola's chilling character study of San Francisco surveillance expert Harry Caul is one of the best films of the paranoid Watergate era.

Dim Sum: A Little Bit of Heart (Wayne Wang, 1985). Set among San Francisco's Chinese community, Wayne Wang's appealing comedy of manners about assimilation and family ties is a modest and rewarding treat. His earlier sleeper *Chan is Missing* (1982) also shows a Chinatown tourists don't usually see.

Dirty Harry (Don Siegel, 1971). Based on the infamous case of the Zodiac Killer, Siegel's morally dubious, sequel-spawning thriller casts Clint Eastwood in his most famous role as a vigilante San Francisco cop. The first and best in a long series.

Escape from Alcatraz (Don Siegel, 1979). Though evocatively portrayed in *Bird Man of Alcatraz, Point Blank, The Rock* and many others, this is the ultimate movie about San Francisco's famously unbreachable offshore penitentiary. Starring Clint Eastwood (again) as a most resourceful con.

Gimme Shelter (Albert and David Maysles, 1969). Excellent documentary about the ill-fated Rolling Stones' concert at Altamont, in which Hell's Angels were hired to provide their own version of "security". Its searing look at home-grown American violence and Vietnam-era chaos at the end of the 1960s includes an on-camera stabbing.

Greed (Erich von Stroheim, 1924). Legendary silent masterpiece about the downfall of Polk Street dentist Doc McTeague was shot mostly on location in the Bay Area, and remains, even in its notoriously truncated version, a wonderful time-capsule of working-class San Francisco in the 1920s.

Invasion of the Body Snatchers (Philip Kaufman, 1978). Great remake of a classic 1956 paranoid chiller, in which aliens replicate by taking the shape of humans in the form of "pod people". This quite atmospheric and eerie version is set in San Francisco, which is used to great effect, and has Donald Sutherland as the health-inspector protagonist.

Pal Joey (George Sidney, 1957). Based on the hit musical, this Frank Sinatra vehicle presents its title character as a womanizer with few limits, using Kim Novak and Rita Hayworth to his own ends, in the swinging city by the bay.

Petulia (Richard Lester, 1968). Julie Christie is dazzling in this fragmented puzzle of a movie about a vivacious and unpredictable married woman who has an affair with a divorced doctor (George C. Scott). Set against the wittily described background of psychedelic-era San Francisco, and superbly shot by Nicolas Roeg.

Play It Again, Sam (Herbert Ross, 1972). A strike in Manhattan led to one of Woody Allen's uncommon visits to the West Coast for this hilarious film about a neurotic San Francisco film critic in love with his best friend's wife and obsessed with Humphrey Bogart in *Casablanca*.

The Times of Harvey Milk (Robert Epstein, 1984). This powerful and moving documentary about America's first openly gay politician chronicles his career in San Francisco and the aftermath of his 1978 assassination. Based on the book by Randy Shilts (see p.713). Gus Van Sant's 2008 dramatic adaptation, *Milk*, won Sean Penn an Oscar for best actor.

The Towering Inferno (John Guillermin, 1974). Classic skyscraper-on-fire flick that ushered in the 1970s wave of disaster spectaculars, for better or worse, with this version featuring a cast of grizzled Hollywood old-timers and pulse-pounding action as a 138-storey building blazes away on the San Francisco skyline.

"Way out" West

Beach Blanket Bingo (William Asher, 1965). A cult favourite – the epitome of sun-and-surf movies, with Frankie Avalon and Annette Funicello singing and cavorting amid hordes of wild-eyed teenagers.

Bob & Carol & Ted & Alice (Paul Mazursky, 1969). Once daring, but still funny zeitgeist satire about wife-swapping and bed-hopping in hedonistic Southern California, starring Natalie Wood, Robert Culp, Elliott Gould and Dyan Cannon as the titular foursome.

Boogie Nights (Paul Thomas Anderson, 1997). A suburban kid from Torrance hits the big time in LA – as a porn star. Mark Wahlberg, Julianne Moore and Burt Reynolds tread through a sex-drenched San Fernando Valley landscape in the disco years.

House on Haunted Hill (William Castle, 1958). Not the clumsy remake, but the ghoulish Vincent Price original, with the King of Horror as a master of ceremonies for a scary party thrown at his Hollywood Hills estate

Vertigo (Alfred Hitchcock, 1958). Hitchcock's sombre, agonized, twisted love story is the San Francisco movie nonpareil, and one of the greatest films ever made. From James Stewart's wordless drives around the city to the film's climax at the San Juan Bautista Mission, Hitchcock takes us on a mesmerizing tour of a city haunted by its past.

Zodiac (David Fincher, 2007). Pulse-pounder covering a lone cartoonist's search for the infamous Zodiac Killer, who still hasn't been caught after almost forty years. Jake Gyllenhaal is good as the cartoonist; Robert Downey Jr is his usual brilliant and bizarre self as a crime reporter.

– actually, Frank Lloyd Wright's Ennis House (see p.96).

Modern Romance (Albert Brooks, 1981). Brooks – the Woody Allen of the West Coast – stars in this comedy about a neurotic film editor who dumps his girlfriend and instantly regrets it. Full of early 80s LA signifiers, from Quaaludes to jogging suits.

Point Break (Kathryn Bigelow, 1991). Pop favourite set in the surfer-dude world with Keanu Reeves as a robbery-investigating FBI agent and Patrick Swayze as his rebel-surfer quarry.

Rebel Without a Cause (Nicholas Ray, 1955). Fine, brash colours and widescreen composition in this troubled-youth film, starring, of course, James Dean. A Hollywood classic with many memorable images, notably the use of the Griffith Park Observatory as a shooting location.

Repo Man (Alex Cox, 1984). Emilio Estevez is a surly young punk who repossesses cars for Harry Dean Stanton. Very imaginative and fun, and darkly comic.

Shampoo (Hal Ashby, 1975). Using LA as his private playground, priapic hairdresser Warren Beatty freely acts on his formidable, though nonchalant, libido. A period piece memorable for its washed-out look.

Valley Girl (Martha Coolidge, 1983). Early Nicolas Cage flick, in which he winningly plays a new-wave freak trying to woo the title character (Debra Foreman) in a clash of LA cultures. Good soundtrack, too.

Off the beaten track

Bagdad Café (Percy Adlon, 1988). Inspiring fable about a German tourist who arrives at a dusty roadside diner in the Mojave Desert and magically transforms the place with her larger-than-life charm.

The Birds (Alfred Hitchcock, 1963). Set in Bodega Bay, just north of San Francisco, Hitchcock's terrifying allegory about a small town besieged by a plague of vicious birds features indelible bird's-eye views of the Northern California coastline.

Citizen Kane (Orson Welles, 1941). In this pinnacle of American filmmaking, director Welles successfully copies the baroque splendour and frightful vulgarity of William Randolph Hearst's legendary prison-like palace in San Simeon on the Central Coast (see p.393). Here, it's called "Xanadu" and shot in San Diego's Balboa Park.

Faster, Pussycat! Kill! Kill! (Russ Meyer, 1965). Meyer's wonderfully lurid, camp, action flick unleashes a trio of depraved go-go girls upon an unsuspecting California desert. One of a kind.

Fat City (John Huston, 1972). Stacy Keach and Jeff Bridges star in one of the last great films from Huston, a realistic, grim depiction of the lives of small-time Stockton boxers. Based on an equally acclaimed novel (see p.716).

The Graduate (Mike Nichols, 1967). Although usually more identified with youthful 1960s anomie than California per se, there are many evocative images in this generational comedy,

including those of campus life at Berkeley and USC and middle-class suburban complacency.

High Plains Drifter (Clint Eastwood, 1972). Spooky Mono Lake is one of the bleak, disturbing settings for this tale of a mysterious gunslinger who comes back to a dusty burg to avenge a wrongful death – before drenching the town in blood and renaming it "Hell".

One-Eyed Jacks (Marlon Brando, 1961). Set, unusually for a Western, on the roaring shores of Monterey, where Brando tracks down Karl Malden – the bank-robbing partner who betrayed him five years earlier in Mexico – only to find him reformed and comfortably ensconced as sheriff.

Play Misty for Me (Clint Eastwood, 1971). Another Monterey movie, Eastwood's directorial debut, a thriller about the consequences of a DJ's affair with a psychotic fan, was shot in Clint's hometown of Carmel, and on his own two hundred acres of Monterey coastland.

Riding Giants (Stacy Peralta, 2004). One of the best of the surfing documentaries, showing the glories of the sport (with modern, high-tech equipment), the life stories of some of its bigger names, and that perennial California backdrop of sun and waves.

Sideways (Alexander Payne, 2004). Two vino-slurping pals take a trip to the Central Coast's wine country, one of them seeking a last fling before he gets married, the other wallowing in shame and self-pity. The golden landscapes often resemble a two-hour ad by the California tourism board.

Some Like It Hot (Billy Wilder, 1959). The film some claim as the best comedy ever, set around a luxurious Florida resort that's actually San Diego's own *Hotel del Coronado* (see p.187), itself dripping with swank beachfront elegance.

Three Women (Robert Altman, 1977). A fascinating, hypnotic and unique film in which Sissy Spacek and Shelley Duvall, co-workers at a geriatric centre in Desert Springs, mysteriously absorb each other's identity.

Books

C alifornia has been the subject of more **books** than any other US state outside of New York, and for contemporary culture it's clearly drawn the most ink. Most of the state's stories tend to revolve around the Spanish Mission era, Gold Rush, movie industry, and modern politics and cultural mores. LA and San Francisco are predictably well covered, though other major cities appear much less often, with San Diego in particular yet to find an insightful chronicler on the order of Carey McWilliams (LA), Herb Caen (SF) or Kevin Starr (the entire state). The note "o/p" signifies an out-of-print title – which you may be able to find through one of the many secondhand-book merchants in LA or on the internet.

Travel and specialist guides

Steve Grody *Graffiti LA*. If you're inclined to probe LA's poorer neighbourhoods, you might discover many of the colourful pieces of home-grown art depicted here, which the author dissects according to their ethnic, cultural, and (in places) gang affiliation. Includes CD-ROM.

Tom Kirkendall and Vicky Spring *Bicycling the Pacific Coast*. Excellent, detailed guide to the bike routes all the way along the coast, from Mexico up to Canada.

Eric Mahoney *Walking L.A.: 38 Walking Tours*. A bevy of fascinating treks through the city, from the well-trod districts to obscure places off the radar of most locals and all tourists; well worth the journey.

Leonard Pitt and Dale Pitt *Los Angeles A to Z*. If you're truly enthralled by the city, this is the tome for you: six hundred pages of encyclopedic references covering everything from conquistadors to movie stars.

Ray Riegert *Hidden Coast of California*. A detailed and interesting guide, now in its eleventh edition, to the nooks and crannies along the California state beaches and parks, told from the perspective of a recreational enthusiast who tracks down all his favourite underrated beaches.

John R. Soares *100 Classic Hikes in Northern California*. An engaging presentation of wilderness hiking in the northern part of the state, from the Bay Area up to the Oregon border. Also good is the author's *100 Hikes in Yosemite National Park*.

Surfer Magazine's Guide to Southern California Surf Spots A handy, comprehensive reference to the best places in the state to ride the pipeline and find a killer break – even better, the pages are waterproof.

History

Oscar Zeta Acosta *Autobiography of a Brown Buffalo, Revolt of the Cockroach People* (Vintage). The legendary model for Hunter S. Thompson's bloated D. Gonzo, this author was in reality a trailblazing Hispanic lawyer who used all manner of colourful tactics to defend oppressed and indigent defendants. Two vivid portraits of late-1960s California, written just before the author mysteriously vanished in 1971.

Mark Arax and Rick Wartzman *The King of California: J.G. Boswell and the Making of a Secret*

American Empire. Essential reading for anyone interested in the real history of the state, focusing on how a family of Georgia farmers migrated to the San Joaquin Valley and created the nation's biggest cotton empire with hardly anyone noticing.

H.W. Brands *The Age of Gold*. Excellent introduction to Gold Rush-era California, highlighting the immigrants from around the world who came to mine the ore, the unexpected fortunes of a lucky few, and the political and social repercussions of this unprecedented event – the first glimmer of the Gilded Age.

Gray Brechin *Imperial San Francisco: Urban Power, Earthly Ruin*. Long-overdue puncturing of myths about the City by the Bay, showing how dubious mining and financial schemes led to its rise, and how its history, strangely enough, parallels that of ancient Rome and other classical cities.

Vincent Bugliosi *Helter Skelter: The True Story of the Manson Murders*. The late 1960s wouldn't have been complete without the Manson Family, and here the prosecutor-author lays out the full story of the horrifying crimes carried out by the gang, inspired by their cult leader, formerly a Sunset Strip hippy and would-be pop songwriter.

Carey McWilliams *Southern California: an Island on the Land* (Gibbs Smith). The bible of Southern California histories, focusing on the key years between the two world wars and written by a lawyer and social activist involved in much of the drama of the time. Also excellent is McWilliams' broader *California: The Great Exception*.

Mark Reisner *Cadillac Desert* (Penguin, US). An essential guide to water problems in the American West, with special emphasis on LA's schemes to bring upstate California water to the metropolis. One of the best renderings of this sordid tale.

Dennis Smith *San Francisco Is Burning: The Untold Story of the 1906 Earthquake and Fires* (o/p). An excellent, detailed examination – published on the hundredth anniversary of the event – of the infamous cataclysm, with a good mix of scientific and historical analysis and personal stories of some of the figures involved.

Kevin Starr *Golden Dreams: California in an Age of Abundance, 1950-1963*. The latest round of Golden State history from the state's pre-eminent chronicler, one in a series of eight such volumes. Of those, the best overall is *Material Dreams: Southern California through the 1920s*, on the city's boom interwar years of celebrities and scandals.

Politics and society

James Conaway *Napa: the Story of an American Eden*. Compelling tale of how Napa Valley vintners attained international glory through clever science and down-and-dirty politics.

Mike Davis *City of Quartz*. The most important modern history of LA, in this case from a leftist perspective, vividly covering cops, riots, politicians, movies and architecture. The latest edition provides a modern update. Other volumes, *Ecology of Fear* and *Under the Perfect Sun*, respectively tell of LA's apocalyptic bent and of the corruption at the core of sunny San Diego.

Lisa McGirr *Suburban Warriors: the Origins of the New American Right*. The tale of how once-fringe right-wing activists in Southern California rose from the ashes of the 1960s to dominate state and, later, national politics, culminating with the presidency of Ronald Reagan and his acolytes.

Ethan Rarick *California Rising: The Life and Times of Pat Brown*. More than even Nixon or Reagan, Pat Brown was the most influential political figure for modern California, from building aqueducts and freeways to curbing racial discrimination, and this impressive volume details the man and his empire-building legacy.

Randy Shilts *The Mayor of Castro Street: the Life and Times of Harvey Milk*. Overview of the life, career and martyrdom of one of America's most famous gay-rights advocates, presented as an emblem for the rise of identity politics and social activism in 1970s California.

Architecture

Reyner Banham *Los Angeles: the Architecture of Four Ecologies*. The most lucid account of how LA's history has shaped its present form; the trenchant British author's enthusiasms are infectious.

Susan Cerny *Architectural Guidebook to San Francisco and the Bay Area*. Fine overview in text and photography of the key structures in the Bay Area, and their historic and cultural importance, along with their architectural value. A long-awaited volume.

David Gebhard and Robert Winter *Architectural Guidebook to Los Angeles*. For many years the essential guide to LA architecture, from historical treasures to contemporary quirks. Some of the quality has been lost with Gebhard's death, so try the 1994 edition (his last) for the best writing on modernist structures.

Jim Heimann *California Crazy and Beyond: Roadside Vernacular Architecture* (o/p). This fun volume is still a favourite after twenty years, and has now been updated to include the latest of the state's bizarre-chitecture, from diners shaped like hot dogs to wigwam motels, and the influence it has had nationally.

Randy Leffingwell *California Missions and Presidios*. Its attractive photos draw the eye, but this valuable pictorial is also good for its detailed story of the chequered history and architectural background of the state's signature spiritual outposts.

Elizabeth Pomada *Painted Ladies Revisited* (o/p). One in a series of volumes on Victorian mansions (in San Francisco and beyond) that you'll see in bookstores throughout the region, and well worth a look as a photo glossy and architecture guide.

Elizabeth A.T. Smith *Case Study Houses: the Complete CSH Program*. An excellent compendium of essays, photos and articles about the modernist homes of a pioneering 1950s design programme. A huge, expensive ($200) book, but essential for architecture buffs.

Hollywood and the movies

Kenneth Anger *Hollywood Babylon*. Deliciously dark and lurid stories of sex scandals, bad behaviour and murder in Tinseltown, written by the *enfant terrible* of 1960s experimental film.

Jeanine Basinger *Silent Stars*. Great ode to the still-famous and long-forgotten Hollywood figures of the silent era, with brief biographies that outline the careers of movie cowboys, vamps and sheiks. The same author's

The Star Machine explains how the studio system created movie icons out of unknowns – and how it kept its stars under a tight rein.

Robert Evans *The Kid Stays in the Picture*. Spellbinding insider's view of the machinations of Hollywood after the demise of the studio system, written with verve and flash by one of LA's biggest egos and, it turns out, most compelling authors – the head of Paramount when that company was at its modern peak.

Otto Friedrich *City of Nets*. Evocative descriptions of the major actors, directors and studio bosses of the last good years of the studio system,

before TV, antitrust actions and Joe McCarthy ruined it all.

Ephraim Katz *The Film Encyclopedia*. The essential reference guide for anyone interested in the movies, providing valuable information on the old movie companies and countless studio-system bit players, along with more contemporary figures.

Jerry Stahl *Permanent Midnight*. When his employers heard star scriptwriter Stahl (*Moonlighting*, *thirtysomething*) was spending his already-huge paycheck to support his heroin and other habits, they gave him a raise to cover the difference and keep him on the job. A gritty descent into Tinseltown drug hell.

Music and culture

Erik Davis *Visionary State: A Journey Through California's Spiritual Landscape*. Quite a journey, indeed, focusing on the various cults, New Agers and Zen philosophers who have illuminated the state in recent decades, along with older shamans and showmen, all highlighted by evocative, tantalizing photographs.

Joan Didion *Slouching Towards Bethlehem*. One of California's best and most polarizing writers takes a critical look at 1960s California, from the acid culture of San Francisco to American tough guy John Wayne. In a similar style, *The White Album* traces the West Coast characters and events that shaped the 1960s and 70s.

Barney Hoskyns *Beneath the Diamond Sky: Haight-Ashbury 1965–1970*. A vivid account of the glory days of mid-1960s psychedelia, with evocative pictures of seminal rock bands such as the Jefferson Airplane, Grateful Dead and Charlatans, and a narrative that describes how the hippy paradise was lost.

Robert Koenig *Mouse Tales*. All the Disneyland dirt that's fit to print: a

behind-the-scenes look at the ugly little secrets – from disenchanted workers to vermin infestations – that lurk behind the happy walls of the Magic Kingdom.

Kevin Nelson *Wheels of Change: From Zero to 600 MPH, the Story of California and the Automobile*. If you love the glorious epoch of auto worship – and salt-flat and drag racing, modified hot rods, car shows and other shrines to the mechanical beast – you'll love this sweeping overview of California's seemingly indispensible icon.

Danny Sugarman *Wonderland Avenue*. Publicist for The Doors and other seminal US rock bands from the late 60s on, Sugarman delivers a raunchy, autobiographical account of sex, drugs and LA rock'n'roll.

Tom Wolfe *The Electric Kool-Aid Acid Test*. Take an LSD-fuelled bus trip with Ken Kesey and his Merry Pranksters as they travel through mid-1960s California, before the counterculture was discovered, and co-opted, by corporate America.

Fiction and literature

T. Coraghessan Boyle *The Tortilla Curtain*. Set in LA, this novel boldly borrows its premise – a privileged white man running down a member of the city's ethnic underclass – from Tom Wolfe's *The Bonfire of the Vanities*, and carries it off to bleak satiric effect.

Richard Brautigan Tacoma-born writer often associated with the California Beat writers of the 50s and 60s, his surreal work is overlaid with cultural references. His most successful book, *Trout Fishing in America*, although designed as a fishing handbook, stealthily creates a disturbing image of contemporary life. Part of a comprehensive volume that includes *The Pill Versus the Springhill Mine Disaster* and *In Watermelon Sugar*.

James Brown *The Los Angeles Diaries*. Difficult-to-stomach but strangely compelling memoir about life in the dark underbelly of the state, awash in drug abuse, child molestation, arson, suicide and Hollywood striving. A memorable self-view from a talented author and screenwriter.

Charles Bukowski *Post Office*. An alcohol- and sex-soaked romp through some of LA's more festering back alleys, with a mailman surrogate for Bukowski as your guide. One of several books the author wrote exploring his encounters with the city's dark side.

James M. Cain *Double Indemnity*; *The Postman Always Rings Twice*; *Mildred Pierce*. Along with Raymond Chandler, Cain is one of the finest writers of dark, tough-guy novels. His entire oeuvre is excellent reading, but these three are the best explorations of LA's underside.

Raymond Chandler *Farewell My Lovely*; *Lady in the Lake*; *The Big Sleep*. Famous books adapted into classic movies, but Chandler's prose is still inimitable: terse, pointed and vivid. More than just detective stories (centred on gumshoe detective Philip Marlowe), these are masterpieces of fiction.

Philip K. Dick *A Scanner Darkly*. Erratic but brilliant author who evokes the mid-1990s split between the Straights, the Dopers and the Narks – a dizzying study of identity, authority and drugs. Among the pick of the rest of Dick's vast legacy is *Do Androids Dream of Electric Sheep?*, set in San Francisco, which gave rise to the film *Blade Runner*, set in LA.

Joan Didion *Play It as It Lays*. Hollywood rendered in all its booze-guzzling, pill-popping, sex-craving terror. Oddly, the author went on to write the uninspired script for the third adaptation of *A Star Is Born*.

James Ellroy *The Black Dahlia*; *The Big Nowhere*; *LA Confidential*; *White Jazz*. The LA Quartet: an excellent saga of city cops from the postwar era to the 1960s, with each novel progressively more complex and elliptical in style. The author's other LA-based works are also excellent – but start here.

John Fante *Ask the Dust*. The first and still the best of the author's stories of itinerant poet Arturo Bandini, whose wanderings during the Depression highlight California's faded glory and struggling residents.

F. Scott Fitzgerald *The Last Tycoon*. The legendary author's unfinished final work, on the power and glory of Hollywood. Intriguing reading that gives a view of the studio system at its height. The US edition features a reconstruction of what the finished version may have looked like.

Leonard Gardner *Fat City*. Poignant account of small-time Stockton boxing, following the initiation and fitful progress of a young hopeful and the parallel decline of an old contender. Painfully exact on the confused, murky emotions of its men as their lives stagnate in the heat of the town and the surrounding country.

Molly Giles *Iron Shoes*. A sobering but fascinating look into the life of a Northern California woman, busy caring for her dying mother while trying to juggle the absurd and dismal characters in her life.

Dashiell Hammett *Five Complete Novels: Red Harvest, The Dain Curse, The Maltese Falcon, The Glass Key, and The Thin Man*. Seminal detective novels featuring Sam Spade, the private investigator working out of San Francisco.

Chester Himes *If He Hollers Let Him Go*. A fine literary introduction to mid-twentieth-century race relations in LA, narrated by one Bob Jones, whose struggles mirrored those of author Himes, who eventually ended up living in Spain.

Helen Hunt Jackson *Ramona*. Ultra-romanticized depiction of mission life that criticizes America's treatment of Indians while showing the natives to be noble savages and glorifying the Spanish exploiters. A valuable period piece – perhaps the most influential work of fiction ever written about California.

Jack Kerouac *Desolation Angels*; *The Dharma Bums*. The most influential of the Beat writers on the rampage in California. See also his first novel *On the Road*, which has a little of San Francisco and a lot of the rest of the US.

Elmore Leonard *Get Shorty*. Ice-cool mobster Chili Palmer is a Miami debt collector who follows a client to

Hollywood, and finds that the increasing intricacies of his own situation are translating themselves into a movie script.

Ross MacDonald *Black Money*; *The Blue Hammer*; *The Zebra-Striped Hearse*; *The Doomsters*; *The Instant Enemy*. Following in the footsteps of Spade and Marlowe, private detective Lew Archer looks behind the glitzy masks of Southern California life to reveal the underlying nastiness of creepy sexuality and manipulation.

Armistead Maupin *Tales of the City*; *Further Tales of the City*; *More Tales of the City*. Lively and witty soap operas detailing the sexual antics of a select group of archetypal San Francisco characters of the late 70s and early 80s.

Walter Mosley *Devil in a Blue Dress*; *A Red Death*; *White Butterfly*; *Black Betty*; *A Little Yellow Dog*; *Bad Boy Brawly Brown*. Excellent modern noir novels that involve black private detective Easy Rawlins, who "does favors" from his South Central base. Mosley compellingly brings to life pre-riots Watts and, later, Compton.

Frank Norris *Novels and Essays*. One of the great naturalist writers presents a bleak, uncompromising view of the state at the turn of the last century; *McTeague* has a San Francisco dentist face social struggle and his own violence, while *The Octopus* is an epic battle in the San Joaquin Valley between railroad robber barons and heroic wheat-farmers.

Kem Nunn *Tapping the Source*. One of the most unexpected novels to emerge from California beach culture, an eerie murder-mystery set among the surfing landscape of Orange County's Huntington Beach.

Thomas Pynchon *The Crying of Lot 49*. Pynchon's celebrated – and most readable – excursion into modern paranoia follows the hilarious adventures of techno-freaks and potheads in 60s California, and reveals the sexy side of stamp collecting. His later, lesser *Vineland* and *Inherent Vice* are set in Northern and Southern California, respectively.

Luis J. Rodriguez *Republic of East LA.* Stark, memorable tales of life in the barrio, where struggling romantics and working-class strivers face the inequities of class and race, and gang crime looms ever-present.

Theodore Roszak *Flicker.* In an old LA movie house, Jonathan Gates discovers cinema and becomes obsessed by the director Max Castle – a genius of the silent era who disappeared in mysterious circumstances in the 40s – leading Gates into a labyrinthine conspiracy with its roots in medieval heresy.

Danny Santiago *Famous All Over Town.* Coming-of-age novel set among the street gangs of East LA, vividly depicting life in the Hispanic community.

Budd Schulberg *What Makes Sammy Run?* Classic anti-Hollywood vitriol by one of its insiders, a novelist and screenwriter whose acidic portrait of the movie business is unmatched.

Upton Sinclair *The Brass Check.* The failed California gubernatorial candidate and activist vigorously criticizes LA's yellow journalism and its underhanded practices. Sinclair also wrote *Oil!*, about California's 1920s oil rush.

Terry Southern *Blue Movie.* Sordid, frequently hilarious take on the overlap between high-budget moviemaking and pornography, with the author's vulgar themes and characters cheerfully slashing through politically correct literary conventions.

John Steinbeck *The Grapes of Wrath.* The classic account of a migrant family forsaking the Midwest for the Promised Land. The light-hearted but crisply observed novella, *Cannery Row*, captures daily life on the prewar Monterey waterfront, and the epic *East of Eden* updates and resets the Bible in the Salinas Valley.

Robert Louis Stevenson *The Silverado Squatters.* Portrays the splendour of the San Francisco hills and the cast of eccentrics and immigrants that populate them, as well as the strange atmosphere of Silverado itself, a deserted former Gold Rush settlement.

Amy Tan *The Joy Luck Club.* Four Chinese women – new arrivals in 1940s San Francisco – come together to play mahjong and tell their stories. They have four daughters, divided between Chinese and American identities, who also tell their tales, from childhood and from their often troubled present.

Michael Tolkin *The Player.* A convincing look at the depravity and moral twilight of the filmmaking community, with special scorn for venal movie execs. Made into a classic flick by Robert Altman (see p.703).

Gore Vidal *Hollywood.* The fifth volume in the author's "Empire" series about emerging US power on the world stage, this one focusing on the movie industry, its interaction with Washington bigwigs, and its boundless capacity for propaganda.

D.J. Waldie *Holy Land.* Strangely evocative memoir of growing up in the master-planned super-suburb of Lakewood in the 1950s, written in spare, haunting fragments by a poet who also happens to be the town's public information officer – though you'd never know it.

C

CONTEXTS | Books

Evelyn Waugh *The Loved One*. The essential literary companion to take with you on a trip to Forest Lawn – here rendered as Whispering Glades, the apex of funerary pretension and a telling symbol of LA's postmortem status mania.

Nathanael West *The Day of the Locust*. The best book about LA not involving detectives, an apocalyptic story of the fringe characters at the edge of the film industry, which culminates in a glorious riot and utter chaos.

Travel
store

Books change lives

Book Aid International
www.bookaid.org

Poverty and illiteracy go hand in hand. But in sub-Saharan Africa, books are a luxury few can afford. Many children leave school functionally illiterate, and adults often fall back into illiteracy in adulthood due to a lack of available reading material.

Book Aid International knows that books change lives.

Every year we send over half a million books to partners in 12 countries in sub-Saharan Africa, to stock libraries in schools, refugee camps, prisons, universities and communities. Literally millions of readers have access to books and information that could teach them new skills – from keeping chickens to getting a degree in Business Studies or learning how to protect against HIV/AIDS.

What can you do?

Join our Reverse Book Club and with your donation of only £6 a month, we can send 36 books every year to some of the poorest countries in the world. For every two pounds extra you can give, we can send another book!

Support Book Aid International today!

 Online. Go to our website at **www.bookaid.org**, and click on 'donate'

 By telephone. Start a Direct Debit or give a donation on your card by calling us on 020 7733 3577

Book Aid International is a charity and a limited company registered in England and Wales.
Charity No. 313869 Company No. 880754   39-41 Coldharbour Lane, Camberwell, London SE5 9NR
T +44 (0)20 7733 3577   F +44 (0)20 7978 8006   E info@bookaid.org   www.bookaid.org

FAIR FARES from
NORTH SOUTH TRAVEL

Our great-value air fares cover the world, from Abuja to Zanzibar and from Zurich to Anchorage. North South Travel is a fund-raising travel agency, owned by the NST Development Trust.

ALL our profits go to development organisations.

Call 01245 608 291 (or +44 1245 608 291 if outside UK) to speak to a friendly advisor. Your money is safe (ATOL 5401). For more information, visit northsouthtravel.co.uk. Free Rough Guide of your choice for every booking over £500.

EVERY FLIGHT A FIGHT AGAINST POVERTY

ROUGH GUIDES

World Coverage

Travel

Andorra The Pyrenees, Pyrenees & Andorra Map, Spain
Antigua The Caribbean
Argentina Argentina, Argentina Map, Buenos Aires, South America on a Budget
Aruba The Caribbean
Australia Australia, Australia Map, East Coast Australia, Melbourne, Sydney, Tasmania
Austria Austria, Europe on a Budget, Vienna
Bahamas The Bahamas, The Caribbean
Barbados Barbados DIR, The Caribbean
Belgium Belgium & Luxembourg, Bruges DIR, Brussels, Brussels Map, Europe on a Budget
Belize Belize, Central America on a Budget, Guatemala & Belize Map
Benin West Africa
Bolivia Bolivia, South America on a Budget
Brazil Brazil, Rio, South America on a Budget
British Virgin Islands The Caribbean
Brunei Malaysia, Singapore & Brunei [1 title], Southeast Asia on a Budget
Bulgaria Bulgaria, Europe on a Budget
Burkina Faso West Africa
Cambodia Cambodia, Southeast Asia on a Budget, Vietnam, Laos & Cambodia Map [1 Map]
Cameroon West Africa
Canada Canada, Pacific Northwest, Toronto, Toronto Map, Vancouver
Cape Verde West Africa
Cayman Islands The Caribbean
Chile Chile, Chile Map, South America on a Budget
China Beijing, China,

Hong Kong & Macau, Hong Kong & Macau DIR, Shanghai
Colombia South America on a Budget
Costa Rica Central America on a Budget, Costa Rica, Costa Rica & Panama Map
Croatia Croatia, Croatia Map, Europe on a Budget
Cuba Cuba, Cuba Map, The Caribbean, Havana
Cyprus Cyprus, Cyprus Map
Czech Republic The Czech Republic, Czech & Slovak Republics, Europe on a Budget, Prague, Prague DIR, Prague Map
Denmark Copenhagen, Denmark, Europe on a Budget, Scandinavia
Dominica The Caribbean
Dominican Republic Dominican Republic, The Caribbean
Ecuador Ecuador, South America on a Budget
Egypt Egypt, Egypt Map
El Salvador Central America on a Budget
England Britain, Camping in Britain, Devon & Cornwall, Dorset, Hampshire and The Isle of Wight [1 title], England, Europe on a Budget, The Lake District, London, London DIR, London Map, London Mini Guide, Walks In London & Southeast England
Estonia The Baltic States, Europe on a Budget
Fiji Fiji
Finland Europe on a Budget, Finland, Scandinavia
France Brittany & Normandy, Corsica, Corsica Map, The Dordogne & the Lot, Europe on a Budget, France, France Map, Languedoc & Roussillon, The Loire, Paris, Paris DIR,

Paris Map, Paris Mini Guide, Provence & the Côte d'Azur, The Pyrenees, Pyrenees & Andorra Map
French Guiana South America on a Budget
Gambia The Gambia, West Africa
Germany Berlin, Berlin Map, Europe on a Budget, Germany, Germany Map
Ghana West Africa
Gibraltar Spain
Greece Athens Map, Crete, Crete Map, Europe on a Budget, Greece, Greece Map, Greek Islands, Ionian Islands
Guadeloupe The Caribbean
Guatemala Central America on a Budget, Guatemala, Guatemala & Belize Map
Guinea West Africa
Guinea-Bissau West Africa
Guyana South America on a Budget
Holland see The Netherlands
Honduras Central America on a Budget
Hungary Budapest, Europe on a Budget, Hungary
Iceland Iceland, Iceland Map
India Goa, India, India Map, Kerala, Rajasthan, Delhi & Agra [1 title], South India, South India Map
Indonesia Bali & Lombok, Southeast Asia on a Budget
Ireland Dublin DIR, Dublin Map, Europe on a Budget, Ireland, Ireland Map
Israel Jerusalem
Italy Europe on a Budget, Florence DIR, Florence & Siena Map, Florence & the best of Tuscany, Italy, The Italian Lakes, Naples & the Amalfi Coast, Rome, Rome DIR, Rome Map, Sardinia, Sicily, Sicily Map, Tuscany & Umbria, Tuscany Map,

Venice, Venice DIR, Venice Map
Jamaica Jamaica, The Caribbean
Japan Japan, Tokyo
Jordan Jordan
Kenya Kenya, Kenya Map
Korea Korea
Laos Laos, Southeast Asia on a Budget, Vietnam, Laos & Cambodia Map [1 Map]
Latvia The Baltic States, Europe on a Budget
Lithuania The Baltic States, Europe on a Budget
Luxembourg Belgium & Luxembourg, Europe on a Budget
Malaysia Malaysia Map, Malaysia, Singapore & Brunei [1 title], Southeast Asia on a Budget
Mali West Africa
Malta Malta & Gozo DIR
Martinique The Caribbean
Mauritania West Africa
Mexico Baja California, Baja California, Cancún & Cozumel DIR, Mexico, Mexico Map, Yucatán, Yucatán Peninsula Map
Monaco France, Provence & the Côte d'Azur
Montenegro Montenegro
Morocco Europe on a Budget, Marrakesh DIR, Marrakesh Map, Morocco, Morocco Map,
Nepal Nepal
Netherlands Amsterdam, Amsterdam DIR, Amsterdam Map, Europe on a Budget, The Netherlands
Netherlands Antilles The Caribbean
New Zealand New Zealand, New Zealand Map

DIR: Rough Guide DIRECTIONS for short breaks

Available from all good bookstores

For more information go to www.roughguides.com

Visit us online

www.roughguides.com

Information on over 25,000 destinations around the world

- **Read** Rough Guides' trusted travel info
- **Access** exclusive articles from Rough Guides authors
- **Update** yourself on new books, maps, CDs and other products
- **Enter** our competitions and win travel prizes
- **Share** ideas, journals, photos & travel advice with other users
- **Earn** points every time you contribute to the Rough Guide community and get rewards

NOTES

Small print and
Index

A Rough Guide to Rough Guides

SMALL PRINT

Published in 1982, the first Rough Guide – to Greece – was a student scheme that became a publishing phenomenon. Mark Ellingham, a recent graduate in English from Bristol University, had been travelling in Greece the previous summer and couldn't find the right guidebook. With a small group of friends he wrote his own guide, combining a highly contemporary, journalistic style with a thoroughly practical approach to travellers' needs.

The immediate success of the book spawned a series that rapidly covered dozens of destinations. And, in addition to impecunious backpackers, Rough Guides soon acquired a much broader and older readership that relished the guides' wit and inquisitiveness as much as their enthusiastic, critical approach and value-for-money ethos.

These days, Rough Guides include recommendations from shoestring to luxury and cover more than 200 destinations around the globe, including almost every country in the Americas and Europe, more than half of Africa and most of Asia and Australasia. Our ever-growing team of authors and photographers is spread all over the world, particularly in Europe, the US and Australia.

In the early 1990s, Rough Guides branched out of travel, with the publication of Rough Guides to World Music, Classical Music and the Internet. All three have become benchmark titles in their fields, spearheading the publication of a wide range of books under the Rough Guide name.

Including the travel series, Rough Guides now number more than 350 titles, covering: phrasebooks, waterproof maps, music guides from Opera to Heavy Metal, reference works as diverse as Conspiracy Theories and Shakespeare, and popular culture books from iPods to Poker. Rough Guides also produce a series of more than 120 World Music CDs in partnership with World Music Network.

Visit www.roughguides.com to see our latest publications.

Rough Guide credits

Text editors: Natasha Foges, Helen Ochyra
Layout: Anita Singh
Cartography: Animesh Pathak
Picture editor: Mark Thomas
Production: Rebecca Short
Proofreader: Diane Margolis
Cover design: Nicole Newman, Dan May
Photographer: Paul Whitfield
Editorial: London Andy Turner, Keith Drew, Edward Aves, Alice Park, Lucy White, Jo Kirby, James Smart, James Rice, Emma Beatson, Emma Gibbs, Kathryn Lane, Monica Woods, Mani Ramaswamy, Harry Wilson, Lucy Cowie, Alison Roberts, Lara Kavanagh, Eleanor Aldridge, Ian Blenkinsop, Charlotte Melville, Joe Staines, Matthew Milton, Tracy Hopkins; **Delhi** Madhavi Singh, Jalpreen Kaur Chhatwal, Jubbi Francis
Design & Pictures: London Scott Stickland, Dan May, Diana Jarvis, Nicole Newman,

Sarah Cummins; **Delhi** Umesh Aggarwal, Ajay Verma, Jessica Subramanian, Ankur Guha, Pradeep Thapliyal, Sachin Tanwar, Nikhil Agarwal, Sachin Gupta
Production: Liz Cherry, Louise Minihane, Erika Pepe
Cartography: London Ed Wright, Katie Lloyd-Jones; **Delhi** Rajesh Chhibber, Ashutosh Bharti, Rajesh Mishra, Jasbir Sandhu, Swati Handoo, Deshpal Dabas, Lokamata Sahu
Marketing, Publicity & roughguides.com: Liz Statham
Digital Travel Publisher: Peter Buckley
Reference Director: Andrew Lockett
Operations Coordinator: Becky Doyle
Operations Assistant: Johanna Wurm
Publishing Director (Travel): Clare Currie
Commercial Manager: Gino Magnotta
Managing Director: John Duhigg

Publishing information

This tenth edition published May 2011 by
Rough Guides Ltd,
80 Strand, London WC2R 0RL

11, Community Centre, Panchsheel Park, New Delhi 110017, India

Distributed by the Penguin Group
Penguin Books Ltd,
80 Strand, London WC2R 0RL

Penguin Group (USA)
375 Hudson Street, NY 10014, USA

Penguin Group (Australia)
250 Camberwell Road, Camberwell, Victoria 3124, Australia

Penguin Group (NZ)
67 Apollo Drive, Mairangi Bay, Auckland 1310, New Zealand

Rough Guides is represented in Canada by Tourmaline Editions Inc. 662 King Street West, Suite 304, Toronto, Ontario M5V 1M7

Cover concept by Peter Dyer.

Typeset in Bembo and Helvetica to an original design by Henry Iles.

Printed in Italy by L.E.G.O. S.p.A, Lavis (TN)
© J.D. Dickey, Nick Edwards, Charles Hodgkins and Paul Whitfield, 2011
Maps © Rough Guides
No part of this book may be reproduced in any form without permission from the publisher except for the quotation of brief passages in reviews.
744pp includes index
A catalogue record for this book is available from the British Library
ISBN: 978-1-84836-862-0
The publishers and authors have done their best to ensure the accuracy and currency of all the information in **The Rough Guide to California**, however, they can accept no responsibility for any loss, injury, or inconvenience sustained by any traveller as a result of information or advice contained in the guide.

1   3   5   7   9   8   6   4   2

MIX
Paper from responsible sources
FSC   www.fsc.org   FSC™ C018179

Help us update

We've gone to a lot of effort to ensure that the tenth edition of **The Rough Guide to California** is accurate and up-to-date. However, things change – places get "discovered", opening hours are notoriously fickle, restaurants and rooms raise prices or lower standards. If you feel we've got it wrong or left something out, we'd like to know, and if you can remember the address, the price, the hours, the phone number, so much the better.

Please send your comments with the subject line "**Rough Guide California Update**" to ® mail @uk.roughguides.com. We'll credit all contributions and send a copy of the next edition (or any other Rough Guide if you prefer) for the very best emails.

Find more travel information, connect with fellow travellers and book your trip on ® www .roughguides.com

Acknowledgements

J.D. would like to thank his editor Natasha Foges for successfully guiding this book and providing valuable suggestions and improvements. Thanks also to all those who have provided current and ongoing help in the research of this book. Some of these names include Marcia Murphy, Allison Goldstein, Lisa Scarpelli, Leopoldo Marino, Aaron Wong, Eric Macey, Dennis Holifena, Kim Partlow, David Cohen, David Rodriguez, Doug Camp and Michael Grochau. Also, the assistance of LACVB and other visitor bureau staff is much appreciated. Finally, thanks to everyone on the Rough Guide staff who have worked so assiduously, including Animesh Pathak for the maps and typesetter Anita Singh.

Nick would like to thank all the staff of the various tourist authorities, especially Barbara Hillman in Berkeley, Kelly Chamberlin of Half Moon Bay, Emily Polsby of Mendocino, Bob Warren & Karen Whitaker of Shasta Cascades and my good friend Richard Stenger of Humboldt County. Thanks also to Natasha Foges and Helen Ochyra for eagle-eyed editing. Much gratitude for hospitality and excellent company to the merry fellows of Bonita Hollow in Berkeley and Nikki & Eric in them thar hills. Finally, as ever, heartfelt thanks for support from afar to my dearest Maria.

Charles thanks: Mani and Keith at Rough Guides HQ for the opportunity to cover my home state;

my co-authors Nick, Jeff and Paul, and our editors, Natasha and Helen; Rough Guides' editorial, production and cartography staff for their invaluable contributions; Tom Walton at Fortune PR; Gregory, Jeff and Andrew for helping get me into this mess in the first place; Linda for all the understanding and cooperation; Todd, Emily, Tyler and Aaron for being pals among pals; Mom for the memories and Dad for the support; and Sonja, for the love, affection, laughs...and patience.

Paul would like to thank all those who contributed to this book in any way; sharing hikes and bar-room tales, voicing opinions, and helping out with logistics. The assistance of park rangers and visitor centre staff is particularly appreciated: you know who you are. And cheers to Jade Nelson for Palm Springs insights. Special thanks go out to Chris Kapka for a home from home in San Fran and to those at the Rough Guide office in London, particularly to Natasha Foges and Helen Ochyra who helped make this edition what it is, as well as Anita Singh for setting the guide, Animesh Pathak for the maps and Mark Thomas for taking care of the photos. And lastly to Marion for fortitude through long absences, and support back home when the writing days got long and indexing became mind-numbingly boring. Thanks.

Readers' letters

Thanks to all the readers who have taken the time to write in with comments and suggestions (and apologies if we've inadvertently omitted or misspelt anyone's name):

Stuart Ballard, Sabine Boesz, Mike Cussen, Olwen Greany, Patrick Harrington, Alfred Jacobsen, Matthijs Moeken, Erin Pope,

Sarah Riches, Michaela Riesen, Rob Sawyer, Ed Shaw, Debbie Wood.

Photo credits

All photos © Rough Guides except the following:

Introduction

Joshua Tree National Park © Olivier Grunewald/
 Photolibrary
Newport Beach © Richard Cummins/Superstock
Californian poppies © Adam Jones/Getty Images
San Francisco street scene © Jon Arnold Images/
 Alamy
Napa Valley vineyard © Brad Perks/Alamy
Yosemite Valley © David W Hamilton/Alamy
Restaurant, Beverly Hills © Jonathan Alcorn/
 Axiom
Golden Gate Bridge © Mitchell Funk

Things not to miss

01 Big Sur coastline © Don Smith/Getty Images
02 Santa Monica Mountains © Aurora Photos/
 Alamy
03 Lava Beds National Monument © Greg
 Vaughn/Alamy
04 Surfer near the Golden Gate Bridge © Deanne
 Fitzmaurice/Getty Images
05 Hearst Castle © Anders Blomqvist/Getty
 Images
06 Sunset Strip © John Shearer/Getty Images
07 Burrito © Robert Llewelyn/Getty Images
11 Red Rock Canyon © Dennis Frates/Alamy
12 Gay Pride parade © David Paul Morris/Getty
 Images
13 Yosemite Valley © Jo Son/Getty Images
14 La Jolla © Chris Selby/Alamy
17 Disney Hall © Anthony Arendt/Alamy
19 Cable car © Jenny Acheson/Axiom
20 Redwood National Park © Jim Corwin/Alamy
21 Balboa Park © Marco Simoni/Getty Images
22 Mount Whitney © David Sanger/Alamy
24 Rafting, Kern River © Witold Skrypczak/Alamy
25 Whale-watching © Wildlife GmbH/Alamy
26 Chinese Theatre © David McNew/Getty
 Images
27 The *Coast Starlight* © Della Huff/Alamy
28 Golden Gate Park © Harald Sund/Getty
 Images

Exploring the outdoors colour section

Snowboarding, Lake Tahoe © Corey Rich/Getty
 Images
Cross-country skiing © David Madison/Getty
 Images
Surfing, Half Moon Bay © Bob Stanton/Alamy
Climbing, El Capitan © Corey Rich/Getty Images
Hiking, Zabriskie Point © Jason O Watson/Alamy
Sea-kayaking © Bill Stevenson/Getty Images

Epicurean California colour section

Californian grapes © Garry Gay/Getty Images
Spago, Beverly Hills © Look/Alamy
Mel's Diner © Ian Dagnall/Alamy
In N Out Burger © Stars and Stripes/Alamy
Fish tacos © Livia Corona/Getty Images
Chinese restaurant sign © PCl/Alamy
Grape harvesting © Fine Wine Stock
Napa Valley vineyard © Thomas Hallstein/Alamy

West Coast sounds colour section

The Beach Boys © Michael Ochs/Getty Images
1960s promo poster © Blank Archives/Getty
 Images
Snoop Dogg © David Livingston/Getty Images
Red Hot Chili Peppers © Jo Hale/Getty Images
The Hollywood Bowl © Visions of America/Alamy
NWA © LGI Stock/Corbis
The Doors © Henry Diltz/Corbis
Otis Redding © Giles Petard/Getty Images

Black and whites

p.66 Getty Centre for the Arts © Robert Landau/
 Alamy
p.162 Mission Basilica San Diego de Alcalá
 © Getty Images
p.550 Lake Tahoe © Michelle McCarron/Getty
 Images
p.602 Mount Shasta © Richard Price/Getty
 Images

Map symbols

maps are listed in the full index using coloured text

------	International border		🛈	Immigration post
--⋅--⋅--	Province/US state border		🏠	Ranger station
----	Chapter division boundary		🏛	Stately home/Palace
80	Interstate highway		⬇	Viewpoint
30	State highway		✶	Windmill
1	Highway		✶	Lighthouse
=====	Secondary highway		⬧	Church (regional maps)
⸺	Local road		✈	Airport
▬▬▬	Pedestrianized road		★	Bus stop
⊞⊞⊞⊞	Steps		⛽	Fuel station
⸺	Unpaved road		◆	Point of interest
⸻	Railway		●	Museum
··········	River		@	Internet café
– – –	Ferry route		ⓘ	Tourist information
⸻	Muni/Bart		✉	Post office
– –⋅	Tramline		⊞	Hospital/medical center
⸻	Light rail		⊠	Gate/Park entrance
- - - -	Footpath		◉	Accommodation
⸻	Wall		⛺	Campsite
◓	Cave		🏊	Swimming pool
⋏⋏	Mountain range		⚔	Battlefield
▲	Mountain peak		🎿	Ski area
⊛	Crater		)(	Bridge
⚘	Waterfall		⚑	Golf course
⬉	Marshland/swamp		▬	Building
⊬	Dam		⊞	Church (town maps)
⌐⌐⌐	Rocks		⊹	Cemetery
↟	Sequoia grove		▒	Park/Forest
↟↟	Oasis		░	Beach
∿∿	Spring		▨	Marine base
⊥	Wind farm		◨	Restricted zone

So now we've told you about the things not to miss, the best places to stay, the top restaurants, the liveliest bars and the most spectacular sights, it only seems fair to tell you about the best travel insurance around

WorldNomads.com
keep travelling safely

Recommended by Rough Guides

www.roughguides.com
MAKE THE MOST OF YOUR TIME ON EARTH
ROUGH
GUIDES